LITERARY NEVADA

Western Literature Series

Literary
Nevada

WRITINGS FROM THE SILVER STATE

EDITED BY
CHERYLL GLOTFELTY

UNIVERSITY OF
NEVADA PRESS
RENO &
LAS VEGAS

This project is funded in part by a grant from the Nevada Arts Council, a division of the Department of Cultural Affairs, and the National Endowment for the Arts, a federal agency.

University of Nevada Press, Reno, Nevada 89557 USA
Copyright © 2008 by University of Nevada Press
Manufactured in the United States of America
Design by Kathleen Szawiola

Library of Congress Cataloging-in-Publication Data

Literary Nevada : writings from the Silver State / edited by
  Cheryll Glotfelty.
       p. cm. — (Western literature series)
    Includes bibliographical references and index.
    ISBN 978-0-87417-755-8 (hardcover : alk. paper) —
    ISBN 978-0-87417-759-6 (pbk. : alk. paper)
    1. Nevada—Literary collections. 2. American literature—
  Nevada. I. Glotfelty, Cheryll.
  PS571.N3L57 2008
   810.8'09793--dc22   2008014377

The paper used in this book is a recycled stock made from 30 percent post-consumer waste materials, certified by FSC, and meets the requirements of American National Standard for Information Sciences—Permanence of Paper for Printed Library Materials, ANSI/NISO Z39.48–1992 (R2002). Binding materials were selected for strength and durability.
FIRST PRINTING

17   16   15   14   13   12   11   10   09   08
5   4   3   2   1

Publication of Literary Nevada *was made possible by contributions from the following organizations and individuals:*

John Ben Snow Memorial Trust

College of Liberal Arts Scholarly and Creative Activities
Grant Program, University of Nevada, Reno

Department of English, University of Nevada, Reno

Mountain and Desert Research Committee,
University of Nevada, Reno

Center for Environmental Sciences and Engineering,
University of Nevada, Reno

Nevada Arts Council

Nevada Humanities

Friends of Washoe County Library

Charles Redd Center for Western Studies

Loren and Evelyn Acton

Michael P. and Eryn Branch

Paul and Lynn Brosy

Patricia A. Cooper-Smith and Peter J. Smith

David Corkery

Debbie and T. J. Day

Esther Early

Jane and Dr. George Magee

Ann Ronald

William C. and Barbara C. Thornton

Carter and Peggy Twedt

William Wager, DDS

To the great state of Nevada
and to Steve and Rosa

To those who know the Desert's heart, and—through years of closest intimacy—have learned to love it in all its moods, it has for them something that is greater than charm, more lasting than beauty, yet to which no man can give a name. Speech is not needed, for they who are elect to love these things understand one another without words; and the Desert speaks to them through its silence.

IDAH MEACHAM STROBRIDGE,
In Miners' Mirage-Land (1904)

. . . .

As far as we could see, there was nothing but open land. Range upon range of desert mountains followed one upon the other into interminable distance, each with its own hue of rose or gray or violet, until they disappeared finally into a haze. . . . When we had lowered ourselves down, my father said, "Well, that's your Nevada out there."

ROBERT LAXALT, *Nevada* (1970)

. . . .

Step out onto the Planet.
Draw a circle a hundred feet round.
Inside the circle are
300 things nobody understands, and, maybe
nobody's ever really seen.
How many can you find?
LEW WELCH, *Ring of Bone* (1973)

CONTENTS

List of Illustrations   *xxv*

Preface   *xxvii*

Acknowledgments   *xxxi*

ONE

VOICES FROM THE HOMELAND

Native American Stories and Myths   1

WESTERN SHOSHONE   5

Origin Tale   5

Coyote Wants to Be Chief   7

Bungling Host   7

Tso'apittse   9

NORTHERN PAIUTE   11

Stone Mother   11

Water Babies at Coo yu e Lake   12

Pa-o-ha   14

Porcupine and Coyote   15

SOUTHERN PAIUTE   16

The Creation of the Indians   17

Cŭnā´waʙⁱ   19

Cŭnā´waʙⁱ's Grandson   20

Salt   23

WASHOE   23

Wolf and Coyote—Origin of Death   24

Damollale and the Black Widow Spider   25

Damollale and the Water Baby   26

Story of the *Ong*   27

TWO
GREAT BASIN RANGINGS
Journals of Exploration   29

JEDEDIAH S. SMITH   31
   from *The Southwest Expedition of Jedediah S. Smith*   31
PETER SKENE OGDEN   37
   from *Journal of the Snake Country Expedition, 1828–29*   37
ZENAS LEONARD   40
   from *Adventures of Zenas Leonard, Fur Trader*   40
JOHN C. FRÉMONT   45
   from *A Report of the Exploring Expedition to the Rocky
   Mountains in the Year 1842, and to Oregon and North California
   in the Years 1843–44*   45
JOSEPH C. IVES   52
   from *Report upon the Colorado River of the West*   53
JAMES H. SIMPSON   58
   from *Report of Explorations across the Great Basin of the
   Territory of Utah in 1859*   59
GEORGE M. WHEELER   62
   Cave in Cave Valley   63

THREE
FEARFUL CROSSINGS
Emigrant Encounters and Indian Responses   65

VIRGINIA REED MURPHY   67
   Across the Plains in the Donner Party (1846)   67
J. QUINN THORNTON   71
   from *Oregon and California in 1848*   72
WILLIAM GRAHAM JOHNSTON   74
   from *Experiences of a Forty-Niner*   75
SARAH ROYCE   78
   from *A Frontier Lady*   79
ADDISON PRATT   83
   Diary   84
WILLIAM LEWIS MANLY   87
   from *Death Valley in '49*   88

SARAH WINNEMUCCA   92
from *Life among the Piutes*   93
WOVOKA   98
The Messiah Letter   99

FOUR

LITERARY RICHES FROM THE MINING FRONTIER   101

J. ROSS BROWNE   103
A Peep at Washoe   103
DAN DE QUILLE   109
Underground Business Arrangements   109
Fun and Frolic   114
MARK TWAIN   117
from *Roughing It*   118
Information for the Millions   121
ALFRED DOTEN   125
Nevada Correspondence   126
MARY MCNAIR MATHEWS   129
from *Ten Years in Nevada*   130
SAM DAVIS   133
The First Piano in Camp   133
FRED H. HART   139
from *The Sazerac Lying Club*   139
IDAH MEACHAM STROBRIDGE   142
The Quest of Old Man Berry   143
MRS. HUGH BROWN   149
from *Lady in Boomtown*   149
ANNE ELLIS   153
from *The Life of an Ordinary Woman*   154
NELL MURBARGER   157
Queen of the Black Rock Country   157
LUCIUS BEEBE   165
Going for the Mail   165
SALLY ZANJANI   168
Making History   168

FIVE

THE OTHER NEVADA

Reflections on Rural Life   179

HOWARD R. EGAN   181
  Mountain Rat, Food for Indians   181
  Pine-Nut Harvest   182
  Hunting for Water   183
MARY ANN HAFEN   185
  A New Home in Nevada   186
SARAH E. OLDS   190
  from *Twenty Miles from a Match*   190
WILL JAMES   195
  from *Lone Cowboy: My Life Story*   195
WALLACE STEGNER   200
  Mormon Trees   200
OWEN ULPH   202
  The Critter   203
MOLLY FLAGG KNUDTSEN   208
  Preface to *Under the Mountain*   209
  A Flake of Flint, A Sherd of Earthenware   209
JEAN McELRATH   212
  Rabbit Fighter   212
  Natcherly Dumb   215
DENNIS PARKS   218
  from *Living in the Country Growing Weird*   218
SOPHIE SHEPPARD   225
  Airspace   225
CAROLYN DUFURRENA   231
  from *Fifty Miles from Home*   231
GREGORY MARTIN   236
  from *Mountain City*   236

SIX

A GATHERING OF COWBOY POETRY   243

OLEPHIA KING   245
  The Dappled Grey Mustang   245

R. GUILD GRAY   247

   In Defense of Cattlemen   248

JACK WALTHER   249

   The Longhorn's Short Career   249

GEORGIE CONNELL SICKING   250

   Nevada's Subtle Beauty   251

ERNIE FANNING   251

   The Vanishing Valley   252

LINDA HUSSA   253

   Ride the Silence   254

ERIC SPRADO   254

   Wait 'til You Become a Man   255

WADDIE MITCHELL   256

   Story with a Moral   257

   Typical   258

ROD McQUEARY   259

   Life and Times   259

SUE WALLIS   260

   Coyote Bitch   261

SEVEN

THE BIGGEST LITTLE CITY

Writings About Reno   263

JACK LONDON   265

   Confession   265

ARTHUR RUHL   269

   The Fight in the Desert   270

LESLIE CURTIS   273

   Reno   274

   Our Alphabet   274

   As Others See Us   276

CORNELIUS VANDERBILT JR.   277

   from *Reno*   277

MAX MILLER   281

   from *Reno*   281

WALTER VAN TILBURG CLARK   286

   from *The City of Trembling Leaves*   287

WILLIAM STAFFORD   293
   Reno   293
JILL STERN   294
   from *Not in Our Stars*   294
ARTHUR MILLER   299
   from *The Misfits*   300
ROLLAN MELTON   302
   Reno Visitors Center   302
   Truckee Treasures   304
WILLIAM A. DOUGLASS   306
   The End of the Line   306
EMMA SEPÚLVEDA   314
   from *From Border Crossings to Campaign Trail*   314
   Here Am I Now   320
   If I Renounce the Word   322
MARY WEBB   323
   from *A Doubtful River*   323
VERITA BLACK PROTHRO   329
   Porched Suitcases   329

EIGHT

LIVING LAS VEGAS
Inside the Entertainment Capital of the World   339

MARIO PUZO   341
   from *Inside Las Vegas*   341
SAMMY DAVIS JR., JANE AND BURT BOYAR   343
   from *Yes I Can: The Story of Sammy Davis Jr.*   343
HUNTER S. THOMPSON   346
   from *Fear and Loathing in Las Vegas*   347
WILLIAM J. PLUMMER   349
   from *A Quail in the Family*   350
SUSAN BERMAN   355
   from *Easy Street*   355
A. WILBER STEVENS   363
   Vegas: A Few Scruples   364
   Paradise Crest   364
PHYLLIS BARBER   365
   Mormon Levis   366

DAVE HICKEY   373
    A Home in the Neon 373
JOHN L. SMITH   378
    "Flying Nun" Stunt Double Lands on Her Feet in Las Vegas 379
    Kidney Caper: The Making of a Myth Nobody Can Miss 381
DAYVID FIGLER   383
    The Shrimp Manifesto 383
    Zamboni 384
HARRY FAGEL   386
    Jaywalker 386
    L.S.D. (Street Talk Pt. 4) 388
BRUCE ISAACSON   389
    Life in Las Vegas 389
    Lucky 390
BILL BRANON   392
    Seven-Out Sally Is Loose with the Rent 392
HART WEGNER   393
    The Blue Line 394
JOHN H. IRSFELD   402
    Stop, Rewind, and Play 403
DOUGLAS UNGER   410
    Second Chances 410
GREGORY CROSBY   423
    The Long Shot 424

NINE
IN OUR BACKYARD
Notes from Nuclear Nevada 427

FRANK WATERS   429
    from *The Woman at Otowi Crossing* 429
WILLIAM STAFFORD   436
    At the Bomb Testing Site 436
DENISE LEVERTOV   437
    Watching *Dark Circle* 437
ROBERT VASQUEZ   438
    Early Morning Test Light over Nevada, 1955 439
TERRY TEMPEST WILLIAMS   440
    The Clan of One-Breasted Women 441

LYNN EMANUEL   447
    The Planet Krypton   447
ADRIAN C. LOUIS   448
    Nevada Red Blues   449
CAROLE GALLAGHER   450
    from *American Ground Zero*   450
REBECCA SOLNIT   453
    from *Savage Dreams*   454
GARY SHORT   458
    Tidings   458
CURTIS OBERHANSLY AND DIANNE NELSON
OBERHANSLY   459
    from *Downwinders: An Atomic Tale*   460
CORBIN HARNEY   465
    from *The Way It Is*   465
WILLIAM KITTREDGE   468
    In My Backyard   469
SHAUN T. GRIFFIN   473
    Nevada No Longer   474
RICHARD RAWLES   475
    Coyote Learns to Glow   476
JAMES CONRAD   479
    from *Making Love to the Minor Poets of Chicago*   480

TEN

THE LONELIEST ROADS IN AMERICA
Contemporary Travel Writing   485

JOAN DIDION   487
    At the Dam   487
WILLIAM LEAST HEAT-MOON   489
    from *Blue Highways*   490
CHARLES BOWDEN   494
    Tortoises   495
JAMES CONAWAY   500
    from *The Kingdom in the Country*   501
TOM ROBBINS   507
    The Real Valley of the Dolls   508

DAVID DARLINGTON   514

    from *Area 51: The Dreamland Chronicles*   515

BRUCE STERLING   523

    Greetings from Burning Man!   523

WILLIAM L. FOX   531

    from *Driving By Memory*   531

DAVID THOMSON   536

    from *In Nevada: The Land, the People, God, and Chance*   537

BILL DONAHUE   541

    Boomtown   541

JANICE EMILY BOWERS   545

    Remains of the Day   545

ELEVEN

A DESERT BLOOMS

Contemporary Poetry   551

IRENE BRUCE   553

    Virginia City, Nevada   553

    Arrowhead   554

MILDRED BREEDLOVE   554

    What Hills Are These?   555

    Camping   555

JOANNE DE LONGCHAMPS   556

    Snowmountain   556

    Bat   557

    Becoming Crippled   558

HAROLD WITT   558

    Pyramid   559

    Light on the Subject at Lehman Caves   560

STEPHEN S. N. LIU   560

    A Mid-July Invitation   561

    August Mirage   562

    Monologue from the Chicken Ranch   562

GARY SNYDER   563

    Hitch Haiku   564

    Magpie's Song   564

    Old Woodrat's Stinky House   565

ELAINE DALLMAN   567

    Sparks for a 24/7 Week   568

    Desert   568

TOM MESCHERY   569

    Trucks   570

    Weeds—Teaching Poetry at Wittenburg Juvenile Hall   570

BILL COWEE   571

    More Than Worms Slip through Worm Holes   572

    To the Austrolorps in Wild Abandon   573

ADRIAN C. LOUIS   574

    excerpt from "Earth Bone Connected to the Spirit Bone"   575

    The Boy Hears Distant Drums from across the Sierras   576

    Coyote's Circle   577

KIRK ROBERTSON   579

    Adjusting to the Desert   580

    Fallon   581

    Lure   582

LYNN EMANUEL   583

    Chinoisserie   584

    For Me at Sunday Sermons, the Serpent   584

    What Ely Was   585

WILLIAM L. FOX   586

    untitled poem from *Monody*   586

    untitled poem from *Reading Sand*   586

    disowning   588

JIM HUSKEY   590

    Stone Koan   591

    Building the Pumphouse   591

BRUCE LAXALT   592

    Work in Progress   593

    Autumn Fire   594

NILA NORTHSUN   594

    sweat preparation checklist   595

    lost in the woods   596

    i gotta be indian tomorrow   596

SHAUN T. GRIFFIN   598

    A Place of Stone   598

    Trash Run   599

    Those People   600

GARY SHORT   601

    Toward Morning   601

    Flying over Sonny Liston   602

    What I Believed   603

DONALD REVELL   605

    The Little River Wants to Kee   605

    My Mojave   606

ALIKI BARNSTONE   607

    You Pray to Rain Falling on the Desert   608

    The Lights of Las Vegas   609

    Freeway Love Poem   611

GAILMARIE PAHMEIER   613

    The Promise of Good Food   613

    When You Love Someone for a Long Time   614

CLAUDIA KEELAN   616

    Blue Diamond   616

    Relinquish   617

TWELVE

ANYTHING IS POSSIBLE

Contemporary Fiction   619

ROBERT LAXALT   621

    from *The Basque Hotel*   621

DAVID KRANES   626

    The Phantom Mercury of Nevada   627

JOANNE MESCHERY   636

    An Otherwise Happy Life   637

BERNARD SCHOPEN   644

    from *The Big Silence*   645

    from *The Desert Look*   646

    from *The Iris Deception*   648

FRANK BERGON   649

    from *Wild Game*   650

THOMAS SANCHEZ   657

    from *Rabbit Boss*   657

H. LEE BARNES   662

    from *The Lucky*   662

DARRELL SPENCER   671
    My Home State of Nevada   672
STEVEN NIGHTINGALE   673
    from *The Lost Coast*   673
ART GIBNEY   680
    The Manure Spreader   681
MONIQUE LAXALT   689
    from *The Deep Blue Memory*   690
TERESA JORDAN   694
    St. Francis of Tobacco   694
SAM MICHEL   703
    Seeing Hunter Creek   704
JEFFREY CHISUM   711
    The Middle of Nowhere   711

THIRTEEN

WILD NEVADA

Lessons of the Land   723

MARK TWAIN   725
    from *Roughing It*   725
JOHN MUIR   727
    Nevada Forests   728
ISRAEL C. RUSSELL   732
    The Great Basin   732
GEORGE R. STEWART   735
    from *Sheep Rock*   735
SESSIONS S. WHEELER   738
    from *The Nevada Desert*   738
JOHN McPHEE   741
    from *Basin and Range*   741
STEPHEN TRIMBLE   746
    from *The Sagebrush Ocean*   747
ANN HAYMOND ZWINGER   750
    Of Blackbrush and Sagebrush   750
DIANA KAPPEL-SMITH   753
    Fossil Water   754
JOE ELY   756
    More Than Romance   757

JIM SLOAN   762
  The Oldest Living Thing   763
ANN RONALD   769
  Water   770
MICHAEL P. COHEN   774
  The Future of the Great Basin   775
JON CHRISTENSEN   777
  from *Nevada*   777
ROBERT LEONARD REID   782
  West, to the Future   783

  Further Reading   787
  Chronological List of Contents   797
  Sources and Credits   809
  Index   825

ILLUSTRATIONS

MAP

State of Nevada   xxxvi

PHOTOGRAPHS (following page 426)

John C. Frémont

Dan De Quille

Mark Twain (Samuel L. Clemens)

John Muir

Sarah Winnemucca (Thocmetony)

Sam P. Davis

Idah Meacham Strobridge

Wovoka

Will James

Lucius Beebe

Walter Van Tilburg Clark

Nell Murbarger

Sessions S. Wheeler

Arthur Miller

Jean McElrath

Corbin Harney

A. Wilber Stevens

Georgie C. Sicking

Joanne de Longchamps

Robert Laxalt

Sammy Davis Jr.

Stephen S. N. Liu

Rollan Melton

Dennis Parks

Ann Ronald

Frank Bergon

Phyllis Barber
H. Lee Barnes
Susan Berman
Adrian C. Louis
Kirk Robertson
William L. Fox
Waddie Mitchell
nila northSun
Shaun T. Griffin

PREFACE

Eighteenth-century maps of North America show a mysterious blank space lying between the Rocky Mountains and the Sierra Nevada, labeled *Tierra Incognita*—unknown land. Three hundred years later, as we enter the twenty-first century, Nevada occupies that space. One of the leading tourist destinations in the world, for the last two decades this once-unknown land has been the fastest-growing state in the United States. Today Nevada is well known—but not known well. Its literary heritage, for example, is virtually *incognita*. Who *are* Nevada's authors? How has Nevada been imaginatively explored and construed? What are its stories? Where are its poems? This anthology answers these questions and fills in perhaps the last remaining blank space on the *literary* map of America.

In the early 1990s my department chair asked me to revive a course that was listed in the university catalog as "Literature of the Far West and Nevada." By assigning my students the task of finding and reporting on a Nevada book, I figured I had fulfilled the expectations of the "and Nevada" portion of the course. To my surprise, the class reports changed my life. The books my students read and talked about sparked my interest and imagination. As I wrote the titles down on my "Must Read" list, I noticed that the students were deeply invested in talking about regional books. Nevada literature mattered to them in a way that other literature did not. It was personal. So I began my new career of reading and teaching Nevada literature. I soon realized that there were too many good books to fit into one course, and I wondered why there was so little knowledge of these works, even among specialists of western American literature. As a new champion of Nevada writing, I decided to put together this anthology, to make Nevada's literature more widely known and readily available to Nevadans and to anyone who reads with a spirit of curiosity and a taste for adventure.

I have spent many happy hours—and more than ten years—prowling around in libraries and bookstores, talking to authors, archivists, and avid readers of western Americana, poring over bibliographies, surfing the Internet, and tracking down leads. My favorite hours took place in my office behind a closed door, on my couch with a cup of tea, nose in a book. When friends asked about the anthology's progress, I was evasive, replying that I was still . . . uh . . . in the "research" phase. It has been a wonderful and enormous project. I've experienced the quiet euphoria of many *Eureka! I've found it!* moments, discovering golden words lying in wait between the drab covers of a dusty book.

Now the time has come to go public, to stop researching and share the spoils. First, a few words about selection criteria and organization. My overriding purpose is to enable readers to discover Nevada through stories and poems, to explore this interesting and paradoxical place via its literary trails. Every piece in this book is either set in Nevada or is about Nevada or Nevadans. The result is an unusually wide range of authors. This anthology features Nevada's best-known authors, such as Mark Twain, Sarah Winnemucca, Walter Van Tilburg Clark, and Robert Laxalt. These writers left us enduring works that have shaped our imaginative understanding of Nevada and its people. Also included are established and emerging Nevada writers from all parts of the state whose work has been recognized with prestigious literary awards, such as the Pushcart Prize, the Drue Heinz Prize, the *New York Times* Notable Book selection, Guggenheim Fellowships, National Endowment for the Arts grants, the Western States Book Award, and the Nevada Writers Hall of Fame and Silver Pen Awards.

Beyond these obvious choices, you'll find some surprises. Few people, for example, would think of Jack London as a Nevada author; however, his reminiscence of conning a Reno homemaker into a free dinner explores vintage Nevada themes of deception, gullibility, opportunity, and luck and recalls the hobo experience of Reno in the early 1900s, when it was known as a railroad town. "Confession," therefore, made the cut, as did good writing by nonresident authors such as John Muir, Arthur Miller, Hunter S. Thompson, Joan Didion, and Gary Snyder, writers whose fine work illuminates important facets of Nevada experience.

While I have made a strong effort to find and feature writing by authors who live in Nevada, I've left out the work of resident writers whose subjects and settings lie outside the state. Within the borders of this chosen literary terrain, the stories and poems included here provide imaginative access to virtually every corner of Nevada and give voice to many points of view. You'll read about Las Vegas and Lahontan, ranchers and high-rollers, prospectors and jet pilots, showgirls and schoolteachers, Mormons and reprobates, Basques and Native Americans, Cadillacs and pickup trucks, neon and sagebrush, prehistoric lakes and nuclear blasts. Walt Whitman once proclaimed in *Song of Myself,* "Do I contradict myself? Very well then I contradict myself, (I am large, I contain multitudes.)" Nevada is likewise large, complex, and contradictory, and the selections here illuminate its fascinating incongruities.

This anthology reprints previously published works and, in one or two instances, prints new works by established authors; it does not premier unpublished writers, however promising. With just a few exceptions, the anthology does not include genre fiction, drama, history, or children's literature. I have edited this book to flow smoothly, with the enjoyment of general readers in mind. Therefore, I've omitted scholarly footnotes that may have been present in certain editions. Pertinent information from those footnotes appears here in the headnotes and in square brackets in the text. Authors who write under pseudonyms are identified by their pen names (e.g., Mark Twain); their birth names are revealed in the headnotes.

Size considerations often required cutting text even from within excerpts. Cuts are signaled by ellipses for brief passages and by extended ellipses for elisions of a paragraph or more. Illustrated works appear here without illustrations. For the sake of authenticity, irregular spellings, odd punctuation, and nonstandard English usage in the originals are preserved here. Typographical errors in the published works have been corrected with the authors' permission or, generally, retained in the case of deceased authors. Serious students and scholars should consult the original sources, whose publication information is provided in the Sources and Credits section in the back matter.

The book is divided into a lucky thirteen chapters, each of which can stand on its own as a manageable reading cluster for personal enjoyment, a thought-provoking focus for a book club discussion, or a teachable unit. Within each chapter, writings are arranged in chronological sequence, unless otherwise noted. The chapters themselves follow the course of history, beginning with traditional Native American tales, progressing through the exploration and emigration periods, chronicling Nevada's mining booms and busts, covering the settlement and evoking the spirit of rural Nevada, Reno, and Las Vegas respectively, and concluding with chapters on contemporary poetry and fiction. A brief essay introduces each chapter, establishing the historical and literary contexts that help one more fully understand the selections in that chapter. Read sequentially, the chapter introductions tell the story of the evolution of Nevada's literature.

A handful of topical chapters interspersed throughout the book reflect distinctive elements of the Nevada experience. Cowboy poetry, for example, is closely allied with rural Nevada but has become a cultural phenomenon—indeed, a literary genre—in its own right, deserving a special chapter. The Nevada Test Site, a world within a state, is off-limits to most civilians, but the activities there—atomic testing, weapons research, and proposed nuclear waste storage—have ignited powerful literary protests that can be instructively read as a set. A contemporary travel writing chapter features the impressions of incisive outsiders, recognizing the fact that still today the most widely read writing about Nevada is written by temporary visitors for a national audience. Finally, a concluding chapter on wild Nevada re-turns our attention to the land itself—the bedrock upon which cultures stand or fall—revealing the secret beauty of Nevada's mountains and deserts.

In some cases a given work could reasonably have been placed in two or three different chapters. Final placement was made with an eye to balance among chapters and resonance within chapters, as well as to teaching considerations. For readers who prefer to follow a linear trail through time, the Chronological List of Contents at the back of the book traces the origins and development of Nevada's literary tradition.

If you are like me, even this substantial book will not satisfy your craving for Nevada writing. You are in luck—the literature presented in here is only a small fraction of what lies *out there*, awaiting discovery. To point you in the direction of future literary rambles, I offer a "Further Reading" section that furnishes enough promising leads to last a lifetime. "To ramble," incidentally, derives from the Middle Dutch *rammelen*, meaning, of animals, "to wander around in heat"—a splendid image for Nevada exploration, literary or otherwise.

ACKNOWLEDGMENTS

O ne of the most rewarding aspects of this project is that it brought me into company with so many likable people. First, my sincere thanks to the authors themselves, who are the heart of this book. They have been generous in their support of this collection. My gratitude extends to the families of deceased authors for their heart-warming enthusiasm and encouragement. This book would not have seen the light of day without the exceptional work, terrierlike tenacity, and amazing skills of my ace assistant, Patricia Cooper-Smith. Patti helped me with research, typing, editing, proofing, permissions paperwork, and more. Patti's friendly reminder of Anne Lamott's phrase "bird by bird" and her commitment to seeing this book to publication gave me hope at critical times, and ultimately prevailed.

At the University of Nevada, Reno, I wish to thank a succession of chairs of the English Department for their leadership and support—Bob Merrill, Steve Tchudi, and Stacy Burton—and the classified staff for their reliable assistance: Geri McVeigh, Linda Gorelangton, Cami Allen, and Alec Ausbrooks. I am grateful to UNR colleagues who have offered expertise and encouragement—Ann Ronald, Scott Slovic, Mike Branch, Terre Ryan, David Fenimore, Bill Jacobsen, Michael Cohen, Mary Webb, Gailmarie Pahmeier, Susan Palwick, Richard Brown, Bill Wilborn, Ann Keniston, Bernie Schopen, Lorena Stookey, Lee Thomas, Bill Rowley, Elizabeth Raymond, Jerry Edwards, Jim Hulse, Richard Davies, Katherine Fowler, Don Fowler, Glenn Miller, Paul Starrs, Peter Goin, Steve Jenkins, and Pete Brussard. At the UNR Oral History Program, thanks to Tom King, Mary Larson, and Kathleen Coles. In public relations, Andrea Turman and Jean Dixon have been wonderful champions. Special thanks to university administrators for their dedication and leadership—Bob Mead, Eric Herzik, Heather Hardy, John Frederick, Bill Cathey, Steve Zink, Joe Crowley, John Lilley, and Milton Glick. Sincere thanks to my students, too numerous to name, whose response to Nevada readings taught me about the transformative power of regional literature, and whose own writing talent promises some interesting Nevada literature still to come. At UNR, I have been blessed with excellent research assistants, Paul Bogard and Meg Cooke. Typist extraordinaire, for whom I am eternally grateful, is Amy Bartlow.

My research has been greatly aided by the skill and helpfulness of many librarians. At UNR, I would like to thank Bob Blesse, Betty Glass, Jacquelyn Sundstrand, Kathryn Totton, Donnelyn Curtis, Bonnie Ragains, Susan Searcy, Maggie Ressel, Victor Atkocaitus, Carole Keith, Kris Dondero, Millie Syring, and Victoria Pascucci. At the Nevada Historical Society, special thanks to Eric Moody and Michael Maher. Washoe County librarians have gone the extra mile for me. Thanks to Tim Gorelangton, Julie Machado, Sandie Sheldon, Barbara Kaufman, and Ian Campbell. At the Nevada State Library, thanks to archivist and living legend Guy Rocha, Sara Jones, and Karen Starr. At the UNLV library, thanks to Kathy War. The independently owned Sundance Bookstore in Reno is a stalwart sponsor of the greater Nevada literary community.

Fund-raising for this project required me to learn new skills. UNR development officers Michele Basta and Robyn Powers kindly coached me in the art of development and helped me make valuable contacts. Thanks to UNR employees Lynda Buhlig, Emi Weldon, Joyce Duncan, Sharon Brush, and Megan Denio for their tactful and timely assistance. At the Washoe County Libraries, Sharon Honig-Bear and director Nancy Cummings provided helpful advice. Thanks to Nevada Humanities for a research grant, and to Judy Winzeler and Steve Davis in particular. The inspiring Esther Early offered immense moral support as well as a generous early donation; thanks, Esther. I am deeply grateful for financial support from major donors, acknowledged on the donors page, and from many other supporters, starting with the very first gift of all, from my daughter Rosa, who donated her two-dollar allowance, and including gifts from Sherrie Clark and Peggy Shepperson.

Editors of other anthologies have been enormously helpful in offering feedback and indispensable advice. I am indebted to Jack Hicks and his assistant Katie Rodger, William Kittredge, Diane Quantic, Jane Hafen, Mike Branch, Shaun Griffin, Jim Maguire, Bill Fox, Barney Nelson, Mike Tronnes, and John Bradley. Professional colleagues have led me to literature, shared their research, reviewed drafts, written letters of support, and been fine friends—thanks to Nancy Cook, Allison Wallace, Sue Rosowski, Joe Flora, Jim Dwyer, Glen Love, Mark Schlenz, David Mazel, Larry Berkove, Bill Stobb, William Howarth, David Robertson, Laurie Ricou, Melody Graulich, Alvin McLane, Hal Klieforth, Stan Paher, James Hulse, Michon Mackedon, Katherine Fowler, Bill Jacobsen, William Freudenburg, Michael McDowell, Jon Christensen, Richard Logsdon, Susan Boskoff, Ed Vogel, Carolyn Loftis, Catherine Lavender, Laura Bush, Forrest Robinson, Ed Smith, Donald Scott, Bill Handley, John Elder, Morris Brownell, Susan Baker, Bill Fox, Kirk Robertson, and Shaun Griffin. Artist Valerie Cohen offered keen ideas about design elements. A small army of volunteers helped shoulder the work of proofreading—my thanks to Virginia Ewick, Gregory Hayes, Peter Smith, and Eric Wershing.

I would like to thank the University of Nevada Press for their coaching, attention to detail, and commitment to excellence—Joanne O'Hare, Ron Latimer, Tom Radko, Margaret F. Dalrymple, Sara Vélez Mallea, Gerry Anders, Kathleen Szawiola, Carrie House, Vicki Davies, Charlotte Heatherly, and Sheryl Laguna. Thank you to Valerie Cohen for drawing the sagebrush ornament in the front matter.

Warm thanks to my family and friends, who have shared this life through thick and thin—Loren and Evelyn Acton, Stan Acton and Rebecca Evans, Phil and Marlene Glotfelty, Eileen Pape, Laura Koeninger, Gretchen Diether, Sondra Herbert, the Ruckstuhl family, the Ellsworth family, Alvin McLane, Ann Ronald, Lois Snedden, Mike and Eryn Branch, Michael and Valerie Cohen, and Scott Slovic and Susie Bender. Finally, I would like to thank my husband, Steve, and daughter, Rosa—and our animals—for home, sweet home.

LITERARY NEVADA

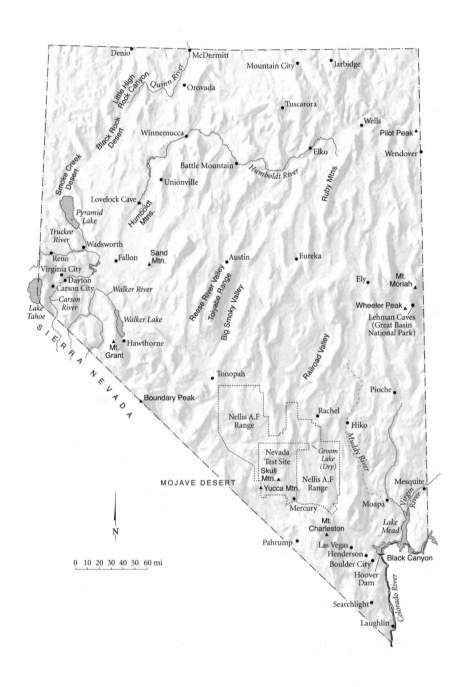

Denio •   • McDermitt
                                    Mountain City •   • Jarbidge

Little High   Quinn River
Rock Canyon   • Orovada
                                                   • Tuscarora
Black Rock
Desert   • Wells
                          Winnemucca •   Pilot Peak ▲
Smoke Creek   • Elko   • Wendover
Desert   Battle Mountain •   Humboldt River
                                    • Unionville   Ruby Mtns.
Pyramid   Lovelock Cave •
Lake   Humboldt
Truckee   Mtns.
River   • Wadsworth
Reno •   • Austin   • Eureka
Virginia City •   • Fallon   Sand   Ely •   Mt.
  • Dayton   Mtn.   Moriah ▲
Carson City •   Wheeler Peak ▲ ■
Carson   Walker River   Lehman Caves
River   (Great Basin
Lake   National Park)
Tahoe   • Walker Lake

SIERRA   Mt. • Hawthorne
                Grant ▲

                                                                Railroad Valley
N E V A D A
                          • Tonopah   • Pioche

            ▲ Boundary Peak   • Rachel

                              Nellis A.F   • Hiko
                              Range
                                                    Muddy River
                              Nevada
                              Test Site   Groom
                              Skull   Lake
                              Mtn. ▲   (Dry)
                              ▲ Yucca Mtn.   Nellis A.F   • Mesquite
        MOJAVE DESERT   • Mercury   Range
                                                        • Moapa   Virgin River

                                          Mt.   Lake
                                          Charleston   Mead
        0 10 20 30 40 50 60 mi   ▲
                                  • Pahrump • Las Vegas
                                            Henderson •
          N   Boulder City •   • Black Canyon
                                            Hoover
                                            Dam
                                  • Searchlight   Colorado River

                                            • Laughlin

Reese River Valley
Toiyabe Range
Big Smoky Valley

ONE

VOICES FROM THE HOMELAND

Native American Stories and Myths

The land that we call Nevada has been home to people for at least twelve thousand years, an extraordinarily long time when you consider that Las Vegas
recently celebrated its mere centennial. In terms of human occupation, then, Nevada is both a new place and an ancient one. The most recent tribal groups are extremely old, their range extending well beyond Nevada's present borders to include
most of the Great Basin as it is defined by anthropologists. These tribes, the true
native Nevadans—Western Shoshone, Northern Paiute, Southern Paiute, and
Washoe—were culturally similar, practicing similar subsistence methods and
trading with one another. The languages of all but the Washoe tribe belong to the
Numic, or northern, branch of the Uto-Aztecan language family, while Washoe
appears to be an isolated language, not closely related to any other in the vicinity,
but perhaps distantly to some in California.

Patterns of life for Great Basin Indians were dictated by the land itself—a desert, where no single place could support people year round. People thus developed
seminomadic lifestyles, a subsistence pattern that required a detailed knowledge of
a particular territory. The annual diet included many varieties of plants, mammals,
fish, birds, reptiles, and insects—so many different menu items that one historian
has likened the Great Basin to a supermarket, offering an abundance of choices
to those with sufficient knowledge and without food prejudices. Nuts from the
piñon pine were an especially important staple food, harvested and stored every
fall for consumption during the winter. Close-knit Numic bands of a hundred to

two hundred people were identified with a particular place and its major food source—the "grass seed eaters," the "squirrel eaters," the "cui-ui eaters." In each band, the family formed the basic economic unit, the men responsible for hunting, fishing, and toolmaking, the women for plant gathering, food preparation, sewing, and child care. The Great Basin is dotted with springs and seeps, and blessed with a few lakes and rivers, water sources that were well known to the Indians and became the sites of annual temporary encampments. Until the calamitous arrival of Euro-Americans in the nineteenth century, time passed cyclically, with a sequential round of specific activities occurring every season, one year closely resembling another.

Great Basin Indians considered winter the proper time for storytelling, after dark, when the day's chores were done. At these times, elders took turns telling stories that had been told to them when they were children, an enjoyable way of preserving knowledge, teaching proper behavior, and maintaining cultural identity. Some stories take place in a timeless mythical age when animals were human-like and had the power of speech. Others are legends about events supposed to have occurred in times within memory.

Anthropologists have identified incidents, motifs, and elements common to Great Basin stories and have categorized stories characteristic of the region, four major types of which are included in this chapter. Creation tales narrate the origins of the land and the people. Etiological, or "just so," stories tell how certain things came to be, for example, why salt is found near St. Thomas. Cannibal tales feature scary monsters that eat people, but also caution against venturing too far from a social network. And trickster tales—the most common Great Basin story type—follow the funny misadventures of a mischievous, selfish, perverse, and lovable character, most often Coyote. These entertaining trickster stories show the consequences of wise and unwise behavior, and they add comic relief to cultures that valued conformity and time-honored mores. Great Basin stories, known for their frequent use of humor, are often sexual or scatological. "They don't sound dirty in Indian," one interpreter remarked, "but they sound pretty dirty in English." It is worth remembering that the stories in this chapter are both translations and transcriptions. Inevitably, translation conveys only a partial meaning, while transcription imposes artificial fixity on an organic, oral form that permitted multiple variants for each story.

The Numic term for storytelling translates literally as "telling each other stories," emphasizing the reciprocal and social nature of this activity, the storyteller pausing now and then for others to ask questions, make corrections, or give assent, after which the story would resume. Upon seeing stories written on paper for the first time, one Shoshone woman said that it was an isolating experience.

She missed the live setting and group participation that she remembered from her girlhood. The stories collected here are reprinted from ethnographies, folklore journals, tribal histories, and published story collections. Keep their original context in mind. Outside it is cold and dark. In the security of a shelter, warmed by a small fire and rabbit-skin blankets, you are with your family, by turns laughing, nodding, cringing, sighing, and then . . . drifting off to sleep as the sound of your grandfather's voice grows ever softer.

WESTERN SHOSHONE

The Western Shoshone called themselves "Newe," a term that means "the People." Newe terri-
tory covered parts of California, Nevada, Idaho, Montana, and Utah. The range of the Western
Shoshone cut a wide diagonal swath across Nevada from southwest to northeast, including
the headwaters and upper half of the Humboldt River. The Humboldt and its tributaries sup-
ported an abundance of wildlife and birds, such as deer, antelope, mountain sheep, rabbits,
beaver, ducks, geese, grouse, and sage hens. The Newe lived well and in harmony with the land,
developing effective techniques for hunting, fishing, and plant gathering, careful not to deplete
renewable resources. Wild onions, watercress, cattails, wild carrots, camas root, wild rye grass
seeds, sunflower seeds, currants, buckberries, and serviceberries were among the many plants
used for food and medicine. In the late fall, scattered bands joined together for an annual
celebration and harvest of pine nuts, eaten raw or roasted, and ground into flour for making
nutritious gravies and soups.

Newe legends dealt with all aspects of life, telling how people were created, conveying rules
of conduct, and recalling past events. The characters were usually animals, each of which
displayed a certain character trait that he or she shared with humans. Coyote was a favorite
character, a walking disaster who exhibited the very traits discouraged in Newe culture. The
stories collected here come from a book called Shoshone Tales, *edited by Anne M. Smith. Smith*
earned her PHD *in anthropology from Yale University in 1939. For her graduate fieldwork she*
traveled throughout central and eastern Nevada and western Utah, recording stories from
twenty different narrators, some who told the stories in English, some requiring translation,
each with his or her own distinctive style. Narrators and translators are identified at the end
of each story.

Origin Tale

Coyote lived by himself. He was making a rabbit net and while he was working, a
girl peeked in the door. She was pretty. She didn't say a word, but left right away.
Coyote thought that she was beautiful, so he left his net and followed her. He
chased her but he couldn't see her—he just followed her tracks. He almost caught
up with her but she kept ahead of him going over the little hills. When they came
to the water, Coyote caught up with her. She told him to get on her back and she
would take him across the water. Coyote wouldn't sit on her back very well but
kept slipping down. So the girl let him slip off into the water.

Coyote turned himself into a water-strider and swam ahead of her, he got way
ahead and got to the girl's mother's house before her. The girl told her mother, "I
let Coyote go and he fell in the water. He didn't behave himself." Her mother said,

"Don't talk so loud, Coyote is already here sitting in the house and he might hear you." The women cooked some ducks for supper and they ate outside while Coyote ate inside, lying on the bed.

He heard a great crunching of bones outside and Coyote thought maybe they had a dog. So he made a dog and sent it outside to see what all the noise was. The dog came back quietly, so Coyote knew that there were no dogs outside. The women were throwing the bones underneath them and there was something there chewing the bones. Coyote saw them through a little crack in the house. After a while they all went to bed in the house and the women stretched a net around so that Coyote couldn't get out. Coyote wished for a pocket gopher so he could chew the net.

They all went to bed and fastened the door. Coyote got in bed with the daughter. He felt something between her legs with teeth in it. He stuck his thumb in there and jerked it back quick when the teeth snapped. Coyote got scared and ran outside. They wanted to kill him but he was too smart for them. He hunted and found a pestle to put in there. He stuck it in and when the teeth snapped, it broke them all off. Then he went over to the old woman and did the same thing and pulled all the teeth out of the hole. So they had a good time when they got into bed again. The next night when they all went to bed nothing bothered him and he did what he liked. When they got up the next morning the girl was already swollen up big. In two or three days they had young ones. The old woman gave Coyote a jug to go fetch some water in. He went down to the springs but the jug leaked, so he had to put it in the water to soak until it would hold water.

After a while he brought the water home but he was too late. The children were all grown. The women had divided them into two bands and had taken all of the handsome ones and gone away. Coyote kept the band of ugly kids. They were Shoshones. The others were other kinds of Indians. That is where the Indians came from. Coyote is the father of the Indians. Coyote put the Shoshones into the water jug and started for his home with the jug on his back. Soon he heard a lot of racket in the jug—laughing, hollering, and raising hell. He was tired of packing the jug, so he set it down and opened it. Some of the littler ones got out and ran away. They were in Arizona and they speak just like Shoshones. The rest of them stayed in the jug and Coyote brought them home, washed and cleaned them and let them go.

The woman that Coyote followed was called Paa Naipi, Water Girl.

—Jim Tybo
Battle Mountain, Nevada

Coyote Wants to Be Chief

People from all over the country—all kinds of animals, even Stink Bug—gathered together in a valley for a council. Rumors were going around that a lot of them wanted to make Coyote the head man. Meadowlark told Coyote that Coyote was going to be a great chief. As he was going along, Coyote met Skunk, who told him the same thing, that Coyote was going to be the biggest chief there ever was. Then Coyote met Badger and he said the same thing. Every time Coyote heard this he got so swelled and he wished he would meet some more people who would tell him the same things.

Coyote wanted to find his brother. Wolf had been away for a long time. Coyote ran around that valley so fast, looking for Wolf, that he got all tired out.

The council was to start before the sun came up. Coyote didn't sleep the night before, he was so weary. In the middle of the night Coyote got sleepy. He still had a long way to go to get to the council. Coyote sat down to rest a little while in some timber. He didn't want to go to sleep but he was very weary. His eyes began to close. He picked up some little yellow flowers and propped his eyelids open with them. He fought sleep but he was so tired. Finally he fell asleep and didn't wake up till noon the next day. He got up and ran toward the valley. To his surprise he began meeting people. They were coming back from the council. He started asking, "What did you talk about? Who became a chief?" And they all told him, "Your brother did. He is the biggest man in the country now. He is the chief."

Coyote wanted to find his brother. Then Coyote found his brother and asked him if he were the biggest chief. Wolf said, "Yes." The people all wanted him to be the biggest chief.

—Anna Premo
Owyhee, Nevada

Bungling Host

Jackrabbit had a camp and Coyote came and visited him. Jackrabbit said, "What can I cook for us?" He had his bow and arrow on the wall. He took it and shot under every sagebrush and when he came back he pulled out all the sagebrush and laid them on the coals of the fire. When he took them out of the ashes they were nice fat rabbits and they had a fine meal.

In return, Jackrabbit came and visited Coyote. Coyote remembered what Jackrabbit had done and said, "What will we have to eat?" He took his bow and arrow and shot all the sagebrush and pulled them up in the same way Jackrabbit had done and then he laid them on the fire. To his surprise, when he took them out of the fire they were smoking sagebrush stumps. Jackrabbit went home.

So Coyote went and visited Otter where he was camped near the creek. After visiting a while, Otter said, "What can I get for us to eat?" He took a short twig of willow, split it and dove into the water with it. When he came up, the twig had speared a lot of fish. So they boiled them and had a fine feast.

Otter came to visit Coyote. Coyote said, "What will I find for us to eat?" He took a willow twig as Otter had done and jumped into the water. But he started to drown. He filled up with water and he only got out by his magic. But when he got out he had no fish. Otter went home.

Coyote went to visit Beaver in his camp by the creek. Beaver said, "I don't know what we'll have to eat." But he heard his children playing on the bank, so he killed a couple of them and cooked them. He said, "Don't touch the bones with your teeth, but lay them aside right here." After they finished, Beaver threw the bones in the creek and soon Coyote heard the little beavers playing on the bank again.

Beaver returned Coyote's visit. Coyote said, "What can I get for us to eat?" But he heard his children playing outside. He went and killed them and boiled them for supper. Beaver wouldn't eat any because it smelled so bad while it was cooking. Coyote ate some and then threw the bones in the river. The bones sank to the bottom, much to his surprise.

Coyote went to visit Mountain Sheep. Mountain Sheep said, "Let's see what I can find for supper." He took his bow and arrow and went off. He shot his arrow straight up in the air. When the arrow turned to come down he turned around and put his rear end up and the arrow shot him in the anus. He put down a tray and twisted the arrow and pulled all his fat out. They had it for supper.

Mountain Sheep went to visit Coyote. Coyote said, "What will we have for supper?" But he remembered what Mountain Sheep had done. He shot his arrow up in the air and turned around so the arrow would hit him in the anus. He was scared and shook but the arrow hit him in the right place all right. He bawled and ran around. Whenever he touched the arrow he cried like a child. Finally he pulled it out but it was only a bloody arrow. Mountain Sheep had to go home hungry.

Coyote got disgusted and left the country so guests wouldn't bother him. On his way he found a nest of little sage chickens. He urinated on them, threw dirt on them and went on. The mother hen found what he had done and followed him. When he was coming along the river, she hid by the bank to scare him. When Coyote was opposite she started to fly up and scared Coyote so he fell into the water.

The reason sage chickens look speckled and dirty is because Coyote threw dirt on the chicks. Sage hens always fly out and scare people that hunt them the same way the mother hen did to Coyote.

Coyote got mad and got his bow all ready to shoot. He said, "If she tries that again I am going to shoot her." So he traveled along with his bow ready. Again Sage Hen scared him, so he dropped his weapons and fell in the water again.

He went on and soon he came upon a wildcat sleeping. It was daytime. Coyote pushed Wildcat's nose in and the tail, too. That is why Wildcat looks that way to-day. When Wildcat woke up he found his nose gone. He followed Coyote's tracks and soon found him asleep. He rolled Coyote's nose between his palms to make it sharp and then he pulled his tail out long. Coyote woke and saw the shadow of his nose, so he felt it and it was real long. When he got up he felt something behind him. It was his tail and it scared him.

—Johnny Dick
(*Tom Premo, translator*)
Owyhee, Nevada

Tso'apittse

Tso'apittse started from his house to hunt for people. When he walked, the mountains shook. He sang, "I wonder if there are any Pine Nut Wood people here." He was walking in the forest to look for people to eat. As he came through the trees he saw a couple of fresh human tracks. The people were hunting cottontails. Tso'apittse said, "Ah, human cottontails have been here," and he looked to see which way the tracks went. He started at a trot to trail them. The people heard Tso'apittse coming and saying, "Whi, whi, whi, whi." That scared them. The only way they could get away was to climb up. So they started to climb up the hill and down the other side. When they got to the foot of the hill, there was an old woman camping there and they made for her house. The old woman said, "You keep on going. I'll use my club on him." She dreamed that she was a monster-fighter.

Tso'apittse was already coming down, still hot on the tracks. The old woman was in the back of the house. Tso'apittse sat down and said, "Hudu." Then he got up and the old woman jumped up too and they had a hand-to-hand fight. Tso'apittse had a conical basket for packing things in. It was lined with pitch. He threw people inside and they stuck and couldn't escape. He tried to put the old woman in but he failed. The old woman finally threw Tso'apittse on his behind. He got up and saw the print of his behind on the ground. He got up crying and went home because he wasn't allowed to have the print of his behind on the ground.

So afterward, Tso'apittse tried to make another hunt. He looked for more human tracks. As he went over the saddle of the mountain he came near a man who was traveling. The man stood still and froze with his arms outstretched like a tree. Tso'apittse walked right by him. Tso'apittse looked at the man then went on. He stopped again and looked. He was suspicious. He would go away and look back to see if it moved. The man was still there. Tso'apittse said, "What is it? A burnt stump?" He went back a way and looked again. He couldn't make up his mind what it was. Tso'apittse came right up close. The man just froze and didn't dare breathe. Tso'apittse said, "He has a penis and a nose." He tickled him but the man didn't move. Tso'apittse pushed him over and the man fell with his arms out and he didn't move. Tso'apittse went away and said, "Oh, it's just a burned stump." The man didn't get up until Tso'apittse was gone. Tso'apittse kept going on down to the valley.

Near a big pine a couple of boys ran into him. Tso'apittse said, "Young human cottontails." He chased them around the junipers panting, "Tsoa whi whi, tsoa whi whi." They kept on chasing around in the junipers. He said, "I'm going to have a feast." They kept on running and the two boys hid behind a tree. When Tso'apittse wasn't looking they ran to another tree. They got up to the summit and looked back and saw Tso'apittse still running around the tree saying, "Whi, whi, whi." After a while when they were a long way off he started trailing them again. They went down the other side of the mountain and came to an old man's house and said to the old man and his wife, "Tso'apittse is chasing us." The old man was a doctor and he sat down and started singing and said, "You'd better go along home." The old man was calling on all his spirit helpers. He was calling the last one when Tso'apittse came in at a trot. Tso'apittse had big red eyes and he popped them out to look fierce. Tso'apittse sat down and said, "Hudu." The old man's wife was hiding back of the house. The doctor had all his spirit helpers. Tso'apittse was looking back the way he had come. The doctor made some waving motions with his hands over Tso'apittse's head and took out Tso'apittse's spirit and threw it back up the trail. Tso'apittse saw his spirit going up the trail and he jumped up and chased it back up the mountain.

Around Eureka on the hillside is a big rock that looks like a person. They say that is Tso'apittse's body where he died chasing his spirit.

—Herbert Holly
(*Tom Premo, translator*)
Owyhee, Nevada

NORTHERN PAIUTE

The Northern Paiute people refer to themselves as "Numa" or "Neh-muh," which, like the Shoshone "Newe," means "the People," a common naming convention among hunter-gatherer societies. Their traditional range encompassed the western third of Nevada (with the exception of the Reno–Carson City–Tahoe region), much of southeastern Oregon, and portions of southern Idaho and eastern California. Pyramid Lake and Walker Lake were especially important fisheries for the Numa and remain in tribal ownership to this day. The Numa were widely dispersed over their territory, living in kinship-based groups that were seminomadic, camping for varying lengths of time according to seasonal availability of a particular food and congregating in larger groups at specific times of the year to fish the spawning runs, hunt coots, participate in rabbit drives, and harvest pine nuts. Animals were regarded as intelligent, each species possessing an individual personality that the Numa knew in detail. Power was believed to reside in nearly all plants, animals, and natural objects, most of which could serve as sources of power for humans, with shamans being exceptionally gifted in accessing this power to do good or harm to others.

In stories from the Great Basin Indians, it is unusual to mention a specific locale; however, the first three stories below are about Pyramid Lake, known to the Numa as the lake of the cui-ui fish—"Coo-yu-ee Pah" or "Ku-yu-i-wai," depending on the transcription. The first two stories appear in a 1974 history of the Pyramid Lake Indians by Nellie Shaw Harnar, a Paiute born on the Pyramid Lake Paiute Indian Reservation and educated in Indian schools, who earned a master's degree at the University of Nevada, Reno and worked for thirty-seven years as a teacher and counselor in Indian schools. "Stone Mother" explains how Coo-yu-ee Pah and a tufa formation on its shores came to be, while "Water Babies at Coo yu e Lake" tells the origin of the legendary water babies whose personified spirits live in the lake and molest the Numa. "Pa-o-ha," was collected in 1873 by ethnographer John Wesley Powell; it tells about how one of these water babies tormented a woman. "Porcupine and Coyote" appeared in a 1938 issue of Journal of American Folklore *in a set of Northern Paiute tales recorded by anthropologist Isabel T. Kelly.*

Stone Mother

Long ago in the Great Basin lived one large family. This was known as the Neh-muh family or the Northern Paiutes as they are known today.

These people were gentle and kind, but one brother was quarrelsome. He swayed some of his sisters and brothers to his bad manners. The children then divided into two sides. There was a continuous bickering from day to day that led to blows, counterblows, and much physical harm.

When the parents saw that their counseling was of no avail they decided to separate the children. This was a bitter decision, but had to be taken before murder was committed.

The father told the children that they had to move away from the parental home. He designated the quarrelsome leader to the land over the tall Sierra Mountains into what today is California. This brother and his family became the Pitt River Indians.

A brother who favored the quarrelsome one was designated to the land in the cold north—today's Idaho. He and his group became the Bannocks.

Another brother was asked to go to the southland beyond the Sierra Nevada to Owens Valley in modern California. These became known as the southern Paiutes or the Pe tah neh quad.

Others of this family were dispersed into bands to lands near rivers and lakes.

The parents remained but were very sad. They were truly heartbroken when the Pitt River band returned to fight the remaining groups.

The father passed on to the Great Milky Way. Then there seemed no consolation for the wife and mother. Even at her chores of seed gathering she wailed and mourned. No one checked her whereabouts when she did not return to her canee at night.

Notice was made only when a large body of salt water appeared. Near this pah nun a du was the form of the mother. She still had her burden basket on her back. She had been turned to a stone. The lake was the tears she had shed.

The Stone Mother is one of the Coo yu e Lake's tufa formations. It can be seen close to the Woh noh (Pyramid) today.

The area around the Stone Mother is a sacred place to the Neh-muh for their meditation and prayer.

Water Babies at Coo yu e Lake

In the Long Ago, the Neh-muh traded with the Indians living beyond the snow-clad mountains to the West (Sierra Nevada). Generally, these traders were composed of groups of men only, but occasionally, they took their families with them.

One party of traders, after visiting several tribes in the Land-near-the-Ocean, made ready to return to the Neh-muh country.

One of their members was not accounted for, so they waited over for several days. The youth never reappeared. Finally, the leader decided that the return home would have to be made with or without his presence. That evening, they remained in camp longer than usual in the hopes that the absent one would overtake them.

Several nights later the young man did appear. They were exultant at the sight of him, although overjoyed at the reunion the straggler was noticeably depressed.

The other traders exchanged tales of their adventure, but the youth made no comment. As the evening progressed into night, one by one the people retired. When only the leader and the youth remained, the leader asked, "Is there something you would like to tell me?" After a long moment the youth answered in the affirmative, and revealed he was planning to bring a wife back with him. The leader was not too surprised, and said, "Bring her to our camp so that we can all leave together in the morning."

The groom then left to fetch his bride as the leader waited to welcome them. He was astounded when the youth emerged bearing a mermaid in his arms. After the leader designated a place for the young couple to stay that night, he beckoned the husband and he begged him to return the wife to her home. The young man replied that he loved her and wanted to take her to his home in the Neh-muh country.

Because he was persistent, the leader retired filled with misgivings. Before falling asleep he pictured the troubles the pair would encounter. The Neh-muh people did not relish the idea of strange wives for their young men as the mother in the Neh-muh family was its head, and they would certainly doubly resent a Woman-from-the-Sea.

After a restless night the leader got up early to inform the others of the new woman traveler in their midst.

None of the group would consent to taking the girl back to their homeland. One after another they tried to persuade the husband to return her to the sea. Some men volunteered to help him return her to her new home. After each night of the new couple's stay the men found that much water was beginning to surround the camp. Each morning they found it was necessary to move briskly ahead of the ever encroaching water. Eventually the frightened leader decided to tell the pair that they must remain behind, as they were endangering the lives of the other tribal members in the party.

The majority hurried home in the hope that they would never see the mermaid again!

Days passed!

Then one morning the groom arrived with his bride at the village. News of the strange woman had been spread throughout the band. The people were terrified!

As kind and friendly as were the Neh-muh, they were also very superstitious. They could not allow a Woman-of-the-Sea to live with them. The chiefs demanded that the relatives refuse to permit the young couple to live with them.

As the young couple advanced water was already trickling in their wake. This was even more alarming! When the relatives insisted, the couple moved to the outskirts of the village.

Those who visited the couple reported a body of water had appeared close by the domicile of the newlyweds, and that the bride spent much time immersed. Later the relatives, in apprehension, stopped their visitations altogether.

Today the descendants of the couple may be encountered at the north of the Coo-yu-ee Pah. Water baby crying has been heard, small children's foot tracks have been seen on the beaches, and they themselves have been visible on many occasions.

Since the mother was not accepted by the Neh-muh, in retaliation she cast a spell over her babies and her abode. If any Neh-muh sees these water babies he may become very ill and may even die. To counteract the spell the Neh-muh prays to the Great Spirit to be cleansed of the spell.

Only individual medicine men (poo ha gum) can communicate with the water babies who are their medicine-helpers.

Lake Tahoe was created when the travelers camped with the bride and groom, the Truckee River was created on their journey, and Coo-yu-ee Pah was created at the final residence of the couple.

Pa-o-ha

Two women were walking along the shore of Ku-yu-i-wai [Pyramid Lake] and one carried with her a babe which was lulled to sleep by the noise of the waters. When the mother was weary of carrying the child, she wrapped it in a little robe and left it in the cradle among the reeds and with her companion wandered away to a distance.

Now all this time Pa-o-ha was watching their actions, and when the woman was quite out of sight she stole quietly up to where the child was lying and, placing her hand over the infant's mouth and stifling its cries, she strangled and devoured it.

When this was done she wrapped the robe about herself and laid down in the cradle instead of the child. After a time the mother returned and took up Pa-o-ha supposing it to be her child, and held it to her breast that it might nurse.

Now Pa-o-ha greatly enjoyed this feast for a time until in her eagerness she bit the woman. Then the mother mused to herself, "Has my little one got teeth so soon?" And turning back the robe she beheld in it a wonderful being. Filled with terror she turned to throw it down, but Pa-o-ha clung to her breast with her teeth, and the woman fled to her companion for assistance, but they, together could not disengage Pa-o-ha. When the woman tried to pull her away, the strange being would take a new and deeper grasp until she swallowed the whole breast.

Baffled in this way, the woman returned to camp and all the people gathered about with great curiosity to see this child of the water, though terrified and indignant.

They brought fire and put [it] on the back [of] Pa-o-ha, but at this the nymph only laughed for fire would not burn her. Then they tried to cut her throat with a knife and still she laughed for the knife would not penetrate her flesh.

Now the people consulted among themselves concerning some plan by which to be rid of this dangerous enemy and an old woman said, "Go get me a knife." This was done and when it was handed her she put it in the fire and heated to redness and with that she essayed to cut off the head of Pa-o-ha who only laughed in derision at their folly.

So at last they sent for a renowned sorcerer and when he came he told them his art had no power over such a being, so he took a knife and severed the woman's breast from her body and with it still in her mouth the mermaid ran back to the water.

Porcupine and Coyote

Elk was going across a big river. Porcupine wanted to go with him. "Where shall I sit?" he asked. "Where shall I sit, on your back, under your neck, or under your tail?" So he sat under his tail. Then Elk went across the water. When he was nearly there, Porcupine went into his anus and up into his intestines. He was going to kill Elk. That Elk died as soon as he reached shore. Then Porcupine came out.

He was walking around talking. He was saying, "What can I use to skin him?" He was looking for an obsidian knife. Pretty soon Coyote came up. He said, "What are you talking about? It sounds as though you had killed something." Porcupine said, "Oh no, I'm just talking." Then Porcupine told Coyote what he had. Coyote said, "Let's go and look." When they came there, he said, "What shall we do? Let's have a race. Let's run and jump over that Elk. The one who jumps best can take him." Porcupine said, "All right." They both ran. Coyote jumped clear over. Porcupine tried to jump, but he fell back. So Coyote said, "This is mine; I beat you." He started to take it away. Porcupine said, "No, that's mine." Coyote thought he would kill this Porcupine. He fought hard before he could kill him.

Coyote went home. He left his cap where he had killed Porcupine. He told his cap, "You wait here. If one of them moves, you say, 'Move,' and I'll come." Coyote went home to bring his family. When he was nearly home, his hat said, "It's moving; it's moving; it's moving." It was Porcupine moving.

Porcupine got up. He took that cap. He said, "Well, I have never seen a hat that could talk," and he threw that cap in the water. Then he started to skin and butcher that Elk. He hung all the meat high on a juniper.

Pretty soon Coyote came with his wife and his children. Porcupine was up in the tree. There, that Elk was gone; Porcupine was gone; Coyote's cap was gone. Coyote trailed that Porcupine and found him way up on top of the tree.

"My nephew, give me a piece of meat," he said. Porcupine said, "I'll give you a piece. Have your wife and all your children stand under me. I'll give them a big piece." Then he said, "I'll give them a great big piece so they can catch it." They all stood together under him. Then that Porcupine threw a great big piece of meat on them and killed them all.

This happened when Coyote was an Indian.

So he ate that meat all by himself, that Porcupine, way up on top of the tree.

—Tom Anderson
(*Nellie Townsend, translator*)

SOUTHERN PAIUTE

Southern Paiute (also known as Ute) territory extends from southeastern California through southern Nevada to southwestern Utah and northwestern Arizona, the many subgroups in this large region speaking dialects of a common language and considering themselves one people, the "Nuwuvi." Later observers called their land in Nevada's Mojave Desert "harsh," but the Nuwuvi were well adapted to this place and revered the sheer power of the land that surrounded them, areas that included present-day Mount Charleston, Valley of Fire State Park, Red Rock Canyon, and the Virgin River Valley—today's Lake Mead. The Nuwuvi followed a hunting and gathering lifestyle, with plants providing the bulk of their diet. Among the many palatable plants were mesquite and screwbeans, whose pods were gathered, winnowed, parched, and ground on a flat stone to make flour. The sweet-tasting heart of the agave plant was roasted and baked, and the yucca supplied soap and fiber for rope and shoes. Pine nuts were an essential food, stored in caches for winter. In spring, food stores could run low, and the Nuwuvi might resort to less palatable foods, such as juniper berries, Joshua tree blossoms, caterpillars, locusts, and rattlesnakes. Native agriculture was introduced several decades before the coming of the whites, supplementing wild foods with corn, squash, beans, pumpkins, and sunflowers.

Like other Great Basin Indians, the Nuwuvi enjoyed playing games and gambling. The psychologically challenging "hand game" was popular, one team arranging two pairs of bones (marked and unmarked) in their hands or under a basket, the other team guessing their position, usually with a wager at stake. Storytelling was a winter activity, for a sidewinder might bite you if you told stories in summer. Good storytellers enlivened their performance by mimicking the sounds of nature, singing, and calling on listeners to participate. Conversational

parts of a story were often sung, each character associated with a particular song, a song that
accompanied this character from one story to the next. The trickster Coyote (Cŭnā´waʙⁱ in
the stories below) appears frequently, sometimes in human form. The stories collected here
were recorded in the Moapa region by Austrian-born Dr. Robert H. Lowie, who worked for the
American Museum of Natural History, later becoming professor of anthropology at uc *Berke-*
ley. They were published in a 1924 volume of the Journal of American Folklore.

The Creation of the Indians

Long ago an old woman, named Cō´tsi'pamā´pŏt, made the whole country. No one
lived here at all anywhere except this old woman, her son, and her daughter. The
entire country was flooded with water except one little spot where Cō´tsi'pamā´pŏt
stayed. At last she scattered earth all over, seed-fashion. Then she sent her daughter to see how much land there was. When the girl came back, she said, "It is not
enough yet." Her mother kept sending her, and the girl always came back reporting
that there was not yet enough. At last the girl went a great distance and when she
came back she said there was now enough land. The old woman said, "See whether
you can find some people, look everywhere, go up to the mountains, and see." So
the girl went and looked everywhere but she saw nothing. The old woman said to
her, "I don't think you looked very much." So she went again and found just one
man. She traversed the entire country in a very short time. She returned and told
her mother, "I have found only one man."—"Well, that will be well, get him." The
girl went to the man and said, "My mother wants you to come to where we live."
He agreed to come.

Cō´tsi'pamā´pŏt lived in the middle of a wide stretch of water. The girl laid a
stick across from the shore and walked ahead. When she was nearly across, she
tipped the stick so as to topple the man into the water, but he flew up, unseen by
her, and reached camp first. When the girl arrived, she told her mother, "I called
him and he was drowned." She had one lodge while her mother lived in another.
Her mother said, "That man is in your lodge." The girl did not know that he had
flown there.

Cō´tsi'pamā´pŏt made deer, cottontail rabbits, bears, antelope, and every kind
of animal out of mud, threw them off and bade them take to the mountains. She
said to her daughter, "You had better stay with him, you can't find anyone else,
keep him for a husband." So the man and the girl lay together, but the man, though
eager to possess her, was afraid. The old woman said to him, "Since you can do
nothing with her, you had better go to get some deer; kill it and bring the first vertebra." The man went off, killed a deer, and brought the first, hard vertebra. "Well,"
said Cō´tsi'pamā´pŏt, "You had better use this, don't let her see this. This may fix

it, perhaps she will bite it, then you can have your will of her." Night fell. He took the vertebra and put it by his *membrum virile*. The girl had a toothed vagina, but the teeth could not bite the bone and broke off. Then he had his will of her and she bit no more. He lay with her every night now.

After a while the young woman was big with child. Her mother made a big sack and into this the daughter dropped her children so that the bag was full of them. Cō´tsi'pamā´pŏt said to the man, "You had better take this bag to the center of the world. Don't open it till you get there, no matter what noise you may hear from within." So the man set out with the sack and went on. After a while his load grew heavy and he heard a noise inside. He thought he would like to see the inside. He took off the bag, sat down and listened to the noise. He was eager to see what it was. At last he opened the bag and saw nothing. The babies got out and scattered all over the country. Most of them escaped. When he tied up the sack again, there were only a few left. He sat down and gave tribal names to the different babies. "You go up there, you shall be called by such a name," and so forth. To those few that remained at the bottom he said, "These are my people." All the babies in the sack were Indians.

The man had a long stone knife and an awl of hard bone. He had a rabbitskin blanket wide enough for two to sleep under. He had nothing with which to start fire, except a rock on which he would place his food. After a while he saw ashes falling down. "Where did this come from?" He sent several men far up, but they could see no fire anywhere. Others went higher still, and yet they could find no fire. Finally one of them went higher still and reported, "It looks like fire over there."—"Well, I think we had better all go and get that fire by gambling or some other way." He got all of them to come with him. They went to the people who had fire and gambled with them. Before daylight Cŭnā´waвi took a piece of bark, tied it round his head, stuck it into the fire, and then ran off. The people who owned the fire ran after him, but did not catch him. Then he took some root and said, "Make fire out of this." So he made fire from it, and after a while he threw away the rock he had used to cook on. He cooked seeds in the fire now.

He named all the hills and waters and rocks and bushes, so that people knew what to call them. He was the first to name them.

After a while the people who had come from the sack fought among themselves.

Cō´tsi'pamā´pŏt, the old woman who made the earth, is still living. She made all the tribes speak different languages. She saw what all the people were doing. When Indians died they went to her, and she made new ones. People did not know where the dead went to; we don't know it, but she knows it all.

Cŭnā´waвi had a brother, Tŏвa´ts. He thought that somebody should kill him and somebody killed him. Tŏʙa´ts left a small package. Cŭnā´waʙⁱ untied it, and after a while he could see nothing there. It suddenly became dark. He groped about, found some feathers and threw them up to the sky, then it was daylight and the sun shone. He tried several feathers, and one of them made the Sun. When it was day, he heard his brother crying and started to look for him.

Cŭnā´waʙⁱ made all kinds of sickness by thinking that people should be sick. He called the different mountains and everything else by distinct names.

The Mᵘ´qwits tribe used to live here and moved away a long time ago. After a while the white people came here.

The old woman gave people all kinds of seed to eat. She thought of the seeds and the people went to the place she pointed out and would find the seeds and eat them. "Live on this, boys," she would say; "this is yours to eat."

All the birds, big and small, talked Indian once. Duck was a doctor long ago. When a boy was sick, his relatives sent for Duck and gave him a spoon for fee. Duck said, "I'd better try the spoon for my nose.—This is all right." He put it on his nose and so he has it now on his face.

Cŭnā´waʙⁱ

Cŭnā´waʙⁱ wanted to go and gamble with people against whom he had always lost. His brother Tŏʙa´ts, and others accompanied him. Tŏʙa´ts asked, "How did you lose every time?"—"Before gambling they gave me some mush to eat."—"That was not mush, that food was no good. If they give it to you again, don't eat it but throw it back at them." Cŭnā´waʙⁱ and his followers got to camp. Two old women prepared mush for Cŭnā´waʙⁱ and brought it to him. "Here is some mush for you, Cŭnā´waʙⁱ." He took it and threw it back at them. They prepared another kind of bad food for him, but he threw that at them also.

They now began to gamble. The two old women had two sons who would gamble indoors while their mothers stayed outside. As soon as the boys won a game, they would cut off their opponents' heads and throw them to their mothers. These would then say, "Our boys have won." Cottontail, of Cŭnā´waʙⁱ's party, played against the boys and won. The boys said, "We don't want to lose our lives." But Cottontail said, "No, that's not the way we were to play." He cut off their heads and threw them to the old women. These, without looking, said, "Our boys have won again." When they looked they said, "These are our boys' heads," and began to cry. The people killed them, too, and went home.

After a while Cŭnā´waʙⁱ said, "Let us go and gamble with some other people." They went further this time and got to another camp. Cŭnā´waʙⁱ said, "We are coming here to gamble, let us gamble all night." They made a fire and agreed to gamble all night. They gambled and Cŭnā´waʙⁱ won all the property they had in camp. Then they bet their pine nuts, and he won those. But the pine nuts were in a bag on a high, branchless tree, and Cŭnā´waʙⁱ could not get them down. He said to Mouse, "Mouse, get them." Mouse went up and brought the pine nuts down. Then he and his party went homeward. They were attacked by the people who had lost, but Cŭnā´waʙⁱ carried the pine nuts to the other side of Las Vegas, where there is a big mountain. There he left them on the trees, saying, "Pine nuts belong here." The enemy could not get them back. "We can't do anything, let us go home." So they went home.

Turtle had a spring where mountain sheep came for water. He told one of his boys, "It's raining over there, I think. Go to the top of the hill and look, I want to kill sheep." The boy came back and said, "Yes, it is raining." So Turtle went and killed a sheep. When he was ready to skin it, Cŭnā´waʙⁱ got there. He said, "Let us jump over him; the one who jumps across shall have the hide." Turtle landed on the middle of the body, but Cŭnā´waʙⁱ got across and thus won the hide. He skinned it, then said, "I have nothing to pack it with." Turtle said, "Get some joss weed and make a string of it." So Cŭnā´waʙⁱ went for it. In the meantime Turtle packed the whole sheep and went off. When Cŭnā´waʙⁱ tried to get the weed for his rope, it moved away and kept moving away, thus delaying him. Turtle thus got near his home before Cŭnā´waʙⁱ got the weeds needed. When he found that Turtle had gone with the sheep, he tracked him, but could not catch him for he was inside his house.

Cŭnā´waʙⁱ went home furious. Then he said to his sons, "My boys, do you ever dream of anything bad, any of you?" One of them said, "I sometimes dream of a heavy rain and flood."—"Well, that's it, let us make a hard rain and kill Turtle by flooding his house." It began to rain, and the flood washed away Turtle's wife and children, but Turtle stayed inside and was not carried away. When the rain ceased, Turtle came out. He found the rest of his family and when all had gathered he asked, "Does any of you boys ever have a dream?" One of them answered, "I sometimes dream that it is very hot all over."—"Well, let us make it hot so that the water will boil." Then they made it hot even in the shade. Cŭnā´waʙⁱ said, "It's pretty hot this morning." It was hot even in the shade, and his wife and boys perished from the heat. He went toward the water. "It's always cool there." He ran down and jumped in, but never came out, for it was boiling hot and he died.

Cŭnā´waʙⁱ's Grandson

Cŭnā´waʙⁱ said to himself, "I am going to be a doctor; I am old, but I'll be one anyway. My wife is sometimes ill and I will doctor her." He saw some geese flying and thought they were doctors. "Come down, I'll be with you." They were traveling far away but came down to the ground where he was. They stayed with him. Each gave him one feather. He now looked like a goose. "Fly down a little ways, don't get over it, fly down and wait for us." He flew down but disobeyed, going over. When he came down, he stopped. "He doesn't do it right, let us take our feathers away." Each took his feathers away, then they killed him and took out his brains, departed and left his body there. After a while he got up again and saw his brain in mush form. He ate it. "They are good fellows, they left me some food," he said. Then he felt that he had no brains. "This is too bad." He put a white rock in place of his brain, followed the birds' tracks and overtook them, but they gave him no more feathers. He had to walk on the ground but looked up at the geese and accompanied them for a great distance. The geese were singing about something they were going to eat. They came down to the ground and got to Cǔnā´waʙⁱ, who said, "They are going to fight far down." They sent three or four scouts towards the enemy and Cǔnā´waʙⁱ went with them. "We'll camp down there for tonight. You shall meet us in that place after having located the camp, near Yuma." The scouts left, the rest stayed there. The scouts camped near the Yuma people. In the night they said, "We'll go around and kill them." About daylight they came near. Then they killed all of them. There was one woman who had just given birth to a baby. They killed the mother but Cǔnā´waʙⁱ took the baby. The rest left him alone there.

Later Cǔnā´waʙⁱ returned home by himself. When he came nearer, he made mud teats for himself. The next morning he had milk like a woman and nursed the baby on his way home. It was a great distance. After a while the infant began to grow very fast. Then it began to talk and was soon big enough to walk. They went far. It talked about everything and knew everything. Cǔnā´waʙⁱ said, "We still have a long walk." The baby was now walking with him. When they got home, she was a big girl. He killed a small mountain-sheep to feed her. He now threw away his teats, having no more use for them. This girl was angry at Cǔnā´waʙⁱ. He said to her, "You had better get wood to cook the meat." She went far away, left her basket, and went off without bringing any wood. This young woman had a cane, which she threw away. She traveled far. After a while she met a young man. She did not talk to him but lowered her head. After a while he said, "What's the matter? Why don't you talk? Don't you know me? I am your son. Don't you remember the cane? That is myself, you are my mother." Then she said, "Yes, you are my boy." Then they talked to each other. The boy came down. "You had better go down." She went up the other way and said, "When it rains, you may get wet. If you find a cave, don't sleep inside, stay and sleep outside; don't enter it." The boy went down and his mother went in the opposite direction. It began to rain. He was near a cave and saw nothing inside. "Why doesn't she want me to go inside?" So he went in.

"I see nothing inside." He fell asleep. After a while he woke up, before daylight. "I see nothing to trouble me." He fell asleep again. The sun rose. He woke up. "I don't know what is the matter with me, I feel differently." He opened his eyes. "I feel differently in my heart, I don't know what is the matter." He looked at his hand, it had changed into a mountain-sheep's foot. All over he was transformed into a mountain-sheep with horns. He felt badly about it, there was nothing of the Indian about his body, he was a mountain-sheep. He got up. He had been traveling down to Cŭnā´waʙⁱ's camp, but now he went up the mountains and joined the other sheep. At last he went with them to Cŭnā´waʙⁱ who said, "I saw mountain-sheep here. No, that biggest one is not a sheep, that belongs here." The transformed boy brought them down close to his grandfather Cŭnā´waʙⁱ who killed the sheep. Then the transformed boy went up-hill to bring more game down. For two days he did this and Cŭnā´waʙⁱ killed more game. The boy lured them down three or four times. He said to his grandfather, "I was transformed up there. My mother told me not to enter a cave. I disobeyed and before sunrise I was transformed and went up the mountain. Maternal grandfather, go up, look at the cave, and see why I was changed there."

So Cŭnā´waʙⁱ went there, for his grandchild had a big bundle there. He returned, saying it was too heavy for him to carry it. His grandchild went up to get more sheep. Some boys from another camp wanted to hunt sheep. Two boys saw him and wanted to kill the biggest in the flock. They followed and got close, then they shot the biggest in the herd. The sheep ran down some distance and fell down. Following him the hunter found a man lying dead. He felt badly about it. His companion asked, "What is the matter?"—"I told you it was no sheep but a man." The other said nothing, but felt badly about it.

Cŭnā´waʙⁱ was camping with Tŏʙa´ts, who said to him, "You had better see where he got killed." Cŭnā´waʙⁱ returned. "Let us get someone to dry up all the water so as to punish those who killed him." So the water was all dried up, and when the two hunters looked for some there was none left. They went high up into the air to look for some; they were very dry. They could not see any water anywhere. Cŭnā´waʙⁱ had left just one place with water and they did not see that one.

Tŏʙa´ts was also angry about the boy's death. He sent Cŭnā´waʙⁱ to get another man who should make a net for him. With this he made a snare to catch the two hunters in the air. At last these found the remaining waterhole. Cŭnā´waʙⁱ hid nearby to kill them; he made a mud house for himself by the water. Tŏʙa´ts told him to heat a rock red-hot. "Don't hit them with it till it is red-hot. They watch the water." They did come down to drink but were afraid. Cŭnā´waʙⁱ waited for the rock to get hot. When they were very thirsty, they began to drink, taking a big draught. Cŭnā´waʙⁱ threw the rock, which went through one boy and struck the other without piercing him. This boy went up into the air, but Tŏʙaʹts caught him with his net and killed him too. Thus both were dead now.

The next morning Tŏʙaʹts said, "I want to go where the boy was killed. I'll go over there to see him." So he went. At first he saw nothing, then a little blood. He picked it up but saw nothing else. Then he found some hair and picked it up. He brought it home and restored the boy from his hair.

Salt

Salt used to be far away. He was a man and was traveling through the country. The Indians never used salt then. He looked ugly all over, and the people did not like him. He came to a camp and said, "Let me put my hand in there, then the food will taste well."—"No," said the cook, "I want to eat this, you look too ugly." He went off to another band and said, "Let me put my hand in here, it will taste well."—"No, it is too dirty." He came to Moapa and said the same thing, but people declined his offer. So he went on and got to a camp about thirty-five miles away. There he found a cook and said, "I want to put my hand into the food, then it will taste better." The cook allowed him to do so and he put in his hand. "Now taste it." The Indian tasted it and it was fine. Salt settled right there and stayed forever about ten or twelve miles from St. Thomas.

WASHOE

While located in the geographical Great Basin, the Washoe culture has the least in common with other Great Basin Indian tribes, possibly bearing greater similarity to California tribes to the west. The Washoe language, a distant relative of the Hokan languages scattered around California, is unrelated to the Numic languages of the other Great Basin Indians. Neither the Washoe territory nor its population is large, but evidence suggests that Washoes have resided in their place longer than other Great Basin tribes have in theirs, possibly as long as nine thousand years. Washoe territory straddles present-day Nevada and California, bounded on the west by the Sierra Nevada and on the east by the Pine Nut and Virginia ranges, extending north to Honey Lake and south to Sonora Pass. Kinship-based groups of Washoe established permanent residences near valley streams, close to reliable food sources, especially fish. When seasonal foods became available elsewhere, Washoe groups left their homes for food-gathering camping trips. Every spring, all the Washoe groups came together at Lake Tahoe, Tahoe being a Euro-American variation of the Washoe word for lake, da-ow. There they fished, hunted, and gathered the roots of native plants such as the camas lily, sego lily, and bitterroot. Washoe groups converged again in the Pine Nut Range for annual pine nut harvests in the fall, each household storing up to a ton of nuts for winter. Washoe parties also trekked to the western slopes of the Sierra to collect acorns, another important winter staple. In the autumn, an elected "rabbit boss" organized cooperative rabbit drives in the sagebrush valleys, where the Washoe caught thousands of rabbits for food and rabbit-skin blankets.

Lake Tahoe was a spiritual center of Washoe life, and many stories pertain to the lake and surrounding features. Two parallel sets of brothers recur in these stories, Wolf and his younger brother Coyote, and Long-tailed Weasel and his younger brother Short-tailed Weasel, an impudent character named Damollale, who sometimes appears as a squirrel. The first story in this section, where Coyote is responsible for death, has multiple variants; the one reprinted here was recorded by anthropologist Robert H. Lowie and published in 1939. The other three stories are traditional tales retold by Washoe tribal member Jo Ann Nevers in her 1976 book Wa She Shu: A Washo Tribal History. *(*Washo *and* Washoe *are variant spellings, the latter version becoming more common;* Washo *is used primarily by anthropologists and linguists,* Washoe *in government and legal documents, place names, and as the spelling of the Washoe tribe today.)*

Wolf and Coyote—Origin of Death

Wolf and Coyote were talking to each other. They were brothers. Wolf spoke first. He said, "Now, my brother, what shall we do when these Washo get old? I think I am the head of all kinds of wolf and other animals. I should like to save the Washo when they get old. Now, what do you think of that my brother?" Coyote answered, "Well, you are the head of everything; you can do anything you have a mind to; I listen to you." Wolf said, "I think we'll save the old people; we'll dig a well for the Indians on top of De.oku´lum (Job's Peak). We'll dig as deep as we can. Whenever a Washo gets old and ready to die, he'll go up to the top of the mountain and take a bath in that water and he'll begin to be young again." Coyote said, "Oh, no! I like to see dead people. I can't do anything to kill animals, I'll go hungry if Indian bodies grow young again. Don't say that, my brother, for I eat anything dead that smells rotten. It's the only thing I live on, you know." Wolf said, "That is so; you are right. When Indian people get old, let them die. That's all. You and I, we travel well, so we can get jackrabbits, squirrels, and all animals of that kind. We can catch them faster than anyone else." Coyote answered, "Oh, yes, we don't do it regularly, only sometimes: dead people are the best thing (to feed on)."

—Dave Cheney
Minden, Nevada

Damollale and the Black Widow Spider

The day began early for the two brothers. *Pawetsile* rose early, prepared a quick meal, and roused *Damollale*. He urged his brother to hurry so that they could begin to hunt before the animals were fully awake. *Damollale*, who had difficulty even opening his eyes to greet the new day, told his brother that he wanted to stay in bed a little longer, at least until mid-day. As far as he was concerned, there were no animals around. *Pawetsile* tried to rouse his brother, but eventually gave up the effort. He instructed *Damollale* not to stray too far from the camp, for there were many dangers a young person could encounter. *Damollale* promised not to leave the camp; he told his brother he would clean the campsite and do many other things. Hearing *Damollale's* promises, *Pawetsile* left to hunt.

As soon as *Pawetsile* was out of sight, *Damollale* began to play, straying further and further from the camp. He saw a den that intrigued him and began to explore its entrance. Looking in, he saw a black widow spider patiently weaving her web. The curious squirrel began to pester the spider, asking question after question. When *Damollale* thought she wasn't paying attention, he threw dirt at the web. The spider replied that she was minding her own business and he should mind his. She told him to leave her alone and play in the trees. But *Damollale* did not go away. Finally, when the spider completed her web, she began to explain how the web was made. Listening to the details, *Damollale* ventured deeper into the den. When he had come in far enough, the spider leaped over him, blocking the entrance. As he tried to escape, the black widow pounced on him and bit him. When *Damollale* died from her poison, the spider scraped the coals and ashes away from her fire and buried him in a hole. Then she replaced the rocks and coals so it looked as if nothing had been disturbed.

When *Pawetsile* returned to camp, he called his brother many times, but to no avail. Circling the camp, he picked up *Damollale's* tracks, which led straight to the spider's den. He asked the spider if she had seen his little brother, *Damollale*. She maintained that she had been working on her web all day and had seen no one. When *Pawetsile* told the spider that his brother's tracks came straight to the entrance of her den, she became very angry and shouted at the weasel. *Pawetsile*, who realized he would not get any answers from the black widow, returned to the campsite and began to pray.

He spoke to the Great Creator, who knows all, hears all, and sees all. When the weasel had explained his difficulties, a rainbow extended from the sky. A big voice, which came from all around, told the weasel to get on the rainbow. The moment the weasel climbed on the rainbow, he was brought before the Great Creator. The

Spirit told the weasel that he knew what the black widow had done, and that it was not proper for anyone to lie to another individual. He gave *Pawetsile* a small pouch which contained tobacco and explained its proper use. Just before he sent the weasel back to earth, the Creator gave him the power to restore a life one time. Then he placed *Pawetsile* on the rainbow and carried him back to his campsite.

Pawetsile returned to the spider's den and asked the spider again if she had seen his little brother. The spider shouted that she had not seen anyone and if the weasel did not leave he would suffer the consequences. Then *Pawetsile* took out the tobacco pouch the Great Creator had given him and began to make a smoke. Growing more and more nervous, the spider jumped up into the corner of her den and asked the weasel not to light the smoke. The weasel questioned her once more, but she still maintained that she had not seen his little brother, so *Pawetsile* lighted the tobacco and began to puff on the smoke. Perspiring heavily, the spider jumped from corner to corner. Continuing to smoke, the weasel repeated his question at intervals. The spider answered that she had seen no one. Finally the weasel blocked the entrance to the den and puffed so hard on the tobacco that the room filled with smoke. Eventually, when the temperature got very hot, the spider popped and died.

The weasel, who had been told where his brother was, dug beneath the coals and lifted his little brother from the hole. He carried *Damollale* outside and placed his head toward the east, where the sun rises. Using the power vested in him by the Creator, *Pawetsile* stepped over his brother, saying "*Geahgesha*," which means, "Live again." *Damollale* awoke, rubbing his eyes. The mischievous brother, who had never realized the serious consequences of disobeying his brother, told *Pawetsile* that he had had a good rest, and asked how long he had slept.

Damollale and the Water Baby

Pawetsile had just killed a deer. He told his brother, the mischievous one, to fetch some water from Lake Tahoe while he built a fire. When *Damollale* reached the lake, he saw a young water baby combing her long, beautiful hair. Looking at the water baby sitting on Cave Rock, he thought, "My brother always wanted long, beautiful hair like that." The water baby, who knew what he was thinking, said to him, "If you try to take my hair, the lake will swallow you." Then *Damollale* began to wrestle with the water baby. They rolled around the lake to the place on the south shore where the Little Truckee runs into the lake. There, *Damollale* killed the water baby. That is why the creek is always red.

When *Damollale* killed the water baby, the lake began to boil. As *Damollale* started up the mountain to escape, he pulled a strand of hair from the water baby's scalp. The lake advanced behind him; each time he plucked a hair it rose up and then receded. Finally *Damollale* reached Job's Peak, where his brother was. *Pawetsile* told him to give the water baby's hair back to the lake before the water swallowed them. *Damollale* protested, "But I thought you wanted her hair." Since by this time the water had reached their necks, *Pawetsile* insisted that his brother throw the hair back. Finally, he convinced his younger brother, who did what he was told. Then the lake returned to its original bed, but as it retreated it left water in all the depressions in the area. That is why there are many small lakes in the mountains near Lake Tahoe.

Story of the *Ong*

A long time ago, a monstrous bird called the *Ong* lived in a big nest in the middle of Lake Tahoe. This gigantic man-eating bird picked up unsuspecting Washo. These people, who had not heeded persistent warnings, ventured into open areas where the monster could easily see and capture them. The Washo greatly feared this monster, who was so powerful that the wind from his wings could bend the trees when he flew near shore.

One day the *Ong* snatched a Washo and took him to the huge nest in the middle of the lake. The Washo pretended to be dead, but watched the *Ong* carefully all the time. Luckily, the monster was not very hungry and had another person to eat. As the Washo watched, he noticed that the *Ong* closed his eyes to chew. This curious habit gave the Washo an idea. Each time the monster took a bite and closed his eyes, the Washo threw several arrowheads into his mouth. By nightfall, all these arrowheads had made the beast very sick. As the monster moaned and groaned with pain, a terrible storm raged. By morning the *Ong* was dead, so the Washo pulled a feather from its tail. Using the feather as a boat, he reached shore and returned to his home.

GREAT BASIN RANGINGS

Journals of Exploration

The first writing about the place now called Nevada was made by working men in the line of duty, trespassing on foreign soil. When Mexico gained independence in 1821, Nevada—formerly claimed by Spain—became part of Mexico. In 1848, after the Mexican-American War, Nevada's lands were transferred to the United States, forming in 1850 the western half of the newly created Utah Territory. It split off in 1861 to become the Nevada Territory, achieving statehood in 1864. For a long time Nevada remained "terra incognita," as explorer John C. Frémont dubbed it, or "Great American Desert," as it was sometimes labeled on maps. Although Indians had lived in Nevada for thousands of years and were intimately familiar with its geography, to Euro-Americans, Nevada was as alien and forbidding as another planet might be to us today.

The first whites to enter this unknown region were gun-toting men looking for beaver. By the mid-1820s, fur trading was a lucrative enterprise, and fur companies were competing for control of beaver country. As the more productive areas were trapped out, mountain men pushed into new country, some of them keeping journals of their routes and pelt yields. The first two men to record their impressions of Nevada were Peter Ogden, employed by the British-owned Hudson's Bay Company, and Jedediah Smith, co-owner of its rival, the Rocky Mountain Fur Company of St. Louis, Missouri. Both men entered present-day Nevada in 1826, but their journals were not published until the twentieth century.

Although Ogden had reasonable success in the northern part of the state, most of Nevada was a sore disappointment to beaver trappers, who described the land as "barren," "unpromising," "desolate," and "unhospitable." Nevada's native peoples fare no better in these accounts. Trappers described them as "miserable looking wretches," "poor and dejected," and "like wild animals." Smith speculated that the Indians formed "a connecting link between the animal and intelectual [*sic*] creation and quite in keeping with the country in which they are located." These "savage" Indians saved the trappers' lives on more than one occasion by giving them food and directing them to water sources. Stylistically, trappers' journals are rough, grammatically irregular, but they nonetheless are significant in the literary record as they document Euro-Americans' first impressions of Nevada and its native residents.

Military men were next on the scene, beginning in the early 1840s. They were employed by the U.S. government in the spirit of Manifest Destiny to explore and map the West, paving the way for westward expansion, transcontinental communication, and resource extraction. In our own time, government reports seldom appeal to a mass audience, but in the nineteenth century publications of the U.S. Government Printing Office about the West were eagerly consumed by the public, emboldening some of them to emigrate. Government explorers typically traveled in heavily armed parties (Frémont brought a cannon), a mix of soldier escorts and civilian cartographers and scientists, sometimes guided by a mountain man. While not expected to be literary masterpieces, these reports—based on field notes, amplified and polished later—remain highly readable and occasionally share the author's emotions and reflections as he contemplates the landscapes before him. Less vulnerable than the beaver trappers, government explorers with their military escorts tended to be more favorably impressed with Nevada's Indians, communicating with them through translators and trading goods for fresh food. Government explorers named features (features that already had Indian names), filling in the Nevada map with names such as Pyramid Lake, Humboldt River, Wheeler Peak, Reese River Valley, Walker Lake, Carson River, and Simpson Park Canyon.

The journals and reports collected here, arranged chronologically by year of exploration, form an interesting and historically significant set of travel narratives by men confronting the unknown. By turns afraid, disappointed, repulsed, thirsty, disoriented, desperate, curious, and inflamed by desire, these early chroniclers evoke the wonder and terror of an uncharted land and, in the same stroke, chart it.

JEDEDIAH S. SMITH [1799–1831]

Born in Bainbridge (then Jericho), New York, and reared on stories of the Lewis and Clark expedition, Jedediah Strong Smith determined at a young age to become an explorer. Making his way to St. Louis in 1822, he signed on with General William H. Ashley's fur-trading company (later renamed the Rocky Mountain Fur Company), becoming its co-owner in 1825. Smith was tough and religious, always carrying his Bible and remaining bonded to his Methodist ways. A survivor of multiple Indian attacks, he was killed by Comanches on May 27, 1831, while en route to Santa Fe. Certainly one of the greatest explorers of the early West, Smith was the first American to journey overland to California; the first to cross the Sierra; and the first to traverse the Great Basin. In 1826–27 he led a beaver-trapping expedition into country virtually unknown by Anglo-Americans at the time. From the Great Salt Lake they traveled southwest to cross the present south tip of Nevada and continued across the Mojave Desert to San Bernardino before turning north and crossing the Sierra Nevada at Ebbetts Pass. In the Great Basin, Smith passed south of Walker Lake, crossed Big Smoky and Railroad valleys, and then passed north of Wheeler Peak in the Great Basin National Park before returning to the Great Salt Lake. A manuscript of this expedition was discovered in St. Louis in 1967. George R. Brooks edited these papers in 1977 under the title The Southwest Expedition of Jedediah S. Smith, *which depicts his route across Nevada.*

from *The Southwest Expedition of Jedediah S. Smith*
[Smith near the Virgin River, September 1826]

On the evening of the second day I had advanced a little ahead of the company to look for a place to encamp. near a small Creek coming in from the west and at the distance of 200 yeards I observed an Indian on a hill and made signs for him to come to me but he presented his bow and arrows and in a moment I saw 15 or 20 appear. not considering it safe to remain here I hastened back to the party and then proceeded on to the selected encampment. By this time 20 or 30 were seen skulking around among the Rocks. I therefore had every thing prepared for the worst and advancing alone before the camp by making signs and speaking in a friendly tone of voice I finally succeeded in persuading one of them to come to me. The poor fellow the bravest in the band advanced with evident signs of fear his limbs trembling and his voice faltering. holding out in his hand a hare or rabbit to offer as a token of friendship. I took it and carrassed him and he immediately set down. When the others saw that he was not hurt 10 or 12 of them came bringing in their hands an ear of corn as an emblem of peace—(a pleasing sight to starving men) they set down Began to talk and make signs. As provisions was our greatest present desire we were much pleased to hear that they had corn and pumpkins close at hand. I gave them some small presents among which I found that pieces of Iron were verry acceptable and started some of them off for corn & pumpkins. they soon returned well loaded and indifferent as this may seem to him who never made his pillow of the sand of the plain or him who would consider it a hardship to go without his dinner yet to us weary and hungry in the solitary desert it was a feast a treat that made my party in their sudden hilarity and Glee present a lively contrast to the moody desponding silence of the night before. As both men and horses required rest I thought it advisable to remain here 2 or three days during which time I sent some men down to the river to see what the prospect was ahead and 2 men back on the trail for 2 horses that had been left behind. In the mean time I was trading for Corn in order to have a small stock of provision when I started again. My men from below returned and told me that the river about 10 m below entered the mountain which we could see from camp and that we could not follow the River through the Mt unless we traveled in the water as the Rocks rise from the water perpendicularly on both sides. The river being wide and shallow there is no chance for Beaver but there being a great many willows cut on the banks it appeared that they came here in high water and the Indians by signals told me that there were plenty below. The two men returned on the third day with the tired horses. The weather while here was verry warm the Mercury rising above blood heat. I visited some indian lodges a mile above our camp on the creek for the purpose of seeing how they farm. Their little corn patch is close on the bank of the creek for the convenience of water. The Creek is damed about and the water is conducted in a trunk to a place where it can be spread over the surface. For a hoe they use a piece of wood 3 in Broad and 4 feet Long. The pumpkins and Corn were not quite ripe. Their small Lodges are covered with weeds and cane grass the fires being on the out side. They kept their women and children secreted so that I did not see one while with them. They have some Crockery which is thiner than common Brown earthen colored yellow lead Color and like stone ware. I saw no Iron among them so that any piece that could be converted into a knife or an arrow point was a great acquisition. They have pipes made of fine clouded marble and a kind of Tobacco of their own like that which we in the Mountains call snake Tobacco. Each man smokes for himself not passing the pipe around the circle as is the custom among the Mt Indians. They care verry little about our Tobacco. A good many of these Indians were the scalp of an antelope or Mt sheep with the ears on for a hat. . . . Having somewhat recruited both men and horses I moved on down the River to the foot of the Mt and then turned off to the right the course of the river still s w winding about among the rocks and ravines. I succeeded in gaining the Summit of the Mountain composed of Ridges of Rock and gravel. But although

I was so high that I could see the low ground beyond the mountain yet there was a deep ravine before me which I was obliged to cross the descent was extremely steep and as we had had no water since morning I was obliged to follow down the Ravine to the River & as it was then nearly night encamped without any grass for my horses. I killed an Ibex in good order and one of the men killed another. These relished verry well with men who had been for several days deprived of their accustomed rations of meat. Early the next morning we started down in the bed of the general shallowness of the water. By the meanderings of the stream it was about 12 m through the rocks rising perpendicularly from the waters edge in most places to the heighth of 3 or 400 feet. A good many hot springs but not as hot as some I have seen at the Salt Lake and on the Big horn. Some appearance of Iron ore. At one place I was obliged to unload and swim the horses. Moved about 3 miles after getting through the mountain to the bed of a stream coming in from the west on which there was some good sized cotton wood trees. There is verry little appearance of Indians in this vicinity. The country is not so rough as on the other side of the mountain but extremely barren and the river continues wide and shoal. At this place I saw a new kind of quail some smaller than the atlantic quail. The male has three or four feathers an inch long rising from the top of the head. For four days traveling down the River nothing new or material occured. After passing the Mt the River turns more south keeping nearly parallel with the mountain and at the distance of 5 miles. The grass has been somewhat plentier along the river, and in two or three places a few small cotton wood trees. No game since we left the Mt. On the evening of the fourth day from the Mt I saw an Indian at a distance called to him and after a little hesitation he came to me and understanding by his signals that there was some lodges near by we went on to the mouth of a creek from the sw small but apparently unfailing on the bank of which was several Lodges of Indians like those on corn Creek. They had corn (which was gathered) Pumpkins squashes and some small green Water Melons. I soon purchased some pumpkins and squashes and encamped. As I was weary of traveling in this barren country I of course made many enquiries of the Indians as to the country ahead. They told me there was a large river not far off and of course plenty of Beaver for it is a general characteristic of indians to answer your questions in the manner that they think will please you but without any regard to the truth. There are however some individuals of different tribes in the Mts on whose word you may depend. These Indians are Pa utch but not as wild as those above the Mt. their women and children did not run off. I saw at their Lodges a large cake of rock salt weighting 12 or 15 lbs and on enquiry found that they procured it a cave not far distant. I engaged an indian and sent one of my men to ascertain the truth. The men reported it as true. I saw Ochre among these Indians which was procured from the N E about 30 m. I thought I had some reason to believe these indians in relation to the beaver as they had moccasins made of the skins. It happened that there were two indians here from another tribe apparently for the purpose of trading for salt and ochre. They told me that a days travel below here this river entered another large River coming from the North East and several days journey Below the mouth of this river they resided where there is plenty of beaver and the indians have horses. I saw on these indians some blue yarn and a small piece or two of Iron from which I judged they had some intercourse with the Spanish provinces. I engaged these indians as guides for I might as well go on as undertake to return. Some of my horses had given out and were left and others were so poor as not to be able to carry a load. The prospect ahead was if the indians told me the truth that I might in this moderate Climate trap all winter and also purchase some horses. these considerations induced me to abandon the idea of returning to the mountains until I should have gone somewhat further in exploring the secrets of this thus far unpromising country.

[Smith in Central Nevada, June 1827]

8th   As my horses were much fatigued and the grass was tolerable good I concluded to rest. The general Character and appearance of the country I have passed is extremely Barren. High Rocky hills afford the only relief to the desolate waste for at the feet of these are found water and some vegetation While the intervals between are sand barren Plains.

9th   S S E 12 miles and finding it necessary to change my course to E N E I traveled 12 miles Leaving a high hill on the North and found a little spring in the plain by which I encamped. In the course of the day saw fresh sign of indians.

10th   28 miles E at 10 O Clock found the water and grass in the plain & stopped for the horses to eat. I there found an Indian and 2 squaws who had no opportunity of running away. I endeavored to talk a little with them by signs but found them too stupid or wilful. They had a piece of a Buffalo robe and a Beaver skin which last I bought of them—at 11 O Clock I continued my course E. Our remaining horses had now become so weak that we were general obliged to walk. At 3 O Clock one of them gave out and was left in the plain. Having crossed two Ranges of hills Just after dark I discovered a fire and steered towards it. and found an Indian Squaw and 2 children who were of course much frightened. They appeared to be travelers having with them some water which they divided with us.

I then for the first time saw scorpions prepared to eat. I went a short distance and encamped without water. During the night it rained which of course refreshed the horses.

11th   E 20 miles across a valley. Soon after starting I found a little water in some holes collected from the last rain. I encamped in a range of high hills where I found water. At that time we were on allowance of 4 ounces of dried meat per day and hardly the possibility of killing anything.

12th   25 miles East Crossed over the range of hills on the top of which I found some Aspin and service Bushes. then crossing a valley I found a little water and encamped but without grass. In the course of the day I killed a hare. I mention this for in this country game is so scarce and wild that it is a most hopeless task to kill anything. An Antelope or Black tailed deer may sometimes be seen solitary and wild as the wind.

. . . .

16th   I lay by to rest. for 12 days I have been with my two men on an allowance of   ounces of dried meat per day and the last of it was eat for supper last night. No possibility of killing any game. My horses extremely poor and one so lame in his hind feet as to be unable to travel. He was shod before but his hind feet were worn to the quick. As a last resource for provision I determined to kill this horse and dry some of the best of his meat. Accordingly in the morning I had him killed. It was bad eating but we were hungry enough to eat almost any thing.

17th   E N E 30 miles crossing 2 ranges of Rocky hills and the intervening valleys and encamp in a 3d range of hills without water having seen none since morning.

18th   E 10 miles starting early I crossed the chain on whic[h I] was encamped but seeing no prospect of water Eastwardly I turned N E and after traveling 10 miles I fell in with some indians 14 in number. we were the[n] close to water which happened verry well for one of my men had stoped a short distance back being able to proceed no further. The Indians went with me to the spring and I sent one of them with a little kettle of water to the man that was left behind. After drinking he was sufficiently refreshed to come up. The Indians gave me two small ground squirrels which we found somewhat better than the horse meat. They likewise showed me a kind of water rush which they ate. I tasted of it and found it pleasant. I had three horns for the purpose of carrying water. In these sandy plains we filled them at every opportunity But I seldom drank more than half a pint before they were exhausted for neither of my men could do as well without water as myself.

19th   15 miles N E as a high range of hills lay on the East I was obliged to travel N E to a low gape in the chain and then crossing over encamped on the East side we there found some onions which made the horse meat relish much better.

20th   N E 20 miles along a valley sandy as usual and just at night found water. In this part of the plain almost all the high hills have snow on their tops. But for these snowy Peaks the country would be utterly impassible as they furnish almost the only grass or water of this unhospitable land. They are to this plain like the island of the Ocean. Rising but a short distance from the sandy base the snowy region commences which is an evidence of the great elevation of this plain.

[The]re after encamping some Indians came to me. They appeared verry friendly. These as well as those last mentioned I supposed were somewhat acquainted with whites as I saw among them some Iron arrow points and some Beads. They gave me some squirrels and in return I gave them presents of such little things as I had after which they went to their camp and we our rest.

21st   25 miles North. Early this morning the indians that were at the camp last night returned and with them several others. They seemed to have come out of mere curiosity and as I was ready for starting they accompanied me a short distance. Some of them I presume had never before seen a white man and as they were handling and examining almost every thing I fired off my gun as one of them was fingering about the double triggers. At the sound some fell flat on the ground and some sought safety in flight. The indian who had hold of the gun alone stood still although he appeared at first thunder struck yet on finding that he was not hurt he called out to his companions to return. I endeavored to learn from those indians by signs something in relation to the distance and course to the Salt Lake But from them I could get no satisfaction whatever for instead of answering my signs they would imitate them as nearly as possible. After vexing myself for some time with those children of nature I left them and continued on my way. All the indians I had seen since leaving the Lake had been the same unintelligent kind of beings. Nearly naked having at most a scanty robe formed from the skin of the hare peculiar to this plain which is cut into narrow strips and interwover with a kind of twine or cord made apparently from wild flax or hemp. They form a connecting link between the animal and intelectual creation and quite in keeping with the country in which they are located.

PETER SKENE OGDEN [1790–1854]

A descendant of prominent British loyalists in colonial New Jersey who fled the United States after the Revolutionary War, Peter Skene Ogden was born in Quebec. He received a legal education but declined to follow his father into law. Instead, he joined the British-owned North West Company in 1810 in its thriving fur trade. In 1821, when North West merged with its former rival the Hudson's Bay Company, Ogden was denied employment due to his North West loyalties. However, in 1823, with the support of the governor, Sir George Simpson, Ogden was reemployed. Simpson later described Ogden as "keen" and "sharp," "very Wild and thoughtless and . . . fond of coarse practical jokes, but . . . a very cool calculating fellow who is capable of doing anything to gain his own ends." Between 1824 and 1830, Ogden led six expeditions into the Snake River country, ranging across what are now the states of Washington, Oregon, California, Nevada, Utah, Idaho, and Montana. These large beaver-trapping brigades sometimes consisted of over one hundred people, including women and children. A major objective was to create a "fur desert" between the American territory and the Columbia River to discourage American trappers from encroaching into the rich Pacific Northwest. Ogden's journals—sparse field notes recorded on "small sheets of beaver skin often indifferently cured and tied with a thong; and the writing . . . done with a quill under very uncertain conditions of weather or comfort"—are among the earliest descriptions of the region's flora, fauna, and native people. Ogden is believed to be the first Anglo to enter present-day Nevada, exploring its northernmost reaches in the spring of 1826, a few months before Jedediah Smith traversed its southern tip. The journal entries below, however, were made on Ogden's fifth Snake Country expedition (1828–29), on which he discovered what he called the Unknown River, today's Humboldt River.

from *Journal of the Snake Country Expedition, 1828–29*
Tuesday 4th Nov. [1828]

The three men in advance discovered 4 Indians one of whom directed them to follow the trail to a large river and he advanced some distance with them, then deserted. A cold night. Reached a bend of the river and camped. Indians are most numerous, their subsistence grass roots and wild fowl. They fly in all directions. We are the first whites they have seen and they think we have come with no good intentions.

Wednesday 5th Nov.
Sent out 6 men to ascend the mountains in the highest parts and reconnoitre, followed the Indian back to the sources of the river. Passed the night without supper or sleep unable to come back to camp.

Friday 7 Nov.

At 7 AM we crossed over the river wh. from running thro' a number of lakes I have named River of the Lakes [Quinn River], although not a wide stream certainly a long one.

Saturday 8 Nov.

Crossed a plain and reached a stream similar in size to the River of the Lakes. The banks of the river are lined with huts and the river has natives most numerous.

Sunday 9th Nov.

One of the hunters in advance returned with word this river discharges into a lake no water or grass beyond only hills of sand. Reached the lake and camped. Surprised to find tho' the river discharges in the lake and takes a subterranean passage it appears again taking an easterly course. Had not advanced 4 miles when a large stream appeared lined with willows [Humboldt River]. So glad was I to see it that at the risk of my life, over swamps, hills and rocks, I made all speed to reach it and the first thing I saw was a beaver house well stocked.

Monday 10th Nov.

Long before dawn of day every trap, trapper was in motion. As dawn came the camp was deserted, success to them. I gave orders for all to ascend the river as the season is now advanced we may expect the river to be frozen. Should this river flow to Sandwich Island River I trust we shall have full time to trap it.

Tuesday 11th

To ascertain if possible what course this river takes, I started at daylight and continued down the river till one PM. As far as I could see, it must return from whence it came. Found trappers had arrived at night with 50 beavers.

Thursday 13th

Had a cold night. Half our trappers absent. Those that came in brought 30 beaver. 6 Indians paid us a visit and traded 3 beaver. On asking what they had done with other skins, they pointed to their shoes and examination showed them to be made of beaver. This accounts for beaver being so wild. They told us toward the sources we shall find beaver more numerous.

Monday 17th Nov.

Started with the camp to find grass for the horses. Advanced 6 miles 6 of the trappers came in with 41 beaver. The river is scarce of wood.

Tuesday 18 Nov.

At this season last year, we were surrounded by snow and ice. Weather is mild as September and the rattlesnakes have not yet gone. This gives us hope the winter will be mild.

Wednesday 19th Nov.

At 8 AM we started following the stream advanced 10 miles and encamped as usual on the banks of the river lined with deserted Indian villages, no less than 50 tents. 150 Indians paid us a visit, miserable looking wretches, with scarcely any covering, the greater part without bows and arrows without any defence. They were fat and in good condition. Six trappers came in with 58 beaver, and 10 traded from the Indians make 68. They report the river lined with Indians. On our arrival, they took us for a war party but are now convinced we war only on the beaver. They annoy us and have stolen 2 traps. By following us they make the beaver very wild.

Thursday 20th Nov.

Again 60 beaver to skin and dress. I wish the same cause may often detain us. Recovered one trap. 300 Indians around our camp: very peaceable. This river takes a southern course.

Saturday 22nd

52 beaver; the river still fine; dead water and willows in abundance: gale of wind from the south and appearances of rain.

Sunday 23rd

Rain: three Snake Indians arrived and informed us they were from the Twin Falls of the Snakes and that 2 mos. since 6 Americans had been killed there, by the Snake camp. I am confident it is not Payette's Party, as they were not to go in that direction. Course south, mountains visible in all directions. We need 200 to complete our 1st thousand beaver.

ZENAS LEONARD [1809–1857]

The first battle between Indians and whites in present-day Nevada took place in 1833, when Nevada was the northern frontier of Mexico. A party of about forty beaver trappers under the command of Joseph Walker entered northeastern Nevada near Pilot Peak, the first white party to cross northern Nevada from east to west, traveling along the Humboldt River, then called the Unknown River, Ogden's River, or Mary's River. Unaware that Peter Ogden and his men had taken about one thousand beaver from the Humboldt River area several years earlier, the Walker party found the river destitute and named it the Barren River. Accounts of the "Battle of the Lakes," which took place near the Humboldt Sink, differ considerably in the number of casualties reported and in the character and motives imputed to both sides. Washington Irving's 1837 The Adventures of Captain Bonneville u.s.a. *condemns the Walker party for their unprovoked, vicious massacre of peaceful and merely curious Indians. However, Zenas Leonard, who was a participant in the conflict, explains in his 1839 account that Walker's defensive strike was justified. Leonard was one of nine children born to a farming family near Clearfield, Pennsylvania. Wild and daring, he left home at twenty-one and made his way to St. Louis, where he joined a westbound trapping expedition in 1831, switching to the Walker party in 1833. Leonard returned home in 1835 to the surprise of his family, who had presumed him dead. His book, initially published in installments in a Clearfield newspaper, fell out of sight for the rest of the century, a rare copy rediscovered by a St. Louis librarian in the early 1900s. Subsequently republished several times, Leonard's account is valued for its firsthand observations of the western fur trade in the 1830s.*

from *Adventures of Zenas Leonard, Fur Trader*

The other division, under the command of a Mr. Walker, was ordered to steer through an unknown country, towards the Pacific, and if he did not find beaver, he should return to the Great s. l. in the following summer. Mr. Walker was a man well calculated to undertake a business of this kind. He was well hardened to the hardships of the wilderness—understood the character of the Indians very well—was kind and affable to his men, but at the same time at liberty to command without giving offense—and to explore unknown regions was his chief delight. I was anxious to go to the coast of the Pacific, and for that purpose hired with Mr. Walker as clerk for a certain sum per year.

. . . .

After traveling a few days longer through these barren plains; we came to the mountain described by the Indian as having its peak covered with snow. It presents a most singular appearance—being entirely unconnected with any other chain. It is surrounded on either side by level plains, and rises abruptly to a great height, rugged and hard to ascend. To take a view of the surrounding country from this mountain, the eye meets with nothing but a smooth, sandy, level plain. On the whole, this mountain may be set down as one of the most remarkable phenomena of nature. Its top is covered with the pinone tree, bearing a kind of must, which the natives are very fond of, and which they collect for winter provision. This hill is nearly round, and looks like a hill or mound, such as may be met with in the prairies on the east side of the mountain.

Not far from our encampment we found the source of the river mentioned by the Indian. After we all got tired gazing at this mountain and the adjacent curiosities, we left it and followed down the river, in order to find water and grass for our horses. On this stream we found old signs of beaver, and we supposed that, as game was scarce in this country, the Indians had caught them for provision. The natives which we occasionally met with, still continued to be of the most poor and dejected kind—being entirely naked and very filthy. We came to the hut of one of these Indians who happened to have a considerable quantity of fur collected. At this hut we obtained a large robe composed of beaver skins fastened together, in exchange for two awls and one fish hook. This robe was worth from thirty to forty dollars. We continued traveling down this river, now and then catching a few beaver. But, as we continued to extend our acquaintance with the natives, they began to practice their national failing of stealing. So eager were they to possess themselves of our traps, that we were forced to quit trapping in this vicinity and make for some other quarter. The great annoyance we sustained in this respect greatly displeased some of our men, and they were for taking vengeance before we left the country—but this was not the disposition of Captain Walker. These discontents being out hunting one day, fell in with a few Indians, two or three of whom they killed, and then returned to camp, not daring to let the Captain know it. The next day while hunting, they repeated the same violation—but this time not quite so successful, for the Captain found it out, and immediately took measures for its effectual suppression.

At this place, all the branches of this stream is collected from the mountain into the main channel, which forms quite a large stream; and to which we gave the name of Barren River—a name which we thought would be quite appropriate, as the country, natives and everything belonging to it, justly deserves the name. You may travel for many days on the banks of this river, without finding a stick large enough to make a walking cane. While we were on its margin, we were compelled to do without fire, unless we chanced to come across some drift that had collected together on the beach. As we proceeded down the river we found that the trails of the Indians began to look as if their numbers were increasing, ever since our men had killed some of their brethren. The further we descended the river, the more promising the country began to appear, although it still retained its dry, sandy nature. We had now arrived within view of a cluster of hills or mounds, which presented the appearance, from a distance, of a number of beautiful cities built up together. Here we had the pleasure of seeing timber, which grew in very sparing quantities some places along the river beach.

On the 4th of September we arrived at some lakes, formed by this river, which we supposed to be those mentioned by the Indian chief whom we met at the Great Salt Lake. Here the country is low and swampy, producing an abundance of very fine grass—which was very acceptable to our horses, as it was the first good grazing they had been in for a long time—and here, on the borders of one of these lakes, we encamped, for the purpose of spending the night and letting our horses have their satisfaction. A little before sunset, on taking a view of the surrounding waste with a spy-glass we discovered smoke issuing from the high grass in every direction. This was sufficient to convince us that we were in the midst of a large body of Indians; but as we could see no timber to go to, we concluded that it would be as well to remain in our present situation and defend ourselves as well as we could. We readily guessed that these Indians were in arms to revenge the death of those which our men had killed up the river; and if they could succeed in getting any advantage over us, we had no expectation that they would give us any quarter. Our first care, therefore, was to secure our horses, which we did by fastening them all together, and then hitching them to pickets drove into the ground. This done, we commenced constructing something for our own safety. The lake was immediately in our rear, and piling up all our baggage in front, we had quite a substantial breastwork—which would have been as impregnable to the Indian's arrow as were the cotton bags to the British bullets at New Orleans in 1815. Before we had got everything completed, however, the Indians issued from their hiding places in the grass, to the number, as near as I could guess, of eight or nine hundred, and marched straight toward us, dancing and singing in the greatest glee. When within about 150 yards of us, they all sat down on the ground, and despatched five of their chiefs to our camp to inquire whether their people might come in and smoke with us. This request Captain Walker very prudently refused, as they evidently had no good intentions, but told them that he was willing to meet them halfway between our breastwork, and where their people were then sitting. This appeared to displease them very much, and they went back not the least bit pleased with the reception they had met with.

After the five deputies related the result of their visit to their constituents, a part of them rose up and signed to us (which was the only mode of communicating with them) that they were coming to our camp. At this ten or twelve of our men mounted the breastwork and made signs to them that if they advanced a step further it was at the peril of their lives. They wanted to know in what way we would do it. Our guns were exhibited as the weapons of death. This they seemed to discredit and only laughed at us. They then wanted to see what effect our guns would have on some ducks that were then swimming in the lake, not far from the shore. We then fired at the ducks—thinking by this means to strike terror into the savages and drive them away. The ducks were killed, which astonished the Indians a good deal, though not so much as the noise of the guns—which caused them to fall flat to the ground. After this they put up a beaver skin on a bank for us to shoot at for their gratification—when they left us for the night. This night we stationed a strong guard, but no Indians made their appearance, and were permitted to pass the night in pleasant dreams.

Early in the morning we resumed our journey along the lakes without seeing any signs of the Indians until after sunrise, when we discovered them issuing from the high grass in front, rear, and on either side of us. This created great alarm among our men, at first, as we thought they had surrounded us on purpose, but it appeared that we had only *happened* amongst them, and they were as much frightened as us. From this we turned our course from the border of the lake into the plain. We had not traveled far until the Indians began to move after us—first in small numbers, but presently in large companies. They did not approach near until we had traveled in this way for several hours, when they began to send small parties in advance, who would solicit us most earnestly to stop and smoke with them. After they repeated this several times, we began to understand their motive— which was to detain us in order to let their whole force come up and surround us, or to get into close quarters with us, when their bows and arrows would be as fatal and more effective than our firearms. We now began to be a little stern with them, and gave them to understand that if they continued to trouble us they would do it at their own risk. In this manner we were teased until a party of eighty or one hundred came forward, who appeared more saucy and bold than any others. This greatly excited Captain Walker, who was naturally of a very cool temperament, and he gave orders for the charge, saying that there was nothing equal to a good start in such a case. This was sufficient. A number of our men had never been engaged in any fighting with the Indians, and were anxious to try their skill. When our commander gave his consent to chastise these Indians, and give them an idea of our strength, 32 of us dismounted and prepared ourselves to give a severe blow. We tied our extra horses to some shrubs and left them with the main body of our company, and then selected each a choice steed, mounted and surrounded this party of Indians. We closed in on them and fired, leaving thirty-nine dead on the field—which was nearly the half—the remainder were overwhelmed with dismay—running into the high grass in every direction, howling in the most lamentable manner.

Captain Walker then gave orders to some of the men to take the bows of the fallen Indians and put the wounded out of misery. The severity with which we dealt with these Indians may be revolting to the heart of the philanthropist; but the circumstances of the case altogether atones for the cruelty. It must be borne in mind that we were far removed from the hope of any succor in case we were surrounded, and that the country we were in was swarming with hostile savages, sufficiently numerous to devour us. Our object was to strike a decisive blow. This we did—even to a greater extent than we had intended.

These Indians are totally naked—both male and female—with the exception of a shield of grass, which they wear around their loins. They are generally small and weak, and some of them very hairy. They subsist upon grass-seed, frogs, fish, &c.— Fish, however, are very scarce—their manner of catching which is somewhat novel and singular. They take the leg-bone of a sandhill crane, which is generally about eighteen inches long, this is fastened in the end of a pole—they then, by means of a raft made of rushes, which are very plenty—float along the surface of these lakes and spear the fish. They exhibit great dexterity with this simple structure— sometimes killing a fish with it at a great distance. They also have a kind of hook by which they sometimes are very successful, but it does not afford them as much sport as the spear. This hook is formed of a small bone, ground down on a sand-stone, and a double beard cut in it with a flint—they then have a line made of wild flax. This line is tied nearest the beard end of the hook, by pulling the line the sharp end with the beard, catches, and turns the bone crossways in its mouth.

These lakes are all joined together by means of the river which passes from one to another, until it reaches the largest, which has no outlet. The water in this lake becomes stagnant and very disagreeable—its surface being covered with a green substance, similar to a stagnant frog pond. In warm weather there is a fly, about the size and similar to a grain of wheat, on this lake, in great numbers. When the wind rolls the waters onto the shore, these flies are left on the beach—the female Indians then carefully gather them into baskets made of willow branches, and lay them exposed to the sun until they become perfectly dry, when they are laid away for winter provender. These flies, together with grass seed, and a few rabbits, is their principal food during the winter season.

Their habitations are formed of a round hole dug in the ground, over which sticks are placed, giving it the shape of a potato hole—this is covered with grass and earth—the door at one side and the fire at the other. They cook in a pot made of stiff mud, which they lay upon the fire and burn; but from the sandy nature of the mud, after cooking a few times, it falls to pieces, when they make a new one.

These Indians call themselves Shoshocoes; and the Lakes have been named Battle Lakes.

JOHN C. FRÉMONT [1813–1890]

It is difficult to separate the writing of John C. Frémont from that of his wife, Jessie Benton Frémont, his "secretary and other self," whose hand, as early as 1842, polished his reports and later his memoirs for submission. Daughter of a U.S senator, Jessie gave John the prestige and support he craved, himself an illegitimate son of an itinerant Frenchman and a southern aristocratic mother. Frémont's family background may explain his need to move, to explore. Like many people important to the history of Nevada, Frémont merely passed through; nevertheless, he found the Great Basin to be more than meets the eye, "a sandy plain, barren, without water, and without grass." His engineering and surveying experience with the U.S. Corps of Topographical Engineers gave Frémont the skills to measure, survey, and describe a space "demanding the qualification of great expectations." The excerpt below, from Frémont's expedition to Oregon and Northern California in 1843–44, describes a land of extremes, between wide open basins and snow-capped mountain ranges, desert lakes with barren edges and boiling springs, sweet cottonwood and a myriad of flora and fauna that surprised and delighted the explorer. Frémont's life took the same extremes. He was an explorer, national hero, gold-rush millionaire, Civil War general, presidential candidate, and governor of the Arizona Territory—and he lost everything but a legacy that, thanks to Jessie's hand, endures. Frémont was not the first to explore the western routes he helped establish, but he was the first to survey, describe, and often to name them, "Great Basin" and "Pyramid Lake" being just two among many enduring labels he left in passing. Frémont's reports paved the way for settlement of the American West—"from the ashes of his campfires have sprung cities."

from *A Report of the Exploring Expedition to the Rocky Mountains in the Year 1842, and to Oregon and North California in the Years 1843–44*

The camp was now occupied in making the necessary preparations for our homeward journey, which, though homeward, contemplated a new route, and a great circuit to the south and southeast, and the exploration of the Great Basin between the Rocky mountains and the *Sierra Nevada.* . . . This was our projected line of return—a great part of it absolutely new to geographical, botanical, and geological science—and the subject of reports in relation to lakes, rivers, deserts, and savages hardly above the condition of mere wild animals, which inflamed desire to know what this *terra incognita* really contained. It was a serious enterprise, at the commencement of winter, to undertake the traverse of such a region, and with a party consisting only of twenty-five persons, and they of many nations—American, French, German, Canadian, Indian, and colored—and most of them young, several being under twenty-one years of age. All knew that a strange country was to be explored, and dangers and hardships to be encountered; but no one blenched at the prospect. On the contrary, courage and confidence animated the whole party. Cheerfulness, readiness, subordination, prompt obedience, characterized all; nor did any extremity of peril and privation, to which we were afterwards exposed, ever belie, or derogate from, the fine spirit of this brave and generous commencement.

. . . .

January 3.—A fog, so dense that we could not see a hundred yards, covered the country, and the men that were sent out after the horses were bewildered and lost; and we were consequently detained at camp until late in the day. Our situation had now become a serious one. We had reached and run over the position where, according to the best maps in my possession, we should have found Mary's lake, or river. We were evidently on the verge of the desert which had been reported to us; and the appearance of the country was so forbidding, that I was afraid to enter it, and determined to bear away to the southward, keeping close along the mountains, in the full expectation of reaching the Buenaventura river. This morning I put every man in the camp on foot—myself, of course, among the rest—and in this manner lightened by distribution the loads of the animals. We travelled seven or eight miles along the ridge bordering the valley, and encamped where there were a few bunches of grass on the bed of a hill torrent, without water. There were some large artemisias; but the principal plants are chenopodiaceous shrubs. The rock composing the mountains is here changed suddenly into white granite [Granite Range]. The fog showed the tops of the hills at sunset, and stars enough for observations in the early evening, and then closed over us as before. Latitude by observation, 40° 48′ 15″.

. . . .

January 5.—Same dense fog continued, and one of the mules died in camp this morning. I have had occasion to remark, on such occasions as these, that animals which are about to die leave the band, and coming into the camp, lie down about the fires. We moved to a place where there was a little better grass, about two miles distant. Taplin, one of our best men, who had gone out on a scouting excursion, ascended a mountain nearby, and to his great surprise emerged into a region of bright sunshine, in which the upper parts of the mountain were glowing, while below all was obscured in the darkest fog.

January 6.—The fog continued the same, and, with Mr. Preuss and Carson, I ascended the mountain, to sketch the leading features of the country, as some indication of our future route, while Mr. Fitzpatrick explored the country below. In a very short distance we had ascended above the mist, but the view obtained was not very gratifying. The fog had partially cleared off from below when we reached the summit; and in the southwest corner of a basin communicating with that in which we had encamped, we saw a lofty column of smoke, 16 miles distant, indicating the presence of hot springs. There, also, appeared to be the outlet of those draining channels of the country; and, as such places afforded always more or less grass, I determined to steer in that direction. The ridge we had ascended appeared to be composed of fragments of white granite. We saw here traces of sheep and antelope.

Entering the neighboring valley, and crossing the bed of another lake, after a hard day's travel over ground of yielding mud and sand, we reached the springs, where we found an abundance of grass, which, though only tolerably good, made this place, with reference to the past, a refreshing and agreeable spot.

This is the most extraordinary locality of hot springs we had met during the journey. The basin of the largest one has a circumference of several hundred feet; but there is at one extremity a circular space of about fifteen feet in diameter, entirely occupied by the boiling water. It boils up at irregular intervals, and with much noise. The water is clear, and the spring deep; a pole about sixteen feet long was easily immersed in the centre, but we had no means of forming a good idea of the depth. It was surrounded on the margin with a border of *green* grass, and near the shore the temperature of the water was 206°. We had no means of ascertaining that of the center, where the heat was greatest; but, by dispersing the water with a pole, the temperature at the margin was increased to 208°, and in the centre it was doubtless higher. By driving the pole towards the bottom, the water was made to boil up with increased force and noise. There are several other interesting places, where water and smoke or gas escape, but they would require a long description. The water is impregnated with common salt, but not so much as to render it unfit for general cooking; and a mixture of snow made it pleasant to drink [the hot springs at Gerlach, Nev.].

. . . .

Our situation now required caution. Including those which gave out from the injured condition of their feet, and those stolen by Indians, we had lost, since leaving the Dalles of the Columbia, fifteen animals; and of these, nine had been left in the last few days. I therefore determined, until we reach a country of water and vegetation, to feel our way ahead, by having the line of route explored some fifteen or twenty miles in advance, and only to leave a present encampment when the succeeding one was known.

Taking with me Godey and Carson, I made to-day a thorough exploration of the neighboring valleys, and found in a ravine in the bordering mountains a good camping place, where was water in springs, and a sufficient quantity of grass for a night. Overshading the springs were some trees of the sweet cottonwood, which, after a long interval of absence, we saw again with pleasure, regarding them as harbingers of a better country. To us, they were eloquent of green prairies and buffalo. We found here a broad and plainly marked trail, on which there were tracks of horses, and we appeared to have regained one of the thoroughfares which pass by the watering places of the country. On the western mountains [Lake Mountains] of the valley, with which this of the boiling spring communicates, we remarked scattered cedars—probably an indication that we were on the borders of the timbered region extending to the Pacific. We reached the camp at sunset after a day's ride of about forty miles. The horses we rode were in good order, being of some that were kept for emergencies, and rarely used.

Mr. Preuss had ascended one of the mountains, and occupied the day in sketching the country; and Mr. Fitzpatrick had found, a few miles distant, a hollow of excellent grass and pure water, to which the animals were driven, as I remained another day to give them an opportunity to recruit their strength. Indians appear to be everywhere prowling about like wild animals, and there is a fresh trail across the snow in the valley near.

Latitude of the boiling springs, 40° 39' 46".

On the 9th we crossed over to the cottonwood camp. Among the shrubs on the hills were a few bushes of *ephedra occidentalis,* which afterwards occurred frequently along our road, and, as usual, the lowlands were occupied with artemisia. While the party proceeded to this place, Carson and myself reconnoitered the road in advance, and found another good encampment for the following day.

January 10.—We continued our reconnaissance ahead, pursuing a south direction in the basin along the ridge; the camp following slowly after. On a large trail there is never any doubt of finding suitable places for encampments. We reached the end of the basin, where we found, in a hollow of the mountain which enclosed it, an abundance of good bunch grass. Leaving a signal for the party to encamp, we continued our way up the hollow, intending to see what lay beyond the mountain. The hollow was several miles long, forming a good pass [Fremont Pass], the snow deepening to about a foot as we neared the summit. Beyond, a defile between the mountains descended rapidly about two thousand feet; and, filling up all the lower space, was a sheet of green water, some twenty miles broad. It broke upon our eyes like the ocean. The neighboring peaks rose high above us, and we ascended one of them to obtain a better view. The waves were curling in the breeze, and their dark-green color showed it to be a body of deep water. For a long time we sat enjoying the view, for we had become fatigued with mountains, and the free expanse of moving waves was very grateful. It was set like a gem in the mountains, which, from our position, seemed to enclose it almost entirely. At the western end it communicated with the line of basins we had left a few days since; and on the opposite side it swept a ridge of snowy mountains, the foot of the great Sierra. Its position at first inclined us to believe it Mary's lake, but the rugged mountains were so entirely discordant with descriptions of its low rushy shores and open country, that we concluded it some unknown body of water; which it afterwards proved to be.

On our road down, the next day, we saw herds of mountain sheep, and encamped on a little stream at the mouth of the defile, about a mile from the margin of the water, to which we hurried down immediately. The water is so slightly salt, that, at first, we thought it fresh, and would be pleasant to drink when no other could be had. The shore was rocky—a handsome beach, which reminded us of the sea. On some large *granite* boulders that were scattered about the shore, I remarked a coating of a calcareous substance, in some places a few inches and in others a foot in thickness. Near our camp, the hills, which were of primitive rock, were also covered with this substance, which was in too great quantity on the mountains along the shore of the lake to have been deposited by water, and has the appearance of having been spread over the rocks in mass.

Where we had halted, appeared to be a favorite camping place for Indians.

January 13.—We followed again a broad Indian trail along the shore of the lake to the southward. For a short space we had room enough in the bottom; but, after travelling a short distance, the water swept the foot of precipitous mountains, the peaks of which are about 3,000 feet above the lake. The trail wound along the base of these precipices, against which the water dashed below, by a way nearly impracticable for the howitzer. During a greater part of the morning the lake was nearly hid by a snowstorm, and the waves broken on the narrow beach in a long line of foaming surf, five or six feet high. The day was unpleasantly cold, the wind driving the snow sharp against our faces; and, having advanced only about 12 miles, we encamped in a bottom formed by a ravine, covered with good grass, which was fresh and green.

We did not get the howitzer into camp, but were obliged to leave it on the rocks until morning. We saw several flocks of sheep, but did not succeed in killing any. Ducks were riding on the waves, and several large fish were seen. The mountain sides were crusted with the calcareous cement previously mentioned. There were chenopodiaceous and other shrubs along the beach; and, at the foot of the rocks, an abundance of *ephedra occidentalis,* whose dark-green color makes them evergreens among the shrubby growth of the lake. Towards evening the snow began to fall heavily, and the country had a wintry appearance.

The next morning the snow was rapidly melting under a warm sun. Part of the morning was occupied in bringing up the gun; and, making only nine miles, we encamped on the shore, opposite a very remarkable rock in the lake, which had attracted our attention for many miles. It rose, according to our estimate, 600 feet above the water; and, from the point we viewed it, presented a pretty exact outline of the great pyramid of Cheops. . . . Like other rocks along the shore, it seemed to be incrusted with calcareous cement. This striking feature suggested a name for the lake; and I called it Pyramid lake; and though it may be deemed by some a fanciful resemblance, I can undertake to say that the future traveller will find a much more striking resemblance between this rock and the pyramids of Egypt, than there is between them and the object from which they take their name.

The elevation of this lake above the sea is 4,890 feet, being nearly 700 feet higher than the Great Salt lake, from which it lies nearly west, and distant about eight degrees of longitude. The position and elevation of this lake make it an object of geographical interest. It is the nearest lake to the western rim, as the Great Salt lake is to the eastern rim, of the Great Basin which lies between the base of the Rocky mountains and the Sierra Nevada; and the extent and character of which, its whole circumference and contents, it is so desirable to know.

The last of the cattle which had been driven from the Dalles was killed here for food, and was still in good condition.

January 15.—A few poor-looking Indians made their appearance this morning, and we succeeded in getting one into the camp. He was naked, with the exception of a tunic of hare skins. He told us that there was a river at the end of the lake, but that he lived in the rocks nearby. From the few words our people could understand, he spoke a dialect of the Snake language; but we were not able to understand enough to know whether the river ran in or out, or what was its course; consequently, there still remained a chance that this might be Mary's lake.

Groves of large cottonwood, which we could see at the mouth of the river, indicated that it was a stream of considerable size; and, at all events, we had the pleasure to know that now we were in a country where human beings could live. Accompanied by the Indian, we resumed our road, passing on the way several caves in the rock where there were baskets and seeds; but the people had disappeared. We saw also horse tracks along the shore.

Early in the afternoon, when we were approaching the groves at the mouth of

the river, three or four Indians met us on the trail. We had an explanatory conversation in signs, and then moved on together towards the village, which the chief
said was encamped on the bottom.

Reaching the groves, we found the *inlet* of a large fresh-water stream, and all
at once were satisfied that it was neither Mary's river nor the waters of the Sacramento, but that we had discovered a large interior lake, which the Indians informed
us had no outlet. It is about 35 miles long; and, by the mark of the water line along
the shores, the spring level is about 12 feet above its present waters. The chief commenced speaking in a loud voice as we approached; and parties of Indians armed
with bows and arrows issued from the thickets. We selected a strong place for our
encampment—a grassy bottom, nearly enclosed by the river, and furnished with
abundant firewood. The village, a collection of straw huts, was a few hundred yards
higher up. An Indian brought in a large fish to trade, which we had the inexpress-
ible satisfaction to find was a salmon trout; we gathered round him eagerly. The
Indians were amused with our delight, and immediately brought in numbers; so
that the camp was soon stocked. Their flavor was excellent—superior, in fact, to
that of any fish I have ever known. They were of extraordinary size—about as large
as the Columbia river salmon—generally from two to four feet in length. From
the information of Mr. Walker, who passed among some lakes lying more to the
eastward, this fish is common to the streams of the inland lakes. He subsequently
informed me that he had obtained them weighing six pounds when cleaned and
the head taken off; which corresponds very well with the size of those obtained at
this place. They doubtless formed the subsistence of these people, who hold the
fishery in exclusive possession.

I remarked that one of them gave a fish to the Indian we had first seen, which he
carried off to his family. To them it was probably a feast; being of the Digger tribe,
and having no share in the fishery, living generally on seeds and roots. Although
this was a time of the year when the fish have not yet become fat, they were excellent, and we could only imagine what they are at the proper season. These Indians
were very fat, and appeared to live an easy and happy life. They crowded into the
camp more than was consistent with our safety, retaining always their arms; and,
as they made some unsatisfactory demonstrations, they were given to understand
that they would not be permitted to come armed into the camp; and strong guards
were kept with the horses. Strict vigilance was maintained among the people, and
one-third at a time were kept on guard during the night. There is no reason to
doubt that these dispositions, uniformly preserved, conducted our party securely
through Indians famed for treachery.

In the meantime, such a salmon-trout feast as is seldom seen was going on in
our camp; and every variety of manner in which fish could be prepared—boiled,

fried, and roasted in the ashes—was put into requisition; and every few minutes an Indian would be seen running off to spear a fresh one. Whether these Indians had seen whites before, we could not be certain; but they were evidently in communication with others who had, as one of them had some brass buttons, and we noticed several other articles of civilized manufacture. We could obtain from them but little information respecting the country. They made on the ground a drawing of the river, which they represented as issuing from another lake in the mountains three or four days distant, in a direction a little west of south; beyond which, they drew a mountain; and further still, two rivers; on one of which they told us that people like ourselves travelled. Whether they alluded to the settlements on the Sacramento, or to a party from the United States which had crossed the Sierra about three degrees to the southward, a few years since, I am unable to determine.

I tried unsuccessfully to prevail on some of them to guide us for a few days on the road, but they only looked at each other and laughed.

JOSEPH C. IVES [1828–1868]

In 1857, with a Mormon rebellion brewing in Utah against the United States, the U.S. War Department was keen to scout routes and possible supply lines into the Great Basin should troops need to be deployed there. First Lieutenant Joseph Christmas Ives was chosen to lead an expedition from the Gulf of California up the Colorado River to determine its feasibility for steamboat travel. Born in New York on Christmas Day, Ives graduated from Yale and West Point and in 1853 had traveled the Southwest, working for the Pacific Railroad Survey. For the 1857–58 Colorado River expedition, Ives, who later talked of the trip as "the event of his life," assembled exceptional talent in geology (John Strong Newberry), topography (F. W. Egloffstein), and art (Heinrich Baldwin Möllhausen). His illustrated Report upon the Colorado River of the West (1861) stands as a classic of exploration literature, conveying vivid descriptions of landscape and camp life, interesting encounters with Indians, hair-raising adventures, and moments of pure sublimity. The party's steamboat struck a rock at "the mighty defile" of Black Canyon (below today's Hoover Dam), which Ives deemed the northernmost limit of navigability. Nevertheless, with a smaller crew, he pressed on in a skiff, becoming the first white party to visit the floor of the Grand Canyon. Returning to Washington, DC, Ives was the engineer and architect for the Washington Monument. During the Civil War he declined an offer to be captain in the Union army, instead serving the Confederacy, ultimately as aide-de-camp to President Jefferson Davis. Ives may have sided with the South due to his marriage into a

prominent southern family, his admiration for Robert E. Lee, who had been his commander at
West Point, or his friendship with Davis, whom he had known in Washington, DC. Regardless
of his reasons, historians speculate that Ives's southern sympathies and early death have led to
a regrettable oblivion for this important explorer and talented writer.

from Report upon the Colorado River of the West

As we steamed away from the Mojave villages we passed a conspicuous conical peak, a few miles east of the river, which stands almost upon the 35th parallel, opposite the initial point of the California boundary. Cairook soon after bid us goodbye, and returned home. Ireteba is to remain; and unwilling to be entirely bereft of the society of his tribe, has brought along a lad of sixteen, by the name of Nah-vah-roo-pa, to keep him company. Since the meeting with Cairook, our relations with the Mojaves have been of the most friendly description. They have, at every stopping place, brought provisions to trade, and of beans and corn we have now an adequate supply. Our original rations will be exhausted in a few days, and I have made every exertion to procure some wheat, in order to vary, as much as possible, the fare, but of this they have a limited quantity. The little flour they have brought is mixed with corn meal. It makes an excellent bread.

The zoological collections have been largely added to. Fish, squirrels, rabbits, rats, mice, lizards, snakes, &c., &c., have been brought in—many of them alive.

The behavior of the Indians has been orderly, and every evening, exactly at sunset, they have retired in a body from camp. Mariano and Capitan are delighted with the pacific relations that have been established, and no longer manifest any impatience to return, though, a few days ago, they were becoming importunate upon the subject. Capitan is a great favorite with the Mojaves, particularly with the young ladies. For several nights he has been absent at entertainments given in his honor, and, if what Ireteba says is true, has been taking advantage of his absence from Mrs. Capitan to be altogether too much of a gallant.

There has been a great deal to interest us among the people of this valley, and I regret that we have had to pass so hurriedly, and that we have been unable to learn more in regard to their habits and customs. Very few parties of whites have visited them, and none have remained longer than a few days. They are, therefore, in their native state, as they have existed for centuries. Of their religion or superstitions, I have not been able to learn anything. Government, they have so little of, that there cannot be much to learn. They are not at all communicative concerning their institutions. The marriage tie seems to be respected in more than an ordinary degree among Indians. I think that few, if any, have more than one wife.

Their minds are active and intelligent, but I have been surprised to find how little idea of the superiority of the whites they have derived from seeing the appliances of civilization that surround those whom they have met.

Fire-arms, and the Explorer's steam-whistle, are the only objects that appear to excite their envy. In most respects they think us their inferiors. I had a large crowd about me one day, and exhibited several things that I supposed would interest them, among others a mariner's compass. They soon learned its use, and thought we must be very stupid to be obliged to have recourse to artificial aid in order to find our way. Some daguerreotypes were shown to them, but these they disliked, and were rather afraid of. I heard one or two muttering, in their own language, that they were "very bad." There being a few musicians and instruments in the party, the effect of harmony was tried, but they disapproved of the entertainment, as of everything else, and when the sounds died away, appointed two or three of their own musicians to show ours how the thing ought to be done. These artists performed a kind of chant, in a discordant, monotonous tone, and after making some of the most unearthly noises that I ever listened to, regarded us with an air of satisfied triumph. I tried, by showing them the boundaries upon a map, to make them comprehend the extent of our nation, as compared with their own, and to explain the relative numbers of the inhabitants. The statements were received simply as a piece of absurd gasconade, and had the same effect as the visits of some of the chiefs of the northwestern Indians to the Atlantic cities, which have resulted in destroying the influence of the unfortunate ambassadors, by stamping them forever, in the estimation of their own tribes, as egregious liars.

. . . .

It is somewhat remarkable that these Indians should thrive so well upon the diet to which they are compelled to adhere. There is no game in the valley. The fish are scarce and of very inferior quality. They subsist almost exclusively upon beans and corn, with occasional watermelons and pumpkins, and are probably as fine a race, physically, as there is in existence.

Before leaving Washington, the late Secretary of War, Mr. Davis, proposed to me to carry out varieties of seeds for distribution to the Mojave tribe, and in accordance with this humane suggestion I provided an assortment of vegetable and fruit seeds, and have given them to the chiefs and some of the leading men, who have promised to try this season the experiment of planting them.

The annual overflow of the river enables them to raise, with little labor, an abundant supply of provisions for the year, which they improvidently consume, allowing the future to take care of itself. The failure of a crop is, therefore, an irremediable calamity. During one season, a few years since, the Colorado did not overflow its banks; there were consequently no crops and great numbers of the Mojaves perished from starvation. It is quite possible that such visitations are of periodical occurrence, and are among the means adopted by nature to prevent the population of the valley, as there is no outlet for it nor room for its expansion, from increasing beyond the capacity of the country to sustain it. There is no question but that for several centuries, since the first visits of the early Spanish explorers, there has been little or no increase in the number of inhabitants. This number is apt to be overrated. I have discovered that the crowds seen collected at the different points passed during our progress up the river have been composed, to a considerable extent, of the same set of individuals, and suspect that the chiefs in their first formal visits have enhanced their apparent state and importance by borrowing recruits from their neighbors.

A system of irrigation and an improved method of agriculture would make the valley far more productive, but it is not certain that it could ever be a profitable place for white settlements. The shifting of the river bed, which, to the Indians who have a certain community of property, is a matter of little importance, would occasion serious embarrassment to settlers who had established permanent locations and improvements. The rapidity and extent of the changes in the position of the Colorado can scarcely be imagined by one who has not witnessed them.

. . . .

Camp 53, Round island, March 1.—The Cottonwood valley was found to be only five or six miles in length and completely hemmed in by wild-looking mountains. The belt of bottom land is narrow, and dotted with graceful clusters of stately cottonwood in full and brilliant leaf. The river flows sometimes through green meadows, bordered with purple and gold rushes, and then between high banks, where rich masses of foliage overhang the stream, and afford a cool and inviting shade. From the edges of this garden-like precinct sterile slopes extend to the bases of the surrounding mountain chains. A few isolated black hills break the monotony of the ascent. There is no vegetation; the barren surfaces reach to the very summits of the lofty ranges and impart to the grandeur of the scene an air of painful desolation.

We have now entered a region that has never, as far as any records show, been visited by whites, and are approaching a locality where it is supposed that the famous "Big Cañon" of the Colorado commences; every point of the view is scanned with eager interest. We can distinctly see to the north the steep wall of one side of the gorge where the Colorado breaks through the Black mountains. Whether this is the "Big Cañon" or not it is certainly of far grander proportions than any which we have thus far traversed.

At the head of the Cottonwood valley we threaded a cañon formed by the passage of the river through a spur that connects the Black and Dead mountain ranges. It was only two or three miles in extent, and the sides were of moderate height, but the gorgeous contrast and intensity of color exhibited upon the rocks exceeded in beauty anything that had been witnessed of a similar character. Various and vivid tints of blue, brown, white, purple, and crimson, were blended with exquisite shading upon the gateways and inner walls, producing effects so novel and surprising as to make the cañon, in some respects, the most picturesque and striking of any of these wonderful mountain passes.

. . . .

Camp 57, mouth of Black cañon, March 8.—The twenty miles of distance between Round island and the present camp required five days to accomplish. A dozen or more rapids, of all descriptions, had to be passed; some were violent and deep, others shallow. At a few the bed of the stream was sandy; but generally it was composed of gravel and pebbles. Below the crest of one rapid the current forked, forming two eddies. Several attempts were made to ascend; but the bow was not pointed exactly towards the centre of the fork, and, being thrown off by the eddy, the boat would go down stream, whirling around like a teetotum. After four or five unsuccessful trials, Captain Robinson struck the right point, and we got through without further trouble. The worst places encountered have been where the banks were low and destitute of vegetation, and the rocky bed of the river afforded no holding ground nearby for an anchor. The lines have become almost worn out by hard service; the skiff is badly battered, and scarcely able to float, and all the oars are broken. The last seventy miles will, perhaps, be the best part of the Colorado to navigate when the water is not at so exceedingly low a stage. The rapids will be less violent, and the bottom being gravelly no new bars will be formed as the river rises.

Between Mount Davis and the Black mountains the river flows between gravel bluffs and the foot-hills of the latter chain. The view in all directions was intercepted, and before we were conscious of its neighborhood a sudden turn around the base of a conical peak disclosed the southern portal of the Black cañon directly in front. The Black mountains were piled overhead in grand confusion, and through a narrow gateway flanked by walls many hundreds of feet in height, rising perpendicularly out of the water, the Colorado emerged from the bowels of the range.

A rapid, a hundred yards below the mouth of the cañon, created a short detention; and a strong head of steam was put on to make the ascent. After passing the crest the current became slack, the soundings were unusually favorable, and we were shooting swiftly past the entrance, eagerly gazing into the mysterious depths beyond, when the Explorer, with a stunning crash, brought up abruptly and instantaneously against a sunken rock. For a second the impression was that the cañon had fallen in. The concussion was so violent that the men near the bow were thrown overboard; the doctor, Mr. Mollhausen, and myself, having been seated in front of the upper deck, were precipitated head foremost into the bottom of the boat; the fireman, who was pitching a log into the fire, went half-way in with it; the boiler was thrown out of place; the steam pipe doubled up; the wheel-house torn away; and it was expected that the boat would fill and sink instantly by all, but Mr. Carroll, who was looking for an explosion from the injured steam pipes. Finding, after a few moments had passed, that she still floated, Captain Robinson had a line taken into the skiff, and the steamer was towed alongside of a gravelly spit a little below; it was then ascertained that the stem of the boat, where the iron flanges of the two bow sections were joined, had struck fair upon the rock, and that, although the flanges were torn away, no hold had been made, and the hull was uninjured. The other damages were such as a day or two of labor could repair.

After making these unexpected and welcome discoveries, the captain and myself went out in the skiff and examined the rock. It stands in the centre of the channel; has steep sides and a conical shape. The summit, which comes almost to a point, is about four inches below the surface of the water; and if the boat had struck half an inch to one side or the other of the flanges, the sheet of iron that forms the bow would have been torn open as though it had been a strip of pasteboard.

Nearly three days have elapsed since the accident, and everything is restored to its former condition. I have thought it would be imprudent, after this experience of sunken rocks, to attempt the passage of the cañon without making a preliminary reconnaissance in the skiff. A second escape of the boat, in the event of a similar encounter with a rock, would be too much to hope for; and should she be sunk in the cañon, and there be nothing to swim to but perpendicular walls five hundred or a thousand feet high, the individuals on board would be likely to share the fate of the steamer. The carpenter has been working at the skiff, to put it in a more serviceable condition, and two or three oars have been mended; to-morrow the captain, the mate, and myself, are going to make an attempt to ascend the cañon.

The arrival of the pack-train is looked forward to with much eagerness. Rockets were sent up this evening from the summit of the cliff above camp, and the southern horizon was watched for the appearance of similar signals in that direction, but without result. For two or three weeks we have been subsisting upon the corn and beans obtained from the Indians; the corn is ground in coffee-mills, and makes a tolerable bread, upon which and boiled beans, washed down with water from the river, we breakfast, dine, and sup. This diet agrees wonderfully with the Mojaves;

but either our stomachs are not sufficiently trained to it, or it is not wholesome fare for whites, for some of the men suffer a good deal. The labor for the past two or three weeks has been excessive, involving the necessity of standing, sometimes for hours, waist-deep in the chilling water; and strong food has been particularly craved. The want of coffee is generally found, on such occasions, to be the severest privation, even more so than that of meat. But the greatest trouble our party has had to put up with has been the absence of salt. The bag containing the whole supply was lost or stolen a fortnight ago. No one can imagine, who has not tried the experiment, how tasteless and disagreeable food may become when prepared without this common but indispensable ingredient. A well-salted dog or mule soup would be received with delight in exchange for the insipid dishes of beans and corn which we are compelled daily to swallow.

. . . .

The mountains west of the river are rich in mineral curiosities. Along the bottoms of the ravines are found crystals of quartz, in curiously grouped clusters, and great numbers of opals. Some of the latter are of considerable size, and promise to prove, when polished, valuable gems.

JAMES H. SIMPSON [1813–1883]

Known for his conservative judgment and scrupulous attention to his duties, in ten years of exploration James Hervey Simpson marched over more western country in the 1850s than any other of the army's topographers. Captain Simpson's Report of Explorations across the Great Basin of the Territory of Utah in 1859 *details his observations while surveying a route that approximates present-day U.S. Highway 50. On May 2, 1859, Simpson led a company of sixty-four men due west out of Camp Floyd, Utah, and across present-day Nevada to Genoa. With the party were a geologist, a taxidermist, a meteorologist, and an artist, and when Simpson's report was published, it included a complete survey of the botany, zoology, and meteorology of the region. Although the Civil War delayed actual publication of the report until 1876, its impact was immediate. Simpson's newly explored route cut some two hundred miles from the existing Humboldt River route, a difference of several days' travel. The trail soon became the Pony Express route, the telegraph route, and an emigrant route. While Simpson offers a formal description of the route, he does so with a personable writing style. He is notable for his careful and sympathetic description of Indians and his understanding that a "great many of the difficulties our country has had with the Indians . . . have grown out of the bad treatment they have received at the hands of insolent and cowardly men."* In an age when some government explorers took strictly scientific inventory of the lands they'd been commissioned to explore, Simpson sometimes waxed philosophical, pausing halfway up a mountain for reflection: "these distant views have, at least to my mind a decidedly moral and religious effect . . . accustoming the mind to large conceptions, and thus giving it power and capacity."

from *Report of Explorations across the Great Basin of the Territory of Utah in 1859*

The first thing which will strike one, on looking at the map, will be the *great number of mountain ranges* which the routes cross in the Great Basin; and this will appear to him the more remarkable, as the idea has been generally entertained, since the explorations of Frémont in 1843 and 1844 (though, as before remarked, he corrected the error in his succeeding expedition), that this Great Basin was a *flat country, scattered over with a system of small lakes and rivers,* and destitute of mountains. The fact, on the contrary, is that it is the most mountainous region, considering its extent, we have probably within the limits of our domain; and so far from being scattered over with a system of small lakes and rivers, which seem to imply a considerable number of this kind of water area, it has but a limited number of lakes, and they almost entirely confined to the bases of the great Sierra which bound the Basin.

. . . .

May 18, *Camp No.* 15, *Ruby Valley.*—Altitude, 5,953 feet. The mules ran against the cords of the barometer-tent early this morning and prostrated it, carrying with it the two barometers, which were suspended from the tripod. Fortunately, only one was affected by the accident, a little air getting into the tube, which can be easily remedied.

. . . .

Several Sho-sho-nees joined us on our route. One of them amused the party very much by his awkward attempts to mount a mule, and, when he got on, his rabbit-skin dress frightened the animal so much as to cause him to run off with his nondescript load, much to the merriment of the men. They wear their skin capes summer and winter, and on such a hot day as this I should suppose the warmth of it would be insupportable. I notice that before they venture to join us they take a good look at us from distant prominent points.

. . . .

Among the Sho-sho-nees who have visited our camp is Cho-kup, the chief of the Humboldt River band of the Sho-sho-nees. It is to be regretted, as I have before remarked, that I am obliged to let Indian Pete, the interpreter, go with my guide ahead, in order to talk with the Indians they may meet. I am thus deprived of the advantages of the information I might otherwise obtain from this chief respecting his tribe. I have had a sketch of him taken. He is a very respectable, intelligent, well-behaved Indian, and seems to have gained the approbation of the California Mail Company. In age I should suppose he was about thirty-five years. He is dressed in buckskin pants, a check under, and a woolen over shirt; has a handkerchief tied around his neck, wears shoes, and has a yellowish felt hat. His air is that of a man who, while knowing his own powers, is capable of scanning those of others. He showed me a letter of Mr. Chorpenning, recommending him as a good Indian, &c. This, together with my intercourse with him, has induced me, from motives of policy as well as justice, to give him the following paper:

"Camp No. 17, Cho-Kup's Pass,
"*May* 19, 1859.

"To all whom it may concern:

"This is to inform persons that the bearer of this paper is Cho-kup, chief of the Sho-sho-nees south of the Humboldt River, and as he is represented, and from my intercourse with him, I believe him, to be a friend of the white man, and a good, respectable, and well-behaved Indian, I bespeak for him and his people the kind treatment at the hands of the travelers through their country that their recent good conduct entitle them to, and which, if they continue to receive, will insure all who may pass through their country safety to their persons and property.

"J.H. Simpson,
"*Captain Topographical Engineers.*"

I have made it a point to treat the Indians I meet kindly, making them small presents, which I trust will not be without their use in securing their friendly feeling and conduct. A great many of the difficulties our country has had with the Indians, according to my observation and experience, have grown out of the bad treatment they have received at the hands of insolent and cowardly men, who, not gifted with the bravery which is perfectly consistent with a kind and generous heart, have, when they thought they could do it with impunity, maltreated them; the consequence resulting that the very next body of whites they have met have not unfrequently been made to suffer the penalties which in this way they are almost always sure to inflict indiscriminately on parties, whether they deserve it or not.

. . . .

The damaged barometer cleaned and refitted with fresh mercury by Mr. Engelmann. At sunset ascended high peak, back or west of camp, to view the pass we have been aiming at. It looks favorable. From this peak had a most magnificent view of the mountains in every quarter of the horizon—the Humboldt range, to the east of north, showing its white snowy summits far above the intervening ones. These distant views have, at least on my mind, a decidedly moral and religious effect; and I cannot but believe that they are not less productive of emotions of value in this respect than they are of use in accustoming the mind to large conceptions, and thus giving it power and capacity. The mysterious property of nature to develop the whole man, including the mind, soul, and body, is a subject which I think has not received the attention from philosophers which its importance demands; and though Professor Arnold Guyot, of Princeton, has written a most capital work on the theme, "Earth and Man," yet a great deal remains to be done to bring the matter to the profit of the world at large, which, it seems to me, a wise and beneficent Creator has ordained should be gathered from the contemplation and proper use of his works.

But then the question arises, Do we rise from the contemplation of nature to nature's God, and therefore to a realization of the amplitude and reach to which our minds are capable, by our own unaided spirit; or is it by the superinduced Spirit of the Almighty Himself, which we have received, it may be, on account of His only Son? But these speculations may be considered as foreign to the necessary rigor of an official report; and I, therefore, will indulge in them no further than to say that, according to my notions, the latter I believe to be the true theory.

. . . .

May 26, Camp No. 22.—Altitude above the sea, 6,373 feet. Up to this morning fifteen persons, nearly one-fourth of the command, have reported sick. A portion, however, have been returned to duty. Morning fine, but cool. Thermometer at 5 AM, 29°. Night sensibly colder than any we have had, caused, doubtless, by the vicinity of the snow mountains, the Pe-er-re-ah range, to the west of us. Our morning departure very exhilarating. The crack of the whip, the "gee! get up!" of the teamsters, the merry laugh, the sudden shout from the exuberance of spirits, the clinking of armor, the long array of civil, military, and economic *personnel,* in due order, moving with hope to our destined end, coupled with the bright, bracing morning, and, at times, twittering of birds, make our morning departure from camp very pleasing.

. . . .

May 28, Camp No. 24, Simpson's Park, Pe-er-re-ah range.—Longitude, 116° 49'; latitude, 39° 30' 32". Altitude above the sea, 6,355 feet. Thermometer at 5 AM, 30°. Morning somewhat cloudy. Renewed journey at 10 minutes to 6 AM. Leave valley of Won-a-ho-nupe Creek and strike west for Simpson's Pass, which we reach by a very easy ascent in 4.7 miles; altitude above the sea, 7,104 feet. The grass in the pass very abundant and of the finest character. This fine mountain bunch-grass fattens and strengthens our animals like oats. The pass at summit is as much as a mile wide, and both backward and forward the views are beautiful. The mountains near our camp of May 25 are seen very conspicuously back of us; and ahead of us, limiting Reese Valley, which we are approaching, is a low range trending generally north and south, and beyond them a very high range covered with snow, called by the Indians the Se-day-e or Lookout Mountains. The Pe-er-re-ah Mountains, which we are now about to leave, are composed, up Won-a-ho-nupe Cañon, of quartzite, altered slates, and granite rocks; and near Simpson's Park the rocks are highly metamorphosed, semifused and stratified. At the pass they are granitic.

. . . .

The valley in which we are encamped, as well as its creek, I call after Mr. Reese, our guide, who, with two other men, discovered it some years since in their per-egrinations between Salt Lake City and Carson Valley. They gave it the name of New River; but as Mr. Reese has been of considerable service, and discovers very laudable zeal in examining the country ahead in our explorations, I have thought it is but just to call the river and valley after him. The Indian name of the river is Pang-que-o-whop-pe, or Fish Creek.

GEORGE M. WHEELER [1842–1905]

There are an estimated three hundred caves in Nevada, maybe more, forming a subterranean world foreign to most people. Some caves are vast, some contain ancient artifacts, while others are merely cramped tunnels, reeking of pack-rat urine. George Montague Wheeler and his reconnaissance team did not set out looking for caves, but they explored one, described below, known today as Cave Valley Cave. George Wheeler's inscription can still be found on the cave walls. Wheeler, a native of Massachusetts, worked for the U.S. Army Corps of Engineers, having graduated sixth in his class at West Point in 1866. In 1869 Wheeler led a five-month expedition from Camp Ruby, Nevada, in present-day Ruby Valley, south through eastern Nevada, through Pioche, and ending at a Mormon village on the Muddy River. They were dispatched to make military maps of the area, select sites for military posts, ascertain the disposition of the Indians, and record natural history information. Silver had been discovered in Virginia City ten years earlier, and new mining districts were being aggressively developed throughout the state. Some historians theorize that Wheeler's reconnaissance trip was a cover for prospecting, obliging powerful mining capitalists in San Francisco. Tellingly, Wheeler devoted most of his report—Preliminary Report upon a Reconnaissance through Southern and Southeastern Nevada, Made in 1869 *(published in 1875)*—*to mining districts and mining opportunities. This party was the first to determine the elevation of eponymous Wheeler Peak (13,063 ft), Nevada's second-highest mountain. From 1872 to 1879 Wheeler directed a much more ambitious survey—one of four U.S. Geographical Surveys west of the 100th meridian—that produced topographic maps of 326,891 square miles of the mountainous West. On this survey, geologist Grove Karl Gilbert named the Basin and Range Province, recognizing its fundamental difference from the folded Appalachians.*

Cave in Cave Valley

Our anticipations had been greatly aroused by varied reports of a cave near the Patterson Mining District, for the greater part unexplored, and supposed to be of grand magnitude. Accordingly, upon arriving in its vicinity and pitching our tents within some three hundred yards, our next efforts were toward fitting up a party to make a thorough exploration. We were fortunate in securing the services of an old Indian of the Gosiute tribe, named Anzip, who professed a thorough knowledge of the subterranean windings, and to be conversant also with the various Indian traditions that attribute strange characteristics to the locality.

As we gather round the camp-fire dinner he relates to our interpreter in his native tongue the various wonders of this underground world. The principal tradition runs that far within the cave they come upon a new and grand world where a race of white people live having fair fields and flowers, grassy lawns and cool fountains, with a vast profusion of magnificence; that at one time and another the Indians who have ventured within their confines have been taken and made prisoners, never being allowed to return to their tribes. In all during his remembrance six had been so taken, and the various lodges mourned their loss and were desirous that some strong power like our own should go to demand their return.

The intense excitement of Anzip's imagination depicted so truthfully upon his swarthy features was highly interesting, connected with his earnest and gesticulating manner. When we would seem to doubt his re-asserted tale he was so terribly angry that, being afraid that he would abandon us as guide, we gave tacit consent to his various narrations. Our old guide "Pogo" has told us that within the memory of his mother, now very aged, two squaws had been taken upon entering the cave, and, after an absence of four years, were sent back to the outer world, clad in the finest of buckskin, covered with hieroglyphics of the race who had for that time held them in bondage. They professed to have been well treated and to have lived in a pleasant land. Again two more had disappeared in the same way and were never heard from again.

These and various other stories served to while away the twilight hour of the evening before our visit to the above locality. Our party numbered twenty-three, well supplied with all necessaries, such as candles, ropes, and arrangements for measuring and making a survey. We made an early start, and were out of the light of day between six and seven hours. Our measurings made the cave no longer than 3,000 feet, and for the last 1,000 feet the novelty had greatly worn away, when we found ourselves crawling among the slime of some of the worst imaginable clayey sediment. For 700 or 800 feet from the entrance everything was dry, the walls high, and several compartments were quite interesting; beyond that the humidity and mud commenced, and upon our returning to the outer air our persons were more of a curiosity than the cave itself.

Our guide got along very well for about two thousand feet; then he commenced to get excited and bewildered, constantly threading various labyrinths and returning to the place of departure. This mistake could have happened to any one, only that we had left marks here and there easily to be recognized.

Every channel was closely examined, and all were found to exhaust in the solid wall of the surrounding lime. One deep well was found that apparently extended downward for seventy feet, at which point the lead sinker struck either the bottom or a projecting shoulder.

A plan of the cave, as well as a view of the buttes in which it is situated, will appear in Vol. I of the Survey Reports. The sketch indicates that the subterranean opening extends as far as these buttes, which are situated some three or four miles from the high peaks of the adjacent Schell Creek range.

We came out and returned to our camp, weary, covered with mud and slime, and with every particle of romance eliminated from us, and to wonder that there ever could be a race so imaginative and speculative in everything that is absurd as the Indian.

FEARFUL CROSSINGS

Emigrant Encounters and Indian Responses

Enthusiasts of extreme sports and survival games would have been in their element in the 1840s in the company of wagon trains going west. Except that there was no safety net and no production crew to evacuate the losers. The game was real and the stakes were high. If you survived, you won a chance to own land in balmy California or find a gold nugget and become instantly wealthy. If you didn't make it, oh well, yours would be one of the shallow graves decorating the trail. Many Americans chose to try their luck and gamble all for the big chance. An estimated 25,000 emigrants made their way to California via the Overland Trail in 1849 alone—not just able-bodied men, but women, children, babies, and the elderly. These bold travelers knew that they were witnessing a migration of epic proportion, and hundreds of them kept diaries and wrote reminiscences. Much of this extensive body of literature has subsequently been published; probably still more sits in library archives and family trunks. The sampling of excerpts reprinted here begins with northern accounts both before and during the gold rush of 1849, includes two accounts of southern routes, and concludes with two Indian responses to this disastrous Anglo invasion of their homeland.

Roughly five hundred miles of the Overland Trail—one quarter of the two-thousand-mile trek from the Missouri River to Sacramento—traversed present-day Nevada, the worst part of the entire trip. Entering Nevada via southern Idaho or the Great Salt Lake, emigrants had to find their way through mountainous country to the Humboldt River, a west-flowing, meandering watercourse that threaded its way for three hundred miles through Nevada's north-south-running mountain ranges. Although the Humboldt was a lifeline, emigrants cursed it, calling it the "Barren River," decrying its lack of trees—"without . . . a stick large enough to make a walking cane"—fearing its "thieving" Indians, bogging down in its swamps, being tormented by swarms of mosquitoes, sweltering in the heat, and gagging on the Humboldt's "brackish" and "bitter" alkaline waters.

But if the Humboldt River was bad, the dreaded forty-mile desert that came next was worse. This was the true test. Emigrants pitied their poor, gaunt animals—oxen, cattle, horses, mules—as their heads drooped and many gave out entirely. Emigrants grew so inured to the carnage that one man ate his lunch while perched on the corpse of a dead horse, and parties took their meals "amidst the effluvia of a hundred putrescent carcasses." As their animals expired, emigrants were forced to jettison possessions, abandon entire wagons, carry only what was essential. Journals and memoirs frequently describe how the dire predicaments became a test of character, revealing both the best and the worst in the "tired and exhausted," "anxious and distressed" travelers. Should the faster members of a party leave the slower ones behind? Is an ailing member nursed or left to die? Does one share one's last drops of water? How do you deal justice to someone who has stolen food? Disagreements, divisions, and even violence erupted under the strain. Should we follow the northern route along the Humboldt and risk being caught in winter storms like the Donner party, or detour south, joining the much longer Old Spanish Trail from Santa Fe to Los Angeles, far from the gold fields? Should we try the tantalizing, dubious cutoff or stick to the miserable, known route? And—in the greatest extremity—do I eat the body of my fallen friend?

Few emigrants extolled the beauty of Nevada's scenery. On the contrary, they described it as "dreary beyond description," "parched and arid," "a wide waste of desolation," "wearisome, dull, and melancholy," and "the valley of the shadow of death." One account of crossing Nevada begins with the epigraph, "Who enters here, leaves hope behind." It would not be until the 1850s that any Anglos would consider living in Nevada, and not until 1859 that they would actually stampede to get there.

VIRGINIA REED MURPHY [1833–1921]

Perhaps no story of the westward movement is better known than that of the Donner party, whose members were forced to resort to cannibalism to survive in the Sierra Nevadas during the winter of 1846–47. But in her "Across the Plains in the Donner Party (1846)," one of the few firsthand accounts of the ordeal, Virginia Reed Murphy makes clear that cannibalism was only the last and most extreme episode of a journey filled with extraordinary effort and events. Murphy, who was twelve years old during the journey, first shared her account soon after the fateful winter in a letter written in May 1847 and printed in the Illinois Journal with the understated headline "Deeply Interesting Letter." "Across the Plains in the Donner Party" appeared in Century magazine in 1891, forty-five years after the events it describes. While not without historical inaccuracies, Murphy's account remains an indispensable record of an almost unimaginable experience. With vividness and a sense of drama, Murphy recounts the momentous banishment of her father, James Reed, at "Gravelly Ford" (in today's Nevada) after he killed a man in self-defense. She tells of the "doomed" party, with "heavy hearts," so tired that "they declared they could not take another step." Murphy's own determined spirit shows through in the story as her father's absence "seemed suddenly to make a woman of me. I realized that I must be strong and help mama bear her sorrows." Her subsequent years proved just as vibrant, as she and her husband had nine children, and she lived to be eighty-seven. A sense of gratitude for life echoes in her writing. "At Donner Lake," she wrote, "we seemed especially favored by the Almighty as not one of our family perished, and we were the only family no one member of which was forced to eat of human flesh to keep body and soul together."

Across the Plains in the Donner Party (1846)

I now come to that part of my narrative which delicacy of feeling for both the dead and the living would induce me to pass over in silence, but which a correct and lucid chronicle of subsequent events of historical importance will not suffer to be omitted. On the 5th day of October, 1846, at Gravelly Ford, a tragedy was enacted which affected the subsequent lives and fortunes of more than one member of our company. At this point in our journey we were compelled to double our teams in order to ascend a steep, sandy hill. Milton Elliott, who was driving our wagon, and John Snyder, who was driving one of Mr. Graves's, became involved in a quarrel over the management of their oxen. Snyder was beating his cattle over the head with the butt end of his whip, when my father, returning on horse-back from a hunting trip, arrived and, appreciating the great importance of saving the remainder of the oxen, remonstrated with Snyder, telling him that they were our main dependence, and at the same time offering the assistance of our team. Snyder having taken offense at something Elliott had said declared that his team could pull up alone, and kept on using abusive language. Father tried to quiet the enraged man. Hard words followed. Then my father said: "We can settle this, John, when we get up the hill." "No," replied Snyder with an oath, "we will settle it now," and springing upon the tongue of a wagon, he struck my father a violent blow over the head with his heavy whip-stock. One blow followed another. Father was stunned for a moment and blinded by the blood streaming from the gashes in his head. Another blow was descending when my mother ran in between the men. Father saw the uplifted whip, but had only time to cry: "John, John," when down came the stroke upon mother. Quick as a thought my father's hunting knife was out and Snyder fell, fatally wounded. He was caught in the arms of W. C. Graves, carried up the hillside, and laid on the ground. My father regretted the act, and dashing the blood from his eyes went quickly to the assistance of the dying man. I can see him now, as he knelt over Snyder, trying to stanch the wound, while the blood from the gashes in his own head, trickling down his face, mingled with that of the dying man. In a few moments Snyder expired. Camp was pitched immediately, our wagon being some distance from the others. My father, anxious to do what he could for the dead, offered the boards of our wagon, from which to make a coffin. Then, coming to me, he said: "Daughter, do you think you can dress these wounds in my head? Your mother is not able, and they must be attended to." I answered by saying: "Yes, if you will tell me what to do." I brought a basin of water and sponge, and we went into the wagon, so that we might not be disturbed. When my work was at last finished, I burst out crying. Papa clasped me in his arms, saying: "I should not have asked so much of you," and talked to me until I controlled my feelings, so that we could go to the tent where mama was lying.

We then learned that trouble was brewing in the camp where Snyder's body lay. At the funeral my father stood sorrowfully by until the last clod was placed upon the grave. He and John Snyder had been good friends, and no one could have regretted the taking of that young life more than my father.

The members of the Donner party then held a council to decide upon the fate of my father, while we anxiously awaited the verdict. They refused to accept the plea of self-defense and decided that my father should be banished from the company and sent into the wilderness alone. It was a cruel sentence. And all this animosity towards my father was caused by Louis Keseburg, a German who had joined our company away back on the plains. Keseburg was married to a young and pretty German girl, and used to abuse her, and was in the habit of beating her till she was black and blue. This aroused all the manhood in my father and he took Keseburg to task—telling him it must be stopped or measures would be taken to that effect. Keseburg did not dare to strike his wife again, but he hated my father and nursed his wrath until papa was so unfortunate as to have to take the life of a fellow-creature in self-defense. Then Keseburg's hour for revenge had come. But how a man like Keseburg, brutal and overbearing by nature, although highly educated, could have such influence over the company is more than I can tell. I have thought the subject over for hours but failed to arrive at a conclusion. The feeling against my father at one time was so strong that lynching was proposed. He was no coward and he bared his neck, saying, "Come on, gentlemen," but no one moved. It was thought more humane, perhaps, to send him into the wilderness to die of slow starvation or be murdered by the Indians; but my father did not die. God took care of him and his family, and at Donner Lake we seemed especially favored by the Almighty as not one of our family perished, and we were the only family no one member of which was forced to eat of human flesh to keep body and soul together. When the sentence of banishment was communicated to my father, he refused to go, feeling that he was justified before God and man, as he had only acted in self-defense.

Then came a sacrifice on the part of my mother. Knowing only too well what her life would be without him, yet fearful that if he remained he would meet with violence at the hands of his enemies, she implored him to go, but all to no avail until she urged him to remember the destitution of the company, saying that if he remained and escaped violence at their hands, he might nevertheless see his children starving and be helpless to aid them, while if he went on he could return and meet them with food. It was a fearful struggle; at last he consented, but not before he had secured a promise from the company to care for his wife and little ones.

My father was sent out into an unknown country without provisions or arms— even his horse was at first denied him. When we learned of this decision, I followed him through the darkness, taking Elliott with me, and carried him his rifle, pistols, ammunition and some food. I had determined to stay with him, and begged him to let me stay, but he would listen to no argument, saying that it was impossible. Finally, unclasping my arms from around him, he placed me in charge of Elliott, who started back to camp with me—and papa was left alone. I had cried until I had hardly strength to walk, but when we reached camp and I saw the distress of my mother, with the little ones clinging around her and no arm to lean upon, it seemed suddenly to make a woman of me. I realized that I must be strong and help mama bear her sorrows.

We traveled on, but all life seemed to have left the party, and the hours dragged slowly along. Every day we would search for some sign of papa, who would leave a letter by the way-side in the top of a bush or in a split stick, and when he succeeded in killing geese or birds would scatter the feathers about so that we might know that he was not suffering for food. When possible, our fire would always be kindled on the spot where his had been. But a time came when we found no letter, and no trace of him. Had he starved by the way-side, or been murdered by the Indians?

My mother's despair was pitiful. Patty and I thought we would be bereft of her also. But life and energy were again aroused by the danger that her children would starve. It was apparent that the whole company would soon be put on a short allowance of food, and the snow-capped mountains gave an ominous hint of the fate that really befell us in the Sierra. Our wagon was found to be too heavy, and was abandoned with everything we could spare, and the remaining things were packed in part of another wagon. We had two horses left from the wreck, which could hardly drag themselves along, but they managed to carry my two little brothers. The rest of us had to walk, one going beside the horse to hold on my youngest brother who was only two and a half years of age. The Donners were not with us when my father was banished, but were several days in advance of our train. Walter Herron, one of our drivers, who was traveling with the Donners, left the wagons and joined my father.

On the 19th of October, while traveling along the Truckee, our hearts were gladdened by the return of Stanton, with seven mules loaded with provisions. Mr. McClutchen was ill and could not travel, but Captain Sutter had sent two of his Indian vaqueros, Luis and Salvador with Stanton. Hungry as we were, Stanton brought us something better than food—news that my father was alive. Stanton had met him not far from Sutter's Fort; he had been three days without food, and his horse was not able to carry him. Stanton had given him a horse and some provisions and he had gone on. We now packed what little we had left on one mule and started with Stanton. My mother rode on a mule, carrying Tommy in her lap; Patty and Jim rode behind the two Indians, and I behind Mr. Stanton, and in this way we journeyed on through the rain, looking up with fear towards the mountains, where snow was already falling although it was only the last week in October. Winter had set in a month earlier than usual. All trails and roads were covered; and our only guide was the summit which it seemed we would never reach. Despair drove many nearly frantic. Each family tried to cross the mountains but found it impossible. When it was seen that the wagons could not be dragged through the snow, their goods and provisions were packed on oxen and another start was made, men and women walking in the snow up to their waists, carrying their children in their arms and trying to drive their cattle. The Indians said they could find no road, so a halt was called, and Stanton went ahead with the guides, and came back and reported that we could get across if we kept right on, but that it would be impossible if snow fell. He was in favor of a forced march until the other side of the summit should be reached, but some of our party were so tired and exhausted with the day's labor that they declared they could not take another step; so the few who knew the danger that the night might bring yielded to the many, and we camped within three miles of the summit.

That night came the dreaded snow. Around the camp-fires under the trees great feathery flakes came whirling down. The air was so full of them that one could see objects only a few feet away. The Indians knew we were doomed, and one of them wrapped his blanket about him and stood all night under a tree. We children slept soundly on our cold bed of snow with a soft white mantle falling over us so thickly that every few moments my mother would have to shake the shawl—our only covering—to keep us from being buried alive. In the morning the snow lay deep on mountain and valley. With heavy hearts we turned back to a cabin that had been built by the Murphy-Schallenberger party two years before. We built more cabins and prepared as best we could for the winter. That camp, which proved the camp of death to many in our company, was made on the shore of a lake, since known as "Donner Lake."

J. QUINN THORNTON [1810–1888]

Born in West Virginia, Jessy Quinn Thornton grew up in Ohio, became a lawyer, and began his career in Missouri. An abolitionist, Thornton left Missouri because of its proslavery stance, resettling in Illinois. In 1846, Thornton and his wife, Nancy, both in ill health, joined a wagon train bound for the salubrious climate of Oregon. Once underway, their party joined the infamous Donner-Reed party until the Oregon-bound wagons, including the Thorntons,' separated from the ill-fated California-bound wagons. The Thorntons and their party were persuaded to try the newly discovered Applegate Cutoff, touted as sparing emigrants a very dangerous stretch in the Columbia River Gorge. The Applegate Cutoff left the Humboldt River some miles downstream from today's Winnemucca, headed northwest, crossed the Black Rock Desert, passed Tule and Goose Lake valleys in northern California, and crossed the Cascades near Klamath Lake. For the Thorntons this southern route to Oregon was a nightmare—"dreary beyond description"—and they spent the parched miles cursing the fiend who duped them into taking it. The ordeal initiated an acrimonious dispute between Thornton and Applegate, preserved in a lively record of published attacks and defenses. Thornton's account often reads like a legal brief, wherein he carefully articulates the facts and vents his anger at Jesse Applegate's purported lies. Thornton settled in the Oregon country, was appointed to the supreme court of the provisional government in 1847, and was sent to Washington, DC—by sea—to present the petition for Oregon's territorial status, which passed in 1848, the same year that the discredited

Applegate Cutoff fell into disuse. Thereafter, Thornton practiced law throughout Oregon, was active in public affairs, and died in Salem.

from *Oregon and California in 1848*

August 8. In the forenoon one Jesse Applegate came into camp. . . .

Applegate affirmed the following things, among others: 1. That the distance to Oregon, via the Dalles Mission was from 800 to 850 miles. 2. That the distance by his cut-off was estimated by him to be at least 200 miles less than that route. 3. That the party who had explored the new road with him, estimated it at even 300 miles nearer. 4. That the whole distance was better supplied with water and grass than the old road. 5. That it was not more than 190 or 200 miles to the point at which his cut-off left Ogden's River. 6. That the road was generally smooth, and, with the exception of a dry drive of thirty miles, well supplied with an abundance of good water, grass, and fuel. "These things, which now seem frivolous and slight, will prove of serious consequence:" and if the total absence of all truth in each of these affirmations affords any means by which to judge of the principles of the man making them, he may unhesitatingly be said to be *Parthis mendacior* [a line from Horace meaning "more mendacious than the Parthians"].

. . . .

Applegate had informed us, that at the place where his road left Ogden's River, we should enter upon a dry drive of thirty miles, ending at the Black Rock; and that this was the only one we would have. It is unnecessary to state that we had now no confidence in any thing that had been affirmed by him. That we were about to enter upon a perfectly untried and unknown desert, there could be no doubt; but, judging from the extent to which his assertions as to the previous part of the road differed from facts, we very naturally inferred, that we should find this drive to be sixty, or even eighty miles, instead of thirty. Accordingly, after filling our kegs with water, we entered this desert, with heavy and desponding hearts, having no longer any assurance as to the real character or length of the road, between one watering place and another. . . . We continued to travel very rapidly all day over a desert that appeared to be boundless, having nothing growing upon it but a few scattered bushes of artemisia, at long intervals. The earth appeared to be as destitute of moisture, as if a drop of rain or dew had never fallen upon it from the brazen heavens above. We encamped for the night upon the side of a mountain; and there being neither water nor grass for our poor, toil-worn cattle, they were carefully guarded through the night. I had gone forward in the morning, and found, within about three-fourths of a mile of our encampment, and far up the side of the mountain, a very small vein of water, that moistened the ground a few yards around. I removed a considerable quantity of earth with my spade, so as to make a little reservoir. Into this the water very slowly collected, and enough was obtained for tea; and from it, a few of the cattle received, perhaps, half a pint of water apiece. I divided among the poor fellows of my team a keg of water I had brought from Ogden's River. The weary emigrants at length retired to their tents for rest; but I took my now empty keg up the side of the mountain, where, by remaining until between one and two o'clock in the morning, I succeeded in obtaining enough of the precious fluid to fill my vessel.

We resumed our journey very early on the following morning, and traveled with great rapidity over a rolling, arid, and barren country, until about half an hour before sunset, when we halted to rest our cattle a little, and to take some food. The oxen looked wild and famished. We had now traveled about forty-five miles, instead of thirty, and we knew not how far it was yet to water or grass.

The country over which we had passed was dreary beyond description. There were in it no diversities of color or form, to relieve the mind by their variety. The earth was iron, and the heavens brass. Every thing was parched and arid; and all those sources of beauty, which, from their being so generally diffused through nature, are usually regarded as things of course, were here dried up by a hot sun beaming down upon sand and rocks. Here was none of the living luster of a gay and beautiful spring, dressed in robes of the richest green, smiling upon the wooded hills and the grain-covered valleys, or laughing and dancing along the brooks and rivers. Here were none of the rich glories of autumn, laden with delicious fruits. There were neither sounds of melody to charm the ear, nor sights of beauty or grandeur to please the eye, and delight the heart.

Just as the sun was sinking, we resumed our journey, and after descending a little hill we entered a country more forbidding and repulsive than even that I have described. There we occasionally saw a stray and solitary bush of artemisia. It was a country which had nothing of a redeeming character. Nothing presented itself to the eye, but a broad expanse of a uniform dead-level plain, which conveyed to the mind the idea that it had been the muddy and sandy bottom of a former lake; and, that after the water had suddenly sunk through the fissures, leaving the bottom in a state of muddy fusion, streams of gas had broken out in ten thousand places, and had thrown up sand and mud, so as to form cones, rising from a common plane, and ranging from three to twenty feet in height. It seemed to be the River of Death dried up, and having its muddy bottom jetted into cones by the force of the fires of perdition. It was enlivened by the murmur of no streams, but was a wide waste of desolation, where even the winds had died. It was a wearisome, dull, and melancholy scene, that had been cheered by the beauty of no verdure since the waters of the flood had subsided, and the dove left the patriarch's window to return no more.

The oxen hurried forward with a rapidity, which will be considered great, if we remember that they had now been two days and one night without either water or grass. Some cattle had already perished, and we hastened forward, anxious and distressed, amidst the silence of the night.

At length, about half an hour before daylight, in the morning, myself, and four others, arrived at the Black Rock, where we found an immense spring of scalding hot water, which cooled after flowing off to a place where it spread out upon a plain; and afforded moisture to sufficient grass for our cattle during a short stay. Other wagons continued to come up until 10 o'clock. Mr. Crump's team was so reduced that it became necessary to send back aid to him. Mr. David Butterfield brought him into camp about sunset. His team had then been without water and grass three days and two nights, during a drive the length of which was variously estimated at from sixty to seventy miles; but which a man, abhorred for the sufferings occasioned by his heartless untruths, had caused us to believe was no more than thirty miles. Some of our cattle perished in the desert, and all that survived were greatly injured. And now, that we had got to water, it was greatly impregnated with mixed alkaline salts, that made it unfit for use at the springs, even had it been cool there. But, in addition to this, it flowed off over ground filled with the carbonate and bi-carbonate of potash, which imparted to the water a taste which caused it to be known among the emigrants as saleratus-water.

. . . .

I believe it can be demonstrated that the wanton liar always unites the fool with the knave. Falsehood never fails to defeat its own end. For, although it may possibly succeed in a single instance, as in the present case, yet the thing will be sure to become notorious, and then, his character for veracity being gone, his power to deceive goes with it.

WILLIAM GRAHAM JOHNSTON [1828–1913]

The year was 1849. California or Bust! was the clarion call to young men throughout the world, compelling them west to seek El Dorado. William Graham Johnston was no exception. Joseph Sullivan, in his foreword to the 1948 edition of Johnston's Experiences of a Forty-Niner *(1892), republished as* Overland to California, *comments that "the party was very well equipped and one of the finest planned that started for California" and that "their amazing average of 22-½ miles a day . . . is a record that probably has never been equaled." Written forty years after the events described, Johnston's account—privately printed in a small edition in 1892—depicts hardship and joy, tempered with the reflection of time passed. In a Great Race, under the able leadership of the well-known guide Jim Stewart, their party brought the first forty-niner wagons to Placerville and Sacramento. Only a mule train beat them there that year. Johnston was born August 22, 1828, in Pittsburgh, Pennsylvania, with ancestors in the Revolutionary War and in the publishing business, early proprietors of the Pittsburgh Gazette newspaper. He attended public and private schools, filling in gaps in his education by working in a bookstore. By his own account he walked most of the way from Pennsylvania to California, despite a childhood hip injury that left him periodically lame. Returning east in 1857, Johnston became a captain of industry and a financial and civic leader of Pittsburgh. With the same spirit that drove him west, he founded the still existent printing and bookbinding house William G. Johnston, an insurance company, a bank, America's first steel-casting company, two telegraph companies later taken over by Western Union, and the Woodruff Sleeping Car Company, which later merged with the Pullman Company. His memoir,* Life and Reminiscences: From Birth to Manhood *(1901), capped a successful American life and story.*

from *Experiences of a Forty-Niner*

> "Seest thou yon dreary plain
> Forlorn and wild,
> The seat of desolation . . .
> . . . Hail horrors. Hail!"

Sunday, July 15th.—A march of five hours brought us to the vicinity of the Sink of Humboldt River, at about nine o'clock; and continuing over a well beaten sandy trail until noon, we encamped on the edge of the Great Desert. Of late the region through which we journey had been growing more and more desolate; but here was reached what might be aptly termed "the valley of the shadow of death," and over its portals might be inscribed:

"Who enters here, leaves hope behind."

Towards the south—for in that direction the road bent, was a vast solitude covered with loose sand, which the wind heaped in hillocks, like waves of the sea. Scarce any vegetation existed; at long intervals might be seen a stalk of sage or greasewood, gnarled, blackened, and looking as if well nigh exhausted in its hard struggle for life. Eastwardly lay the great marshy plain which as in ages past continued to swallow the ever flowing stream, which but for this quenchless thirst might have expanded into a mighty river. Over it hung a veil of mist, impenetrable now, and for anything that I know to the contrary it may be ever thus to the eye of man; as doubtless the heat of the sun over the broad, shallow expanse of water causes a constant evaporation. Where we encamped, we found it necessary to dig wells for water. These wells, about four feet in diameter and of a trifle less depth, furnished an abundant supply of water, but intensely brackish, bitter with salt and sulphur. Some mules, and men also refused to drink of it; but, with nothing else to quench the thirst, we were painfully conscious that all would eventually use it, before better could be found. Every cask and canteen was filled with these alkaline waters, in expectation of a night's journey on the desert. Some men boiled coffee and filled their canteens with it, as in this form it was more palatable. My canteen having sprung a leak, I filled a bottle instead, rinsing it well, as it had contained turpentine. In a neighboring slough we found a sort of flag-like grass growing, which none but well nigh famished mules would have eaten; such ours must have been, for they ate of it as though it were choicest clover. Finding this the case we cut a supply to carry with us.

In the morning we had passed the Platte City Company, and at the Sink caught up to another, led by General Marney. The wagons of both were drawn by mules. In company with the latter we set out upon the desert at six o'clock in the evening. A few miles out we crossed a small stream, excessively salt and utterly unfit to drink. Here the trail forked, the road to the right leading to the northern pass of the Sierra Nevada, via Truckee River; while the other, a newer route, led to Carson River, and a more southerly pass. The latter we pursued. The day was warm and cloudy, but the night was pleasant. At midnight we encamped, tying the mules to the wagons, giving them the wiry grass we brought with us, also water from the casks. Under the circumstances it was deemed unnecessary to have on guard more than one man, and the task for the two hours of rest which we intended taking was determined by lot. Distance, thirty-six miles.

Monday, July 16th.—Contrary to design, we did not get started at two o'clock; for the solitary guardsman, having no one to *watch him*, fell asleep. A restless fellow, to whom conscience or possibly some evil spirit would not grant unbroken rest, happening to awake sufficiently, discovered the situation and aroused the camp. This was at four o'clock; soon after we were jogging along. In the early morning the temperature of the air was pleasant, but towards nine o'clock the sun blazed fiercely upon us. Our thirst soon became excessive, and we drank water, brinish as it was, freely. In spite of the rinsing, the taste of turpentine still clung to the bottle which I had brought, and I was compelled to fling it away; and the canteen of Mr. Scully, who walked with me, had to do double duty, until it became exhausted, which was not long.

It was early ascertained that a terrible blunder had been committed—*every cask was found to be empty.* Before the morning start the mules had been watered; and those having this duty in charge left untouched a certain cask, which they intended for the use of the men through the day. But when too late, the discovery was made that the contents of that particular cask had been given to the mules in the night.

It was a fearful condition to be placed in; a hot sun overhead, burning sands beneath our feet, while our thirst was perhaps intensified by a knowledge of our helplessness.

Trudging along on foot was excessively wearisome, for at every step we sank in the deep sand; and were compelled often to seek rest by sitting down on the desolate wayside; and as drowning men are said to grasp at straws, so for the few grains of comfort to be derived from a contact with the less heated layers of sand beneath, we brushed aside those which overspread the surface, and tried to imagine we were thus made cooler. The wagons dragged heavily, taxing the mules to the utmost of their strength. The poor, dumb beasts, oppressed with heat and toil, excited whatever of compassion we could spare from a review of our situation.

As if in cruel mockery to torture us whilst thus already suffering sufficiently, again and again mirages arose, deceiving with their pleasing enchantments. Hopes thus elevated by appearances of bodies of water, margined by waving forests, were sometimes suddenly dashed by their instantaneous disappearance; at others gradually dispelled, by the slowly fading of these mimic landscapes. No form of deception could more nearly approach reality; and no trick of conjurer could possibly be more complete.

About midday the heat having increased to an intense degree, a wind began to sweep across the arid waste; but there was no refreshment in its breath; rather it seemed as a blast vomited from a stygian furnace.

When within a few miles of Carson River we were met by some of our company, who having ridden to the stream, were returning with supplies of water for those who were famishing. Words are meager to express the relief thus afforded. Many spoke of it as the most refreshing draught that had ever crossed their lips. After relieving our wants there were yet numbers further back, full as much in need as we had been, to whom they went.

It was two o'clock when we reached the river, and many leaped instantly down its steep banks into the rushing current, and drank an amount of water that would seem incredible. Notwithstanding this imprudent excess, no apparent injury was sustained. An hour later Sweigler rode into camp with his mules, having left his wagon on the desert, intending to return for it after obtaining rest and refreshment. From a party encamped near us we learned that some men in crossing the desert yesterday approached quite close to the "dusky shades," one of whom having become frantic from thirst buried himself in the sand, and but for the untiring efforts of companions, would have perished. A wayside message left by Captain Paul informed us that whilst at this place, a few nights since, he lost a mule; it having been shot with a poisoned arrow by some prowling Digger.

Carson River, where we struck it, was about thirty yards in width, deep and rapid. A few cottonwoods were scattered along its banks, but none were near our camp. We used willows for fuel, dense thickets of which lined both banks of the stream. After a rest of two hours, we moved a few miles farther up the stream, and found excellent pasture. Wild sage of unusual size was abundant; some stalks were fully six feet high, and proportionately thick.

We passed a train glorying in the name of "Jews-Harp Company"; and what was more curious, their wagons were hauled by oxen, and yet they had outstripped a host possessing the great advantages derived from the use of mules.

Although it might seem a small matter to pass an ox train, a feat often previously performed with but little exertion, it was now a matter of considerable importance, for we had at length reached the goal for which we had long been contending, being in the lead of all wagon trains; the pack trains of our friends, Paul and Blakey, alone being in advance of us.

Dr. Pearis and Judge Townsend, whom we had met a week since, joined our train today. In addition to a wagon and mules, an appendage consists of Mr. Fink, previously mentioned as having abandoned the role of pedestrian to assume the positions of driver and cook with these gentlemen. Fink is an odd sort of fish; witty, yet half-witted; not altogether foolish, and yet none too wise. Good natured, constantly grinning, his light-heartedness was infectious. Explaining why he had been induced to change his mode of travel, he said, "Emegration in a foot train arnt a hard way of drivin' to Californy, but tain't jes the thing for a feller to be a pair of dividers to span the continent; as Shakespeare says, 'to what base uses we sometimes *turn*.'" Distance, twenty-seven miles.

SARAH ROYCE [1819–1891]

"Have you seen the elephant?" Such was the question the forty-niners asked of returning, east-bound travelers on the California route. On April 30, 1849, Sarah Eleanor Bayliss Royce left Council Bluffs, Iowa, with her husband, Josiah, and their two-year-old daughter. The family "suffered the usual dangers and hardships," mostly journeying alone because they insisted on observing the Sabbath. Mrs. Royce, guided by a puritanical Christian faith that at times became

mystical, traveled with her Bible and her "Pilgrimage Diary." According to her daughter-in-law,
Katharine Royce, in the foreword to A Frontier Lady: Recollections of the Gold Rush and
Early California *(1932), Royce's writing is "straightforward and sincere as well as vivid." Sarah*
Royce's recollections were written for her son Josiah Jr. with no intent of publication. Born in
England and raised in the United States with a "careful, old-style academy education," Sarah
Royce was undaunted by the overland journey and her primitive new home in Grass Valley,
California. When no suitable school was available for her three daughters and son, she estab-
lished one and taught it herself, using "astronomical charts, histories, and an encyclopedia of
common and scientific knowledge." Josiah Jr. became a leading American philosopher, histo-
rian, and Harvard professor. Sarah Royce's memories illustrate the danger, the drudgery, and
the unexpected epiphanies of the overland journey. At the western edge of the desert, Sarah
Royce said simply, "We had conquered the desert."

from *A Frontier Lady*

When the explorers returned from their walk to the ridge, it was only to report,
no discovery: nothing to be seen on all sides but sand and scattered sagebrush
interspersed with the carcasses of dead cattle. So there was nothing to be done
but to turn back and try to find the meadows. Turn back! What a chill the words
sent through one. *Turn back,* on a journey like that; in which every mile had been
gained by most earnest labor, growing more and more intense, until, of late, it had
seemed that the certainty of *advance* with every step, was all that made the next
step possible. And now for miles we were to *go back.* In all that long journey no
steps ever seemed so heavy, so hard to take, as those with which I turned my back
to the sun that afternoon of October 4th, 1849.

. . . .

I found no difficulty this morning in keeping up with the team. They went so
slowly, and I was so preternaturally stimulated by anxiety to get forward, that,
before I was aware of it I would be some rods ahead of the cattle, straining my gaze
as if expecting to see a land of promise, long before I had any rational hope of the
kind. My imagination acted intensely. I seemed to see Hagar, in the wilderness
walking wearily away from her fainting child among the dried up bushes, and seating herself in the hot sand. I seemed to become Hagar myself, and when my little
one, from the wagon behind me, called out, "Mamma I want a drink"—I stopped,
gave her some, noted that there were but a few swallows left, then mechanically
pressed onward again, alone, repeating, over and over, the words, "Let me not see
the death of the child."

Just in the heat of noon-day we came to where the sage bushes were nearer together; and a fire, left by campers or Indians, had spread for some distance, leaving beds of ashes, and occasionally charred skeletons of bushes to make the scene more dreary. Smoke was still sluggishly curling up here and there, but no fire was visible; when suddenly just before me to my right a bright flame sprang up at the foot of a small bush, ran rapidly up it, leaped from one little branch to another till all, for a few seconds, were ablaze together, then went out, leaving nothing but a few ashes and a little smouldering trunk. It was a small incident, easily accounted for, but to my then over-wrought fancy it made more vivid the illusion of being a wanderer in a far off, old time desert, and myself witnessing a wonderful phenomenon. For a few moments I stood with bowed head worshiping the God of Horeb, and I was strengthened thereby.

. . . .

On Monday morning we loaded up, but did not hurry, for the cattle had not rested any too long; another day would have been better; but we dared not linger. So, giving them time that morning thoroughly to satisfy themselves with grass and water we once more set forward toward the formidable desert, and, at that late season, with our equipment, the scarcely less formidable Sierras. The feeling that we were once more going forward instead of backward, gave an animation to every step which we could never have felt but by contrast. By night we were again at the Sink where we once more camped; but we durst not, the following morning, launch out upon the desert with the whole day before us; for, though it was now the 9th of October, the sun was still powerful for some hours daily, and the arid sand doubled its heat. Not much after noon, however, we ventured out upon the sea of sand; this time to cross or die.

Not far from the edge of night we stopped to bait [to feed], at no great distance from the scene of our last week's bitter disappointment. Once beyond that, I began to feel renewed courage, as though the worst were passed; and, as I had walked much of the afternoon, and knew I must walk again by and by, I was persuaded to get into the wagon and lie down by Mary, who was sleeping soundly. By a strong effort of will, backed by the soothing influence of prayer, I fell asleep, but only for a few minutes. I was roused by the stopping of the wagon, and then my husband's voice said, "So you've given out, have you Tom?" and at the same moment I knew by the rattling chains and yokes that some of the cattle were being loosed from the team. I was out of the wagon in a minute. One of the oxen was prostrate on the ground, and his companion, from whose neck the yoke was just being removed, looked very likely soon to follow him. It had been the weak couple all along. Now we had but two yoke. How soon would they, one by one, follow?

Nothing could induce me to get into the wagon again. I said I would walk by the team, and for awhile I did; but by and by I found myself yards ahead. An inward power urged me forward; and the poor cattle were so slow, it seemed every minute as if they were going to stop. When I got so far off as to miss the sound of footsteps and wheels, I would pause, startled, wait and listen, dreading lest they had stopped, then as they came near, I would again walk beside them awhile, watching, through the darkness, the dim outlines of their heads and horns to see if they drooped lower. But soon I found myself again forward and alone. There was no moon yet, but by starlight we had for some time seen, only too plainly, the dead bodies of cattle lying here and there on both sides of the road. As we advanced they increased in numbers, and presently we saw two or three wagons. At first we thought we had overtaken a company, but coming close, no sign of life appeared. We had candles with us, so, as there was not the least breeze, we lit one or two and examined. Everything indicated a complete break down, and a hasty flight. Some animals were lying nearly in front of a wagon, apparently just as they had dropped down, while loose yokes and chains indicated that part of the teams had been driven on, laden probably with some necessaries of life; for the contents of the wagons were scattered in confusion, the most essential articles alone evidently having been thought worth carrying. "Ah," we said, "some belated little company has been obliged to pack what they could, and hurry to the river. Maybe it was the little company we met the other day." It was not a very encouraging scene but our four oxen still kept their feet; we would drive on a little farther, out of this scene of ruin, bait them, rest ourselves and go on. We did so, but soon found that what we had supposed an exceptional misfortune must have been the common fate of many companies; for at still shortening intervals, scenes of ruin similar to that just described kept recurring till we seemed to be but the last, little, feeble, struggling band at the rear of a routed army.

From near midnight, on through the small hours, it appeared necessary to stop more frequently, for both man and beast were sadly weary, and craved frequent nourishment. Soon after midnight we finished the last bit of meat we had; but there was still enough of the biscuit, rice and dried fruit to give us two or three more little baits. The waning moon now gave us a little melancholy light, showing still the bodies of dead cattle, and the forms of forsaken wagons as our grim waymarks. In one or two instances they had been left in the very middle of the road; and we had to turn out into the untracked sand to pass them. Soon we came upon a scene of wreck that surpassed anything preceding it. As we neared it, we wondered at the size of the wagons, which, in the dim light, looked tall as houses, against the sky. Coming to them, we found three or four of them to be of the make that the early Mississippi Valley emigrants used to call "Prairie Schooners": having deep beds, with projecting backs and high tops. One of them was specially immense, and, useless as we felt it to be to spend time in examining these warning relics of those who had gone before us, curiosity led us to lift the front curtain, which hung down, and by the light of our candle that we had again lit, look in. There from the strong, high bows, hung several sides of well cured bacon, much better in quality than that we had finished, at our last resting place. So we had but a short interval in which to say we were destitute of meat, for, though warned by all we saw not to add a useless pound to our load, we thought it wise to take a little, to eke out our scanty supply of food. And, as to the young men, who had so rarely, since they joined us, had a bit of meat they could call their own, they were very glad to bear the burden of a few pounds of bacon slung over their shoulders.

After this little episode, the only cheering incident for many hours, we turned to look at what lay round these monster wagons. It would be impossible to describe the motley collection of things of various sorts, strewed all about. The greater part of the materials, however, were pasteboard boxes, some complete, but most of them broken, and pieces of wrapping paper still creased, partially in the form of packages. But the most prominent objects were two or three, perhaps more, very beautifully finished trunks of various sizes, some of them standing open, their pretty trays lying on the ground, and all rifled of their contents; save that occasionally a few pamphlets, or, here and there, a book remained in the corners. We concluded that this must have been a company of merchants hauling a load of goods to California, that some of their animals had given out, and, fearing the rest would they had packed such things as they could, and had fled for their lives toward the river. There was only one thing, (besides the few pounds of bacon) that, in all these varied heaps of things, many of which, in civilized scenes, would have been valuable, I thought worth picking up. That was a little book, bound in cloth and illustrated with a number of small engravings. Its title was "Little Ella." I thought it would please Mary, so I put it in my pocket. It was an easily carried souvenir of the desert; and more than one pair of young eyes learned to read its pages in after years.

Morning was now approaching, and we hoped, when full daylight came, to see some signs of the river. But, for two or three weary hours after sunrise nothing of the kind appeared. The last of the water had been given to the cattle before daylight. When the sun was up we gave them the remainder of their hay, took a little breakfast and pressed forward. For a long time not a word was spoken save occasionally to the cattle. I had again, unconsciously, got in advance; my eyes scanning the horizon to catch the first glimpse of any change; though I had no definite idea in my mind what first to expect. But now there was surely something. Was it a cloud? It was very low at first and I feared it might evaporate as the sun warmed it. But it became rather more distinct and a little higher. I paused, and stood till the team came up. Then walking beside it I asked my husband what he thought that low dark line could be. "I think," he said, "it must be the timber on Carson River." Again we were silent and for a while I watched anxiously the heads of the two leading cattle. They were rather unusually fine animals, often showing considerable intelligence, and so faithful had they been, through so many trying scenes, I could not help feeling a sort of attachment to them; and I pitied them, as I observed how low their heads drooped as they pressed their shoulders so resolutely and yet so wearily against the bows. Another glance at the horizon. Surely there was now visible a little unevenness in the top of that dark line, as though it might indeed be trees. "How far off do you think that is now?" I said. "About five or six miles I guess," was the reply. At that moment the white-faced leader raised his head, stretched forward his nose and uttered a low "Moo-o-oo." I was startled fearing it was the sign for him to fall, exhausted. "What is the matter with him?" I said. "I think he smells the water" was the answer. "How can he at such a distance?" As I spoke, the other leader raised his head, stretched out his nose, and uttered the same sound. The hinder cattle seemed to catch the idea, whatever it was; they all somewhat increased their pace, and from that time, showed renewed animation.

But we had yet many weary steps to take, and noon had passed before we stood in the shade of those longed-for trees, beside the Carson River. As soon as the yokes were removed the oxen walked into the stream, and stood a few moments, apparently enjoying its coolness, then drank as they chose, came out, and soon found feed that satisfied them for the present, though at this point it was not abundant. The remainder of that day was spent in much needed rest. The next day we did not travel many miles, for our team showed decided signs of weakness, and the sand became deeper as we advanced, binding the wheels so as to make hauling very hard. We had conquered the desert.

ADDISON PRATT [1802–1872]

Addison Pratt left his native New Hampshire at age nineteen to work on a whaling ship. He spent ten years as a sailor before returning and marrying Louisa Barnes, a seamstress and schoolteacher. In 1838, with four daughters, the Pratts converted to the Mormon faith and in 1841 moved to Nauvoo, Illinois, the headquarters of Joseph Smith's Latter-day Saints. In 1847, with Addison on a church mission in the Sandwich Islands, Louisa traveled to Salt Lake City, and Addison joined them the following year. Pratt's "Diary" (1849), reported in Journals of Forty-Niners: Salt Lake to Los Angeles *(1954), is the account of the family's journey from Salt*

Lake City to California via the southern route to Los Angeles, a route that crossed through present-day Mesquite, Moapa, Las Vegas, Barstow, Victorville, and San Bernardino. In the excerpted section, Pratt details the "Big Springs" at Las Vegas. According to Frank Wright, a curator with the Nevada State Museum, Las Vegas, these were the springs where John C. Frémont and Kit Carson camped in 1844 and where the Mormon settlers grazed cattle in the 1850s. The springs fed Las Vegas Creek, creating the vegas *(Spanish for "meadows") downstream, making the founding of Las Vegas possible. Pratt described the area as "a large valley, covered with immense quantities of good grass . . . [that] would support a great number of cattle, and the soil appears to be very rich." The Pratts settled in the Mormon community at San Bernardino, California.*

Diary

Tuesday, Nov. 13   In the morning we were visited by men belonging to the [Gruwell-Derr] company traveling ahead of us; they were hunting cattle which had been stolen by the Indians. When they left us, going ahead, we followed them, and before noon we met a cow with an Indian's arrow sticking in her thigh. We extracted the arrow, but the flint with which it was pointed still remained in the flesh, and so we made an incision with a knife large enough to admit the finger and took it out. We then took the animal along with us. When we approached, we saw an Indian driving the cow, but as he espied us, he dodged behind the willows, which grew thick on either side of the road. At first, the poor cow was so badly frightened that we could not get near her; but when she saw that we were white men, she became perfectly gentle and stood still while we cut out the arrow. We traveled 8 miles, when we went into camp as some of the cattle were getting worn out; one cow gave entirely out, and several of our animals are becoming very weak and thin, and yet the most of the journey is yet before us.

Wednesday, Nov. 14   We continued our journey down the river and before noon we came to a canyon through which the road leads away from the Virgin. As there was neither grass nor water between this point and the next stream called the Muddy, we stopped and turned our animals out to graze. We were visited by a severe squall of rain and wind, and Brother James S. Brown and I, who guarded the cattle on that day, sought shelter in a cave. In continuing our journey up the canyon, we overtook Mr. Dallas, the owner of the cow we had found. He also owned seven wagons who had gone on ahead to the Muddy; he hailed from Galena and was on his way to the California gold mines with men and means and his family. The road in the canyon was very sandy, which made the pulling very hard on our weak cattle. In the evening we came to a steep hill which we had to ascend in order to reach the bench land above. This hill is about two hundred yards long and rises with a circular sweep near the top it is rocky and nearly perpendicular. We drove as far up as our teams were able to pull the wagons, when we blocked the wheels of each wagon and put ten or twelve yoke of oxen on the forward vehicle, and thus we got up with much difficulty; it was so steep near the top that an ox could barely stand without pulling at all. Mr. Dallas told us that he had chains enough with his teams on the Muddy to reach down the hill from the top and hook onto the wagons below, in which case the cattle pulling on the top of the hill could draw them up. But we knew that our cattle could not stand it long without grass and water. By the use of a coil of 2-inch rope found in one of the wagons and all of our lighter chains, we managed to pull all our wagons up. Mr. Dallas told us that a wagon belonging to a doctor in the company ahead had gotten nearly to the top when a chain broke and the wagon, with almost lightning speed, ran to the bottom of the hill where it was smashed to pieces, and the things with which it was loaded destroyed. It had taken Dallas and his men two days to get up the hill; but we were all up by 3 o'clock in the morning. We camped on top of the hill till daylight, nine miles from the Virgin.

November 15, 1849   At daylight, we hitched up our teams and drove ahead three miles, where we unexpectedly found some bunch grass, here we stopped an hour and hunted our cattle, the cows that belonged to Mr. Dallas, and the one belonging to Mr. Sowderwager were left in the canyon, as they were so feeble that they could not get them up the hill. The rain that fell the day before had moistened the grass so that the cattle ate very readily without water, after they had eaten we started over the fourteen mile desert that lies between the head of the canyon and the Far muddy creek, and arrived there a little after noon. . . . We stayed here the next day. This creek is fed by warm springs and the water is warm and pleasant to bath in this time of year, I found some fish in the creek much resembling a well known fish in the rivers of New England, called carp. They bite readily at a hook, the largest of them weighing near a pound. As I saw lumps on some of their sides, I cut them open and found them sacks, containing a sort of wireworm.

17th   Moved up the creek three miles and went into camp again, as we had a fifty mile desert to cross when we left here, we thought it best to recruit our teams as there is plenty of grass here; on the morning of the 18th I was out in pursuit of some ducks that frequented a pool there was in some grass, as I was creeping through the grass I espied Bro. Rich and Brown, on the side of the pool, they discovered me at the same time, and Bro. Rich called out, at the top of his voice "good morning Bro. Pratt" at the sound of the voice the ducks arose out of the water and flew toward me and as I returned the salute and said, "good morning Bro. Rich" I at the same time discharged my fowling piece at the ducks, where two fell from the flock, and Bro. Rich often laughed at me afterwards about the oddity of the occurrence. Bro. Rich had just before arrived in camp with his company of packers from the mountains and reported great distress among the wagons that had taken the cut off.

. . . .

We are all very much rejoiced to see Bro. Rich and his company of "Mormon Boys," they have had very hard times in the mountains, had lost some of their animals and expended nearly all of the provisions. . . .

As we had such a long desert to cross it was thought best to travel in the night so that our cattle would not suffer so much thirst as they would in the daytime. Consequently we had everything arranged and on the 20th at noon we left the creek and started up a canyon [California Wash] that led us out into the desert, on one side of this is a sort of barrier prepared by the Indians, and from this they attacked a pack company, that was the first that passed here this fall. The first part of our road was sandy, after that it was good, at two o'clock in the morning we had traveled twenty-two miles, a little off of the road, at this place we unexpectedly found a little grass and water, the last rains we found would facilitate our crossing deserts very much.

21st   At ten o'clock in the morning we started ahead again, and at ten in the evening the wagons reached Vegas Creek, this rises from some large springs and runs down through a large valley, covered with immense quantities of good grass. This would support a great number of cattle, and the soil appears to be very rich. As I went ahead with the horsemen we reached there about sunset, and before coming on to the edge of the grass we passed over a wide mud flat covered with meskeet trees, the largest I had seen.

We had seen no horses for several days, and as our provisions were getting low, it was our object to get all the wild game we could, and as we were stringing in a line, I heard someone ahead cry out "A hare." I looked ahead and saw a hare at the top of his speed coming nearly in a parallel line with the road, those on ahead shot as he passed, but he escaped unhurt until he came on a line with me, when I gave him a shot that keeled him over. We went into a camp and soon had him roasted, and as Bro. Rich, Hunt, and myself were picking his bones, "This," said Bro. Hunt, "is a sort of God send, for the wagons will not be up with us until midnight and we could get nothing to eat until they came," but they did arrive about ten o'clock, when we got supper. This place is about 450 miles from the Council house at Salt Lake City.

22nd   Traveled six miles and camped on the head of the Vegas. Here we began to see the sacrifices of property made by those that were on ahead of us, they [Gruwell-Derr Company] had camped here, and lightened their wagons of clothing and feather beds, there were piles of goose feathers and down lying in heaps, as if it had got to be troublesome times with them. The head of this stream is a curiosity, we found the water running in tolerable streams, from several of those wells [springs] that I have heretofore described, and were filled with[in] six or eight feet of the surface with quicksand and this was kept in perpetual motion, caused by the sand settling back into the channel and stopping the water until it had gathered force enough to burst its way through the sand, and as the water did not come to the surface at the same point, at such time, it kept the sand continually rolling and shifting from side to side in grand commotion. In one of them there were some lumps of hard load about the size of turtles and as they were lighter than the sand they were kept diving about in it until we thought they had life and could not be satisfied until we got one out.

WILLIAM LEWIS MANLY [1820–1903]

"Away out in the center of the Great American Desert, with an empty stomach . . . and parched throat," William Lewis Manly knew he "must succeed or perish." Originally published in 1894, Death Valley in '49 remains the classic account of pioneers lost in an unknown desert, a desert that in the wake of their harrowing ordeal would be named Death Valley. Born in Vermont, Manly was bitten by the California gold rush bug in 1848 and joined a wagon train one hundred wagons strong on the Oregon/California Trail. Reaching Salt Lake late in the season, the party was advised to veer south and follow the Old Spanish Trail to Los Angeles to avoid the Donner party's tragic fate. But the travelers grew impatient with the southern route, and that winter Manly joined a wagon party that left the known trail to head directly west. In their attempt to find a shortcut, this splinter group became completely lost in what is today southern Nevada, a bewildering experience reprinted here. The party, which included women and children, eventually straggled into Death Valley, near starvation. Manly, age twenty-nine, battled his conscience. Alone he could reach safety—and gold—quickly, but he chose to remain dedicated to the fellow members of his party, even if it meant his own death. So dehydrated they could not eat, so thirsty they could not sleep, Manly and a companion traveled fourteen days—and 270 miles—before finding help, bringing food back to their companions, and leading them to safety. Manly's plainspoken account, written in what has been described as a "meat-and-potatoes" style, contains such accurate detail about landforms that later scholars have mapped his route. Manly eventually married and became a farmer in San Jose. Today Death Valley is a National Park that attracts more than one million visitors per year.

from *Death Valley in '49*

We walked fast down the hill and reached the camp about dark to find it a most unhappy one indeed. Mrs. Bennett and Mrs. Arcane were in heart-rending distress. The four children were crying for water but there was not a drop to give them, and none could be reached before some time next day. The mothers were nearly crazy, for they expected the children would choke with thirst and die in their arms, and would rather perish themselves than suffer the agony of seeing their little ones gasp and slowly die. They reproached themselves as being the cause of all this trouble. For the love of gold they had left homes where hunger had never come, and often in sleep dreamed of the bounteous tables of their old homes only to be woefully disappointed in the morning. There was great gladness when John Rogers and I appeared in the camp and gave the mothers full canteens of water for themselves and little ones, and there was tears of joy and thankfulness upon their cheeks as they blessed us over and over again.

The oxen fared very hard. The ground was made up of broken stone, and all that grew was a dry and stunted brush not more than six inches high, of which the poor animals took an occasional dainty bite, and seemed hardly able to drag along.

It was only seven or eight miles to the warm spring and all felt better to know for a certainty that we would soon be safe again. We started early, even the women walked, so as to favor the poor oxen all we could. When within two miles of the water some of the oxen lay down and refused to rise again, so we had to leave them and a wagon, while the rest pushed on and reached the spring soon after noon. We took water and went back to the oxen left behind, and gave them some to drink. They were somewhat rested and got up, and we tried to drive them in without the wagons, but they were not inclined to travel without the yoke, so we put it on them and hitched to the wagon again. The yoke and the wagon seemed to brace them up a good deal, and they went along thus much better than when alone and scattered about, with nothing to lean upon.

The warm spring was quite large and ran a hundred yards or more before the water sank down into the dry and thirsty desert. The dry cornstalks of last years crop, some small willows, sage brush, weeds and grass suited our animals very well, and they ate better than for a long time, and we thought it best to remain two or three days to give them a chance to get rest. The Indian we left here the evening before had gone and left nothing behind but a chunk of crystallized rock salt. He seemed to be afraid of his friends.

The range we had been traveling nearly parallel with seemed to come to an end here where this snow peak stood, and immediately north and south of this peak there seemed to be a lower pass. The continuous range north was too low to hold snow. In the morning I concluded to go to the summit of that pass and with my glass have an extensive view. Two other boys started with me, and as we moved along the snow line we saw tracks of our runaway Indian in the snow, passing over a low ridge. As we went on up hill our boys began to fall behind, and long before night I could see nothing of them. The ground was quite soft, and I saw many tracks of Indians which put me on my guard. I reached the summit and as the shade of its mountain began to make it a little dark, I built a fire of sage brush, ate my grub, and when it was fairly dark, renewed the fire and passed on a mile, where in a small ravine with banks two feet high I lay down sheltered from the wind and slept till morning. I did this to beat the Indian in his own cunning.

Next morning I reached the summit about nine o'clock, and had the grandest view I ever saw. I could see north and south almost forever. The surrounding region seemed lower, but much of it black, mountainous and barren. On the west the snow peak shut out the view in that direction. To the south the mountains seemed to descend for more than twenty miles, and near the base, perhaps ten miles away, were several smokes, apparently from camp fires, and as I could see no animals or camp wagons anywhere I presumed them to be Indians. A few miles to the north and east of where I stood, and somewhat higher, was the roughest piece of ground I ever saw. It stood in sharp peaks and was of many colors, some of them so red that the mountain looked red hot, I imagined it to be a true volcanic point, and had never been so near one before, and the most wonderful picture of grand desolation one could ever see.

Toward the north I could see the desert the Jayhawkers and their comrades had under taken to cross, and if their journey was as troublesome as ours and very much longer, they might by this time be all dead of thirst. I remained on this summit an hour or so bringing my glass to bear on all points within my view, and scanning closely for everything that might help us or prove an obstacle to our progress. The more I looked the more I satisfied myself that we were yet a long way from California and the serious question of our ever living to get there presented itself to me as I tramped along down the grade to camp. I put down at least another month of heavy weary travel before we could hope to make the land of gold, and our stock of strength and provisions were both pretty small for so great a tax upon them. I thought so little about anything else that the Indians might have captured me easily, for I jogged along without a thought of them. I thought of the bounteous stock of bread and beans upon my father's table, to say nothing about all the other good things, and here was I, the oldest son, away out in the center of the Great American Desert, with an empty stomach and a dry and parched throat, and clothes fast wearing out with constant wear. And perhaps I had not yet seen the worst of it. I might be forced to see men, and the women and children of our party, choke and die, powerless to help them. It was a darker, gloomier day than I had ever known could be, and alone I wept aloud, for I believed I could see the future, and the results were bitter to contemplate. I hope no reader of this history may ever be placed in a position to be thus tried for I am not ashamed to say that I have a weak point to show under such circumstances. It is not in my power to tell how much I suffered in my lonely trips, lasting sometimes days and nights that I might give the best advice to those of my party. I believed that I could escape at any time myself, but all must be brought through or perish, and with this all I knew I must not discourage the others. I could tell them the truth, but I must keep my worst apprehensions to myself lest they lose heart and hope and faith needlessly.

I reached the camp on the third day where I found the boys who went part way with me and whom I had out-walked. I related to the whole camp what I had seen, and when all was told it appeared that the route from the mountains westerly was the only route that could be taken, they told me of a discovery they had made of a pile of squashes probably raised upon the place, and sufficient in number so that every person could have one. I did not approve of this for we had no title to this produce, and might be depriving the rightful owner of the means of life. I told them not only was it wrong to rob them of their food, but they could easily revenge themselves on us by shooting our cattle, or scalp us, by gathering a company of their own people together. They had no experience with red men and were slow to see the results I spoke of as possible.

During my absence an ox had been killed, for some were nearly out of provisions, and flesh was the only means to prevent starvation. The meat was distributed amongst the entire camp, with the understanding that when it became necessary to kill another it should be divided in the same way. Some one of the wagons would have to be left for lack of animals to draw it. Our animals were so poor that one would not last long as food. No fat could be found on the entire carcass, and the marrow of the great bones was a thick liquid, streaked with blood resembling corruption.

Our road led us around the base of the mountain; There were many large rocks in our way, some as large as houses, but we wound around among them in a very crooked way and managed to get along. The feet of the oxen became so sore that we made moccasins for them from the hide of the ox that was killed, and with this protection they got along very well. Our trains now consisted of seven wagons. Bennett had two; Arcane two; Earhart Bros. one. Culverwell, Fish and others one; and there was one other, the owners of which I have forgotten. The second night we had a fair camp with water and pretty fair grass and brush for the oxen. We were not very far from the snow line and this had some effect on the country.

When Bennett retired that night he put on a camp kettle of the fresh beef and so arranged the fire that it would cook slowly and be done by daylight for breakfast. After an hour or so Mr. Bennett went out to replenish the fire and see how the cooking was coming on, and when I went to put more water in the kettle, he found that to his disappointment, the most of the meat was gone. I was rolled up in my blanket under his wagon and awoke when he came to the fire and saw him stand and look around as if to fasten the crime on the right party if possible, but soon he came to me, and in a whisper said: "Did you see anyone around the fire after we went to bed?" I assured him I did not, and then he told me some one had taken his meat. "Do you think," said he "that any one is so near out of food as to be starving?" "I know the meat is poor, and who ever took it must be nearly starving." After a whispered conversation we went to bed, but we both rose at daylight and, as we sat by the fire, kept watch of those who got up and came around. We thought we knew the right man, but were not sure, and could not imagine what might happen if stealing grub should begin and continue. It is a sort of unwritten law that in parties such as ours, he who steals provisions forfeits his life. We knew we must keep watch and if the offense was repeated the guilty one might be compelled to suffer. Bennett watched closely and for a few days I kept closely with the wagons for fear there might be trouble. It was really the most critical point in our experience. After three or four days all hope of detecting the criminal had passed, and all danger was over out of any difficulty.

One night we had a fair camp, as we were close to the base of the snow butte, and found a hole of clear or what seemed to be living water. There were a few minnows in it not much more than an inch long. This was among a big pile of rocks, and around these the oxen found some grass.

There now appeared to be a pass away to the south as a sort of outlet to the great plain which lay to the north of us, but immediately west and across the desert waste, extending to the foot of a low black range of mountains, through which there seemed to be no pass, the distant snowy peak lay still farther on, with Martin's pass over it still a long way off though we had been steering toward it for a month. Now as we were compelled to go west this impassable barrier was in our way and if no pass could be found in it we would be compelled to go south and make no progress in a westerly direction.

Our trail was now descending to the bottom of what seemed to be the narrowest part of the plain, the same one the Jayhawkers had started across, further north, ten days before. When we reached the lowest part of this valley we came to a running stream, and, as dead grass could be seen in the bed where the water ran very slowly, I concluded it only had water in it after hard rains in the mountains, perhaps a hundred miles, to the north. This water was not pure; it had a bitter taste, and no doubt in dry weather was a rank poison. Those who partook of it were affected about as if they had taken a big dose of salts.

A short distance above this we found the trail of the Jayhawkers going west, and thus we knew they had got safely across the great plain and then turned southward. I hurried along their trail for several miles and looked the country over with field glass becoming fully satisfied we should find no water til we reached the summit, of the next range, and then fearing the party had not taken the precaution to bring along some water I went back to them and found they had none. I told them they would not see a drop for the next forty miles, and they unloaded the lightest wagon and drove back with everything they had which would hold water, to get a good supply.

I turned back again on the Jayhawker's road, and followed it so rapidly that well toward night I was pretty near the summit, where a pass through this rocky range had been found and on this mountain not a tree a shrub or spear of grass could be found—desolation beyond conception. I carried my gun along every day, but for the want of a chance to kill any game a single load would remain in my gun for a month. Very seldom a rabbit could be seen, but not a bird of any kind, not even a hawk buzzard or crow made their appearance here.

When near the steep part of the mountain, I found a dead ox the Jayhawkers had left, as no camp could be made here for lack of water and grass, the meat could not be saved. I found the body of the animal badly shrunken, but in condition, as far as putrefaction was concerned, as perfect as when alive. A big gash had been cut in the ham clear to the bone and the sun had dried the flesh in this. I was so awful hungry that I took my sheath knife and cut a big steak which I devoured as I walked along, without cooking or salt. Some may say they would starve before eating such meat, but if they have ever experienced hunger till it begins to draw down the life itself, they will find the impulse of self preservation something not to be controlled by mere reason. It is an instinct that takes possession of one in spite of himself.

SARAH WINNEMUCCA [CA. 1844–1891]

"I was born somewhere near 1844," writes Sarah Winnemucca (Hopkins) in Life among the Piutes: Their Wrongs and Claims (1883), a blend of autobiography, tribal history, ethnography, and political argument that is believed to be the first book by a Native American woman. Born near Lovelock, Nevada, Thocmetony—"Shell-Flower" in English—was about five when the *forty-niners stampeded through her homeland. Both her grandfather, Captain Truckee, and her father, Winnemucca, were prominent Paiute leaders who urged peaceful coexistence with the unstoppable white tide. At thirteen Thocmetony was sent to live with the Ormsby family in what is now Genoa, Nevada. There she was known as "Sarah" and quickly learned English, reading, and writing. Thereafter, Winnemucca mediated between two cultures, comfortable in neither. Her three marriages—two to white men—were likewise difficult, the last to Lewis Hopkins. As interpreter between the Paiutes and U.S. officials, Winnemucca witnessed war, forced relocation, gross injustices, and corruption. Incensed, she became a courageous "word warrior" for her people, delivering more than four hundred speeches throughout America and meeting, in 1880, with both Secretary of the Interior Carl Schurz and President Rutherford B. Hayes. She wrote* Life among the Piutes *to make the plight of her people more widely known and to apply pressure on Congress for redress of wrongs. In 1885 Winnemucca opened an innovative bilingual school, encouraging Paiute children to function in both worlds. Sadly, events beyond her control forced the school to close in 1889. Although Winnemucca died discouraged and misunderstood, history is tending to vindicate her actions and honor her heroic efforts on behalf of her people. Winnemucca was the first woman to have a Nevada state historic marker erected in her honor; she was named to the Nevada Writers Hall of Fame and inducted into the National Women's Hall of Fame; and in 2005 her statue was installed in the National Statuary Hall in the U.S. Capitol.*

from Life among the Piutes

I was born somewhere near 1844, but am not sure of the precise time. I was a very small child when the first white people came into our country. They came like a lion, yes, like a roaring lion, and have continued so ever since, and I have never forgotten their first coming. My people were scattered at that time over nearly all the territory now known as Nevada. My grandfather was chief of the entire Piute nation, and was camped near Humboldt Lake, with a small portion of his tribe, when a party traveling eastward from California was seen coming. When the news was brought to my grandfather, he asked what they looked like? When told that they had hair on their faces, and were white, he jumped up and clasped his hands together, and cried aloud,—

"My white brothers,—my long-looked for white brothers have come at last!"

He immediately gathered some of his leading men, and went to the place where the party had gone into camp. Arriving near them, he was commanded to halt in a manner that was readily understood without an interpreter. Grandpa at once made signs of friendship by throwing down his robe and throwing up his arms to show them he had no weapons; but in vain,—they kept him at a distance. He knew not what to do. He had expected so much pleasure in welcoming his white brothers to the best in the land, that after looking at them sorrowfully for a little while, he came away quite unhappy. But he would not give them up so easily. He took some of his most trustworthy men and followed them day after day, camping near them at night, and travelling in sight of them by day, hoping in this way to gain their confidence. But he was disappointed, poor dear old soul!

I can imagine his feelings, for I have drank deeply from the same cup. When I think of my past life, and the bitter trials I have endured, I can scarcely believe I live, and yet I do; and, with the help of Him who notes the sparrow's fall, I mean to fight for my down-trodden race while life lasts.

Seeing they would not trust him, my grandfather left them, saying, "Perhaps they will come again next year." Then he summoned his whole people, and told them this tradition:—

"In the beginning of the world there were only four, two girls and two boys. Our forefather and mother were only two, and we are their children. You all know that a great while ago there was a happy family in this world. One girl and one boy were dark and the others were white. For a time they got along together without quarrelling, but soon they disagreed, and there was trouble. They were cross to one another and fought, and our parents were very much grieved. They prayed that their children might learn better, but it did not do any good; and afterwards the whole household was made so unhappy that the father and mother saw that they must separate their children; and then our father took the dark boy and girl, and the white boy and girl, and asked them, 'Why are you so cruel to each other?' They hung down their heads, and would not speak. They were ashamed. He said to them, 'Have I not been kind to you all, and given you everything your hearts wished for? You do not have to hunt and kill your own game to live upon. You see, my dear children, I have power to call whatsoever kind of game we want to eat; and I also have the power to separate my dear children, if they are not good to each other.' So he separated his children by a word. He said, 'Depart from each other, you cruel children;—go across the mighty ocean and do not seek each other's lives.'

"So the light girl and boy disappeared by that one word, and their parents saw them no more, and they were grieved, although they knew their children were happy. And by-and-by the dark children grew into a large nation; and we believe it is the one we belong to, and that the nation that sprung from the white children will some time send some one to meet us and heal all the old trouble. Now, the white people we saw a few days ago must certainly be our white brothers, and I want to welcome them. I want to love them as I love all of you. But they would not let me; they were afraid. But they will come again, and I want you one and all to promise that, should I not live to welcome them myself, you will not hurt a hair on their heads, but welcome them as I tried to do."

How good of him to try and heal the wound, and how vain were his efforts! My people had never seen a white man, and yet they existed, and were a strong race. The people promised as he wished, and they all went back to their work.

· · · · · · · · ·

The following spring, before my grandfather returned home, there was a great excitement among my people on account of fearful news coming from different tribes, that the people whom they called their white brothers were killing everybody that came in their way, and all the Indian tribes had gone into the mountains to save their lives. So my father told all his people to go into the mountains and hunt and lay up food for the coming winter. Then we all went into the mountains. There was a fearful story they told us children. Our mothers told us that the whites were killing everybody and eating them. So we were all afraid of them. Every dust that we could see blowing in the valleys we would say it was the white people. In the late fall my father told his people to go to the rivers and fish, and we all went to Humboldt River, and the women went to work gathering wild seed, which they grind between the rocks. The stones are round, big enough to hold in the hands. The women did this when they got back, and when they had gathered all they could they put it in one place and covered it with grass, and then over the grass mud. After it is covered it looks like an Indian wigwam.

Oh, what a fright we all got one morning to hear some white people were coming. Every one ran as best they could. My poor mother was left with my little sister and me. Oh, I never can forget it. My poor mother was carrying my little sister on her back, and trying to make me run; but I was so frightened I could not move my feet, and while my poor mother was trying to get me along my aunt overtook us, and she said to my mother: "Let us bury our girls, or we shall all be killed and eaten up." So they went to work and buried us, and told us if we heard any noise not to cry out, for if we did they would surely kill us and eat us. So our mothers buried me and my cousin, planting sage bushes over our faces to keep the sun from burning them, and there we were left all day.

Oh, can any one imagine my feelings *buried alive,* thinking every minute that I was to be unburied and eaten up by the people that my grandfather loved so much? With my heart throbbing, and not daring to breathe, we lay there all day. It seemed that the night would never come. Thanks be to God! the night came at last. Oh, how I cried and said: "Oh, father, have you forgotten me? Are you never coming for me?" I cried so I thought my very heartstrings would break.

At last we heard some whispering. We did not dare to whisper to each other, so we lay still. I could hear their footsteps coming nearer and nearer. I thought my heart was coming right out of my mouth. Then I heard my mother say, "'T is right here!" Oh, can any one in this world ever imagine what were my feelings when I was dug up by my poor mother and father? My cousin and I were once more happy in our mothers' and fathers' care, and we were taken to where all the rest were.

I was once buried alive; but my second burial shall be for ever, where no father or mother will come and dig me up. It shall not be with throbbing heart that I shall listen for coming footsteps. I shall be in the sweet rest of peace,—I, the chieftain's weary daughter.

Well, while we were in the mountains hiding, the people that my grandfather called our white brothers came along to where our winter supplies were. They set everything we had left on fire. It was a fearful sight. It was all we had for the winter, and it was all burnt during that night. My father took some of his men during the night to try and save some of it, but they could not; it had burnt down before they got there.

These were the last white men that came along that fall. My people talked fearfully that winter about those they called our white brothers. My people said they had something like awful thunder and lightning, and with that they killed everything that came in their way.

This whole band of white people perished in the mountains, for it was too late to cross them. We could have saved them, only my people were afraid of them. We never knew who they were, or where they came from. So, poor things, they must have suffered fearfully, for they all starved there. The snow was too deep.

Early in the following spring, my father told all his people to go to the mountains, for there would be a great emigration that summer. He told them he had had a wonderful dream, and wanted to tell them all about it.

He said, "Within ten days come together at the sink of Carson, and I will tell you my dream."

The sub-chiefs went everywhere to tell their people what my father had told them to say; and when the time came we all went to the sink of Carson.

Just about noon, while we were on the way, a great many of our men came to meet us, all on their horses. Oh, what a beautiful song they sang for my father as they came near us! We passed them, and they followed us, and as we came near to the encampment, every man, woman, and child were out looking for us. They had a place all ready for us. Oh, how happy everybody was! One could hear laughter everywhere, and songs were sung by happy women and children.

My father stood up and told his people to be merry and happy for five days. It is a rule among our people always to have five days to settle anything. My father told them to dance at night, and that the men should hunt rabbits and fish, and some were to have games of football, or any kind of sport or playthings they wished, and the women could do the same, as they had nothing else to do. My people were so happy during the five days,—the women ran races, and the men ran races on foot and on horses.

My father got up very early one morning, and told his people the time had come,—that we could no longer be happy as of old, as the white people we called our brothers had brought a great trouble and sorrow among us already. He went on and said,—

"These white people must be a great nation, as they have houses that move. It is wonderful to see them move along. I fear we will suffer greatly by their coming to our country; they come for no good to us, although my father said they were our brothers, but they do not seem to think we are like them. What do you all think about it? Maybe I am wrong. My dear children, there is something telling me that I am not wrong, because I am sure they have minds like us, and think as we do; and I know that they were doing wrong when they set fire to our winter supplies. They surely knew it was our food."

And this was the first wrong done to us by our white brothers.

Now comes the end of our merrymaking.

Then my father told his people his fearful dream, as he called it. He said,—

"I dreamt this same thing three nights,—the very same. I saw the greatest emigration that has yet been through our country. I looked North and South and East and West, and saw nothing but dust, and I heard a great weeping. I saw women crying, and I also saw my men shot down by the white people. They were killing my people with something that made a great noise like thunder and lightning, and I saw the blood streaming from the mouths of my men that lay all around me. I saw it as if it was real. Oh, my dear children! You may all think it is only a dream,—nevertheless, I feel that it will come to pass. And to avoid bloodshed, we must all go to the mountains during the summer, or till my father comes back from California. He will then tell us what to do. Let us keep away from the emigrant roads and stay in the mountains all summer. There are to be a great many pine-nuts this summer, and we can lay up great supplies for the coming winter, and if the emigrants don't come too early, we can take a run down and fish for a month, and lay up dried fish. I know we can dry a great many in a month, and young men can go into the valleys on hunting excursions, and kill as many rabbits as they can. In that way we can live in the mountains all summer and all winter too."

So ended my father's dream. During that day one could see old women getting together talking over what they had heard my father say. They said,—

"It is true what our great chief has said, for it was shown to him by a higher power. It is not a dream. Oh, it surely will come to pass. We shall no longer be a happy people, as we now are; we shall no longer go here and there as of old; we shall no longer build our big fires as a signal to our friends, for we shall always be afraid of being seen by those bad people."

"Surely they don't eat people?"

"Yes, they do eat people, because they ate each other up in the mountains last winter."

WOVOKA [CA. 1856–1932]

More than two hundred men, women, and children were massacred at Wounded Knee, South Dakota, in December 1890, a tragic slaughter that ended the Indian wars of the West. Nevada is tied to this landmark battle through the Paiute prophet Wovoka, whose Ghost Dance religion swept across western America in the late 1880s. Representatives from many Indian nations traveled to Wovoka's home on the Walker River near Yerington to hear his message from God and learn the Ghost Dance, a ceremony that promised to restore better days. Military officers interpreted the Plains Indians' "frenzied" dancing as a precursor to war and ordered soldiers to suppress the dance, resulting in the massacre at Wounded Knee. In 1891 the U.S. government sent ethnologist James Mooney to Nevada to meet Wovoka and determine if his teachings were dangerous. Mooney's published report completely absolves Wovoka, finding him "a mild-tempered member of a weak and unwarlike tribe" and his doctrine "one of peace." Mooney reprinted Wovoka's message as translated by Casper Edson, an Arapaho; another version written by the daughter of a Cheyenne delegate; and Mooney's own rendering for clarification. Wovoka's peaceful intent is evident, as is his vision of restored health and vitality, a message of hope to people whose lands were taken, ways of life destroyed, and population decimated. Son of a Northern Paiute shaman, Wovoka (meaning "wood cutter") was sent at a young age to live with the Wilson family, white ranchers in Mason Valley, where he became known as Jack Wilson. Throughout his life Wovoka fell into trances in which his body went rigid and he received holy visions. He correctly predicted the end of the severe drought of 1888–89 and was reputed to make ice appear on summer rivers and to be impervious to bullets. After Wounded Knee, the Ghost Dance religion dwindled, but Wovoka continued to dictate letters and meet with Indian delegates for many years.

The Messiah Letter
(Arapaho version)

What you get home you make dance, and will give you the same. when you dance four days and in night one day, dance day time, five days and then fift, will wash five for every body. He likes you flok you give him good many things, he heart been satting feel good. After you get home, will give good cloud, and give you chance to make you feel good. and he give you good spirit. and he give you al a good paint.

You folks want you to come in three [months] here, any tribs from there. There will be good bit snow this year. Sometimes rain's, in fall, this year some rain, never give you any thing like that. grandfather said when he die never no cry. no hurt anybody. no fight, good behave always, it will give you satisfaction, this young man, he is a good Father and mother, dont tell no white man. Jueses was on ground, he just like cloud. Every body is alive again, I don't know when they will [be] here, may be this fall or in spring.

Every body never get sick, be young again,—(if young fellow no sick any more,) work for white men never trouble with him until you leave, when it shake the earth don't be afraid no harm any body.

You make dance for six weeks night, and put you foot [food?] in dance to eat for every body and wash in the water. that is all to tell, I am in to you. and you will received a good words from him some time, Don't tell lie.

(Cheyenne version)
When you get home you have to make dance. You must dance four nights and one day time. You will take bath in the morning before you go to yours homes, for every body, and give you all the same as this. Jackson Wilson likes you all, he is glad to get good many things. His heart satting fully of gladness, after you get home, I will give you a good cloud and give you chance to make you feel good. I give you a good spirit, and give you all good paint, I want you people to come here again, want them in three months any tribs of you from there. There will be a good deal snow this year. Some time rains, in fall this year some rain, never give you any thing like that, grandfather, said, when they were die never cry, no hurt any body, do any harm for it, not to fight. Be a good behave always. It will give a satisfaction in your life. This young man is a good father and mother. Do not tell the white people about this, Juses is on the ground, he just like cloud. Every body is a live again. I don't know when he will be here, may be will be this fall or in spring. When it happen it may be this. There will be no sickness and return to young again. Do not refuse to work for white man or do not make any trouble with them

until you leave them. When the earth shakes do not be afraid it will not hurt you. I want you to make dance for six weeks. Eat and wash good clean yourselves [The rest of the letter had been erased].

(free Rendering)

When you get home you must make a dance to continue five days. Dance four successive nights, and the last night keep up the dance until the morning of the fifth day, when all must bathe in the river and then disperse to their homes. You must all do in the same way.

I, Jack Wilson, love you all, and my heart is full of gladness for the gifts you have brought me. When you get home I shall give you a good cloud [rain?] which will make you feel good. I give you a good spirit and give you all good paint. I want you to come again in three months, some from each tribe there [the Indian Territory].

There will be a good deal of snow this year and some rain. In the fall there will be such a rain as I have never given you before.

Grandfather [a universal title of reverence among Indians and here meaning the messiah] says, when your friends die you must not cry. You must not hurt anybody or do harm to anyone. You must not fight. Do right always. It will give you satisfaction in life. This young man has a good father and mother. [Possibly this refers to Casper Edson, the young Arapaho who wrote down this message of Wovoka for the delegation].

Do not tell the white people about this. Jesus is now upon the earth. He appears like a cloud. The dead are all alive again. I do not know when they will be here; maybe this fall or in the spring. When the time comes there will be no more sickness and everyone will be young again.

Do not refuse to work for the whites and do not make any trouble with them until you leave them. When the earth shakes [at the coming of the new world] do not be afraid. It will not hurt you.

I want you to dance every six weeks. Make a feast at the dance and have food that everybody may eat. Then bathe in the water. That is all. You will receive good words again from me some time. Do not tell lies.

FOUR

LITERARY RICHES FROM THE MINING FRONTIER

From a literary standpoint, the greatest asset of Nevada's mining era is the rich body of writing that it produced. While the gold and silver mines were exhausted long ago, the literature, like a renewable resource, remains vital, awaiting discovery by new generations of readers. And what a contrast you'll see between the emigrant accounts of the 1840s, recorded by weary travelers who feared for their lives, and writing from the mining frontier a decade later, penned by lusty adventurers, living it up. The former experienced Nevada as a terrifying desert where a misstep could mean miserable death, while the latter regarded the same landscape as a deceptive veneer concealing fabulous treasure, a land where a lucky strike could mean magnificent wealth.

The year 1859 may be the most important in Nevada history, marking an abrupt change in the life of the place. By that year, word was out that there were rich gold deposits east of the Sierra, and the "Rush to Washoe" was on. It was soon discovered that the black mud impeding the efficient extraction of gold was, in fact, silver of almost unbelievable purity. The Comstock veins of precious metal proved to be more extensive than anything California could offer, and as thousands rushed in, Virginia City materialized like a pop-up tent; the Nevada Territory was created by Congress in 1861, and statehood followed soon thereafter, in 1864. Money made Nevada and Nevada made money.

Newspapers were key players on the mining frontier, publicizing new discoveries, reporting profits and stock prices, providing grisly details about fires and mining accidents, exposing corruption, announcing meetings, new businesses, and social events, and entertaining an audience hungry for print. Some men became journalists after unsuccessful stints as prospectors, enjoying the steady pay but certainly not immune from risk: Frontier journalists were held personally accountable for their stories, and on occasion had to face down—or fight off—hot-tempered men whom their articles offended. Even in a bustling mining town, however, there were slow news days. Inventive journalists such as Dan De Quille, Mark Twain, and Fred Hart found creative ways to fill columns, employing their considerable wit by writing poems, humorous sketches, tall tales, and outright hoaxes, some of which gained international attention, such as De Quille's "The Rolling Stones of Pahranagat," which elicited a letter of inquiry from a noted scientist in Germany. Indeed the "Sagebrush School," as some literary scholars characterize writers of this period, elevated literary hoax to a high art, no doubt playing on the fraud and gullibility that were such a part of the mining enterprise.

The Comstock bonanza inspired prospectors to buy a burro and, often with a grubstake, wander over formerly spurned desert country in search of another strike. Between 1860 and 1880 dozens of mining camps sprung up throughout the state. Indeed, a map of nineteenth-century mining camps in the Silver State contains more towns than does a road map of Nevada today: Aurora, Star City, Unionville, Austin, Cortez, Silver Peak, Belmont, Tuscarora, Hamilton, Eureka, Treasure City, Pioche, Candelaria. Then came *borrasca,* or bust, a twenty-year hiatus that saw no new strikes, exodus from Nevada, and talk of revoking statehood. Major gold discoveries in Tonopah (1900) and Goldfield (1903) kicked off a new series of camps in the early twentieth century, and towns like Delamar, Searchlight, Bullfrog, Rhyolite, Manhattan, Fairview, Rawhide, Wonder, and Jarbidge appeared. Every substantial mining district quickly had at least one newspaper, and sometimes more. Each camp produced lore as well as ore, tales that form a colorful chapter in Nevada's heritage.

The stories collected here are a small sack full of samples from the much vaster literary terrain from which they were gathered. We start with a cluster from the Comstock, sharing the first impressions of a roving travel writer who saw Virginia City in its infancy, then showcasing several of the Comstock's leading writers, and ending with the memoir of a widowed mother. Next, we visit some other, later, mining camps and prospects—Pioche, Austin, the Black Rock Desert, Tonopah, and Goldfield. The chapter concludes with twentieth-century reconsiderations of Nevada's mining towns and characters.

J. ROSS BROWNE [1821–1875]

The classic account of Virginia City during the earliest days of the Comstock, "A Peep at Washoe," comes from a man who had already traveled far and wide. Born near Dublin, Ireland, in 1821, John Ross Browne moved with his family to the United States in 1833, settling in Louisville, Kentucky. The adventurous Browne left home at seventeen to hire on as a flatboat hand on the Mississippi River. When he was twenty-one Browne joined the crew of a whaler bound for Zanzibar, later producing Etchings of a Whaling Cruise *(1846), believed to be an important source for Herman Melville's* Moby-Dick. *Browne's literary peregrinations crisscrossed the globe—England, Germany, Iceland, Norway, the Mediterranean, Russia, China, the Middle East, Egypt, "Robinson Crusoe's island" off the coast of Chile, and the American Southwest. Becoming a writer to support his wanderlust, he contributed articles to the* Globe, National Intelligencer, Harper's, *and* Overland Monthly, *gathering these pieces into travel books and supplementing this income with government posts as revenue agent, postal inspector, customs agent, and Indian agent. By the time he spent two months in Virginia City in 1860, prospecting for silver in the newly discovered Comstock Lode, he had developed a writing style that blended humor with a sharp eye for detail, a combination often accompanied by his own exquisite drawings. In Virginia City he saw "gangs of miners . . . digging and delving into the earth like so many infatuated gophers," and he penned a memorably infernal impression of the place. "A Peep at Washoe" originally appeared serially in* Harper's *magazine in 1860–61. That series and Browne's 1869 book* Washoe Revisited *likely influenced Mark Twain's* Roughing It. *Browne was a few steps ahead of followers whose reputations would eventually eclipse his own. Married with nine children, he spent the last years of his life with his family outside of Oakland, California, succumbing suddenly to appendicitis in 1875.*

A Peep at Washoe

There was now, of course, an end to all mining excitements. It could never again happen that such an imposition could be practiced upon public credulity. In the whole state there was not another sheep that could be gulled by the cry of wolf. Business would now resume its steady and legitimate course. Property would cease to fluctuate in value. Every branch of industry would become fixed upon a permanent and reliable basis. All these excitements were the natural results of the daring and enterprising character of the people. But now, having worked off their superabundant steam, they would be prepared to go ahead systematically, and develop those resources which they had hitherto neglected. It was a course of medical effervescence highly beneficial to the body politic. All morbid appetite for sudden wealth was now gone forever.

But softly, good friends! What rumor is this? Whence come these silvery strains that are wafted to our ears from the passes of the Sierra Nevada? What dulcet Eolian harmonies—what divine, enchanting ravishment is it

"That with these raptures moves the vocal air"?

As I live, it is a cry of Silver! Silver in WASHOE! Not gold, now, you silly men of Gold Bluff, you Kern Riverites, you daring explorers of British Columbia! But SILVER—solid, pure SILVER! Beds of it ten thousand feet deep! Acres of it! miles of it! hundreds of millions of dollars poking their backs up out of the earth ready to be pocketed!

Do you speak of the mines of Potosí or Golconda? Do you dare to quote the learned Baron Von Tschudi on South America and Mexico? Do you refer me to the ransom of Atahualpa, the unfortunate Inca, in the days of Pizarro? Nothing at all, I assure you, to the silver mines of Washoe! "Sir," said my informant to me, in strict confidence, no later than this morning, "you may rely upon it, for I am personally acquainted with a brother of the gentleman whose most intimate friend saw the man whose partner has just come over the mountains, and he says there never was the like on the face of the earth! The ledges are ten thousand feet deep—solid masses of silver. Let us be off! Now is the time! A pack-mule, pick and shovel, hammer, and frying-pan will do. You need nothing more. HURRAH FOR WASHOE!"

. . . .

I was desirous of seeing as much of the mining region as possible, and with this view took the stage for Virginia City. At Silver City, eight miles from Carson, I dismounted, and proceeded the rest of the way on foot. The road here becomes rough and hilly, and but little is to be seen of the city except a few tents and board shanties. Half a mile beyond is a remarkable gap cut by Nature through the mountain, as if for the express purpose of giving the road an opportunity to visit Virginia City.

As I passed through the Devil's Gate it struck me that there was something ominous in the name. "Let all who enter here—" But I had already reached the other side. It was too late now for repentance. I was about to inquire where the devil—Excuse me, I use the word in no indecorous sense. I was simply about to ask where he lived, when, looking up the road, I saw amid the smoke and din of shivered rocks, where grimy imps were at work blasting for ore, a string of adventurers laden with picks, shovels, and crow-bars; kegs of powder, frying-pans, pitch-forks, and other instruments of torture—all wearily toiling in the same direction; decrepit old men, with avarice imprinted upon their furrowed brows; Jews and Gentiles, foot-weary and haggard; the young and old, the strong and the weak, all alike burning with an unhallowed lust for lucre; and then I shuddered as the truth flashed upon me that they were going straight to—Virginia City.

Every foot of the canyon was claimed, and gangs of miners were at work all along the road, digging and delving into the earth like so many infatuated gophers. Many of these unfortunate creatures lived in holes dug into the side of the hill, and here and there a blanket thrown over a few stakes served as a domicile to shield them from the weather.

At Gold Hill, two miles beyond the Gate, the excitement was quite pitiable to behold. Those who were not at work burrowing holes into the mountain were gathered in gangs around the whisky saloons, pouring liquid fire down their throats, and swearing all the time in a manner so utterly reckless as to satisfy me they had long since bid farewell to hope.

The district is said to be exceedingly rich in gold, and I fancy it may well be so, for it is certainly rich in nothing else. A more barren-looking and forbidding spot could scarcely be found elsewhere on the face of the earth. The whole aspect of the country indicates that it must have been burned up in hot fires many years ago and reduced to a mass of cinders, or scraped up from all the desolate spots in the known world, and thrown over the Sierra Nevada mountains in a confused mass to be out of the way. I do not wish to be understood as speaking disrespectfully of any of the works of creation, but it is inconceivable that this region should ever have been designed as an abode for man.

A short distance beyond Gold Hill we came in sight of the great mining capital of Washoe, the far-famed Virginia City. In the course of a varied existence it had been my fortune to visit the city of Jerusalem, the city of Constantinople, the City of the Sea, the City of the Dead, the Seven Cities, and others of historical celebrity in the Old World, and many famous cities in the New, including Port Townsend, Crescent City, Benicia, and the New York of the Pacific, but I had never yet beheld such a city as that which now burst upon my distended organs of vision.

On a slope of mountains speckled with snow, sage-bushes, and mounds of up-turned earth, without any apparent beginning or end, congruity or regard for the eternal fitness of things, lay outspread the wondrous city of Virginia.

Frame shanties, pitched together as if by accident; tents of canvas, of blankets, of brush, of potato-sacks and old shirts, with empty whisky-barrels for chimneys; smoky hovels of mud and stone; coyote holes in the mountain side forcibly seized and held by men; pits and shafts with smoke issuing from every crevice; piles of goods and rubbish on craggy points, in the hollows, on the rocks, in the mud, in the snow, everywhere, scattered broadcast in pell-mell confusion, as if the clouds had suddenly burst overhead and rained down the dregs of all the flimsy, rickety, filthy little hovels and rubbish of merchandise that had ever undergone the process of evaporation from the earth since the days of Noah. The intervals of space, which may or may not have been streets, were dotted over with human beings of such sort, variety, and numbers, that the famous ant-hills of Africa were as nothing in the comparison. To say that they were rough, muddy, unkempt, and unwashed would be but faintly expressive of their actual appearance; they were all this by reason of exposure to the weather; but they seemed to have caught the very diabolical tint and grime of the whole place. Here and there, to be sure, a San Francisco dandy of the "boiled-shirt" and "stove-pipe" pattern loomed up in proud consciousness of the triumphs of art under adverse circumstances, but they were merely peacocks in the barn-yard.

. . . .

Upon fairly reaching what might be considered the center of the town, it was interesting to observe the manners and customs of the place. Groups of keen speculators were huddled around the corners, in earnest consultation about the rise and fall of stocks; rough customers, with red and blue flannel shirts, were straggling in from the Flowery Diggings, the desert, and other rich points, with specimens of croppings in their hands, or offering bargains in the "Rogers," the "Lady Bryant," the "Mammoth," the "Woolly Horse," and Heaven knows how many other valuable leads, at prices varying from ten to seventy-five dollars a foot. Small knots of the knowing ones were in confidential interchange of thought on the subject of every other man's business; here and there a loose man was caught by the button, and led aside behind a shanty to be "stuffed"; everybody had some grand secret, which nobody else could find out; and the game of "dodge" and "pump" was universally played. Jewish clothing-men were setting out their goods and chattels in front of wretched-looking tenements; monte-dealers, gamblers, thieves, cut-throats, and murderers were mingling miscellaneously in the dense crowds gathered around the bars of the drinking saloons. Now and then a half-starved Pah-Ute or Washoe Indian came tottering along under a heavy press of fagots and whisky. On the main street, where the mass of the population were gathered, a jaunty fellow who had "made a good thing of it" dashed through the crowds on horseback, accoutered in genuine Mexican style, swinging his riata over his head, and yelling like a devil let loose. All this time the wind blew in terrific gusts from the four quarters of the compass, tearing away signs, capsizing tents, scattering the grit from the gravel-banks with blinding force in everybody's eyes, and sweeping furiously around every crook and corner in search of some sinner to smite. Never was such a wind as this—so scathing, so searching, so given to penetrate the very core of suffering humanity; disdaining overcoats, and utterly scornful of shawls and blankets. It actually seemed to double up, twist, pull, push, and screw the unfortunate biped till his muscles cracked and his bones rattled—following him wherever he sought refuge, pursuing him down the back of the neck, up the coat-sleeves, through the legs of his pantaloons, into his boots—in short, it was the most villainous and persecuting wind that ever blew, and I boldly protest that it did nobody good.

Yet, in the midst of the general wreck and crash of matter, the business of trading in claims, "bucking" and "bearing," went on as if the zephyrs of Virginia were as soft and balmy as those of San Francisco.

This was surely—No matter; nothing on earth could aspire to competition with such a place. It was essentially infernal in every aspect, whether viewed from the Comstock Ledge or the summit of Gold Hill. Nobody seemed to own the lots except by right of possession; yet there was trading in lots to an unlimited extent. Nobody had any money, yet everybody was a millionaire in silver claims. Nobody had any credit, yet everybody bought thousands of feet of glittering ore. Sales were made in the "Mammoth," the "Lady Bryant," the "Sacramento," the "Winnebunk," and the innumerable other "outside claims," at the most astounding figures, but not a dime passed hands. All was silver under ground, and deeds and mortgages on top; silver, silver everywhere, but scarce a dollar in coin. The small change had somehow gotten out of the hands of the public into the gambling saloons.

Every speck of ground covered by canvas, boards, baked mud, brush, or other architectural material was jammed to suffocation; there were sleeping houses, twenty feet by thirty, in which from one hundred and fifty to two hundred solid sleepers sought slumber at night, at a dollar a head; tents, eight by ten, offering accommodations to the multitude; any thing or any place, even a stall in a stable, would have been a luxury.

. . . .

In truth, wherever I turned there was much to confirm the forebodings with which I had entered the Devil's Gate. The deep pits on the hillsides; the blasted and barren appearance of the whole country; the unsightly hodge-podge of a town; the horrible confusion of tongues; the roaring, raving drunkards at the bar-rooms, swilling fiery liquids from morning till night; the flaring and flaunting gambling saloons, filled with desperadoes of the vilest sort; the ceaseless torrent of imprecations that shocked the ear on every side; the mad speculations and feverish thirst for gain—all combined to give me a forcible impression of the unhallowed character of the place.

. . . .

Notwithstanding the number of physicians who had already hoisted their "shingles," there was much sickness in Virginia, owing chiefly to exposure and dissipation, but in some measure to the deleterious quality of the water. Nothing more was wanting to confirm my original impressions. The water was certainly the worst ever used by man. Filtered through the Comstock Lead, it carried with it much of the plumbago, arsenic, copperas, and other poisonous minerals alleged to exist in that vein. The citizens of Virginia had discovered what they conceived to be an infallible way of "correcting it"; that is to say, it was their practice to mix a spoonful of water in half a tumbler of whisky, and then drink it. The whisky was supposed to neutralize the bad effects of the water. Sometimes it was considered good to mix it with gin. I was unable to see how any advantage could be gained in this way. The whisky contained strychnine, oil of tobacco, tarantula-juice, and various effective poisons of the same general nature, including a dash of corrosive sublimate; and the gin was manufactured out of turpentine and whisky, with a sprinkling of prussic acid to give it flavor. For my part, I preferred taking poison in its least complicated form, and therefore adhered to the water. With hot saleratus bread, beans fried in grease, and such drink as this, it was no wonder that scores were taken down sick from day to day.

. . . .

I soon felt the bad effects of the water. Possibly I had committed an error in not mixing it with the other poisons; but it was quite poisonous enough alone to give me violent pains in the stomach and a very severe diarrhea. At the same time, I was seized with an acute attack of rheumatism in the shoulder and neuralgic pains in the head. The complication of miseries which I now suffered was beyond all my calculations of the hardships of mining life. As yet I had struck nothing better than "Winn's Restaurant," where I took my meals. The Comstock Ledge was all very fine, but a THOUSAND DOLLARS A FOOT! Who ever had a thousand dollars to put in a running foot of ground, when not even the great Comstock himself could tell where it was running to. On the whole, I did not consider the prospect cheering.

. . . .

The complications of ills which had befallen me soon became so serious that I resolved to get away by hook or crook, if it was possible to cheat the —corporate authorities of their dues. I had not come there to enlist in the service of Mammon at such wages.

Bundling up my pack one dark morning, I paid Zip the customary dollar, and, while the evil powers were roistering about the grog-shops taking their early bitters, made good my escape from the accursed place. Weak as I was, the hope of never seeing it again gave me nerve; and when I ascended the first elevation on the way to Gold Hill, and cast a look back over the confused mass of tents and hovels, and thought of all I had suffered there in the brief space of a few days, I involuntarily exclaimed, "If ever I put foot in that hole again, may the—"

But perhaps I had better not use strong language till I once more get clear of the Devil's Gate.

DAN DE QUILLE [1829–1898]

If you had proposed a bet on the Comstock about who would win immortality, Mark Twain or his friend and mentor Dan De Quille, oddsmakers would have heavily favored De Quille. Indeed, as a chronicler of the Comstock, De Quille remains unsurpassed, and his magnum opus, History of the Big Bonanza *(1876), is still regarded as a basic source book on the history of the Comstock Lode. De Quille was born William Wright in Ohio, the eldest of nine children. In Iowa, Wright married and had five children—two died in infancy—before leaving the Midwest in 1857 to seek his fortune in the West. Joining the rush to Washoe in 1860, he was hired by editor Joseph T. Goodman to work on the* Territorial Enterprise, *which rapidly became one of the most celebrated newspapers of the day. As was popular for writers of this era, Wright took on a nom de plume, Dan De Quille being a clever play on "dandy quill." De Quille had a consuming interest in all aspects of mining operations and a knack for explaining the arcana of mining affairs. He earned a reputation for good reporting, humor, bravery in standing up to offended scoundrels—and heavy drinking. De Quille was fired on a number of occasions and rehired when sober. Unlike most who rushed to the Comstock and left again when the ore played out, De Quille remained in Virginia City for nearly four decades. But in 1897, a few years after the* Enterprise *folded, the aging journalist moved back to Iowa to live out his final days on a pension kindly provided by Comstock silver king John Mackay. Over the course of his career, De Quille contributed articles and stories to numerous periodicals, including the* Overland Monthly, *the* San Francisco Examiner, *and* California Illustrated Magazine. *Many of his essays, stories, and works of humor have been rescued from oblivion by dedicated scholars, in collections such as* Washoe Rambles *(1963),* Dan De Quille: The Washoe Giant *(1990), and* The Fighting Horse of the Stanislaus *(1990).*

Underground Business Arrangements

In order that the reader may obtain something like a correct idea of the appearance of the interior of a first-class mine, let him imagine it hoisted out of the ground and left standing upon the surface. He would then see before him an immense structure, four or five times as large as the greatest hotel in America, about twice or three times as wide, and over two thousand feet high. The several levels of the mine would represent the floors of the building. These floors would be one hundred feet apart—that is, there would be in the building twenty stories, each one hundred feet in height. In a grand hotel communication between these floors would be by means of an elevator; in the mine would be in use the same contrivances, but instead of an "elevator" it would be called a "cage."

Our mine, raised to the surface as we have supposed, would present much the same appearance as would a large building with the side walls removed, allowing a full view of all of its floors to be obtained. As we should see the elevator stopping at various floors to take on and put off passengers and baggage, so we should see the cage stopping at the several levels to take on and put off miners or full of empty ore-cars.

Upon the various floors of our mine we should see hundreds of men at work, but there would be seen between the floors, in many places, a solid mass of ore in which the men were working their way up and rearing their scaffolding of timbers toward the floor above.

Not only would the men be seen thus at work, but there would also be seen at work on the various floors engines and other machinery; with, high above all, the huge pump, swaying up and down its great rod, two thousand feet in length and hung at several points with immense balance-bobs to prevent its being pulled apart by its own weight.

Occasionally, too, we should see all of the men disappear from a floor, and soon after would be heard in rapid succession ten or a dozen stunning reports—the noise of exploding blasts.

When blasts are about to be let off in a mine, after the fuses have been lighted and the miners are retreating to a place of safety, "Fire!" is the startling cry that is heard from them as they fall back along the drifts and crosscuts. The cry is well understood throughout the mine to mean no more than that fire has been set to the fuses and that several blasts will shortly go off.

In the Consolidated Virginia mine, and in all other leading mines, three shifts of men are employed, each shift working eight hours.

. . . .

When the shifts are being changed the men do not rush promiscuously to the shaft, but form in a line and march up to the cages in single file, just as men are seen to form in line in front of the window of a post-office or at the polls on the occasion of an election. On the levels below, when the men are coming up, they form in lines in the same way in front of the shaft. No crowding or disorder of any kind is permitted.

. . . .

The following amounts of timber, wood, and other mining supplies are used per month in the Consolidated Virginia mine, and from this what is used in other leading mines may be surmised: feet of timber per month, 500,000; cords of wood, 550; boxes of candles, 350; giant-powder, 2 tons; 100 gallons of coal-oil, 200 gallons of lard-oil, 800 pounds of tallow, 20,000 feet of fuse, 37 tons of ice, 3,000 bushels of charcoal, 1 ½ tons of steel, 5 tons of round and square iron, 4 tons of hard coal (Cumberland), 50 kegs of nails, and a thousand and one other articles in the same proportion. The amount of timbers buried in the mines of the Comstock is almost beyond computation. It is more than there is in all of the buildings in the State of Nevada.

Nearly all the pine forests on the eastern slope of the Sierra Nevada Mountains for a distance of fifty or sixty miles north and south have been swept away and buried in the lower levels, or consumed under the boilers of the mills and hoisting works. Already the lumbermen are pushing their way beyond the summit of the mountains, and the demand for timber and lumber is increasing every month as new levels and new mines are opened.

In a silver-mine it is not all dark and dismal below, as many persons suppose. On the contrary, the long drifts and crosscuts are lighted up with candles and lamps. It is only in the little-used drifts, in parts of the mine distant from the main workings, that absolute and pitchy darkness prevails.

In the principal levels candles and lamps are always burning. When it is midnight above, and storms and darkness prevail throughout the city, whole acres of ground hundreds of feet below in the bowels of the earth are lighted up; and down there all is calm and silent save when sounds peculiar to the place break the stillness.

In a mine there is neither day nor night; it is always candlelight. If we go into a mine late in the afternoon and remain below for some hours, a gloomy feeling is experienced when we come to the surface and find it is everywhere night above. We almost wish ourselves back in the lower levels of the mine, for when we are there it seems to be always daylight above.

On the principal levels of a mine we have long drifts, galleries, and crosscuts which intersect each other, much as do the streets and alleys in some old-fashioned, overcrowded village—some village seated in a confined place, where encroaching precipices seem to crush it out of shape.

Our underground streets are not wanting in life. As we pass along the highways and byways of the lower levels, we meet with the people of the place at every turn. Our mine connects with another, and so we have streets three miles long. There are employed in a single mine from five hundred to seven hundred men, a number sufficient to populate a town of considerable size. Men meet and pass us, all going about their business as on the surface, and frequently a turn brings us in sight of whole groups of them. We seem to have been suddenly brought face to face with a new and strange race of men. All are naked to the waist, and many from the middle of their thighs to their feet. Superb muscular forms are seen on all sides and in all attitudes, gleaming white as marble in the light of the many candles. We everywhere see men who would delight the eye of the sculptor. These men seem of a different race from those we see above—the clothes-wearers. Before us we have the Troglodytes—the cave-dwellers. We go back in thought to the time when the human race housed in caverns, not only far up the Nile, as the ancients supposed, but in every land at a certain stage of their advancement in the arts of life.

Not infrequently while traveling along a lonely passage in some remote section of the mine, we are suddenly confronted by a man of large stature, huge, spreading beard, and breast covered with shaggy hair, who comes sliding down out of some narrow side-drift, lands in our path, and for a moment stands and gazes curiously upon us, as though half inclined to consider us intruders upon his own peculiar domain. We seem to have before us one of the old cave-dwellers and we should not be at all surprised to see him cut a caper in the air, brandish a ponderous stone ax, and advance upon us with a wild whoop.

The only clothing worn by the men working in the lower levels of a mine are a pair of thin pantaloons or overalls, stout shoes, and a small felt hat or a cap such as cooks are often seen to wear. Not a shirt is seen. From the head to the hips each man is as naked as on the day he was born. All are drenched with perspiration, and their bodies glisten in the light of the candles as though they had just come up through the waters of some subterranean lake.

In places, in some of the mines, the heat is so great that the men do not even wear overalls, but are seen in the breech-clout of the primitive races. Instead of a breech-clout, some of the miners wear a pair of drawers with the legs cut off about the middle of the thighs. Something must be worn on the head to keep the falling sand and dirt out of the hair, and shoes must be worn to protect the feet from the sharp fragments of quartz that strew the floors of the levels. One may be well acquainted with a miner as he appears upon the streets, yet for a time utterly fail to recognize him as found attired in the underground regions of a mine.

When about their work in the mine, the miners have little to say, and in going about in the several levels group after group may be passed and nothing said by anyone, except some question may be asked by the foreman of the level or the superintendent of the mine, who are the usual guides of those who visit these underground regions.

Underground the men all have their respective levels, and there alone they belong. The miner who works on the 1,400-foot level may not venture down upon the 1,500, nor up to the 1,300. Those who are working on one level of a mine know no more of what is going on in the level above or below, when there is anything of special importance being done, than they do of the developments that are being made in the mine of another company. The foreman of one level does not intrude upon the domain of a brother foreman. When, for instance, he has shown a visitor through his own level, he conducts him to the next and turns him over to the foreman or "boss" in charge of that portion of the mine.

In small or newly opened mines this is of course different, as there but little is to be seen, and there is generally but a single officer in charge.

No fighting is allowed among the miners while in the lower levels. No matter how angry they may become, not a blow must be struck. The penalty for a violation of this rule is the immediate discharge of both parties to the quarrel.

It very frequently happens that two men who have had a serious misunderstanding while in the mine repair to some quiet place when they come to the surface and have their fight out, friends on both sides being present and the rules of the prize ring being observed.

Fights growing out of wrangles in the mines are always thus settled with fists; knives or pistols are never used on such occasions. However, there is much less quarreling in the mines than would be supposed, the large number of men and their various and antagonistic nationalities being considered. The fact that nearly all are members of the same society—the Miners' Union—doubtless has much to do with keeping peace among all the large underground families along the Comstock lode.

. . . .

To those not familiar with mines it may appear strange, but the lower levels—indeed, all of the levels—are alive with rats. The miners never kill or molest them; therefore they become quite tame and saucy. As the miners all carry a lunch with them into the mine, the rats live well on the fragments. These rats are really of service, as they devour the scraps of meat and bones thrown upon the ground, which would in a short time create a bad odor in the mine. The decay of the smallest thing in a mine cannot be endured. Should a rat be killed by any accident it must be sent up out of the mine. Should a small piece of cotton cloth be burned in a drift, the miners would smell it throughout the level, and to burn a small splinter of pine would probably cause serious alarm if not a grand stampede among them, as they would think there was a fire in the timbers of the mine.

. . . .

There are frequently rats that are the pets of the men working in a particular part of the mine—a rat known to them by some mark, as his having lost a piece of his tail. To this rat they give some such name as "Bobby" or "Tommy," and they feed and pet him until he becomes so saucy that he can hardly be kept out of the dinner-pails.

When there is about to be a great cave in a mine, the rats give the miners their first warning. They become very uneasy and are seen scampering about at unwonted times and in unusual places. The rats first discover that the mine is settling, and they start out in search of a place of safety. It is supposed that in settling, the waste rock and timbers pinch them in their usual holes and haunts and they are obliged to go forth in search of new quarters in order to escape being crushed to death. A fire in a mine kills them by thousands. The poisonous gases penetrate to every part of the level, and not a rat is left alive. Sometimes after a fire in a mine they are gathered up on the floors by bushels. In trying to jump across the main shaft, a rat occasionally miscalculates the distance and falls to the bottom. A rat falling a thousand feet and striking a miner on the head is sure to knock him down. The rat is killed, of course, as he generally explodes wherever he strikes. Dogs are dangerous about a shaft. Some years since, at Gold Hill, a dog fell into a shaft across which he attempted to jump, and killed two men who were at work at its bottom, three hundred feet below the surface.

So many men have been killed in all of the principal mines that there is hardly a mine on the lead that does not contain ghosts, if we are to believe what the miners say.

Fun and Frolic

As it may be of interest to persons who have never been in the mining regions of the Pacific coast, I shall give an account of a prospecting trip that I took in Washoe in 1860, just after the Indian troubles. Although no grand discovery was made, a sketch of the trip will serve to show the manner in which such expeditions were at one time conducted.

I was at that time camped at Silver City. One day a miner came to my cabin in a great state of excitement and said he had just learned that some men had struck placer-diggings of extraordinary richness on El Dorado Canyon, a large canyon to the southward of the Carson River. He said: "They are getting gold as large as peas, and are making from ten to twenty dollars per man with rockers." A dozen or more in the camp were let into the secret, and we soon had several mules packed with "grub"—flour, beans, bacon, tea, and sugar—and were ready for a start. We wished to reach the new gold region in time to get good claims and in advance of the rush of prospectors that was likely to occur as soon as news of the new strike should leak out. Not a soul in the camp knew where we were going, and as we marched down Gold Canyon, the miners pushed aside the blankets that were hung up as doors to their cabins and gazed in wonder upon our caravan. Each countenance said more plainly than words could have expressed it: "A big strike has been made somewhere. Those fellows know where it is and are going to it. I must find out about it and be off after them!" With a great clatter of pots, kettles, gold-pans, and frying-pans, our mules trotted into Chinatown (now Dayton). In this camp our "grand entry" created something of a sensation, and curiosity was seen in every face. Even the unimpressible Chinamen gazed upon us in almond-eyed astonishment. We were nearly all on foot and carried picks and shovels upon our shoulders and long knives and six-shooters slung to our belts.

All who saw us were dying to ask us what was up; but, evidently feeling that it was a secret expedition, no man ventured to question us. Already we were rich, in imagination, and all felt as jolly as so many millionaires setting off on a pleasure excursion. Indeed, miners generally make these trips a sort of pleasure excursion and give about as much time to deviltry and to wandering about curiously and viewing the wonders of the wilds as they do to the real business of the journey.

. . . .

Continuing our journey up the canyon, we presently arrived at the place where the miners were at work who were reported to be making from ten to twenty dollars per day. They seemed much surprised to see our party and told us that they were making nothing. None of us believed this, and, without waiting to unpack their animals, two or three of our men rushed off up the ravine to secure claims. I asked to see the kind of gold they were getting, and was shown a pan in which were five or six specks about one fourth as large as the head of a pin. The man who had told me in Silver City about the big strike and who had induced me to join the expedition said the men were fooling us; he was sure they had rich diggings. Taking the pan, this man got down into the hole that had been dug by the miners and got a panful of the best-looking gravel he could find. Winking for me to follow, he started down the stream to a small pool. When we were out of hearing, he said he thought the men were trying to "play us." "They don't want it known that there is anything here," said he, "until their friends are all on hand to gobble up the ground. You can bet high that I'll get a good prospect out of this pan of dirt. It looks like the right stuff."

Meanwhile he was washing it down, stopping once in awhile as he neared the bottom to flit the water over it in the expectation of seeing a "chispa" or a "nugget." The less sand there was in the pan, the longer grew his face. At last all was panned out, even to the last grain of "black sand," and naught remained but a few little specks of gold ("colors") originally in the pan.

"Skunked, by the holy spoons," cried he. I then washed out the pan and filled it with earth out of a crevice—the best I could find—panned it down, and had three small colors.

We then went back to the camp of the miners who had dug the prospect-hole and asked how the story got started that they had found gold of the size of peas and were making from ten to twenty dollars per day. They knew nothing about it, but one of them finally recollected that when he went to Silver City for a rocker he had said to someone that from the number and shape of the "colors" they were finding on the surface, he did not doubt they would find them as big as peas when they reached the bedrock. Someone then remarked: "If you do you'll be able to make from ten to twenty dollars per day." From this grew the story of the rich strike in El Dorado Canyon. We all felt rather "cheap" when we heard this explanation, the perfect truthfulness of which we could not doubt. I have known many grand mining excitements that have even less foundation. Even this little "sport" did not end with our visit to the canyon.

After we had been at home a week, and when we supposed it was well understood that the diggings were too poor to pay, parties were still rushing thither. Presently the story crossed the Sierras, and the California papers said that "in the El Dorado Canyon diggings, Nevada, miners are making from $20 to $40 per day with rockers; and the gold is of fine quality, being worth $17 per ounce." Though our ardor was a good deal cooled by what we had learned in regard to the diggings, we were not altogether discouraged. The boys got their picks, pans, and shovels and, dividing into small parties, struck out in various directions up and down the canyon and among the small ravines putting in from the hills, agreeing that wherever the best prospects were found, claims should be staked out for all. At night all hands returned, and nothing had been found that would pay—a few small colors was all that could be found, and they could be obtained almost everywhere. It was something like the present Black Hills mines. Lighting our campfire we baked our slapjacks, fried our bacon, and made a glorious meal, after which pipes were lighted and many stories told of the good old days of "'49," when the pockets of every honest miner overflowed with gold. When each man had spun his yarn it was time to think of sleep, and every man rolled himself in his blankets and stretched himself in the best and softest spot he could find, looking up at the stars in the ceiling of his bedroom until he fell asleep. At daylight we were astir. Pike was among the first up. Tom did not unroll till breakfast was almost ready. He then crawled out and proceeded to pull on his boots, taking a seat on a pack-saddle.

About this time I observed that Pike was closely watching Tom's movements. Tom had got one boot on and his toes started in the other when he stopped and yawned lazily. Rousing himself, he then drew his boot on with a "chuck." His foot had hardly struck bottom before he gave a yell and turned deadly pale. Grasping his foot, he tried to pull his boot off, but lost balance and rolled to the ground.

"Pull off my boot, quick, somebody! There is a scorpion in it!" cried Tom.

Pike managed to be the first to reach Tom and, catching him by the ankle, began tugging desperately, dragging Tom here and there, with nothing but the top of his head touching the ground.

"Your foot is swelled, Tom, and this boot can't be got off!" said Pike.

"Yes, it can," cried Tom. "Pull, confound you, pull! He is stingin' me all the time. Pull, Pike—confound you, pull! He's stingin' me to death!"

Pike gave several desperate plunges, lifting Tom clear off the ground each time; then stopped.

"I tell yer, Tom," said he, "it ain't no use; it'll never come off, your foot is swelled so bad."

"Cut it off then!" roared Tom. "Cut it off, I can't die this way!"

Pike drew his bowie-knife and had ripped the leg of Tom's boot half-way down when, thinking the joke had been carried far enough—for I was satisfied Pike had been playing a trick of some kind—I pushed Pike aside and pulled the boot off at once. When the boot was off, behold! sticking to the bottom of Tom's stocking, a small prickly pear.

On seeing the prickly pear where there should have been a scorpion, all hands laughed, and all were pretty well satisfied that the trick was Pike's, as a good deal of sport had been made of him in regard to his having been snake-bitten. To the surprise of all, Tom neither raved nor swore—said not a word, in fact—but set quietly to work at extracting the spines, which had penetrated his foot in fifty places. He then examined his boot, which was cut down almost to the heel, drew it on, and took his seat in silence at the camp breakfast. This conduct on Tom's part gave Pike great uneasiness, as all could see. At last he said:

"Who in thunder do you suppose put that air cussed par in your boot, Tom?"

"I suppose you know as much about it as anyone here," said Tom.

"Me! Good Lord, I don't purtend to know. I can't account for it nohow, without one of them mountain rats might of done it."

"Yes," said Tom, dryly, "mountain rats are mighty fond of runnin' about with prickly pears in their mouths, so we'll say no more about it."

MARK TWAIN [1835–1910]

Many people know that Mark Twain's real name was Samuel Clemens and that he was born in Missouri, was once a Mississippi riverboat pilot, and eventually wrote the American classic The Adventures of Huckleberry Finn *(1885). Fewer know that Clemens adopted the pen name Mark Twain in Nevada. In 1861 Twain's older brother, Orion, was chosen to be secretary-treasurer of the new territory of Nevada. Sam, lured by dreams of fantastic adventures and fabulous riches in gold and silver, dodged the Civil War and accompanied Orion west. Their arrival was anything but propitious, as Twain recalls in* Roughing It: *"Visibly our new home was a desert, walled in by barren, snow-clad mountains. There was not a tree in sight. There was no vegetation but the endless sagebrush and greasewood. All nature was gray with it. We were plowing through great deeps of powdery alkali dust that rose in thick clouds and floated across the plain like smoke from a burning house. . . . We moved in the midst of solitude, silence, and desolation." When Twain's visions of making a quick fortune in mining evaporated under the harsh heat of reality, he hired on as a newspaperman for Virginia City's Territorial Enterprise, where, under the tutelage of fellow journalist Dan De Quille, Twain developed his famous humorist style, freely mixing news coverage and invented stories. The popular Mississippi explanation of Clemens's choice of "Mark Twain" as a pen name hearkens back to his riverboat days, the term designating water depth. The Nevada version asserts that "Mark Twain" is actually a saloon term, meaning "allow two free drinks," and has its origins in Twain's notorious "on credit" drinking contests. Twain left the Nevada territory in 1864, just months before statehood, but his jaunty memoir of that time,* Roughing It *(1872), helped to launch his writing career and left Nevada with an image it has yet to live down.*

from *Roughing It*

After leaving the Sink, we traveled along the Humboldt River a little way. People accustomed to the monster mile-wide Mississippi grow accustomed to associating the term "river" with a high degree of watery grandeur. Consequently, such people feel rather disappointed when they stand on the shores of the Humboldt or the Carson and find that a "river" in Nevada is a sickly rivulet which is just the counterpart of the Erie Canal in all respects save that the canal is twice as long and four times as deep. One of the pleasantest and most invigorating exercises one can contrive is to run and jump across the Humboldt River till he is overheated, and then drink it dry.

On the fifteenth day we completed our march of two hundred miles and entered Unionville, Humboldt County, in the midst of a driving snowstorm. Unionville consisted of eleven cabins and a liberty pole. Six of the cabins were strung along one side of the deep canyon, and the other five faced them. The rest of the landscape was made up of bleak mountain walls that rose so high into the sky from both sides of the canyon that the village was left, as it were, far down in the bottom of a crevice. It was always daylight on the mountaintops a long time before the darkness lifted and revealed Unionville.

We built a small, rude cabin in the side of the crevice and roofed it with canvas, leaving a corner open to serve as a chimney, through which the cattle used to tumble occasionally, at night, and mash our furniture and interrupt our sleep. It was very cold weather and fuel was scarce. Indians brought brush and bushes

several miles on their backs; and when we could catch a laden Indian it was well—
and when we could not (which was the rule, not the exception), we shivered and
bore it.

I confess, without shame, that I expected to find masses of silver lying all about
the ground. I expected to see it glittering in the sun on the mountain summits. I
said nothing about this, for some instinct told me that I might possibly have an
exaggerated idea about it, and so if I betrayed my thought I might bring derision
upon myself. Yet I was as perfectly satisfied in my own mind, as I could be of
anything, that I was going to gather up, in a day or two, or at furthest a week or
two, silver enough to make me satisfactorily wealthy—and so my fancy was already busy with plans for spending this money. The first opportunity that offered,
I sauntered carelessly away from the cabin, keeping an eye on the other boys, and
stopping and contemplating the sky when they seemed to be observing me; but as
soon as the coast was manifestly clear, I fled away as guiltily as a thief might have
done and never halted till I was far beyond sight and call. Then I began my search
with a feverish excitement that was brimful of expectation—almost of certainty. I
crawled about the ground, seizing and examining bits of stone, blowing the dust
from them or rubbing them on my clothes, and then peering at them with anxious
hope. Presently I found a bright fragment and my heart bounded! I hid behind a
boulder and polished it and scrutinized it with a nervous eagerness and a delight
that was more pronounced than absolute certainty itself could have afforded. The
more I examined the fragment, the more I was convinced that I had found the
door to fortune. I marked the spot and carried away my specimen. Up and down
the rugged mountainside I searched, with always increasing interest and always
augmenting gratitude that I had come to Humboldt and come in time. Of all the
experiences of my life, this secret search among the hidden treasures of silver land
was the nearest to unmarred ecstasy. It was a delirious revel. By and by, in the
bed of a shallow rivulet, I found a deposit of shining yellow scales, and my breath
almost forsook me! A gold mine, and in my simplicity I had been content with
vulgar silver! I was so excited that I half believed my overwrought imagination was
deceiving me. Then a fear came upon me that people might be observing me and
would guess my secret. Moved by this thought, I made a circuit of the place, and
ascended a knoll to reconnoiter. Solitude. No creature was near. Then I returned
to my mine, fortifying myself against possible disappointment, but my fears were
groundless—the shining scales were still there. I set about scooping them out, and
for an hour I toiled down the windings of the stream and robbed its bed. But at last
the descending sun warned me to give up the quest, and I turned homeward laden
with wealth. As I walked along I could not help smiling at the thought of my being

so excited over my fragment of silver when a nobler metal was almost under my nose. In this little time the former had so fallen in my estimation that once or twice I was on the point of throwing it away.

The boys were as hungry as usual, but I could eat nothing. Neither could I talk. I was full of dreams and far away. Their conversation interrupted the flow of my fancy somewhat, and annoyed me a little, too. I despised the sordid and common-place things they talked about. But as they proceeded, it began to amuse me. It grew to be rare fun to hear them planning their poor little economies and sighing over possible privations and distresses when a gold mine, all our own, lay within sight of the cabin and I could point it out at any moment. Smothered hilarity began to oppress me, presently. It was hard to resist the impulse to burst out with exulta-tion and reveal everything; but I did resist. I said within myself that I would filter the great news through my lips calmly and be serene as a summer morning while I watched its effect in their faces. I said:

"Where have you all been?"

"Prospecting."

"What did you find?"

"Nothing."

"Nothing? What do you think of the country?"

"Can't tell, yet," said Mr. Ballou, who was an old gold miner, and had likewise had considerable experience among the silver mines.

"Well, haven't you formed any sort of opinion?"

"Yes, a sort of a one. It's fair enough here, maybe, but overrated. Seven-thousand-dollar ledges are scarce, though. That Sheba may be rich enough, but we don't own it; and besides, the rock is so full of base metals that all the science in the world can't work it. We'll not starve, here, but we'll not get rich, I'm afraid."

"So you think the prospect is pretty poor?"

"No name for it!"

"Well, we'd better go back, hadn't we?"

"Oh, not yet—of course not. We'll try it a riffle, first."

"Suppose, now—this is merely a supposition, you know—suppose you could find a ledge that would yield, say, a hundred and fifty dollars a ton—would that satisfy you?"

"Try us once!" from the whole party.

"Or suppose—merely a supposition, of course—suppose you were to find a ledge that would yield two thousand dollars a ton—would *that* satisfy you?"

"Here—what do you mean? What are you coming at? Is there some mystery behind all this?"

"Never mind. I am not saying anything. You know perfectly well there are no rich mines here—of course you do. Because you have been around and examined for yourselves. Anybody would know that, that had been around. But just for the sake of argument, suppose—in a kind of general way—suppose some person were to tell you that two-thousand-dollar ledges were simply contemptible—contemptible, understand—and that right yonder in sight of this very cabin there were piles of pure gold and pure silver—oceans of it—enough to make you all rich in twenty-four hours! Come!"

"I should say he was as crazy as a loon!" said old Ballou, but wild with excitement, nevertheless.

"Gentlemen," said I, "I don't say anything—*I* haven't been around, you know, and of course don't know anything—but all I ask of you is to cast your eye on *that*, for instance, and tell me what you think of it!" and I tossed my treasure before them.

There was an eager scramble for it, and a closing of heads together over it under the candlelight. Then old Ballou said:

"Think of it? I think it is nothing but a lot of granite rubbish and nasty glittering mica that isn't worth ten cents an acre!"

So vanished my dream. So melted my wealth away. So toppled my airy castle to the earth and left me stricken and forlorn.

Moralizing, I observed, then, that "all that glitters is not gold."

Mr. Ballou said I could go further than that, and lay it up among my treasures of knowledge, that *nothing* that glitters is gold. So I learned then, once for all, that gold in its native state is but dull, unornamental stuff, and that only lowborn metals excite the admiration of the ignorant with an ostentatious glitter. However, like the rest of the world, I still go on underrating men of gold and glorifying men of mica. Commonplace human nature cannot rise above that.

Information for the Millions

A young man anxious for information writes to a friend residing in Virginia City, Nevada, as follows:

Springfield, Missouri
April 12

Dear Sir:

My object in writing to you is to have you give me a full history of Nevada. What is the character of the climate? What are the productions of the earth? Is it healthy? What diseases do they die of mostly? Do you think it would be advisable for a man who can make a living in Missouri to emigrate to that part of the country? There are several of us who would emigrate there in the spring if we could ascertain to a certainty that it is as much more a country than this. I suppose you know Joel H. Smith? He used to live here; he lives in Nevada now; they say he owns considerable in a mine there. Hoping to hear from you soon, etc., I remain,

Yours truly,

WILLIAM—

The letter was handed in to a newspaper office for reply. For the benefit of all who contemplate moving to Nevada, it is perhaps best to publish the correspondence in its entirety:

Dearest William:

Pardon my familiarity—but that name touchingly reminds me of the loved and lost, whose name was similar. I have taken the contract to answer your letter, and although we are now strangers, I feel we shall cease to be so if we ever become acquainted with each other. The thought is worthy of attention, William. I will now respond to your several propositions in the order in which you have fulminated them.

Your object in writing is to have me give you a full history of Nevada. The flattering confidence you repose in me, William, is only equaled by the modesty of your request. I could detail the history of Nevada in five hundred pages octavo, but as you have never done me any harm, I will spare you, though it will be apparent to everybody that I would be justified in taking advantage of you if I were a mind to. However, I will condense. Nevada was discovered many years ago by Mormons, and was called Carson County. It only became Nevada in 1861, by an act of Congress. There is a popular tradition that the Almighty created it; but when you come to see it, William, you will think differently. Do not let that discourage you, though. The country looks something like a singed cat, owing to the scarcity of shrubbery, and also resembles that animal in the respect that it has more merits than its personal appearance would seem to indicate. The Grosch brothers found the first silver lead here in 1857. They also founded Silver City, I believe. Signify to your friends, however, that all the mines here do not pay dividends as yet; you may make this statement with the utmost inflexibility—it will not be contradicted from this quarter. The population is about thirty-five thousand, one-half of which number reside in the united cities of Virginia City and Gold Hill. However, I will discontinue this history for the present, lest I get you too deeply interested in this distant land, and cause you to neglect your family or your religion. But I will address you again upon the subject next year. In the meantime, allow me to answer your inquiry as to the character of the climate.

It has no character to speak of, William, and alas! in this respect, it resembles many, ah! too many, chambermaids in this wretched world. Sometimes we have the seasons in their regular order, and then again we have winter all the summer, and summer all winter. Consequently, we have never yet come across an almanac that would just exactly fit this latitude. It is mighty regular about not raining, though, William. It will start in here in November and rain about four months, and sometimes as much as seven days on a stretch; after that, you may loan out your umbrella for twelve months, with the serene confidence which a Christian feels in four aces. Sometimes the winter begins in November and winds up in June; and sometimes there is a bare suspicion of winter in March and April, and summer the balance of the year. But as a general thing, William, the climate is good, what there is of it.

"What are the productions of the earth?" You mean in Nevada, of course. On our ranches here anything can be raised that can be produced on the fertile fields of Missouri. But ranches are very scattering—as scattering as lawyers in Heaven. Nevada, for the most part, is a barren waste of sand, and fenced in with snow-clad mountains. But these ghastly features were the salvation of the land, William; for no rightly constituted American would have ever come here if the place had been easy of access, and none of our pioneers would have stayed after they got here, if they had not felt satisfied that they could not find a smaller chance for making a living anywhere else. Such is man, William, as he crops up in America.

"Is it healthy?" Yes, I think it is as healthy here as it is in any part of the West. But never permit a question of that kind to vegetate in your brain, William, because as long as Providence has an eye on you, you will not be likely to die until your time comes.

"What diseases do they die of mostly?" Well, they used to die of conical balls, and cold steel, mostly, but here lately erysipelas and the intoxicating bowl have the bulge on those things, as was very justly remarked by Mr. Rising last Sunday. I will observe for your information that Mr. Rising is our Episcopal minister, and has done as much as any man among us to redeem this community from its pristine state of semi-barbarism. We are inflicted with all the diseases incident to the same latitude in the States, I believe, with one or two added and half a dozen subtracted on account of our superior altitude. However, the doctors are about as successful here, both in killing and curing, as they are anywhere.

Now, as to whether it would be advisable for a man who can make a living in

Missouri to immigrate to Nevada, I confess I am somewhat mixed. If you are not content in your present condition, it naturally follows that you would be entirely satisfied if you could make either more or less than a living. You would exult in the cheerful exhilaration always produced by a change. Well, you can find your opportunity here, where, if you retain your health, and are sober and industrious, you will inevitably make more than a living, and if you don't, you won't. You can rely upon this statement, William. It contemplates any line of business except the selling of tracts. You cannot sell tracts here, William; the people take no interest in tracts; the very best efforts in the tract line—even with pictures on them—have met with no encouragement. Besides, the newspapers have been interfering; a man gets his regular text or so from the Scriptures in his paper, along with the stock sales and the war news, every day now. If you are in the tract business, William, take no chances on Washoe; but you can succeed at anything else here.

"I suppose you know Joel H. Smith?" Well, the fact is, I believe I don't. Now isn't that singular? Isn't it very singular? And he owns "considerable" in a mine here, too. Happy man! Actually owns in a mine here in Nevada Territory, and I never heard of him. Strange—strange—do you know, William, it is the strangest thing that ever happened to me? And then he not only owns in a mine, but owns "considerable"; that is the strangest thing about it. He is a lucky dog, though. But I strongly suspect that you have made a mistake in the name; I am confident you have; you mean John Smith—I know you do; I know it from the fact that he owns considerable in a mine here, because I sold him the property at a ruinous sacrifice on the very day he arrived here from over the plains. That man will be rich one of these days. I am just as well satisfied of it as I am of any precisely similar instance of the kind that has come under my notice. I said as much to him yesterday, and he said he was satisfied of it, also. But he did not say it with that air of triumphant exultation which a heart like mine so delights to behold in one to whom I have endeavored to be a benefactor in a small way. He looked pensive a while, but, finally, says he, "Do you know, I think I'd 'a been a rich man long ago if they'd ever found the d—d ledge?" That was my idea about it. I always thought, and I still think, that if they ever do find that ledge, his chances will be better than they are now. I guess Smith will be right one of these centuries, if he keeps up his assessments—he is a young man yet. Now, William, I have taken a liking to you, and I would like to sell you "considerable" in a mine in Washoe. Let me hear from you on the subject. Greenbacks at par is as good a thing as I want. But seriously, William, don't you ever invest in a mining stock which you don't know anything about; beware of John Smith's experience!

You hope to hear from me soon? Very good. I shall also hope to hear from you soon, about that little matter referred to. Now, William, ponder this epistle well—never mind the sarcasm here and there, and the nonsense, but reflect on the plain facts set forth, because they are facts, and are meant to be so understood and believed.

Remember me affectionately to your friends and relations, and especially to your venerable grandmother, with whom I have not the pleasure to be acquainted—but that is of no consequence, you know. I have been in your town many a time, and all the towns of the neighboring counties—the hotel-keepers will recollect me vividly. Remember me to them—I bear them no animosity.

Yours affectionately.

ALFRED DOTEN [1829–1903]

Carpenter, fisherman, forty-niner, speculator, farmer, rancher, and journalist, Alfred "Alf" Doten, who hailed from Plymouth, Massachusetts, was one of the "good old boys" of the gold rush era. Briefly a colleague of Mark Twain and a close friend and drinking companion of Dan De Quille, Doten wrote for most of the Comstock's illustrious newspapers—the Territorial Enterprise, *the* Virginia Daily News, *and the* Gold Hill Daily News. *But Alf Doten's diary is his true magnum opus: one-and-a-half million words, filling seventy-nine leather-bound volumes from March 18, 1849, to his death November 11, 1903, with scarcely a day missing. The acclaimed twentieth-century Nevada author Robert Laxalt, himself a former journalist, called it "the blood and guts from a newspaperman." The diary is a little of everything: notebooks and reminders both public and personal, scrapbooks, political handbills, stock certificates, letters, playbills, theater programs, subpoenas, a reward poster, and remarks on the weather. Doten was enamored by "firsts," "lasts," and "onlies." After his death, his diary was moved from one family attic to another for half a century, finally purchased by a book dealer, and in 1961 acquired by the University of Nevada, Reno, where it was painstakingly edited for publication by the distinguished author Walter Van Tilburg Clark. Clark dedicated the remainder of his life to the arduous task, to the detriment of his own writing. Journalist Cy Ryan noted that Doten was "one of the most influential and wealthiest newspaper owners on the Comstock. . . . [He] died penniless and an alcoholic in Carson City." In a private manner that became public property, Doten's is the voice and memory of early Nevada. The newspaper articles excerpted below—Nevada Correspondence to Doten's hometown newspaper,* Old Colony Memorial and Plymouth Rock—*cover Nevada's statehood, the end of the Civil War, and the wonders of the telegraph.*

Nevada Correspondence

No. XXXVII. Virginia, Nev. Nov. 15th, 1864. *Editor Memorial and Rock:*

VIRGINIA.

This city was commenced in 1859, about the time of the discovery of the great Comstock ledge, and for a time, during the prevalence of the great mining excitement, the population increased very rapidly until it reached nearly 30,000; but the general financial crisis came with crushing force, paralyzing all branches of trade and industry, until we have now only about 20,000 inhabitants. The city is built on the eastern slope of the Sierra Nevada, only some half dozen miles up from the plains of the Carson river, and in full view of the vast interior Basin of the Continent, with its barren wastes of sage-brush, sterile, sandy deserts, alkaline plains, and bleak rocky mountains and hills, upon whose sides scarce a tree or shrub is to be seen. A much more desolate scene one does not often contemplate. Only some half dozen years ago the poor weary half-starved emigrant with his worn out cattle, as he passed through this desolate, unfruitful country, slowly dragging his weary way towards California, unable to find decent feed for his stock, wondered what in the name of Heaven, this unpromising, sterile, barren waste was made for. No one at that time thought it good for anything. But lo! what a change. The wandering adventurer, Comstock—came here among a few explorers and prospectors for gold, and in the course of his examinations he happened to discover the richest and most extensive silver mine known in the world; a ledge, the extent of which is far from being comprehended, and in fact it is but merely prospected, as yet, the deepest shelf on it being but 520 feet in depth. Near this ledge, the miner's cabins formed the first nucleus for the present city, which in a short time extended itself far away down and along the mountain slope. It is laid out in squares, as nearly as the conformation of the country will admit of, and contains a vast number of fine brick and stone buildings, churches, and other public buildings, is supplied with water works, gas works, etc., and in fact is really a fine city, considering the age of it. Many of the buildings are four and five stories in height, and finished off inside and out in splendid style.

. . . .

POLITICAL.

Well at length I am in one the States of the Union again, and the bright silver star Nevada is added to the grand Union constellation. I had the honor of assisting by my vote, to make California a State, and now I have the honor of assisting Nevada into the Union. And a true and loyal State, too, she is, for as you have probably learned long 'ere this, by telegraph, we went for Uncle Abe, strong; and so far, claim to be the banner State, for the largest Union majority in proportion to our total vote. The whole vote for the State, including the soldiers' vote, will be about 11,000, and the Union majority, 3,200. And another thing, too, we can well afford to brag of: *Every officer, State and Legislative, is a sound Republican Union man.* The snakes many of them, are about to leave for Mexico, thinking justly that this is no good country for them.

Your friend, A. D.

No. XXXIX. Virginia, Nev. July 11th, 1865. Eds. Memorial and Rock.

THE GLORIOUS FOURTH

Has come and gone, but in the hurry and bustle consequent on the preparations for and celebration of that grand national day, I came near forgetting you, but you see I have not. We celebrated the day here with far more than usual *spirit* in every sense of the word, as is shown by the records of the police court the next day, although the officers were as lenient as their conscience would allow, and took none to the station house except those who were disorderly as well as very drunk.

. . . .

PATRIOTISM.

When the news of Lee's surrender arrived, this whole excitable city went as "mad as a March hare." All the bells were rung for six hours, and guns and everything that could make a noise were brought into requisition, old men danced like children, and waved their hats and hurrahed till their old throats were hoarse. Everybody went wild drunk with joy, for well they knew the war was now ended, and the long prayed for peace had come at last.

Only a week later, and all the flags were draped in crape, at half-mast, one building after another was hung with the symbols of grief and the whole city was in mourning. Men stood in knots about the corners and along the sidewalks, conversing in low but eager and excited tones that boded no good to traitors, or those who approved the foul deed of the black-hearted assassin. Every saloon and place of business was closed, and no man seemed to know what to do or how to act, but the deep under current of determination was apparent, and woe be to the traitor that should dare raise a voice of rejoicing over the hellish deed. The old men now were the most excitable, and with bared heads, and tears in their eyes, they cursed the hand that had stricken down the Saviour of his country—Abraham Lincoln. Yes, men walked the streets with weapons of death in their hands, seeking but for a reason to use them, and the military companies assembled at their armories. Well was it that secessionists and traitors "haunted their holes" that day. Well was it that their mouths were dumb, for had a collision once taken place in Virginia, it would have ended in a fearful fight of extermination.

. . . .

No. XLII. Virginia, Nev. May, 13, 1867.

Editor Memorial and Rock:—Time rolls on; and the days, months, and years, like so many chips, still go ever floating onward, ceaselessly borne on the bosom of the great broad tide which empties into the illimitable sea of eternity. The mighty Mississippi still pours its vast volume of many stenched waters into the blue Atlantic, Hobbs' Hole brook and Eel River continue to contribute their aqueous torrents towards the general good and welfare of this mundane world, as they did in ages past, when ye gentle savage roamed undisturbedly in all his primeval innocence along their grassy banks, fishing for trout and herrings; and so, too, I in course of time resume the thread of my somewhat chronic correspondence. (How's that, now, for a starter?)

. . . .

TELEGRAPHIC.

This telegraph is certainly the greatest and most wonderful contrivance known of in the world. Time and space are literally nowhere—annihilated—wiped out. We know here all about what they are doing in London just as soon as the cockneys themselves do; yes, even sooner we may say. For instance, owing to the difference of latitudinal time, should Smith "bust Brown in the snoot," near the Queen's palace, we receive the full account with all the aggravating particulars, by telegraph, and have it published in the evening papers some hours before the thing has happened at all, or the pugilistic Smith has even begun to wax belligerent. In fact we are even better posted as to the New York and Boston news than you Plymoutheans are, for we read them every morning in the daily papers, and you don't. Speaking about news this is a glorious country to make up a newspaper in. We have plenty of exchanges, all prolific and constantly pregnant with matters of interest, and the local department is always very readable, containing items in profusion relative to new and exciting discoveries, sensational accidents, choice robberies, elopements, rich mineral yields, etc. Our readers however, in addition, require a goodly supply of blood-curdling news items every day, such as will induce their eyes to protrude with horror, and their hair to rise on end in a healthy manner; single murders, double suicides, whole families with throats cut, aggravating rapes, sensational seductions, wholesale burglaries, bank robberies, startling rascalities and all that sort of thing. For these we scissorize our eastern exchanges, and never fail of a plentifully desirable supply to suit all. Why bless you, we are a much more moral, decent, peaceable, and upright people than you of the Atlantic side. When we do manage to dish up an original shooting or cutting scrape, a big dog fight, a stage robbery, or even a real murder among us, we feel that we have struck a rich lead, and publish glowing accounts thereof, well displayed, with sensational headings in big type, exclamation points, etc.

....

There is one other Plymouthean, (E. H. Morton) a fixture in the City besides myself, and let me assure you that the *Memorial and Rock* comes to us as a familiar and welcome old friend. We receive it with all reasonable regularity, and always read it through from beginning to end, advertisements and all. With its friendly pages to refresh our memories, we can never become in any degree oblivious of our childhood's happy home, or the loved friends and companions of our youthful days. In conclusion let me now bid you good-bye until you hear again from your friend, A. D.

MARY MCNAIR MATHEWS [1834–1903]

In the flush years of the Comstock Lode, men outnumbered women by more than two to one. Of these women, stories have been told about prostitutes, on the one hand, and millionaires' wives, on the other. Rarely do we glimpse what it was like to be a middle-class woman on the Comstock, much less a single mother. Mary McNair Mathews's memoir tells that story in color-ful detail and with sometimes shocking bigotry. "I have been frequently requested by my East-ern and Western friends to write up my life in Nevada, and tell them how I managed to sustain myself and child, carry on law, and lay up property." So begins Ten Years in Nevada; or, Life on the Pacific Coast *(1880). Born in 1834 in Livingston County, New York, Mathews was widowed early and never remarried. In 1869 she sold her hometown hoop-skirt factory and hastened to Nevada after hearing the news of her beloved younger brother's fatal shooting in Virginia City. Intent on sorting out his affairs, she set forth with her nine-year-old son, Charlie, on a journey by train of some nineteen days. Arriving nearly penniless, the intrepid and entrepreneurial Mathews soon found work and managed over the course of her years in the West to—among other things—keep her own school, invest in mining stocks, run a boardinghouse, and establish a soup kitchen for the destitute. In* Ten Years in Nevada *Mathews was determined that her readers see "with what tenacity I clung to my purpose, never allowing any obstacle to hinder, or fear deter me. They will see that while accomplishing it we had to endure a great deal of sickness, privations, trials, and hard work." At the same time, she was equally determined that her readers understand that "few people ever enjoyed life more than we did."*

from *Ten Years in Nevada*

The people of Virginia City are great gamblers. Two-thirds of the city gamble. The gambling dens are perfectly magnificent in style. They are gotten up to attract people to them. Some are kept very orderly, while others are not.

They have a very good law in Virginia City to prevent young men from gambling. Every young man under twenty-one years of age is prohibited; and if he is allowed to gamble in any saloon, the proprietors can be held accountable for the act. But it lacks good officers to put the law in force, for half of the boys from twelve to twenty-one in the city gamble. It is astonishing how this law is violated by nearly everybody. Boys from twelve to fifteen have already acquired such a passion for gambling that they will pawn any article of jewelry in their possession, such as rings, pins, sleeve-buttons, and even their sister's gold watch and chain.

I knew one of the finest boys in Virginia City to do this, so great was his appetite for gambling. And yet their parents will not put the law in force.

At one time, when my son was but twelve years old, he had just drawn his wages, and was on his way home from the *Chronicle* office. Some of his mates called him to a child's gambling den. They had what they called a stick game, I believe. They bought a stick of candy for $1, with the inducement held out to them that they might get $3 or $4 wrapped up with the stick.

The proprietor had been there about three months swindling the boys in town out of all the money they could get. He had let some boy win $5. This was enough to set every boy wild with the hope of gain. Charlie had $14. He went in and bought one stick, but lost, and, like older gamblers, wanted to win it back. He bought another, and lost again. He then got excited, and bought until he lost $8. He then turned and fled from the place, for fear of losing the rest of his money, for the man kept telling him to try again—he might gain the next time, perhaps.

He came home and laid his money on the table by me, and said: "Mamma, I have done something awful; I have been gambling."

I asked him where. He told me the place, and how much he had lost. I told him to come with me. I went to the den and told the man to refund the $8 to my child. He denied ever seeing him, and ordered me out.

I told him I would go, but I would come again with a power he did not dare to disobey.

I then went to the district attorney, Mr. Thomas Stephens, and asked him if there was not a law to protect children from being swindled. I stated the case to him. He said there was, and he would see that they were protected every time there was a complaint made to him.

He wrote a note to the person having the den, ordering him to refund the money to Charlie, and also to the other boys he had robbed, or he would have him in the lock-up before four o'clock. It was now about eleven.

I took the note and went back. As I entered the building, I said: You see I have kept my word. *Here is my authority.*

He took the note and read it, and, turning to Charlie, said: "Come in here and get your money."

He went in the office part, and I heard him say to Charlie as he counted out the money: "You d—d fool, what made you tell your mother? If I ever catch you around here again, I will kick you out!"

"You may," said Charlie, "if you catch me here again."

As we came out of the office, I told him it would not be very healthy for him to touch my boy, and it would also be well for him to refund the money to the other boys before the time expired. I told him I would know whether he did or not, for I was well acquainted with them all.

About four o'clock I happened to pass that way, and the place was empty. He had packed up and left town, as he probably had no idea of refunding the money he had swindled the boys out of. He saw by the note that Mr. Stephens meant business. And he did. By his promptness in this case, Virginia City was minus one villain. He was never heard of there again.

Virginia City is a very hard city in which to bring up children, for all classes drink, high and low. They keep beer by the keg, and wine and other spirits by the case, in their houses. Nearly all play and gamble. Two-thirds swear, and the other third uses by-words of every kind—some very laughable ones—while others use coarse and rough ones.

It seemed very odd to me to hear people in the best social circles of society in the city betting their "bottom dollar," or their "loose change," or "your sweet life," or "all your stock that is not in soak," and such like expressions in large assemblies of people. Yet it was never noticed any more than if you had said "Thank you," for nearly everybody uses by-words.

I do not think anyone ever enjoys life better than they do. When they go anywhere, which is every night in the week, they go for a good time, and they manage to have it, too.

The ladies, as a class, never allow anything to prevent their going anywhere they wish to. Sick children and sick friends never keep them. Of course there are exceptions; but if they can get anyone to take care of them, they are off to the theater or dance.

The men are just as bad. They will bury a friend in the afternoon, and go to a dance the same night.

If persons die, they will bury them in style. The funerals in Virginia City are conducted differently, and are superior to any I ever witnessed, and also larger than I ever saw in any other place.

. . . .

When we left Virginia City I thought our trials were over, for I now had enough for myself and family to live on without ever lifting our hands to work again. But it seems our cup of sorrow was not yet filled; for alas! our greatest trials and troubles were yet to come after we reached home.

But, reader, after all I have suffered in the land of sage, I would much rather live there than in the East, for several reasons. First of all, my health was much better there than here; second, if I dealt with a person, I knew what to expect. I like a person better who will show his hand than a sneaking hypocrite with whom I do not know how to deal. Third, if I transact my own business, I can make more money in three months that I can in the East in a year; and I never saw the time while there that I could not borrow from $1,000 to $2,000 on one day's notice; and the parties lending it would never think of asking me about my indebtedness, or how much property I owned, if it was a small sum of $200 or $300, or less. My word was always quite sufficient for them. But I find it a common practice in the East for persons to inquire into your private affairs if you only wish to borrow $5 of them.

As I have said before, there are no misers or penny-mites in Nevada. Even the bonanza men, who are the hardest crowd to get money out of on a small scale, are sometimes princely in their donations for charitable purposes.

And if we live out our money fast, we make it fast.

Now, kind reader, if I have given the Western people a worse name than they deserve, I have done it unintentionally. If I have given any too much credit (which I doubt), it is because my love for them has blinded me to their faults.

If I have seemingly spoken too highly in praise of my son, the reader will pardon a mother's pride in an only child; and though I may never meet again any of my kind Pacific friends, let them ever bear in mind that though absent they are not forgotten; that the garden of my heart has ever been kept green by the blossoms of their love, the memory of each and all their many acts of kindness bestowed on me, a stranger, while sojourning in their land of sage and silver.

SAM DAVIS [1850–1918]

Few of the hordes who flocked to the Comstock Lode in its heyday lingered in the state when bonanza turned to borrasca. Sam Davis stayed and became an influential Nevadan. Davis was born in Connecticut, raised in various states, and sent to Racine College in Wisconsin to prepare for the clergy like his father, an Episcopal priest. Sam was expelled due to lackluster academic performance coupled with a genius for pranks. Davis had edited the college newspaper, and he now pursued that vocation. In Nebraska, where he began his career, his harsh exposés of legislators aroused the electorate. The unscrupulous legislators hired thugs to kill Davis, but the wily reporter escaped out a window, continuing the exposés from hiding. Heading west, Davis worked for the San Francisco Chronicle *and other Bay Area papers for several years before moving to boisterous Virginia City, Nevada, in 1875, to work for the* Virginia City Evening Chronicle. *In 1879 he settled in Carson City to edit the* Morning Appeal *after the death of its editor, Henry R. Mighels. He married Mighels's widow, Nellie, becoming stepfather to her four children and adding two more. He continued to be a fearless political reporter and humorist, famously lampooning a fictitious rival newspaper called the* Wabuska Mangler. *A promoter of agriculture, Davis introduced the first Holstein cows to Nevada, from Holland, and initiated the observance of Arbor Day. He became involved in the Silver Party, advocating the unlimited coinage of silver, and served two terms as state controller, forcing integrity in the insurance industry. In addition to reams of newspaper columns, Davis penned fiction, poetry, memoir, and history. A selection of this work was published as* Short Stories, California Sketches, Bright, Humorous *(1886). He edited* The History of Nevada *(1913), which favored reminiscence and anecdote over "dry and uninteresting statistics." "The First Piano in Camp," originally titled "A Christmas Carol," is Davis's most famous story.*

The First Piano in Camp

In 1858—it might have been five years earlier or later; this is not the history for the public schools—there was a little camp about ten miles from Pioche, occupied by upward of three hundred miners, every one of whom might have packed his prospecting implements and left for more inviting fields any time before sunset.

When the day was over these men did not rest from their labors, like honest New England agriculturists, but sang, danced, gambled, and shot one another, as the mood seized them.

One evening the report spread along the main street (which was the only street) that three men had been killed at Silver Reef and that the bodies were coming in. Presently a lumbering old conveyance labored up the hill, drawn by a couple of horses well worn out with their pull. The cart contained a good-sized box, and no sooner did its outlines become visible through the glimmer of a stray light than it began to affect the idlers.

Death always enforces respect, and, even though no one had caught sight of the remains, the crowd gradually became subdued, and when the horses came to a standstill the cart was immediately surrounded. The driver, however, was not in the least impressed with the solemnity of his commission.

"All there?" asked one.

"Haven't examined. Guess so."

The driver filled his pipe and lit it as he continued:

"Wish the bones and load had gone over the grade!"

A man who had been looking on stepped up to the driver at once.

"I don't know who you have in that box, but if they happen to be any friends of mine I'll lay you alongside."

"We can mighty soon see," said the teamster, coolly. "Just burst the lid off, and if they happen to be the men you want, I'm here."

The two looked at each other for a moment, and then the crowd gathered a little closer, anticipating trouble.

"I believe that dead men are entitled to good treatment, and when you talk about hoping to see corpses go over a bank, all I have to say is that it will be better for you if the late lamented ain't my friends."

"We'll open the box. I don't take back what I said, and if my language don't suit your ways of thinking, I guess I can stand it."

With these words the teamster began to pry up the lid. He got a board off, and then pulled out some rags. A strip of something dark, like rosewood, presented itself.

"Eastern coffins, by thunder!" said several, and the crowd looked quite astonished.

Some more boards flew up, and the man who was ready to defend his friend's memory shifted his weapon a little. The cool manner of the teamster had so irritated him that he had made up his mind to pull his weapon at the first sight of the dead, even if the deceased was his worst and oldest enemy. Presently the whole of the box cover was off, and the teamster, clearing away the packing, revealed to the astonished group the top of something which puzzled all alike.

"Boys," said he, "this is a pianner!"

A general shout of laughter went up, and the man who had been so anxious to enforce respect for the dead muttered something about feeling dry, and the keeper of the nearest bar was several ounces better off by the time the boys had given the joke all the attention it called for.

Had a dozen dead men been in the box, their presence in the camp could not have occasioned half the excitement that the arrival of the lonely piano caused. By the next morning it was known that the instrument was to grace a hurdy-gurdy saloon owned by Tom Goskin, the leading gambler in the place. It took nearly a week to get this wonder on its legs, and the owner was the proudest individual in the State. It rose gradually from a recumbent to an upright position amid a confusion of tongues, after the manner of the Tower of Babel.

Of course everybody knew just how such an instrument should be put up. One knew where the "off hind leg" should go, and another was posted on the "front piece."

Scores of men came to the place every day to assist.

"I'll put the bones in good order."

"If you want the wires tuned up, I'm the boy."

"I've got music to feed it for a month."

Another brought a pair of blankets for a cover, and all took the liveliest interest in it. It was at last in a condition for business.

"It's been showin' its teeth all the week. We'd like to have it spit out something."

Alas! there wasn't a man to be found who could play upon the instrument. Goskin began to realize that he had a losing speculation on his hands. He had a fiddler and a Mexican who thrummed a guitar. A pianist would have made his orchestra complete. One day a three-card-monte player told a friend confidentially that he could "knock any amount of music out of the piano if he only had it alone a few hours to get his hand in." This report spread about the camp, but on being questioned he vowed that he didn't know a note of music. It was noted, however, as a suspicious circumstance that he often hung about the instrument and looked upon it longingly, like a hungry man gloating over a beefsteak in a restaurant window. There was no doubt that this man had music in his soul, perhaps in his finger ends, but did not dare to make trial of his strength after the rules of harmony had suffered so many years of neglect. So the fiddler kept on with his jigs, and the greasy Mexican pawed his discordant guitar, but no man had the nerve to touch the piano. There were doubtless scores of men in the camp who would have given ten ounces of gold dust to have been half an hour alone with it, but every man's nerve shrank from the jeers which the crowd would shower upon him should his first attempt prove a failure. It got to be generally understood that the hand which first essayed to draw music from the keys must not slouch its work.

It was Christmas Eve, and Goskin, according to his custom, had decorated his gambling-hell with sprigs of mountain cedar and a shrub whose crimson berries did not seem a bad imitation of English holly. The piano was covered with evergreens, and all that was wanting to completely fill the cup of Goskin's contentment was a man to play the instrument.

"Christmas night and no piano-pounder," he said. "This is a nice country for a Christian to live in."

Getting a piece of paper, he scrawled the words:

$20 Reward

To a compitant Pianer Player

This he stuck up on the music-rack, and, though the inscription glared at the frequenters of the room till midnight, it failed to draw any musician from his shell.

So the merrymaking went on; the hilarity grew apace. Men danced and sang to the music of the squeaky fiddle and worn-out guitar as the jolly crowd within tried to drown the howling of the storm without. Suddenly they became aware of the presence of a white-haired man crouching near the fireplace. His garments—such as were left—were wet with melting snow, and he had a half-starved, half-crazed expression. He held his thin, trembling hands toward the fire, and the light of the blazing wood made them almost transparent. He looked about him once in awhile as if in search of something, and his presence cast such a chill over the place that gradually the sound of the revelry was hushed, and it seemed that this waif of the storm had brought in with it all the gloom and coldness of the warring elements. Goskin, mixing up a cup of hot eggnog, advanced and remarked cheerily:

"Here, stranger, brace up! This is the real stuff."

The man drained the cup, smacked his lips, and seemed more at home.

"Been prospecting, eh? Out in the mountains—caught in the storm? Lively night, this! . . . Must feel pretty dry?"

The man looked at his streaming clothes and laughed, as if Goskin's remark was a sarcasm.

"How long out?"

"Four days."

"Hungry?"

The man rose up and, walking over to the lunch-counter, fell to work upon some roast bear, devouring it like any wild animal would have done. As meat and drink and warmth began to permeate the stranger, he seemed to expand and lighten up. His features lost their pallor and he grew more and more content with the idea that he was not in the grave. As he underwent these changes, the people about him got merrier and happier and threw off the temporary feeling of depression which he had laid upon them.

"Do you always have your place decorated like this?" he finally asked of Goskin.

"This is Christmas Eve," was the reply.

The stranger was startled. "December twenty-fourth, sure enough."

"That's the way I put it up, pard."

"When I was in England I always kept Christmas. But I had forgotten that this was the night. I've been wandering about in the mountains until I've lost track of the feasts of the Church."

Presently his eye fell upon the piano.

"Where's the player?" he asked.

"Never had any," said Goskin, blushing at the expression.

"I used to play when I was young."

Goskin almost fainted at the admission. "Stranger, do tackle it and give us a tune! Nary man in this camp ever had the nerve to wrestle with that music-box." His pulse beat faster, for he feared that the man would refuse.

"I'll do the best I can," he said.

There was no stool, but, seizing a candle-box, he drew it up and seated himself before the instrument. It only required a few seconds for a hush to come over the room.

"That old coon is going to give the thing a rattle."

The sight of a man at the piano was something so unusual that even the faro dealer, who was about to take in a fifty-dollar bet on the trey, paused and did not reach for the money. Men stopped drinking, with the glasses at their lips. Conversation appeared to have been struck with a sort of paralysis, and cards were no longer shuffled.

The old man brushed back his long, white locks, looked up to the ceiling, half closed his eyes, and in a mystic sort of reverie passed his fingers over the keys. He touched but a single note, yet the sound thrilled the room. It was the key to his improvisation, and as he wove his chords together the music laid its spell upon every ear and heart. He felt his way along the keys like a man treading uncertain paths, but he gained confidence as he progressed, and presently bent to his work like a master. The instrument was not in exact tune, but the ears of his audience did not detect anything radically wrong. They heard a succession of chords, a suggestion of paradise, melodies here and there, and it was enough.

"See him counter with his left!" said an old rough, enraptured.

"He calls the turn every time on the upper end of the board," responded a man with a stack of chips in his hand.

The player wandered off into the old ballads they had heard at home. All the sad and melancholy and touching songs, that came up like dreams of childhood, this unknown player drew from the keys. His hands kneaded their hearts like dough, and squeezed out tears as from a wet sponge.

As the strains flowed one upon the other, the listeners saw their homes of long ago reared again; they were playing once more where the apple blossoms sank through the soft air to join the violets on the green turf of the old New England states; they saw the glories of the Wisconsin maples and the haze of the Indian summer blending their hues together; they recalled the heather of Scottish hills, the white cliffs of Britain, and heard the sullen roar of the sea as it beat upon their memories vaguely. Then came all the old Christmas carols, such as they had sung in church thirty years before; the subtle music that brings up the glimmer of wax tapers, the solemn shrines, the evergreen, holly, mistletoe, and surpliced choirs. Then the remorseless performer planted his final stab in every heart with "Home, Sweet Home."

When the player ceased, the crowd slunk away from him. There was no more revelry and devilment left in his audience. Each man wanted to sneak off to his cabin and write the old folks a letter. The day was breaking as the last man left the place, and the player, with his head on the piano, fell asleep.

"I say, pard," said Goskin, "don't you want a little rest?"

"I feel tired," the old man said. "Perhaps you'll let me rest here for the matter of a day or so."

He walked behind the bar, where some old blankets were lying, and stretched himself upon them.

"I feel pretty sick. I guess I won't last long. I've got a brother down in the ravine—his name's Driscoll. He don't know I'm here. Can you get him before morning? I'd like to see his face once before I die."

Goskin started up at the mention of the name. He knew Driscoll well.

"He your brother! I'll have him here in half an hour."

As Goskin dashed out into the storm, the musician pressed his hand to his side and groaned. Goskin heard the word "Hurry!" and sped down the ravine to Driscoll's cabin. It was quite light in the room when the two men returned. Driscoll was pale as death.

"My God! I hope he's alive! I wronged him when we lived in England, twenty years ago."

They saw the old man had drawn the blanket over his face. The two stood a moment, awed by the thought that he might be dead. Goskin lifted the blanket and pulled it down, astonished. There was no one there!

"Gone!" cried Driscoll, wildly.

"Gone!" echoed Goskin, pulling out his cash drawer. "Ten thousand dollars in the sack, and the Lord knows how much loose change in the drawer!"

The next day the boys got out, followed a horse's track through the snow, and lost it in the trail leading toward Pioche.

There was a man missing from the camp. It was the three-card-monte man who used to deny point-blank that he could play the scale. One day they found a wig of white hair, and called to mind when the "stranger" had pushed those locks back when he looked toward the ceiling for inspiration on the night of December 24, 1858.

FRED H. HART [CA. 1840–1897]

Like Virginia City's Territorial Enterprise, Austin's Reese River Reveille, founded in 1863, gained fame well beyond the state. Fred H. Hart was an editor for the Reveille from 1873 to 1878. Originally from New York, Hart came west in the early 1860s, chasing mining strikes across several states but finding steadier pay by working the newspapers. In the early 1870s Hart lived in Carson City, covering the Nevada state legislature for the Gold Hill Daily News. His lively articles attracted the attention of the Reveille's owner, who recruited Hart to work for him. The telegraph made it easy to fill up the national news columns, but concocting the local stories could tax one's powers of invention. One night, desperate for material, Hart made up a fictional club and reported on its formation. Named the Sazerac Lying Club, after the Sazerac saloon in Austin—itself named after a brandy label—the club consisted of old-timers who engaged in lying competitions. For several years, Hart entertained readers by printing the lies supposedly told by the fictitious club members. Hart's stories were reprinted throughout the country and in Germany. A San Francisco publisher invited him to collect these stories and others, resulting in The Sazerac Lying Club: A Nevada Book (1878), dedicated to "each and every person who may purchase it, and pay cash for it." Hart completed his career in Nevada journalism with the Territorial Enterprise, where he worked briefly in 1880. He was run out of town when two vituperative editorials he authored—accusing a local politician and a mining company of lying and stealing—enraged the newspaper's backers. Fellow journalist Alf Doten wrote that Hart's "journalistic ship was wrecked forever, and he drifted about [in San Francisco], picking up little jobs of reporting by way of precarious subsistence , . . finally dying August 30, 1897, in the Sacramento County Hospital," age fifty-seven.

from *The Sazerac Lying Club*
Life in a Mining Town

One day, while out in search of an item, I asked a fellow-citizen, "What's the news?" "Nothing startling," he replied. Nothing startling! That man would never do for a newspaper reporter in a small interior town. Nothing startling, indeed! Why, as he made the remark, two dogs were preparing to sign articles for a prize-fight right in front of his store; a wagon loaded with wood could be seen in the distance, which was sure to pass his way during the day, if something did not break down. Two women, whom he knew to be mortal enemies, were approaching each other on the corner above; a doctor was hurrying across the street, and a man who always kicks up a fuss and gets arrested when drunk was just entering the door of a saloon a block below. If that fellow-citizen had had the soul of a reporter within his bosom—or in any other part of his body where a reporter's expansive soul can find lodgment—he would have got out his jack-knife, picked up a chip, and, sitting down on the first convenient dry goods box, have whittled, and waited for something startling. Nothing came of all the incidents, however. The dogs signed a peace protocol and formed an alliance to bark at a passing horse; the load of wood was delivered lower down the street, the women merely swept their skirts aside from each other as they passed, the doctor only wanted to borrow ten dollars of the man on the other side of the street, and the fellow who makes a noise when he gets drunk simply went into the saloon to inquire what time the Battle Mountain stage started.

It is such disappointments as these that sour the reportorial milk of human kindness, and force the country newspaper man to fill up his columns with incidents evolved from his own imagination—incidents that are invariably tinged with the humor born of worldly wisdom, and the practical as opposed to the sentimental view of men, life, and things. I have before explained the origin of the Sazerac Lying Club; and to the same want of "local" the following actual occurrences owe their appearance in print:

A Sunday-School Story

"Yes, my boy, to be virtuous is to be happy. It gladdens your old father's heart and causes it to swell with pride when he beholds your name published in the REVEILLE as having attained the maximum figure awarded for deportment in your school. Keep on in the pursuit of knowledge; refrain from the vile practice of playing hooky; do not allow the example of bad boys to induce you to throw spit-balls at your teacher; never, never swear; and you will grow up worthy of the name handed down to you by your Puritan ancestors. Bring me my slippers, my son, and I will hear you recite your lessons, and see what progress you have made."

Johnny stood one hundred in deportment on the last roll of honor of the Austin Public School, which shows that he is a very good boy; and when he dropped a dozen tacks into his father's slippers, it was done in a fit of abstraction. He had worked out several abstruse mathematical problems on his slate since then, and his mind had been so absorbed that he forgot all about such a trivial matter as a few tacks in his father's slippers. He did not intend to be around when the old man put on the slippers, but the circumstance of the tacks having slipped his memory, he brought and laid them at his father's feet in all the confiding innocence of un-suspecting youth.

"As I was saying, my son—Ooch! Owch! Gewhilikens! Thunder'nlightnin'! Hellfire'nbrimstone! What'nthunder'sthat!"

"Did you step on a pin, sir?"

"'Step on a pin!' I'll pin you, you young rapscallion of thunderation, you! Come out here in the wood-shed, and I'll show you what I stepped on."

Then Johnny's father took him out in the wood-shed and talked to him, and the boy in the next house took his fingers out of the jar of jam in the pantry, and remarked, "Jersey District and the Black Hills, aint he a-catchin' it, though?" And Johnny remarked that he "wouldn't never do it no more."

Moral—The fact of a boy's name being on the roll of honor is not a sure sign that he is truly good.

· · · · · · · ·

"What's the news up your way?" asked a down-town woman of an Upper Austin woman in a Main Street store to-day.

"Oh, not a thing in the world," replied the one questioned; "you see, we're awful quiet, peaceable people up our way, and of course I stay to home so much I don't know what's going on, anyhow, 'cause I have so much to do to 'tend to my children, and the sewing, and washing, and cooking; but they do say that Mrs. Bustem has got a brand-new silk dress, and nobody knows how she got it, and her husband only a common chlorider, and hasn't had a crushing in four months, and his last rock didn't pay for milling; and that Mrs. Gabble and Mrs. Tattle has had the worst kind of a fight, and when Mrs. Tattle made a grab at Mrs. Gabble's hair it was false, and all came out, and two-thirds of it was jute; and Mr. Squeezem chucked his wife out of doors 'cause she lammed the servant girl for letting him kiss her in the wood-shed; and that Mr. Sinchem drew a six-shooter on Mr. Bilkem for saying his wife said that his wife couldn't have no new bonnet this fall, 'cause her husband was poorer than Job's turkey, and couldn't pay ninety cents on the dollar if his creditors was to come down on him to-morrow and sell him out at forced sale. Oh, I tell you, we're awful peaceable people up our way; only it's tedious living in a neighborhood where there aint nothing going on."

· · · · · · · ·

County Assessor Spires discovered a mouse in his office in the courthouse, yes-terday. Instead of getting up on top of his high desk-stool and gathering his skirts about his ankles and screaming, he took down the assessment-roll and let it drop on the mouse. As this was only a one-hundred-and-forty-two quire book, it merely stunned the animal; and as it lay on the floor unconscious, he pounded it on the head with the bullion-tax book and Vol. 1 of the Compiled Laws. Then he went out and got a broom and shovel to remove the corpse, and just got back to the office in time to see the mouse's tail disappearing in a hole in the base-board. The remarks addressed to the retreating mouse can be found in almost any orthodox prayer-book, but not connected in the exact sequence in which Spires framed the words.

. . . .

We have heard a number of people complain that this has been a dull day; but we have failed to see it. A freight team arrived; several loads of wood passed up Main Street; seventeen dogs were all barking at once at a cow, on Court Street; a woman stubbed her toe against a plank, on Union Street; a man dropped a four-bit piece through a crack in the sidewalk, on Cedar Street; a clothes-line full of clean linen was blown down, on South Street; a cat had fits, on Overland Street; two little boys had a fight, on Sixth Street; a cow ate up a whole garden, on Pine Street; and there was a whirlwind on Virginia Street. If the day was dull with all these stirring events, we would like to see what some folks call a lively one. But some men would say times were dull if their grandmother was to fall three thousand feet down a mining shaft.

IDAH MEACHAM STROBRIDGE [1855–1932]

Idah Meacham Strobridge was born into a prospecting family, grew up among prospectors, and was herself a prospector. Her father, George Washington Meacham, shipped around the Horn to San Francisco in the rush of '49. In 1864 Meacham homesteaded with his family in Lassen Meadows, between Lovelock and Winnemucca, future path of the Central Pacific Railroad. There he built the Humboldt House, a hotel and restaurant for train passengers. An only child, young Idah became an omnivorous reader. One delightfully cool reading haunt was an old mine whose walls were white gypsum and yellow sulfur. At twenty-three Idah was sent off to Mills Seminary in Oakland, where she met Samuel Strobridge. After graduation, they married and returned to Lassen Meadows to start a family and begin a life of ranching. Fate, however, dealt a cruel blow. Idah's first son died the day after he was born, and her next two sons and husband succumbed to pneumonia during the terrible winter of 1888–89. Left a childless widow by age thirty-four, Strobridge threw herself into a variety of endeavors. A visiting news correspondent wrote an article calling Strobridge a "New Woman," impressed that she had staked five claims, laid out a new mining camp, superintended four men, ranched, and routinely climbed "precipitous cliffs." Strobridge's father helped her set up a bookbindery in the attic, the Artemisia Bindery. Bookbinding led Strobridge to writing, and in 1901 she and her elderly parents moved to Los Angeles, where she befriended Mary Austin and joined the literary circle of editor Charles Lummis. Strobridge wrote numerous articles and published three self-bound books—In Miners' Mirage-Land (1904), The Loom of the Desert (1907), and The Land of Purple Shadows (1909)—that express the powerful lure of Nevada's deserts. These works were reprinted in 1990 as The Sagebrush Trilogy.

The Quest of Old Man Berry

The faith of the old prospectors! There is no other such blind faith in the world.

Take up your map of the Western States. There, where the great Oregon lava flow laps over the State line of Nevada, in the northwestern corner, lies the Black Rock country. Out there in that sweep of gray sand and sage-levels, and grim heights—the scaling of which—taxes the soul sorely, I found him—the typical prospector, "Old Man Berry," or "Uncle Berry," they called him. Over eighty years old he was, and for more than fifty years of his life led by the lure of a mirage.

All day I had been traveling over alkali flats and greasewood-covered mesas, to reach—in late afternoon—the upper tablelands. They were dotted with mountain mahogany, and slashed with cañons where streams ran bordered with cottonwood and aspen.

It was already dusk when we began our descent of one of the larger cañons, and quite dark when we stopped at the ranch-house doorway, through which the lamp-light streamed—the friendliest sight a Desert wayfarer ever "meets up with."

We had come upon one of those small ranches that are tucked away in the heights, where old prospectors are as sure to drift to, when not out in the mountains with poll-pick and hammer, as though they—like the ranchman's collie or the cat curled up on the bunk—were among the assets of the place.

He was tall and spare—gaunt, you would have called him; and you would have noticed at once how bowed he was. But not as other old men on whom age has rested a heavy hand. It was the head, not the back, that was bowed—as though he had walked long years, and far, with his eyes upon the ground. When he lifted them quickly—looking directly into your own—you found they were bright and piercing, with a keenness that belonged to a man forty years his junior; and you felt that his sight reached away beyond—to things not of your reckoning.

We speak of beards that are "snow-white," and usually it is a misapplied term. His was really white as snow—white as freshly fallen snow is white, with thick and long hair to match. A patriarch of the mountains, he; you would have declared.

Except as you noted his trembling hands, and saw how heavily he leaned his weight against the staff he carried as he walked, you did not feel he was old—rather it was as though, of his own choice, he wrapped himself in a dignity of years—wearing it as a monarch wears his robes of state, in no wise to be counted as the mark of flying Time.

Indeed, there was something royal about the old man; and you might join the others (the ranch hands, and the teamsters, and the cowboy crew) in good-humored scoffing at the old man himself, as well as his hobbies, when his back was turned. Yet, not you, nor any man among them dared to jest ever so lightly to his face. He commanded your respect. And you, too, would have shown him the same deference as they did, whenever he spoke. Somehow, one feels more or less a coward to try to disabuse a man of his faith in a thing that he has believed in with all his soul for a lifetime. So it is the kinder way, even as it is the easier way, to listen as they tell of such things as you, perhaps, may doubt.

That night, after the supper dishes had been cleared away, and the others had gone out to sit in the darkness, and smoke, and talk over the day's work and the plans for the morrow, while the crickets sang their night-song to the stars, Old Man Berry and I sat by the bare pine table, by the wind-blown flame of a flaring kerosene lamp, while he told me of his quest for a mine he had been seeking for more than half a hundred years.

Back in the days of the young century when he had crossed the plains, while camping at the point of Black Rock, he had found a bit of "float." Small, it was, but so rich in gold that it scarcely seemed real. It was lying at the edge of the well-traveled road where it almost touches the foothills. He looked about everywhere for others of the same sort. That one wonderful nugget was all that he found.

The old man unfastened his shirt-front, and drew from his breast a buckskin bag—a crudely constructed affair that bespoke his own handiwork. It hung suspended from his neck by a buckskin string. Old Man Berry handled it as though it were something holy, turning it over and over, as though weighing it. Finally he untied the string, and turned the bag upside down. The nugget struck heavily on the boards of the table. It was a wonder! Enough, and more than enough to drive any man mad with the gold fever.

"Nuggets like these don't just happen anywhere—as if they were made in the sky, and let fall," he said. "They come from a ledge—carried down to the flats by the forces of Nature. They are like strangers down there—their home is in the mountains. This came from the mountains—the mountain back of Black Rock. There is a ledge there somewhere. Where—in what cañon or on what ridge? Maybe it is a long, long way from there; for 'float' travels a long way sometimes. Where is it—where? Where will I find it, and when? But I will find it! I'll find it, so help me God! Why, I have almost found it now—almost, but not quite. . . . I may find it next week; and it will be MINE! There are tons and tons of gold like this, where this came from."

He was talking fast and feverishly, and I saw he was no longer talking to me, but rather thinking aloud. He had forgotten me—his surroundings—everything, except the one thing he never forgot, sleeping or waking.

For a long time he sat there, turning his fetish over and over in his knotty and weathered hands. I hardly breathed as I watched him—never moving, my eyes on the nugget, too. Somehow I had caught sight of the face of the Siren, and was one with him, for the time.

Suddenly he seemed to remember me, and he hastily put the nugget back in the little bag, and slipped it again into his breast. I could hear the men lazily talking where they leaned back against the walls of the sod house; and an owl hooted over at the barn. The chirping of the crickets sounded shriller than ever from their cover in the tall weeds and nettles down by the creek. I heard it all as in a dream. There was something unreal in all the sounds. Nothing seemed real and believable, except the sight of the nugget of virgin gold, and the tale of Old Man Berry.

By and by, I heard him talking again—telling me how, at that time, he had ventured to stay in the country for a few days, to prospect in the hope of finding the ledge. Not for long, however; for he dare not risk the savages, or draw too heavily on his food supply which was barely enough to see him through to California. The delay brought him no reward. He found no ledge; neither did he find any sign of mineral in all the district. He was forced to abandon, for the time being at least, his quest, and to push on to the sea. Once there, however, he was impatient to get back; and again he returned to the sagebrush country. Once more his quest brought him nothing, and he was forced to return to the coast. So he went back and forth between the sea and the sagebrush; and finally he came to stay. Now he had been here for so long, that he could not count the years. And, anyway, what did it matter? Few, or many, it was all the same to him.

. . . .

The next morning, after I had gone down to the cabin from where I had slept the sleep of those who are elect to find rest under the arching, star-studded sky, I found myself the last one at the breakfast table. So that, when I had finished, and had gone outside again, I found the others gathered about the corral where they were assisting "Uncle Berry" get his horses hitched to what passed for a wagon. Such a marvel of inadequacy I never have seen, as the "team" he was to use in getting off into the Desert where the lure of the gold—a veritable mirage—was calling him!

Originally intended for a small delivery wagon, it had long borne no likeness to any sort of a vehicle whatever. There was no dashboard. There was no seat. The double-trees were home-made; and the tongue was a cottonwood pole. Missing spokes in the wheels were replaced by the limbs of the quaking asp; and the reach itself was pieced with a pole used as a splice. The tires were wired on with baling wire—wound round and round with the wire, till the tire itself was scarcely to be seen. Wire all over the wagon; wire to mend the harness. The reins were of bits of old straps fastened together; and wouldn't have held a runaway pair of kittens. He had a dry willow switch for a whip. One of the horses was too old to have been properly apportioned to anything in this world, except to the filling of a grave in a horse-graveyard. The other was a half-broken colt.

Again, he was starting off for Black Rock. Alone, of course; for he would have none with him on a trip like this, lest they see where he went, and so—perhaps— some time wrest the Mine of the World from him. No; there were none he would trust. Did not a nephew come out of the East to pave the way to becoming his heir, against the hour the old man should discover the ledge and—then die. And did not this same nephew, who began by calling him "Dear Uncle Berry," end by cursing him for an "old fool," and then go away leaving the old man laid up with a crushed ankle—Did he not, all the while, and secretly, try to find the ledge for himself? No; he would have none of them. He was sufficient unto himself. He needed no one.

The colt was acting badly, and two of the cowboys were getting him into the harness—lightly dodging his heels which he lashed out viciously at them, or springing quickly aside as he reared and came down "spiking" at them with his fore-legs.

After a good deal of manoeuvering, they got him blindfolded, and finally into the harness. One of the men held the colt by the head, while old "Uncle Berry" climbed up and seated himself on his roll of blankets, which—in lieu of any other—served as a seat.

There was a look of determination on his face that did me good to see. It was the grim look that a face takes on when its owner has the knowledge that he has met a worthy foe, yet he has willed to fight to the end. It stirred my blood with admiration to see him.

There he was—more than eighty-four years of age, and yet able to climb cliffs, and peck away at the rock that lies at the tops of the mountains. Why! they told me, he would ride this unbroken colt—and did, often—if the men would help him to mount.

Such goods as he got for his small needs, must come from towns a hundred miles distant; and to them (through the winter's snow-drifts, or under the Desert's dizzying sun)—alone—in that old rattletrap of a wagon, would he go. Truly, the old man was the personification of "Western pluck."

He was thinly clad, and through the threadbare cotton shirt he wore, one could see the framework of the great, gaunt body. Somehow, the other men standing about (cowboys, and ranch hands, and teamsters), seemed puny beside him,—feeble though he was, and an octogenarian.

He nodded "good by" to us. Then—"Ready!" and a pause. "Let them go!" he said; and the man at the young horse's head, pulled off the blind and jumped back. The colt reared on his haunches—pawed the air with his hoofs, and leaped forward—almost jerking the old buckskin horse off his feet, as he went. Old Man Berry sat there—his feet braced far apart; his gray hair blowing back in the rush of wind that came up the cañon; his knotted hands gripping the reins; and that grim look on his face that made you feel that he, after all, was master of whatever he undertook.

So, down the steep cañon, through a cloud of alkali dust he went. And every instant I expected to see the old wagon go to pieces.

"God! but he's got pluck!" said one of the cowboys, turning away as "Uncle Berry" went out of sight round a bend. "They ain't nary thing that old feller won't tackle, just give him the chanst. He's clean grit, through and through!"

He was grit.

Two days later, when we came down to the ranch after a day of deer-hunting on the heights, there—at the haystack, contentedly feeding—stood Old Man Berry's horses. They were necked together just as he had left them when he had turned them out at night, to graze on the scant growth of artemisia down on the Desert, and they—led by the instinct that guides home-lovers—had come straightaway to their mountain home. The horses were well and safe, but—Where was Old Man Berry?

There was not one of us who did not feel (though no one dared voice that fear) that down on the alkali flats somewhere—far from water—they would find Something that would be a horror to see.

The ranchman ordered work in the corrals stopped, and hurried the men on swift errands he directed. To the creek, to fill canteens and demijohns with water; to the house for blankets; to the barn for horses to be put to the wagon, and others to be saddled. Every man was to aid in the work of rescue. Scarcely one of them spoke, but all wore sobered faces. Not one among them but that loved the old man; "loco" though they declared him to be.

I watched them go down the cañon, as I had watched him go such a short time before. Then I went back to the sod-house, and wondered where they would find him, and how. Ah! that is the thought—when we know some one is astray in the Desert—that grips one's throat, making it hard for them to swallow. It is as though one's mouth was parched, and without moisture; and as though one had been long without water to drink. Strange, is it not? that our fears for another should in that way hold the prophecy of what is to come to them.

After an hour or two of restless wandering about the place, I, too, went down the road that led to the Desert. I wanted to sight, if I could, the coming of the men. Then—less than a hundred yards down the cañon —I came upon them. They were bringing Old Man Berry.

Alive. And quite determined to go back, just as soon as he could arrange with some one for another wagon. Pluck to the last!

When he found his horses had gone, he started back on foot after them, thinking to find them but a short distance away. Following their tracks, for twenty-five miles he went up and down gullies—weary and faint for want of food; over sun-baked alkali flats where the warped mud-crust had dried in up-curled flakes like feathers blown forward on the back of some wind-buffeted fowl—(it showed where water had been); along foothills where he stumbled and fell, while the sharp stones cut into and bruised his flesh; through the burning sand where the sun seethed and bubbled in his brain, and he wondered if he was going mad.

It was the old story of the earth in those places where it is far between water-holes. He fought with Death in the Desert. Fought, and won!

The cowboys, after the fashion of their kind, cursed him roundly (but with a ring of tender feeling for the old man in every word they said), and they called him many kinds of an old fool for getting lost. All of which he took in the spirit in which it was meant. Yet more than one of them had wet eyes as he tried to talk to them with thickened tongue that was still black between his lips; and we saw that his palms—which he tried to hide from us—were all bruised and blood-stained from sharp stones where he had fallen.

He was pluck itself—yes, sheer grit; for he fought his way through to victory over age, and infirmities, and Death. Yet, the end is not yet. Some day—there on the sun-bleached levels—they will find him—Old Man Berry—when the Desert has taken its toll.

MRS. HUGH BROWN [1884–1987]

When Marjorie Brown arrived in Tonopah, Nevada, in 1904 as a young bride, she beheld the
frontier scene with a youthful sense of adventure. "I had been born in San Francisco, had lived
all my life in the green fragrance of that moisture-laden air," she recalls in Lady in Boomtown:
Miners and Manners on the Nevada Frontier *(1968), "and yet this dry, rarified atmosphere, so*
sparkling, this vast expanse of open country were overpoweringly lovely." Her husband, Hugh,
freshly graduated from Stanford, was sent by his law firm to open an office in Nevada's largest
boomtown. Tonopah's rich silver rescued Nevada from a twenty-year economic depression that
depopulated the state, even raising a constitutional question of whether statehood could be
revoked. Jim Butler's discovery set in motion a twentieth-century mining boom in south-central
Nevada, and capital poured in to finance mines, mills, banks, hotels, and railroads. As the wife
of a prominent lawyer—Hugh became the first president of the Nevada Bar Association—Mrs.
Brown befriended Tonopah's leading citizens, including Tasker Oddie, a future governor of Ne-
vada, and Key Pittman, a future U.S. senator. Her memoir captures in words and photographs
the social life of the town's well-to-do. Lavish parties, parades, ladies' club meetings, formal
dinners, theater, celebrity visits, even a banquet and dance in the Mizpah mine, three hundred
feet below the surface. Mrs. Brown took the train to San Francisco to give birth to her first child
and was in the Palace Hotel during the 1906 earthquake that not only shook the City by the
Bay but undermined the financial capital that supported Tonopah. Despite their plummeting
fortunes, the Browns stayed in Tonopah until 1922. Mrs. Brown's memoir of their time, written
for her three children, is an engrossing record of the growth and development of Tonopah and
Goldfield. A lady to the last, Mrs. Brown died in San Francisco at age 103, outliving Hugh by
more than fifty years.

from *Lady in Boomtown*

Hugh's voice at the other end of the telephone was serious and urgent. Would I
meet him at the Occidental Hotel at four o'clock? It was near his office, and he was
pressed for time.

"I'm going to Tonopah tonight, and I want to talk to you."

"*Tonopah?* Where's Tonopah?"

For sixty years people have been asking the same question. Only those who
have been there seem to be aware of its existence.

"It's a mining camp in southern Nevada," Hugh answered. "They've discovered
ore there—gold and silver. A boom's on."

Like any other young lady in San Francisco in 1903 who wanted to meet a man
in a downtown hotel, I had to request my mother's permission, which she gave
with just the right amount of reluctance. I suspected that she was not unmindful

of the fact that Hugh Brown was a very eligible young man, a graduate of Stanford University law school, serving the usual internship in a prominent firm, Campbell, Metson, and Campbell. If I was in love with him, it might quiet the agitation caused by my famous uncle, Theodore Roberts, a leading character actor of the era who was determined to lure me to New York for a career on the stage. No lady became an actress, my family insisted, even if she had talent. But, after all, I had already been graduated from Mills Seminary, and I was eighteen and not always sweetly amenable.

Hugh met me at the door of the hotel looking excited and happy—a tall, slender young man in a light grey suit with a blue stock tie. We walked up a flight of red-carpeted stairs to the "Ladies' Parlor," a large elegant room hung with dark red drapery and filled with massive furniture upholstered in the red plush and fringe made fashionable two decades before by riches that poured into San Francisco from Virginia City.

Briefly Hugh told me what had happened. A prospector had discovered rich ore out in the middle of the Nevada desert, and the rush was on. Hugh's firm had decided to open a law office there, and to his delight, he had been selected to represent the firm in the new town—Tonopah. He'd be gone maybe a year, not a day longer. With no further preliminaries he plunged on: would I marry him? I raised my eyes to his sweet serious face.

Of course I would.

He waved his hand to include the drawing room. "It won't be like this," he said. "It will mean hard work and rough living, but it will be exciting. There'll be no running water, and there'll be Indians."

With the wide smile that brought out the characteristic lines around his mouth, he added, "And you'd better get used to canned milk, for that's all you'll get." I threw back my head and laughed with the confidence of extreme youth.

Then we became grave as he held out his hand. "My bags are downstairs, and my ferry leaves in thirty minutes."

With a glance around the room—there were only two other people in the parlor—Hugh drew a newspaper from his pocket, unfolded it, and whispered, "Here, take this end. I haven't kissed my promised bride."

I took the edge of the newspaper, and we held it up as a shield. For the first time I kissed my future husband. Then he touched the chatelaine watch pinned on my breast and turned it over to read the inscription: *Animo et fide* (WITH COURAGE AND FAITH). It was my mother's motto, engraved on the watch she had given me as a graduation gift. As I look back to that moment, with more than sixty years between that time and this, I know Hugh needed the motto more than I, for this young man of twenty-eight was about to assume the hazard of taking to the frontier a bride of nineteen, a girl who had always been completely sheltered and was entirely unprepared for hardship—trained for nothing except how to be a lady.

. . . .

When my thoughts return to the women of Tonopah, I recall how my sympathy went out to the brides. As soon as a young man made a stake, he invariably went back for the girl he had left behind. Many were entirely unfitted for the life of a mining camp. The older women, wives of engineers, mine officials, and tradesmen, seemed adequate, but you could almost tell by looking at the brides whether they would be able to stick it out.

The problems of housekeeping on the desert were very real. During the bitter cold winters the wind moaned and whistled through the cracks in the board-and-batten houses. In the terrific summer heat, you had to cook over a wood stove with one eye always watchful for insects. Have you ever inadvertently crushed a stink bug and lived with that stench for days? Have you ever turned suddenly to look at your baby on the floor and found a scorpion on his arm? Have you ever found a bedbug on your pillow and faced the task of getting rid of the pests? The women used to say it was no disgrace to get bedbugs, but it was certainly a disgrace to keep them.

We were successors to that wonderful race of pioneer women who have been scattered over the West since the western trek began, women who brought their babies into the world in lonely places, women who cooked for their sick neighbors. These were women who washed the dead and laid them out, and rode horseback for miles to help a beleaguered home.

Jen Stock and her mother belonged to that race of women. Jen became my most intimate friend. She had a keen mind and a grand sense of humor. She did much to smooth that first year when I wrestled with new problems. She taught me to darn, to make soap, to wet paper and sprinkle the bits over the floor before I swept so that the fine talc-like dust would be kept down; and best of all, she taught me to make bread. But there was one thing she didn't teach me. She didn't teach me how to wash clothes, because I was ashamed to confess my ignorance to my more experienced neighbor.

Once I had called in Annie, an Indian woman, who looked a thousand years old though she was probably not as old as my own mother, but things were in such disorder by the time she was through that I could not think of having her in my neat little kitchen again. I watched Jen and other neighbors hang out sheets, tablecloths, pajamas, shirts, until every bit of linen I owned had been used up in an effort to postpone the evil day. At last I tackled it. If other women could do the washing, I could.

The water, remember, was in a big barrel in the kitchen. Once a week a man came up the hill behind a team of mules struggling against the weight of a wagon loaded with six huge barrels full of water. He'd stop as close to the front of the house as the uneven ground would allow, prop the back wheels with a wooden wedge, and empty one of the barrels through a bunghole into buckets. Then he came teetering into my kitchen, carrying two buckets at a time, from which water spilled across the floor, but ultimately most went into my barrel. Each week I paid him a silver dollar.

Every bit of water we used was lifted out of that barrel. Bathing was not too difficult, for we had two oversize tea kettles. One of these, heated to boiling, then poured into the big galvanized iron tub on the floor and cooled with more water, was not too hard to handle. But for laundering I had to lift the kettle from the stove to a tub balanced between two kitchen chairs, scrub the clothes as I had seen Annie do, then dip the water out with a pitcher until the tub was light enough to drag along the floor and empty out the back door. I repeated the filling process to rinse the wet, heavy sheets, not to mention the terrific effort of getting them hung on the line, and then mopped up the water that had splashed on the floor! This was more than I had ever bargained for.

The task was not half complete before I had rubbed the skin off the backs of my fingers, and when the job was done, my body ached in every joint.

When Hugh came home, I cried in his arms. Poor man, he didn't know what to do with me; but that night, when I lay in bed, my hands throbbing with pain, I made a vow: I would never try it again! Tomorrow I'd go down to the little cubbyhole on Main Street that passed for a dry goods store and buy bed linen. My husband (as if it were his fault) would have to get his shirts washed in the same way he had managed before I arrived, and everything else would go to a Reno laundry and back by stage.

Reno was two hundred miles away. It took two days for the laundry to get there and a little less than three weeks for it to return, but I've never been ashamed to confess I didn't do my washing myself. After I maneuvered Hugh into carrying the package down to the stage office, he decided to send his own linen to Reno, too. For the next two years the arrangement was a great comfort to both of us.

Washing my windows was the next source of humiliation for me though without quite serious repercussions. I had been reared by a Victorian mother who insisted that no lady should ever be seen doing menial labor. I had no hesitancy about doing the necessary scrubbing and polishing indoors—in fact I loved it—but it did give me a sense of degradation to realize I would have to go out on the porch in full sight of the whole town to wash those windows. Should I hire old Annie? Unthinkable. I'd have to do it.

So I went at it, making myself as small as possible and hoping no one would notice me. But alas for foolish wishes, that afternoon a lady knocked at the door. She was the wife of the bank cashier, and, I had been told, the granddaughter of a Virginia City millionaire. That day she was elegantly dressed in soft brown wool under a sealskin coat.

"Oh, Mrs. Brown," she announced gaily, "I've wanted to come to see you ever since you arrived, and when I saw you out washing your windows this morning, I said to myself, 'There now, I'll go this very afternoon.'"

I'm sure she washed her own windows, and I was relieved to think she didn't know how mortified I was. But gradually I learned it was not the doing of the menial labor that was "déclassé," but the *not* doing it. I learned to discount the toll of my complexion and the awful things that happened to my fingernails (Hugh never did get over regretting the condition of my hands), and never since have I been able to recapture the importance of such things. There is very little in the way of physical labor I haven't done, even chopping wood for the cook stove. I *love* to swing an ax!

ANNE ELLIS [1875–1938]

Anne Ellis's Life of an Ordinary Woman (1929) provides a glimpse of the working class in western mining towns. Ellis's life was never easy. Born in Missouri, as a small child she crossed the Great Plains in an oxcart with her extended family, bound for Bonanza, Colorado. There, her father deserted the family, her mother died, and at age eighteen Anne left her six younger siblings to marry a miner in hopes of bettering her station in life. A mining explosion killed her husband, leaving Anne and her two small children penniless in Cripple Creek, Colorado. She gained a measure of financial stability by running a boardinghouse for miners, where she met and married Herbert Ellis and had a third child. Ambitious to improve her lot, Anne pressured Herbert into moving to the boomtown of Goldfield, Nevada. Supplies were short in this crude frontier town, and winters were cold. Her husband took ill, her daughter Joy died of diphtheria, and the 1907 labor strike terminated Herbert's income. Destitute, the Ellises scraped their way back to Colorado, whereupon Herbert died. Twice widowed, Anne Ellis supported herself and her two remaining children by cooking for construction crews, sheep shearers, and hay farmers. Then, in a far-fetched scheme, she ran for treasurer of Saguache County, winning the election and retaining the job for six years, long enough to send her children to college. Finally, Ellis's chronic asthma forced her to move to a sanitorium in Albuquerque, New Mexico, where, again nearly broke, she was encouraged by a friend to write about her life. The Life of an Ordinary

Woman *(1929),* Plain Anne Ellis *(1931), and* Sunshine Preferred *(1933) offer a moving portrait of the thoughts, hopes, and struggles of folks who live close to the poverty line. Thankfully, the books generated a modest income that cushioned the final years of Ellis's hard life.*

from *The Life of an Ordinary Woman*

> A swarming of human bees and no one to beat on a pan in order to hive them.
>
> A. E.

I am getting tired of this little mining camp (had I only known it, I was eating my white bread then), wanting to get a start in life and seeing no chance here. I am afraid I harped on this one string a good deal, as one day Herbert said, "There is no satisfying you. You no more than get one thing than you want another."

"Sure I do. This is what makes progress, men trying to satisfy women."

. . . .

I have been getting letters from a family in Goldfield, Nevada—a new booming gold camp, and it all sounds so interesting and prosperous that I urge Herbert to go. He is slow to make a change, but does consent to give up his job, sell the furniture (at a loss), and again we are on the road. This move was entirely my fault, and all that followed I had to swallow without a word of complaint. Herbert was big enough never once to say, "It is because of you we are here."

The Goldfield train was just pulling out as we came into Hazen, so we had to spend the night there, in a green-lumber, just-put-up hotel, crowded with people going to this gold boom town. Outside along the railroad track was the largest pile of goods that I had ever seen—tools of all kinds, tents, bedding, provision, merchandise, lumber, barrels of whiskey, and everything, the owners frantic to get it into Goldfield. In the big bare office where we crowded around an enormous heating stove, we all talked of gold and Goldfield. Miners, mining men, prospectors, business men, promoters, and men of every sort were there; not so many women, but what there were, were more excited than the men. Mine were the only children in this adventuring crowd.

That day as I sat there I thought, "I wish I could write about these people and describe their actions, faces, and clothes"; and I considered getting a pencil and doing it, but writing seemed impossible to me then. Here we saw our first big automobiles owned by very rich men. We, too, expected to have one soon; I had even bought a big automobile veil so as to be ready. In all the pictures they had their heads wrapped in a veil, the long ends blowing straight out behind them.

The doctor at home had one of the first automobiles. It had to be pulled up the hill every time he came to Bonanza. It was 1910 before I ever rode in one, and then and always my seat has been a back one, the guest's seat.

. . . .

After searching, we find a small one-room tent which had been boarded up, then covered with tar paper. For this we give three hundred and seventy-five dollars and move in. Our beds are made of bed springs which during the day can be closed against the wall; in one corner is a tiny inkstand stove; between the foot of the bed and table is one trunk, which two children can sit on while they eat. (On wash days this trunk is used for a bench.) The big box is unpacked and used for a dresser, lending quite an air when it is draped with a piece of Battenberg on top, with the old mirror hanging above. I hemstitch curtains for the one window and door, and after the books are unpacked and put on a shelf, and the few pictures tacked up, we are quite cosy.

Now I am seeing life in big gobs; fortunes made or lost each day on the stock exchange, in the saloons, at the mines, or at stealing, buying, and selling high-grade. I knew men who made, in addition to their wages, from twenty to fifty dollars per day, depending on how rich the ore was where they were working. The ore was a dark porous formation, no gold showing till it was roasted. In almost every family, either in the oven or on the back of the stove, there were pieces of this ore roasting; then, when you poured water over the hot ore, blisters of gold came out.

. . . .

Fuel is very scarce and expensive; at one time there is a real famine and people suffer. Coal and timbers are stolen from the mines; a car of coal is taken right off the tracks, and guards are put out to take care of it. During this time Herbert is sick, and we try in every way to get fuel, but there is none, only promises from day to day, then talk of the coal being shipped elsewhere, or of other towns taking over whole trainloads. Finally, through the influence of some one in power, a car does come to Goldfield—I just have to have some of this, so go early in the morning to the Tonopah freight yards, over a mile through slush and mud, to find a huge crowd—all of the same mind—before me, all talking and arguing. We form in some kind of line, trying to slip and squirm nearer. After standing for hours, I come to where the man is doling it out, only to find that there is none left. I tell him, "There is no use in talking, I just have to have coal; a sick husband at home," etc., and make it pretty strong. He gives me a gunnysack full—supposed to be one hundred pounds, for which I pay three dollars and a half. Then begins the search for an expressman to take it home.

During this lack of fuel, Herbert "lifted" the foundation from a vacant tent, bringing it home in the night. He sawed it into blocks and hid it under the bed, but we were punished at once, as the blocks were so green they were hard to saw, and brought forth much puffing and sweating. They never did dry out enough to burn. So was justice meted out.

This time that Herbert was sick, we were so frightened of dread pneumonia, people dying like flies with it—nurses being rushed in on every train. But I kept him well plastered in onions and one morning was delighted to have him turn in bed and say, "The bacon smells good; I think I can eat some."

. . . .

Now comes the strike. I never did understand what it was all about. . . . Some strikes may be all right, but it seemed to me this one was uncalled for, and, oh, how it dragged out!

Day after day, week after week, and the money almost gone. During a strike all suffer, but I think it must be harder on the wife. The husband, tramping and looking for work, sees other men and can talk matters over with them, thereby forgetting himself and gaining a sort of courage, but she, at home, is planning what and how to feed her children in the cheapest and most nourishing way possible— counting and recounting each penny, so much for fuel, so much for water, so much for a soup bone. They told of a woman who asked a neighbor if she could borrow her yesterday's soup bone. The answer was, "No. Mrs. So-and-So has it to-day." The wife worries every hour of the day, not knowing which way to turn, and in the evening, when the man returns from his hopeless wanderings, she, looking up at his gray face, can tell at a glance that there is no good news.

I try to get any kind of work as do so many others. One day I have sewed and got two dollars, which goes into the family exchequer, we having only one pocket-book in our family, kept in a common place, so that there was no asking or giving of money. When I go to pay the water man, the two dollars is gone. I ask, "Herbert, did you take any money?"

He answers, red-faced, "Why, yes, I didn't think the two dollars would help much, so bet it on a horse race, four to one."

"And did you win?"

"No; it was a muddy track. Luck seems to be against us. Others were winning all around."

I turn away, but do not say anything, as I see he is about desperate, and besides keeping myself in order I must not let him lose hope.

NELL MURBARGER [1909–1991]

If you have ever been "ghost-towning" or thought about ghost towns, it may be because of Nell Murbarger, the self-styled "roving reporter of the desert." Born in the Black Hills of South Dakota and home-schooled through the eighth grade, Nell married Wilbur Murbarger at twenty-two, divorced him at thirty, and never looked back. She worked for several western newspapers before becoming a freelance writer. With four books and over one thousand magazine articles on every conceivable desert subject, Murbarger was a desert rat extraordinaire. Her books reflected her interests: Ghosts of the Glory Trail: Intimate Glimpses into the Past and Present of 275 Western Ghosttowns *(1956);* Sovereigns of the Sage: True Stories of People and Places in the Great Sagebrush Kingdom of the Western United States *(1958);* 30,000 Miles in Mexico: Adventures of Two Women and a Pick-up Camper in Twenty-eight Mexican States *(1961); and* Ghosts of the Adobe Walls: Human Interest and Historical Highlights from 400 Ghost Haunts of Old Arizona *(1964). Murbarger dedicated* Ghosts of the Glory Trail *to "my Father and Mother who taught me to love the out-of-doors, to respect old things and old people, to find peace in aloneness, and beauty everywhere," and signed her foreword, "Nell Murbarger, Somewhere-in-the-Great Basin." This excerpt from* Sovereigns of the Sage *depicts Josie Pearl, the "Queen of the Black Rock Country," a legend and enigma of that "upper left-hand corner of Nevada." Pearl declared she was "close to 100 years old, dearie—and I've led about as strange a life as any person living." Murbarger ends Josie's story with the observation that meeting Josie "was like looking at the last free antelope, or the last piece of open range." Murbarger may have seen her own reflection in that image.*

Queen of the Black Rock Country

Spiraling out of the north, a sinuous dust devil lurched across the desert, swelling in volume as it gathered into itself more thistles and broken sage, more dust. As the dancing column dissolved in the heat haze to the south, the yellow flat slipped back under its briefly-broken hush. Once again there was only vastness, hemmed by rugged hills and stitched by the thin tracery of the road.

As a roving reporter of the desert I was not a stranger to this upper left-hand corner of Nevada. In the course of filling half-a-dozen magazine and newspaper assignments in the Black Rock country, I had been through here enough times to know that the nearest town to the northwest was the little way-station of Denio, on the Nevada-Oregon border, 72 miles distant; and that to the west there was no town nearer than Cedarville, California, 170 miles. Between those outposts and Winnemucca spread 10,000 square miles of highland desert—a territory more than a fourth as large as the entire state of Indiana, but without either a post office or point of supply.

Somewhere in the heart of that arid immensity I hoped to locate a woman described to me as one of the most remarkable characters in the West—a true Sovereign of the Sage.

Until two days previously, my acquaintance with Josie Pearl had been limited to a few pages in Ernie Pyle's book, *Home Country,* a collection of his best newspaper columns originally written and published in the 1930s.

> *"Josie Pearl was a woman of the West,"* Pyle had written. *"Her dress was calico, with an apron over it; on her head was a farmer's straw hat, on her feet a mismatched pair of men's shoes, and on her left hand and wrist six thousand dollars worth of diamonds! That was Josie—contradiction all over, and a sort of Tugboat Annie of the desert. Her whole life had been spent . . . hunting for gold in the ground. She was a prospector. She had been at it since she was nine, playing a man's part in a man's game . . ."*

Several years after reading that description of this unique desert character, I had been in Winnemucca covering a magazine assignment when one of the folks there asked why I didn't "do" a story on Josie Pearl. My memory did a flip-flop and I recalled the book I had read so long before.

"You can't mean that woman miner Ernie Pyle wrote about in *Home Country?*" I exclaimed. "Don't tell me she's *still alive?*"

"And going strong!" said my friend. "But she's far more than a 'woman miner.' She's a great personality straight out of the pages of the Old West—and the last of her kind!"

If I had been told Kit Carson was waiting to take me to a dance I could scarcely have been more astounded! Nearly 20 years had elapsed since Pyle had written his story of this woman. Even then, he had planted the impression that she was almost as old as Adam. To learn she was still "going strong" was just about more than I could believe.

Although my Winnemucca friend was well acquainted with Josie, he couldn't tell me how to reach her home—a situation I was to find quite prevalent during the next two days. Everyone around town seemed to know her, but no one I contacted could give explicit directions for finding her.

"Sure, I know Old Josie!" they would say. "But I've never been out to her mining claim . . ." or maybe they would tell me she lived "somewhere near the north end of Black Rock Desert," or "up in the vicinity of Summit Lake," or "over beyond the Quinn River country." No matter how they expressed it, the directions were uniformly vague.

Because it seemed the logical approach to any of the geographical points mentioned, I drove north from Winnemucca, 33 miles, to the junction of State Route

8-A that leads westerly across the desert to Denio and Cedarville. Hesitating, momentarily, at the turn-off, I ranged my eyes over that wide and lonely land spreading ahead; then, I eased my foot from the clutch pedal and my old car was rolling down that long, empty road.

Human inhabitants are few in this part of Nevada and the first chance I had to check my navigation was at Quinn River ranch, 38 miles west of the turn-off. Only the ranch cook was in evidence. Like everyone with whom I had talked at Winnemucca, the cook was acquainted with Josie Pearl, but not with where she lived.

"When she goes to town, she comes up from the south," he said, meditatively stroking his nose with a flour-dusted forefinger. "If it was me, I'd take the Leonard Creek road to the next ranch—the Montoya place—and ask there. It's not far. Mebbe 25 miles . . ."

The Leonard Creek road was a primitive sort, not hazardous so long as speed was held down, but generally narrow, given to sharp turns, and always dusty. Dodging sand pockets and shuttling though hedge-like aisles of sagebrush, I thought of Ernie Pyle traveling that same trail all those years before.

"There really wasn't any road to Josie Pearl's cabin," he had written. *"Merely a trail across space. Your creeping car was the center of an appalling cloud of dust, and the sage scratched long streaks on the fender . . ."*

After skirting the southeasterly foot of Pine Forest range and rounding its tip, the little "trail across space" struck out over the northern fringe of Black Rock Desert. Stretching away for more than 100 miles, this bleak playa is a place of expansive silence. At its widest point the old lakebed is close to 15 miles across; but here at its upper tip the road soon left it behind and went climbing into the rough brown hills beyond. Another few miles revealed the Montoya ranch—officially, the Pine Range Livestock company. Here, for the first time since leaving Winnemucca, 95 miles earlier, I learned I was actually on the right course! Josie's place was only five or six miles father back in the hills.

Following a twisty road up the canyon, I soon came in sight of a small house set in a clump of poplars, about 100 yards off the trail.

"Josie Pearl," Pyle had written, *"lived all alone in a little tar-paper cabin surrounded by nothing but desert. From a mile away you could hardly see the cabin amidst the knee-high sagebrush. But when you got there it seemed almost like a community—it was such a contrast in a space filled only with white sun and empty distance . . ."*

Bringing my dust-layered car to a halt in the yard, I looked about me. Everywhere were tables and boxes and benches, each piled with ore samples, rocks, petrified wood, geodes, rusty relics, purple glass, miners' picks and candlesticks, prospectors' pans, parts for cars, and miscellaneous trivia. At one of the tables a woman was mortaring a piece of ore. Her face was screened from view by the brim of a man's felt hat that was jammed solidly on her head.

"Pardon me," I ventured. "I'm looking for Josie Pearl."

"Yeah?" said the woman, gruffly. "Well, you've found her. I'm Josie. What's on your mind?"

As she spoke the question she glanced up for the first time since my arrival, and I found myself looking into one of the most unforgettable faces I have ever seen. Years were in that face—many years—but it mirrored also some strange quality that far transcended the casual importance of age. The eyes that bored into mine were neither friendly nor unfriendly. Rather, they were shrewd and appraising; as steady as the eyes of a gunfighter, as inscrutable as those of a poker player. She was not a large woman but was healthy-looking and robust, with determination and self-sufficiency written all over her. I felt instinctively that should she decide to move one of the surrounding mountains to the other side of the canyon, she would go about it calmly and deliberately, some evening after supper, perhaps. And she would move it—every stick and stone of it—and would ask no help from either God or man.

That was my first impression of Josie. It still stands.

She wasn't sure she wanted her life story written for *Desert Magazine*.

"Not that I don't like *Desert*," she hastened to assure me. "I do. Good magazine. Down-to-earth stuff in it. I just don't 'go much' on publicity . . ."

But persistence and persuasion eventually won the day.

"Okay," she agreed. "Since you put it that way, I'll give you the story . . . but don't be surprised if you find some of it hard to believe. I'm close to 100 years old, dearie—and I've led about as strange a life as any person living!"

As we started across the yard toward her cabin, Josie glanced at my car. "You travelin' alone? Good! Then you'll stay overnight." There was no question mark at the end of that statement.

"*Her cabin,*" to again quote Ernie Pyle's observation, "*was the wildest hodge-podge of riches and rubbish I'd ever seen. The walls were thick with pinned-up letters from friends, assay receipts on ore, receipts from Montgomery Ward. Letters and boxes and clothing and pans were just thrown—everywhere. And in the middle of it all sat an expensive wardrobe trunk, with a seven thousand dollar sealskin coat inside . . .*"

It was all there, just as Ernie had described it—assay reports and newspaper clippings and letters and picture postcards and tax receipts and cash register slips.

During the considerable lapse of time between Ernie's visit and mine, I'm sure the collection on the walls had grown progressively deeper; and while I didn't actually *see* the sealskin coat, I'm willing to concede its presence, somewhere in the chaos.

"Have a chair," said Josie. "Any one you like. Here—this is the best one." With a vigorous sweep of her arm she sent avalanching to the floor several weeks' accumulation of newspapers and magazines. "Now," she said, motioning me to the cleared seat. "What is it you want to know?"

The story of Josie's life was presented with as much chronological order as may be expected in a freshly-shuffled pack of cards. It was presented while we were out in her small garden cutting lettuce and lamb's-quarter greens for supper, and gathering rhubarb for a pie. It was presented while Josie was rattling the grate and building a roaring fire in the big cookstove, and concocting the aforementioned pie, and grinding meat for hash, and making hot cornbread; while she was out in the chicken yard feeding her assorted fowls and rabbits, and gathering eggs, and getting in wood for the night, and filling the kerosene lamps and cleaning their chimneys, and shooing flies away from the door, and screaming at her dogs.

The story Josie told me, against this backdrop of confusion, was not an easy story to record; and, as Josie had forewarned, it was not an easy story to believe. Yet, I believe it.

It had its beginning away back when Josie was still a small child and her parents left their Eastern home to settle in New Mexico. There her father became interested in mining. It was an interest that quickly communicated itself to Josie and, at 13 years of age, when most little girls of that hoop-skirted era were still embroidering samplers, she found her first mine and sold it for $5000. By the time of the mining boom at Creede, Colorado, Josie was a young woman and nothing could stop her from joining the stampede.

"Was that ever a time!" she shook her head with the memory. "Guess maybe you've heard Cy Warman's poem:

"The cliffs are solid silver,
    With won'drous wealth untold,
    And the beds of the running rivers
    Are lined with purest gold.
    While the world is filled with sorrow,
    And hearts must break and bleed—
    It's day all day in the daytime
    And there is no night in Creede!

"That's how it was—roaring night and day. Gambling, shootings, knifings. I got a job slinging hash. Bob Ford and Soapy Smith always ate at one of my tables.

Every Sunday morning each of 'em would leave a five dollar gold piece under his coffee cup for me. Fine fellows, both of 'em. I never could understand how Bob could have killed Jesse James as he did . . ."

I asked if she was in Creede when Ford was murdered.

"Indeed, I was!" said Josie. "I was waiting table when I heard the shooting and folks began yelling. I ran outside to see what was happening . . . and there lay Bob, all bloody and still. Yes," she nodded, "I was there . . ."

In 1892 Josie became the wife of Lane Pearl, a young mining engineer and Stanford graduate. For awhile she operated a boarding house patronized largely by men from the Chance, Del Monte, Amethyst and Bachelor mines, of Creede vicinity. Later, she and her husband moved to California; thence to Reno, where she worked for a time at Whittaker hospital. And then came the strike at Goldfield.

"We were among the first ones there," she recalled. "I got a job at the Palm restaurant, owned by a Mr. French, from Alaska. He paid me four dollars a day, plus two meals and my tips. There was no end of gold in circulation, and the men tipped as if it were burning holes in their pockets.

"Mr. French had a rule against hiring married women, so I had taken the job under my maiden name. Lane would come in and sit down at one of my tables and eat, but we never let on we were husband and wife. One day, Mr. French said, 'Y'know, Josie, I think that young mining engineer is sort of stuck on you!' They never caught on."

With Goldfield beginning to languish, Lane Pearl took a job with the leading mine at Ward, Nevada, where he was still employed when the influenza epidemic of 1918 claimed his life. Although she was by then a middle-aged woman, not even the loss of her idolized husband could kill Josie's love for the rocky soil of Nevada and its mining towns. Restlessly she began drifting from camp to camp, operating miners' boarding houses.

"When I had a boarding house at Senator Getchell's Betty O'Neal mine, near Battle Mountain, I cleared $35,000 in three years—and then sunk the whole thing in another mine and lost it all. More than once I've been worth $100,000 one day and next day would be cooking in some ratty mining camp at $30 a month! But I always managed to keep my credit good. Right today," she declared, "I could walk into any bank in this part of the state and borrow $5000 on five minutes' notice!"

The older she grew, the more mining became an obsession. Eventually, she gravitated toward northern Humboldt County where she acquired some claims in the hills, and had been working them ever since.

"Of course," said Josie, "I still do a bit of prospecting, now and then. Just knock off work, jump in my old pickup, and head out to see what I can find. Last week I was up in Idaho, looking at a uranium prospect. Scads of money in some of this new stuff . . . Scads of money!"

At Winnemucca I had been told that Josie nursed half the sick miners in northern Nevada, and had spent thousands of dollars grub-staking old washed-up prospectors who were eating their hearts out for one last fling at the canyons. When I referred to this phase of her activities, she brushed it aside impatiently.

"My real hobby," she brightened, "is boys. Homeless boys. Lord knows how many I've taken in, and fed and clothed, and given educations. Lots of 'em were rough little badgers when I got 'em. Penitentiary fodder. What they needed was love and understanding, and to know somebody was interested in what they did. Every boy I've helped turned into a fine man; not one of 'em has gone wrong. Most of 'em have good jobs. Some are with the armed forces; some are married and have families."

The dream of her life, she confided, was to make enough money to build and endow a home for boys. "Like Father Flanagan's Boys' Town," she explained. "That's all I'm working for, now."

When I asked how she happened to meet Ernie Pyle, she said she had gone to Albuquerque to visit her sister, who lived near the Pyles and had been nursing Ernie's wife through an illness.

"Naturally, I met 'em both. Ernie and I talked a lot about the West, and Nevada, and mining, and I told him to come and see me. He said he would—and he did. He was out here several times, and we corresponded all the rest of his life. In the last letter he wrote me, he said: 'The happiest I will ever be again is the day I stick my feet under your table and eat a pot of those Boston Baked Beans!'

"Thirteen hours later," said Josie quietly, "he was dead—cut down by a lousy sniper's bullet, in the South Pacific . . ."

All afternoon dark clouds had been bunching over the bare hills to the northwest and before we finished supper a biting wind was sweeping through the desert ravine and the air had turned bitterly cold. With the dishes washed, the assorted livestock fed and sheltered, and the lamp lighted, we drew our chairs close to the glowing cook stove and talked until far in the night.

Josie seemed to draw upon an inexhaustible fountain of experiences. She told of loneliness; of what it meant to be the only woman in mining camps numbering hundreds of men. She told of packing grub on her back through 20-below-zero blizzards, of wading snow, and sharpening drill steel, and loading shots; of defending her successive mines against high-graders and claim jumpers and faithless partners.

"More than once," she said, "I've spent a long, cold night huddled in a mine tunnel with a .30-30 across my knees . . ."

And there had been lawsuits. Lawsuits without end.

"She said gold brought you nothing but trouble and yet you couldn't stop looking for it," Ernie Pyle had written. *"The minute you had gold, somebody started cheating you, or suing you, or cutting your throat. She couldn't even count the lawsuits she had been in. She had lost $15,000 and $60,000 and $8,000 and $10,000, and I don't know how much more. 'But what's $8,000?' she said. 'Why eight thousand doesn't amount to a hill of beans. What's eight thousand?'"*

Late that night, long after Josie and I had retired and the fire in the cook stove had died to gray embers, I lay wakefully in the darkness, listening to the wind as it pummeled the windows and doors, and whistled down the stove pipe, and tore at a piece of loose canvas, and flung gravel against the side of the cabin. Now and then a jagged flash of lightning split the dark sky and distant thunder rolled and rumbled across the ranges.

Some time, on the day to follow, I would return to Winnemucca—to electric lights and sidewalks and dime stores and super-markets—and Josie Pearl would be left to face alone the bitter storms of this high, desert land. Alone she would cope with possible illness and accident, with primitive roads and drought and failing springs. Most particularly, she would be left alone to cope with the problem of daily needs—that Frankenstein's monster that forever roosts on the doorstep of persons who live 100 miles from the nearest town.

It was impossible to imagine a stranger sort of existence for a woman—particularly one who, by her own admission, was "almost 100 years old." Yet, even this one day, I had seen enough of Josie to believe that as long as she retained her good health she would stand tall and fiercely proud, facing the multiple challenges of each new morning with hope and courage and a wonderful enthusiasm for whatever that day might bring.

Now that I had met and talked with this strange woman of the West, I could understand what my friend had meant when he called her "the last of her kind."

That was one reason I couldn't sleep. I was afraid my friend was right, and something about that thought was terribly sobering and saddening.

It was like looking at the last free antelope, or the last piece of open range.

LUCIUS BEEBE [1902–1966]

American newspaper columnist, railroad historian, author, editor, publisher, gourmand, oeno-
phile, and self-proclaimed snob, Lucius Beebe was a legend in his own time. With impeccable
manners, his 6'4" frame fastidiously clad in suit, gloves, top hat, and gold-knobbed cane, "Mr.
New York" could apparently whisk into the finest restaurants in America and be instantly
ushered to the best table—without a reservation. A dignified Edwardian gentleman despite
his anachronistic birth in the twentieth century, Beebe loathed airplanes—"thrice-damned
flying machines"—but was passionately devoted to trains. He and his partner Charles Clegg
purchased one of the last private railcars, spent a fortune to have it fitted with lavish Venetian
décor, fireplace, wine cellar, and Turkish bath, and, with their St. Bernard, Mr. T-Bone, rode
in style throughout the land. Outspoken, flamboyant, a master of hijinks, Beebe was expelled
from Yale and suspended from Harvard before commencing a long career in journalism. As
syndicated columnist for the New York Herald Tribune, *his vignettes in "This New York" about*
the uppity "Café Society" entertained Depression-era readers. In 1950, Beebe abruptly moved to
Virginia City, Nevada, where he lived until his death. Why? The little ghost town had twenty
gorgeous Victorian saloons for a population of about four hundred. Smitten, Beebe exclaimed
to Clegg, "Why, the alcoholic proof here is so high, and the moral tone so low, that we can be
absolutely inconspicuous." But behind the bon vivant lurked a fiendishly hard worker. In 1952
Beebe and Clegg bought the once illustrious Territorial Enterprise *and turned it into the high-*
est circulation weekly on the West Coast. Beebe churned out a book a year for forty years in ad-
dition to his weekly newspaper columns and magazine features for Gourmet, Cosmopolitan,
Esquire, American Heritage, Saturday Review, Newsweek, Playboy, *and others.*

Going for the Mail

A tie with the American past establishing continuity with a simpler age, the morning walk to the post office is still the identifying hallmark of the fast-vanishing
country village. Going in person for the mail is one of the few American folk habits that connect the urban here and now with the country ways that were evident
almost everywhere in the United States a century or so ago.

In such small towns as Virginia City (where I make my legal residence and
spend the clement months of the year), going for the mail is almost the only common bond between the somewhat haphazard citizenry of this abode of the ancient
glories of the Comstock Lode. Meetings of Their Honors, the Storey County Commissioners, are apt to be slimly attended unless matters of great moment, such as
the annual debate over licensing the girls in Six Mile Canyon, are to be discussed.
The subject of the girls is brought up every summer when one group of insur-
gent taxpayers insists they be licensed for county revenue, while another group

demands their suppression on moral grounds. The result is always the same. The district attorney rules that licensing them is illegal but that the maintenance of love stores is in itself no violation of Nevada law. So the girls remain *in situ*, doing a roaring summer-month trade in a disreputable trailer camp down Sutro way.

Even the great community drunks on the occasion of the full moon, once common in many towns where the old frontier has died slowly, have now fallen into the discard. A full Comstock moon, than which there is none fuller or more mysterious anywhere on earth, used to set the patrons of C Street's saloons and other resorts at each other's throats to such a degree that the maimed and contused lay all night in the gutters and had to be swept up in the morning amidst general cries of "What seems to have happened?" Now the old-timers who liked to wrap a bar stool around each other's heads are all in the town's several cemeteries.

Only the nine o'clock walk to the post office for the morning mail remains. One must take part in this ritual in person, since sending an emissary or surrogate is invariably taken as a sign that a Comstocker is *in extremis* and won't last the day. Preferably one goes on foot to participate in the exchange of news (fallacious) and views (malicious) that takes place among the enlightened electorate on the sidewalk while waiting for Tex and Marion Gladding to finish putting up the second class.

In the West, where we all like to imagine vestigial traces of the Old West still linger in the most palpable tourist traps, the mail has an even greater significance than it does in, say, Vermont or Nantucket. The time when Horace Greeley's *Tribune* took eight weeks out of Missouri to get here is only yesterday in the general awareness. The well-known sketches, in all the Western histories, of the first San Francisco settlers waiting in long lines at the post office for the arrival of a steamer from Panama are evidence of a heritage of dependence on the safe arrival of mail. The morning ritual in Virginia City in 1966 has the best imaginable bloodlines.

Nine o'clock, when Virginia City sets its face toward the post office, finds an almost full tally of its first citizens hastening, ambling, or slouching (as their several natures suggest) toward the lockboxes. First on the scene, in her official capacity of picking up the county business, is Shirley Andreasen, the all-powerful functionary who, as Clerk, administers the county's affairs in their remotest detail. Nominally, the commissioners are the regulatory body, but in practical fact authority rests in the Clerk's office in the vast and venerable Storey County Court House near Piper's Opera. The courthouse was built in the seventies, when the Comstock still boasted 25,000 permanent residents, and now absorbs the microscopic taxes and records the deeds and legal business of a scant 350.

Hard on Mrs. Andreasen's heels comes Judge Edward Colletti, former partner and senior barman at the Delta Saloon now elevated to the magistracy, and as formal of attire and habit as any Montgomery Street broker over the hill in San Francisco. The town takes pride in Judge Colletti's decisions, but regrets his loss as a bartender.

In the early van of Virginia City's notables will be Florence Edwards, proprietor of the Silver Dollar Hotel and perhaps the community's most celebrated character. Mrs. Edwards, whose middle name is Ballou and who, on its basis, claims elevated connections in the East, came to Virginia City twenty years ago on a sight-seeing bus and awakened next morning in the Silver Dollar with a deed to the property, all properly sworn and attested, in her hand. Florence has never been away since. One day a week, she takes off for Reno and the hairdresser in her museum-piece motorcar, "The Spirit of Nausea," and the town makes book on whether she'll get it back up the hill by dinnertime.

Early on the scene, too, will be the town's only certified artist, Cal Bromond, whose Western canvases, mostly on a heroic scale, command really startling figures and can be discovered behind the bars of some of Reno's best sluicing places.

By nine-thirty the daily rite of picking up the mail is over, and the news of the day has been circulated with far greater celerity than in larger communities served by the rotary press. Everybody knows who is in jail for what from the night before, and Florence Edwards has recited the entire register of her guests at the Silver Dollar, together with their pedigrees, incomes, and social connections.

With this observance of the rite of going for the mail, Virginia City does more than pay its respects to a ceremony deep-rooted in the Western consciousness. It also prepares itself to honor an even more compulsive tradition. In the days of the deep mines of the Comstock, the town's multiple saloons were crowded with workers of the night shift who went off duty at eight in the morning, pausing on their way for an "after-shifter." The custom, which would raise scandalized eyebrows in New England, still obtains. Everyone of consequence still has an after-shifter when the mail has been cleared.

Occasionally, when the mail is late, the after-shifter takes on overtones of mild abandon, because the most natural place to wait for the mail is the place where one is eventually going anyway. "An old Western custom," everyone assures everyone else, as they teeter out into the cold light of day.

SALLY ZANJANI [B. 1937]

Shortly after earning her PHD in political science from New York University, Sally Zanjani and her scientist husband traveled to a series of scientific meetings around the world. A family illness forced them to miss one flight, a plane that crashed into the sea off the coast of Greece, target of a terrorist bomb. That narrow escape made her stop and ask what she had left undone in her life. Zanjani had been intending to write a memoir of her pioneer family in Nevada, the Springmeyers, and she decided to begin that project immediately, writing her first book, The Unspiked Rail: Memoir of a Nevada Rebel *(1981), and getting so hooked on Nevada history that she never wanted to do anything else. Sally Zanjani's grandfather emigrated from Germany in 1868 and settled in the Carson Valley, south of Reno. Her father, George Springmeyer, joined the gold rush to Goldfield in 1906. In eight books and more than forty articles, Zanjani unearths interesting Nevada stories for the delight and education of her readers, an accomplishment formally recognized by the Nevada Writers Hall of Fame Award in 2000. Her book* The Ignoble Conspiracy: Radicalism on Trial in Nevada *(1986), coauthored with Guy Louis Rocha, led to the posthumous pardons of two Goldfield miners and radical union members who were unfairly convicted of murder in 1907.* A Mine of Her Own: Women Prospectors in the American West, 1850–1950 *(1997), named one of the top ten books of all time by the Mining History Association, recovers the forgotten stories of nearly one hundred women prospectors, correcting the common misconception that all miners were men.* Sarah Winnemucca *(2001), Zanjani's biography of the renowned Native American activist, received the Evans Biography Award and the Westerners International Co-Founders Award. The short story reprinted below is one of the few occasions when Zanjani adopts a fictional form, allowing her to speculate about the story behind the story of gold rushers.*

Making History

Inside the black tape recorder, tiny wheels turned busily. Satisfied that the tape was still running, the interviewer leaned toward Henry once more, fixed her intent gray-green eyes on his face, and asked, "Why did you go?"

Henry shifted uncomfortably on the plaid couch. The boy he was more than seventy years ago would have squirmed and ducked his head. The young man who had left for Goldfield in 1906 might have averted his eyes and turned sullen. The eighty-two-year-old that Henry had become in 1969, his blue eyes faded, his hair a white shock falling over the brow of a leonine head, his once powerful body a big shell, gave little sign that the question had struck home, except that his gnarled fingers gripped the cane more tightly.

"Went to make my fortune," he said. "Same as everybody else." That was the usual answer, the one that nobody questioned.

The interviewer sensed that there was more to be said. She was good that way. A little too good. "It must have been a big change for a nineteen-year-old boy who'd been clerking in a dry goods store in Iowa to go dashing off to Goldfield," she said helpfully, trying to bring him along with her.

"It was," said Henry, clamping his wide mouth shut. He did not want to be brought. In fact, just now he was sorry he had agreed to be interviewed. She'd started asking questions he didn't want to answer.

"What did your parents say when you told them you were joining a gold rush?" she asked, coming toward him from another angle.

Henry coughed and looked away from the intent gray-green eyes. There was something hypnotic about those eyes. They could draw the words right out of you if you weren't careful. You'd find yourself saying things you never meant to say. And there they would stay, in the little machine with the turning wheels, where you couldn't get them back.

"Said I was a young fool. They were right." There was more, of course. The sign ALTMAN & SON, DRY GOODS & SUNDRIES painted only a year earlier and hung proudly over the store. His father's anger and hurt, his mother's sobs, almost as though she had known, in spite of all his promises, that she would never see his face again.

"Did you ever go back to Iowa?"

"No, I never did. My parents came down with pneumonia that winter—the winter of 1906—while I was in Goldfield. By the time I heard they were sick, they were dead and buried. My uncle took over the dry goods business. There wasn't much to go back for after my folks were gone."

The guilt still wrenched him after more than sixty years. Not taking the time to stand for an hour or two in the mail line at the post office. Not even hiring a boy to do it for him because he'd been spending all his money at Jake's. Allowing the letter that told him of his parents' illness to wait there uncollected for weeks. Not being with them when they needed him.

She seemed to sense his pain and decently turned away. Henry liked her for that. Sometimes he had a feeling that she'd been working him over pretty smart, asking the ordinary questions she knew would start an old gaffer talking and then sliding in with the ones that cut to the bone. All the same, she'd taken the trouble to read up on Goldfield in the old newspapers, which was more than you could say for most of the young folks with tape recorders and notepads who came down to Tonopah to poke and prod at the last of the old gold rushers left alive. Nowadays that came down to Henry and his friend Chester, who lived next door in the tumble-down shack beside Henry's neat cabin.

"By the way, you said you went to make a fortune. Did you make one?"

"Guess not. Wouldn't be here if I did." Henry smiled grimly. It was a damn silly question, in his opinion. If he'd made a fortune, he wouldn't be sitting in a tiny cabin on a hillside in Tonopah. He'd be taking his ease in a mansion by the sea in Long Beach or San Francisco, where the nabobs went after they'd made a killing in the mines. Maybe she knew that and just kept circling back, by different ways, to the thing he didn't want to talk about. Couldn't talk about. It would have felt like taking his clothes off on Main Street.

"Did many people make fortunes in those gold rushes?"

"Very few. And even those who made money—well, mostly it went back into the ground."

She liked this phrase. "Went back into the ground," she repeated, cocking her head, with the straight brown hair clipped almost as short as a boy. "Now what does that mean?"

"Means you couldn't stay satisfied. Kept thinking you'd strike it rich again. Sank all the money you made into worthless mines."

She nodded. "Before I leave, I'd like to ask you a few follow-up questions about Goldfield in the boom days around 1906. You mentioned a dance hall called Jake's. What was it like in there?"

Henry relaxed. Now she was moving into safer territory.

"Jake's was noisy," he said. "People drinking and talking and laughing. Little band sawing away. And crowded. They had a fine maple wood floor down at Jake's, but we were squeezed in so tight we couldn't hardly get around. Of course, there were the girls, lots of pretty girls. That's what we came for."

He smiled at her and knew he didn't have the words to make her understand the way it was, the eerie desert stillness of the Malapai outside, with the ghostly shapes of joshua trees in the dim starlight, and the glowing warmth, the gay music, and the laughing voices that tugged you into Jake's. Tugged like a magnet to the iron nail that was you. You might have thought you'd be going somewhere else after coming in from the mines, having a wash, and starting out from your tent cabin of an evening, but you always ended up at Jake's. He remembered it still, the burn of whiskey in his throat, the stubbled faces of the miners and prospectors around him, the sweet curved body of a girl nestling in his arms for a dance. Gus in a green silk dress.

"About how often would you go to Jake's?"

"Pretty often." Actually, it was damn near every night.

"What kind of names did the girls have? I'm assuming they didn't use their real names."

Henry nodded. "None of them used their real names. Men's names were the fashion in those days—and boxers. Names like Jimmie Britt and Bat Nelson and

Gus and Ray and Fighting Bill. Others too, Klondike Kitty and Maizie and Swivel Hips Sue."

He watched carefully to see if she would react to Gus's name. He had noticed during their interviews over the last three days that when she was hot on the trail of something she'd lean a fraction closer toward him, as though listening with her whole body, not just her ears, and the large gray-green eyes would widen and then narrow just a little. But she showed none of these signs. Maybe she wasn't on to Gus.

"How long did a dance last?" the interviewer continued.

"Not near long enough if you had one of the dance hall queens in your arms," said Henry, still remembering Gus. Some of the girls had their glasses filled with colored water when you bought them drinks, but not Gus. She could drink you under the table with the real stuff, dance all night, and then, if you were lucky, lead you by the hand to her cabin out back and love you till noon. "Jake kept the dances pretty short to make more money," he added.

"How much did those dance hall queens make? I've heard they made as much as five hundred dollars a night."

"I believe that's an exaggeration. But they did pretty well."

How well would *you* have done back in Jake's, thought Henry to himself, letting his eyes skate skeptically over the interviewer. First you'd have to grow you some hair, enough so it takes a good ten minutes to take all the hairpins out and a man can bury his face in it like a hog in a wallow, hair like Gus's long dark brown mane. And you'd have to put some meat on, so you'd be more than an armful of bones. You'd have to move altogether different. He thought of the smooth kind of wiggle, like a fish twitching its tail in a stream, that was Gus moving toward him across the crowded dance floor and the way her body seemed to flow around a man.

"How did the girls dress?"

"Bright colors. Pretty skimpy. They didn't wear overly much."

That's another thing you'd have to change, he thought, eyeing the woman's jeans with disapproval. You'd have had to dress like a female, in something like the green silk outfit that had clung to Gus's waist and switched from her hips. Henry hadn't minded when he woke up in the twenties to find a lot of female knees staring him in the face, as Will Rogers put it, and again in the sixties. Skirts could go up or down for all he cared, and best of all over a woman's head, but pants did nothing for the female form.

"Did any romances develop?"

"Might have. Can't rightly say." Henry knew himself for a barefaced liar.

"I've wondered if some of these girls might have had an appeal that a respectable woman, say a school teacher, didn't have?"

"They were pretty, some of them," said Henry, dodging the question.

"Do you know what happened to the girls after Goldfield went into decline and Jake's closed down?"

She was leaning forward now, eyes a little narrowed.

"I really can't say," said Henry, on guard.

"I've been told that some of the dance hall queens, as you call them, made good marriages and moved away and turned into pillars of society. Can you tell me any more about that?"

"I don't believe I can," said Henry, looking vague.

Somebody must have told her something. Maybe that fool Chester, who didn't know when to stop talking. But not Gus's married name, not where she lived, if she was still living, and Henry didn't want to imagine Gus any other way. He'd learned to live with how Goldfield was now, since the big fire of '23 left the better part of it a blackened smoking ruin, but he liked to picture Gus as the toast of high society, as once she'd been the toast of Jake's. Necessarily an older Gus, with a few streaks of gray in the dark brown mass of her hair, but still very much the same. He'd seen her photograph a few times in the society pages of a big-city newspaper, and that was how he wanted to think of her, laden with jewels at a charity ball, skimming over sunny seas in a yacht, sashaying down the aisle at the opera with just a touch of the old fish tail wiggle. When she married the tycoon who carried her off on the same kind of sudden whim that made her throw everything she had on the roulette wheel when she felt lucky or spur her horse to a thundering gallop when she fancied a ride at dawn, Henry had wished her well. He knew she'd favored him, but Gus was never just his girl. Only the best he ever had.

"I could turn off the tape recorder if there's anything you'd like to tell me in confidence, Mr. Altman," coaxed the interviewer.

"Think I've told you just about everything I know." Just about. Never Gus. And not the other, which was kind of mixed up with Gus, in a way.

"I guess I haven't asked you if you found what you were looking for in Goldfield?"

She had asked him, several different ways, and they both knew it. He wondered briefly if she had figured out the answer and only wanted him to say she was right. The intent eyes had softened. Henry sensed that she would press him no further.

"Told you I never made much," he muttered, sticking to his story.

"I guess that about wraps it up then," she said. She snapped off the tape recorder and put it carefully in her carrying bag. Noticing that Henry was working to gather his strength, she added, "Please don't bother to get up."

She stepped quickly over to him, gripped his hand, and said shyly, in a sudden rush, "Thank you so much for talking with me, Mr. Altman. You know, you guys were making history down there in Goldfield, and you've helped me understand how it was. I'll let you know when the book comes out."

Henry shook her hand, feeling subtly rebuked. Making history. That was why he talked to these people who came down from the University up north in Reno. When he read some of the fool nonsense they were writing these days about the great rush to Goldfield, it made him so mad he'd cracked his cane on the doorpost. So when these writers came around wanting to see him, he tried to set them right about how the union got busted and how Goldfield was in the wild days before the mine owners turned it into a company town.

But if he was trying to set them right, why had he pointed her wrong with that easy answer about making his fortune? She hadn't believed it either. He wondered if he should have tried to explain. Looking out the window, he watched her dark green car making its way slowly down the hill toward Main Street and wondered if he should ask her to come back. Maybe phone her at the motel. She would doubtless be gone, though, speeding along the highway north to Reno. That was the trouble with these writers. They never stayed long enough to find out what it was really like in Tonopah, or thirty miles down the highway in Goldfield. And if you lived here long enough to learn how the mirages shimmered across the white sands of the Clayton Playa, how the wind blew when a storm was coming in, or how the hills turned into melting strawberry ice cream in the late afternoon light, then you probably didn't know how to write books.

With more effort than it had once taken him to demolish a hard rock ledge in the mines with his drill, Henry hoisted himself to his feet, leaning heavily on his cane. Every movement seemed like such an effort today that Henry was inclined to think he might not be around to see this latest book come out. Sometimes these writers took years to squeeze out a skimpy little book you could read in less time than it took to play a decent game of poker. Other times no book showed up at all. Maybe somebody ought to interview them and make them explain why this writing business took so long. Slowly, with faltering steps, he made his way to the door. It was almost three o'clock, the time of day when he always sat outside for a while with Chester, and Henry did not like to have his routine interrupted.

After he had negotiated the door, Henry saw Chester already waiting for him in an old kitchen chair on the porch in front of the cabin next door. The well-nailed tightly set boards and trim railing of Henry's porch, kept in good repair by the young man down the street, were decidedly better than the cracked uneven boards with widening gaps, set just a foot or so above the ground, that Chester called a porch, but Chester liked to sit on his own porch because two years ago he had seen a rattler slither under the boards. Ever since, he had been waiting to decapitate it with his shovel. Lean and wizened, his thin chest caved in like an old barrel, his bald head mottled, and his shapeless nose reddened by years of hard drinking, Chester sat out on the porch, coughing, smoking the cigarettes long forbidden to him by the doctor, stubbing them out in an empty can, and tapping on the boards now and then with the shovel he kept by his side. "I can hear him. He's still rustling around under there," he would say to Henry, and Henry humored him. Waiting for the snake lent a certain excitement to their afternoons.

Henry lowered himself with difficulty into the sagging seat of the dilapidated rocking chair beside Chester and sat looking silently over the rooftops and the abandoned mines of Tonopah below them. New places had gone up here and there, but some of the old buildings like the Mizpah Hotel still stood on Main Street. To Henry's way of thinking, that meant that Tonopah had grown old in the right way, like a person losing his hair and wrinkling up but still recognizably himself. Not like Reno and Las Vegas, so changed now that a man could walk down the street and feel he'd never been there before.

Henry turned his glance to Chester, seeing in the mottled ancient beside him a shade of the wild and wiry youngster, dark hair pasted to his skull like shoe polish and cigarette pasted to his lip, who used to pour drinks at Jake's over sixty years ago. "She been to see you?" he inquired.

"Came and went this morning," said Chester. "Told her all about me and Wyatt Earp. I even drew her a picture. Said I was standing here"—he tapped with the shovel—"and old Wyatt was over there, cool as you please, and them claim jumpers busted into the mine right there with guns a-blazin'. You got to draw 'em a picture, Henry. It gets 'em every time."

"She was just too polite to tell you what an old liar you are," said Henry. "She probably knows Wyatt Earp was long gone for California before you ever got here."

Chester chuckled. "I'm tellin' you, Henry, I had her goin'. And the fella with the big concha belt and the little bitty mustache that come by last year—he swallered it whole. All you got to do is draw 'em a picture. Now here's ole Wyatt . . ." His chuckles hoarsened into a prolonged fit of coughing.

"Did she ask about Gus?" asked Henry when the coughs had subsided.

"She asked about them dance hall queens. Told her some of 'em married nabobs and moved away and turned into society queens. A course I didn't point to no places, and I didn't name no names." He looked at Henry with a teasing twinkle in his bleary eyes.

"You sure you didn't let that mouth of yours run away with you?" demanded Henry, eyeing him severely.

"I wouldn't tell on your girlfriend, Henry. Don't I know you'd split my head wide open with that cane of yours if I did?"

Henry leaned back in the rocking chair, feeling easier in his mind. Gus was safe from the black tape recorders and the prying eyes of history. None of the old crowd who used to watch her shimmy across the floor at Jake's was left to tell but him and Chester. She'd go to her grave a fine lady, with no one any the wiser.

He watched the shadows move down the slope over Tonopah, washing over the pale hillocks of tailings across the highway. Down below a rancher's pickup rattled nosily up the street, loaded with supplies. That was part of what had drawn Henry back to Tonopah, after he'd finally "played his string out," as the old Comstockers used to say in Goldfield. If Tonopah wasn't clotted with burros and prospectors and freight wagons the way he'd first seen it, at least it was still a real place, not fancied up for tourists like Virginia City. No strangers with maps and cameras cluttering up the sidewalks and pointing at things. Most everybody you met on Main Street had business there, which was the way Henry liked it to be. Tonopah was still a working town, done with silver mining maybe, but a supply center for ranches and mines in the country all around and a main stop on the highway south from Reno. The kind of place where Henry could keep his bearings, without feeling as if he was turning into the display in a lighted glass case in a museum.

"She ask why you went to Goldfield?" he said to Chester after a while. It was a question he had never put to Chester in all these years. To Henry's way of thinking, your reasons—your real reasons—were as much a part of you as your arm. Maybe that was why he didn't like this writer probing at him any better than he liked the doctor pressing and testing the hurtful places in his naked flesh. And why he never thought about his reasons any more than he thought about his other parts until something started aching. Like now.

"She asked why we come right enough," said Chester. "Told her Pap said we was goin', so we just up'n went."

"Did your dad figure on striking it rich there?"

"Don't know if he thought so big as all that. Don't b'lieve he hardly gave no thought to it at all. It come on him more like an itch. Everybody in Cripple Creek was goin' to Goldfield, and so was we. We was like geese flyin' south, or grasshoppers, or them ratty little creeturs that runs into the sea all in a bunch. We was just goin'. When folks was movin', Pap couldn't stay put."

A sudden thought struck him. "I should've thought quicker," he said, chuckling. "When she asked why we come, I should've said it was Wyatt. Now Wyatt wrote me this letter, see. He says, 'Chester, I'm in a tight spot, and I need your help real bad . . .'"

Henry wasn't listening. He was thinking about going to the gold rushes to make your fortune. That had made sense to people, when he told them the stories he'd read about the nabobs who made millions in the mining booms. John Mackay, who was nothing but a poor Irish miner when he started and came out of the Comstock with money to burn. Or Al Myers, so poor he had to hock his trunk before Goldfield turned him into a millionaire.

Mining booms were risky, of course. He'd admitted that, sitting at the kitchen table back in Iowa with the newspaper stories about Goldfield spread out in front of him. His father had listened, hurt darkening his eyes, while his mother sat with her handkerchief to her face. But when he explained how with no capital and a lot of hard work you stood a good chance of making a fortune in a gold rush, it sounded like a dollars-and-cents decision. A way to make money that they could understand if not approve. Almost logical.

What he couldn't tell his father, or the interviewer, or anyone else, was the yearning that had curled in the heart of a young man and left him wide-awake at night, staring at the forked shadows cast on his bedroom window by the old elm tree and thinking of the world out beyond the elm tree that he would never see. Not unless he cut himself loose from Altman & Son and all that was safe and familiar in the little town where he had grown up. He had spoken to his father of mining millionaires and dollars and cents because he couldn't talk about the truth, the secret wishes and the pictures in his head that couldn't come out in words. Pacing in his room at night, he had imagined himself riding through vast deserts and pitching his tent on the empty plain like the first explorers. The sun glittered on the icy peaks of the far Sierra. Hawks wheeled overhead. Herds of mustangs, sorrel, black, and white galloped through the canyons of purple mountain ranges. The spicy smell of sagebrush filled the air. The moon rose over silver sands by night as coyotes howled eerily in the distance, and mirages of impossible castles and gardens trembled over the horizon by day.

He would pause in his pacing to read the newspaper clippings he already knew by heart and look at the books about the West that stood stacked in the same spot on this bedside table where his mother had kept the Bible. The dream grew stronger by the day. He saw himself with his pants tucked into his boot tops in the miner's way striding into the saloons of an evening. He would listen to the stories the grizzled prospectors told, drink raw whiskey that smoldered like live coals in his belly, and throw his dice at a green table with adventurers from all the four corners of the world. He wouldn't care if he won or lost, and neither would anyone else. No trickle of whispers running through the neighborhood about what he did and what time he came home. No watchful eyes peeping out from behind the curtains. No more evenings spent in a parlor on a stiff little chair not half his size trying to make small talk and wondering if later on he might have the chance to hold a woman's hand.

The women in that saloon flickered through his daydreams, a bevy of beauties dressed in brilliant colors. They'd never worry about what was nice and proper or what folks might say, not if they had the grit to follow a gold rush. These would be the wild and wanton ones he could never meet at a church social in Iowa. He saw their gleaming naked shoulders. They had a way of moving to make a man stare and met the stares with bold eyes. Women whose touch could make a man's blood sing.

Gus, long before he knew her name.

FIVE

THE OTHER NEVADA

Reflections on Rural Life

In 1974 Robert Laxalt published an article in *National Geographic* entitled "The Other Nevada," illustrated with photographs of cowboys branding cattle, a female buckaroo smiling over a hearty lunch, a herd of galloping mustangs, and a small saloon in Austin. As Laxalt described it, the "other" Nevada "is a Nevada of small communities, livestock towns like Elko and Yerington, isolated ranches and Indian reservations, and ghost towns surrounded by an overpowering vastness of land." There, in the hinterland beyond the neon sprawl of Las Vegas and Reno, lies "the old heart of Nevada," a land whose people embody a spirit of independence to match the "great sweeps of pungent sagebrush desert," where "the silence is broken only by the moan of the desert wind." "It's not an easy life but I like it," one backcountry woman told Laxalt, a comment likely to draw nods on down the line of Nevada's ranches, farms, and small towns.

Native peoples, as we've seen, have been at home in this land for millennia. The first non-Indian settlers arrived in the 1850s, some of them establishing trading posts along the emigrant trails. Farmers and ranchers found a ready market for their products in the mining camps. Mormons established footholds throughout present-day Nevada, including Carson Valley in 1851 and towns in eastern and southern Nevada, places like Panaca, Callville, Bunkerville, St. Thomas, St. Joseph, Moapa, West Point, Overton, and Mesquite. Staunch Mormon communities in the valleys contrasted sharply with the rowdy, mostly male mining camps in the mountains, creating a moral topography, where family values settled to the lower elevations.

Then as now water was the limiting resource. Early settlers selected homesites where water was accessible—in Reese River Valley, Paradise Valley, Pleasant Valley, Clover Valley, Spring Valley, and others. Despite the pleasing, verdant images these names evoke, homesteading was no picnic. Memoirs of the early settlers are a record of hard work. Pioneers cleared brush, planted a garden, hauled water, dug ditches and wells, chopped wood, strung fences, built a house and barn, hunted, trapped, cared for their animals, put up food, delivered babies, educated children, nursed the sick, and buried the dead. One wonders if we could do the same today. Plunk yourself down in a remote corner of Nevada, with no electricity, no cars, no grocery stores, no computers, no telephones, and no TV. Would you survive?

Most prose about rural Nevada is nonfiction, written by relative newcomers for future generations and/or urban readers. The pieces in this chapter—by nineteenth-century settlers and modern-day transplants—explain in detail the work and rewards of living on the land. Whereas stories from the mining frontier fixate on money, here you'll find an emphasis on food, noting how it was procured, preserved, and prepared, activities synchronized to nature's seasonal rhythms. Living in the country means living with animals, and these pages are populated with them. Perhaps because human neighbors are few and far between, community events—such as Fourth of July celebrations, steak fries, town meetings, roundups, and rabbit drives—feature prominently in these narratives.

Life in Nevada's heartland has never been easy. If early arrivals struggled to get a start, today's residents struggle to stay. Population density in rural Nevada is a mere 1.4 persons per square mile, officially classifiable as a frontier. Today ranching and farming use 77 percent of Nevada's annual water budget but contribute only 1 percent to its economy and employ only 1.5 percent of its workers. Nearly 90 percent of the state's population lives in the urban areas of Clark and Washoe counties and Carson City, making Nevada the most urban state in the nation. The 2002 Nevada Natural Resource Status Report frankly states, "Increasingly, rural area resources will be sought to meet urban area needs for water supply, waste disposal sites, and industries with large pollutant discharges, and outdoor recreation." Not to mention military air space. The pieces in this chapter preserve Nevada's agricultural heritage and argue for the continuing value of this endangered way of life.

HOWARD R. EGAN [1840–1916]

One of the most fascinating accounts of pioneer life in the Great Basin is a rare, out-of-print book entitled Pioneering the West, 1846 to 1878, Major Howard Egan's Diary, also Thrilling Experiences of Pre-Frontier Life among Indians; Their Traits, Civil and Savage, and Part of Autobiography, Inter-Related to His Father's, *by Howard R. Egan. This 302-page book was laboriously "Edited, Compiled, and Connected in Nearly Chronological Order" by Wm. M. Egan and privately printed by the Howard R. Egan Estate, Richmond, Utah, in 1917. The thin, glossy pages of this small volume contain print as tiny as you might find on a medicine bottle, interspersed with vintage photographs of wagon trains, Indians, and members of the Egan family, and facsimiles of diary entries and letters. In the appendix a genealogy of the Egans extends back to Adam and Eve. This family book combines the diary of Major Howard Egan with reminiscences by his son Howard Ransom Egan. Major Egan led one of the original bands of Mormon pioneers from Nauvoo, Illinois, to Salt Lake City. He also scouted a route from Salt Lake City to California for the Overland Mail—today's Lincoln Highway—and, in a record ride, rode muleback in 1855 from Salt Lake City to Sacramento in only ten days. Son Howard R. Egan, from whom the following reminiscences are taken, was a Pony Express rider, Overland Mail driver, and stage stop manager, based out of Deep Creek (today's Ibapah), near the Nevada-Utah border. He established the first farm in Ruby Valley and befriended local Indians, learning their language, customs, and survival techniques. His vivid sketches describe food gathering and preparation for a wide range of culinary dishes, including ants, crickets, rabbits, rats, antelope, pine nuts, and moles, as well as sharing riveting tales of pioneer life, Indian medicine, and death-defying Pony Express exploits. Perhaps someday this wonderful book will be reprinted.*

Mountain Rat, Food for Indians

On one of my days out I came across an old Indian going home with his day's catch of rats. He had a large sheet iron camp kettle nearly filled with them. They had all been caught the night before by dead falls, as we call them, which consists of two sticks about three and a half or four inches long fastened together at their centers by a string that will allow them to spread apart about four or five inches in the shape of the letter "H." One of these, with any convenient flat rock heavy enough to smash and kill a rat, is one dead fall. This Indian had over a hundred of the triggers that he hadn't used, but said he had set the most of them.

His plan was to go up one side of the canyon, setting the traps wherever he saw the sign of rats, and the same down the other side. The next day, taking the same route, gathering the catch and resetting the traps. The rats the Indian had were six to eight inches long, two and a half inches wide and half an inch thick. They were packed as close as he could pack them in the kettle and were quite heavy for the old man to pack to camp, so I carried them for him. At his camp was where I first saw the squaws making rabbit skin robes. This is how it was done:

They had a lot of twine, that had been made of some fiberous bark or grass, and a pile of rabbit skins that had been dried and then rubbed pliable. But it must have been done with care, for a rabbit skin is very tender. These squaws were not making a new robe, but patching up and making an old one larger. The robes are of length to reach from the neck to about the middle of the thighs, say about three or four feet long, and wide enough to reach around the body at the shoulders.

One of the squaws was twisting the strips of skin around a twine that was stretched to two stakes, placed a little past the length of the robe, and as she proceeded the other was following her up and tying that fur rope thus made and laid alongside the previous one close together at about every four inches. They worked back and forth in this fashion till the skins were all used up. There was a strip about two feet wide of new robe attached to the old one. I examined it and found that the tie strings were placed in a straight line across the robe, with the ends of the ties left to attach more robe or to be used to tie the robe together as wanted.

When hung around the neck the person so clothed can stand in a hard rain or snow storm and not one drop of wet will pass through the robe. They are wind and rain proof and almost cold proof. There is no right or wrong side, as both sides are just the same—one solid piece of fur that will stand the wear of years, used as a mattress or bed covering or wind brake. In fact, they never completely wear out.

When the fur at any place gets worn off it is replaced with a few strands of new. This makes an old robe look striped and of different colors. The squaws while at work seemed as happy as a party of white women at a quilting and were talking and laughing just as fast. After spending some time chatting and smoking with the old man, he gave me the location of another family. I gave him a little tobacco and left them much pleased with my visit.

Pine-Nut Harvest

Jack and I were taking a scouting trip high up in the Shell Creek range of mountains, when we came across an Indian who, with his squaw and children, were busily engaged gathering pine-nuts. The man had a long pole with a strong hook fastened to one end. He would reach up in the tree to the pine cones, hook the crook around the branch on which they hung and pull branch and all down, the squaw and children carrying them to a place and piling them up in a heap. When they had collected as many as they wanted that day, the buck had finished his part of the work and could pass the rest of the time sleeping or hunting squirrels just as he pleased.

The squaws and children gathered a little dry brush, which was thrown loosely over the pile of cones and set fire to. The cones are thickly covered all over with pitch, for this reason they make a hot fire, the squaw watching and stirring it up as needed to keep the nuts from burning, as all she wants is to burn the pitch off. When this is done she rakes them back from the fire as a man would do when drawing charcoal.

When the pitch was all burned off the burs, or cones, the squaw spreads a blanket down close to the pile, then taking up one cone at a time, would press them end ways between her hands, which opens the leaves, under which there were two nuts to every leaf. Then shaking the cone over the blanket the nuts would all fall out as clean as you please.

We stayed with them to see the finish, which was not so very long. When the nuts had all been cleaned from the cones they were put in a large basket that would hold over two bushels and was nearly full, the squaw carrying that on her back to a place where they were to be cached and left till wanted. These caches were placed all through the pine-nut grove to save carrying them too far and save time, for the harvest does not last long, for a heavy frost will cause the cones to open and the nuts drop to the ground, where the squirrels and coyotes feast on them.

A pine-nut cone looks like a green pineapple, but some smaller and covered with pitch, that protects them from insects and squirrels. The Indians put them in caches holding about ten bushels or less.

Once on a time when Jack and I were passing along a range where there were a good many pine-nut trees, and as we were getting hungry I asked him if he thought there was any nuts cached there. He said he didn't think they were all cleaned out and would look around. He was not long in locating one, and pushing the large stick of wood aside that was placed on top of the small raise in which the nuts were to be found, he moved off about six inches of dirt and found a tight layer of cedar bark about two inches thick. He dug a hole through this big enough to pass his arm through, which he did, and pulled out a handful of very fine nuts, as fresh as when first put in.

Well, we took about two gallons, covered and left the cache as we found it, minus the few nuts taken.

Hunting for Water

In traveling through Go-Shute Valley (later called Flower Lake Valley), we were getting very thirsty, having been traveling five or six hours from the last water hole and it being a dry hot and sultry day I and the horses needed water. The nearest I knew of was about twelve miles distance and that not in the direction of our travel, and our one canteen being empty, I thought we would have to change our course to get water. I asked Jack, "How far to water this way," pointing the way I wanted to go. He said, "I do not know, maybe no water." "Well, are you thirsty?" "Yes." "Well then, think fast and locate water or Indian no better than white man."

We were about the middle of the valley, facing southeasterly, and were among the sand-dunes, which spread a few miles in width and many miles in length through the valley. We had not gone far after this talk when Jack said, "Wait," and pointing to some rat or gopher holes in the side of the sand-dunes, said, "They must have water, I see." Dismounting, he picked a place between the dunes and with his hands scraped off the loose sand to a depth of about six or eight inches to water. He then made the hole nearly a foot deeper and a foot wide, which quickly filled to the water level. Waiting for it to settle, we then tasted it and found it to be a little brackish, but still nice and cool and quite drinkable. Having drank what we wanted, filling the canteen, we let the horses have their turn. They got some, but soon caved the sand in and made the water so riley they would drink no more.

Jack filled the hole up and leveled the sand over it as it was before and said if he did not do it there could not be any more water ever found anywhere near there (Superstition), and I think he actually believed what he said.

Towards evening we were traveling along the foothills, going in the direction of where we knew there was a water hole five or six miles distance. Where we were the limestone formation lay very flat and in some places was washed clean of all soil for large areas and but few cracks or breaks all along the lower edge of these limestone beds.

I noticed that the grass and brush was thicker and stronger than farther down. I asked Jack if he thought we could get water near the edge by digging. "No," he said, "too deep; but wait, see the coyote tracks. They get water somewhere close to here." So hunting around a while I got off my horse and sat on a little raise watching Jack. He zig-zagged around till he had worked off about one hundred yards from me. I went to where he was standing and said, "Did you find water?" he said, smiling; "Come and see," leading the way to the bottom of a large saucer shaped swag, and what I saw was an oblong hole about four feet across the narrowest way and about twelve feet deep. There was eight or nine feet of water in it and so clear that we could see the bottom and sides very plainly and all the walls were solid limestone.

The water was cold and not a bit brackish, so I proposed to camp there that night. Jack said, "Yes," for he was very tired; but said, "We must go a little way off so the wild animals can come and drink." How were we to water the horses here? They could not reach it and if one fell in, it would be good-by, as we could never get him out, except in pieces. Well, we watered the horses and gave them all they wanted by using my hat for a bucket.

. . . .

The next day we, having crossed the summit of the desert range of mountains, about noon, as we were riding along the base of the mountain or about half a mile above the white alkali desert (the most desolate and dreary country I ever saw) seeing a poor, pretty near hairless coyote, I asked Jack what he was doing so far from water. "Maybe not far," he said. "We will try and find his drinking hole." So in riding along he pointed up the mountain a little way and farther along our way to where the limestone ledges dipped at a very steep angle into the mountains, he said, "We will go along that way."

We came to a place where a thick ledge about thirty feet high hung over a thinner one that was about eight or ten feet high and from two to six feet from the higher one, that hung completely over it. Jack went to one end of the ledge, or to where he could get on top of the smaller ledge, gave a whoop and said, "Plenty of water." I was soon at his side and saw a pool of clear water (no scum or dirt) that extended from ledge to ledge and some thirty feet long. At the ends the bottom sloped toward the center, at which place there was no way to judge the depth, as the bottom could be seen only a few feet from the ends, but there was thousands of gallons of water held there, as good, too, as any you ever tasted. But let me tell you, a person might ride or walk within six feet of it and still think it was miles, and hot ones, to the nearest water. A tenderfoot would die of thirst leaning his back against the four-foot wall that separated him from enough water to supply an army. One could not see the least sign of water, every spot all around being sunburned and browned.

MARY ANN HAFEN [1854–1946]

Born in Switzerland, Mary Ann Hafen immigrated to America at the age of six, when her parents, who had converted to Mormonism, decided to settle in Zion. In 1860 the family became members of the "handcart pioneers," early Mormons who walked west across America to the promised land of Utah, carrying their belongings in wooden carts pulled by hand. In southern Utah, Hafen grew up in a culture that encouraged plural marriages and large families to "build up Zion," and at age nineteen she became her uncle's second wife. He was killed in a runaway-team accident only a week after their marriage, and Mary, following her parents' wishes, then married John Hafen, becoming the second of his four wives. In 1891, partly to evade federal raids against polygamists, John Hafen moved Mary and their growing family away from her home in Santa Clara, Utah, transplanting them to Bunkerville, Nevada, a small Mormon settlement on the Virgin River, where Mary was left to raise and support seven children pretty much on her own. Hafen and her children pitched together to grow fruit and vegetables and maintain a cow, a couple of pigs, and chickens, coping with blistering hot summers, devastating flash floods, and deadly illnesses. In 1938, when she was eighty-four, Hafen's memoirs were privately printed for her descendants as Recollections of a Handcart Pioneer of 1860; with Some Account of Frontier Life in Utah and Nevada. *The book was republished by the University of Nebraska Press in 1983, with a new paperback edition in 2004. Hafen's youngest child, LeRoy, earned his* PHD *from the University of California, Berkeley, and became an eminent historian of the American West, with books on the Spanish Trail, the forty-niners, fur trappers, and other frontier topics. His autobiography,* The Joyous Journey *(1973), recalls growing up in Bunkerville.*

A New Home in Nevada

Because Santa Clara had so little land for so many settlers, we decided it would be best for me to take my young family and move to Bunkerville, where a settlement had been started and where there was more and cheaper land. My son Albert was already down there helping John's other wife, Anna.

. . . .

On May 6, 1891, with me and our five children tucked into a covered wagon, John clucked at the horses and drove away from our old home town. Another wagon, driven by young Johnnie, conveyed our household effects. As neighbors, relatives, and friends crowded about to see us off, I with others shed a few tears. I knew I was going to something of the same hardships I had known in childhood days; that my children were to grow up in a strange land with scarcely a relative near; and that they too would have to share in the hardships of subduing a new country.

Our drive was not unpleasant, however. The country was all new to me as I had never been beyond Santa Clara westward. Past Conger Farm, up Conger Hill, and on to Camp Springs Flat we traveled and there camped for the night. The next day we drove past the Cliffs, and down the long Slope where great Joshua trees looked like soldiers with their helmets and spears. The second night we spent at the Beaver Dams on a clear little creek where gnawed young cottonwoods gave evidence of beaver being present. The next day we passed the beginnings of Littlefield. Then we followed the Virgin River bed, crossed Mesquite flat, where a few farms and shanties showed settlement, again crossed the river, and arrived at Bunkerville.

The little town was rather inviting. In the early dusk the numerous young cottonwoods along the field canals and along the town ditches looked like an oasis in a desert. There was only one fence in the whole town and that was around Samuel Wittwer's lot.

Albert was overjoyed to see us. John's other wife, Anna, had supper waiting for us when we arrived. Among other things she served alfalfa greens dressed with white sauce. It was quite a tasty dish.

The next morning we went up to the little place that John had purchased from a Danishman, Brother Jorgensen. It was a two-roomed adobe house with dirt floors and dirt roof. That did not look so inviting, but John promised that he would see that it was soon finished off with a good roof and floors, and probably would put a second story on the house to make more bedrooms.

The big lot already had five or six almond trees growing, and a nice vineyard of grapes. But there was a little wash running through the side of the lot which had to be filled in; and there was only a makeshift fence of mesquite brush piled about three feet high. Besides, the lot was covered with rocks, because it was close to the gravel hill. Our twenty-five-acre farm, about a mile and a half above town, was only partly cleared of arrow weeds and mesquite. It was sandy land with some large sand knolls to be leveled.

The cow we had brought down was dry so John turned her in as part payment on the land. Later another was brought down from Santa Clara. Because of his duties as Bishop in Santa Clara my husband had to hurry back and left Albert, our sixteen-year-old son, in charge of the planting.

As soon as we could we planted corn, cane, cotton, squashes and melons in the field; and vegetables in the town lot. The brush fences were but poor protection from the stray animals that went foraging about. However we got a pretty good crop from everything planted that year. Albert dug up three young mulberry trees from Mesquite and planted them around our shadeless house. Now, after forty-seven years of growth, those mulberry trees completely shade the old place.

I remember how in those earliest years we were disturbed by the hot winds that swept over the dry bench lands from the south.

That first fall John came back bringing a load of lumber to finish off the house. During the winter he and Albert put in the floors and ceiling; built up the adobe walls to make a second story; and put on a shingle roof. There was no stairway up so the children used a ladder out of doors.

. . . .

About every year I managed to make the trip up to see my relatives. And for a while John came down every month or so to help Albert and to make small improvements around the place. But being Bishop at Santa Clara, and with his other three families, he could not be with us much. So I had to care for my seven children mostly by myself. He had provided us a house, lot, and land and he furnished some supplies. But it was a new country and we had a hard time to make a go of it.

Though we almost always had grain on hand, we sometimes found ourselves without flour. At such times we had to grind the wheat in a coffee mill until we could take a grist to the mill at Washington, sixty-five miles away. We also ground corn in the coffee mill and made mush of it. With molasses and milk on the mush it made our breakfasts for years.

We hauled our loads of cotton to the cotton factory at Washington and received cloth in exchange. I think we got about twelve and one-half cents per pound for cotton in the seed, and paid fifty to sixty cents a yard for jeans—a cotton and woolen mixed cloth.

Sugar, or sorghum, cane we took to the town sorghum mill and got our year's supply of molasses. Sugar and honey were almost unknown in those times, so sorghum served as sweetening. Candy pulls around the shining molasses mill were favorite evening pastimes for the young people. Most every year we made a practice of putting up twenty-gallon barrels of preserves—peaches or green tomatoes. The peaches were washed, dumped whole and unpeeled into the big vats of sorghum. After cooking to a preserves they were put into barrels. Green tomatoes were generally gathered just before frost, soaked over night in salt water, and then cooked over the furnace fire with sorghum as sweetener.

After we had been in Bunkerville about two years, my last child was born—December 8, 1893. He was a fine husky boy, weighing 12 ½ pounds. Aunt Mary Bunker, wife of the Bishop, was the acting mid-wife of the town. She came the customary ten days to bathe the baby while I was in bed. We called him Reuben LeRoy. As soon as his father learned of the birth, he came down to Bunkerville. I have never had a doctor at the birth of any of my children, nor at any other time for that matter, and I have never paid more than five dollars for the services of a mid-wife.

. . . .

I did not want to be a burden on my husband, but tried with my family to be self-supporting. I picked cotton on shares to add to our income; would take my baby to the fields while the other children were at school, for I never took the children out of school if it could possibly be avoided. That cotton picking was very tiresome, back-breaking work but it helped to clothe my children.

I always kept a garden so we could have green things to eat. Keeping that free from weeds and watering it twice a week took lots of time. With a couple of pigs, a cow, and some chickens, we got along pretty well.

In the spring of the year, when the grass sprang up on the hills, almost everybody turned their cows out to graze for the day. Sometimes they failed to return at night, unless there was a young calf to call them back. Often I have walked almost to the mountains, to hunt for and bring back the straying cows. We had alfalfa, or lucern as we called it, in the lot and the children or I always cut it with a sickle or scythe throughout the summer to feed the cows. In the early spring, before the lucern was high enough to cut, we would go to the field and fill sacks with young sweet clover and bring it home to the cows. This clover or young lucern we would mix with straw so the cows would not bloat on it.

We made good use of the grapes on the lot. The thinskins we dried into raisins on the roof of the kitchen. I always made some batches of jam, usually out of the Californias. The Lady Downings and tough-skins we usually sent fresh with peddlers to the mining camps. Albert frequently took them to Delamar or Pioche.

The year after Mother died, my oldest girl married—September 3, 1895. She was only seventeen and I hated to see her go, but she got a good husband and has raised a fine family since.

In the spring of 1896 I took my three youngest children and went up to the March conference. Now that Mother was dead, I always stayed with my sister Rosie whenever I visited Santa Clara. When I walked in with my babies there lay Ella, Rosie's little girl, all blotched with red measles.

A week after I got back home with my family they all broke out with measles. One night when I was weary from caring for the sick children, I fell asleep on top of the bed. My boy Wilford, eight years old, crawled out of bed and took a big drink of cold water. The measles went in on him and do what we would we were unable to help him. Smothering spells came on and he jumped up fighting for breath. Shortly before he died he kept looking up to the corner of the ceiling and saying, "I'm coming." And then he left us. I felt somewhat reconciled to his going because of the dream I had had when he was a baby. I believed that his time had come; that God wanted him on the other side.

SARAH E. OLDS [1875–1963]

For most of her life, Sarah Olds was too engaged in living to write a book. However, in the late 1920s when her children were grown and out of the nest, she found an opportunity to reflect on the last twenty years and record her memories of homesteading in Nevada early in the century. Still later, when she was a widow and grandmother living in Reno, she polished these reminiscences. They were brought to the attention of the University of Nevada Press after her death and published in 1978 as Twenty Miles from a Match: Homesteading in Western Nevada. *This captivating memoir reveals Sarah's zestful personality, her determination, resourcefulness, optimism, and robust health, the very qualities of a successful pioneer. Born on an Iowa farm, the youngest daughter of nine children, Sarah dutifully studied dressmaking and nursed her elderly parents. When they died, Sarah, age twenty-one, much to the consternation of her relatives, joined an older sister in the West and supported herself as a seamstress. In the small mining camp of Stent, California, Sarah had just returned from a boisterous snowball fight when a gruff old man scolded, "Why in hell don't you get down in the back yard or some back alley if you're going to yell around here like a pack of Piutes?" Notwithstanding the hostility of their initial meeting, Sarah and Albert J. Olds married shortly thereafter, maintaining a bickering affection through six children and many moves, he calling her "Old lady," she referring to him as "A.J." or, later, "Daddy." The couple and their growing brood moved from mining camp to mining camp throughout the West until A.J. became too weakened by silicosis to continue mining. Having strength enough for both of them, Sarah in 1908 persuaded A.J. to homestead about twenty miles north of Reno. The adventures recounted below give a taste of the challenges of that life.*

from *Twenty Miles from a Match*

Our vegetable garden was our first need. Everything was painfully slow, for we had no plow, harrow, or scraper, and only one old horse. We had to work by hand with spade, shovel, mattock, pick, and hand rake.

Since A.J. was a miner, his greatest knowledge and contribution to the place was in developing water. He went to work digging and developing to bring three small springs together, which made a good spring of water to irrigate with. Then with pick, shovel, spade, and wheelbarrow he laboriously dug a small reservoir. The springs and reservoir were both on high ground, and underneath were acres of good virgin sagebrush land. While Daddy was employed developing water, the children and I cleared the sagebrush off a space of ground about one hundred feet square. Then Edson and I with mattock and spade turned over the ground for our new garden. It was slow work, but what a happy time we all had working together there in the sunshine. Even the baby was there, for the garden was a quarter of a mile from the cabin and none of the children could be left behind. When our garden was all planted we turned our attention to well digging.

Until now we had been hauling water clear from the garden reservoir. We dug our well just a few feet in back of the house, and we were able to strike water at a shallow depth. A.J. hit water at six feet, and at nine feet the flow was too strong to allow him to dig anymore.

We walled the well up with rocks within two feet of the surface of the ground. There we built a wide shelf all around the inside, and then finished walling the well to the surface.

The shelf was a godsend. It was our only refrigerator for years. Cream, butter, left-overs from the table—everything that needed cooling went into the well on that shelf.

Of course, we had to fence our garden with woven wire to keep out the jackrabbits, which necessitated a trip to town to buy wire. What were we going to use for money with which to buy the wire, I wondered. We had an early spring and the sage hens had hatched early and were now big enough to eat. I suggested that instead of going in debt for the wire, Daddy should kill a couple dozen birds, and I should take them to Reno to sell them. At first he objected, "How do you know you can sell them?"

"Well, there are ten thousand people living in Reno, and out of that number, I'll bet there are two dozen who'll be willing to buy sage hens. It'll be my job to find that two dozen." That was the beginning of a new venture. What a wonderful thing it is to have confidence in one's self. I never for a moment doubted my ability to sell those birds. It was many years before I realized I had any sales ability. Later I was to remark boastfully, "I've sold everything from our ranch from a quart of gooseberries to a wagon-load of manure."

. . . .

In making our homestead plans we had some friendly advice. One neighbor said, "Don't ever kill gopher snakes. You just can't raise a garden without 'em. They kill gophers and ground squirrels." We learned to distinguish the difference between a gopher snake and a rattler. Although their markings are much the same, the rattler is much brighter in coloring, and has a more beautiful, slender body with, of course, the string of rattles at the end of his tail. Legend has it that a rattler grows one rattle for each year. I don't know how true that is, but a snake is likely to lose some of his rattles in crawling through our sharp Nevada rocks and sagebrush.

We vowed not to kill gopher snakes. One day a distant neighbor lady was down helping me tack a quilt. We hadn't yet hung up the screens at the front and back kitchen doors. Our quilt was laid across our long, homemade pine table, and we were busily working away, when in crawled a whalin' big gopher snake. I screamed. There's simply something repulsive and uncanny looking about a snake. I didn't want to hurt it, so I got the broom and began very gently to sweep it out, talking to it all the time. "Come now, old fellow. I don't want to hurt you. Shoo! Shoo on out." It was determined to stay in. I suppose it was the first contact it had ever had with human beings and didn't know how mean we could be. It kept raising its head from the floor and trying to dodge around my broom, first one side, and then the other. I was persistent in giving him gentle little sweeps, and finally succeeded in sweeping him out and down the path. Coming back in, I went on with my quilt tacking. Our work was now in the center of the quilt and we had to stand in a stooping position to tack it. We had been working steadily for about an hour when I straightened up and without looking, backed to my chair and sat down on something soft and squirmy.

I jumped clear across the floor and let out another bloodcurdling scream. There in my chair was that immense big gopher snake coiled round and round on the cushion of the chair, his head hanging over the edge as nonchalantly as though he really belonged there. And there sat Daddy on the front doorstep laughing with all his might. He said, "Remember, old lady! It's a gopher snake." I was standing there almost paralyzed with fear—cold chills running up and down my spine uttering exclamations of, "Oh! Ugh!" I was so angry with Daddy for laughing, for it's awful to be laughed at when you're as badly frightened as I was.

I picked up the chair and gingerly carried it to the back door, giving it a good hard jerk, and dumping the snake to the ground. Then I grabbed the broom and swatted him through the air ten feet at a swat. No gentle treatment this time. I got him outside the gate and down the gully, telling him he'd better stay there. When I came back into the house, Daddy was still chuckling. I looked at him belligerently and said, "If that thing comes back in here I'm gonna chop his head off. You just see if I don't!" With that I grabbed the darning needle and went furiously to work. All this time, my friend sat there with a smile on her face, but I think she was afraid to laugh out loud. When we finished the quilt it was noon and time to get dinner. When I reached into the woodbox for fuel for the cook stove, the piece of wood I pulled out held that horrible big gopher snake. By now my patience was exhausted. I screamed again, slamming him outside the door. Then I picked up a garden hoe and cut off his head, and carried him out into the sagebrush. When I came in, Daddy was still looking quite pleased. I shook my head at him and said, "A gopher snake may be a rancher's friend, but I'm not going to live in the same house with them."

"Well, old lady, that one did get a little too sociable. Maybe the rest won't be that friendly." That and one other, were the only gopher snakes we ever killed. We found they were truly the rancher's friend.

. . . .

As there was an abundance of game in the country, it naturally followed that there were many predatory animals. There was usually a good market for the skins of coyotes and bobcats, besides the bounty of two and a half dollars per head.

If Edson could learn to trap, that would be another source of income. That fall he put in a few weeks with an old trapper. We bought him a couple of dozen of number three steel traps, and he very proudly and confidently set them out. A few days later he came running in all big-eyed and excited to tell me that he had caught a coyote in one of his traps. Would I come quick and help him skin it? He would kill it immediately, and we would skin it while it was still warm. The only knife we had was a dull butcher knife—I never owned any other kind.

Daddy had gone to town that morning with the only pocket knife we had in his pocket. I went with Edson to skin the coyote. He killed it with a club, while I turned my back and cried.

Then we started on our first skinning job. First we cut it up the belly, which was not the correct way. I would cut and skin for awhile, making too many slices in the hide, then Edson, thinking he could do better than I, would take the knife and try his hand. All the time, one of us pulling as hard as possible on the hide. We made an awful mess of it.

Finally after three hours of hard work we got the hide off. It was full of holes. There wasn't a six inch square on the whole skin that wasn't cut. It might have been worth a few dollars when we started, but it wasn't worth ten cents when we finished. We had learned something, however. We had learned that we didn't know how to skin coyotes.

Edson went back to the trapper to learn the skill—and it is a skill—of skinning, in which Edson became very efficient. He learned to skin one in three minutes and often used to laugh at the three hours it had taken us on our first try. He became very good at trapping, and the income from his hides was our greatest help in early homestead days. That first year he sold one hundred and fifty dollars worth of raw skins.

. . . .

I had raised all eight of my little turkeys. When they were about three months old one of them got sick. It drooped around for days. I had given it grains of black pepper and all the home remedies I had ever heard of, but it looked like it was really going to die. I picked it up one day, and there seemed to be a rock in its craw the size of a walnut. I thought, "Well, the darn thing's going to die anyway. I'm going to open its craw and see what that is."

I plucked out a few breast feathers, got Daddy's razor, cut the outside skin of the craw, and then cut open the craw proper. There was the hard lump all right—as hard as a rock. It looked like grass matted down into a solid substance. I removed it, then with a sterilized needle and white silk thread I sewed up the craw and the outside skin. I then banded the turkey's leg for future reference. The turkey got well.

Now it was Thanksgiving time. I wanted to save two hens and a tom for next year's stock, which left me three to sell and two to eat—one for Thanksgiving and one for Christmas. I took good care to sell the banded turkey and was anxious to see what kind of scar the operation had left. Much to my surprise the skin was smooth—there was no scar. The operation had evidently been a perfect success. Then the day before Thanksgiving one of our remaining turkeys died. We had to make a quick decision as to whether to do without turkey for Thanksgiving or for Christmas. We decided to have our turkey dinner on Christmas, for that's what the children wanted. We had already invited the cowboys and old Goshie, the foreman of the sheep ranch for dinner. Goshie, a French Basque whose real name was Juan Barrandegui, was a big fat fellow with a stomach that hung over the edge of his trousers, which he constantly tried to pull up. He had a kind old face with almost liquid brown eyes. He thought the world of the children and I never went to town without Goshie sending some money along with me so that I could buy a special treat for them.

We had to have something special for dinner, so Daddy went out and killed a number of mountain quail. We all feasted on stuffed, roasted quail and never missed the turkey.

Edson took the dead turkey for coyote bait, wired it to a juniper tree across the flat and caught three coyotes with it. The coyotes ate all the flesh off the bird, but it was years before the ligaments disintegrated and let the bones drop. Now after half a century has passed the leg bones of that turkey are still wired to the juniper tree.

WILL JAMES [1892–1942]

Cowboy and illustrator, Will James invented his life story. If you read his classic Lone Cowboy: My Life Story *(1930), you will learn that James was born on an emigrant trail in Montana. Orphaned at age four, James fell in with an old French trapper named Jean Beaupre who tutored him in the ways of the wild. After the trapper's death, the young James drifted all over the West, from Canada to Mexico, hiring on to cattle outfits, breaking broncs, punching cows, and leaving behind a trail of sketches. Arrested for cattle rustling near Ely, Nevada, James did time in the state prison in Carson City, where he seriously contemplated changing vocations. After his release, however, James went right back to cowpunching, that is until an ornery horse named Happy bucked him onto some railroad tracks that smashed his head, then proceeded to step on his back. A lovely young lady named Alice nursed the mangled cowboy back to health in Reno, accepted his proposal to marry, and convinced him to write stories to accompany his drawings of range life. The New York publishing giant Scribner's accepted his first book,* Cowboys North and South *(1924), and went on to publish more than twenty more, most famously* Smoky, the Cowhorse *(1926), which won the coveted Newbery Medal for children's literature. James was an enormously popular writer, Hollywood stunt rider, and celebrity, prized for his authenticity. However, twenty years after James's death, biographer Anthony Amaral discovered that "Will James" was born Joseph-Ernest-Nephtali Dufault in Quebec, Canada, to a French-speaking merchant family. Amaral speculates that the stress of maintaining a false identity in the limelight drove James to heavy drinking, which killed him by age fifty. No one denies, however, that James was indeed a skilled cowboy and master storyteller whose illustrated tales about life on the open range have captivated generations of readers.*

from *Lone Cowboy: My Life Story*

I met the old cowman in the same desert town where he'd hired me near two years before. . . .

. . . Along the next morning, . . . me and the old cowman started for the stables to get the horses and ride out. I walked in there and, as is my habit, I went to looking over all the horses that was in the stalls. The stocking hind feet of a horse caught my eye, so did his color. Some picture away back in my mind was trying to make itself fit in as I went on to sizing up the horse. I went in the stall, looked at his head, and the picture begin to fit more. But, I thought, it couldn't be, not after all this time. I untied the horse, led him out of the stall and looked at the brand on his thigh. It had been worked over, but I could see the original brand there. It was the brand that had been on good old Smoky, and the horse *was* Smoky.

"What's the matter with you there?" hollers the old cowman as he hears me letting out a whoop.

"This is my horse Smoky. Been stole from me four or five years ago."

The stable man came up about then and heard what I'd just said. He asked me, if it was my horse, where did I get him in the first place, where was he stole from, and many other questions, and when I answered 'em all and showed him the original brand that had been made by a stamp iron and how it had been worked over by a running iron, he seemed convinced that that mouse-colored horse was mine sure enough.

"This boy has worked for me long enough so I know he wouldn't lie about that horse," says the old cowman. That settled it.

. . . .

Now I was happy to have him again and I just wanted to go away with him to where both him and me belonged, back to the range.

I didn't ride Smoky out. He was looking old and weary and he wasn't in the good shape I used to keep him. I led him behind the horse the old cowman had brought for me, and when I got him to the main camp I begin shoving hay and crushed barley to him. Hay and grain was expensive because that had to be shipped into the country by rail and then freighted out of town by teams. The old man had got quite a few tons of hay and some grain freighted in for the bronks I was going to break for him. He'd wanted to keep 'em up while I was breaking 'em. I paid for Smoky's feed and I was mighty glad to do that. I floated the old pony's teeth, got him condition-powders and got his hoofs in shape. Poor shoeing had caused 'em to contract pretty bad.

In a month's time I had him looking slick as a whistle. His hide had loosened up and begin to shine like it always had before he'd been stolen from me. I kept him around for a few weeks longer, and every day, after I'd get thru stomping out my string of bronks, I'd go to looking him over and wondering what more I could do for him. The old man used to say that he'd seen plenty of cowboys act like daggone fools over a horse but that he'd never seen such a big daggone fool as I was over that old smoke-color horse.

"You'd think he was a ten-thousand-dollar race horse," he'd say.

"A heap more than that to me," I'd come back at him.

I took a lot of pains putting new shoes on Smoky one day, and when a bunch of mixed horses came at the spring to water, I turned him loose with 'em. The feed was good and strong where that bunch ranged, but it was mighty rocky, and I shod Smoky so he wouldn't get sore-footed while going back and forth from range to water. A sore-footed horse never picks up much fat. There was colts and yearlings in the bunch, and when I turned old Smoky loose he begin to buck and play, just like them colts and yearlings did. He mixed right in with 'em, and soon the bunch went to running, over one ridge and another and out of sight. Smoky stopped and looked back just before going over the last ridge, and he acted like he would turn back. But soon he went to playing again and headed for the bunch and wide open range.

I got to see him every day or two after that, when him and the bunch would come to water. He'd leave the bunch then for a time and stick his head over the corral fence where I was always busy edducating one bronk or another, and he'd nicker a hello to me. I'd always have crushed barley in a morral (nose bag) and ready for him when he came, and while he'd chew away on that, I'd get to feel his slick hide and talk to him. Often the bunch he was with would water and leave before he got thru eating his grain, but he didn't seem worried about that, and when I'd take the morral off his head and turn him out of the corral he'd sometimes stick around for an hour or two, just as tho he wanted to confab with me.

Smoky was a great horse. If any man ever said a word by mouth, that pony done near as much by the way he'd cock his little pin-ears. I knowed the language of them ears mighty well. I'd seen a lot of country over them, and if ever I was dubious about what was ahead while riding in dark nights, I could tell by the feel of 'em if I should go ahead or turn back. My hand on his neck would tell me a lot of things his horse-sense knowed, and that way him and me talked to one another.

I never rode Smoky after I found him again at the livery stable. He'd done his work, I had more than plenty other horses to ride, and now all I wanted to do was to have that pony around, see him once in awhile and see him feeling good.

. . . .

Smoky was like a big spoilt old kid, with nothing to do but eat and play and stick his nose into whatever I was doing when I was around camp. He was more company to me than I can tell, and during the two years I worked for that outfit and while he was around he made this cowboy mighty contented and pleased to stay in that one country. I never stayed so long in one country, not since I was left alone. But now I somehow didn't care to drift no more. It was mostly because I didn't want to take Smoky on any long trips, and I sure didn't want to leave him behind.

. . . .

Like with most all cow outfits I'd ever rode for, my working hours wasn't very regular. They're less regular with desert outfits on account of water holes being far apart and where riding is mostly done from permanent camps. It's not like riding for prairie outfits and where the round-up wagon follows the works. While riding for the old cowman I'd sometimes be in the saddle twenty out of twenty-four hours, with nothing to eat during that time. That would be when a snow or rain storm would come. Cattle would then drift to fresh range and where there was no spring water. I'd have to see that they didn't drift too far, so they could get back to the springs again when the snow and rain-water was all gone. Cattle that I'd sometimes miss would barely make it in to the springs and when they did, if I wasn't around to watch 'em, they'd near kill themselves with water. A few would, once in a while. Sometimes big thirsty herds would drift in to troughs that could water only fifty head at a time, and many a time, after a long day's ride, I'd have to get up in the middle of the night, get on a night horse that I always kept up, split the herd and scatter it to other springs. It was hard work to get the thirsty cattle away from the troughs, and sometimes the sun would be high when I'd get back to my camp. I'd heat up some coffee then, swallow a cold biscuit, catch a fresh horse, and go a hunting for more cattle that was holding out on far-away range and feeding till thirst drove 'em in.

With such work that has to be done, a cowboy can't form no union and go by no union hours. If a rider was to quit when a certain hour come and there was work still to be done, he wouldn't be no cowboy, and in some countries there wouldn't be no range cattle. . . . Sunday is no day of rest for the cowboy, and there's no celebrating of holidays. They're just days like all others.

But it wasn't always long hours in the saddle. There was whole weeks at a time when I'd ride out of camp after sun-up and could easy get back in the middle of the afternoon. That was when there was no water in the flats and cattle watered at the springs. Before leaving camp in the morning I'd always wrap a big can of tomatoes with gunny sack and plant it by the spring or slip it under a trough where water would drip on it. When I'd get back from my day's ride the first thing I'd do was to open up the can, sprinkle a little salt on the tomatoes and take the whole canful down. That was sure what I called refreshing. Then I'd ride to where my horses was hobbled, change to a fresh one, ride back to camp and go to cooking me a bait. My day's work was done, unless cattle came to water and there was calves in the bunch that needed branding.

I sure always liked them late afternoons and evenings at the camps. Everything was sure peaceful, and I'd stretch out either on my bunk or under a cedar tree, looking at saddle-makers' catalogs and old magazines or at the distance. When dark come I'd light a candle and draw a bit by it. I thought I was getting to draw pretty good about that time, but no new ambition of me trying to be an artist came to me.

· · · · · · · ·

One evening, after I'd tied up one of the bronks for a night horse, I happened to look up a draw where I'd took the hobbled horses up thru, and sees old Smoky all by himself and poking along down towards camp. I'd never seen him leave the bunch during the evening, before. I laughed as I watched him come and I says to myself, "That old bum wants another biscuit."

But Smoky didn't want no biscuit. He refused the one I held out to him, and for the first time. He didn't seem to want anything, and there was a kind of far-away look in his eyes. I thought then that he was sick. I felt of his ears but they was warm and I couldn't find any signs of anything being the matter with him. I figgured he just wanted company, and after I talked to him a spell I went to making some cedar kindling to start the morning fire with. I didn't pay no attention to him while doing that and when I got thru I looked to see him laying down by a cedar tree and with his head propped against it. I went to him again then to watch for signs of sickness, but he was breathing easy and regular and he seemed all at peace. He sure didn't look sick, and he was round and fat as a butter ball.

I squatted by him, rolled me a smoke and while taking the burrs out of his foretop I went to talking to him. He seemed to enjoy that a whole lot, he liked me to rub his ears too. I sat by him there thru the whole evening and till dark come, and then after one more pat on his slick neck I left him to go into the cabin and crawl in between my soogans. There was a long ride ahead for me on the next day.

It was sure some surprise when, waking up the next morning, I looked out the opened door to see Smoky still laying where I'd left him the night before, still in the same position and with his head propped against the tree. He looked asleep, but I jumped out of bed into my boots, pulled up the pants they was always left inside of, and hit out to Smoky's side. He didn't move an ear nor open an eye when I came near, and as I layed a hand on his neck it felt cold . . . with the cold of death.

Old Smoky had just went to sleep thru that. I don't think he ever felt a pain or that a muscle even twitched when he drawed his last breath, and far as I know he might of passed away while I was talking to him the evening before.

I didn't go on that long ride that I'd planned on. Instead I dug a deep hole right by where Smoky layed, rolled him in and buried him, and stacked rocks on his grave so the cayotes wouldn't dig him out.

Smoky's going made me feel down-the-mouth quite a bit, and now that I couldn't do no more for him, I wanted to ride and ride, in one straight line and for many miles. It was noon that day when I caught the two horses the old cowman had made me a present of. I put my bed on one, my saddle on the other, and taking the hobbles off the other horses, I started 'em out of the corral and turned 'em towards the headquarters of the company. It was late that night when I got there. I asked for my time check the next morning and rode on again, a looking ahead for new ridges to cross.

WALLACE STEGNER [1909–1993]

Widely acknowledged as the dean of western writers, Dr. Wallace Stegner casts a long shadow in the American West. In a career spanning more than fifty years and more than thirty books, Stegner won both the Pulitzer Prize (for Angle of Repose, *1971) and the National Book Award (for* The Spectator Bird, *1976). In 1945 he left a position at Harvard to launch Stanford University's creative writing graduate program, which became one of the nation's top programs, training many noted writers, including Ken Kesey, Edward Abbey, Larry McMurtry, Tillie Olsen, William Kittredge, Frank Bergon, and Gary Short, among others. Although Stegner never set an entire book in Nevada, many of his works "pass through" Nevada, and his understanding of the West as foremost a land of aridity applies especially well to Nevada, the country's most arid state. From his humble roots—or, rather, rootlessness—Stegner had a long way to climb to reach literary prominence. His father was a nomadic dream chaser, always in search of "the big rock candy mountain," as one of Stegner's novels is titled. Born in Iowa, young Wally was dragged all over the West, eventually staying put in East End, Saskatchewan, for six formative years, immortalized in his history/memoir* Wolf Willow *(1962). Such permanence was not to last, however, and the family took to the road again, bouncing around the West until they alighted in Salt Lake City, where Stegner attended high school. Although he never became a Mormon, Stegner admired aspects of Mormon culture, especially the strong sense of place and community. For the rest of his life, Stegner debunked the cowboy myth of rugged individualism, instead emphasizing westerners' mutual dependence and advocating an ethic of cooperation and stewardship of the land. In "Mormon Trees" from* Mormon Country *(1942), Stegner reveals his abiding interest in American places as he "reads" the cultural history of Lombardy poplars.*

Mormon Trees

Wherever you go in the Mormon country, whether through the irrigated Snake River Plains of eastern and southern Idaho, the infrequent oases among the Great Basin ranges of Nevada, the desert springs and flash-flood river bottoms of northern and central Arizona, or the mountain valleys of Utah, western Wyoming and western Colorado, you see the characteristic marks of Mormon settlement: the typical, intensively-cultivated fields of alfalfa and sugar beets and Bermuda onions and celery, the orchards of cherry and apple and peach and apricot (and it is not local pride which says that there is no better fruit grown anywhere), the irrigation ditches, the solid houses, the wide-streeted, sleepy green towns. Especially you see the characteristic trees, long lines of them along ditches, along streets, as boundaries between fields and farms. They are as typical as English hedgerows; perhaps, to the predominantly English converts of the early days, they had some force as a substitute, copying in the desert, under conditions vastly different from those of the old country, the angled and bisected and neatly-blocked landscape of their first home.

These are the "Mormon trees," Lombardy poplars. Wherever they went the Mormons planted them. They grew boldly and fast, without much tending, and they make the landscape of the long valleys of the Mormon Country something special and distinctive. The view across one of those valleys from the alluvial aprons of the mountains, when the wind is bending the tall poplars and the whole land leans a little tipsily and even the shadows yaw on tight alfalfa fields and brown pasture land, is a view one does not immediately forget. There are Lombardy poplars elsewhere in the world; there are few places where there are so many, and there is no place where the peculiar combination of desert valley and dark lines of trees exists as it does in this country.

They give a quality to the land so definite that it is almost possible to mark the limits of the Mormon Country by the trees. They do not grow in the mountains, but neither do the Mormons, except for scattered sheepherders and cowpunchers who by their very profession are cut off from the typical Mormon way of life. Mormons and Mormon trees are both valley races. And once in a while the presence of Lombardy poplars reveals surviving centers of Mormon population where one would never have suspected them. I was driving with a friend through Nevada some years ago and came through Sparks, just a short way down the Truckee from Reno—almost a suburb of that "biggest little city on earth." My companion looked at the roadside lined with poplars and said, "For God's sake, is this a Mormon town?" He had forgotten, if he ever knew, that Nevada was part of the old State of Deseret, that its first farmers were Mormons, that the Carson Valley towns under the lee of the Sierra were founded by Mormon colonists. He had forgotten that the Mormons once reached much farther than they do now, that Mormons participated in the gold strike at Sutter's Mill, that even Eilley Bowers, that fantastic wife of Sandy Bowers, himself one of the most fantastic figures in the history of western mining camps, was a twice-divorced Mormon wife when she married Sandy, and that she came to Nevada with her second husband as one of a colonizing group. The Carson Valley towns were abandoned early, for political reasons, but the stamp of the early settlers remains here and there far outside the reaches of the present Mormon Country. The trees in Sparks are a dead give-away that Nevada is not merely the home of sin and shame and cheap divorces and open gambling and Basque sheepherders and the Wingfield banks. It was and to some extent still is a part of the Mormon Country, and even in the biggest little city on earth there is a sizable Mormon population. That may, as a matter of fact, have something to do with the quiet and sobriety of Reno's residential section.

There are not as many Mormon trees as there used to be; it seems a pity. Trees of other varieties, wherever there has been developed a dependable water-supply, break up the clear patterns that existed in many parts of the Mormon country only a generation ago. Some of the rows of poplars have been cut down in Salt Lake City streets and along the edges of fields east of the city, because their age and possible heart-rot made them a hazard. They are not a particularly long-lived tree. Increasingly, too, people have wanted wider-crowned trees that would throw more shade. But still in the rural districts, in the places where unreconstructed Mormonism maintains itself comparatively untouched, the Lombardy poplars line the ditch banks and the fields.

Perhaps it is fanciful to judge a people by its trees. Probably the predominance of poplars is the result of nothing more interesting than climatic conditions or the lack of other kinds of seeds and seedlings. Probably it is pure nonsense to see a reflection of Mormon group life in the fact that the poplars were practically never planted singly, but always in groups, and that the groups took the form of straight lines and ranks. Perhaps it is even more nonsensical to speculate that the straight, tall verticality of the Mormon trees appealed obscurely to the rigid sense of order of the settlers, and that a marching row of plumed poplars was symbolic, somehow, of the planter's walking with God and his solidarity with his neighbors.

Nonsensical or not, it is not an unpleasant thought. Institutions must have their art forms, their symbolic representations, and if the Heavenward aspirations of medieval Christianity found their expression in cathedrals and spires, the more mundane aspirations of the Latter-day Saints may just as readily be discovered in the widespread plantings of Mormon trees. They look Heavenward, but their roots are in earth. The Mormon looked toward Heaven, but his Heaven was a Heaven on earth and he would inherit bliss in the flesh.

OWEN ULPH [1914–2003]

The best way to introduce Owen Ulph is to let him speak for himself: "The truth is that horses exhibit, in an exaggerated form, many of the worst characteristics of people. They are greedy, envious, spiteful, malicious, slothful, superstitious, and stupid. They are congenital hysterics and each one is, ominously, a prospective homicide. If horses could talk, they would lie!" In his essay collection The Fiddleback: Lore of the Line Camp *(1981) and roman à clef* The Leather Throne *(1984), Ulph's subject is cowboys, his setting is central Nevada, and his style is pungent* *and impertinent. As a historian, Ulph is well aware that the cowboy has been written into the ground and mythologized beyond recognition. His genius is to present cowhands—and their animals—as distinct individuals, mingling range lingo and profanity with his own cultivated prose. On his home range of academia, Ulph was a maverick. An Englishman by birth, Ulph came to America at age five, grew up in Oakland, California, earned all his degrees—*BA, MA, PHD—*in history at Stanford, and spent most of his thirty-five-year teaching career at Reed College, interrupted by brief stints at a half dozen other universities in the West, including the University of Nevada, Reno (1948–51). Ulph's scholarship grazed wildly diverse fields, including medieval French history, Russian literature, the history of military science, and the western frontier. Despite plaudits earned for his teaching, Ulph described his academic career as "doing time" and fondly recalled five halcyon years in the early 1950s when he ditched the professoriate to take up the saddle as a cowhand in Big Smoky Valley, Nevada. Retiring from Reed in 1979, Ulph moved to his Bear Trap Ranch in Lamoille, Nevada, where he lived with dogs and horses and cats and llamas, mended fences and irrigated, and penned two cowboy classics.*

The Critter

It was the time we were working out of the Diamond Hook, Davy Stevens' starve-out operation at Cloverdale in northern Nevada. Cloverdale was the cluster of sod and tarpaper shanties the Fiddleback was using as a line camp late that particular fall, and Davy Stevens was the eighty-year-old cowman who held title to the spread. The Fiddleback and the Diamond Hook outfits shared a corridor of range through the San Antone sand hills, and we used to help Davy with his riding. Holly Richardson and I had cut three hundred two-year-old heifers from the Fiddleback bunch and had herded them down to Miller's Flat where they could winter on rabbit brush, browse, and alkali. The range down that way was usually free from snow cover. They would scrounge and learn to make out.

We had dropped them, loaded our tired horses into the stock truck that had been left for us, and, with indecent haste, bumped back to Cloverdale, where we submerged ourselves in the luxury of lumpy, rat-stained mattresses in place of gravel, downy sage, and rabbit pellets.

Long before daylight had wiped out all but a couple of lingering stars, we were awakened by old Jean Daniels' gruff chuckle. (He never slept beyond 3 AM.) "Your girls is back."

How Jean could tell the bellowing of a heifer from that of a full-grown cow was something I never figured out, but sure enough, there they were, bawling outside the west pasture fence. Let me make the situation clear: we had all but taken root in our saddles inching those surly laggards along the dusty flat at a pace that would

have made a snail impatient. Fifty frying miles. Three forty-hour days. And now
in a single night the ornery brutes had retraced the full distance it had taken those
three days to travel!

"You should've stayed with 'em until they was settled," Jean said.

"Kee-rist, Jean," Holly protested, "we located 'em on water an' everything . . ."

"You don't never trust 'em," Jean muttered, giving us the benefit of his experience. "They're critters."

. . . .

"*Critter*" is a term seldom found in action-packed oaters in which the cowboys usually manage to avoid encountering cows. But to the hand with no time for draw-
downs and shoot-outs at dawn or sunset because he has been pounding leather
long before and long after these approved hours for gunplay, "critter" was an indispensable part of his working vocabulary.

. . . .

"Cows" and "critters" are not synonymous terms. The former is a neutral noun, the
latter packs a judgment on the animal's character. Unless the speck on the ridge
was a perverse bunch-quitting stray, it could not have been a critter; it had to be
a cow. Cattlemen, by which is meant bucolic capitalists, would refer to their stock
as "cows," thinking of them collectively as marketable units of beef-on-the-hoof. It
was only the cowboy who called cows "critters" and then only when he was dealing with them as willful entities reacting with varying degrees of obstinacy to his
efforts to educate them. No cowboy would ask a rancher, "How many critters do
you run?" but he could easily remark, "John Casey runs the worst bunch of critters
that ever busted out of hell's corral!"

. . . .

A long list of philanthropic services rendered the ungrateful critter by the company
of mounted friars who minister to her incessant needs can be added: inoculation
against a plethora of potential diseases; dipping and spraying against the afflic-
tions of flies, grubs, and assorted pests; doctoring for pinkeye, foot rot, lump-jaw,
gotch ear, blue tail, bloat, red water, staggers, and spangs; pumping water during
droughts, breaking ice on frozen water holes in sub-zero weather, and constructing windbreaks against northers; planting trees for back scratching, rump rubbing,
and shade—all these plus a myriad of unique, nonclassifiable acts of attention such
as the time Henry Steen rescued a critter that had wedged itself upside down in a
trough, or the time Zane Hyatt sawed another loose from the outhouse at Cloverdale that it had no business investigating in the first place.

Despite such abundant benevolence, the cow has very little to be thankful for, and gratitude toward mankind is not a virtue one should reasonably expect it to display. Any generosity shown the cow is strictly utilitarian. Hay pitched when the drifts were deep was not forked out as an act of charity. Starved cows produce no return on investment, and all the cures inflicted without anesthetics are something the animal would willingly forgo. All the sinister grooming is directed toward ultimate butchery. Cows instinctively know this (there is much evidence that cows possess ESP), and consequently their reluctance to cooperate in their own eventual destruction should not be regarded as an indication of defective character. "Critter," though a derogatory expression, is not entirely an epithet. The critter was the cowboy's Miltonic Satan—a salty adversary. Until this luckless victim of man's carnivorous greed was roped at both ends and pinioned by a member of the ground crew, one knee thrust against its neck, one hand gripping a foreleg and the other yanking up its snout, it was not safe to relax in the saddle. Anchored to the prostrate critter and temporarily secure in his leather throne, the cowboy could reflect upon the diverse imbroglios of existence.

Pat Fee, who would haul the devil from a live volcano, skin him, and throw him back if I were to refer to her as a "cowperson," once wrote to me from her remote spread on the fringe of the Black Rock Desert: "Cattle have formed the character of the American cowboy. Old cowboys are usually sour, profane, disdainful, and skeptical. Why? From dealing with obnoxious cows and homicidal horses. Everything that has been said about cowboys needs re-examining! Has anybody ever written that most cowboys have ulcers? Chuckwagon food, too much raw whiskey, bad water, but above all, worry and frustration from contending with the goddam cows."

. . . .

On one memorable occasion Holly and I were bringing a batch of recalcitrant heifers off the head of Reese River. The country is rough, precipitous, and the slopes of the steep canyons are strewn alternately with groves of mahogany and great patches of tightly matted quaking aspen. We wanted to bring them down into the relatively open stream bed of South Twin. Cattle under herd in mountainous terrain have a tendency to set a brisk pace directly along the contours of the ridges. They are difficult to control, because they are picking the game trails while the rider is bounding about on his snorting horse, fighting brush and shale, trying to keep above and abreast of the leaders simultaneously. If a rider loses his bunch, they can skirt the side hills and slip over a divide into another drainage basin. If they ever emerge onto the flat, they can be forty miles from where he wanted them—over a hundred miles as a cow horse travels and if they happen to be Fiddlebacks.

This bunch had made up its collective mind to elude us, but we had them outfoxed. We thought. Ahead was a mammoth talus slope about a quarter of a mile wide at the base and narrowing to a point at its apex. Between the peak of the talus and the foot of the cliff that rose sharply above it was a skirt of stunted aspen. If the leaders crashed this thicket before we headed them off, they could worm through the brush for Mexico. We could not have turned them, because there would have been no way to get in front of them. Hampered by the talus below and the cliff above, we could only helplessly have followed their tails. Cows make tunnels through thickets which afford them snug escape routes while horse and rider, their heads tangled in a network of branches, are effectively checked. The critters knew all this and were cunningly edging toward their little green gateway to freedom. But while they were reading our minds, we were reading theirs.

"Stay on their ass," Holly shouted confidently. "I'll scoot ahead. All we have to do is keep above 'em. When they hit that rockslide, they won't have no place to go but down."

I agreed. The talus slope was an effective barrier. It would have stopped a mountain goat.

Only it didn't stop our critters. The leaders hit the slide, hesitated while they eyed Holly poised vigilantly above, cast a backward glance at me, and proceeded to stumble deliberately into the rock.

"Them dirty, festerin', no-good, sonsabitching foddermuckers . . . !" Holly cut loose a torrent of profanity that would stupefy the current generation that seems to suffer from the delusion that it discovered the four-letter word.

The critters reached the middle of the slide and came to a standstill. All we had to do was figure how to get them out. One thing for sure was that we didn't want them to continue across onto the far shore. They had to be brought *back*. We had two advantages. Goaded by a man on foot behind them, they could scent their way over their own tracks. Also, they would be enticed by the horses stationed at the edge of the slide as decoys. Even had the horses been able to mince their way through the slide without crippling themselves, they would have been no use in the rocks.

Holly argued that one of us should stick with his horse to prevent the critters from bolting uphill and into the quakers if they decided to come out, so I worked around the stranded cattle on foot to get into position to haze them back. They wouldn't budge. They let me push, poke, prod, and lather their rumps with my coiled rope. No go. After meditation and consultation (we hadn't yet gotten around to prayer), we agreed that Holly's presence on his horse was spooking them. So he climbed down and joined me, leaving Roany with dropped reins in a spot that he could get to fast should the critters suddenly plunge out. Everything had been calculated as fine as a tanned snakeskin. Except that a half hour later when they began an unheralded exodus, they headed straight for us, ignoring our flailing ropes, our fanning hats, and our angry hollers. Right on past us they went, and out the far side as if we had been of no more account than a pair of juniper stumps. Off for the Matto Grosso. The Panama Canal wasn't going to stop them. Holly squatted down and *bawled*. My delirious laughter was akin to his tears.

We limped back to the horses, who nickered with sympathy. When it concerns the critter, a cow horse shares its rider's sentiments.

Hours later, as we neared camp, we met Jean descending another canyon with our runaways in tow. He'd spotted a plume of dust along the shoulder of a ridge where "it hadn't orter had been." He knew they were critters that had dodged some bedeviled rider and he cut their caper short. The way a top hand can appear from nowhere in time to stop the hanging is uncanny.

This episode was routine compared to many—some accompanied by sinister consequences. It should be clear, at any rate, that cowboy fortitude didn't come from the Boy Scout's manual. It was a product of constant confrontation with un-reasoning reality. It was the only attitude left that made sense after every possible response to adversity—rage, disgust, self-pity—failed to pay off. Instead of hunt-ing up a dog to kick, the cowboy learned to keep his wits in easy reach. He real-ized, too, that there were a lot of times when that "didn't help none neither." His thoroughgoing skepticism went so far as to support his innocent superstitions. "It may not do no good," Henry Steen admitted when Jean raked him over for tucking a rabbit's foot into his shirt pocket every time he climbed aboard a raw bronc, "but it sure don't do no harm."

. . . .

Mother Nature is not one of religion's effective missionaries. Atheists may or may not have occupied foxholes, but it can be stated with certainty that a high tally of infidels could be run up among those who rode the range. Routine cattle work presented riders with so many grisly tasks and so much horror that the notion of justice, sacred or profane, was plainly absurd. A compassionate deity was as com-prehensible as a softhearted horsefly. The same brand of rational empiricism that supported Henry Steen's defense of his rabbit's foot led the cowboy to reject the existence of God but to acknowledge the existence of the Devil. "Evidence is a mite lean for the former, but a hand wouldn't have no trouble proving up his claim for the latter," Jean Daniels would argue during sessions of cow-camp theology.

The range presented an inexhaustible record of unwitnessed tragedy. Every-where, withered hides clung to the crumbling scaffoldings of gray-white bones— midget tents pitched across the arid wasteland, visited only by the ubiquitous magpie and other scavengers of the purple sage. Carcasses in bogs, ravines, and caved-in mine shafts, carcasses heaped against corners of drift fences where blizzard-trapped animals, their backs to the scourging wind, perished in mass misery, carcasses strewn around water holes baked into yellow crusts by years of drought, carcasses in the buckbrush, in swampy meadows, amid the mountain timber—these and countless other testaments to the savagery of the elements constantly sharpened the cowboy's awareness of the harshness of life. The surface inclemency of the cowhand was a psychological necessity. His morbid wit cloaked repressed sensitivity. It was a defiant assertion of immunity to the outrages perpetuated by the forces of evil and a device for scoring a moral victory over them.

MOLLY FLAGG KNUDTSEN [1915–2001]

Born Thyrza Benson Flagg in New York City to a wealthy and socially prominent family, "Molly," as she preferred to be called, attended exclusive boarding schools for girls, obtained an equitation diploma from the Royal Institute of the Horse in London, and made formal debuts in New York and London. She studied the metaphysical Elizabethan poets at King's College, University of London, shared a mews apartment with a countess, and vacationed in Europe. Marrying one of many suitors, Bill Knudtsen, in 1937, Molly landed in Reno in 1941 for a divorce. The required six-week residency stretched to a sixty-year residence when she met and married Dick Magee, a handsome trainer of thoroughbred horses. The newlyweds settled on Magee's ranch in Grass Valley, Nevada, twenty miles north of Austin, where Knudtsen found herself cooking for almost thirty hired hands. Terrified by the cadaver of a cow, Molly asked her husband, "What do I do with it?" "Cut it up and cook it," he said, and walked away. Although she loathed the job of crew cook, Molly grew to love Grass Valley, where she managed a herd of purebred Hereford cattle. In 1969 Molly bought out Dick Magee and the two divorced, she remarrying Bill Knudtsen. Meanwhile, Molly Flagg Knudtsen researched the history of Grass Valley, led historical preservation efforts, and became an amateur archaeologist, recording local lore in articles for the Reese River Reveille, American Antiquity, Vogue, Family Circle, *and others, and in her books* Here Is Our Valley *(1975),* Cow Sense *(1980),* Under the Mountain *(1982), and* Joe Dean and Other Pioneers *(1985). Desiring to be an advocate for rural children, Knudtsen became the first woman elected to the Nevada Board of Regents, serving for twenty years (1960–80) and helping to establish community colleges, the University of Nevada Press, and the Department of Anthropology at* UNR.

Preface to *Under the Mountain*

On a still day in January you can hear the mountain talking to itself. Rumbling. Grumbling. The sound comes from deep in its huge body. Mount Callaghan is an old mountain. It mourns aloud, like an old man, for the days of its youth, when rocks danced in the sky and the world was a wonder of fire and ice. All that has come after is only erosion.

Time has left the mountain bald, stoop-shouldered, dying down eternity. The glacial snows have melted, leaving great scars along its flanks. The warm waters have receded until only the fossilized starfish remain.

White clouds cap the top of the mountain, extending soft fingers down canyons and ridges. Wild storms scream through the passes, rage into the long valley, flattening the quaking aspens and twisting the trunks of the mahogany trees.

In summer the sun sinks late in the cleft of Skull Creek Pass. In winter it veers south behind Callaghan Canyon. Summer solstice. Winter solstice. The rock cairns on the peaks mark the year's passage.

Mount Callaghan lies like a giant hand on my life. From the day I came to live under its shadow in Grass Valley, I have felt its terrible strength; sustaining, restraining.

"Where do you live?" they ask.

What else can I say but, "I live under the mountain. . . ."

A Flake of Flint, A Sherd of Earthenware

There is a world beyond the world we know. A shadow world, where men move silently on naked feet. A world of flickering fires and long nights. A world of snarling predators with gleaming fangs. A world of hunger, cold, and nameless fears. A simple world, whose deep simplicity mystifies the inhabitants of more complex civilizations as a still pool lost in a deep canyon mystifies the observer with its wavering, inverted reflections of overhanging branches.

The greenery reflected in this deep pool is not more evanescent, more intriguing, more beautiful than is the world of prehistory, illumined for a fleeting instant by a pottery sherd or a translucent fragment of flaked flint.

. . . .

Before I came to live in Nevada, my life had been spent either on the eastern seaboard of the Atlantic, in Western Europe, or traveling in North Africa and parts of Asia. It was quite a contrast from these places to living on a cattle ranch in Central Nevada.

I think the most difficult adjustment I had to make was accustoming myself to the newness of my surroundings. Fresh from the temples of Angkor Wat, the tombs of the Valley of the Kings, the rain-drenched gardens of Versailles, from all such monuments to olden times, I had come to live in a world where history seemed never to go back further than human memory, and where people acted as though a hundred years was an eternity.

The transition tested my powers of adaptability to their limit. I sought salvation in local history and literature. I tried to familiarize myself with the story of the Fur Trade. I studied westerly migration. I researched the early settlements of the surrounding country. I read Angel and Mighels and Sam Davis. I read Mark Twain. I read Bret Harte. I even read his cousin, Fred Hart.

And then one day, driving a bunch of cows and calves up the horse pasture toward the ranch, I stopped my horse in a clump of buck brush to give the slow-moving cattle time to rest. Idly, I glanced at the ground and saw, lying at my horse's feet, a small, leaf-shaped point.

It had a basal notch and bifacial, transverse flaking. Its edges were serrated. And it was made of flint in two tones of light grey. It was about an inch and a half long, and about half an inch broad at its widest point. It is a fairly common type of point for the area. But on that day, when I first saw it, I had never seen anything like it before.

I slipped off my horse and picked it up, holding it cradled in the palm of my hand. As I stared at the leaf-shaped projectile point I felt the past stir around me, with all its rustle of unanswered questions. And I lifted my eyes to a valley which suddenly was peopled with unknown shadows.

What hand had shaped that point? Where? When? Why?

There was nothing stirring in the valley except the cattle, my horse, my dog, and I. But the stone tool in my hand was evidence that people had been there before us. Long, long before.

I dropped the grey point in my pocket, remounted, and slowly followed the cattle up the pasture, wondering as I rode if the flint in my pocket was just an isolated find or if there might be other artifacts in the valley, other traces of a world older than local history's hundred years. Older, perhaps, than a thousand. Perhaps even old as the Pleistocene.

The questions I asked myself that day have not all been answered. But of the people who lived in Grass Valley in pre-Caucasian times I know more than I would have dreamed possible when I found that first projectile point.

I know now where the Grass Valley people lived, what they ate, how they died, where they lie buried, their strange, high monuments. I know now their goings and their comings up and down the valley. I have found where they quarried the red chert and where the flesh-toned quartz. I know the slopes where they gathered grass seed, the forests where they harvested pine nuts. I have followed the deer trails and stumbled on the haunts of the mountain sheep they stalked. I know their sacred springs, and the high cliffs covered with their petroglyph carvings. I can walk through their winter villages, finding my way from house cluster to house cluster as easily as a suburban housewife visiting friends in a nearby street.

This knowledge came to me gradually over the years. It did not reveal itself all at once. And some evidence that was there I failed to interpret, or even to see, because I did not know enough to look for it. For years I remained blind to bedrock mortars and stone men, looking at them without knowing what I was seeing.

. . . .

In the years since I found the grey projectile point in the horse pasture buck brush, I have uncovered the remarkably complete evidence of a classic neolithic society inhabiting Grass Valley. What gives this discovery significance is the fact that Grass Valley is located in the "empty quarter" of Nevada, a sparsely populated, little-visited area where it was taken for granted few if any prehistoric remains existed. My discovery of pottery to the extent and in the variety in which it exists in Grass Valley has significantly changed any future archaeological estimates concerning Central Nevada prehistory.

Archaeology aside, the personal satisfactions of my work have been enormous. The days, the weeks, the months, the years I have spent in Nevada have been immeasurably happier because of what I have learned about the past of this country I love so well.

When I am working to reconstruct a shattered vessel, I sense beside mine the smooth, agile, brown fingers of the Shoshone woman who modelled the clay a hundred, a thousand, perhaps two thousand years ago. Then all the valley was filled with her people. Then sage hen strutted in the sage flats, and fat, greasy pine nuts roasted in the camp fires of the winter villages.

I have no monopoly on this wonderful world of prehistory, nor is Grass Valley the only place where the long dead may be called back to tell us how they lived their lives. But to those who would turn back the centuries, a word of caution.

Remember to deal gently with the ghosts you wake.

JEAN MCELRATH [1917–1967]

"In the history of Wells, no individual contributed more to bringing alive its past and giving it a place in Nevada than Jean McElrath," according to Nevada's Northeast Frontier, a history. *McElrath's is a remarkable story. From the mining camp of Chloride, Arizona, her family moved to Wells when she was seven. At sixteen, she fell and injured her spine, causing the onset of progressive rheumatoid arthritis. By age twenty-one she was unable to walk, and she was blind at thirty-three. Taking her handicaps in stride, McElrath and her devoted family set up a "newsroom" in her bedroom, consisting of a telephone, tape recorder, and typewriter, fitted with Braille keys. From her bed, McElrath sent dispatches to the* Salt Lake City Tribune, the Nevada State Journal, *and the* Elko Daily Free Press. *Thanks to a wide circle of loyal informants, McElrath often broke the news of Wells and Elko County before other reporters caught wind of the story. She also contributed feature stories to* Desert *magazine, the* San Francisco Chronicle, Nevada Highways, Grit, *the* Wall Street Journal, American Family, Better Farming, *and others. Her much-loved weekly column "Tumbleweeds" ran in the* Wells Progress *from 1940 to 1967, the longest-running column in Nevada at that time. McElrath kept a file of anecdotes and vignettes about northeast Nevada's early days, gleaned from old newspaper articles, histories, archives, and old-timers. Despite McElrath's protestations that "books don't pay, and I like to eat," a friend persuaded her to write a book.* Aged in Sage *(1964) "pins down" thirty-six of these tales from Wells, Elko, Berlin, Tonopah, Battle Mountain, Jarbidge, and other out-of-the-way places. In 1971* Tumbleweeds, *a selection of her* Wells Progress *columns, was published posthumously, thanks to the efforts of McElrath's many friends.*

Rabbit Fighter

Metropolis was at war in the autumn of 1917 and the strife lent unique flavor to schoolteaching there. Sounds of martial distress from other troubled spots on the globe only faintly reached Metropolite ears, tuned to a dry wind's ceaseless keening and the rustling menace of a jackrabbit invasion.

"Sorry, Miss. This week's train to Metrop has gone," the Southern Pacific's agent told Eleanor Hasenkamp when she stepped off the Overland Limited one Indian summer day in Wells.

"Hazy" tucked soft brown hair out of the wind's reach and considered. Drought and rabbits couldn't daunt a Nebraska-bred girl, but the pretty first grade teacher wasn't prepared for any ten-mile trudge across the wilds of northeast Nevada.

"Today's mail stage has gone too," the agent contributed.

The girl smiled wryly, remembering the brochure that less than six years before had extolled Metropolis' paved and electrically lighted streets, its busy railroad station and $100,000 hotel as the "best between San Francisco and Ogden, Utah."

Now, with the land in drought's vise, station and hotel were closed. Bishop Dam's promised 30,000 cultivated acres had dropped to an advertised 12,000 acres, then settled, without fanfare, to a realistic 2,000.

"I'm headin' for Metrop, Miss," a wind-leathered farmer cut in and drew a smiling thanks for this offered "lift."

The Model T shot northward along a road scraggle-bordered with gray sage. It leaped into tub-size chuck holes, and creamy dust boiled up around them, flowing liquidly back as the jitney bucked out. Jack rabbits, big as young coyotes, skittered ahead, zig-zagging with as much agility as the Model T. Neither yielded a dust mote of the right-of-way.

"Powerful lot of 'em, this year," the jitney jockey made lung-top conversation. "Bob Steele, out in Clover Valley, says he sat on top of one of his haystacks, knockin' jacks over as fast as he could pull the trigger and still they ate the stack from under him. Left him sittin' high and dry on air."

The new teacher shot him an appreciative grin but kept a firm grip on her hat and the jitney door.

"Metrop's a Mormon town, you know," the chauffeur offered next. "Mormon," he reaffirmed, enjoying hazel eyes startled wide in a dust-whitened face. "School Board likes gentile teachers. They won't bother you none," he concluded, dexterously wrestling flivver wheels slewed by a rut.

. . . .

"Ever see a Saint?" her pilot asked as the panting Ford stopped before the Pacific Reclamation Company's office and Hazy stepped down.

"I met some missionaries back home once," she replied. "They were Elders."

"Only difference between an Elder and a Mormon Bishop is that the Bishop has horns," he cited a popular legend and rattled off.

. . . .

Lavender-blue twilight brought another surprise in Miss Hasenkamp's Metropolis initiation. Bulging amber eyes glowed, ogling her through the small bedroom window. While he sat on his heels to stare, the great jackrabbit bent one enormously long ear with a forepaw and scratched, leaving the other standing like an exclamation point. These fellows, the children later told teacher, could leap 20 feet at a bound and, running, make fools of wise old coyotes.

When Mr. Neely, the school principal, kept a blunderbus at school for the teachers, boarding house banter predicted Wild West sharp-shooting careers for Miss Hasenkamp and associates. Hazy delighted in the spirit that converted small things to laughter in the face of the relentless struggle with rabbits to get even slim pickings for Metropolis families from the drought-stinted harvest. The six-and-a-

half foot oat stands and fabulous Turkey Red wheat acreages recorded during the
project's first water-blessed years could have made them rich in war years. Thousands of rabbits fell to poisoning and shooting, but the "hollow belly" population
flourished.

Even so, announcement that school would be dismissed Friday so students *and*
teachers could help with a rabbit drive was a jolt. That sounded like brutal business
for children. Besides, what made Metropolis farmers think those slip-and-dodge
experts could be "driven"? Government agricultural authorities said they could.

Miss Hasenkamp said, "No."

Two husky young farmers exchanged glances over her head, picked her up,
and set her firmly on the back seat of the inevitable "Tin Lizzie." Presently, stick in
hand, she moved with a long, ragged line of men, women, and children, fanning
across the width of a 640-acre section to be driven. Rabbits leaped from every sagebrush as whacking, whooping beaters closed ranks to send them scrambling and
bounding along the wire netting wings of the great V-shaped trap, to be clubbed
to death by the men.

Autumn was brittle with chill, and rabbit hordes seemed undiminished when
L. F. Hatch received the letter from a produce company in San Francisco. Their
firm would pay 14 cents apiece for all rabbits shipped to them from Metropolis.
The pace of the weekly drives increased. So did the rabbits.

Snow swept down from Emigrant Canyon, and rounded canvas tops were shifted
from school wagons to sleigh beds. Nearly 100 farm children rode to school tightly
packed on the long benches inside the five sleds, and every sled was warmed by
its little wood-stove. Harness jingled and the driver's voice was a white puff in the
frosty air as he gave orders to the team through his small sliding window in front.

One last big one would have to shut down the rabbit drives for the winter.

About then, a "drummer" from San Francisco reported that those mangy Metropolis jacks were selling in a meat-short war market on fancy restaurant menus—
and for fancy prices—as "Nevada Hare."

Metropolites were incredulous. Tough as times might get, no Metropolite would
knowingly eat jackrabbit. But if San Franciscans wanted jackrabbits, jackrabbits
they should have. Between drives, men, women, and children stalked the pests
with guns and clubs and exchanged them at Mr. Astle's store for "a jackrabbit's
worth" of either goodies or necessities.

As winter neared, droves of gaunt rabbits blackened the snow nightly, fighting to get at haystacks already resembling giant toadstools where jacks, standing
upright, had eaten away as high as they could reach, tunneling them into collapse.
Not a wisp remained for ribby livestock when the winter moon turned away.

Cheers greeted the count when the final drive netted 1106 "hares" to be thrown, beheaded and drawn, into an empty room of the railroad station to freeze. Jubilation, too, anticipated the $10 bounty to be collected on the two coyotes that had popped up among the long-ears and were herded into the trap.

Only Hatch, his dark eyes twinkling, and Carlos Lambert, Extension agent, grumbled mildly over the record haul. They were weary of being left with the whole shipping job once the drive's excitement was over.

The lady schoolteachers generously offered to help whisk through that little task. After cold hours of holding gunnysack maws wide while the men crammed them with frozen rabbits, all the lumpy sacks finally lay in a great brown mound. The lady educators humbly took their aching backs and stiffened hands to bed. Then, in six AM blackness, came the cheerful "up-and-at-'em" cry of the rabbit shippers. Someone had to tag all those sacks. The school ma'ams could write, couldn't they?

All Metropolites, including the lady teachers, were at hand for the caper-cutting weekly dance when, with a resounding piano chord, it was announced that the final shipment had cleared $150.72.

"I move we give the 72 cents to them that sacked 'em—the teachers!" some joker shouted from the rear.

"I second that motion!" came Hazy's clear voice.

A burst of laughter and a lilt on Fred Calton's fiddle set the dance awhirl.

Natcherly Dumb

Opening Coon Creek Road over the summit to Jarbidge for the Fourth of July has been a point of honor with Jarbidge citizens ever since that upward looping mountain drag was built in the summer of 1911. Jarbidge traditionally hosts a tremendous fish or steak fry on the Fourth, inviting everybody within traveling distance. Only washtubs are big enough to hold the necessary amounts of potato salad and sheepherder beans. There are mounds of hot rolls, gallons of black coffee and the spirits flow as merrily as the snow water chortling down Bear Creek.

Consequently, in late June, to keep a sparkling reputation for hospitality untarnished, Jarbidgites have tackled granite solid snowdrifts, sometimes 10 to 14 feet high, with pick and shovel, dynamite and, in late years, mechanized snow removal equipment. Once, along about 1921 or '22 the road was burned open. That time, The Twins did it. "Natcherly," they said.

"People thought the Crisp Twins were kinda dumb, just naturally that way," Coley Brown mused, remembering the incident more than 40 years after he'd put in a stint working in the "Long Hike" mine at Jarbidge. "But I never could be sure about that."

The Twins, Jim and George, had arrived in Jarbidge along about 1910, when only pack trails snaked down into the bottom of the canyon already blossoming with tent houses like a field of mushrooms. By the spring of 1911, they'd staked claims north of Jarbidge Peak and near the head of Jennie Creek.

"Everybody else went to Jarbidge for gold, but The Twins never mined that I heard of," Coley said. "Mostly they cut logs off their claims, or leased 'em to somebody wanting to work." With a chuckle, too, Coley recalled the little dry farm The Twins homesteaded on the Diamond A Desert. "They figured on getting rich raisin' spuds out there and sellin' them in Jarbidge."

Jim and George were identical twins—middle-aged bachelors when they hit Jarbidge. In their blue and white bib-overalls and heavy, high-top shoes, with their sandy, straight hair awry, and candid blue eyes in wind-reddened faces, they looked "natcherly dumb." Nobody could tell them apart, and a standing joke in camp was the question of whether they themselves could or not. They said they could.

"Easy!" Jim (or was it George?) earnestly assured any questioner. "Ever since he taken to chawin' *Star* plug, and I chaw *Horseshoe*, if'n ye jes' look to see who's got which, there ain't never no mistakn' which is who."

They'd come from the Missouri hills to help build Twin Falls and the irrigation ditches, radiating out around it in southern Idaho, in the early 1900's. Neither could read nor write. They said they'd had a "commin school idjicashun," and they had never found that they needed more. They never had to sign their names to written contracts or promises. Their word was good.

Jarbidge would be The Twins' home for more than 30 years, until their death. And for a quarter-century after that, the legends built up around their long, loose-gaited figures were being retold to the joy of summer resort and hunting season visitors. More tangible mementos of the days when gold was king and Jarbidge not a summer resort, were sturdy timbers cut by The Twins to shore up now silent mines, and fine pine logs felled on the Crisp claims to help build the homes that replaced the tents.

But it was when they were fresh from the new agricultural development in Idaho that The Twins tried the spud venture on the Diamond A dry farm. They dug a well and put up a windmill, but it wouldn't pump enough water to keep green all the potato plots they had planted, enough to supply expanding Jarbidge for a year. About then, as Jarbidgites merrily remember one version, a windmill salesman came along. Craftily the fellow suggested that if The Twins dug another well and put up a second windmill, they'd have twice the water.

"Nope." Gravely as one, Jim and George shook their heads and explained, "'Twouldn't never work. They's just about enough wind to work thet one windmill good—sometimes not even that. They'd never be enough for two."

When the spud-growing flyer petered out, The Twins concentrated on logging. One day Jim took his false teeth out and laid them on a stump for a moment to rest his mouth. The Twins' teeth were by all odds the fanciest teeth in camp. In fact, they had so many gold crowns, so prominently displayed, that there was a rumor around that they were solid gold. Well, Jim and George got busy burning off some brush and forgot the teeth. Official records say more than ten million dollars in gold was taken out of the Jarbidge mountains, but this does not include that sifted out of the ashes by Jim and George that tragic day.

"Por ol' Jim would set there lookin' at me so miserble-like, havin' to gum his grub while I et," George explained later, "that it got so's I et in a hurry while Jim waited fer me to pass my choppers across the table."

Having one of The Twins toothless was no help in identification. They switched their single set back and forth, as they savored their "tobacky chaws" between meals. Catching one with a plug of *Star* or of *Horseshoe* in hand, continued to be the only way to know which was George and which Jim.

"The boys were all swarmed up in the bar, one night before the Fourth of July," Coley Brown recalled. "Don Steele was superintendent then. They'd done everything they could, but there was still one deep, narrow cut on that Coon Creek grade they hadn't been able to open. Snow packs in there like rock, 10 to 12 feet high, and the sun never gets to it.

"So this night, Don says, 'Boys, I'd give 50 dollars to anybody who'd get that road open before the Fourth!'"

Coley chuckled, remembering how as one man the Crisps had drawled, "Wal, Mr. Steele, if you really want that there cut cleaned, we'll do 'er—fer 50 dollars."

Don Steele looked at them and grinned, "Okeh, boys. You do 'er, and the 50's yours."

The evening wore on and The Twins stayed on in the bar, talking, listening, fooling around. When they did step out onto Jarbidge's one street, it was moonlight on Bear Creek summit at the top of Coon Creek grade, 2000 feet above them.

The next morning they were downtown early, sitting on the bench outside the store, watching the world go by, and someone said, "When are you boys gonna open up that road? The women's beginnin' to get the grub ready for the big feed."

The Twins looked at each other, then up at the summer sky.

"She must be about open by now," they reckoned simultaneously, and would explain no more than, "We done 'er natcherly."

"Well, Don Steele and a bunch of the boys went boomin' up there to see," Coley Brown continued. "Sure enough, that road was open! Them dumb Crisp Twins had gone up there the night before, rememberin' a big, old, dead pine tree astandin' on the high bank above the cut. They chopped it down so it fell along the top of that snow bank and set fire to it. By the time that big old dry pine had burned itself all up, the road was open. They got their 50 dollars. And that's why I never was quite sure about how dumb they really were."

DENNIS PARKS [B. 1936]

People in China, Poland, Hungary, the Czech Republic, Latvia, and Uzbekistan have heard of Tuscarora, Nevada, population 14. Why? Because Dennis Parks lives there, establishing the Tuscarora Pottery School in 1972. Internationally renowned as a ceramic artist, Parks has lectured, taught, or exhibited in the above countries and more, and his works have been purchased by museums in Italy, Belgium, England, and Russia. Parks is known not only for his art, but for technical innovations in the ancient craft of ceramic production, innovations that, like his life, favor simplicity and follow a scavenger ethic. Clay, for example, he procures with shovel and gunnysack from local tailings piles left behind from Tuscarora's mining days. He pioneered a time-saving technique to apply glaze to raw, dry clay and fire pieces a single time in a kiln fueled by recycled motor oil. His findings were published by Scribner's as A Potter's Guide to Raw Glazing and Oil Firing *(1979), which sold more than ten thousand copies worldwide, helping innumerable artists build their own kilns. So how did Parks end up in Tuscarora? That story is artfully told in* Living in the Country Growing Weird: A Deep Rural Adventure *(2001), a "funny, funky, and wise memoir" that shares the idealism and survival skills of a family who left the rat race for the quiet pace of a ghost town. Just as Parks often incorporates bits of local detritus into his sculptures,* Living in the Country Growing Weird *is a well-wrought, recycled conglomeration of scraps gathered in thirty years of Tuscarora residence—literary quotations, rural witticisms, newspaper clippings, photographs, recipes, epitaphs—artfully embedded in the clay of Parks's prose. "I think in terms of clay," Parks once remarked, "I dream of clay. . . . Ideas come into my head wet and soggy. I just firm them up a bit, glaze and fire."*

from *Living in the Country Growing Weird*

Summer 1972: Julie sang softly, and I steered east toward Nevada. Our two young sons, Ben and Greg, fought each other in the backseat. The car surfaced above the LA Basin at the summit of Cajon Pass; we would sleep the night in our mountain home. Yesterday was a simile for our tomorrow: the simple preindustrial life. A potter and his family scratching their message in the dirt. I could visualize the mountains and the sagebrush clearly in black and white or sepia, no neon and no blood.

. . . .

A long drive. From time to time Julie knelt on the front seat and ministered to the needs of our boys in the back: adjudicating questions of ownership, wiping a bloody nose, distributing bribes. I did not know what she was thinking, though I trusted that she had a better grasp of detail than I did.

I was staring at the broken yellow line on asphalt ahead and glancing occasionally at the speedometer below. No accident or arrest should slow us down. My attention drifted to the animals I would soon be acquiring: rabbits, chickens, ducks, geese, pigs and goats . . . and a garden with a compost heap here, fruit trees there, berry bushes and all. I had no original thoughts or survival skills.

From 1968 through 1972 I had been employed as an assistant professor of art at Pitzer College, a progressive liberal arts college southeast of downtown Los Angeles. Full-time faculty members were required to teach three classes one semester and two the next. Most colleges classify such a light load as part time. Pitzer also had a generous sabbatical program: the first was automatic after four years; subsequent sabbaticals came every three years.

I was promised early tenure when I returned. Job security appealed to a middle-class core while challenging what was left of rebelliousness in a thirty-five-year-old latter born. Julie is also latter born, and we agreed that tenure looked like a life sentence.

Recalling the slogan "If you're not part of the solution, you're part of the problem" eased my conscience as we left the crowds, smog, and traffic jams. Southern California, the land of contrasts: Disneyland and the Watts Towers; brush fires in Malibu and fire bombs in Compton; ghosts of Aimee Semple McPherson and Charles Manson cohabitating. The population was diminished by four.

. . . .

No map of the town [Tuscarora] existed, but my survey calculated eight city blocks defined by an unpaved grid of Gold Street, Silver, West Avenue, California Street, Argenta, Clay, Weed, and Main. Mostly empty lots covered in desert weeds, rusty machinery, vintage automobiles minus wheels, and the occasional stack of bleached, splintered lumber. A few colorful travel trailers and mobile homes, less than a decade old, interjected that certain modernity that precluded Tuscarora's value as a setting for cowboy films.

Shape rather than color was the memorable quality about the houses: small squares and rectangles with shotgun additions. A few with quaint false fronts, but mostly no-frills utilitarian. One or two had a veneer of flattened five-gallon metal cans shingling the walls and roof. After decades of little moisture the surface patina was reminiscent of contemporary skyscrapers in Cor-ten steel.

Architectural exception stood out. The tavern was a massive stone structure constructed from local rock. The hotel down the street had been moved twice from failed mine camps before reaching Tuscarora. This two-story building looked at home surrounded by a picket fence and towering Chinese elms and Lombardy poplars. On the far west end of Weed Street was a small elegant, high-ceilinged, red-brick home, best viewed from a block away. The front porch was only a skeleton, and the wooden addition out back had a collapsed roof. Uninhabited for half a century, yet emitting a whiff of potential. Definitely a fixer-upper town.

This town and the valley made me restive: the sunshine and the big sky, the quiet pace and potential.

. . . .

When I coaxed my family into moving high above pollution and population, gardening was in the back of my mind.

. . . .

I wasn't planning to stake my livelihood on gardening. I fantasized only a small fenced plot cultivated to fulfill modest physical and spiritual goals. Cycles of effort followed by idleness. Most of my time was to be spent watching little plants grow bigger.

> It's amazing how easily and naturally the inner springs resume their functioning once you surrender to sheer idleness. (Henry Miller, *Big Sur and the Oranges of Hieronymus Bosch*, 102)

. . . .

I selected seeds touted by catalogs to be precocious and tough: quick to maturity and frost hardy. My baby fruit trees and berry bushes arrived sealed in plastic wrap stamped with the guarantee "Good to thirty below zero." After I bought coils of water hose and an assortment of sprinkler heads, I thought I was prepared.

In *Living the Good Life*, Helen and Scott Nearing stress the importance of a cash crop. Theirs was maple syrup; mine would be pottery. Tuscarora could never attract many acquisitive tourists, but our family's wants were few. Over time a fiscal equilibrium established itself.

The processes involved in both gardening and pottery impose considerable down time: freshly thrown pots must dry a bit before being trimmed and more before being glazed and fired; in the garden even weeds need an undisturbed period to germinate. These respites allowed leisure time for me to explore in and around town and see what Nature was up to. Initially, I researched popular field guides to help identify the choice and edible from the nasty. Unfortunately these texts concentrated on plants growing in lush, humid climates. A few illustrations looked familiar, but black-and-white drawings gave this novice no confidence.

Fortunately my close neighbors were eager to teach.

"Have you seen those mushrooms coming up in the meadow?"

"No."

"You picked a mess of fuzzy britches yet?"

"No."

"Bushes up McCann full of chokecherries this year."

"Where?"

Knowledge of wild plants and topography of the area came as I examined samples on kitchen tables and watched maps being drawn on paper napkins. Nona, a widow, ex-miner, and ex-rancher, even told me the day and time when she would take me out and show me where everything was.

Three miles driving on dusty roads in an arc south and west of Tuscarora brought us to a halt at the edge of a step-over stream, McCann Crick.

"Boy, we're not fishing today, but there're some good holes . . . like there . . . back in those willows. Some morning you bring those boys of yours. All you need're worms. Won't bite on fancy bait."

Nona remained seated in the pickup shouting directions and pointing until I was standing by a mixed thicket of elderberry and chokecherry bushes. She noted that my trousers were entangled in primrose. "I'm going to show you what you do when the fish aren't biting."

Since none of the berries were ripe, she gave the approximate months when I should return to harvest and added very general instructions for making jam, wine, and tea. Before I walked back to the truck she pointed streamside to a patch of wild spearmint that she wanted picked.

Nona's Elderberry Wine

Loosely pack a clean clear-glass gallon jar with as many clusters of ripe elderberries as will fit. Pour over these two quarts boiling water. (Place jar in pan of warm water so that the boiling water won't break it.) Cover with plastic wrap then screw on lid one and a half turns. Set in a sunny place outside for three days or until all berries have risen to top. Strain and squeeze through a jelly bag and return juice to jar. Stir in 6 cups of sugar until dissolved, then 1 cup chopped raisins. Cover lightly again and set in warm place inside for three weeks. Strain through several thicknesses of cheesecloth and siphon into clean sterilized wine bottles. Cork lightly and leave until there are no small bubbles inside bottles. Cork tightly. Store for one year.

. . . .

Potential buyers can be intuited on sight because they do not arrive in period vw buses or on motorcycles. Also sales are rarely made to graying owners of motor homes or tobacco-chewing cowboys in pickup trucks hauling a horse trailer. For some years I also predicted the likelihood of a sale by the color of the arriving car. I discovered empirically, with no aesthetic or psychological underpinnings, that drivers of red cars were the most likely. Unfortunately, today touring the Western states is most often done in a rental; the driver has little or no choice of model or color. Travelers fly into Salt Lake City or Reno, sign up for a car, and purchase a guidebook.

Currently, the probability of a sale is gauged by the proximity of a parked car to my front gate. If the driver has stopped on our side of Main Street, close to the gate, prospects are good. If the car rests on the far side, but opposite the gate, the probability is strong. But any driver who parks two or more car-lengths away only wants to ask questions about my life in Tuscarora.

The historian Arthur Schlesinger says questions that no one has a right to ask are not entitled to a truthful answer. I agree with him if awkward questions come at me in a crowded cocktail party, but out here sophistication mellows and the threshold is lower for both asking and answering intrusive questions. My Tuscarora answers may be a simple yes or no, or a grunt, and Julie says that sometimes I give a flippant reply. But in all instances I am attempting to be honest.

Visitors usually pop questions after I have given them a free docent tour of the showroom up front and then guided them out back through the studios and around the kiln yard. We return to the front of the hotel by way of the long lawn I manicure on the north side. Mowing, fertilizing, and watering are justified on the theory that the bright green landscape distracts from the run-down wood exterior of the building. Visitors meander slowly among pedestaled sculptures on the path shaded by a mature apple tree. Questions begin:

1. "Why do you live so far away?"
2. "Were you born here?"
3. "You must like it?"
4. "Have you ever been to Pittsburgh?"
5. "Don't you ever get bored?"

"No," I answered to the last question. I have thought of elaborating with a string of my own questions: How could I get bored when I have no proper job? How could I get bored working in the studio making whatever whenever I please? I can stretch out on my sofa by a wood stove and read the weekly *New Yorker* from cover to cover before the next issue arrives, or explore above town looking for the makings of a salad, or spend my day with a fishing rod. How could I be bored when each day is filled with all those activities a regularly employed worker dreams of indulging in after sixty-five?

Only once when I was very impatient I answered, "Hey, if I want to get bored, I can buy myself a TV satellite dish." The visitor beamed and replied, "Really, so you can have entertainment up here. That's good." This encouraged me to revert to short answers.

. . . .

Naturally, I am taken aback when an outsider asks about my financial health. "You and your wife really afford to live year 'round here?" "And you raised children out here?" I speculate that there is some effect on seemingly decent tourists, perhaps the Big Sky and the quiet, that turns them into Peeping Toms.

I have thought to myself and spoken with Julie about what would constitute a complete and honest explanation. With close urban friends, who are too polite to ask, I still sense the submerged question: "How the hell do Parkses survive?" Rurals can appear aberrant to urban couples who are both employed at serious jobs with regular paychecks and have never doubted the prevailing American ethos that financial security buffered with weekends of popular entertainment is the basis of a normal, well-rounded life. Our old friends seem tolerant of others who have chosen a different road to travel, but on occasion I catch a hint that they detect an underlying recklessness, mild irresponsibility, and a possible self-indulgence. Other friends who aspire to personal goals less economic than most, but more spiritual than mine, refer to our family life in Tuscarora as being blessed. Both camps agree that those Parkses stumbled onto a lot of good luck.

Truth is we have survived from the sale of pottery and Julie's part-time employment at the post office and aided by summer student fees, which were not sufficient for salary but supported a year-round studio. Our combined income was probably never greater than that of a beginning public school teacher in Mississippi.

. . . .

During the Nixon era the government classified our income below the poverty line, and for two years in a row we received unrequested, supplementary income checks. The amount would not have saved the truly poor from hunger, but we were joyous for a little extra. Poverty is a relative term; we never felt poor.

. . . .

Our level of relative poverty probably did contribute to Ben and Greg growing up resourceful and independent. At the beginning of our first winter in the mountains, they disparaged the perfectly good, clean, warm coats Julie had picked out in a thrift store. The boys circled goose down arctic jackets in an REI catalog and would buy them with their own money, which they planned to earn after school by trapping muskrats in the Owyhee River. I had no experience that would help them in this enterprise.

Our neighbor, Butters, invited them across the street to a shed behind his house where he gave them a dozen small, vicious, steel-jawed traps and an introductory lecture on how to set them in action. Randy, the schoolmarm's husband, had given up on small animals in favor of coyotes and bobcats, and contributed additional small traps and also led the boys on a field trip down along the river, instructing them on subtleties.

Ben and Greg were in the independent fur business. The first Euro-Americans who explored northeastern Nevada were doing the same, but on horseback. Ben drove a Land Rover, and Greg, with legs too short, but wearing the longer irrigator boots, was responsible for wading into the water when emergencies arose.

They targeted muskrats, though occasionally a mink was bagged, and only once they intentionally trapped a beaver, which proved very tiresome to skin. Then by mistake they caught one mean river otter. Standard bait was a slice of apple, enhanced with drops of anise oil, impaled on a willow stick, which was stuck into the shoreline and overhung shallow water.

The little dead animals were skinned in our backyard and the pelts stretched on boards like inside-out stockings. Remaining fat was scraped from the skin, and then these hides were propped inside a shed to dry for several days before being stuffed into a gunny sack and mailed to a buyer in Salt Lake City. By late winter, Ben and Greg were wearing down-filled coats.

. . . .

Occasionally I would accompany them for an afternoon walk along the riverbank as they collected their bounty and reset traps. I watched Greg pull a trap out of the water which had by happenstance snapped shut on the tail of a small brook trout. The boys laughed and then Greg smashed the fish dead on a rock. Next he replaced the apple bait with an impaled fish. "Dad, you'll see . . . tomorrow I'll have a mink here."

The next day, sure enough, when they came home, in their sack of muskrats was one long mink. "I told you so, Dad," Greg said as they began the task of skinning. I stood around, curious to see them loosen pelts with a new technique they had just learned from a friend at school. Instead of laboriously separating fur from meat with sharp knives, Ben made just a small incision on a back leg and inserted a sports needle, the common variety used to inflate playground balls. A bicycle pump was activated, and the animal quickly swelled up double in size. Once deflated, with the pelt loosened from the flesh, only a minimum of cutting and scraping finished the job. A father raised in suburbia was astonished.

SOPHIE SHEPPARD [B. 1946]

An artist from a prominent family of artists, Sophie Sheppard is currently better known for her paintings than for her prose. Sheppard grew up in Reno, but never strongly identified with the city, which "ran on money, money with a capital M," preferring, instead, the Nevada backcountry that her father introduced her to on family camping trips. While still a girl, Sheppard spent three years traveling in Norway and France with her painter/professor father and sculptor mother, returning on her own to study at the Ecole des Beaux Arts in Paris before earning her BA from the University of Nevada, Reno, and master's degree from Central Washington University. She married and had a son, Jason, relocating throughout the West—twelve houses in eight years—for temporary university teaching jobs. After a divorce, Sheppard and her son returned to a rapidly growing Reno but felt pressed in by buildings and cement. In 1980 she and a friend, archaeologist Lynn Nardella, attended a barn dance in the northwest corner of the Great Basin. They stayed, married, and raised Jason in Lake City, California, near the Nevada border, a town of "sixty-two people and forty-two dogs." Sheppard continued her art, illustrating books and showing her paintings in galleries throughout the West. She is a dedicated activist, working on environmental and community issues in the northwest Great Basin. Sheppard's essays in Sharing Fencelines: Three Friends Write from Nevada's Sagebrush Corner *(2002; coauthored with Linda Hussa and Carolyn Dufurrena) represent a new medium for her, but she has discovered that "writing is like painting: you have to figure out what to put into the piece, how big it's going to be, where to put it, and what color it will be." The following selection is from* Sharing Fencelines.

Airspace

The jets had never come at night before. Nor had they come to town.

It was a summer evening. We were enjoying a barbecue at our neighbors,' Hugh, Sara, with the kids, on their deck that looked out over the valley. Everywhere, that peaceful, just-before-dark mauve glow and the whistle of the night hawks diving down out of the sky, falling, falling to the fields, then swooping upward at the last minute above the willow patch. Soaring, diving, swooping again.

It took a moment to figure.

Two military jets spiraling toward us in a screaming dogfight, a tight vortex just above our little town. The horses in the fields panicked, bolted, tried to outrun the sudden wall of sound that had surrounded them. They ran toward the teeth of the barbed-wire fences. Two-year-old Madeline opened her perfect pink-rosebud mouth, but her fear could produce no sound until Sara picked her up and cradled her. Even then, we couldn't hear her cries, masked by the howling jets.

Always before it had been in daylight and only when we were across the border in Nevada. One time when Tina and I and the children were riding back from the hot springs together in my pickup, I could see the three blond heads reflected in my rearview mirror. Jason and Tina's two girls sat in the truck bed, side by side, close to the cab. Creaking and rattling, we slowly bounced along the back road from Eagleville out to the Long Ranch on the Nevada side of the valley. Tina and I deep in conversation, were enjoying our time together.

Then the sound hit, at first barely audible over the complaints from the chassis of my old truck and the rumble of the worn engine. It seemed to come from no particular direction, was just suddenly there, an engulfing roar swelling louder, too fast for my senses to absorb. I glimpsed the jet coming up over the horizon, coming at us, low to the ground. At the exact moment that I saw it, the pilot must have seen us, for the jet took aim, veered, and dove toward us, head on. My body took over and I drove the truck off the gravel road down into the thick creosote brush. By then the jet had passed us by and my logical brain had engaged again as the roar receded behind us. I knew the jet wouldn't have hit us, but as it was happening . . . it was all too fast, too loud, too much. The kids were a little shaken but unhurt. I shook my fist ineffectually at the dot in the sky. And I got angry. Very, very angry.

It wasn't the first time. One autumn morning out on the Sheldon Antelope Refuge, Lynn and I had carried our first cup of coffee up a little knoll above our camp, seeking the early-morning sun. We sat sheltered, leaning against the rim-rock, above the frost, warming. Suddenly the desert morning silence turned into its opposite, the sound too loud, coming from where? from where? I remember looking down in disbelief, down from the knoll onto the top surface of the wings of the jet that was strafing our camp in mock combat, down over the pilot's head clearly silhouetted in the plastic canopy of the cockpit. There was something in his posture of a teenage boy crouched behind the handlebars of a fast, sleek motorcycle. Yet the sudden, overwhelming power of sound from his terrible screaming machine could not possibly be compared to a motorcycle. The jet was, after all, a very expensive machine designed for killing. At the instant of our understanding of the nature of this beast, the attacker was already gone. That time, too, we had shaken our fists at the departing speck in the sky. Don Quixote. Pathetic. Other military jets had buzzed Lynn's old red truck, the truck that we called the Tomato Can, because when we camped in the bed we made in the back, we felt like tiny cartoon mice tucked in all cozy inside a cartoon soup can. But that morning on the knoll I hadn't been as fearful or as angry as I was the afternoon on the dirt road. That morning it was just Lynn and I, just two mice; that morning I didn't have three children tucked in the back to worry about.

Everyone we knew who went out into Nevada to camp or to buckaroo told similar stories. Of camps used as targets in mock but nonetheless scary attacks from the jets. Of being knocked to the ground by a wall of sound. Of cows scattered over the scab rock, of horses bolting and losing a rider.

A few weeks after the incident on the knoll, Mary, a friend of ours who lived in the Smoke Creek Desert, called. She asked if I had heard the rumors about a new proposal for a military takeover of airspace. She was worried and I knew why. The jets were worse on their edge of that desert one hundred miles to the south of us. I had heard a rumor and didn't know what to make of it. We promised to let each other know if we learned anything more.

. . . .

Shortly afterward, Citizen Alert, a fledgling environmental organization from Reno, called to tell me that the air force was proposing a Military Operations Area, known as an MOA in the official parlance, just to the east of us. The MOA would extend from the Hart Wildlife Refuge in Oregon, down over the Sheldon Antelope Refuge in northern Nevada, and over a portion of the Black Rock Desert to the southeast. Citizen Alert sent us a copy of the one-page "Categorical Exclusion" prepared by the air national guard. The "Exclusion" claimed exemption from any environmental analysis. We scanned down that one meager page. In it was no mention of the treasures we know in that area, no mention of the towns, of the ranches dependent on the Nevada summer grazing. Nothing about the antelope or the sage hens. And nothing of the big silent sky over the high sagebrush steppes that open to the east of us.

A jet strafing the desert there would be as much a sacrilege as a hoodlum roaring around inside Chartres cathedral doing wheelies on a dirt bike. But with the exception of the Native American Sacred Places Act, our culture has yet to give legal recognition to the idea of sacred place in nature. After all, how could a wild, unimproved place deserve the same protection afforded a religious edifice?

We let our neighbors know about the MOA. We called all the friends we consider neighbors a hundred miles to the north, a hundred miles to the east, and a hundred miles to the south. We worried that the ranchers, often fierce in their patriotism, would think we were Commie-pinko-ratfinks in opposing the American military. I asked Bettie for her opinion. She told me more stories of cows scattered, of horses bolting while ranchers were out buckarooing in the rough country under the proposed new military airspace. My friend Pat, a teacher and local historian, told me of the flyboys and their flight-training runs during World War II and how they had strafed the antelope herds with live ammunition, decimating the pronghorn population in the Sheldon Refuge. How even then, during the height of fervent patriotism in the area, many in the valley had found the slain antelope hard to overlook and forgive.

I thought of all the empty fifty-caliber casings we had seen out there east of our valley in Nevada, the brass acquiring a turquoise-blue patina over time. Wherever we walked we would find a line of blue dashes spaced about twenty or thirty yards apart, a tracery of death drawn fifty years before.

On her ranch at the north end of the Black Rock Desert, Dale told me that her barn had been bombed once, killing their best milk cow. She said later she had picked up a fallen military parachute on their winter range. For years she had made silk cowboy shirts for all her kids, using Rit to dye that white silk every color of the rainbow. She chuckled then.

I learned that the ranchers might indeed be highly patriotic, but that many of them who had cows in Nevada had a highly jaundiced view of the military pilots. And their jets.

In August, Citizen Alert called Mary to request that she testify before the Nevada Legislative Committee on Public Lands concerning the impending takeover of yet another huge piece of the sky above Nevada. Mary asked if we wanted to go too, though we lived in California. She knew the ranchers in Surprise Valley depended on the range in Nevada for their summer feed and were in many ways more connected to Nevada's politics than to California's.

When we arrived at the capitol building in Carson City, we made a hurried detour to the ladies' room. We had driven the two-hundred-mile trip without the benefit of air-conditioning, and the day was hot. We needed to tidy up, wash our sweaty faces, and run a comb through our windblown hair.

I listened to the speakers scheduled ahead of me: some people from Dixie Valley. Located near Fallon Naval Air Base, this remote valley was much like ours and had had a Military Operations Area created over it several years before. I heard them tell of sonic booms that imploded windows, of cows run through fences. The stories sounded fantastic, but I had my own experience from home to give them credence. Now, they told the committee their land was being condemned. The military was extending its operations from the sky to the Dixie Valley floor. They were being forced to leave the valley and the lives they loved. It was obvious from the questions asked by the committee that they had seen these people from Dixie Valley before.

I had never spoken into a microphone. When my turn came after Mary's to address the panel, the tremor in my voice surprised me. I raced through the telling: the threat to ranchers' summer range, the intent to locate the new airspace over the Sheldon Antelope Refuge, the current low-level flight violations, how helpless we felt in the face of those violations and this new MOA proposal. I sat down with relief when I had finished my nervous, rapid-fire delivery. The committee chairman banged his gavel at the buzz of conversation that started up at the news of the new airspace proposal. He called an immediate recess.

The chairman collared us in the hallway of the legislative building as we were preparing to leave. He told us we needed to get our California legislators and county supervisors involved in fighting this thing. He offered to fly to Cedarville to help.

We organized a town meeting about the proposed MOA. We served cookies and coffee and listened to guest speakers from Dixie Valley who were determined to thwart the military's efforts to ruin more rural lives. More people in our own community were involved now. Our efforts had gathered some momentum.

Finally we received an answer from the air force to our inquiries about how to comment on their "Categorical Exclusion." That answer was the clincher. There was to be no further environmental analysis. There was no comment period to the "Categorical Exclusion." It was final. There was no way to get the air force to recognize the issues we had raised. *Yes, we could comment,* they said, *on the Federal Aviation Administration's (FAA) final decision. There would be a forty-five-day comment period. The FAA would allow comments to be made on their decision. But only on aeronautical issues. Environmental issues would not be considered.* We read that the only hearing to be conducted by the air force and FAA would be in Reno, far from any of us who would be affected. We wrote and called and complained. Finally the air force agreed to hold a hearing in Lakeview, across the state line, in Oregon, only a little more than an hour away for us and a four-hour drive for the folks in the Black Rock area or from the north around Denio. I called Mary. She called Carolyn. The telephone alert extended out across the desert.

When we arrived at the hearing, I was surprised to see the solid chain of cars parked around the block at the Lakeview Federal Building. So many had driven so far, all the way from the far-flung edges of the perimeter defining the huge airspace the military planned to take over: ranchers from California, from Nevada, and from Oregon, the whole vast area under the skies that the military wanted.

We asked the young air force captain who conducted the meeting why they needed to put the operations area over us. He answered that they had chosen it because nobody lived there. The moment he uttered it, he realized his mistake. There was a low, angry growl from all the people who had driven so far to come there to sit on the stiff metal folding chairs, filling that room, standing to overflow out into the entrance hall. We understood him to mean that nobody who *mattered* lived under the proposed MOA.

. . . .

Foolishly, we were elated at the end of the meeting. Our numbers and logic had won, we thought. We had shown up and shown them: people did live under the airspace the military wanted, people who mattered.

. . . .

Heading north for home, we top the rise at Sand Pass, the place where the whole length of the Smoke Creek Desert is suddenly visible. The pale-blue shadow of the Granite Range holds up the sky and keeps it from touching the north end of the huge playa. We like to take this road sometimes. The Smoke Creek playa can be treacherous. Compared to the white surface of the Black Rock playa, Smoke Creek is tan: it holds moisture in a different way. There is only one route across the playa that we know of. It is so seldom traveled that you have to look hard to see the faint track. It is easy to find yourself stranded here in the mud hidden under the dry salt crust, so we take the gravel road. It is poorly maintained, skirting the western edge of the dry lake.

There is usually no traffic up the gravel road. It is slower than the pavement along the Winnemucca Lake route, but here we can pull over anywhere to indulge our curiosity and wander on a whim.

As we drop down the rise at Sand Pass, we catch the glint of a windshield about four miles up the road. Another truck. We can see that it is stopped at the lowest place on the road, the place where the road meets the edge of the playa, a place that once tempted us to walk out on the flat surface, shimmering with mirages in the midday sun. But a few steps out onto the seemingly bone-dry cracks brought us back, our feet breaking through the crust, slipping, skidding, sinking into the hot, wet clay just below. This year the playa is even wetter. We can see the reflection of standing water.

We watch the truck pull away from where it had been parked at the edge of the playa. It heads in our direction and eventually passes us, a new silver-gray pickup driven by a couple of guys in their late twenties, early thirties. A loaded gun rack fills the rear window.

And when we reach the place where they had parked, there on the edge of the playa, we see the delicate bodies, the broken, shattered bodies of the avocets they had shot. Cinnamon, pearl, white, and black, the dead birds litter the damp playa. Red spatters glisten. Picked off, one by one, I suppose because they were there.

Imagine: in the desert how each life stands out, visible, so clearly outlined by what seems a blank, uninhabitable place. Life for the taking. Life to take for the sport of it. Life that couldn't possibly count. Mere targets. The wing of one lifeless avocet points skyward, into the empty, silent blue.

CAROLYN DUFURRENA [B. 1953]

Carolyn Dufurrena fell in love with Nevada as a college student, working with an archaeology crew from the Peabody Museum in Cambridge, Massachusetts. That summer of fieldwork, skinny-dipping in hot springs, and getting drunk at the Basque festival in Elko was "the antithesis of my safe, intellectual, urban life," Dufurrena recalls, and when she returned east she told her mother that she'd never really leave Nevada again. She earned a BA in geology from Wellesley College and an MS in geology from the University of Texas at Austin. Degrees in hand, Carolyn returned to Nevada as a corporate geologist for Exxon, looking for uranium and finding Tim Dufurrena, a bearded man with "the far horizon in his eyes." Thus began Carolyn's initiation into sheep and cattle ranching and, after their marriage, into the daunting job of rancher's wife, which includes cooking lunch for hungry work crews. In order to make ends meet on the Quinn River Ranch in Denio, where the Dufurrenas live, she returned to school yet again, this time to earn a teaching certificate and become a teacher in a two-room schoolhouse in rural Humboldt County. Dufurrena ranches on weekends, writes for Nevada *and* Range *magazines on the side, and is a guide for D & D Adventures, which she cofounded with her mother-in-law, Linda Dufurrena. Carolyn and Linda Dufurrena collaborated on a photo-essay book entitled* Fifty Miles from Home: Riding the Long Circle on a Nevada Family Ranch *(2002), which captures the rhythm, joy, and hardship of rural ranching. Carolyn's work has appeared in several essay and poetry collections, and she is coauthor with Linda Hussa and Sophie Sheppard of* Sharing Fencelines: Three Friends Write from Nevada's Sagebrush Corner *(2002), contributing thoughtful essays on rural weddings, raising her son, teaching school, making cherry pie, and testifying before government boards on behalf of ranchers' concerns.*

from *Fifty Miles from Home*

It is time for marking lambs, late enough in the spring for there to be snakes. On the road through the red canyon, someone has hung a huge dead rattler head-high in the sagebrush beside the road. His tail drags the earth, a warning to travelers—and perhaps a herder's victory statement.

The ring of sagebrush where we will mark the lambs is perhaps four feet tall, its walls as thick as they are wide. Living sagebrush grows in the walls, the manmade fence and the living desert woven together almost seamlessly. It is an oval ring high on a sloping ridge, built tilted into the rising sun, sheltering the animals inside it from the wind, warming them with the dawn. No one knows who built it, or how long ago. We use it once or twice a year. The rest of the time it is an artifact, a structure so subtle you might not even notice it when you drive by, in a place you would never drive by. It is the last of its kind, although there were once many like it in this country.

We sleep in cots, up off the ground, but not in tents this year. Canvas and heavy denim quilts cover our blankets and bedrolls to keep off frost. It is very early in the morning. Black silhouettes of family and friends who have come to help are backed with a few late stars against the clear purple of the coming morning. We dress quickly inside our bedrolls, stick our feet into frozen boots. There is no fire yet. We will eat after.

We spread out silently around the little cup-shaped basin, tilted to accept the sun's liquid warmth. The sagebrush oval is on the hill above us. We take positions in the tall, sharp-smelling brush, listening for the sheep. It is important to stay quiet, not to startle them as we turn them into the corral. We wait, and finally they come. The herder brings them slowly, just before the sun creeps down the red rock ridge. Dusky white shapes mutter to each other; brass bells sound in sagebrush. They move slowly, easing away from the human shapes standing silently, guiding them toward the corral. The sun pours light through the dust as they funnel through the gate, mill around softly, calling their lambs.

Our children comb the hillside, looking for dead branches to make the fire. It will keep the red branding paint liquid in the cold morning and warm their cold fingers and toes. They pile brush into a heap taller than they are, feed the little fire until it is roaring.

Below the corral is a series of small paneled enclosures, into which are funneled bunches of thirty or so sheep and lambs from the big pen for marking. This big bunch stays quieter this way, as the dogs and herders and kids don't go into the big pen as often through the morning. The young boys leap over the fences into the marking pen, wade thigh-deep through lambs, looking for the ones they can hold. The old Bascos stand outside the pen, their musical blend of English and Basque, Spanish and French a beautiful low murmur of language on the steam of their breath in the early sun. "A little frosty this morning," Frank always says, r's rolling.

And it always is. This is the day the sheepman learns how his year will go. How many ewes have twinned, how many lambs the coyotes and cougars have taken. Anticipation floats in the frosty puffs of breath above our heads. "Good-looking lambs," the Bascos say. "Big, stout lambs."

We line up outside the pen, behind the men who do the docking and castrating. They wrap adhesive tape around their thumbs, and face the holders, line up inside the pens in a sea of white wool. They are the only ones whose legs are warm. We give shots, stamp a red circle brand with paint between the lambs' shoulder blades. It goes on and on, trying to be quick, and still gentle with them. The holders' hands grow stiff and sore from holding thousands of squirming legs. We begin at dawn, finish when the sun is high. There are no breaks.

After the pen is empty of lambs, the ewes are counted out, to run anxiously for their children in the brush and grass nearby. The little cup-shaped basin echoes with the sound, mothers calling children, children answering.

Knives are folded, adhesive tape stripped from thumbs. The children bury empty vaccine bottles deep in abandoned badger holes. A second fire is kindled, near the paint fire. Loaves of French bread appear, home-cured ham sliced thin and wrapped in aluminum foil, chorizo, blood sausage from the front seats of pickups. There are hard cheeses, red wine. We slice onions into the huge two-handled sauté pan, cook potatoes, eggs. We stir the pan with long-handled spoons, turning our faces away from the heat of the fire. Voices rise and fall in Basque, French, Spanish. The docked tails are counted and checked and figured against the lines of numbers on a piece of cardboard box lid, representing the ewes counted out. Pete shows me how he learned to divide the numbers as a boy in the French Pyrenees. It is a mysterious, tidy algorithm, long division arranged around the quadrants of a central cross. We get the same answer, 125 percent.

Soon it will be clear how the rest of the year will go, whether there will be worry-creased foreheads or quiet celebration. One year it snowed at marking. One year the lambs were raked by a lion that came through the band the night before the marking, batting and playing until in the morning fifty of them lay dead. One year the front of the pickup was full of wobbly-necked babies gathered from the bed ground, their necks and heads oozing blood from the puncture wounds of bobcats. We took them to the ranch, to be bottle-fed and cleaned up, nurtured. Most of them died.

Marking time is a turning point. The lambs that come in to marking have made it through the first six weeks of life. They have survived the transition from April to May, from winter to spring, and have survived the desert, which will become their home. These are the lambs we count; we see roughly those ewe lambs that will be taken into the band, the wethers that will be fed this fall and sent to market. Marking is a look forward, and a look back. Each year we repeat our tasks, sometimes in another place, on a different day, variations on a timeless theme. Each year our children grow taller, our friends a bit frostier around the temples. The brush corral is mended and left till next year, the territory of ground squirrels and badgers, snakes and hawks. It will be there, the oval on the red rock hillside, changeless as the mountain.

· · · · · · · ·

The children of ranchers know what their fathers do all day, because their fathers take them along. They teach them the tools of their trade and how to use them. I watch my son tie a knot with leather saddle strings, slowly, methodically, the way you do something before it becomes second nature. I've never seen this knot before. His father has taught him. There are other lessons, some apparently trivial, some not: this is the way to coil your lead rope; work your horse through the herd this way. Gather cows across a flat like this. Never ride your horse through the bog after that one stubborn cow in the willows; get off and throw things at her. You might get in trouble here; go around the long way. Dad can see the places where trouble lurks. He's been in that bog up to his horse's chest, or his dad was once. The men weave a skein of knowledge and concern and jokes, punctuated by memory and the far vision that comes from looking down the long years on the land.

· · · · · · · ·

Women's territory tends to shift with the age of children. When the little ones are old enough to begin to learn the larger territory outside the house, it frees their mothers also. Maryjo drives the tractor on weekends, but the rest of the time she's teaching at her two-room school in Oregon or helping a little group of preschoolers at the Denio Community Hall. They come once a week to learn their colors, how to count, how to shape their letters. Hank's wife tends goats and the leppy lambs, drives the book mobile in town, reads meters for the local power company. I try to cowboy on the weekends when I'm not teaching school, and I write about the desert. Linda teaches photography and sells her images of this life all over this country and Europe. It's all quietly about survival.

Our family ranches are disappearing as surely as the carrier pigeon, with less fanfare than the leopard frog. There are fewer grandparents each year, fewer ranch kids who can afford to stay, or want to. Life is not always kind out here. But families, working together, learn who they are, what kind of men and women they will be, determined by the hardships, and the joy, of living here. Every decision has a consequence, every mistake its price.

. . . .

The desert is a difficult environment to live in and to nurture. It will flourish, but it takes patience and knowledge of when to act, when to wait in the shade until it's time to act. Each of us is nurtured, in our own way, by the deep rhythm of the seasons on the land, the motion of light on the hills, the simple joy of a season of rain after drought. We draw a kind of sustenance from the way a sagebrush flings seed, the manic growth of its offspring in a wet winter, getting the tiny start that will bring them through the hot months of summer, when everything seems to hunker down and wait.

Most of the desert is hidden inside time. It is not possible to see it in a season, maybe not in a lifetime. The waves of plant and animal life, the way wet seasons move boulders off the mountain, give a glimpse of a much larger pattern in the fabric, moving over our circle like shadows of ripples move across the sand in shallow water. Control of this land has long since passed from the people who have cared for it. Tom's ranch was taken for wildlife refuge, the Pine Forest lands for wilderness, Alex's home place passed into the hands of wealthy men who live far away. The vast majority of the land is public, controlled by the whim of politicians and, lately, the muscle of corporate environmentalism.

The powerful have always pushed the less powerful into history. We are a culture on the cusp of extinction, not just the ranching culture, but the culture that permits the generations to mingle, allows grandsons to work shoulder to shoulder with grandfathers. The relationship with the land has less to do with ownership than with covenant, as does the relationship between the generations. For these Basque people, a Stone Age people transplanted from ancient roots, the covenant with the new landscape is, in a sense, a continuation of the covenant with the old. The tenacious love of life and land, work and family, that they bring with them has responded to this empty place. And so the land owns us, not the other way around. We are part and parcel of the ridges and the soggy meadows, the dusty alkali and the storms that cross the emptiness. The circle of family continues, part of the landscape. The landscape feeds our circle, permits it to remain.

GREGORY MARTIN [B. 1971]

When Gregory Martin graduated from the University of Virginia with a BA in philosophy, he knew that he wanted to be a writer, and he knew that he wanted to write about Mountain City, Nevada, where he had summered with his relatives, but he didn't know what kind of book to write, and he didn't have formal training in creative writing. Undeterred, he moved to Mountain City, a dilapidated mining town located eighty-four miles north of Elko, whose population bumped up to thirty-four with his arrival. He worked for a year in his Aunt Lou and Uncle Mel's grocery store, scribbling notes on whatever scrap of paper was at hand—even on the back of produce slips—to capture nuances of conversation, character, and scene. Taking his sack of notes to Tucson, he earned an MFA in creative writing from the University of Arizona, mentored by the distinguished writers Richard Shelton and Alison Hawthorne Deming. His memoir Mountain City *is a prose mosaic, cast in a stoic tone that is paradoxically understated and affecting at once. Martin's portrait of this remote Nevada town and its elderly residents found a respected East Coast publisher (North Point Press, 2000), received eloquent endorsements from major western writers William Kittredge and Ivan Doig, and was catapulted to prominence when it was named a Notable Book of the Year by the* New York Times. *But perhaps the biggest compliment paid to* Mountain City *was from Uncle Mel Basañez himself, who likes the book, has since sold the store, and occasionally accompanies his nephew on book tours. Martin is currently a professor of English and creative writing at the University of New Mexico and is working on a novel.*

from *Mountain City*

My uncle Mel is telling a joke.

"This old Basco from Winnemucca got tired of herding sheep and decides to fly home to the Basque Country. He takes a seat on the plane, settles into it, and then a little before takeoff a stewardess comes over and says, 'Excuse me, sir, but this is first class. Your seat's back in row twenty-six.' But that Basco says, 'My name is-a Aitor Uberuaga, and I am-a going back to Bilbao. And I like-a this seat right here!'"

Mel's finger points down and pokes the checkout counter firmly, as if the store were the plane and the counter the seat in first class. Melvin Basañez is short, a little chubby, and has salt-and-pepper hair and a large, slightly hooked Basque nose. His accent now is that of his father, a man who at fourteen came from the Basque Country to northern Nevada to herd sheep. He came without speaking a word of English and in fifty years never learned to read or write. In fifty years he never once returned home.

"The stewardess doesn't know what to do, so she gets the copilot, who comes

out and says to the Basco, 'Sir, I'm sorry, but this seat has been assigned to someone else. Your seat's back in row twenty-six. It's a fine seat.' Well that Basco's pretty
steamed up by now. When they're off alone with all them sheep, they're not used
to getting bossed around. So he says again, 'My name is-a Aitor Uberuaga, and I
am-a going back to Bilbao. And I like-a this seat right here!'"

Mel's finger is this time pounding on the counter and his eyes are gleaming.

"So the stewardess and the copilot go back into the cockpit, and after a minute
or two, here comes the captain. The captain leans over and says something to the
Basco which the others can't make out, cause the captain's talking to him in confidence. Then, when the captain's done, the Basco nods his head, slaps the captain
on the arm, and goes back and takes his seat in row twenty-six.

"Now this surprises that stewardess and copilot, and they ask the captain,
'What'd you say to him that made him change his mind?' And the captain says,
'Well, now, you got to know how to handle them Bascos. I told him that *this* sec-
tion of the plane wasn't going to Bilbao.'"

The Frito-Lay man laughs, looking up from the jars of salsas and dips he's been
stocking. Gramps and I shake our heads, trying not to grin, and my aunt Lou turns
back to the produce case from the aisle where she was standing, listening. And for
a short while Tremewan's Store rests suspended in the atmosphere of the joke, the
same joke Mel told Jerry, the UPS man, the day before, and Bert, the school bus
driver, the day before that. It's eight-thirty in the morning in December, and no
customers have yet arrived. The soda pop case hums. Outside the two wide front
windows, in the store's reflected light, magpies gather on the opposite shoulder of
the highway where earlier Gramps scattered the day-old popcorn. The ignition of
the Frito-Lay truck catches, its diesel engine turns over in the cold, and the magpies startle into the predawn dark. Inside, Mel, Gramps, and I haven't moved from
our spots by the front counters, and Lou is the only one working at something, but
leisurely, picking out the tired grapes and placing them in the pocket of her green
apron.

· · · · · · · ·

My uncle Mel has a Basco joke for nearly every occasion, and he tells them so often
that they become highly refined. . . .

The Basco never makes out too well in these jokes. In a culture where much of
the humor relies on a more familiar race or ethnic group for the butt of its jokes,
and in a culture where these jokes are almost always told by someone from outside
that group, the Bascos provide their own butts for their own jokes. Case in point:
Lou recently won a horse trailer in a 4-H raffle. Lou and Mel don't own any horses
and neither has ever been a rancher. Lou just thought she'd enter to support the

4-H. When Lou found out she'd won, the first thing she said was, "Well, I don't have a horse, but I got part of one."

In response to this, Mel later said, "You know, it's not clear what she meant by that. She could have been talking about either a part of her or all of me."

Lou smiled and said nothing, which made it more clear.

. . . .

Mountain City is one mile long, limit to limit. Birch and golden willow shade the yards and porches of low framed houses and trailer homes, and rusted chain-link fences separate lawn from sage. In the meadow below town, the east fork of the Owyhee meanders north, past willows and ryegrass and fence posts and wire, and above everything, like a low, uneven wall, rounded hills rise up and circle the town, obscuring the view of higher mountains.

At the north end of town is Mountain City's "commercial district." Seven buildings. The Forest Service building, the post office, and the Steakhouse on the west side of the highway, closest to the river. On the east side, the Chambers' Motel, the Miner's Club, Reed's Service Station, and Tremewan's Store.

Highway 225 is Mountain City's Main Street, but no one calls it that. As it enters town, the highway slows and becomes Davidson Street, after a man who used to run a mining store in town before the turn of the century, before the bust and abandonment. The name is posted on a few white wooden signs, but no one uses that name either. People call it "the highway" or "the road." There are no stoplights and no stop signs. Eighty-four miles south, the highway ends in Elko, and there are no towns in between. North from Mountain City, it's four miles to the Duck Valley Indian Reservation, thirteen miles to Owyhee, the only town on the reservation, and sixteen miles to Idaho, where the road becomes Highway 51.

Thirty-three people live in Mountain City. I come and go, but when I'm here that makes thirty-four.

. . . .

Only a few people who shop regularly at Tremewan's Store pay at each purchase; that includes residents in town, the area's ranchers and miners, and the Indians from the Duck Valley Reservation. Customers keep a copy of their receipt, the store keeps a copy stapled in a book under the customer's name, and then most customers pay their bill at the end of each month. Some people, like the Thompsons and the Donnelsons, pay once a year in the fall, after they've sold off their cows.

The store doesn't accept credit cards—only cash, check, or Tremewan's Store credit. One older woman in town writes rubber checks for all her groceries. After she's gone, one of us takes the check from the till and staples it and the receipt to her page in the credit book. At the end of the month, Lou totals the checks and mails the receipts and a bill to the woman's sister in Reno. The sister pays the bill, and the process begins again. I don't know how long this has gone on. When she writes her checks, neither party to the transaction suggests by any comment or gesture that things are not entirely as they seem.

. . . .

Mel sometimes calls Tremewan's Store "Melbertson's." He employs supermarket lingo. "Glazed donuts are over in bakery," he says, or "You'll find that back in dairy," or "Let me ask the manager of our produce department." He cups his hands over his mouth and, in a loud, muffled voice, he imitates an intercom: "Louise, Louise, price check on aisle twenty-nine, Louise." He subjects customers to the same treatment: "Coleen James, Coleen James, come to the butcher's counter please, Coleen James. Your children are playing with the meat slicer." Coleen James, a Paiute woman who runs the Head Start program in Owyhee, is standing in front of the cereals, considering her options. Mel can see the top of her head above the Cheerios. Her children are hiding behind the meat counter, playing along.

. . . .

A wealthy, middle-aged California couple comes into the store. The man's wearing a suit, which, in Mountain City, is like wearing a Halloween costume. The woman is wearing more glittery ornaments than a Christmas tree. Her eyelids are mauve. She glances around, notes the rustic, provincial charm.

"I really like your little store."

"How much do you like it?" Mel asks sharply. His eyes narrow.

"Quite a lot."

"No, I mean, how *much*? There's a price for everything, you know. And me and the wife, well, we've been thinking about unloading this pork and beans operation, moving to the big city, soak up some of that culture you got there."

"No. Not really, would you?"

"Really. Would *you* be interested in this place? Free groceries. T-bone steaks every night." Mel is insistent, pushy.

"Well, no," she says, her enthusiasm gone. She doesn't understand Mel's tone.

"Oh. Oh. Okay. Just thought I'd ask." Mel nods knowingly to himself, like he's just proven a point.

The couple buys two bottled waters and then they leave.

"Did you see me give her the old 'aw shucks' routine?" Mel asks me.

"I saw it."

"You don't like that too much, do you? You think it's mean."

"I didn't say that."

I've seen Mel do this before. He doesn't do it too often, because he knows it drives away customers, but at times he can't seem to help himself.

Over the past few years, for some reason, I've taken to playing the role of Mel's conscience. We have these conversations frequently, where Mel asks me, "You don't think I should say that, do you?" Most of the time, I'm righteous in my responses, indignant, as if my uncle needs "civilizing," and I'm the one for the job. Sometimes, after Mel says something insensitive, he looks my way slyly, and winks. He's trying to get a rise out of me, to see if I'll jump on my soapbox.

But in this particular case, I didn't like the couple any more than Mel did. I had already imagined them back at their gated community, saying, "You should have seen the quaint country store we discovered in Nevada," as if the store, and our ingenuous, uncomplicated lives in it, existed solely for their aesthetic pleasure, for their sentimental appropriation.

. . . .

At five o'clock each day Mel pours his first highball into a tall, clear glass. Ice, Black Velvet, 7UP from a small seven-ounce can. He drinks behind the butcher's counter. He sets the glass on the polished top of the stainless-steel meat grinder, and he slices ham, baloney, cheese. He packages hot dogs or hamburger. He sips whiskey. A sign Mel has hung on the wall behind him reads, NO WORKIN' DURING DRINKIN' HOURS. It's a rule he can't follow. He'll pour a second drink before we close at six.

If Kenny Kohones or Larry Otheim or any one of a few other men happen to be in the store in the hour before closing, Mel will pour them a highball, without offering, and set it out for them on the meat counter. The two men will drink and chat, and Larry or Kenny or whoever will stand a little to the side so Mel can take orders. One such time, as Lou walked past the men on her way to the front, she muttered, "We ought to get barstools."

Mel called after her, "I want the kind that spin around."

. . . .

Mice are a problem in Mountain City. At my grandparents' place, they run between the apartment walls and up above the ceiling tiles. Some nights at dinner, when the mice start scampering above us, Mel says, "And . . . they're off!"

. . . .

Tremewan's Store has its own mice troubles, but Mel looks upon the matter philosophically:

"Animals have all the time in the world. *That's* why they're so mischievous. They don't have anybody telling them to get something done by noon, or to be someplace and not be late. They can just work at a problem until they get her done. Take the mice we get in the store here. The Macaroni Bandits. They know we got the place sealed up pretty good, but that don't worry them. If it takes them all day to get through the floor and into the macaroni, that's just fine. They're not punching the clock. Take the cows out in the meadow. They only hustle around when Jim's out there hollering at them to get a move on, and his dog's nipping at their heels. Mice, on the other hand, having never been domesticated, don't have that anxiety. They don't stand around worrying about mousetraps and all the things they got to get done before their number gets called. That's an advantage.

"Animals excel at relaxation. Sure they work at surviving. But when that's squared away, they let up some. Not us. We always have to be doing something. Producing. Time's money. I've got it figured out. I've been studying this. I know it doesn't look like it, but I have. Pretty soon I won't be wearing this green apron every day. Stick around and watch. Pretty soon this Basco's gonna start exercising his animal nature."

SIX

A GATHERING OF COWBOY POETRY

I magine eight thousand people converging on a small cow town in northeastern Nevada in the middle of winter. Temperatures may not climb above freezing, and snow piles mound up several feet tall. They come in planes, trains, and automobiles—oh, and pickup trucks—from points throughout the American West, some from the East Coast and Canada, and a smattering from abroad—Germany, Switzerland, and Australia, even Mongolia. Along the town's main street, hotels and motels big and small flash NO VACANCY signs. What on earth could induce so many people to make such an effort to get to Elko, Nevada, in late January, early February? The superabundance of cowboy hats is a clue. Yes, these folks are here for the annual National Cowboy Poetry Gathering. At the heart of the Gathering are ranchers, who look forward to this week in winter, when ranch work is slow, to get together, confabulate, and listen to recitations of poetry that springs from the rugged work of ranch life.

Cowboy poetry could be considered a subgenre of rural literature, but whereas much rural literature is written by transplanted city folk for urban readers, cowboy poetry is by and for ranch folk. Furthermore, in the beginning at least, it was not written down. It was not even called poetry. Cowboy poetry is an oral tradition, a folk art, if you will. It originated shortly after the Civil War on the long cattle drives from Texas to points north, mostly to railroad shipping yards in Kansas and Missouri. These drives took several months—dust-eating, fly-swatting, shirt-sweating, manure-smelling, saddle-creaking months—during which cowboys would entertain one another by telling stories around a campfire. Stories were more easily remembered and enjoyably repeated if they were set to rhyme. A simple four-line ballad verse form, with a regular beat and rhyming couplets, lent itself well to memorization; thus evolved traditional cowboy poetry, much of which traveled from cow camp to cow camp anonymously, its original author forgotten.

Folklorists were the first to collect and record these work poems and, later, to organize the first Cowboy Poetry Gathering in 1985. When folklorist and organizer Hal Cannon and his cowboy poet friend Waddie Mitchell were getting things ready that first year, they felt sheepish setting up two hundred chairs, a number that seemed wildly optimistic. Waddie told Hal they should take some of them down. To everyone's amazement five hundred people showed up for that first gathering, a hundred poets and about four hundred friends. The event was covered by national magazines, with playful headlines such as *People Weekly*'s "Out Where the Sages Bloom, 120 Rhyme-Stoned Cowboys Show How the West Was Spun." The Gathering was repeated the following year and has become an annual tradition, pumping an estimated seven million dollars into Elko's economy and inspiring 150 spinoffs throughout the West. More important to participants, however, the Cowboy Poetry Gathering gave the cowboy culture a voice and boosted morale. Cowboys are an American icon, thoroughly commercialized and mythologized, but most people have little idea of who real cowboys are or what their work entails, how much skill it demands but how low-paid it is.

The Elko gatherings have created a renaissance in cowboy poetry, stimulating the production of new poems, anthologies, albums, and Web sites and encouraging the emergence of talented women poets. Experimentation in subject and form have generated lively debates within the field about whether cowboy poetry must rhyme, whether its subject must be ranch life, whether its authors must be cowboys, whether the poetry should be intended for recitation, whether cowboy poetry is folk art or art, and whether cowboy poetry is evolving or has lost its way.

Perhaps because cowboy poetry is essentially a poetry of vocation, and because cowboys themselves may work for many outfits throughout the West in their lifetimes, cowboy poetry tends to lack reference to specific places, making it difficult to find poems with clear Nevada settings. The poems collected here are by poets who have ranched in Nevada and most of whom have recited their work at the Cowboy Poetry Gathering in Elko. The poems represent a wide range of styles and themes, from traditional verses about horses, cattle, and nature's beauty to more recent poems with a political edge. They give outsiders a feel for the life and values of the cowboy way, and they help urban readers reconnect with their roots in the earth.

OLEPHIA KING [1905–1988]

"I've always been glad I was raised a cowgirl out on the range," writes Olephia "Leafy" King. "The freedom that exists on the range of Nevada, Nature's beauty, the wide open spaces have a tendency to live on, and flow deep in one's blood, once you have known the contentment of outdoors life." Leafy and her sister, Emma, were raised on the Barley Creek Ranch, in Monitor Valley, ten miles east of the old mining town of Belmont. King attended a few years of school in little country schoolhouses with her Indian friends but got most of her tutoring directly from nature, observing deer, chipmunks, birds, and wild horses, delighting in spring wildflowers, drinking in the beauty of brilliant sunsets, and gazing out atop her horse from the rimrock to contemplate God's country. Although remote from world events, there was never a dull moment, King recalls, and she wouldn't have changed places with a millionaire. There were exciting spring and fall roundups with one's spurs jingling against the sagebrush, the delicious smell of beans and bacon from the chuckwagon, songs and stories around the campfire before rolling out the bedrolls for a night under the starry sky. There were scary encounters with rattlesnakes, exhilarating races with wild mustangs, and the fun of getting caught in a hard thundershower. King's poetry, most of which was written when she was a grandmother, living in Fallon, preserves the precious memories of her girlhood on the range. Her first book, Western Poems *(1965), illustrated by herself, was so popular that it went into a second printing, and she was encouraged by friends and family to write another book, publishing* Western Poems No. 2 *in 1967. Her books predate the first Cowboy Poetry Gathering of 1985 by twenty years, making her a precursor of the revival of this art form.*

The Dappled Grey Mustang

"Snap" was a dappled grey cowhorse,
　　Just a mustang from the Monitor range.
　　　　So fast he could turn on a pancake,
　　　　　　But his old mustang ways wouldn't change.

One ear tipped back as he watched you,
　　From the corner of one snappy eye,
　　　　No wild range cow could out run him,
　　　　　　But the worst fault he had was to shy.

I slapped my rig on him one morning,
　　And busted him out down the flat.
　　　　His long mane waved like dark silver,
　　　　　　His trim legs were quick as a cat.

I was trailing a bunch of wild range cows,
That had broke down the cross fence that night.
A high horned bunch of old Herefords,
When I jumped them they got on the fight.

They took off in every direction,
Their fat curly calves bucked and played.
I was turning the lop horned old leader,
Of that wild ornery bunch that had strayed.

As we raced through a clump of scrub sagebrush,
A rattle snake buzzed near "Snaps" feet.
He darted out swift as an arrow,
I felt my self leaving the seat.

I had lost my old right stirrup,
Was hanging far down on his side.
Could feel the wind of his hoof beats,
Sure thought that would be my last ride.

I clung to his mane and the saddle,
Far down near his fast mustang feet.
I must have done some trick riding,
Some how I swung back in the seat.

I thanked the Good Lord for kind favors,
It still was a mystery that day,
Just how I got back in the saddle,
On the back of that fast dappled grey.

My old flop hat had gone rolling,
In the brush where the big rattler hid.
Both me and that mustang were spooky,
As we sneaked back to rescue my lid.

Once again we turned those wild Herefords,
And headed them homeward again.
Even the green fields looked greener,
As I turned them in Barley Creek lane.

"Snaps" nose sort of rippled the water,
    As he drank from the cool mountain stream.
        The ride that had seemed like a nightmare,
           Fled away like a bright sunbeam.

I pulled off my saddle and bridle,
    Tied "Snap" near the old barn door.
        I could hear him nicker so softly,
           As I filled up his manger once more.

He rubbed his sweaty head on my shoulder,
    As I stroked his dark silver mane.
        That mustang knew I still loved him,
           And we'd both roam that old range again . . .

R. GUILD GRAY [1911–1998]

"He had a mad love affair going with the state of Nevada," observed one of Gray's friends after his death. Gray's family moved to Nevada in 1913, when he was just two years old and when Nevada's population averaged less than one person per square mile. Gray grew up with the state and helped to shape it, earning numerous honors and having an elementary school in Las Vegas named after him. With the exception of years spent in the navy in World War II and time at Stanford University, where he earned a doctor of education degree, Gray lived and worked in Nevada for the better part of a century. Known as "a dead-square, level man," Gray held a wide range of jobs, beginning at age sixteen when he rode a mule named Nicotine, working for a survey crew that chained off the state into thirty-six-square-mile townships. Gray went on to be a teacher and principal of Reno High School, the first school superintendent of the Clark County School District, a state legislator, and manager of Boulder City. In addition, he chaired the committee that established Nevada Southern University, which started as a one-room schoolhouse and evolved into UNLV. Complementing Gray's active civic life was his avocation as an outdoorsman and writer. When not working, Gray could be found exploring the mountains and valleys of the Great Basin, taking the photographs and writing the poems that are collected in his book Nature Sings: Great Basin Scenes with Verse *(1996). In 1998, just before his death, Gray was a featured poet at the Cowboy Poetry Gathering in Elko. He also wrote an epic-scale historical novel,* The Treble V: The Legacy of a Cattle Baron of the Old West *(1986), spanning three generations of a pioneering Nevada ranch family in the Ruby Valley.*

In Defense of Cattlemen

The cattlemen don't rape the land,
At least the ones I know.
They've spread the streams that sank in sand
To make their grasses grow,
Then shared their fields with hungry deer,
Wild antelope and hare.
Their reservoirs hold waters clear
For ducks and fish to share
Their windmills make life possible,
As even quail can tell
That live in lands untenable
Without a rancher's well.
Their fields of crested wheat grass, greens
What once was sage and sand;
And in so changing desert scenes
Make useful, feral land.

Extremists have befuddled minds,
At least the ones I know,
Especially 'vironmental kinds
Who worship status quo—
A status quo of their design
Where men would ever be
Subservient to a place and time
They'd choose from history.
The cattlemen must go they say
Because the Western range
No longer is just like the way
It was ere human change.
How thoughtless of them to ignore
Earth's ever changing scene.
How foolish of them to deplore
Man's place in Nature's scheme.

JACK WALTHER [B. 1919]

Jack Walther has worked and owned cattle ranches in Elko County all his life, having been delivered by a midwife back in the years "before calendars were made." His sense of humor and storytelling flair have made him a local favorite and a featured presenter at the Cowboy Poetry Gathering in Elko. He and his wife, Irene, raise registered Red Angus cattle—"Ruby Red Angus"—as well as Suffolk draft horses, and they enjoy restoring buggies. Walther has always used a horse-drawn wagon to feed his cattle in the winter, and he enjoys a national reputation as a saddle-horse and workhorse trainer. The more printable of Walther's poetry is published in his book Ruby Mountain Rhymes *(1987). His contentment is well expressed in "Ruby Mountains," which begins, "I am a part of this range of waving grass, / Part of the evening breeze, the gentle rains that pass. / I am the horse or range cow that moves out there so free, / Deep down within, they seem a part of me." While "Ruby Mountains" is reverent, the poem reprinted here displays Walther's humorous side. As Walther tells the story, a retired professor who "had it all figured out" bought some land near Walther's ranch. Dreaming of self-sufficiency, the professor bought goats for meat, horses for power, and some longhorn cattle (supposedly low in cholesterol and requiring minimal feed), and he planted a garden and fruit trees. The goats got into the garden and ate up the trees, one of the horses died and the other balked, and a longhorn bull jumped a fence and mingled with another neighbor's cows. The professor asked Walther if he thought the neighbor would mind about the longhorn bull. Walther replied that, oh, he probably wouldn't mind since he had a good roping horse and a pocket knife.*

The Longhorn's Short Career

> If my lot was to be a longhorn bull,
> I would live my life complete and full.
> There are heifers in the field next door.
> I must be what they are waiting for.
>
> A fence between them and me?
> It doesn't seem that this should be.
> A fragrance of such depth and surge
> Gave me a very determined urge.
>
> Nature's urge was so intense
> In one big leap I cleared that fence.
> Then I was happy as could be
> Doing what comes naturally.

Two riders came in on a lope,
Swinging each a long strong rope.
On horn and heels I felt their sting.
They're stretched out tight as a violin string.

An operation soon was done.
I heard them say, "We'll stop his fun."
My career is over. This I fear,
Unless to be a Marlboro steer.

I did what I felt I had to do.
The neighbor is mad, my owner too.
When I look back it makes no sense
Why did I ever jump that fence?

Because of man's temper and rage,
My life has turned a sad sad page.
Man's anger on me has been spent,
But look, those heifers seem content.

GEORGIE CONNELL SICKING [B. 1921]

*"I've spent a lifetime of doin' things that couldn't be done," observes Georgie Sicking. Given a boy's name and raised like a boy on a rough ranch outside of Kingman, Arizona, Georgie learned to ride a horse by age two and was moving cattle by age three. To mount her horse, she threw a biscuit on the ground, and when Buster lowered his head to get the biscuit, Sicking climbed on his head, and crawled up his neck. It wasn't easy to be "a mare among the geldings," but Georgie continually proved her worth by doing all the things a "top hand" was expected to do—break horses, herd and doctor cattle, brand and castrate, mend fence, shoe horses, rope and tie cows, and gather mustangs. Furthermore, flouting warnings that no man would marry a tomboy, Georgie married Frank Sicking—she met him at a rodeo—and they had three children. In 1954 she and Frank bought a ranch near Fallon, Nevada, which remained her home for more than forty years. As a girl, Sicking began to write poetry with a stub of a pencil on any scrap of paper she could find, including an old feed bag, continuing this practice throughout her life. She was chosen to represent Nevada at the first Cowboy Poetry Gathering in Elko, in 1985. Three collections of her poetry have been published—*Just Thinking *(1985),* More Thinking *(1992), and* Just More Thinking *(2004). She was the first woman in Nevada to be inducted*

into the Cowgirl Hall of Fame, she won the Gail Gardner Working Cowboy Poet Award, and
she was presented with a plaque by the Nevada Cattlemen's Association for 100,000 miles on
horseback. At age eighty-one she was still taking part in cattle roundups.

Nevada's Subtle Beauty

Did you ever see a dusty trail just weavin' and a'windin'
Made by a car or pickup goin' across an open valley
To a ranch or mine location many miles from town?
If you have, my guess would be, you could be in Nevada.

Have you ever watched the mustangs comin' in to water
For miles and miles a'walkin.' And the dust behind them risin,'
And seen their manes and tails a'wavin' against a settin' sun?
The sight sets your pulse to beating, and you will long remember
Nevada is the state you saw it in.

Have you gone outdoors one morning after a summer rain,
With a gentle breeze blowing across a black sage valley
And smelled the earthy sagey freshness, none like it on this earth.
It sure makes life worth livin,' and you know when God was givin,'
He didn't short-change Nevada.

Have you ever in the afternoon watched the mountains changing colors
From the shadows as they grow from brown and black and tan to violet,
Or sometimes the deepest blue.
Ever changin,' ever different, they seem to smile, then frown,
Waitin' for sky colors to be added as the sun goes down.

If these things I mention you have seen and felt and known,
"Beware," for Nevada has a hold on you, and will claim you for her own.

ERNIE FANNING [1935–2006]

Although few people these days are ranchers, just about everyone has felt the effects of change.
Witnessing the "cows to condos" transformation of the landscape makes cowboys shake their
heads and lament the disappearance of natural beauty. Ernie Fanning's "Vanishing Valley,"
collected in Hal Cannon's Cowboy Poetry: A Gathering *(1985), reminds us that the Truckee*

Meadows were once meadows. *Another poem by Fanning, "One Red Rose," recalls a vanishing way of life and gives thanks for being able to see and do things that his grandchildren will never see: "I've seen 5,000 head of steers / Stretch for miles and miles, / . . . Or just watch a bunch of mustangs / When they leave a water hole, / Or set on the edge of a crick / With an old skillet and pan for gold." Ernie, who learned his first poem at age six and began writing poetry at twenty-nine, lived in northern Nevada from 1948, and for many years he owned the 102 Ranch in the Carson Valley. Until his death in 2006, he lived with his wife, Kay, in Gardnerville and earned a living by breaking and training carriage and draft horses and building horse-drawn vehicles, carts and wagons, for his Classic Carriage Company. Fanning was a popular performer who was featured at the Cowboy Poetry Gathering in Elko and appeared every November at the Carson Valley Inn's Rhymers Rodeer. He and musician Tony Ilardi teamed up as the Grubline Riders and performed throughout northern Nevada. Fanning made a tape of his poetry, entitled* Beatin' the Brush with Ern & Friends, *and he wrote a monthly column under that byline for the Gardnerville-based newspaper* Horse Tales.

The Vanishing Valley

Out on a Nevada mountain
While lookin' for his stock,
A cowboy stopped to rest his horse
A-top a big rimrock.

And as he set and looked
At the valley floor below,
He asked himself this question:
Where the hell did the valley go?

Whatever happened to the fields of spuds
And onions that the old degos used to raise,
And where have gone the lush green meadows
Where the fat cattle used to graze?

For as he set and looked down
Through the smog in the shimmering summer's heat,
What filled his vision most
Were mounds of steel and gray concrete.

And he knew there was no way to slow,
Much less halt,
The spreading of the buildings
And the ribbons of asphalt.

He could still remember when every man
In the valley helped pull his neighbor's load,
When Kietzke Lane was nothing more
Than a gravel country road,

When they drove fat cattle from the Humphrey lots
to the shippin' pens at Stanford Way.
Oh yeah, Cowboy,
But that was yesterday.

Well the cowboy stepped across his horse
And he started to the valley floor below,
And once more he asked himself a question:
Why the hell did this valley have to go?

LINDA HUSSA [B. 1941]

*"Each of us—if we are lucky enough to find our home country and community, the place where
we belong—must do what we can to return the gift," writes Linda Hussa in her introduction
to* Sharing Fencelines: Three Friends Write from Nevada's Sagebrush Corner *(2002). Hussa,
born to horse trainers in eastern Oregon and raised in Walnut Creek, California, found her
home place in Surprise Valley, California, just over the Nevada border, on the edge of the Great
Basin. She and her husband, third-generation rancher John Hussa, work side by side raising
cattle, sheep, horses, and the hay to feed them. Linda Hussa has given back to the "sagebrush
corner" through her community involvement and her writing, which conveys a powerful sense
of place and deep respect for the people who live there, giving voice to an area that many
Americans assume is uninhabited. While Hussa writes about ranch life and has been a featured poet at the National Cowboy Poetry Gathering in Elko, her work cannot be pigeonholed
as "Cowboy Poetry" in the narrow sense of the term. Hussa's themes are universal, and she
prefers to think of her work as poetry or, perhaps, "Poetry from the Land." Hussa was invited
to read at the Library of Congress in 1994, and the Nevada Writers Hall of Fame presented
her with the Silver Pen Award in 1999. Hussa's biography* Lige Langston: Sweet Iron *(1999), a
creative blend of oral history, storytelling, and poetry, pays tribute to the extraordinary skill
and integrity of a Nevada buckaroo who was born at the turn of the century on a homestead
at Duck Flat. Her third collection of poetry,* Blood Sister, I Am to These Fields *(2001), won
the Wrangler (National Cowboy and Western Heritage Museum), the Spur (Western Writers
of America), and the Willa (Women Writing the West) awards.*

Ride the Silence

This land asks for quiet passion.
The surface still,
beneath   a thunderous shake
of underground rivers grinding
through bed rock of the earth's own form.
No one knows the torment knotted,
gnarled beneath their daily feet.

Life on this land where we tend stock
against relentless heat and tearing storms
must be steady.
We ride the crust of earth with its hot arteries
flowing molten stone and we are calm
we are silent and watch the land as a placid sea, biding
agonies that will undo blouses and trousers of the depths.
Passion chained back
when ice storms blow snow down throats of cows—
they drown on white and frozen land,
or sickness cuts the tally,
or men of power bleed the poor ones pale.

The torture turns passion to petty heights,
pulls the juice,
the raging juice that lies below—
lets it loose when night comes
and no one hears the back door close.

ERIC SPRADO [B. 1945]

Home meant Nevada. There are those who couldn't afford to stay. Eric Sprado's "Wait 'til You Become a Man," published in Hal Cannon's New Cowboy Poetry: A Contemporary Gathering (1990), has become a well-known poem in cowboy poetry circles because it so effectively conveys the precariousness of ranch economics and the pain of defeat. Ranchers have always had to contend with vagaries of weather, drought, disease, and fluctuating markets. On top of all that, today's ranchers face pressures from changing federal grazing policies, land develop-

ers who drive up real estate prices and subdivide the range into ranchettes, and urban envi-
ronmentalists who want cattle removed from public lands. All these forces make ranchers an
endangered species. Eric Sprado speaks for the cowboy who was forced off the range. Son of a
German father and Russian mother, Sprado was born in an immigrant community on the East
Coast but grew up on desert ranches near Anza Borego, California. Sprado became a skilled
horseshoer and worked as a farrier for the Kansas State Vet School before moving to Montana,
Alaska, and in the mid-1970s, Nevada, where he bought a remote ranch between Wells and
Ely and named it the Plumb Bob. Sprado participated in the Pioneer Arts and Crafts Folklife
Festivals in Elko, precursors to the Cowboy Poetry Gathering, where he has also performed as
a poet and musician. Harsh economic conditions forced him to sell out and move on in 1982.
Since 1991 he has worked as a real estate broker representing buyers, based in Eugene, Oregon,
specializing in rural properties. Sprado also cuts a memorable figure as a fiddle player and
vocalist whose towering form animates a country-swing band called the Leftovers, which has
played together for more than a decade, releasing its first disc, Entrée, *in 1998.*

Wait 'til You Become a Man

I remember seeing men
Who lost their farms in the thirties—
Deep lines and haunted looks
Carved into those faces.

Why do those men look angry and sad?
I asked as a little boy.
You're too young to understand, son;
Wait 'til you're a man.

I grew up and forgot that look.
Good times were here to stay.
Drifting around, having fun,
Still, putting money away.

Finally, my dream come true.
A ranch of my own.

In harsh sagebrush country,
Hot in the summer, cold in the winter,
A country that makes you feel big and small,
Covered with alkali dust, I could
Break off a piece of sagebrush and say,
    "I love you."

Herding cows in a blizzard, I could
Lay back my head and
    Laugh like a madman.

Now it's gone.
The deep, deep lines and haunted look
I think I understand.
Maybe I've become a man.

WADDIE MITCHELL [B. 1950]

Waddie Mitchell is the man on stage with the twinkle in his eye, the flamboyant handlebar mustache, and the energetic, in-your-face delivery style. Nevada's most famous and beloved cowboy poet—who has performed on Johnny Carson's Tonight Show, *at Carnegie Hall, and around the world—was born Bruce Douglas Mitchell on a remote ranch in northeastern Nevada. Nicknamed Waddie by his father (*waddie *is an old term for "cowboy"), the young lad enjoyed listening to the talk of working cowboys, who entertained one another by telling stories, sometimes put to rhyme. Back then Mitchell never thought of these oral recitations as poetry—"Poetry's for sissies and womens," he used to think. Mitchell was a working cowboy for twenty-six years, managing ranches so remote that he was lucky if he made it into town once a month. He helped his friend Hal Cannon organize the first Cowboy Poetry Gathering, held in Elko in January 1985. Over the years, Mitchell won a large following at the annual Gathering, and he was signed by Warner Brothers to make the CD* Lone Driftin' Rider *(1992). Mitchell then left the range to become a touring cowboy poet and entertainer. At the height of his career as a performer, he spent approximately three hundred days a year on the road and has been featured in* People, Life, USA Today, Fortune, National Geographic, *the official program for Super Bowl XXX, and the* Wall Street Journal. *He has recorded numerous albums, starred in documentaries, published two books—*Waddie Mitchell's Christmas Poems *(1987) and* Waddie's Whole Load *(1994)—and has been inducted to the Cowboy Poets and Singers Hall of Fame, all the while maintaining an Elko home address. Mitchell once claimed that his goal was to earn enough money to buy his own ranch: "I'm hoping for the opportunity to go broke on a ranch by myself instead of helping somebody else do it!" Thanks to his success in the limelight, in 1997 Mitchell purchased a ranch in the foothills of the Ruby Mountains, where he began building a ranchstead that is off the electric-power grid.*

Story with a Moral

I know there's things worse
      that make cowpunchers curse,
And I reckon it's happened to us all.
Though it's been years, since, you can bet,
      when I think of it yet,
It still makes my old innards crawl.

I was making a ride
      to bring in one hide
That hadn't showed up in the gather;
I was riding upstream,
      daydreaming a dream,
When I caught there was something the matter.

Near some quaking asp trees,
      I had caught in the breeze
A stench that was raunchy and mean,
And I reckoned as how
      it might be that old cow,
So I rode to a bend in the stream.

Sure enough, that cow lied
      in the creek there and died.
Hard telling how long she'd been there.
She was bloated and tight—
      was a horrible sight!
She was oozing and slipping her hair.

Her eye sockets were alive
      with maggots that thrive
On dead flesh, putrid yellow and green,
An' the hot sun burning down,
      turnin' pink things to brown,
Spewing oily gunk in the stream.

I spurred upwind fast
      to get away from the blast
Of the heavy stink that cow made.

And I felt bad seein's how
    I had lost the old cow,
So I pulled up near a tree in the shade—

Then, I got sick to the core,
    rememberin' just moments before
I'd done something that made me feel worse:
Not thirty yards down,
    I'd stepped off to the ground
And drank till my belly near burst!

For months after it,
    just the thought made me spit,
And I'd live it over like a bad dream.
And the moral, I think,
    is if you must take a drink,
Never, ever remount and ride upstream.

Typical

Out on the cliff's edge further than he'd ever been before
He sat with legs a danglin' high above the valley's floor.
He was lost in thought while drinking in the grandeur of it all,
When a gust of wind unseated him and he began to fall.
'Twas a drastic situation and he didn't dare think slow,
For certain death awaited in the rocky crags below.
So he called upon a friend (I guess the only one he could)—
The one we all forget about when things are going good.
He said, "God, if you will help me now, I'll quit my sinful ways;
I will do those things you'd have me do and work hard all my days;
I will quit the booze and cigarettes and help my loving wife;
I will spend time with my children and I'll turn around my life;
I will work to help the needy and I promise to repent."
Just then, a tree limb caught his coat and stopped his fast descent.
And while hanging from the tree that grew upon that rocky shelf
He looked skyward saying, "Never mind, I handled it myself!"

ROD MCQUEARY [B. 1951]

More Vietnam soldiers committed suicide after the war than died in combat. A third-generation cattle rancher from Ruby Valley, Nevada, Rod McQueary, a widely anthologized cowboy poet, was saved by poetry. McQueary left the UX Livestock Ranch, where he had lived all his life, to serve in Vietnam with the First Marine Division as a military policeman near Da Nang. After the war, he returned to the lovely UX, but his mental landscape was devastated. For more than twenty years, McQueary suffered from harrowing nightmares and grisly memories. His marriage broke up, he drank heavily, and were it not for poetry, he says, "I would've taken some Rompin, climbed onto this rank horse I had and headed for the hills." But he didn't. Instead, he wrote. By facing his demons and defeating them, McQueary found the trail home. Blood Trails (Dry Crik Press, 1993), a powerful poetry collection that McQueary cowrote with fellow veteran Bill Jones, cuts a swath from torment to healing, telling other Vietnam vets, "It is imperative / my Legion, / my Brothers / that you know / it is Possible." Besides writing about the war, McQueary writes both humorous and serious poetry on behalf of embattled ranchers, fourteen million of whom have left ranches and farms for the city in McQueary's lifetime. "My poetry tries to tell the truth about my culture and my profession," McQueary observes, "The only thing ranch families can be sure of is that they are misunderstood."

Life and Times

> *When they ask of Life,*
> *What will I say?*
> *Can I describe time that swirls,*
> *Flits with fickle castanets,*
> *And disappears?*
> *A shrinking, self-swallowing serpent?*

> Sometimes in spring
> When ropes with eyes
> Fly to heads and heels

> The smokey celebration of
> Surviving another winter
> Buys the seven-way and Bud

> Dusty faces crack from laughing
> Bloody hands pass Copenhagen
> Back and forth

No furtive glances hopefully
Caress snowless ridges
Today
The future is studiously ignored
For the intensity of
Now

Ground crew limps—unnoticed
Tomorrow's hips and rope-arm
Shoulders
Get no second
Thought

If
By God
We are a primitive
Futureless band

At least we avoid
That flatland
Urban trap
Of measuring life
With
Time

SUE WALLIS [B. 1957]

Sue Wallis's Nevada years were hard but ultimately rewarding. Raised on a cattle ranch in the Powder River Breaks of northern Wyoming, "a string of hard left turns" brought Wallis to Elko in the early 1990s to work as an administrator for the Western Folklife Center, which organizes the annual Cowboy Poetry Gathering. A divorced single mother of three young children at the time, Wallis had already been a cowboy, ranch manager, horse trainer, coal miner, and uranium prospector. In her poem "The Big Lonely," Wallis asks why she never felt lonesome riding her horse alone over vast, empty landscapes, yet "a trailer house / In town, full of closed-in kids / Too many neighbors and too much noise / Is more . . . lonely / Than anything I've ever known." At this time in her life, Wallis must have fantasized about her free-spirited great-aunts Marge and Alice, the "Riding Greenoughs," who were champion saddle-bronc riders early in the

*century, eventually inducted into the Cowboy Hall of Fame, with Alice journeying on to Aus-
tralia and then Spain, where she rode fighting bulls in the bullrings. "Coyote Bitch," reprinted
below, springs from Wallis's difficult Nevada years. In Elko, Wallis and some friends would get
together to trade poems and stories. Wallis wrote "Coyote Bitch" for fun, out of a mood, and
she shared it with her friends. To her surprise, the poem took off, and she got fan letters and
e-mail from women as far away as New York. Happily, one of those Elko friends was Nevada
rancher and cowboy poet Rod McQueary, whom Wallis married in 1994. In Wallis's two collections of poetry—*The Exalted Ones *(1991) and *Another Green Grass Lover *(1994)—*she
strives for a "clear, strong, positive female voice that speaks to, and for, the feminine concerns
in ranching culture."*

Coyote Bitch

> Tonight . . .
>
> I feel like a Coyote Bitch
> (in heat)
> Do not annoy me, tempt me, or toy with me
> I have been lonely too long.
>
> An old bitch will wait with native intellect
> Run just below the ridges
> You won't see her 'til she catches
> That first waft of
> Rottenness
>
> She'll linger ruthless
> Over the carrion carcass
> Of some uncaring
> Wild Steer
>
> Then drag the stinking skin
> Back to her solitary den
> To chew and slobber and maul the hide
> Long after all hint of flesh is dried
>
> Just for comfort
> Mangling idle dreams of regal wolfish lovers
> Strong and smart and beautiful
>
> . . . Who never appear.

SEVEN

THE BIGGEST LITTLE CITY

Writings About Reno

"Where are the Truckee Meadows?" new Reno residents wonder, puzzled by weather reports for the Truckee Meadows on Reno radio stations. As they learn, Reno is *in* the so-called Truckee Meadows, even though one would be hard pressed to find a meadow anywhere in the suburban sprawl of the Reno-Sparks metropolitan area. New subdivisions and developments are equally deceiving, named after the very things they have obliterated: Kiley Ranch, Caughlin Ranch, Quail Park, Pebble Creek, Juniper Ridge, Wingfield Springs, Double Diamond, Hidden Valley, and many more. This contrast between old Reno and new Reno, this sense of there being two Renos, creates tension in the literary tradition of the "Biggest Little City in the World." Is Reno big? Is it little? It is both, depending on how you look at it.

Unlike many Nevada towns, Reno did not originate as a mining camp. Located on the Truckee River, the city grew around a toll bridge named Lake's Crossing, established in 1861, a crossroads for emigrant trails. Reno, incorporated in 1868 and named after Jesse Lee Reno, a Union officer in the Civil War, remains a transportation hub today, lying at the junction of east-west Interstate 80 and north-south Highway 395. In 1868 the Central Pacific railroad reached Reno, and one year later the newly platted town serviced the newly completed transcontinental railroad. Located only thirty miles from Virginia City, Reno prospered as a supply and shipping center while the Comstock boomed. By the late nineteenth century, however,

Nevada's mining industry had virtually collapsed, and Reno cast about for other means of support. While the Tonopah-Goldfield gold discoveries in 1900 and 1903 rescued Nevada's economy, Reno made a start in promoting tourism by hosting the famous Johnson-Jeffries prizefight in 1910, witnessed by 22,000 spectators. Just two weeks before the celebrated fight San Francisco had canceled its plans to host the event due to pressure from reformers who objected to professional boxing. Reno grabbed the opportunity, discovering the big money to be made in sanctioning activities that were discouraged elsewhere. In the ensuing decades, gambling, prostitution, easy divorce, and quickie marriage joined prizefights as profitable ventures, giving Reno a naughty national reputation as the "Divorce Capital of the World," an image at odds with the way local author Walter Van Tilburg Clark characterized it, as the "City of Trembling Leaves." Two Renos.

The divorce industry inspired Reno's first literary flowering. To obtain an "easy" Nevada divorce, divorce-seekers were required to be residents of the state, establishing an address and residing there continuously for six months. In 1927 the residency requirement was lowered to three months, and in 1931 to a scandalous six weeks. Nevada has had some high-profile "resident" authors, including Nobel Prize winner Saul Bellow, playwrights Arthur Miller and Clare Boothe Luce, *New Yorker* journalist A. J. Liebling, novelist Jill Stern, and international intellectual C. L. R. James. A special vocabulary of euphemisms arose among the "colonists": divorce was referred to as "the cure," culminating on "graduation day" when one earned one's "diploma." An "affinity" was a Reno lover, perhaps a rugged cowboy hired to entertain lonely women at the popular "dude" (divorce) ranches. In the voluminous literature of divorce, produced from the 1920s through the mid-1960s, Reno itself is described variously as a pleasant party town or as a kind of purgatory in the desert, and as a real place or a symbol. Two Renos.

Reno natives and permanent residents write about the city quite differently than the temporary residents described above. Walter Van Tilburg Clark studiously focused his attention, not on downtown Reno, but on the neighborhoods where normal people carry on normal lives. Others, such as William A. Douglass, wax nostalgic for a Reno that used to be—the quiet, small town, bisected by the lovely Truckee River, where mink, beaver, and otter were evidence of Reno's wild heart. Spanish-speaking immigrant Emma Sepúlveda experienced a "white-faced, red-necked" Reno, hostile to foreigners, while African American Verita Prothro reveals a vibrant subculture-of-color within the larger culture. One place, many Renos.

JACK LONDON [1876–1916]

Born out of wedlock, Jack London got his surname from his stepfather, John London, whom his mother married after Jack's biological father, an itinerant astrologer, left them. London dropped out of school after eighth grade to embark on a life of adventure, enjoying a fling as an oyster pirate in the San Francisco Bay before switching sides to work for the fish patrol. In 1893 he sailed the North Pacific on a sealing schooner, returning to work in a salmon cannery and shovel coal for a power plant, hard labor that he found mentally deadening. At eighteen London joined a western contingent of Coxey's Army, unemployed workers bound for Washington, DC, to protest. He was arrested in Niagara Falls for vagrancy and spent a month in jail, where he resolved to make something of himself. Returning to Oakland, London enrolled in high school and steamrolled his way to graduation in eighteen months. Determined to become a successful writer, he began pumping out stories, essays, light verse, and jokes, netting two years' worth of rejections. Undeterred, he drilled himself on vocabulary words and developed a lifetime regimen of composing one thousand words each morning, six days a week, remarking to a friend that "I am writing for money. . . . every time I sit down to write it is with great disgust." Nevertheless, London persisted, gaining valuable material when he joined the Klondike gold rush in 1897. In 1900 Houghton Mifflin accepted his first book, The Son of the Wolf, *a collection of Alaska tales.* The Call of the Wild *(1903) became world famous, and thereafter London enjoyed a ready market. By the time he died at age forty, he had published over fifty books, hundreds of articles, and dozens of stories, the first American to become a millionaire by writing. The following sketch, from* The Road *(1907), recalls the penniless, hobo days of his youth.*

Confession

There is a woman in the state of Nevada to whom I once lied continuously, consistently, and shamelessly, for the matter of a couple of hours. I don't want to apologize to her. Far be it from me. But I do want to explain. Unfortunately, I do not know her name, much less her present address. If her eyes should chance upon these lines, I hope she will write to me.

It was in Reno, Nevada, in the summer of 1892. Also, it was fair-time, and the town was filled with petty crooks and tin-horns, to say nothing of a vast and hungry horde of hoboes. It was the hungry hoboes that made the town a "hungry" town. They "battered" the back doors of the homes of the citizens until the back doors became unresponsive.

A hard town for "scoffings," was what the hoboes called it at that time. I know that I missed many a meal, in spite of the fact that I could "throw my feet" with the next one when it came to "slamming a gate" for a "poke-out" or a "set-down," or hitting for a "light piece" on the street.

. . . .

But to return to the woman to whom I so shamelessly lied. It was in the evening of my last day in Reno. I had been out to the race-track watching the ponies run, and had missed my dinner (*i.e.* the midday meal). I was hungry, and, furthermore, a committee of public safety had just been organized to rid the town of just such hungry mortals as I. Already a lot of my brother hoboes had been gathered in by John Law, and I could hear the sunny valleys of California calling to me over the cold crests of the Sierras. Two acts remained for me to perform before I shook the dust of Reno from my feet. One was to catch the blind baggage on the westbound overland that night. The other was first to get something to eat. Even youth will hesitate at an all-night ride, on an empty stomach, outside a train that is tearing the atmosphere through the snow-sheds, tunnels, and eternal snows of heaven-aspiring mountains.

But that something to eat was a hard proposition. I was "turned down" at a dozen houses. Sometimes I received insulting remarks and was informed of the barred domicile that should be mine if I had my just desserts. The worst of it was that such assertions were only too true. That was why I was pulling west that night. John Law was abroad in the town, seeking eagerly for the hungry and homeless, for by such was his barred domicile tenanted.

At other houses the doors were slammed in my face, cutting short my politely and humbly couched request for something to eat. At one house they did not open the door. I stood on the porch and knocked, and they looked out at me through the window. They even held one sturdy little boy aloft so that he could see over the shoulders of his elders the tramp who wasn't going to get anything to eat at their house.

. . . .

By this time I had lost heart. I passed many houses by without venturing up to them. All houses looked alike, and none looked "good." After walking half a dozen blocks I shook off my despondency and gathered my "nerve." This begging for food was all a game, and if I didn't like the cards, I could always call for a new deal. I made up my mind to tackle the next house. I approached it in the deepening twilight, going around to the kitchen door.

I knocked softly, and when I saw the kind face of the middle-aged woman who answered, as by inspiration came to me the "story" I was to tell. For know that upon his ability to tell a good story depends the success of the beggar. First of all, and on the instant, the beggar must "size up" his victim. After that, he must tell a story that will appeal to the peculiar personality and temperament of that particular victim. And right here arises the great difficulty: in the instant that he is sizing up the victim he must begin his story. Not a minute is allowed for preparation. As in a lightning flash he must divine the nature of the victim and conceive a tale that will hit home. The successful hobo must be an artist. He must create spontaneously and instantaneously—and not upon a theme selected from the plenitude of his own imagination, but upon the theme he reads in the face of the person who opens the door, be it man, woman, or child, sweet or crabbed, generous or miserly, good-natured or cantankerous, Jew or Gentile, black or white, race-prejudiced or brotherly, provincial or universal, or whatever else it may be. I have often thought that to this training of my tramp days is due much of my success as a story-writer. In order to get the food whereby I lived, I was compelled to tell tales that rang true. At the back door, out of inexorable necessity, is developed the convincingness and sincerity laid down by all authorities on the art of the short-story. Also, I quite believe it was my tramp-apprenticeship that made a realist out of me. Realism constitutes the only goods one can exchange at the kitchen door for grub.

. . . .

But to return to the woman in Reno who opened her door to me in the deepening twilight. At the first glimpse of her kindly face I took my cue. I became a sweet, innocent, unfortunate lad. I couldn't speak. I opened my mouth and closed it again. Never in my life before had I asked any one for food. My embarrassment was painful, extreme. I was ashamed. I, who looked upon begging as a delightful whimsicality, thumbed myself over into a true son of Mrs. Grundy, burdened with all her bourgeois morality. Only the harsh pangs of the belly-need could compel me to do so degraded and ignoble a thing as beg for food. And into my face I strove to throw all the wan wistfulness of famished and ingenuous youth unused to mendicancy.

"You are hungry, my poor boy," she said.

I had made her speak first.

I nodded my head and gulped.

"It is the first time I have ever . . . asked," I faltered.

"Come right in." The door swung open. "We have already finished eating, but the fire is burning and I can get something up for you."

She looked at me closely when she got me into the light.

"I wish my boy were as healthy and strong as you," she said. "But he is not strong. He sometimes falls down. He just fell down this afternoon and hurt himself badly, the poor dear."

She mothered him with her voice, with an ineffable tenderness in it that I yearned to appropriate. I glanced at him. He sat across the table, slender and pale, his head swathed in bandages. He did not move, but his eyes, bright in the lamplight, were fixed upon me in a steady and wondering stare.

"Just like my poor father," I said. "He had the falling sickness. Some kind of vertigo. It puzzled the doctors. They never could make out what was the matter with him."

"He is dead?" she queried gently, setting before me half a dozen soft-boiled eggs.

"Dead," I gulped. "Two weeks ago. I was with him when it happened. We were crossing the street together. He fell right down. He was never conscious again. They carried him into a drug-store. He died there."

And thereat I developed the pitiful tale of my father—how, after my mother's death, he and I had gone to San Francisco from the ranch; how his pension (he was an old soldier), and the little other money he had, was not enough; and how he had tried book-canvassing. Also, I narrated my own woes during the few days after his death that I had spent alone and forlorn on the streets of San Francisco. While that good woman warmed up biscuits, fried bacon, and cooked more eggs, and while I kept pace with her in taking care of all that she placed before me, I enlarged the picture of that poor orphan boy and filled in the details. I became that poor boy. I believed in him as I believed in the beautiful eggs I was devouring. I could have wept for myself. I know the tears did get into my voice at times. It was very effective.

In fact, with every touch I added to the picture, that kind soul gave me something also. She made up a lunch for me to carry away. She put in many boiled eggs, pepper and salt, and other things, and a big apple. She provided me with three pairs of thick red woolen socks. She gave me clean handkerchiefs and other things which I have since forgotten. And all the time she cooked more and more and I ate more and more. I gorged like a savage; but then it was a far cry across the Sierras on a blind baggage, and I knew not when nor where I should find my next meal. And all the while, like a death's-head at the feast, silent and motionless, her own unfortunate boy sat and stared at me across the table. I suppose I represented to him mystery, and romance, and adventure—all that was denied the feeble flicker of life that was in him. And yet I could not forbear, once or twice, from wondering if he saw through me down to the bottom of my mendacious heart.

"But where are you going to?" she asked me.

"Salt Lake City," said I. "I have a sister there—a married sister." (I debated if I should make a Mormon out of her, and decided against it.) "Her husband is a plumber—a contracting plumber."

Now I knew that contracting plumbers were usually credited with making lots of money. But I had spoken. It was up to me to qualify.

"They would have sent me the money for my fare if I had asked for it," I explained, "but they have had sickness and business troubles. His partner cheated him. And so I wouldn't write for the money. I knew I could make my way there somehow. I let them think I had enough to get me to Salt Lake City. She is lovely, and so kind. She was always kind to me. I guess I'll go into the shop and learn the trade. She has two daughters. They are younger than I. One is only a baby."

Of all my married sisters that I have distributed among the cities of the United States, that Salt Lake sister is my favorite. She is quite real, too. When I tell about her, I can see her, and her two little girls, and her plumber husband. She is a large, motherly woman, just verging on beneficent stoutness—the kind, you know, that always cooks nice things and that never gets angry. She is a brunette. Her husband is a quiet, easy-going fellow. Sometimes I almost know him quite well. And who knows but some day I may meet him? . . .

On the other hand, I have a feeling of certitude within me that I shall never meet in the flesh my many parents and grandparents—you see, I invariably killed them off. Heart disease was my favorite way of getting rid of my mother, though on occasion I did away with her by means of consumption, pneumonia, and typhoid fever. . . .

I hope that woman in Reno will read these lines and forgive me my gracelessness and unveracity. I do not apologize, for I am unashamed. It was youth, delight in life, zest for experience, that brought me to her door. It did me good. It taught me the intrinsic kindliness of human nature. I hope it did her good. Anyway, she may get a good laugh out of it now that she learns the real inwardness of the situation.

ARTHUR RUHL [1876–1935]

For one week in 1910, the eyes of the world were on Reno, Nevada, for the "Battle of the Century," a prizefight between Jack Johnson, who in 1908 became the first black man to win the world heavyweight championship, and Jim Jeffries, a white "colossus" who had won the title in 1899. The public persuaded Jeffries to come out of retirement as the "Great White Hope." The fight was scheduled for July 4 in San Francisco, but moral reformers pressured the governor of California to cancel it. Promoter "Tex" Rickard then appealed to Nevada's governor Denver Dickerson, who gave his assent. Timbers for the arena arrived in Reno by train at midnight, June 27, whereupon frenzied construction began, and an estimated seventeen thousand people poured into the town of ten thousand. As Halley's comet shone in the night sky, every bed was full, pool tables became makeshift bunks, and people slept in train cars and automobiles. Among the more than three hundred reporters on the scene was Arthur Brown Ruhl, writing for Collier's. *Born in Rockford, Illinois, Ruhl attended Harvard, where he served on the editorial staffs of the* Lampoon *and* Advocate. *Graduating in 1899, Ruhl became a reporter for the* New York Evening Sun, *commencing a thirty-year career in journalism, during which he worked for many New York newspapers and magazines as a sports reporter, drama critic, and foreign affairs correspondent, earning a reputation as a meticulous observer and discerning writer, a respected authority on Latin America, the Caribbean, Germany, and Russia. Of his eight books, his best known is* Antwerp to Gallipoli: A Year of War on Many Fronts—and behind Them *(1916), a compilation of his World War I dispatches from Europe, where he reported from both sides of the front. Ruhl's Nevada pieces include a 1905 article on the Newlands irrigation project and a 1911 piece entitled "Reno and the Rush for Divorce."*

The Fight in the Desert
"Reno or Bust"

Well, no ride with Tom Turtle on top a stage-coach through the finest English country in the snappiest fall weather could have been more splendid and exciting than the morning of the fight. The day dawned spotlessly clear, one of those still crystalline mornings which come in the thin dry air of the mountain desert country. The town was jammed. Miles, it seemed, of dusty Pullmans stretched down the tracks, above their dining-car roofs the blue smoke of the breakfast fires. From east and west other trains kept pouring in, and dustier still and honking gaily as they came, touring cars with ragged signs of "Reno, or Bust."

There were Indians, Chinamen, Hindus, New York wine-agents, and other queer fish, but above all it was a man's crowd—of husky men, boyish, in high spirits, talking at a great rate, and in the liveliest good humor, about the difficulties of getting breakfast, getting a shave, and about the prospects of the fight.

You must imagine a bright green little oasis, ten or fifteen miles across, set in a sort of dish of bare enclosing mountains—brown mountains with patches of yellow and olive-green and exquisite veils of mauve and amethyst, and at their tops, blazing white through the clear air, patches of austere snow. In the center of all this a great pine bear pit had been raised, glaring white and hot in the blazing desert sun, and into this at 1.30 o'clock that afternoon 20,000 men were crowded with their eyes fixed on a little roped square in the center.

The betting was 10 to 6 or 7 on Jeffries and the talk about 1,000 to 1. You couldn't hurt him—Fitzsimmons had landed enough times to kill an ordinary man in the first few rounds, and Jeffries had only shaken his head like a bull and bored in.

The negro might be a clever boxer, but he has never been up against a real fighter before. He had a yellow streak, there was nothing to it, and anyway, "let's hope he kills the coon."

A Scowling Brown Colossus

That was about the mental atmosphere as Lil' Artha,' wrapped in a dressing-gown and smiling his half-puzzled, rather pleading smile, climbed into the ring. Old Billy Jordan, who has been announcing fights for fifty years or so, was just introducing the negro to the buzzing, hostile audience, when Jeffries, with a cloud of seconds and camp-followers behind him, climbed through the ropes.

I had a seat at the ringside, directly opposite him, and I can unhesitatingly state that I have never seen a human being more calculated to strike terror into an opponent's heart than this scowling brown Colossus as he came through the ropes, stamped like a bull pawing the ground before his charge, and, chewing gum rapidly, glared at the black man across the ring.

If looks could have throttled, burned, and torn to pieces, Mr. Jack Arthur Johnson would have disappeared that instant into a few specks of inanimate dust. The negro had his back turned at the moment, as he was being presented to the crowd on the opposite side. He did not turn round, and as he took his corner and his trainer and seconds, crowding in front of him, concealed the white man, a sort of hoot, wolfish and rather terrible, went up from the crowd. "He darsen't look at him! O-o-o! Don't let him see him! Don't let him see him!" And when Jeffries pulled off his clothes with a vicious jerk, and standing erect and throwing out his chest, jabbed his great arms above his head once or twice, I don't suppose that one man in a hundred in that crowd would have given two cents for the negro's chances.

Nor did many suspect until Johnson's left shot across to the white man's right eye in the sixth round and closed it—so strong and convincing was the Jeffries tradition, the contagion of the atmosphere, and that crouching, scowling gladiator—that the negro's finish was anything but a matter of time.

They had all seen or heard of that short, rather slow, piston-rod-like punch which the white man knew how to send with a tremendous, if not spectacular, force into his opponent's side just under the lower right ribs. They saw him send it in, time and again apparently, and each time the crowd gave a sort of subdued, exultant grunt. When Johnson merely smiled his far-away smile, people supposed he must be shamming, and when those upper-cuts of his shot up like lighting, they thought it was merely pretty, but didn't hurt.

When that blow got across in the sixth round, however, the cynicism of the white man's glare suddenly went dead and changed. His right eye blackened and closed, and the blood began to run down from his right nostril. He was fighting after that not to finish his opponent, but to save himself, to stave off what he probably knew, if the crowd did not yet suspect, nothing but chance could save him from. Mr. Jim Corbett, who, as Jeffries' second and following the quaint sportsmanship of the ring, had gone across to the corner nearest the negro between each of the earlier rounds to fix him with a sneering eye and wittily taunt and terrify him, lost his bright vaudeville smile. Once, when he called out to Johnson during a round, the negro, laughing across Jeffries' shoulder, gave him as good as he sent. Once a man far up in the seats called down to Johnson, "Why don't you smile now?" and the negro, who seemed to know everything that was going on in and out of the ring without at any time paying close attention, deliberately turned his head and smiled. He looked fierce occasionally, but that was only when he feinted. When something real and dangerous was to be done, he was apparently dreaming placidly as the flowers of May.

A Mirage for the Multitude

The rest is an old story now—how the big man, bleeding, beaten, but glaring stubbornly out of his one good eye, bored steadily in as the bull charges the matador toward the end of his fight; how, suddenly, the main drama about which had gathered such a curiously modern and top-heavy mountain of accessories, rushed to its swift and unexpected conclusion. In the thirteenth round the crafty black turned loose for a moment, and it was all over then but the shouting.

In the fourteenth and fifteenth rounds, however, the old champion came crouching back, groggy but willing; in the fifteenth there was a quick clash, and all at once his tree-like legs caved in, and the great hairy brown hulk, which had never been knocked down before nor beaten, sank close to the ropes. The crowd didn't cheer. It rose and stood and stared, as if the solid ground beneath it were turning to a mirage.

At the count of nine Jeffries got to his feet, only to be sent back again, this time between the ropes. His camp followers, forgetting themselves in the desperation of the moment, pushed him to his feet, but it was only to stagger across the ring and go down again, and for the last time, on the other side.

They lifted the fallen idol and slapped his big shoulders and led him away; men rushed down and hopped over the sputtering telegraph instruments, to cut the ropes and floor canvas into souvenirs, and Mr. Jack Arthur Johnson, with only a slightly cut lip, rode back to camp in his automobile with a harder road ahead of him than any he ever yet has traveled—the gilded, beguiling pathway of him who is not climbing but has arrived.

The After-Effect

The white race, whose supremacy this contest was going to establish, must, naturally, have been as dead as the Aztecs or the Incas; but the representatives of it in
Reno seemed to battle their way into the overflowing restaurants to-night with
their usual interest, to smoke their black cigars with their customary zest, and
gaze out at the pink and lavender lights turning to purple and ashes in the distant
mountains with the usual air of equanimity. They reasoned, I believe, that there
hadn't been any fight, that Jeffries was only a shell of a man, and it wasn't certain
that they were convinced that he even *had* any arms.

That was all very well after the event and for those who forget how things stood
when the battle opened. But any one who happened to see, from Johnson's corner,
the face of Jim Jeffries as he climbed into the ring, and felt the focused mind and
heard the taunts and jeers of the hostile crowd, knows that it took something more
than boxing skill for that black man to go out and meet his fate; that he had concentration right enough if it didn't show on the outside, and stood on his own feet
and thought for himself, and fought and vanquished a brave opponent cleanly and
like a brave man.

LESLIE CURTIS [1882–1962]

Epigrams by Curtis:

    "Reno is a co-educational Turkish Bath for matrimonial drunkards."

    "Jones—What do you think is the cause of divorce? Bones—Matrimony."

    "A millionaire on hand is worth two of his sons."

    *In the early 1900s, when Reno's divorce industry was just beginning to attract national at-
tention, newcomer Leslie Curtis won considerable distinction as a clever young writer. Curtis
originally hailed from Denver but arrived in Reno in 1909 from New York City, where she
had been a showgirl and then a newspaper writer. In Reno, Curtis wrote for local newspapers and dispatched witty, divorce-related epigrams, poems, stories, one-act plays, song lyrics,
and articles to* Snappy Stories, Theater *magazine,* Smart Set, Life, Judge, Satire, Overland
Monthly, *and other venues, quipping that "the successful author rises from a bed of rejection
slips." In 1910 she published a collection of this material under the title* Reno Reveries, *one of
the first books ever written about Reno. Curtis's focus on the divorce mill led some readers to
assume that she had come to Reno to dissolve a marriage. Chagrined, Curtis placed an ad in
the* Nevada State Journal, *insisting that she had never been married and had "no intentions
of inflicting herself upon the sterner sex." Nevertheless, headlines later that year, in December*

1910, announced, "Miss Curtis to Become Bride." Indeed, Leslie Curtis married a millionaire twenty-five years her senior, the recently divorced Alva Kitselman, president of the Indiana Wire and Steel Company. In 1936 the Kitselmans purchased a ranch at Sutcliffe on the shores of Pyramid Lake, where their three children spent much of their childhood. After Alva's death in 1940, Leslie Curtis Kitselman managed the Pyramid Lake guest ranch, the only privately owned resort in the Paiute Indian Reservation. In 1942 she married a visiting artist named Fidel Figueroa and spent her remaining years at his home in Taxco, Mexico, in a beautifully restored palace.

Reno

Reno is a haven for the heart that breaks.
Reno is the clearing house for all mistakes.
    The climate is attractive,
    The legal lights are active,
And everyone—yes, everyone
    Is glad to come to Reno!

Reno! Reno! Biggest little city on the map!
Reno! Reno! Just the place to end a silly scrap!
Where the sunshine is eternal and the dark clouds
    roll away,
Where the broken hearts are mended at the Courthouse
    every day,
Where the moon shines bright on the Truckee
    every night,
It's a great little place,
It's a great little place,
It's a great little place to stay!

Our Alphabet

A—Stands for ALIMONY, ANSWERS, and AIM,
    Also AFFINITY (whisper his name!).
B—for the BLUFF, which we hand out so strong,
    And BRIEF an affair sometimes awfully long.
C—stands for CLIENT, COMPLAINANT and COURT
    CHARGES OF CRUELTY (any old sort).
D—for DEFENDANT, DIVORCE and DECREE,

DESERTION, DENIAL and DESTITUTE. See?
E—stands for EVIDENCE, ERROR and EASE,
    EVERYONE striving to ENTER decrees.
F—stands for FAILURE to FAIRLY provide,
    (FRIENDS and the FAMILY all on one side).
G—For the GIRLIES who Reno-wards roam,
    Then the word "GRANTED," which hurries them home.
H—for HER HUSBAND, a HORRIBLE brute!
    Also HER HAMMER which knocks the poor mute.
I—for INTENTIONS to live here awhile,
    IMMEDIATE cause for an INNOCENT (?) smile.
J—for JOY, JOURNALIST, JURY and JUDGE,
    Also for JEALOUSY born of a grudge.
K—for KIDNAPPING—quite usual now—
    And KISSES as well (Reno laddies know how!).
L—for the LAWYERS who worry us through,
    Also the LOVERS we telegraph to.
M—stands for MARRIAGE, a bothersome state!
    And MONEY extracted from grouchy ex-MATE.
N—for NEGLECT—the cause of much woe,
    To NEVADA for NERVOUS disorders we go.
O—for the OATH we must everyone face,
    "Honest, dear Judge! there's no man in the case!"
P—stands for PROPERTY, PLAINTIFF and PRAY,
    PREJUDICE, PAINT (which is seen every day).
Q—for QUEER QUIBBLES, while fair plaintiffs pout,
    At the QUESTIONS His Merciless Honor calls out.
R—for RELIEF from the marital yoke,
    Also RE-MARRIAGE (and this is no joke!).
S—stands for SACRIFICE, SORROW and SIGH,
    SAD SEPARATION—"Write Reno, Goodbye!"
T—stands for TRIAL, TESTIMONY and TEARS.
    And later, TRANQUILITY, missing for years.
U—for UXORICIDE, quite the style now,
V—is for VENUE, VICE, VIRTUE and VOW,
W—for WITNESSES WIVES we endow.
X—for ex-anything, just as you please!
Y—for YOUTH'S YEARNING to capture decrees.
Z—ZESTFUL ZEALOTS, who hustle for fees!

As Others See Us

Reno is situated on an island in the Sea of Matrimony. It is parted in the middle by the Truckee River, which flows from the Reef of Many Causes to the Harbor of Renewed Hope and More Trouble. The tide comes in regularly by the Southern Pacific and the untied depart the same way.

Reno is a winter resort for some people and a last resort for others. It consists of well-defined grounds both outside and inside of a courthouse. The town is laid out in sub-divisions and the inhabitants are laid out in court. The population is mixed, consisting of men, women and lawyers.

Hotel Refuge, on Evidence avenue, contains separate suites and individual pillow cases. Rates dependent upon alimony. Affinities and other luxuries, extra. Special department for family skeletons.

The principal industries are divorce and mining. Judges and legal lights control the most profitable mines. The main shaft extends to the level of desperation and is crossed by the drifts of non-support and cruelty. Hundreds of lawyers are engaged in sorting high and low grade domestic ore. Considerable brass is discovered and is in evidence daily. A rich vein of humor pervades the situation.

The divorce mill is situated on Alimony avenue, near Separation street. It is used for grinding grounds and pulverizing reputations. Scandal is a by-product which is devoured while fresh by a species of buzzard known as "the journalist." Painless extraction of fees, life histories and dramatic episodes a specialty. One bottle of our deadly divorce dope will eliminate husbands, wives and other insects in six months. Assumed names, new or second-hand, delivered at your door upon request. Phone 23.

The style of dressing in Reno is distinctive. Neckties, home-ties and railroad ties are being gradually eliminated. Separate skirts and waists are all the rage. Wardrobes consist in most cases of two suits, Sunday and legal. Contested varieties occasionally in evidence, but are not popular. Hair is worn parted. Double chins not encouraged.

The Reno city government is unduly severe. All trains arriving in the city are uncoupled according to city ordinance. All wagons affect single-trees. Persons doubled up with pain are requested to redouble their efforts to leave the city. Broken hearts mended at the Double Cross hospital.

Left over husbands and wives may re-enter the United State(s) by collusion and a conference with the license clerk.

Bonds of matrimony discounted at the courthouse. No interest after six months.

Children possessing progressive parentage must be labeled with their right names.

Motto of Reno—"Part the speeding guest."

CORNELIUS VANDERBILT JR. [1898–1974]

By his own admission, Cornelius Vanderbilt Jr. was born into this world with a golden spoon. As an heir to one of America's wealthiest and best-connected families, he was well schooled, well heeled, and had the opportunity to dabble in just about anything he wanted. In addition to serving in the U.S. Army Intelligence Corps in both world wars, he was a journalist, travel writer, business executive, radio commentator, novelist, biographer, and memoir writer. His memoirs include Personal Experiences of a Cub Reporter *(1922),* Personal Experiences of a Legislative Correspondent *(1922),* Personal Experiences of a Washington Correspondent *(1923), and* Man of the World: My Life on Five Continents *(1959). He crossed the Atlantic 158 times, the Pacific forty-six, and traveled around the world twelve times. Seven times married, six times divorced, and author of the book* Too Many Wives *(1940), Vanderbilt was a poster boy for the Nevada "quickie" divorce, and he "took the cure" in Reno. One result was the divorce novel* Reno *(1929), which, according to scholar Ann Ronald, "infuriated the natives" even though Vanderbilt's book was kinder to the city than other novels of its genre. In a memoir Vanderbilt said, "Reno had charm and I fell in love with the Nevada country," but apparently Reno did not appreciate being portrayed as a dissolute city with "divorce colonies" and permissive laws. In Nevada, Vanderbilt "decided to become a rancher," but he was more a "drugstore cowboy." In the 1920s he owned a dude ranch near Pyramid Lake, and a divorce ranch—the* Lazy Me Guest Ranch—*south of Reno. Vanderbilt continued to write novels and nonfiction, such as* Park Avenue *(1930),* Palm Beach *(1931),* Farewell to Fifth Avenue *(1935),* A Woman of Washington *(1937),* Children of Divorce *(1939),* The Living Past of America *(1955),* Ranches and Ranch Life in America *(1968), and others in a long writing career.*

from *Reno*

Dick and J.B. arose late. They had an "eye-opener," then sauntered down to the dining room for breakfast. As they passed through the lobby, a pretty, fair-haired girl, with dancing eyes set off by a dress of firecracker-red chiffon, caught J.B.'s arm.

"Hello, there, J.B. How ah you'all?" A sweet drawling voice, heavy with the accent of the Far South. "We'ah th'owin' a pahty tonight, J.B.—Lola Penny's graduating!" Dick did not know that graduating meant legal freedom, freedom of marriage, an event invincibly celebrated in Reno.

J.B. acknowledged the greeting with a careless "Hello, Sweetness," and good-naturedly responded to the girl's obvious desire for an introduction to Dick.

"Mrs. Rita Rogers, of Savannah, Georgia, recently arrived."

"You heah fo' the Cuah, too?" she asked flippantly.

Dick was torn between irritation and amusement, it was none of *her* business why he was here! But this was Reno. It would be silly to pretend, so he nodded.

"You'all must be suah an' come to the pahty!" her smile was for Dick, alone. "Don' you fo'get, Big Boy!"

But a "party" was about the last thing Dick cared to contemplate. His career had been punctuated by parties, both at college and in the subsequent life in which it had pleased his god to place him. Parties! No! Sleep had restored to him his normal, healthy outlook upon life, and besides he was beginning to feel the tang of the clear crispy and bracing Nevada air.

He was in Reno on business—serious business, that had had its roots in parties. Now he wanted to get away from everything even suggesting the life that had wrecked his romance and left him, thirty years of age, a spiritual failure.

"J.B.," he said, as he returned from the rack with his cap. "Jackasses have one peculiar trait not shown by horses. If a jackass stops on the trail for the night, his first thought is for his orientation, while the horse starts right to eating, he sets out to get an eyeful of the country."

"What has all this to do with anything in particular?" asked J.B. quizzically.

"Well, in this respect—and perhaps others, I am like a jackass. If I am surrounded by the dangers you recounted last night, and the one I've just seen looming up, I'd like to get my bearings. In other words, I'd like to see Reno."

"You couldn't have chosen a more intelligent rubberneck guide than your Uncle John," replied J.B. reaching for his hat. "Come along, there's a lot that will surprise you."

And surprise there was, for preconceptives are usually mental-habit fulfillments and Dick had pictured Reno, until his first glimpse last night, as a blazing, sunburnt, railroad town, set down in the immensity of the Nevada desert. In fact, having traveled across fifteen hundred miles of beautiful but dreadful Inferno, he had landed in Reno, not knowing he had reached the end of the bleached-bone trail, and that the city lay piled almost under the shadow of the High Sierras that piled precipitously up toward the West.

"I feel like Wrigley when he first approached Catalina Island for which he had paid three million dollars," said Dick.

"My God!" he exclaimed, "it's a mountain! I thought it was flat!"

"And those mountains are from ten to fourteen thousand feet high," added J.B. "Reno itself is more than forty-five hundred feet above sea level."

It was not the mountains to the West, nor the desert toward the East, however, that challenged Dick's interest as he strolled about the town. First of all, it was the people, swank Easterners who might have been right off Fifth Avenue, rubbing elbows with silent taciturn men from the mountains and the garrulous, gregarious 'rats' from the desert.

Another feature Dick noted was that the town was bisected by Virginia Street, running North and South, and by the Truckee River, running from West to East. And running was the proper word, for it was a roaring, turbulent river of pure mountain water tumbling right through the city's heart.

"That's what I heard last night," said Dick. "I thought it was all imaginary noise like that in a sea shell."

"Just as the Ganges is supposed to wash away Hindu sins," observed J.B. as they stood on one of the concrete bridges spanning the swirling waters, "so the Truckee is supposed to wash out one's marital past. The moment a divorcée is granted her final decree of freedom, she hurries to the river with her friends—and often the man she is to marry on the morrow—and standing upon the bank, and with some sort of prayer beginning: 'Here goes nothing,' she throws the wedding ring into the enveloping waters.—They say there is more gold now in the river's bed than was taken out by all the placer miners of the early days."

Virginia Street, too, was a surprise. The broad pavement upon which were diagonally parked myriads of cars—not Fords and Chevrolets, as one might expect, but high-priced cars, many of foreign make—was flanked by substantial brick stores. In fact, Reno was a city of brick and concrete.

In only one thing did Virginia Street suggest the West. Business places, with that typically American expression of local pride of homesickness, bore such signs as: "The Denver Market," "The St. Paul Cleaners," "The Texas Toy Shop,"—names which make of every Western city a cosmopolis.

Furthermore, as a means of relieving the nostalgia of the divorce colony, there were branch stores of all the great metropolitan emporiums of trade—Hughes,' Brooks' Bros., Knox, Spalding, Dobbs, etc.

But the one store that removed Reno far from the ranks of the wild and woolly west was "The Betty Bloom Chocolate Shoppe," no cowboy or desert rat would stand for a "shoppe."

"In one way this is a hick town!" exclaimed Dick as he noted the swarms of people entering the post office. "Hasn't Reno any delivery service?"

"Oh yes," laughed J.B. "for the local population, but the hard-boiled 'Renoite' prefers general delivery. You see it's not pleasant to have your address known, if your husband back East is a snoopy gentleman who wishes to have you watched. Most of the ladies choose to keep their hide-outs a secret."

"Then General Delivery holds much charm for masculine inquisitiver," continued J.B. "It is true one may not learn the lady's favorite flower or telephone number by hanging 'round, but he may learn her name, and sometime her real address. I learned something there one day that was delightfully exciting for a week, but it cost me my watch and two perfectly good cuff-links." And J.B. sighed reminiscently.

Then suddenly they came upon the famous court house that has been the scene of many of America's greatest dramas—and comedies.

"There's another bit of color, Dick, peculiar to this little city," and J.B. led the newly arrived searcher for happiness up the steps to where he stood beside one of the high white columns of the court-house façade.

"You see this smudge of pink just head-high?" smiled J.B. "Rouge!" he added cryptically. Then in answer to Dick's questioning eyes he went on to explain.

"The Blarney Stone is a joke compared to this. For it is one of the fixed customs of Reno that when a lady gets her final decree and starts for the river to throw her wedding ring in, she first stops here and kisses the dear old court-house that gave her her freedom. They wash it occasionally, but the pink persists!"

Thus, thought Dick, do customs develop into folkways.

. . . .

Dick was suddenly conscious of the startling contrasts in the environment of Reno. It seemed to be a sort of beautiful Purgatory standing between Heaven and Hell, with a much firmer grip in Heaven.

Driving back through the city he was further impressed with another contrast—that of the green lawns and huge shade trees of the suburbs, a distinctly small-town atmosphere, and the metropolitan air of the large hotels and gaudy apartment houses. He noted the same contrast in the people. A scattering of big-city fashionables but with the larger part of the population going about its affairs apparently as unaware of the presence of these outlanders as the Versailles clams are of their barnacles.

Evidently there were two Renos—one, a city of quiet homes, bright-eyed school children and contented parents; the other a group of hotel and apartment house inmates merely stalling around until their short tenure should have passed, or gregariously "throwing parties" in a sad and tragic effort to forget their troubles. The latter group was, however, a social entity as distinct from the real Reno as "Holly-wood" is from the immense social life of Los Angeles.

MAX MILLER [1899–1967]

By 1941, Reno was accustomed to publicity. An article in the Nevada State Journal *from that year observed that Reno "has had the spotlight turned on it from many sources, it has been lied about and praised, it has been the setting for sensational stories and it has been condemned for sins of omission and commission." In contrast to writers who sensationalized Reno, journalist Max Miller won the* Journal's *approval for debunking: "He picks up many of the stories spread by less industrious writers, who colored their stories to get them printed, and supplants them with facts that weave into a continuous, interesting and many times an affectionate chronicle of what goes on here and why." Miller's well-informed* Reno *(1941) ably covers the region's history, natural features, quirks, lore, notable people, and tourist attractions. While Miller's main focus is on the "One Thing"—the divorce industry—he remains keenly aware of the "wilderness" surrounding Reno, the "air-cleansed desolation" integral to the Reno experience.*

Max Carlton Miller grew up in Traverse City, Michigan, was educated at the University of Washington, and became a newspaper reporter for the Seattle Sun, *the* Melbourne Herald *in Australia, and the* San Diego Sun, *where he was the waterfront reporter. His* I Cover the Waterfront *(1932) became a best seller and in 1933 was made into a movie starring Claudette Colbert. That book's success allowed Miller to quit the newspaper business and become an independent writer, producing more than twenty-five books over the next thirty-five years, often about regions of Southern California and the Baja Peninsula. As a young man Miller served in the U.S. Navy during World War I and was on active duty in the naval reserves during World War II and the Korean War. In the following scene, the onset of World War II clearly troubles Miller, even as he describes women undone by their own domestic conflicts.*

from *Reno*

Maybe Reno is not important to the nation. Or maybe Reno is exceptionally important to the nation. One wonders about these things. But the place to wonder is not so much within the town itself, over the town bars, but off a bit on one of the elaborately silent hills somewhere overlooking Reno, perhaps.

For within a few minutes out of Reno in any direction whatsoever the world becomes the epitome of peace, of calmness, the epitome of air-cleansed desolation. The world becomes our conception of the moon should ever we visit it.

So, if we must have a national clinic for wrecked domestic nerves, this region may as well be the site for such a clinic, I suppose. The shock of space, and the shock of endless horizons with signs neither of man nor of house, certainly must work its share in jarring back to saneness those tortured souls whose lives presumably have ended back in an apartment house when a husband said: "You go to Reno and get it. I can't spare the time from business."

For it is a fact that nine of the ten women who come to Reno for a divorce are doing so under order of their husbands. Nine of the ten women—so the Reno lawyers tell us—do not want what they are sent to get. But the axe has fallen. The expense account is furnished. And the women, for the sake of their own pride, must do the rest.

This is speaking with the broadest of generalities. But these generalities are the ABC's of Reno, the basic groundwork if one is to understand the nightly scenes around Reno bars or the daytime scenes around these dude ranches.

A good Reno lawyer has to be both a doctor and a father confessor, and from such Reno lawyers (a dozen of the 180 in town have ninety per cent of the business) one learns more about life and sex and marriage than in all the volumes by the late Havelock Ellis. For he did have, after all, rather a Sunday-school boy outlook. He perpetually was astounded by the obvious. But these lawyers of Reno are astounded by nothing. And they let us know, too, with brisk frankness, that when a man approaches his dangerous years, his own menopause, the bedroom suddenly becomes more important than the kitchen. He suddenly becomes fearful that, while concentrating on making money for his family's security, he may have lost out on something terrific which more careless men have had all the time. Or at least they say they have had. And man, the same as woman, is a greedy beast. He wants everything. First he wanted a home, we will say. He has it, and has found it wanting. He would as soon have some of that romance, too, "which other guys have talked about."

He meets up with some specialist, some girl or some young woman who knows all the tricks of making him feel that—until he met her—his bedroom talents had gone unappreciated. She can make him feel he is a robust bull indeed. For, like a well-arranged war campaign, she has to fight only on one front, allowing her to muster her skill splendidly. But the wife has had to be a mother, too, perhaps. And a cook. And a manager. And a sweeper-out-of-kitchens. She has had to hold her fight on many fronts, and the part of a lover has been only one of them. The specialist, for a fact, is a dangerous little animal, and because of her there is a Reno.

And because of her the wife one day is told that she is repulsive, that she doesn't know how to dress, that she has no warmth, and that rather than wait until the coolness between them turns to downright hate she had better go right out to Reno "so that we still can be friends at least. And here's a check."

. . . .

The gods of the volcanoes, of the ice age, of the seas, earthquakes and molten lava overplayed their hands a little—just a little—when they threw things around so robustly in preparing the region where today sits this little town.

After the gods had their big fling they did not bother to pick up the pieces, or allow drainage for the melting ice to reach the oceans. With the coming of the three-toed horses, tigers, rhinoceri, sloths, monster birds, mastodons, and finally man, the gods simply gave up and scampered, it would seem, leaving this land in a topsy-turvy free-for-all the same as it is today—a lofty birdbath without an outlet and gradually drying up under the sun.

The magic word Reno, then, means more than the name of this concentrated little Byzantium. The word, in a way, stands for all this surrounding region too, for which Reno is the crossroads, the trading center, the watering hole, the meeting place. And Reno's laws are founded on the theory that each man should be capable of looking out for himself. The desert on three sides, and the Sierra on the west side, have been the ancient task-masters.

This is why there is more to Reno than the constant clinking of its eight hundred slot-machines.

This is why there is more to Reno than its seventy-four bars in winter, eighty in summer.

This is why there is more to Reno than its roulette wheels, its race-horse keno, its chuck-a-luck, its faro. This is why there is more to Reno than the Celebrated Thing which accounts for so many of the dude ranches and for so many of the town's lawyers. For Reno is the mouthpiece of a wilderness which, all in all— though the state is the sixth largest in the United States—does not contain enough citizens to fill the Pasadena Rose Bowl.

And so, in such a wilderness, the tempo is—always has been—that each man should be capable of looking out for himself. If he is not capable he can get out, he can go "over the hill," meaning over the Sierra to California. If he wants to gamble, the prerogative is his own. But he must not hang around whining if he loses, nor ask the state for recompense, nor for a free living ever afterwards.

But in this Nevada the word gambling is a broad term. The word reaches beyond the Methodists' conception of it. Cattlemen are gamblers. Each season in this dry land is a gamble with them. The same with sheepmen, miners, and certainly with prospectors. Not to gamble in Nevada would mean not to be working for a living.

. . . .

Pyramid Lake with its scorched mineral cliffs is but thirty or forty minutes from Reno and across such manless desolation that the trip may as well be to Upper Tibet. Yet Pyramid Lake is as essential to the Clinic of Reno as iodine in a medicine chest.

The more humane of the Reno lawyers, and therefore the smarter of the Reno lawyers, long have used Pyramid Lake as an opiate for their hysterical clients arriving in town directly from the apartment-house quarrels of the east. For these lawyers, the best of them, are obliged to be not only doctors, not only psychologists, but also nerve specialists.

"Let's get out of this office," the lawyer will say to his shaking client whose world has just splintered, whose husband has shoved her off to Reno to do the work. "Let's get out of this office." He may use the excuse he has business at Pyramid Lake. He may use any sort of excuse, even the excuse he has to see an Indian at Pyramid about a fishing license.

This would sound legitimate, too, for Pyramid is on an Indian reservation, and, therefore, its shores today are not open to white settlers. The Indians own the lake, and from them the special fishing licenses must be obtained. Anyway, regardless of how the lawyer gets her there, we will assume this is her first trip to what in my opinion is the strangest lake of its size on earth, a so-called fresh water lake (at least fresh enough to support the world's largest trout) in the midst of a baked desert, with no foliage, and scarcely any habitation. She may have seen lakes and lakes, but if she is from the east she has not seen before a lake like this one—forty-five miles long, ten miles wide—and the colorings of its rocky walls are those of the Grand Canyon.

The lake is approached by surprise. The car turns a quick bend between two desert hills, and there the lake rests naked and calm, as naked and calm as in pre-history. The lawyer, knowing his business, will say nothing for a while. He merely will sit there silently, allowing this new world, this different world, this world-without-man, to soak itself into his client. For the lawyer, the same as the rest of us, is only too well aware that one cannot easily forget one's troubles in a city where mankind's own importance is everything, where mankind is held kingpin of the earth, the sole purpose of the earth having been built.

He knows the same as we know that when one is submerged in the squirming tangle of dressed-up flesh of New York, of Chicago, of Pittsburgh, of Los Angeles that one also must become a part of this squirming tangle of dressed-up flesh. For our own survival it seems most important for any of us to do so.

For our own safety—except when in the solitude of a wasteland—we never dare release our guard long enough to realize that perhaps other creatures may be fully as important to this world as man. And that they, too, may be truly as responsible for its well-being as are we. Nor are we to blame, either, for this vain presumption that the conduct of the world is entirely our own doings, our full responsibility. We are manufactured to believe so, we are manufactured with this vain presumption as a part of our sinews, our blood, our brains. Yet, somehow, so helpless are we before forces beyond us, that we no more could be to blame, even for our own conduct as mankind, than the grass is to blame for its conduct as grass, or the chipmunks for their conduct as chipmunks. Nobody, so far as I know, has given us outright the full management of The World Incorporated. In our own stubbornness to exist we merely imagine this has been done, and we feel wretched each time the supposed management so bluntly is yanked beyond our control—as during wars.

The joke always seems to be on us.

And only when on a desert, with no other humans around, can the more slug-gish of us finally be brought face-up to the fact that—yes, there still would be an earth whether man was on it or was not on it. There still would be an earth, and it would be the same size, and it still would be answering the same astronomical laws, the same tides, the same winds. The lawyer is not responsible for the world. She is not responsible for the world. I am not responsible. We are as helpless, in the long run, as any other natural item upon it. We and the lemmings, I often feel, are brothers in our own blind helplessness, in our own blind instincts for wholesale suicides, periodically. You promise to kill me and I'll promise to kill you. Our own inventions in which we take such pride are used finally for our own finish.

The space surrounding Reno can bring all this to mind the moment one leaves town. He or she can, for the moment, become the only person on earth and can taste, for a moment, the sensation of having nobody with whom to quarrel, no-body with whom to be jealous, no other nations with which to fight, no boundar-ies to consider, and no factories, and even "that woman he's with now" back in Baltimore—even she for the moment may seem but a retrospective speck and not the entire cosmos of one's concentration.

Pyramid Lake.

I say all this, though poorly, because the sensation must be explained somehow, poorly or not. It must at least be hinted, even repeated, because it is most impor-tant to Reno. It remains, with repeated emphasis, so much the reason the shattered women return to the region of Reno for their repeat cures. They themselves may not be able to word just why, though frequently they do try to word it. But the reason, as I say, is not Reno itself so much as the weird space surrounding Reno, the space which can permeate the town if need be, and despite the noise going on around here. The space is here, it is everywhere around here, and it is medicine.

. . . .

And so there is Pyramid Lake with its silence. Pyramid with its blue, green and obsidian black silence. The greatness of the silent lake so startles her that she does not know what to do. She sees upon the walls and the shores the strata upon strata of earth-formations before man—her man or anybody else's man—came on earth. And the formations probably will be there, just as sturdy and just as indifferent, after man—her man or anybody else's man—has left earth.

Those geological strata, with their tier on tier of reds and purples and cherry and pink, can do plenty towards pounding into her mind that five hundred million years of workmanship are a lot of years to be used only for man's brief moment exclusively, and for her brief second exclusively, in hate.

The tiny desert squirrels with their light tufts (even the desert squirrels around Pyramid are of a separate species) must be certain that all these silent formations of Pyramid were built expressly for them, too. One could think so, as the diminutive devils scramble around the porous rocks, really enjoying them. The squirrels perhaps wonder, too, just who or what she is. But anyway—

—she has stopped crying.

WALTER VAN TILBURG CLARK [1909–1971]

When the Nevada Writers Hall of Fame was established in 1988, Walter Van Tilburg Clark and Robert Laxalt, whom Clark mentored, were the first two honorees. Born in Maine, Clark was raised in Reno, where his father was president of the University of Nevada (1918–38). Clark earned a BA and MA from the University of Nevada, Reno, and a second MA from the University of Vermont. Thereafter, he taught English and creative writing at numerous universities throughout the United States. A "writer's writer," Clark composed poems, novels, essays, and short stories. In a letter to his son he reflected that "writing is not an occupation, it is a way of life, in a sense not altogether unlike that of a religious devotion." With The Ox-Bow Incident (1940), an allegorical novel of a lynch mob in the American West, he became a national literary figure. Ox-Bow was followed by The City of Trembling Leaves (1945) and The Track of the Cat (1949). Fellow writer Wallace Stegner observed that The City of Trembling Leaves "chronicles the development of a sensitive adolescent into an artist. It is preoccupied with the relationship between art and life." City is a slow novel, like slow food. Patiently savored, it never disappoints. The novel's Prelude, reprinted here, establishes the symbolic geography of Reno from the perspective of protagonist Timothy Hazard, who grows up there, a poignantly different view of the city than the ones reproduced in divorce novels of the same period. Clark lived in the East during his golden decade of writing western-set novels (1940–50). After the instant success and film adaptations of Ox-Bow and Track of the Cat, Clark dusted off and rewrote earlier stories, but by 1962 he had produced little new work. By his own admission, he spent his last years bogged down, editing the voluminous diaries of Alfred Doten, a writer and editor on the Comstock Lode.

from *The City of Trembling Leaves*

This is the story of the lives and loves of Timothy Hazard, and so, indirectly, a token biography of Reno, Nevada, as well. Now, whatever else Reno may be, and it is many things, it is the city of trembling leaves. The most important meaning of leaves is the same everywhere in Reno, of course, and everywhere else, for that matter, which is what Tim implies when he calls moribund any city containing a region in which you can look all around and not see a tree. Such a city is drawing out of its alliance with the eternal, with the Jurassic Swamps and the Green Mansions, and in time it will also choke out the trees in the magic wilderness of the spirit. In Reno, however, this universal importance of trees is intensified, for Reno is in the Great Basin of America, between the Rockies and the Sierras, where the vigor of the sun and the height of the mountains, to say nothing of the denuding activities of mining booms, have created a latter-day race of tree worshippers. Furthermore, to such tree worshippers, and Tim Hazard is high in the cult, the trees of Reno have regional meanings within their one meaning, like the themes and transitions of a one-movement symphony. It would be impossible to understand Tim Hazard without hearing these motifs played separately before you hear them in the whole.

The trees of the Wingfield Park–Court Street region dispense an air of antique melancholy. You become sad and old as you walk under these trees, even on a bright, winter day when all the leaves are gone and the branches make only narrow shadows across homes covered with sunlight.

The park is not large, yet it feels like the edge of a wilderness of infinite extent, so that if you lie on the grass there on Sunday, or sit on one of the green benches (this is in the summer now), you don't even have to close your eyes to believe in a great depth of forest and shadow of time. In part this is due to the illusion that the treetops of Reno are continuous, one elevated pampas of stirring leaves, unconcerned with houses and streets below, so that the park, actually a ledge between the Truckee River and the bluff of Court Street, does not seem set apart. Even more it is due to the spacious shadow and the quiet under the trees. No rush of wind and leaves, no slow snowing of cottonwood-down, or cries of playing children, or running on the tennis courts can really disturb this quiet. It is an everlasting late-afternoon somnolence, the mood of a Watteau painting, if you can imagine the beribboned courtiers much smaller under their trees, like Corot's wood nymphs, and completely dreamy, not even toying with flutes, mandolins, fruit or amorous preliminaries. This applies only to the older part of the park, of course. The newer part, on the island breasting the Truckee, is out in the sun, and its trees are younger and more susceptible to vagrant airs. It is like a light motif dropped into the melancholy central movement in anticipation of the theme of the outskirts.

The mood of the Court Street trees is heavy with the homes, some of which can be seen from below, staring northward from the bluff out of tired windows. Among their lawns, shaded by their trees and their pasts, these houses do not wholly despair, but they have reason to. Their doors seem closed, their windows empty and still, and they appear to meditate upon longer, more intricate and more pathetic pasts than any of them could possibly have accumulated. The vitality of these houses, compounded of memory and discontent, is inconsiderable compared with their resignation. Even though it would not be statistically accurate, you must think of all the houses in Court Street in terms of high-ceilinged rooms with the shades drawn in late afternoon in summer, or with the shades up but the windows closed in a windy, moonlit night in winter. And you must be alone in the room and in the house. It makes no difference any more who lives in these houses, or what they do; they cannot change this nature, which has been accepted and expressed by the trees of Court Street.

Beyond Court Street to the south, this mood goes through a gradual and almost constant brightening. The Court Street theme still dominates the region of Flint, Hill, Liberty, Granite and California, all that height and slope between Belmont Road and Virginia Street, the region of big rooming houses and apartments, which owes allegiance to the Washoe County Court House, and may be called the Court House Quarter. Even the private homes of this region are sunk under the Court Street theme, and its big and beautiful trees give the impression that they should be motionless, even in a plateau gale, and that only their topmost leaves should accept sunlight, and tremble. Tim's best friend, Lawrence Black, whose life will at times seem almost synonymous with Tim's, lived in this quarter when he was a boy, and Tim says that his home echoed the theme, and was gently and completely haunted from attic to basement. Its liveliest time was the bearable melancholy of six o'clock in the afternoon in June. Tim's great single love, Rachel Wells, also lived in this quarter, in a big house with a porte-cochere and an air of dark yesterdays, until she had finished high school.

From here out, to the south and west, spreads a high region of increasingly new homes, bungalows, ornamented brick structures of greater size, a number of which it would be difficult to describe fairly, and white, Spanish houses. This region seems to become steadily more open, windy and sunlit as you move out, and at some point you will realize that the Court Street theme has become inaudible, and that you have truly entered what may be called the Mt. Rose Quarter. Here there are many new trees, no taller than a man, always trembling so they nearly dance, and most of the grown trees are marching files of poplars, in love with wind and heavens. Here, no matter how many houses rear up, stark in the sunlight, you remain more aware of the sweeping domes of earth which hold them down, and no matter how long you stay in one of the houses, you will still be more aware of Mt. Rose aloft upon the west, than of anything in the house: furniture, silver, books, or even people. Even at night, when the summit of the mountain is only a starlit glimmer, detached from earth, it is the strong pole of all waking minds in that quarter.

. . . .

On the north side of the Truckee River, the Court Street theme continues, but in a higher and sharper key, interrupted by short, ominous passages from the middle of the city. Also it moves toward the north edge more rapidly and with a quickening tempo, for in this district of the McKinley Park and Mary S. Doten schools, the dominant houses are, from the first, the dying miniature Victorian and the bungalows, and they don't influence the trees.

When you reach the little trees of the north edge, where Virginia Street becomes the Purdy Road, or the region of upper Ralston Street west of the hilltop cemeteries, there is a new theme, higher, clearer and sharper than that of the south edge. Here the city is thinner, and not expanding so rapidly, for it is already on the mountains. From windows on the heights, University Terrace, College Drive, Fourteenth and Fifteenth Streets, you look down across the whole billowing sea of the treetops of Reno, and feel more removed from the downtown section than in any other place in the city, because you are off any main streets, away from the sound of them even, and because you can see the tops of downtown places, the Medico-Dental Building, the roof sign of the Riverside Hotel, the gray breasts of the Catholic Church, like strange and tiny islands in that sea, and realize how far you are from them.

There is another difference, too, which indirectly affects the meaning of the trees. The University of Nevada is on the climbing north edge, and it is an even better place than any of the parks for glens and stretches of lawn, and clumps and avenues of trees. It has a tone of active, enduring quiet, and is big enough to impart much of this tone to all the north end except the eastern corner, which is drawn into the influence of the race track. For Tim Hazard, after his boyhood, the university quarter was foreign country, the city of the hills seen from the plains. He went up there only once in a while, to hear some music, or see a play, or watch a game in the gymnasium or on Mackay Field. Yet he says that he always felt that in going north, toward the university, he should walk, but in going south, until he had passed the last service station on the South Virginia Road, he should drive, and drive like hell.

A further and, perhaps, in the course of time, even more important, difference between the high north edge, and the low south edge, is that Mt. Rose is the sole, white, exalted patron angel and fountain of wind and storm to south Reno, while in north Reno, her reign is strongly contested by black Peavine Mountain, less austere, wilder, and the home of two winds. Mt. Rose is a detached goal of the spirit, requiring a lofty and difficult worship. Peavine is the great, humped child of desert. He is barren, and often lowering, but he reaches out and brings unto him, while Rose stands aloof. He is part of the great plateau which is the land of the city, while Rose is part of the western barrier. Rose begets reverence, but Peavine begets love. There is a liveliness in his quarter which gets into everything.

. . . .

The north-east quarter of Reno, with the ranching valley on the east of it and the yellow hills with a few old mines on the north, is drawn out of the influence of the university and Peavine into the vortex of the race track. Even in Tim's boyhood the race track was alive only two or three weeks out of a year, yet it seems a fast-moving place. The trembling of the leaves in its sphere rises easily into a roaring through tall Lombardies set in rows in dust and open sunlight. This quality of thin, hasty brightness persists clear down through the quarter, where the trees close in and the small, white houses fill the blocks, in the lumber yard beyond, and even down to the Western Pacific Depot and the grimy edge of Fourth Street. It is a theme almost strident, and saved from being as intolerable as persistent whistles only by the yellow hills, like cats asleep in the north, and by the greater and darker Virginia Range in the east, through which the Truckee cuts its red and shadowy gorge. Sunset on those hills is also a very important subduer.

It was in this quarter that Tim Hazard lived when he was a boy, on the street right next to the track, so that he got to see a good many horse races and rodeos, and even circuses that set up their tents outside the fence. He lived in a square, white-board house with a shallow porch with a dirt walk and three big poplars in front of it. His bedroom was upstairs in front, and when he was in bed he heard the poplars, winter and summer, windy and quiet, and saw them, morning and night, cloudy and clear, moonlight and starlight and dark.

. . . .

The south-east quarter of Reno combines the qualities of the north-east and south-west, yet has a quite different, quieter and more uniform tone, because it is dedicated to the valley, into which it is slowly spreading, and is not much influenced by any mountain. Daybreak and sunset are the test times of any region's allegiance, and at daybreak and sunset the south-east quarter thinks toward the valley, where the light spreads widely, and is more aware of that level spaciousness than of the mountains beyond it. None of the themes of Reno is isolated, however. They merge one into another, and so one corner of this quarter, the Mill Street toward Virginia Street corner, echoes the Court Street theme and the rumbling and cries of the center of the city.

Reno began with Lake's Crossing on the Truckee, and in its beginnings was divided by the Truckee, but as it grew the activity of men quartered it by the intersection of Virginia Street, running more or less north and south, and Fourth Street, running more or less east and west. Virginia Street and Fourth Street are what is commonly called the main arteries, or the purveyors of the life-blood of the city. They are the streets which continue on out and tie Reno into the world, as the others fade away or blend into each other. The only important difference between them and the purveyors of the life-blood of any city arises from the fact that Reno has sheltered itself in the north-west corner of its valley, so that it has stretched along Virginia Street only to the south, where it becomes the highway to Carson, and along Fourth Street only to the east, where Reno and Sparks have become practically one city. It is more important, however, to the Reno of Tim Hazard, that on the west, Fourth Street plunges quickly into the foothills of the Sierras, and that North Virginia Street promptly becomes the Purdy Road, which goes away lonesomely across passes and great desert valleys into a land of timber, fine cattle, deep upland meadows and secret lakes. It is notable, for instance, that on the Purdy Road hawks, and even eagles, may be seen perching for long periods on fence posts and telephone poles.

Mary Turner lived in a frame bungalow on North Virginia Street, opposite the university, while she and Tim were going to the Orvis Ring School. The Orvis Ring is the school for the north-east quarter. The Western Pacific tracks run right behind it, but the Western Pacific there is a quiet, single line, and doesn't disturb the school, or have much effect on the quarter, except as a dividing line between the university region and the race-track region.

This is not the case with the big Southern Pacific lines, but since they run through the downtown section, and only a block south of Fourth Street, they don't create a separate zone. Aside from the fact that they make a railroad street of Commercial Row, their effect is one with that of Fourth Street. Yet they have a subtle influence in Reno, whether it is heeded or not, aside, that is, from the obvious results of carrying thousands of people and cattle, and thousands of tons of freight, into and out of and through Reno. The gigantic freight engines of the SP, often two to a train when headed into the mountains, gently shake all the windows in the city in their passage. At night their tremendous mushrooms of smoke, lighted from beneath by the center of the city, may be seen from the hills of the north edge, swelling above the trees. Their wild whistles cry in the night, and echo mournfully all round the mountain walls of the valley. Thus Reno is reminded constantly that it is only one small stop on the road of the human world, that it trembles with the comings and goings of that world, and yet that the greatest cry of that world is only a brief echo against mountains.

. . . .

There is also, of course, the treeless center of the city, which we have worked all around, though not without hearing it several times, in sudden, shrill bursts from the brass or deep mutterings in the rhythm section. This, however, is the region about which the world already knows or imagines more, in a Sunday-supplement way, than is true, and it will do, for the present, to suggest that it is not unlike any moribund city, or the moribund region of any city. It is the ersatz jungle, where the human animals, uneasy in the light, dart from cave to cave under steel and neon branches, where the voice of the croupier halloos in the secret glades, and high and far, like light among the top leaves, gleam the names of lawyers and hairdressers on upstairs windows. In short, this is the region which may be truly entered by passing under the arch which says, RENO, THE BIGGEST LITTLE CITY IN THE WORLD.

Yet there is one important difference between even this region and the truly moribund cities of the world, the difference which makes Reno a city of adolescence, a city of dissonant themes, sawing against each other with a kind of piercing beauty like that of fourteen-year-old girl or a seventeen-year-old boy, the beauty of everything promised and nothing resolved. Even from the very center of Reno, from the intersection of Virginia and Second Streets, and even at night, when restless club lights mask the stars, one can look in any direction and see the infinite shoals of the leaves hovering about the first lone crossing light.

WILLIAM STAFFORD [1914–1993]

Once described as "a western Robert Frost," William Stafford published more than fifty books over his career and earned some of America's highest distinctions, including a National Book Award in 1963 for Traveling through the Dark *and an appointment as consultant in poetry for the Library of Congress in 1970, a position that later became known as poet laureate. Born January 17, 1914, in Hutchinson, Kansas, Stafford earned his* BA *from the University of Kansas in 1937. Five years later he lived in Washoe Valley, Nevada, in a camp for conscientious objectors to World War II. It was his four-year experience in four different such camps that formed a life-long early-morning habit. Too tired at the end of each day of manual labor—building fences, fighting fires—Stafford made himself get up early enough to write before having to work. He later described his habit as sitting alone and writing whatever occurred to him, following his impulses. Writing "is like fishing," he said, and one must be receptive and "willing to fail." Stafford held a long teaching career at Lewis and Clark College in Portland, Oregon, where he was fondly remembered by students for emphasizing process over product, helping writers overcome crippling self-censorship by enjoining them to "lower your standards." Stafford wrote often of western subjects and scenes, and, like Frost's, his deceptively short and simple poems often hide complex anxieties and ambiguities below their surface. He visited Reno fairly frequently on family trips through the Great Basin and to give readings at the university. "Reno" appears in his collection* Going Places: Poems, *published in 1974 by West Coast Poetry Review in Reno. Stafford died at his home in Lake Oswego, Oregon, on August 28, 1993. The poem he had been working on that morning includes the words "Be ready for what God sends."*

Reno

     Mouth, hands, and cascade hair—
     in dim bedrooms the hopeful wait.

     Flown here to their ebbing tide, they find
     horizons more cruel than laws can name.

     Finessed by ads, they follow their pictures,
     pay for themselves, buy identities.

     No matter how young they are, if no one
     calls tonight, they hear winter far away,
          one little slit snowflake.

JILL STERN [1915–2005]

"I spent six weeks in wonderment . . . thinking what will the sociologists 100 years hence say of this," observed author Jill Stern to the Nevada State Journal *in 1957, after her brief residency in Reno to obtain a divorce. Through Stern's eyes, Reno represented a "cross-section of the unhappy everywhere. It is the symbol of those of us who have tried and failed to make necessary adjustment to family life. It is a carnival of the lost." Born in Illinois, Stern was raised in a prominent publishing family. Her father, Julius David Stern Jr., was a close friend of Franklin D. Roosevelt and published the* Camden Courier, Philadelphia Record, New York Post, *and a book,* Memoirs of a Maverick Publisher. *Jill's older brother David Stern III, also a newspaper executive, is better known for his 1946 novels starring Francis the Talking Mule, inspiration for Donald O'Connor's Francis the Mule movies as well as the later television take-off,* Mr. Ed. *Jill Stern attended Wellesley and Bryn Mawr colleges, acted on Broadway, served in the* WAVES *during World War II, and copublished the* Hartford Gazette *with her then-husband Paul Capron. After her divorce Stern and her daughter Janet moved to New York, where Stern continued to write. Stern's novel* Not in Our Stars *(1957), reissued as* Nine Miles to Reno *(1958), follows Sara Winston and her young son, Joey, during their stay at the Jolly-J Guest Ranch, nine miles west of Reno, where they learn the stories of other "colonists." Sara and a divorce-seeker named Van from Long Island fall passionately in love, but Van ultimately returns to the long-suffering Hilda back home, who has waited ten years for him to leave his wife.* Not in Our Stars *explores the psychological complexity and emotional nuance of divorce, examining why marriages fail and what happens to people who seek the "cure" in divorce centers such as Reno.*

from *Not in Our Stars*
D-Day

Reno isn't a place, Sara thought as she had on the day of her arrival. It's just a symbol to America and the rest of the world; a symbol of failure to some, of release to others, of despair to the unloved, of the promised land to the domestically trapped. It meant quick marriage to impatient lovers, quick divorce to those who had found more desirable mates, the possibility of a quick killing for those with a lust for the wheel and the dice and the cards. *Could be, might be, maybe this time, maybe next time. . . .* Yes, Reno was a symbol of the second chance and the chance after that which every man always believed awaited him—as he never really believed that death would come to him. In America, everybody had a chance—and if they muffed it there was always the second chance. Reno had given a second chance to Jean Trolley, to Terrie and Bert, to Aileen Wilson ("I'm one of the ones who came out and never went back"); it would give a second chance to Van and perhaps to her.

But to Maggie and Belle, to all the Maggies and Belles, the thousands who were cast off each year by unloving husbands—what did Reno mean to them? To them, Sara thought, it was a symbol of the restlessness, the rootlessness, the heartlessness of mid-twentieth-century America, maybe of the world, itself. Reno, Las Vegas: gamble while you sit out your six weeks' residence. Gamble and drink and dance. Don't for one minute stop to shed a tear. It isn't being done these days. Reno, Las Vegas: each year a few swankier hotels and gambling casinos to take care of the growing pilgrimage from every state in the Union. Reno, Las Vegas: and in between the desert where the atom bomb was tested, each year a bigger and deadlier one. Each year a more destructive bomb to be released upon the sands, a few more divorces, a few more suicides, a few thousand more mentally disturbed patients to be supported by the government than the year before. . . .

What had produced a Reno? Where had it all started? What made it the strange modern melting pot that it was? The ranchers, the miners, the engineers, the promoters, the cowboys, the Nevada politicians who had reduced the residence requirements for divorce from six months to six weeks to encourage business, the dude ranch owners who served as witnesses at the trials, the divorce lawyers and the gambling club proprietors, the tourists who came to gape and gamble, the soda jerks who doubled as shills at night, the movie stars who entertained at the Riverside while sitting out their own six weeks, the divorcees-to-be from East Orange and Little Rock and Los Angeles and Westchester—they were all America. Reno wasn't a place. It was a state of mind, a general state of the collective American mind.

. . . .

"This is case No. 143,629—Winston v. Winston."

"May we have a private hearing?" from Bill Nelson, her lawyer.

"Upon application of counsel for the plaintiff, it is ordered that the trial of this case be private and heard behind closed doors," the judge directed.

"Ready on the part of the plaintiff," said Bill Nelson.

"Ready on the part of the defendant," said a strange, pasty-faced man in a salt-and-pepper suit, who must be Wade's counsel, she realized.

Then the judge said: "You may proceed."

(Why did she think of the time they took out her tonsils twenty years ago? She had been rather pleased at the prospect until she found herself in the little operating room with the doctor and the nurse and the anesthetist who clamped that horrible mask over her face and kept saying: "Now just breathe in slowly. Just breathe in slowly." Too late then to stop all of the terrible process. Too late now to—)

Then one of the bit part characters was calling Teresa Matthews to the witness stand. Bill Nelson asked her to state her name and place of residence.

"The Jolly-J Guest Ranch, Washoe County, Nevada," Terrie mumbled the words a little like a child repeating an oft-told tale. Sara wondered how many times she'd repeated these same lines, in this same room, before this very judge and these very lawyers. She, herself, must be the only fresh note in the whole proceeding.

"You and your husband operate that ranch, do you?"

"We do."

"Do you know Sara Winston, the plaintiff in this case?"

"I do."

"When did you meet Mrs. Winston?"

"September 3 of this year."

"From September 3 to the present time, has she been actually, physically residing in Nevada each and every day to your knowledge?"

"Yes."

"Have you seen her in Washoe County, Nevada, each and every day since that time?"

"Yes, I have."

"That is all," from Bill Nelson.

"No questions," said the pasty-faced man in the salt-and-pepper suit who, she was sure now, must be Wade's lawyer in absentia.

The judge excused Terrie and then went through the same set of questions with Bert Matthews. Then she found herself swearing on a Bible to tell the truth, the whole truth, and nothing but the truth. Those tired, old words, she thought with a kind of horror. They mean nothing to me, nothing to that judge or those lawyers or the witnesses. Everybody knows I'll be lying in this testimony, that I didn't come to Nevada to establish a permanent residence. And there'll be other half-truths, twisted truths. It was all a formality—a travesty of the law and the legal process. Well, there was no such thing as absolute truth. Everybody knew that. And yet— yet what kind of a country was it which condoned its citizens lying glibly under oath in a district court of one of its forty-eight states? And what kind of a citizen am I, she asked herself, who can do it so easily? Well, all of us break laws all the time, most of the time without realizing it—and yet to have to swear. There was something corrosive in the act.

"Will you state your name, please?"

For the fraction of a second, her mind became a blank, as it did sometimes when she woke suddenly in the night. She had no identity. Then she said:

"Sara Deering Winston."

"You are the plaintiff in this action?"

"I am."

"What relation is Wade Joel Winston, the defendant to you?"

"My husband."

The questions went on. Where and when had they been married? The present status of the marriage? The date of her arrival in Reno? Her place of residence while in Reno? Then—

"When you came to Nevada, did you come with the intention of making Nevada your home for an indefinite period?"

"Yes," she said.

"Has that intention continued with you since that time?"

"Yes."

"Is it your present intention?"

"Yes. . . ."

"Is there any child, or are there any children the issue of the marriage?"

"There is."

She went on stating Joel's full name, his age, date and place of birth, confirming the fact that he had been residing with her in Nevada, that she was requesting his custody with the right of the defendant to have reasonable rights of visitation at reasonable times and places; that there was no community property belonging to her and the defendant; that, yes, she felt that one hundred dollars a month was a reasonable sum for the defendant to pay her for the support of the minor child.

Then Bill Nelson was asking her, unexpectedly:

"You have alleged the defendant has treated you with extreme mental cruelty. Is this allegation true?"

"Yes." (Oh, no, cried a voice from her heart. It's a lie. Wade couldn't treat anyone with extreme mental cruelty, with cruelty of any kind. Well, maybe, sometimes. But all humans were cruel to each other sometimes. It is an axiom of life and loving and coming close that people must sometimes be cruel to one another. Must it be pronounced thus, so starkly, so darkly, pronounced and summed up and publicized, signed, sealed and delivered? It was, to be sure, merely a form, a meaningless ceremony to be enacted, a little play to be performed. And yet—and yet—words had a life of their own, whether they be spoken or in print. Why couldn't she tell them the truth, the plain and simple truth? Wade and I don't love each other anymore, never can love each other, never can understand each other, never should try to live together. Why did it have to be twisted and disguised? Why make this ridiculous farce into more of a mockery?)

"What was his attitude after returning from the war?"

"He—he was extremely critical. It was—we seemed to argue continuously. He was neglectful, moody. It was exceedingly difficult." (But he'd fought through a long, hard war, she wanted to explain. Any man is allowed to be critical and moody and unstrung when he's returned from the war. . . .)

"He didn't show any great amount of attention toward you: is that correct?"

"That is correct." (No, no, the little voice from her heart cried, he showed me plenty of attention in those days . . . for, certainly, criticism, hostility is attention of a kind. It was only later that—.)

"During the course of these arguments did he frequently use abusive language?"

"Yes, he had quite a violent temper."

"And this was a continuous course of conduct on the part of the defendant from the time he returned from the war to the time of the separation?"

"Yes." (Oh, no, no. Nothing in life or love is continuous. Things are subtle and complicated; things change, live and grow and quiver and decline. Why must you ask me all these stupid questions? And why must I be forced to give you all these stupid, insensitive, oversimplified answers?)

"You never gave the defendant any cause for or justification for his conduct, did you?"

Ah, there it was. The question to end all questions. With this one the lights should all go on at once as in those pin-ball games in the drug stores. As if anybody, anywhere, could honestly say that they never gave the defendant cause for being critical, neglectful, moody. Of course I gave him cause, she yearned to shout at them, plenty of cause. That's the whole point. That's why I'm here, because I couldn't stop giving him cause and he couldn't stop and it went on and on until our life together became like a nightmare with no waking moments.)

"No, I did not," she answered primly.

"Do you believe if you had to continue living with the defendant that your health would be permanently impaired?"

"Yes." (Well, that was true, wasn't it? Her emotional health and his emotional health would certainly be affected—and emotional disturbances were supposedly the cause of many physiological ailments.)

"You were very nervous and upset on account of his conduct toward you?"

"Yes." (Well, she was. And now she only wanted to have it all over with, quickly. Just breathe in deeply, deeply, deeply. Be still, my soul.)

"You were under the doctor's care?"

"Yes." (Well, that Baltimore psychiatrist was a doctor and he had given her care of a sort. Not enough care. There wasn't enough anywhere of that kind of care. Only Van could—.)

"Is there any possibly of a reconciliation with the defendant?"

"No, there is not." ("Why, you little bitch. You little bitch in heat. I wouldn't take you back now if you begged me.")

"That is all," from Bill Nelson.

"No questions," from Wade's counsel.

"That is all. You may be excused," from the judge.

She returned to her seat next to Terrie, feeling somehow like a little girl who had passed an examination by the skin of her teeth. And yet she had answered everything correctly. Perhaps it was the examination, itself, which was wrong. And yet she had asked for it. It was she, herself, who was the author of this whole tawdry little playlet. You are all a pack of cards, she wanted to cry like Alice before the Queen of Hearts. Until the realization struck her sadly that it was she and Wade, now, who were no longer real, the she and Wade who had once been an entity. The figures in the courtroom knew what they were about all right. What did she know except that she was running away from her life, from an old part of her life to—. The judge's words cut like a saw through the dead wood of her memories.

"It is ordered, adjudged, and decreed that the bonds of matrimony heretofore and now existing between plaintiff and defendant be, and the same hereby are, dissolved, and each of said parties is restored to the status of a single person on the ground of extreme cruelty on the part of the defendant. . . .

"It is further ordered, adjudged, and decreed that the sole care, custody and control of the minor child of said parties be, and the same hereby are, awarded to plaintiff, subject to. . . . The testimony will be transcribed, sealed and filed. Next case."

ARTHUR MILLER [1915–2005]

Over his lifetime, Arthur Miller received almost every literary and drama award available, including a Pulitzer Prize and a Drama Critics Circle Award. How did this renowned, eastern-based playwright find himself writing about Reno, Nevada? Born in New York City to Jewish parents, Arthur Miller studied journalism at the University of Michigan. As a sophomore he wrote The Villain *(1936) in six days, received the Hopwood Award in Drama, and transferred from journalism to English. In its* American Masters *series, PBS notes that in the period following World War II, "American theater was transformed by the work of . . . Miller. Profoundly influenced by the Depression and the war that immediately followed it, Miller tapped into a sense of dissatisfaction and unrest within the greater American psyche." In the*

1950s Miller was subpoenaed before the House Un-American Activities Committee, refused to
"name names," and was convicted of contempt of Congress, a ruling subsequently overturned.
In 1956 the author of All My Sons *(1947),* Death of a Salesman *(1949),* The Crucible *(1953),*
and many others came to Nevada for a divorce so he could marry Marilyn Monroe. He wrote
a story entitled "The Misfits," subtitled "Chicken feed: the last frontier of the quixotic cowboy"
(1957), which focuses on a group of Nevada mustangers who capture wild horses and sell them
to feed companies. He later expanded the story into a novel "conceived as a film," which in
fact was shot, starring Marilyn Monroe and Clark Gable, directed by John Huston. Monroe
played beautiful Roslyn Tabor from Chicago, who comes to Reno to get a divorce. By the time
filming began, Miller's marriage to Monroe was itself deteriorating, Clark Gable was in fragile
health, and the heat and desolation of the desert near Pyramid Lake affected everyone. The
Misfits *(1961) was a box office failure but enjoys a loyal following today as a classic, a so-called*
"eastern Western."

from The Misfits

Roslyn's rented station wagon is speeding along a straight, endless highway a quarter of a mile behind Gay's ten-year-old pickup truck. Except for the two vehicles
the highway is deserted. On both sides the bare Nevada hills are spread out, range
beyond range. An occasional dirt trail winding into them raises the surprising
thought that one could follow it and arrive at a human place in the interior. No
house shows; only an occasional line of fence indicates that cattle range here sometimes. The hills front the highway like great giants' chests; to the eye speeding
past, their undulating crests rise and fall as though the earth were silently breathing. The noon sun is lighting up red woundlike stains on their surfaces, a sudden
blush of purple on one, the next faintly pink, another buff. Despite the hum of the
engines the land seems undisturbed in its silence, a silence that grows in the mind
until it become a wordless voice.

Roslyn, driving with Isabelle beside her, constantly turns from the road to stare
at the great round hills. Her look is inward, her eyes widened by an air of respect.

Roslyn: "What's behind them?"

Isabelle: "More hills."

"What's that beautiful smell? It's like some kind of green perfume."

"Sage, darling."

"Oh, sure! I never smelled it except in a bottle!" Laughing: "Oh, Isabelle, it's
beautiful here, isn't it?"

Isabelle, sensing Roslyn's excitement: "I better tell you something about cowboys, dear."

Roslyn laughs warmly: "You really worry about me, don't you!"

"You're too believing, dear. Cowboys are the last real men in the world, but they're as reliable as jackrabbits."

. . . .

Guido jumps up into the room with a small bag of groceries and a bottle. He looks at them and at Isabelle drying glasses on her sling and calls out: "Boy, it's nice to see people in here! Come on, folks, let's get a drink." Going to Isabelle in the kitchen area: "I'll start the refrigerator. It makes ice quick."

"Ice!" Isabelle calls through the open studs to Roslyn: "We stayin' that long?"

"I don't know. . . ."

She unwittingly looks to Gay for the decision, and he speaks to her uncertainty.

"Sure! come on, there's no better place to be! And you couldn't find better company, either!"

"All right!" Roslyn laughs.

"That's it, sport!" Gay calls to the kitchen: "Turn on that ice, Guido boy!"

Isabelle comes in, balancing a tray and glasses, which Gay leaps up to take— along with the bottle from her sling. Gay pours.

Gay: "Let's get this stuff a-flowin' and make the desert bloom."

Isabelle: "Flow it slow. We only got the one bottle."

Gay grasps Roslyn's wrist and puts the glass into her hand. "There you are, now! Put that in your thoughts and see how you come out."

She smiles at him, warmed by his persistence.

Guido enters and takes a glass. "Come on, sit down, everybody! Let's get comfortable."

Roslyn sits on the couch, Isabelle beside her. The two men take chairs.

Guido addresses Roslyn, his hope flying: "Say, I'm really glad you like this place."

Isabelle: "Well, here's to Nevada, the leave-it state."

Roslyn: "The what state?"

They are already starting to chuckle.

"The leave-it state. You want to gamble your money, leave it here. A wife to get rid of? Get rid of her here. Extra atom bomb you don't need? Just blow it up here and nobody will mind in the slightest. The slogan of Nevada is, 'Anything goes, but don't complain if it went!'"

Gay: "God, that's no lie!"

Guido: "How come you never went back home, Isabelle? You came out here for your divorce, didn't you? Originally?"

Isabelle drinks, glances diffidently at Roslyn. "Tell you the truth, I wasn't beautiful enough to go home."

Roslyn: "Oh, Isabelle!"

"It's true, darling. Beauty helps anywhere, but in Virginia it's a necessity. You practically need it for a driver's license. I love Nevada. Why, they don't even have mealtimes here. I never met so many people didn't own a watch. Might have two wives at the same time, but no watch. Bless 'em all!"

ROLLAN MELTON [1931–2002]

If you picked up the Reno Gazette-Journal *anytime between 1978 and 2001, chances are you saw one of Rollan Melton's nearly four thousand thrice-weekly columns chronicling the lives of northern Nevadans, both the eminent and the everyday. Melton's own remarkable life is recounted in* Sonny's Story: A Journalist's Memoir *(1999), creatively formatted as headline stories. Melton was born into a troubled family in Idaho. When he was four his mother, "Rusty," divorced his father, and she, "Sonny," and his sister, "Brownie," became hoboes, evading rent collectors, sometimes getting evicted, once living in a converted chicken coop. Before his fifteenth birthday, Melton had attended eighteen schools. His fortunes began to perk up when Rusty landed a job at the Owl Café-Casino in Fallon. Stable at last, Melton played football and got an after-school job as a printer's devil for the* Fallon Standard, *his entree to the newspaper world. He credits his teachers and the Fallon community for nurturing him, and he was a loyal benefactor to Nevada for the rest of his life. On scholarship, Melton attended the University of Nevada, Reno, where he majored in journalism and eloped with Marilyn Royle, a beloved lifetime companion. Thereafter, hard work and some lucky breaks propelled Melton's meteoric rise from sportswriter, to wartime public information officer (1955–57), to general assignment reporter for the* Reno Evening Gazette, *to editor, to publisher of that paper and its sister paper the* Nevada State Journal, *to vice president and then president of Speidel Newspapers, to a senior vice president of Gannett Corporation. By 1978, feeling "executive burnout," Melton voluntarily stepped down to columnist, beginning his twenty-three-year dream job, stopped only by death itself. Selected columns from 1978 to 1988 are reprinted in* Nevadans *(1988), while those culled between 1988 and 2001 appear in* 101 Nevada Columns *(2001).*

Reno Visitors Center

Things are never dull at the Visitors Center of the Greater Reno-Sparks Chamber of Commerce.

The staff of the center, located on the lower level at 135 N. Sierra Street, juggles a gaggle of incoming telephone calls. Mail volume approaches 500 letters a month. The walk-in traffic can get brisk, and sometimes tipsy.

The lady in charge is visitors desk coordinator Jacqueline Herrmann. She has manned the position two years. She is a slender five-foot-three and has brown eyes, with silver in her hair, "some of which I spray in there myself." She is a frank and witty person. When I asked if I might give her age, she answered, "No. Go climb a tree."

Anyway, to hear Jacqueline Herrmann tell it, a lot of the incoming letters and calls are routine and usually fall into two categories: people considering relocating to Reno or Sparks and people who plan to visit.

People want to know about living accommodations, schools, shopping areas, costs. They ask for information on churches, banks, the weather. They're curious about how to get married or how to get unhitched.

A few writers forecast the future—one not long ago said Jesus Christ will be returning in April 1985. Calls are not always routine. One gentleman rang up the desk on a late afternoon and told Herrmann, "If you'll be there awhile, I'll come right over and marry you." A woman called long-distance. She wondered if she kept a diary of personal expenses during her forthcoming trip to Reno, "Would the Chamber of Commerce reimburse me?"

Recently, an out-of-state man sent Herrmann and colleagues a shopping list. He wanted somebody to fetch him a bunch of clothes. He listed all his sizes, including the trouser leg inseam length. His final command to Herrmann: "Please send the clothes to me COD."

One Saturday came a long-distance call from a man who identified himself as a leader of a Boy Scout troop. He said someone had recommended he take his scouts on an encampment at a place called Mustang Ranch. He was quickly convinced that Mustang isn't the type of place to write home to the folks about.

Some of the mail is in other languages—one came the other day from Tahiti, written in French. Herrmann could make out only two words—matrimony and divorce.

Staffers have a smattering of knowledge of foreign languages and usually figure out the message. Perhaps eighty percent of calls to the visitors center are long-distance, including one from a man three days ago who wanted to know where he could secure ten camels so "I can start my own camel race." Staff member Dottie Boatwright put in him touch with the fellow who runs the Virginia City camel sprints.

Mail from abroad is heaviest from Italy, France and Japan.

Many writers and callers check in, asking how to track down missing relatives.

There is much fascination about prostitution: a letter the other day asked if prostitutes are "available in Reno" and "if not, why not?"

One inquiry: "How do I become a prostitute? How much does a license for a prostitute cost? How long must a prostitute practice before she can be considered a professional? After I am licensed, how many 'houses' may I practice in? What kind of income can I anticipate? If you can't help me with the answers, who can?" Hermann answered that prostitution is illegal in Reno and referred the woman to the sheriff's department for other information.

Once a man called on behalf of his wife. He wondered where "she should go to get tattooed above and below her eyes, so she'll no longer have to wear eyeliner." The staff had no answer.

The greater percentage of mail, calls and drop-in traffic is polite and is unfailingly treated in kind. The phone call volume reflects growth in the Greater Reno area—an average of 500 calls a day in recent weeks. The experienced Herrmann and her four part-time helpers can meet most challenges successfully. To them, most questions are routine: "How far is New York City?" "How much will I have to pay in customs to get this stuff home to Canada?" "What's the distance from Reno to Yellowstone National Park?"

Herrmann says a lot of couples visit the Sierra Street office and you can determine very easily who is married and who is not. "The people abusing each other are married."

One happy couple strolled in, arm in arm, last week.

The front of his T-shirt said, "I only sleep with the best."

Her T-shirt said, "I'm the best."

Ron Watson, Chamber executive vice-president, has headed the Reno-Sparks office for a year and a half and has twenty-three years' experience in Chamber management. His comment on "different" calls and/or inquiries?

"Everything seems to be based on the cycle of the moon. When it's full—watch out!"

Truckee Treasures

In the summer of 1976, three Reno men climbed into wet suits and began dredging the Truckee River at the downtown bridges, to find what they could find, In the beginning, it was merely a hobby for Darrell Garman, Walt Dulaney and Jerry Felesina. A wet and different way to idle away a Sunday; a casual method of capturing the curious gawks of passersby. Judy Garman thought husband Darrell a bit crazy. But only at first.

Now, much of what the men extracted from the Truckee is being shown in a Washoe County Library exhibit. The show is so popular, it's been held over through November. Inside the glass cases are memorabilia, trivia and physical testimony that some undying love does die.

See what Darrell and Walt and Jerry found:

Tie clasps, a Southern Pacific Company padlock, a Harrah's Club lucky token, screwdrivers, cuff links and a hot-metal Linotype matrix.

And 250 pounds of pennies, some as green as the roof of Reno City Hall; silver dollars; foreign coins from as far away as Switzerland; a dime valued at $800; one railroad spike and a beer can opener; fishing tackle and Laura F. Fooster's Harrah's check-cashing courtesy card.

The blue $1 chip from Gold Dust West; the key to Mapes Hotel room No. 316; knives, a dagger, eyeglasses, dice, and Donald H. Clark's plasticized Social Security card, 006-26-6111; two gold-capped teeth, an eyeglass case (Dr. Banks, Optometrist, Wilmington, Delaware); a St. Christopher's medal.

Empty ammunition cartridges, unexpended bullets, a plastic clothespin, men's and women's watches and the key to Mapes Hotel room No. 511; a toenail clipper; a ball and chain; nuts, bolts, screws, washers and a horseshoe.

Keys, keys, keys and more keys; a gold-plated Elks Lodge pin; a $5 gaming chip from the Horseshoe Club; earrings; a University of Nevada–Reno tie clasp, a pair of scissors, and scores of rings found during three summers of Truckee probing; a Masonic ring valued at $250; worthless rings, diamond rings, handsome men's and women's wedding rings; a diamond ring valued by three appraisers at a Lake Tahoe swap meet at between $1,200 and $1,250.

Rings engraved "Love eternal," "Forever," "Become One."

Spark plugs, bracelets, a marble and a .45 revolver, inscribed "M.D. Wyatt, Redding, CA," and Wyatt's black holster.

Wrenches, safety pins and bus tokens from Salt Lake City, Sacramento and Denver; the plasticized driver's license of Robert Lewis Babb, listed at a Sparks address, born August 18, 1913; Mr. Babb's unsmiling face, peeking off the card—he is five-foot-nine, 185 pounds, hazel eyes—the card is valid until Mr. Babb's birthday in 1980.

A sewing thimble, teaspoons, tablespoons, buttons, a drink token from the Corner Bar ("Have one on us") and a yellow plastic name tag from the Comstock Hotel that says "I'm Bob."

Finally, a lovely gold ring with a garnet stone. The engraving says, "Love is as strong as death—1890."

WILLIAM A. DOUGLASS [B. 1939]

William Douglass grew up in a Reno most of us will never know. When he was a boy, Reno was bigger than Las Vegas, the v&t Railroad ran from Reno to Carson City, and neither the Reno-Tahoe Airport nor I-80 yet existed. Douglass attended the "Old Manogue" school located on the Truckee River in east Sparks, but his real classroom was the surrounding countryside, where he avidly learned to trap beaver, muskrats, and sometimes the elusive mink. Douglass's four-hundred-mile trapline paid his way through the University of Nevada, Reno, for his BA in Spanish literature. After studying abroad and spending several summers doing fieldwork in the Basque country of Spain, Douglass received his PHD in anthropology in 1967 from the University of Chicago. He turned down several prestigious teaching offers to return to Reno, where he was hired by the University of Nevada System to found the Center for Basque Studies, which he directed for thirty-three years, building the largest Basque library in the Western Hemisphere and becoming one of the world's leading experts in Basque studies. Simply to list Douglass's honors, grants, and publications would take more than ten single-spaced pages. A few highlights are the Lagun Onari Award, presented to Douglass in 1999 by the Basque government for distinguished service to the Basque people, his major book Amerikanuak: Basques in the New World *(1975, with Jon Bilbao), and the oral histories* Beltran, Basque Sheepman of the American West *(1979) and* Tap Dancing on Ice: The Life and Times of a Nevada Gaming Pioneer *(1996), about Douglass's father, one of the founding partners of Reno's Club Cal Neva and the Comstock Hotel-Casino. The semiautobiographical story below is one of Douglass's only fictional works. Whereas the story's protagonist traps right up until the end, Douglass himself switched to catch-and-release fly-fishing years ago, and he recently cochaired the northern Nevada chapter of the Nature Conservancy.*

The End of the Line

"God, I love this," Jerry mused. "I must!" he snorted aloud, shivering in the December pre-dawn while making his preparations by the feeble beam of the car's trunk light. A skinned carcass to replace the bait of a raccoon set, a killer Conibear for the muskrat den he had found the last time over his trapline, an axe, gunnysack, drowning wire, and a powerful number four Victor steel trap should he run across fresh beaver sign all went into the wicker pack basket.

He felt warmer as he descended the familiar trail leading to the Truckee River nearly a quarter of a mile below. In the distance the headlights of a lone traveler appeared on the interstate, reminiscent of the eyes of an elusive nocturnal beast.

Why did he continue? As a boy the sale of his catch meant freedom and the ability to own a car. It also meant pride of accomplishment. It had taken him four years to catch his first mink, despite reading hundreds of how-to articles in *Fur Fish and Game* magazine and three or four trapping manuals. It was only after Einar had taken him under his wing that Jerry truly became proficient.

Einar was a former professional trapper who had spent several winters running a snowshoe line in the Sierra Nevada before California protected the pine marten. He had lost an arm in a sawmill accident and welcomed the assistance and the youthful enthusiasm of his protégé.

Under Einar's direction Jerry learned to read nature. No longer was a stream-bank merely a place where land met water. Rather it was a marriage between the aquatic and terrestrial realms, two porous worlds linked by trails, tunnels and dens. Tree branches served as bridges and rocks as promontories. To the trained eye, tracks, feces, bent grass, disturbed leaves and the remains of a meal all betrayed the presence and movements of furbearers. To understand these signs was to possess their spirit and control their destiny. It was the essential expertise that translated into the "green" skins drying on wire stretchers in his shed.

Yet for Jerry trapping was much more than killing for financial gain. It was the communion with Einar forged out of an apprentice's respect and a master's pride. It also facilitated the bond with Stan, cemented by an oath of mutual fealty and a plan to journey together to Venezuela to search for diamonds, yet fated to dissolve when Stan met Mary. Above all there was the communion with self. Perhaps that best explained why Jerry was still trapping years after Einar was felled by a stroke and he had all but lost touch with Stan.

For Jerry was a loner and never more content than when immersed in the solitude of his trapline. He could not even express his sense of satisfaction as he skinned his catch with great care. The tactile earthiness of the act corresponded to a part of human essence that was all but extinguished in his fellow office work-ers. Sometimes, while he sat by his wood stove with a damp beaver pelt spread over his lap sewing it to the round stretcher, his spirit merged with the former generations of fur trappers who had opened up a continent. This was his private reverie.

Jerry had always felt like an anachronism, which did not displease him, but then he had come to know fear. When the state required each trap to bear a name and address tag he groused over the minor inconvenience; one morning he awoke to find his living room window shattered by a trap lying on the floor. As he removed the message from its jaws and read the vague and anonymous threat of worse to come he had his first real taste of personal violation. On his next trip to his beloved San Francisco he was befuddled by the vehemence of the protesters who picketed the furrier on Union Square and verbally assaulted any passer-by wearing a fur coat.

By the time Jerry reached the railroad tracks the first hint of dawn suffused the eastern sky, obliterating the glow of Reno's distant neon lights. A gust of wind and the scudding clouds which caused the still visible stars to flicker in the western firmament confirmed the weather report he had watched while skinning yesterday's catch. The winter storm warning promised to make the day difficult. The thought quickened his pace as he traversed the railroad bed.

For more than twenty years Jerry had covered this same ground, as regular in his pattern as a mink running a riverbank. He knew that by stepping on every other tie 950 paces would bring him to the rock slide where he had his first set. Usually he counted them as a way of passing the time, but today his mind wandered.

"I don't buy fur anymore, lads! No price, don't you know? The market's poor and going down." Jerry's schoolboy indecision welled up inside him as he contemplated Johnny O'Keefe, Reno's premier junk dealer and only furbuyer. A large truck and tractor rumbled past the front door, shaking the establishment. In the pre-interstate days Fourth Street doubled as the Lincoln Highway, the main roadlink between Chicago and the coast.

The old Irishman continued to sort pieces of copper and brass in silence. Jerry's gaze met Stan's and a hint of desperation flitted across both faces. "You're sure, Johnny?" Jerry mumbled, irritated at the obvious quiver in his voice. After an appropriately agonizing pause O'Keefe looked up from his task. His blue eyes darted like starlings behind his otherwise impassive, soot-covered mask.

"Well, you're good lads, I must say. I shouldn't even consider it, but at least I could look at your 'rats.'" The thick Irish brogue delivered in a soprano, choirboy-crystalline voice seemed incongruous.

Jerry and Stan dashed to the car and returned with two hundred muskrat pelts and a sprinkling of other skins. Ignoring the few mink, raccoons and beavers, O'Keefe sized the muskrats into discrete piles. Occasionally, he ran his hand into the recess of a cased hide to see if its fur was prime. The broad, blue stripe on the flesh side was a tell-tale sign of an early-season catch made before the winter weather had fully thickened the coat. Jerry and Stan flinched visibly as a border-line decision relegated a skin to the un-prime pile, but then Johnny would shrug and reassign it to a more valuable category.

"Tea lads?" The hardest part of the transaction was the hospitality before the final negotiation. The cubicle in one corner of the junk shop that served as living quarters scarcely accommodated a bed, stove and wash basin. Concerned not to offend, Jerry and Stan struggled to contain their revulsion at the surroundings as they sipped the brew from cups caked with years of service and little soap.

"Want to see my coyotes, lads?" This was the signal that endgame was approaching. Pleased to escape the squalor of teatime, they dutifully scrambled down the stairwell leading to the dirt-floor basement. O'Keefe held a flashlight as Jerry and Stan surveyed several hundred coyote pelts criss-crossed neatly into an impressive tower. His voice assumed a near-sacred tone as he re-told the story of his monument to furbuyers' folly.

"Paid six dollars apiece for them, I did. Back in the twenties; nineteen twenty-six it was. By the time I shipped them to New York they were worth three. Had to pay the freight both ways and here they sit thirty years later. Not worth a dollar today, but who knows—maybe someday. That's the fur business, lads!"

"Seventy-five cents apiece, Johnny? The market report says extra-large 'rats' are selling for a dollar and a quarter," Jerry protested.

"Can't pay attention to that lads. But you should try shipping them East. I'll give you an address. You can send your 'rats' there and see what happens. It would be a favor to me. I don't really buy furs anymore. Too risky." As Jerry and Stan gathered their wares, fearful that they would really have to test the unknown, Johnny changed the subject to the poor price of scrap metal.

"Maybe we'll see you next year, Johnny," Jerry said by way of leave- taking. "I hope to be here, lads. But I've been thinking that maybe I could give you eighty cents for old times' sake." There was some satisfaction in the pending instant gratification once O'Keefe's in-pocket check could be cashed, but it was tempered by the thought that they had acceded to his first offer for their mink, 'coon and beaver.

Once in college Jerry extended his trapline as far north as the headwaters of the Feather River and south to the West Walker. He was trapping alone and it took him three days to cover the four hundred mile circuit. While his classwork suffered, in the three weeks from mid-November until the freeze-up in early December he could earn his year's expense money.

By then he was making an annual trip to California to sell his catch to Joe Garcia in Hollister. It was as much an adventure as a transaction. Garcia paid the market price so there was nothing to haggle over. While the furbuyer sorted his catch Jerry wandered wide-eyed through the warehouse fingering Alaskan pale wolf, white fox, lynx and wolverine skins.

After the sale he would drive frenetically to San Francisco, check into a hotel and begin his rites of passage. There was the zoo, the aquarium, the de Young Museum and the first realization of the extraordinary beauty of both the bridge and park which bore the magical name of Golden Gate. The cacophony of Chinatown contrasted with the staid consumerism of Macy's. Both expanded his adolescent horizons and informed his dreams. Then there were the largely fruitless attempts to assault the barricades of the seamier side of the adult world with a fake ID. To his

amusement, Jerry's ears burned anew as he recalled the maternal streetwalker's refusal of a nineteen-year-old and the response, "You must not o' fought very hard,"
by the doorman at a North Beach night club when informed that Jerry was thirty
and a veteran of the Korean War.

Jerry left the tracks and descended the rock slide. Experience had taught him how
to negotiate the loose matter that sloughed away beneath his feed. Even in hip
boots, down jacket and top heavy with pack basket his movements were so nimble
as to border upon dance. At stream's edge he peered into the tunnel formed by the
jumbled boulders. The trap was gone; the wire leading to its chain was drawn taut,
pointing into the depths. Jerry tugged and after momentary resistance a silky buck
mink rose to the surface. As he swirled it in the current to wash the sand from
the fur he recalled that over the years this set had produced more than a dozen
catches.

He depressed the double springs, removed the paw and re-set the steel trap. He
carefully adjusted the pan so that it was level with the jaws and hair-triggered to
respond to the slightest brush of the nimble mink. He placed the trap under three
inches of water about a foot from the muskrat carcass which served as bait, taking
care to seat it firmly by rearranging the pebbles on the stream bottom. He then
stood back and splashed water over the area, remembering Einar's advice that it
was the best way to remove human scent.

As he walked to his next set, Jerry squeezed the water from the mink's fur and
then reached over his shoulder to drop it into his pack basket. Day had dawned
but was laden with gathering clouds. The first flakes of snow mingled with the
hoarfrost of the winterscape.

He came to a beaver set and again the trap was missing. Jerry could make
out the dark form beneath the surface of the clear water. Its tail pointed downstream, undulating in the current. He retrieved the drowning rig and removed the
thirty-pound beaver. It was too small to be of much value. But then he shrugged
with the realization that it didn't really matter. Long gone were the days when his
fur trapping made a financial difference.

Pearce had been right thirty years earlier when he predicted that one day the
mountain streams would be overrun with beavers. The retired Reno rancher had
trapped the Truckee near the turn of the century when the population was held
in check by the predations on beaver kits by river otter. But he caught his last one
in 1920. When the average price of beaver pelts fell to ten dollars, which failed to
cover expenses let alone compensate for time and effort, most trappers quit or

directed their attentions to other species. Now the river was swarming with the prolific rodents, as evidenced by the scores of girded and felled trees.

The next two sets were empty and Jerry amused himself by reading the sign of a raccoon that had meandered along the river the previous evening. Where it had entered the water the faint traces in the mud bottom were like the ghost of an image still barely discernible on a palimpsest. Along the bank the accumulating snow acted like an eraser, gradually obliterating the tracks.

Jerry reached the ford and selected a stick to serve as a wading staff. Despite the poor light and swift current he strode confidently into the water. Years of winter trapping and summer fishing had given him intimate knowledge of the stream bed. At times on a summer's night, after flyfishing beyond dusk, he had crossed here in utter darkness "seeing" with his feet and ankles. He paused in mid-stream, resting against the boulder that was his favorite perch while waiting for trout to rise to an evening hatch. It was then that he might see his next winter's quarry if a beaver swam by holding in its mouth a freshly-cut sapling to be added to the food pile. The sight always delighted yet saddened him, in much the same vein that a farmer contemplates his new-born lamb or calf, enthralled by the miracle of life while sobered by the certain knowledge that he would be the agent of its death.

On the far shore Jerry unholstered his .22 pistol. When he had first begun trapping, bobcats and coyotes were all but worthless—so Einar hadn't bothered to include them in his training. Later long-haired furs became fashionable and their value soared. Jerry learned to catch the unsophisticated bobcat on his own, but he had been largely stalemated by the cagey coyote.

The rocky outcropping was at a point where two ride lines converged, swerving as a funnel through which any animal intending to reach the river would likely pass. Jerry checked the empty set from a distance so as to avoid leaving his scent. Here he had trapped his first bobcat years earlier and the memory was fresh. That day he had approached casually and was almost within range when the spitting, snarling feline lunged at him from behind a manzanita bush. It had taken a harrowing two hours of circling and feinting before he was able to dispatch it with a lucky blow from a stick. Since then he always carried a firearm.

As he descended toward the river he passed the spot where he had caught his only coyote. Unsuccessful with traps, he had purchased snares and a manual to outsmart the wily animal. He set two snares along the trail and on his next visit the first was missing. The small sagebrush to which it was anchored had been wrenched out of the ground. At the second set there was a huge coyote which silently lunged away from him in a desperate try to escape. It was caught around the midriff and the first snare and sagebrush hung from its neck like a garland. Its gorgeous fur was cream-colored and tipped in gray. Jerry was so overwhelmed by its majesty that had there been a way he would have released it. But things had gone too far. The coyote was spent yet too dangerous to approach. It lay down and fixed him with a gaze of resignation as he raised his pistol. It was the last time that Jerry used a snare.

"Got eighty dollars, twenty apiece," Einar chortled while handing Jerry his half. "Sold 'em to a dealer in Harold's Club. Walked right up to her table with 'em and she couldn't resist. She's gonna have a choker made."

Jerry fought back his remorse as he contemplated his share. He felt guilty for the nagging of Einar that led to their setting six traps for pine marten on the ridge above Webber Lake. He felt guilty for the lie that he had spotted a game warden following his tracks and therefore doubled back to his car without running the illicit line when, in fact, he had lost his way in a world so transformed by a fresh snowfall that he was unable to find the traps. Einar had pulled them by moonlight to avoid possible detection. That he had donated a marten's skeleton to the Biology Department for its collection did nothing to assuage Jerry's shame.

The rupture came shortly thereafter. The stain of the dishonesty of the poaching spread to the rest of their relationship. Jerry was obsessed with saving money for his pending South American venture, so he stepped up his activity to include every likely trapping spot in the valley. As his catch mounted he became aware that Einar was contributing little more than advice.

One day he found a fur cache hidden in a corner of Einar's basement. Jerry's hands and voice trembled with anger as he demanded an explanation. Einar's claim that the skins belonged to his cousin in Susanville and had been sent along with the request for help with marketing scarcely registered as Jerry stormed out of the house. A few days later they divided their furs and their lives in silence. It was years before Jerry saw Einar again, and only then after his mentor was immobile and inchoate.

Crossing the river Jerry retrieved his pack basket and continued on to a spot where he anticipated fresh beaver sign. One slide on the river bank was ice-covered—a certain clue that it had been used the night before by a wet animal emerging from the water. He followed its trail and found a half-girded tree. The wound was nearly three feet off the ground, evidence that the beaver was blanket-sized.

Jerry took the gunnysack from his pack basket and filled it with rocks, adding extra ones for good measure. Securing the weight to a twelve foot length of heavy drowning wire he hurled it into the depths of the deep run. Jerry then slipped the L-bracket attached to the trap chain onto the wire which he anchored firmly around a tree root on the shore. Once caught a panicked animal dove for safety, taking the trap to the gunnysack. When it realized its mistake and tried to surface the bracket locked on the wire, sealing its fate. It was over in a matter of minutes. The system was nearly foolproof, and in all his years of trapping he had only encountered two beavers alive in his traps.

Jerry cut three willow saplings to jam into the mud slide. He serrated them with the axe blade to simulate beaver gnawing, and then daubed them with a lure made from castors and oil of anise. It was Einar's opinion that such baiting and luring couldn't hurt, but that the real purpose of the saplings was to make the animal drop its front feet while approaching the bank. Otherwise it might trigger the trap with its chest, leaving behind a few hairs in exchange for the wisdom to avoid the spot at all costs.

At this point Jerry entered the stream gingerly to position himself to adjust the set properly. The large and powerful double longspring trap was more than sufficient to hold any beaver, even the occasional eighty or hundred-pounder. The footing was slippery and treacherous on the narrow mud ledge next to the shore, and he shuddered at the thought of falling in over his hip boots. It was snowing hard and he was two miles from the car. He maneuvered the trap into place, seating it under five inches of water and slightly off center to compensate for the beaver's straddle. He then remembered the extraordinary size of this particular one and reached out to adjust the placement.

Jerry lost his footing and was thrust forward against the bank. His right hand grasped a willow but his left exploded in pain as if smashed by a hammer. He jerked it out of the water trailing the trap. "For Christ's sake!" he shouted aloud, as he realized that four of his fingers were caught. Fearing that they might be broken he tried to move them, but they were already numb from the shock and cold. His cheek throbbed with pain as the blood trickled down from a mud-smeared wound. He felt icy water work its way down the inside of his boots.

He grabbed a trap spring with his right hand and depressed it, but the other held firm. The ill-conceived attempt caused the bracket to slip further down the wire, thwarting his efforts to move the trap toward shore. He paused to think, struggling to ignore the penetrating chill from his soaked Levi's and socks. He grasped the trap in his good hand and tried to pull the heavy sack of rocks from the river bottom, but it wouldn't budge and he almost lost his footing. He realized that he must somehow reach the bracket, now well beneath the surface, to release its purchase on the drowning wire.

Jerry took a deep breath, shuddered to steel himself against the shock, and plunged into the swift current. He groped for the bracket and found that it had moved yet further down the wire. For a brief moment he surfaced and fought to inhale a breath of air, but was stymied by the gasping from his uncontrollable chest spasms.

Once more he was underwater, weighted down by his saturated jacket. His feet touched the stream bottom and he made one last panicked lurch toward shore. Jerked up short by his imprisoned hand he rolled over on his back. He was aware of the dim dawn several feet above him. The gray light then flashed white and he felt a peace that was so profound as to be sensual—". . . must not o' fought. . . ." His feet pointed downstream, undulating in the current.

EMMA SEPÚLVEDA [B. 1950]

Born in Argentina and raised in Chile, Emma Sepúlveda's life changed forever on September 11, 1973, when Augusto Pinochet overthrew the democratically elected government of Salvador Allende and established a brutal military dictatorship known for "disappearing" political dissidents. Sepúlveda was a vocal supporter of Allende in college, and when her close friends began disappearing, she made the anguished decision to flee Chile. She arrived in 1974 in Reno, where the language barrier reduced her options to menial labor at first. But she eventually earned a BA at the University of Nevada and a PHD in Spanish literature at the University of California, Davis, writing a dissertation on silence in poetry. Indeed, as the title of her poetry collection Death to Silence, Muerto al silencio (1997) suggests, silence is one of Sepúlveda's obsessions—the inexpressibility of certain feelings, the choice not to be silent politically, the yearning for silence in a world of chaos. Sepúlveda teaches Spanish literature at UNR and is a tireless community activist. Her Practicum course puts students' Spanish skills to work in the community; she founded Latinos for Political Education, has directed Nevada Hispanic Services, and served on the U.S. Senate's Hispanic Task Force. In 1994 Sepúlveda ran an energetic campaign for Nevada state senate, an experience vividly recounted in From Border Crossings to Campaign Trail: Chronicle of a Latina in Politics (1998). A prolific writer in both Spanish and English, Sepúlveda has published several books of poetry, several nonfiction works, journal articles, and regular newspaper columns. Her poetry was first translated into English by Shaun T. Griffin for Desert Wood: An Anthology of Nevada Poets (1991).

from *From Border Crossings to Campaign Trail*

Shortly after we arrived in Reno, I went to the state of Nevada employment office in search of prospects. I had an interview in Spanish, but the official who conducted the interview only knew a few phrases in Spanish. After he reviewed my qualifications, he told Michael I had two choices: I could be a maid, or I could be a dishwasher. How ironic—I hadn't even made my own bed when I was growing up. I had the finest private high school education and four-and-a-half years of college, yet I was told that I was only qualified to start at menial labor.

America hardly seemed the "land of opportunity" at that moment. I was no longer a privileged, educated young woman. I was now an immigrant—dumb, dark and ignorant.

. . . .

It was the end of June 1974. Summer had arrived in Reno, in the dusty high-desert. I thought it was hell. We had come from the southern half of the hemisphere where it was winter. My body was not prepared for this drastic transition, and especially not for the humidity-free air of the Great Basin. I felt like my skin and my whole body was cracking. Nor was I ready for Reno itself. Santiago, with its smog, public transportation and crush of humanity, was an active, bustling city of four million people. It had been my life-long reference point for the definition of "city." But Reno was a small, rural town that proclaimed itself "The Biggest Little City in the World." It had barely 100,000 people. It seemed an outpost at the end of the world, and where practically everyone was white.

That was one of the first realities about Reno I absorbed. There were only one or two small areas of town where I could drive and encounter African-Americans. Latinos were relatively few. There were maybe one or two Mexican restaurants.

Everything was so white. Even the people looked like the desert. Their faces totally lacked color. Something of the surrounding sagebrush was in their constitution. They were like sagebrush—tough, growing obstinately in a harsh environment, without colorful bloom or lush foliage. Their manners and dress seemed so stiff and staid, much like the original pioneers and cowboys.

It appeared to me that these citizens went about their business stoically, disconnected from one another. The glaring exception to this mundane world was the handful of blocks in the middle of downtown, where casino neon flashed day and night, players smoked and drank and wagered non-stop, and female workers were scantily clad revealing the tops of their breasts and bottoms of their butts. Reno had a split personality.

My first venture inside one of these gambling madhouses was enough to dissuade me from returning. The clang and clamor of machines and lights and buzzers going off were cacophony, a garish and offensive sensory assault, a distortion of reality, submerged in a swirl of cigarette smoke and cocktail waitresses dispensing libations at a robotic pace. For an instant, standing there bewildered, time seemed to stand still. I was bathed in the artificial light of a netherworld whose occupants were passionately engaged in a willful escape.

Unlike everyone else in Reno, I walked everywhere. It was my only way of getting around, even in the July sun! We had a little apartment on Taylor Street, about a mile south of the University of Nevada campus, and perhaps a half-mile east of the downtown casino core. I walked through the sweltering heat to the supermarket as pickup trucks rumbled by. I yearned for a little four-cylinder car, a Fiat maybe, or a Citröen, to whiz past to remind me of Santiago. I couldn't get used to seeing people driving pickups with shotgun racks. They'd climb down from the trucks in cowboy boots, and I'd grow very nervous, wondering, "My God, are they going to start shooting each other?"

I knew next to nothing about Reno. I knew of its ultra-liberal marriage and divorce laws. My mental picture before arriving was that Reno was a mining town out of the Old West teeming with cowboys—a peculiar place. The television show *Bonanza,* set at nearby Lake Tahoe and on the Comstock, was very popular in Chile. I imagined I would encounter Hoss, Little Joe and the other Cartwrights. I had some dreamy idea that Virginia Street, the main drag, would be a sun-blanched boardwalk lined by saloons, where a cowboy would kick the swinging doors open and step out, six-shooters in holsters, to peer beneath the brim of his Stetson toward a road lined by horses and buckboards. Somewhere a tinny piano or a harmonica would be playing.

This reverie was not so far from wrong as one might think. I arrived eleven decades after Virginia City's mid-nineteenth century heyday. Virginia Street and all the other streets were paved, modern and full of cars. There was a small airport and a land-grant university, which was the center of what little cultural life existed. Reno was a gambling town; the economy depended on it. The city ebbed and flowed with the stream of gamblers and tourists coming east over the Sierra from California on the new Interstate 80. There was limited shopping with only one mall (Park Lane) and almost no fine restaurants and few apartment houses.

Overall, Reno seemed to me, at that time, to be white-faced, red-necked, and still reeking of leather. I felt like a Latina extra inserted into a movie script for comic relief.

There was the matter of finding a job. My interview at the state employment office had been horrifying. Fortunately, a friend of my husband had a wonderful idea to spare me from making beds or scrubbing pots for a living. He suggested that we check prospects at the Mexican restaurants. I was game for anything that would land me a job. It seemed only natural that I should seek a job that wouldn't require a knowledge of English.

Our friend and I walked into a Mexican restaurant on the main street in Reno. I didn't have a clue what my friend discussed with the woman at the cashier's stand, but suddenly a lovely man, very short, a bit pudgy, walked up with a big smile on his face and started speaking to me in very basic, broken Spanish. It was the language of someone who had very little formal education in Spanish. "You know, you're so cute that I think I have a job for you," he said. "You can be a hostess."

I had no clue what a hostess was. The man, the owner of the restaurant, didn't know the word for it in Spanish. He merely said, "*una hostess*." He explained that I had to smile a lot, greet people as they came into the restaurant and escort them to their table. I was as offended as when I had been asked to run for homecoming queen in college. I hadn't imagined that my looks would land me my first job in the United States.

The pay was around $1 an hour.

"Make sure not to take any tips, because the tips are for the waitress," he said, still smiling.

So I gave it a try.

In those years, the mini-skirt was in vogue. My hair went down my back past the hem. I had to wear big heels. I remember walking in on my first day with four phrases written on my hand: "Good evening"; "How many in your party?"; "Follow me"; and after I escorted patrons to their table and distributed menus "Have a nice dinner." I repeated these phrases hundreds of times that first day. If anybody said anything to me I just smiled, because I had no idea what they were saying.

It was a huge restaurant. As the hours went by I found my feet giving out, crammed as they were into unwieldy high heels. The cashier was a woman named Roberta. She spoke no Spanish, but communicated through a bilingual waitress. Roberta innocently asked if my feet were aching because it was the first time I'd worn shoes. Roberta had the idea people from South America normally went bare-foot. It may have been a Mexican restaurant, but all the workers out front and in the bar were Anglos. The kitchen workers were from Mexico and Central America. From the first day, the cooks and dishwashers called me "*chingada*." I had no idea what *chingada* meant. I figured it referred to people from Chile.

On my second day, I was joined by a hostess who had started before me, 16-year-old Yolanda. She had been born in Mexico and spoke Spanish. "Oh, it's nice that you're going to be working here," she said. "We're going to be a pair of hostesses. What's your name?"

"Emma," I chirped, and added, proudly, "but you can call me *la chingada*." She started laughing so hard that I was embarrassed.

Then she told me that *chingada* meant fucker.

A few months later, I was standing in the kitchen of the restaurant getting a glass of water, when suddenly I heard screams of, "*La migra! La migra!*" In no time, the kitchen was empty. My co-workers ran outside. I had no idea what was going on, so I ran, too. I didn't know what "*la migra*" meant; it wasn't a phrase we used in Chile. But in Chile there are many earthquakes, so the first thing that came to my mind in my desperation was that they must have felt an earthquake. Whatever it was, it was a major crisis. I knew I had to flee like everyone else.

Out the back door and into the parking lot behind Virginia Street we ran. Some of my co-workers got into cars and sped away. Others bolted down the street at top speed. I stood on the asphalt, anxious and perplexed, calling out, "*Que pasa? Que pasa?*" I was lost, and no one would explain to me what was going on. "*Corre!*" (run) they yelled. So I started running. Then I realized it would be smarter to drive. My keys were still inside the restaurant. I went inside. Roberta was still there and so were the people waiting on tables. The restaurant was not abandoned. What strange panic had gripped the others? Unfortunately, Yolanda, my security blanket, wasn't scheduled that day, so no one could explain to me what had just happened.

I hunted for my purse. Roberta asked me what was going on. "*La migra,*" I said, hastening to leave. "Emma, no," Roberta said, stopping me. She tried to explain to me why I didn't need to leave. She called another waitress over, one who had mastered basic Spanish to communicate with the cooks in the kitchen. "*Tarjeta verde, tarjeta verde* (green card, green card)," the waitress said. I told her that I didn't have any green card. She translated that for Roberta who looked at me and said, "Run fast, Emma." So, like a jackrabbit, I took off across the restaurant, in front of all the customers. As I was approaching the back door, the semi-bilingual waitress grabbed my arm and dragged me to where my purse was kept. I still didn't understand what was happening. She grabbed my purse, pulled out my wallet and went through it. She held up a blue immigration card and said, "*tarjeta verde* (green card)."

It was at that moment I realized how important that little card was. No matter what they called it or what its real color was, its lack kept undocumented workers—such as the kitchen staff and busboys—in a constant state of apprehension. In addition, they were vulnerable to the pranks of co-workers who would sound the alarm of "*la migra*" to clear out half our work force.

I began to learn about the underground world of the undocumented workers, people who worked without the necessary papers. Sometimes one would want to return to their country to see family. So he would do something, perhaps commit a small crime, to cause immigration officials to detain and deport him. He would later return north, often leading a dozen or so friends. These workers never had qualms about telling me they didn't have their papers. Some couldn't read or write.

When I was promoted from hostess to cashier, they would cash their paychecks and I would help them sign.

My boss, Miquel Ribera, was quite a character. His main claim to fame in Reno was that he'd arrived around 1960, with hardly a dime to his name but an incredible talent as a Mexican chef. He had bought his first restaurant with only $135 and faith in God, and ended up owning five.

He could see how miserable I was, going home in tears each night. He knew my goal was to finish school, but I would never be able to save the money for tuition earning menial wages. He decided that when the time was right he would pay for my tuition, books and health insurance.

But as I toiled along, all I felt was despair in my dashed ambitions that had been buried beneath the weight of expectations. I worked five or six days a week, sometimes seven when I could substitute for somebody. As an immigrant, I was immediately and painfully made aware of how people in my new land perceived me. My appearance invited two stock reactions from customers: "Look at this little Mexican, I wish I could take her home!" or "You're so stupid, why can't you communicate? What are you doing here if you can't speak the language?" Even my fellow native speakers took advantage of this. I had become, "*la chingada.*"

There is a story from those days that I still tell my Spanish-language students. When you learn a language in a cursory course in high school—as I had learned a few words of English—you are never taught the dirty words. So I had never heard the foul words most Americans freely use. Indeed, I gamely struggled to serve the restaurant patrons as a perpetually smiling hostess, eager to please. When I would find myself adrift in a sea of incomprehensible English, I would do what non-lingo speakers do everywhere: I would guess at the meaning. After navigating enough close calls, a certain confidence develops.

I was a sponge, quickly picking up English through exposure by reading or watching television in my spare time. I began to lose my bashfulness. I started taking chances.

I should note that the restaurant's bar was an active sector of the establishment. The restaurant did a booming business in margaritas. After imbibing an unlimited amount, guests would sometimes reel from the bar to the dining room, to be guided by me to their seats.

Late one night, when I was still a hostess, an older woman made her way to the dining room entrance, barely balancing a large margarita glass, and asked for a table. I led her to one with two chairs near the entrance to the kitchen. She looked at me and said, "I don't want this fucking table."

I didn't understand exactly what she was saying—no one had used this word with me before. But with my increasing confidence in my English, I quickly decided the adjective, "fucking" must mean, "close to the kitchen." Customers never liked to be seated next to the kitchen. So I merrily led her to a big table right in the middle of the restaurant, laid the menu beside her and asked loudly, with a big smile on my face, "Is this fucking table? Is this fucking table?"

The woman began screaming at me. The customers at the surrounding tables erupted in laughter. "Call in the manager!" the woman roared, red-faced. "Call in the manager!" She was making quite a scene.

Unfortunately for me, the owner was still at the restaurant that night. He rushed over. "*Que dijiste?!*" he demanded. What did you say?!

"Well, I just asked her if this is a fucking table."

He could not believe it. "How could you possibly say that?" he exclaimed. "Punch out! Punch out!"

That was his standard response when he got pissed off at an employee. "Punch out." Take your time card, punch out on the time clock and go home.

Back in the kitchen, I was in tears. Everyone wanted to know what the *chingada* had said. "I said nothing," I told them. "I just asked this lady if that was a fucking table."

They couldn't believe it, either. "Emma, where did you learn that?" they said.

Finally, I said, "She told me first."

And so, though at great expense, I learned a new word in English. On the positive side, I now knew how to be insulting whether I was in Mexico or the United States.

Here Am I Now
> *for Ana María*
> *Reno, Nevada, 1987*

> Here
> am
> I
> now
> Emma
> laden
> with
> last names
> with nothing from my past
> a fine lot of nothing, waiting
> for them to answer

an exile who has endured much
and nothing cleanses, waiting
for them to give me a certificate
that says I cannot go
and cannot return
until my bones decide
if it's here
or there
the place where the dead speak
and the crosses are silent.

Aquí estoy yo ahora
Para Ana María
Reno, Nevada, 1987

Aquí
estoy
yo
ahora
Emma
y
una
suerte
de
apellidos
sin nada de lo que traje
y bien poco de todo
esperando que me den respuesta
a un exilio que tanto dura
y nada borra
esperando que me den un certificado
que diga que no me voy
y que no vuelvo
hasta que los huesos decidan
si es aquí
o es allá
el lugar en donde las cruces callan
y son los muertos los que hablan.

If I Renounce the Word

> If I scratch out what I write
> do not convey my thoughts
> if I do not say what I desire
> if I can be half silent
> if I submit to orders
> not discuss truth
> if I accept silence
> if I decide to speak no more
> if I renounce the word
> do not write it
> do not tell it
> if I do not ever read it . . .

> Could we find each other again?

Si renuncio a la palabra

> Si borro lo que escribo
> no escribo lo que pienso
> si no digo lo que quiero
> si me callo la mitad
> si acato las órdenes
> no discuto la verdad
> si acepto el silencio
> si decido nunca más hablar
> si renuncio a la palabra
> no la escribo
> no la digo
> si no la vuelvo a leer . . .

> ¿Nos volveríamos a encontrar?

MARY WEBB [B. 1956]

The Truckee River, the liquid heart of Reno, once watered real meadows in the now urban Truckee Meadows. With the passage of the Newlands Reclamation Act in 1902, the Truckee became the first western river to be dammed, diverted, and divided by the federal government, and its many users include Reno residents and businesses, power generators in California and Nevada, Fallon farmers and ranchers, recreationalists, the Pyramid Lake Paiute Tribe, and fish and wildlife agencies. Alas, more people have claims on the Truckee than there are drops of water to fill them. The litigation history of this oversubscribed river could fill a thick book. But who would read it? Instead, photographers Robert Dawson and Peter Goin and author Mary Webb collaborated on a cultural history of the Truckee, entitled A Doubtful River *(2000). The book, which won the Wilbur S. Shepperson prize from the Nevada Humanities Committee, follows the Truckee on its one-hundred-mile journey from Lake Tahoe to its desert terminus at Pyramid Lake. Webb tells the stories of people who depend on and adjudicate the river's precious water, including a Federal Water Master, a fifth-generation Fallon rancher, the Pyramid Lake Paiute tribal chairman, and suburban homeowners. While Webb gives voice to many different perspectives, her own sympathies lie with nature and wildlife, and she urges readers to respect the natural limits that aridity imposes. Originally from the humid environs of St. Louis, Missouri, Webb learned to love the desert when she went West to earn an* MA *in English at Northern Arizona University. She joined the faculty at the University of Nevada, Reno, in 1985, and has developed courses in desert literature and nature writing.*

from *A Doubtful River*

Despite consecutive years of drought from 1987 through 1992, one can stroll any neighborhood in Reno and be amazed, as my Los Angelean sister was during one particularly hot July day, at the verdant lawns, the shade trees, and thirsty, water-dependent landscaping. As Wallace Stegner points out in "Living Dry," what we do about aridity in our culture is to "deny it for awhile. Then you must either try to engineer it out of existence or adapt to it."

When my neighbor and her husband moved in, they went right to work on their yard. Each weekend they mowed, trimmed, weeded, and fertilized their lawn. They planted flowers. They proved, unlike me on the other side of the fence we shared, to be model homeowners. Approving smiles of the neighbors began to shine upon their tidy corner, an immaculately groomed expanse of green that hummed with the whine of their power mower.

Through the drought summers, the daily hissing of their sprinklers evoke my hostility.

In that summer of 1992, the sixth consecutive drought summer, Lake Tahoe was below its natural rim, which meant that no water would spill over the dam at Tahoe City into the river. The ultimate contrast, the greening of lawns within sight of the diminished river, seemed not to register with many people, particularly my neighbor. Although she was born and raised in this area, she does not understand the limits of a desert environment; she has much in common with the transplanted easterners who find the desert frightening.

My neighbor's lawn, like others in the area, demonstrates our long history of "civilizing" nature by carpeting the desert with green grass. And like others who defend lawns, she blames growth, not a limited water supply: "When we bought this house, there was plenty of water. I am not letting my grass die."

She keeps the desert as far to the edges of their lot as possible. We talked one morning over breakfast, after yet another long, dry summer; by September, Stage 3 (one day per week) watering restrictions were in place, yet I still heard that hiss each morning. The Carson Ridge of the Sierra peeked through the large window near our table, showing stands of aspen beginning to turn gold on the sides of the mountains. We discussed another neighbor's lawn, which was slowly being converted to xeriscape, replacing the lawn with drought-resistant plants and rocks.

"It's ugly," she said, referring to the other neighbor's indigenous boulder and sagebrush yard. "And it doesn't go with the houses here. I mean, look around—the reason we bought in this neighborhood was that it looks so quaint, with the trees and lawns and older brick homes," she said, aptly describing the charm of our neighborhood.

I disagreed. "His yard will look great next year. But it *does* take awhile for the desert plants to take hold, and from what he has told me, it's expensive to take out the lawn, put in these native plants, and then hook up the drip system." I silently envied his garden of poppies and lupine that would bloom in later summers.

She continued, "Anyway, I'm not fond of rocks. And besides, why should *we* go to that expense when people keep moving here and using up more water? I plan to sell this house in another year, and that will be tough to do if it looks like a desert."

The words "But it *is* one" fell on deaf ears.

"I think the whole thing is a bunch of crap," she said.

"The drought?" I asked, pancake dangling from my fork.

"No, this watering restriction nonsense. I am not going to let my lawn die if *they* are going to keep letting people from California move in and do here what they have done in LA."

I paused. "So what you're saying is that it's okay for you to be here, to have a lawn, a garden and so on, but it's not okay for anyone else to come here and do the same?"

"Yeah, exactly. As long as they are still issuing building permits, still letting people come here in droves and not controlling the growth of this place, to hell with it. Why should I suffer so that more people can come here and ruin it for everyone? People want to come here and enjoy the cleaner air without giving up anything," she said.

As we talked, I realized she articulated exactly the view I heard from an old-timer when the drought first began: "Why conserve water when it will just be gobbled up by casinos and developers? Might as well use it till it's gone," he'd said.

She summed up her argument: "Can't you see the contradiction of conservation? *We* conserve water, while doing so makes more water available for new growth. You can call me selfish, but I am not going to espouse some phony desire that others have the same opportunities I have. There're too many of us here already."

What she said illustrated yet another change to the landscape: The Truckee Meadows used to be just that—a meadow, full of riparian habitat, otter, fish, birds. Driving across town offers a strange version of the Jeffersonian dream. Not yeoman farmers, as Jefferson once envisioned, but a tourist-town mix of casino workers, university personnel, and middle managers live amid those manicured swaths of fescue, within those high privacy fences. Reminiscent of pioneer stockades, these quadrants divide residents from each other; but more important, the fences impose on those who live within them a kind of blindness to the world beyond.

A friend from New Mexico, his family descended from pioneers, reminded me that lawns were a way of demonstrating to relatives back east that this uncivilized, wild landscape could in fact be tamed. "Lawns were always kind of a status symbol," he said. "It took a lot of money to get a lawn going in Albuquerque. People from our home, back in Illinois, came out to visit, and you had to show them that you were doing okay in what they saw as a forsaken place. You had to transform the desert to make it habitable."

Lawns demonstrate on a small scale what happens when we import a lifestyle that clashes with available natural resources. Our predecessors, whether they came west ten years or five generations before us, brought with them their taste for lush green lawns and the belief that land should be tamed and brought under human control.

The new developments spreading into the hills encompassing Reno vary in design and price, but most will be surrounded by green lawns. All are marked by the small flags, whipping in the wind, that draw the eye to advertisements; the signs promise not just houses but entire lifestyles, new beginnings. An advertisement appearing in the *Wall Street Journal* uses John Muir to sell exclusive real estate. A quotation from Muir tops the ads: "'Thousands of tired, nerve-shaken, over-civilized people are beginning to find out that going to the mountains is going home.' Muir knew this a century ago," the ad goes on to claim. "You know it has never been truer than now. You've moved up the ladder. Now move up the mountain."

I lived for a time in one of the then-new developments that scored the lower foothills of Peavine Mountain. Housesitting for friends, I could enjoy their delightful redwood deck and hot tub in that tiny backyard, without the responsibility of owning and maintaining them. My evening soaks in the tub allowed me to study the ways in which maximum profit is extracted from the land, by stacking houses upon each other.

Any memory of the sage-covered foothills had been bulldozed and scraped beneath these expensive tract homes with their pastel siding and curved windows. Hearing the spring wind whine on those evenings was something of a sacrilege, for I had walked every ravine and hummock of that very hill, had climbed up to dramatic rock formations each evening to forget the multitude of sins and responsibilities in my life. I had napped up there between the piles of boulders, interwoven with green lichen and red paintbrush; I checked out the clouds, the spring wildflowers, the silver light of a November afternoon, seemingly high above the brown layer of air on a "green (okay to burn) day." All that has been leveled, replaced with yet another generic tract, carpeted by sod. As the development slopes gently toward the street, the small flags wave, announcing Stone Ridge or Vista Meadows or Juniper Hills. Only in name is there the vaguest recollection of the original terrain.

Suburban sprawl, new or middle-aged, represents more than just growth. It registers our appetite for ready-made community, convenience, and, in an odd way, conformity. Wandering through the new development, we might feel comforted by the familiarity of the same old strip malls, the same state-of-the-art landscaping, a few spindly tress and tatty marigolds. But we feel suddenly dislocated in the midst of these signs of progress, these advanced sprinkler systems and the orderly once-a-week mowings. We could be anywhere—Reno, Phoenix, Walnut Creek; all are contributors to the yearly diversions of western water supplies. The Truckee, the Colorado, the Hetch Hetchy—all compromised to green up these municipal areas.

A friend recently provided another view of development as we spent an afternoon driving a visitor around town, showing him the sights of urban Reno. As our route soon revealed, we were to take our visitor to the "good neighborhoods." We drove south, toward the foothills of the Sierra, where the larger, exclusive homes have been built on luxurious parcels of land. Our visitor whistled appreciatively at the ponds and streams flowing near impressive Tudor-style homes with four- and five-car garages. As we followed the curving, two-laned road through pastureland, a feeling of grace seemed to descend upon the three of us. It was relaxing, driving past these older homes, each with its own private pond populated by a pair or two of Canada geese. A bicyclist whizzed past. "This is nice," our visitor commented.

In a while, our road dead-ended at the southern end of town, where we had to rejoin the busy four-lane traffic on the business route. The feeling of ease disappeared. Traffic and noise increased while the scenery changed. Old trailer parks, run-down motels, and palm readers clung to their original sites along what had formerly been the two-lane highway (old 395), while more contemporary enterprises like Home Depot and industrial parks began to occupy more and more of the highway frontage.

My friend gestured with her hand toward one old brick motel and remarked to our visitor, "See? All of Reno used to look like this." I found her comment interesting in its ambiguity. The nostalgia I felt toward the tacky, unsophisticated metal trailers and the neon signs evoked a different response in my friend. Where I saw remnants of a bygone era in a classic neon sign, a woman's figure swan-diving into space, announcing "Pool," she saw a past to be forgotten. These seedy indicators of the small town Reno once had been were being erased, replaced by new industry. My friend saw these changes as progress, a definite improvement over the original.

. . . .

At the summer solstice, Peavine Mountain appears out my office window, now clothed in the customary browns of summer. Despite the moisture of the past winter and spring, the desert mountains surrounding Reno are swathed in their summer tans. "Mount Peavine," as this basin-shaped peak is called, is the last peak of the Carson Range. It rose with the Sierra Nevada and moved sharply, leaving a steep fault scarp on its northeast flank. Both the Washoe Indians and the Northern Paiutes considered it sacred; the Washoe called it "the upside-down mountain," and the Paiutes, "Sunflower Mountain." They traveled along this ancient lifeway to gather sunflower seeds from Mount Peavine. It stands 8,264 feet tall; the Anglo name comes from the wild peavine, a type of vetch that grows on its upper slopes.

After a summer of dry, hot days, Peavine is still rich with water. Small, ephemeral streams are flowing, and lush green grasses and wildflowers abound. Sego lilies, red Indian paintbrush (and yellow and orange), lupine, sunflowers, primrose, globe mallow, and penstemon flourish. Peavine Mountain, draining to the Truckee River just a few miles away, provides a fitting, though frightening, image with which to conclude this narrative.

"Normal" precipitation in the Truckee Meadows totals about seven inches annually. Wet cycles, like the winters of 1994–1998, brought additional precipitation, averaging four to five inches beyond the norm. Such moisture, such winters, incline us to forget about periods of drought, but experience tells us that the dry periods will return. The snow and ensuing floods have diluted any willingness to restrict our consumption of water as the Truckee Meadows continues to grow. We have survived the immediate crisis, and some of us even changed our water-using habits, but the city's growth has not changed because of it.

Developments proliferate; some are built on landfill—where once a wild ravine carried runoff from Peavine, now fill dirt and machine sculpt the land for future homes and tamp down foundations for yet another shopping center. The economy thrives, and newcomers arrive daily to take jobs in construction or wait for prospective ones in downtown's newer casinos. The feeling, at least at city hall, is enthusiastic, though the sentiments among my neighbors and acquaintances seem more cynical then ever. If anyone mentions growth in Las Vegas, we all shiver and reckon that things here aren't as bad as they could be. As one woman I chatted with at the dentist's office remarked, "Yes, there are more jobs now, but what *sort* of jobs are they offering to people? Minimum-wage jobs. People can barely rent a place to live, much less buy one. What kind of community are we building here?"

This current boom cycle, like others before it, brings up the same questions for people living in arid lands—how do we live within the context of aridity?

. . . .

Now, as nearly a century before, profit and optimism motivate our actions rather than empathy for the land and the river. The consequences of our heedlessness surround us. Drive into the sunset on the interstate highway and notice as the last rays of sunlight reflect on the myriad of broken bottles, fast-food cups, and wrappers. Randomly check nearby desert hills and mark the abandoned bedsprings, bullet-ridden shells of former automobiles, television sets, and washing machines. The glittering remnants of human consumption declare, this land *is* not our land at all; this is land for which we feel no kinship.

. . . .

We cannot undevelop the open spaces. What we can do is learn from the Truckee River. We can learn to live with aridity, which in fact is our only choice. . . . We can listen to the river and to the landscape it drains. This doubtful river has much to teach us.

When I leave my office, I will walk on Peavine. Doing so brings me an awareness of the mountain and the changes each day, each season brings. I will study the rocks themselves, a combination of volcanic rocks and granite boulders, their gray surfaces veined with yellows and lavenders, glowing in the lengthening shadows. I'll breathe the spicy aroma of sagebrush, which covers the mountain, and notice the trash that has been dumped, and look toward town, see the winding green that marks the Truckee River, and know how intricately tied we all are.

Go out and listen; only then can we understand ourselves and the limits of our own backyards, wherever they may be.

VERITA BLACK PROTHRO [B. 1964]

According to 2000 census data, only a tiny fraction—about 2 percent—of Washoe County's population is African American. Thus, the experience of being black in Reno-Sparks is not one that is widely shared or even known. Verita Black Prothro, who directs the northern Nevada office of U.S. Senator John Ensign, is one of the area's most prominent African Americans. In 2001 she was one of eleven "success story" featured speakers at the First Annual Empowerment Panel at the University of Nevada, Reno; in 2003 she won a "Woman of Achievement" award from the Nevada Women's Fund; and she is an active member of the Greater New Hope Baptist Church. A Reno native and graduate of Wooster High School, Prothro grew up in a neighborhood of "blacks and Italians, collard greens or lasagna," as she puts it. She earned a degree in journalism from the University of Nevada, Reno, and a masters in education from Lesley College and has served as the editor of the National Judicial College alumni magazine and written many freelance articles. At UNR Prothro took a class from the distinguished writer Robert Laxalt. "We had to do a writing assignment," Prothro recalls, "and he kept telling me, 'Verita, this isn't your voice.' He said, 'You should write from the heart. You're writing from your head.' He told me to try writing at different times of the day. He told me to write in the middle of the night or early in the morning. He told me to write while I was sipping tea or when I was having a glass of wine." With his encouragement, Prothro eventually wrote a story that he loved—"Porched Suitcases"—selected for Shaun T. Griffin's The River Underground: An Anthology of Nevada Fiction *(2001). The story invites us into the houses—and the hearts—of Reno's small community of color.*

Porched Suitcases

"I had another dream last night. I dreamed that ol' hussy was throwing grenades at me. She was pullin' 'em right out of that ol' raggedy suitcase. Them grenades would come right up on me and I was tryin' to get out of the way but they just kept on comin' but they didn't hurt me. Ain't God good? I sure hope that heifa ain't tryin' to work no root on me," said Mama Jenkins as she sat in her ripped pine-green vinyl recliner and talked on the phone to her sister friend, Mrs. Carrington. Part of the reason they didn't like Loodybelle was, although she attended Mission Society, she never came to church and she gambled in the casinos.

"Girl, that dream was as clear as day. I never did like that ol' nappy-headed heifa. I better get my sista to send me a geeree bag from Louisiana to put around my neck at night, just in case she's tryin' to work a root on me." (Geeree bags were supposed to keep away bad spirits, but they were most successful in keeping away people because of their high garlic and dead weed content.)

Mama Jenkins seemed to have always been old. Everyone called her Mama even though she never had any children. She was feisty. She moved to Reno from a small country town in Louisiana in the early forties in an attempt to make her life better. She was never a pretty woman, but she had always been striking because of her odd combination of features. Her skin was smooth as silk and black as night, and her baby blue eyes could peer right through you, especially when she was angry. The years had changed her bone-straight hair to a salt-and-pepper color, but she wore it as she had done for a thousand years—French-braided back into a roll that looked like a cinnamon bun.

She and Mrs. Carrington had been friends since they first came to Reno. They couldn't remember how or when they met, only that they couldn't stand each other at first, but now they loved one another more than sisters could.

Mrs. Carrington was fiery (her first name was Ollie but she refused to let anyone call her anything other than Mrs. Carrington). She had one daughter who lived in New York. They didn't talk because they didn't get along; they were too similar. Mrs. Carrington was nearly as old as Mama Jenkins, but she had had many advantages that most black women of her day weren't afforded: education, travel, and fine clothes. She was still fairly attractive. Her creamy yellow skin had few wrinkles, and her silver hair and perfect English made her look and sound as distinguished and as uppity as most people thought her to be. Despite being opposites in looks and backgrounds, they were both black women, their experiences were common and their struggles were what bonded them.

"Girl, my rheumatism is bothering me today but Mission Society is tonight, so I'll press my way. You better bring your ol' self. You know that hussy Loodybelle will be there, tryin' to be cute and workin' on my nerves."

Mrs. Carrington replied, "You know I never miss."

The Mission Society, a Bible study for the church ladies, met every Tuesday evening at six o'clock at one of the ladies' homes. Mama Jenkins and Mrs. Carrington played host more than most because they didn't drive and it was just more convenient that way. Mission Society was mostly just an excuse for these ladies to talk about the old days.

Mama Jenkins loved to cook and play hostess because it gave her a reason to bake one of her famous butter-laden, melt-in-your-mouth pound cakes. She loved to add an extra stick of butter and an extra half cup of powdered sugar to make it even richer and sweeter.

It was a clear, hot summer evening in the Truckee Meadows. The ladies began to file in at exactly 5:55 PM. About fifteen minutes were spent on the Bible lesson. The ladies were so predictable. One never wore her false teeth because "they hurt somethin' awful." Another one pretended she left her glasses every week; everyone had figured out long ago she couldn't read, but they played along—they would never damage her pride. Mama Jenkins trudged into the kitchen to bring out the pound cake and iced tea she'd made for the meeting.

They were spending the remaining hour reminiscing about life down South and about loves they'd once had, when Loodybelle made her entrance. The room grew quiet as she sauntered in with that old suitcase. The truth be told, no one liked her because she was so pretty and so strange. She didn't have one wrinkle in her cocoa-brown skin. All of the ladies thought she must be working a root to make herself look so young. She obviously dyed her heavy hang-down hair—it didn't have a hint of gray, but it looked so natural, it glistened. Even though she was in her early seventies, many men would snub a young woman to be with her. She was one of the first and few black women to work in a casino, and not as a maid. She worked as the powder room girl, and rumor had it she used to mess around with the white men. She always angrily denied this accusation. She claimed she was a beauty queen down South, and no one doubted it. But with all of her beauty, she had sullen eyes.

"Glad you could make it! And your black ass knows not to bring that suitcase mess in *my* house," snapped Mama Jenkins.

"Chile, I'm sorry to be late but I see I'm in time for some of your good ol' down-home pound cake. Girl, that cake will make you hurt yourself," she replied as she walked back outside to set the suitcase on the porch.

"What was the Bible lesson about?" she inquired, pleasantly, considering she was a woman under attack.

"It was about letting your light shine. Bearing fruit of the spirit. You know, like not gambling and drinking and carrying on, so that people will know you *got* the Lord," Mrs. Carrington replied, knowing this would irritate Loodybelle.

"Sounds like it was a right nice lesson, Ollie!" Loodybelle snapped.

"*No-You-Did-Not-Call-Me-Ollie!*" She stood up and put her hands on her hips.

"My name is Mrs. Carrington and you best not forget that. You might be old as black pepper and your memory might not be that long"—she quickly snapped her fingers—"but nobody calls me Ollie." By this time Mrs. Carrington was apple red. "Don't make me get my pistol out." She looked around for her pocketbook.

"You know, Mrs. Carrington, they didn't stop making .38s when they made yours!"

Mama Jenkins interrupted, "Now listen here, I won't have this dog mess in my house. This here is a Christian home and we respect folks up in here. I tell you I've never seen the likes—Christian women carrying on." All the other ladies looked relieved.

Loodybelle had steam coming out of her ears, but she took one bite of the cake and pretended to cool off. She could understand why Mrs. Carrington insisted on the white folks calling her Mrs. Carrington, but she couldn't understand why they all had to.

One of the women tried to ease the tension. She started talking about her grandchildren. "You know my little grandbaby, Malcolm? He's going to play Frederick Douglass in the community center play. He's smart as a whip and only five years old. You know he's the one who was born the day Dr. King was killed."

"Ain't he the one with the white mama?" someone asked.

"Yeh, girl. She's white but she sure is nice. And as long as my son is happy, I'm tickled."

Like calling Mrs. Carrington "Ollie," white people were a subject that sent Loodybelle through the roof.

"If that don't beat the bugs fightin'! That's what's wrong with church folks now. They is too complacent—'if he's happy, I'm tickled.' What you gonna do when she turns on him? Will you be tickled then . . ."

And as always, when she would go into a tirade, someone would break into the monologue and ask the same question. This time it was Mama Jenkins. "Loodybelle, ain't none of us in here crazy about white folks, but girl, you got a problem. Why you hate white folks so much?"

"I told y'all a hundred times—I don't hate nobody."

They all had seconds of the pound cake and continued to reminisce. Some talked about how rough it was leaving the South to come to an unknown place. Many talked about how they liked living in Herlong better because it was small and more like the South. Mama Jenkins always lamented, "But when that 'dog' Eisenhower got in office and cut all the jobs, everybody had to move to Reno to make a living. Just don't make no sense."

An hour or so later, everyone left, except Mrs. Carrington. She always stayed late so they could gossip about Loodybelle. Everywhere she went Loodybelle toted this old small suitcase, and these ladies desperately wanted to know what was in it. Mama Jenkins blurted out, "I bet she has all kinds of mess in there. I once knew a woman from down home who used to carry a bag like that. Everybody knew she was working roots. People would go to her and buy potions—potions to make people love you, to make people get sick if you hated them, and potions to make people fall dead if you owed them money. I never went around her. I was scared to death of that old woman."

Mrs. Carrington added her part. "A woman I knew of in New York used to write people's names in red pepper and fry them up in a skillet, when she got mad at them. Sure enough, those people would fall dead when they heard she'd done that. Everybody was scared to walk by her house."

"Do you think that old she-devil has a man's privates in there?" Mama Jenkins wondered.

"Girl, she might. She might have an old dead man in that thing," Mrs. Carrington retorted.

"No, it would stink to high heaven if it was a body and 'sides, it ain't big enough for a whole damn body," snapped Mama Jenkins.

Mrs. Carrington looked puzzled. "I wonder if she really keeps a mojo in there?"

"I don't know, but that's why I won't let her bring that mess in my house. I make her ol' self keep it right out there." Mama Jenkins pointed wildly to the porch.

Mrs. Carrington scratched her head and looked even more awestruck. "Child, she might have some money in that thing."

"Well, if that old heifa has some money she oughta pay somebody else to carry it around for her sorry self. She looks as crazy as I don't know what, carrying that thing around *all* the time. It's so raggedy. It has more tape on it than leather."

Mrs. Carrington replied, "Think it don't! She's just pitiful," and they roared in unison.

They agreed as usual that one day they were going to find out what was in the old suitcase.

The week was a typical one of much prayer and gossip.

Sunday morning rolled around, and Mama Jenkins and Mrs. Carrington headed for morning worship service. They lived next door to each other on Quincy Street, and for years one of the younger women in the church had been picking them up every Sunday.

Mrs. Carrington always looked like she had just stepped out of a fashion magazine on Sunday morning. She would always go over to Miss Ema Jean's to get her hair done up on Saturday night so the curls and finger waves would look fresh for church. She always wore a small flowered head ornament and gloves, and she had shoes to match every outfit. She said that's the way they did it in New York. She was the only one who wasn't from down South. And she was proud of that. She was also proud that everyone knew she could never have been a sharecropper's wife or child.

Mama Jenkins tried to wear nice clothes, but she never looked nice because every Sunday before she would go into church she would dip snuff. As the deacons would start singing the hymn "What a Friend We Have in Jesus" to signal that devotion was beginning, she would spit it into her snuffbox, an old Del Monte green bean can with a partially ripped label. She'd stuff a wad of tissue in the can and tuck it in her purse. She looked much like a man because of her thick moustache and the snuffbox, but the gaudy hat, big purse, and tacky fur stole let everyone know she wasn't.

She and Mrs. Carrington always sat on the Mothers' Bench. It was a place of honor in the church. For most of these women, it was the only honor they would ever receive. They sat proudly, as erect as Father Time would allow, flaunting their hats and sporting their pretty togs.

As the church clerk got up to read the weekly announcements, Mrs. Carrington's jaw tightened, as it did every Sunday at this time. "It doesn't make any sense for them to have her up there," she fumed quietly. The clerk continued to stumble horribly through her reading. "They just shouldn't have her country, 'Bama self up there *trying* to read those announcements. You just wouldn't see this country mess in New York. . . ."

She was about to continue when Mama Jenkins hunched her in the side and told her to hush up. She conceded, albeit unwillingly.

The choir sang their newest song, "Oh Happy Day," and then the offering plate was passed. Mama Jenkins and Mrs. Carrington were always stretching their necks and their eyes trying to see what people around them were giving. Later they would gossip about how cheap Sister So-and-So was; it was a Sunday afternoon ritual.

After the offering the choir sang "We Have Come This Far by Faith." That is when the Holy Ghost entered the building. Sisters started shouting and speaking in tongues, especially Sister Smith. Every Sunday, she would knock the pews over in her excitement over God's goodness. Many people thought most of her spirit came out of a bottle. While the choir was singing, the mood of the entire church changed. Suddenly sisters who'd spent a lot of money on their wigs didn't care if they flew off—in fact, they would snatch them off. Women who spent countless hours selecting shoes would run right out of them. People would yell, "Ain't God good?" "Thank ya, Jesus!" and "Won't he make a way, y'all?"

After the choir sang, Pastor Gibbons got up to give his sermon; but he felt too good to talk, so he just sang, "Amazing Grace, how sweet the sound, that saved a wretch like me. . . ." Whenever Pastor sang that song, Mama Jenkins would stand up, wave her white lace handkerchief, and cry. Those who knew Him understood; those who didn't sat in bewilderment.

She would declare, "I thank ya, Jesus, I just thank ya, Jesus, because last night my covers didn't become my winding sheet. I just thank ya."

Pastor would always wait for her to get her issue of the Holy Spirit before he would move on.

"Today, I'd like you to turn with me to the Gospel According to Saint Matthew seventh chapter, seventh verse. 'Ask and it shall be given to you. Seek and ye shall find. Knock and it will be opened unto you.' My subject for today is 'Why Don'tcha Just Ask Him?' Before I start my sermon, I would like my lovely wife to bless our souls with a solo."

The pastor's wife hopped up to the front microphone and began to sing, "It's a highway to heaven, none can walk up there, but the pure in heart . . ."

"Now she's gonna chase the Holy Ghost out of here, with her no-singin' self. Bless her heart, she sure can't sing," Mama Jenkins said as she began to come off of her spiritual high.

After the song, the preacher whooped and hollered and put on quite a show for the congregation at the Greater First Baptist Church. After the sermon he offered the Invitation to Christian Discipleship; no one accepted. There was one more offering and church was dismissed.

People fellowshipped outside for a while, catching up on the week's news. By twos and threes they all left.

During the ride home, Mama Jenkins was still complaining about the pastor's wife chasing the Holy Spirit away.

"She's simple as the day is long. She oughta know she can't sing no better than me. Poor soul. She's right pitiful, gettin' up with that solo mess," she complained.

Mrs. Carrington wouldn't let a good complaint session go without adding her two bits: "I don't know what's wrong with him, putting her up there all the time. Poor thing, he must be pussy-whipped. Ooooo, God forgive me, I should not talk about Pastor like that, he's a good man and he sure did preach today. Blessed my soul."

When the car stopped at Mrs. Carrington's house, they both got out. They'd already decided to have dinner there. Mrs. Carrington's house was ragged and old from the outside, and the inside too. It was dimly lit because she never opened the drapes; the walls looked like poorly done papier-mâché, and the floors creaked when you walked. But she had fine antique cherry-wood furniture, sterling silver utensils, the finest china, and European crystal stemware.

Mrs. Carrington walked with the assistance of a four-pronged cane. She always wore long dresses to cover her knees, which time and arthritis had grossly mis-shapen. Mama Jenkins, on the other hand, was at least a hundred pounds over-weight and moved very slowly. No one could be as patient with them as they were with each other. They *always* helped each other along.

Mrs. Carrington didn't like to cook, and she didn't cook nearly as well as Mama Jenkins. So today, thanks to Mama Jenkins, they feasted on Southern fried chicken, homemade macaroni and cheese, freshly snapped green beans with a little salt pork added for flavor, cornbread, and lemonade.

It was another excruciatingly hot day. After dinner the weather turned moody and electric as a thunderstorm moved across the heavens. The ladies knew the danger of storms and as soon as the first flicker of lightning raced across the sky, everything electrical was turned off and they sat in silence. As children, both had seen schoolmates struck by lightning and killed. Each time the thunder would roar, the ladies would quietly call "Sweet Jesus" in unison. Mama Jenkins slept in the guest room that night.

Tuesday rolled around again and the Sisters were meeting at Pastor's house. He was out of town, the church sent him to the national Baptist convention. The pastor's wife picked the old women up.

"How are you ladies doing tonight?" she asked.

"Baby, I ain't a bit of good today," Mama Jenkins answered.

"Oh, I'm fine today, but I'm not as young as I used to be," Mrs. Carrington mused.

Mama Jenkins said, "Girl, you sure did sing that solo Sunday."

Mrs. Carrington could barely hold back her laughter.

When they arrived at the house, the other ladies were arriving also. Loodybelle appeared later. She brought the old suitcase in, and Mama Jenkins started rubbing her hands together and rocking back and forth like a parent waiting on a delin-quent teenager. She knew she couldn't tell her to take the case outside because it wasn't her house or Mrs. Carrington's, but she didn't want that thing near her. Finally she could no longer take it.

"Girl, why don't you take that mess outside?"

"If Pastor's wife wants me to, I will."

The pastor's wife pretended not to hear the exchange.

This week the Bible lesson was forty-five minutes long since it was at Pastor's house. His wife served store-bought cake and the ladies took a piece to be courte-ous. But later they would gossip about her being too lazy and trifling to bake a homemade cake.

"Sister Gibbons, I'm not the meddling type, but you need to stop spoiling Pastor so much," one of the ladies said.

Mama Jenkins was glad to jump in on a man-bashing conversation, "Yeh, girl, you are young and one thang you needs to know is that the two easiest things in the world to spoil is a dog and a man."

They all laughed hysterically.

Sister Gibbons was curious. "But didn't you ladies spoil your men when you were young? You know it's so hard being a black man in a white man's world. I just want him to feel extra special when he's at home. That might be the only time he feels special."

Mrs. Carrington jumped in and answered before anyone else. She loved to talk about her late husband. "Yeh, girl, my husband was a good man. The best one God ever put on the earth. And I spoiled him somethin' terrible. Folks said he worked himself to death." Her eyes filled with tears. "All I know is, when he died—well, I've never been the same. And I tell you *one* thing, another man better not come up in my face trying to be too friendly. That's all I know."

Mama Jenkins loved to talk about her love-affair battle wounds. "Well, my man was a skunk. Hear me what I say? He drank *and* chased women. I thought if I spoiled him he would leave those other women alone and only love me. He wasn't worth two dead flies. He hurt me real bad. And it sure hurt me real bad when I had to chase his black ass away with the rifle that day, but, girl, I'd had enough. I tell you, I'd had enough. I say, you just can't spoil 'em, you just have to be slouchy and nasty. That's all. Men love slouchy, nasty women, I don't know what it is about 'em, but men love themselves a no-good woman."

"What about you, Miss Loodybelle, did you spoil your man?" Sister Gibbons was the only person who called her Miss Loodybelle.

"She probably killed him off with that mojo mess she carries around," Mrs. Carrington jabbered out.

Just as she said that, a flash of lightning streaked across the sky and thunder roared wrathfully.

"My man was a good man." The storm apparently didn't frighten her. She kept on talking and the other women listened. "He was the best man God ever made. *He* was fine, dark and tall, and his eyes—oooo, they were the kindest, prettiest eyes in the whole world. I mean, all the women wanted him. He was also strong and kind. And he only loved me."

"Well, I don't think they make men like that. Sounds like that Superfly fella, if you ask me. If he's so good, where is he?" Mama Jenkins asked, obviously forgetting the storm.

Loodybelle looked out toward the thunder and just talked.

"One day he didn't come home. That wasn't right. We hadn't married yet and his mama, she was so worried. He was reliable. Late that night the sheriff came and told his mama her boy was hangin' from a tree down Thompson Road. He told *her* to go cut *him* down. Lord, that woman hollered, screamed, and called on Jesus. Everybody came runnin' when they heard all the commotion.

"The pastor, he said my man must have done something—talked crazy to the white folks, looked at a white woman—something. I knew he hadn't done nothing. They cut him down. Since we weren't married, I couldn't even sit close at the funeral, so I went back and got that long rope they hung him with."

"Is that what you carry in the suitcase, Miss Loodybelle?"

Miss Loodybelle just looked off in the distance, not crying, just gazing.

They shared each other's pain, but she was too strange for them to share hers. Loodybelle's pain was too deep and too close to home for them to acknowledge it. So, seemingly ignoring her, they went on talking about church business and the weather.

After the meeting, Pastor's wife took the ladies home. They sat in Mama Jenkin's house and talked about the night's conversation.

"You know why that ol' crazy-behind heifa wouldn't answer, don'tcha? 'Cause she got root workin's in that suitcase and she didn't wanna admit it in the Man of God's house. That's what it is," Mama Jenkins insisted.

Mrs. Carrington had sorrow in her eyes. "That ol' woman needs to learn to pray. We've all been hurt, but we don't carry it around with us all the time. Won't do any good. Next thing you know, she'll be at the nuthouse over in Sparks."

EIGHT

LIVING LAS VEGAS

Inside the Entertainment Capital of the World

I n 1900 the population of Las Vegas Valley was thirty. By 2000, in just a century, the Las Vegas metroplex had reached a population of 1.4 million and spilled beyond the valley. Today growth in Clark County is so rapid that five to ten new schools open every year, road construction is a way of life, and maps are outdated upon publication. From three o'clock to seven, traffic on Las Vegas Boulevard is gridlocked, one guidebook joking that women have been known to go through menopause during the wait. Las Vegas is the driest and one of the hottest metropolitan areas in the United States, with summer temperatures in the triple digits— you really *can* fry an egg on the sidewalk—low humidity, and an annual precipitation of only 4.19 inches. Vegas Valley gets slammed by fierce windstorms that torment contact-lens wearers, sandblast car paint jobs, and set everyone's nerves on edge. Not to mention that Las Vegas is surrounded by blistering desert, a waterless moonscape where unnumbered early emigrants perished. Yet just beyond these barren plains rise snow-capped, alpine mountains. Indeed, in this place of extremes it is possible to go snow skiing in the morning on Mount Charleston and water skiing in the afternoon on Lake Mead. Many people flee the Las Vegas area but even more arrive, producing a staggering net increase of six thousand new residents *per month*, not to mention the 30 million tourists who visit annually. Pundits call Las Vegas America's last great boomtown and liken it to Monaco, Byzantium, and Babylon. How did such a place come to be? What are the odds?

Early humans are thought to have lived in the Las Vegas Valley ten thousand years ago, during the last ice age. Fast forward to the 1800s, when "Las Vegas"—Spanish for "The Meadows"—became known for its big springs and abundant grass, a refreshing stop on the Old Spanish Trail. Although a ranch was established near the springs, Las Vegas did not become a town until a railroad laid tracks from Salt Lake City to Los Angeles, auctioning off lots on a sizzling spring day in 1905. Construction of Hoover Dam in the 1930s boosted Las Vegas's economy, as did the Basic Magnesium plant in nearby Henderson during World War II. But the real shot in the arm was the arrival of organized crime throughout the '40s and '50s, attracted to Nevada precisely because running a gambling joint, well, wasn't a crime. Thanks to Mob financing and the hubris of men like Benjamin "Bugsy" Siegel, and thanks to air-conditioning, made possible by new technology and cheap electricity from Hoover Dam, Las Vegas metamorphosed from a watering hole to a resort destination. When the eccentric billionaire Howard Hughes arrived on the scene in 1966 and began buying up properties, corporations soon replaced the Syndicate, and Kirk Kerkorian and Steve Wynn led a new pack of visionary entrepreneurs.

Writers have been fascinated by Las Vegas ever since it became "Sin City." Log on to amazon.com, enter "Las Vegas," and you can scroll through literally thousands of titles. You'll discover that most Las Vegas books are guidebooks, proffering tips on getting comped, finding meal deals, playing craps, and locating the loosest slots. Other prominent Las Vegas genres include exposés of the underworld, erudite cultural studies, gonzo travel journalism, and dark stories of troubled sojourns. These books are authored by outsiders who analyze, dissect, interpret, excoriate, celebrate, and wallow, depicting Las Vegas through their own preoccupations and pathologies. Understandably, Las Vegans may resent it when outside commentators are cited as the authorities on their town, earning fame and fat contracts from major trade presses. Since the 1990s, regional presses have sponsored a countermovement to publish books about living and working in Las Vegas. This chapter begins with three classic pieces by renowned visitors from the '60s and '70s: Mario Puzo, Sammy Davis Jr., and Hunter S. Thompson. The later pieces, constituting the bulk of the chapter and appearing in order of publication, are part of the movement to give Las Vegans themselves a voice, listen to those who call it home, and go backstage and inside the entertainment capital of the world.

MARIO PUZO [1920–1999]

"Why do I believe that gambling has bettered my character, kept me out of prison, helped me to bring up five children pleasurably and, I think, more or less successfully?" asks Mario Puzo in Inside Las Vegas *(1977), "Well, gambling has helped preserve my marriage for thirty years by keeping me too busy to chase other women and too guilty to resent my wife and children for having to support them, has forced me to write more by putting me into debt, and has improved my health by forcing me to learn how to play tennis at gambling resorts in order to stay out of casinos." This mix of honesty, knowledge of human nature, and nonjudgmental view is authentic Puzo, who is a self-proclaimed "degenerate gambler" and lover of Las Vegas. One of seven children of a poor Italian family in a rough neighborhood of New York City called Hell's Kitchen, Puzo is best known for his Mafia novel* The Godfather *(1969), which was on the* New York Times *best-seller list for sixty-seven weeks and was made into an Academy Award–winning movie, directed by Francis Ford Coppola, with screenplay by Puzo. Before* The Godfather *Puzo was $20,000 in debt, despite the critical success of two prior novels,* The Dark Arena *(1955) and* The Fortunate Pilgrim *(1964). He decided to become rich and famous. On cue,* The Godfather *book and movie netted Puzo over a million dollars, after which he gave up gambling because he had too much to lose. Nevertheless,* Inside Las Vegas *argues that gambling is one of the primary drives of mankind, bringing "solace and pleasure" to "countless millions living in worlds without hope and without those dreams essential to life." Two of Puzo's eight novels—*Fools Die *(1978) and* The Last Don *(1996)—depict gamblers, Las Vegas, and organized crime.*

from *Inside Las Vegas*

How lonely old people are. How hard it is to make close friends. When you are past a certain age the juice to love your fellow man seems to evaporate. And we all know, no matter what our age, that younger people find older relatives burdensome.

· · · · · · · ·

There was a woman from Brooklyn. She lived a full life. She married and she had children. Her sons became successful professional men. Her daughters gave her grandchildren. Her husband operated one of the most successful delicatessens in Coney Island. She was a model hausfrau, a loving mother, and a faithful wife.

When she reached the age of sixty five her husband died. She knitted a great deal, she visited her grandchildren. Friends took her to Florida—Miami Beach. She found the people there too old. She visited a married daughter in California. She found the people there too young. On the way back to New York she stopped over in Las Vegas. And there she became a penny ante degenerate gambler, a not-so-rare species in America. She took a small apartment and settled down for a life of "sin."

. . . .

In Vegas the Brooklyn lady gambled all day long. She read up on roulette systems. She played the slot machines until her shoulders ached. She accumulated treasure boxes full of nickels and dimes and quarters. She made friends with fellow penny ante degenerate gamblers and went for picnic lunches with them to Hoover Dam and the Grand Canyon. She never dipped into her savings. She used her Social Security and pension money to pay her rent and the rest she gambled on a daily budget.

It is not enough to say she was happy. She was in a state of bliss, entranced all day with the whirring slots of the casino, the red and black swirling numbers of the roulette wheel. The diamond-backed blackjack cards unfolding before her. She could forget her approaching death. She did this for fifteen years.

Her sons and daughters came to visit her twice a year. They brought her grand-children to see her and receive presents from her. (She refused to leave Las Vegas for a single day.) But then, finally one of those old-age diseases began to grind her out like a casino percentage. She was bedridden and became frailer and frailer. But every day her cronies gathered around her bedside to play gin rummy and that is how she died, with a hand full of playing cards and an 87¢ loser on the sheet.

. . . .

When I am too old for sex, when age withers my appetite for pizza and Peking duck, when my paranoia reaches the point that no human being arouses my trust or love, when my mind dries up so that I will no longer be interested in reading books, I will settle in Las Vegas. I will watch the ivory roulette ball spin, place my tiny bets on red and black numbers and some sort of magic will return again. I will throw the square red dice and hold my breath as they roll and roll along the green felt. I will sit down at the blackjack table and baccarat and wait for my own magical Ace of Spades to appear and I will be a lucky child again.

Should I go to heaven, give me no haloed angels riding snow-white clouds, no, not even the sultry houris of the Moslems. Give me rather a vaulting red-walled casino with bright lights, bring on horned devils as dealers. Let there be a Pit Boss in the Sky who will give me unlimited credit. And if there is a merciful God in our Universe he will decree that the Player have for *all* eternity, an Edge against the House.

SAMMY DAVIS JR. [1925–1990]
Jane and Burt Boyar

From a vaudeville song-and-dance, Stepin Fetchit shuffle to Las Vegas headliner, Broadway star, and Hollywood actor, Sammy Davis Jr. was the most famous African American entertainer of the 1950s and '60s. Born in Harlem, Davis was a mere three years old when his showman father took him on the road to perform. Sammy's formal education was minimal, but chutzpah *he had. He faced segregation and deep-seated racism in the U.S. Army during World War II. In early Las Vegas, then called the "Mississippi of the West," Davis was not allowed to sleep or gamble in the hotels where he starred. Davis's 1960 interracial marriage to Swedish actress May Britt, his conversion to Judaism, and his friendships with the Kennedys and Richard Nixon were atypical for a black man. He enjoyed saying, "I'm colored, Jewish and Puerto Rican. When I move into a neighborhood, I wipe it out!" His autobiographies,* Yes I Can: The Story of Sammy Davis, Jr. *(1965) and* Sammy *(2000), both cowritten with Jane Boyar and Burt Boyar, offer candid observations of the bittersweet life of a black performer in segregated America, his ambivalence toward the black pride movement, the end of his marriage to Britt, his flamboyant and sometimes self-destructive lifestyle, and membership in Frank Sinatra's Rat Pack. Garry Giddins, reviewing two Davis biographies, summed up the man, saying that Davis was "trying to live life as though color did not matter." Davis's film and stage work is extensive, but he may be best remembered for* Ocean's 11 *(1960) and the Broadway musical* Golden Boy *(1964). By 1990, when Davis died of throat cancer, Giddins observed that "if the tap-dance revival, jewelry-decked hip-hop moguls, interracial marriage, integrated nightclub acts and black Republicans are now too commonplace to merit comment, more than a little credit must go to Sammy Davis, Jr."*

from *Yes I Can: The Story of Sammy Davis Jr.*

The trade papers were bursting with news about Las Vegas. It was starting to become a show town. El Rancho and the Last Frontier were the first luxury hotels and there was talk about new hotels being planned to go up near them.

My father was heating coffee on the hot plate. "The word is they're payin' acts twice as much as anywheres else. Free suites and food tabs." Will said, "They're out to make it the number one show town." I listened to them like I was watching a ping-pong game. ". . . flyin' customers in . . ." "*Variety* says . . ." "The whole business is watching what's happening in Vegas."

. . . .

I looked around backstage while we waited to rehearse. The band was the biggest we'd ever worked with, the floor of the stage was springy and slick, the lighting was the most modern I'd ever seen. I was standing next to the stage manager. I asked, "Do I have it right about our rooms, that they're a part of our deal here?"

The manager came over to us as we finished rehearsing. "Sorry. We can't let you have rooms here. House rules. You'll have to find a place in the—uh, on the other side of town."

I picked up our suitcases. "Let's go, Dad, Will."

The hotels we'd passed in the town itself looked awful compared to El Rancho but even they were out of bounds to us. The cab driver said, "There's a woman name of Cartwright over in Westside takes in you people."

It was Tobacco Road. A three- or four-year-old baby, naked, was standing in front of a shack made of wooden crates and cardboard that was unfit for human life. None of us spoke.

The driver sounded almost embarrassed. "Guess y'can't say a lot for housing out here. Been hardly any call for labor 'round these parts. Just a handful of porters and dishwashers they use over on the Strip. Not much cause for you people t'come to Vegas."

The cab stopped in front of one of the few decent houses. A woman was standing in the doorway. "Come right in, folks. You boys with one of the shows? Well, I got three nice rooms for you."

When she told us the price Will almost choked. "But that's probably twice what it would cost at El Rancho Vegas."

"Then why don't you go live at El Rancho Vegas?"

"Pay her the money, Massey. It's not important."

Will counted out the first week's rent. My father smiled sardonically at her. "Looks like if the ofays don't get us, then our own will."

"Business is business. I've got my own troubles."

My father followed me into my room. "Not half bad." I nodded and started unpacking. He sat down and I could feel him watching me. I threw a shirt into a drawer and slammed it closed. "All right, Dad, for God's sake what is it?"

"*That's* what it is. Exactly what you're doin', eatin' yourself up, grindin' your teeth. Y'can't let it get t'you, Poppa. I know how you feels. But the fact is, when it comes time to lay your head down at night what's the difference if it's here or in a room at El Rancho?"

"Dad, I don't give a damn about their lousy rooms, I really don't. Right now, the only thing in this world that I want is their stage!"

As I danced, I did Satchmo. I shuffled across the stage like Step'n Fetchit. Then I spun around and came back doing the Jimmy Cagney walk to the center of the stage and stood there, facing my father and Will, doing Cagney's legs-apart stance, the face, and then "All right . . . you dirty rats!" For a moment there was no sound from out front—then they roared.

In the wings Will smiled warmly. "I'm glad I was wrong, Sammy." My father laughed and hugged me. "Poppa, you was *great!*" He put me down. "Whattya say we get dressed after the next show and go look around the casino. I got fifty dollars that's bustin' t'grow into a hundred."

We went out the stage door and around the building. The desert all around us was as dark as night can be but the casino was blazing with light. The door opened and as some people came out there was an outpour of sounds such as I'd never before heard: slot machines clanging, dealers droning, a woman shrieking with joy—and behind it all, a background of the liveliest, gayest music I'd ever heard. As I held the door open for my father, my head went in all directions to slot machines, dice tables, waiters rushing around with drinks, a man carrying a tray full of silver dollars.

I saw a hand on my father's shoulder. A deputy sheriff was holding him, shaking his head.

We rode to Mrs. Cartwright's in silence. They got out of the cab and I continued on downtown where there was a movie theater, where for a few hours I could lose myself in other people's lives.

A hand gripped my arm like a circle of steel, yanking me out of my seat, half-dragging me out to the lobby. "What're you, boy? A wise guy?" He was a sheriff, wearing a star badge and the big Western hat. His hand came up from nowhere and slapped across my face. He'd done it effortlessly but my jaw felt like it had been torn loose from my head. "Speak up when I talk to you!"

"What'd I do?"

"Don't bull me, boy. You know the law."

When I explained I'd just gotten to town and had never been there before, he pointed to a sign. "Coloreds sit in the last three rows. You're in Nevada now, not New York. Mind our rules and you'll be treated square. Go on back and enjoy the movie, boy."

I had no choice but to go in. A Mickey Rooney picture was on. After awhile I glanced up to catch a song he was doing and I looked away, still steaming. Then I looked up again and I forgot the cop and the theater and the rules and I was dancing across the campus in a college musical. An hour later I was Danny Kaye git-gat-gattling my way through the army. Then the lights went on and I was sitting in the last row of an almost empty movie theater, and again I was a Negro in a Jim Crow town.

I went back to Mrs. Cartwright's and slammed her dirty, gouging door and swore to myself that someday it would be different. I tried reading but I couldn't keep my mind on the book. I felt closed in so I went out for a walk but the sight of all the poorness drove me back to my room. I stared out the window at the glow of the lights from the Strip in the distance until it faded into the morning sun.

I should have been tired the next night but as eight o'clock drew near I was vibrating with energy and I couldn't wait to get on the stage. I worked with the strength of ten men.

We did our shows and went out to get a cab to Mrs. Cartwright's. I looked away from the lights of the casino but I couldn't avoid hearing the sounds. Night after night I had to pass that door to get a cab. Once, between shows, I stood around the corner where nobody would see me, and waited for the door to open so I could catch the short bursts of gaiety that escaped as people went in and came out. I sat on the ground for an hour, listening and wondering what it must be like to be able to just walk in anywhere.

HUNTER S. THOMPSON [1937–2005]

"Politics: Anarchist. Religion: None. Hobbies and other interests: Collecting guns." For better or for worse, arguably the best-known book ever written about Las Vegas is Fear and Loathing in Las Vegas: A Savage Journey to the Heart of the American Dream *(1971), by Hunter S. Thompson. In 1970* Sports Illustrated *commissioned Thompson to cover the Mint 400 motorcycle race in Las Vegas.* SI *"aggressively rejected" the high-speed, drug-trip log that Thompson disgorged from his all-expenses-paid gig, but* Rolling Stone *magazine sensed its sensational potential and ran it in two installments, outrageously illustrated by the British cartoonist Ralph Steadman. The story was acquired by Random House and hailed as "Best Book on the Dope Decade," its status as an American masterpiece secured with a Modern Library edition in 1996 and a Universal film version in 1998, starring Johnny Depp. A prolific writer from an early age, Thompson wrote more than a dozen books on topics as wide-ranging as the Hell's Angels, the 1972 Nixon-McGovern presidential campaign, and the 1980 Honolulu Marathon in Hawaii, all reeking of his unique blend of iconoclasm, vandalism, hallucinogenic hilarity, political invective, and nightmarish paranoia. Literary history credits Thompson with pioneering gonzo reporting, an extreme form of New Journalism that fuses fiction and fact, starring the writer as central protagonist. "To find myself at this age is just baffling," Thompson told an interviewer in 2002 at his home in Woody Creek, Colorado, when he was in his mid-sixties. "I always counted on dying young and violently." As for Las Vegas, its own baffling longevity has been won by cashing in on, rather than repudiating, the image as the main nerve of the American Dream*

so memorably articulated more than a quarter-century ago by the outlaw journalist "Dr. Gonzo." Thompson shot himself in the head in 2005, dying violently if not young.

from *Fear and Loathing in Las Vegas*

Mainline gambling is a very heavy business—and Las Vegas makes Reno seem like your friendly neighborhood grocery store. For a loser, Vegas is the meanest town on earth. Until about a year ago, there was a giant billboard on the outskirts of Las Vegas, saying:

DON'T GAMBLE WITH MARIJUANA!

IN NEVADA: POSSESSION—20 YEARS

SALE—LIFE!

So I was not entirely at ease drifting around the casinos on this Saturday night with a car full of marijuana and head full of acid. We had several narrow escapes: at one point I tried to drive the Great Red Shark into the laundry room of the Landmark Hotel—but the door was too narrow, and the people inside seemed dangerously excited.

. . . .

I drove around to the Circus-Circus Casino and parked near the back door. "This is the place," I said. "They'll never fuck with us here."

"Where's the ether?" said my attorney. "This mescaline isn't working."

I gave him the key to the trunk while I lit up the hash pipe. He came back with the ether-bottle, un-capped it, then poured some into a Kleenex and mashed it under his nose, breathing heavily. I soaked another Kleenex and fouled my own nose. The smell was overwhelming, even with the top down. Soon we were staggering up the stairs towards the entrance, laughing stupidly and dragging each other along, like drunks.

This is the main advantage of ether: it makes you behave like the village drunkard in some early Irish novel . . . total loss of all basic motor skills: blurred vision, no balance, numb tongue—severance of all connection between the body and the brain. Which is interesting, because the brain continues to function more or less normally . . . you can actually *watch* yourself behaving in this terrible way, but you can't control it.

You approach the turnstiles leading into the Circus-Circus and you know that when you get there, you have to give the man two dollars or he won't let you inside . . . but when you get there, everything goes wrong: you misjudge the distance to the turnstile and slam against it, bounce off and grab hold of an old woman to keep from falling, some angry Rotarian shoves you and you think: What's happening here? What's going on? Then you hear yourself mumbling: "Dogs fucked the Pope, no fault of mine. Watch out! . . . Why money? My name is Brinks; I was born . . . born? Get sheep over side . . . women and children to armored car . . . orders from Captain Zeep."

Ah, devil ether—a total body drug. The mind recoils in horror, unable to communicate with the spinal column. The hands flap crazily, unable to get money out of the pocket . . . garbled laughter and hissing from the mouth . . . always smiling.

Ether is the perfect drug for Las Vegas. In this town they love a drunk. Fresh meat. So they put us through the turnstiles and turned us loose inside.

The Circus-Circus is what the whole hep world would be doing on Saturday night if the Nazis had won the war. This is the Sixth Reich. The ground floor is full of gambling tables, like all the other casinos . . . but the place is about four stories high, in the style of a circus tent, and all manner of strange County-Fair/Polish Carnival madness is going on up in this space. Right above the gambling tables the Forty Flying Carazito Brothers are doing a high-wire trapeze act, along with four muzzled Wolverines and the Six Nymphet Sisters from San Diego . . . so you're down on the main floor playing blackjack, and the stakes are getting high when suddenly you chance to look up, and there, right smack above your head is a half-naked fourteen-year-old girl being chased through the air by a snarling wolverine, which is suddenly locked in a death battle with two silver-painted Polacks who come swinging down from opposite balconies and meet in mid-air on the wolverine's neck . . . both Polacks seize the animal as they fall straight down towards the crap tables—but they bounce off the net; they separate and spring back up towards the roof in three different directions, and just as they're about to fall again they are grabbed out of the air by three Korean Kittens and trapezed off to one of the balconies.

This madness goes on and on, but nobody seems to notice. The gambling action runs twenty-four hours a day on the main floor, and the circus never ends. Meanwhile, on all the upstairs balconies, the customers are being hustled by every conceivable kind of bizarre shuck. All kinds of funhouse-type booths. Shoot the pasties off the nipples of a ten-foot bull-dyke and win a cotton-candy goat. Stand in front of this fantastic machine, my friend, and for just 99¢ your likeness will appear, two hundred feet tall, on a screen above downtown Las Vegas. Ninety-nine cents more for a voice message. "Say whatever you want, fella. They'll hear you, don't worry about that. Remember you'll be two hundred feet tall."

Jesus Christ. I could see myself lying in bed in the Mint Hotel, half-asleep and staring idly out the window, when suddenly a vicious nazi drunkard appears two hundred feet tall in the midnight sky, screaming gibberish at the world: "*Wood-stock Über Alles!*"

We will close the drapes tonight. A thing like that could send a drug person careening around the room like a ping-pong ball. Hallucinations are bad enough. But after a while you learn to cope with things like seeing your dead grandmother crawling up your leg with a knife in her teeth. Most acid fanciers can handle this sort of thing.

But *nobody* can handle that other trip—the possibility that any freak with $1.98 can walk into the Circus-Circus and suddenly appear in the sky over downtown Las Vegas twelve times the size of God, howling anything that comes into his head. No, this is not a good town for psychedelic drugs. Reality itself is too twisted.

. . . .

What were we doing out here? What was the meaning of this trip? Did I actually have a big red convertible out there on the street? Was I just roaming around these Mint Hotel escalators in a drug frenzy of some kind, or had I really come out here to Las Vegas to work on a *story?*

I reached in my pocket for the room key; "1850," it said. At least that much was real. So my immediate task was to deal with the car and get back to that room . . . and then hopefully get straight enough to cope with whatever might happen at dawn.

Now off the escalator and into the casino, big crowds still tight around the crap tables. Who *are* these people? These faces! Where do they come from? They look like caricatures of used-car dealers from Dallas. But they're *real.* And, sweet Jesus, there are a hell of a *lot* of them—still screaming around these desert-city crap tables at four-thirty on a Sunday morning. Still humping the American Dream, that vision of the Big Winner somehow emerging from the last-minute pre-dawn chaos of a stale Vegas casino.

WILLIAM J. PLUMMER [B. 1927]

Although Gambel's quail do not gamble in the usual sense, this aptly named bird makes its home in the Las Vegas area, a high-stakes gamble where the odds favor urban development over desert habitat. Dazzled by the showy spectacle of the Strip, it is easy to forget that Vegas Valley is home to species other than our own. William Plummer's A Quail in the Family (1974) describes a poignant encounter with the natural world that in Las Vegas is so often upstaged by

culture. Plummer's book, whose reviews compare it favorably to Cry Wolf *and* Ring of Bright
Water, *is the story of Peep, an orphaned Gambel's quail that the Plummer family adopted.
Characterized as "sweet and sober, modest, wholesome," the book further challenges Las Vegas
stereotypes by chronicling a healthy family living a sane life. Before one tiny quail entered the
picture, William Plummer had never seriously considered writing. Originally a midwesterner,
he earned* BS *and* EE *degrees from the University of Wisconsin and spent his career as an elec-
trical/instrumentation engineer, working for Los Alamos Scientific Laboratory in New Mexico
in the 1950s and, after 1962, working in management for* EG&G, *an engineering firm supporting
the Nevada Test Site. But at age forty-six, while on leave from his job to get a business degree
from* UNLV, *he wrote* A Quail in the Family *"simply because the story needed telling." Two
more books about other members of the Plummers' menagerie followed—Friends of the Family (1975) and* Five of a Kind *(1976)—before other priorities reasserted themselves. William
Plummer and his wife, Wanda, who have been married for more than fifty years, retired in the
1980s to Spring Creek in northern Nevada, where they enjoy watching a delightful variety of
"friends," including a mixed flock of Gambel's and California quail.*

from *A Quail in the Family*

It was a Saturday morning in May of 1969 and already warm, even for Las Vegas.
The spring winds and blowing sand had subsided, leaving the air clean and light.
In the distance, calico mountains were outlined sharply against the clear, unbroken blue, while a few blocks away the Sahara tower sparkled in the sunlight. Its
flashing sign marked the start of the Strip, and against the bright sky it was barely
readable as it alternately announced: 11:00—95°. A little farther on, the Riviera
and the Stardust clamored for attention; then came the new Frontier, boasting of
Jimmy Durante in its show room. Frank Sinatra was appearing at Caesars Palace,
and, in a penthouse atop the Desert Inn, the enigmatic Mr. Hughes was pondering
additional acquisitions for his Nevada empire.

Working on the shrubs around the pool, I had stripped off my shirt to savor the
southwestern sun on my midwestern back. Pausing to study the palms, their new
fronds just emerging in tight accordion pleats, I shuddered a little. It was time to
remove last year's growth, hanging dead and dry against the trunks, but I knew
that my gloves would be useless against those hooked, shark's-tooth thorns. Still,
the old fronds had to come off.

As I debated with myself, Mike, the youngest of our three boys, came slamming
out into the backyard.

"Hey, Dad, I found another baby bird!"

I responded to his obvious enthusiasm with a small sigh of resignation.
"Couldn't you put it back in its nest?"

"There was no nest around. He was all by himself on the ground."

As Mike came up to me and carefully uncupped his dusty hands, I expected to see the usual quasi embryo, naked and pink and wrinkled. Instead, his unfolding fingers revealed a captivating little chick the size of my thumb. He was no more than a striped fuzz-ball in beige and brown, but cute as a cartoon character. A tiny top-knot was already evident, and his feet were like outsized snowshoes, almost as big as his body.

More by intuition than by recognition I exclaimed, "Why, that's not a bird, it's a quail!" The illogical distinction seemed somehow appropriate.

Mike, who was nearly nine, was genuinely surprised at my observation, but I scolded him anyway for removing wildlife from its natural environment. The fact was he had found the baby in the desert only a block away and had looked about carefully for a family before retrieving it. Apparently the chick had hatched late or had become separated through some crisis or other. It could hardly have been more than a few hours out of its shell, and easy prey for a hawk or fox.

The sudden sun dazzled the wee fellow, and he closed his eyes a moment to bask in its warmth. Then in a wink he was up and squirming to be free. Incredibly small and fragile, he was so active that we were afraid he would injure himself.

"Well, I suppose he hasn't much chance of survival," I commented, "but at this point, his only hope is with us. We'd better do our best for him."

So my gardening was put aside while Mike and I mobilized the family to accommodate our newest boarder.

In those days our house often served as an animal refuge. On any given day there was sure to be more than one small creature enjoying our care and custody. The list might include a stunned songbird deceived by an exceptionally clean picture window or a venturesome lizard rescued from the bottom of the pool. Guarding our entrance light was a great praying mantis, fattening up on miller moths, and in the den a kangaroo rat named Squeaky had resided comfortably in his special bookshelf for five years.

Although many of our little guests were wild, it was not because we lived in a remote area. Ours was a typical suburban plot in a well-established residential neighborhood, but in Las Vegas the desert is always close at hand. Like many cities in the Southwest, Las Vegas had grown by sprawling out in an irregular checkerboard pattern, leaving numerous patches of undeveloped real estate interspersed among the developments. These remained rough and rugged, lying idle while their capital value appreciated. Typically, they were sandhills covered with sage and thistle, tumbleweed, mesquite, and creosote bush, and within their boundaries wildlife flourished. No wonder that an occasional roadrunner, rabbit, or even a desert fox might cross the wrong street and crash an afternoon pool party.

At our house he'd find himself encouraged to stay. The boys were forever adopting snakes, insects, and lizards. My wife, Wanda, drew the line at scorpions and tarantulas, but even so we entered the boys' rooms with some trepidation. And anyone poking around the house late at night had better have a flashlight and slippers!

Mike's sister Leslie was our eldest, just fourteen and with appreciable experience at managing the animal ménage. Her credits included fish, frogs and turtles, hamsters and mice, parakeets, canaries, a duck, and even, briefly, a baby alligator.

It was Leslie to whom we turned now for help with Mike's foundling. She promptly produced a surplus five-gallon aquarium. In it we deposited sand, gravel, weeds, and the baby quail, in that order. The little chick began at once to pace rapidly along the front of the glass, looking for an exit. His incessant peeping led us to christen him, rather unimaginatively, "Peep." Subsequent elaboration made it "Beau Peep," but this proved too cumbersome for regular use.

Peep understood at once how to drink water from a bottle cap, but we were temporarily at a loss to provide him with acceptable food. After a series of rejections we gained his endorsement for cherry pie filling, and eventually cornmeal and flour found his approval too. In a pinch, he seemed able to locate minuscule edibles among the litter.

By now we were a committee of six attending to the baby bird's welfare, but our combined credentials were singularly unimpressive. Despite many exposures to wildlife, we were almost completely ignorant of the ways of desert quail. We had sighted them frequently in the desert, but our observations were inevitably brief and distant. I am afraid, too, that as naturalists our approach was haphazard—rather more empirical than academic. Unless circumstances focused our interest upon a given species, we were not likely to refer to the literature.

Thus it was that none of us had any concrete idea of how to get Peep through that first night. Presumably some pseudo-maternal source of warmth was required, but we worried that he might burn or smother. We settled finally upon a cigar box wired with two small Christmas tree lights. This was propped up at one end of the enclosure with a discarded sock tacked over its open side.

As evening approached, we covered the aquarium with a towel, leaving the corners open for air and observation. The Christmas tree bulbs provided a faint rosy glow, while steady, radiant warmth filtered through the old brown-checked sock. Peep took to the arrangement right away, sprawling up onto the box rather than nestling against it.

For the first hour or two we checked on him frequently. He appeared to be doing just fine, comfortable and content, with no evident problems. Warning ourselves that he'd probably not make it through the night anyway, we tiptoed off to watch television.

. . . .

Our skepticism was very likely justified. In the wild, a great many baby quail are weeded out naturally soon after hatching, and even in captivity many die in the first few days. One local breeder stated that with Gambel's quail (which we subsequently found Peep to be) only about 15 percent of any that hatch are likely to reach adolescence. Even this requires starting them out in carefully controlled brooders—disinfected with ultraviolet light, temperature maintained at 98°—and feeding them a special mash containing antibiotics. Apparently the breeders haven't discovered the power of cherry pie filling!

Beau Peep had, however, and when we uncovered his aquarium the next day, he was already up and tromping happily about in it. He looked very chipper—bright-eyed and hungry. Resuming an inventory of the pantry, we added pancake mix to his list of edibles, and he devoted the morning to eating, pacing, and napping.

We resisted the impulse to handle him, but by midafternoon we were sufficiently encouraged at his obvious vigor to take him outside. Making a little procession to the shady patio area, we arranged ourselves as an enclosure with Peep in the middle. He was delighted with his new freedom and darted about this way and that, pecking at bits of dirt and grass with great enthusiasm.

He was such a little charmer, unbelievably tiny in the huge outdoors. Tripping himself repeatedly, he raced eagerly about on his great snowshoe feet, looking for all the world like Tweetie Bird of the Warner Brothers cartoons. Peeping and pecking constantly, he managed to find minute insects on the paving, so small that we had to look closely even to see them.

It was Sunday afternoon, and our good friends Ted and Marie dropped by for their weekly visit. They were enthralled by our new foster child. Ted and I took movies to document the little bird's frenetic activities, but he moved so rapidly we could hardly keep him in view, much less in focus.

After a half hour we put him back in the aquarium, where he drank from the bottle cap and almost immediately went to sleep, atop the lighted box. By the time our friends left, he was up and pacing again, so we took him out once more in the cool twilight.

After that he was exercised several times a day, making no effort to run off. If he found himself more than a few yards from us, he came scurrying back; if we moved away, he would follow close behind until we settled into a new location. We discovered he would stay with any one of us, so we could spell each other off at quail-sitting, passing the duty from one to the other without unsettling him.

Within a few days, he had explored most of the backyard, and we had seen it from an entirely new point of view. It was much larger and more interesting than we had thought.

. . . .

It was nearly four years since that May day when Mike had come bursting out into the backyard with a little ball of down cupped in his grimy hands, excited about finding a baby bird, yet not quite realizing what he had. In many ways four years is quite a long time. For a quail, it is fifteen times longer than it takes him to grow into maturity. And yet that first three months after hatch-out must itself be a marvelously rich, full period, for in that short time he discovers and subdues a whole, exciting world.

For the rest of us, many things had changed in four years. Mike was nearly thirteen now; Leslie was eighteen and engaged. Outside near a different pool, a new set of palm trees was challenging me to tackle last year's barbed fronds. Over the back wall we could still see the calico-colored mountains, but often now they were obscured by a brown smudge. On the Strip, MGM's new Grand Hotel was pushing up and out, striving to rob the Dunes of its eminence. Howard Hughes was thrice removed, and Frank Sinatra was actually in retirement.

It was an unusual year, 1973. In the first few months, the Las Vegas area had already received its total average annual precipitation, and it had all come in well-spaced, slow, soaking rains. The desert was responding with its most luxurious growth in fifteen years; some said in fifty. Soon there would be blooms everywhere, incredibly profuse: wild poppies and verbena, thistle, forget-me-nots, Indian paintbrush, lupines, cane cactus, and prickly pears. Slopes that had been brown for years would suddenly turn green, and the area would come alive with birds, lizards, and insects.

Undeniably, southern Nevada residents were due for a very special year. It would be a good spring to start a lawn; it would be a splendid summer for water sports on Lake Mead; it would be an outstanding season for growing roses and day lilies.

And this time there could be no doubt: it was going to be an especially good year for the desert quail.

SUSAN BERMAN [1945–2000]

Susan Berman was the sheltered only child of prominent Las Vegas hotel owner and philan-
thropist Davie Berman. "Susie" grew up beside the pool at the Flamingo, did her homework
in casino backrooms, played gin rummy with the family's bodyguard, and was serenaded by
Liberace on her twelfth birthday. Shortly thereafter her father died, and within two years her
mother committed suicide, leaving Susie in the care of Uncle Chickie, famed gambler and
bookie. Berman, who once remarked that she was "born to write," earned a BA from UCLA
and an MA in journalism from UC Berkeley. She was a staff reporter for the San Francisco Ex-
aminer—known for getting the "impossible" interview—and a writer for "The Evening Show"
on KPIX-TV in San Francisco, a journalist for New York magazine, an editor, screenwriter,
playwright, and novelist. Berman did not learn of her father's criminal past until she was an
adult, when a brash journalist handed her a stack of FBI files that revealed him to be a former
bootlegger, murderer, ex-con, and close associate of Syndicate leaders Meyer Lansky and Frank
Costello. Utterly devastated, Berman began a period of feverish investigative journalism into
her own roots, culminating in the acclaimed memoir Easy Street (1981), in which she poi-
gnantly reveals the true stories of her parents' lives, reassesses her own childhood, and narrates
the coming of age of her glamorous "older sister," Las Vegas. Berman was a writer for the A&E
Network documentary The Real Las Vegas (1996). Her accompanying book, Lady Las Vegas:
The Inside Story behind America's Neon Oasis (1996), interweaves her family's story with
that of the growing city. Berman made headline news when she was found murdered gangland
style in her Beverly Hills home on Christmas Eve 2000. Cathy Scott's true crime book Murder
of a Mafia Daughter (2002) points to murder suspect millionaire Bobby Durst in a case that
remains unprosecuted.

from *Easy Street*

It snowed in Las Vegas once when I was eight. The weather forecasters had been predicting it for days, and it was heralded as an almost unheard of event. As the magical white powder began to sprinkle the ground, I ran into my father's room to drag him outside.

When he looked at the light snowfall, he smiled and said, "Susie, I hope this is the only snow you ever see." Then he went inside, totally uninterested.

He loved the sunny hot weather Las Vegas usually had and one of his constant retorts to his friends asking, "Davie, how are you?" was "It's eighty degrees outside, how bad can things be?"

He never mentioned that he had grown up in another place, a place so cold that weather was a constant enemy. In later years, when Aunt Lil identified the place as Ashley, North Dakota, she laughed bitterly as she remembered it. "It was so cold that our feet froze on the way to school, one of our brothers died of pneumonia, and one winter our farmhouse burned down and we spent the night outside, all thinking we would die. If Davie hadn't gotten us out of that town soon after that, we never would have survived it."

. . . .

Most days after school the driver would take me to the Flamingo Hotel to be with my father.

I'd run into the casino and head for the pit, ducking under the burgundy velvet cord, yelling, "Daddy, Daddy, I'm here." Gamblers would look annoyed at hearing a child's shrill voice in this most grown-up of places but once they saw whose child it was, they acted delighted.

My father was always dressed in a stylish suit. He had a ruby mezuzah that hung on a gold chain from his pocket and he always smelled of French cologne.

His eyes twinkling, he'd reach down and throw me in the air, catching me and hugging me on the way down. Then he'd lead me off to the counting room in back of the pit where we'd get down to the serious business of homework. The counting room always smelled awful to me, odors of old cigarette butts and paper money clung to the walls. He'd clear off a space and we'd begin.

"A story about a duck? Well, let's see, what do ducks think about, Susie? Try to write a story about what's important to ducks." Geography, history, arithmetic? He knew it all and would make it come alive. Italy? He had been there in the war. He always said, "Education is the one thing they can't take away from you, Susie," and I thought, Who's "they"? and why would anyone want to take anything away from me?

He expected all As and he got them. He told me school was like a contest. If you chose to enter the contest, you should fight to win. He drilled me on spelling-bee words endlessly until I won the All Las Vegas Spelling Bee almost every year.

Fifth Street School was dismal. There was constant war between the white, Indian, and black children. Learning was secondary to fighting, so for a while my father decided that I should be flown down to Los Angeles for school. He found a private elementary school in the Hollywood Hills and for about six months my mother and I flew down every week until he decided I was too far from his watchful eye.

Once I was back, he concentrated on improving my math, never my best subject. He hit on an inventive solution—he started a coin collection for me. He bought me the coin books and had hotel sheriff Dave Schuman bring in handfuls of change from the slots for me to sort, catalogue, and add up. It was a lesson in casino economics.

. . . .

My father was extremely proud of being Jewish. He took every opportunity to tell me I was Jewish and just what that meant. He felt that for a Jewish child to be properly brought up, there must be a synagogue, a rabbi, and a cantor in evidence. So he started the first and imported the latter two.

He convinced Moey Sedway and Willie Alderman that all their kids needed to go to Friday-night services and Sunday-morning lessons. At first he designated a vacant house as the shul; for a year we went to services and sat on card-table chairs. Then he and his friends built a real shul on the corner of 13th and Carson in the residential area of Las Vegas. He brought in Rabbi Arthur Leibowitz.

Every Sunday morning he would wake me very excited. He loved to talk about the ancestors Esther and Moses. He was the only parent who stayed through lessons, with the occasional exception of Willie who sometimes came with him. Although they did have the courtesy not to sit in my actual class, they sat three rows back. I never understood why the weekly event seemed to make my father so happy. Later his friends told me he had been a staunch supporter of Israel and had raised a great deal of money for the Irgun. He had even personally organized and financed a plane flight of weapons to Israel during the War for Independence.

Soon after he started the synagogue he had an idea for Passover services. Since none of our mothers were Jewish, and no one lived in a big enough house to hold a Seder, he decided that it should be held at the Last Frontier Hotel. My father even brought Bubby in for it; she taught our mothers to make charosis and other traditional foods.

He'd have special matzohs for Passover sent to us from New York and he'd always take me with him to pick up the shipment at the airport. My father would see to it that any employees who were Jewish would be invited, and on the way to the hotel he read their names to the rabbi so that he would be familiar with their children.

He would walk me through the casino, where as usual I'd be straining to see who was winning a jackpot, but my father would say, "Not tonight, Susie. Tonight is special, it's Passover."

The dining room would be transformed; all the small tables would be lined up in long rows. In their shiksa zest, our naive mothers decorated the ceiling with streamers from all the Jewish holidays and silver decorations picturing dreidels and Hanukkah lights mixed with those of Passover and Rosh Hashanah. The rabbi would introduce himself to any new children and those of us who knew him trailed along to meet the new celebrants.

When the rabbi walked onto the stage and yelled the four questions into the microphone—"Why is this night different from all other nights? . . ." —my father led us in the answers. A few other men had imported their small fat mothers, too. Yiddish accents, the recitation of the four questions, and our two or three attempts at Jewish songs led by the cantor like "David Melech, King of Israel" and "*Mayim*" spewed from this room. Occasionally confused guests would wander in and inquire why there was no floor show that night and we kids would laugh hysterically at their mistake.

I found the whole experience exhausting and usually wound up falling asleep on my father's lap. I'd be awakened from my slumber when he whispered in my ear, "Susie, the *afikomen*." This was the highlight of the evening; whoever discovered the hidden matzoh in the napkin got a picture book on Israel. As soon as Rabbi Leibowitz told us to get started, the thirty or so of us dived into the dining room. Trouble was, Rabbi Leibowitz didn't have much of an imagination, he always hid the *afikomen* in one of three places: under the microphone stand, in the orchestra pit, or backstage. I never got there first, a fact which I blamed on my father. He held on to my dress sash until the rabbi said "Go," and there were two other girls who always got a head start. When it was over, we all pitched in to take the decorations down off the sparkly ceiling because the second floor show was going on as usual after we left. In fact the guests were already lining up. I always gave them a superior grin, they were mere tourists, we *were* Las Vegas.

. . . .

My mother had loved Las Vegas, too—at first. She was twenty-six and I was a two-month-old baby when she brought me with her on the train from Minneapolis.

My father was living in the bungalow at the El Rancho Hotel (the only place hotel owners could get a war-rationed phone) and he could see the train depot from his window. The pink flat desert skyline was then completely empty. As soon as he saw the smoke from the locomotive he had his driver take him to the station.

It was the middle of a sweltering July; my mother had dressed for her arrival in a white linen suit and big-brimmed hat and had put me in a white silk dress. She got off the train and handed me to him with a look of shock on her face. She uttered the words any Midwestern wife might say: "Where is the town?" staring around at nothing but miles of sagebrush, cactus, and carcasses of prairie dogs. She had expected something more like Los Angeles.

The "town" was only firmly established in my father's mind. With the greatest passion, he told her it was going to be the jewel of the desert.

"Gladys, honey, this is only the backdrop," he said standing on the platform that day in his tailored suit.

Las Vegas was still a cowboy town of sixteen thousand people when my mother first saw it. Men with perpetual sunburns, sweaty underarms, and silver stirrups walked the streets. Grizzled prospectors and out-of-luck gamblers looked up with wonder as my father and his partners brought their fancy city manners and suits to town. Alligator shoes were beginning to take the place of cowboy boots. The city was composed of just two areas: a small residential section and "Glitter Gulch," the raggedy downtown where my father owned his clubs. Many residents lived in trailers and cinderblock houses, there was a large Indian reservation on the outskirts of town, and all the town's blacks lived on the west side under a cement underpass called the Cement Curtain.

Most of the action was at the downtown gambling clubs, but the Western Union office always held some drama. There, cast-off mates hoped for a second chance; divorce and marriage were second to gambling as a town attraction. The entrances to both ends of the town were lined with wedding chapels.

We moved into the El Rancho's yellow and royal-blue bungalows with my father, while my mother scoured the town for a suitable house. She finally found one: a small brown and white Tudor home with a real fireplace in the living room, maybe the only house with a fireplace in all of Las Vegas. It was surrounded by a white picket fence and she said it reminded her of the house she grew up in in St. Paul. My father laid down fifteen thousand dollars cash and bought it for her. She flew back to Minneapolis to get furniture and clothes and shoes for me. There were no real stores in Las Vegas yet. The town had few amenities. Besides the downtown club coffee shops, there were only two restaurants, the Green Shack, and Fong's, a Chinese restaurant we used to frequent run by Big Fong and Little Fong.

While my father worked his fourteen hours a day, my mother embraced the western culture. She rented horses at the Day Dream Ranch behind the Last Frontier Hotel and loped across the empty land, land that now holds the Strip hotels. When I was old enough she had the drivers take us to the ghost towns surrounding Las Vegas, and we collected rocks, saw abandoned silver mines, went fishing at Lake Mead. She bought us western clothes at Smith and Chandler's Western shop; she and I had matching brown suede fringed jackets.

She tried to keep herself occupied with me at home. She played her piano constantly; my first few Christmases were memorable for the times she played and sang "White Christmas" and "Frosty the Snow Man." She had a piano bench stuffed with sheet music from many Broadway musicals and she could sing all the tunes. She bought a sewing machine and sewed us matching dresses.

But very soon the violence of my father's life began to destroy her. He told her nothing, but she perceived enough to know that her husband and child were not safe. She knew that we were living on the enchanted edge of a dark reality. She was not allowed to make friends freely, her movements were guarded. The two or three wives of my father's partners that she had known from before were as isolated in their homes as she was in hers. She had no interest in gambling or drinking, frequent escapes for Mob wives.

Then several catastrophic events occurred. First Ben Siegel was killed, and death threats were made to friends of my father's. She never knew if my father might be threatened or killed. She could trust no one; she'd thought respectability in Las Vegas would bring safety, it didn't.

The constant family peril was too overpowering for her, silence sucked her in. Her daily life was constricted by caution and fear. The stress of living in a violent, unpredictable world broke her. She became obsessed with getting out of Las Vegas, away from the Mob.

. . . .

My father pretended to us that the dark side of his life didn't exist. If he had any fear, he never showed it. He had lived in a state of war all his life. The possibility of an instant death went with the territory and he thought he was smart enough to avoid it.

He showed me only the public side of his life. He liked to concentrate my attention on city events, like the Helldorado Parade. I still remember the night before each parade when he would take me to see the float being prepared in back of the hotel. It would be a gigantic mixture of crepe paper, tissue paper, and props. One year I was a butterfly in a moving simulated forest, another year a swimmer in a "Sports" theme parade. I always waved at my father and all of his friends who were watching out of a window in the El Cortez Hotel.

As time went on, my father became involved more and more in civic activities. But my mother didn't see his increasing power as success. She perceived only the ominous atmosphere of the town and everything about it was frightful. My father worked all day and night; she was left alone to worry and go mad.

. . . .

She was obsessed with my safety. One day when I was eight, I was dragged into a car near Fifth Street School by a middle-aged man. He threw me in the back with a bunch of comic books and I knew he was no friend. He had only driven a block when I hit him in the face and jumped out of the car yelling all the way. Two policemen heard me and brought me home. It was a blow my mother's friends say she never recovered from. The man was never heard from again and never caught. There was no evidence it was Mob kidnap, it could have been a crank or a pervert. But it happened to be a time of Mob tension. My mother was convinced that I had just escaped death. She screamed and cried in her bedroom for three weeks after that and my father had to keep coming home from the hotel.

The worst had happened; her private world had been violated. I was her total identity, her only reason for living, and now she had proof that something could happen to me.

Two years before, my father had heard about analysis, the new "miracle cure." He found the best doctor in Los Angeles "that money could buy," Dr. Ralph Greenson, who saw my mother but was too busy to take her case himself. She tried other analysts for the next four years. She would fly down to Los Angeles three times a week. It seemed to sap all her energy to even make the trip, and sometimes she'd end up staying at the Beverly Wilshire for months and my father and I would fly down to visit her on weekends. She would always hold me very tightly when we were together. It was as if she felt she was protecting me from something, but from what? From traffic? From strangers? My father seemed to make no sense at all during these visits. He just kept asking, "Gladys, baby, what can I do to make you feel better. Honey, what do you need?" He looked like he was in pain. When we'd go back he, too, would hold on to me very tightly and hug me a lot—not to protect me but because to him I was all that was left of her. I began to wonder if she would ever come home again.

. . . .

During the next year my mother made a brief rally. She said she felt well enough to have me live with her in Los Angeles, that I must get out of Las Vegas. My father said he would try to extricate himself from Las Vegas, but that it would take a year.

He went down to rent us an apartment in Westwood, on Wilshire Boulevard. But he wouldn't let us move in until there was another apartment available so that a friend of his could live next door to us. We stayed at the Westward Ho! Motel for a month waiting for two vacancies in the same building to open up.

Once we were settled in the apartment, I had never seen my mother so happy. That terrible dread she associated with Las Vegas seemed to vanish here. I had a somewhat normal life for the first time. I went to Fairburn public school for the fifth grade, still walked back and forth by Lou, but I was allowed to visit friends after school and sell lemonade on the corner like any other kid. I didn't understand that the life in Las Vegas had been isolating and different from most others; I just knew that this felt good.

. . . .

My father came down every weekend for at least a day and she cherished that visit. She was careful to tell me time and time again that "You know Daddy loves you, you have a family like other girls. Daddy and I love each other very much and we're not getting a divorce, I just have to live down here to go to the doctor. Daddy will be living here soon; we'll all be together." My father called every night and my mother and I bubbled over with the small events of our lives, while my father was reduced to saying "So, what else" every five minutes. He always asked my mother if I could go home for a vacation but she said no, that I had to stay in Los Angeles. She'd remind him that he promised to move down with us the next year.

Then everything good and joyous went out of our lives. One day in the spring I came home to the apartment on Wilshire Boulevard to find my father looking very upset. My mother was crying. My father kept saying, "I can't leave now, Gladys, you've got to understand. I just can't do it." My mother sat silently crying, accepting her fate.

After that visit, my mother got worse again. She seemed to lose interest in everything and took to her bed. She talked about her visits to the psychiatrist constantly and began to look like she had in Las Vegas. When my father called there were tears and she'd say softly, "I can't live if I have to worry about you there—and Susan, what will happen to Susan?"

Right after school let out in June my father came home and took me back to Las Vegas. I knew something was very wrong with my mother again, but I didn't know what. Whenever she would get sick and stop eating, I would do the same. They both seemed to feel that I would be better off in Las Vegas with my father.

There were very few happy occasions during that year. All my father was interested in discussing was my mother's condition, with doctors, friends, anyone who would listen. He was begging for a shred of hope. She was in a sanitarium, allowed no visitors. At one point he must have accepted the possibility that he could wind up my only parent. He went for his yearly checkup at the doctor's and took me along. When he came out of the office, he crumbled his pack of Chesterfields and threw them in the basket.

"The doctor says these aren't good for me," he told me as he kicked an entire lifetime of chain-smoking three packs a day cold turkey. True to his self-discipline, he never took another puff. He told one of his friends that week, "Now I've got to take care of myself. What if Gladys never gets better?"

As I was growing older, so was Las Vegas. When I came back at age eleven in 1956, I was free to come and go in my house for the first time. There were no longer two or three men living with us, only Lou. New hotels blossomed on the Strip where I had ridden horses over empty desert—now the Sands, the Sahara, Last Frontier, and Desert Inn were built and the Dunes, Stardust, and Tropicana were in various stages of construction. When the Dunes had its official opening, my father took me and asked his friend, an owner, to let me have the story-book doll collection from every state when they were through exhibiting it. Production shows were now as common as big-name stars, Charleston and North Las Vegas became subdivisions and little McCarran Field became a regular airport. Churches, schools, and movie theaters sprouted up and Las Vegas became a real city. The Minsky's Revue and the Latin Quarter Revue premiered. The dancing waters with their colored lights became a regular attraction on the Strip, and the Strip even had its own police force with one hundred fifty armed guards.

On my twelfth birthday, my father gave me a party at the Riviera Hotel. He had invited ten of my girlfriends from owners' families and Liberace sang "Happy Birthday." My father had a special cake made up, all chocolate, and bought out the hotel gift shop for me. He sat in a booth behind our table to watch the whole extravaganza with pride.

One month later he was dead.

A. WILBER STEVENS [1921–1996]

A westerner by temperament if not by birth, Arthur Wilber Stevens—"Wil" to his friends— was born in Brooklyn, New York, grew up in Manhattan, and attended Brown University. Going west for graduate study, Stevens earned an MA and PHD from the University of Washington, where he studied with the poets Theodore Roethke, Richard Hugo, and Carolyn Kizer. In Seattle, as a graduate student, Stevens founded the literary journal Interim *in 1944, editing it for the next ten years. In one memorable adventure from that period, Stevens hitchhiked in a mail and grocery truck to Big Sur in order to get a piece from Henry Miller for* Interim. *After graduation, Stevens took college teaching and administrative positions throughout the West, won Fulbright professorships to Burma, Thailand, and Brazil, and eventually settled in Las Vegas in 1973, where he began a twenty-year distinguished teaching career at UNLV. Stevens acted in and directed local theater productions and wrote theater and music reviews for the* Las Vegas Sun *and* Las Vegas Review-Journal. *He resurrected* Interim *in 1986 and gained a reputation as a tireless, judicious, and generous editor, in contrast to an editor of another journal who rejected one of Stevens's poems without a word of explanation, enclosing only a little pile of ashes in the return envelope. Stevens urged* Interim's *authors to be "naughty," to risk "miracle hoping defiance" rather than "informed despair." His own poetry defied passing fashions and easy categorization as it probed urban and suburban lives. With minimal punctuation and ambiguous imagery, his poems are difficult to paraphrase but curiously quotable. Considered one of Nevada's most accomplished and influential poets, Stevens published more than one hundred poems, more than fifteen scholarly articles, and eight book-length works, earning the Nevada Writers Hall of Fame Award in 1992. The following poems appear in the "Las Vegas" section of Stevens's collected poems,* From the Still Empty Grave *(1995).*

Vegas: A Few Scruples

> Under scrutiny of hills in the hot sun
> A woman crazed has cut her lover
> Hacked at his privacies kicked
> Glass at him broken glass is the thing
> Here where the children at the lower
> Elementary levels have one of the best
> Systems and more daysleeping parents
> Than Monaco it's a tight town
> Full of churches rampant cars like
> Pimples mapping the alleys behind
> The Strip a wonderment of sullen searchers
> Planted firmly on the shifty earth looking.
>
> When Brigham sent his band here
> He did not foresee what the sun could
> Do but burn for the Faith it does burn
> Indeed burn right for the Saved of which
> There are many species transient and nested
> And too there are the lesser breeds the manic
> The levitated professors who floated
> Into this crude escrow like bad seeds vagrant
> Talent dumped from the more thoughtful cities
> All sorts of burning bushes in dry tide
> Now by gardens and pools the natives half watch
> The cuffed change girl shuffle to the cool blue car.

Paradise Crest

> The pit boss wives and a few other lady
> Connections parade their ways together
> Urgently marching their arms
> Talking and testing the early sun
> Occasionally a drained man will pass them

Puffing his way toward eternity
It is hard on my bones to watch them
Grouping buzzing somehow they look
So confident so proud of something
They seem to have found while over my oatmeal
I wonder what that treasure may be
These pilgrims seem to be importuning an answer
To a prayer they look as if they've
Been pimping for the recent dawn "Amazing"
I think I hear one varicose Brunhilde cry
Slapping firmly her entrenched purple
Walking shorts as she flips her cigarette
Into a pansy patch nodding at her then the
Neighbor neurosurgeon appears tugged by "Angel"
His straining pitbull the shifts keep changing
All this before seven the TWA wife happily joins one
Babbling troop her husband when not
Flying to Amsterdam works religiously on a yellow
Chris Craft now the high roller's son
Is picked up for private school two good neighbors
From work in Boylesque depart their
Porsche quarreling the Mormon Bishop zings along
Waving the truck of Mexican *campesinos* (four in
Front) negotiate the confident promenades
They too have come to greet the streets of Paradise.

PHYLLIS BARBER [B. 1943]

"I lived in Boulder City until I was twelve, before my family moved twenty-five miles away to another planet called Las Vegas," writes Phyllis Barber in How I Got Cultured: A Nevada Memoir *(1992), winner of the Associated Writing Programs award in creative nonfiction. Barber's father served in the navy, helped to build Hoover Dam, and became an insurance salesman and a bishop in the Boulder City Ward of the LDS church. As Barber recalls in her preface to* Parting the Veil: Stories from a Mormon Imagination *(1999), "it was as common to think of an angel appearing by my bed as it was to drink orange juice for breakfast." The Mormon values for women of purity, modesty, and chastity were seriously challenged, however, when*

the family moved to Las Vegas just as Barber reached adolescence. There, in the "Forbidden City," yearning for action, Barber joined the Rhythmettes, a kick-line dance team similar to the Rockettes, and she quenched her thirst for high culture through piano lessons, ultimately becoming a professional pianist. Despite the lure of worldly attractions, Barber fulfilled the role of dutiful Mormon wife—she attended Brigham Young University, married a lawyer, had four sons, and volunteered in the community. Barber, who cofounded the Writers at Work conference in Park City, Utah, and has taught creative writing at several colleges, began writing at age thirty-two, after her fourth son was born. Her critically acclaimed work, which includes two children's books, a novel about the building of Hoover Dam (And the Desert Shall Blossom, 1991), a memoir, and two short story collections, captures the individual variety, moral dilemmas, and complexity of Mormon life in the West.

Mormon Levis

Tight, like two long cigarettes rolled in denim. We call them white Levis, Mormon Levis, but they're actually albino beige. I suck in my stomach, zip up my pants on the way to the window in my bedroom, split the venetian blinds to check the night and see if Shelley's pulling into my driveway. Not yet. I walk down the stairs and see my long legs reflected in the mirror at the bottom. Daddy Long Legs. Leggy legs. Legs made for walking and dancing the whole night through.

Where did you say you were going, Mattie? my mother asks as she pretends to dust the piano with the dishtowel in her hands.

To the movie.

What's playing?

A western.

I hear Shelley's horn. Thank heavens. I'm out of here. Out the door. Bye, Mom.

Remember your curfew, Mattie. And don't be chasing after those boys you think are so cool. You know better.

My eyes brush past my mother's eyes and the picture of Jesus on the wall behind her. Sunrays coming out of his head. Light like the sun on his forehead. Jesus is always looking over someone's shoulder it seems. Sure, Mom. Bye.

The door sounds final as I slam it, sealing me off from my house. I'm released into Friday night.

Hey, Wondah Woman, Shelley says after I slam the door of her brown Plymouth that looks like a tank. She backs into the street that separates me from the desert: the rim of Las Vegas, the edge of the plate. My house is in the last subdivision in town. The desert is my front yard.

Hey, Wondah Woman yourself, I say. Tonight's the night.

Shelley turns the radio up until the sound is bigger than the car and the street. *Stairway to Heaven.* I settle back against the seat and drape my arm over the open window. We're off to hunt for Rod and The King, our non-Mormon, forbidden boyfriends. Forget the movie. Find somebody who knows the plot. We're off to the Bright Spot to wait for the boys.

They're at the Tracks right now, the place where the manly men of Las Vegas High drink on Friday nights, throwing Teddy Beer cans off the trestle while the Ch-Ch-Chiquitas of LVHS cruise the Spot, in and out of the driveway, circling, trolling.

As me and Shelley turn into the magic driveway under the blinking, rotating sign where the BRIGHT shines brighter than the SPOT, we're looking for the heart of something that probably won't be here until the boys are. We check out who's with who, who's not with who, who's in their own car, who borrowed from M and D. We cruise some more, floating on shock absorbers, big tires, the night pouring into the windows, waiting.

It's 8:45. They're usually back from the Tracks about 9:30. So after we bump over the drive-in's speed traps for the sixth time, we dip into the gutter and out onto Charleston. We head for Fremont Street, past Anderson's Dairy, past the Little Chapel of the West, then turn left onto Fremont, toward the big vortex of light near the Union Pacific depot. The razzle dazzle that never fails to take the words out of my mouth. The Golden Nugget. The Horseshoe. Those zillion bulbs of light.

. . . .

Shelley's the best, even if my mother thinks she's a bad influence on her rare gem of a daughter. It's good Shelley isn't afraid of my mother—the Lioness of Righteousness, the Defender of All Virtue. God bless Shelley. The Primo Chiquita.

A car full of shaveheads from Nellis pulls up next to us and pins us with their air force eyes, like we're ground targets in the desert. One whistles a two-finger whistle. Another sticks out his tongue and wiggles it. Yuk, Shelley says. She tries to speed up when the light changes, but the traffic is packed like sardines. She's bumper to bumper with a Dodge wearing Iowa plates.

I've seen enough rubber-neckers from Iowa, she says as she tap dances her foot on the brake.

We're stuck in the intersection, and I feel squirmy like an amoeba under a microscope. Horns honking. Everyone stalled. The Nellis boys next to us, a bunch of prying eyes. I keep my head forward, but notice with my side eyes that one of them is opening the back door of their dull black car and is lunging toward our Plymouth, making like a primate for the entertainment of his friends. I roll up my window and lock my door just before the primate lands on the side of the car and plants a blowfish kiss on the glass. I can hear the rest of the guys in the car laughing like crazy.

Hey girls, he's yelling in between planting slobbery circles across the window. Pussy for me, girls? He puts his hand over his crotch, jiggles his family jewels, sucks in his breath with his teeth tight together.

Don't pay him any attention, I whisper as I turn away from the window, maintaining my cool, hardly breathing.

The blowfish moves over to the windshield and mashes one side of his face against the glass. I act as if I'm talking to Shelley with a permanent left hand angle to my head. He mounts the hood of the car. He's crawling on his hands and knees, panting like a dog in 120-degree heat.

Go find another fireplug, I shout as loud as I can which isn't too loud, then cover my face with the side of my hand. I'm laughing. I shouldn't be.

This isn't all that funny, Shelley says to me. Get off the car, she yells to him. You stupid jerk.

I'm trying to fold up in my elbows and arms, trying to be serious and angry like Shelley, but the flyboy's eyes. They're hollow. There's a famine there.

Luckily, the traffic starts to move, and, as Shelley creeps forward, she hits the brake, hard. He slides back, almost loses his balance, then leaps into the street. He gives us the finger before he becomes a reflection of the flashing lights.

My heart is beating in my throat. There's not enough air in Shelley's car. Shelley, let's get out of here.

Mattie, I'm doing the best I can. One more block.

In one block we'll hit Main Street, the end of Fremont Street, the place where we can turn left and get back to the Bright Spot, where we can hold our breath for something important, like Rod and The King, even though they'll be drunk. Drunk enough to give the finger to all worldly inhabitants plus the moon and the stars as they speed down the highway. Drunk enough to call us Bitch One and Bitch Two.

I love it when they talk like that, words from the Forbidden City. Their words are like bold fingers on my neck, brushing over my breasts, down to my belly button. I can taste their words, and it doesn't matter what they call us, because they need us—our arms, our lips, our necks, our breasts, though we don't plan to give them anything past the neck. We are, after all, Mormon girls in Mormon Levis, saving our sacred bodies for The Big Event called temple marriage.

. . . .

The jumping neon on the Bright Spot's sign is still going round and round the circular sign. The lights keep traveling the same old same old, and I wonder if there will ever be a moment when something will interfere with this geometrical pattern—six bulbs to a row, each row marching one by one into the light? Could these bulbs ever try another route? Is this world made of uninterruptable patterns? Unleavable sockets? Can anything or anybody dare to be different?

Shelley parks in stall #16. The carhop slides a cardboard ticket under the windshield wiper. Cherry Lime Rickey, we both say in unison. We'd both like to add french-fried onion rings, but we don't have enough money. We don't care about food, anyway. We're still waiting, listening to all the radios as cars cruise the Bright Spot. *You Are So Beautiful. Lady of the Blue Rose.*

When do you think they'll get here? Shelley asks as she guzzles the last of her Cherry-Lime Rickey through her straw. Her red hair reflects the lights on the Bright Spot sign, speckles of light dance across her bangs.

I tap the bottom of my glass to coax the last of the shaved ice to fall in my mouth. They better hurry, I say, getting tough, like I'll leave if they don't show. Fat chance.

And suddenly they're back, leaning into the windows of Shelley's Plymouth. Rod and The King. Their faces are red. They look like they're feelin' good. Park your car, they say. Come with us, you women, you broads.

I gotta take a whiz first, The King says. Too many Teddy Beers. He laughs. He makes a move with his hand like he's gonna whip his jewels out from behind his zipper right then and there and do it in the bright lights. But he winks at me and walks off for the bathroom. He's so lanky and tall and knows how to move those thin hips of his. I'm holding my breath again. Hurry back, I whisper, then think about the science of pelvises.

Too much hard work at the Tracks, Rod says as we walk toward The King's car. Lifting those cans takes a lot of muscle. Like Olympic weight lifters, you better believe.

As soon as The King returns, we all slip into the magic car, the silver streak, Shelley and I in the back seat, Rod at shotgun, The King driving. I wish I was up there with him. I'd slide so close to him, I'd barely leave him room. I want body contact. But instead I watch the back of his head as he drives, the steady rhythm of the street lights lighting up his olive neck, his dark hair like a Bedouin's, the perfect desert boyfriend, someone who might ride a camel and wrap scarves around his head if he had some.

Why don't you get your ten-pound weakling body to the gym? The King is shouting to Rod as we pass Health World, the new gym in town, punching him in the shoulder.

Muscles, Rod says as he pushes a beer can against his bicep. The only kind of muscle I need, he says.

The King is slapping the seat with his hand. He's laughing as if Rod just told the last joke on earth. He's punching his buddy in the arm and the car is running on auto-pilot.

Watch where you're going, I want to say, but don't. I bite my tongue. I want to fit this time and this moment. Our Mutual Improvement Association teachers gave us cards that said "Dare to Be Different." They thought this would encourage us to be daring enough not to fall into the morass of the world and the pit of the hell-bound, daring enough to live by The Truth. But I took the cards to mean I should be different from the way anybody told me I had to live life. Dare to be different from everything.

So I don't care if our car is weaving slightly as The King drives from street light to street light. Life is to be lived now, so why spend it preparing for the next one, hoping I'll be God's Little Darlin'? He holds the steering wheel with two thumbs, and I wish again I could be by his shoulder and see into the night better than I can from the back seat. The stars are shining more brightly the farther we pull away from the center of Las Vegas.

Where are we going? I ask as I lean on my elbows against the front seat.

The Lake, The King says. Something new.

What would really be new, I say, is to drive to the stars.

Well, aren't you something? The King says to me.

Did my voice sound sexy when I said "stars"? I wonder. Is that what he means? Or does he think it's a cool idea to drive to the stars? When we get to the lake, maybe he'll want to change places with Shelley. Sit in the back seat with me.

Today's the day, Rod sings, the Teddy Beers have their picnic.

Tonight's the night, I say.

The radio blasts as we whip down Boulder Highway toward the man-made lake called Mead which buries skeletons of Moapa Indians and Mormon pioneers and the bones of their houses. I've heard about this in Sunday school. The King accelerates. I close my eyes and imagine we could leave the ground any minute and take an aerial highway and blast through the stringy night clouds highlighted by the moon. I feel the power of speed, the moan of the tires spinning faster than light traveling.

I look over at my best friend Shelley whose jaw is tight. We both laugh, and yet steel-nerve Shelley's gripping the seat with claw-like hands. Her face looks white in this light. The desert hills whip by like ghosts, the marker posts by the sides of the road, white dominoes falling behind the path of the car. *Chances Are,* I hum.

I like the idea of leaving the ground, leaving my father's Dale Carnegie and Norman Vincent Peale speeches. He won't allow me to say anything unkind about someone unless I say three nice things. We live The Golden Rule at home. We believe in all good things, we seek after these things. Life is one big bud of goodness, I've been told, and yet, sometimes it's a maximum security prison to have to smile and be loving all the time. To be inside those invisible bars of goodness that catch sunlight and keep me true to my word, true to the covenants with God. A cage of golden sunlight, golden plates, and golden birds who can't sing because their feathers are solid. Golden angels who can't fly because they're made of gold.

I think of myself giving my testimony in sacrament meeting. "I know this church is the only true church on the face of the earth and that Joseph Smith is the Only True Prophet." Believing, believing, and yet here I am, the velour air rubbing across my face and arms and making me want to unbutton my shirt. Open up to the night air. Save me, somebody.

Maybe tonight we'll bust free to the new religion of time and space. We're going fast enough. Fly, King, I whisper so he can't hear me. Step on the accelerator. My veins are drunk with you.

Have a swig, Rod says, reaching across the seat and handing his Teddy Beer to The King. He takes a long swig and heads into the night.

Shelley and I are leaning against the back seat, our legs spread wide. I'm looking at two large white vs. Our legs in the shadow of the car. Our legs that look like bones in this moonlight. I love the wind that's whipping my hair and tangling it and blinding me with its thickness. Hair in my mouth, whipping around my ears. Hair is the only thing I can feel right now. Sometimes it slaps my cheek and stings, but I like the almost feel of cutting into my innocent skin. I'm a pharisee. A white sepulchre in white Levis. Me. I touch my mouth. It can't wait until we stop somewhere so it can kiss The King. French kiss him. Feel his tongue in my mouth. It can't wait to be bruised from kissing too hard, and I feel throbbing against the tight seam between my legs. Our bodies will wrangle with each other, roll on some sand at the lake, though I know it's only a rocky beach. I can't wait for him to get hard and push against me and my pelvis bone and the cloth of the Mormon Levis.

But I know I'm still a good girl. I want to live with Jesus some day. Shelley, too. We're saving ourselves like stamps or coins or something valuable, even though we're crashing through the night, headlights cutting the dark into ribbons. I have a hunch we're both thinking that some day soon we'll be more careful. Do what our parents ask us. But this Nevada night. It sucks us in like a Hoover, and we're on the edge of something big.

The King takes another sip of the beer, tossing his head back for one second too long. The car swerves onto the gravelly shoulder of the road and fishtails from side to side. Careening, lurching, jerking, tipping, swaying, righting itself. The King finally gets control and pulls the silver Pontiac back into the southbound lane of the two-lane highway. We're still headed south. Both Shelley and I have one hand flat against our chests. With the other hand, we're holding each other's arms tighter than a fistful of cash.

Damn, that was beautiful, Rod says. Damn, damn. He's slapping his knees and pulling the ring top of another beer. Sweet little Teddy Beer, he says. Good little Teddy. Take care of me. Make me happy. He's stroking the side of the can as if it were a stuffed animal he had when he was a kid.

Give me another sip, The King says. Rod reaches across the front seat, his arm silhouetted against the windshield and the passing rocks and hills that look like grotesque shapes of elephants and desert camels we're passing on the lake road. Beer, beer, wonderful beer, he chants while The King takes more time with this swig. The King accelerates even more. We're heading for a rise in the road, the mound of the railroad track looming large ahead of us, and suddenly the sharp definition of double yellow stripes seems to be rising straight up to the sky.

Jesus and Mary, Rod says. Holy shit! Will you look at that Monster Rise in the Road? Holy holy shit. Rod's eyes are big as he holds his beer can mid-air and looks at The King with a mouth caught by the hook of surprise.

Hey you women back there, The King is yelling. You want love, do you? You want excitement? Well, hold onto your seats. We're gonna take air. A little foreplay, girls and boys.

Floor it, Rod says, leaning into the windshield to watch the ground rise. Go for it.

Maybe we'll sail when we hit the top of the mound because our car isn't a car anymore. I look at Shelley who looks back at me. Our faces are blanks. We're here. On the ride. We accept our fate as The King steps on the pedal, pushes it to the floor, and we head for the high point in the road, the place with a railroad cross shining back at us. The radio is blasting.

I grab Shelley's hand and hold it tight and together we lay our heads back and surrender, just like we used to do on the Roll-O-Plane at the carnival. Maybe we'll land like a jet on the other side. Maybe we'll keep flying. If that's the case, maybe Jesus will be waiting for us with open arms.

I squeeze my eyes shut. I squeeze Shelley's hand and brace my feet against the floor. I love you, Shelley, I whisper. You're my best friend ever. If I don't have anything else that matters, I have you.

You're the best, Shelley says, wrinkling her nose as she squeezes her eyes tightly. I peek at the black mountain of road soaring in front of the headlights, then slam my eyes shut again.

Jesus, we just might be coming to you. Hold those arms wide open. We're leaving the desert and maybe we'll get to look into your eyes and see if they really are sad, and if they are, we can ask you why.

DAVE HICKEY [B. 1940]

What would an internationally renowned art critic say about Las Vegas? Someone who has been director of an art gallery in New York City, executive editor of Art in America, *contributing editor to* Art Issues *magazine in Los Angeles and to* Parkett *magazine in Zurich, and recipient of a MacArthur Foundation "genius" fellowship in 2001. From such a sophisticated thinker, one might expect a witty, highbrow putdown of all that is unartistic about the glitzy spectacle of mass culture that is Las Vegas. Instead, Dave Hickey, who prefers "honest fakery" to "fake honesty," cleverly outwits convention, and in smart essays on topics such as the Liberace Museum, Siegfried and Roy, and Godiva (a lady wrestler), he defends Las Vegas as America's Saturnalia, "the nonstop, year-round, 24-hour, American equivalent of that ancient Roman festival during which slaves took the roles of masters." "People revel here who suffer at home," he contends, "are free here who would otherwise languish in bondage." Hickey, who never defended his 1967* PHD *dissertation on literature and linguistics at the University of Texas, Austin, has worked in record stores, honky-tonks, commercial art galleries, jazz clubs, cocktail lounges, bookstores, and rock-and-roll bars, all the while writing for major publications such as* Rolling Stone, Art News, Harper's *magazine, the* Village Voice, Vanity Fair, *and the* New York Times, *to name a few. Gravitating in midlife to a job with health insurance, he spent the 1990s as a professor of art criticism and theory at the University of Nevada, Las Vegas. An academic who relishes popular culture, an intellectual who detests intellectual snobbery, Dave Hickey received the Nevada Writers Hall of Fame Award in 2003 for his fiction and criticism, including the works* Prior Convictions: Stories from the Sixties *(1989),* The Invisible Dragon: Four Essays on Beauty *(1993),* Air Guitar: Essays on Art & Democracy *(1997), and* Stardumb *(1999).*

A Home in the Neon

It's the strangest thing. I have lived in a lot of cities, some of them for substantial lengths of time, but I have never thought of any of them as home. I thought of them as "where I'm living now." Then, the other morning, I woke up and realized that Las Vegas has, indeed, become my home—that I routinely think of it as such. Somehow, in the few years that I have been living here and traveling out of here, this most un-homelike of cities has come to function for me as a kind of moral bottom-line—as a secular refuge and a source of comforts and reassurances that are unavailable elsewhere—as a home, in other words.

Even as I write this, however, I realize that claiming Las Vegas as my home while practicing "art criticism" in the hyper-textualized, super-virtuous high culture of the nineteen nineties probably sounds a little studied—a bit calculatedly exotic— as if I were trying to make a "statement," or something. In truth, this condition of feeling at home in Las Vegas makes me wonder just how far back things really go, since, when I was a child, whenever I heard about Las Vegas, it was always being discussed as a potential home by my dad's jazz-musician buddies and their "so-called wives" (as my mom invariably referred to them).

This was back in the nineteen fifties, when Las Vegas was rapidly becoming the only city in the American West where a professional musician might hold down a steady gig without living out of a suitcase. So, for my dad's pals, Vegas shone out there in the desert like a grail, as a kind of outlaw town, like Butch Cassidy's Hole in the Wall or Fritz Lang's Rancho Notorious, where a tiring swing musician or a jive-talking bopster might find a refuge from the road and from respectability as well. A player might work steadily in Vegas, and perhaps get a taste of Fat America, might rent a house in the suburbs, for instance—with a two-car garage and a yard, even—and still be able to play Charlie Parker in the kitchen at 4:00 AM and roll the occasional funny cigarette. The only time I was ever *in* Las Vegas as a child, we spent a hot afternoon in the dark kitchen of a pink-stucco bungalow doing approximately that.

While the sun glared outside, my dad and his friend Shelton drank beer out of tall brown bottles and played Billie Holiday's *Gloomy Sunday* about a zillion times. The whole afternoon, Shelton kept marveling at the ease with which he would pick up his axe later that evening, put it in the trunk of his Pontiac, and drive down to his gig at the Desert Inn. He pantomimed this procedure two or three times, just to show us how easy it was. That night, we got to go with him to the Desert Inn, where there were a million lights, roulette wheels clicking, and guys in tuxedos who looked like Cornel Wilde. Through the plate-glass windows, we could see a turquoise swimming pool surrounded by rich, green grass, and there were white tablecloths on the tables in the lounge, where we sat with other sophisticates and grooved to the music. I thought it was *great,* but my dad got progressively grumpier as the evening wore on. He kept making remarks about Shelton's musicianship, and I could tell that he was envious of his friend's steady gig.

So, having told you this, if I tell you that I now have a steady gig in Vegas, that I live two blocks from the Desert Inn and eat lunch there about once a week, you will understand my reservations about the possibility of our ever growing up—because, even though the days of steady gigs for sax maniacs are long gone, I still think of Vegas the way Shelton did: as a town where outsiders can still get work, three shifts a day, around the clock, seven days a week—and, when not at work, may walk unmolested down the sidewalk in their choice of apparel. My brother calls Vegas a "cowboy town," because fifty-year-old heterosexual guys still room together here, and pairs of married couples share suburban homes, dividing up the bedrooms and filling the communal areas with beer cans and pizza boxes.

Most importantly for me, Vegas is a town that can serve as the heart's destination—a town where half the pick-up trucks stolen in Arizona, Utah, Montana, and Wyoming are routinely recovered in casino parking lots—where the vast majority of the population arises every morning absolutely delighted to have escaped Hometown, America and the necessity of chatting with Mom over the back fence. This lightens the tone of social intercourse considerably. To cite an example: While I was having breakfast at the local IHOP the other morning, my waitress confided in me that, even though the International House of Pancakes wasn't the *greatest* organization in the world, they *had* transferred her out of Ogden, Utah, and she was thankful for that. But not so thankful, she said, that she planned to stay in "food." As soon as she got Lance in school, she was moving up to "cocktail," where the tips were better.

She was looking forward to that, she said; and, to be honest, it's moments like this that have led me to adopt Las Vegas as *mi varrio*. I mean, here was an *American,* in the nineties, who was thankful for something and looking forward to something else. So, now, I affectionately exchange stories of Vegas's little quirks with my fellow homies. I chuckle over the legendary teddy bear in the gift shop at Caesars Palace that was reputedly sold five hundred times. Every night, it seems, some john would buy it for a hooker. Every morning, the hooker would bring it back for cash. That night another john would buy it for another hooker—and thus the cycle continued until Herr Teddy, that fuzzy emblem of middle-aged desire, became irretrievably shopworn. I also defend my adopted hometown against its detractors—a great many of whom are disconsolate colleagues of mine down at the University—lost souls whom I must count among those who are *not* looking forward to moving up from "food" to "cocktail," who do *not* arise from their slumber thanking their lucky stars to have escaped Mom and Dad and fucking Ithaca.

These exiles, it seems, find Las Vegas lacking in culture. (Define culture!) They think it is all about money, which, I always agree, is the worst way of discriminating among individuals, except for all the others. They also deplore the fact that Las Vegas exploits people's weaknesses—although, in my view, Vegas rather theatrically *fails* to exploit that most plangent American weakness, for being parented into senility. This is probably why so many of them regard Vegas as an unfit atmosphere in which to raise children—although judging by my students, the town turns out an amazingly resilient and insouciant brand of American adolescent, one whose penchant for body decoration seems to me a healthier way of theatricalizing one's lack of prospects than the narcotics that performed this function for my generation.

Most of all, I suspect that my unhappy colleagues are appalled by the fact that Vegas presents them with a flat-line social hierarchy—that, having ascended from "food" to "cocktail" in Las Vegas, there is hardly anywhere else to go (except, perhaps, up to "magician"), and being a *professore* in this environment doesn't feel nearly as special as it might in Cambridge or Bloomington, simply because the rich (the traditional clients of the *professore* class) are not *special* in Las Vegas, because money here is just money. You can make a lot of it here, but there are no socially sanctioned forms of status to ennoble one's *having* made it—nor any predetermined socio-cultural agendas that one might pursue as a consequence of having been so ennobled.

Membership in the University Club will not get you comped at Caesars, unless you play baccarat. Thus, in the absence of vertical options, one is pretty much thrown back onto one's own cultural resources, and, for me, this has not been the worst place to be thrown. At least I have begun to wonder if the privilege of living in a community with a culture does not outweigh the absence of a "cultural community" and, to a certain extent, explain its absence. (Actually, it's not so bad. My *TLS* and *LRB* come in the mail every week, regular as clockwork, and just the other day, I took down my grandfather's Cicero and read for nearly an hour without anyone breaking down my door and forcing me to listen to Wayne Newton.)

This deficiency of haut bourgeois perks, I should note, also confuses visiting Easterners whom I have docented down the Strip. So attentive are they to signifiers of status and exclusivity that they become restless and frustrated. The long, lateral blend of Vegas iconography unrolls before them, and they are looking for the unmarked door through which the cognoscenti pass. They want the "secret Vegas." But Vegas is about stakes, not status—real action, not covert connections. The "high-roller" rooms with satin walls are secure areas for high-stakes gambling, not hideouts for high-profile dilettantes. If Bruce Willis and Shannen Doherty just want to get their feet wet, they shoot dice with the rest of us. This seems to confuse my visitors, who don't, of course, *believe* in celebrity, but still, the idea of People with Names gambling in public offends their sense of order—and mitigates their aspirations as well, I suspect.

In any case, when visiting culturati actually start shivering in the horizontal flux, I take them to one of the restaurants in town where tank-tops are (sort of) discouraged. This is the best I can do to restore their sense of propriety, because the "secret of Vegas" is that there are no secrets. And there are only two rules: (1) Post the odds, and (2) Treat everybody the same. Just as one might in a democracy (What a concept!), and this deficiency of secrets and economy of rules drives writers crazy! They come here to write about Vegas. They are trained in depth-analysis. They have ripped the lid off seamy scandals by getting behind the scenes, and Las Vegas is invisible to them. They see the lights, of course, but they end up writing stories about white people who are so unused to regulating their own behavior that they gamble away the farm, get drunk, throw up on their loafers, and wind up in custody within six hours of their arrival. Or they write profiles of the color-ful Runyonesque characters they meet in casinos, oblivious to the fact that such characters populate half the barrooms in America, that, in truth, they need only have driven a few blocks for their "colorful characters," had they been inclined to transgress the rigid stratifications that (in *their* hometowns) stack the classes like liqueurs in a dessert drink.

America, in other words, is a very poor lens through which to view Las Vegas, while Las Vegas is a wonderful lens through which to view America. What is hid-den elsewhere exists here in quotidian visibility. So when you fly out of Las Vegas to, say, Milwaukee, the absences imposed by repression are like holes in your vi-sion. They become breathtakingly perceptible, and, as a consequence, there is no better place than Las Vegas for a traveler to feel at home. The town has a quick, feral glamour that is hard to localize—and it arises, I think, out of the suppression of social differences rather than their exacerbation. The whole city floats on a sleek *frisson* of anxiety and promise that those of us addicted to such distraction must otherwise induce by motion or medication.

Moreover, since I must regularly venture out of Vegas onto the bleak savannas of high culture, and there, like an aging gigolo, generate bodily responses to in-creasingly abject objects of desire, there is nothing quite as bracing as the prospect of flying home, of swooping down into that ardent explosion of lights in the heart of the pitch-black desert—of coming home to the only indigenous visual culture on the North American continent, a town bereft of dead white walls, gray wool carpets, ficus plants, and Barcelona chairs—where there is everything to see and not a single pretentious object demanding to be scrutinized.

I remember one particular evening in the spring. I was flying back from Wash-ington, DC after serving on a National Endowment for the Arts panel. For four solid days, I had been seated on a wooden chair in a dark room looking at racks of slides, five at a time. Blam, blam, blam, blam, blam, ad infinitum. All hope de-parted somewhere near the end of the second day, and I started counting popular iconography: skulls, little houses, little boats, altars, things in jars, etc. By the end of the third day, despair had become a very real option, but we finally selected the correct number of winners—and a number of these actually won. The rest won the privilege of having their awards overturned by a higher court on the grounds of propriety.

The moment I stepped off the plane, I sat down in the terminal to play video poker. Basically, I was doing the same thing I had been doing in Washington: look-ing at banks of five images, one after another, interpreting finite permutations of a limited iconography, looking for a winner. Sitting there at the slot machine, how-ever, I was comfortable in the knowledge that Vegas cheats you fair—that, unlike the rest of America (and Washington in particular), the payoffs are posted and the odds easily calculable. I knew how much of a chance I had to win. It was slim, of course, but it was a real chance nevertheless, not some vague promise of parental benevolence contingent on my behavior.

In the reality of that chance, Vegas lives—in those fluttery moments of faint but rising hope, in the possibility of wonder, in the swell of desire while the dice are still bouncing, just before the card flips face-up. And win or lose, you always have that instant of genuine, *justifiable* hope. It is always there. Even though we know the rules governing random events are always overtaken by the law of large numbers, there is always that window of opportunity, that statistical crazy zone, before this happens, when *anything* can happen. And what's more, if you win, you win! You can take it home. You cannot be deemed unworthy after the fact—as we all were in Washington, where we played our hearts out and never had a fucking chance. So right there in the airport, I could make a little wager, and there was a real chance that luck and foolish courage might, just for the moment, just for a couple of bucks, override the quagmire of status and virtue in which we daily languish. And if I got *really* lucky, I might move up from food to cocktail. Hey, don't laugh. It could happen.

JOHN L. SMITH [B. 1960]

Las Vegas Review-Journal columnist John L. Smith pitches his words primarily to the home crowd, and he has become, for many, a favorite Las Vegas voice and an influential crusading journalist, fighting for truth, justice, and accountability. Just when Smith begins to wonder why he keeps up the grueling pace of writing a daily column—for a career total of more than two thousand articles—he might chance to sit down in a local bar and glimpse someone unfold their newspaper, turn straight to his column, and laugh out loud. As a fourth-generation Nevadan who grew up in Henderson, Smith has seen Las Vegas metastasize, and in twenty years of reporting he has never been at a loss for subjects, from colorful characters to hot political issues, sports, crime, and urban legends. The best of these columns are collected in On the Boulevard *(1999), capturing "the odd but indefatigable spirit of one of the world's toughest and most intriguing cities." In a town where everyone seems to be in someone's pocket and where dead bodies are buried in the desert, Smith has chosen the dangerous path of investigative reporter, publishing book-length exposés of the most powerful men in the city. The marketing of his unauthorized biography of billionaire Steve Wynn—*Running Scared: The Life and Treacherous Times of Las Vegas Casino King Steve Wynn *(1995)—resulted in a multimillion-dollar libel suit that threatened to bankrupt the original publisher. Other books about Vegas kingpins include* No Limit: The Rise and Fall of Bob Stupak and Las Vegas' Stratosphere Tower *(1997),* Quicksilver: The Ted Binion Murder Case *(2001), and* Of Rats and Men: Oscar Goodman's Life from Mob Mouthpiece to Mayor of Las Vegas *(2003). In 1998 Smith was voted "Nevada's Outstanding Journalist" by the Nevada Press Association and was awarded third place in the National Headliner Awards.*

"Flying Nun" Stunt Double Lands on Her Feet in Las Vegas
April 10, 1994

Visitors may think they know what makes Las Vegas a place apart, but it's not the Dali-on-steroids architecture or the endless sea of $2 steaks.

It's the people.

Every color and kind, thrown together like pigments in a Jackson Pollock painting, all seeking a slice of secular salvation in America's last great boomtown. They save this city's neon soul.

Over the years I have met gangsters and governors, chiselers and champions in this maddening metropolis in the making.

If memory serves, Jenny Malcomb is my first stunt nun.

Yes, stunt nun.

What a town.

Malcomb's work history reads like a script from "Saturday Night Live" when it was funny or "Monty Python's Flying Circus" any time: She has been a stunt sister to the stars, a Disneyland dancer, a psychedelic babe in a go-go cage, a backup singer to Steely Dan, a leading member of an almost successful pop ensemble.

In short, a bit player in a world that only rewards big stars.

Today Malcomb sells wholesale goods at Valley Foods, but her story is no teary lament of a fame that faded. Fact is, Malcomb embodies the best of Las Vegas. But I'm getting ahead of myself.

In the late 1960s, Malcomb was an azure-eyed California girl with blonde pigtails and little interest in the hustle of Hollywood. She loved singing and dancing and only auditioned for the movie *Harlow* as a favor to a girlfriend.

Fate was kind. She won a place in the crowd, joined the union, and eventually wound up on the set of "The Flying Nun."

Sally Field was the star, but one bit part remained.

Stunt nun.

Malcomb had little experience but even less fear. She faked it.

"I said, 'Do I do aerial work? Of course I do aerial work,'" she says, laughing. "He said, 'Show up Monday morning.' I showed up. They fit me into a leather harness. I signed a six-year contract and never looked back."

Or down, for that matter.

Malcomb sailed over land and sea as the stunt double for Field. The situation comedy featured Field as Sister Bertrille, who spent her days doing the Lord's work with just enough time left over to fly her way into trouble.

Trouble was Malcomb's business. With the harness in place, she was outfitted in a nun's habit and was suspended up to 100 feet in the air by hair-thin piano wire. Rigged to a construction crane, she was cast over the bay like a large fishing lure. It was enough to make a California girl recite the rosary, but Malcomb wasn't scared.

"I guess I was too young to realize that what I was doing was dangerous," she says. "I was a carefree kid. What did I know? Off I went, flying over Marina Del Rey."

Sister Bertrille was a frequent flier. After Field was finished with the close-ups, Malcomb winged into action wearing her habit and cornet. In one scene, she was perched on the pinnacle of a sailboat mast 60 feet up. She soared over a church steeple, and swooped inches from the breaking waves.

The fact that she came away without breaking bones is just short of a miracle.

It was not her only role. She wore considerably less clothing in episodes of "Mannix," "Mission Impossible," and "Run for Your Life." She was a dancer, remember, and those male-dominated shows rarely made it through a week without setting a scene in a funky nightclub featuring go-go girls behind bars.

"I was in a lot of cages," she says.

She won other parts and for a while had steady work. When the work went away, she reached a crossroads. Malcomb had her dreams, but she also had two children, no husband, and no income.

Sound familiar?

It's the neon story.

A dozen years ago fate brought her to Las Vegas, where go-go jobs are plentiful, but the nuns perform their own stunts. She sang awhile with *Legends in Concert* at the Imperial Palace, but gravitated toward steady work. After flying for a living, she landed on her feet, remarried, and took a job selling food to restaurants and resorts.

It's not as glamorous as Hollywood, but then stunt-nun jobs don't come along all the time.

As I said, Jenny Malcomb embodies what is right about Las Vegas. It's a second-chance town in a long-shot world.

Despite its reputation, this is a place to call home for go-go girls and sisters of every habit.

Kidney Caper: The Making of a Myth Nobody Can Miss
March 30, 1997

It's the ultimate Las Vegas vacation offer:

Three days, two nights, one kidney removal.

Why, not even Bob Stupak in his heyday could have offered such a deal.

The city is known for its off-the-wall marketing concepts, but something tells me the Discount Kidney Junket is destined not to catch on. It turns out that when people take vacations, they don't mind dropping their money, but they hate to leave behind internal organs.

Cash, yes.

Kidneys, no, sir.

Surely by now you have heard the one about the Las Vegas tourist who meets the willing woman and escorts her to his hotel room, only to be drugged, knocked out, and become yet another Man Without a Kidney.

Hey, why doesn't this ever happen in Reno?

Anyway, after his kidney is plucked out, the dupe is stitched up, bandaged, and set in a bathtub of ice. You know, to prevent the pain and discomfort that often accompany such surgical procedures.

By the time he wakes up, his kidney is being brokered hundreds of miles away on the human-organ black market, where this week there's a two-for-one special on hearts and livers. Personally, I don't shop there because they don't take coupons and their produce is weird, but that's another subject.

As it turns out, the kidney incident always happens to a friend of a friend.

Ah, urban legends. You gotta love 'em.

As fast as you can put a puppy in a microwave and sing "Pop goes the weasel," the Las Vegas kidney-kidnapping story has circulated the planet.

Las Vegas Convention and Visitors Authority spokesman Rob Powers continues to field inquiries from curious travelers and travel agents regarding the secret kidney-snatching story. So far, his bosses aren't considering changing the convention authority's current slogan, "Las Vegas: Open 24 Hours," to "Las Vegas: You've got to be Kidney," "Las Vegas: Urine the Money," or even "Las Vegas: Bladder Ask Your Travel Agent."

As an aside, the "I Lost My Kidney in Las Vegas" T-shirt is an anemic seller at downtown gift shops.

But I digress.

"The vast majority of people with common sense would realize that it's a silly story that has no basis in fact," Powers says. "We see it as one of those urban folklore things that the vast majority of people with common sense will see for what it is—a silly story."

But then it figures he'd say something like that. The guy works for the convention bureau.

The fact is, this silly story has gone off dialysis and taken on a life of its own. Powers says virtually every call his office has received has come after the caller has encountered the tale floating on the Internet. At least some of the Internet stories have appeared under the heading "Traveler's Warning." Apparently that attracts more attention from browsers than "Suckers, Read This."

The Las Vegas police homicide section is aware of the kidney story, too. Its detectives have heard breathless tourists and head-scratching cops from out of state report the tale of the hooker who knocks out her customer and swipes his kidney but, apparently, leaves his wallet and watch. (A fact which surely proves the story is not based in reality.)

After many years investigating real stories of mayhem, mutilation, and murder, Sergeant Bill Keeton shrugs at the urban legends that buzz like gnats around the city. The frequency of the kidney story did, however, lead him to place a call to the convention authority to inform its officials of the bad news.

Keeton, the homicide section's unofficial urban myths curator, likens the kidney caper to the smelly old story of the dead prostitute stuffed under the bed at the Strip resort and discovered after she began to get gamy. The story was false—do you really believe union housekeepers never vacuum under the bed?—but it has persisted in various versions for a decade.

For my part, I have been contacted on the subject by journalists from out of state, at least one of whom figured she had entered Pulitzer territory with the kidney story. She was pretty disappointed when I told her there was no truth to it. I imagine the British author who recently wrote to the newspaper for assistance in researching the American kidney-theft phenomenon will be downright depressed when he finds out there is no big story.

Meanwhile, the calls keep coming.

"It's absolutely ridiculous," Keeton says.

Easy for him to say. He didn't have a friend of a friend lose a kidney in Vegas.

DAYVID FIGLER [B. 1967]

Las Vegas native and whiz kid Dayvid Figler, son of a Sahara casino card dealer, double dips as an attorney and slam poet. Passing the bar exam at age twenty-three, Figler became one of the youngest lawyers in Nevada history. He has worked for Clark County since 1997, specializing in defending accused killers, including death penalty cases. His record of acquittals, dismissed charges, converted sentences, and state supreme court reversals testifies to his courtroom prowess, and in 2003 Figler was appointed a judge of the Las Vegas Municipal Court. Dropping suit and tie for a T-shirt that reads, "Corporate Poetry Still Sucks," Figler after hours transforms into one of the funniest slam poets in the country. His 1998 comedy tour de force "Dayvid Figler is Jim Morrison in Hello, I Love You (Where You Folks From?)" played to a sold-out crowd of four hundred at its premier in Las Vegas and was featured at the 1999 Bumbershoot Festival in Seattle. He wrote a weekly food review parody for the Las Vegas Mercury, *airs his off-kilter commentary on* KNPR's *weekly* Ain't Necessarily So, *and has been a frequent guest on National Public Radio's* All Things Considered, *entertaining an audience of 10 million with his poetic, dryly humored monologues. Figler is a favorite performer at slam poetry festivals around the country, including Lollapalooza,* SXSW, NXNW, *and the National Slam Poetry competition, to name a few. His poems have appeared in* SPIN *magazine,* Exquisite Corpse, Pearl, Chiron Review, Free Lunch, Red Rock Review, *and others, and his first book,* Merry Christmas, Jewboy, *was released from Kapow! Press in 2002. Figler's performances, columns, radio commentary, punk band "Tippy Elvis," and civic go-getting have enlivened Las Vegas culture, and he once told a reporter, "I'm proud to be a voice in our community for justice, tolerance—and cultural intrigue."*

The Shrimp Manifesto

Do not ask

Where the shrimp come from
What kind of shrimp they are
Why they are only 99 cents

Do not use

quotation marks

when referring to the shrimp
either orally or

in writing

Do not suggest
to tourists that they

avoid the shrimp

Do not mock
taunt or
challenge the shrimp or
the cocktail sauce or
the shredded lettuce bed

This is the SHRIMP MANIFESTO

It is clearly posted in your
casino employees' cafeteria
and restrooms

We have been driven
to zero tolerance

Apparently some people
can't help ruining

a good thing.

Zamboni

And beyond the mountains
surrounding Las Vegas
lies the land of clocks

All the people here,
come from there

Once arrived, they protest like
arrogant white tigers getting fed
chow chow chow from a bag

We will not assimilate.
We will not assimilate

Their toes are rooted,
seeking ground water
like mad

They chase the darkness
on the lonely roads

to their new homes
(which are only slightly different
from everyone elses' new homes)

They throb in
sleepless nights
that are
frustratingly tainted with sunlight

Awake,
they recline,
toes cooled in free rivers

"Action is its own reward," chants
one of the new spinning voices in their heads.

(Sometimes
they really miss the
whole idea
of "last call.")

Friends watch friends
decompose
before their eyes

We can eat sushi in the
middle of the summer

We can watch hockey
in the desert

We can build dreams
on the shells of tortoises

We can throw buckets of
water on the sand for fun

We can eat and drink nickels,
regally not waiting in lines

No one intervenes
because it might be them;

No matter where they came from
They belong here.

HARRY FAGEL [B. 1968]

Known as the preeminent poet cop of Las Vegas, Harry Fagel achieved local fame in 1999 when
Street Talk *was published. The biographical note reads, "Harry Fagel has lived in Las Vegas for*
thirty years. He's a Police Officer with Las Vegas Metro. He has also been a bartender, a black
jack dealer, a college student, and a madman. He can often be seen rollerblading around town,
or lurking in Alternate Reality Comics. He loves his wife and son more than anything." Six years
later Fagel was working in the Robbery Division, had added another son to his family, contin-
*ued to read his poems at public events, had completed a new poetry book—*Undercover*—and*
maintained a Web site (www.fagelman.com) where he posts new poems, photos, and blogs.
The language of Street Talk *is the lingo of the gutter, and its graphic imagery centers on drug*
addicts, death scenes, sex crimes, crazies, suicides, robbers, gangbangers, homeless people, pros-
titutes, and pimps. The poems lay bare a human soul behind the bulletproof vest and offer a
cop's-eye view of Las Vegas. Fellow poet Dayvid Figler advises readers, "Enjoy the safety of your
armchair, now, the streets will look very different from now on." Fagel wrote most of the poems
in Street Talk *at Café Roma, a hip coffeehouse near* UNLV, *where he ran the Monday Night*
Open Mic poetry for a while, played pinball, and typed up search warrants. Seediness, danger,
gridlock, and all, Fagel loves Las Vegas and has been an imposing figure in its cultural growth.
One of his poems begins, "I am so sick So Terribly Sick So Incredibly sick / (and tired) / Of all
this Vegas-bashing." He continues, "I mean C'mon Man / This wasteland is just beginnin' to
cook and us / The errant Artists . . . / We get to Shape it / Shape it / Shape it."

Jaywalker

> Like Pond bugs
> Skimmin'
> Across a Black Lagoon
> The Jaywalkers Dance on
> Maryland Parkway
> Matadors in black clothes
> Swishin' at the furiously passing cars
> Whose honks are like elephants
> Farting
> Loud and Rude and Often
> Cars are like cave bats blind and
> Hungry and seeking sustenance from the
> Teeming insects that swirl and whoop in the
> Darkness

The Jaywalker's mission is simple mostly
To score a forty ounce bliss bottle from the
7–11 and to get away from the crack house
heat and 7 kid stink that
Permeates the cheap apartment that serves as
Flop space for sadness
Sometimes
The Jaywalkers feel so tired that they blithely
March in front of the starving cars
Hopin' for a quicker release than a bottle or a pipe can bring
and the sound of a wall hittin' a person is louder than Kiss
And bones snap like graveyard fingers and shoes sit still a
Testament to the last place they stood before the impact
and the tell tale shattered windshield glares like an angry
Cyclops
With blood for tears that streak down the glass like
raindrops
and the drivers always sob and wish they hadn't left the
party or
the job or whatever and limbs akimbo cannot do the vision
of a person flung like a squoosh ball to break upon the
pavement justice
The Jaywalkers look like rubbermen with leaky brains
or Fruit Rollups that someone crumpled like toilet paper and
Discarded with their cigarette butts
And we do our thing and close down Maryland Parkway for
a
While and people curse cause they were in Fuckin' Hurry
for Crissakes
and newspeople take their minutes and the other Jaywalkers
Stand on the Curb for a change and nod and nod and
commiserate
about how dangerous crossing the street is in this town and
Pretty soon the Free Jaywalker is scraped up and the driver
is in
Therapy and traffic resumes and that's why I wrote you the
Fuckin' Ticket.

L.S.D. (Street Talk Pt. 4)

I met a crazy woman
Next to a swimming pool
She told me the people who live in the trees the
"Tree People"
were trying to kill her so that is why she was banging on
various apartment doors with a medium no-stick frying pan
I couldn't help but notice this young shapely woman was
probably
Pretty once
Before the doctors
and Institutions
and Prozac
and Xanax
and Lithium
and Radium
and Who-knows-what-um
But now her hollowed darkened eyes spun with madness
and
the question burns me—Is madness contagious?
She goes on to tell me that the "Monkey Men" who live in
the "Tree People's" branches
were trying to have sex with her—
"I know they are real!" she beseeched me, "I sat on one and
could feel his heart beating and could feel his limbs,
although I could not see him."
Is madness contagious?
As they loaded her into the ambulance I stood next to a
bowl of fruit and noticed the banana ringing so I answered
it.
It was for her.

BRUCE ISAACSON [B. 1956]

Bruce Isaacson moved to Las Vegas in 1995 and quickly enlivened local poetry. Isaacson, who holds degrees in theater and financial economics from Claremont McKenna and Dartmouth, earned an MFA at Brooklyn College, where he submitted a thesis to Beat poet Allen Ginsberg. A generation after Ginsberg, Isaacson was a mobilizing presence in the San Francisco poetry scene. He founded Zeitgeist Press, which has published more than sixty poetry books, and he helped revive spoken word poetry at the Café Babar series. Spoken word is a predecessor to slam poetry; in both, poets entertain with in-your-face subject matter delivered in an unpretentious, animated, even aggressive style. Isaacson participated extensively in poetry communities in New York, particularly the nationally known Nuyorican Poets Café, where he was a surprise finalist of the inaugural poetry slam season. He was also involved in Hollywood, where he read poetry with Alec Baldwin, Harry Dean Stanton, and Moon Zappa. In Las Vegas, Isaacson joined the editorial team of Red Rock Review *and has been a passionate voice for poetry and free speech. He made the news in 2000 when Zeitgeist Press author Harry Fagel was ejected from Barnes & Noble for using "the f-word" in a poetry reading. Isaacson was also ejected for disputing Barnes & Noble. Weeks later, nine civil guerrillas—the "Bookstore Nine"— selected classics from Barnes & Noble shelves (all containing profanity) and began reading aloud to protest censorship. In a 2003 opinion piece for* Las Vegas Weekly, *Isaacson wrote: "To defend poetry is to express hope for a human future beyond the dictatorship of dollars that runs us all so completely and efficiently until death." Isaacson has published criticism, opinion, and six books of poems, among which are* Bad Dog Blues *(1988),* Love Affairs with Barely Any People in Them *(1990),* Error Is an Enlightened State *(1992), and* Ghosts among the Neon *(2005).*

Life in Las Vegas

Even in the shadow of Casinosaurus
Life springs irrepressible from the sands
Artists, poets, lovers, children
Dream of the seventh gold city . . .
To those who see in Vegas always what is small
We contain strange multitudes
Old west gun-racked in a pickup
The Liberace Museum
Street dudes lined up to work
New west corporate Disneysaurus
Every great nation's culture presented in a buffet cuisine
Las Vegas—LA extended east to absurdity

A strip of Hollywood Babylon spread-eagled over the Sierra
Las Vegas—the only town with twisted enough imagination
to conceive a life size replica of New York
and the humor to call that a resort
Casinosaurus gold flashes in teeth
But maybe here will be raised up the new man—
beautiful, sexual, immune to breasts on a billboard
Casinosaurus drowses in the dawn
after a typical night on the kill
Later the sun will plump up like a tomato going bad
Later the beast will stretch its talons in advertising
roar back about blackjack, insurance and family fun
But there's also the gathering of the art tribe on the sands
Or I'm alone 6 AM writing poems
in the natural light of the desert
In a moment before the desert begins
When casino neon still outshines the sun
Here I am—a jew in the desert—found
in the fabled seven cities of gold
Flamingo . . . Dunes . . . Sahara . . .
We are shimmering.

Lucky

At the grocery store in Las Vegas
You fall in line behind
A hefty woman in a tank top
Freckled, chubby, curvy,
Stained bra strap showing & too tight jeans
As she leans down to set her things on the conveyor
You see a red & blue flaming sun tattoo from spine to . . .
And in a minute her titties look so good
You can hardly restrain yourself
You see she's a smoker—you're an ex-smoker
You know she's been working strip clubs
You know your love life has already resulted in
More court time than a rash of muggings
In short, you will do anything to be with her

She leans over & gives you a small vacant smile
With perfect crooked teeth
Instead you start a conversation with her 3 yr old daughter
In short, you are washed up, finished,
Suicidal desperate for affection
You can do econometrics, bar dips
And computer network protocols
But you'd trade it for one sweaty lip lock
You're ready to retire with the caved in mother
Of the twenty year old blond girl who
Lives like a strawberry in the apartment upstairs
Mom's face age-spotted a thing growing on her chin
But her breasts slink like cats beneath her Las Vegas tank top
The only reason not to spend your life together is
You're too ashamed to go to her and propose
Sex
You will say nothing because that is how you feel
You're in the middle of the food chain in
The richest plentitude in history
This is Las Vegas—Sex is for the tourists
You see the gamblers, even in Lucky, entranced in
Slot machines & you're dying to care like that
You've seen 12 yr old kids on the basketball court bragging
About how they whiffed rock
There are gang killings and police killings and
14 yr olds who bond by defending you to the pack
Then greet you with hi-fives &
slang you can't even understand
Their parents—divorced, drugged, disappeared,
disassociated, dis'd & deserve it
My generation got what it wanted—itself.
When you think of all the love lost
You want to die, but—
Your son must have his father
And he won't be losing himself in donuts
He won't be drugged out, money drunk,
cruel power monster
He won't settle for love that isn't

This is what beauty means in Babylon
The boy sits so comfortable in my lap he doesn't notice me
Even in the grocery caught staring at my own desperation
The feeling of loving him protects me
I'm ready to die
And I'm Lucky.

BILL BRANON [B. 1937]

Bill Branon must be the envy of every aspiring novelist. After receiving two rejections for his first novel manuscript, he published it himself in 1992. Against staggering odds, Let Us Prey *was discovered and named a* New York Times *Notable Book of the Year. Branon then became so bombarded with orders that he unplugged his fax machine to stay sane and quickly accepted HarperCollins's offer to buy publication rights. The book became a best-selling selection of the Book-of-the-Month Club and Quality Paperback Book Club.* Let Us Prey *is a "raw and visceral" political thriller, set in Las Vegas and the Mojave Desert, about a group of revolutionaries who set out to destroy the U.S. government by eradicating the Internal Revenue Service. The book warned of the potential for domestic terrorism, a message that seems prophetic in the wake of the Oklahoma City bombings two years later. Branon himself is as high-octane as his characters. Educated at Harvard (BA 1959) and the University of Pennsylvania dental school (DDS 1963), Branon served in the navy for twenty-three years, an expert in weaponry, demolitions, and state-of-the-art surveillance. He is also a proficient marksman, champion ocean sailor, pro-level golfer, and resident of Las Vegas, who once told an interviewer, "If I wasn't writing, I'd probably be passed out under some sawdust-joint craps table." Branon has written two other thrillers,* Devil's Hole *(1995), about a murderer-for-hire in Las Vegas, and* Spider Snatch *(2000), about a covert operation to destroy a drug lord near the Panama Canal. In addition to thrillers, Branon has written poetry and a philosophical meditation on loss,* Timesong *(1998), featuring a three-legged coyote who befriends an autistic boy and helps him to reconcile the death of his father.*

Seven-Out-Sally Is Loose with the Rent

Not the Red Rock lumps to the west.
Not snow-capped Sheep and Potosi.
Not the paradox of Mead corked by concrete.
Not the prime rib delaminating in slabs of hot pink;
    not the neon; not the tigers.

Not Riviera butts or Alta hill or Siegfried's Roy.

Not even the air-pus on Friday's horizon.

None of those.

The ebonite chatter of dice doing preflight in a hot cup of palm.

The whisper of face cards on felt.

The unwinding grind of Monday night's till as it spits out another crippled parlay.

The smack-babble-clack of roulette frets bitch-slapping their indentured white ball.

The heart-kicking *ding* of three bars in a row.

The necklace of *beeps* as a flush counts up quarters.

The tick of the Big Wheel as it slows to one more empty conclusion.

These.

And Sally down on her knees.

"God, please help me."

HART WEGNER [B. 1931]

"The Blue Line," like much of Wegner's fiction, "involves Las Vegas as a geographical site where the characters 'dwell,' but not live," he explains, *"because the immigrants of my stories live somewhere else, in their memories and surrounded by bits and pieces of their former lives."* As reviewer Richard Wiley notes, Wegner writes *"with the amazing sense of something you might call 'place misplaced.' The people in his fiction are at home and not at home."* Wegner was born and raised in Silesia, a mountainous region between Germany and Poland, educated in Breslau at an ancient school, founded two hundred years before the voyage of Columbus. In the wake of World War II, when Eastern Europe was under Communist rule, Wegner immigrated to America, earning a BA and MA at the University of Utah, and a PHD in German language and literature from Harvard, with a dissertation entitled "Die dichterischen Bilder im Frühwerk Brechts" [The Poetic Images in the Early Work of Brecht] (1970). Since 1968 Wegner has been a professor at UNLV, teaching German, comparative literature, and film studies. He founded and has chaired UNLV's Department of Film, has published two film studies textbooks and more than fifty scholarly articles and reviews, and for more than thirty seasons hosted UNLV's International Film Series, which at times was the only venue in the state dedicated to screening foreign films. To this foreign-born scholar, winning the Nevada Writers Hall of Fame

Award (1990) and the University of Nevada Regents' Award for Creative Activities (1994) is welcome recognition. As Wegner once remarked, "First, I had to learn English. Then I had to learn to use it creatively." His stories, collected in Houses of Ivory *(1988) and* Off Paradise *(2001), show émigrés clinging to memory and to each other to preserve their Old World identities as they struggle to adapt to the New World.*

The Blue Line

When Martin parked his car behind the privet hedge, he could see that his father had already driven the Toronado out of the carport. It stood on the wet driveway, where Mother was drying a fender while Father, from a lawn chair, pointed his walking stick at a spot Mother had missed.

"We'd best go inside," Father said when he saw Martin walking over from the street.

Mother gathered up the wet rags and dropped them in a green plastic bucket. "Come inside and have breakfast before you go."

His parents went in ahead of Martin while he stopped on the porch for another look at Father's car. How old was it now? Seventeen, eighteen years? The Toronado had been the best of the cars his parents had been able to afford in America, and they had taken good care of it. The golden metallic paint glowed in the spring sun as if it were a car waiting for a king.

"You . . . look handsome . . . this morning." His mother shouted from the kitchen over the clatter of the juicer.

"How do I look on other days?" Martin dropped the morning newspaper on the sofa by his father's side and bent down to kiss him.

"Other mornings . . . you might not . . . wear a tie." When Martin cocked his head, she shouted, "In a moment . . . I'll be finished with the juice."

"You didn't have to wash the car. I looked at it yesterday and I didn't see one speck of dust on it."

"*Ordnung muss sein.* You know how much we like things to be orderly."

"Papa isn't even taking a driving test, just a reading examination." Sitting down in an easy chair, Martin propped his legs on a footstool.

"Somebody from church might see you driving in a dirty automobile." Mother set a breakfast tray in his lap. "Besides, the car should look beautiful on such an important day."

For at least two weeks they had talked of Father's having to renew his driver's license. Mother was worried that the authorities wouldn't give a license to a man whose eighty-sixth birthday was coming up next month. "We really need this license. You think they would understand that we have to go to church and that we want to buy groceries on our own, get our checks cashed." Although Martin kept correcting her, now and then she still pronounced it "grosheries."

"And be free," she added. "We still want to be free."

"Why don't you stop polishing your shoes?" Martin asked his father. "They are already gleaming like chestnuts."

Bent over his shoes, Father wiped them gently with an old woolen sock. After awhile he folded the sock carefully and put it on top of the shoeshine kit. "Ah, the chestnuts," he said, looking over at his son eating breakfast from a tray in his lap.

Martin remembered when the wind shook the chestnut trees lining the road near their house in the Old Country. Bouncing on the ground, the spiky green shells split open and the chestnuts rolled sleek and moist into the dust. He gathered them into a pillowcase. Then, at the round table in the living room, he made chestnut men, chestnut animals with legs made from wooden matches, chestnut boats, and heavy chestnut necklaces. It didn't matter how beautiful the things looked that he had made because every year the sleek shiny chestnuts always shriveled into dull brown stones.

Father stood up and put on his jacket.

"You don't have to do that yet," Mother said. "You'll be sweaty even before you leave the house. Martin is still eating. But since you have your coat on, let me look at you." Walking around Father, she inspected his shirt collar, slid the knot of his tie up, pulled his jacket down in back, then brushed the shoulders of his dark blue blazer.

"Take off your jacket, your hair's too long. People will think that you're Ben Gurion."

"No, more Old Testament," Martin said. "More like Moses on Mount Sinai."

From her sewing box Mother took a pair of scissors and clipped some of Father's white locks from the back of his neck. "Don't move, I have to cut over the ears too." Then she brushed his hair once more. Stepping back, she looked at him and shook her head. She licked her fingertips and smoothed back a wisp touching the top of his ear. Then she helped him back into his jacket. "Just one more thing." Not knowing what to expect, Father obediently stood as if at attention. Mother tiptoed up to him, with a pink can of hair spray hidden behind her back. When she squirted twice at Father's neck he sneezed and pulled his head into his collar like a threatened turtle. "Don't touch your hair," she said. Standing behind his back, she waited until he raised his head and then squirted him once more. "This way you'll look tidy and orderly for the photographer."

. . . .

When Martin saw that Father kept glancing at his wristwatch, he took his breakfast dishes into the kitchen and pulled on his jacket. He hadn't finished eating his breakfast, but he didn't want Father to worry about time and he wanted his mother to see how he looked by Father's side. At the door he stood next to him. Although his father was a head shorter than Martin, both men looked very much alike, even down to their gray mustaches, except that Father trimmed his until it lay flat against his upper lip.

"Why do you cut your mustache so short?" Martin asked, although he knew how their church felt about facial hair.

"I want to look orderly."

"The beautiful sunshine we have in America." Mother looked around from the porch. "And the car shines too, as if it were the chariot of Israel . . ."

"And the horsemen of Elias," Father added with a smile.

"You are so *Bibelfest*," admired Mother.

"Elijah," Martin wanted to correct, but didn't. Both of his parents could quote readily and correctly from the Bible—as long as it was the German Luther translation—verses that they had learned by heart when they were children in school. The English Bible had never taken with either one of them. Even now Mother still followed the Sunday school lessons in her German Bible.

She kissed husband and son as if they were setting out on a long journey. "You drive," she told Martin, "so he can save his strength for the examination."

Martin drove slowly past the privet hedge so that they could wave at Mother from the open windows of the car. Father pointed back at the hedge.

"You saw that the *Liguster* wasn't cut evenly?"

With nothing more than a yardstick, a ball of string, and hand clippers, Father used to sculpt a sharp-edged wall from the privet bushes. Now, the man who mowed the lawn also took a few minutes to go over the hedge with an electric trimmer. When Father complained that the hedge wasn't evenly cut, the man looked at him with incomprehension, as if Father talked to him in a language of aliens.

"I saw it. The privet is sloping toward the right." Martin nodded. "I noticed it." He used the German expression "it fell into my eye." His father had taught him to let things fall into his eye. As a child, Martin had often been taken to construction sites where his father's company was building apartments for the railroaders in town. It was then that Martin had learned to spot anything that wasn't straight, level, or true to plumb. Father would ask, "How long is this wall?" and Martin would sight along the edge of the concrete foundation and guess. Then they both paced off the distance, Martin having to stretch the steps of his shorter legs as best he could. When Martin's estimate was close, they would both laugh and walk on. As he thought about it now, night always seemed to have fallen quickly so that they hurried home where Mother waited with supper.

When he stopped at the first intersection, he glanced into the rearview mirror and saw that his mother stood in the middle of the street, still waving.

He took St. Louis Avenue because its broadness reminded him of a grand boulevard in a city with real history. Here in Las Vegas, the only old building had been the icehouse by the Union Pacific tracks until someone had set fire to it. There had been talk of arson. In this town, it was almost as if anything old made people uncomfortable.

. . . .

As soon as Martin turned into the parking lot he saw the long line.

"Look at all of these people."

From the end of the line Father counted the people between them and the olive tree standing in front of the double glass doors. "There are fifty people ahead of us. We should have left earlier."

"It's not so bad." Martin tried to soothe his father. "When they open the doors, people are going to line up at different counters."

When they got inside, Father shook his head when he saw the long lines of people snaking in different directions through the big hall. "We should have left earlier."

"This is like Ellis Island," Martin said.

"What do you know about Ellis Island? You never had to go there."

"True, but I've seen pictures, and I know what it looked like."

Father walked to the end of the nearest line.

"Wait!" Martin kept pointing to a large overhead board.

"Black, blue, green, red, and yellow lines. This reminds me of the control panel at the railroad, of the office in the shunting yard."

"Let's see if we can shunt ourselves in the right direction." Martin kept pointing at the overhead board. "The lines are color coded. Yellow line, information; black line, truck plates; red line, license plate for the first time; green line, license plate transfer. Here. Blue line, drivers license renewals."

Martin began to read aloud the placards posted on the buff-colored walls. "Thumbs-Up to Seat Belts," he read from a poster showing policemen in different uniforms. "Give a Chance at Life—Be an Organ Donor."

The line moved slowly and stopped altogether in front of a corkboard displaying special license plates.

"This is for a state legislator, that one for former prisoners of war, and this over here is for soldiers who were awarded the Medal of Honor. I wonder how many people in the state of Nevada are eligible for that plate?"

"How about this one for me?" Father pointed at one of the silver license plates.

"'Disabled Veteran,'" Martin read aloud. "You certainly are that, but they may say that you fought on the wrong side." When his father was hit by shell fragments during a French artillery barrage in World War I, how old had he been? Nineteen? Twenty?

"Maybe this one?"

"No. 'Old-timer' is for old cars, not old people."

"And this? I can't see what's on it."

"It's a scenic plate. You can get it for an extra ten dollars. It shows a mountain with a Joshua tree. You must have seen them when you and Mother used to drive down from Salt Lake City, before you moved here. After you pass through St. George, you must have seen a whole field of Joshua trees. With their arms raised up, they always made me think of an army surrendering in the desert."

"Under Joshua the children of Israel never surrendered to anyone, not at Jericho or when they were on the midnight side of Ai."

"I didn't mean that. . . . The other items on the license plate are the usual Nevada stuff, like a bighorn sheep, our state animal. I think that it's the same as Aries, your horoscope sign."

"It is?" Father smiled. "But of course this horoscope thing is nonsense."

At the counter, more windows were being opened. To pass the time, Martin speculated which would be theirs. Finally, a woman waved to them to step forward from the end of the blue line.

"This nice lady will help us." Father shook hands with the examiner, an older woman who wore her dyed black hair in a beehive. Looking from one to the other, she smiled at the two men dressed identically in jackets and ties as if they were aliens from another world who happened to be stranded in a colorful crowd wearing T-shirts, halter tops, and shorts. She was still smiling when she dropped the card with the reading test into the machine.

Martin squeezed his father's shoulder, although it wasn't necessary. Already thirty years ago his father had known all the road signs when he taught his son how to drive along the loop of Liberty Park, and he hadn't forgotten them since.

His father drew himself up and stood with his eyes closed, as if he were praying, then he bent down to peer into the machine. And he called out the signs, he saw the woman's powdered face turn sad as she checked the list in front of her. Then she glanced again at Father's application on the counter.

"All of your answers were wrong." She didn't raise her eyes from the application.

"Did you understand everything?" Martin asked his father in German. He nodded. "I'll translate for you." Martin looked apologetically at the examiner, as he always did when he spoke German in front of others.

"Take your time." The examiner flicked to another row.

"It's going to be all right," Martin said in German.

Clearing his throat, Father began to read. He spoke slower now, as if he wanted to make sure that he would not be misunderstood.

"Wrong again." The examiner gave Martin a reproachful look, as if she wanted to say, "Martin, why are you putting your father through this torture?" "Everything is wrong again."

His father stood alone, although only an arm's length away from his son. Martin could see the perspiration beading among the brown spots on his father's forehead.

"He is nervous because he has to take this test." Martin spoke softly to the examiner so that his father wouldn't hear that his son was making excuses for him.

The examiner clicked in another row of signs. "Tell your father to take a deep breath and to read more slowly what he sees."

Martin translated the examiner's instructions, although he could see by the look in his eyes that he had understood.

"He's nervous. His English is usually much better." The moment he had finished speaking, he knew that he had betrayed his father by apologizing for him. Martin put his arm around his father's shoulder. The wool of the jacket felt warm and moist to his touch. He kept his arm on his father's shoulder while he read the signs as he had been told to do in two languages.

When he stopped reading, the woman looked pleadingly at Martin. "I don't know how to tell you this."

Martin took his father's arm as if he were leading an invalid. It has come to this, he thought. Finally it has come to this. The beginning of the end.

"No," Martin said aloud.

His father looked up at him with a face that was serene, not nervous or sad. Martin dropped his father's arm. "I am going to check the machine," he said in German, while his father stepped back to the end of the blue line.

The red, green, and yellow road signs stood out from the dark depth projected by the machine, sharply defined, as if they and the darkness were part of a memory of home.

"Is *this* what you see?" The examiner's eyes were filled with such sadness as if she were about to cry. "All of your answers were wrong, too."

Martin straightened up from the machine. "No, I had no difficulty recognizing the signs." He spoke louder than before. "All the answers should be correct."

As Martin's voice rose angrily, Father looked at his son and pulled at his sleeve. "Don't make trouble because of me."

Martin gently drew his sleeve out of his father's grip.

"No, this is wrong." Now he spoke English to his father.

Puzzled by the challenge in Martin's voice, the woman looked first at Martin, then at her fellow workers at their desks, and finally down at her machine. She pulled up the card with the road signs and read aloud its title and number, reassuring those at the desks that she couldn't possibly have made a mistake. Then she slowly reread the card. As if it were a close-up on a movie screen, Martin watched as her lips began to quiver. Then she looked with relief at the two men on the other side of the counter.

"I'm sorry. This was the wrong card." She waved to Father. "Please, step to the counter and look into the machine. It was a mistake."

This time Martin didn't translate the instructions. Instead he stared angrily at the woman, ready to tell her what he thought, when out of the corner of his eye, he saw that his father was smiling.

"Press your forehead against the pad."

Martin didn't dare to breathe as his father obediently pushed his face into the machine. Then he called out the signs in a clear voice as he calmly pronounced each foreign word.

"Perfect! Congratulations. You don't have to read anymore."

Father straightened up, and Martin wondered how his heart was bearing up under the strain of the examination. He remembered him in the hospital bed after his first heart attack. Martin had flown in from Denver to find his father in the intensive care unit of a Salt Lake City Hospital. Tubes were coming out of his father's nose. Martin was sure that he was dying. That had been fifteen years ago.

"Put your signature on your new driver's license."

Martin watched over his father's shoulder as he signed with the old fountain pen he had brought to America. Writing his name clearly and evenly, he filled the assigned spaces without going beyond the borders set for him.

. . . .

They followed the blue line to the photographer's station. When Martin put his father into the low chair in front of the yellow backdrop of the booth, he saw that the woman behind the camera was the one who had examined him.

"The photographer is taking a break, and I didn't want your father to wait any longer than necessary." She smiled at him. "No, that won't do! Smile a little, but not too much. We're not supposed to take smiling pictures."

The camera flashed twice, and his father got up.

. . . .

When they picked up the license, both men shook hands with the examiner. Martin didn't bow, but his father did, and the woman smiled at him as if he were a Continental gentleman calling on her.

At they walked toward the exit, Father stopped and pointed toward the golden car parked under the olive tree with two trunks and the sunshine and the blue sky. With his circle of white hair, he might have been Moses on a rocky ledge of Mount Nebo gazing into the land of promise.

"Look at that golden background behind your head," Mother said. "Something special for Papa."

Martin didn't have the heart to tell her that everybody in the state would be photographed for a whole year in front of the same yellow background.

"You could have smiled."

"I did. When they were through with me."

"Look at him! Now he smiles."

They laughed as if with one voice.

"I'll lie down for a while."

Martin embraced his father.

"Either you're still growing or I'm getting smaller."

Martin didn't answer, but he kissed his father and watched him walk down the corridor to the bedroom. Then he picked up the plastic card from the kitchen table.

"Be careful!" Mother warned. "The license might still be wet."

"I'm just checking for mistakes. Height: five-ten," Martin read aloud. "Hair: gray; eyes: green." He examined the picture more closely. "You know, his eyes don't really show green in the photo." But for some reason he couldn't put down the card from which his father's eyes were looking at him, not unkindly but without any lightheartedness. And under the mustache that looked so much like his son's, the line of his mouth ran straight and level to its corners.

"That's it, I guess," Martin said, but he still didn't let go of the card. He was shocked when he saw how deep his father's head had sunk into his shoulders. Had his father declined so much, unnoticed by his son, who saw him every day? Although his neck may have shrunk into the collar of his jacket, the bent of his nose made him look even more fierce. It was as if his shoulders had been frozen in the upward motion of a defiant shrug that said, "No, I will not." And then, of course, there was his signature, which moved evenly along the line under the old face, as if the letters were soldiers drilled to march in formation.

"I guess that's it," repeated Martin as he turned toward the door.

He stopped in the carport by the Toronado. For the drive home from the test, he had asked his father if he wanted to take the wheel. He had driven smoothly and swiftly, so much so that the speedometer had rolled above the speed limit. Martin had tapped his hand in the air in imitation of his father's cautioning motion, but he had pretended not to notice. Martin stroked the sloping rear deck of the car. He could see how the metallic paint had faded in the desert sun.

"'*My father, my father,*'" he said, recalling the quote that neither of his parents had been able to remember fully. "*And Elisha saw and cried, 'My father, my father . . .'*" Then he too faltered and all he remembered was the last line: "'*And he saw him no more.*'"

JOHN H. IRSFELD [B. 1937]

"The world is a playground and it is always recess," John Henry Irsfeld once told an interviewer, adding, "If I weren't doing this, I'd be doing something else." Irsfeld, who received the Nevada Governor's Arts Award in 1994 and was inducted into the Nevada Writers Hall of Fame in 2003, has done many things in his life. Raised in Texas, he taught high school Spanish and English in Calallen, Texas, and served three years in the army infantry. He earned a PHD from the University of Texas, Austin, in 1969, whereupon he left the Lone Star State to become an English professor at the University of Nevada, Las Vegas. At UNLV Irsfeld started out in the classroom, became chair of the English Department, executive assistant to the academic vice president, deputy to the president, and then vice president and deputy to the president in the 1990s. Irsfeld's writing career began promisingly with the publication of his novels Coming Through *(1975) and* Little Kingdoms *(1976). Administrative work consumed the next decade, delaying publication of his third novel,* Rats Alley, *until 1987. After another decade slipped by, Irsfeld noticed all the unpublished fiction stored in binders on his shelves, and he decided to write again, issuing* Radio Elvis and Other Stories *in 2002. The title story, "Radio Elvis," imagines what would happen if Elvis Presley were alive today and visited—or not—a convention of Elvis impersonators. As reviewer Tom Doyal notes of this collection, Irsfeld "captures the lives of the grifters and drifters, losers and loners of the Nevada desert." Irsfeld also served as senior editor for both* Las Vegan *and* LV *city magazines and has published critical essays on Las Vegas fiction.*

Stop, Rewind, and Play

Lilla gave herself one day off a week. She was firm about it. Even if she thought she needed the money or had nothing to do but stay around her apartment and read, she still took one day off. Ordinarily it was Saturday. Most of the other girls she knew told her she was crazy. Saturday was the best business day of the week. Some girls claimed they made as much on Saturdays as they did the rest of the week put together. "That's fine, hon," Lilla would say. "I'll just leave that for your delectation." Lilla wasn't quite sure what that word meant; she had heard it somewhere, perhaps from a customer, and she liked the sound of it. None of the girls ever asked her.

Her argument was that Saturday was the good business day it was because of the incursion of unacceptable clientele. She didn't like patrons whose breath stank of too much alcohol, or who took too long because the booze slowed them down, or who passed out on her. And on Saturdays that kind came out of the woodwork. So she took Saturdays off and let her professional colleagues join with the amateurs and have all the business they wanted. The only time she violated the rule and worked on Saturdays was when she had what she termed "a touch of the ring." If she had such a touch, there was no point in trying to spend the day by herself; she couldn't. Mostly she had the ring on those days when the wind blew in from the southwest and clouded the valley with sand. Then the static electricity crackled, and Lilla paced her apartment like an animal. Nothing could calm her down on those days.

When she experienced her first dust storm she tried to drink to allay the tensions of the energy that ran through her like alternating current, but it didn't help. She was still jumpy as a whore, as she sardonically put it. And she knew what that word meant. When a windstorm occurred on Saturday, Lilla went ahead and put in an evening's work. She worked harder than usual, in fact, trying to dull with fatigue the needling of the nerves that was worse than anything else she had to contend with in life.

Today was a Saturday, and it was calm. Lilla had not worked late the night before, however, and so she was up fairly early in the day. It was now only eleven o'clock. She had already had her juice and one cup of coffee and was settled in with her second cup, reading her second newspaper. Neither paper was very good, but Lilla read them both every day. It was from these sources primarily that she drew the information she used as grist for her small-talk mill in the evenings when she worked. The other girls who knew her either accused her of pretensions or admired her because she worked so hard at trying to sound where it's at, as they put it.

She turned to the editorial page and read the editor's column, as she habitually did. When she finished it her eyes strayed to a story about the boyhood life of a famous singer playing at one of the big hotels on the Strip. He was handsome and had a lovely wife and family, and Lilla knew for a fact he was gay, having seen him operate at a small party. The story in the newspaper told how the singer had hunted and fished under the name of Huckleberry Finn when he was a boy back home. "Oh brother," Lilla said, shaking her head. Anyway, what did she care? When you're hot, you're hot, and that includes who you're hot for.

She turned the page and scanned the ads on the left. She did not get to the bottom before she skipped over to the other side. It was a full-page ad for a hardware store. Lilla liked their ads. All the merchandise they had for sale yelled, "Everything is all right!" There was only one thing in the ad today that she really wanted: a big color television set.

Lilla had the nine hundred dollars it cost and six times more than that beyond. It was all in the bank, in five certificates of deposit at six-and-a-quarter percent, and in a passbook account at five-and-a-half. She was conscientious about her savings. The lure of a color television set was not strong enough to sway her from her financial duty to herself. Furthermore, since she was gone all the other nights, Saturday was the only night of the week she could watch television, and she wasn't that strong on the afternoon soaps.

So, not only could she not watch a color television set if she had one, she would, furthermore, be obliged in the bargain to get one too big for a burglar to carry away. Her place had already been broken into three times, but she had lost nothing after the few dollars taken the first time. Lilla learned easily.

She turned the page and reached for her coffee cup. The paper edge fell over itself. When she put her cup down and straightened the paper out, her eyes immediately went to the hidden corner. The first thing she saw was an ad for a promotional function at Benny Binion's Horseshoe Club downtown: drawings from noon to midnight. And the big prize every hour was a giant 23-inch color TV. That tickled Lilla's fancy. She didn't go downtown much, but she knew the big places and she knew the Horseshoe. They had good Mexican food. A junketeer from Houston had taken her there one evening and ordered their supper in Spanish, which she thought quite elegant.

Impulsively she dropped her newspaper and got up. She looked at her watch. It was five after eleven. She headed toward the bathroom. She took off her peignoir and looked at herself in the mirror that made up the whole far wall of the bathroom beyond the toilet seat. She still looked good; she probably would for some time. She might get off her ass and make something out of herself yet. Or, she might get lucky.

"That kind of talk goes nowhere," she said harshly to herself. "And pull your stomach in," she added to her image in the mirror. She liked her bathroom a great deal; it had been the deciding factor in her taking the apartment. The mirrored wall wasn't all of it. Around the corner, behind her to the left, was the shower bath. And in the wall just outside the end of the shower bath there was a sliding glass door that opened to a patio. The patio, a good ten by twenty-five feet in size, was surrounded by an eight-foot high rough cedar fence. There was a shower outside too, with a drain set neatly in the concrete floor below the head.

Soon after she moved into the apartment Lilla had placed several plants in red cedar pots about the patio. Then she had bought a rope net hammock and a plastic web chaise lounge. The last thing she got was a small wrought-iron table and two matching ice-cream chairs. The table had a glass top; the rest of it was painted white like the chairs. The patio was Lilla's favorite spot. This was where she sunned herself in the hot Nevada summers and lazily dreamed about the future and how nice and quiet it was going to be.

Lilla came to herself and went around the corner and out through the sliding door into her little garden.

It was a beautiful hot spring morning, very clear and bright. Lilla stretched again, facing up toward the sun with her eyes closed. She made a soft, furry sound. "Well," she said to herself, as if in gentle remonstrance. She smiled again and went to her outside shower. This was the best of all: soaping and washing and rinsing outside produced a complex sensation that was both immensely dirty and commensurately clean. In the end, it was purifying.

By twelve o'clock she was dressed in a white double-knit pantsuit, with white shoes and purse, ready to go. She tried on three pairs of sunglasses until she found the ones that suited her, silver-rimmed, mannish Ray-Bans. She was going to miss the first drawing, but she would not hurry on her day off; if she missed a drawing, she missed it.

She drove over to the Strip and then north toward downtown. It was not long before she was picking up a ticket from the electric ticket machine at Binion's garage. She had to drive to the fifth floor before she found a place to park. She waited patiently for the elevator to come fetch her back down.

In the casino things were already buzzing. Lilla liked the way heads turned as she walked into the room and then down past the restaurant and the little bar, toward the center of the gaming. When she was working she did not like to be too conspicuous; it wasn't safe. Sheriff's men and city detectives were crawling all over the place. But on Saturdays she was just another pretty girl, and she loved the attention she got. She was attractive enough, striking enough, that even women turned to look at her.

That was fine with Lilla; homage paid was homage taken. When you're hot. . . .

The drawing was being held at the end of the horseshoe bar that divided the table games from the slot machines. The bar extended out from the restaurant area toward Fremont Street, which was not twenty feet from the outside bank of slots. Off toward the front corner of the room, in the no-man's land between craps and slots, Lilla saw the large glass case in the horseshoe frame filled with 100 ten-thousand-dollar bills. A photo girl stood near a camera on a tripod aimed at the million dollars.

Lilla walked down by the table side of the horseshoe bar until she was within a few feet of the million dollars. She had seen it before, the night she ate Mexican food with the man from Houston, but since he had been impressed by it, she hadn't looked at it. She knew men liked it more if she were a little haughty, a little reserved. The photo girl didn't ask Lilla if she wanted her picture taken. She and Lilla smiled distantly at each other. Lilla heard a man at the bar behind her to her right talking about her: "I'd wear that son of a bitch like a face mask," he said, and then his voice got swallowed up in a sudden babble from one of the craps tables behind her on the other side.

"Where's the drawing?" she asked the photo girl.

"There," the girl said, nodding toward the end of the bar at a big wire drum set in brackets. The drum, full of tickets, had replaced two bar stools. Blank forms were stacked on the bar top nearby.

"Thank you," Lilla said to the girl.

"Yeah," said the girl, "don't mention it."

Lilla looked at her watch as she walked toward the end of the bar. It was already twelve thirty-five.

She took a Cross ballpoint pen from her small white handbag, twisted the point out, and neatly filled in one of the blank forms. She folded it square and dropped it in the slot at the top of the wire drum. Then she went to the nearest bar stool and sat to wait. She ordered a Scotch and soda in a tall glass and nursed it until one o'clock. Her name was not drawn; she did not even get an honorable mention.

Lilla decided to move around. She could not sit at the bar until the two o'clock drawing. She left the Horseshoe and went next door to the Mint Hotel that made up the rest of that block downtown. She rented a room and toked the desk clerk five dollars to ensure that he would get someone out to the airport to locate her misplaced bags. Then she bought a bottle of Scotch and some magazines and went upstairs to wait for the next drawing. By one-thirty the bellboy had brought her ice and she had mixed herself a drink. It made her feel lewd to be in a hotel room by herself, fully dressed. She touched herself on the breasts and, delicately, her flanks, looking in the mirror. Maybe she would pick someone up . . . just for fun, not a trick. Maybe she would see a girl who looked okay. That might do. Of course it wasn't part of the program. But after working all week with men, and trying, the gentler outlines of a woman's body seemed attractive to her. But a waste.

When she finished her drink it was time to go back to the Horseshoe to see if she would win. She put the "Do Not Disturb" sign on the doorknob and took the elevator downstairs. The man in charge was just drawing the first name as she worked herself through the growing crowd of slot players toward the barrel. Hers was not the first one called. It was not long, however.

When it was called over the P.A. system she was startled. For a moment she was at a loss. She stopped where she was, motionless; then she looked up at the man who was calling her name again, and she waved her white purse daintily.

She had not won the 23-inch color TV. She had not won the fur stole. She had not won even the stereo record player. She had won, however, as the fourth person named who was present, a fancy executive's cassette tape recorder. She accepted it with thanks, pleased that she had won anything at all; but she retained her mask of relative indifference. She did not wish to crack her Saturday makeup; she wished to remain beautiful and distant. She could tell that every eye was on her when she stepped up on the little platform to take her prize. She held her belly flat and kept her expression noncommittal.

When she had accepted the recorder and stepped back down on the worn red carpeting, a ripple of applause rolled through the crowd. It pleased Lilla; for a moment her face almost flushed, but she caught herself and kept it pale.

As she started away the man in charge of the drawing called to her. "Wait a sec, doll," he said. "Hang on there a minute."

Lilla stopped and turned around, expecting a proposition. Instead the announcer handed her a cardboard box.

"Here," he said. "Trade you. That's our window dressing."

"Oh," Lilla said.

After they had exchanged recorders, Lilla headed straight toward her room in the Mint. Even in the elevator she did not look at the package she held. She had a funny feeling of excitement, as if something important were about to happen.

First she mixed a new drink. Then she took off her shoes and the white pantsuit. She draped the clothes neatly across the easy chair and took her drink and the boxed tape recorder over to the bed.

"All right," she said. "Let's take a look at this famous prize." And she began to open the box, tearing away the stapled ends.

Within a quarter of an hour she had figured out how to operate the machine she had won. She had it plugged into the socket next to the lamp cord.

"Testing. One, Two, Three, Four," she said into the microphone. Then she pushed a button marked "Stop," another marked "Rewind," and a third marked "Play."

"Testing," some woman's strange voice said. "One, Two, Three, Four." Lilla frowned. Then she pushed "Stop," "Rewind," and "Play" again. This time the voice sounded more familiar. It still wasn't her voice, but it was not so strange.

A funny feeling passed through Lilla, as if there were something alien inside her. She took a sip from her drink. Then she pushed the "Rewind" button and let all the tape pile up on the left reel.

"What shall I say?" she asked of the room. "How should I begin this?" She could see herself in the mirror over the dresser. There was a window to her right, which looked out on Fremont Street, across toward the Golden Nugget.

"I'll tell a story," she said. There was a funny tone in her voice. She looked again at her reflection across the room. Her white brassiere contracted sharply with her sun-darkened skin. She pushed "Record."

"How did a nice girl like you get into a business like this?" she said into the microphone. "Bad title," she said, frowning again. She waited a moment, thoughtfully.

"I've got it," she said. "This is better. This is it: My life and times." She felt uncomfortable, as if there were something she had forgotten to do.

"My life and times," she said again, picking up her drink and toasting herself in the mirror. She tossed her hair back and began.

There were two sixty-minute tapes with the machine; Lilla finished her story halfway into the second one.

"Oh, what the hell," she said then. "So what? So what's the point? Life is real? Life is hard? So what else is new?"

She looked at herself in the mirror again and drank the last of her drink.

Then she said, "The End," into the microphone and pushed "Stop."

She still felt uncomfortable. Perhaps it was her story—she didn't know. "That's not it," she said aloud. She saw no reason why the story should bother her. Though never to herself, she had told it many times before during her years in the business. It wasn't even true. That is, only some of it was true. She didn't know anymore, in fact, which parts were true and which were false. There had been, for a long time, no need to distinguish between them: a high school romance, the Vietnam war, her fiancé a prisoner and then dead. It had all been so horrible.

Well, it had all been horrible. At least that part was the truth.

Lilla got up and went around the bed to the window that overlooked the street. Beyond the top of the Golden Nugget and between some buildings a couple of blocks away she could see what might have been the early signs of a dust storm rising.

"Crap," she said.

She let the window curtain fall and went back around the bed. She picked up her drink to take a sip, but the glass was empty. Outside in the hallway she heard some tourists going toward the elevator. If the wind was coming up, she supposed she ought to go to work. She already knew that Scotch was no defense against the wind. But that meant she would have to go home and change and then go over to the Strip. She didn't work downtown; she was class. And it would all be such a lot of trouble.

"Class's ass!" she said sharply, surprising herself. "You're just another hooker. A whore. Just another . . . just another whore. . . ."

And at that, a tear popped up unexpectedly in her right eye. It creased the makeup down along the line of her nose as it fell. It cut off at the upper lip and ran around to the edge of the mouth and then exhausted itself somewhere between her jaw and her neck. The others after it, just as unexpected, came so fast they went straight down her face, across her lips, and onto her chin. Lilla felt some of them fall on the tops of her breasts and on her lap. So many tears, after so long, and where did they come from?

After a while she picked up the microphone again, and with the index finger of the same hand pushed "Record."

"When I was sixteen I got pregnant. My boyfriend and I went to Mexico, and I got an abortion there. We were going to get married, but we never did. He went away. I grew up. I started sleeping around a little, looking for someone to marry, trying to get pregnant again. That's all I want. But nobody ever asked me. And I never got pregnant. That's how I got into this. That's all." Then she pushed "Stop."

She got up and slipped on her white pantsuit and her white shoes. She sat in front of the mirror above the dresser and fixed her face again, avoiding her eyes as much as possible. It was not yet five o'clock. She would collect her car at Binion's garage, go home and shower, catch a nap, and then get dressed and go to work. She would be rocking on Cleopatra's Barge at Caesars Palace by nine o'clock.

At the door Lilla turned and looked back at the room. She had her magazines with her and her Scotch in the paper bag it had come in. The two cassette tapes were in her white purse, but the drawing prize itself was still there on the bed where she had left it.

"That's ridiculous," she said and sighed in exasperation.

But she left it where it was. While the tape recorder was innocent of blame, still she probably would not have made up any stories at all had she not had it there to confide in. And, she thought, as she saw it lying there on the bed, passive but potential, the bed was as good a place as any for it.

DOUGLAS UNGER [B. 1952]

Douglas Unger garnered national attention when his first novel, Leaving the Land *(1984), was a finalist for a Pulitzer Prize. This novel and a related one,* The Turkey War *(1988), chronicle the breakdown of a small community in South Dakota in the decades following World War II, as family farms are gobbled up by corporate ownership. Unger himself grew up on struggling farms in the West, choosing education as his ticket out. In the late 1960s he was an exchange student in Argentina, where he witnessed the political unrest, military dictatorship, and tragic "disappearances" of dissidents. His novels* El Yanqui *(1986) and* Voices from Silence *(1995) tell the stories of Argentineans living under a repressive regime. Deeply concerned with social issues, Unger's novels and story collection* Looking for War *(2004) reflect his experiences, skirt the border between nonfiction and fiction, and as one critic observed, "center [on] themes of displacement and exile." After earning a* BA *from the University of Chicago, and an* MFA *from the University of Iowa, Unger held several teaching positions before settling in Las Vegas in 1991, where he is a professor at* UNLV. *He cofounded and has directed* UNLV's *innovative* MFA *in Creative Writing International Program, explaining that the program makes sense in Las Vegas, possibly the most international city in the United States. Unger, who likes the action of Las Vegas, has contributed significantly to its cultural standing. He has been managing editor of the* Chicago Review, *associate editor for* Point of Contact, *a book reviewer for the* New York Times, *recipient of a Guggenheim Fellowship, an essayist for the* MacNeil/Lehrer News Hour, *radio commentator, screenwriter, and board member of the International Institute of Modern Letters, the Las Vegas–based supporting organization for literary arts around the world. "Second Chances," a genre-blending "life tale," offers a new angle on Unger's persistent theme of displacement and exile.*

Second Chances

The two most abiding memories about Merle Richards might be his talk of guns and that he had ended up in Las Vegas. This would be how his daughter-in-law Grace—Kyle Richards' wife—summed up his time on earth. Kyle bristled every time, knowing his Dad had been more complex than that. He had lived a whole other story than in Las Vegas that Grace never even pretended to appreciate. On the other hand, wasn't some natural friction with the in-laws expected in a marriage?

Grace had been born and raised on Long Island, on wealthy Sands Point, a short train ride away from the sophistications of New York. She still considered her sixteen-year residency in the housing tracts under the photogenic sunsets of the Mojave Desert and in the shadows of the spectacular light shows of the mega-resorts to be a mere temporary condition—as if Kyle were ready to sell his construction business any minute and take them off properly back East. Back East, there were actually four seasons in a year, and she wouldn't have to cup her mouth to the telephone and say to distant family and friends, lowering her voice, "Yes, you know, in Vegas . . . ," her tone apologizing for the embarrassing oddities of some primitive culture in a foreign land. "Nothing stays here," she would say. "They blow it up when they're done. And in a place so notorious for its mobster history, can you believe you still can't find a decent pizza?"

Kyle long ago quit showing his irritation, and there were times when he wasn't sure if Grace might be right—that nobody really lived here, not in any rooted sense, certainly not the way he ever would have thought of himself as living, years ago, when he and his brother Jeb would stretch out for a rest in one of Merle's thorny hay fields in South Dakota. They blue-skied about what kind of futures they would make—which piece of short grass prairie they would add to the Richards family holdings, what kind of new steel barn and feed lot complete with Harvestore silo they would build in that gumbo bottom land by the best sweet water for miles around; how they would improve their pastures with that new tri-grass and clover mix, switch over from raising sheep to much easier and more profitable cattle, planning how their place would gradually spread out as neighbors inevitably moved on or died off. Their land would be linked through their fraternal labors into one contiguous mammoth ranch so big no bank would dare bring it down. They'd go off to college to find wives, bring their wives back to the homeplace, raise their kids. The brothers would spell each other for two shopping trips a year over to the Twin Cities to keep their women happy—five days at most, no more—where they would eat out at restaurants, go to shows, get their fix of urban life. Then it would be back to that blessed nowhere of near limitless grasslands between Buffalo and Faith, where the Richards family would continue on a roll—this was the essence of their dream—just plain living on their own time, managing their lives like two brotherly kings.

That was before a draft board lottery number came up with Jeb. He returned from the last month of that lost war with a shattered spine from a fall out the door of a helicopter on which he'd been ordered to kick off fleeing refugees, so many of them clinging in dark human knots to the struts that the helicopter could barely lift up into the air. One of the refugees grabbed at Jeb's boot, and that was that—he fell. Jeb would be planted in a wheelchair and hooked up to a colostomy bag for the rest of his days. He came home just in time to watch Merle's third wife carry her suitcases out of their picturebook ranch house in the middle of nowhere. Jill was on her way to leaving him for a Presbyterian minister who had just moved into Buffalo. "A goddamned minister," his father said. "Some kind of Puritan! No man alive can live that one down."

Merle stood in the ranch house living room, simmering as he watched her lining up those suitcases in the gravel drive. Kyle saw it coming but was too far across the living room to stop him, when, on impulse, Merle pulled his custom grip 9mm Beretta out from under the couch cushions. He stepped onto the front stoop and started plugging Jill's suitcases full of holes. Jeb was close enough he could wheel into him from behind, knocking Merle's knees out from under him so he went sprawling into Jeb's lap. Kyle also jumped over and grabbed at his arm before Merle could swing the barrel enough to take the last shot left in the clip straight into his wife's cowering, cheating ass—which family legend had it Merle was surely meaning to do—so it was Jeb who had saved him from a prison term. Still, after that, nobody could save the ranch from Jill's lawyers, at least not on top of the already merciless pressure from the banks.

So began three years of fending off that final loss, years when the bottom dropped clear out of the grain and meat markets, the seasons marked by dwindling auction sales of almost everything they owned. Merle started raging off with increasing regularity in his pickup for twenty-eight-hour drives across Wyoming and down into Utah then that long straight shot through the empty desert to Las Vegas, Merle carrying with him whatever money he could scrape up, later on even borrowed money, like he didn't give a damn. Kyle and Jeb understood this, though they were resentful the old man never once invited them along. These Vegas escapes were never planned trips, almost always started in the middle of the night when Merle was at his worst with the messy tragedy of legal paperwork and unpayable bills piled all around him in his office in the back of the feed room. Besides, what else could the old man do to give him hope? And he didn't always lose. So, after the ranch was finally sold off, it seemed somehow logical that Las Vegas would be the place where Merle Richards chose to move. "Nothing a man needs to be ashamed of in Las Vegas," he would say. "You toss a chip out on the table, you're treated the same as anybody else. Nobody gives a damn where you come from, where you're going is all that counts. How about a place where a woman is discouraged from breast feeding in public yet it's perfectly legal for her to carry not one but *two* concealed weapons? There's not a single hour of the day or night when you can't get a cup of coffee and a shot of Jim Beam."

The story of how Merle had decided to move to Las Vegas would be told again and again at Grace's elegant dinner table set festively for the holidays with her Spode Butternut china and her Tiffany Audubon silverware—"turkey ware," Merle called it, pointing out the raised bird patterns to his grandkids just to get Grace's goat. The cutlery was arrayed in neat ranks and files on either side of his plate, and Grace would watch disdainfully as Merle's thick rancher's fingers awkwardly picked through its complexities before he just grabbed up the biggest knife and

fork and gripped them in his fists. Before his grandkids were born and Grace prohibited gunplay in her house, Merle might even pull out the Beretta tucked in his
belt and show it off. "It was either murder my third wife or move to Las Vegas," he'd
sum up. This became his line about himself even to strangers, delivered deadpan,
serious, "that's how I'm here," he'd say, then he'd break through the tension with a
laugh and call for a round.

The dining room of Grace and Kyle's new house in the Anthem Hills looked
out through a high bay window at the incomparable gorgeous spill of lights over
the valley floor below, a view resplendent with the colorful jewels of hotel towers
on the Las Vegas strip. Grace always sat at the head, regally, with this spectacular
view behind her, and Kyle could see her cringe as she looked them all over—the
two Richards brothers with their barely presentable Dad—regarding them like
the peasants they were, on each occasion an expression of surprise, as if she kept
forgetting the kind of people she had married into. Her face would twist into a
strained composure. She assumed the attitude of patient forbearance that was her
custom around her in-laws—as if she were visiting royalty condescending to serve
a holiday meal at a shelter for the homeless.

Jeb had little tolerance for this. He searched his ragged jean jacket covered with
POW-MIA and unit veterans' patches for little toys from casino gift shops he had
brought over for Kyle's kids—Tommy and little Suze—rubber insects he'd toss in
a handful on their plates to make them squeal, light-up yo-yos that could knock
chips out of Grace's cherrywood table, dinosaur wind-up toys he'd aim straight into
the butter dish. Jeb delighted in egging the kids on to whatever chaos he could.
Merle and Jeb's talk at the table would be of point-spreads on next Sunday's NFL,
which casinos had the best lines and most tolerable buffets. Then they'd turn to
how many Clark County Commissioners were taking bribes on valley development, "goddamned corrupt Republicans," Merle would complain. Both topics
would send Grace off to the kitchen at least twice to bang her pots around. After
the meal, Merle invariably would take his youngest son aside and say, "Let's hope
she don't act like she got barbed wire up her ass in your bed."

The family settled into a routine of gathering together mainly for holiday or occasional Sunday meals. Kyle wished they could be closer than this, but he was busy
with work, and Grace would only put up with so much. Kyle would think back to
that day he helped move Merle and Jeb into their used doublewide in the Sunrise
Trailer Park over by Stewart and Lamb—what Merle and Jeb together could afford, in the only park in town that would take a dog that weighed over twenty
pounds. He measured the steps front and back, made runs for plywood, built two
switch-back ramps covered in Astroturf for Jeb's wheelchair, all the while understanding, without his father or brother saying a word, that it would be the two of

them living there together, scraping along on Jeb's VA disability and Merle's early, thus reduced, Social Security checks. Their life plan was to hit the craps tables and lunch buffets every day, live like there was no tomorrow—which, after three generations of sweat and toil building up the stock and fields Merle had finally lost, Kyle guessed there really wasn't anymore.

Kyle was odd man out. He had the grades to get into college. A last-minute wrestling scholarship offer would pay part of his freight to Syracuse University—a place back East he had only heard of vaguely during winters listening to basketball games on his car radio. He and Merle humped a few sticks of battered ranch furniture out of the U-Haul into the doublewide while Jeb wheeled around outside in the heat, trying to get his young sheepdog he'd named "Sinner" used to a leash. As they unpacked, they could hear Jeb calling out there, "Sinner! Good boy, Sinner! Heel, Sinner!"

Merle and Kyle set up the two TVs on their stands and a gun rack in each bedroom—every rifle in them loaded, on Merle's insistence—then Kyle installed handicap rails in the bathroom for Jeb. Pictures seemed too crowded on the walls—mostly of Jeb and Kyle in various stages of growing up, in grade school, at 4-H with fat lambs, at their high school graduations, Jeb in his dress army uniform, Merle's cracked photo from the Navy in World War Two. And there was that one in the hallway of their mother, Ruth, when she was young, with a curly '40s perm, before she married Merle and he moved her out to the ranch where their kids were born. Even then she was a scared-looking woman, Kyle thought, her wide gray eyes starting to one side of the frame as if the cattle truck that would years later T-Bone her car and wipe her off the planet was already barreling toward her from that direction.

As a last touch, Merle asked Kyle to pound a few nails into the flimsy fake oak paneling in the living area over the couch. He hung up his old square-bladed irrigation shovel with its handle shiny from use—like a kind of gleaming, utilitarian sculpture—his one reminder any of them had ever worked the land. "I'll look at that old shovel and know I've hung it up," Merle said. "That's it now, damnit. We're done. Let's get over to the Golden Nugget before they switch over to the dinner price."

In downtown Las Vegas, Kyle left them behind—the old man pushing his elder son in a wheelchair over that broad sidewalk in the white hot breath of desert heat amid the honky-tonk daytime party Glitter Gulch was in those days before they covered Fremont Street over with a mammoth high-tech light show and messed it up with cheap souvenir booths, popcorn stands, and recorded noise. "It's either cowboy paradise or a perfect vision of hell, take your pick," Jeb said.

After following them downtown in the old Plymouth Valiant he and Merle had fixed up for his long drive East, Kyle decided against joining them for the buffet—not wanting to face such long highway miles loaded down with all that ballast. Merle shook his hand, once, roughly, as was his way. "Some of us get a chance in this life and some of us don't," he said. "Wish us luck now. Let's all come up winners."

Kyle waved goodbye as his father and brother rolled on into the welcoming air-conditioned promise of the buffet at the Golden Nugget, his old man bumping Jeb's wheelchair through the wide entryway onto the plush carpet, a little American flag tied to an old whip car antenna Jeb had fastened to his wheelchair puffing up with a blast of cool air. They vanished into the clanking and ringing of the slot machines amid milling people, the craps and card tables stretching off all around them like a glimmering mirage of fertile green fields.

Kyle often wondered now: had his father been happy with him? Had he done "right enough"—that old saying of Merle's when he was satisfied? He wasn't sure. He couldn't remember even what his Dad's last words had been to him, unless they were something like, "Maybe I'll go for the over-under on the Broncos next Sunday, what do you think?" He knew Kyle didn't gamble and could only shrug. His Dad had been unhappy with Grace, considered her a stuck-up prig, which she was, though to be fair to her, she was aware enough of this fault in herself to work at it with her in-laws, and who didn't have faults? Besides which, how could a man who bragged about nearly murdering his third wife be taken seriously for his opinions on marriage?

Reviewing their lives, Kyle couldn't help but be irritated that Grace never expressed any happiness or even comfort with the idea that they had landed in Las Vegas and even prospered here. After their romance as students at SU and her wealthy parents staged such an elegant wedding at the Little Church Around the Corner in New York—the same church where her parents had married then Grace's Dad had stepped onto and easily succeeded at the conservative ladder-climbing of investment banking on Wall Street—Grace maybe naturally expected a similar pattern to their own lives, that Kyle might take his SU business degree and accept a leg up into the three-piece-suited world of young corporate insiders in New York whose sole ambition was money and its swiftest possible accumulation. Grace should have known that wasn't for Kyle—how choked and stifled he felt in that crowd. He had little talent for schmoozing at lunches in Manhattan trading contacts and tips, courting fund managers and fat cats, and he was no good at all at fast-talking sales pitches over the telephone. He was no salesman, never would be, didn't have the knack or the required capacity to tell lies. He lost three jobs. He failed—it was that simple.

Grace also failed, in her own way—picking up an MA in English at NYU then not able to do much with it but manage a bookstore in the West Village that went suddenly bankrupt when the owner was diagnosed with lung cancer. He cleaned out the accounts behind her back and took off for Tahiti, stiffing distributors and publishers out of three seasons' worth of invoices. Grace was left with the nightmare of getting herself out of the lawsuits, and—though none of it was her fault—she still ended up smeared with a reputation as a deadbeat.

That winter, snow piled high in the city streets, breaking records, locking New Yorkers into a grim dreary survival mode of slogging icily through the gray freezing mornings then down into the stale air of the subways, barely able to make it to work. Then it was back again through the wind-whipped nights, bundled up like Siberian refugees, clutching wet bags of groceries to their chests. Between jobs, Kyle and Grace hid out, depressed, feeling luckless in their trendy, one-bedroom apartment in Chelsea. "Thousands a month for a space no bigger than six lambing pens with a tacked-on kitchen the size of your average closet," Kyle later described it, "and us eating nothing but pasta until it was coming out our ears." They soon quit being able to make rent without the "ultimate humiliation" of Grace having to ask her banker Dad for monthly loans. Truth was, they both had failed.

Still, what neither one of them would say anything about except by glancing at each other in a conspiratorial ebullience of a shared secret whenever either one was telling their story at a dinner party with friends—charging these tales of their dark days in New York with an erotic energy anyone listening would pick up on and not know why—some of their best memories as a young couple were of those winter nights and days spent in bed. Grace fixed her hair, made herself up, put on one of her gauzy negligees cut like an exotic dancer's. She spread out clean sheets, made them tight with hospital corners, lit a row of candles, poured cheap jug wine into her Steuben crystal. Then she propped herself up on a big mound of goose-down pillows and posed there on their bed like what she really was—a Long Island princess waiting to be pulled off her throne. Kyle understood that this royal posing by Grace represented an essence of his first attraction to her—she was the girl who displayed a promise of wealth and possibility of that urban life that had been sold to him and every other country boy since he became aware there was some other world beyond the dust and silage and manure of where he had been born. And what other fantasy did the culture offer a tough farm boy to project himself into after his cropland blew away than those glossy urban glamor-shots of anorexic women hungry with lust spread all over the magazine racks, movie, and TV screens—all gazing out at him as if what they truly desired was to be messed up first then royally screwed?

Kyle more than obliged Grace in these fantasies that bordered on the rapine, even rough—the way she later admitted she imagined him to be ever since she first watched him on a wrestling mat taking his opponent down with a hard fall then pinning him in an NCAA competition at the Carrier Dome. They were shy, at first, in expressing these desires to one another. Grace acted on their first date as if she merely deigned to go out with him from a missionary sense of generosity to the lower castes—as though she might tutor him in the ways of the privileged, talking to him of art museums, trendy books, which wine went with what entrée at the expensive restaurant she was insisting on paying for with her father's credit card. She talked and talked, too quickly, too much. Grace was a talker when she was nervous. Kyle responded with instinctive moves. In slow stages, he reached for her leg underneath the table. He let her feel the strength in his hands. When the check came, he stood up—a foot taller than the waiter—and tossed a roll of cash on the table with a cowboy bravado that said he would brook no arguments. Outside, Grace tried to get him to take her share of the bill, struggling to press money into his coat while Kyle was scraping the ice off the windshield of her bright orange Saab. He turned suddenly, pulled her head back by her hair. He planted a long kiss on her mouth that took her breath away. He was surprised at his roughness with her. He let her go, her mouth opening and closing like she wanted to say something more but she was speechless. "That sure stopped you talking," he said, as if apologizing, then they both laughed.

They were total opposites, and, in the way of this, they fell in love. Later, spending those dark jobless nights together in New York stripped them of any further hesitation. What they discovered about each other became more or less their rhythm from then on—Grace preferred Kyle unshaven, sweaty, unwashed from work or looking for work, talking obscenities into her ears. She arranged their bedroom like a gauzy stage set from the Arabian Nights. He would enter it like a pirate carrying off his prize. As their love games deepened, pushed to an edge just short of pain, Kyle was still uneasy about their role-playing—it felt against his nature, somehow. Then he made peace with it as what his wife desired—not lovemaking so much as him kidnapping her then subjecting her to a kind of gently controlled beating.

Kyle wondered if this evolution in their married life had something to do with their move that spring to Las Vegas—though Grace at first believed it was just for a visit to see Merle and Jeb, a well-deserved break from their hardest year so they could regroup and try it once more back East. Not that there was any reason to think so, still, Kyle just naturally associated the two life developments. Wasn't Las Vegas the place where anything goes? Open to all comers? Welcome to all kinds?

Not really—Kyle knew this was just hype from the ad agencies and Convention Authority. What drew people to live here was something else. Las Vegas was the best place in America for second chances. Losers were welcomed here. And America sorely needed such a place. More than half of all married couples split up in ruinous divorces, workers were being laid off from jobs at plants and factories by the thousands, four out of five small businesses went belly up, nine out of ten farmers lost their farms, three out of every twenty professionals failed at their practices or, worse, lost their licenses in other states. People were going bankrupt and getting stripped of everything with increasing frequency. The untold truth of America was that for every success story it was possible to find five-fold testimonies of people who had failed. If Las Vegas didn't exist already, the country would have had to invent it all over again just to relieve the pressure. Merle was right when he claimed that in Las Vegas it didn't matter what a person had been so much as what he was heading toward. It was simple casino logic and the very essence of gaming that, with each new bet placed, the past ceased to exist, it was the future that counted. Las Vegas was a city that had invented itself only by its own improbable vision for the future.

With a stake from his brother, Kyle and Grace rented a battered two-bedroom in the Sunrise Trailer Park near Merle and Jeb. "Impossible," Grace's Mom said when she found out, but they weren't there long. In the normal course of moving around town—asking a few tired-looking guys at Paddy's Pub who were just getting off work—Kyle landed a job punching a nail gun for a framing contractor busy tossing up cheap stucco tract homes in the scorpion and rattlesnake-infested hardpan that stretched off into the northwest of the Las Vegas Valley.

In those days of the boom, almost anyone with an able body could find work, and it took little enough ambition on Kyle's part to figure out he would be good at putting together his own crews. The trick in such a transient place was to develop an instinct for picking the kind of guys willing to work who would stay on for long enough. Kyle knew such men just by the expressions on their faces—he had seen it on his own face—that darkly troubled tiredness of the guy just barely making it here from someplace else, fully meaning to climb up out of defeat, powered by the earnestness of knowing he had less than a quarter tank of gas left in his car. And so at first it was three guys, then eight, then twelve, then finally up to sixty under Kyle's supervision knocking out stick frames one after another like stapling big cardboard boxes together and bolting them to concrete slab after slab after slab, the worst part of it the dizzying, exhausting heat in the summer months when their bodies evaporated out more water than they could keep down. His expanding crews subcontracted out in The Lakes then in Summerlin then Green Valley then Sun City then in the more luxurious tracts that gradually crawled and grew southeast into the black rock hills on the other side of which was the craggy slope down into Boulder City and the sapphire blue of Lake Mead.

And so Kyle's business grew as the city grew. He followed certain rules—never get too big, never be too greedy, no matter the pressure, don't ever go so fast as to leave behind mistakes; finally and above all, never pretend to be anything more than what you are. He believed this last rule was a key to the way the whole city was growing up around him, though it was also the Las Vegas paradox. With so many faux themed resorts rising up on the strip and becoming emblematic of the place—a scale-model Eiffel Tower over a plasterboard Paris, a stage set façade of the New York skyline, robot pirate ships, gas-powered volcanoes, indoor canals complete with singing gondoliers, and on and on with so much more, all of it with such patent-medicine fakeness and over-layering of designs so baroque and busy they clashed beyond any human capacity to take them in all at once—paradoxically, for all this fakeness, Las Vegas never pretended to be anything other than what it was. Even its gambling was thoroughly honest—odds were published and easily available for any slot machine and table game, all anybody had to do was ask for them on a casino floor. Las Vegas made no claim at offering anything real. With its hoopla of advertising, its chaos of fantasies, its games of chance, Las Vegas promised just exactly what it delivered—nothing less, little more. It was a city of representations. Underneath them, Las Vegas was the most honest city on earth.

Gradually—something he would never brag about—Kyle took on this sense of civic pride and vision of place as the city grew around him. He put in ten and twelve hour days, season after season, working with Richards Construction's ever growing crews spitting out their millions of nails in a moving assembly-line of strenuous labor and knuckle-scraping toil, putting up what amounted to the same half dozen basic designs of ranch or two-story structures that spread out in a monotonous simulacrum across a desert wasteland busy transforming itself into real estate and dreams. Kyle cut deals with real estate agents to get in on these developments. He moved Grace into them one after another—six houses in their first fifteen years—seeding in the grass, planting palm trees, digging the swimming pools, laying up the brick barbecues, then just when a neighborhood was finally looking lived in and shedding its dustblown newness with green lawns and streets full of kids, he sold the house for half more than what he paid for it and he and Grace moved again.

In Las Vegas, people rarely stayed in one place. This phenomenon was difficult for Grace to explain at first, "Yes, you know, in Vegas," she'd try to justify to her Mom, who was concerned about the stability of the kids. Grace would shut that up by getting her Dad on the phone to talk equity investments, pitched to him as though they were still putting together a stake big enough that they could move comfortably back to New York. Grace handled their money. Despite her tendency to go off and spend too much on what she always called "the best" in all she bought, she was good at managing money—far better than Kyle with his business degree. And Grace wasn't one to stay at home just mothering Tommy and Suze for very long either, preferring to keep current in her field by teaching at least two classes a semester at the new Community College in Henderson. "Poetry for the huddled masses," she called her courses. "Half these students claim not to know what a poem is, much less ever to have truly read one. Can that really be? Two or three in every class pull down six-figure salaries serving cocktails or tending bar. A valet parker in this town makes more than a junior stock broker in New York. So what use is poetry? In Vegas, this is the challenge."

Kyle heard it all, usually in bed, Grace musing her way toward her renewed sense of mission. "Somebody needs to represent real culture here," she'd say. Then she'd prop up a book in her lap and read poems to Kyle—he considered himself an educated reader, but contemporary poetry seemed increasingly senseless to him, words arranged not in stanzas but scattered like shotgun pellets all over the page. But he was glad enough just to listen to the happy tone of Grace's voice singing out the disattached sounds in her breathy way—like a ringing of just slightly off-key wind chimes—refreshing, lulling him to sleep after his long days out pounding nails with his crews in hellish heat, after he and Grace had put the kids to bed under the humming breezes of the central air conditioning, after he had done his briganding duty as a husband by busting into her palace bedroom in his dusty work boots, roughing her up a little as she desired, carrying her off and away.

All in all, he thought, it was a good life, what they had built here together. Kyle only wished that Grace would admit to how good it was and quit apologizing for the place in that dismissive tone, "Yes, you know, in Vegas . . ."

He had to leave the room every time. He scolded her about it, "Why can't you admit that we live here? That this is our home?"

"Why do you keep moving us?" she asked. "There must be something here that makes people feel they can't possibly be staying."

"Damnit, Grace, we're happy here!"

"I love it when you get mad like this," was all she said.

As much as for Grace to accept their lives, Kyle also wished his brother Jeb could find some happiness, could make a better life. He had tried to get Jeb in on his business, move him into a real house, get him more involved with people. But Jeb persisted stubbornly staying just where he was, taking care of Merle, both of them getting stuck in their same old patterns. After a while, Kyle realized that— save for the occasional holiday or Sunday dinner and the times he dropped the kids off to visit—he hardly saw his father and brother anymore. Kyle began not to see them in other ways too, as if thinking of his brother and father in a kind of blur among all the rest of the numerous but seldom noted in this town—not unlike blackjack slowpokes to catch on to the next turn in the deal, slot junkies left wishing they'd cashed out when, bingo players holding unfilled cards—the ones who crawled back and forth through the six-lane traffic jams in the parade of fortune who found it ever more difficult to raise up their spirits with hope, sitting there frustrated in their cars, totaling up their losses in their heads while waiting for their lane to inch a few feet forward and the next day to bring them more of the same, the same, the same, the same. Jeb was among the ones who had never moved. And if Jeb wouldn't move—or couldn't move—Kyle wished his brother at least could have better settled in and come to terms.

Three days before Christmas, Jeb called from Desert Springs Hospital. "He sat down on the couch to watch TV after his shower like he always did. He said his elbow hurt. Then Dad turned blue and that was it. Gone. Paramedics tried to revive him but no dice," he said.

After Kyle got off the phone, as he was pulling on his clothes to drive off to the hospital, Grace said, "Let's not wake the kids with this. They just finished wrapping Merle's gifts. They'll be up all night." Then, as if she recognized how cold she sounded, she said, "I'm sorry. But it's not as though this is unexpected."

Later, as Kyle was dragging Merle's old stinking couch out into the side yard of that falling-apart doublewide—the couch spooked Jeb, as if he could still see Merle sitting on it, dead—Jeb let loose about how they had lived. "You don't understand, Kyle, how it's been for me. Like a full-time job, setting a clock to get up and go with him to the casinos to play his wrong way dice—you know, gambling on the losers, doubling up his bets on the 'no pass' line until a table just went cold and all the players went away. He'd wheel me into line for the lunch buffets or use his comp coupons at the coffee shops. Afternoons, it was sitting around with him nursing beers at the sports books. Watching him flirt with the cocktail waitresses. Listening to his same old jokes. Every day. Day in, day out. Worse than work, me having to slip him cash at the end of most months to keep staking him. Think about it Kyle, how damned oppressive all that's been. Twenty some odd years since we left the homeplace. Is that any kind of life?"

Kyle didn't say anything about the other things he knew they did—weekly rides out into the desert with their rifles to shoot targets, and that time they took Tommy and Suze to fire a machine gun at the Desert Arms Emporium on Tropicana, where Merle often traded. Grace had had a fit about that one, "Does your Dad really think it's educational to put an automatic weapon in the hands of an eight-year-old?" Then after Suze told her grandma, Grace was on the phone again, "Yes, you know, Mom, in Vegas . . ."

And Merle and Jeb had occasional escapades with those flim-flam exotic dancers advertised in lewd pamphlets "direct to your room" all over town that they'd call up when Merle was especially flush from a banner day at the tables, after one of which Grace wouldn't let Kyle drop the kids off unsupervised at her in-laws for almost a year. "Both of them? Not just Tommy, but Suze, too? Watching Jeb paint a screaming eagle across some cheap dancer's naked breasts? And your Dad saying it was all just harmless fun? Do you realize almost anyplace else they could get arrested for this? Kyle?"

Jesus, Kyle thought, at least the old man got to see his grandkids. Not that this had been much of a life for Jeb—Kyle understood that his brother had done the obligatory duty as a son to Merle, filling in with him in ways Kyle never could have, he wouldn't have had the patience, as if still making up somehow for the old man's loss. Jeb's twenty-two years in Las Vegas must have felt more like a sentence to house arrest than any life of his own.

That night, after driving Jeb back home from Desert Springs, Kyle watched him pushing restlessly back and forth across the carpet worn deep with ruts from his wheelchair, streaks and patches stained with gun oil and engine grease from when Merle used to set up repair projects on the coffee table in front of the TV in the evenings. Kyle noted the stainless steel dog dish still in its place by the refrigerator—gleaming there like a silver dollar—left in its spot after Jeb's dog died of old age. Jeb's face was pasty and pale, showing a bluish veneer of skin kept too long out of the sun. His eyes were red rimmed, hollow looking, unable to focus, as if still staring off into blinking lights on casino floors.

"So . . . what do you think you'll do now?" Kyle asked.

"Get that damned shovel off the wall," Jeb said.

Kyle hunted through drawers to find a hammer, then he stood in the empty space where the couch had been and bent back the nails holding up Merle's old irrigation shovel—even through the greasy dust and cobwebs clinging to it, he felt the slick wear on the handle, how its weight balanced familiarly in his hands. He could see again all those dawns out in the fields, the way they grew up, the three of them laboring together in the irrigation ditches piling dirt on the canvas dams amid the storms of deer flies and mosquitoes, directing glistening streams of water out onto their newly planted fields. The memory was something solid after what they had been through—the grim disorienting paperwork filled out at the emergency room amid the hurt people and their families lining up in pain, and the shock of seeing Merle's death written there in black and white. In the space for "Disposition of the Body," Jeb scrawled, "Palm Mortuary, your basic burn," then signed his name while still clutching a plastic tie bag containing Merle's watch and keys. After all that, the shovel's weight felt grounding somehow, and comforting, like the voice of a friend. Kyle was a little reluctant to let it go.

Jeb reached for the shovel and balanced it across his lap. Kyle followed as Jeb awkwardly jockeyed his wheelchair and the shovel out onto the back steps, metal parts banging angrily into the flimsy frame of the trailer door. For a minute, the two brothers braced themselves at the top of the porch ramp.

"You could move in with us," Kyle said.

"Grace would never put up with me," Jeb said.

"We could make it work," Kyle said.

"Forget it," Jeb said. "Besides, I might like the chance to live on my own."

Kyle shivered, not so much with the chill of the desert night as with the weather of grief Jeb wheeled around everywhere with him, something the events of this night only deepened. Change seemed promised now. Still, nothing could really change for Jeb. He wouldn't move. He would wheel himself four blocks down the avenue from the trailerpark to the supermarket shopping center and fill his lap with his daily needs, then he'd wheel himself back home—there and back again, two times a day, as he had been doing for years. He'd hole up, alone in his bitterness in front of the television, day in, day out, with the only difference that he would hardly get out at all now that Merle was gone. He was stuck here. And Jeb would stay stuck here. Kyle would ask himself if he could have managed things for his brother differently, and how much of his brother's condition was really his fault. He would keep searching through his memories looking for that one crucial moment when he might have intervened to avoid the future he saw spread out before them now—for Jeb mainly filled with loss and regret, and for himself ever wondering why. Why did so few achieve all the success while the others were left stranded out in the desert? Why?

They waited there on the porch landing a long time, it seemed, just breathing in the chill night air. Red aircraft warning lights on the Hilton tower blinked in the distance; a low winter cloud cover lay painted with a vivid orange glow vibrating up from the simmering cauldron of the city. Jeb gripped the shovel, hefting it to his shoulder like a clumsy spear. He flung it off into the night with a primitive cry.

GREGORY CROSBY [B. 1967]

In downtown Las Vegas, between Fourth Street and Las Vegas Boulevard, there is a quiet public plaza with a gurgling stream, reflecting pond, pedestrian bridge, benches, tasteful street-lights, and an outdoor stage for live music, poetry, and art events. Known as the Poet's Bridge, this plaza is the centerpiece of Las Vegas's twenty-first-century downtown revitalization plan, a tiny oasis of high culture for locals, bravely championing community arts, even in the midst of the tourist megalopolis that Las Vegas has become. A bronze plaque near the stage displays the poem by Gregory Crosby reprinted here, entitled "The Long Shot," a tribute to the history and phenomenal growth of this odds-defying desert city. Crosby grew up in Las Vegas and became a poet, editor, and freelance journalist. He wrote a column about Vegas history and art criticism for the Las Vegas Mercury *and* Las Vegas City Life *weekly newspapers and aired arts commentaries on* KNPR. *Winner of a Nevada Arts Council Fellowship, Crosby's work has appeared widely in publications such as* Neon, Red Rock Review, *the* Las Vegas Sun, SCOPE *magazine,* Time Out, *and* Artweek, *and his chapbooks include* Revenge of a Mortal Hand *(1998) and* Satan's Skull Glows White Hot *(2000). In 2004 Crosby moved to New York City to pursue an* MFA *in creative writing at the City College of New York. Reflecting on the entertainment districts of the two cities, Crosby observed: "Everybody's postcard is someone else's backyard. The Strip and Times Square might be gaudy contrivances for wide-eyed visitors, but they're fascinating places, kept running by real people with stories of their own. They are intrinsically interesting even if they are stage-managed by global corporations or merger-crazed gaming companies."*

The Long Shot

> *On the dedication of the Poet's Bridge, Lewis Avenue Corridor, Las Vegas, September 24, 2002*

After the springs that brought them, after the fort, abandoned;
After ranches became grids and lots became cottages and gardens;
After white men in high collars stood in sunlight's oven, checking
Their railroad watches; after the dice began to tumble and the river
Became a lake, subdued by its concrete mansion; after the citizens
Grew whiskers every May, and played the pioneer while a giant
Cowboy of neon greeted them with a *Howdy* like thunder; after
They worked and drank and stopped at that first sign of Permission,
Sign of the Windmill; after the gunners learned their deadly art,
Preparing the sky for the scattering of atoms; after the Psychopath
Brought glamour and death and *businessmen* with strange names
Who skimmed the new sea of green like birds diving at the bounty
Of the oceans; after the Voice became a Chairman, and the lounge
Became a temple; after girls became feathered, legs up to necks,
And fantasy sprung wildly from the arid land in every direction;
After a billionaire scrubbed his thin hands yet again while a King
Re-enacted, nightly, his coronation, and *Our Thing* withered into

The bottom lines of corporations; after white tigers roamed, and
Juice flowed like elixir of life from every connection; after the boom,
The tile and the stucco, sprinkler heads gushing while the turnstile
Spun and 4,000 came each month for new starts, their second and
Third and fourth chances; after the implosions, the unions, the
Retirees, the families that raised their children, the American
Dreamers who beat the odds and those who lost, the suckers, the
Addicted; after all this, when the springs of pleasure and promise,
Of profit and providence have long since expired, dry as the
Font that once drew the thirst of the weary into the valley, and
The cities that line the boulevard of this city fall into ruin,

They will look upon us, saying, They made their own luck.
Selling it to all takers, they built a world like no other,
And lived in it, and thrived there, and shone and sparkled,
Glittering in the sleepless night, each of them a facet,
A brilliance, of the strange diamond they had fashioned;
A million to one that such a place ever happened.

John C. Frémont. Courtesy of Nevada Historical Society.

Dan De Quille. Courtesy of Special
Collections, University of Nevada, Reno
Library.

Mark Twain (Samuel L. Clemens). Photograph by
Bradley & Rulofson, ca. 1860s. Courtesy of Special
Collections, University of Nevada, Reno Library.

John Muir at Yosemite National Park, 1907. Courtesy of the National Park Service, Yosemite National Park. Photograph of John Muir, RL-4398. Photograph by Francis M. Fultz.

Sarah Winnemucca (Thocmetony) in lecture attire of her own design, ca. 1870s.
Courtesy of Nevada Historical Society.

ABOVE: Sam P. Davis. Courtesy of Special
Collections, University of Nevada, Reno
Library.

LEFT: Idah Meacham Strobridge. The cap
by Strobridge reads, "taken by herself 250
from a photograph gallery—otherwise you
should have a more conventionally arrang
picture. Yours—without apology—The
Bookbinder." Courtesy of Nevada Historic
Society.

ABOVE: Wovoka, Paiute prophet. Courtesy of Nevada
Historical Society.

RIGHT: Will James. Courtesy of Special Collections,
University of Nevada, Reno Library.

Lucius Beebe with Mr. T-Bone Towser, Virginia City, 1953. Gift of Lucius Beebe, 1964. Courtesy of Special Collections, University of Nevada, Reno Library.

Walter Van Tilburg Clark. Photograph by Arthur Winfield Knight. Courtesy of Special Collections, University of Nevada, Reno Library.

Nell Murbarger, the "Roving Reporter of the Desert," Grantsville ghost town, Nevada, ca. 1952. Courtesy of Stanley W. Paher Collection.

Sessions S. Wheeler, Pyramid Lake, Nevada. Photograph from *The Desert Lake* (1967), courtesy of Caxton Press, Caldwell, Idaho.

ABOVE LEFT: Arthur Miller. Edward Olsen photograph
collection. Courtesy of Special Collections, University of
Nevada, Reno Library.
RIGHT: Jean McElrath. Courtesy of Jean Wagner.

Corbin Harney, All Nations Healing Ceremony, Nevada Test Site, April 1991. Photograph by Will Powers. Courtesy of Will Powers.

TOP: A. Wilber Stevens. Courtesy of Special Collections, University of Nevada, Las Vegas Library.

BOTTOM: Georgie C. Sicking. Photograph by Reed Bingham. Courtesy of the artist.

Sammy Davis Jr. at the Copa Room,
Sands Hotel, Las Vegas, 1966. Sands Hotel
Collection. Courtesy of Special Collections,
University of Nevada, Las Vegas Library.

Stephen S. N. Liu.
Courtesy of Stephen S. N. Liu.

Rollan Melton. Courtesy of Marilyn R. Melton.

Dennis Parks. Photograph by Valerie Parks. Courtesy of Dennis Parks.

Phyllis Barber. Photograph by John Aldrich. Courtesy of Phyllis Barber.

H. Lee Barnes. Courtesy of H. Lee Barnes.

ABOVE, LEFT: Susan Berman. Photograph by Mary Ellen
Mark. Courtesy of Mary Ellen Mark, Falkland Road, Inc.
RIGHT: Adrian C. Louis. Courtesy of Adrian C. Louis.

Kirk Robertson. Photograph by Valerie J. Serpa. Courtesy of
Kirk Robertson.

ABOVE: Waddie Mitchell, cowboy poet. Photograph by Donald Kallaus.
Courtesy of Western Jubliee Recording Company.

FACING PAGE: William L. Fox. Photograph by Tony Hansen. Courtesy of William L. Fox.

ABOVE, LEFT: nila northSun. Photograph by
Kirk Robertson, ca. 1979. Courtesy of R. L. Crow
Publications, publisher of *love at gunpoint* (2007).
RIGHT: Shaun T. Griffin. Photograph by Media
Production, University of Nevada, Reno.

IN OUR BACKYARD

Notes from Nuclear Nevada

Responsible for creating economic prosperity in a desert state, Nevada's political leaders have endorsed some unconventional projects, sponsoring the Newlands Reclamation Act in 1902 to "make the desert bloom," legalizing gambling in 1931, and bringing atomic testing to Nevada in the early 1950s. Senator Pat McCarran is said to have worked hard to convince the Atomic Energy Commission and President Truman to relocate small-scale, strategic-weapons atomic testing from the Marshall Islands to southern Nevada, a more practical location from a logistics standpoint. Nellis Air Force Range, ninety-five miles northwest of Las Vegas, already occupied a huge restricted area the size of Rhode Island. Why not put all that empty land in Nevada to good use? Nevada could serve national interests, and the federal government would invest millions of dollars and create thousands of jobs in Nevada. A win-win deal, so the thinking went. The first atomic bomb was detonated at the Nevada Test Site in January 1951, kicking off a series of atmospheric blasts—averaging about one a month—until 1963, when the tests continued underground. In 1952 Nevada Governor Charles Russell praised the program: "It's exciting to think that the submarginal land of the proving ground is furthering science and helping national defense. We had long ago written off that terrain as wasteland, and today it's blooming with atoms." Although Nevada was promised that tests would remain small, over the years "kiloton creep" occurred, rendering the atmospheric nuclear tests ever more deadly. The move to underground testing paved the way for even larger, thermonuclear weapons, a movement fueled by cold war deterrence strategy and optimistic hopes that peaceful uses could be found for nuclear weapons.

Initial concerns that atomic testing would discourage tourism were allayed by a brilliant marketing plan that turned the bomb into another Las Vegas attraction. Atomic cocktails, atomic hairdos, and even a Miss Atom Bomb contest made the bomb a lot of fun. Special calendars showed blast dates, casinos offered box lunches for bomb viewing, and an image of a mushroom cloud graced the seal of Clark County. Out at the Test Site, scientists and experimenters gave free play to their imaginations. They constructed "Doom Town" to determine how a nuclear blast would affect an average American house, and in an experiment whimsically called "Charge of the Swine Brigade," they dressed pigs in uniforms and penned them near ground zero to test fire-retardant fabrics.

It stopped being fun when reports reached the public about flocks of sheep killed by fallout, weird radiation burns and mysterious ailments among Test Site workers, and high rates of cancer downwind of the blasts. By the 1970s an antinuclear protest movement was building, and in 1993 President Bush signed a moratorium on U.S. nuclear tests for that fiscal year. To that date, more than nine hundred nuclear bombs had been exploded in Nevada, the most bombed state in America. After 1993, "subcritical" tests continued, as did citizen protest, organized in annual Mother's Day gatherings outside the Test Site, including speeches by elders of the Western Shoshone nation, whose official claim to the ancestral lands occupied by the Test Site dates back to the 1863 Treaty of Ruby Valley.

In the 1980s the U.S. government chose Nevada for yet another important service to the nation, this time to host a proposed high-level radioactive waste repository at Yucca Mountain, within the Test Site, that would provide storage for ten thousand years for seventy thousand metric tons of nuclear waste. Again, beaucoup money would flow to Nevada, and stringent safety precautions would naturally be taken. But once burned, twice shy. This time Nevada's public officials and the vast majority of its citizens balked, employing every means at their disposal to deter the nuke dump. At this writing, the fate of Yucca Mountain hangs in the balance.

This chapter begins with a group of pieces about nuclear testing, presented in the order of their publication, from Frank Waters's *Woman at Otowi Crossing,* first published in 1966, to Curtis Oberhansly and Dianne Nelson Oberhansly's *Downwinders: An Atomic Tale* (2001). Following this group are pieces that treat the Yucca Mountain project, beginning with Corbin Harney's *The Way It Is,* a transition piece about both nuclear testing and nuclear waste, written from a Western Shoshone point of view. From there, pieces proceed chronologically, concluding with James Conrad's *Making Love to the Minor Poets of Chicago* (2000), which features a satirical tour of Yucca Mountain. Some writers included in this chapter also appear elsewhere in the anthology, where their biographical headnotes are located. The brief headnotes here focus exclusively on their nuclear concerns.

FRANK WATERS [1902–1995]

One of the Southwest's most important writers, Frank Waters was born in Colorado Springs, Colorado, to an Anglo mother and a father whom Waters believed to be part Cheyenne. After studying engineering at Colorado College, Waters became a laborer in the oil fields of Wyoming and a telephone engineer in Southern California, near Mexicali, where he wrote his novel The Lizard Woman *(1929) in his spare time. The 1930s saw the semiautobiographical novels* The Wild Earth's Nobility *(1935),* Below Grass Roots *(1937), and* Dust within the Rock *(1940), which all take a serious look at mining in the West and were later edited into the single volume* Pike's Peak *(1971). Waters's move to Taos, New Mexico, in the late 1930s strengthened his interest in Native American culture and religion and the mythos of the Southwest. Criticized by East Coast publishers for his "regional" settings, Waters replied that "all writers are regional writers. . . . Good ones create works that go beyond their 'local color,' imbuing universal values." This he did. A Taos-based patron of the arts, Mabel Dodge Luhan, and her husband Tony Luhan, a Taos Pueblo Indian, befriended Waters and inspired his most popular book,* The Man Who Killed the Deer *(1942), which examines the impact of Euro-American culture on Native Americans, particularly contrasting religious philosophies between the two cultures.* The Woman at Otowi Crossing *(1966), which went through thirteen revisions, explores the meeting of "the Indian drum and the atom smasher" during the time Waters worked as an information consultant for the Los Alamos Scientific Laboratory in New Mexico and at the Nevada Test Site near Las Vegas.*

from *The Woman at Otowi Crossing*

Riding high on an expense account, Turner registered at Aladdin's Palace and walked back across acres of velvet lawn surrounded by tropical palms to his luxurious room.

Next morning, with other members of the national press corps, he drove out to see the obverse side of the ironic paradox that had selected the vicinity of Las Vegas for the site of the nuclear tests. . . . They came to a vast, squalid disarray of tents, makeshift barracks and rubber water tanks: Camp Desert Rock, just established by the Army to quarter troops which would participate in military maneuvers connected with the tests.

A few miles off the highway the reporters were stopped. The road to the test site was barred to unauthorized visitors by a pass gate. Armed security officers in jeeps patrolled the near boundary. The entire perimeter was patrolled by a plane to keep out stray hunters and prospectors. Even air traffic over the area was controlled.

Turner swore. "Just like the Hill! How are we expected to see anything?"

There was only one available vantage point. A rutted mountain road snaked up 12,000-foot Mount Charleston to an open ridge on Angel's Peak. Here, fifty-three miles away, they could look northward into the remote desert valley hemmed in by the landmarks of an almost forgotten era: Specter Range and Skull Mountain, Emigrant Valley, Pahranagat Valley, Arrow Canyon, Pint Water and Papoose Range, and the Sheep Mountains. A tingle of excitement raced up Turner's spine. Down there glistened the ancient lake beds of Yucca Flat, Frenchman's Flat and Jackass Flat. There too protruded the foundations of the old ghost mining camp of Wahmoni that had been one of his Whistle Stops. What was going on down there now? The whole world wanted to know.

So every midnight these pioneer press members of the Atom Bomb Watchers Society, as they called themselves, left the plushy confines of Aladdin's Palace, their bars and casinos, and drove through darkness and bitter cold to the snowdrifts on Angel's Peak. The test shots would be held on undisclosed days at dawn. Cameramen braced their tripods against the howling wind, opened their shutters as the time neared. Swathed in blankets, huddled in coats and gloves, the reporters kept waiting.

Then one morning, just before dawn, it finally came. A flash of blinding light that lit up the crinkled desert mountains, the rocks at their feet. A livid red fireball dangled suspended before them. Murkily changing into a monstrous, convoluting doughnut fried in the satanic fat of blast and heat. Swiftly expanding into a giant mushroom cloud shearing off from its dust stem and slowly rising into the stratosphere like a genie out of an uncorked bottle. It was then the shock wave reached them, gently shaking the rooted mountain.

"Christ Almighty God!" Were there no translators of Government gobbledygook, no fission poets to sing hallelujah to these spectral fungi born of a poisonous age? They flung into their cars and roared down the mountainside to file their feverish announcements at the first telephone. "VEGANS ATOMIZED!" The continental atomic test series had begun.

. . . .

Back in town Turner watched from a rooftop the gorgeous annual parade of Helldorado week. Nine sheriffs' posses on matched palominos with silver-mounted gear, resort hotel floats filled with chorus girls, a band of Paiute Indians, bathing beauties, covered wagons, surries and buckboards, a miniature Boulder Dam, and finally the prize entry—the Twenty Mule Team Borax Wagon that had hauled borax out of Death Valley, and which was driven by the last, aging mule skinner. Over it now swept a squadron of jets. At the exact moment they roared overhead, there burst from the horizon another mushroom cloud. The photographer beside him caught it all in a single frame—the past and future of the gigantic paradox which was America itself.

. . . .

Turner was getting impatient. The frequency of the test shots was increasing and so was their intensity. The power of the detonations had increased to twenty-five times that of the 20,000 tons TNT equivalent of the initial Trinity blast. Photos of the Los Angeles City Hall lit up by the flash no longer made the front pages. The flash was now being reported as seen as far away as Kalispel, Montana. The tests, for the press corps, had lost their novelty and were taking on a practical aspect that a minimum of declassified information would not satisfy.

"To hell with all these paper handouts!" stormed Turner, speaking for the group. "When are we going to be allowed to see a Big Bang itself?"

There was no denying their demands. So one day in March came an announcement from Washington that an inspection tour and an "Open Shot" would be held for the press.

Early on the morning of D-day minus one they left Las Vegas in Security-escorted buses, and this time the pass gate opened to let them through—the first eyes of the outside world permitted to see the Valley Where the Giant Mushrooms Grew.

Turner stared with amazement at the vast array of barracks, mess halls, warehouses and shops that constituted Camp Mercury, the base camp housing the scientists and workers. Twenty miles north, after entering another guard gate to the Forward Area, the buses climbed up the familiar rocky pass separating Frenchman's Flat and Yucca Flat. On it now stood a huge, doubly-reinforced concrete blockhouse without windows save for inch-thick glass portholes. This was Control Point, the electronic nerve center of the test site. Turner got out and with the other correspondents silently paraded through its labyrinth of rooms to the control room. Everything possible had been declassified for their inspection: arrays of electronic equipment, instrument panels, frequency control indicators and gadgetry beyond their comprehension.

"What's the idea of always shooting so early in the morning?" a reporter asked boldly.

Patiently a scientist explained. Darkness was needed to obtain the best possible photography of the second's lifetime of an explosion. For this the fastest high-speed camera in the world had been developed at Los Alamos. It could take successive pictures at the rate of fifteen million frames a second, supplementing other devices that registered impressions every one-hundred-millionth of a second, the standard of measurement called a "shake." But also light was needed for the maneuvering of planes immediately after the detonation. So the shot was scheduled for predawn to meet both requirements.

· · · · · · · ·

[Turner] was relieved when the buses took off for the prize display in the show. They leapt out of the sandy plain with all the human frailty and tragic intensity that forever bespeaks our faulty comprehension, the weakness of our flesh, and the brief tenure of our days; that appeal to the heart of man rather than to his intellect. They were two modern, six-room, frame houses completely furnished, which might have stood on the corner of Main and Elm Street in any little town in America. A town which suddenly and unknowingly at dawn tomorrow was doomed to be blasted forever off the face of the earth. Doom Town, U.S.A.

The house Turner entered, only 3,500 feet from the tower, was occupied by a large family of plaster dummies, completely dressed, with their lifelike faces painted and powdered. All the Mannequins were oblivious of their impending doom. In the living room Mr. Mannequin lounged in his easy chair, watching TV. On the floor beside him sprawled two staring children; a smaller one was bellied out before a book of comics.

Mr. Mannequin was not a man to bother about those queer and complicated atom doings in far off Nevada, nor to worry about the world situation in general. "I'm just too doggone tired when I get home from work," Turner seemed to hear him say. "Taxes, rising prices, all that's enough worry for me. With all the kids we got, it's too expensive to go to the movies too often. Besides, a fellow likes to loaf around his own home."

In the dining room the table was already set. Mrs. Mannequin was out in the kitchen cooking dinner. The refrigerator door was open, showing fresh vegetables, milk, eggs, and the remains of a roast waiting to be made into hash. The pantry shelves were stocked with canned goods, packaged cereals, glasses of jelly and preserves. "Yes, we're getting along right fine now that Mr. Mannequin got a little raise," she seemed to say. "We've paid for the car. Now we can start to set a bit aside for a rainy day. It's a little town that'll never be famous for anything, but we like it. A good place to raise kids. They can ride their bicycles to school."

Upstairs a teen-age daughter was primping for her boy friend; she wanted to look like Mimi de Vere in her latest movie . . . Yes, a nice homey family, these Mannequins, but not without a heartache, too. An older boy, Hank Mannequin, had run away from home and they had not heard from him.

Turner crept out feeling like an interloper. A car was pulled up in the driveway with its door open, and on the ground lay a doll. Turner picked it up and placed it carefully on the seat so the car would not run over it. Somebody in the crowd let out a raucous laugh. For over the Mannequins, over all Doom Town, hung a threat that not even a doll could escape.

Riding back to Las Vegas, Turner heard a correspondent talking in the seat behind. "Now who the hell would steal one of those dummies? And how—out of that house, out of a firing area in the most carefully guarded spot in the whole country! And for what? It beats me!"

That night Turner rolled and tossed in his pink sheets in Aladdin's Palace. He dreamed of Helen Chalmers. Dressed in a white nightgown, she was sitting in an armchair on Angel's Peak and looking down on a simple, homey family that would never see the sun rise.

"Why does it have to be us?" they pleaded. "We've never hurt anybody! Can't you find a better way?"

The telephone rang. It was 2:00 AM, D-day, and time to get up . . .

Again in cold and darkness the buses rushed through the desert night. Past Camp Desert Rock where boy-troops were being loaded into trucks and half-tracks. Past Camp Mercury. Past Control Point ablaze with lights. To unload finally at an abrupt rise of jagged volcanic rock on the shore of the ancient Yucca Lake where an enterprising newsman had stuck up a sign: News Knob.

In the flicker of lights Turner saw rows of benches and tables at which the reporters could pound out their copy. Signal Corps vans providing radio-teletype circuits over which they could file it for transmittal to the nation's waiting press. TV and radio transmitters. A coffee stand. Loud-speaker. A couple of latrines. And stretching out in front of him a dark and naked immensity in which glowed a single light—a 100-watt lamp in the tower cab seven miles away. Doom Town was dark. In their white, two-story house at Main and Elm the Mannequins were peacefully sleeping. Mr. Mannequin faced a hard day at the office. Mrs. Mannequin's face wore a pleasant smile; she had hidden away in the cookie jar $2.80 for her weekly bridge game that afternoon.

The agonizing wait began. Cameramen scurried up News Knob, wedging their tripods between rocks. Reporters got out typewriters with fumbling fingers. The loud-speaker commentary began.

"H-hour minus 15 minutes! Attention please! High density goggles are being issued at the foot of this stand. Last call for dark glasses! Repeat . . ."

Longer and longer lines formed in front of the latrines. "What the hell you doing here again, Turner? You no sooner get to the head of the line till you're back at the foot!"

Shivering with cold nervousness, Turner buttoned up his coat and stared at the desert mountains beginning to take outline against the sky. Above them he could see the dim vapor trails of the planes boring in on their prescribed flight patterns.

The minutes dragged by, each doled out from a dwindling measure. He was before his typewriter on the table now, stiff with cold but feeling a drop of sweat running down his cheek.

"H minus one minute. Put on your high density goggles or face away from the blast. Repeat. Do not face the flash without high density goggles."

Turner flung a quick look around. Men were crouched at tables or backed against rocks, all braced for the shock. The lights went off. In the wan dawn the flat shone like a tranquil sea. Beyond it a Joshua tree bristled weirdly against the horizon.

The count-down began.

"Ten seconds!"

"Five."

Turner leaned forward, gripping the edge of the table. The goggles over his eyes were so dark he could see nothing. It was as if he were shrouded in a blackness that nothing could ever penetrate.

"One!"

He lowered his head, closed his eyes . . . The abrupt, brilliant, and blinding flash of a hundred suns struck his eyeballs. Men, mountains, everything around him stood out insubstantial and without shadow in that silent gush of clear, cold and pitiless white light. He stared transfixed at its focal point. It was ballooning now into what might have been a monstrous, flaming planet suspended in space before him.

A draft of hot air struck his shivering body. Turner did not notice it. For as he jerked off his goggles, he saw the swiftly expanding fireball beginning to boil in writhing convolutions of purple, orange and iodine.

The blast wave rolled in with a jarring shock; simultaneously he heard a sharp crack whose thunderous roar kept echoing from the surrounding desert mountains. Turner could not tear his gaze from the rising fireball. It was clouding over into a giant puff ball, and sucking up from the ground a stem of dust and debris.

From deep in his memory the image leapt immediately from his mind to his fingers. He knew it now! The monstrous *Amanita Virosa*, the Destroying Angel, the most poisonous fungus of its species. There was the frill around the upper stem, the discolored bag at the bottom, the wrinkled blades of the gill hanging down from the underside of the cap. Bigger, higher, it still kept climbing. An ice sheet formed on top of its rounded cap, its glossy whiteness reflecting the first rays of the sun. The Destroying Angel was full formed now. Tall, stately, shimmering with the satiny whiteness of absolute innocence; yet raining down its invisible, poisonous spores upon the earth, the cacti and the lizard in the sand, the rattlesnake and the skittering bird . . . This was the image Turner's mind saw, the head to the story his fingers pecked out on the typewriter. This was the unconscious way a man worked, cold and nervous in the dawn, facing an indescribable reality; as a man must work or not at all.

By the time the mushroom cloud had ascended to 40,000 feet and began its slow drift around the planet, Turner had filed his copy. Now the wait began anew, this time in the blazing sun. The flames of burning Joshua trees died down, but across the barren lake bed clouds of dust still rolled. Not until mid-afternoon did the buses load and take off toward the site of Doom Town.

A few miles out they were stopped by a radiation monitor. He was dressed in his booties, gloves and protective clothing, wearing his oxygen mask, and carrying his detection instrument. In the barren immensity he looked as a man may someday look when he stands for the first time on the barren surface of a new planet in outer space.

"I'm sorry," he said. "The radiation level is too high for you to proceed farther."

Clouds of radioactive dust still hung above the sandy plain. Turner could not see where Doom Town had been. Nor was he disappointed at not being able to view the wreckage on the corner of Main and Elm. Doom Town, like Wahmoni on Jackass Flat, like all the other vanished ghost towns, belonged to the past. All the Mannequins had perished save Hank, the Outcast of Yucca Flat, the boy who had run away from home. Turner wondered what had become of him as he rode back to Las Vegas.

Two weeks later he found out. ANS released a news item datelined Portland, Oregon, stating that Hank Mannequin's headless body had been found in the Willamette River by the Harbor Patrol. A glass jar was tied around his waist. In it was a note which read:

They took my Mom and Pop, my brothers and sisters, to use in the atom bomb test. That's not for me. Goodbye cruel world.

WILLIAM STAFFORD [1914–1993]

Additional biographical information for William Stafford appears on p. 293. As a conscientious objector during World War II, Stafford spent four years in church-supported Civilian Public Service camps, an experience recalled in his 1947 memoir Down in My Heart: *"It was unnerving to wake up in a barracks and find ourselves almost totally alien, proscribed, lost, tagged, orphaned, outlawed. . . . [I]n order to avoid participation in the large violence of our immediate society—and thus to stay true to a larger society—we found it necessary to act in such a way as to arouse the antagonism of our neighbors." Having stood true to his commitment to nonviolence, even under the most difficult of circumstances, Stafford was profoundly troubled by America's postwar development of atomic weapons. "At the Bomb Testing Site," collected in Stafford's* Stories That Could Be True: New and Collected Poems *(1977), conveys his sense of foreboding and epitomizes many of the traits that make Stafford's work so popular, important, and accessible. Chief among these is the way that Stafford personifies elements of the landscape, and many readers have seen the lizard in this poem as a prime example. As one critic has written, "The lizard and human kind . . . are both gripping the sand and wondering what the fallout, literal and figurative, of nuclear technology will produce."*

At the Bomb Testing Site

> At noon in the desert a panting lizard
> waited for history, its elbows tense,
> watching the curve of a particular road
> as if something might happen.
>
> It was looking at something farther off
> than people could see, an important scene
> acted in stone for little selves
> at the flute end of consequences.
>
> There was just a continent without much on it
> under a sky that never cared less.
> Ready for a change, the elbows waited.
> The hands gripped hard on the desert.

DENISE LEVERTOV [1923–1997]

In 1953 the Atomic Energy Commission launched Operation Upshot-Knothole at the Nevada Test Site, detonating a series of eleven nuclear bombs whose combined force totaled over 250 kilotons, about twenty times the power of the atom bomb that destroyed Hiroshima. Thousands of servicemen—later known as "atomic vets"—were exposed to the blasts as they hunkered down in trenches within two miles of the blast site. The government also experimented with nonhuman subjects, confining sheep, rabbits, and pigs at varying distances from ground zero. The pigs were dressed in special clothes, made from the same fabric as army uniforms. These bizarre tests were featured in Chris Beaver's award-winning Dark Circle *(1983), a haunting antinuclear documentary about the effects of plutonium. Denise Levertov wrote the following poem after watching that film. A leading antiwar activist and outspoken opponent of nuclear energy and nuclear testing, Levertov grew up in "a house full of books" in Essex, England, and was home-schooled by her Welsh mother and Russian Jewish father, who later became an Anglican priest. She served as a nurse during World War II and witnessed the terrifying air raids on London. Levertov married the American writer Mitchell Goodman, moving to the United States in 1948, where she became a naturalized citizen, befriended poets Kenneth Rexroth and William Carlos Williams, and earned a reputation as a distinguished American poet, publishing more than twenty-five volumes of poetry along with collections of essays and reviews. Committed to being "a poet in the world," Levertov held professorships at both Tufts and Stanford, joined the "Ban the Bomb" movement of the 1950s, and later protested the Vietnam War, nuclear arms proliferation, American intervention in El Salvador, and the Persian Gulf War. Criticized by some for writing political poetry, Levertov replies that she writes out of her own experience, creating poems that are both politically engaged and lyrical.*

Watching Dark Circle

> *Why, this is hell, nor am I out of it . . .*
> Marlowe, *Dr. Faustus*

Men are willing to observe
the writhing, the bubbling flesh and
swift but protracted charring of bone
while the subject pigs, placed in cages designed for this,
don't pass out but continue to scream as they turn to cinder.
The Pentagon wants to know
something a child could tell it:
it hurts to burn, and even a match
can make you scream, pigs or people,

even the smallest common flame can kill you.
This plutonic calefaction is redundant.

Men are willing
to call the roasting of live pigs
a simulation of certain conditions. It is
not a simulation. The pigs (with their high-rated
        intelligence,
their uncanny precognition of disaster) are real,
their agony real agony, the smell
is not archetypal breakfast nor ancient feasting
but a foul miasma irremovable from the nostrils,
and the simulation of hell these men
have carefully set up
is hell itself,
                and they in it, dead in their lives,
and what can redeem them? What can redeem them?

ROBERT VASQUEZ [B. 1955]

Poet Robert Vasquez was born about 230 miles due west of the Nevada Test Site, in Madera, an agricultural town in California's San Joaquin Valley. Like other children of the American West in the 1950s, Vasquez experienced the blinding light of a nuclear blast before he was even born. "Early Morning Test Light over Nevada, 1955" tells this story as it was told to him by his father, who witnessed the eerie light of the blast from the house in Madera that he shared with his pregnant wife. Vasquez grew up in Fresno, where he began working full-time in a series of menial jobs while still in high school. He worked his way through California State University, Fresno (BA), UC Irvine (MFA), and Stanford University, where he held a Wallace Stegner Poetry Fellowship. Since 1991 he has taught English and creative writing at the College of the Sequoias in Visalia, California. He has won three Academy of American Poets prizes, three National Society of Arts and Letters awards, a National Writers Union award, and—for his book At the Rainbow (1995)—the San Francisco Foundation's James D. Phelan Award. His poems have been widely anthologized and have appeared in various periodicals, including the Los Angeles Times Book Review, Missouri Review, New England Review, Parnassus, Ploughshares, *and the* Village Voice. *A Chicano poet who is known for his visionary word paintings of California landscapes and for his ability to see the extraordinary in the ordinary, Vasquez thinks of himself as a translator from the dialects of the physical world into the printed word. "If the scratched, polished instruments within us are in tune," he believes, "even the darkest notes can sing us home."*

Early Morning Test Light over Nevada, 1955

Your mother slept through it all,
her face turned away
like the dark side of the earth.

We'd heard between *rancheras*
on the radio
that the ladles
and the two bears
that lie among the stars
above Nevada
would fade at 3:15 as though seared
by a false sun.

The stove exhaled all night
a trinity of blue rings. You entered
your fourth month
of floating in the tropical,
star-crossed water
your mother carried under her heart
that opens and closes
like a butterfly.

When the sky flared,
our room lit up. Cobwebs
sparkled on the walls, and a spider
absorbed the light
like a chameleon and began
to inch toward the outer rings
as if a fly trembled.

Roosters crowed. The dog
scratched at the door. I went outside
hearing the hens and thought *weasel*
and found broken eggs, the chicks
spongy, their eyes

stunned and shrouded
by thin veils of skin.

"Don't open your eyes,"
I whispered to you when darkness
returned. I thought of your bones
still a white gel, I remembered the story
of blood smeared on doorways,
and I placed my hand on the balloon
you rode in—that would slowly sink
to your birth. I said
the Old German name your mother already picked
for you, *Robert*. It means *bright fame*.

TERRY TEMPEST WILLIAMS [B. 1955]

Terry Tempest Williams "could change your life," according to the UTNE Reader, *which named Williams on its list of one hundred visionaries. Indeed, both in person and in prose, Williams possesses an extraordinary gift to "pierce the heart." A fifth-generation Utahn and coeditor with Thomas Lyon of* Great and Peculiar Beauty: A Utah Reader *(1995), Williams has been shaped by geography and by her embodiment as a Mormon woman. Her writing—in books such as* Refuge: An Unnatural History of Family and Place *(1991),* An Unspoken Hunger: Stories from the Field *(1994),* Desert Quartet: An Erotic Landscape *(1995),* Leap *(2000), and* Red: Passion in the Desert *(2001)—is always intense, making her one of the most stirring voices on political and environmental issues in the western states. Williams and Stephen Trimble rallied twenty-one major western writers to contribute eloquent pleas on behalf of Utah wilderness. They presented the resulting book,* Testimony: Writers of the West Speak on Behalf of Utah Wilderness *(1996), to every member of Congress, miraculously moving enough hearts to defeat a bill that would have had drastic implications for Utah wilderness. For Williams, citizenship demands that we speak out, question our government, and defend the places we love. Activism, Williams contends, defies the culture of "blind obedience" espoused by the Mormon church, and she has suffered censure from church leaders. As a vital force for reform, however, Williams coedited* New Genesis: A Mormon Reader on Land and Community *(1998) with William B. Smart. "The Clan of One-Breasted Women"—the epilogue to* Refuge—*has been extensively reprinted, standing as one of America's most powerful expressions of nuclear protest.*

The Clan of One-Breasted Women

I belong to a Clan of One-Breasted Women. My mother, my grandmothers, and six aunts have all had mastectomies. Seven are dead. The two who survive have just completed rounds of chemotherapy and radiation.

I've had my own problems: two biopsies for breast cancer and a small tumor between my ribs diagnosed as a "border-line malignancy."

This is my family history.

Most statistics tell us breast cancer is genetic, hereditary, with rising percentages attached to fatty diets, childlessness, or becoming pregnant after thirty. What they don't say is living in Utah may be the greatest hazard of all.

We are a Mormon family with roots in Utah since 1847. The "word of wisdom" in my family aligned us with good foods—no coffee, no tea, tobacco, or alcohol. For the most part, our women were finished having their babies by the time they were thirty. And only one faced breast cancer prior to 1960. Traditionally, as a group of people, Mormons have a low rate of cancer.

Is our family a cultural anomaly? The truth is, we didn't think about it. Those who did, usually the men, simply said, "bad genes." The women's attitude was stoic. Cancer was part of life. On February 16, 1971, the eve of my mother's surgery, I accidentally picked up the telephone and overheard her ask my grandmother what she could expect.

"Diane, it is one of the most spiritual experiences you will ever encounter."

I quietly put down the receiver.

Two days later, my father took my brothers and me to the hospital to visit her. She met us in the lobby in a wheelchair. No bandages were visible. I'll never forget her radiance, the way she held herself in a purple velvet robe, and how she gathered us around her.

"Children, I am fine. I want you to know I felt the arms of God around me."

We believed her. My father cried. Our mother, his wife, was thirty-eight years old.

A little over a year after Mother's death, Dad and I were having dinner together. . . .

Over dessert, I shared a recurring dream of mine. I told my father that for years, as long as I could remember, I saw this flash of light in the night in the desert—that this image had so permeated my being that I could not venture south without seeing it again, on the horizon, illuminating buttes and mesas.

"You did see it," he said.

"Saw what?"

"The bomb. The cloud. We were driving home from Riverside, California. You were sitting on Diane's lap. She was pregnant. In fact, I remember the day, September 7, 1957. We had just gotten out of the Service. We were driving north, past Las Vegas. It was an hour or so before dawn, when this explosion went off. We not only heard it, but felt it. I thought the oil tanker in front of us had blown up. We pulled over and suddenly, rising from the desert floor, we saw it, clearly, this golden-stemmed cloud, the mushroom. The sky seemed to vibrate with an eerie pink glow. Within a few minutes, a light ash was raining on the car."

I stared at my father.

"I thought you knew that," he said. "It was a common occurrence in the fifties."

It was at this moment that I realized the deceit I had been living under. Children growing up in the American Southwest, drinking contaminated milk from contaminated cows, even from the contaminated breasts of their mothers, my mother—members, years later, of the Clan of One-Breasted Women.

It is a well-known story in the Desert West, "The Day We Bombed Utah," or more accurately, the years we bombed Utah: above ground atomic testing in Nevada took place from January 27, 1951, through July 11, 1962. Not only were the winds blowing north covering "low-use segments of the population" with fallout and leaving sheep dead in their tracks, but the climate was right. The United States of the 1950s was red, white, and blue. The Korean War was raging. McCarthyism was rampant. Ike was it, and the cold war was hot. If you were against nuclear testing, you were for a communist regime.

Much has been written about this "American nuclear tragedy." Public health was secondary to national security. The Atomic Energy Commissioner, Thomas Murray, said, "Gentlemen, we must not let anything interfere with this series of tests, nothing."

Again and again, the American public was told by its government, in spite of burns, blisters, and nausea, "It has been found that the tests may be conducted with adequate assurance of safety under conditions prevailing at the bombing reservations." Assuaging public fears was simply a matter of public relations. "Your best action," an Atomic Energy Commission booklet read, "is not to be worried about fallout." A news release typical of the times stated, "We find no basis for concluding that harm to any individual has resulted from radioactive fallout."

On August 30, 1979, during Jimmy Carter's presidency, a suit was filed, *Irene Allen v. The United States of America*. Mrs. Allen's case was the first on an alphabetical list of twenty-four test cases, representative of nearly twelve hundred plaintiffs seeking compensation from the United States government for cancers caused by nuclear testing in Nevada.

Irene Allen lived in Hurricane, Utah. She was the mother of five children and had been widowed twice. Her first husband, with their two oldest boys had watched the tests from the roof of the local high school. He died of leukemia in 1956. Her second husband died of pancreatic cancer in 1978.

In a town meeting conducted by Utah Senator Orrin Hatch, shortly before the suit was filed, Mrs. Allen said, "I am not blaming the government, I want you to know that, Senator Hatch. But I thought if my testimony could help in any way so this wouldn't happen again to any of the generations coming up after us . . . I am happy to be here this day to bear testimony of this."

God-fearing people. This is just one story in an anthology of thousands.

On May 10, 1984, Judge Bruce S. Jenkins handed down his opinion. Ten of the plaintiffs were awarded damages. It was the first time a federal court had determined that nuclear tests had been the cause of cancers. For the remaining fourteen test cases, the proof of causation was not sufficient. In spite of the split decision, it was considered a landmark ruling. It was not to remain so for long.

In April 1987, the Tenth Circuit Court of the Appeals overturned Judge Jenkins's ruling on the ground that the United States was protected from suit by the legal doctrine of sovereign immunity, a centuries-old idea from England in the days of absolute monarchs.

In January 1988, the Supreme Court refused to review the Appeals Court decision. To our court system it does not matter whether the United States government was irresponsible, whether it lied to its citizens, or even that citizens died from the fallout of nuclear testing. What matters is that our government is immune: "The King can do no wrong."

In Mormon culture, authority is respected, obedience is revered, and independent thinking is not. I was taught as a young girl not to "make waves" or "rock the boat."

"Just let it go," Mother would say. "You know how you feel, that's what counts."

For many years, I have done just that—listened, observed, and quietly formed my own opinions, in a culture that rarely asks questions because it has all the answers. But one by one, I have watched the women in my family die common, heroic deaths. We sat in waiting rooms hoping for good news, but always receiving the bad. I cared for them, bathed their scarred bodies, and kept their secrets. I watched beautiful women become bald as Cytoxan, cisplatin, and Adriamycin were injected into their veins. I held their foreheads as they vomited green-black bile, and I shot them with morphine when the pain became inhuman. In the end, I witnessed their last peaceful breaths, becoming a midwife to the rebirth of their souls.

The price of obedience has become too high.

The fear and inability to question authority that ultimately killed rural communities in Utah during atmospheric testing of atomic weapons is the same fear I saw in my mother's body. Sheep. Dead sheep. The evidence is buried.

I cannot prove that my mother, Diane Dixon Tempest, or my grandmothers, Lettie Romney Dixon and Kathryn Blackett Tempest, along with my aunts developed cancer from nuclear fallout in Utah. But I can't prove they didn't.

My father's memory was correct. The September blast we drove through in 1957 was part of Operation Plumbbob, one of the most intensive series of bomb tests to be initiated. The flash of light in the night in the desert, which I had always thought was a dream, developed into a family nightmare. It took fourteen years, from 1957 to 1971, for cancer to manifest in my mother—the same time, Howard L. Andrews, an authority in radioactive fallout at the National Institutes of Health, says radiation cancer requires to become evident. The more I learn about what it means to be a "downwinder," the more questions I drown in.

What I do know, however, is that as a Mormon woman of the fifth generation of Latter-day Saints, I must question everything, even if it means losing my faith, even if it means becoming a member of a border tribe among my own people. Tolerating blind obedience in the name of patriotism or religion ultimately takes our lives.

When the Atomic Energy Commission described the country north of the Nevada Test Site as "virtually uninhabited desert terrain," my family and the birds at Great Salt Lake were some of the "virtual uninhabitants."

One night, I dreamed women from all over the world circled a blazing fire in the desert. They spoke of change, how they hold the moon in their bellies and wax and wane with its phases. They mocked the presumption of even-tempered beings and made promises that they would never fear the witch inside themselves. The women danced wildly as sparks broke away from the flames and entered the night sky as stars.

And they sang a song given to them by Shoshone grandmothers:

Ah ne nah, nah	Consider the rabbits
nin nah nah—	How gently they walk on the earth—
ah ne nah, nah	Consider the rabbits
nin nah nah—	How gently they walk on the earth—
Nyaga mutzi	We remember them
oh ne nay—	We can walk gently also—
Nyaga mutzi	We remember them
oh ne nay—	We can walk gently also—

The women danced and drummed and sang for weeks, preparing themselves for what was to come. They would reclaim the desert for the sake of their children, for the sake of the land.

A few miles downwind from the fire circle, bombs were being tested. Rabbits felt the tremors. Their soft leather pads on paws and feet recognized the shaking sands, while the roots of mesquite and sage were smoldering. Rocks were hot from the inside out and dust devils hummed unnaturally. And each time there was another nuclear test, ravens watched the desert heave. Stretch marks appeared. The land was losing its muscle.

The women couldn't bear it any longer. They were mothers. They had suffered labor pains but always under the promise of birth. The red hot pains beneath the desert promised death only, as each bomb became a stillborn. A contract had been made and broken between human beings and the land. A new contract was being drawn by the women, who understood the fate of the earth as their own.

Under the cover of darkness, ten women slipped under a barbed-wire fence and entered the contaminated country. They were trespassing. They walked toward the town of Mercury, in moonlight, taking their cues from coyote, kit fox, antelope squirrel, and quail. They moved quietly and deliberately through the maze of Joshua trees. When a hint of daylight appeared they rested, drinking tea and sharing their rations of food. The women closed their eyes. The time had come to protest with the heart, that to deny one's genealogy with the earth was to commit treason against one's soul.

At dawn, the women draped themselves in Mylar, wrapping long streamers of silver plastic around their arms to blow in the breeze. They wore clear masks, that became the faces of humanity. And when they arrived at the edge of Mercury, they carried all the butterflies of a summer day in their wombs. They paused to allow their courage to settle.

The town that forbids pregnant women and children to enter because of radiation risks was asleep. The women moved through the streets as winged messengers, twirling around each other in slow motion, peeking inside homes and watching the easy sleep of men and women. They were astonished by such stillness and periodically would utter a shrill note or low cry just to verify life.

The residents finally awoke to these strange apparitions. Some simply stared. Others called authorities, and in time, the women were apprehended by wary soldiers dressed in desert fatigues. They were taken to a white, square building on the other edge of Mercury. When asked who they were and why they were there, the women replied, "We are mothers and we have come to reclaim the desert for our children."

The soldiers arrested them. As the ten women were blindfolded and hand-cuffed, they began singing:

> *You can't forbid us everything*
> *You can't forbid us to think—*
> *You can't forbid our tears to flow*
> *And you can't stop the songs that we sing.*

The women continued to sing louder and louder, until they heard the voices of their sisters moving across the mesa:

> *Ah ne nah, nah*
> *nin nah nah—*
> *Ah ne nah, nah*
> *nin nah nah—*
> *Nyaga mutzi*
> *oh ne nay—*
> *Nyaga mutzi*
> *oh ne nay—*

"Call for reinforcements," one soldier said.

"We have," interrupted one woman, "we have—and you have no idea of our numbers."

I crossed the line at the Nevada Test Site and was arrested with nine other Utahns for trespassing on military lands. They are still conducting nuclear tests in the desert. Ours was an act of civil disobedience. But as I walked toward the town of Mercury, it was more than a gesture of peace. It was a gesture on behalf of the Clan of One-Breasted Women.

As one officer cinched the handcuffs around my wrists, another frisked my body. She found a pen and a pad of paper tucked inside my left boot.

"And these?" she asked sternly.

"Weapons," I replied.

Our eyes met. I smiled. She pulled the leg of my trousers back over my boot.

"Step forward, please," she said as she took my arm.

We were booked under an afternoon sun and bused to Tonopah, Nevada. It was a two-hour ride. This was familiar country. The Joshua trees standing their ground had been named by my ancestors, who believed they looked like prophets pointing west to the Promised Land. These were the same trees that bloomed each spring, flowers appearing like white flames in the Mojave. And I recalled a full moon in

May, when Mother and I had walked among them, flushing out mourning doves
and owls.

The bus stopped short of town. We were released.

The officials thought it was a cruel joke to leave us stranded in the desert with
no way to get home. What they didn't realize was that we were home, soul-centered
and strong, women who recognized the sweet smell of sage as fuel for our spirits.

LYNN EMANUEL [B. 1949]

For biographical information on Lynn Emanuel, see p. 583. In 1995 the first American anthol-
ogy of antinuclear poems was published, Atomic Ghost: Poets Respond to the Nuclear Age,
edited by John Bradley. Lynn Emanuel's "The Planet Krypton," from her poetry collection The
Dig *(1992), is included in* Atomic Ghost. *Emanuel explains, "For me this is a poem about the*
irresistibility of technology. It is also about the impact of technology on labor. The poem opens
with mining and ends in space. It tracks the extinction of one kind of industry by another. I
don't think I would have thought about the bomb in that way except for the fact that I was
living in Pittsburgh during the 1970s–80s when the steel industry was going extinct and being
replaced by the technology of computers and bio-medicine." The poem additionally reminds
us that television itself was an emerging technology during the early years of atomic testing.
Superman comics fans will recognize Krypton as the fictional doomed planet on which the hero
was born. Before the planet exploded, a Kryptonian scientist and his wife placed their infant
son on an experimental rocket ship that eventually arrived on planet Earth, where the infant
grew up to be the superhero Superman, star of the comic strip series first launched in 1939 and
popular throughout the era of atomic testing.

The Planet Krypton

> Outside the window the McGill smelter
> sent a red dust down on the smoking yards of copper,
> on the railroad tracks' frayed ends disappearing
> into the congestion of the afternoon. Ely lay dull
>
> and scuffed: a miner's boot toe worn away and dim,
> while my mother knelt before the Philco to coax
> the detonation from the static. From the Las Vegas
> Tonopah Artillery and Gunnery Range the sound

of the atom bomb came biting like a swarm
of bees. We sat in the hot Nevada dark, delighted,
when the switch was tripped and the bomb hoisted
up its silky, hooded, glittering, uncoiling length;

it hissed and spit, it sizzled like a poker in a toddy.
The bomb was no mind and all body; it sent a fire
of static down the spine. In the dark it glowed like the coils
of an electric stove. It stripped every leaf from every

branch until a willow by a creek was a bouquet
of switches resinous, naked, flexible, and fine.
Bathed in the light of KDWN, Las Vegas,
my crouched mother looked radioactive, swampy,

glaucous, like something from the Planet Krypton.
In the suave, brilliant wattage of the bomb, we were
not poor. In the atom's fizz and pop we heard possibility
uncorked. Taffeta wraps whispered on davenports.

A new planet bloomed above us; in its light
the stumps of cut pine gleamed like dinner plates.
The world was beginning all over again, fresh and hot;
we could have anything we wanted.

ADRIAN C. LOUIS [B. 1946]

For biographical information on Adrian C. Louis, see p. 574. From a Native American perspec-
tive, atomic testing is one more outrage in a centuries-old assault on and desecration of sacred,
ancestral lands by conquerors of European descent. As Louis explains, "in 'Nevada Red Blues'
I was dealing with the surface diseases of Nevada. I was thinking how Nevada seemed to be
a spawning ground for all that is base in man's nature: gambling and the aspect of preying on
human desire to make something from nothing; prostitution, the cathouses that still exist; rape
of the land by mining, and then the ultimate insult to Mother Earth, the testing of A-bombs on
ancestral lands." The poem, reprinted in John Bradley's Atomic Ghost: Poets Respond to the
Nuclear Age *(1995), originally appeared in Louis's collection* Among the Dog Eaters *(1992),*
written while Louis was living and teaching on the Oglala Sioux reservation in South Dakota.
There he shared the despair and demoralization of reservation life, expressing this reality in

poems that are bleak, bitter, hostile, honest, and sometimes darkly humorous. In "Nevada Red Blues," Numa is the Paiute Indian word for "the people," while Taibo means "white man." Louis's epigraph by Chilean poet and Nobel laureate Pablo Neruda (1904–73) is a line from his poem "On Mexico's Walls," where "live fire" refers to the volcanoes that made Mexico's mountains, those subterranean forces still brooding beneath the country's surface topography.

Nevada Red Blues

> *Where live fire began to inhabit you.*
> —Pablo Neruda

We live under
slot machine
stars
that jackpot
into the black
velvet
backdrop
and
mirror the greed
of the creatures who soiled our land.

Numa,
it was
not
enough
for
Taibo
to make
our sacred land
a living
though
pustulous
whore.

He
had
to drop
hydrogen bombs
where

thousands
of years
of our blood
spirits lie.

CAROLE GALLAGHER [B. 1950]

*Having grown up practicing duck-and-cover drills in school, New York City photojournalist
Carole Gallagher has long been fascinated by the Bomb, and in the early 1980s she obtained
recently declassified "top secret" government documents that described the people living downwind of the Nevada Test Site during the years of above-ground atomic testing (1951–63) as "a
low-use segment of the population." The callous bigotry of that phrase impelled Gallagher to
leave a successful career in New York and drive west to document the effects of nuclear testing
on "downwinders," Test Site workers, and military personnel whose maneuvers exposed them
to radiation. Little did Gallagher know that this project would consume the next dozen years
of her life. She recalls that she lived on a shoestring, faced hostility from conservative Mormons,
and battled any war correspondent's predictable depression as she witnessed radiation-caused
leukemias, heart disease, brain tumors, thyroid cancers, miscarriages, sterility, and birth de-
fects, coupled with the U.S. government's thirty-year cover-up of the damages caused by fallout.
Gallagher's collection of photographs and oral histories was rejected by thirty publishers before
MIT Press issued* American Ground Zero: The Secret Nuclear War *in 1993 and called it "a
striking gallery of the undecorated casualties of an undeclared war," a book heralded by reviewers as a monumental achievement. A companion exhibition to the book was organized by the
International Center of Photography in New York and traveled to museums and art galleries
across the country. The photographs were also exhibited at the Hiroshima Peace Museum and
in Kazakhstan, where the Soviet nuclear test site is located. Gallagher received a Pope Foundation award for outstanding individual achievement in investigative journalism. Fearless in
bringing our nation's ugliest secrets to light, Gallagher is currently working on a book that
documents the health problems of veterans of the first Gulf War who were exposed to nerve
agents, depleted uranium, and chemical and biological weapons.*

from *American Ground Zero*
Ken Case, January 1984, North Las Vegas, Nevada

Ken Case had the dubious distinction, he thought, of being called the "Atomic
Cowboy," both by his fellow workers at the Test Site and by the press. Hired on

a horse as a deputy sheriff by 1954, he literally became a cowboy for the Atomic Energy Commission, riding a herd of cattle and horses over ground zero after a nuclear detonation so that the effects of radiation on wildlife could be measured by scientists at Los Alamos. This series of animal experiments continued for seven years. He showed me yellowed photographs from the fifties of himself in that capacity, the complete Marlboro Man, in the saddle and holding up a cattle branding iron with AEC initials measuring almost a foot high. There would be no mistaking a radioactive cow on the range with a 12-inch brand burned into her hide. In another testing era photo he pointed to himself on horseback, and particularly to the dust raised by both horses and cattle. "They got cancer and we got cancer," he said, "only the animals were so much closer to the ground that they died faster."

Case himself had many feet of his intestines removed, and his spleen, and at the time of his interview the cancer had spread through most of the organs of his body. His wife was also dying of cancer, and she had also endured for years the fusion of the disks of her spine, another health effect of high radiation exposure. They both lived in a trailer in North Las Vegas, and among the bric-a-brac hanging on the wall were photographs of two atomic bombs that Case had witnessed at close range, among many others, while he worked at the Test Site. One hung above a plate with a poem "To Mother" on it, glazed with pink roses. He was a kindly bear of a man, and he and his equally endearing wife were, as religious Mormons, preparing themselves for Eternity—they knew they hadn't long to wait.

Your job was to herd cattle on the range. Were you close to the ground zero area?

Went right through it a lot of the times. I had ridden the range all the time on horseback, all the area, checking for feed and water. To start with, in '55 and '57 they brought in 27 or 37 big helicopters, the kind they call the banana type, the big sway-nose with the double props. I think every mission, in the chopper, the pilot and I would be the first ones in ground zero. We were monitoring.

Did the Geiger counters go off-scale? How close to the ground were you, and what did it look like?

We would get over [ground zero] and bang, off-scale. When we went back over about 30 feet off the ground, the sand, it would be melted just like glass. Those ground zeros in the spring, you look out, they bleed a big circle in the snow around ground zero. After a shot and it's cooled down, then they monitor all that area and what's left of the tower [on which the bomb was detonated]. They just melted that tower down. They had a few aerial bombs that planes came in and dropped. They would have just so much time to get away from them. If you happened to watch the plane, it would rock the plane. As quick as it went, the area around the outside of that circle would be on fire. All the weeds and grass, and if there were trees, they were on fire too. Rabbits would run across there and they would be on fire. It was something.

How long were you monitoring from the helicopter, how many shots?

About 15 or 18 aboveground shots, and I was in every one of them. We took samples of the cattle all the time, twice a year, so many out of each herd. I think that as far as having to do that first for results of radiation, they have been wishing away their money for the last ten years. They had all the data they ever needed, had it for a long, long time. They've tried every shot they can think of, over and over and over and over. It's just a way people spend a lot of money.

Many years after this interview, in 1989, I took a "public information tour" of the Test Site that is available to anyone who requests it in advance. The Department of Energy even solicits visitors at conventions in Las Vegas and at old age homes, and so the bus was filled with senior citizens looking forward to a day "out of the city" as well as people from other countries who were just plain curious. No photographs were allowed, and no tape recorders. The tour guide knew who I was and became flustered when I asked about the animal cages still left standing on Frenchman Flat, the site of 27 atomic bomb tests. She denied they were cages. Thinking also of Ken Case, I continued to inquire if there had ever been a program of animal experimentation at the Test Site, say in the fifties, before they knew better. "Oh, no, we wouldn't do that."

What were the viewing conditions when an aboveground detonation would take place?

They had a big crowd out at the observation point, lots of people there and cars. They had gone through and told everybody that before the shot time, they would furnish the glasses like goggles, to wear them or turn their backs to the shot, not to face it. There were a few of them that tried to be smart and try to look without them. They were blinded for quite a while. The bombs were powerful enough that you could turn your back and it would burn the back of your neck from the heat. That was about five or six miles from ground zero from where we was at.

Did you witness what the atomic vets experienced? How many of them did you know?

About two hundred. A bigger share that I knew personally while I was out there, I don't think there's four or six alive today. They were all over. Camp Desert Rock had a lot of them, of course. They went out with machines and dug trenches for them to get into. So many feet or yards away from ground zero. I forget how close. The first ones were pretty close, closer than a mile away. It was where it was hot. There wasn't hardly any of them at that time that didn't get sick. They tried to keep them to say it wasn't, but it was, the effects of it. A lot of it depended on the type of shot it was, what chemicals they used in the device itself. [I've lost] eight or ten friends that I knew quite well.

When I first started getting ready for the shots out there, when they started their series in '55, the only shot I wasn't near was from Control Point, and they had me go out on the highway, patrol the highway from Lathrop Wells to Indian Springs. The winds had changed and brought [the fallout cloud] right back over Control Point. The patrol car we were using was an old Plymouth sedan. They took it into camp later and washed it down. I had a little breakfast, then asked them if it was ready and they said yes. I got partly back to Control Point and my arm started burning. I rolled my sleeve up and I was burned from my hand to my elbow a strip about that wide [about two inches]. There was radiation in the felt pad on the window, because it was wet where they washed it down. We got hold of who was supposed to be the head guy and told him what happened. He said, "Go back to work, nothing to worry about." He wouldn't even look at my arm. That's the way they operated out there. It's a fright, it's terrible.

I've had eleven surgeries. Tumors. The Test Site, as far as I'm concerned, is just nothing but a place for them to spend a hell of a lot of money foolishly.

Ken Case died on July 5, 1985, and his wife, Woody, followed him shortly there-after.

REBECCA SOLNIT [B. 1961]

Political activism is a way of life for essayist, critic, and cultural historian Rebecca Solnit, whose early business cards read, "Rebecca Solnit: flowery prose, ghostwriting, and flaming propaganda." Raised in the San Francisco Bay Area, where she became involved in nuclear, environmental, and human rights issues, Solnit, whose degree is in English literature, first came to Nevada in 1988 to join an antinuclear protest at the Nevada Test Site. Being at the Test Site and meeting Western Shoshone activists put a place and a face to nuclear issues that had previously seemed to be abstractions. Her resulting book, Savage Dreams: A Journey into the Landscape Wars of the American West *(1994), received wide acclaim as a daring critical history of the Test Site—America's Armageddon—and Yosemite National Park—America's Eden. In both places, Solnit argues, indigenous people were erased from the picture.* Savage Dreams, *one of the first books in the growing field of environmental justice, restores their visibility in the ongoing resource wars. Solnit once observed to interviewer Bill Stobb that "there's amazing histories that haven't been told yet and just these huge, colossal things that nobody writes about." It is precisely those unremarked things and forgotten histories that Solnit brilliantly brings to light in her seven books on topics as far-roaming as the cultural practice of walking* (Wanderlust: A History of Walking, 2000), *the development of chronophotography* (River of Shadows: Eadweard Muybridge and the Technological Wild West, 2004), *and the devastation of dot-com gentrification on civic life* (Hollow City: The Siege of San Francisco and the Crisis of American Urbanism, 2000). *As Solnit has noted, these books and her newest books "are united as investigations of the life of the mind in the body and the body in the landscape, of time, place, and presence."*

from *Savage Dreams*

The Test Site was a blank on many maps, a forgotten landscape, off limits to the public and swallowed up in a state which itself seemed sometimes to be overlooked by the rest of the country. Even though Nevada is growing rapidly, its population is still not much over a million, half of it in Las Vegas and most of the rest of it in the Reno–Carson City area. There aren't many people living in all that open space, and few artists and writers have celebrated its qualities. Not very many people were displaced when the land that became Nellis was sealed off in 1941, when the population of Nevada was around 110,000, and not many people objected, because this landscape is widely thought to be worthless already.

Space itself isn't an absolute, or at least the spaciousness of landscapes isn't. Up close, aridity means that even the plants grow far apart from each other; for people and animals, this sparseness means that they too have to spread out to make a living off the land. In the East, a cow can live off a few acres of grass; out here the land is often overgrazed at only a few cows per thousand acres, and where they overgraze the soil erodes back to dust and rock. It is rock—geology—that dominates this landscape. In lusher landscapes, it is as though the skin and bones of the earth are dressed in verdure; here the earth is naked, and geological processes are clearly visible. It is geological time and geological scale that dominate this landscape, dwarfing all the biological processes within the uplift of ranges, the accretion of basins. The very rocks on the ground have lain in place so long around the Test Site that their tops and bottoms are different colors, and any disturbance leaves a lasting scar. Every act out here has to be measured against this scale of change and scope. It is this apparent geology, this bare rock, that makes newcomers read the desert as a dead or barren landscape, though if you spend more time in it, you may come to see the earth itself lives, slowly and grandly, in the metamorphoses of geology.

. . . .

I came to the Test Site four springs in a row, and the third spring, the spring of 1990, the place began to make sense to me. The first year, . . . I walked with friends into the arms of the waiting guards. We had simply climbed through the fence a short distance away from the road entrance to the place, and they had come to get us. The boundary of the site is marked by a barbed-wire fence, and the point at which one is trespassing on the road is the far side of the cattleguard (cattleguard, easterners and urbanites: a set of thick bars running the length of a trench across the road, easy for human feet to cross by stepping on the bars but impossibly treacherous for hooves). It seems typically Western that all the Test Site boundaries are designed to obstruct livestock rather than people, for no serious walker is halted by a cattleguard in the road or a fence across the land.

My second year at the Test Site I went in with a bunch of anarchist women from San Francisco and Seattle. . . . We'd agreed that we would pair off so that no one got abandoned or left at the guards' mercy without a witness, and then we'd hiked northwest up 95 about a mile north of the main gate, so that we'd have time to cover some ground before we were interfered with. I'm not sure what our purpose was— curiosity?—but my own desire was always to walk as long as possible across the land that was off limits. "Reclaim the Test Site," the big American Peace Test action of spring 1988 had been called. Walking claims land not by circumscribing it and fencing it off as property but by moving across it in a line that however long or short connects it to the larger journey of one's life, the surrounding roads and trails, that makes it part of the web of experience, confirmed by every foot that touches the earth.

Actually, that spring afternoon in 1989 the dozen other women and I only got about a quarter mile in, walking in a gully that made it hard to see us from the land, before the helicopters found us, swooping low overhead with men in paramilitary uniforms leaning out ready to jump. If we were conducting our war as a picnic meander, they were conducting their job as a military maneuver. But when the hovering copter got low enough to pelt us with gravel spat from the ground by its gust of air, we ran, and the men leapt out and ran after us. I ran madly in the bad footing of the desert, with its soft patches of sand and crusted-over dust, cobbled stretches, boulders, loose rocks, and low bushes, only slowing down enough to keep pace with the woman with whom I'd paired off. The anarchists were all wearing vivid colors, and I in my dusty khaki regretted that we were so visible. I wondered this time, as I did so many others, whether I could disappear from view if I walked by myself, but solitude was discouraged here—it could be dangerous.

I ran for a ways without looking back, and then I turned my head a little and saw a man in camouflage all but close enough to grab me, far closer than I expected. He must have decided to join another chase, because it seems unlikely that I actually outran him. And running was one of the things that we usually agreed not to do, as it wasn't in keeping with the spirit of nonviolent direct action. Urgent, unpredictable, quick actions threw the security forces into a panic, made it possible for things to go astray.

I gave up easily, letting them handcuff my hands behind my back, but my companion resisted, letting the two guards know why she was here and by what laws she had the right to be here. She cited the fact that the land was stolen from the Western Shoshone in the first place, and that we had permission from them to be here, that she was following the Nuremberg Principles they were violating. Now I can't even remember which of the women she was, only the unwavering conviction with which she refused to cooperate. She refused to walk, too, and so they herded the two of us into another gully and handcuffed us ankle to ankle. One stood guard over us while the other went for reinforcements. The other women were no longer visible. Picture an immensity of flatness populated only by two immobilized women and two men in camouflage, one of whom was rapidly disappearing. There was nothing to say. The Test Site looked exactly like the landscape outside, though we were now unable to stand up in it because of our shackles.

The second guard came back with a third man. While one guard walked behind me to make sure that I didn't attempt to flee, the other two picked her up, each taking one arm and one leg, and carried her. We progressed a couple of hundred yards in this way, when an older, red-faced guard joined our group of five. He snarled at the guards not to indulge her by carrying her. First he got them to drag her by her arms, then he got them to stop going around the obstacles. They began to drag her through thornbushes and over cacti.

He had convinced them to engage in a mild form of torture, and it didn't seem to have occurred to any of them that they could refuse his orders, though it was this kind of mindless obedience that the Nuremberg Principles she cited were made to combat. Finally she gave up and, near tears, asked them to stop. She began to walk, so she wouldn't be dragged. We walked to the dirt road that ran parallel to the Test Site periphery, where a big van was waiting for us, along with several of the other women in our group. The van was there to take us to the huge holding pens the Department of Energy had built a year or so before, next to the main gate. The guards cut off the plastic handcuffs we were bound with and rehandcuffed us with our hands in front, letting the cut pairs lie where they fell. My companion offered me a drink of water from the bota bag they hadn't confiscated, then she took off her hiking boot with awkward double-handed gestures and took out her Swiss army knife. I pulled out as many of the thorns in her foot as I could with the knife's tweezers. Some of them were huge, and one long one broke off deep in her foot.

I have trouble with the abstract and the concrete. In the abstract we were committing civil disobedience in the cause of peace and justice, making a gesture that echoed the gestures of Thoreau in Concord in 1846 and the trials in Nuremberg in 1946, the resistance of the Shoshone and of pacifists in many places and times. In the concrete we were scrabbling around in the scrub, playing tag with a bunch of mercenaries who thought that we were completely demented. My faith wavers. I always had trouble seeing the guards as representatives of the U.S. military policy rather than as rednecks with limited career options, though I think many of the activists at the Test Site had the opposite problem, that perhaps the concrete didn't complicate their abstract ideals. The invisible background to all this, to our plastic handcuffs, to the thorn that broke off in her foot, to the helicopter pelting gravel and the men making a living by wearing camouflage and chasing pacifists, to the whole ramshackle peace camp and direct action, the background we would never see, was even harder to keep in mind: huge nuclear weapons detonations in preparation for international wars and as part of a local nuclear war nearing the forty-year mark.

There is a theory about lines of energy that traverse the earth, running through sacred sites, called "ley lines." The people who have developed this theory demonstrate it by showing the alignment of important sites along straight lines. I'm not sure about ley lines, but I believe in lines of convergence. These lines are no more visible in the landscape than ley lines, and I am not even proposing that they have any existence at all outside our imaginations—which are themselves crucial territories. These lines of convergence are the lines of biography and history and ecology that come together at a site, as the history of nuclear physics, the Arms Race, anti-Communism, civil disobedience, Native American land-rights struggles, the environmental movement, and the mysticism and fanaticism deserts seem to inspire in Judeo-Christians all come together to make the Nevada Test Site, not as a piece of physical geography, but of cultural geography, not merely in the concrete, but in the abstract. Such places bring together histories which may seem unrelated—and when they come together it becomes possible to see new connections in our personal and public histories and stories, collisions even. A spiderweb of stories spreads out from any place, but it takes time to follow the strands.

. . . .

I want to be able to see the history of gestures behind even a voyage into the new, and I want more to be able to remember the lines of convergence that lead to a place like the Nevada Test Site. This is the abstract whose weight I have tried to feel behind every concrete gesture at the Test Site, a place that however few may see it, however invisible it may be, is the hub of so many crucial lines of our history. But it was hard to remember all this while pulling thorns out of someone's sweaty foot with my hands cuffed together.

. . . .

There's something profoundly American about getting arrested at the Nevada Test Site: The very issues are, not cowboys and Indians, but land, war technology, apocalypse, Thoreauvian civil disobedience, bureaucratic obscurity, and Indians, part of the great gory mess of how we will occupy this country, whose questions are as unsettling as its land is unsettled.

GARY SHORT [B. 1953]

For biographical information on Gary Short, see p. 601. As a Nevada poet, Short is keenly attuned to the environmental damage wrought by mining and the military. "I don't set out to write poems on a certain issue," Short explained to interviewer Bill Stobb, "but I always kind of told myself that I would never publish a book that at least didn't talk about or discuss the issue of what happened to Nevada in the 1950s with atomic testing. I mean, we're bombing our own country and people." "Tidings," below, regards both mining and nuclear testing and transport in Nevada as a local fulfillment of an ancient Mayan prophecy. The Maya viewed the world in cyclical terms, believing that the earth is created and destroyed every three thousand to five thousand years, each age ending in great death and destruction. When Short chose a Mayan epigraph for this poem, little did he know that some years later he would be living in the highlands of Guatemala on a lake that reminded him of Lake Tahoe, but "with volcanoes instead of casinos."

Tidings

> *Bitterness will flow*
> *The earth will burn*
> —from a Mayan prophecy

The bloated carcass of a wild horse
is not abstraction
but a specific example—

the cyanide that seeps into the creek
from heaps of dirt leached for microscopic gold,

its residue. The death of a mustang,
wind bristling a fetlock's stiff hair,
is a political statement.

Bitterness will flow

There are well-funded scientists
in a lab in California who breed weapons
delivered & unleashed at the Test Site
near cloud-shadowed Yucca Mountain.
A clacking train shakes the dreams
of a child in Fernley, Nevada.

Waking, she looks out the window. Her breath,
a quivering cell on the cold glass,
grows & then shrinks.
The bow on her white-sheep nightgown
is tied to sign for infinity.
She hears the lurching

boxcars full of harm
now past her. She cannot see
the steel tracks glint on & off in moonlight,
silvery rills of a stream
that runs to the vanishing point . . .

the earth will burn

CURTIS OBERHANSLY [B. 1941]
DIANNE NELSON OBERHANSLY [B. 1954]

Utahns Curtis Oberhansly and Dianne Nelson Oberhansly are downwinders, people who lived on the leeward side of the open-air atomic tests conducted at the Nevada Test Site during the 1950s and 1960s. Dianne Nelson Oberhansly was born on a homestead ranch near Motoqua, Utah, nine miles from the Nevada border and just ninety miles from ground zero. The Oberhanslys became aware that although a great deal of nonfiction has been published about atomic testing, not much fiction is available to put a human face on this subject. Hence, the two, who are married, collaborated on Downwinders: An Atomic Tale *(2001) and established*

Black Ledge Press of Salt Lake City to publish it, on the fiftieth anniversary of Nevada's first atomic bomb test. The novel became the number-one-selling book in Utah and won the 2001 Fiction Award from the Utah Center for the Book. Downwinders *is a gripping historical and legal thriller that tells the truth about some of the more bizarre aspects of atomic testing, including positioning soldiers only two miles from ground zero, with orders to charge into the crater after the explosion—a scene depicted in the excerpt below—and the federal government's cover-up of the suspected dangers of radioactive fallout. Each author brings expertise to the collaboration. Curtis (JD, University of Utah Law School) practiced law in the 1960s and '70s, including pro bono work for the Sierra Club and American Civil Liberties Union. Dianne (MFA in creative writing, Arizona State University) has published fiction in the* Quarterly, Iowa Review, Ploughshares, *and* Red Rock Review *and won the Flannery O'Connor Award for her short story collection* A Brief History of Male Nudes in America *(1993).*

from *Downwinders: An Atomic Tale*
Saluting Ground Zero

August 23, 1952, 5:30 AM.
Yucca Flat, Nevada Test Site
All final procedures for Shot Huey were on track—it was a go at H minus five seconds. The sun was due to break over the mountains at any moment. Expectation and excitement had turned into jitters and sweat.

A button was pushed, sending an electrical current from the control center to the top of a gigantic tower. A single reverberating click shattered the tense calm and then, for one microsecond, a flutter of fluorescence—the Teller Light—bathed the test area in a violet glow, immediately followed by a stark, brilliant glare, cold and gray-green, flashing across southern Nevada, so indescribably bright and powerful that it would have resembled a flashbulb popping off to someone viewing it from the moon.

In that next moment, it seemed as though the entire sky turned liquid as the raving heat of a new sun flared across the desert floor. A double mushroom cloud began to form, one billowing at ground level and the other rising off the top of a gigantic column of smoky debris. The five hundred foot detonation tower, complete with its elevator and room at the top—over three hundred tons of steel—was suddenly gone, flashburned and then vaporized, along with vehicles, dummies, animals, and all other exposed objects within a quarter mile of ground zero. Their minute particles combined with rock and sand, anything near the cloud's vortex, and were sucked upward through the stem into a molten fireball that roiled higher and higher, greedily seeking oxygen—twenty, thirty, then forty thousand feet above the southwestern United States.

Two miles away in the trench, the Marines of First Platoon, Bravo Company, tried to maintain blast position as instructed: down on one knee, head bent forward, eyes tightly closed, right arm wrapped under the helmet brim and tight across the face. They couldn't believe what they were seeing, though. Even with their eyes tightly closed, the bones in their forearms, elbows, and hands—the radiuses, ulnas, and phalanges—clear as any x-ray, glowed a bright, fluorescent green.

But the platoon sergeant, Porkchop, didn't have time to be dazzled or scared shitless by his own bones. The back of his neck was suddenly so hot that he instinctively covered it with his left arm. The first shock wave passed through the ground just after the flash of light and shook the trench with such violence that he was slammed against the narrow sides like a rag in the jaws of some monster dog. Dirt and rocks poured down, and Porkchop seriously thought they might be buried alive. An intense pressure, volumes of compacted air, pushed down on his back, shoving him even lower in the trench. Vaguely, through the dirt and powdery ruckus, Porkchop could hear his men shouting and cursing, could hear his own voice—Jesus-friggin'-Christ-what-the-hell?

The second shock wave came from behind, was a rebound of the first, bouncing off the mountains and subterranean rock formations and back toward ground zero, doubling the trench line's violent whipsawing. Porkchop tried to open his eyes, but the falling sand and debris were so thick he could barely see the Marine next to him. Even so, a light many times brighter than the sun penetrated the dust and he clamped his eyes shut again, held onto his helmet banging from wall to wall, and rode the fury out. After the longest few seconds of his life, he sensed through his gritty daze that it was letting up, that they were only buried knee deep, and that they would probably live to talk about it.

He had once been in a trench at seven miles from ground zero for a smaller shot and found it merely an exciting pyrotechnic display, but this was something else entirely. This went far beyond what he had expected or been prepared for, and he immediately wondered if there was a mistake, a miscalculation by his superiors or the scientists.

Porkchop cautiously stood up and tried to shake off the bad thoughts along with the sand and dust and debris. He heard the muddled clamor of his men as they attempted to orient themselves, calling out each others' names. "Hey, you okay?" and "Shit-a-mighty, what was that?" He waited a couple of minutes and then ordered his platoon out of the trench.

It was reassuring to be out of the ground, to see that daylight itself hadn't been blown to smithereens. The towering cloud suspended above them was an unearthly sight—dense, gray-black vapor expanding in all directions. Porkchop felt shaken and dizzy, but he had his orders: lead the platoon in a direct assault on ground zero. Purpose: gauge if troops could endure an atomic blast in the field and then pursue the enemy. He wondered now, craning his neck toward the atmosphere and back down to the base of the cloud, what enemy could possibly be holed up in the middle of that thing. But his was not to question why.

"Alright, First Platoon, listen up," he said. "Shake it out, move it. Start forming up, squads on line."

There were moans and groans and one dazed Marine, staring up at the hissing cloud, lost his balance, stumbled sideways, and went down on top of his weapon, the side of his helmet slamming into the steel barrel.

One stood with his mouth wide open. "Mother of God! Look at that."

"Son of a bitch, my balls ache," said yet another.

"Christ, my knees and hips are killing me. What is this shit?"

Porchop's own joints were aching too, and what had started as a warm sensation in his groin had turned into prickling pain. He decided to take it slowly, give his men time to come to their senses. "Shake the dirt out of your utilities and gear," he said, stripping to the waist and brushing himself off. Others began to follow his lead. "Walk it out. You'll be okay. We still got work to do."

Porkchop observed the confusion and decided to delay their field maneuver until they could pull themselves together. He stepped a few yards away from the platoon, taking his time to brush off his gear, bending over to reblouse his trousers, and generally trying to shape himself up. His head began to clear, the pounding in his temples eased, and the negative thoughts about what they had been through slowly subsided. Come on, he told himself. They hadn't charged a machine gun nest, just had their cages rattled. As a professional fighting man, he'd seen worse, much worse, he assured himself.

And he knew the boys in his platoon. He had trained them hard, instilled pride and discipline and molded them into a capable fighting unit. Although they were untested in battle, Porkchop had other boys in the past just like these who had followed him, hi-diddle-diddle, straight up the middle, on Guam, Okinawa, and then in Korea. And before that, he himself had been one of these boys, hitting the beaches of the South Pacific behind some hard-bit sergeant. Porkchop bled Marine green; this was his life and he knew who could take what. There were Rodriquez and Chapman, both hard chested and tight-lipped, now helping their buddies, taking the lead and encouraging the others to buck it. PFC Flood, face like a little bulldog and the confirmed screwup of the bunch, had been down on his knees puking in the sand, but even he was calming down, getting reassurances from the others. Today's exercise was just another field maneuver, the second part easier than the first. So just calm down, Porkchop thought; there'll be no Purple Hearts awarded for this business.

The sun, now up over the horizon, was blocked from their view by the towering residue of Shot Huey. Porkchop got his men loosely formed up, squads on line, three abreast in single file, and gave the hand signal to move out. Two miles to ground zero was a piece of cake. They ran three miles almost every morning before it got too hot and occasionally hiked as far as twenty miles on night maneuvers. Now, however, they started out at a walk, needing a moment to work their aching joints and regain the simplicity of movement. After a short forced march, Porkchop signaled again, raised his fist and pumped it twice, gearing the platoon up into a plodding double time.

Around them, things were beginning to clear. The prevailing winds were slowly regaining control from the force of the blast and cleansing the air, breaking up the black cloud and pushing it toward the east, into the sun and away from them. The Marines maintained their pace on a direct line toward the dissipating column of smoke. Near the edge of what had been Doomtown, they passed the waving lady, now reduced to a bent length of steel pipe, some melted plastic, and a little hanging rag of scorched fur. A twisted, pink oven door, its glass front exploded, lay at her feet. Nearby, the Darling house stood completely open, the windows and doors and parts of the walls gone, the upper half of the red brick chimney burst and scattered as if constructed from a child's blocks.

Porkchop led the platoon on a winding course through the twisted debris. All heads turned and looked, but the men passed by. The day was heating up, and rivers of sweat poured from them as they jogged over the warm sand past shards of smoking metal. Usually Porkchop or one of the squad leaders called cadence when they ran in formation, but this morning he maintained silence. It didn't matter. The Marines had run together so much that they automatically fell into perfect step, became one big machine, rifles gripped across their chests in port arms, battle ready for quick response. A mile from their objective, ash began falling, covering them like a light and dirty snow, depositing a soft gray overspread on the sand. The closer in they moved, the thicker the blanket of ash, until it became ankle deep. Each pounding step—eighty thick-soled combat boots in unison—stirred the downy layer.

In a sudden moment that none of them could have imagined, a blind and terrified pig ran straight at them, scalded bright pink and hairless, pieces of smoldering fabric seared to its skin. Blood ran from its nose, ears and mouth, and it almost collided with squad left before sensing something, veering sharply, and squealing in agony. But not one Marine broke ranks; not one boot missed cadence. Forty rights and forty lefts rose and fell as if welded together in fear and awe.

They passed the railroad trestle, gray and skeletal, steel twisted and buckled beyond recognition, the train cars on their sides, mere matchboxes against the force of Huey. The domes of underground shelters had blown off; rebar and concrete and pipes stuck out of the ground as if in some futuristic, junkyard world. Smoky orange sunlight filtered down around the advancing platoon, casting prismatic rainbows over them and the twisted rubble. A ream of paper blew slowly, page by page, out of a demolished shelter.

Porkchop was stunned. He knew about battle stress and this qualified—a half-roasted pig in remnants, a burning no-man's-land. He fought to keep his eyes focused on the objective. Sweat streamed down his face, into his eyes, mouth, and ears; his utility shirt was as wet as if it had been raining. Head radiated off the sand, which had been blistered into a glassy crust, and the soles of his boots were steaming. Ash flecked his face; his mouth tasted like acetylene and his own raw nerves.

Not far off on their left, a white Atomic Energy Commission van came into view, stopped a couple of hundred yards away, and four men slowly climbed out. They were dressed in what looked like space suits—protective boots, body suits, respirators, and sealed hoods—and they carried Geiger counters, small entrenching tools, and lead-lined containers. Anywhere else, Porkchop the hardcore Marine would have snickered—those guys walking around awkwardly like overgrown boys in stifling snowsuits—but out here, the differences between "them" and "us" became dark and threatening. What was it that those men had to be protected from, while his own boys were in everyday field dress? The AEC men froze and watched them like startled deer. The Marines kept chugging noiselessly forward like some phantom locomotive, steamy ash billowing up around their flanks, their destinies joined like the long shadow they now cast over the desert floor.

Finally the platoon left behind the wreckage and entered an area of translucent emptiness. All that lay in front of them for a quarter mile was flat, smoking ground and a dark crater; everything else was gone. Orders were to simulate a direct assault on ground zero and make it secure. Was he supposed to tactically form the squads, some positioned down for covering fire while others zigzagged in, hitting the deck, then up and charging? What? Dive into the smoldering crater? At about three hundred yards out, the heat intensified even further, and Porkchop gave the command to walk, then halt. He turned and absorbed the astonishment and fright on the young Marines in his charge—citizen-soldier-draftees standing in a silent storm of ash. If they wanted more than this from his men, well . . .

Porkchop spun around in a perfectly executed about-face and looked at the crater. He paused and then, alone, advanced twenty rigid steps. He halted, called the platoon to attention without turning, then locked his heels. He saluted smartly and held it, squarely facing ground zero. That was enough. If this damn place wasn't secure, he was one son of a buck sergeant who would never, ever see secure.

CORBIN HARNEY [1920–2007]

The Western Shoshone people have played an important leadership role in protests against nuclear testing. The Nevada Test Site is situated in the Shoshone people's homeland, Newe Segobia, a large geographical area comprising much of Nevada. These Shoshone lands were recognized in the 1863 Treaty of Ruby Valley, which guaranteed white men safe passage but did not cede any Shoshone land to the United States. Western Shoshones argue, therefore, that President Truman illegally seized Shoshone lands to establish the Nevada Test Site in 1951, and Indian claims to the land have been litigated since that time. Corbin Harney, an elder and spiritual leader of the Western Shoshone nation, was involved in peaceful demonstrations at the Test Site for two decades starting in 1985, when he "came out from behind the bush" to speak out for the health of Mother Earth. In 1994 he founded the Shundahai Network, a nonprofit organization dedicated to breaking the nuclear chain by building alliances with indigenous communities and environmental, peace, and human rights movements. As a boy, Harney ran away from a missionary school that punished children for speaking their native language, and he was raised by medicine people of the Owyhee Indian reservation. Consequently, in his later life he was one of the few people who knew the Shoshone language, sacred songs, and medicine. At the Test Site, Harney led a sunrise ceremony, sang traditional songs, played the drums, conducted sweat lodges, and used eagle feathers to pray for sick people, performing valued spirit work at protest gatherings. His book The Way It Is: One Water, One Air, One Mother Earth *(1995) is a compendium of autobiography, native beliefs, history, and activism. Harney was arrested at the Test Site several times and spoke out against nuclear testing and nuclear energy at the White House and in the Republic of Kazakhstan, Japan, Sweden, and England.*

from *The Way It Is*

> "*With over 900 bombs exploded, the Shoshone are the most bombed nation on Earth.*"
>
> —Chief Raymond Yowell, Western Shoshone

> "*We've created a monster, with no means of destroying it or neutralizing its effects, and we have no place to plant it. We cannot put it back into the Mother Earth as it is, since it's not the same as it was when it came out. It's been transformed into a monster.*"
>
> —Bill Rosse, Sr., Western Shoshone

There's a vision I've had from way back. Well, I've had visions about a lot of different things, but for instance, not too long ago, something came to me and talked to me about the water here. One time, when we were having a spiritual gathering, when I was praying for the water, the water said to me, "I'm going to look like water, but pretty soon nobody's going to use me." The Creator, or the Spirit told me this, and I passed it on to the people who were there at the time. Now, wherever I go, the people talk about their water being contaminated, and they can't use it.

One particular vision showed me something at the Test Site (U.S. Nuclear Testing Site in southern Nevada)—where they were drilling holes into the earth, and when they blasted those holes, or set those bombs off underground. The vision showed me that place is now beginning to fill up with water. The water is filling up those holes. I saw what it is doing to our earth, inside the earth itself. That's one vision I have seen.

I've seen a lot of visions, but I don't like to talk about them, because generally nobody believes in what I'm saying. It's very hard for people to believe these things. I don't like to talk about most of them. They are things that I don't think anybody would really understand. But there are visions among all of us, not only Indian people; white men also have visions. . . . People have to realize that we all have visions, and when we have a vision, we have to follow the vision and see for ourselves if it is true.

Some of us understand what a vision is, even though it's something that everybody has. All the living things on this planet of ours, everything has a vision. Even the planet itself has a vision, and now it's beginning to warn us that something's going to become different pretty quick, if we don't do something about it. This kind of vision is given from the earth to the people, but the people aren't paying attention to the visions. We think they're just something that we've dreamed up, or something that we just don't understand.

. . . .

We have one big enemy, a very important one, against which we, the people, have to unite together to stop. That one big enemy is the development of nuclear energy. Nuclear plants throughout the world and nuclear testing throughout the world are going to wipe us out. Once it contaminates our Mother Earth, then Mother Earth cannot produce food for us, or for all the living things on this Earth.

I've been working for the past few years down at the Nevada Test Site. It's on our Shoshone land that they're testing those nuclear weapons. They're using our land for bad things. I've been working with the white people against the Test Site, and the Native people in this part of the country are also saying, "This can't go on." Everybody's beginning to realize this. Forty or fifty years ago, when it started, everybody was hush-hush about radiation danger—until we experienced the effects, and it started taking over our lives.

So our role is in a dangerous place to be, but we're involved in stopping the testing, and somebody has to do it. I guess I was chosen by the Spirit, so I'm out there talking, meeting people, going on the radio, taking pictures, and making videos— anything I can do to make people aware how serious this nuclear contamination has become.

Between the United States and Great Britain, they've exploded almost 1,500 huge bombs down there. They're telling us it's safe on the surface ground, because the blasting is done way down deep. I and other people are asking the DOE, "What is that blasting doing within our Mother Earth?"

. . . .

We have to unite together—as a people—to put a stop to nuclear testing. Nevada might sound like a long ways away from some people's homes, but it's not—the air that we breathe today, is already contaminated. The wind patterns have carried that contamination to all parts of the country and beyond.

The nuclear testing they do within the Earth, drilling holes into it, a mile or two miles deep, and then blasting away—what do they think it's doing to the water table underneath? What does it look like underneath us? We've only got one planet; we've only got one air, one water. So what is this testing doing? And what is the effect? The government people will now admit, "We don't really know."

There are three small towns in northern Nevada where they're already hauling water in because they can't use the water that is there. In Carlin, Nevada, one of those towns, they've already been told, "Your water is contaminated; boil it." But boiling it won't work. Wherever we are, we're going to be drinking the same water that we're drinking here, and breathing the same air. There's no other planet that we can move to; this is our only home.

. . . .

Our water in the lakes comes from springs in the first place. Once those springs and underground lakes are mixed with that dangerous something else, then all our water is going to be dead water.

My people have always said that, when water becomes dead water, you can't revive it at all. That means that everything out there is not going to survive without that water, because the water's got to be alive. It's got to have a spirit. Once you kill that spirit, you have nothing. Once we kill the spirit of what's out there, then we are at a standstill.

. . . .

Yucca Mountain [site for the proposed U.S. Nuclear Waste Repository] lies asleep like a snake. When you walk on top of the mountain, it feels like you are walking on dried snakeskin. Someday, when we wake that snake up, a few of us will have to sit down and talk to that snake. It will get mad and rip open. When it awakens, we will all go to sleep. With his tail, that snake will move the mountain, rip it open, and the poison will come out on the surface. Long ago, the Indians talked about it. They see it is going to happen.

. . . .

As Native people, we're not looking to support ourselves alone, because I think many people throughout the world are already concerned with this nuclear enemy. Soon, everyone is going to be saying that we're going to have to put a stop to all this.

I would like to see people start talking to other people, getting together, and asking questions such as: What are we going to do? Who shall do it? Who wants to talk about what? How can we get together? What can we say to each other? Let's not be ashamed or shy. I used to be ashamed, but here I am, speaking up.

. . . .

I don't see any other way we can change the world, except by the people coming together, praying for the Earth, and then waking up the rest of us. A long time ago, the elders said that there would come a time when the Native people would have to lead everyone else out of this mess, so that's what we're trying to do now.

WILLIAM KITTREDGE [B. 1932]

William Kittredge grew up on the MC cattle ranch in the Warner Valley of southeastern Oregon. In "Buckaroos" Kittredge recalls a time spent as a teenager on the IXL ranch in Guano Valley, Nevada, just south of the Oregon border, rubbing shoulders with work-hardened buckaroos. Kittredge himself, however, never claimed any ability on horseback and had no desire to buckaroo. Instead, after earning a degree in agriculture from Oregon State College and serving in the air force from 1954 to 1957, Kittredge returned to the MC to be farming boss, deploying an arsenal of chemicals—2-4-D ethyl, malathion, parathion, and 1080—to kill pests from clover mites to coyotes. The chemical assault backfired. He writes, "The rodent population exploded and field mice destroyed our alfalfa. We irrigated and re-irrigated, pumped and drained; our peat soil began to go saline." Kittredge has spent a lifetime regretting his role in transforming "paradise" into a valley of death. After an interlude of self-destructive drinking and philandering, Kittredge made a commitment to writing, earning an MFA at the University of Iowa, and becoming an English professor at the University of Montana, Missoula, in 1969. Kittredge's influential The Last Best Place: A Montana Anthology *(1988), coedited with his*

"True Companion," Annick Smith, put Montana on the literary map and inspired other states to preserve their literary heritage in similar volumes. His many books, including Owning It All *(1987),* Hole in the Sky *(1992),* Who Owns the West? *(1996), and* The Willow Field *(2006), and more than 150 articles and stories, have made Kittredge one of the most important voices in the American West as he sounds the clarion call to jettison the machismo mythology of domination—symbolized below by the nuclear, military-industrial complex—and find a new story to inhabit that will guide us toward a respectful and sustainable relationship with each other and the natural world.*

In My Backyard

There was a cold nighttime wind blowing sand down the slope of Highway 95 when we parked outside the Mizpah Hotel in Tonopah. The Mizpah is an elegant old building left from the mining boom of the early 1900s in central Nevada, and it has been refurbished with some nice period furniture and lots of red-and-black whorehouse wallpaper. Jack Dempsey started his career as a bouncer in the Mizpah.

The True Companion and I had first stayed in the Mizpah on the advice of a friend who'd lived a few months in a room on the third floor while he wrote most of a pretty good novel about searching for gold. We ate lobster tail flown in from some coast, and it was terrific. But last spring the carpet on the stairs was worn through, and the dining room was closed.

I grew up knowing Nevada; my family ranched in southeastern Oregon, right on the Nevada border, and I'm one of the rare North Americans who feel at home and centered when I'm traveling the high sagebrush and creosote deserts. My maternal grandfather worked his way north to Oregon through the old mining camps in southern Nevada, Goldfield and Beatty and Rhyolite. But on this drive south from Montana, where I live now, I was taking stock of another Nevada, not the basin and range country that I love, but the Nevada our nation seems to think of as a vast, convenient dumpster out there waiting to be filled. Most recently in this regard, Nevada was designated the proposed site for our national nuclear waste repository.

The search for such a site was begun by the Energy Research and Development Administration in 1975. The kinds of formations seriously considered were bedded salt (the Paradox Basin in Utah and the Permian Basin in Texas); domed salt sites (Vacherie Dome in Louisiana and two sites in Mississippi); fine-grained igneous basalt (Hanford, Washington); and, in southern Nevada, volcanic tuff—rock composed of the finer kinds of volcanic detritus and fused by great heat. Under the Nuclear Waste Policy Act of 1982, the list was narrowed to three sites—Deaf Smith

County, Texas (eliminated: the site was beneath the agriculturally crucial Ogallala Aquifer); Hanford (eliminated: too close to the Columbia River); and the winner, designated by an impatient Congress last fall, the barren desert ridge called Yucca Mountain, north of Las Vegas, maybe fifty miles from California's Death Valley, and a couple of hours' drive south from the Mizpah.

Researchers are just "testing" Yucca Mountain right now, but don't expect them to find any snags. The government proposes spending more than $6.6 billion at Yucca Mountain in order to inter about 77,000 tons of high-level radioactive waste produced by Pentagon bomb-making and nuclear power plants. The junk they want to bury will remain seriously lethal for something toward 10,000 years. I wanted to stop by and have a look and see if I could convince myself that this was not a crazy idea. You might give it some thought yourself; Yucca Mountain is closer to Los Angeles than it is to Carson City.

. . . .

The next morning the True Companion and I drove south from Tonopah, down Highway 95 toward Yucca Mountain, which lies on the western edge of the test site. Traveling through the elegant morning light over those clean distances, with the white-topped shadows of the great California mountains far off on the western edge of things, I thought how unfair it was that this particular stretch of America should be our capital of radioactivity. Nuclear waste is so clearly a problem that belongs to others, people who commute to suburbs on one coast or another. They would be the first to stomp around and yell "Not in My Backyard."

It seems increasingly clear that a lot of people in the nuclear power business have a considerable stake in seeing things work out at Yucca Mountain. The site is in some respects an answer to the crisis in the industry. Electric utilities ordered 231 nuclear power plants in the years before 1975; since then they have ordered 13 (none after 1978), and they have canceled orders on 114, several of which were under construction. There are complex reasons for this decline: a drop in demand for electricity during the mid-1970s, after people began conserving in the wake of the OPEC oil embargo; increasing public awareness of the potential for disaster after the Three Mile Island accident; and a history of indecision about the problem of high-level nuclear waste. The nuclear repository in Nevada is supposed to solve that one.

We checked into a motel in Las Vegas, and an employee of the Department of Energy named Karen Randolph picked me up and drove me over for a visit with Carl Gertz, manager of the Nevada Nuclear Waste Storage Investigations Project. I expected armed guards at the door, and the kind of pomp we so often get when our democracy tries to play superpower. Instead I was led to some windowless offices built into the third floor of a parking garage a couple of blocks off the Las Vegas strip. I was happy: there were lots of maps and cutaway models of Yucca Mountain. There's nothing like schematics to make things look sensible and well planned.

It was the drill for Carl Gertz to brief me before Karen Randolph drove me to Yucca Mountain. "The repository, when filled," he said, "will be no more dangerous than unmined uranium ore." Who says? I wanted to ask. "It's our job," he said, "to inform the public. We're open. This whole thing is an experiment, conducted under public scrutiny. According to law," he said, and I didn't hear the rest. An experiment on what, and on whom? Who is ever going to get to vote on any of these matters?

After the briefing, driving past Nellis Air Force Base on our way to Yucca Mountain, Karen Randolph and I watched a couple of F-16 Thunderbirds (from the Air Force aerobatic team) come in low over Indian Springs, throttled back and looking so casually invincible. Out in these deserts we still find staging grounds for our shoot-out make-believe, as in Westerns.

But that kind of machismo seems almost innocent when compared with the accumulating power of the quiet empire that has taken control of so much of our empty lands in the years since World War II. And "empire" seems like the right word for the intertwining structure represented by the military and the Department of Energy. Not only at the test site in Nevada but in places like Los Alamos and White Sands in New Mexico, we are breeding a secret and enormously well-funded society of scientists and technicians, unseen for the most part, hidden behind fences and Top Secret Clearances, an elite answerable to almost no one except one another. That is not the way we are supposed to do things in our democracy.

Which may sound like another sci-fi paranoid dream.

Or not. Once I was cleared through the gates at Mercury, we headed out across the deserts inside the test site. It was like a trip through a land thick with national memories, names and huge prehistoric-looking monuments left from a heroic and dimly remembered time of greatness. Lost in the distances, looking abandoned for the most part, were clusters of huge stark buildings where our society perfected its secret work: the EMAD Facility; the Engine Test Stand, where they worked on the idea of a nuclear engine; Test Cell C; Test Cell A; RMAD. What did they do in there? The Bren Tower, once used to simulate air-drops, stands thin as a pencil line against the blue skies, taller than the Empire State Building. And beyond, Yucca Mountain. It was a nice day, and Karen Randolph was a person I liked. She had been at Oregon State College only a couple of years after me in the 1950s. We knew some of the same people.

Yucca Mountain is a long, unexceptional-looking desert ridge, composed of layers of volcanic ash-flow tuff deposited 13 to 18 million years ago, some of which have welded into a very dense, nonporous rock. It is in a formation of this type, some 1,200 feet beneath the surface of the mountain, that the repository would be located. At the top of Yucca Mountain Karen Randolph and I were met by a young shaven-headed man name Tony Buono, a hydrologist working for the U.S. Geological Survey. He gave me a whole portfolio of charts and maps, all the detailed information I could ever want about the site, and references in case I wanted more.

Gazing west over the shimmering distances of the Amargosa Valley, you see little volcanic cones, one of which was active no more than 20,000 years ago, and beyond you see faint lines of trees, which would have to mean there is pump agriculture in that country. Somebody out there is using up an aquifer whose water took millennia to accumulate; that must feel like quite a privilege.

The chance of volcanic activity and the presence of that aquifer, with its water and permeable rock, along with the unsettling fact that earthquake fault lines course nearby, represent the main geological concerns about Yucca Mountain as a site for a 10,000-year nuclear repository. Is it truly stable? Is there any way radioactive material might work down to the water table, which is more than 1,900 feet below the mountain top, and at least 700 feet below the base of the proposed repository? Yucca Mountain is one of the driest places in the United States, with an average rainfall of less than six inches a year. But still, we're talking 10,000 years—and a lot can change, and does, in 10,000 years.

After a lot of scientific talk about probabilities, meant to be reassuring, I was left with the idea that these kinds of questions are really unanswerable. While Yucca Mountain is probably going to prove as safe as any nuclear repository could be, nothing geologic is forever. I carried home a sample of welded ash-flow tuff. I see it now, as it sits on my windowsill, gray and dense, and I pray to God, impermeable enough.

"Nothing has been decided," Buono said to me before I left. "That's what we're doing here. We're getting ready to study this site, and see if it's safe. This is a case in which the public has to trust the scientists."

Ah, yes, but. Trust the people who brought us all this in the first place.

Which brings us to the ways trust is earned in southern Nevada. You don't have to spend much time in this region to figure out that Top Secret often means money in the air. The nuclear industry provides jobs and paychecks, and a good life for a lot of decent people. It also attracts those who are perfectly willing to screw each other if there's enough money involved. Which gets us to the story of Bullfrog County.

Congress decided, early on in all this, that the county selected as the site for the repository should be paid "funds in lieu of taxes." Think of this money as a kind of bait. Estimates of the amount involved range from $2 to $40 million, depending on whether DOE or the State of Nevada evaluates the worth of the site. Which is an issue that will no doubt be resolved in the courts. But in the meantime, it looked like great empty Nye County, one of the largest counties in the United States (18,000 square miles, population 14,250, 6,000 registered voters), was coming into a considerable windfall.

As can be imagined, a lot of people wanted in on the action. In one of the last sessions of the 1987 Nevada legislature, with the strong backing of representatives from Clark County (Las Vegas), a new county was created around Yucca Mountain, *entirely* inside Nye County and *completely* unpopulated, which was called Bullfrog County. The seat of government for Bullfrog County was conveniently located in Carson City, in the office of Governor Richard H. Bryan. Which meant the "funds in lieu of taxes" would really go to the state, and would end up being spent primarily in Clark County, where most of the people in Nevada live. But then Nye County sued the State of Nevada, and the whole notion was nixed by the Nevada Supreme Court. As things stand, nobody in Nevada wins, as usual, except maybe comic-opera fans.

SHAUN T. GRIFFIN [B. 1953]

For biographical information on Shaun Griffin, see p. 598. In the early nineties when the federal government advanced plans to build a permanent nuclear waste dump in southern Nevada, poet Shaun Griffin attended the Department of Energy public hearings for many months and read what he recalls as "the endless papers being given out to extol the virtues of Yucca Mountain." Unconvinced, Griffin organized an art show of his watercolors, sculpture, and poems against the nuke dump. At a last hearing in a Reno casino, Griffin learned that the DOE geologist who testified about the scientific safety of the site had been paid to leave her academic position to endorse the project—apparently paid lots. Sometime later Griffin read a statement by hydrologist Tony Buono, admonishing the public to trust the scientists. Griffin responded by writing the poem "Nevada No Longer," quoting Buono for an epigraph. The title of the poem came from Griffin's repeatedly reading indices of culture—bookstores, newspapers, colleges, churches—and never finding Nevada. A silly thing, perhaps, but when, as he says, "the atomic purveyors came knocking, it seemed silly no more." He wrote the poem for his two boys, who, in Griffin's words, "must live here when we leave," and "for all of us who must live here until then." He wrote it when, as he recalls, "I believed words were the equal of governments." "I'm convinced we can put the genie back in the bottle if we choose," Griffin says, "but until we develop a Los Alamos for neutralizing fission with the best and brightest minds today—until we harness a power less toxic—hydrogen or solar—we will pursue the immediate and not the consequences of such a choice." Like many others who have suffered reprisals for trying to do the right thing, Griffin speaks out "to preserve an earth where all can sustain a livelihood."

Nevada No Longer

> *This is a case in which the public has to trust the scientists.*
> —Tony Buono, USGS Hydrologist, Nevada Test Site

Nevada is never on the map, not now,
not ever.
     If only
I could finger a word
for the few who live
        by the sun,
what would it be: itinerant,
sparse dragon people
       who fly
in the sand and spin before the books
that name a cactus to clothe
the loins of uranium down deep?

No, it would not be harsh; rather
we live here.
We raise family, split wood,
shovel snow, and read of our absence.

Nevada is never on the map,
not now, not ever,
       save the day
a green lung percolates
from two miles below volcanic tuff—
then you will recognize us
as the place that kills
or was killed, but for now
I cannot find a way down Alternate 95—
not scholarly, not radical, not
known. And still, faces cling

to the taverns of Beatty,
Tonopah, and Yerington.

Where do I go to lie with the yucca? California?
No, it is many things but quiet.
Oregon? No, it is wet and
dry there, so I remain
home
with states before and aft
coming like insects
to the Test Site, coming
with something to read.

Today, I tell my son
of a desert with no name. He remarks
"Why?" I do not know—Nevada is
never on the map, not now,
not ever.

RICHARD RAWLES [B. 1948]

Born in Southern California during the height of the baby boom, Richard Rawles was forced to make the difficult choices that beset his generation. He refused induction into the military at the height of the Vietnam War and performed alternative service in Santa Cruz and San Luis Obispo, where he began his editing and literary careers. He attended UC Santa Barbara and UC Santa Cruz, graduating from the latter with honors in the creative writing program. Both writer and scholar, Rawles attended graduate school at the University of Canterbury in New Zealand, and his dissertation focuses on William Blake and the Kabbalah. Editor and writer for a variety of publications and technology companies, Rawles has in addition written against ballistic missile defense and deep-geologic nuclear waste burial and has protested activities at the Nevada Test Site from outside the gates of Mercury. Rawles's work has appeared in Sierra, Spectacle, White Heron Poetry Review, Café Solo, Outerbridge, and Bleating Hearts. As part of a powerful husband-wife antinuclear team, he is married to sociologist Valerie L. Kuletz, whose book The Tainted Desert: Environmental Ruin in the American West *(1998) is a theoretically sophisticated ethnoecological study of nuclear landscapes of the Southwest, documenting how nuclear activities have devastated the people and spiritual landscapes of Native America and highlighting ongoing native resistance. Both Rawles and Kuletz have traveled extensively in Nevada, interviewing Western Shoshone and antinuclear activists. Rawles is currently living in Oakland, where he is completing a book of poems, editing a history of biotechnology, and writing his "Countersigns" blog. "Coyote Learns to Glow" is excerpted from John Bradley's* Learning to Glow: A Nuclear Reader *(2000), which also contains Kuletz's "Tragedy at the Center of the Universe."*

Coyote Learns to Glow

A sign near the entrance to the Nevada Test Site reads:

Desert Tortoise Habitat
Threatened Species
It is unlawful to possess, harass, transport,
injure, kill, receive or remove
a threatened or endangered species
16 USC Sec. 1538

By those standards of criminality, the entire Department of Energy (DOE) operation at Mercury, Nevada, should be subject to arrest. The amount of radiation the tortoises have been exposed to should qualify as injury. As part of the department's "bugs and bunnies" environmental research program, the reptiles are routinely rounded up and tagged for monitoring.

. . . .

It's typical of the American government's professed concern for the "environment" that it should regard the desert tortoise as endangered—but not the region's long-time Shoshone inhabitants. . . . Americans prefer to think of their wilderness as uninhabited; it makes it easier to reconcile setting aside certain areas for military activities, such as bomb tests. If their sacrifice is necessary for national security, well, tortoises don't protest their extinction, and if they must go, they go quietly. Put up signs around the perimeter to make it look as though civilians are responsible for their disappearance, not the military. Never mind the fact that the tortoise (*Gopherus agassizii*) is totem to some people who have lived in the region as long as the tortoise has—some ten to twelve thousand years.

The Nevada Test Site and the overlapping Yucca Mountain Project to the north rest on traditional native lands. In fact, despite efforts by the federal government to buy them out, the Western Shoshone hold title to the land based on the 1863 Treaty of Ruby Valley. They have resisted assimilation to varying degrees, often supplementing a subsistence living from diminishing reserves of game animals and pine nuts with ranching and mining jobs. . . .

Far from being an uninhabited wilderness, the desert regions in and around the Nevada Test Site show archaeological evidence of human habitation for thousands of years until the land was withdrawn from public use by the military. These "invisible people" fight the very thing that the tortoise sign warns of: extinction.

. . . .

I have a recurrent fantasy. Drilling into Yucca Mountain, scientists discover a large vault. Teams of archaeologists are called in. An underground city, perhaps? Maybe a rumored golden city of Cibola, a scene reminiscent of recent tomb discoveries in Egypt, unimagined treasures, or of the discovery of the lunar monolith in Kubrick's *2001: A Space Odyssey?* Speculation abounds. Finally workers clear away enough debris for scientists to enter the cavern. What they discover is a vast chamber, vaguely familiar, where large casks of steel, some corroded beyond all recognition, lie in disarray. An eerie glow, like some primeval mist, pervades the cavern, the floor of which is flooded up to the scientists' knees. And then the realization. This is an atomic vault, a radiation waste dump of a civilization long since vanished from the face of the Earth.

Science fiction? Yes, but we easily forget how much science is fiction—how predisposed we are to conceive of problems in certain ways. The scene I envision could easily be enacted ten thousand years hence, during a future waste crisis. The scale of time by which scientists calculate the outcomes of intervention at Yucca Mountain is geologic, longer than recorded history. No man-made container can be guaranteed to stand up for more than a few hundred years. Russian engineers will count their blessings if the specially designed materials they've used to seal the damaged Chernobyl reactor last two hundred years. Any estimates of a material's durability beyond that remain as speculative as any science fiction. Instead scientists are relying on supposedly water-impermeable welded tuff, of which the Yucca Mountain formation is composed, to hold the most toxic waste in check.

No, the crisis is now. Not in some unimaginable past or future.

We are fond of the stories scientists tell us. They are somehow reassuring, comforting in the face of what we don't fully comprehend. (Myth, it is sometimes argued, serves a similar function in less "advanced" cultures.) Chaos theory, for instance, reduces the forces of entropy and disintegration to human scale: something almost imaginable, even manageable, something that we can visualize in computer simulation, rendered harmless by innocuous terms like "the Butterfly Effect." The implication—that small, even infinitesimal anomalies in the initial conditions of a system can magnify over time, with massive repercussions—is ignored when science wants the outcome of its experiments predetermined. The massive "experiment" at Yucca Mountain—testing the feasibility of siting a radioactive dump there—has a foregone conclusion. Theories to the contrary, such as the "critical mass" theory, in which physicists speculate that storing all that plutonium in one place could lead to an explosion, are summarily dismissed.

I read a Louis L'Amour western, I forget its name, written before chaos theory was popularized by James Gleick and *Jurassic Park.* It begins its saga with a coyote scratching at a piece of dirt, which loosens some rocks. After years of erosion, a vein of gold is exposed that would otherwise have remained hidden, perhaps forever, had the coyote not loosened the rock. Discovery of the gold ushers in a gold rush, of course, forever altering the natural history of the West. What chaoticists call the Butterfly Effect, here I would rename the Coyote Principle.

Extrapolating the Coyote Principle to the Yucca Mountain story, the use of a tunnel-boring machine to drill a hundred miles of twenty-five-foot-diameter tunnels into the mountain will have consequences far beyond what we can currently imagine. The site, selected for its relative remoteness and particular geology, is nestled among dozens of known earthquake faults and recently active (within the last fifteen thousand years) volcanoes. Ironically, Yucca Mountain was chosen as the site to house high-level radioactive waste for its inertness, and yet the surrounding area is quite active geologically. A 5.5 temblor shook the area a few years back, damaging facilities at the neighboring Nevada Test Site. Within the mountain itself, water is perched on ledges, ready to seep downward through fissures should conditions change. We can well imagine the current drilling into the mountainside serving as the agent of such a change. And the area is not active just geologically. Until weapons testing ceased in 1992, hundreds of underground nuclear tests rocked the region.

No one can watch a film of an aerial view of an underground nuclear test and go away believing that it has no effect on the land. Spreading outward from the epicenter, the land buckles up like a soufflé before subsiding into a kind of sink. Rocks in the interior of the Earth are subjected to temperatures found only on the surface of the sun. Corbin Harney asks, "What does that do to the groundwater?" The aquifer under the Nevada desert, the third largest in the United States, is already receding due to the demands of a booming Las Vegas. Add possible radiation, and you don't need to worry about the desert tortoise, except for a few possible mutants. Nor do you have to worry about the few troublesome Shoshone who cling to the land. In time, however, the water will drain past Ash Meadows, the oasis twenty miles to the southeast, ultimately affecting the Colorado River that supplies Los Angeles and that, if irradiated, will make the news too late to do anything about it.

The quarter-of-a-million-year legacy (equal to ten half-lives of plutonium) of our fifty-year experiment with nuclear energy is further evidence of the Coyote

Principle. Little could Americans have imagined in 1945 the scope of the problem that attempting to harness the nuclear fire would engender. Little can we imagine it now. But imagine it we must. In thinking about such time scales, which are well beyond the scope of the historical imagination, we must revert to the language of myth. Science offers little help.

Coyote, of course, is the culture bringer, mischief maker par excellence in western Native American Indian traditions, and, like Prometheus in our Western mythology, the bringer of fire, stolen not from gods but from other humans during the time when animals were human—or, as Westerners prefer to think of it, when *humans* were animal. Atomic energy represents another cycle in the myth of the stolen fire. Like Coyote, who lights his tail in order to transport the fire and whose fur consequently catches fire during his getaway, we are experiencing a difficult time putting out the fire. Every attempt to douse the flames only seems to spread them. It is out of control. In one version of the story, the people who are the keepers of the fire eventually catch up with and kill Coyote. Like his cartoon counterpart, Coyote is of course immortal, and goes on to other misadventures. Our species may not be so lucky.

JAMES CONRAD [B. 1964]

Experts agree that nuclear waste will remain dangerously radioactive for ten thousand years, longer than the life spans of most of the world's languages and all of its major civilizations. If the proposed long-term nuclear storage facility at Yucca Mountain is built, what kind of warning signs and systems can be installed that will remain decipherable? James Conrad happened to pick up the New York Times Magazine *on an airplane and read an article on Yucca Mountain, covering proposed solutions that ranged from giant daggers projecting from the ground to artwork conveying universal images of danger. Born and raised in Orono, Minnesota, with a BA in English from Northwestern University, and an MFA from the Columbia Writing Program, Conrad had been thinking of writing some stories on a group of crazy poets in Chicago. The* Times *article struck him as absurd and helped him imagine his first novel,* Making Love to the Minor Poets of Chicago *(2000), as the story of a Chicago poet who is commissioned to write an epic poem about the dangers of nuclear waste. In order to finagle her way into the Nevada Test Site to research material for the poem, the poet volunteers to be a tour guide. The scene reprinted below imagines the training that guides receive—Conrad's sardonic commentary on the marketing of Yucca Mountain. In order to write the scene, Conrad, who has been involved in nuclear freeze protests, underwent a lengthy government clearance process before being permitted to take the very tour he describes. Conrad has published poetry in* Tin House, *the* James White Review, Fruit, *and* Allegheny Review *and is currently working on a new novel from his home in Woodstock, New York, where he supports himself as a graphic designer and co-owner of a knitting store, the Woodstock Wool Company, that offers fiction writing classes, a reading series, and a knitting book club.*

from *Making Love to the Minor Poets of Chicago*

"I can tell right off what a good storyteller you are," Donna Black says, gripping my hand with both of hers with that overenthusiastic condescension that makes me realize why Westerners loathe tourists. "I can just tell you're a woman made up of stories, stories I look forward to hearing sometime. But for now our story is Yucca Mountain, and like your own life, it is a story made up of many different stories."

I nearly fall backward a step when she finally releases my hand and turns to the three other tour guides in training. . . .

It's my first day at the year-old Yucca Mountain Visitors' Center, a one-story building about the size of a Gap store and actually located in a small strip mall. The center is not for the employees of the Yucca Mountain Project but for the people of Nevada and tourists from around the world who want to learn more about the first underground, long-term nuclear waste storage facility. As Donna Black continues telling the other trainees about the stories she's confident they possess, I glance around the single room that serves as a science center made up of maps, photographs, Native American artifacts, and small-scale models of the mountain, the proposed storage facility, and the methods of transportation under consideration to bring nuclear waste to the mountain.

"You'll hate her," Peg told me as she drove us to the center. It had been Peg's idea for me to train as a guide. I had always expressed my desire to go to the site and see for myself the place where it was hoped toxic waste could be safely sealed and left alone for ten thousand years. Once the center opened, it was announced that tours of the site for the public would be conducted one Saturday every month. . . .

"She's one of those overpaid corporate therapists who treats everyone like toddlers when it comes to environmental impact adjustment."

"You mean she whitewashes everything," I say, letting Peg's convertible Miata blow-dry my hair with dust.

"I mean she's a bitch."

"You are the faces of Yucca Mountain," Donna Black tells us, after convincing us to all sit cross-legged on the industrial carpeting in a circle. "There are no issues. There are no politics. There is no right, there is no wrong, and above all, there is no danger." She wears an expensive white business suit that looks Italian, and her red hair is cut in an asymmetrical bob so that her thin face always seems to be at a slight angle, perfectly posed for a camera. I guess her to be younger than me, and I settle down comfortably on the floor in my jeans and T-shirt to enjoy hating her.

"What that leaves us with are stories. A nonjudgmental narrative to tell people what they're seeing and what isn't there to be seen. For example, Bob here," Donna indicates a thin, bearded man who looks like a graduate student in something you can't see the need to graduate in. "Bob is training as a botanist at the site. He will tell people the story of plant life at Yucca Mountain. After showing people the variety of desert life, he will finish his story by explaining how the government plans on restoring exactly all the desert environment that is temporarily being used by workers and machinery. He will show diagrams and timetables explaining how this will be accomplished. Bob has already had extensive training on-site and is, perhaps, a little further along in knowing what kinds of questions to expect from visitors to Yucca Mountain. Let me show you. So, Bob," Donna drops her voice down to mimic a man's, causing nervous laughter from the rest of us. I see Peg walk out the door with a quick hand wave over her shoulder. "Why spend all this money restoring plant life when all that nuclear stuff they're burying here will just kill it all anyway?"

Bob clears his voice and speaks directly to Donna. "There really is no threat to the environment from the proposed storage facility. Evaluations are continuing, and if any potential for leakage is found, the site will be ruled out. The story of plant life at Yucca Mountain will continue with the return of normal desert life once construction is finished."

"Notice his use of *proposed*," Donna says, back in her high-pitched hostess voice. "Though the digging of the tunnel is underway, this is the only method for continued tests on the suitability of the mountain. When all tests have been concluded to favorably show the safety of the site, then storage will start. This is important because we want our visitors not to feel the story has been concluded without them. We are all a part of the story of Yucca Mountain, and by stressing that you will gain the trust of the group. Also, notice how Bob did not resort to words like *nuclear* and *waste*. Avoid these words at all cost. What's that kind of cactus where the needles literally fly out at you when you get too close?" She looks at Bob, who seems caught off guard, unsure whether or not this is one of the potentially sensitive questions he's in training for. "Well, I think those words are like that kind of cactus; get too close and you get pricked."

. . . .

I'm on a tour bus in the middle of a desert, and two armed soldiers in camouflage are walking down the aisle toward me. I feel singled out even though I successfully went through all the clearances necessary to put me on this bus with Donna Black, the three other Yucca Mountain tour-guides-in-training, two certified tour guides, and a couple of dozen displaced Californians (with a few genuine Nevadans) heading to Yucca Mountain with their minds already made up. The soldiers look on the floor between rows of seats and above us in the overhead compartments. They also try to look each of us in the eye as they pass, as if they can determine a potential terrorist from the terrified looks on our faces. The tour guides didn't warn us this would happen once we reached the boundary of the U.S. Testing Site, a literal state within the state of Nevada; and even Donna Black, who has been here before, looks taken aback by this Soviet-style checkpoint. I can already imagine her making mental notes to try and downplay this scenario on future tours. Perhaps the soldiers could wear khaki shorts and Yucca Mountain T-shirts to make them look more like ticket takers at Disneyland. I force myself not to look at Donna (who is across the aisle from me) as I am already nervous enough that they will randomly start questioning me.

. . . .

The soldiers finally get off the bus, and we enter the testing site. Though the barren landscape hasn't changed one bit on the other side of the fence, the tourists are all pushing themselves toward the windows, wide-awake after this brush with the military. I catch Donna's eye, and she too quickly slaps on a smile as if to say well, that was one of those cactus I was warning you about. Get too close, and the needles just fly out at you.

Donna instructed me and the other three tour-guides-in-training to act like normal tourists today, to carefully observe the interactions of the real tourists with the trained guides. We are allowed to ask questions like the tourists; in fact, she has encouraged us to do so; that way we won't look suspicious. Donna has even gone to the trouble of providing us with some sample questions to ask. "How far is the nearest population center to Yucca Mountain?" "What wildlife, if any, make Yucca Mountain their habitat?" "How long would it take a drop of rain to reach the water table below the mountain?" From what I've heard on the first hour of the bus ride, asking such a question would be a bigger giveaway of my training than wearing a name tag. So far the questions have been more like declarative statements. "Why can't they store the stuff in outer space?" "Nevada doesn't even use nuclear power, so why do we have to deal with it?" "If it's so safe, why do they have to drag it all the way out here to bury it?"

The tour guides have done exactly as Donna would do. They calmly answer these questions with the most unthreatening and scientific responses possible. They avoid saying it's absolutely determined that the waste will end up in Yucca

Mountain and that's why we're all out here, to see how suitable the site is. No one seems to believe this. I listen more to the murmuring between passengers than the textbook responses of the guides. There is a general distrust of the military, the government, and the East Coast as being responsible for the stuff in the first place, and everyone reacts in that Western way I've gotten used to. In the minds of people in the West, Washington, DC is as far away as China, and the government's only interest in the West is to strip it of its minerals and use it as a garbage heap for illegal immigrants, weapons, and waste. The guides try to make a game out of the difference of opinion with the more vocal opposition (a couple of middle-aged men who say they served in the military and, thus, claim to know a lot about anything nuclear). The guides don't do a very good job and sound like camp counselors coaxing children away from their homes on their first camping experience. "On the ride back we'll see if our stories of Yucca Mountain haven't convinced some of you of the careful and important work being done out here." From what I can see, nothing in the barren landscape surrounding us will give the skeptic's stories any surprise endings.

TEN

THE LONELIEST ROADS
IN AMERICA

Contemporary Travel Writing

"I saw no one." How often can we say that? Some people journey to Nevada to experience "the nothing that is not there and the nothing that is," to borrow a line from poet Wallace Stevens, not writing about Nevada but somehow capturing the pull of its emptiness. "We traveled for hours and hours along narrow dirt roads through the high emptiness of Nevada. Anybody who is under the impression that the world is becoming too crowded should move into Nevada," penned British writer J. B. Priestley in 1937. "A road there seems to lead endlessly from nothing to nothing." Sixty years later, Steve Roper, in "The Roads," recorded a similar impression: "One look at the road signs and you know you're out in nowhere. Next Services 112 Miles. Deer Crossing Next 78 Miles. Caution: Pavement Ends. Road Not Maintained by County. Road Plowed Only During Daylight Hours. Flash Flood Area: Use Caution. Road Not Maintained: Use at Own Risk. America's Loneliest Highway." "Calm lay over the uncluttered openness," writes another modern-day traveler. "The immensity of sky and desert, their vast absences, reduced me," recalls yet another.

While the masses flock to Reno and Las Vegas, only a select few venture out into the desert beyond the neon oases. An article in *Life* magazine in the late 1980s specifically warned against doing so, noting of U.S. Highway 50: "It's totally empty. There are no points of interest. We don't recommend it. We warn all motorists not to drive there unless they're confident of their survival skills." Nevada turned lemons into lemonade by formally designating Highway 50 "The Loneliest Road in America" and developing a "Route 50 Survival Kit." Travelers who get their "passport" duly validated along the way earn a certificate signed by the governor, a lapel pin, and a bumper sticker that reads, "I Survived the Loneliest Road in America." Indeed, many memoirs of Nevada travel focus on driving, the view out the car window a mélange of monotony and sublimity. Nevada's highways evoke powerful memories, their very numbers emanating distinctive vistas and aromas, miseries and insights—I-80, I-15, 50, 395, 93, 95, 6. The byways are even more unforgettable, occasioning survival stories of their own. Broke down. Spare was flat. Bogged down on a playa. Lost in a snowstorm. Up to the axles in sand. Rolled over. Engine overheated. High-centered. Out of water. No signal. Stuck. Again, Steve Roper: "The roads are schizophrenic. Ten minutes after zooming along at seventy-five on the Interstate, you can be lurching along a sandy track, wondering which of the forks ahead to take. No signs here. Paved roads change without warning to gravel, and then to dirt. High crowns appear between the wheel tracks, and then high crowns crowned with clumps of sagebrush. Your muffler gets a free, aromatic scrubbing. It's time to turn around—if you can find a place."

How long can even the most inventive writer sustain nothing? Generally, travel accounts arrive at an attraction, somewhere to get out of the car and stretch. Nevada offers some, frankly, weird destinations: The Little A'Le'Inn on the Extraterrestrial Highway, "Earthlings Welcome"; the Burning Man festival on the Black Rock Desert, clothing optional; Rhyolite and other ghost towns; bunny ranches; petroglyphs of giant vaginas; Hawthorne, America's largest munitions depot; Winnemucca, whose billboards boast, "City of Paved Streets"; and the Old Spice Festival at Battle Mountain, a town selected by the *Washington Post* in 2001 as "The Armpit of America," where the "only flora consists of nondescript scrub that resembles acres upon acres of toilet brushes buried to the hilt." Nevada travel writing dates back to the earliest fur trappers in the 1820s, picking up speed in the age of the automobile, thanks to a wonderful Depression-era WPA guidebook that was organized by driving tours. The pieces here, from the last twenty-five years, feature brilliant musings on a quirky selection of roadside attractions, triggering existential meditations on technology, modernity, and community.

JOAN DIDION [B. 1934]

No matter where she travels, Joan Didion always describes the same place—the psyche of Joan Didion. But because Didion identifies so strongly with the national condition, her personal essays about breakdown and despair reflect the disintegration of America itself. With charac-teristic dread, Didion interprets Hoover Dam—a monumental American success story—as a premonition of the collapse of civilization. "At the Dam" appears in The White Album *(1979), whose preface shares a 1968 psychiatric report describing Didion as alienated, pessimistic, and depressed. Didion's first essay collection,* Slouching towards Bethlehem *(1968), which estab-lished her as a leading essayist, takes its title from William Butler Yeats's poem "The Second Coming," which warns: "Things fall apart; the center cannot hold; / Mere anarchy is loosed upon the world." Didion's five novels, journalism, and nine nonfiction books express the chaos of modern life and the corruption of American politics. Her notable Nevada works include the nihilistic novel* Play It As It Lays *(1970), nominated for a National Book Award, in which Nevada appears as an existential desert; and "Marrying Absurd," an essay in which Las Ve-gas's quickie wedding chapels signify the absurd loss of meaning in America. Among the most accomplished twentieth-century writers, Didion grew up in Sacramento, in a family whose California roots date back to 1848. Graduating from* UC *Berkeley in 1956, she began working at* Vogue *magazine in New York, where she rose from promotional copywriter to associate feature editor. In 1963 she married John Gregory Dunne, editor of* Time *magazine, and the two moved to Los Angeles to launch their freelance careers, also collaborating on many screenplays.*

At the Dam

Since the afternoon in 1967 when I first saw Hoover Dam, its image has never been entirely absent from my inner eye. I will be talking to someone in Los Angeles, say, or New York, and suddenly the dam will materialize, its pristine concave face gleaming white against the harsh rusts and taupes and mauves of that rock canyon hundreds or thousands of miles from where I am. I will be driving down Sunset Boulevard, or about to enter a freeway, and abruptly those power transmission towers will appear before me, canted vertiginously over the tailrace. Sometimes I am confronted by the intakes and sometimes by the shadow of the heavy cable that spans the canyon and sometimes by the ominous outlets to unused spillways, black in the lunar clarity of the desert light. Quite often I hear the turbines. Frequently I wonder what is happening at the dam this instant, at this precise intersection of time and space, how much water is being released to fill downstream orders and what lights are flashing and which generators are in full use and which just spin-ning free.

I used to wonder what it was about the dam that made me think of it at times

and in places where I once thought of the Mindanao Trench, or of the stars wheeling in their courses, or of the words *As it was in the beginning, is now and ever shall
be, world without end, amen.* Dams, after all, are commonplace: we have all seen
one. This particular dam had existed as an idea in the world's mind for almost
forty years before I saw it. Hoover Dam, showpiece of the Boulder Canyon project,
the several million tons of concrete that made the Southwest plausible, the *fait ac-
compli* that was to convey, in the innocent time of its construction, the notion that
mankind's brightest promise lay in American engineering.

Of course the dam derives some of its emotional effect from precisely that aspect, that sense of being a monument to a faith since misplaced. "They died to
make the desert bloom," reads a plaque dedicated to the 96 men who died building
this first of the great high dams, and in context the worn phrase touches, suggests
all of that trust in harnessing resources, in the meliorative power of the dynamo,
so central to the early Thirties. Boulder City, built in 1931 as the construction town
for the dam, retains the ambience of a model city, a new town, a toy triangular grid
of green lawns and trim bungalows, all fanning out from the Reclamation building.
The bronze sculptures at the dam itself evoke muscular citizens of a tomorrow that
never came, sheaves of wheat clutched heavenward, thunderbolts defied. Winged
Victories guard the flagpole. The flag whips in the canyon wind. An empty Pepsi-
Cola can clatters across the terrazzo. The place is perfectly frozen in time.

But history does not explain it all, does not entirely suggest what makes that
dam so affecting. Nor, even, does energy, the massive involvement with power and
pressure and the transparent sexual overtones to that involvement. Once when I
revisited the dam I walked through it with a man from the Bureau of Reclamation.
For a while we trailed behind a guided tour, and then we went on, went into parts
of the dam where visitors do not generally go. Once in a while he would explain
something, usually in that recondite language having to do with "peaking power,"
with "outages" and "dewatering," but on the whole we spent the afternoon in a
world so alien, so complete and so beautiful unto itself that it was scarcely necessary to speak at all. We saw almost no one. Cranes moved above us as if under their
own volition. Generators roared. Transformers hummed. The gratings on which
we stood vibrated. We watched a hundred-ton steel shaft plunging down to that
place where the water was. And finally we got down to that place where the water
was, where the water sucked out of Lake Mead roared through thirty-foot penstocks and then into thirteen-foot penstocks and finally into the turbines themselves. "Touch it," the Reclamation said, and I did, and for a long time I just stood
there with my hands on the turbine. It was a peculiar moment, but so explicit as to
suggest nothing beyond itself.

There was something beyond all that, something beyond energy, beyond history, something I could not fix in my mind. When I came up from the dam that day the wind was blowing harder, through the canyon and all across the Mojave. Later, toward Henderson and Las Vegas, there would be dust blowing, blowing past the Country-Western Casino FRI & SAT NITES and blowing past the Shrine of Our Lady of Safe Journey STOP & PRAY, but out at the dam there was no dust, only the rock and the dam and a little greasewood and a few garbage cans, their tops chained, banging against a fence. I walked across the marble star map that traces a sidereal revolution of the equinox and fixes forever, the Reclamation man had told me, for all time and for all people who can read the stars, the date the dam was dedicated. The star map was, he had said, for when we were all gone and the dam was left. I had not thought much of it when he said it, but I thought of it then, with the wind whining and the sun dropping behind a mesa with the finality of a sunset in space. Of course that was the image I had seen always, seen it without quite realizing what I saw, a dynamo finally free of man, splendid at last in its absolute isolation, transmitting power and releasing water to a world where no one is.

WILLIAM LEAST HEAT-MOON [B. 1939]

In February 1978 Dr. William Trogdon lost both job and wife. Prior to this fateful month, Trogdon had earned a BA, MA, and PHD in literature from the University of Missouri, Columbia, taught English at Stephens College, and returned to "Mizzou" to earn a BA in photojournalism in 1978. Ready for change, Trogdon took his recently acquired skills on the road, reasoning that a "man who couldn't make things go right could at least go." He and his van, named Ghost Dancing, embarked on a three-month, thirteen-thousand-mile, thirty-eight-state, clockwise circuit of small-town America, sticking to the two-lane roads that appear as wavy blue lines on old maps. Four years later, under the pen name William Least Heat Moon, he published Blue Highways: A Journey into America *(1982), which enjoyed overwhelming critical and popular success, staying on the* New York Times *best-seller list for nearly a year. Hence, out of difficulties, Trogdon emerged as the prominent American writer William Least Heat Moon (later hyphenated to Heat-Moon to avoid being called "Mr. Moon"). Attracted to unusual town names, such as Nameless, Tennessee, and Dime Box, Texas, Heat-Moon chose a pen name that held personal meaning. His scoutmaster father, of Osage Indian ancestry, took the name "Heat Moon"; his eldest son is "Little Heat Moon," and William is "Least Heat Moon." Heat-Moon's* PrairyErth: (a deep map) *(1991) is an intensely concentrated travel book about a single place, Chase County, Kansas, home of an increasingly endangered remnant of tallgrass prairie.* River-Horse: The Logbook of a Boat across America *(1999) is an epic account of*

Heat-Moon's navigating more than five thousand miles of rivers and lakes, from the Atlantic to the Pacific, while Columbus in the Americas *(2002) imaginatively joins Columbus on his adventures, viewing the New World through his eyes but also viewing Columbus through the eyes of our own time.*

from *Blue Highways*

Within a mile of the Nevada stateline, the rabbit brush and sage stopped and a juniper forest began as the road ascended into cooler air. I was struck, as I had been many times, by the way land changes its character within a mile or two of a stateline. I turned north on U.S. 93, an empty highway running from Canada nearly to Mexico. I'm just guessing, but, for its great length, it must have fewer towns per mile than any other federal highway in the country. It goes, for example, the length of Nevada, more than five hundred miles, passing through only seventeen towns—and that's counting Jackpot and Contact.

Pioche, one of the seventeen, was pure Nevada. Its elevation of six thousand feet was ten times its population; but during the peak of the mining boom a century ago, the people and the feet above sea level came to the same number. The story of Pioche repeats itself over Nevada: Indian shows prospector a mountain full of metal; prospector strikes bonanza; town booms for a couple of decades with the four "G's": grubstakes, gamblers, girls, gunmen (seventy-five people died in Pioche before anyone died a natural death); town withers. By 1900, Pioche was on its way to becoming a ghost town like Midas, Wonder, Bullion, Cornucopia. But, even with the silver and gold gone, technological changes in the forties made deposits of lead and zinc valuable, and cheap power from Boulder Dam (as it was then) kept Pioche alive.

A citizen boasted to me about their "Million Dollar Courthouse"—a plain yet pleasing century-old fieldstone building sitting high on the mountainside—albeit a little cynically, since construction cost a fraction of that; but through compound interest and refinancing, the price finally hit a million. The courthouse was condemned three years before the mortgage was paid off.

The highway went down into a narrow and immensely long, thunder-of-hooves valley, then, like a chalkline, headed north, running between two low mountain ranges, the higher eastern one still in snow. A sign: NEXT GAS 80 MILES. In the dusk, the valley showed no evidence of man other than wire fences, highway, and occasional deer-crossing signs that looked like medieval heraldic devices: on a field of ochre, a stag rampant, sable. The signs had been turned into colanders by gunners, almost none of whom hit the upreared bucks.

Squat clumps of white sage, wet from a shower out of the western range, sweetened the air, and gulches had not yet emptied. Calm lay over the uncluttered openness, and a damp wind blew everything clean. I saw no one. I let my speed build to sixty, cut the ignition, shifted to neutral. Although Ghost Dancing had the aerodynamics of an orange crate, it coasted for more than a mile across the flats. When it came to a standstill, I put it back in gear and left it at roadside. There was no one. Listening, I walked into the scrub. The desert does its best talking at night, but on that spring evening it kept God's whopping silence; and that too is a desert voice.

I've read that a naked eye can see six thousand stars in the hundred billion galaxies, but I couldn't believe it, what with the sky white with starlight. I saw a million stars with one eye and two million with both. Galileo proved that the rotation and revolution of the earth give stars their apparent movements. But on that night his evidence wouldn't hold. Any sensible man, lying on his back among new leaves of sage, in the warm sand that had already dried, even he could see Arcturus and Vega and Betelgeuse just above, not far at all, wheeling about the earth. Their paths cut arcs, and there was no doubt about it.

The immensity of sky and desert, their vast absences, reduced me. It was as if I were evaporating, and it was calming and cleansing to be absorbed by that vacancy. Whitman says:

> O to realize space!
> The plenteousness of all, that there are no bounds,
> To emerge and be of the sky, of the sun and moon and flying clouds,
>   as one with them.

On the highway a car came and went, sounding a pitiful brief *whoosh* as it ran the dark valley. When I drove back onto the road, I saw in the headlights a small desert rodent spin across the pavement as if on wheels; from the mountains, my little machine must have looked much the same. Ahead hung the Big Dipper with a million galaxies, they say, inside its cup, and on my port side, atop the western range, the evening star held a fixed position for miles until it swung slowly around in front of me and then back to port. I had followed a curve so long I couldn't see the bend. Only Vesper showed the truth. The highway joined U.S. 6—from Cape Cod to Long Beach, the longest federal route under one number in the days before interstates—then crossed the western mountains. Below lay the mining town of Ely.

Not everything that happens in Ely happens at the Hotel Nevada, but it could. The old place is ready for it. But that night the blackjack tables were empty, the slots nearly so, and the marbleized mirrors reflected the bartender's slump and a waitress swallowing a yawn. Yet I did see these things:

Item: a woman, face as blank as a nickel slug, pulling dutifully on the slot handles. She had stood before the gears so many times she herself had become a mechanism for reaching, dropping, pulling. Her eyes were dark and unmoving as if unplugged. The periodic jangle of change in the winner's cup moved her only to reach into the little coffer without looking and deposit the coins again.

Item: a man moseyed in wearing leather from head to toe; attempting cow-puncher macho, he looked more like a two-legged first baseman's mitt. With him a bored blonde. "I'm a very competitive person. I'm in it to win," he said, and the blonde yawned again.

Item: in a glass case hung a cross-section of bristlecone pine. At its center a card said: 3000 BC BUILDING OF THE PYRAMIDS. A seedling today could be alive in the year 7000. That put a perspective on things.

Over another beer I watched faces that would be lucky to see AD 2000. When I left, a man in a white goatee whispered, "No games of chance, cowboy?"

"Haven't finished losing the first one," I said.

. . . .

The argument whether or not Sand Mountain had crossed the highway made more sense when I saw the thing—a single massive mound of tawny sand, a wavy hump between two larger ridges of sage and rock. It was of such size that, while it wasn't perhaps big enough to be a mountain by everybody's definition, it was surely more than a dune. Nevadans once called it "Singing Sand Mountain" because of the pleasant hum in the blowing sands, but no one has heard the mountain since off-road vehicles from California took it over.

I crossed Eight Mile Flat, a stretch of alkali crusts and shallow winter run-off where a machine scraped up salt crystals. It was near here in 1907, they tell, that a cafe owner, preparing broilers for supper, found two chicken craws laden with golden gravel; he at once butchered all his yard hens and found more nuggets. Because the flat contained no gold, he began looking for the source of the chickens and learned they had been raised on four separate farms before he bought them. Although the search lasted years, the Chicken Craw Goldrush died as it was born.

I stopped for a beer in Salt Wells at a place called Maxi's. If there was more to Salt Wells than that entirely Chinese-red building, I didn't see it. An ornamental wrought-iron fence covered the front; the gate was locked. Turning to leave, I noticed an arrow pointing to a button. Push me. I felt like Alice in Wonderland. I pushed, a dark face peered from a circle scraped on a window (painted red too), the gate clicked open, and I went inside where walls, ceiling, curtains, and light-bulbs were bright red. A sign:

DANCE WITH THE LADIES
50¢
THREE FOR A DOLLAR.

Below was a sticker, GO NAVY. A saloon as peculiar as the desert. That's when I realized it wasn't a desert saloon. It was a desert cathouse. Bold and plain, directly on U.S. 50, and flagrantly red from top to bottom.

Everyone—two Indians, two Negroes, a Chicano, and the bartender—all of them watched me. I ambled to the bar as if I'd known all along. Mirror decals showed the management accepted Visa, Mastercharge, American Express.

"Hey, Joe, what's your name?" she asked. I don't know where she came from.

"Al," I said.

"How about a party, Al?"

"What's *your* name?"

"Tiffany. How do you like it, Al?"

"It's a fine name."

"Not the name, Al baby—your party. How do you like your party? Hot?"

Tiffany, with all due respect, was one of the most facially unfavored women I'd ever seen. Her features would have been woeful on a man, but on a woman who earned her way by sexual attraction they were calamitous. She was a good dose of saltpeter. Yet nature, not withholding everything, had recompensed her with two impressive advertisements that she rested flat on the bar. "How about a dance with a lady? Three for a dollar."

"Dances or ladies?"

"Don't be cute, Allie. Just name your pleasures."

Allie it was now. "I only stopped in to use the phone. You know, engine trouble with my rig. Got to report in to the dispatcher."

She looked at me sympathetically. "Are you gay, honey? Tiffany's helped a hundred of your kind. Your problems show up like the honeymoon virgin."

I think that woman must have been a terrific salesperson. She had backed me into a dialectical corner with three or four sentences and left me only two escapes: admit to deviance or prove a capacity to perform at her standard. The bartender edged over, insinuating a little pressure. Tiffany turned on her stool and one of her portions on the bar followed. Another dancing lady came in. She was quite pretty.

"That's Faith," Tiffany said. "Men prefer her. Maybe you would too. I'm used to it. I mean, it's no surprise to Tiffany." Another tack coming. "I just hope if you have a little girl, she's beautiful, because you men make it so tough on anybody who doesn't look like Debby Boone."

"Debby—I mean Tiffany—I'll tell you the truth. I walked in here not realizing it was—it was a place."

"Sometimes us girls call it a whorehouse."

"Right. When I finish my beer I'll have to get back on the road."

"So you're in a whorehouse. Too good for woman's company, Mister Allen?"

The woman had the tactical mind of General Patton. She blocked me at every move. The bartender leaned in. "Good buddy, let Miss Tiffany help you. She's cured worse cases than yours. Why do you think she's called Tiffany? Pure class. Twenty-four carat."

"My case is okay. I just don't have the money."

"Look, Joe," Tiffany said. "You talk money? It's costing me to sit here trying to give a good time. You think I like crapping around with tweeties?"

I drank my beer and took my case down the road, through the irrigated plain at Fallon, into hills, along the Truckee River, under a shelf of glowing clouds above downtown Reno, past signs offering CANDLE LIGHT WEDDINGS—NO WAITING—FREE WITNESSES. I stopped near the University of Nevada and put my case to bed. The geologist was right. It was one crazy state.

CHARLES BOWDEN [B. 1945]

Tucson-based journalist "Chuck" Bowden traveled to Nevada to cover a conference on the desert tortoise, an endangered species. His report, entitled "Tortoises," appears in the "Beasts" section of Blue Desert *(1986), alongside essays on Mexican free-tail bats, whose populations are drastically plummeting; a tiny remnant population of Sonoran pronghorn antelope; and the nearly extinct Yacqui topminnow. All these creatures have butted up against the rampant development of the Sunbelt, a landscape transformation of biblical proportion. Indeed, Bowden's epigraph is taken from the book of Psalms: "[They] lusted exceedingly in the wilderness, and tempted God in the desert. And he gave them their request; but sent leanness into their soul." The theme of unbridled lust, unchecked desire, monumental greed, and human excess pervades Bowden's work in more than a dozen books on topics such as water use in the desert (*Killing the Hidden Waters, *1977*)*, urban development in Tucson (*Frog Mountain Blues, *1987*)*, paranoid Americans (*Blood Orchid: An Unnatural History of America, *1995*)*, drug wars along the Mexican border (*Down by the River: Drugs, Money, Murder, and Family, *2002*)*, and rapists, drunks, psychopaths, and suicidal artists (*Blues for Cannibals: The Notes from Underground, *2002*). Known for his "frank and charged prose," his "muscular" style, his "rapturous indignation," and his sermonic "rants and rhapsodies," Bowden's is a con-*

flicted voice crying in the wilderness, as infatuated by the seven deadly sins of modern life as he is protective of the tranquility of the natural world. Born in Chicago, Bowden left an academic career path in American intellectual history to settle in Tucson in the 1970s, where, as he says, he "scrounged for a living," working for the local newspaper on the sex crime beat, eventually quitting to pursue freelance writing, an occupation he has described as "practically a free ticket to the asylum."

Tortoises

I once knew a woman who had a pet tortoise named Fluffy and I think of this fact as I face the action.

The blue air hangs over the room of clacking machines as people pack this casino hugging the banks of the Colorado River and wearily pull the levers on the slots.

I am hungry. I check my backpack with the doorman and rub my fingers across the stubble of my beard. The people are very intent and do not look up or around or at one another. Laughlin, Nevada, strings a half dozen casinos along the tame stream and is only a minute by boat from the Arizona shore. Outside the parking lots are packed with campers, trucks, and vans and every machine has a toy poodle yapping at the window. This is a blue collar Las Vegas.

I want bacon and eggs, but I hesitate on the floor of the casino. The players are men in caps and T-shirts, fat-hipped women in polyester stretch pants, retired folks plunging with dimes and quarters. I am pretty much dirty clothes, clumps of greasy hair, and hung-over eyes. Last night I slept in the hills overlooking the valley. Cottontails grazed around my head and hopped along the sides of my sleeping bag. All night the casino signs splashed color and form into the night sky and then at first light, lines of herons and ducks and geese slowly winged down the ribbon of river to the feeding grounds. In this big room of smoke, booze, and slots, sunrise and sunset count for nothing.

Clocks are kept from sight, the pit blocks all views of the outside and the women peddling drinks to the players, God! Those women in black net stockings, thrusting breasts, fresh young faces, and ancient eyes. Well, the women strut through the blue air denying that time or age or bills or tomorrow exists or matters. I love the women and what they are doing for us all. Just savor them, I tell myself, don't speak to them, don't go home with them, just brush them with your eyes. In here, they are the promise of flesh and fun and smiles and I do not want to know about the two kids, the old man that skidaddled, the small trailer where every time you turn around you bump into yourself.

I finally cross the casino floor and walk into the restaurant, a barren that is here and there dotted with tired people pumping coffee and reading the sports pages. I sit down, swallow a couple of cups and start nibbling at the pile of scientific papers I carry. I have come here to listen to experts consider the plight of the desert tortoise and the experts have gathered here from the universities, from the Bureau of Land Management, from the fish and game departments, from all the small offices with gray desks and steady checks, because, hell, why not meet in a casino town?

The desert tortoise itself (*Gopherus agassizii*) has skipped this occasion. In the bright lights and big cities of the Sunbelt this small reptile is no big deal. Loving a desert tortoise is a little bit like bonding with a pet rock—scholars estimate that the beast spends 94.9 percent of its time in dormancy, which means just lying there in its burrow. Today they are being wiped out in the desert, and in Sunbelt cities survive mainly as pets and captives (at least twenty thousand in California and thousands in Tucson and Phoenix). Once upon a time they averaged from ten or twenty up to several hundred per square mile. But this is a new time and a new west.

I thumb through this leviathan study, an 838-page draft report being considered by the Desert Tortoise Council, the cabal of experts zeroing in on this casino for a conference. I discover that *Gopherus agassizii* runs six to fourteen inches, tops the scale at maybe ten pounds and hardly pesters anyone. They endure their slow lives for 50 to 100 years, and I am briefly bewitched by the notion that somewhere out there lumber Methuselah tortoises that have seen the whole western movie, all three reels, from Wyatt Earp to Palm Springs.

The eggs and bacon finally arrive and I devour them. This is a nickel-and-dime trip where I figure on skipping room rent by flopping in the desert, jotting notes during all the weighty sessions of tortoise papers, and hopefully, scribbling a story that will pay the rent.

The tortoise looks to be a perfect foil for a quick hit: they are the innocents, the benign nothings who do not attack cattle, sheep, or hikers, the little rascals who pack no venom and fire up all the fantasies of nature that people relish. Scientists tag them as an indicator species, meaning one that suggests the health of the ecosystem as a whole. Almost stationary in their habits, long-lived, low in reproduction rate and quiet, they function as witnesses to the way human beings in the Southwest treat the land and the forms of life woven into the land.

In short, tortoises have a high potential to evoke human guilt. Box office.

I have been counseled at length by a friend who for decades has flourished as a free-lance writer of nature stories. He warned me to avoid all colorful references to the casino ("none of those clinking ice cubes in glasses of whiskey," he fumed) and play it straight and be rich in technical information. This is good advice that I find hard to follow. I have yet to meet the casino that cannot seduce me. The pits are so full of human greed and human hope and always there are those little touches—

the men in the glass room packing sacks of money and wearing smocks that have no pockets—that make me glad to be a human being. There are few places as honest as the rampant fraud and fantasy of a casino. Here we let down our hair, our pants, our everything and confess to all our secret hungers.

The women working the place are a problem also, busting out of their britches, bending down to pour coffee and slapping my face with deep cleavage. I can think of few things more pleasurable then to sleep on the desert, watch the rabbits bounce around and then at dawn walk into a casino where time has stopped and everything always promises to be juicy.

I pay the bill and move up the stairs to the meeting rooms where plump, contented tortoise experts gather over coffee and doughnuts. I strike up conversations with perfect strangers who are all friendly in this bastion of tortoise love. An elderly couple tells me of their son who is in the grocery business and has a kind of tortoise preserve at his home with eighteen of the beasts thriving on the wilted lettuce he brings home each night. A lady from Phoenix brags on her pet male who taps the patio doors when he wants in the house. The registration table for the conference is a gold mine of tortoise pendants, pens, pins, T-shirts, key chains, wind chimes.

Everyone seems satisfied after an evening of frolicking over steak dinners, trying their luck at blackjack, having a spin in this dab of sin—all at government expense. Finally, the session comes to order and I hunch in my chair busy noting the hard facts of *Gopherus* scholarship.

Being a desert tortoise may not constitute a full-time job. A calendar of the tortoise year, based on a daily time budget (DTB) and annual time budget (ATB), is not full of big events. The animals emerge from their holes in late March to late July when the days begin to be warm. At first, basking (tortoise sunbathing) takes up about 19 percent of the DTB, a figure which declines as the season advances, and only kills 1.5 percent of the ATB. Once out and about tortoises turn to foraging (1.5 percent ATB and love-making (0.08 percent ATB). Even during the friskiest part of the summer season they go dormant 33 percent of the time.

Tortoises spend only three to six months a year actively feeding and moving, and even during this frisky period they devote most of their hours to snoozing in their burrows. Basically, *Gopherus agassizii* is not a Type A personality and this wonderful calm has prevented tortoise scholars from glimpsing much action.

A few tidbits have been gleaned. When picked up and alarmed they are liable to piss all over people. When two male tortoises meet, they bob their heads and often ram each other—the loser being toppled onto his back and left to die in the heat if he cannot right himself. When sprinting they can cover about six yards in a minute but they hardly ever move far from their burrows unless maddened by thirst.

They have very little to say. When disturbed or when mating, they sometimes hiss, grunt, and make pops and poinks. I hesitate in my note-taking and contemplate the ring of a hearty tortoise poink. Dominant males seem to pack a potent punch when they defecate and have been known to send the rest of the boys scurrying from a burrow with one mighty dump.

Sex occurs to a tortoise after reaching the age of fifteen or twenty and the first date begins with the male bobbing his head and then nipping the female a few times on the shell before mounting her. Tortoise women maintain an air of calm and sometimes keep right on eating during copulation. Eggs are laid, buried, and after 100 days, hatch. The young tortoise must face five years of desert life with a soft shell.

Generally, tortoises are homebodies and spend their lives within a few hundred yards of their burrows, wandering off mainly for a little dining, basking, or love-making. Specimens tagged during a study in the late thirties and early forties were found in the same area by scientists in the eighties. They chow down on green herbs, leaves, and blossoms of annuals, succulents, grasses, and cacti.

The papers come one after another and they stand in contrast to the sea of peace that constitutes normal tortoise life. Outside the casino walls in the desert we cannot see well (the meeting room, naturally, has no windows), out there it is holocaust time for tortoises. I look around at conference attendants and see a lot of grim faces.

People, it seems, have been wreaking havoc on tortoises for a long time—they were sold as dog food in Los Angeles during the 1890s—and from this fact has sprung the modern tortoise industry. We shoot them just for the hell of it, hack them to pieces, drive over them with cars, collapse their burrows with off-road vehicles, stomp them to death with our livestock, and starve them to death by running cattle and sheep on their range—beasts which devour all the forage tortoises crave.

Until the 1970s, nobody much cared. Then something new happened—all those federal laws about endangered species and all those new agency mandates demanding environmental impact statements. I take a closer look at the faces in the room and realize I am sitting with the new servants of the desert tortoise. Hacks from the BLM who suddenly must kowtow to a damn reptile because their beloved steers are destroying it. Biologists from game and fish departments who thought they would spend their days keeping tab on deer and antelope and bighorns and elk who now are here fat with statistics about tortoises and management plans for them.

I no longer like the room. I once had a professor who patiently explained to me that I never could stomach any cause once it had become successful. Well, there must be worse sins. I have heartily supported every law, executive order, and petition to salvage the dwindling biological wealth of the earth. But now I see what happens to every decent impulse in my society: they become that ugly thing, government.

I get up and wander out of the meeting. Downstairs time has passed, but mercifully everything has remained the same. I sidle up to the long bar which stares out at the river and sip whiskey as the afternoon sinks toward evening. Others at the bar amuse themselves with electronic poker games and there is an air of deadly serious sport about the place.

The hills bordering the valley bear the traces of Indian trails where tribes of the Colorado once raced north and south for hundreds and hundreds of miles exporting war, magic, and a few hard goods. The ground cover is scant and low and this is not the kind of country most Americans call beautiful. They storm across it in their machines from Phoenix, Tucson, Los Angeles, and more distant parts of the Republic so they, like their fathers before them, can gather at the river. And once here they drink, gamble and feed.

At my back, hunkered over the crap tables, poker tables, and slots, are my fellow citizens hailing from most states in the Union. And none of them are likely to waste much time pondering the plight of a desert tortoise. The couples, ma and pa, tend to wear matching caps and windbreakers. In the gift shop, there is practically nothing to read for sale. The casino seems dedicated to low-level aerobics and no slackers are allowed to pull back and pursue thick books or falter from doing their reps with the slot machines. No pain, no gain.

Denouncing this place would be like coming out against the tooth fairy.

I join the line for the casino cheap feed, a chicken dinner (all you can eat) for a few bucks. Three Indians sit down at my table. Their faces are brown, blank, and immobile. We chomp on the fried birds and slowly words drone from their mouths. They are Navajos working on a stretch of nearby railroad track and they find the casino curious and the food a great bargain. I arrived in the Southwest in 1957 and according to the best reports, my tablemates seized some local turf in the fifteenth century. But we seem to have wound up in the same situation. We ogle the girls, speculate on the thrill of guzzling a few drinks, and say the casino is a real pleasant puzzler.

The Southwest is a place where almost everyone slips their moorings and just drifts. The cities and towns are ugly, the populace footloose, the crime frequent, the marriages disasters, the plans pathetic gestures, the air electric with promise. There is so much space and so much ground that no one can for a single moment doubt the basic American dream that it is possible to make something worthwhile of life. Everything a desert tortoise is—calm, a homebody, long-lived, patient, quiet—the people of the Southwest are not. We don't stay in our burrows much anymore or limit our motion to the cycle of the sun. Just across the road from the casino, a huge powerplant belches smoke into the sky. The facility burns coal mined on Black Mesa in the Navajo and Hopi country of northern Arizona, coal that is piped as a slurry the 278 miles to Laughlin. The electricity generated here is then flashed outward to blaze in the lights of Southern California. Such grids of energy and rivers of energy-flows are the stuff of life in the Southwest and they do not produce a state of mind that cottons to the issue of endangered species. It is not that we are too busy building the empire to tend to details but simply that we are too busy running to ever look back at the ghosts trailing behind us or down at the ground where the writhing beasts shudder with their last convulsion of life. We haven't got time for this nature stuff. We were born to drive, not park.

I walk down the road to a store and buy a pint of whiskey, reclaim my backpack from the doorman, and head back into the hills for another night of stargazing. I lie amid the creosote with my head next to an Ajo lily and study tortoise papers under the flicker of my candle lantern. The documents are grim stuff with the reptile all but gone from the Mojave, being mowed down in Nevada and Utah, still legal game in Arizona. I pour my Sierra cup full of whiskey, blow out the light and witness a falling star.

JAMES CONAWAY [B. 1941]

Winnemucca is a world away from James Conaway's normal beat around Washington, DC's Beltway. Finding himself city-bound at midlife, Conaway began looking at maps of the West, where he noticed vast tracts of federal real estate and wondered what was out there in those empty places. In six months of travel through public lands in the West, Conaway discovers . . . well, people—"repositories of a national myth," as he thinks of them. His book The Kingdom in the Country *(1987) is a social inventory of thinly populated places, profiling a quirky cast of characters that includes a gunslinger, gold miners, marijuana growers, dune buggy fanatics, and helicopter-riding cowboys. Conaway grew up a long way from the Wild West, in Memphis, Tennessee, a childhood recalled in his memoir* Memphis Afternoons *(1993). After graduating from Southwestern at Memphis in 1963, a Wallace Stegner Creative Writing fellowship at Stanford University brought him to California, after which he began a career as a reporter, magazine writer, book author, and editor, starting out as a reporter in Memphis for the* New Orleans Times-Picayune, *working in Europe for the* Rome Daily American, *settling in Pennsylvania where he wrote for the* New York Times *and* Atlantic Monthly, *and serving as Washington editor for* Harper's. *He has published three novels and seven nonfiction books, including the best-selling social histories* Napa *(1990) and its sequel,* The Far Side of Eden: New Money, Old Land, *and the Battle for Napa Valley (2002). Conaway's ambitious, illustrated histories—The* Smithsonian: 150 Years of Adventure, Discovery, and Wonder *(1995) and* America's Library: The Story of the Library of Congress, 1800–2000 *(2000)—and his current position as editor of* Preservation *speak to his ongoing interest in national institutions and historic preservation. The* Kingdom in the Country *shares this spirit, preserving in words a place—a national treasure, really—that is undergoing profound transformation.*

from *The Kingdom in the Country*

Southwest Idaho meets Nevada in alkali flats, dry lakes called playas, and stringy mountain ranges of deceptive height and distance, furred by blue bunchgrass growing on their flanks. The valleys stretch away under sage and greasewood— and squirrel tail and Indian rice grass, if the BLM brochures are to be believed. The BLM owns 86 percent of Nevada, and a lot of the country looks very lean.

On the edge of the Great Basin, roads far from the Interstate run for miles toward some immense stony wrinkle before making an abrupt turn and running for miles more. The lights of Winnemucca, Nevada, floated in a trough of evening shadow, as I came to the end of a long day of desert driving. The casinos on the main drag cast bright nets for passing motor homes. Winnemucca was no tourist attraction, but then gambling is a local pastime in Nevada, where townsfolk drop a five-dollar bill on the roulette table as casually as some people buy a newspaper.

I parked on a side street and ate tuna fish from a can for dinner, watching cowboys and girls in Levi's jackets tromp between the pools of glitter and Winnemucca's grainy darkness. I needed a place to park and sleep, and found my way to the BLM headquarters a couple of blocks from the last casino. I woke up the next morning to a full parking lot and the sight of people working in the offices.

They were expecting me. An hour later, I rode west across more desert with a soft-spoken, intense range con who for two years had been trying to get out of Winnemucca. "If you're a GS twelve, you have to move every four or five years," he said, "or you lose your effectiveness. People at the office get used to looking at the same face. The ranchers you've trespassed think you're an SOB."

A trespass was a citation for grazing more cows on government land than were allowed; judging by the view, any stock at all should have constituted trespass.

He said, "What can I tell you about Nevada? It has its share of unconventional people, is the main thing. We've got outlaws and renegades right here. They stab people, steal things, run mustangs."

Each of the six BLM management areas in Nevada is larger than Massachusetts, and each harbors wild horses that have to be rounded up. That requires a special sort of cowboy.

"This one's the best in the business," said the range con, indicating a collection of trucks isolated in big country at the foot of the Humboldt Range. A steel corral had been set up amidst the sage, and a few lone riders sat casually on their cow ponies, looking toward the mountains. We left the BLM Suburban near the road and hiked up. The contractor's name was Dave Cattoor; he was a small man with a horny hand and a slightly misaligned eye. The brim of his straw cowboy hat had been mended with epoxy, and his jacket bled goose feathers.

His lariat had a piece of chain attached to the end, for looping over the saddle horn after he roped a mustang. "It'll stay on the saddle that way," he said, to no one in particular. "Saddle might not stay on your horse, though."

He and his partner had earned half a million dollars in the last eight months. That seemed a lot of money, he said, until you realized that the weekly fuel bill for the helicopter alone was more than fifteen hundred dollars. Two had crashed since Thanksgiving. The previous year, a big semi belonging to the outfit had overturned in northern Nevada, and Cattoor and his men had set up a corral beside the highway and winched forty live mustangs out of the wreckage.

Cattoor and his partner, the helicopter pilot, paid all those expenses, plus wages and board for four men, and a bonus if things worked out well. They were paid sixty-nine dollars for each mustang they captured, and had to earn two thousand dollars a day to break even. However, they were making money.

The wranglers all bunked at the Two Stiffs Motel, in Lovelock, for weeks. So did the pilot. We could hear him working the canyons, the rhythm of the engine changing as he turned and began to push the sound toward us.

"Here he comes," said Cattoor. "Get behind the horse trailer and stay out of sight."

The chopper flew low to the ground, while half a dozen horses raced ahead of it. They passed a mile to the north, bound for another canyon, but the chopper flanked and gradually turned them. They came charging into full view, coats dark with sweat. Cattoor had tied his horse behind the trailer and led a pony down to the open end of the corral, camouflaged with hay bales and sage. He crouched, waiting for the herd.

"That's the Judas horse," the range con said. The Judas horse stood patiently while the wild ones—a bay stallion, three mares and three ponies—charged past. They wheeled as the chopper cut them off and drove them back toward the trap.

Cattoor released the Judas and it trotted obediently between the fences, followed by all but the stallion. At the last moment it turned and reared, making for the narrow slot between iron bars and that clattering machine. I could see the pilot clearly now inside his glass bubble, in a Windbreaker over an old plaid shirt, faded Levi's, and boots, a technological cowboy unhappy with this recalcitrant stallion forty feet from his rotors. Even I could tell that the horse was not going into the trap.

Men rose up with a long tarpaulin and ran across the mouth of the trap, cutting the rest of the horses off from escape. The stallion charged the helicopter. The pilot performed a sleight of hand inspired by the vision of a severed equine head, buckets of gore, a broken rotor blade, and oily black flames. The chopper swung heavily to port—reeled, really—the pilot silently screaming at an animal that had not known of his existence half an hour before.

Out of my peripheral vision charged two riders, leaning forward in their saddles, at a clip not commonly seen outside racetracks and the speeded-up versions of old TV Westerns. Men and horses seemed to vibrate with the effort, over rough country full of prairie dog holes. The stallion disappeared in a draw, followed by the riders, then emerged, a little smaller, the men seemingly close enough to reach out and put a hand on that sweaty flank. One tossed his lariat and missed, then Cattoor tossed his and the stallion came up hard at the end of it, pawing the air.

The range con beside me said, "Goddamn, he got him."

The lariat cut off the mustang's breath, bringing it gradually to its knees. It rolled over, and Cattoor dismounted and cautiously approached. With a hank of rope he tied fore and hind hooves together before the horse revived, then left it to be picked up when the truck came around collecting hog-tied animals as if they were battle casualties.

"That Judas horse almost ironed me out," Cattoor said a few minutes later, seeking shelter in the horse trailer from some rare Nevada rain. The horse had kicked at him when he released it.

Another BLM agent had brought more observers to the roundup. One was a wild horse advocate from Austin, Texas, named Deedee. She stood for a while with her hands deep in the pockets of her jeans, watching Cattoor. Then she told him that she had a special interest in his profession, being a founder of the American Mustang and Burro Association, which was a relative newcomer to the extensive wild horse lobby.

"We have members in thirty-eight states," she said. "We're one of the fastest-growing wild horse interest groups."

Someone said, "It ain't supposed to rain in Nevada."

Deedee's organization had joined the much larger American Wild Equine Council, and had paid for her to fly to Nevada. In addition to exercising influence there, she was on the lookout for another mare for her Texas household. She planned to adopt one of the mustangs. "We like the idea of horses running free, their manes flying in the wind," she said.

The range con later told me he badly wanted out of wild horse work, one of the most time-consuming and frustrating tasks in the BLM. "You can't imagine how much coordination goes into it."

I asked how many roamed Nevada. He thought there might be as many as forty thousand.

"Forty thousand?"

Mustangs are destroying what's left of the range, but public interest groups prevent the government from dealing with them the way it deals with other, less harmful creatures. Coyotes are shot from helicopters or poisoned, but wild horses roam free, eating four and five times as much of the sparse ground cover as a cow. Some are trapped and shipped to feedlots, at ruinous expense, where they live until they drop of old age. Thousands of horses behind government fences eat their way through government forage because a few people consider them related to the old Spanish war mounts, and a symbol of wildness. So they cannot be sold as meat or turned into dog food, as an old steer might be.

The horses may be adopted, and for a year government agents have to visit these orphans to make sure they are being properly cared for. This part of the program, like the expense and the ban on productive use of wild horseflesh, arouses ridicule in the men who round up mustangs.

Mustangs aren't a good symbol of the wild, unspoiled West. They have nothing to do with the conquistadors but are the progeny of mares and studs turned out on public land during the Depression, when their owners couldn't afford to feed them. A few may be descended from draft horses let loose when the cavalry disbanded in the 1890s. Yet there are sixty-nine organizations fighting for their rights.

Behind Deedee, in the corral, tattered, bony, murderous animals with bloody legs, white scars on flanks and withers, and chunks missing from their own hides routinely sank their teeth in other horses. The fighting went on more or less continuously, and not just in captivity. Now the whinnying reverberated for a mile and more, hooves rattling against the metal bars and drumming on other equine rib cages.

A wrangler urged them into the collecting pen, careful to stay clear. Once the roundup was complete, the animals would be trucked to Palomino Ranch, a BLM feedlot north of Reno set up just for mustangs, where they would be processed, inoculated, and fed. Prospective adopters occasionally came by; most were discouraged by the sight of equine orphans kicking one another and demolishing the odd horse trailer.

A little mare lay in the weeds. A wild horse had stood on her neck until some-one noticed and moved him. Now the mare's eyes assumed a terminal glassiness.

"Shock," the range con said.

"Our sign fell down," said one of the cowboys.

He dragged the dead horse away, tied to the pickup, and left her in a sage clump where predators would take over.

I later found out that in fiscal 1985 the BLM had spent $17 million on wild horses. Congress had passed the Wild Horse and Burro Act fifteen years before, at the urg-ing of the wild horse lobby, stipulating that mustangs had a place on the range. The BLM operates its wild horse program under a continuing resolution; the program includes squiring around visiting journalists and horse lobbyists, holding public meetings, hiring permanent wild horse and burro specialists, conducting envi-ronmental studies and horse counts, and hiring cowboy entrepreneurs like Dave Cattoor. It also involves publishing expensive brochures that reflect the political reality of wild horse sentiment: "Like the relics left by ancient Indian tribes," says the BLM's Special Wild Horse Issue of *Our Public Lands,* "and the still visible ruts made by wagon trains, wild horses and burros are important links to our heri-tage." The wild horse program provides high visibility for the BLM's new role as preservationists at relatively little cost, while overgrazing, mining, and timbering continue.

Cattoor asked the BLM range con for a time extension. Ordinarily roundups stopped at one o'clock, to keep the wild horses from overheating, but it was damp and cold now, and Dave had not made his minimum. The range con radioed the BLM's wild horse specialist, who was sitting in his Suburban down on the highway, and got permission. Within half an hour the chopper was pushing forty more mus-tangs down out of the Humboldts.

A BLM investigator with a carbine under the seat of his Bronco would spend the night there, to guard the herd from renegades. The horses would be loaded and trucked the next day. Dave and the others drove back to Lovelock, and I followed them. They seemed close to the real notion of cowboys, in a state that in one way, at least, closely approximated the Old West: Nevada was still largely unfenced. I suspected that the men who went after mustangs were similarly unrestricted, but my questions about their occupation were met with disbelief, and amusement. Cowboys don't like talking about what they do when they are doing it, because the work is hard and exacting. They don't like talking to strangers about it when it's over, because those who have never done it can't imagine what it's like. Also, cowboys see almost everybody else as aliens, opposed to their way of life or, at best, unsympathetic.

We ate a quick meal full of cryptic references and plate-rattling silences in Love-lock, around the corner from Rose's Chapel of Love.

"Some guys say they dally-rope mustangs," said a wrangler.

"Sure, and watch their fingers fly off."

"I used a sloppy loop on that ole chicken-necked sorrel."

"You think that tarp'll hold 'em if they decide to turn around?"

"Sure it will."

"When they put the hammer back," said Cattoor, "you'll know it."

Talk turned to recreation. Someone said, "I hear they're having them camel races in Virginia City this weekend."

"I didn't see any camels last year, but I saw a lot of drunk people."

"They had some mighty friendly whiskey up there. Wasn't nobody on the fight, or nothing."

"I told myself then," said Cattoor, "that if I was ever in Nevada when the camel races were going on, I'd be there."

"Not many colts today," said Jim Hicks, the chopper pilot. His face and arms were covered with scar tissue left by burns, and the backs of his hands bore the permanent imprint of bandages. "Mountain lion's working the hills, or maybe a human type."

"You said you couldn't herd no more," said Dave. "Then you came down with a whole shitload of mustangs. That's attitude improvement."

They had been working together for eight years and had collected twenty-five thousand wild horses. Jim had flown in the Vietnam War, doing low-level recon-naissance over the Cambodian border in the late sixties. Back in this country, he flew predator control over public lands in the West. One night when driving a fuel truck outside Elko, Nevada, bound for his helicopter, he blew a front tire and the truck turned over. Gasoline covered the highway and ignited. He crawled out the window and through the flames in a T-shirt; the only part of him that wasn't burned was the palms of his hands.

When he got out of the hospital, he tried selling asphalt roofing but couldn't stand it, and was soon back in the wild horse business. "There's a challenge to this. These old horses are wild, and smart. You can't fly a helicopter like a cutting horse—it's too hard on the machine. And once those horses realize a helicopter can't hurt 'em, then you're in trouble. Then you need a roper."

"It's high risk," said Dave. "It's hard to work around wild horses day after day and not get hurt. You've got to go full speed over them dog holes. These old horses kick and bite. We've been lucky."

"Been a bad year for helicopters, though. In November I had engine failure at forty feet. Rotors cut off the tail boom when I hit. That's standard. We had it re-built, and the exact same thing happened two months later."

I asked how he had escaped unhurt.

"Oh, you just wait for things to stop flying around. Then you jump out."

"The insurance companies don't love us no more," Dave said. "The premiums are horrendous. Sometimes we don't collect from the government until we're sixty thousand dollars in debt. The credit card people get mighty nervous," he added, handing his American Express card to the waitress.

TOM ROBBINS [B. 1936]

One of Tom Robbins's ex-girlfriends reputedly told him, "The trouble with you, Tom, is you have too much fun." Robbins's eight novels, including the underground classics Another Road-side Attraction *(1971) and* Even Cowgirls Get the Blues *(1976), also have earned him a repu-tation for playfulness and wit, manifested in exuberant characters, surprising plots, and a flamboyant style. Robbins's first novel,* Another Roadside Attraction, *for example, follows the antics of a group of hippies who come into possession of the mummified corpse of Jesus Christ and display it in a funky hot-dog stand and roadside zoo in Skagit Valley, Washington; while* Half Asleep in Frog Pajamas *(1994) introduces two erotically enmeshed stockbrokers who become involved in the mystery of the planet's disappearing frogs. Although critics often associate him with West Coast writers such as Ken Kesey and Richard Brautigan, Robbins was born in Blowing Rock, North Carolina, and later moved to Virginia, where in high school he was voted "most mischievous boy." Still unruly, Robbins dropped out of Washington and Lee University after being expelled from his fraternity for tossing biscuits at the housemother during a food fight. Relinquishing any notion of becoming a southern gentleman, Robbins hitchhiked around the United States and then served in Korea as an air force meteorologist. Back home, Robbins graduated from college with academic honors and began his career as a journalist for a conservative newspaper in Virginia, later moving to the more liberal Seattle after annoying editors by repeatedly inserting into the paper pictures of Sammy Davis Jr. In Seattle, Robbins studied Eastern philosophy and took psychedelic drugs, which helped him move fluidly between different levels of reality. Robbins's playfulness represents a consciously chosen path of "crazy wisdom" in a paradoxical world. Thus, his quest for the "Canyon of the Vaginas" in Nevada is both irreverent and reverent, complementary states of being in Rob-bins's philosophical stance. His piece speaks to the continuing attraction and uncanny power of Nevada's ancient petroglyphs.*

The Real Valley of the Dolls

When one is on a pilgrimage to the Canyon of the Vaginas, one has to be careful about asking directions.

I mean, there're some pretty rough ol' dudes in west-central Nevada. One knows the ol' dudes are rough when one observes that they eat with their hats on.

Nine days I was in the high desert between Winnemucca and Las Vegas, during which time I never witnessed a male Homo sapiens take his noontide nor his evening repast with an exposed bean. In every instance, a grimy bill or brim shaded the fellow's victuals from the vulgar eye of light. I assumed that they breakfasted *en chapeau* as well, but by the hour that your pilgrim sat down to *his* flapjacks, the rough ol' dudes had already gone off to try to strike it rich.

When a man's brain is constantly heated by thoughts of striking it rich, thoughts that don't fade much at mealtime, perhaps he requires some sort of perpetual head cover to cool the cerebral machinery. On the other hand, since they live in relatively close proximity to America's major nuclear test site, a nerve-gas depot, several mysterious airfields, and numerous depositories for our government's nasty toxic secrets, maybe the rough ol' dudes are just trying to prevent their haircuts from ever flickering in the dark. If I lived in west-central Nevada, I might dine in gloves and a Mylex suit.

Naturally, one has to wonder if the men of Nevada also sleep in their hats. More pointedly, do they sleep with their wives, girlfriends, and thoroughly legal prostitutes in their hats? I intended to interview a Nevada woman or two on the subject, but never quite got around to it. However, something at the Canyon of the Vaginas gave me reason to believe that the answer is affirmative. Of that, more later.

Getting back on course, beneath those baseball caps that advertise brands of beer or heavy equipment, under those genuine imitation Stetsons, there're some rough ol' hangovers being processed and some rough ol' ideas being entertained. One simply does not approach a miner, a wrangler, a prospector, a gambler, a Stealth pilot, a construction sweat hog, or sandblasted freebooter and interrupt his thoughts about big, fast bucks and those forces—environmental legislation, social change, loaded dice, et cetera—that could stand between him and big, fast bucks; one simply does not march up to such a man, a man who lifts his crusty lid to no one, and ask:

"Sir, might you possibly direct me to the Canyon of the Vaginas?"

. . . .

I can disclose this much: to arrive at the Canyon of the Vaginas, your pilgrim had to travel a ways on Highway 50, a blue guitar string of asphalt accurately described by postcards and brochures as the Most Lonesome Road in America. It will impress some readers as poignantly correct that so many vaginas are reached only by a route of almost legendary loneliness. Others won't have that reaction at all.

. . . .

It delighted me that the Canyon of the Vaginas was out here smack dab in the middle of the Wild American West. How swell that in the Old West of gunfights and land grabs, massacres and gold rushes, bushwhackings and horsewhippings, missions, saloons, boot hills, and forts, there existed a culture that celebrated with artistic eloquence and spiritual fervor the most intimate feature of the feminine anatomy.

Imagine Custer's cavalry troop thundering innocently over a ridge, only to come face-to-face with (gasp!) the pink, the moist, the yielding, the delicately curly. Imagine a Saturday matinee: *Roy Rogers at the Canyon of the Vaginas.*

Mentally, emotionally, my pilgrimage began back in my late twenties or early thirties, whenever it was that it first occurred to me that the female genitals were literally divine. In the Orient, especially in the religious systems of Tibet and India, that notion has prevailed since dimmest antiquity, and as a matter of fact, there are yonic symbols in the caves of Paleolithic Europe (dating back twenty thousand years) that are indistinguishable from those venerated today by the tantric cults of the Himalayas.

When I read how, among the practitioners of tantra, the vulva is adored as the organ for the generation of world and time, it struck a resonant chord. From that day on, I have been seeking the American tantra, which is to say, I've been seeking American images that promote that inner intensity of feminine sexuality, whose source is the Goddess of Creation.

. . . .

It phased me only a smidgen to discover that what may be the ultimate tantric tribute on our continent is located in west-central Nevada. Even that trace of skepticism vanished when I remembered that the Goddess of Creation also serves as the Goddess of Destruction.

. . . .

Alas, on that May afternoon when finally we neared the canyon, Ms. Destruction appeared to be directing the show. The wind was gusting at 70 miles an hour, and with every windshieldful of sand and snow, the chiropractic Mercedes whined as if its back hurt.

. . . .

Through rents in the curtain of snowy dust, we could see that we were entering the foothills of a low mountain range. "According to the map, we're only a pubic hair away," said I, and moments later, Alexa stopped the car. Well, if there was holy real estate in the vicinity, it wasn't exactly advertised. Nothing caught our vision beyond the boundlessness of space. The silence was so deep that even the gale seemed to be wearing moccasins. And when we opened the doors, a great essence of sage rushed in. It smelled as if every grandmother in the U.S.A. were simultaneously stuffing a turkey.

We stumbled about pessimistically in that Thanksgivingscape for a while. And abruptly, there it was! There was no mistaking it. We couldn't make out details, but the site was so charged it practically had an aura around it. The three of us glanced at one another knowingly, then, bucking the wind, took off at a fast trot. And we didn't slow down until we were surrounded by a plenitude of pudenda.

I looked one of the specimens right in the eye. "Doctor Vagina, I presume?"

The official name of the place is innocuous: North Canyon. It's quite narrow and fewer than two hundred yards long. The entire canyon is rather vaginal in shape, terminating in a scooped-out basin of white alkali that those so inclined could read as *uterus* or *womb*. The canyon floor is hirsute with juniper and sage.

According to Jon's compass, North Canyon lies on a perfect east-west axis. The entrance is at the east end, where it's most narrow. Obviously, there's a strong solar connection. When the sun rises each morning, it passes through the natural gateway, moving up the passage to the "womb." The volcanic-ash-flow walls are a yellowish orangish reddish tan, which is to say, the palette of the sun.

Both facing walls of the canyon entrance are covered with petroglyphs. No, somehow "covered" doesn't do them justice. They are *singing* with petroglyphs.

A petroplyph is a drawing that has been pecked, incised, or scratched into stone. Frequently, as is the case at North Canyon, the rock exposed by the pecking is appreciably lighter in color than the outer surfaces, which have been patinated by millennia of oxidation. This affords the design excellent contrast, although as the centuries hop along, the uncovered rock, too, gradually darkens.

There are innumerable examples of petroglyphs in the western U.S., some of them ceremonial in intention, some mnemonic, some totemic (clan symbols), and some, it would appear, just an outburst of pleasurable doodling. The majority of the drawings are concerned with game, for the artists who chipped them were hunter-gatherers, and they may or may not include human figures. In addition, there are highly mannered petroglyphs and examples that are completely abstract.

The rock panels at the portal to North Canyon support a smattering of curvilinear abstractions, including the mysterious dot patterns that are characteristic of Great Basin rock art. There are a goodly number of enlarged bird tracks, apparently the symbol of the Bird Clan. And there is a European-style house and a miner's charcoal kiln, proving that Indians were still pecking at the site well into the nineteenth century. By far the dominant motif of North Canyon, however, is the stylized vagina.

The vagina glyph is not exactly rare on the rocks of the West, but at no other site is it found in such concentration or profusion. In an old shaman's cave on nearby Hickison Summit, there's a lone yoni of great loveliness, but North Canyon, oh mama! North Canyon is a *festival* of female genitalia, a labial showcase, a vulval jubilee, and clearly the wellspring of our indigenous tantra.

Rome wasn't built in a day, to coin a phrase, and neither was this vaginal display. Worn, overlapped, and overlaid, the drawings were pecked over a long period of time. Human habitation in the region dates back ten thousand years. Volcanic ash is too soft to hold an image for such a lengthy period, but one of the few archaeologists to give North Canyon more than a passing nod has estimated that it could maintain a vulva in fairly good condition for about five centuries. Shelley Winters, eat your heart out.

Although the Paiute may have had a finger in them, the best guess is that North Canyon's murals are the work of the Shoshoni, a seminomadic civilization of underestimated complexity. The question is, Why? Why did they adorn the sun gate of Nevada's high desert with scores of mannered pudenda? Perhaps North Canyon was a fertility motel that Shoshoni couples checked into in order to ensure conception. Perhaps it involved a type of coming-of-age ritual. Perhaps—and your pilgrim favors this theory—it was intended as an homage to that feminine principle that the Shoshoni recognized to be the genesis of continuous creation: Earth herself; mother of deer, mother of trout, mother of grass seeds, bulbs, and roots, mother of the ground on which they walked and the cliffs that sheltered them. Maybe, on the other hand, North Canyon was purely sexual, a horny pecking of individual lust into the enduring dimension of stone.

It's reported that there are heterosexual males who can stare down a vulva, real or rendered, and register not an erg of prurience, but, honestly now, do you trust these guys? Would you want your daughter to marry one?

At any rate, many of North Canyon's vaginas are bull's-eyed with holes that have been "worried" by sticks. Assuming that the sticks were surrogate penises, there definitely was some sort of copulative magic going on. The energy of the place is openly erotic, and at the same time keenly spiritual. Presumably, the Shoshoni would have found no contradiction.

We stood there in a whirl of white flakes, eating a full ration of grit, letting the wind paint our ligaments blue, feeling somewhat sexy and somewhat religious, feeling a little like laughing and a little like weeping, until we got so cold we could no longer feel anything but the necessity of a steaming bath. Since the nearest public lodging was more than a hundred miles away, we set out for it at once, saving a closer examination of the curious canyon for a more hospitable day.

That evening, in the dining room of Tonopah's Mizpah Hotel, the chicken-fried steak was delivered to Alexa, a vegetarian, while Jon, a raging carnivore, received the bowl of iceberg lettuce. The aging waitress grinned, and tugged at the lapels of her dotted-swiss uniform. "Does the right table count for anything?" she asked. Apparently not, for the hot turkey sandwich that your pilgrim ordered (all that sagebrush had awakened a most nostalgic craving) landed on a table across the room, where it was instantly devoured by a man wearing a hat.

While our waitress labored to correct the mix-up, the lights went off. Then, on again. Off. On. Off. On. At least four times. "Happens all the time," said the waitress. "Not to worry. It's just the wind knocking two wires together."

Jon found the explanation less than plausible, but as I suffered the long wait for a turkey sandwich to call my own, it occurred to me that here was a pretty good metaphor for west-central Nevada: two wires knocking together in the wind. In the high desert, the present knocks against the past, development knocks against nature, repression against indulgence, reality against dream, masculine against feminine, the Goddess of Destruction against the Goddess of Creation, the Atomic Proving Grounds against the Canyon of the Vaginas.

For two blustery days, we holed up in the hotel, chasing fruit around the cylinder of a slot machine and watching garbage-can lids UFO past the leaded windows. On the third day, the wind fell over dead and the temperature rose 40 degrees. When we drove back to North Canyon, the sky was as blue as our waitress's beehive, and a silky calm lay upon the land. Inside the canyon, the peace index tripled. It struck us as a haven, a refuge, a place where even the undeserving might be safe. Small and sweet, the canyon was nonetheless so powerful that its vectors held one's soul upright, afloat, as if in metaphysical brine.

Obviously, the Shoshoni hadn't settled on this spot arbitrarily. On a practical level, it offered protection and water, for its cliffs are high and there's a spring at the "uterus" end. Then, there's the matter of its solar alignment. These facts fail to explain its magic, however, an intrinsic presence that was merely enhanced by the hanging of vaginal wallpaper.

Incapable of solving the greater mystery, we were content to sit, stroll, and loll in private communion with the disembodied organs that surrounded us there. I could almost smell the sea in them, feel their merry, saline humidity against my cheek. Like a dolphin, a vagina wears a perpetual smile, a grin as sloppy and loving as the cradle we all rocked out of. Even in the desert, such bogs do not dry up but glisten invitingly enough to make one suspect that little warm marshes dominate the topography of Paradise.

Later in the day, exploring the canyon's middle section, we came upon what might have been Paradise Swamp itself. There on the southern wall (it seemed impossible that we'd missed it earlier) was the queen of the yonis. It was eighteen feet tall (the other vulval images seldom topped ten inches), circular, with a dark vertical gash and a broadcast wattage that could've carried its salty song to the moon. Truly the grandma, the great-grandma of vaginas, it had been embellished by pecking tools, but apparently was a natural formation.

We debated whether this geological yoni might not have been the inspiration for the petroglyphs. It carried life in it—that life that is self-renewing and outside history—the way a bomb carries death. This goddess-size orifice must have filled the Shoshoni with wonder, binding them to the flesh that was their origin and to the earth in which their journey ultimately would end.

Jon with his camera and sketch pads, Alexa with her tarot cards, and your pilgrim with his catalog of quirks, each of us would leave North Canyon with the profound impression that contemporary society lacks any equivalent of it, and that we're the poorer for that. We sensed, moreover, that in our remove from nature and those forces that our ancestors knew intimately yet seldom named, we've lost something so important that its loss is akin to literal amputation. Without a Canyon of the Vaginas in which to peck our American tantra, in which to connect our hormones to the stars, we may be becoming psychological paraplegics.

Toward the close of day, we strolled up to the western end of the canyon to observe, as the Shoshoni certainly did before us, the setting sun. Mountain bluebirds were caroling from the juniper bushes, lizards were using their tails to write love letters in the sand, and I was meditating on Lawrence of Arabia's remark that he adored the desert because it was clean, when I stepped in a pile of regrettably fresh antelope dung. While scraping my shoe, I glanced up an incline and spotted a suspiciously marked boulder sitting off to one side.

Upon inspection, the rock proved to have been graced with what may have been the oldest vaginal glyph at the site. It was both more eroded and more naturalistic than the stylized clusters at the entrance. That, however, wasn't what caught my eye. It turned out that this rock, and it alone, had been pecked upon by white men.

There were a couple of English words cut in the stone. They were less than legible, but from their dark color and serif lettering, we could tell that they'd been inscribed by settlers, perhaps at the turn of the century. There was also a figure on the boulder. A caucasian figure. A male figure. And how.

The honky dude sported a massive, saw-log erection (doesn't phallic graffiti invariably distort in the direction of largeness?), and it was pointed at the vagina like a cannon at a clam. The clumsiness of the execution, the image's total lack of emotional subtlety or spiritual dimension underscores the difference between so-called primitive cultures and those of the European invaders. It's the difference between harmony and aggression, wisdom and shallowness, art and pornography.

Although safely out of the state now, I still wouldn't want to say that the figure is indicative of a "dick first" attitude that continues to epitomize west-central Nevada. Nevertheless, I should mention one further thing about the man carved on the rock. As he moves to possess the object of his sexual passion, the ol' dude is wearing a hat.

DAVID DARLINGTON [B. 1951]

In April 1996 a windy unveiling ceremony took place in the desert of south-central Nevada as Governor Bob Miller officially christened Highway 375 "The Extraterrestrial Highway." While the lieutenant governor greeted the crowd with "Good afternoon, Earthlings," Governor Miller held up road signs bearing "Speed Limit Warp 7" and declared Nevada's interest in tapping a new market, intergalactic tourism. The ninety-eight-mile, two-lane highway skirts the north border of the infamous "Area 51," a classified military base where cutting-edge aircraft and weapons systems are tested, creating otherworldly displays of light in the night skies above the little town of Rachel. In the early 1990s, the area became a mecca for UFO buffs, who suspect that the U.S. government harbors aliens and recovered alien spacecraft at top secret Papoose Lake within the base. Berkeley-based writer David Darlington, who specializes in examining the relationship between people and landscapes, first heard about Area 51 at a cocktail party in 1993 and immediately smelled a good story. His book Area 51: The Dreamland Chronicles *(1997) has been praised by Glenn Campbell, director of the Area 51 Research Center and author of* "Area 51" Viewer's Guide, *who writes, "This is the first published book on Area 51 among several currently in the pipeline, and it will surely be known as the best." As Campbell notes, Darlington's strategy is to interview "the sundry characters who lurk along the base's borders," leaving it up to the reader to deduce where the truth lies. Darlington's other books include* In Condor Country *(1987), about the controversies over managing the last wild population of the California condor;* Angels' Visits: An Inquiry into the Mystery of Zinfandel *(1991), about the history, geography, and people involved in the making of fine wine; and* The Mojave: A Portrait of the Definitive American Desert *(1996), about the human impact and prickly politics of this surprisingly vulnerable landscape.*

from *Area 51: The Dreamland Chronicles*

One day in October 1993, I left my home in northern California and drove east through the Great Central Valley, through the burnished Gold Rush foothills, past the polished granite of Yosemite, over the vertiginous Sierra Nevada crest, past the blue expanse of Mono Lake and streaked cinder slopes of its adjoining craters, through the forests that give way to sagebrush west of Benton Hot Springs, below cloud-capped Boundary Peak in the bristlecone-dotted White Mountains, and into that vast and vacant territory, that wide-open alternation of elevation and depression, that enormous interior drainage bowl of dry-lake-dotted desert—that congenitally uncontrolled kingdom which despite being composed almost wholly of federal land and a vociferously patriotic American populace hardly seems part of the United States, realm of the piñon pine and juniper, scourge of gamblers and forty-niners, home to untamed mustangs, unreined brothels, and unbridled atomic bombs: the fastest-growing state in the Union, the Silver State, that sovereign state of mind called Nevada.

The welcome sign to Tonopah High School said HOME OF THE MUCKERS. East of town along U.S. Highway 6 was the missile-flanked entrance to the Tonopah Test Range, from which squadrons of stealth fighters embarked for the Persian Gulf in 1990. The most common road sign contained the black silhouette of a prancing bull within the customary yellow diamond, underscored by the words OPEN RANGE. Wild horses gamboled on the plains; fighter jets carved the sky with contrails; mountains sucked streaks out of the clouds to pummel the darkened earth with storms. In places where rain had recently fallen, the surface of the two-lane blacktop steamed in the sun. Rainbows shimmered above shining mesas. The air was redolent of sage.

As I turned south on Nevada 375 at Warm Springs—an unpeopled intersection with a collection of cottonwoods and an abandoned pool of hot water—I entered the fallout zone: the swath of the West that took the brunt of atmospheric testing in the 1950s, when nuclear bombs were detonated only if the wind was blowing this way. As I topped plutonium-tinged Queen City Summit and crossed the line between Nye and Lincoln counties, ahead and below in the gathering dusk, adjacent to an unnamed playa, I could see the scattered trailer homes that comprise the town of Rachel: population 100, elevation 4970 feet, established approximately 1978. Within the enormity of Sand Springs Valley, it looked like some research compound on a distant planet.

Luckily, the red-white-and-blue sign in front of the Little A'Le'Inn said EARTH-LINGS WELCOME. I pulled into the parking lot and went inside the building, which was actually a double-wide house trailer. The only people in the room were a stout, pretty, dark-haired barmaid and a guy in a baseball hat who was playing the slot machine. The jukebox had a few recent pop tunes augmenting its staple diet of Hank Williams, Dolly Parton, Merle Haggard, and Randy Travis. The walls were decorated with pictures of fighter planes from nearby Nellis Air Force Range, little gray aliens with big dark eyes, and local terrestrial luminaries: the science buff Bob Lazar, the pilot John Lear, the TV reporter George Knapp, the radio host Anthony Hilder, the funeral director Norio Hayakawa, and the self-proclaimed "world's foremost UFO researcher" Sean David Morton, who was shown meditating beneath a pyramid. T-shirts, bumper stickers, and U.S. Geological Survey maps of the area were for sale. On one wall was a six-foot panoramic photo of the secret base at Area 51, located twenty-five miles to the south. There was also an extensive library containing books and magazines and a stack of binders: UFO Papers and Reports, the International UFO Reporter, Skeptics UFO Newsletter, MUFON Local Chapters, Bob Lazar Paranet Printouts, Black Mailbox Magazine Articles, Newsletters and Press Releases, Roswell and General Reference, Crop Circles, Black Budget Aircraft, UFO Intelligence and International UFO Library. Most of this was the property of one Glenn Campbell (*not* the noted pop-country troubadour, who spells his name with only one N).

I asked the guy in the baseball cap if he'd ever been near the secret base. He said that one night when he was drunk, he'd crossed the boundary and been caught by the guards, but they decided to let him go. He showed me a copy of a form he'd signed admitting that what he'd done was illegal and subject to a five-hundred-dollar fine.

I went back outside and drove half a mile down the road to another trailer whose sign said AREA 51 RESEARCH CENTER. The yard was filled with cacti, cattle skulls, a miniature windmill, a pair of plastic "Smokey Sam" rockets, and a piece of airplane fuselage bearing the letters AF 51. A camper was parked in the driveway, and a bald, mustachioed man in his thirties was out in front. This was Glenn Campbell, whose voice betrayed northeastern roots when he said, "Welcome to Rachel."

I had phoned Campbell ahead of time to tell him I was coming. I had never met him, but knew him as the author of the *Area 51 Viewer's Guide*—a collection of information about the base and region, beginning with "Commonly Asked Questions" ("What is the best time to look for flying saucers?"— "What will happen if I intrude into the restricted zone?") and continuing with advice to visitors, a mile-by-mile guide to points along Highway 375, and meditations on everything from local government to extraterrestrial intelligence.

I had learned about Area 51 at a cocktail party a few months earlier. At the time, I was working on a book about the Mojave Desert; one of its chapters concerned a structure in California called the Integratron, which had served as a focal point for the UFO craze of the 1950s. When I mentioned this at the party, a woman asked if I knew about Rachel and the Little A'Le'Inn. I soon learned that the town, the bar, and the base had been featured on *A Current Affair*, in the *Los Angeles Times*, even in *Business Week* ("Little Gray Men Made My Eyes Turn Red"). Within the next few months, the subject would also find its way into the *New York Times Magazine* and onto the cover of *Popular Science*, and within a couple of years would be investigated on *60 Minutes*, portrayed in the movie *Independence Day*, and chosen as the location for a three-hour UFO special on *Larry King Live*. There wasn't much consistency to these dispatches, some of which focused on flying saucers while some didn't mention UFOs at all, choosing instead to dwell on issues involving government secrecy. But there seemed to be something here for everybody, all piqued by the allure (in the words of the *New York Times*) of a "base so secret that it doesn't exist."

As I pieced it together over time, the outline of the overall story went like this: Area 51 was located next door to the Nevada Test Site, where the government had experimented with nuclear bombs since 1951. Although it has never appeared on aviation charts or U.S. Geological Survey maps, a base was built in the mid-fifties alongside Groom Lake, a remote playa ringed by parched mountains, for the U-2 spyplane. After Francis Gary Powers was shot down over the Soviet Union in 1960, the place continued to serve as the test site for Black Budget (secretly funded) intelligence and defense projects, including the A-12 and SR-71 Blackbirds, the F-117 Stealth fighter, and a rumored hypersonic spyplane called the Aurora. For decades it was known to insiders as Watertown Strip or the Ranch, to aircraft buffs and military pilots as Dreamland or the Box—the latter names referring respectively to the call sign of its control tower and its off-limits status on aeronautical maps. Even Nellis fighter pilots taking part in "Red Flag" war games were grounded and interrogated if they overflew the restricted airspace. The base had also reportedly been used for Strategic Defense Initiative (SDI) research and NASA and commando training, which, combined with the Nellis aeronautical activity, sometimes rendered the local night skies a virtual fireworks display of flashing and streaming lights. Unmarked 737 flights from Las Vegas (one hundred miles to the south) and Palmdale, California (location of the "Skunk Works," headquarters for Lockheed Advanced Development Projects), dispensed a daily workforce of between one and two thousand employees, who were required to sign security oaths prohibiting them from even mentioning the place, violation subject to ten years in jail and a fine of ten thousand dollars.

In 1984, without the required approval of Congress, the Air Force seized control of 89,000 acres of public land around the base to prevent people from coming near it. This inspired a series of hearings in Washington, DC, during which the Air Force representative, John Rittenhouse, told the chairman of the House Subcommittee on Lands and National Parks, Representative John Seiberling of Ohio, that he could explain the reasons for the withdrawal only in a closed briefing. When Rittenhouse said that the decision to take the land had been made at a higher level than his, Seiberling responded that "there is no higher level than the laws of the United States"—signifying, in the minds of some, that Area 51 was outside the control of the U.S. government and, by extension, the American people. The controversy was exacerbated by the Air Force's ongoing refusal to acknowledge the existence of any military facility in the area.

The intrigue escalated to a new and different level in 1989, when an obscure Las Vegas technician named Bob Lazar appeared on a local television news show and claimed that, on the recommendation of Edward Teller, the so-called father of the hydrogen bomb and chief proponent of SDI ("Star Wars") defense technology, he had been hired to work at Area 51. Lazar said that when he reported to the base, he was taken in a bus with blacked-out windows to another, smaller playa called Papoose Lake ("S-4" in alleged classified parlance), where he learned that his task was to research the propulsion systems of recovered alien spacecraft. With disarming lucidity, Lazar delivered a detailed recital of a fantastic story, touching off a frenzy in the UFO subculture. Seekers from around the world soon began making pilgrimages to Rachel, where they gathered at a black mailbox in the desert south of town, near the spot on Highway 375 where Lazar said he'd taken his friends to watch flight tests of the spacecraft on Wednesday nights—a misstep that supposedly led to his severance from the program. Quick on the uptake, the Rachel Bar and Grill expeditiously renamed itself the Little A'Le'Inn, declaring its candidacy as Mecca to UFO believers.

Meanwhile, back in Washington, DC, a class-action suit was filed alleging that Area 51 employees had sustained long-term health damage from toxic materials illegally burned in open pits at the base. Claiming that any disclosures about classified activities would jeopardize national security, the government declined to address the charges, adding yet more acetylene to the inferno.

Unfortunately for the Air Force, its 1984 land withdrawal had neglected a promontory called White Sides Mountain, an unobstructed viewpoint just outside the border of Area 51. Photos of hangars, runways, and towers at the "nonexistent" base soon began appearing in magazines as curious hikers and correspondents converged on the peak. A private enterprise called Secret Saucer Base Expeditions even offered guided tours, promising disclosure of previously withheld government information on extraterrestrials. Whenever people were at large in the area, operations at the base had to be delayed or canceled, playing havoc with operations. Hence, in 1993, the Air Force filed a new application for four thousand more restricted acres, citing the need "to ensure the public safety and the safe and secure operation of activities in the Nellis Air Force Range Complex."

This time, watchdogs were waiting. Citizen Alert, an antinuclear organization in Reno and Las Vegas that had protested the earlier closure, and an ad-hoc group called the Rural Alliance for Military Accountability lobbied actively against the new withdrawal. Proponents of the neo–Sagebrush Rebellion, which holds that the federal government has no legal claim to Western lands, declared the proposal unconstitutional. Lincoln County—99 percent of which is public property and whose commissioners hadn't initially been notified of the plan—registered a formal protest. And citizen Glenn Campbell, lured by the legends, moved from his home in Boston to Rachel, where, operating from a corner table in the Little A'Le'Inn, he set up the Secrecy Oversight Council and White Sides Defense Committee, both of which consisted entirely of he, himself, and him.

In the forays along the border that culminated in his *Viewer's Guide,* Campbell succeeded in becoming a good-sized thorn in the side of the government. He furnished visitors with directions to the border and counseled them about their rights if they were challenged. He tied ribbons around Joshua trees to mark the route up White Sides Mountain; when those were removed, he spray-painted arrows on the rocks, and when those were eradicated, he replaced them with larger, more numerous ones. He dismantled motion sensors on public land along the Groom Lake access road ("a buffer zone for the buffer zone," he charged) and published the arrival and departure times for the flights that shuttled workers to the base, as well as the radio frequencies used by the Groom Lake air control tower, the security guards, and the Lincoln County sheriff. In short, he pushed the jurisdiction of the government as far as he could within in the limits of the law and framework of the Constitution.

Most irksome of all to authorities, Campbell discovered an even better vantage point than White Sides Mountain: a ridgeline only a dozen miles from Groom Lake, with a bleacher-seat view of the base. In October 1993, he announced that he would lead a campout on this legal overlook, which he had christened Freedom Ridge. I had driven to Rachel in order to take part.

Inside the Area 51 Research Center, shelves and cartons overflowed with files: "Freedom of Information Act," "UFO Catalogs," "Las Vegas Newspaper Articles," "Nevada Test Site & Nellis AFB." In one corner was a copy machine, in another a computer. A poster display of "Modern Warplanes" adorned one wall, while a model army helicopter rested on a table. (At least once, Campbell had been sought out and sandblasted by an unmarked Blackhawk on White Sides Mountain.) Affixed to the refrigerator was the "Rachel phone book": a single sheet of paper containing thirty or forty names and numbers. The place had the atmosphere of a bunker or bivouac. In a back room, Campbell cleared a space for himself to sleep. Perusing the accommodations, I asked what had motivated him to move from Boston to a trailer in Rachel.

"I regard myself as an irritant," he explained. "I'm a lobbyist for openness. The military's job is to protect national security, which to them means not to let the enemy in on what you're doing. I agree that you can't let a Saddam Hussein know what you have, but wherever there are secrets, there are going to be abuses. The military is always pushing for more secrecy and more land; they could probably make a case that they need all of Nevada and the rest of the western states if we let them get away with it. But somebody has to push from the other direction. Fate has given me that job."

As we departed the trailer to have dinner, I noticed that Campbell left his door unlocked. We went back up the road to the A'Le'Inn, which in observance of Nevada custom serves a low-priced buffet on weekends. Accordingly, the place was now packed with Rachel residents, many of whom were reputedly employed at the "Test Site," a catch-all term for the conglomerate comprised of Nellis, Area 51, and the A-bomb center itself—a total region as large as Switzerland.

As Campbell and I sat down, an elderly man paused alongside us on his way to the bar. Shielding the contents from the view of others in the room, he opened his wallet to show Glenn an ID card from Wackenhut. This was the high-level CIA-affiliated security firm rumored to supply the guards who patrol the base's border.

"Where did you get that?" Campbell asked.

The man grinned. "If I told you, I'd have to kill you," he answered.

Campbell merely laughed and nodded. "That's the traditional response to questions about the base," he told me after the man had departed. "People who work there unilaterally won't talk about it. You might catch them in an offhand remark, but if you press them, they clam up and get real nervous."

Campbell himself had a somewhat peculiar way of speaking. In the midst of explaining something, he would occasionally close his eyes, apparently concentrating while continuing to talk. His voice, however, was fluid and articulate, his eyes dark and bright in a full, square face. By contrast, his clothing—jeans, old jogging shoes, and hooded sweatshirt—was no more formal or composed than the inside of his trailer. He didn't seem much concerned with matters that weren't mental.

Campbell told me that he'd grown up near Boston, but had never left New England until he was twenty years old, at which point he "traveled everywhere," transferring from one college to another (Brown University, the University of Alaska, the University of Southern California) as a way of getting funded to explore contrasting environments. In the summers he'd worked for the National Park Service, though his tenure there has been controversial. For one thing, he'd tried to organize an employee's union in Glacier National Park.

"When I was twenty-two, I worked on the north rim of the Grand Canyon. I was hired to be a stock clerk, but they also gave me the job of putting out the employee newsletter, which was called *As the Rim Turns*. I changed it to the *North Rim Guardian* and began agitating in favor of things the employees needed, like toilet paper. The Park Service came down on me for publishing an unauthorized newsletter, and finally fired me for insubordination. Another time, when I was working in an office-supply store, I wrote the manager a note suggesting ways to improve the business and retard shoplifting. He went ballistic, but since I was just a young kid, he let me keep my job. So I started acting according to my knowledge and squirreled away enough office supplies to last several years."

As a boy, Glenn had been interested in computers before he ever touched one. "I was very fond of Hal in *2001*," he said. Later he got a job programming the Apple II, and after that the IBM PC. Eventually he joined a start-up software company, designing a program that enabled bank treasuries to track their commerce efficiently. "At one point we were down to only two people—the boss and me," Campbell said. "I lived at the office and got paid in stock instead of money. Later the company became successful and expanded to about twenty employees. But I'm not a long-term company man, so when it became an organization I phased myself out, collected back salary, and sold all my stock."

Faced with the resulting "excess of funds," Campbell needed a new project. "I'd been interested in UFOs when I was a kid," he said. "I was introverted and unhappy as a teenager, but I was into science fiction and really liked Kurt Vonnegut. I drank up all the popular UFO books, but it was really just escapism—I was hoping the saucers would relieve me of this mortal coil. Eventually I realized that they were irrelevant: even if UFOs *were* orbiting the planet, I still had to live my life here on Earth. But in '91 or '92, I realized that the subject represented an intellectual challenge, a way to explore the nature of truth. The field is full of nuts and ridiculous folklore, but that doesn't mean there isn't some truth hiding behind it. The situation is intriguing precisely because there's no physical evidence. It's so vague and ambiguous, Sherlock Holmes would love it. UFOs are like a Rorschach test: When people look at a light in the sky, what they see indicates something about what's inside them. And Rachel is the place to look at people looking at UFOs."

Campbell said he first visited Rachel because of Richard Boylan, a psychologist who said he'd witnessed unexplainable phenomena there. Glenn had also heard

Sean Morton proclaim on a videotape that in Rachel you could see saucers flying on a timetable basis. "I went out to the Black Mailbox and saw some hanging golden orbs," Campbell remembered. "After a couple of nights, though, I realized they were just military flares. The Nellis Range is the nation's premier testing and training area for aviation warfare, so there are all kinds of things in the sky around here. By the time I went home, I could explain every sighting of Boylan's except one: dots that jumped through space a quarter of a mile at a time. I decided I had to come back, and when I did, I met the aviation writer Jim Goodall and John Andrews, the model designer for the Testor Corporation who had come out with the first replica of the Stealth—reputable people who, I was surprised to learn, considered Bob Lazar to be credible."

Though he had no interest in aircraft technology, nor any evidence of extraterrestrial craft, Campbell began to see potential in Area 51. "I don't have any means to investigate what the aliens might be up to," he said. "But what the *government* is up to—the land grab, the cover-up—that's something I can relate to. From the beginning with the Groom Lake base, I said: This is something I can have fun with, something that can drive a creative structure. I'd begun noting mileage markers and collecting data as soon as I got here; after all, if you're looking for UFOs at night, what do you do during the day? So I started compiling the *Viewer's Guide* and cataloguing the culture of the area. The base was the core, the kernel that it was all built around. But even that's really just a sidelight—an excuse to explore these subjects and see how society works."

Between sentences, Campbell cleaned his plate of the A'Le'Inn's steam-table fare: stir-fried vegetables, Salisbury steak, chicken à la king. "If it turned out that UFOs were real," he said, "it would certainly be a turning point for humanity. But my real interest would be in helping people adjust to it. It would be like discovering another culture in Africa—the aliens might know things we don't know, but once we learned them, we'd just say, 'Oh, we should have seen that before.' I'm not into UFOs; I'm into humanity and philosophy. I'm a philosophical warrior. I have the existential view that as soon as you're born you're faced with problems and the purpose of life is simply to solve them as efficiently as possible. In the process, I try to go about shooting down icons as best I can."

Outside, the last light threw the Sand Springs Valley into otherworldly relief, a rosy sunburst shooting up behind the range that concealed the base. As Campbell and I went back toward the Research Center, I asked him how he liked the West.

"This is where I belong," he said. "There's a great deal of optimism here. The cities and towns are all brand-new, so they're very efficient. It clears the mind of extraneous stuff." As he pushed open the door to his trailer, he said, "There's no clutter."

BRUCE STERLING [B. 1954]

The four hundred square miles of playa on the Black Rock Desert in northern Nevada is be-
lieved to be the largest flat spot on earth, thought of by some as the World's Largest Stage.
This featureless desert has become one of Nevada's most popular seasonal attractions, as every
Labor Day legions of hipsters converge on the playa to revel in the week-long Burning Man
festival, reputedly the largest venue for performance art and environmental sculpture in North
America. The rites of the Burning Man began on a San Francisco beach in 1986, when Larry
Harvey and some friends built and then burned a wooden man, the fiery spectacle helping the
lovelorn Harvey recover from a recent breakup. The ritual was reenacted every year to growing
numbers, relocating to the Black Rock Desert in 1990. By 2001 more than twenty-five thousand
people, including a hefty percentage of Silicon Valley techies, camped at Burning Man, making
it briefly the fifth largest city in Nevada. An enactment of community, a venue for eccentric
self-expression, an immersion in the surreal, the event's cardinal rule is PARTICIPATE. *Who*
better to help readers construe this experiment in alternative reality than a writer of science
fiction? Bruce Sterling is widely acclaimed as a progenitor of cyberpunk, cutting-edge science
fiction adapted to a revolutionary new era of biotechnology, information technology, and pop
culture. Sterling's influential Mirrorshades: The Cyberpunk Anthology *(1986) has been called*
"the definitive document of the cyberpunk movement," and his novel Schismatrix *(1986) is*
hailed as "one of the landmark works of modern science fiction." Sterling lives in Austin—the
Silicon Valley of Texas—and has authored more than a dozen works of dazzlingly inven-
tive fiction and nonfiction, also contributing stories to Omni, Isaac Asimov's Science Fiction
Magazine, *the* Magazine of Fantasy and Science Fiction, *and* Interzone.

Greetings from Burning Man!
Thursday, August 29

Stopped at the gas station for directions to the Burning Man Festival. Grizzled,
portly Nevadan local growls: "If ya have to ask, you *don't belong* there!"

As if anybody was gonna drive all the way to Gerlach, Nevada (population 340),
for some other reason. The gas station was packed with mobile homes and junker
slackermobiles. The guy relented and gave us directions. Seems a multiple-pierced
and tattooed lovely in a clingy peach taffeta costume had melted his heart.

Drove 16 miles. Then drove another 12 miles across the bottom of a very dead
lake. Driving across the playa is like space travel: you point the front of the vehicle
into emptiness and launch. Gaseous tails of flying white dust spurt up like jet exhaust. Cars and trucks leave huge wakes on the horizon, like white prairie fires. If
the wind kicks up, the world becomes a twilight zone of milky haze. Driving fast
in a whiteout dust fog is an excellent way to get killed.

We're in a 22-foot Ford recreational vehicle, in which I've brought the family to Burning Man: Nancy Sterling (wife, mom), Amy Sterling (9 years), and the littlest desert fox, Laura of Arabia, a hardened travel veteran at 4 months. We've never lived in an RV before. It's a mutant cross between an aircraft and a small chunk of suburbia. It's brand-new, but it shudders, moans, vibrates, rattles, squeaks, and emits foul generator exhaust.

Reached the camp, found a place to park, got out to walk around. Maybe 500 vehicles here already. People are setting up tents, parachutes, awnings, tiki torches, tribal flags. The lake bed is a Euclidean plane with zillions of dry fractal cracks. The parched Nevada mountains of the Black Rock Desert rise on three sides. Weary treeless hills full of sullen majesty.

Friday, August 30

A guy got killed last night. He rear-ended a truck while zooming along the darkened playa on a blacked-out motorcycle.

The place feels like the afterlife. When you walk across it, you just drift over endless cracked whiteness, lifting your feet maybe a quarter inch from the surface. It's all mobile; it's all temporary. Twist the ignition key and drift with the wind.

Burning Man is an art gig by tradition. Over the longer term it's evolved into something else; maybe something like a physical version of the Internet. The art here is like fan art. It's very throwaway, very appropriative, very cut-and-paste. The camp is like a giant swap meet where no one sells stuff, but people trade postures, clip art, and attitude. People come here in clumps: performance people, drumming enthusiasts, site-specific sculptors, sailplane people, ravers, journalists, cops. I'm a journalist and a newbie, but even I can tell the pros from my fellow newbies. The veterans have brought their own pennants, bicycles, flashlights, and tiki torches, plus enough water for anything.

The alkali dust is like a fine and bitter talcum. It gets into everything, so why fight it? Just throw off your clothes. Keep maybe a straw hat, shades, and boots. Throwing off all your clothes is the cheapest, quickest way that was ever invented to cop an attitude. It's also a cool youth-culture solidarity move. Young people look great without clothes. Young people don't need 'em.

Vehicles have scattered all over the playa. It's as if a giant bowl of mixed nuts had dropped off a kitchen counter onto white linoleum. The parachute-covered Central Camp does duty as the broken bowl. All around it are cashews, peanuts, and sunflower seeds: dinky pup tents, some bigger pop tents, RVs, pickups, trailers. There's even an honest-to-goodness geodome erected by some ambitious guys who have brought a crane. Their towering construction crane arouses much envy, and they get to boast of having "the biggest tech on the playa."

The streets are vaporous formalities. They're premarked with tiny colored plastic flags: the flags get bent, they get stepped on, they even get run over. But once the *idea* of a street is established, the community standard holds.

You're not supposed to throw anything away on the playa. You're supposed to leave nothing at all. The idea of leaving no visible trace is a central part of the Burning Man zeitgeist, a performance-art process move. The organizers are very specifically eco-correct—maybe because they're so lighthearted about tolerating most anything else.

We're new here, and as a married couple with kids we are very adult and polite. So we dutifully follow orders, and we don't dump anything. It's a quick and brutal lesson in the gross inconvenience of modern convenience. Everything we own or want to get rid of becomes a burden: toilet paper, snack bags, beer cartons, dirty diapers, our unwashed clothes. Nancy and I take to wolfing down Amy's food so that we won't have to store it in malodorous twist-tie bags.

There's some good art here. When you see the good art—even though it is very temporary—it's like finding a pearl in a bag of salted peanuts. The Burning Man is good art. Flat on his back, he looks like a giant abandoned packing crate, but when he's catapulted into standing position, he becomes a striking neon symbol of pretty much everything that matters. You can sit on a hay bale at the foot of the Burning Man and the whole world passes by. It's like hanging out on the Venetian Rialto.

Had a long chat with a guy about Moscow. I'd never met this guy except through email, but he recognized me, and we immediately struck up a conversation. We talked about Russians and their literature for an hour, as we sat in a desert—bathing blue neon glow from the 40-foot Burning Man. We ruminated thoughtfully on the fate of Eastern Europe as people drove past on motorcycles that looked like aardvarks and bananas. Witchy pagan chicks stalked by in coats of body paint. Crypto-Arab hippies sauntered by arm in arm with bearded punks wearing devil horns. It felt very soothing and cosmopolitan.

The Stupa is also real art. It's constructed of books, mud, water, and wood. It's about 15 feet high. It's very majestic and spiritual. To the east there's a Forest of Meditation that is also real art. It's made of black rocks and twisted pieces of plumbing pipe, and it's about a mile across. People keep trying to camp inside that art. It's beautiful.

Had a few words with the justly legendary Larry Harvey today. Ten years ago, Larry went out and set fire to a big wooden statue on a beach. Kind of a private act of purgation and cleansing, by all accounts, but his idea caught on big time. Larry is a heavy hipster dude. He's beyond mere trendiness. Guys of his ilk can create social trends at will, out of straw, hot air, and attitude. Larry is an artist, but under these circumstances he looks just like you would expect the mayor of an impromptu city of 10,000 people to look. Larry looks real busy. He's wearing his trademark fedora, and he hasn't shaved, and his eyes are red-rimmed with dust. He's biting his lips a lot. Larry's puttering around on his battered motorcycle, putting out impromptu social fires: diverting ego trips and freak-outs, coordinating the uncoordinatable.

Larry appears to have a couple dozen city councillor running buddies who he can trust to mortar over the cracks. They all have this certain *look,* these tribal elder hippie-guru characters. Time has given them the faces they deserve. They all end up with this spacey Crowleyan smirk . . . not *seamy* exactly, but some kind of terrible wisdom, like a cross between Gandalf and Nietzsche. It's truly a very interesting way to live, but you get to where you can smell it after a while. You don't want to clutch your wallet when you're around these guys, it's not like they're as degraded as, say, car salesmen or members of Congress. But when you're in their company you feel a distinct witch-doctor vibe. I kinda suspect that Larry Harvey could do interesting and terrible things to the soul of '90s America, if he really put his mind to it. And if '90s America had more soul for Larry and his friends to work with.

Burning Man is a standard hippie tribal thing, except for the highly nonstandard fact that it is not kitschy '60s nostalgia. This event is very '90s, very big, and very much alive. It's a Tim Leary, Wavy Gravy, Deadhead caravan, grab-the-mike-at-Woodstock kind of event. Feels lovely and enormously persuasive. Nonbureaucratic, participative, solidarity-driven, noncommercial, arty. With all those manifest virtues, you have to wonder why a setup like this can't seem to last any longer than a Labor Day weekend.

Maybe it's because *real* tribes aren't tattooed postmodern termite artists like the Burning Man people are. Actual, no-kidding tribes were tattooed hunter-gatherers, who lived in a world where nothing ever, ever changed. A world where witch doctors made all the important decisions.

There's another thing really different and novel about Burning Man. It's a hippie gig, but it's swarming with cops. The Nevada cops have been in from the get-go. There are plenty of concert-security type Danger Rangers, too. Security people are all over the place, and they could give two pins that people are running around naked, setting fires, and blowing things up. I think this proves that Temporary Autonomous Zones really can work in real life—as long as the cops help create them.

Saturday, the last day of August
Fiends in human guise greeted the dawn by wailing for half an hour on didgeridoos. This should be a capital offense.

Woke up, had breakfast. Looked out my RV window and saw a guy sitting on a toilet. He was skidding by at about 45 MPH in a massive trail of dust. He had his toilet mounted on a wooden sled, and he was being towed by a pickup. His pants were around his ankles, and he was reading a magazine as he skidded along. It was the magazine reading that made this truly a memorable gesture.

Left "town" for a while to fetch more water. Can't take risks. We've got a baby on board. Came across a spectacular highway casualty. Bunch of Nevada sheriffs and paramedics were pounding on the rib cage of a guy sprawled right in the middle of the highway. He was lying there in a sea of shattered glass amid his violently scattered possessions: a mattress, assorted camping gear. The cab of his little Toyota truck was crushed like a bug. I can't say for certain that this dead or dying kid was headed out to Burning Man, but a hell of a lot of the traffic stacked up behind him certainly was.

People think it's good that Burning Man is difficult and rather dangerous to reach. This keeps the gawking frat boys and the sodden alcoholics at bay. To get this far Out Here you've got to pay some dues and take some risks. Gotta live on the edge, at least a little. "Survival is a matter of personal choice," as the Burning Man official tabloid puts it. But when there are 10,000 people making risky choices, cold statistics dictate that some will surely croak.

Ran into Danny Hillis, the supercomputer designer, today. Hillis was standing in the coffee line. He's here with his wife and their three little kids. His two twin toddler sons are real chips off the block. They have a real engineer's mind-set. With absolute desolation around and nothing much to play with, they ingeniously began pelting each other with dust.

Not a lot of little kids in this burg. Scarcely any old people. With a babe in arms, you're an instant public attraction. Got two shots of tequila from a crew of friendly Australians merely for allowing a young woman to dandle my infant. My baby's wearing a red tie-dyed onesie for the sake of local color, and she's coming across like The Littlest Deadhead. I'm wearing a nuclear-power-plant worker's jumpsuit, shades, sandals, and a cowboy hat with a bandanna. Nancy and Amy have flowing tie-dyed seraglio robes with veils and canteens. We're passing for normal.

Visited the i-STORM trailer where the World Wide Web contingent is putting together the live Burning Man Web site, *www.istorm.com/burningman/*. I enjoy hanging with these happening GenX Web entrepreneurs. They're nice guys just fizzing with creativity. It's like meeting Walt Disney when he was still drawing on a tabletop in Kansas City, Missouri. Before Walt Disney became the scary, litigious, freeze-dried media titan. OK, maybe I shouldn't give Disney any lip. Danny Hillis works for Disney these days.

Walking around the playa with my family at night. This is the time to tour the site, because Burning Man is truly weird then. "Black Rock City" has no power system, so at night it's all lanterns and chugging generators and tiki torches and lots of chemglow. Colored strings of chemglow out in the desert, woven through the spokes of bicycles and mysteriously revolving. Looming figures in costume. Huge dramatic bowl of desert stars overhead. Fireworks and flying flares casting a lurid trench-warfare glow above the massive camp. Drum-pounding maniacs with guys dancing in the grip of hallucinogens, nerdy guys capering with out-of-it clumsiness, as if they had never danced in their lives. Daughter Amy starts grumbling and complaining. It dawns on us that she's getting scared. Something to do with the evil Helco pavilion with its saw-edged performance machines and the gruesome cutout movie stars from the LA Cacophony Society. Amy is a sensitive and imaginative child. She bursts out suddenly: "This is awful! It's like a LIVING NIGHTMARE!"

It *is*, too, which is pretty much why we jaded adults are really living it up. But Amy won't be comforted and has to go back to the RV with Mom. It's getting late. I hitch a ride on the Aggravator, a monstrous steam-punk contraption with a flame-thrower and four sets of bicycle pedals.

I then sit on the Aggravator's iron tractor seat and watch an astounding presentation, over by the sinister temple towers of the City of Dis. A formal procession begins with honks, rattles, and electronic squeaks. Pagan hierophants in tall headdresses and silver lamé march in slow step, toting flaming standards of arcane device. Swarms of nude dancers, male and female, caper up in bizarre sword-and-sorcery bondage gear. The soundtrack switches to repeated, insane, bestial screaming. An awe-inspiring insect goddess—a hunchbacked bug on red stilts—comes towering and tipping and tottering into the firelight, like a mad Kafkaesque advent. It's like a cross between Vatican ceremony, Cirque du Soleil, and a necro-erotic cannibal mantis mating ritual. The performers seem ready to burst into a flagellant orgy at any instant, in front of a solid milling crowd of at least 3,000.

This sure isn't the sort of thing one sees every day. It's something that a desperately horny sci-fi fan might see on acid and cough syrup. Then the performers set fire to the set. The tall rebar towers, turned to instant chimneys, glow white-hot and vent livid five-story flames. I'm really enjoying this.

OK, so they're not professional exotic dancers. They're eager amateurs. They dance the way '50s B-movie starlets danced in some cheesy lost-race epic. "OK, Jim, Cindy, you guys are pagan babes at the palace orgy, so just go out there and lose it, get really lusty!" They caper and dance very lustily for more than an hour, and then they get pretty tired and out of breath, and they have to sit down. But it's a lot of fun watching these tattooed San Franciscans flinging the dour garments of repentance. It's sweet to watch them lose themselves in the moment.

After the towers buckle and collapse, the screaming and chanting Greek chorus takes a well-deserved rest. The dancers hug each other, all bright-eyed and happy, and the crowd dissipates into the desert.

Then a bunch of drummers wander in and take over by the smoldering bonfire. There are swarms of drummers here. Most can't beat a steady rhythm worth a dang. But we've got a cadre of guys who really *can* drum, accompanied by some crazy dancers who are not half bad, either. They go at it hot and heavy, booming-banging-boogying. The drummers are really savoring the joy of life. It's worth coming a long way to see this.

Sunday, September 1

Our noses are parched and crusty. Our lips are chapped. Our lungs are lined with a fine layer of alkali dust. We haven't slept much. We decide to go out to the hot springs.

Fabulous place. It's got a geyser. Eerie maroon towers of hot mineral concretion. The water's hot enough to hard-boil eggs, but it flows out into a broad series of weedy muddy pools, so you can pick your temperature. There are about 200 hippies here, naked and covered with mud.

A nude woman covered with mud is an interesting sight, but mostly she looks like she's undergoing a spa treatment. But take some nude muscular young guy and armor him face-to-foot in black and gray sulfurous muck and he looks genuinely impressive, like a New Guinea head-hunting Mud Warrior. Hey, Nancy and I are with this. It works for us. We strip the dusty clothes from our middle-aged, married-couple carcasses and we cover ourselves with mud. The baby skips the mud bath, and my 9-year-old's not real thrilled at this prospect either, but Nancy and I are getting seriously hot, down, and slimy.

The sky is blue, and the water is poaching our desert-parched hides with deeply gratifying effect, and for the first time we really feel like we're on vacation.

A lot of air stuff today. Hot air balloon, paragliders, a skywriter plane. At night somebody constructs a fake constellation. It's a glowing mass like the Little Dipper, and it looks just like stars, except they're moving across the night sky without visible means of support. Faking the stars, cutting-and-pasting the desert sky—now that's a good trick. It's good art. I truly can't believe what I'm seeing.

Then night falls, and it's time to finally burn the Man. I've got Amy up on my shoulders videotaping this, in the midst of an enormous, boisterous, cheering crowd. A procession marches up, solemn, freakish, and deeply hilarious. Then they fire up the guy, and he explodes in sheets of colored fireworks and giant livid gouts of flames. This spectacle seriously lights my fourth-grader's circuits. "BURN HIM!" Amy is screaming, wriggling like an eel. It's without doubt the most exciting thing she's ever witnessed. "Look at him BURN! This is AMAZING! I can't BELIEVE IT! WOW!!!"

When the man's about to collapse from sheer conflagration, some brave and hefty folks grab a pair of dangling steel cables from the Burning Man's shoulders. They tug and yank. The giant wooden man goes into a weird spastic dance, pointy arms upraised and shedding massive showers of fire. A 40-foot-high wooden doll dancing in flames is a sight that really hits the 9-year-old demographic. My kid is in ecstasy, she's loudly swearing that she'll remember this for the rest of her life. I'm sure this is true.

Baby's asleep in mother's arms. It's OK. She can see it when she's older. We've got it all on tape.

Monday, September 2

Back to Reno. There are places in Reno that are seriously weird. There are lessons here. Las Vegas is a major family destination. Nevada casinos have become American family values now. It's considered just fine to go into one of these windowless scary gambling-malls, drink yourself silly, lose your ass at roulette, and then go ogle showgirls with breast implants. Republicans do this now. Working-class folks do it in polyester stretch pants. It's normal.

Meanwhile, if you want to get high and be a naked hippie, you're under suspicion of engaging in the moral equivalent of terrorism. You've got to haul out into the middle of some godforsaken desert and hope that not too many people find out about it.

It's all exactly backward. If you want to have a naked pagan art fair, you ought to have it in the padded comfort of a sealed, air-conditioned casino. It would be perfect for this kind of activity. If you want to divorce somebody or feed the gambling bug or lick your chops over paid nudity, then you ought to have to creep off to do that in some remote boondocks where the rest of us don't have to witness your gross behavior. I wonder how our culture got into this oxymoronic situation. It can't be good for us.

I went to Burning Man. I took my kids. It's not scary, it's not pagan, it's not devilish or satanic. There's no public orgies, nobody gets branded or hit with whips. Hell, it's less pagan than the Shriners. It's just big happy crowds of harmless arty people expressing themselves and breaking a few pointless shibboleths that only serve to ulcerate young people anyway. There ought to be Burning Man festivals held downtown once a year in every major city in America. It would be good for us. We need it. In fact, until we can just relax every once in a while and learn how to do this properly, we're probably never gonna get well.

WILLIAM L. FOX [B. 1949]

For a discussion of William L. Fox's poetry, see p. 586. William Fox describes the focus of his nonfiction as "cognitive dissonance in isotropic environments," by which he means the unnerving sense of disorientation that humans experience in flat, featureless landscapes. This interest has taken Fox to Nevada's Black Rock Desert, to the Bonneville Salt Flats outside Wendover, and to the cold deserts of Antarctica and the Arctic, where he observed scientists operate in the closest earthly analog to Mars. The work has plunged him into the intellectual domains of cartography, cultural geography, and cognitive psychology, and informed many of his books, including The Void, the Grid, and the Sign *(2000),* Playa Works *(2002), and, with photographer Mark Klett,* The Black Rock Desert *(2002), among others. Fox, who currently lives in Los Angeles, first came to Nevada from San Diego at the age of ten, when his mother settled in Reno after a divorce. The open vistas gave him a sense of freedom, and he returned to Reno after earning a BA in English at Claremont McKenna College. His thirty-three-year residence in Nevada included working at the Nevada Museum of Art and for the Nevada Arts Council, where he served as executive director from 1984 to 1993. In a remarkably productive and influential career, Fox has been a writer, artist, critic, editor, arts administrator, and arts consultant, promoting the arts at both the regional and national levels, serving as literature consultant for the Western States Arts Federation and on the literature panel of the National Endowment for the Arts. In* Mapping the Empty *(1998), Fox analyzes how artists have responded to the emptiness of the Great Basin. In the excerpt reprinted below, from* Driving by Memory *(1999), he views military installations as another response to those same landscapes of void.*

from *Driving By Memory*

To drive from Reno to Las Vegas is to feel as if you're a message vibrating along a string between two tin cans. There's a close connection between the two places, but it's definitely low tech, all but forgotten when the two towns outgrew each others' friendship. In 1959 when I moved to Reno, its population of 50,000 still exceeded that of Las Vegas, and for years the political power in Carson City's legislative roundhouse was held by Reno and the rural counties. By the 1990s, Reno's citizenry could maybe be stretched to 150,000—but Las Vegas was fast closing in on the one million mark and had all but completely rebalanced the powers of state government. And US 95, the most direct route between the two cities, couldn't help bridge the gap of economic envy and political frustration. In fact, the highway doesn't even pass through Reno, but sixty miles to the east in Fallon.

9:23 AM: Fallon

Outside, the air is fresh and cool, the morning continuing to warm, and I turn over the keys to Beth, who quickly and efficiently gets headed south on US 95, the road to Las Vegas. Before leaving town we pass a house with a flooded yard, several geese paddling around.

Straight and with a progressively higher speed posted as we enter the farmlands, we level off at the new legal limit, 70 MPH. We're surprised, given that it's only a two-lane road. New Mexico has kept its two-lane highways capped at 55 and California at 65, both states only letting the interstates go any higher at 75. It's a realistic speed for this road, though, given the distance between towns and the long stretches of straight and level blacktop. You stand more danger of killing yourself while driving to Las Vegas by falling asleep at 55 than you do by hitting something at 70.

. . . .

The fields end, and now it's sagebrush that's flooded. At the far end of the valley the road climbs up toward Russell Pass and we sight the "Top Gun Drag Strip," which presumably means a place to race cars and not F-18s, its dirt track about the only dry piece of level ground we can see. On the other side of the pass, the landscape to the east unfolds in a series of hazy ridges. The nearest peaks, the Blow Sand Mountains, are within the purview of the naval air station, and signs arrayed along the road warn of "Low Flying Aircraft." It's a caution found throughout Nevada, though a trifle insufficient when a jet flies a hundred feet over your car at night firing rockets at a target a few hundred yards off the road, as happens in Dixie Valley just east of Fallon.

Over 80 percent of Nevada is owned by the federal government, and 16 percent of the entire country's military lands are within the state, some four million acres in all. Superlatives accumulate: Fallon is not only the largest naval air station in the West, but the largest electronic warfare range in the world. While Nevada is the most urban state in the union, with well over 85 percent of its population living in or adjacent to Reno or Las Vegas, its landscape is also the most militarized. Nellis Air Force Range, the largest peacetime military ground and airspace in the Western world, is three million acres on the ground with control over more than ten million acres of airspace, a territory that's been compared in size to Switzerland. The military drops bombs out here, shoots off rockets and airborne cannon rounds, and fires lasers (one of the nearby "Warning: Approved Laser Range" signs was once involuntarily donated to our family art collection). From here to Las Vegas the military installations are a patchwork terrain of forbidden parcels either within sight or close by and just over a hill.

We cross the boundary of the Walker River Indian Reservation, and the top of Mt. Grant, at 11,239 feet the highest point of the Wassuk Range, comes into view. It's always impressive to see the peak, which looms over Walker Lake and the town of Hawthorne, two features still hidden from view. First we have to pass through Schurz, elevation 4,126 feet, which we reach at 10:54 AM, diving into the cool green of the cottonwoods lining the very full Walker River. On the other side of the bridge this morning, both of the Nevada Highway Patrol cars responsible for all of west-central Nevada are parked in front of the local restaurant, the officers presumably meeting over coffee. David points out that the nearby Church of Latter-day Saints is a mobile home, while Beth directs my attention to four guys wearing baseball caps and sweatshirts sitting in a boat parked to one side of the house next door. Maybe they're waiting for the really Big Flood, having the means for both spiritual and bodily salvation at hand. Except for the trees growing alongside the Walker River, everything in town looks ready to pick up and move.

The road climbs over a short rise, then soon dips into the Walker Lake basin, which holds one of the most supremely surreal earthworks on the planet. Looming under a high thin scrim of gray cloud to our right is Mt. Grant, much closer now, and the birthplace of the Ghost Dance, that late nineteenth-century visionary Indian cult that foretold the expulsion of white men from the continent. Sweeping above and below us are eleven stepped terraces, ancient beaches from the prehistoric times demonstrating all too vividly the slow death of the lake. And in front us, covering 147,000 acres, are arrayed the bunkers of the largest ammunition depot in the hemisphere, if not the entire world. We pull off the road above the lake, David uncorking himself from the back seat with a slewing sideways motion that almost produces an audible Pop! of relief as he squeezes out. Except for the occasional vehicle passing by, it's entirely silent.

The rim of Walker Lake at this point is defined by 20 Mile Beach, a camping and boating shore that remains popular with fishing parties—or will remain popular until the fish are gone. The lake level had dropped almost a hundred feet between 1930 and 1994, a quarter of the shrinkage taking place just since 1976, the combined effect of continual drought and serious overcommitment of the water rights in the Walker River system. The rapidly increasing salinity of the remaining water was supposed to kill off the last of the fish no later than the year 2000, but the three wet winters have given them a reprieve. As it is for the majority of the farmers around Fallon, it's a losing battle for the cutthroat trout, but this morning David counts two dozen boats with fishermen in just our quadrant of the lake.

Descending three of the shoreline benches in about twenty yards, down to the edge of a particularly steep drop off to the next terrace, we turn and slowly pick our way back to the car in a more or less straight line, inventorying the litter as we go. Despite that fact we've picked a small and inconspicuous pullout, the survey results are impressive: four rusted tin cans, fourteen broken bottles, one plastic drink top, a dried orange peel, and one toddler's size tennis shoe; a foot-long section of truck tire (tread in good condition), one gas cap, one Brisk Iced Tea plastic bottle, a Budweiser can, and a transparent blue plastic lighter with fuel (which sparks but doesn't light); two empty motor oil jugs (Castrol 20W-50W), one tire inflator/sealant can (empty), one Salem cigarette pack (empty), one blue straw (same color as the lighter), two Polaroid film packs (empty); and two copies of a receipt with carbon from the American Building Company in Carson City for "13 out of 182 of part #95212, 33'0" long."

What this quick roadside archeology reveals is a cross-section of the traffic by the lake, from families traveling with their children to truckers hauling pipe, from old cars overheating on the grades to tourists in RVs stopping for a smoke and a beer. Back on the shoulder most of the junk is hidden, slowly subsiding into the ground and forming a new layer within the geology for future reading.

11:38 AM: Hawthorne. Two miles south a sheriff has a Range Rover with California plates pulled over. The entrance to the beach below displays, according to David, about one hundred recreational vehicles in various stages of disarray for the weekend. On a nearby boulder a fresh Valentine has been painted, its red heart outlined in white tracery, almost too nice to label as graffiti, and then we're on the edge of the Hawthorne Army Ammunition Depot. Parked as a decoy at the boundary is a decommissioned black-and-white, the retired patrol car resting on low tires. Signs instruct explosive-laden trucks to avoid the main gate of the base, and Beth prudently drops a little speed.

Hawthorne was a railroad town in the late 1800s, has been an on-again off-again county seat since 1883, and nearly burned to the ground in 1926. It might have simply become another sandy beach at the southern end of the lake but for its selection that same year to become a safely remote site for the storage of bombs, hand grenades, mines, bullets, artillery shells, and mustard gas. Subsequently, the town's economy has been almost totally dependent on the fortunes of war, thriving when the ammo trade is in full swing during conflicts, and shrinking in between. In the mid-1980s things looked pretty dismal, and all the depot did was store weapons and run a salvage and demilitarization operation dismantling munitions. The end of the Cold War early the next decade could have again killed the town, but lately, due to the budget cutting of the bipartisan Base Realignment and Closure Commission, the Hawthorne Depot has been receiving relocated munitions from bases being closed in Oregon, Arizona, and New Mexico, states which are apparently held in greater scenic esteem than central Nevada.

To the east, dozens of newly painted yellow army freight cars with bright red doors are parked on sidings, perhaps evidence of fresh deliveries. Information about the depot is notoriously difficult to obtain, so we're not sure. To our west the crisply laid out officers' houses with their rectangular lawns and empty flagpoles are occupied by local residents. The depot is now run by a civilian contractor and only two military personnel are on site, but the integration of the town and military remains evident by the cemetery, where a dozen large artillery casings and a double-barreled antiaircraft gun mark the entrance to downtown, such as it is. The bars, casinos, markets, and gas stations in Hawthorne are remarkable only for their lack of distinction, a quasi-urban architecture with only the smallest pretense to anything other than factual signage. In a reversal of the normal order of things, the built environment of the town is overshadowed by the military signage, and once through town, the extent of the bunkers becomes apparent.

High and steeply graded parallelograms of dirt, many with sagebrush growing on their sides, most of the "igloos," as they're designated by the army, are bisected at both ends by driveways cut down to ground level. The bunkers themselves have large metal loading doors at either end, which face concrete blast shields built into the dirt across the driveways. We park off the road by one of the numerous and seemingly undefended entrances to the base, and I ask both Beth and David to estimate the number of bunkers in the valley. Stretching in every direction into the foothills, the relentless and very visible military grid of dirt roads and two hundred miles of railroad tracks makes apparent how large the valley really is, how immense the territory we're traversing today.

Beth shakes her head, speechless. David gropes for a number—*1,000—2,000—5,000?* None of us can guess. It takes a printout from the Center for Land Use Interpretation in Los Angeles to inform us that there are 2,427 of the igloos with a storage capacity exceeding 7.6 million square feet, that as of March 1996 was 74 percent utilized.

We're about to leave when we realize that the gate in front of us leads into the "NUWC Detachment." Putting a "Naval Underwater Warfare Center" at a lake everyone knows is drying up rapidly seems a bit odd. A model of the submarine USS *Nevada,* fashioned from an old torpedo and painted matte black, acts as a mascot to one side, while on the other a large sign warns us that photographing, sketching, or taking notes about this facility is strictly forbidden, that everyone is subject to search at any time, and persons caught violating the rules will be subject to prosecution. There's also a polite request to leave all matches and lighters with security personnel at the gate, none of whom are in evidence. Just outside the sentry post a white sign reading "Threat Condition" has the word "Normal" in green letters attached to it, an odd parody of forest fire warning signs throughout the West. We give up trying to decipher any of this and drive off, only to come to a screeching u-turn thirty seconds later when one of the blue Adopt-a-Road signs catches my eye. Underneath, the name of the sponsor is listed as the "*Nuclear* Underwater Warfare Center," which carries with it a distinctly different and more ominous meaning than simply "Naval." We wonder which one is correct.

As we leave the valley, Beth still driving and David writing furiously in his journal, I turn to catch a last glimpse of Mt. Grant. Despite the fact that it's within the jurisdiction of the military, which appropriated the peak to protect the depot from attacks launched off higher ground, and that there's a dirt road leading to the top, I've always wanted to hike it. It's not that I would expect to reexperience the vision of Wovoka, the Paiute prophet of the Ghost Dance, but to be physically on the site out of which such a powerful story emanated is always sobering. It's a very nearly apocryphal metaphor for the summit—where Wovoka supposedly received his visions of the whites being consumed by cataclysm—that it is included by the military within their largest preserve of explosives.

DAVID THOMSON [B. 1941]

Having spent much of his life in the dark, the distinguished film critic David Thomson, who has seen about twenty thousand movies, is drawn to Nevada for its light. Having lived most of his life in crowded cities—born and raised in London, a San Francisco resident since the 1980s—Thomson feels a magnetic attraction to the "sublime distances" and "the deep and ultimate vacancy" of Nevada, its "beautiful emptiness and the just as tranquil, patient uneventfulness." And having led the life of an intellectual, Thomson is as interested in the idea of Nevada as in its physicality. For him, Nevada is the place where America experiments, testing not just weapons but also social ideas, such as divorce, gambling, and prostitution. In Nevada: The Land, the People, God, and Chance (1999) is a combination travelogue and popular history, covering topics as varied as the Burning Man Festival, Frank Sinatra, prizefighting, gambling, nuclear waste, atom bombs, the Comstock Lode, the history of Nevada's boundaries, the Pony Express Trail, Bravo 20, Lake Tahoe, Hoover Dam, and Howard Hughes. The book—if not Nevada itself—received high praise in the national press. Kirkus Reviews calls it a "well-researched portrait of a state that is not a network of vital places so much as an intermittently and briefly interrupted nullity." While Nevadans may prefer to think of their state in terms other than nullity, In Nevada, *like other travel writing, affords an enlightening view of the state from the outside in. Thomson is best known as "the Dr. Johnson of film," with his* Biographical Dictionary of Film *(1975) now in its fourth edition. In addition he has published three novels, a story collection, biographies of David O. Selznick and Orson Welles, several books of film criticism, and film commentary for the* New York Times, New Republic, Salon, Esquire, Vanity Fair, *and the* Independent.

from In Nevada: The Land, the People, God, and Chance

I am going north again—the way I began this book. But farther this time, past Gerlach, all the way to the straight line of Nevada's northern border. It is the part of the state I love the most, the part I see when anyone says "Nevada." Yet time and again as I worked on this book, saying "Nevada" made most people answer "Las Vegas," as if that's all there was to it.

For myself, I am quite content to abide by southern Nevada, the spike driven into the Southwest, and the gathering of Las Vegas, Hoover Dam, Henderson, and even Laughlin. That is where the people and the power are, that is where the affairs of state are determined, and that is where business and progress test their flimsy hold on the ground. I like to be in Las Vegas—for a few days at a time; I see no point in disapproving of its gambling, when our world is caught up in so many larger games of hazard and chance.

But I insist on the north—and not only Reno, Winnemucca, and Elko, smaller places that seem more secure than Las Vegas and which are as old and plain as the small cities to be found all over the West, places that have dug in and learned to put up with the hardship, the severity, the isolation, and the eternity of provincialism. No, I mean the north beyond those towns, the north that has only itself to offer, the land that has so few people, no power, and not even the long-shot chance of being "discovered." For even as I extol the place, and may tempt you, it is a long way to go to get within striking reach of it. And there are next to no comforts there, no facilities. Yet all the rest of the state, from Boundary Peak to Wheeler, all the way along Highway 50, all the way along I-80, and all there is north of that—from Jackpot to Jarbidge to McDermitt to Denio to the last bit of the northwest quarter, where there is not even one small place to name—is Nevada, too. And the emptiness is vital, even it if exists only as a warning or a signal to the bustling, expanding south.

I know: You can step out of the Luxor, say, and feel the closeness of the desert; that is part of the advertised Egyptian experience. But more than that, I relish the way in which some of the most fabulous, outrageous, and moderne gestures of Americana are loomed over by the silent emptiness of the sustaining state. Nevada is the north and the south; it is the greatest concentration of hotel rooms in the world and the expanses in which there is no bed to be found. And, in the end, the corridors of the Mirage, say, make an unexpected rhyming with those stretches of waiting highway in the north.

Not that the north of Nevada is, as they say, "staggeringly beautiful," so demandingly spectacular that tourists make a journey there for its own sake. There is nothing as exquisite as the Canyon de Chelly or as epic as the Grand Canyon. I have driven the Burr Trail in southern Utah, and that and many other places in that state are like savage stage sets or the perfect places for Western drama. Yellowstone is more awesome. The chocolate mesas of Wyoming and the greasy grass rolling prairies of Montana are more picturesque. California itself, as one might expect of the ideal catalog of narrative locations, has Carmel, Death Valley, Shasta, Yosemite, and the Sierra, which are all more gorgeous, more extreme, more more than northern Nevada.

I love all those places, but in hardly any of them is it possible to be alone. I was born and raised in England, where, sometimes, you feel the island is one traffic jam fidgeting its way here and there beneath overcast skies. I had not seen anything like desert until I came to live in California and a friend, Tom Luddy, offered to drive me from Las Vegas to Telluride, Colorado. We went for the film festival there, and it was a good festival, but the landscape and its light meant more to me than being in the dark.

What I am about to say comes with very little scientific explanation, and I am shy about offering it as a therapeutic easing for others—after all, I do not want to find northern Nevada crowded. But I believe, for myself, that there is something beneficial, uplifting, and calming in being out and about in the sunlight and emptiness of that place. I know there are such things as "light therapy," and I know there is an odd tradition of depressed, or repressed, Englishmen—"mad dogs and Englishmen," remember?—finding themselves, or feeling better in the desert and its glowing silence. That's maybe why I prefer to be there alone, or with someone I can show the wonder to, a novice. And the being alone is a kind of modest gamble, too: You make sure your car is serviced; you have some water in the trunk; you never quite lose the thoughts of what you would do—once you had gone thirty or forty miles up the dirt road—if the car died. Would the light protect you, or burn away the very calm it had instilled?

So I am driving north, out of Winnemucca—you'd have to get there, or Boise, Idaho, really, before you could begin this journey by road.

I take Route 95 north out of Winnemucca, for I want to go to McDermitt first, on the Oregon border. It's a long, curving road north, seventy miles or so, with Paradise Valley—a farming enclave—off to the east, and Orovada the only town on the way, poised beneath Sawtooth Mountain in the Santa Rosa Range. McDermitt is not much more than a dot on the ground. In 1940, the district population was around 560; it can't be more today, even if there's the "Say When" Casino, its neon faded in the sunlight.

McDermitt is named after a Col. Charles McDermit, commander of the military outpost there, which was intended to guard settlers and travelers. But those buildings were turned over to the local Indians—Paiutes—in 1886, once a state of peace had been established. There's a supermarket, a filling station, and a few old "Western" buildings, but you can go through the town without changing gears or finishing a sentence. Then you're in Oregon, and it's another hundred miles or so to Boise. But as Boiseans I've known will admit, Boise ain't much.

I stop in McDermitt for coffee and a break, and read the local paper—the *Humboldt*; no other papers get here, it seems, and the TV reception out of Boise is pretty shaky, unless you've got a dish.

So I go back down Route 95 until I reach the Route 140 turnoff to the west. You wonder why such a road exists, for it goes a mighty long way from nowhere to nowhere. And if on the map it seems like the way to Denio, when you get to Denio, there seems to have been no reason for coming.

But Route 140 is near enough ninety miles, looping west and then northwest to Denio. Before you come to the turnoff, you see the road like a ruler through the scrub and the sage, monotonously straight ahead, a place to test your car's power. And it's a well-made road, all the way, with dirt roads off it to the west, one of which could take you to Summit Lake and the ruins of Camp McGarry—a fort that lasted from 1867 to 1871. Summit Lake is not just lovely; it's surreal and haunting—Why a lake with nothing else? you wonder. More than fifty years ago, an old Paiute or Shoshone told the writer of a guidebook, "Summit Lake much better to sit. There can sit long time, can see very far." And the idea has lasted that the Indians went there sometimes just because of the desolation.

It turns out to be a special day, I mean in terms of light, and as the afternoon sun drops—it is mid-September, and ninety degrees—I see the secret color in the Nevada landscape. Here and there, I'm sure, I have called it gray, purple, slate, and mauve. And all those colors, and more, are there. But there is another color that appears only in certain light, and seems to be drawn up to the surface by a low sun, as if it were moisture, feeling, or the kind of primer wash that painters use.

You could call it grass, khaki, gold, or dun, but this day I see, without question, that it is the color of a lion's skin—not the mane, but that skin drawn tight over the ribs and the stomach. It is a dry color, ocher and sage and dunglike, yet glowing, as if you could feel the heart pulsing within the lion's body. It is a color that holds back until the end of the day, and I have never seen it elsewhere.

Route 140 heads due north nearly, but just a few miles short of Denio it turns off to the west again. You can go on and see Denio, on the Oregon line again, with one bar—the Diamond—that has a few slot machines and a low ceiling papered with money. Then it's back on Route 140, going west and seeming to climb.

But first you pass one of those small, wondrous Nevada lakes—Continental Lake—maybe three miles long and a mile and a half across. It has a pink, pearly sheen to it—why not? opal is sometimes mined in the area—and it is large enough to hold the full mountain range nearby upside down on its smooth surface.

The road climbs, and you begin to see the mountains flatten off into buttes or mesas, browner than that lion's color. We are in the Sheldon National Wildlife Refuge by now, a place where you may see antelope, wild mules, and even wild horses sometimes. The next town down the road is Lakeview, Oregon, and that is another sixty miles away.

There is no one on the road as I pass Big Spring Butte to the north, and I can see the sliver of the small reservoir beneath it. We are in the Sage Hen Hills, and the actual border with Oregon comes next at around six thousand feet. But I will go on a little farther, just a few miles, keeping the spirit of Nevada until I reach the place where the land suddenly drops off. I do admit this is a place in Oregon, but you cannot resist the natural boundary, the sense of the great plateau, with the lowlands beyond.

It is still warm at five o'clock, still bright, and the road is so good, you could think that the emptiness was abandonment, that everything else is over—for the day at least. I use binoculars to look down on the parchment of Oregon spread out below, and I can see no life or movement. There are no places there, and if there are a few farms, there is no sign of life or work on them.

This is the only major road coming across Nevada's border without a casino of some sort within three or four miles. The state tries to make its big gift available as soon as possible. Here, there would be no point. There are no people who live here who need to keep in touch with luck. Sometimes gliders use the place to launch out into the spirals, but there is no one here this day.

In Oregon, I am on the edge of Nevada, the most natural, precipitate brink, with a view that is as close to primeval as any you will find in America. But the wind and the air are modern, as well as the tawny hue in the ground. The wind eases and the prickly silence of Nevada comes in on me like an embrace. I can hear myself breathing, hear my heart.

And then from out there, over the crumpled plain of Oregon, looking north, there comes the gong and thud of a sonic boom as some aircraft breaks the sound barrier. The plane is too fast to see. But the sound is slow, grand, and sad, like a tree falling, or a cello string bursting—sound unheard by anyone else, maybe. But I am here to hear it and I cannot tell whether—as an omen—it means beginning or end.

BILL DONAHUE [B. 1964]

Pahrump, a Southern Paiute ancestral home, whose name means "water" (pah) and "flowing from rock" (rimpi), was first settled by whites in the 1880s, growing slowly over the years to become a bedroom community for Las Vegas, with the dubious distinction of being "the place where the whorehouses are." Bill Donahue's dispatch from Pahrump—"Boomtown"—first appeared in DoubleTake *in 1999 and was reprinted in* Neon: Artcetera *from the Nevada Arts Council. Donahue grew up in Farmington, Connecticut, where his mother, Barbara Donahue, wrote history books on a typewriter in the kitchen. He attended Colby College in Maine, where he majored in English while writing for the campus paper. After graduating in 1986, Donahue moved to Oregon, determined to be a freelance writer. He got a break in 1992, becoming a correspondent for* People *magazine. Since then, he has published in the* New Yorker, *the* New York Times Magazine, National Geographic Adventure, Atlantic Monthly, Outside, *for which he is a contributing editor, and* Mother Jones, *which calls him "the magazine's chief chronicler of off-kilter urban environments"; his essays have been featured in* Best American Sports Writing *and* Best American Travel Writing. *He is currently working on* Drive Thru Church, *a book of essays that ask, "Can Americans live wholly in unholy places?" It will include accounts of his adventures kayaking the concrete ditch of the Los Angeles River, touring the fetid sewer tunnels beneath Minneapolis, and, yes, visiting Pahrump, "an urban planner's nightmare." Donahue lives in Portland, Oregon, where he and his daughter, Allie, publish* biff: *the zine for kids and their parents.*

Boomtown

The road stretching east from Death Valley is desolate, lined with nothing but cacti and rocks, but once I got to the rim of the Pahrump Valley, the scenery changed. All I could see then, on the bleached desert below, were mobile homes. Double-wides, triple-wides, whole little colonies of trailers surrounded by satellite dishes and large dogs yanking on chains. The sprawl in the valley, which encompasses 350 square miles, is so crazy it looks like someone just ripped open a bag of popcorn and let it spill in the wind.

The strip on Highway 160 goes on for ten miles. First there is a smattering of bars and convenience stores, and then a cacophony of commerce: Burger King, Baskin-Robbins, Blimpie, Pizza Hut, Hollywood Video, a McDonald's whose arch is perched a hundred feet high. Everything's new and chaos is prevalent. In the vacant stretches in between parking lots, for instance, there is a forest of hip-high signs screaming slogans at one another: "White Ark Reptiles," "Two Gals Clean'n," "Super Pawn," "Bubba's Tool and Supply, Your Neighbor and Friend." There are no zoning laws in Pahrump. Building codes are a new innovation, and the unincorporated town is blossoming in the frenzied, random manner of the World Wide Web. Seven thousand people lived here in 1990; now there are over 27,000 inhabiting this—what? Can we really call Pahrump a community? The place has almost no history and, it seems, no core at all. When I stopped at a gas station, I asked the clerk where I could find the center of town. She said, "They just put in a Lucky over there and Smith's is over there, so I guess right between them, *that's* the center."

I was there in Pahrump for the annual Harvest Festival, and on Saturday morning I saw the parade roll down 160, drenched in the roar of unmuffled engines. The procession was dominated by the Shriners from the Zelzah Shrine in Las Vegas— middle-aged men who buzzed about the street in miniature cars. The crowd favorite, though, was the camo-green military transport vehicle that bore a crude handpainted sign reading, "Acme Pawn and Gun. Firearm Rentals. 751-BANG." Everyone cheered, and the applause that rang from the lawn chairs at roadside was not, surprisingly, an aggression-thick noise. No, it was the polite patter of small-town parade-goers—the hoot and holler of neighbors and friends. Acme won a blue ribbon, and that afternoon I went down to the store to see how the owners were celebrating. They were out, shooting blanks in a gravel pit, but their business shares a dingy single-wide with a sister concern, Acme Feed, and the door was open. I stepped in to find a couple of cheap guns on a pegboard, an untuned piano, and a flier relating how, for a hundred dollars or so, you could spend a supervised afternoon taking target practice with novelty weapons like AK-47s and sawed-off shotguns. Agricultural chow took up most of the retail space, and Vince Tucker, a robust, bearded guy in pinstripe overalls stamped ACME FEED, sat behind the counter. Guardedly, he explained the connection between the two Acmes.

"We're friends," he said. "Five or six years ago, we all started a salvage operation. We bought stuff from the Nevada Test Site and sold it—desks, tables, file cabinets, ammo boxes. It was an opportunity to make a little money." The five partners, three single men and a couple, all lived together on an emu/ostrich ranch in the hills just west of the valley and discussed their dreams. Tucker, who'd always raised rabbits, wanted to open a feed store. Gary Miller yearned to rent the eighty guns stored in his vault. And so on. By 1995, the collective had grown to nine people, all of whom pitched in to buy the single-wide, which soon housed (for a few months) the world's only tattoo parlor to sell bullets and kitty litter. Today, the Acme crew still pools its earnings and, on the side, sells emu eggs and runs a truck-repair shop. A full array of business cards was displayed by the counter, and when I acted curious, Tucker just shrugged. "I guess we just help each other out," he said, and then he wandered away, to watch TV in the back room.

The word "community" has, I'll admit, always held a precise meaning for me. I think of a town in New Hampshire where my family has gone each summer for over a century. Every person I encounter on the street there is tied to me not only by common experience, but by the common experience of our ancestors—by, say, a wild party held in a ramshackle barn five decades before I was born. But I don't live in that town (year-round, I mean), and Norman Rockwell, were he alive, probably wouldn't either. He'd be as unrooted as the rest of us. He'd be flying to Atlanta for an afternoon meeting with a grantor, I imagine, and checking his E-mail from the computer kiosk at Gate C 64. If Americans were ever anchored to place— ancestrally, inextricably—they aren't now. And so everywhere these days people are groping for "connectedness," "a sense of belonging."

In Pahrump, you'd get run over by a monster truck if you used such language. The valley, with its anarchic clutter of cheap architecture, is a humanist's nightmare. And yet a human impulse prevails. Community is sprouting here as it sprouts everywhere—organically, illogically, almost in spite of the urban planners' predictions. The Harvest Festival was a generic event, a fair featuring cotton candy and rides, but still it was a blast. In the grassy park beside the Lucky, under the floodlights, high school kids grooved to the twangy sound of a southern rock band. Old folks whooped it up in the American Legion's beer garden, and politicians wheeled about, dispensing buttons and bumper stickers as they pumped people's hands.

I talked to forty-eight-year-old Harley Kulkin, who was running for county commissioner and wearing a T-shirt that implored, "Save Our Communities." Kulkin, an air conditioner repairman, moved to Pahrump four years ago, so he could work undisturbed on his thirty-five ancient cars, his 1930 caboose, and his Harleys. "Everywhere else I've lived," he said, "I've been a neighbors' nightmare. I get here, and I'm free to do whatever I want on my property. I felt, right away, like I'd been here in spirit my whole life. But then these people come here from Los Angeles or wherever, and they've got the condo mentality. They want to crowd you; they want to dictate what their neighbors can do."

Kulkin, who'd never been politically active, felt compelled to defend Pahrump.

He started speaking out at town board meetings, calling vehemently for a minimum property lot size. "The local TV station is sick of me," he lamented. "They always cut to a commercial break when I go up to the mike."

Kulkin does have his fans, though, and one of them, an earnest young man with blue eyes, meandered toward us to talk auto mechanics. This youth hung on Kulkin's every word, absorbing each tale as though it were wisdom, and then, quite abruptly, he said, "You know why I'd vote for you—your truth, honesty, and candor." It was a bald comment and, for a second or two, a pained awkwardness enveloped us all. But when the chat sputtered forward again, it was deeper somehow. We had, it seemed, shared something fine—the first blush of kinship.

On my last day in Pahrump, I visited a guy I'd met at the fair. Bill Dailey, seventy-four, is a longtime Legion member with the hat to prove it. He'd been in town for just a few months, but the spanking new home that he shares with his wife of fifty years, Peggy, is a fortress. Just before a Legion meeting, he gave me a tour. In the living room, there was a pile of faux logs that glowed orange. In the three-car garage, we climbed up a ladder to inspect crossbeams on the ceiling. "Everything's caulked," Dailey said. "My son built this home, and he's a perfectionist."

We went outside, and there on the desert was Bill Dailey's masterpiece. The yard, all one and a quarter acres, was three inches deep in gravel. With another Legionnaire, Dailey had shoveled and spread every rock, to smother the tumbleweed. The project took three months, and Dailey did it in summer. "I'd start work at five," he said. "Walter would come over at seven-thirty and we'd go for three hours. And then he'd leave and I'd keep working. I'd shovel for fifteen minutes, then go inside and sit and drink water, then come back out—like that all day long."

The stones were light brown mostly, and gray on the driveway, and they were everywhere. There was nothing green in that yard. And now, for a moment, Dailey just stood there—shirtless, in golf shorts—savoring his finished stone project. He realized, I think, that he'd built something almost permanent amid the blowing dust of the desert. This square of rocks, this house—they would outlast him. Indeed, in some form, they could outlast Pahrump. The whole sprawling settlement sits on an aquifer, but the water table is dropping, dangerously fast. Pahrump could dry up, become just another western place that boomed for a while, then died. I've been to such places: Copper Hill, Arizona; Goldpoint, Nevada; Diamond, Utah. Ghost towns. You drive in, and the once-bright signs on the main street are now faded gray; the saloon has no walls. What remains—vitally, in a way that gives you goosebumps as you stand there, peering in through the windows—is the story the ruins deliver: People *lived* here. No matter how garish and flimsy the town, life carried on.

Eventually, Dailey's wife appeared on the patio to daub the dust off the vinyl seat covers.

"ok?" Dailey said to her after a while.

"ok," she said. And slowly, they gathered up the keys and the shirt and the purse and the wallet, and then they got in their car and drove off to the Legion hall.

JANICE EMILY BOWERS [B. 1950]

The future of most Nevada boomtowns is to become ghost towns as ore bodies play out, water sources dry up, or external investment comes to an end. "Ghost-towning" has become a popular tourist sport, attracting people to places abandoned by an earlier generation. One of the most popular Nevada ghost towns is Rhyolite, located just off the road between Beatty and Death Valley, whose population fluctuated from zero to ten thousand and back to almost zero, all in about six years. Writers have construed a range of meanings in Rhyolite. Historian Patricia Nelson Limerick, for example, in "Haunted by Rhyolite: Learning from the Landscape of Failure" (1994), argues that Rhyolite should be a warning to other western boomtowns to develop sustainably or they, too, will fall victim to "urban infant mortality." Naturalist Janice Emily Bowers reads the ruins of Rhyolite in more positive terms, celebrating the spirited adaptability of the plants and animals who are reclaiming the town site for their own. Bowers, whose training is in botany (BS, University of Arizona, 1976), is a longtime resident of Tucson and has written a dozen books and interpretive guides of natural history, plant life, wildflower identification, and gardening that speak eloquently of the Sonoran Desert that she knows intimately. Her recent books A Full Life in a Small Place and Other Essays from a Desert Garden *(1993) and* Fear Falls Away and Other Essays from Hard and Rocky Places *(1997) have been praised for their fluid style and astute scientific insight, and for illuminating internal as well as external landscapes. When she writes about the Mojave Desert, she confesses, "I am keenly aware of being a tourist." Nevertheless, her collaboration with Pulitzer Prize–winning landscape photographer Jack Dykinga in* Desert: The Mojave and Death Valley *(1999), from which the following excerpt is taken, is an arrestingly beautiful portrait of the life and unexpected beauty of this forbidding desert.*

Remains of the Day

I am not the first to have noticed that something happens to rubbish as it ages. Ordinary and undistinguished objects become rare, or at least interesting. They acquire historical significance. We become grateful that people were so thoughtful as to scatter bits of their lives across the landscape. The Mojave Desert is rich in romantic litter of this sort. Even in the wildest places, a remote canyon, say, where you would swear no one had set foot before, you might find rusted cans so old that they crumble in your hands, or pieces of lavender-tinted glass that have become smaller and smaller with time but never disappeared altogether.

In just such a place, I found an old padlock of a type no longer in use. Its rusty brown body was about the size of a silver dollar, its hasp rectangular in cross section. Only a key with a cylindrical barrel could have opened the lock, but even had there been such a key, the hasp could no longer be shoved home, and the locking mechanism itself was hopelessly rusted. The day I figure out the appeal of such objects will be the day I stop collecting them. In the meantime, I remain a finder of things and a keeper of things found. I slipped the padlock into the pocket of my jeans, and I have it still, along with a jelly jar half filled with pieces of lavender-tinted glass, a handmade spike from an abandoned railway, two lids from old tins of cinnamon or some other spice, and some pieces of broken crockery, one of which, my favorite, is patterned in blue on white in a curvilinear, trellislike design.

Another time, having parked beside a dirt road in the eastern Mojave, I set out across the plain to look at some low hills that struck my fancy. A tongue of sand climbed the near side of the closest hill, and I wondered if it also spilled down the other side. Underfoot, the substrate was like cobblestone pavement except that no human labor had been involved in setting the cobbles side by side in a matrix of fine sand. As I walked, my feet pressed the pebbles deep into the sand, leaving them helter skelter instead of jigsaw-puzzle neat. A flock of sage sparrows played hide and seek with me. Twittering, they flew well ahead, then like sparse snowflakes they settled invisibly among the bushes. Rabbit tracks in long, straight lines angled across my path. I saw lots of animal tracks, in fact, but no human footprints, and why would there be? No reason to come here, which was no place in particular.

Rodents had dug burrows under the creosote bushes. Spider webs hung in the entrances of the numerous abandoned burrows. Fresh paw prints distinguished those few burrows in active use. Dish-shaped hollows in the sand held miscellaneous collections of seeds. Looking more closely, I saw that most of the "seeds" were actually empty husks. The hollows were evidently workstations where kangaroo rats or mice had accumulated and processed batches of seeds.

Certain rodents bury seeds in small caches, then sniff them out at a later date. This is hardly a foolproof way to store food: other rodents can sniff out the seeds just as easily, and although the odds are against it, there might be enough rain to make the seeds germinate, which would deplete the larder in one fell swoop. This happens sometimes with creosote bush seeds. Creosote bush seeds are notoriously difficult to germinate in the laboratory—it is not a matter of simply dropping them on filter paper and keeping them wet—and they are also quite picky out of doors. What they want is a substantial autumn rainstorm when the temperatures are neither too hot nor too cold. What they usually get is the chance to be eaten by some rodent or bird.

In 1998, however, creosote bush had won the lottery, probably when Hurricane Nora swept across the Mojave Desert, and creosote bush seedlings were scattered across the sandy plain, especially under big creosote bushes and also near small obstructions such as fallen twigs. Here and there, densely clustered seedlings marked former seed caches, now well beyond recovery. Most of the seedlings had a single pair of seed-leaves, shaped like tiny scimitars, and another pair of true leaves. None was more than an inch or two in height. Their roots, however, were already five or six inches long. Seedlings of desert shrubs tend not to waste energy on making foliage until they have secured a water supply. Even then survival is far from certain, and all but a small fraction of the seedlings here would probably die from drought stress when summer came. Some had already wilted and probably would not survive the winter.

As I neared the low hills, I stumbled over a broken wooden stake that was poking out of the ground. Odd, I thought, until I noticed more stakes on the hillslope. The stakes obviously marked the corners of a mining claim, and now I could see that what had appeared to be a jumble of rocks was actually a tailings pile outside the mine. Or what would have been a mine if it had not been abandoned: the shaft penetrated perhaps five feet into the slope and ended at a bedrock slab. I would have sworn that no person had ever visited this nondescript hill, but someone had not only beat me to the spot, but had worked a claim and camped here. Scattered between the creosote bushes were rusted food cans, among them the lid to a one-pound can of baking powder. A pound of baking powder—that is a lot of biscuits. There was a rusted and corroded skillet about a stone's throw away, as if the last batch of biscuits had been so bad that the cook had hurled the pan (along with a mighty oath) into the night.

Looking at the site as if I were a miner in the late nineteenth century, I saw that the sandy substrate would make a good sleeping pad, and that dead stems of white bursage could be piled together for a little campfire. The presence of kerosene cans suggested that lanterns had been available for working or reading after dark. There were no springs or creeks within miles and miles, so the miner doubtless hauled water, perhaps in barrels, meaning that there must have been a mule, or a wagon. I tried to imagine what it would be like to stay at this spot for months at a time, how the stars would change overhead at night, how the moon would wax and wane, how the labor of every day would be to chop and dig at that hillside, turning the continuous fabric of bedrock into a jumble of tailings.

I saw how lonely it must have been.

More to my taste are the small, abandoned settlements we call ghost towns. I could imagine living in Rhyolite, say, which in its heyday was the largest town in southern Nevada, a cultural center more important than Las Vegas just one hundred miles to the southwest. Population estimates of Rhyolite at its peak vary from 3,500 to 10,000. In any case, several thousand people lived in Rhyolite by the end of 1907. Eighteen months later, as one historian noted, "it was well on its way to total oblivion." Silver was the key to Rhyolite's prosperity and to its decline. The discovery of rich silver lodes in 1905 attracted miners, first of all, then families, doctors, bankers, school teachers, bakers, hoteliers, stock brokers, prostitutes, journalists—an entire cityful of people who needed clapboard houses, banks, a three-story schoolhouse, a large hotel, a jail, saloons, an elaborate railway depot. And then, when the panic of 1907 hit, Rhyolite's undercapitalized mines could not attract enough investments for further development. Public confidence in the mines lagged. Unemployed miners relocated to other districts. Businesses failed. The newspapers stopped publishing. By 1910, the population of Rhyolite had dropped by eighty percent, and in 1919 the post office finally closed.

Odd to imagine people buying bread at the bakery and making deposits at the bank, unaware that in another few years the streets would be empty, and that a decade after that, without human hands to patch and mend, the town would begin to tumble upon itself.

You can see it happen in successive photographs. Three walls of the bank fall, leaving only the splendid facade. Brick by brick the schoolhouse crumbles until only half of it remains. The jail, more sturdily constructed, loses only its roof and windows. Houses, reduced to piles of rubble and board, drop out of the pictures entirely.

I have visited the town site several times now, and each time a little more of Rhyolite lies on the ground than the time before—more walls collapsed, more beams fallen, more adobe blocks dissolved in rain and snow. Each time there is also less of Rhyolite than there was before, because people carry parts of it away. There must be several hundred pits where—what shall we call ourselves? finder-keepers? antique hunters? looters?--have dug for bottles, crockery, tins, and anything else of financial or sentimental value. Now what remains is mostly broken or badly rusted or both: bottle necks, tin cans, bedsprings, stovepipes, barrel staves, washtubs, bottle caps, and of course an infinite number of pieces of glass, glass being one thing that time can fracture but not obliterate.

Now that its human inhabitants have left, the desert is reclaiming Rhyolite for its own. Pack rats make ingenious use of the ruins, improvising shelter from broken concrete blocks, weathered boards, and assorted rocks. Shadscale, a kind of saltbush, has colonized rubbish piles all over town. Rabbits take cover among the shrubs, and in spring, sage sparrows sit in them and sing. Sometimes their song sounds like *Tck? Chirpy-chirp,* and sometimes like *Ch-chirpy-dee? Chirpy-chirp.* Shadscale grows on the once-bare railroad bed, too, and in the borrow pit beside it. The railroad bed serves as a corridor for coyotes and bobcats, which come to hunt the rabbits and rodents. Rock wrens bob and trill from rubble piles. Ravens scavenge in basements that have been open to sky for decades.

There is something reassuring about a ghost town; it is good to know that the marks humans make on the landscape do not last forever. Grasses and weeds grow between the floor boards; roads disappear into brush; banks, schools, and hotels disintegrate. Plants and animals thrive where people did not and maybe should not. Only our technology lets us enjoy the desert in such large numbers. We invented the padlock, but they, it turns out, have the key.

ELEVEN

A DESERT BLOOMS

Contemporary Poetry

I n the late 1970s two friends intrepidly scoured Nevada in a borrowed pickup
truck, searching for poets. Regional literature was then in vogue, and regional
anthologies were appearing throughout the country. These friends, themselves
poets, wondered whether Nevada had a distinctive poetic spirit. Funded by a grant
from the Nevada Arts Council, Gary Short and Roger Smith aspired to produce a
regional poetry anthology that would define and illustrate the poetic sensibility of
the entire state throughout its history. In their resulting book, *The Nevada Poet:
An Anthology* (1981), they report being "pleasantly disappointed." For while they
discovered dozens of poets, they could discern "no continuity or development of
subject, tone, or style." In other words, they found good poems in surprising abundance, but no poetic tradition or homogeneous development that Nevada could
call its own. They speculate that the great variety in Nevada poetry—the lack of a
center, if you will—owes itself to the mobility and heterogeneity of its people: "The
Silver State has attracted [people] virtually from the first as a magnet attracts iron
filings: indiscriminately, from all directions. First for mining and more recently
for the gaming and divorce industries, people came from all parts of the country
and from throughout the world. Nevada is a demographic anthology of its own."
Of the twelve poets whom Short and Smith identify as Nevada's most proficient,
not one was born in Nevada.

Nevada's poetic landscape has flowered considerably in the quarter-century
since Short and Smith's pioneering inventory, but their conclusions are as true

today as they were then. Nevada poets have produced a significant body of good work, but in no sense does it add up to a cohesive, regional tradition in the way, for example, that Comstock journalists form the "Sagebrush School." It is still the case that the vast majority of Nevada poets—nineteen of the twenty-two collected below—were not born in Nevada; and two of the three Nevada natives subsequently moved away. What we have, then, are poets in exile, or—as one poet describes herself—Nevadans at heart who were born in exile. Furthermore, a safe guess is that every Nevada poet collected here owes his or her chief literary influence to a poet outside the state, sometimes outside the country. Naturally, just because a poet lives in Nevada does not mean that Nevada is the subject of his or her poems. Often poets write about things that have no reference to place at all. They write about love and death, about truth and beauty, about good and evil, and about language and poetry itself. Shaun T. Griffin's excellent 1991 collection *Desert Wood: An Anthology of Nevada Poets* showcases a wide range of poems from forty-nine poets, expressing a full spectrum of human experience and set in places as far flung as Kathmandu.

The purpose of this chapter is slightly different. Rather than being primarily interested in poets who live in Nevada, it features poems with clear Nevada settings, even if the poet lives elsewhere. Here we are primarily interested in understanding Nevada through poetry. Short and Smith found that among those poets who do exhibit an imaginative concern for Nevada, "loneliness, awe, and uneasy attraction almost become a vocabulary of response." In the same vein, the poet and editor William L. Fox has insightfully observed:

> Nevada is a mythical sinkhole, the Great Basin into which water and dreams pour, all tracking right into disappearance. It's an adverse, perverse place to make art.
>
> Much as sculptors here assemble rust, bone and other remnants of arrested decay into totems of great power, Nevada poets seem to collect shards of sanity left turning purple in the sun. The results resemble strands of pearls less than they do medicine pouches. The kind you hesitate to open.

In this anthology, you will find poems stashed in multiple places—in the Reno and Las Vegas chapters, the Nuclear Nevada chapter, and the Cowboy Poetry chapter. Below are gathered contemporary poems from greater Nevada, refracting the state through the poetic prism of multifaceted imaginations.

IRENE BRUCE [1903–1987]

Originally from Tulsa, Oklahoma, Irene Bruce worked in a telegraph office in Texas before she moved to Reno in 1936 and took up writing. She attended the University of Nevada, but finding no course that would teach her how to write poetry, she founded the Reno Poetry Workshop in the 1940s. Always active, Bruce was secretary of the Reno branch of the National League of American Pen Women, hosted a weekly poetry broadcast on KOH radio, and became poetry editor for Nevada Magazine. *She published more than 500 poems in the* Christian Science Monitor, New Mexico Quarterly Review, Nevada *magazine, the* Penwoman, Sunset, *the* San Francisco Examiner, *and others. Her first book,* Crag and Sand *(1945), was self-published, but it paid for itself within the first two weeks of publication and sold out in two years. Her second book,* Night Cry *(1950), was the first publication of Poetry West of Reno, founded by fellow poet Joanne de Longchamps. A favorable review in the* Berkeley Gazelle *called Bruce a "modern writer whose phrases are not always logical, but who strives for coherence by making articulate the effect of the experience upon the senses," further noting that "it is seldom that the West with its desert, ghost towns, and Indians comes so alive as in the descriptive and well-disciplined verse of Irene Bruce." Her poem "City on the Truckee" from that collection describes Reno as "Neon city of chance, / weighs bright pawn-jewels at night, / consorts by day with desert space." In the 1950s Bruce lived in the old mining town of Virginia City, which had attracted several writers, most notably Walter Van Tilburg Clark. She was married for more than twenty-five years to Harry Bruce of Reno, and his death occasioned her privately printed book* Sonnets for Harry *(1976).*

Virginia City, Nevada

The contrived glamour of tourists
glitters palely into this sudden village,
finding dregs of history scattered obscurely
over the rim of a high mountain canyon.
The travelers shiver as the sun stares at them bleakly,
and the tip of the wind catches their garments.

Images here are seldom seen
through pity-taunting eyes of tourists;—
for while they dip lightly into quarter history,
jerking at handles of coin-famished machines,
the embers of dust are stirring
the deeds of men whose deaths
laugh at their modern gestures.

Arrowhead

A flight, now cold, you lie within a frame
Above a mantle, where the glance of years
Records your pageantry in place. One hears
Beyond the prisms of a hearth-warmed flame,
Behind historic volumes flush with shame:
Once smeared grimaces over grudging tears
Hard hands that sharpened you into their fears
And lost their courage in a savage name.

Today you speak a specimen of time,
And fear-swift deer no longer leap from you;
Your feathers in the wind no longer mean
The hunter's hidden track, or warrior's crime:
Your agony and water-moon canoe
Are stoic shadows that are never seen.

MILDRED BREEDLOVE [1904–1994]

Born in Coal Mill, Arkansas, Mildred Breedlove grew up poor but was uplifted by poetry. In those days, as she later recalled, poetry was an everyday presence in most American homes, frequently printed in newspapers and magazines. Women traded poetry as they traded garden seeds, recipes, and remedies. Breedlove quit school in 1920, at age sixteen, to marry. After her two children were grown she reentered the literary world, only to discover that by 1949 most Americans didn't read poetry anymore. She attributed poetry's waning popularity to the obscurity of the Moderns, whose poetry she deemed "unintelligible rubbish." Her strong preference was for accessible verse that adhered to traditional forms of rhyme and meter. She and her husband moved to Las Vegas in 1949, where she became active in the Las Vegas branch of National Pen Women, also lecturing on poetry, her mission to "bring beauty back to the people." Her first collection of poetry, Those Desert Hills and Other Poems *(1959), traces Breedlove's changing response to southern Nevada, from initial repulsion by "endless miles of barren waste" to eventual enchantment by the desert's bewitching beauty. In 1957 Governor Russell appointed Breedlove poet laureate of Nevada, and Governor Sawyer reappointed her in 1959 and commissioned her to write a poem to commemorate the state's centennial. Her epic* Nevada: A Poem *(1964), thirty pages long, is a singular attempt to cast Nevada's geography, history, people, and scenic wonders into poetic form. Three years in the making,* Nevada *demanded heroic effort, as Breedlove was legally blind by then, relying on friends and relatives to drive her around the state and describe what they saw. She typed the poem on an Underwood typewriter in a cabin without electricity or running water. Breedlove spent her final years in Ferron, Utah, where she continued to champion poetry for the people until her death at age ninety.*

What Hills Are These?

    What hills are these that leave a heart enchained?
    Though neither grass, nor underbrush nor trees
    Spread roots above the zinc and manganese
    Nor hide the scars where lead and gold were veined.
    One might not guess how long my heart was trained
    In woodland ways; where wild anemones
    Divided time with jays and chickadees
    And summer left the grasses golden-skeined.

    What magic do these barren hills possess
    That they deliver me to sun and sand?
    No season comes to mountains made of stone—
    And yet their ever-changing rainbow dress
    Wields power that I do not understand . . .
    And I no longer call my heart . . . my own.

Camping

    When the desert dawn is breaking,
    Clear and cold—
    And the ravens, early-waking,
    Fuss and scold—
    What could any man desire
    If he has a greasewood fire
    Brewing coffee in a pot;
    And potatoes piping-hot?

    Or, when twilight is beginning
    In the east,
    And a slim new moon is grinning,
    Would a feast

Need another single thing
To be fit for any king,
If there's sourdough for rolls
And some bacon on the coals?

JOANNE DE LONGCHAMPS [1923–1983]

Joanne de Longchamps's third book of poetry, The Hungry Lions *(1963), was published in the prestigious Indiana University Press Poetry Series, whose authors included Carolyn Kizer, David Wagoner, Conrad Aiken, Josephine Miles, and Theodore Roethke. That Joanne de Longchamps has not achieved the national stature of these other writers can be attributed to geography. As Shaun T. Griffin explains, "She was a Nevadan, and that came to define her existence as being separate and apart from mainstream literary America." Griffin, himself a Nevada poet, has done much to resurrect the poetry and reputation of de Longchamps, editing* Torn by Light: Selected Poems *(1993), drawn from her seven published books and one unpublished manuscript. De Longchamps precipitously moved to Nevada from Southern California at age eighteen, after falling in love with and marrying Galen Edward de Longchamps, son of a noted Reno architect. She participated in the Reno Poetry Workshop in the 1940s, took art and literature courses at* UNR, *and published her work in* Poetry, Prairie Schooner, *the* New York Times, Poetry Northwest, *the* Antioch Review, American Scholar, *and others. Greek mythology, animals, and personal experience figure prominently in her poems, and her last two books are illustrated with stunning collages assembled from colorful scraps of paper. She possessed an uncanny ability to tell love's story: "Lovers die but caution kills / the living while they move." De Longchamps's later poetry bares the crippling personal tragedies of cancer, multiple sclerosis, alcoholism, her son's suicide, and the acrimonious breakup of her marriage. Although she once lamented that "Nevada hardly knows me as a poet," in fact, although America has yet to recognize her genius, Nevada granted her an honorary doctorate from the University of Nevada, Reno, and the Governor's Art Award for literature, both in 1983. In 1989, Joanne de Longchamps became the first woman to be inducted into the Nevada Writers Hall of Fame.*

Snowmountain

From valley floor and smokestack town
we came to this mountain dimension,
the cold fact of winter as eye would have it
in white script, a fable of snow

alive with groved aspen, grave pine
in each part burnished and blazing.

Clean here; high bright precipitous
and struck with pure sunfall.
Our tears glaze the dazzlement:
lungs test the knives of the air
and blood's small warmth, our animal fire
seems threatened. We crouch in our bones.

Soundless down vertical acres
a skier drops like a spider, spins out
sudden tracks in a web of descent.
He has skimmed the new cream of the snow
and released us, glossed over the menace,
crossed over the sheer malevolent mountain.

The warm dumb beast that cowers in blood
sensed death in alpland. But we are saved
by the way a landscape alters with figures,
is reduced to a backdrop. We seem to conquer—
This motion restores us: motion the catalyst
changing the primitive pause of fear
to sudden joy. We shout to the mountain.

Bat

I have come from the dark,
bloodbeat echoing the pulse
of a small beast that deciphers echoes—
I held it in both hands.
It was a many-pointed kite,
a child's glove, black leather,
geometry that breathed—such triangles
for snout and ears and parasol wings.
From moth-mazed summer night,
Bat blundered into hell—
walls not of air, deranging light
where the delicate sonar failed.
It fell—did the sharp bones break?

I made a cup of hands, a sling,
and carried back to the dark
a shape supernally strange and still,
released it to the grass.

Do I tremble for its sake?

Becoming Crippled

The time comes. I feel
earth fall, failing me
with no footholds, toe and heel
betrayed by slippery grass,
by stones forbidding trespass—
Of course it is I who am falling.

I feel it come, pressing near,
pillow and chair-time.
It is almost here
beyond all courage or act
but a matter of fact—
so simple, a matter of failing.

I choose my masks,
opt for dry elegance,
a sedentary dance.
When these, and wry humor, fail
find me curled inward, still,
steel-trapped, a creature—waiting.

HAROLD WITT [1923–1995]

During World War II, Harold Witt, a California native, hitchhiked into Nevada with his dog and his pal Paul Woodford to check into a service camp for conscientious objectors, at Galena Creek, outside Reno. With the Selective Training and Service Act of 1940, Congress for the first time recognized "CO Status" as a legitimate moral stand and gave conscientious objectors the option to perform alternative public service, often on conservation projects. Objectors received no pay or benefits and had to rely on relatives and churches for support. During his stay, Witt befriended Nevada poets Irene Bruce and Joanne de Longchamps and became active in the Reno Poetry Workshop, contributing prefaces to their early books. Witt had earned a BA *from the University of California, Berkeley, in 1943, and after the war he received an* MA *from the University of Michigan in 1947. In 1953 he obtained a degree in library science from* UC *Berkeley and worked for the next two years in Nevada as a reference librarian for the Washoe County Library. Returning to California, Witt worked for the San Jose State College library before becoming a freelance writer in 1959. He enjoyed steady success as a poet and editor, winning several awards, including the Emily Dickinson Award in 1972 from the Poetry Society of America, publishing more than a dozen books of poetry, founding the poetry journal* Blue Unicorn, *and seeing his poems appear in* Atlantic, *the* New Yorker, Saturday Review, *the* Nation, New Republic, Hudson Review, Harper's, *and others. Several of Witt's books contain one or two Nevada poems.* Beasts in Clothes *(1961), for example, includes "Pyramid," while* Surprised by Others at Fort Cronkhite *(1975) contains a poem about hitchhiking to Nevada and one about meeting an Indian in the library. Witt's extensive correspondence with Joanne de Longchamps is housed in the Special Collections Department of the University of Nevada, Reno.*

Pyramid

> The desert cries with gulls, the dry is wet—
> in violence like this, disciples might
> toss and toss until toward their boat
> a raying savior walked through wests of light.
> Then radiance of aftermath might lap
> shores like these, pelicans resurrect
> and, where swans slide too, farfetchedly flap
> beaks, wings, webs, applauding their own éclat.
>
> Beside weird shapes of tufa where they slept,
> snakes might unwind and faintly castanet,
> cui-uis leap through lavenders of quiet,
> the purple pyramid turn to burning red—
>
> Marvelous loaves, and water into wine,
> infinities of fin where none had swum—
> miracles as likely as this shine
> and shadow-shattered coming of the night
> to such a lake, a place where nature seems
> —raying with changing ranges, windrow-lined—

symbolic splendor; suspending disbelief,
we walk the Christ-calmed mirrors of that deep.

Light on the Subject at Lehman Caves

Amazed in a maze, led on by a ranger,
we went through stone curtains patience had dripped
to Xanadu rooms—chapel and chamber,
towers that tilted as centuries slipped,

corridor, archway, pale floor of flowing—
the dark pronged beneath and pooled for whom?—
light on the subject—the ranger was showing
stalactites below in a watery room—

a purpose revealed, in pallid perfection
sharp shapes upreaching, deep in the pool,
and from the roof, reaching down toward reflection
like splinters of light at the heart of a jewel.

He turned out the light, on an edge of our knowing,
as death does—and loveliness changed to a pit—
where we had come from and where we were going
arrested in blackness, negated by that,

but we laughed, and went on, the way we had come,
climbers on dimness, hiking toward what
we had left at the top—a sense of the sun—
and winding behind us, grottos of thought.

STEPHEN S. N. LIU [B. 1930]

Stephen Shu Ning Liu bridges the gulf between East and West. Who else could place the Yang-tze River and the Mojave Desert into the same poem? Son of an aristocratic painter of lotus blossoms, Stephen Liu was born and raised in Fu Ling, Sichuan, China, near the Yangtze River. Having been taught the Chinese classics by his grandfather, Liu majored in Chinese at Nanking University, teaching Chinese in Taiwan after his graduation in 1948. After the Com-

munist revolution of 1949, Liu sailed for San Francisco in 1953 and studied in the United States for the next twenty years, earning his BA and MA in English from universities in Texas, and his PHD in 1973 from the University of North Dakota. During these years he supported himself as a dishwasher, hamburger cook, janitor, and caretaker of white mice. In 1973 he joined the faculty at the Community College of Southern Nevada, in Las Vegas, teaching world literature and creative writing until his retirement in 2001. Liu wrote prodigiously, publishing more than 250 poems, stories, and translations in magazines, anthologies, and college texts. In 1981–82 he was the first Nevadan to receive a Creative Writing Fellowship from the National Endowment for the Arts; he won a Pushcart Prize for poetry in 1982; he won the Nevada Governor's Arts Award in literature in 1985; and he was inducted in the Nevada Writers Hall of Fame in 1993. Liu's first collection of poetry, Dream Journeys to China *(1982), was published in China in bilingual format, and his most recent collection,* My Father's Martial Art, *appeared from the University of Nevada Press in 2000. Richard Logsdon, editor of* Red Rock Review, *describes Liu's poetry as "melodic at times and frequently melancholic. It is his heart's melancholy, along with his painful longing for his father and his homeland that joins with language to give Stephen's poetry its richness." Liu refers to himself as an "old, old desert rat."*

A Mid-July Invitation

The energy crisis is over. Lights are back on the Strip.
Name the place: Sahara, Caesars Palace, Casino de Paris.
This way, please. Come, my people; drink on the house.
You, Great-grandpa, dice-thrower from Sichuan, casting away
one hundred acres of our land overnight, be of good cheer,
this satchel of gold will last you a long while;
and you, Uncle Lu, widower and recluse of Fu Ling, accost
this Dixie belle, dare what you've never dared before:
this bottle will make you bold; and you, Da Shing, you
longed for a journey, you read by midnight lamps and drained
your blood between Confucius' pages and Newton's first law
of motion. Don't despair, little brother. I'll see you
enter a college this fall. And you, ah Shu Ying, how your
windows framed those lonely mountains. How winter light cast
pallor on your skin and bones. How you withered in spring wind.
Like our lily pond, your eyes had never reflected a stranger's
face. Come to the party, my sister. I'll teach you to dance.

Let me hear your moans, let me feel your bony hand.
Come, I know you all. Come, away from the Yellow Springs.

It's mid-July: clouds cross the moon, the earth shudders,
and the mice must not catch you sleeping under the wormwood.

August Mirage

Driving across Death Valley and past Ghost Town,
I'm back from my desert home to those
wind-tousled banks of the Yangtze:
each cactus down the furrow is a bristly head
of a peasant, each rock a water buffalo.
Each road sign leads me to the Apricot Inn,
which Li Bai frequented, carousing through the night,
and the freeway shimmers, liquefying fast
into the old river I knew.

In the sky a single cloud glides on.
I take it for a sampan that carries me
all the way back to Chongqing, Fu Ling,
and discharges me into a farmhouse,
like a package returning for a better address.

Monologue from the Chicken Ranch

Someone set fire on us last year, burned down our trailers,
but four days later we rose again from the ashes.
Come, you world travelers, old bachelors, dilapidated
politicians, family men whose egos have been beaten up
by your kids and your wives. Come, you petty officers
who suffer the oppressor's wrong, you construction workers
who grunt and sweat under a weary life. We've a sauna bath
for you, a water bed and a love machine. Don't call this place
a whorehouse. We're doing better than any college dormitory
in the country. Our ranch is a haven of humanity, a garden
of Eden in the desert, and a shelter for the low and the weak
ones wounded by the arrows of outrageous fortune.
Most of our girls never had a family, never had a home.
They were dumped out as babies on the street. They were abused
as children, but now they're living in a palace of luxury,
a place like Cleopatra's barge, but by Zeus, even the Queen

didn't have a clean, air-conditioned house like this. You know
our girls are humanitarians. There's a blind guy who comes in
here regularly for a physical release. You social workers,
psychiatrists, educators, country preachers, hear this:
We've a bus coming up here from the VA hospital in Los Angeles
about once a month. Those guys don't have any arms or legs,
and yet they're men. Why should you deprive any guy of an
opportunity to be a man?
Now you see that we've no class conscience, no racial prejudice.
Even the guilty-looking Karl Marx was here. After washing
a sea of blood off his little hand, he said, "I see
no hatred in here, no warfare, no spy. You have done something
that would shame the Russians."
Yes, the Silver State may someday shift into the Pacific,
the city of Las Vegas may be gone with the nuclear smoke,
but my pretty chicks will cluck, my Ranch will shine.
If you think I'm phony, speaking with my tongue in cheek,
I've never told the truth
and no man's ever whored.

GARY SNYDER [B. 1930]

*In "Finding the Space in the Heart," Gary Snyder, one of the most significant authors of the
twentieth century, writes that he first saw northern Nevada's Black Rock Desert in the sixties,
in "a Volkswagen camper / with a fierce gay poet and a / lovely but dangerous girl." Suddenly,
"O, ah! the / awareness of emptiness / brings forth a heart of compassion!" Snyder has returned
to Nevada many times every decade, as if to a touchstone, marking stages in his own matu-
ration and charting changes in the national consciousness. The "Hitch Haiku" sequence in
Snyder's early book* The Back Country *(1967) exhibits the freedom of his beatnik, on-the-road
days as well as reveals his interest in Japanese poetic forms and Mahayana Buddhism—Snyder
spent much of 1956–68 in Japan, studying at a Zen temple. "Magpie's Song" from his Pulitzer
Prize–winning book* Turtle Island *(1974) was composed about a dozen miles east of Elko, en
route to a stressful political meeting in Utah where land use issues would be debated. And
"Old Woodrat's Stinky House," which appears in Snyder's magnum opus* Mountains and Rivers without End *(1996), reflects Snyder's later years, having spent a lifetime studying Native
American cultures, Eastern metaphysics, and the ecology and prehistory of North America.*

Throughout his long and influential life, Snyder's abiding concern has been "reinhabitation," that is, learning how to "become native" to our planetary home, finding ways to live in tune with nature, such as natives peoples did. Snyder, who for thirty years has reinhabited the San Juan Ridge in northern California, has written seventeen books of poetry and prose and been honored with prizes too numerous to mention, including the Bollingen Prize in 1997, the nation's most distinguished poetry prize.

Hitch Haiku

•   •   •

A truck went by
                three hours ago:
Smoke Creek desert

•   •   •

Jackrabbit eyes all night
        breakfast in Elko.

•   •   •

Pronghorn country

Steering into the sun
            glittering jewel-road
shattered obsidian

•   •   •

A great freight truck
            lit like a town
through the dark stony desert

•   •   •

Magpie's Song

Six A.M.,
Sat down on excavation gravel
by juniper and desert S.P. tracks
interstate 80 not far off
        between trucks
Coyotes—maybe three
            howling and yapping from a rise.

Magpie on a bough
Tipped his head and said,

"Here in the mind, brother
Turquoise blue.
I wouldn't fool you.
Smell the breeze
It came through all the trees
No need to fear
What's ahead
Snow up on the hills west
Will be there every year
be at rest.
A feather on the ground—
The wind sound—

Here in the Mind, Brother,
Turquoise Blue"

Old Woodrat's Stinky House

The whole universe is an ocean of dazzling light
On it dance the waves of life and death.
            —service for the spirits of the dead

•

Coyote and Earthmaker whirling about in the world winds
found a meadowlark nest floating and drifting; stretched it to
cover the waters and made us an earth—

Us critters hanging out together
something like two billion years

Ice ages come one hundred fifty million years apart
last about ten million
then warmer days return—

all the free water in the world flies up and falls again
within two million years—

A venerable desert woodrat nest of twigs and shreds
plastered down with amber'd urine
a family house in use eight thousand years,
        & four thousand years of using writing equals
the life of a bristlecone pine—

A spoken language works
for about five centuries,
lifespan of a douglas fir;
big floods, big fires, every couple hundred years,
a human life lasts eighty,
a generation twenty.

Hot summers every eight or ten,
four seasons every year
twenty-eight days for the moon
day/night   the twenty-four hours

& a song might last four minutes,

a breath is a breath.

.

Pocket gopher, elk, elk-calf, deer, field mouse,
snowshoe hare, ground squirrel, jackrabbit, deer mouse,
pine squirrel, beaver.
Jumping mouse, chipmunk, woodrat, pika.
House-cat, flying squirrel. Duck, jay, owl, grebe,
fish, snake, grasshopper, cricket, grass. Pine nuts, rose seeds,
mushrooms, paper, rag, twine, orange peel, matches, rubber,
tinfoil, shoestring, paint rag, two pieces of a shirt—
                    from 5,086 coyote droppings—

—And around the Great Basin
        human people living eating cattail pollen,
        bullrush seeds, raw baby birds,
        cooked ducks and geese,
        antelope, squirrel, beetles, chub, and suckers—
        ten thousand years of living
                        from the
        Lovelock Cave—

Great tall woodrat nests. Shale-flakes, sheep-scats, thorns,
heaped up for centuries
placed under overhangs—caves in cliffs—
at the bottom, antique fecal pellets;

orange-yellow urine-amber.
Shred of a bush that grew eight thousand years ago,
       another rain, another name.

    Cottontail boy said "woodrat makes me puke!
    Shitting on his grandmother's blankets—
    stinking everything up—pissing on everything—
    yucky old woodrat!
    Makes his whole house stink!"

—Coyote says "You people should stay put here,
    learn your place,
        do good things. Me, I'm travelling on."

ELAINE DALLMAN [B. 1934]

Poet, editor, educator, and activist, Elaine Dallman embodies the modern women's movement. Born and raised in Sacramento and educated at Stanford University, where she double-majored in psychology and education, Dallman followed a traditional path of marrying and raising children before she recognized her talent and need for poetry. Following the poetic impulse, Dallman earned a master's degree in creative writing from San Francisco State University and a PHD in creative writing and English literature from Southern Illinois University, where she designed and taught SIU's first women's studies course. An inveterate traveler, wherever she goes Dallman puts into action her belief that "the poet must interact with the community to demonstrate the relationship of poetry to life." Dallman moved to Reno in 1977 and founded the nationally recognized independent publishing house Women in Literature, Inc., which produced, under Dallman's direction, the prominent Woman Poet *regional anthology series (1980–91), with volumes on* The West, The East, The Midwest, *and* The South. *These books introduced readers to a wealth of women poets during years when the poetry scene was dominated by men. For more than thirty years Dallman was active in public arts programs in Nevada, teaching in Dayton and Ely through the Nevada poet-in-residence program, developing experimental creative writing classes for Reno area preteens, offering literature information workshops in Nevada libraries, and teaching English at the University of Nevada, Reno. Some 185 of Dallman's poems have been published in a broad variety of literary anthologies and literary journals. Her book* A Parallel Cut of Air, *forthcoming in a special edition, "activates women's studies," exploring aspects of women's experience from childhood through old age. The two poems featured below are from Dallman's chapbook* Nevadans *(2005).*

Sparks for a 24/7 Week

Ping! Shining up into spectacles.
Part of the light comes
from what's in a glass case
in the Sparks Railroad Museum:
2 gold spikes, 1 silver,
1 gold and silver with iron.

In Sparks' evening sky
the filtering of Nevada minerals.
Sun spreads a band of gold
around our rhomboid state borders.
Silver paved galaxies give uneven burnings.
Spirits shovel the iron red mountain,
mine it to darkness.

One 1850 midnight turns into an echo:
"Dod drat a black night."
Soon another miner:
"Time for a spade & pick axe."

Day comes at railroad speed.
Piles of loot
filling up and over the mountain.

Desert

This land is sand grains;
under walking feet Nevada shifts.

A rock resembles a toothed wall.
Desert stones drip shadows, real and felt.
The women call, "See the people's shadows joining
hands!"

In the middle of this valley,
wild wasps entangled in crazy coils fertilize
stamens.
Crowned in gold dust they swarm off.

Wind slams against rock,
a yellow sage blizzard blows;
rain drums like a demigod who holds the faith of its
people.
Rain cannot wash the circle of day away.

Fall suns accumulate beyond the town borders.

Soon, winter emits its slow hungering light.
One circle doesn't notice the sky's tired black.
The circle moves, ever so lightly.
Again winter at winter's center.
Awakening, a yellow eye flies beyond.

TOM MESCHERY [B. 1938]

*Surely Tom Meschery is the first person to be inducted into a writers hall of fame one year and
a sports hall of fame the next. In 2002 poet Tom Meschery was inducted into the Nevada Writers Hall of Fame, and in 2003 into the Bay Area Sports Hall of Fame. At six-foot-six, Meschery
can survey his immigrant past with justifiable pride. Born Tomislav Nickolaevich Mescheria-
koff in Manchuria, China, to Russian parents who had fled the Russian Revolution, Meschery
spent World War II in a Tokyo prison camp for women and children. After the war, it took a
year of travel through the Philippines and Hawaii for Meschery's mother and her children to
rejoin their father in San Francisco. There, eager to blend in, Meschery played basketball as a
way to become American, and he strove to master English, graduating from St. Mary's College
in 1961. Drafted in the first round by the Philadelphia Warriors, Meschery played for ten years
in the NBA, for the Golden State Warriors and the Seattle Supersonics. After one too many
injuries, Meschery retired from basketball and earned an MFA from the University of Iowa in
1974, moved to Truckee, California, with his wife, the author Joanne Meschery, and eventually
embarked on a second career, teaching English at Reno High School and creative writing at
Sierra College. Meschery's first book of poetry,* Over the Rim *(1970), captures images, events,
and people from his basketball days, while his three-part collection* Nothing We Lose Can
Be Replaced *(1999) begins with Russian heritage, covers the basketball years, and ends with
teaching the next generation. Although what is lost can never be replaced, loss in Meschery's
poetry, as reviewer Brad Summerhill has noted, never leads to despair, but, rather, to wisdom
and redemption.*

Trucks

Out of the morning half-light,
they come upon you suddenly
like a headache or that dog
your neighbor never leashes
that stops inches from your knee-cap,
its teeth bared and snarling.

Bumper to bumper, their grills
rise above you in the rear view
mirror: silver, emblematic,
as towerful and American
as Madison Square Garden.

That's when you wish for Guatemala
or the rain soaked roads of West Africa
after a sudden monsoon
to slow everything down, the pace
of your heart, to tropical.

That's when you pray for sixteen wheelers
stuck up to their hubs in mud,
reduced to life forever in the Third World,
without respect, like teachers going to work,
or small four-cylinder used cars.

Weeds — Teaching Poetry at Wittenburg Juvenile Hall

None go nameless: little shit-head,
long neck, ouch! for the tiny thorns
along their stems. If I know them:
dandelion (poor cousin of the flower),
crabgrass, oxalis, their persistent roots
impossible to find and dig out
even in the soft spring earth, to kill before
they, as gardeners like to say, take over —
take over your tulips, the early crocus
and spread into midsummer columbine.

Then, you'll pay the price, bending
on your knees in the hot sun trying to find
their hiding places among gailardia,
beds of iris, mountain lupine, coreopsis.
Spurges, henbit, out to strangle your perennials.
That's when you'll forgo names except the one
these students rhyme with mother, a slant rhyme
that slants the same direction weed roots take
trying to avoid being caught and troweled.

In class when I read these lines
to them to show how poems travel
from one subject to another—the word
I use is "leaping"—some tell me
Man, that's totally poetic. Others look
totally worried. *So that means*
I can go from flowers to fucking,
right? And what if I want to fuck
among the flowers, is that ok too?

I wave off the approaching guard.
This boy, homeless at ten, rapist
and murderer by sixteen, understands
but not enough. I tell the entire class
but mostly him; yes, it's almost always
about passion. Flowers you want to touch
like breasts can't grow unless you weed first.
For a moment, the room goes silent.
It's windowless and hot. In a week
he'll be in court, tried as an adult.

BILL COWEE [B. 1942]

Here is how poet Bill Cowee describes himself in the biographical note to his first book, Bones
Set against the Drift *(Black Rock Press, 1998): "Bill Cowee earns his living as an accountant in
Mound House, Nevada, but spends the good parts of his life reading and writing poetry, partic-
ularly about the West and the people who find this a quality place to live." Born in Milwaukee,*

Wisconsin, Cowee grew up in Montana, and studied at the University of Nevada, Reno, and the University of Southern California. He lived in Southern California, and Phoenix, Arizona, for the next twenty-three years, working as a comptroller for a major grocery chain. Moving to Nevada in 1987, he became a founding member of the Ash Canyon Poets, a Carson City–based group that has been meeting at seven o'clock every Friday evening since 1987 to read and offer constructive feedback on one another's writing. Like Cowee, most of the poets in the group have day jobs, writing poetry after hours. Many members have published their work, and some have won awards, including Cowee himself, who has won both a Nevada Arts Council Literary Fellowship and a Governor's Arts Award. Cowee has served as poetry editor for Bristlecone *and as codirector of the Western Mountain Writer's Conference. His work has appeared in small presses and periodicals in thirty-four states, Great Britain, Ireland, and Wales. Uniquely able to capture the life of an accountant in poetry, Cowee, who now lives in Dayton, Nevada, writes about the people he meets—"the convenience store owner / who includes the bags of pig food / as a deduction because everyone likes / to pet his pig"—and about the desert landscapes that help him maintain composure. Through work poems, love poems, nature lyrics, and philosophical meditations, Cowee gives voice to the poet within.*

More Than Worms Slip through Worm Holes

> Theoreticians weave their parallel universes,
> large nets connected by passageways called
> wormholes. Any hard rock miner knows wormholes,
> the way ore veins weave in and out of heat
> inside a lode, the way purple-blue sand heavy
> with silver is there one minute and then only
> the black promise of rock and chisel echoing
> shaft names that stop to catch like magma
> in a mountain's throat: Yellow Jacket, Virginian,
> wormholes named Chollar, Union and Little China,
> parallel universes ten foot wide and a mile deep.
>
> Kin of forgotten particles, the Double Peak Ranch,
> Lousetown don't exist anymore. Or perhaps they tend
> to exist for those who know where to look, small
> tracings on photographic plates, sandy depressions,
> long wheel ruts beneath the grey sagebrush like
> quark tracks across a steamed bell jar's breast.
>
> Sand and clay, the black holes of wind-driven
> history, give up constellations of obsidian

shards after a fierce storm, arrowhead debris
a gravity of Native American past, heavy
silent, volcanic tears thrown from a black heaven.

Birds nest in the eyes of place names, wooden
bones search vainly for the crumbled foundations
of their existence among star-clusters of Russian
thistle, purple nebulae of locoweed, galaxies
strung with lavender webs of salt cedar. Roads
and time proven by the mathematics of deviant lines
in an infinite universe of parallel universes.

To the Austrolorps in Wild Abandon

The Austrolorps are into the sagebrush
again, their bituminous bodies pecking
at a new bug hatch, feast for the raw red
heads darting like new flames among coal.
A flock of chickens delirious with joy,
swirl in a ground-based funnel cloud
oblivious to the wild dogs that hunt there
and without thought of the scent they
spread for coyotes that slink in the night.
To lose it all for the moment. No dictated
instinct, no codes of decorum or societal
norm, only the bumping, flapping cackle
of poultry gone mad.

        When he was fourteen,
unaware of the accountant hidden within him,
a boy took his chickens one by one, set
them on the ground and hypnotized them by
drawing divergent lines out from their
sight until each sat totally motionless,
a flock of concrete chickens in the dirt.
One by one they awoke, came slowly to life,
shook their heads, and staggered back to
the henhouse.

Now grown, he watches from his office
as hens strut across the horse corral, chests
thrust out, stepping ever faster until they
scatter, rush to determine who will arrive
at their arbitrary destination first, like a black
chattering of numbers in the columns of his work.
All morning the chickens call him. He sees
nothing but rows of diverging ledger lines.

ADRIAN C. LOUIS [B. 1946]

"O Grandfather," writes Adrian C. Louis in a poem entitled "Medicine Song," "is my life to be miserable / from here on in? More miserable / than the miserable it has always been?" A mixed-blood Indian and enrolled member of the Lovelock Paiute tribe, Adrian Louis was born in Lovelock and raised in Yerington, Nevada, the eldest of twelve children in a dirt-poor family. Louis flunked out of the University of Nevada, Reno, and drifted over to the Haight-Ashbury district of San Francisco, where he joined the "white Indians" of the counterculture, worshipping sex, drugs, and rock 'n' roll. Hitchhiking with a friend to Boston, Louis earned a BA and MA in writing from Brown University, after which he returned west and edited a series of native newspapers, including Indian Country Today. *From 1984 to 1998 he taught at Oglala Lakota College on the Pine Ridge Reservation of South Dakota, years of misery that spawned many poetry collections about reservation life, "Cowturdville, Nebraska," alcoholism, illness, and despair. Louis's fierce, uncensored, and flagrantly politically incorrect poems in* Fire Water World *(1989),* Among the Dog Eaters *(1992),* Blood Thirsty Savages *(1994),* Ceremonies of the Damned *(1997),* Ancient Acid Flashes Back *(2000),* Bone and Juice *(2001), and others speak for the downtrodden, offending some readers and inspiring others. Notwithstanding his unsparing self-pity, Louis has written prodigiously (a dozen books of poetry and two works of fiction) and garnered numerous honors and awards, including two nominations for Print Journalist of the Year, a Pushcart Prize, fellowships from the Bush Foundation, National Endowment for the Arts, and Lila Wallace–Reader's Digest Foundation, and his 1999 induction into the Nevada Writers Hall of Fame. Currently Louis is associate professor and director of creative writing at Southwest Minnesota State University, where his writing details his current state of affairs, which is, as he says, "Oh, just chaos and sadness."*

excerpt from "Earth Bone Connected to the Spirit Bone"

I, Adrian, live in the land of the common
doorbell. Every time the doorbell rings
on a TV commercial, my dogs go wild and I
jump up off the couch looking for a place to hide.
Me, a middle-aged man acting like it's 1962.
1962 and I'm a sophomore in high school.
It's Saturday and I'm in my cubby hole of a room
off the enclosed porch of the old railroad house
whacking off when the dogs start barking.
I see a pickup churning up our dirt road.
I'm in my sanctuary, connecting my groin
bone to the heaven bone.
I do not worry until there is a pounding
on the small pine door to my room.
My Nutty-Putty heart ricochets around
my halfbreed ribcage. I pull up my pegged Levi's
and peek out the door. There is Chris Brandon,
fellow soph. A white boy, dressed in his usual
crisply starched button-down clothes.
I smell the Vitalis on his flat-top with wings.
He's no friend, just someone I pass in the halls,
but what the hell is he doing here?
On the porch outside my room is a bucket
of soiled diapers from one of my little sisters.
The entire corridor is swamped with shit-smell.
The whole house is in dirty disarray.
Burning shame makes my eyeballs flutter.
In the living room I can see my illiterate,
drunken, white stepfather making small talk
with Brandon's father. My brown mother
is scurrying after the smaller kids
and she's wearing a tattered gingham dress.
Her black hair is electric and she's pregnant,
although the baby she's holding is less
than a year old and the flypaper above
my head is so covered with flies

that it couldn't hold another and worst of all,
I've still got a boner, and Brandon looks
down and spots it.
At that instant I pray for nuclear attack.
A complete devastation of mankind,
of Adrian, of Brandon, of my entire known
world existing in the midst
of that Nevada Indian poverty
thirty-three years ago.

The Boy Hears Distant Drums from across the Sierras

Yerington, Nevada. July '66
& *Naatsi* is newly nineteen,
laboring for Anaconda Copper
Mine, guiding house-sized
Dart dump trucks along
a dirt road to belch
their loads at an ore crusher
or pour the leached rock
over the tailings slopes
& once or twice a shift
giving the drivers a break,
taking their trucks up
from the ancient depths, up
the inclines of the pit mine
(sixth largest in the world!)
& he thinks he's got it made,
sunshine, company bunk, commissary
credit, & plenty of cash, enough
left over come Friday night
for the cathouse ladies
to do him real nice.

He watches the line of yellow
dump trucks parade upon
the earth like a shimmering
herd of fallen chunks of sun.
They puke green rock

into the ore crusher until
the noon air whistle
screams a bolt of calm
that rips open thermoses
& steel lunchbuckets.

Finished with his Spam
sandwiches & Kool-Aid,
Naatsi ambles away
from the sun.
The dust devils pester
like the nagging, dry wives
the older miners complain of
& he searches for shade
to become brothers
with lizards: lean & cosmic,
dozing & silent & in
the queer desert quiet
he hears distant drums
from across the Sierras.
They call him to leave
his home spirit-soil
& join up with renegade
seekers of freedom
& other enemies
of the state.

Coyote's Circle

for Linda, who ended up East

I

In South Dakota and heading
west, Coyote was hurtling down
the highway and wishing
for a drink, watching a fly trapped
inside the air-conditioned tomb
smash its head again and again
against the invisible God

of the windshield, so he stopped
his Thunderbird and chased
the fly from front to back
with his cigarette lighter
until the concept wearied him
and he wasted it with his fist.

II

Near Provo, Utah, the squeaky
clean, hardass State Storm Trooper
who pulls Coyote over for speeding
also fines him for not wearing his seat
belt and glares at his brilliant white
dentures on the front seat.
He tells Coyote to remove
the eagle feather dangling
from his rearview mirror
because it "impedes vision"
and to put his choppers back
into his hairy head.
"What kinda feather?" the cop asks,
and Coyote says, "Turkey."
Coyote bites his lip to keep from
giggling or starting a shootout
in the loopy land of Brigham Young.
Oy vey, these people claim Indians to
be one of the lost tribes of Israel.
Coyote's fangs pierce his lip
and he smiles at the taste
of his own warm, canine blood.
Nothing matters, he's headed for home.
Home, where his ancestors lie buried.

III

Home, northern Nevada. July baking.
He's zipping down the desert interstate
between Lovelock and Fernley
when a spew of foam in the corner
of his eye shoots ten feet into the air

and Coyote's got the only car around
so he slams on the brakes.
He shakes his head to make sure
he's not having an acid flashback
and prays that the oddity of a geyser
on the barren, baked land won't be
a precursor to alien spaceship landings.
He slowly backs the car up the hot tar
until he comes to the spot where white
foam shot high into the sky.
He gets out with pistol in hand
and sees three cans of Coors
on the scorched sand.
One has exploded
and the other two
are due any second.
Coyote releases the safety
and fires, freeing warm spirits
born to be ice-cold.

Beer, blood, soil, home.

So many lost years connecting crazy.
So many lost years connecting crazy
and love and memories
and love and forgotten memories.

KIRK ROBERTSON [B. 1946]

A drive through the titles of Kirk Robertson's poems reveals much about the landscape of his imagination— "Finding Stillwater," "Fallon," "Adjusting to the Desert," "Driving to Vegas," "Lovelock to Twin Falls," "West Nevada Waltz," "Tonopah," "The Mizpah Sonnet," "The Misfits," and "Talkin' Cow-Calf Pairs at the Coney Island Bar," a two-line poem that reads, "The bigger the hat / The smaller the ranch." Robertson has published more than twenty books of poetry, including his retrospective collection, Just Past Labor Day: Selected and New Poems, 1969–1995 *(1996). His work, which has appeared in a great number of magazines and anthologies, exhibits a spare, unforgiving style, a painterly vision, an interest in connecting exterior and interior landscapes, and an ability to invest the mundane details of an ordinary day with special portent. "Poems are like antennae," he explains. "They enable us to see or perceive . . . things that we aren't quite aware of yet." Kirk Robertson has been a major force for the arts in Nevada, founding Duck Down Press, editing* neon, *the art journal of the Nevada Arts Council, serving as program coordinator for the Churchill Arts Council, and writing art criticism for* Artweek *and* Reno News & Review. *He received the Nevada Governor's Arts Award in literature in 1981 and the Nevada Writers Hall of Fame award in 1994 and is currently writing a book of essays on art and artists. Having grown up in Southern California and graduated from California State University, Long Beach, Robertson roamed around the West until arriving in the Lahontan Valley. "It felt right," he says. "I could live here," he recalls thinking. Robertson still feels the same way about the place where he has lived for a quarter of a century. As he explains, there is a certain quality of light that holds him.*

Adjusting to the Desert

> It's been getting dark earlier
> the light slipping away
> before you notice winter
> comes cruising up to the dock
>
> You wonder as you watch
> the light fade just how
> that ship you've been expecting
> can come in here where even
> the memories of the sea
> have long since dried up
> and blown away   just then
>
> Three stools down the moon
> crosses her legs high
> lights a cigarette and
>
> Right at that moment
> you know what it is
> the coyotes keep askin' for
>
> She leaves early after
> driving everyone crazy
> with the sound of her legs
> drinking up their money
> and making these promises

about how she'll show you
so much *more* tomorrow night

You listen to the broken
hearted cowboys *just so lonesome*
they could cry while outside
the stiff October wind tears
at the petals of a neon rose
spinning everything in sight
like some nervous kid
his first time on a bar stool

After closing you stand
on the ditchbank think
that by not expecting a great deal
or believing too strongly

In things that are either too much
or not enough here and counting

Only on the dizzy sense
of well being you get
under this totally
irrational sky

That *shit*
you just might get by

After all

Fallon

You've driven over
nine hundred miles
just to be here
for a few days
where it's warm
enough
dry enough
to sit on the porch
in the sun on the day
after Christmas

under a sky
you'd almost forgotten
could be so blue

The few clouds
are so high and thin
that when they pass
in front of the sun
there's no change
in the light and
it takes a while
for you to feel
your shirt growing
cold against your skin

But the chill
passes quickly
like a first snow
that sticks around
only in the shadows
of the ditchbank

So you decide
to walk up
get the mail
with the sky
the only coat
around you

Lure

Just what is it
what thing so
hooks my eye

The neon blacklit
swollen web of
her amber hair

The rhythm
her heels beat
on the sidewalk

Or is it a glimpse
just the glimpse
briefly through

The slit skirt
the tops of her
black stockings

That snags my
mind pulls it
toward a sense

Other than common
filled with thoughts
of just what might be

LYNN EMANUEL [B. 1949]

The unsuspecting reader of Lynn Emanuel's The Dig *(1992) may infer that Emanuel grew up in Ely, Nevada. By connecting the dots among these autobiographical poems, one may deduce that Emanuel's mother packed young Lynn into a stolen car and drove to Ely in the 1950s to flee a hot-tempered husband. Choosing poverty over tyranny, they lived in tacky motel rooms and cheap apartments, barely scraping by. Lynn had chronic influenza and a heart stutter, and her mother drank too much. Those years, in the poems, are relentlessly squalid, epitomized by images of repulsive food on a greasy Formica dinner table. At eighteen Lynn escaped and made her way to Italy, where she supported herself by modeling. To read these poems as the literal truth, however, would be to miss the point, for* The Dig, *which was a National Poetry Series winner, is a stunning performance of autobiography, inviting the reader to consider the problematic and slippery nature of autobiography, especially as it is configured in contemporary American poetry.* The Dig *thus complicates the notion of poetry as a window through which one sees the author's real life. In fact, although Lynn Emanuel did visit her grandparents' hotel in Ely as a child, she was born and raised in the East, a graduate of Bennington College (BA), City College of New York (MA), and the University of Iowa (MFA). Emanuel is a professor of English at the University of Pittsburgh, where she teaches in the MFA Writing program. She has*

written three books of poetry, Hotel Fiesta *(1984),* The Dig, *and* Then, Suddenly— *(1999),*
which received the Eric Matthieu King Award from the Academy of American Poets. Her work
has been published in major national journals and has been featured five times in the Pushcart
Prize Anthology *and in* Best American Poetry.

Chinoisserie

    My mother in her dress of red Viyella, teetering like a tiny idol
    on three-inch lacquered spikes, chignon dressed with little gold-
    throated bells that chirped more sweetly than the cricket,
    held her small, perfect hands to the torrent pouring from the slots.
    Money went like water through our fingers: was dammed
    by budgets, released, then abruptly gone at the China Starr,
    that grotto, festooned with red and vivid lanterns.
    Dark as the inside of a limousine, that saloon was where
    our lives, dulled by the copper barons, were cleansed,
    where we bade good-bye to the limp and stutter
    of bad goods, to the wince of the creaky rocker, to the vast
    grandmother dying in its clutch, to the dirty, wrinkled ones
    and tens pieced together to cover the week. Hello, we said,
    to the beautiful dark starlit bar and the luxury therein:
    the runcible spoons with their slippery cargo: the snarled silk
    of tinned bean sprout, the wrinkled flame of the dried lily.
    Hunched over our beakers of jasmine tea, we let the exotic
    rinse over us—impractical and non-negotiable.

For Me at Sunday Sermons, the Serpent

    coming lightly, perfectly
       into the garden
          was as smart as Eve was

    pink, fat & pliant,
       was tough as a root,
          but blue

  or green:
    a reed, a stem;
       the uninterruptedness of him

from tail to lip, all
   one thing, consistent
      as a walking stick.

Or he was a ruby
   cummerbund, a glove
      on its way to the opera

dropped
  in the dust
    of this godforsaken town.

Beside his motionless chill,
   Ely, Nevada,
      was as dull as two buttons.

He was the green
   light, the go-ahead,
      the spark, the road,

the ticket out.

What Ely Was

The mauve, the ocher of canned tamales, the dark silt
of gravy burning, the hominy's white knuckles;
fats that made a surface gleam like a pigeon's neck,
like a spill of gasoline, melt-down crusts of oleo
on the tuna casserole, toast that was blackened
to a piece of macadam, a singed field, a roof shingle.
The cool unguent of jam upon a spoon, but every sweet
thing has a sting. It was good for you, this needle, this pin.
Under the beautiful blue glass dome of plum preserves
was the bite of penicillin. I longed for chocolate both
sweet and bitter, fried green plantain, mustard, onion,
red tomato, rice and black beans in a pot, Moroccan olives
with cayenne, Haut-Brion, cabbage, ham. Somewhere
some green coast exported all I wanted of all I wanted,
a kingdom where my hunger fit, both mind and body, all of it.

WILLIAM L. FOX [B. 1949]

Biographical information for William L. Fox appears on page 531. Picture a lone man on top of Sand Mountain in north-central Nevada. The man inscribes the word wind *into the sand with his finger. The word is quickly erased by the wind itself. The man is William Fox, who had been a traditional lyric poet for several years before this incident in 1974. But this moment, as he explains in the preface to his retrospective collection* Reading Sand: Selected Desert Poems, 1975–2000, *"made me wonder how to make poems about the desert that would be just as physical and immediate" as a word in sand. Thus began a series of experiments creating severely literal poems, grounded in the landscape around him. In Fox's minimalist poems, the words on the page seem to evolve into elements of the landscape, such that the page itself morphs into a dry alkali lakebed. This translation of desert into concrete poetry maps a mind in the act of perception, paring down language to its most basic units. As Fox once explained, most of his fifteen books of poetry "are concerned with walking up to the edge of language to see where we fall off of it." The poems are highly repetitive, much like the recursive character of basin-and-range topography, perhaps resembling minimalist art or music more than mainstream poetry. The fractured syntax and empty white space slow the reader down to picture the terrain in the mind's eye. Among Fox's Great Basin poetry books are* Monody *(1977),* Time by Distance *(1985),* Leaving Elko *(1993), and* geograph *(1994). Fox has encouraged the poetry of others as well, editing two regional poetry anthologies—*Seven Nevada Poets *(1991) and* TumbleWords: Writers Reading the West *(1995)—and being editor/publisher of the avant-garde* West Coast Poetry Review *and Press from 1972 to 1988.*

untitled poem from *Monody*

     sweet   water

     salt   sweat

untitled poem from *Reading Sand*

    1.
    red
    sand

    red
    sun

neon
neon

white
sand

white
sun

neon
neon

2.
blue
sky

blue
sand

one
on

one
off

3.
black
night

black
night

red
on

red
off

blue
one

blue
off

disowning

1.

go   to   the   desert
lie   down   on
what   the   map
would   show   to
be   a   line

pick   yourself   up
find   another   line
lie   down
get   up

erase   all   the
lines   this   way
and   that

think   of   it   as
a   poem   without
line   without
lines   between

lines

think   of   it   as
picking   up
a   lie

2.

train   your   eyes
on   the   horizon
of   the   page

walk   away   from
it   and   every
thing   else

train   your   eyes
to   look   down   to
where   words
fall   away
beneath   you

run   your   finger
down   the   page
and   away   from
the   horizon

your   eye   follows
the   finger   the
horizon   follows
your   eyes

3.
stop   to   look
around   now
and   then   to
take   back   what
you   said

the   names
on   all   the
peaks   and
valleys

the   small
burrows
and   thin
shrubs
burning
on   the   desert
floor

pick   up   after
yourself   and
the   shadow   of
others   who
departed
before   you

the   loose
punctuation
blowing   by
in   the   wind

4.

a   blank   page

think   of   a   blank
page   at   the
end   of   a   book

closing   the   book
and   picking   up
your   steps   as

backwards
you   go

closing   up
the   mountains
and   sand   as
you   walk   off
the   land   and   out
of   the   words.

JIM HUSKEY [1949–2004]

In the late 1970s and early 1980s, the Reno-Fallon area experienced an extraordinary conflu-ence of poetic energy and activity, with the publication of West Coast Poetry Review, *the establishment of Duck Down Press, the poetic experimentation of William L. Fox, Kirk Robert-son, Gary Short, Shaun T. Griffin, and others, and the cultural infusion of a stream of visiting poets. Jim Huskey, whose fledgling A Frosty Morning Press published Gary Short and Roger Smith's anthology* The Nevada Poet *(1981), was right in the middle of the Reno poetry scene. Born in Colorado and raised in Yerington, Nevada, Huskey went east to earn a BA in English from Harvard, staying on the East Coast to teach in the Boston and Washington, DC, areas. In 1978, newly married, Huskey returned to Reno, where he pursued a master's degree in English at UNR, graduating in 1985 with a thesis on the poet James Merrill. During these years Huskey, with Roger Smith, organized the "Poet as Humanist" series that brought in gifted writers such as James Welch, William Stafford, and Howard Nemerov. There was a reading on Fridays, a workshop on Saturdays, and a big party afterward, with cocktails, dinner, and dancing. Saying farewell after these good times was tough, as Huskey recalls in his poem "For Howard*

Nemerov, Summer 1979": "But in the end, poetry comes down / To this: a lonely old man and two / Lonely young people, standing / On a gaudy Reno street corner / Not really wanting to part just yet." Huskey's collection Portfolio I: Poems *(1980) and his poems in Shaun T. Griffin's* Desert Wood *capture this energetic period in Reno's literary history and in his own life. Huskey relocated to Seattle, where he was employed in computer graphic design and counseling. He continued to write, as he said, "to find out who I am."*

Stone Koan

> *for Roger Smith*

The rock stands broad shouldered there,
Stable, aged, aging. The climber
Clambers among it, chiseling his path
Like some Gothic cathedral stone mason.
Gently, calmly, he feels with feet,
With hands for unseen spurs,
Fingernail-thick scores on which
To trust his next push, his next pull.
In time, with the grace of the wind,
He flows up the rock side, and finding
The pulse of the stone, tirelessly tops
The face and sits in sweat feeling
At peace with himself and watching an ant
Scramble among the six pebbles at his feet.

Building the Pumphouse

Crosscut saws, two-by-fours, three-penny nails,
Blue chalkline slapping plywood planks, what's true
And plumb and straight, my father taught me once.
He'd bought an acre—alkali, buck brush,
Salt grass—a lot to build a home on. I'd
Come back to find a summer job. Too smart
To handle tools, I'd grown apart, had learned
A tongue so strange, Dad feared we'd never talk
Again. Fighting for me the only way
He knew, he showed me how to use my hands.

I learned:

> The litany of carpentry: blisters, sweat
> Handsaw's quick trochaic rhythms, Dad's voice
> Filled with the wheat fields and ballparks of his youth,
> The heat of nail after damn bloody bastard nail
> That bent halfway into Masonite sheets,
> Steel spikes that, hammered into pine, rose in pitch,
> Winds soughing in cattails and cottonwoods,
> How nights brought black thumbs, errant saw strokes, hands
> That failed, hammers that fell, mosquito blood,
> Hot showers, cold soda, long dreamless sleep.

September rushed upon us, wood unstained,
Roof half shingled, pipe, pump and water tank
Still undelivered. Sun had beat us down,
Rain had held us up. We might have rushed—
Painted the door, sealed drafts under the walls—
But as I boxed pants and packed books, I felt good
Knowing we'd finish the job another day.

BRUCE LAXALT [B. 1951]

*On Bruce Laxalt's desk there is an ashtray that appears to be made from a circle of small hu-
man skulls—*memento mori, *remember that you have to die. By his early fifties, Laxalt had
already outlived his doctor's predictions of life expectancy by several years. In 2001 this Reno
native was diagnosed with* ALS, *commonly called Lou Gehrig's disease, a progressive degenera-
tive condition that causes muscle atrophy. Writing poetry helped Laxalt to keep "my eyes wide
open and not play games with myself mentally," he told a reporter after the release of his poetry
collection* Songs of Mourning and Worship *(2005). "It has been an interesting trip to be along
for the ride in a self-destructing body," he added. Cofounder of the statewide law firm of Laxalt
and Nomura, Laxalt has practiced law for thirty years, first as a homicide prosecutor, later as a
highly successful civil litigator. For a prominent lawyer to publish poems that are in some cases
painfully private surely required courage, but the act is not wholly unaccountable. Laxalt took
creative writing classes at Stanford University and comes from a family that includes writers
Robert Laxalt (his father) and Monique Laxalt (his sister). Bruce Laxalt's poems express the
hard realities of working in his chosen profession and living in his given body. The law poems*

reveal the thoughts and emotions of an attorney who has faced corpses in the morgue and
murderers on the stand, and who has confounded the devious strategies of his opposition. The
poems on illness share with unflinching honesty how he is making that journey. In courtroom
and wheelchair, Laxalt steers a course between valor and vulnerability.

Work in Progress

    There you sit, lost among the trophies on the office shelves,
    In the dusty detritus of a quarter century's thrusts and parries,
    More of interest to clients now than me.
    There in the back, you are a shy one—a 5x7 photo, peeking out.
    Ignored, it seems, by the nightly cleaning staff,
    Untended, the dust grown highest and unkempt around you.
    Slowly lost, over the years, in the cluttered and momentary exhibitionism
    Of last month's trials and verdicts.

    "What's that?" an occasional more curious visitor will exclaim.
    "Many years ago," I reply, "a work in progress."
    "A beauty," they'll say. And indeed it is.
    Red orb suspended in the black of space, a delicate planet.
    The rivers, in deeper tint, wend their elegant way through the highlands,
    This way and that, in graceful contretemps,
    To the planet's edge and beyond, to the velvet black of void.
    "That's the back of a child's eyeball," I add. "In hemorrhage."

    A work in progress, indeed it is, sweet child.
    As were you, at three.
    Eager eyes and sun-tinged hair, a soap-sudded grin from the porcelain tub,
    The only photo we could find to show the jury
    Of the work of art you were, and would have become.

    The neighbors heard your nightly screams, muffled by the apartment wall.
        They never called in.
    Your case worker broke down on the stand.
        Did you know you'd been on the schedule
        for a next-week's visit?
    Your bartender mother's boyfriend, his own sweet scared eyes open wide
    In silent supplication to the jury box, begged for merciful belief:
    "She fell in the tub."
    I and the jury thought not.

The doctors said you might as well have hit concrete
    in a three-story fall,
And showed the jury the photo of your bleeding retina—
Sad beauty—staring blindly out of the glossy color print,
Caught unawares in the private act of dying.

Autumn Fire

Precious less is much.
The scent of sudden rain in the newly-fallen dusk
Unburdened by the trappings of light,
Borne silkily through the window on silent evening air
To kiss the smoke of the first fall fire.
Round warmth and reed-like cold
In dissonant duet.

Precious little time is long
When longer still than promised once.
The flames still flicker late at night.
Refusing the call to dim to coals.
The smoke still rises in shrinking wisps,
The light still dances on the walls,
Inevitable darkness held briefly at bay.

NILA NORTHSUN [B. 1951]

nila northSun, who was a powwow princess in her youth, may be the first Native American writer to mention Diet Pepsi, nacho cheese, and corn dogs in poetry. Defying expectations of appropriate Native American subject matter and tone, northSun, who is of Shoshone, Chippewa, and Swedish ancestry and is an enrolled member of the Shoshone tribe, employs an informal style to expose the ironies of being a postmodern Indian—the sweat lodge participants whose contact lenses get uncomfortable, the kids who wait for Santa Claus to visit the tribal gym, the elders who tap their feet to polka on the Lawrence Welk TV show. Formerly married to poet Kirk Robertson and coeditor with him for many years of Scree, an avant-garde poetry magazine, northSun even unmasks the craft of writing, telling interviewer Bill Stobb, "I take bits of reality and I mishmash them together, then I throw in some gossip and put a spin on it." *Winner of the Silver Pen Award in 2000, northSun claims to shun capital letters in her poems because she is too lazy to hit the shift key; she may have inherited a trickster personality from her father, Adam Fortunate Eagle, an Indian activist famous for his publicity stunts in the San Francisco Bay Area, such as orchestrating the takeover of Alcatraz Island. Born in an Indian hospital in Schurz, Nevada, northSun grew up in the Bay Area and earned a* BA *at the University of Montana. Her poetry appears in many anthologies, and she has published five poetry books—including her retrospective* a snake in her mouth: poems 1974–96 *and her 2007 release* love at gunpoint. *In addition to writing poetry, northSun coauthored a tribal history. For more than twenty years, northSun made her home on the Stillwater Indian Reservation in Fallon, where she directed a crisis shelter for Native American teens.*

sweat preparation checklist

no alcohol 24 hours before sweat
bring a towel
wear a bathing suit underneath clothing

any additional food
or special food if you're vegetarian
or have special needs is appreciated

contacts may become uncomfortable
jewelry may become hot

women if you're on your moon
(your period) you may not enter the sweat
nor prepare food
but may be present to watch goings-on
and participate after

sweats go in four rounds
when the flap is lifted
and you're getting claustrophobic
or just can't take it anymore
it's no shame to ask to exit

anybody that can come earlier in the day
to chop wood
to prepare the sweat
to prepare the fire
to help cook
is appreciated

lost in the woods

    the lake glistens in the distance
    they can't talk
    lost in their separate thoughts
    ultimately the goal is the same
    among thousands of people
    among roads and trails known
    like the back of their hands
    to somehow lose themselves
    to become invisible to everything
    but the trees
    if they believe hard enough
    they can make it real
    a separate reality
    from cars and hot dog stands
    from day glo biking shorts
    maybe like the indians that were here first
    that return
    and gaze over the lake
    and remember how it used to be
    like wovoka saying pray hard
    pray hard for the return of our ghosts
    and how it used to be
    pray hard
    and we can make it real
    pray hard
    and you can become invisible to their bullets
    pray hard
    and suddenly
    they were alone in the woods.

i gotta be indian tomorrow

    i came back to nevada
    because somebody decided
    they needed a native american
    on their radio show
    & i came to mind

i'm flattered
& my ego drove me
200 miles over snow packed mountains
but now
before the 8 am
interview/reading
i'm panicked
i haven't written an "indian poem"
in a long time
maybe only 1 out of 100 poems
even touch my tribal-ness
they think just because
i am native
means
anything
i write somehow is rooted
in native-ness
but in flipping the pages of
my 3-ring binder
i find nothing mentioning
mother earth or feathers or reservations
even though
i stand on mother earth
& my rearview mirror has
an eagle feather tied to it
and after the interview
i'll be going back to the reservation
to see my family
is that "enough" indian
for them? i don't know
i guess it will have to be
tomorrow
i'll think deeper
about being indian.

SHAUN T. GRIFFIN [B. 1953]

Shaun Griffin has often wondered how to wake America from its slumber. Why do we toler-
ate poverty, hunger, and homelessness? Griffin, who holds a master's degree in counseling, has
dedicated his life to creating a caring community. In 1991 he and his wife, Deborah, founded
Community Chest, a nonprofit organization that directs more than twenty community devel-
opment programs for northwestern Nevada, including hunger relief, shelter, drug and alcohol
counseling, service learning, childhood education, and art and social justice projects. Born and
raised in Southern California, Griffin chose to settle in the old mining town of Virginia City,
where he can see sixty miles, straight east, to a range of purple mountains. A Nevada resident
for more than twenty years, Shaun Griffin "has certainly without question been Nevada's most
important advocate of poetry," avers Robert Blesse, director of the Black Rock Press, noting that
Griffin has taught poetry in the Northern Nevada Correctional Center (editing Razor Wire *for*
fourteen years), has organized the Piñon Poetry Festival, has been a poet-in-the-schools, and
has given readings across the state with TumbleWords, a project of the Nevada Arts Council.
Griffin's Desert Wood: An Anthology of Nevada Poets *(1991) proves unequivocally that poetry*
is alive in Nevada, while his The River Underground: An Anthology of Nevada Fiction *(2001)*
testifies to the vitality of its prose. A gifted translator of Emma Sepúlveda and editor of Joanne
de Longchamps, whose brilliant work he has rescued from oblivion, Griffin is a distinguished
poet in his own right, honored with the Silver Pen Award in 1998. His books of poetry, which
include Snowmelt *(1994),* Bathing in the River of Ashes *(1999), and two chapbooks, flow like*
blood from a soul who daily encounters human suffering but who finds profound sustenance
in Nevada's beauty, in his family, and in poetry itself.

A Place of Stone

    for Ben and Karen

     I come for the wooded dance of the Comstock:
     the piñon pine, harsh as the face of an owl,
     juniper, a scruff beard on the high desert,
     and locust, spent, with purr of cicadas.

     I come alone, in a blue-black forest of night,
     steal my way into the folds of darkness,
     risk ruin under the light of a star. I come
     as so many others must, for that which is missing
     from the stencil of the city: the outline of a face

on the back of a horse, the quiet rocks
that grow and grow in the sun's burnt strokes,
and the pine nuts glazed with sap in the fall.

I come for the fissures that ripple through this land:
the empty spell of a mine shaft, water
dripping in like a slow clock from above;
the breaking, the chipping, the bloody salt smells
that ride the canyons. A trail of ashen dreams
flake the golden skin of Nevada.

I come to fill the fallow contours of my mind
with a place of stone, yet nearly everything
has been stripped from these slopes.
Even the cornflowers cower in the tailings.
Cattle graze on winter roots and a farmer
fingers heat from the stove.
Fences crawl over half-bleached plains,
touch the moon's corrosive light

and I return, a wisp of desert wood.

Trash Run

He hopped a gray prison truck
to the Flint Drive Dump Site,
freedom on a flatbed,
wedged between leaf and carton
for moments unending until
the hydraulic arm lifted,
shot debris to bedsprings
and bicycles bent from hauling.

There in the cool of Carson's refuse
he lay still as rock. The guard
closed in, clicked fingers, and the bed
fell. Dual tires rolled back and forth,
each bag collapsed in a pop
and his eyes, the salty moons
that never rose to ride the road again.

Later that day, the count cleared
save one. They fumbled through archives
to unearth his picture, the sum of years
broken in slow desperate motion.
No time will tell who fed the throttle,
who ordered the tires to roll
the field of Caterpillars and paper.

Those People

Those people on the street
soiled with the grain of hunger
and thrift store bins, those people
lying next to you on cold red bricks
go to work, break bread, and eat
in the plum stairwell of Reno's dry lights.

Those people dream darkness will slip
from the fingers of their children,
and the shelter will stay open one more night.
Those people, hardened in the rafters
of downtown lines, hand their best smiles
to soup kitchen chefs every morning,
drown hope in foolish talk of California,
bus rides, and relatives that curl with each passing
    day.

Those people lying next to you
wear my shoes, your hat, and no name.
Come, let us breathe the steam table
smoking in their eyes.
If mercy can be shown
let us not forget the place-keepers
addled with keys and coffers,
who collect small dreams from children—
football, cribbage, and rag dolls,

we who deduct those people in food bank ledgers,
and still they blow like ice into our lives.

GARY SHORT [B. 1953]

To consider Gary Short's trajectory is to realize that some poets lead wandering lives. Raised in small towns in Calaveras and Placer counties in California, educated in Fresno (BA), Sacramento (MA), and Tempe, Arizona (MFA), Short has held visiting professorships in Norfolk, Virginia, and Fairbanks, Alaska, instructorships in Modesto, California, and Arequipa, Peru, and writer's residencies at the MacDowell Colony for the Arts, the Fine Arts Work Center at Provincetown, and Stanford University. In 2003 he was in Albania collaborating with the poet Luljeta Lleshanaku, and he has lived in Guatemala, on Lake Atitlán. To understand why Short received the 1997 Silver Pen Award for Nevada writers, one has only to read his books of poetry, Theory of Twilight *(1994) and* Flying over Sonny Liston *(1996)—which won the Western States Book Award in 1996—and* 10 Moons and 13 Horses *(2004). "I keep trying to write about something other than Nevada—the moon, coyotes and wild horses—but I look out my door and there they are," he told a journalist. Short taught for six years in Wells and Storey County high schools (1976–82), coedited a pioneering anthology of Nevada poets (*The Nevada Poet, *1981), and was a Nevada Arts Council artist-in-residence from 1985 to 1996. He once lived in the rented office of a closed leach-mining operation in American Flat, Nevada—"leach-front property," he jokes. Short's humor is usually at his own expense, and his humility—in the face of stunning talent and national recognition—can be felt throughout his poetry, which has been praised by reviewers for being "gentle," "compassionate," "honest," and "tender." Having suffered the deaths of his brother, his best friend, and his mother, and the despoliation of places he has loved, Short's work often takes an elegiac tone and attempts to save, if only in memory, people and places he has cared about.*

Toward Morning

The sky sleek as the coat of a blue roan
in the moonquiet of two thousand stars
falling on Fourth Street in Panaca.
The smell of dust in October air.
A horse whinnies, dreams she is the wind.
On highway 319 a haytruck shifts toward Cedar City

and the night grows huge. I remember Basho,
   Deep autumn,
     my neighbors,
      how do they live?—

The high school basketball coach
dreaming a six foot five transfer student;

the county road supervisor, his stubbled face
creased by the white sheet;
the short-order cook at the Silver Cafe
asleep with the smell of onions on her hand.

Flying over Sonny Liston

    Sonny Liston is on all fours,
    trying to rise, a flame of pain
    in the center of his head.

    The crowd noise blurs,
    then distances, as though he is shut
    in a room by himself.

    In his face there is silence.
    His skin glistens with sweat,
    & the glare & flurry of camera flashes

    are far-away lights in his eyes.
    Cassius Clay thin & sharp, stands
    above him, arms a recited W.

    The airplane rises over the cemetery
    where Liston is buried
    next to the runway at McCarran Airport.

    What I recall is his bad press—
    how he learned to box in prison,
    how he hung out with the worst people.
    His violence & his size,

    a film clip of him
    sullenly jumping rope
    to a record of "Night Train."

    A woman in a pink blouse sits next to me.
    Her fingers try to memorize a thick crucifix
    on a chain around her neck.

    She's nervous. But from this safe distance,
    looking out the oval window

& beyond the wing, I see the cross
of the airplane shadowing grave sites.

A boxer knows momentum
can suddenly shift. One blow
changes everything.
The plane lifts. Closing my eyes, I hear

the referee's eight-count, the knockout signaled.
Liston is out of time & still on his knees,
suffering & silent, "Inarticulate

in the way we all are," James Baldwin wrote,
"when more has happened to us
than we know how to express."

In eight seconds an aircraft can bank into
& fly through fists of clouds
above the city of Las Vegas
& the grave of Sonny Liston.

He died alone in a motel room.
His life was nothing like mine,
& so we share a solitariness,

like the passengers on this plane who rise
or fall together
& individually, each with defeats.
The fight for survival is the fight.

What I Believed

Today I brought home a rock
found on the Lake Tahoe shore.
The water has worn
into the rock a face.

I hold it in my hand and think back
to what I believed in my youth:
if I skipped a flat stone
across the skin of the lake

the stone would sing the shape of wind
and water.

And if late at night
I stood under the wandering light of stars
beneath a certain second-story window
near Dayton, Nevada, and took a pebble
and tossed it up and let it click
against the dark glass, the face of a girl
would appear in the black square above.

She'd come out to me and we'd cross the field
through the sweet reek of wet hay
to the neighbor's barn where the horses
were restless with our presence.
It was there that I came to regard
sex as a large, nervous animal.

The girl's father didn't understand
how the flowers were wrecked
beneath his daughter's window,
the broken tiger lilies I'd stepped on.
Afterwards, we laughed that he was so upset,
but maybe those bright lilies
stood for something he believed in.

In the barn, when I lit the votive candle
I'd brought to light the musky dark,
we saw the powder on my jeans,
vivid-orange where my thighs had brushed
the pollen-laden stems of the taller flowers.
Later, I thought the shape of shadows
trembled with the pitch of our excitement.

In the twisting light of candle flame,
she read the smooth skin
of my face with her fingers.
I wouldn't guess
what time could do.
I think I thought I was already
who I was going to be.

Not knowing yet
that the years would shape, change,
and reveal me.

DONALD REVELL [B. 1954]

It may seem ironic that one of America's leading language poets is the son of a man who never learned to read or write, but this fact is not irrelevant to Revell's poetic goals. Simply put, language poets write about the nature of language itself. Paradoxically, through the medium of language Revell aims to arrive at an unmediated experience of the present moment, similar to the prelinguistic awareness of the world that animals have. In his case, however, the impossibility of achieving a prelinguistic vantage point, when one's consciousness has already been so thoroughly shaped by language, leads him to imagine a postlinguistic state. Therefore, using language as an unavoidable tool, Revell seeks to disrupt language and "write my way out of language." Revell freely admits that some of his greatest teachers have been books—linguistic artifacts. He claims to carry three books with him at all times: Thoreau's Walden, *Whitman's* Song of Myself, *and the* New Testament. *Critics have noted these influences in his writing, praising his books* Arcady (2002) *and* My Mojave (2003), *for example, for renewing a poetry of the spirit while also—like Thoreau—displaying an equally strong attachment to the world of nature and fact. Revell has received numerous awards and grants for his nine books, including a Guggenheim, an* NEA, *and a Gertrude Stein Award in Innovative American Poetry. Until 2007 when he was hired by* UNLV, *Revell was a frequent flyer, commuting from his job as a professor at the University of Utah in Salt Lake City back home to the desert outside Las Vegas, where he lives with his wife—poet Claudia Keelan—and their two children. Born in the Bronx, Revell once told an interviewer: "Living in Utah and Nevada, I take my current instruction from snow and sand. They are heavenly forms—substantial and effortless. May poems be so."*

The Little River Wants to Kee

> The little river wants to kee   (P
> Wind romantically transforming the tree   (S
>
>   Us
>
> The joshua tree
> Is a true lily
> It calls and we follow

We descend below
Our hats over the stones
To a dry river bed
And then to a river

Shall we be there
For keeps for
Us

Including the child and his new shoes full of water

My Mojave

Sha-
Dow,
As of
A meteor
At mid-
Day: it goes
From there.

A perfect circle falls
Onto white imperfections.
(Consider the black road,
How it seems white the entire
Length of a sunshine day.)

Or I could say
Shadows and mirage
Compensate the world,
Completing its changes
With no change.

In the morning after a storm,
We used brooms. Out front,
There was broken glass to collect.
In the backyard, the sand
Was covered with transparent wings.
The insects could not use them in the wind
And so abandoned them. Why
Hadn't the wings scattered? Why

Did they lie so stilly where they'd dropped?
It can only be the wind passed through them.

Jealous lover,
Your desire
Passes the same way.

And jealous earth,
There is a shadow you cannot keep
To yourself alone.
At midday,
My soul wants only to go
The black road which is the white road.
I'm not needed
Like wings in a storm,
And God is the storm.

ALIKI BARNSTONE [B. 1956]

Growing up in a family of artists—her father a poet and professor of comparative literature, her Greek mother a painter—Aliki Barnstone began writing poetry at an early age. She made the news as a child prodigy when Macmillan published her book of poems The Real Tin Flower *(1968) when she was twelve. Anne Sexton's introduction called the work "a marvel, . . . in every sense spanking new." To reporters, who descended upon her hometown of Bloomington, Indiana, Barnstone said that she wrote her best poems—"a whole gob of them"—at school during recess. A second collection,* Windows in Providence *(1981), appeared after Barnstone earned a* BA *in semiotics from Brown University, receiving an* MA *in 1983, and a* PHD *from the University of California, Berkeley, in 1995. Barnstone's 1997 poetry collection,* Madly in Love, *nominated for a Pulitzer Prize, shares the concerns of her earliest work—home, family, the seasons, companionship. Gerald Stern noted in her poems a "weird intimacy, the eerie closeness, that absolute confession of soul" reminiscent of Emily Dickinson. Barnstone's recent books include* Wild with It *(2002) and* Blue Earth *(2004). A widely published poet and critic, with a forthcoming book on Emily Dickinson, Aliki Barnstone has also edited* A Book of Women Poets from Antiquity to Now *(1980; 2nd ed. 1992) with her father, Willis Barnstone, and* The Shambhala Anthology of Women's Spiritual Poetry *(2003). For these and other collections, Barnstone translated poems from modern and ancient Greek, Latin, French, Spanish, German, Swedish, Egyptian, Sumerian, Indian, and Chinese. Her translation from the modern Greek,*

The Collected Poems of C. P. Cavafy: A New Translation, appeared to positive reviews in 2006. From 1999 to 2007 Barnstone was a professor of English at the University of Nevada, Las Vegas, in the Creative Writing International Program. Her current book manuscript, Bright Body, contains many Nevada poems, whose imagery includes freeways, lights, subdivisions, and "the same daily blue" sky.

You Pray to Rain Falling on the Desert

>because it is a Sunday where the sky is blue nearly every day
>and you might forget to be sad.
>
>Because you don't sing with a choir, except the quiet
>rain intoning on the backyard patio—
>and the raindrops outside are not the human voices
>you must listen to.
>
>Because in March rains wake up desert flowers
>and globe mallow blooms everywhere—burning bushes
>in the Valley of Fire and vacant lots waiting for gas stations.
>You will see their orange blossoms flaring through your windshield,
>and no voice will say *I am.*
>
>Because the rain will swell Lake Mead with our water for drinking
>and bathtubs and gardens full of thirsty grass, roses, and oleander.
>Because the fatal bacteria will die in treatment plants.
>Because there are no mosquitoes here, no malaria.
>Because the Children's Hospital is stocked with medicine.
>
>Because the rain will wash away dust and misery
>and channel toxins from spent bombs into the ground water.
>
>Because your daughter wanted to walk instead of drive
>and she spun in her orange dress, pointed her pink-sneakered foot,
>and curtseyed in the driveway
>because rain on the desert is a multitude of tender hands
>applauding new life.
>
>It is the eve of war
>and you don't believe the broadcast on radio and on television:
>*I will rid you out of their bondage*
>*and I will redeem you with a stretched out arm,*
>*and with great judgments.**

Because the rain keeps you inward, attending
to the outward hiss of traffic on boulevards.
Because the rain is unclear, a vast gray erasing demarcation.
Because the rain makes you tired of the word because,
tired of causes becoming effects, tired of causes, tired of tired reasons.

*This quotation is from Exodus 6:6, when God speaks to Moses.

The Lights of Las Vegas

I'm driving my daughter to the ice cream shop. She's singing along
the words of a song I listened to half my life ago.

No, this isn't a poem about the past. The full moon
that jangled my dreams a couple of days ago is waning now

and the sky is full of planes, those starloads full of people
I can't imagine—can't help imagining—who read

our valley of lights receding beneath the plane, these mercury lights
guiding me down suburban boulevards, a traffic light winking

red to green, these windows lit with televisions and reading lamps,
swimming pools' blue eyes beaming up at the busy freeway of air,

my headlights pushing aside the darknesses so I see asphalt gleam
like a moonless sea though it's only toxic oil and filth,

so I see some rooms from my car because my daughter's singing
a song called "This Flight Tonight" so I can fly off and see

the altar I made in a milk crate, the candle burning and a yellow rose,
postcards of Frida Kahlo's monkey and skull propped up

against the honeycomb of royal blue plastic. Yes, I lay on a futon
on the floor, mourning the end of—I don't want to name it.

I was alone and couldn't sleep. No, this poem isn't turning back.
Outside the rain-sloppy streets hissed a prayer to the tires

who ran over them. Inside I showered till the hot water gave out.
Have you ever tried to end the past? Made a torch of love letters?

I was free on my bed. I could invite anyone to lie down,
and maybe I did. If I slept, I dreamt my bed was outside

where dogs snarled at the chainlink fence and every bark
was a star in my ear. If I cried, the rain didn't let up all day,

all night, all day. If the sun shone, I saw the double clearly
while my dreams walked beside me. There's no self here.

There's no story here. No, this poem won't confess.
This poem is in couplets because it is not about love,

because it knows that form is the body urging
and the mind muttering make love make love make love.

I'm driving to the ice cream store with my daughter.
I see her dreamy look in the rear view mirror as she sings.

Outside the car windows the brightest constellation of stars
is called a flight path. Inside the planes the tourists spot

this valley, a light-spangled carpet unrolling to their hotels,
and they burst out, "Hey, is that the Strip? I can't believe it!"

Here in Vegas nothing is old but the mountains silently observing.
Here is the brand-new ice cream shop. See the patio of concrete tables,

the umbrellas with misting systems ! cooling the air, the parents
sitting on benches while the kids press their hands to strip mall windows,

yell delight when the owner of the closed toy store
throws open his doors, and all the children run inside

—my daughter, too—and we follow them into the brave new world
where we rediscover spaceships, supermen, baby dolls,

scooters, posters and bath toys and flashcards that teach the alphabet
and how to read. This poem is not retrospective.

This poem is driving home past subdivisions and houses surrounded
by walls to keep neighbor from neighbor, to keep the desert away

from automatic lawn sprinklers and drip irrigation, to block wind and fire.
This poem is half a mile from my home where all the streets are the same,

a grid of lights expanding into panic when I lose the narrative
of my driving and my star is one of millions in the galaxy on the ground,

when for a flash of mind I'm stuck in the present with no direction—
this sudden monotony, this now built of cinder block, stucco, and tile.

Freeway Love Poem

Tonight these lines talk to me and you. I don't know what will come next.
Listen

to quiet and to the sad, waning moon
covered in dreary veils. I understand

her lonely countenance, her gravity,
there above the billboards' come-ons,

the woman lounging in a black lace bra
before a platter of sushi, and ready

to share her fleshy feast, the illumined
icons of the Wheel of Fortune, promises

of riches and luck for all the unlucky
speeding crazily across

each others' lanes, desperate for their exit,
regardless, regardless.

Oh, I know better than to converse
with the moon or call it a she,

claim to understand its expression,
which is just craters on a sphere of stone.

Because I'm in a vehicle flashing along
the utopian freeway to a new tenor

of thought. The radio's off. And I listen
to something I call *myself*

when I should be erasing *I,* should be
shutting those voids, the moon's eyes.

I love you. You question
whether the soul has a mate.

I take the back way home,
to the extent there is a back way,

still some dark spaces,
where shadows

of horses rock on desert dust under
only a few streetlights in a city

that shines brighter than the moon, my love,
where nature barely exists in our racing

minds, where epiphany is a projection
onto a gray screen or billboard maybe,

biochemistry or a fluke of genetic
inheritance. Yet I love you, though love

is dumb. Dum de dum dum. Doomed and loony
old moon (I mean me). I'm too sensitive

to sounds, which I adore and make me mad.
I can hear what you're *not* saying. Say it,

damn it. Because, as the saying goes,
to close the distance between us,

I'm driving too fast, driving! to the end
of my poem or the road

home (as if there were one), though
I want no end, no closure.

I listen for you to come close, your soul
to speak out of nothing or things I see—

supermarkets and full parking lots
below the persistent moon

that keeps following along.
I can almost feel you in my breath,

my solitary breath, boxed in by glass.

GAILMARIE PAHMEIER [B. 1957]

Gailmarie Pahmeier engages an audience, be they beer-slugging baseball fans in a 4th Street bar in Reno, notebook-toting college students, dusty ranchers in the rural West, underserved communities in the Alaska Interior, or inmates of a Nevada prison. When she walks into a room with her cowboy boots, swishy skirt, faded Levi jacket, and jangling silver jewelry, and when she gives you that look and begins flirting in that deep, sensuous voice, reading poems about women and the men they love, the poetry will flush cheeks. As a reader, Pahmeier is provocative, and her poetry about the "world of the waitress" and "the unsung lives of the pink collar workers" awakens something tender in her audience. Calling her work "crafted gossip, but gossip informed by compassion and forgiveness," and employing female voices, Pahmeier's work is accessible. Indeed, readers become attached to the characters of her narrative poetry, especially Emma, who appears so often that people ask Pahmeier how Emma is doing. Joking that she is a "Nevadan born in exile," Pahmeier always knew that she was meant to live in the West. Nevertheless, reviewers describe her work as having a southern sensibility, perhaps reflecting Pahmeier's blue-collar upbringing in the Ozarks and MFA *degree from the University of Arkansas. Her books include* With Respect for Distance *(1992),* What Emma Loves *(1995), and* The House on Breakaheart Road *(1998). Pahmeier has won many awards for her poetry—including the Silver Pen Award in 1999—and for her teaching at the University of Nevada, Reno, where she has taught since 1985, coaching hundreds of writing students to trust their own responses and "lie their way to the truth."*

The Promise of Good Food

Emma sizzles through Sparks, through Fernley
and Wadsworth and on through Oreana
and Mill City. By the time she gets
to Lovelock, she knows he'll be worried,
think she's on her way to Elko

where a serial killer haunts
the highway. But she's not going that far,
not this time. See, when Emma flies, she flies
toward food. By dark she'll make Winnemucca,
the Hotel Martin where she'll share chilled
red wine, wet salad, tongue soup, porterhouse

with people she'd never have imagined
knowing—a cowboy perhaps or a retired
couple from Sault Ste. Marie. They'll laugh

a bit and tell stories, and all
the while Emma will know that he's at home

searching through her stuff. When she takes
her second helping, he will have found
the red lace panties she's never worn,
the antique tray of Mexican rings,
the photographs of her godmother's
handsome husbands: the one who died

of gunshot, the one who fell from his horse,
the one that woman left by bus
for the city. By sherbet, he'll be
hunting for her diaries, little
locked books she pretends to keep. He'll tire

by early light, sleep heavily
and love her hard when she gets home.
This is just the way it is, and Emma
pleasures in the patterns of their life,
knows he'll stay on as long as it takes,
as long as it takes him to find something.

When You Love Someone for a Long Time

—for Ruth

He has planned this road trip for no reason
except he loves her and it is summer
and he needs something to do. She sits beside
him in the truck, a basket of apples
on the floorboard, a map across her lap.
He loves Nevada, loves leaving their Midwest
home for the spare embrace of desert, open
light, loves the way the land here allows
a man to feel as if he has potential.

They've driven through Currant and Warm Springs
and he has promised that when they get
to Tonopah he will buy her dinner
in the old hotel where gamblers and boxers

have left their stories and the ghost
of a jilted woman in a red dress
wanders the third floor. He tells her next time
they will travel out to Tuscarora
or down to Boundary Peak. He does love

the land, this man. He does the driving, most
of the talk. He's trying to teach her things,
bring her closer to the world outside
of kitchen and bedroom and yard. She listens,
her hand resting on his inner thigh.
If she spoke there would be things she could tell,
things a man just somehow misses when he
travels, no matter how large his heart:

Somewhere in Smith Valley there is a road
called Breakaheart, and along its washboard
rests a greying farmhouse. She has often
imagined the woman who must live there,
perhaps her name is Hannah, how her husband
may have one day taken down the gun
and driven off. Although she would be sad,
Hannah wouldn't be surprised to hear the hounds,
the good men come to tell her she's now alone.
For three days Hannah neglects to brush her hair,
but on the fourth she is up, hanging
laundry, forgiving everyone she's ever
known and looking up into the sweet, strong sun.

But he drives, hums along to the country
stations, talks, ask her if steak will be good
tonight, a fat rare one. She smiles and nods.
These road trips are worth their dust, their
unfamiliar beds, their exaggerated
hope. These are the only times she lives
in long, luxurious stretches of time,
when she lives, utterly complete, without him.

CLAUDIA KEELAN [B. 1959]

Claudia Keelan, winner of the 2001 Silver Pen Award and numerous national poetry awards, is known as a L-A-N-G-U-A-G-E poet who is intensely aware of the limitations and potential of human language. Keelan uses poetry to push language to evolve into an instrument that can express what she regards as the greatest idea ever made and articulated, the idea that "I is another." As Keelan explained to interviewer Bill Stobb, part of the logic of her poetry is to commit grammatical and syntactical errors, so that "I" and "you" will be suffused; accordingly, her experimental poetry is also politically engaged with civil rights activism, attempting to "change the language for the future." She strongly agrees with John Keats's notion of "negative capability," that is, that the poet is capable of having no identity in order to fill in for and give expression to other people and things. She has seen this process enacted in great leaders, such as Martin Luther King Jr. and Gandhi, and she strives in her books of poetry—Refinery (1994), The Secularist (1997), Utopic (2000), The Devotion Field (2004)—by pushing and interrogating language, to move "towards a possible language where the community can exist," a world in which, as she told Stobb, "I and you are not the same, but are together." Having grown up in Half Moon Bay, California, studied music and English at Humboldt State University, earned an MFA at the University of Iowa, and lived in Boston and Memphis, Keelan now finds herself feeling protective of the deserts of southern Nevada, with its history of bomb testing and its current unabashed development. Some of her poems are written out of an almost primordial urge to save Nevada, where she has lived since 1996, when she began her current professorship at UNLV.

Blue Diamond

I am virtually gone

                              author or victim
I wanted   in you   to be nothing
      to be a solitude
attached   by emptiness   to everything

Last night   one coyote
            this morning two   They were nature

Keep the children close
          author or victim
The desert looks flat, lies
    flat   what does realism save?
They were animals running across the surface
They are gone

Relinquish

The real world was inaccessible
to us *noumenon, noumenon.*
Not only not real
but not significant,
noumenon, noumenon.

The end of the century THE MEADOWS,
end of THE MEADOWS
a desert, vision itself
a mirage, *noumenon,*
noumenon. The Illusionist

leashes his tiger. The Illusionist
is his tiger. You think
to resist it
noumenon, noumenon?

You vanished an hour ago.
What is lost
in many windows.
Roaring fogging the glass.

TWELVE

ANYTHING IS POSSIBLE

Contemporary Fiction

Because fiction is a mainstay of literature, works of fiction appear liberally throughout this anthology. Stories with clear affinities to specific places or times are located in chapters that most closely reflect their content, whether they be tales from the mining frontier, stories about Reno or Las Vegas, or fictional treatments of nuclear controversies. What we have in *this* chapter are stories that seem to require a category of their own, based not on locale or content but, rather, on their genre, contemporary fiction. Some critics might prefer that *all* writers of contemporary prose—fiction and nonfiction—be in this chapter, among their peers. I invite readers who share this opinion to use the chronological list of contents, located in the appendix. A glance at that list impresses one with the extraordinary blossoming of Nevada writing in recent years, creating a veritable Nevada Renaissance.

Beyond the fact that all the pieces collected in this chapter are fiction, published in the last thirty years, and set in Nevada, we might ask what else, if anything, they have in common, for they vary considerably in mode and intent. Eudora Welty, a master of the short story, once pronounced that "human life is fiction's only theme," an interesting remark, considering that most of Welty's fiction is set in Mississippi and she is esteemed as a major southern writer. The novelist Willa Cather once wrote that "there are only two or three human stories, and they go on repeating themselves as fiercely as if they had never happened before," again an intriguing statement, given Cather's strong association with the midwestern prairie, immortalized in novels that evoke a strong sense of place. These remarks might lead one to conclude that place is merely an incidental element of fiction, a stage set that lends veracity to a fundamentally universal human drama. This line of reasoning could be amply supported by the stories collected here. Frank Bergon, for example, highlights the tension between individual freedom and the law. Teresa Jordan explores the nuances of an extramarital attraction. Art Gibney reveals the mixed emotions of a young man upon the death of his father. H. Lee Barnes studies the maneuvers of a powerful man. These basic human stories could be set just about anywhere at any time. On one level, then, the stories gathered here all appeal to human experience broadly and transcend their anchoring in Nevada.

Still, it is not incidental that these stories are set in Nevada, for a universal property of human experience is that it takes place *in* place. As Eudora Welty further stated, "fiction is all bound up in the local. The internal reason for that is surely that *feelings* are bound up in place." We might ask, then, what is specifically local about these stories? The answers are easily apprehended. Bergon's imagined clash between individual freedom and the law is based on the true story of a poacher who murdered two game wardens, a confrontation that resonates with Nevadans' ambivalence about government. In Jordan's story, a white woman ranch owner is drawn to a hired Mexican ranch hand in northern Nevada; the story thus reflects upon the changing demographics of Nevada ranching. Gibney's young man sells the family ranch—located near the Nevada Test Site—when his father dies, the story a witness to both the loss-of-the-family-ranch trend in Nevada and the state's weird conjunction of ranching and radioactivity. The self-made man in Barnes's novel is cut closely to the mold of real-life Benny Binion, owner of the Horseshoe casino.

These stories, then, encourage us to think about how human nature realizes itself through the particularities of place and time. And just as they explore widely shared aspects of human experience, so too they illuminate distinctive elements of Nevada experience, such as the lives of Basque immigrant families and modern-day Indians, the entrenched but tenuous ranching culture, the "big silence" of the Great Basin desert, the people behind the gaming industry, and the strangeness of living near off-limits, top-secret military installations. Nevada literature likewise probes the less tangible but no less distinctive themes of luck and law, isolation and illusion. Bernard Schopen's opening lines to *The Big Silence* make a good warning label for contemporary Nevada fiction:

In Nevada, anything is possible.

In Nevada, nothing is as it seems.

In Nevada, nothing abounds, nothing signifies, anything is possible.

ROBERT LAXALT [1923–2001]

"My father was a sheepherder, and his home was the hills." So begins Robert Laxalt's master-
piece, Sweet Promised Land *(1957), the story of his Basque father's immigration to America.*
Nevada's most distinguished writer spent his first years in sheep camps of the American West,
speaking Basque, later moving with his family to Carson City, where he learned English and
attended school. While his outdoorsman father returned to sheepherding, Laxalt's mother, also
a Basque immigrant, ran a small hotel and raised their six children. Laxalt attended a Jesuit
college in California, interrupted his studies to serve in World War II, and completed his degree
on a GI bill at the University of Nevada, Reno, where he met his wife, Joyce. After graduating,
Laxalt became a newspaper reporter in Carson City, writing magazine articles on the side in
the pre-dawn hours of the morning. Frequently his articles featured Nevada, notably "The
Other Nevada," the rural hinterland "that few people see, where personal freedom and the
chance to be an individual thrive in an uncrowded landscape." Sweet Promised Land was an
immediate success, triggering a surge of Basque pride that spawned the first National Basque
Festival in Sparks, Nevada, prototype for similar festivals held throughout the West today. In
1961 Laxalt helped to found the University of Nevada Press, directing it for more than twenty
years. He was instrumental in establishing the university's Basque Studies Program in 1966,
and he was a beloved writing teacher at UNR, which created the Robert Laxalt Distinguished
Writers Program in 2004. Despite a demanding career, Laxalt wrote seventeen books, earning
two Pulitzer Prize nominations, numerous national honors, and induction into the Nevada
Writers Hall of Fame. Laxalt's spare, elegant style has led readers to call him "Nevada's answer
to Ernest Hemingway," and his preeminent literary expression of Basque culture won him
Spain's prestigious Tambor de Oro (Golden Drum Award). The following excerpt is taken from
the autobiographical novel The Basque Hotel *(1989), the first novel in Laxalt's Basque family*
trilogy, which also includes Child of the Holy Ghost *(1992) and* The Governor's Mansion
(1994).

from *The Basque Hotel*

When they reached the depot, it was to see the black, steaming hulk of the v & t
already at the city limits on its daily run to Reno. Dodging the rumbling handcarts
pushed by men in black cloth arm gauntlets and little caps, they streaked across
the wooden platform to the tracks. With trembling hands, Pete placed his penny
and Tony his nails on the track. The v & t let go an ear-splitting blast of warning
and they leaped back onto the platform. The engine rumbled dutifully over the
penny and nails and came to a stop with a great hiss of steam. Mike arrived in time
to stand with Pete and Tony in the wet boiler-smelling vapor that rose up around

them like clouds. From his high seat, the engineer in his cap and red bandanna wagged a finger and shouted something incomprehensible.

When the steam had evaporated, they went to the side of the depot to begin their patient wait for the train's departure. Old man Castle, who had been retired from the railroad, was there as always to observe the coming and going of the train with watery eyes and a sad, lost face. Sam the butcher had come down the street to watch, too. Oblivious of the grimaces of the boys, he stood wiping his hands on his blood-smeared apron.

"Oh Christ! Those bastards again," Sam muttered aloud, and Pete turned his head to see whom Sam the butcher was talking about.

Two men in business suits and snap-brim hats were getting off the train. Their faces were stern and intent, and they glanced suspiciously to the right and left as they stepped onto the platform. One of them was thin, with wire-rimmed glasses and a bitter mouth, as if he had tasted something bad.

Sam the butcher noticed Pete for the first time. He leaned over and said ominously into Pete's ear. "You better tell your folks the Prohis are in town." He turned to go and whispered back conspiratorially, "I'll pass the word downtown."

Pete felt his face freeze and the breath catch in his throat. He did not know what the word Prohi stood for, but he knew that it was a word filled with terror and ruin and nightmares of jail. Without a word to Tony, he grasped Mike by the hand and fled over the depot platform and out into the street.

When they reached the hotel, Tristant the sheepherder was standing out in front. Tristant was in good humor. He tried to tease Pete by blocking the doorway. Pete screamed at him and Tristant stood aside, his expression gone sober with the awareness of trouble. When they were inside the hotel, Pete let go of little Mike and ran down the length of the long dining room. The table was already set for the boarders' dinner, and there were wine glasses in front of each plate. Pete scooped up two of the wine glasses on his way through the swinging doors.

The kitchen was sweltering and his mother's face was wet with perspiration when she turned away from the stove. Whatever she was going to say to him for his noisy entrance was stilled when she saw the wine glasses he was holding.

"Prohis!" Pete gasped.

His mother's hand went to her head and her body swayed as if she were going to faint. Then, with an effort of will that shook her frame like a leaf in the wind, she straightened. "Inside?"

Pete shook his head. "Depot!"

Her eyes closed and fluttered open again. "Lock the front door," she said, and then thought better of it. "No! Go tell your father!" Gathering up her long white apron, she ran into the dining room. Pete waited until he heard her footsteps stop.

When the lock on the front door clicked shut, Pete took the back route through the bedrooms into the saloon. His big brother, Leon, was sprawled on a bed and his two sisters were playing jacks on the floor. He paused only long enough to shout, "Prohis! Put the wine glasses away!" He caught one glimpse of Leon raising himself bolt upright on the bed and the blanching faces of his sisters, and then Pete was gone through the back door.

His father, black haired and tall, was standing behind the high old bar in the saloon, serving whiskey in shot glasses to a few politicians and Mizoo, the big cowboy with the ten-gallon hat. Pete was not afraid of Mizoo, but he was intimidated by the politicians in their suits and neckties and shined, knobby shoes. He stood in the doorway, trying to catch his father's attention. It was a while before his father recognized the agonized plea in Pete's face. He left the group at the bar and stood over Pete. "What's the matter?"

"Prohis!" Pete whispered.

"Why didn't you say so?" his father said fiercely. He took two long steps to the bar and spoke in low warning. As one, the men downed their shots of whiskey and passed through the intervening door into the dining room. Pete's father rinsed out the glasses and put them away in a drawer. Whipping the bottle of whiskey off the bar, he corked it and went into the bathroom. Pete heard the splash of the bottle sinking into the water cabinet on the wall high above the toilet and went limp with relief. The peremptory knocking by the Prohis on the front door of the hotel did not bother him. They were safe now.

. . . .

It was the strangest dinner Pete could ever remember. The boarders sipped their soup grumpily and with little conversation. His mother served the rich beef stew, apologizing to the boarders and muttering that it was a scandal to serve a French dinner like this without wine. Tristant the sheepherder nodded in solemn agreement. His father sat at the head of the table, scowling and speaking to no one.

The Prohis came back when the stew was being served. They looked thwarted and angry, and they were almost rude when they asked Pete's mother if they could eat dinner. Pete glanced apprehensively toward the head of the table. His father's hands were clenched into fists beside his plate and the murderous look was in his eyes again. He might have done something violent if Pete's mother had not put her hand warningly on his shoulder.

Neither the big cowboy, Mizoo, nor Mickey McCluskey, who was an old prospector, were to be put off so easily. Mizoo at least had had his shot of whiskey before dinner, but Mickey McCluskey had arrived too late, and he felt his loss sorely. A puckish gleam of revenge shone in his eyes.

"What a terrible thing it is, this goddam Prohibition," he said in his Irish brogue. "A man can't even wash the dust out of his throat properly after a hard day's work. It's the saddest thing in town, I'm telling ye."

Aghast, Pete leaned over to peek at the Prohis. Both of them had stiffened, and the thin one with the wire-rimmed glasses looked as if he had heard blasphemy.

Mizoo set down his knife and fork carefully on his plate. His eyes met Mickey McCluskey's across the table, and then narrowed. "Well, there's some as knows how to get all the booze they wants," he drawled.

"Ye don't say!" said Mickey McCluskey.

"I do say," said Mizoo.

"And where would that be, lad?"

"Not in a house like this," drawled Mizoo. "It's a respectable place. Downright too respectable for my tastes."

"We all know that," said Mickey McCluskey. "But you're not answering my question."

"Well, I hear tell," drawled Mizoo, "the ones who got all the booze are the Prohis."

There was a clatter of a fork from the end of the table, but Pete did not dare look. Keeping his eyes riveted on his plate, he pretended not to hear what was going on.

"That makes sense," said Mickey McCluskey. "Indeed it do. But how does one go about getting acquainted with them Prohi boys?"

"Aw, that's easy," said Mizoo. "You just keep your eyes peeled for a Presbyterian whose face says he's out to reform the world. You can spot 'em every time."

"And what d'ye do when you've spotted one?" said Mickey McCluskey innocently.

"You just get 'em aside and make your proposition."

"D'ye mean offer them money?" said Mickey McCluskey. "That don't seem to me to be hardly legal."

"Aw!" said Mizoo. "Everybody knows that's how they make their money. They make a raid, they sell the booze."

There was a harsh scraping of chairs on the wooden floor, and this time, Pete dared to look. The two Prohis were on their feet. One of them was putting money for the dinner on the table, and the other, the one with the wire-rimmed glasses, looked as if he were going to be sick. His mouth worked like a fish out of water and then he said in a constricted voice, "We will have you know that we are Presbyterian agents." He faltered, "I mean Prohibition agents."

"Ye don't say!" said Mickey McCluskey, his eyes alight as if in genuine surprise.

"Pleased to have ye with us, I'm sure. And would ye be telling me if you've got some booze for sale? I'll make ye a fair offer, I'm that thirsty."

Pete did not watch the Prohis leave. He was staring at Mickey McCluskey and Mizoo, unashamed of the worship he knew was in his eyes.

. . . .

Mickey McCluskey and Mizoo had done for the Prohis in their fashion at dinner, but Pete still needed to strike a blow against the government before the day ended, for what it had made his mother suffer.

Since it was a family affair, he had tried to recruit his big brother, Leon, as his accomplice. Leon, whom their mother considered the only one in the family with no nonsense in his head, had argued that the Prohis were federal government and Pete's intended victim was state government, which didn't have anything to do with Prohibition.

Pete had shouted at him that it was *all* government, federal or state, and that it was *his* mother, too, who had suffered, but Leon had walked away saying the whole idea was pretty silly. So Pete had recruited Tony, who didn't have to have revenge explained to him.

It was dusk and they were huddled like conspirators behind the trunk of an elm that was black and bleeding with summer sap. They had made their way there by a devious route, creeping along the iron fence with its spear-tipped points, following the night shade of other elms, and sprinting across those patches of open grass that the moonlight had gotten to.

All that lay between them and the capitol's big doors was a short stretch of sidewalk and a flight of stone steps. On his hands and knees, Pete crept along the sidewalk and up the stone steps. When he reached the doors, he raised himself up just enough to peer over the dividing line between wood and glass. In order to see through the glass, he had to cup his hands alongside his eyes like a horse with blinkers. They were in luck and he dropped down again and waved his arm to Tony in a signal.

They edged through one of the doors, and Pete said quiet thanks in his heart to the janitor who had finally gotten around to oiling the hinges. But he was also afraid now for the first time, because of the presence of the white-haired watchman at the crossing of the corridors. The fact that the watchman was asleep with his chair tipped back against the wall did not allay Pete's fears, because after all he was a man with a man's hard hands and if he woke up too soon, there would be the dickens to pay.

But the watchman did not wake up until they had made it on tiptoe to the crossing of the corridors. They turned the corner undetected and saw in front of them the long corridor with marble floors and marble walls gleaming in the half light. The corridor stretched invitingly all the long way to the other doors at the side entrance.

Pete knew the watchman would come awake in a hurry when they started to run, but that was unimportant now. They poised themselves like sprinters. "Go!" hissed Pete, and they went. The leather heels that they had supplemented with brass taps cracked with the staccato rattle of machine gun fire, and the echoes bounced with purest ecstasy off the marble walls.

The worry of the watchman was behind them, but there was another obstacle to pass, and Tony shouted out in a strangled voice, "Don't look! Don't look!"

But that was the best insurance that they would look. And both of them turned their heads and looked upwards at the dead old man with a long gray-streaked beard and furious eyes staring down out of the dark oil portrait where he had been fixed in time. With moans of fear, they hurled themselves against the doors and scrambled into the safety of the night.

By the time they had fled down the sidewalk and through the aperture in the iron fence, they had forgotten their fear. The dark expanse of grass and trees, the domed fortress of stone, the fearful portrait of a dead old man Governor, and even the night watchman's hoarsely-shouted threats of things to come were all behind them now, and could hurt them no longer.

When they parted, Tony at a trot because it was past curfew at the Orphans Home, Pete sauntered casually down Main Street to the little hotel, reflecting on the day.

It had been long and puzzling. But at least it had started out right with the sunrise and ended right with the coming of darkness and his blow against authority. He sensed now that vengeance was a part of his makeup that he could do nothing about, but he was not sure whether he liked that. Everything else could bear thinking about when he was in bed. Somewhere within Pete, he felt a vague awareness of lessons learned and a premonition that he was beginning to discover his world.

DAVID KRANES [B. 1937]

David Kranes, who has written many plays and stories set in Nevada, has never actually resided in Nevada. Instead, from his home in Salt Lake City, Kranes has made many forays into Nevada, where he relishes assuming another state of mind every time he crosses the border from the "state" of Utah into the "state" of Nevada. "If you can 'cross over,' you can change," he explains,

"If you can assume another 'state,' you can assume another life: reimagine yourself." Nevada invites players to escape their everyday identity and be transported to a destination of fantasy, Kranes believes. Stories, likewise, transport readers to the world of "what if." Although certainly out of the ordinary, it is not inexplicable, then, that Kranes is both a writer and a consultant for casino space design. In both endeavors, what he seeks—in a world that has become increasingly technological and rational—is a means of accessing the mythic, providing a place to experience "the wild, the ecstatic and outrageous." He aims his writing, to quote from theorist of play Johan Huizinga, "somewhere between the barely imaginable and the clearly impossible." He has written five novels, two books of stories, and many plays, including the Nevada-set works Nevada, *starring John Ritter in its Mark Taper Forum production;* Keno Runner: A Romance *(1989); and* Low Tide in the Desert: Nevada Stories *(1996). Originally an eastern boy, Kranes earned his* PHD *from the Yale School of Drama and moved west in 1967 to teach twentieth-century theater, fiction writing, and play writing at the University of Utah, where, in a career spanning more than thirty years, he won every teaching award offered by the university. His plays have been performed in many major theaters in the United States and abroad, and for fourteen years he served as artistic director for the prestigious Sundance Playwrights' Lab.*

The Phantom Mercury of Nevada

This is not science fiction. This is real! I swear. Real as light spreading over the desert, real as thunder in the Tuscaroras. Real as friendship: me and Ross and LaVelle. Real as any Mercury that ever grew to being in Detroit, its ignition firing, its spoked wheels making a blur, its radio blaring an all-night station miles away. Real as losing a nickel in a slot machine, or a dog under the wheels of a backing Bronco. *Real*—and such a mystery!

Still, I vowed I would keep it to myself. And I made LaVelle swear. I said, "LaVelle—whatever happens; if you and I get married or don't get married; if you decide to go off to Winnemucca and sing with that group at the Star; or if you go with Mr. Forbes to Dallas—whatever. Please! Don't tell!" I had taken her on my trail bike up Mount Lewis and we had spent the night there, "engaged." The sun, blood-red, was just climbing in the east, beyond Dunphy, and reaching toward our own streets in Battle Mountain. I took a bluish-veined rock and nearly crushed my left pinkie finger to impress upon LaVelle that I meant what I said. *It was real! Ross Haine was missing.* That was all we knew or should ever say. He'd gone *off*. Maybe he'd gone to be a busboy, down at Stockman's in Elko, like he sometimes said he would. But we should never breathe a word about what we felt had happened to Ross with the Phantom Mercury. Who knew? And LaVelle cried. And she sucked away the blood from my struck pinkie. And she said, "Yes, Jason! I promise! Yes!" But now LaVelle's gone. And my dreams are just about exploding. So . . .

My parents own the Owl Motel on Front Street. I live in unit 23; my younger brother, Richie, lives in unit 17; and my parents room behind the office. We're never full, but the motel, I guess, makes money; I've never heard anyone complain. I clerk seven to midnight, Mondays, Wednesdays, and Fridays; Richie, Tuesdays and Thursdays. And when my Grandfather Tombes comes up to visit from Arizona, *he* always clerks. We chip in. It really used to be fun. I could watch the Zenith or have Ross Haine over and we could both watch the Zenith. And checking people in, that was interesting. One time a man had driven all the way without stopping from Guatemala, South America. "Is this *the* Battle Mountain?" he asked. "Battle Mountain turquoise?" And I told him yes, it was; and he just lit up. And then I told him that I cut stones myself, that I had some really nice green-and-brown spiderwebbed pieces and a brand-new diamond micro drill and an MT-4s compact tumbler; and we talked rocks. He was a dark man. But now, of course, my shift is terrible. All the stuff on the Zenith is about Death. And Ross is gone. And now LaVelle. And so about all there is to do is sit there, scared really, wondering if the Phantom Mercury is going to come down again out of the Tuscarora Mountains.

I never want to drive. It sounds funny to say that, because I always wanted to. I mean, I'd be going to bed in my unit at maybe one AM, and a guest would pull his Pontiac or Chevy in and the lights would burn through my curtains, and I'd think, *God! Three more years!* Then: *Two more!* Then: *A year and a half!* Then: *November!* And I would actually *dream* about this one particular Torino, three lanes wide, with its high beams on, climbing through the Humboldts toward Sparks. But now—Jeez!

Some cattle went. That was first. A family named Pollito had a small range on the Dunphy side of Battle Mountain up Rock Creek. And they started missing head. Their son, Lyle, knew Richie and Richie told me.

"How many are gone?" I asked.

"Six."

The next day Richie said eight. And the next, eleven. I talked to Ross Haine, and he and I took our bikes up to the Pollitos' land. It was early September, dry, the north creek barely running. Everything seemed brittle. And there was a flinty smell in the air.

We parked. Ross had gotten a quart of beer and we opened that. We sat down by some yews. We knew something was going to happen. We didn't say anything to each other before, but we talked about it afterward—and we *knew.* We picked yewberries, rolled them around between our fingers and tossed them, and watched the sun fall somewhere beyond Reno.

"Would you ever shoot anyone?" Ross asked me.

The insects and the tree frogs had started up. I didn't say anything; I just threw about three yewberries into where it was dark.

"I hope I get to be in a war," Ross went on. He said it felt like he and I were on sentry duty. We'd both shot chukar and grouse. I wasn't sure what made him think of it.

But then . . . both of us leaned forward and looked up. Neither talked. There was something . . . I don't even know if I can describe it any better than that: something high and far away in the Tuscaroras. And it was coming down. And it was coming down . . . and it was coming down . . . and it was coming down. And we were both leaning forward straining for it. And whatever it was—we never knew what that night—*increased;* that was the word we could both agree on; it *increased.* And it increased enough so that at one point we weren't looking up and away any more; we were looking all around us. "Shit! I wish I'd brought my gun!" I heard Ross whisper. And then we found ourselves looking up again—because, whatever it was, it was going home, up, away, *decreasing* now, ridge to ridge, canyon to canyon.

The next day Richie told me that three more of the Pollitos' steers had gone, and I didn't say anything to him about our being up there. I just found Ross.

We tried to agree. We tried to write down some things that both of us could say we'd seen or felt, or that had happened. We made a list. "Rumbling" was on the list, slight rumbling; we thought a while about the word "vibration," but "rumbling" won. I was near a slide once, a rock slide close to Tonopah, and it was like that. And there was a . . . we hit upon the word "fluorescent": a fluorescent glow. It wasn't bright. We argued that it could have been just kind of the after-sunset glow, but then we had to say that it wasn't; it was whiter, greener, like the light in Mr. Iatammi's welding shop, seen maybe a mile away. And there was a chemical smell, just *slight.* All of these things were just slight; it took us nearly three hours just to get the four of them down, to agree. But we'd both coughed at least once. So Ross wrote "sulphur." And the last item was the weirdest of all. I mentioned it kind of as a joke, but then Ross agreed and said that, right, his teeth had hurt him too—when whatever-it-was was the closest. So that was it: a rumbling, a fluorescent glow, sulphur, and our teeth hurt.

LaVelle and I were friends. It hadn't gotten physical yet, except, I know, in my head. Some of the kids called her Frenchie—LaVelle Barrett—which was kind of exciting anyway; but she had a really nice singing voice and played okay on the guitar. We joked. She kept asking when I was going to take her to my motel, and I'd say something back and we'd laugh. But we also talked about serious things. Her father had shot a man, and the man had died, and so her father was serving out a term for it in the Wyoming state prison. LaVelle opened up to me about it one day when we were walking by the Reese River, and she cried, and I just held her and let her, and I guess that was the main reason for our friendship. Her mother was strict. She made LaVelle keep pretty exact hours. Her mother dealt at the Owl Club Casino (no relationship to our Owl Motel), but she always checked on her. Anyway, after Ross and I experienced what we experienced that first night, I told LaVelle.

"Take me!"

"Well . . ."

"I'd like to see!"

I spoke to Ross. He said sure, but let's the three of us keep it at that. So we decided on the following Thursday night.

We went up at just the same time. LaVelle had a horse named Tar (she was supposed to just be out riding), and we met her at a certain place, east on I-80; and then the three of us, on Tar—poor Tar! It was crowded—rode on up.

It wasn't quite sundown, so we investigated. "What if Mr. Pollito sees us and shoots at us?" LaVelle asked. I said, "I'll just tell him I'm Richie's brother and that we're trying to catch his rustlers. He'll be grateful." Then LaVelle found a rock with a long white-silver scrape mark along it.

"That's paint!" Ross said.

"No," I disagreed. "That's just bruised quartz crystals in the rock."

"The hell you say!" Ross, for some reason, got angry. "That's paint!"

At sunset we all gathered back at the same yew bushes. Ross pointed high to the north. "It'll start up there," he told LaVelle. LaVelle looked at me. She started stroking Tar's neck. She fed him a piece of sugar. Then it began, just like the time before—everything on our list, *everything*: rumbling, fluorescent glow, sulphur, our teeth hurt. Tar spooked. For a minute we thought he was going to run off. He shook his head. It must have hurt *his* teeth. LaVelle had taken my hand. It made me sweat a little. "Gol! What was that?" she asked.

The next day Richie told me, "Another steer!"

We knew we were on to something. Ross, LaVelle, and I talked. We wanted to see whether we could add anything else to our list. "Did it trace a path?" I asked them because I sort of had that in my mind.

"Yeah!" Ross said. His eyes just got *large*.

"Yes," LaVelle nodded.

"Coming down—and going up!" Ross moved his hand in a kind of oval.

So that was the fifth thing on our list: "an oval path."

We tried to decide whether we should tell Mr. Pollito what we were up to, so that he wouldn't pick us off by accident—you know, shoot us. But LaVelle was concerned about her mother. So we agreed that we would just all try very hard to be careful. I went walking with LaVelle after our discussion that day, and we wandered into the woods and stood for a while and kissed. It was the very first time. I was very aware of birds there, for some reason, and I asked LaVelle later if she was. "Not particularly," she said.

Our next trip to Pollitos', we decided to locate a little more north and west. It was closer to the grazing areas, where the cattle were. LaVelle was worried about Tar. He had shied the last mile and a half at least; he had tried very much to get his own head and lead us totally someplace else. "Look at his flanks," LaVelle pointed. His flanks were jumping. "And his mane!" She said the hair was taller than usual there, stiffer. But I couldn't see it.

"Why don't we ride him back a ways?" I suggested. "Where he's more relaxed. Tie him. Then you and I can jog on back to here. We've got another half hour or so—before dark."

So we did. We tied him and left him where he could reach a good amount of grass. I kissed LaVelle again. She was kind of against a tree, and she pressed herself, it seemed really hard, against me and I let one hand slip down from her shoulder, and she made a sound that I had never heard before. But then we ran together, holding hands, back to where Ross was, anxious. "Hurry!" he said when he saw us.

That night everything happened—and *more*. To our list we added: "always just after sunset" (which we could have added after the second time), "heat" (we all agreed we'd felt a rise in heat), and—LaVelle was the one who pointed this out, but when she said it, both Ross and I had to go along—"music"; there was some kind of tinny or metal or something *music*. And that was the night of the first really great discovery: *tire tracks*. There were tire tracks in a meadow nearby where some steers still were. LaVelle suggested that they belonged to Mr. Pollito's pickup maybe, but working in a motel and being as interested in driving as I was, I knew they were not pickup tracks; they were *car* tracks. And they were fresh. And they were *real*. Again, I tell you this is not science fiction. Somehow a car had come down through that meadow. And not long ago! Also, Ross thought he saw something. "I saw something, I *know* it!" he said. "Kind of a *car* or something like that shape!" But neither LaVelle nor I could honestly go along with it, so we didn't write it down.

The next day, trying to be casual, I said, "Hey, Rich! How're the Pollitos doing with their stock?"

"Weirdest things!" he said to me. "Last night . . . !"

"Lose more?"

"No, but they found one this morning—*weird*—dead! Lyle said it looked as if it had been hit by a huge rock. Or a *car*."

Oh, and one more kind of connected thing happened before the *true* time, before the time when we actually stood there in the yellow-and-almost-black light, stood with no breath in us at all and actually *saw* the Phantom Mercury. A Mr. Forbes came into town from Dallas. He stayed at the Big Chief Motel and not the Owl, and so I hardly saw him. But his reason for coming to Battle Mountain was LaVelle. He found her and told her that he had promised her father—who he knew very well and respected—that he would do all that he could to bring her back with him from Battle Mountain to Dallas. He told her that there were quite a few what he called "peripheral circumstances" connected with her father's shooting and killing of the other man. And that he felt that it would really be "to her best advantage" (LaVelle's, that is) to get what she could get out of the house here and return there, to Dallas, with him. They talked for several days, and she would report it back to me. She told him that what she wanted, she thought, was to be a lead singer with a group; and he had told her that that was fine, that was a good ambition, and that he would do all that he could for her. At first she thought the whole thing was just ridiculous, but after a couple days, she began to look on it, kind of, as a dilemma.

Ross got a gun. It was a .45 pistol, made in Peru, he said, but he wouldn't tell us where he got it. "Guns are available." That was it! That was all he'd say. He nailed a Clorox jug to a stump near the Reese River and marked it up worse than a keno card with shots. I asked him what he thought he would shoot at when whatever-it-was went by the next time. He said he didn't know.

Meanwhile, LaVelle and I got on. She asked me to listen to her sing. She'd bring her guitar, and we'd climb Mount Lewis, then sit, and she'd play "Leavin' on a Jet Plane" or "Killin' Me Softly," and I'd undo the back buttons on her blouse slowly and when she finished, she'd lean forward so that the two halves of her blouse would fall to either side and she'd just stare out toward Winnemucca and Reno, west, and say to me, "Jason? Do you think I'm good enough?" And I'd say, "LaVelle, I don't know." But before I could finish saying that, she'd ask another question, insert it: "What do you think of Mr. Forbes?" And so I'd just have to tell her again: "I don't know, LaVelle. I don't know what to tell you. He seems short." And then I'd look at her, at her undone blouse kind of riffling in the mountain wind. And at about that same time she'd stand up and walk forward and press one cheek against an aspen tree, and then reach in back of her and do her blouse up again. She was making up her mind.

On the final night—I call it *the final night,* although that was true only for Ross, and even then not exactly true—we all told our parents we were going back to the school auditorium after supper to attend the annual Battle Mountain Gem Show. We lied. We left early. Ross brought his gun. LaVelle was humming. We rode Tar partway, but on the edge of the Pollitos' property, we left him tied and then hiked on.

"I'm planning to stand right where the tire tracks were," Ross told us. "How about you?"

We looked at him. He was carrying his gun. It was a warm night. It felt like summer coming on, sort of, instead of fall. The sky was that color green.

"Have you two gone together yet?" Ross asked us, out of nowhere. LaVelle looked off. I shook my head. "Geez," he said. "It's just a question!" And he pointed his gun off at an old gray junked refrigerator door. We heard our boots and LaVelle's clogs especially, pressing down on rocks all along the creek bed.

When we got there, where the marks had been, we stood. It was . . . I don't know. Except for insects and the diesel sound of a semi down somewhere on I-80 below, it was quiet. Dark was close. And there was the smell—I guess they'd been there earlier—of Pollito's stock. It made me want to be beside LaVelle, to touch her, even her Levi's, which I tried but didn't manage too well.

We checked the air. We looked up as far as we could into the Tuscaroras. They seemed to change their shape. I'd heard a story once about a cougar that was supposed to live high up in them, one that nobody had been able, ever, to kill. His fur looked blue. And somebody had started the rumor—maybe it was an Indian, maybe it was a Shoshone story—anyway, that you could bring him down only with an arrowhead chipped out of black matrix Battle Mountain turquoise.

Ross stationed himself in the path. "I'm ready," he said. LaVelle and I stood on either side, a little away from the tracks. The Tuscaroras got dim. The sun set. The tree frogs started. I heard Ross checking the cylinder of his gun. I heard LaVelle and myself, across from each other, breathing.

"We're going to see it," I said. I don't know what, even, brought the words out.

"I know," LaVelle whispered.

"I saw it last time." Ross picked up the low, quiet tone of LaVelle. We were waiting.

Then things began. Way up. No sound, but a greenish-yellow flare, like heat lightning. The first time not so bright; the second time, much brighter.

We were quiet.

Then the heat lightning or whatever it was flared again, this time down a ways, closer in. "I know," both Ross and I said together. Ross called out, "Touch the stones!" We saw him in the shadows reaching down and touching the stones in the creek bed. So we both reached down and touched the stones ourselves, and when we did, we could feel them shaking. "Gol!" LaVelle said. It was like the stones had little motors.

Then it flashed a fourth time. It was down now, coming down, increasing. And there was that chemical smell that we had all agreed on—but not just slight. I heard LaVelle say, "Jason!" I said, "It's all right." But Ross didn't say anything. I touched my jaw. I could taste my fillings, along with the chemical smell all along the top of my mouth and in my nose. Everything grew. I heard LaVelle making sounds, halfway between crying and the sounds she'd made the night I touched her against the tree. "Get down," I said. "Tar!" she called out. "Tar!" and then: "Jason!" Ross was keeping quiet. It got warmer. Then warmer still.

The glow was coming. LaVelle fell down. It was sort of that welding light. And I could barely stand up myself because of the shaking in the stones. There was an engine sound—and then another sound, like the sound of guitar music turned way up late at night, coming from far away, from some place like Maine or West Virginia on a car radio. "*It's a car!*" I called out "*You bet it is!*" Ross called back. We could see the shape. The shape was coming down the creek bed, glowing, rumbling, giving off showered light, then crossing the meadow just above us. Ross started piling stones up in a dam. The shape went out of sight behind some trees. "Look out!" I called. He said, "Don't worry!" LaVelle was screaming. Then it broke through the trees where we were. "Get back!" I cried. LaVelle was screaming with every breath. "It's a Mercury!" I yelled to Ross. I recognized its grille. God, it was traveling! Then Ross's gun started, again and again, exploding! I smelled gunpowder and hot rubber and transmission oil all at once, and my own body, and, I swear, LaVelle's. I saw the Mercury go by us down the creek bed, and it was all silver and dented white, pitted all over like the moon. *God, it was real!* Ross's gun rang out, then stopped. The Mercury revved once, then entered some trees just below. *It was huge, man!* It was the hugest Mercury I know I've ever seen. It was more huge than a Lincoln even, or a Pontiac!

It was dark. I was sweating. The radio music was in the air, moving, traveling always with the Phantom Mercury. LaVelle was stretched out, rocking, making a kind of sob. There was no moon visible. And I couldn't see Ross. "Ross! It's turned!" I called out. "Ross!" But he didn't answer. I saw the light, saw it turn its oval and start up north, through a meadow, then begin to climb. "It's going back!" I shouted. LaVelle seemed in pain. I went to her. I knelt. She grabbed hold of me and held me; she was strong. She smelled like Tar. She tried to but couldn't form any words. I said, "That's all right," and I kissed her. She was full of sounds.

I turned my head to one side and called out, "Ross!" again. But nothing came. Everything was fading. The light was flickering up into the Tuscaroras. I could see it. And it didn't look huge anymore. It just looked like some backpackers with a Coleman lamp. And the stones were nearly still. And the air tasted burnt. That remained most, and the heat. My skin was dry in places, and wet in others. LaVelle calmed down. The first words she said to me, looking up, were ". . . the music!" I didn't know what she meant; I didn't know what to say. I kissed her on the mouth again. We held it. Then I heard a stone turn, down from us, and I tried again: "Hey, Ross . . . ?"

Someone was standing in the dark. I helped LaVelle and we walked along the dry and now-empty creek bed where the Mercury had come. And Ross was there. He was standing in it, staring up through the night.

"Hi," I said. I squeezed LaVelle. I wanted her to feel that I was there.

Ross nodded.

"You okay?" I asked.

He was quiet. He picked up a stone and threw it. It was a white stone and I could see it leaving his hand for just a second or two. But then it went out, like a candle. And we heard it land maybe a hundred feet away. "I shot the driver," Ross told us.

"Are you serious?" LaVelle asked.

"I shot him." He was straight-faced. "That driver's got to be dead." He picked up another stone and threw it; this one was dark.

We hiked to Tar. We didn't talk. He seemed happy to see us. We mounted him and rode him back down into town. It was maybe nine o'clock.

What happened next was chance. We hadn't planned it, but none of us really wanted to go on along to our places and go to bed, so we decided to go to the Cascade Bowling Alleys and Roller Skating Rink and skate a bit. So we did. LaVelle took Tar home. She said her mother probably would be mad, but that it didn't matter. Ross and I understood.

Inside the Cascade it was pretty wonderful, in fact. It's nice to go around in what's not really dark, but not really light either, with one of those mirror balls in the middle tossing off spots of colored light. It's nice to skate. It's nice just to have records on, too, and to be going around, just be going around and around and around *together*, with your girl in the middle and your very best friend from all your years in school on the other side. And to not be touching the ground! Do you know what I mean? Do you know what I'm talking about? I mean, to be circling and floating there in the Cascade Bowling Alleys and Roller Skating Rink with just *ball bearings* under your toes and heels is *nice*.

We went outside after ten and just stood together. I'll always remember our feet on the ground again in the dark. It had gotten cool. Ross was quietest. We said, "See you in school tomorrow," all of us. I remember. "See you in school," each one; and then, each one: "Yeah" . . . "Yeah" . . . "Right" . . . "See you." Then Ross turned away. And we watched him. His Levi's jacket looked like it had been chipped from stone. I hugged LaVelle, sort of. *Why weren't we talking? Any of us? Why?* And then I walked her home. The next day Ross wasn't in school or anywhere. Then, four months later . . . LaVelle. I know the Mercury got them. Ross especially. I see that heat lightning high in the Tuscaroras now at dusk, and I think, *Maybe he's driving it!* That could be. *Maybe he's the driver now.* And if I go up to the Pollitos' meadow at the end of some afternoon and wait—for the rumbling to start and the welding light and for my teeth to hurt—then Ross will come! And LaVelle! And we can all drive the Phantom Mercury down to the Cascade and skate. And Ross will be wearing his chiseled Levi's jacket. And LaVelle's voice and guitar will be in the air. And I can touch LaVelle again. And taste her. And be Ross's friend. It would be better than seeing Mr. Forbes eating broasted chicken in the Miner's Room at the Owl Club all by himself. Or waking up at headlights.

In fact, I'm sorry that I was ever curious, actually. About the world and about the real things that are in it. I mean . . . why do people disappear?

JOANNE MESCHERY [B. 1941]

A reviewer described Joanne Meschery's novel Home and Away *(1994) as "a believable and moving story of ordinary people coping with the challenges of private and public life" (Mary Carroll,* BookList*). That description aptly characterizes Meschery's entire oeuvre. In a High Place (1981) follows the struggles of a mother who has left her husband and taken her three children to settle in a small town in the Sierra Nevada mountains. A Gentleman's Guide to the Frontier (1990)—a finalist for the* PEN/*Faulkner Award for fiction—charts the interior journey of a recent widower who takes a road trip in an* RV *across America.* Home and Away *(1994) dramatizes the conflicts of a working mother coping with an absentee husband, a teenage daughter, and a conservative community during the years of the Gulf War. Meschery deftly reveals the internal tensions that strain apparently normal families and relationships. Her keen insight can be traced to Meschery's childhood as one of five children of a Methodist minister and his frustrated, self-sacrificing wife. Despite never-ending money worries and a father who was continually called away to minister to others, the family learned to project an image of a model Christian family, the smiling preacher's wife and his smiling children. Meschery has devoted a distinguished writing career to revealing the private truths underlying public appearance. Born in Texas and raised throughout the West, Joanne Meschery attended high school in Fallon, Nevada, and earned degrees from the University of Nevada, Reno, and from the Iowa Writers' Workshop. She is married to poet Tom Meschery, lives in Truckee, California, has raised three children, and has written a history of Truckee. Meschery received the Nevada Writers Hall of Fame Award in 1999 and has taught creative writing at the University of Arkansas and San Diego State University.*

An Otherwise Happy Life

Eunice Packwood opened the screen door at the front of the house as wide as she could and then pulled it shut with a bang. She did this three times. "Shoo," she said loudly, her lips pressed against the screen. "Shoo."

Across the street, Eunice's neighbor, Cynthia Ridge, looked up from the rock garden she'd been working at all spring. Eunice stepped back quickly from the doorway and shut her eyes as if she were still a child pretending no one could see her. When she opened her eyes, Cynthia Ridge had returned to her work.

I'm being silly, Eunice thought as she went to the kitchen. Silly. She wondered if her husband, Chauncey, was right. Maybe she was approaching menopause.

She poured another cup of coffee and walked out onto the patio in the back-yard. The day was so bright and clear that the Sierras seemed to rise abruptly from behind the fence. A year ago, Eunice and Chauncey had moved farther out of town to this smaller house. The last housing development north of town. It was no lon-ger important to be near the schools, the public library, or the big municipal pool where she'd spent summer afternoons watching the boys swim.

There were just the two of them now, as in the beginning. Chauncey said it was like being on a honeymoon all over again, except better. He had bought two new suits and the deluxe edition of a sex manual, which he kept in the nightstand beside their bed. Chauncey was happy; Eunice was bewildered. This morning she was disturbed.

"Childish," she said aloud and walked around to the front of the house. There, to the right of the screen door and just below the mailbox, two giant Polyphemus moths clung fast to the yellow siding and to each other.

Earlier that morning, when she'd gone out for the newspaper, there had been only one of these moths. She'd caught her breath at the sight. The moth's markings were as lovely as the flame-print design inside the cover of an old book. It hung beneath the mailbox, wings spread nearly six inches. Eunice had hurried inside, wishing that Chauncey hadn't left for work or that the children were still little and she could pull them out the door to see.

But a moment later, when she stepped out to look at the moth again, there were two. Eunice had stared at the moths, her face inches from them, so that their shiny black eyes seemed magnified a thousand times. Once, the female tried to break away, and the male moved before her, playing his wings slowly up and down as though to calm her. Something about the movement of the wings disturbed Eu-nice, had seemed both ominous and embarrassing to her. When the male again took the female, she had fled inside the house.

Eunice glanced across the street, relieved that Cynthia Ridge was no longer working in the rock garden. She opened the mailbox and tapped the lid shut several times. The sun fell hot and full against the front of the house, and the lid of the mailbox was warm in her hand. The moths moved only slightly. Their wings dipped to one side, brushed the wooden siding.

Cynthia would think she was crazy, acting this way. Cynthia was a basic person. Only a few days ago she had told Eunice she was getting back to her animal. Eunice thought Chauncey must be getting back to his animal, as well. He had given up smoking in order to smell things better. "Scent has a great deal to do with sexual attraction," he told Eunice. "It's all in the olfactory nerves." Eunice found this hard to believe. On the day she was married, her mother had given her a white pocket-sized Bible to carry with her bridal bouquet and said, "Keep your sights high, Eunice, and never forget you're a step beneath the angels."

"You're looking for mail awful early this morning," Roy Netzel called, tapping his leather mailbag as he turned up the sidewalk to the house next door.

"Just cleaning," Eunice said and laughed loudly. Out of the corner of her eye she saw the wings, up and down, slowly, like a warning. If only they weren't so big, she thought. Anyone walking by would notice them. If only they would go away. She hurried down the sidewalk to meet Mr. Netzel.

"Sorry to disappoint you," Roy Netzel said, looking down at Eunice, his face already brown from the sun, the mail divided between his fingers. "Got another book for your husband, though. He read all these books, your husband?"

Eunice stood very close to Mr. Netzel. She kept her eyes fixed on his face, fearing he would look beyond her to the house. "Mr. Packwood reads nearly every day," she said. "I guess you could say it's his hobby."

Mr. Netzel laughed, and the buckle on the strap of his mailbag flashed in the sun. "That's the kind of hobby to have," he said. "A man can't get into trouble with a hobby like that, now can he?" He laughed again, then stopped. His eyes narrowed in a squint, and Eunice turned as if she were seeing the moths for the first time. Their wings shimmered like things seen through intense heat. The single yellow eyespots on each hind wing seemed to stare back at her as she followed Mr. Netzel to the mailbox.

He put his hands to his hips. "What you've got here, Eunice, is a wonder," he said. "A phenomenon."

A flush ran from Eunice's face down her neck. "During the period of menopause some women experience a sensation known as 'hot flashes,'" Chauncey had read to Eunice one evening, looking at her closely.

"You'll never see a thing like this again in your lifetime, Eunice," Mr. Netzel said, shaking his head. "Neither will I, for that matter. Even when I had the route out in Jack's Valley, I never saw a thing like this. Biggest butterflies I've ever seen."

"They're moths," Eunice said and felt her face grow red again. She started at the circles of sweat staining Mr. Netzel's blue shirt as he stood with his hands on his hips. "Polyphemus moths," she said.

"Is that so?" Mr. Netzel said, turning to look at Eunice. "You ought to tell some-body about this, Eunice. Jessup Phelps down at the paper. He'd be out here in ten minutes. What'd you say they were, again?"

"Polyphemus moths," Eunice said as she moved to go inside. "Like the myth. The Greek myth."

"Well," Mr. Netzel said, "if that isn't a rare sight, I don't know what is."

Something's the matter with me, Eunice thought as she sat in the living room holding Chauncey's new book in her lap. She hadn't unwrapped the book. Chauncey liked to do that himself. He had so many books. All different. All com-ing through the mail. Encyclopedias. Collections of old books. Series after series from Time-Life. Limited editions. Chauncey read them all, curious about every-thing. Even her. Especially her.

Lately she'd caught him looking at her, watching her. Fascinated. He took an unnatural interest in her body. Christmas day the boys had come home, Robert with his wife and the baby. Chauncey had removed Eunice's earrings during the dinner. "You have vestigial ear lobes," he whispered, kissing first one ear lobe, then the other, as if it were a foreign custom. "Vestigial ear lobes are uncommon," he told their little grandchild in the highchair beside him. Eunice had been unable to finish her meal. Another day as Eunice was dressing, Chauncey had dropped to his knees and begun sucking her toes. Eunice went rigid, unable to move. Chauncey had sucked each toe separately, his eyes closed. After that Eunice dressed in the bathroom. Chauncey no longer cared that she was plump. He called her his little buttercup. "The doctor says you're healthy fat," he told her. "That's good enough for me."

Chauncey's book slipped from her lap as she pushed herself out of the chair. "Dear God," she said, peering out of the screen door, seeing the moths, their posi-tion unchanged. How long, she wondered, can they do it? "It is not known," Eunice had read that morning, "for what length of time the male and female remain so united, but on one occasion such a pair was found an hour and a half later on the same tree and in the same position."

Eunice went to the kitchen and began rinsing the breakfast dishes. This must be a record, she thought. She guessed Mr. Netzel was right. Somebody should be told. If she called the *Carson Valley News*, Jessup Phelps would come out and take pictures. He would place a ruler or his hand beside the moths to show that they were extraordinary in size. Or perhaps he would have Eunice stand beside them, like the picture she'd seen when Evans Charley caught the twenty-one inch German brown trout. Eunice went into the living room and pulled the drapes, then returned to the kitchen sink.

She seldom read Chauncey's books. That morning she'd looked in the encyclopedias and through the nature series until she'd found the moths. She doubted even Chauncey knew more about moths than she did. Or myths. A one-eyed giant, Polyphemus, the eye in the center of his forehead gorged out, a great, bloodied orifice. Eunice shivered at the thought of it. She shook the soapsuds from her arms and sat down at the kitchen table.

They had always told one another that sex wasn't the only thing. Certainly not the most important thing. Eunice believed this. She had remarked, sometimes a little angrily, that she didn't know what the fuss was about, all this talk regarding sex. There had been so many other things to think of then, to do.

When her boys were little they were skinny and straight. She had nicknamed them Frick and Frack. At bedtime she'd chased them through the house and had wiggled them into pajamas. Sometimes, when they pulled away, laughing and jumping out of her reach, she was struck by the sight of them. Their muscles small, like knots. Their soft yellow hair. Though she had never doubted she would mother such children, she was astonished.

She wished, now, that the boys were still at home, that she wasn't there all alone in the house with Chauncey. But Chauncey was happy with the way things were. Like a bridegroom, he had carried Eunice across the threshold of their new house. "Just the two of us," he'd said, refusing to put her down, kicking the door closed behind them with his foot. "From now on."

"Who is it?" Eunice called, startled by the tapping at the front door. Her voice cracked as though she hadn't spoken for a long time.

"Did you see these butterflies on your house, Eunice?" Cynthia Ridge asked as Eunice went to the screen door.

"They're not butterflies," Eunice said. She leaned for a moment against the screen. "They're moths."

"They're screwing, Eunice," Cynthia Ridge said. "Come out and take a look. I never saw anything like it."

"Come in, Cynthia," Eunice said. "It's too hot to be standing out there in the sun. I'll fix some iced tea."

"Oh, the sun doesn't bother me," Cynthia answered, brushing sand from her white cotton shorts. "I thought butterflies just laid eggs," she said. "The sun feels good, in fact. Wish I could spend every day like this instead of being cooped up in that damned office. Listen Eunice, have you got a magnifying glass?"

Cynthia looked up from the moths and smiled at Eunice through the screen. Eunice was surprised at how pretty Cynthia looked, her blond hair pulled back from her face with a red bandana. She was a tall woman, younger than Eunice. Her face, as she smiled, was open and relaxed, as though nothing bad had ever happened to her, as though she expected nothing ever would.

"Never mind," Cynthia said. "I've got one at home."

Eunice went to the kitchen and fixed two iced teas with lemon. Almost every day since Cynthia had started her vacation, Eunice had fixed them iced tea. Before that, she'd scarcely spoken to Cynthia. Sometimes in the morning she saw Cynthia leaving for work, rushing out the door, her high heels a hollow echo down the sidewalk to her car. And once, Eunice had seen a man standing just inside Cynthia's doorway, watching her as she pulled away from the curb.

"You want to see something beautiful, come out and take a look through this magnifying glass," Cynthia called as Eunice put the iced teas on the coffee table. "It's like a painting," she said. Then she stood up straight and laughed, pressing the magnifying glass to her nose. "You're not going to believe this, Eunice, but this butterfly's got a black pecker."

Cynthia stepped inside and took a long swallow of her iced tea before she sat down on the sofa beside Eunice. "God, it's dark in here," she said. She pulled the bandana from her hair, shaking the curls loose about her shoulders. "Mind if I open the drapes?"

Eunice frowned against the glare. Particles of dust drifted in the sunlight, settled on the coffee table.

Cynthia sat down again and propped one leg on her knee. She looked at Eunice and giggled. "I'm sorry, Eunice," she said, making her mouth serious. "I can't help it. The idea of it, a little black pecker. Reminds me of when I decided to leave Louis."

Eunice wondered if she would ever sleep well again. She had heard of women who suffered from vertigo during menopause. These women lay awake nights, afraid to move, afraid they would fall off the edge of the bed.

"My dog attacked me," Cynthia said. "It was the last straw. We were living in Chicago, awful place, and my dog got loose. Went after the cocker spaniel down the street. I tore over there and turned the hose on them. They were locked together, tight as a vise." Cynthia looked at Eunice and sucked her lower lip. "The bitch got loose and my dog headed for home. I had a feeling he'd be waiting for me and sure enough, when I hit the front yard he was on me. Meanest dogs in the world, fox terriers. My neighbor had to call an ambulance. On the way to the hospital I said to myself, 'That's it, girl. If you can survive this, you can divorce Louis.'" Cynthia tapped the heel of her tennis shoe with the magnifying glass. "Something like that happens and you see everything in a whole new light. You know what I mean, Eunice?"

Eunice pressed her lips hard against the tea glass. Tears ran down her face, through her fingers, and along the glass like the sweat from the ice cubes.

"Eunice, what's wrong? What's wrong, hon?" Cynthia said, shifting on the sofa to face Eunice. "Oh, Eunice," she said, "don't cry. I didn't mean to make you cry." She pushed Eunice's face into her shoulder and stroked her hair, her cheek. "Don't cry, Eunice," she said.

Cynthia's knit shirt smelled of sun tan lotion, of sand and the heat. Eunice felt very warm against Cynthia's chest. Her temples burned, as though the magnifying glass in Cynthia's hand had caught the sun and trained it at the sides of her head.

"It's all right," Eunice said after a while. She leaned back on the sofa and tucked in her blouse. "It's just my time of life. My time."

"God, Eunice, you sound like you're going to die," Cynthia said.

"I feel like I'm going to die," Eunice said. She swallowed hard, then smiled at Cynthia. A tiny nerve pulled erratically at the corner of her mouth.

"Bullshit," Cynthia said, tossing the magnifying glass onto the coffee table. She looked for a moment at the crack she'd put across the face of the glass. Then she shrugged. "That's all in your head, Eunice. You need to get in touch with your primitive self. Listen to your animal, Eunice."

"I guess you're right," Eunice said after a minute. "It's just been one of those days. A bad day."

"Maybe you ought to try screaming," Cynthia said. "It's like having a good cry except you feel better afterward. I scream for a few minutes every morning when I'm in the bathroom, and I feel better all day." She laughed. "Of course, it's a little hard on your voice. I can't talk above a whisper for a half hour after I get to work. But I'm so relaxed. You just have to do things to make yourself feel better. Some people never learn that."

Eunice went into the kitchen and poured them each another glass of iced tea.

"I've got this book I'll bring over sometime," Cynthia called from the living room. "It covers everything."

Eunice stood at the screen door and watched Cynthia as she rocked a slab of sandstone into place in her garden. It was growing late and the sun had moved behind the house. Eunice opened the door a crack and looked out at the one Polyphemus moth that remained. In a little while this moth would be gone, too. Eunice had read that the female was known to fly for miles in search of a place to leave her eggs. She's gathering her strength, Eunice thought, and at that moment the moth was in the air. It flew low, its shadow ragged on the street. Then it sailed over Cynthia Ridge's house and was gone.

Eunice went back to the living room and pulled the drapes shut again. She thought of thousands of Polyphemus moths emerging from silk cocoons. Millions, the book had said, from the return of one female. Eunice imagined her house covered with Polyphemus moths as though it were a float decorated for a parade. She looked down at her bare arms. She went to the bedroom for a sweater.

She sat on the edge of the bed, the side where Chauncey slept, and pulled the book from his nightstand drawer. "A gourmet guide to the art of love-making," she read and turned the page. The pages of the book were illustrated with drawings of a man and a woman, the same man and woman on each page. The woman was very young. She was slender and beautiful with long dark hair. Her breasts were small and firm, her belly flat, her pelvis shaded in hollows. Eunice looked nothing like this woman. The man was young also, his hair curling at the nape of his neck, curling at his thighs. He looked to Eunice like one of her sons. She stared at an inset in the center of a page which labeled the parts of the man's penis.

She turned page after page, looking at the pictures. "It is important to become aware of your sensuality," she read. "Some women experience great sensual pleasure in wearing clear plastic raincoats when they shower." Eunice turned back to the first page wondering where she'd missed the point.

Once, after a Chinese dinner, Eunice got a fortune that said, "You have at your command the wisdom of the ages." A whole lifetime, she thought and shook her head. What if she'd had all of it wrong?

She hadn't heard Chauncey come in. She looked up and saw him standing in the doorway. He smiled and put his finger to his lips. Then he winked and closed the bedroom door.

"Hello, hello," he whispered, taking the book from her lap.

Eunice kept her head bent, her eyes fixed on her hands as though she still held the book. She heard the soft jingling of car keys and loose change as Chauncey let his slacks fall to the carpet.

Eunice's fingers worked crazily in her lap. "It's a fact, each finger has five bumps," Chauncey had told her. But she'd never counted five.

"Lie back, sweetheart," Chauncey said. He bent over her, lifting her head to put a pillow beneath it. He kissed her forehead, and then her lips, as she opened them to speak. He laid his head on her chest and she felt his fingers at her waist, the sound of the zipper.

"What a funny one you are," he said softly. "The hottest day in June and you have on a sweater. You're a love, Eunice. Such a love."

"It's so warm, Chauncey," she said. She strained to sit up. "It's too warm."

"Don't take off your sweater. A cool bath," he said, "in a minute."

Eunice lay back again on the bed, and Chauncey slid her pale blue slacks and white panties to her ankles. She closed her eyes tight.

Chauncey grasped her hips, pulling her closer to the edge of the bed, so that her feet brushed the carpet. His shoulders came between her legs, spreading them until the elastic of her panties was taut around her ankles.

She felt his tongue along her thighs. Then his breath in her hair, the tip of his tongue parting the folds.

Her eyes opened wide. A terrible heaviness, an enormous weight, seemed to shift inside her, moving down as if her whole body were being sucked away. She pressed the back of her hand against her teeth.

Relax, she thought. Try to relax.

"Listen to your animal," Cynthia had told her. "Relax."

Chauncey's hands cupped and kneaded her hips, moving to her thighs and back again.

There was an animal once that got into their garage. An opossum, Chauncey said. "Why doesn't it move?" Eunice had asked. "Possums feign death when they're afraid," Chauncey had said. He had prodded it with the broom. Then the opossum's eyes came open, small and black, and its mouth with teeth sharp and bright, like a kitten's. Its mouth opened wide but it made no sound.

Eunice turned her face to the ceiling. The flat white paint had become warm and golden, stippled with the last light of the day. There seemed to be no more air in the room. Eunice's sweater bunched hot under her breasts and around her chin. The thick wool carried a faint odor, a smell that was familiar. For an instant Eunice felt sick, as though the wind had been slammed out of her. She arched her back. Chauncey looked up, his face red and moist, and she clapped her hands hard to his ears so he wouldn't hear her scream.

BERNARD SCHOPEN [B. 1942]

As geographers and mystery aficionados are aware, detective fiction often excels at conveying sense of place. Frequently, solving a mystery hinges upon knowing where to search for clues, and, in order to achieve plausibility, authors must create a believable locale. For Bernard Schopen, honoree of the Nevada Writers Hall of Fame Award for 2000, interest in place is primary, and the detective genre provides a compelling way to write about Nevada. Schopen's

three novels—The Big Silence *(1989),* The Desert Look *(1990), and* The Iris Deception
(1996)—catapult private investigator Jack Ross into remote corners of the state, on the trail
of missing bodies. Readers view Nevada through the eyes of Ross, a man of few illusions who
generally prefers his landscapes à la carte, without people. Schopen's mysteries—like those
of Ross Macdonald, about whom he has written a critical book—contain the psychological
and artistic complexity of a novel. Schopen explores issues of identity, environmental change,
and the New West, while entertaining readers with a suspenseful plot and eccentric cast of
gamblers, prostitutes, ranchers, hippies, hermits, and Mafia thugs. Connoisseur of Nevada's
empty quarter, Schopen spent his boyhood in Deadwood, South Dakota, earned a BA *and* MA
in Seattle, and moved to Reno in 1971 to pursue a PHD *Although it was not love at first sight,*
Nevada eventually got to Schopen, who stayed on after graduation to teach in the English De-
partment and the Core Humanities program at the University of Nevada, where he is known
for his inquisitive mind and deadpan humor. Schopen has been spotted around town wearing
a cheery T-shirt that reads, "Have a Nice Day" and depicts a bloody bullet hole in the forehead
of a bright yellow smiley face. As he once told an interviewer, "there are too many people [in
Reno], and I think everybody ought to leave. You first!" The excerpts reprinted here, extracted
from their mystery plots, represent a gallery of Jack Ross's views of Nevada.

from *The Big Silence*

In Nevada, anything is possible.

In Nevada, nothing is as it seems.

In Nevada, nothing abounds, nothing signifies, anything is possible.

. . . .

Then I made myself a drink and sat on the fender and looked at the desert. The late
afternoon sun spread golden light on the land, the silence.

It was a big silence, soothing, serene, made bigger, more soothing, more serene
by the sounds that whispered in it: shush of wind, clack of rock, scrape of brush,
hiss of sand. Beat of heart.

It was what I had come for, the big silence.

I sipped scotch and thought of nothing, let the desert take me, let the gritty
wind scour the faces from my mind, the blackness from my heart, the blood from
my hands.

Silence and emptiness. And time. Silent, empty time—epochs, eras, eons of
time compressed into the rock, carved into the hillsides—so much time that the
past in which human life did not exist became the present, as did the future in
which all trace of humanity has vanished from the universe. In the big silence under the empty sky, time itself became meaningless, and death, and life.

Silence, emptiness, time. Nothingness. Abounding. And nothing mattered. Not even me.

My drink was finished. I had another, reluctant to leave. It wasn't enough, this brief communion. I needed not merely to experience it, the grand nothing, but to become it.

But I didn't have time.

from *The Desert Look*

Everyone in the Nevada desert has a story to tell.

. . . .

She took the cup, looked over the rim at me. "The people I talked to about you, they said you were a private investigator, that you were good at it."

"Good enough," I said.

"And then you . . . just walked away from it, from what you were, from your life. I—why?"

"I got tired of looking for people and finding bodies. Or worse."

"So you . . . came out here. Alone. You came out here alone for . . ." She moved the cup in a long slow arc across what lay beyond the lean-to. "For what?"

For what.

Distant dark rugged ranges, their snow cover graying in the gathering dusk to backdrop the scattered sleet flurries that trailed from ragged clouds; a flat patch of pale playa, filled to the sky with nothing; brown desert foothills traced with ghost roads leading nowhere, dappled with snow and gray sage and dark juniper; a hillside spring a hundred yards away in a clump of willows; three rows of dead apple trees planted and tended and abandoned by some long-gone desert dreamer; a natural juniper blind behind which I'd found dozens of obsidian chips.

For what.

A calm that the flutter of the sage in the wind, the scurry of predator and prey over the sandy earth, the muffled hoofbeats of the mustangs only deepened. A silence that the rush of wind and clatter of sleet and flap of tarp only enlarged.

Her disturbed voice disturbed that silence. "You really like it out here, don't you? Alone."

"Yes."

. . . .

The next morning I tried to shower and stretch the ache out of my body, got breakfast in the coffee shop and some information and directions and curious looks in the sheriff's office, gassed up the Wagoneer, and drove out of Tonopah, east.

Once past the whorehouse and the shacks and trailers and hay sheds and corrals that trickled down a gully to the local fairgrounds, past the airport, past the
turnoff to the not-very-secret government installation where the military was testing Stealth aircraft, past the turnoff to the Big Smoky Valley, the highway cut a
course through a land of marvelous desolation.

Under a pale empty sky, the pale empty earth buckled and swelled into huge
alkali-centered bowls and yawning valleys; rock and patches of cheat grass and stubby
gnarled sage lay scattered as if flung down by the hand of some disgusted god.

Miles and miles of moonscape, space, time.

And to the north, massive mountain ranges—drab bases, dark flanks, bright
white crests under the pale-yellow sun, the pale-blue sky. Mountains split from
each other by wide desert valleys, mountains somehow alone, detached from the
land itself.

Human beings lived in this land, traced it with twisting rutted dirt roads, fenced
it here and there in geometrical shapes that would ignore and thus dominate the
physics of the earth, staked it with white plastic tubes that promised minerals,
drilled it for water, drilled it for oil.

Human beings lived in this land, but not many: at the base of a distant mountain, a ranch huddling against a row of spring-fed poplars; halfway up a slope,
a shack oozing smoke into the still air; at a turnoff, a sudden flowering of silver
mailboxes.

Crazy people lived in this land.

I felt right at home.

. . . .

A hundred yards into the trees the ruts narrowed, in shadows disappeared under
hard-crusted snow, in the sunlight became a spongy sump. I followed them up
through the pine and juniper and rocks and sage, slipping on the ice, stumbling on
the earth. I'd exchanged my tweed for a down-filled coat, and soon I was hot and
sweating in the sun, shivering and sweating in the shade.

And so enjoying the mountain—the juniper-stained air, the crisp silence, the
chill stillness, the bright white snow and black shadows—that I could almost forget
why I was on it.

. . . .

At the aspen grove I stopped to catch my breath.

The silence on the mountain was vast. Nothing sounded but the hush of my
breathing, the squeak of the snow under my boots.

And something else, whispers, voices that weren't voices, sounds that were images flickering at the edge of my mind.

Slowly I perceived what it was, what the grove was.

I crunched closer to the aspens, read the iconographic tales carved into their skin, carved into the meat of trunk and limbs.

Some of the black on the white bark was natural, scars of growth and weather. Some was not, scars of the knives and minds of lonely men.

Initials, names, dates, obscure truncated messages in strange tongues.

Drawings. Stylized meditations on the female form—breasts, hips, thighs. Proud rigid phalluses. Stick figures or bloated beings in eternal coitus.

Sculpture. Breast and phallus, phallus and breast, carved into the limbs of the trees, carved out of chunks of trunks.

And all swollen, distended, distorted by the continued growth of the savaged trees into a nightmare of sexual yearning, as if life had transformed the crude signs of human longing into mocking monstrous symbols of the futility of all human desire.

I'd heard about these aspen groves, the living legacy of long-dead sheepherders, most of them Basque, most of them young and achingly alone in a strange land full of strange things.

This one reminded me of Las Vegas.

. . . .

Nevada by starlight: shades of darkness, shadows, solitary distant specks of light, confused clusters of lights in silent little towns; along the highway brief flashes of lights in predatory eyes, on the highway lumps of bloody furry death.

from *The Iris Deception*

We were finally beyond pavement and concrete and plywood, a mile past Red Rock Estates. The desert was still, silent, dun in the light and frosted gray in the shadows. The slanting morning sun was bright but without warmth.

. . . .

"What am I supposed to be seeing out here that's beautiful? It's so . . . drab. Brown. Dead looking."

The dry land in drought in dying time.

"You want green," I said, checking the mirror again.

"I . . . suppose so."

"The trick is to see what's there, not what isn't, or what you think should be."

What was there was not green but greens, specks and splashes under the dust, subtle, subdued. Gray-green sage, deep olive bitterbrush, yellow-green ephedra.

Shadscale and winterfat, greasewood and hopsage, mule-ear and rabbitbrush and desert thorn.

There was brown. Except when you really looked, the brown was shades of gold and yellow and red and lavender, ocher and umber, pale, quiet.

What wasn't there was people, man.

What was there was the brief history of man, written in the scars on the earth.

What was there was the long history of the earth, written in the strata of rocks and the shapes of hills, water traced, wind scoured.

What was there was silence, into which the desert silently spoke of deep time, eons and eternities, and the utter inconsequentiality of all life.

Yet what was also there was life, ignoring the message of the desert, struggling, surviving.

We drove through it. Martha looked at it.

"Oh," she said.

Then, finally, seeing what was really there, she said, slowly, "Aaah."

FRANK BERGON [B. 1943]

In 1981 in southern Idaho, wildlife poacher Claude Dallas killed two Fish and Game officers who were placing him under arrest. Dallas soon became a folk hero, prized as a likable young outlaw who stood up to authority, a man who wanted only to be left alone to live off the land. Dallas's popularity says a lot about westerners' antagonism toward the federal government and about the enduring myth of the West. Novelist Frank Bergon, however, set the events in northern Nevada and imagined the story from the point of view of a close friend of one of the slain game wardens. From that perspective, Claude Dallas—named Billy Crockett in Bergon's novel Wild Game *(1995)—is an immature punk, a threat not only to law and order but to nature, which he ransacked wantonly. Like Bergon's other novels,* Wild Game *presents a controversy from multiple perspectives, is based on extensive research, features a Nevada setting and Basque characters, and presents the landscape as a chief protagonist and source of values. Bergon's* Shoshone Mike *(1987) depicts the last Indian massacre in the United States, which took place—bizarrely—in 1911, in the age of the automobile.* The Temptations of St. Ed and Brother S *(1993) imagines a Cistercian monastery near the Nevada Test Site and stages a battle between spiritual energy and nuclear energy. This trilogy of novels spans one hundred years of Nevada history, from the late nineteenth-century to the millennium. For his exceptional contributions to Nevada literature, Bergon, who was born in Ely, Nevada, and who has Basque*

relatives throughout the state, received the Nevada Writers Hall of Fame Award in 1998. A pro-
fessor at Vassar College in Poughkeepsie, New York, educated at Boston College (BA), Stanford,
and Harvard (PHD), Frank Bergon is both a novelist and a distinguished scholar, with a book
on Stephen Crane and major editorial works on Crane, John Burroughs, the journals of Lewis
and Clark, and wilderness writing.

from *Wild Game*

Jack knew that Crockett had joined hundreds of trappers who'd flooded into the deserts and mountains since the price of pelts had shot up. Despite Brigitte Bardot, the European market for furs was growing. A warden could only do so much. Tighter quotas on game animals gave guides . . . a steady trade with illegal trophy hunters. At one time Bob had taken it as his mission to cite or arrest every poacher in the state. But he'd mellowed since marrying Cindy. Since he was one of two men trying to cover nine thousand square miles, the most he could do was make the occasional arrest of a flagrant violator stand as a warning to others. And the slaughter went on.

A little after nine Jack and Bob reached the mouth of Little High Rock, a rough volcanic canyon of steep basalt cliffs that cut through the desert for seven miles. They put on down jackets and tramped through shoulder-high sagebrush to where Scotty told them he'd seen trap sets. "Over there," Jack said, his eyes sharper than Bob's. Hanging from a greasewood bush, a brown sage-hen wing fluttered in the wind where it might attract a curious bobcat. The bait was tied to the brush with colorless nylon leader. Under the wing lay an unmarked trap set without spacers to protect the legs of accidentally captured hawks or eagles. Hanging visible bait— mustang meat, rabbit fur, sage-hen wings—was illegal because it attracted raptors, who depended on their eyesight rather than their noses. Here were four violations: no identification on the trap, no spacers, hanging bait, and illegal possession of game bird parts.

"Son of a bitch," Bob said, and pulled the trap. They went farther into the canyon, the basalt cliffs rising higher, and found another set of traps against the rimrock. A captured red-tailed hawk frantically flapped its wings trying to jerk its broken leg free from the jaws of the trap. Without its hunting claws this bird was doomed. The hawk blinked as Jack grabbed its neck and released the trap from the torn leg. Holding the hawk by the head Jack swung it around, its wings flapping as it tried to get away, until he heard the neck break. A bead of blood hung on its beak, and its eyes turned cloudy. He tossed the dead bird into the sagebrush.

"Let's go," Bob said.

They hauled the traps back to the truck and drove along the canyon's north rim, parked, and scoured the sage. Jack spotted another hanging wing. He felt himself getting as angry as Bob. Trash-trapping is what they called it—what Crockett did. Crockett wanted people to think he was a big-time trapper, but he always cut corners. It was easier to use body parts than to go to the trouble of scenting steel the way real trappers did, by using Cat's Passion or making their own scent from bobcat glands or coyote urine or rotted fish or whatever.

"Oh, Christ," Bob said. "He's got a pup." A kit fox, its mangled front paw clamped in the staked trap, tried to scramble across the exposed ground toward the brush, dragging the trap as far as the taut chain allowed. It had begun chewing through its leg just above where the jaws of the trap clung to its paw. The fox glared at the men with intense, frightened eyes and snarled. Bob reached down and jerked it up by its bushy tail, lifting it off the ground. It was a female. "Cut it," he said.

Jack snapped open the blade of his pocketknife and sawed into the bloody leg where the fox had been chewing. The kit fox squalled angrily in his ear. The sharp blade sliced through gristle, then the bone snapped free. The trap dropped into the dirt with the little paw still sticking out of it.

Bob swung the fox by her tail and tossed her several feet through the air. The fox hit the ground in a defensive crouch, her pointed ears erect, staring with dark, alert eyes. Jack looked at the fox. She looked at him. She rose and hobbled over the rocky ground, stopped, glanced back, then began a quick three-legged stumbling trot into the sagebrush, her silvery back and blond legs blending into the desert shades.

"She'll be all right," Bob sighed. "Let's go get that punk."

They walked back to the truck with the pulled traps and continued driving slowly along the rocky rim, stopping now and then to scan the canyon floor with binoculars. It was nearing eleven in the morning when they approached the far end of the canyon and saw a red Ford Bronco parked on the rim.

"Who the hell's that?" Bob blurted out.

A man stood behind the Bronco wearing a red deerhunter's cap with flaps and a woolen red-and-black checkered mackinaw. Bob and Scotty were big, but this man was fat. He was about thirty with rosy cheeks and an expansive pale forehead. He leaned backward to counterbalance the pull of gravity on his bulging stomach.

"How're you doing?" Jack said, not wanting to startle the man. "What's your name?"

"Larry Hughes," the man answered, sounding jumpy. His billowy khaki pants cuffed around new blue Gore-Tex hiking boots.

"Give me that pistol," Bob ordered, pointing toward the holster at the man's hip. "Butt first."

Bob swung open the loaded cylinder and shook the cartridges into his palm.

He dropped the cartridges into the front pocket of the man's jacket and handed back the revolver.

"What are you doing with a .357 Smith?" Bob asked.

Hughes's ruddy face glistened. He was breathing heavily. "Eddie Dodd, the barkeep, loaned it to me. I needed it to signal a friend, to let him know I was here. I was bringing him some supplies from Eddie."

"Where's your friend?" Jack asked calmly, as though he were only casually interested in the answer. He didn't want the man to get any jumpier than he was.

"He went to reset some traps. I was just about to haul the rest of this stuff down." He nodded toward the Styrofoam cooler at his feet. "This is my second trip. I didn't know it was so fucking far down there."

Jack flipped up the lid of the cooler. It was packed with cans of Dr Pepper and Squirt, some chocolate-chip cookies in Saran Wrap, oranges, apples, and a plastic Cool Whip container.

"There's butterscotch pudding in there," Hughes explained, pointing to the Cool Whip container. "My wife made it."

"Does your friend Billy have any game hanging down there?" Bob asked.

The mention of Billy Crockett's name startled Hughes. "Look, you guys, I just came out here for a little outing, to look for some arrowheads and things. Eddie Dodd asked me to drop this stuff off. I don't know what's going on here. I'd like to leave right now."

"Were you planning to take back some pelts with you?" Jack asked. He saw it was too late to sidle up to Hughes calmly; the man was already too agitated.

"Oh, hell. Don't try to set me up. Just let me go down there and get my coin shooter and I'll be on my way. I don't want to be here when Billy gets back."

"Here he comes now," Bob said.

At first Jack couldn't recognize Billy Crockett striding along the rim. It had been four years since he'd last seen the trapper. Crockett had grown a beard and was wearing a long yellow rubber slicker, the kind Marlboro Men wear in ads. When Jack had known him Billy had always been clean-shaven. But he still wore his blond hair in a long neat ponytail swinging from under a high-crowned old-style buckaroo hat. Like Jack, he was about thirty now, but his round steel-rimmed spectacles gave him the look of a college boy, which is why Jack's uncle Pete had nicknamed him "Berkeley" when Billy had showed up looking for work at his ranch a decade ago. Under the unbuttoned raincoat Billy wore clean Levi's and an Eddie Bauer chamois shirt. His clothes almost looked pressed.

Crockett's nose, delicate at the bridge, flared into prominent uptilted nostrils. Sensuous lips curled into a smirk. Behind the steel-rimmed glasses his flat eyes remained rigid, like blue pebbles in ice.

"How do you get rid of a mule you don't want?" he asked nonchalantly. "I got two to give away."

Bob held out his hand, ignoring the question. "Give me your pistol, Billy."

Crockett hesitated a moment, then reached behind the lapel of his yellow slicker and withdrew the pistol from his shoulder holster. It was a .22 caliber, forceful enough to finish off a trapped animal without seriously damaging the pelt. A powerful .357 Magnum, like the one Larry Hughes was wearing on his hip, would ruin a coyote pelt. A less bloody way favored by trappers was simply to stomp on a coyote's rib cage with a boot heel and burst the animal's heart.

"We've got a report on you," Bob told Crockett, "that you've been knocking down game out of season. We want to check your camp."

"I have some meat hung up," Crockett admitted in a calm voice. "If I didn't, I'd have starved to death by now."

"Deer season is over, Billy," Jack said.

"If you guys came all the way out here just to cite me for knocking down a deer, I can't see it. Don't you have anything better to do?"

"You're setting illegal traps," Bob said. "Let's get going."

Crockett turned and glared at Larry Hughes.

The fat man lifted his hands in a defensive posture. "I didn't say anything, Billy. I didn't know they were coming out here."

Air burst from Crockett's nostrils in a dismissive snort. His accusatory look told Jack that he thought the fat man had squealed on him.

"A lot of guys could've told us you were out here," Jack said, trying to cover for Hughes.

Crockett smiled. "Remember what I told you, Jack, when I invited you into my camp?"

Clearly he was talking about the time, four years ago, when Jack had confiscated Crockett's guns and traps. Jack had come across some unmarked traps, and while following the trapper's tracks, he found a parked Jeep with two loaded rifles in the cab. At the time Jack had a feeling of dread that he was being watched, but loaded guns in a vehicle were a misdemeanor that allowed him to confiscate them. Then he saw the outline of a man in a buckaroo hat with a rifle looking down at him from the rimrock. Jack went to his pickup and called Bob, who drove out right away. Two days later Crockett showed up in town to get back his rifles. His hair hung in a single braid down his back. He was polite and soft-spoken, although he wouldn't admit that the unmarked traps were his. Jack told him he'd always been taught that when you get caught with your hand in the cookie jar, you should fess up. But Crockett wouldn't. He only asked in a polite, submissive voice whether he could have his guns back. Jack knew that without a confession he couldn't make any charges stick, and he thought that if he could get on Crockett's good side, the kid might straighten up. They talked about Jack's uncle Pete; Crockett said he'd never worked for a better man in his life. He'd still be buckarooing if Pete's ranch hadn't gone under. Jack told him he could do just as well trapping legally as illegally. "I'm just asking you to play fair," Jack said. Crockett then promised that Jack wouldn't ever see any of his traps baited or unmarked. They shook hands, and Crockett said, "You're always welcome in my camp, Jack, but leave your badge behind."

"You know I can't do that, Billy," Jack had told him.

His eyes had gotten hard. "Well, then stay out of my camps," Crockett had warned.

Crockett was still looking at Jack when Bob ordered him to lead the way from the canyon rim to the camp.

"Can I at least haul down some of this grub?"

Bob said okay, and Crockett swung the heavy Styrofoam cooler to his shoulder and set out at a quick clip. Jack and Larry Hughes followed, and Bob brought up the rear.

The trail switchbacked down the steep canyon wall. Jack was sweating when they hit a sloping scree field of volcanic rock. He took off his coat. The scraping sound of sliding stones echoed from the opposite wall as he scrambled and skidded down the scree field, trying to keep up with Crockett, even though the young trapper's feet swung out in a typical urban dweller's splayfooted duck walk.

On the canyon floor the sagebrush grew shoulder high. Prime cat country. A meandering line of red willows marked the banks of a creek. In a clearing Crockett had pitched a canvas sheepherder's wall tent, tall enough for a man to stand up in. His camp, as always, was orderly; wood was stacked neatly by a fire ring covered with a metal grate. On a foldout table, a frying pan, tin plate, and pots rested upside down on a dish towel. A washstand had been fashioned on a tripod of juniper branches. On another tripod in the shade hung the hindquarters of a deer. On the metal poles behind the tent hung another set of deer's legs from which he had carved slices of meat for himself or his traps. In the brush at the edge of the camp was a third set of venison quarters. On the ground lay a deer's head, with a four-point set of antlers. What the hell did he need with the three deer, if he was only killing for sustenance? Jack knew Bob was thinking the same thing when he asked to see Crockett's trapping license.

"You're still an Idaho resident," Bob said.

Crockett objected. "I've got a nonresident trapping license for here."

"But you've got no license for these deer."

"I never said I did."

"I'm going to write you up."

"What's the point? I'm a hundred miles from civilization. If I obeyed city people's laws, I'd starve to death."

"Those laws still apply to you," Jack said. He wanted to cite Billy and get out of there, but he could see that the three slaughtered deer were causing Bob's temper to crackle.

"A man who lives off the land as I do should have some rights. Game laws don't apply to Indians around here."

"You're no Indian, buddy," Bob snapped.

Crockett remained calm. He seemed to feel a need to explain his way of life, to justify the rightness of his hunter's code. "It's a matter of survival," he said with unforced patience. "I can't buy groceries down the canyon. I either eat venison or a man's cow. And I've never stolen another man's beef."

"What do you have in the tent?" Bob asked.

Billy stiffened. "You're off limits there. This tent is my home."

"Maybe Larry can go in and get the pelts you have in there."

Crockett threw an angry glare toward Larry Hughes. "I don't know what he told you," Crockett said, "but I have a license to trap cats."

Larry protested. The fat man's pale face was splotched from the quick hike down the canyon trail. He looked ripe for a stroke. "I didn't say anything, Billy."

"You have a nonresident license," Bob said, sounding tough. "If you've got illegal game, I have a duty to arrest you."

"Let us see what you have," Jack said, trying to calm the situation. He hoped they wouldn't have to arrest Billy. Since they knew him, and where he lived, they had grounds to write a ticket instead. He hoped Billy would cooperate.

"If you don't have a search warrant," Crockett warned, "I don't want you in my home."

Jack stood between Billy and his tent. Larry Hughes backed away. The front of the tent was tied shut, so Jack couldn't see into it. "Come on, Billy," Jack said. "Let's not make this hard. You know this camp isn't your home. It's temporary. We have a right to search it."

"You show us what you've got," Bob told Crockett, "or we can go in ourselves."

"You're out of line," Crockett's voice snapped, hot now. "This is my home. You're not going in there."

"Okay, Jack," Bob said, "check out what's inside."

Bob stood with his back to the tent. Crockett faced him about six feet away. Jack untied the tent flaps. He wished Billy would quit balking. Whatever tough-guy scenario he had running through his head was only going to get him in more trouble with Bob. The warden wasn't going to put up with an overage adolescent acting out some lunatic mountain-man fantasies—Bob had slammed the lid on tougher poachers than Crockett.

As Jack untied the flap strings, he heard Bob saying, "You know the law, Billy. We have the right to check out any camp." Then Crockett replied in a weak, pleading voice, sounding like a little boy, "Are you going to take me in?"

Inside the shadowy tent, Jack noticed a portable kerosene heater near a canvas cot. A blue North Point sleeping bag and a foam pad lay on the cot. The guy sure liked his comforts. The smell of warm canvas filled the tent. Against the sunlit back wall of the tent leaned two bobcat hides on stretching boards and a raccoon skin drying on a third board. Nothing necessarily illegal except that they had been taken with baited traps—a misdemeanor, though hard to prove. Then along the side of the tent Jack saw the tawny fur of what looked to be the rolled pelt of a mountain lion. Shot or trapped, a mountain lion was illegal at this time of year.

Outside the tent, Bob's voice burst into a shout, "Oh, no!" Jack whirled. Pistol shots cracked. Jack flung back the flaps of the tent and saw Crockett in a crouched police stance, firing a pistol gripped in both hands. The exploding handgun thundered, as Bob fell backward, his face spattered with blood, a coil of smoke snaking up from his chest. Larry Hughes slumped forward, his big body crashing through sagebrush. Crockett swung his arms back and forth, blasting bullets into both falling men. Then, still in his crouched stance, knees bent, he whipped the barrel of the abruptly silent pistol toward Jack.

"Come out here," he yelled.

Jack walked as if trying to push through the thick cloud left by the noise of exploding cartridges. He didn't know whether Crockett's pistol was still loaded. He thought he'd heard it last click on an empty cylinder, but Crockett kept it pointed at his chest. Bob lay on his back. His bloody head lifted up from the ground, his desperate eyes searching in Jack's direction, then plopped back. Jack realized with a stunning jolt of fear that he was helpless. He was defenseless. In the excitement on the canyon ridge he'd forgotten to strap on his pistol. He'd left the damn, hateful gun under the seat of the truck up on the rim.

Crockett ducked into the tent and reappeared carrying a .22 rifle with a leather shoulder sling. Jack watched without believing what he was seeing. "Billy, don't," he shouted. His hands floated up in a hopeless gesture. Crockett shot Bob in the head, then aimed at Larry Hughes, pointing the barrel an inch from the fat man's skull just behind the ear, as if finishing off an animal in a trap. "Billy!" Jack screamed, his fluttering hands futilely extended outward. Jack shut his eyes just as the bullet cracked through bone. Bob and Larry lay in the dirt motionless. Then Jack saw the rifle pointed at his face.

THOMAS SANCHEZ [B. 1944]

A novelist of remarkable range, Thomas Sanchez has published five novels, variously set in the California-Nevada border country (Rabbit Boss, 1973), Los Angeles (Zoot-Suit Murders, 1978), Key West (Mile Zero, 1989), France and Spain (Day of the Bees, 2000), and Cuba (King Bongo, 2003), spanning time frames from the mid-nineteenth century to the post-Vietnam era. His first novel, Rabbit Boss, excerpted below, was written when Sanchez was in his early twenties. He became interested in the Washoe Indians through a professor at American River College in Sacramento, who had done ethnographic fieldwork for a class at the University of Nevada, Reno. Rabbit Boss has been called an American epic, "a landmark work of twentieth-century American literature" that chronicles the changing fortunes of four generations of a Washoe Indian family. The novel opens with a chilling image of the Donner party: "The Washo watched. The Washo watched through the trees. The Washo watched through the trees as they ate themselves." Cannibalism becomes emblematic of the colonizing culture that invades the Washoe's territory and destroys their traditional way of life, ultimately "cannibalizing . . . an entire race," as Sanchez observes. Sanchez's Hispanic surname leads many readers to assume that he is Mexican-American. But in fact his mother and stepfather were Anglo, and his biological father (killed in World War II) was from Spain. Nevertheless, based on his surname, the elementary school that Sanchez attended in California placed him in remedial English classes, while his stepbrother, whose last name was Harden, was placed in the top classes. This and other instances of discrimination sensitized Sanchez to the minority issues that charge his fiction. During the 1960s Sanchez was active in human rights organizations such as the Congress of Racial Equality and the United Farm Workers. At great personal risk, he covered the 1973 takeover at Wounded Knee, and he wrote and hosted a five-part ABC-TV special on the California Hispanic community.

from *Rabbit Boss*

His head was up. The Sun was up. The Birds were out. The yellowmen were everywhere. From the deep squint of his eyes the Indian watched their gold sweatbacks bang steel into solid ground. Behind him the Iron Road was nailed down to the mountain cliff of the Sierra. In front of him was the burntland, waiting for the yellowmen to bang their way across the swollen faces of brown hills. Beneath his boots the Earth would not stop trembling with the rhythm of steel driving into its skin. The higher the Sun pulled itself up the more relentless the rhythm of the yellowmen became. The full hammer weight of their sledges swung and poised above their heads, cascading down in a perfect rain of strength, pounding the Iron Road for all time into the Earth's crust. Beneath the thickness of his checkered jacket he sweated and watched, moving back along the ironrails that had just been laid. The rhythmic driving of slamming steel filled the air like the breath of two hundred yellowmen chained into a relentless iron beast; the sound of slapping steel roared from their lungs as the Iron Road grew. The Indian followed back along the iron-rails toward the wall of mountains until the yellowmen appeared far behind him on the horizon, the single movement of their massed bodies balanced over the hotland like a human blade searching the soft spot to plunge through into the Earth's heart, cutting the vital muscle throbbing blood through their own heads, releasing them from the pounding rhythm of their bodies. The sight of the yellow-men swelled everyday in his head like a cloud. The cloud pushed all other thoughts from him. There became only the single yellow beast sucking the air with iron lungs, feeding off the fierce heat thrown down by the Sun, piercing through the days with a straight Iron Road. The fire-eating Engine crashing down the ironrails threw black smoke into the blur of Sky as it followed the track laid by yellowmen. The yellowmen led the way into the desert, pounding a new time in the heat, all movement swung with sledges lifted over small yellow shoulders. The yellowmen had no Spirit, they gave birth to the fire-eating Engines. Never did they look back to the mountains or to the flatland slapped out to their sides. Their eyes saw only straight ahead and down, where they nailed the hide of the Earth. They were not to be trusted. Between their legs were yellow Snakes. If a woman had the Snake in her it would poison her. The blood would run from her until she died. The yellow-men together had many pieces of metal coin. They would give two bags of gold coins for the meat of the Cat in the mountains. The meat gave poison to their Snakes. He himself during the white days had followed a big Cat in the snow, com-ing close behind the Dogs howling through ravines. There was a night with no stars, just a Moon and the snarling sound of Dogs clawing at the trunk of a tree. At the top of the tree sat the Cat, golden and deep within the fur branches until the blast of the rifle ripped open his side and dropped his bleeding weight in the snow, the silence of his open eyes reflecting the Moon. It took him three days to pack the Cat out of the ravines to the Chinese camp outside Truckee. When the yellowmen handed over the two sacks of metal coin the Cat lay at his feet with the blood of its body frozen through the golden fur like red stone. *Red Cat* the yellowmen called him. Captain Red Cat. He buried one of the sacks of metal beneath snow in the hollowed root of a tree and took the other into Truckee where he spent half of it on six glasses of whiskey and five hands of Blackjack before going down to the big house where the candles burned and the women with skin that smelled like flowers waited. He bought the one with the red hair between her legs. He gave her the half sack of metal in the dark room before he put his hands all over her body and kissed her under the arms until she laughed so hard he threw her down on the floor next to the bed, feeling the silent spread of her flesh going out beneath him while his hands covered the swell of her breasts. In the morning he woke up on the floor, he could hear the woman snoring from beneath the blanket on the bed. His eyes burned in his aching head from the glare of Sun that came through the window and hit the opposite wall. He left the house and walked down through the place where the huge boxcars with ironwheels stood on the silver track in a line against the Sun. He picked his way through the dump, kicking at the fresh heaps for food. It was early for his people to have come and searched through the previous night's waste. Beneath a yellowed layer of scattered lettuce and the black sog of cof-feegrinds he kicked up the hide of the Cat. The yellowmen had quickly stripped out the meat for their poison and tossed the ragged fur away. On a pile of chicken bones rotting back into the Earth rested the severed head, its eyes glazed white and blank in the Sun. He raised the hide and shook it free of garbage. He went down through the trees past his canvas shack and dipped the hide in the river, the blood washing free as he knelt at the bank, watching the red stains melt and disappear in the cold blue. He laid the hide face down on a rock and raked the skin clean of fat and dark tangled clots of meat. He tacked it high in the Sun on the bark of a pin-etree. When the Sun had seared the skin brown he took it down and worked it soft in his hands with the juice of a root before he took it back up the hill to Truckee and bet it against one of the Mexicans who laid down two ten-dollar pieces of metal. The Mexican cut the deck and shuffled the cards, then slammed them on the table and told the Indian to draw. The card the Indian pulled from the closed deck was the King's son. He thought the skin was still his and he could put the gold metal in his pocket, but the Mexican drew the very King himself, flipping the painted card on the gold fur of the skin draped over the table. The Mexican laughed and shouted across the room to the man behind the bar, "A whiskey for the Cap-tain! Two shots of whiskey for Capitan Rex, a born gambler!" Captain Rex gulped the glasses set before him and the ancient song of Birds fluttered in his blood. He threw his head back to let the wings beat from his lips and his eyes caught on the crescent cut of the glass pieces swaying from the chandelier, their clear images re-flecting off one another like a thousand Moons. He sang at the Moons like every nightbird in the forest had been captured and set free in the square of the room. Only the light shining through the cut glass bore witness to his dark song. When the song died on his lips the Birds settled down in his chest, their ancient sound still clinging to the bare walls until it echoed itself into silence. The Mexican brought his fist down on the table, clanking the two empty glasses as his laughter roared into the face of the Indian, he wiped the tears from his eyes as he shouted, "Feed this Injun Capitan a firewater! He sings like the hummingbird, crows like the owl, croons like a woodpecker and shits like the hawk! The christdamn things these hombres won't do!" The Indian stayed in the saloon until the Sun dropped out of the Sky. His lungs raw from bellowing the songs of Birds that scattered from his lips after each whiskey bought for him washed into his body with a sudden knot of heat. He stumbled outside through the door and reeled only for an instant before his boot hooked on the stub of a nail in the boardwalk and tripped him face down in the mud slush of the street. He staggered his way down the road below the town past the silent bulk of the boxcars and over the hills of human waste growing out of the dump. Pieces of snow began to fall from the Sky like dumb gentle white flowers. The rolls and peaks of the dump glistened in the blurred swirl before him. The dark shapes of the women floated like shadows between the scattered cans and broken glass glowing from the touch of iced air. The bandannas wrapped around the women's heads and across their mouths left only the brown slash of their eyes exposed as they bent and dipped into the piles of rubbish with numbed fingers hooking up useful prizes quickly hidden from sight in the weighted gunnysacks slung over their shoulders. The women looked across to the stumbling man, their outlines obscured in the quickening gentle fall from the Sky. They watched him as one as he moved hot and clumsy through their territory, his clothing dark with mud, the wild toss of his black hair turning white from trapped bits of snow. He could see the one who was his mother. She stood inseparable from the others, one of the flock. No sign passed from her to the man who was now almost gone from sight, weaving down through the pines toward the sound of the river racing itself through sharp rocks.

After the snow had covered everything it left the Earth quiet. The Moon cut open the darkness, the slap of canvas over the shack's opening was pushed back. His mother came into the hut. She sat herself on the skinworn Rabbit-blanket and knotted rags of her bed. The cold that she brought with her woke him. He reached out for the bottle that earlier dropped to the dirt floor when his hand had become too shaky to hold it. He quickly raised the bottle to his lips, it was empty. His mouth sucked out the fumes of whiskey from the glass hollow before he let the bottle slip from his grasp to the floor. The woman said nothing. The wind blowing outside in the clear night flapped the loose pieces of canvas stretched over the boarded frame of the hut. He had lost in his memory the day when the woman stopped her talking. She had once been full of words, they had come quickly and often to her lips. The world before the Whites was always in her brown eyes. She ceased to see the new world she had been forced into. She had gone blind to the places her body took her throughout the days. She had long since stopped seeing the man her son had become. There were no words for him. Once she had much talk about the man who put three babies into her body. When she spoke about this husband of her heart called Gayabuc all the happiness out of a time long since gone dead caught on her face and turned it young. She told of the watercress that grew from the shallow streams and how he would go into the water for her, standing brown as a buck, gently pulling the shoots from their bed of water. He would bring them dripping to her so she could suck the green taste from the damp white roots. She told of the small Rabbits he would trap in the snow and bring to her, the bodies still warm as she stripped their fur and staked them over the coals, the hot rising smell of wild flesh swelling in the hut as the husband of her heart lay next to her with his want, his hand tracing the high brown curve of her hip and between her legs to force her open to the thickness of his body. Her face fired as she would talk of her Girl's Dance and how on the mountaintop Gayabuc wrestled with the smoke, forcing its white tongue into the night Sky, forcing it to give its sign to the people gathered below, to write in the Sky that she had acted true and according to the ways of a girl going into a Woman, that her life would be long and straight. She was proud that he had fought the power of the smoke, but to force the sign was against the ways of the past, it was an act that made the animals flee his bow. It was an act that would kill his days short. But that was before *they* came. Before the fences of sharp wire went up and the husband of her heart was shot down. The Ancestors did not forget. It was because Gayabuc had violated the way of the Girl's Dance and forced the smoke to give up a false sign for her that the ancestors punished all the people and brought out of the burntlands those with skin the color of snow. The day of the people was ended, buried beneath a white burden. And Gayabuc had been the first to see *them*. He had watched through the trees. He had watched down to the high snow on the frozen shore of the yonder lake. He watched them moving slowing on the snow, clumsy, like Bears in water. He had been watching silently all that morning, had seen, had seen *them* hunched, away from each other, mouths tearing at knots of flesh, faces smeared the color of a dying Sun. He watched through the trees as *they* ate *themselves*. It was as if he had found *them* in dream and they had followed him into life. Coming one after the other, first in small tired groups, pushing the weight of their heavy bodies up and over the barrier of mountains reaching to the Sky, then in long sluggish lines with hunger burning in their eyes and their great tamed beasts pulling whole billowing tent houses behind on high wooden wheels that creaked in the mountain air, breaking the stones beneath their immense burden to powder. Leaving the Earth behind rutted and used. And still they came, up out of the burntlands, down along the spine of the mountains from the north, up from the hidden valleys of the south. They came closer one upon the other until their line was unbroken and flowed steadily like the sap from a fatal wound in the heart of a great tree. And the man Gayabuc had brought *them*. *They* were born in his eyes as he saw *them* eat of *their* own flesh. *They* were born from his violation of the clear path cut by the Ancestors. The smoke in the Sky at the Girl's Dance died, and he had made it into a false sign for all the people below to see. It began with this lie on the mountaintop, the end of her people. The bones of her people would be crushed like powder beneath the bulk of the iron wheels of *those* who ate of *their* own flesh.

H. LEE BARNES [B. 1944]

Always a hungry reader, Lee Barnes became a writer relatively late in life, publishing his first book when he was fifty-five. Barnes has lived hard, witnessed a lot, and acquired an experiential inventory that sets him apart from most fiction writers today. Born in Idaho, son of a wheat farmer he never met, Barnes and his older sister trailed around the West with their waitress mother, who later married a radio broadcaster, whose career took them from Colorado Springs to Roswell to Tularosa to Alamogordo to El Paso. "Wherever we moved, I was always an outsider," Barnes recalls in the preface to Talk to Me, James Dean: Stories of the Southwest *(2004), "so it seems only natural that I would develop both the voice and the eye of the outsider." When Barnes was nineteen, he fought in Vietnam, earning a Combat Infantry Badge and the Vietnamese Gallantry Cross for his service in the Green Berets. What he observed of human nature in Vietnam informs Barnes's acclaimed short story collection* Gunning for Ho *(2000), followed by* Minimal Damage: Stories of Veterans *(2007) about those who returned. After the war, Barnes held some tough jobs, including deputy sheriff, narcotics agent, private investigator, and martial arts instructor. In Las Vegas, Barnes worked seventeen years as a dealer and supervisor in casinos, becoming an insider qualified to write* Dummy Up and Deal: Inside the Culture of Casino Dealing *(2002). He escaped "the green felt jungle" to return to school, earning a BA at UNLV and an MFA at Arizona State University. Barnes is now a professor at the Community College of Southern Nevada and a writer with the stamina of a marathoner. "I don't have a TV," he explains to account for his high productivity. His work has received four Pushcart nominations and many other honors. The following selection is from his novel* The Lucky *(2003), a brilliant epic of the contemporary West, whose central character, Willy Bobbins, resembles Benny Binion, legendary owner of Las Vegas's Horseshoe casino.*

from *The Lucky*

That Thursday a high roller from Houston lost nearby half a million at the roulette wheel. Willy sat by the gambler the whole time and told stories as the Texan forged his own downfall by constantly asking that the table limits be raised. When the man's bankroll at last flattened out, Willy put him in a limousine to the airport and slumped down in his booth.

"Pete, bring chili and lots of crackers," he said.

"Right away," I said.

"I'm a lucky man. You know why, Pete?"

"No, Willy."

He tilted his hat back with his thumb. "Neither do I."

. . . .

Willy had told me to pack an overnight bag and said, "Let's take a ride." He chewed on a dead cigar as we pulled into a parking space. It was December 27th and cold, and why we were at McCarran Airport was a mystery to me. He slipped his .45 under the seat and cracked his door.

"Still, can't figger that Jack Ruby. Weren't nothing but a two-bit pimp when I met him," Willy said.

"Maybe he's crazy," I said.

"No, don't think so."

I changed the subject. I'd become intrigued with microscopes and the things that fit between slides. Insects took on complex patterns and vivid detail, especially the wings. Assuming his curiosity would be aroused, I described the cell structure of a dragonfly's wing to Willy.

He listened patiently and said, "Get them classes done good, but don't get no ideas about bein no scientist. You're too smart for that stuff. No money in it."

"But . . ."

"Now, listen, Pete. I'm meetin a man who don't know I'm meetin him. It's going to be a surprise. Don't let on no different."

"Okay."

"I figger Jack, who never done nothin, wanted to be remembered for somethin is all. 'Course the whole world is crazy. People killin the President. Well, if you ain't from Dallas, you can't unnerstand." He opened the door, stood up and stretched. "Come on, an bring your bag."

The terminal was swamped with arrivals. Willy approached the United Airlines counter and asked if the flight from Dallas was on time. The ticket clerk pointed to the schedule board. "'S up there, sir."

Willy shook his head. "Didn't ask the board. I ask't you."

The man looked at Willy for a second, then quickly looked away. "Yes, sir, it's on time."

"Good for you," Willy said.

Carrying my overnight bag, I followed Willy through the maze of people to the baggage claim. He asked me to find where the baggage from the Dallas flight would be coming in. I located the sign and motioned him over.

"What other flights're arrivin?" he asked.

I looked again at the signs. "Reno."

"Good."

"Why're we here, Willy?"

"A man 'sposed to kill me," he said.

"Kill you?"

"Yep. 'At's why you gotta carry his bag."

"Me?"

"Trust me, Pete."

Willy leaned against a pillar where he could see the escalator. Looking to all the world unconcerned, he bit on his cigar. A group of travelers from Reno milled about the luggage area. As bags emerged on the conveyor, the people turned into a crowd of half-frenzied grabbers. Arms folded over his chest, Willy chewed on his dead cigar and kept watch.

Fifteen minutes passed before the passengers from the Dallas flight began to show. More and more turned the corner, but Willy's man didn't seem to be among them. The luggage feed spat bags out on the carousel. In minutes most of the tourists claimed their luggage and headed for the door, but a few unclaimed bags circled about like rafts floating in an eddy.

"Maybe he's not coming," I said.

"Probably watchin to see if he's bein watched."

Willy muttered under his breath and chewed harder on the cigar, his eyes unblinking as he scanned the escalator ferrying people to the luggage area. Then he smiled and, using the pillar for cover, turned away as the sliding doors opened. A tall, slim man of about forty wearing a white Stetson rounded the corner. He gazed about as if searching the wallpaper for enemies. His skin seemed immutably tan, as if tattooed brown, and his hawkish face had a composed, dangerous look. He'd slipped by Willy, gone outside, and doubled back.

Willy said, "I'll do the talkin."

Willy came up as the man bent over the conveyor belt. "Art. Art Mosley," Willy said.

The man jerked his head around at hearing the name. "Mr. Bobbins, Mr. Bobbins," he said and stood tall as he smiled down at Willy, almost a head shorter. He had a seducer's smile, practiced and direct, and a mouth full of straight white teeth.

"Call me Willy, Art. What brings you?" he offered his hand, which Art shook.

"It's Las Vegas, ain't it? Little gambling, Willy," he said, hiding behind that plaster smile.

Despite the smiles, Willy and the man who'd come to kill him stared at one another.

Willy said, "Ain't this a coincidence, me here to meet Pete. Pete, this here's Art Mosley."

I shook hands with him.

"Pete kind'a lives with us. Where you stayin, Art?"

"The Algiers," he said and started toward the carousel, where his luggage was on about the twentieth trip around.

Willy followed. "Won't have it, Art."

Art stopped in his tracks. "Won't have what, Willy?"

"Won't have you stayin any place but mine."

"The Lucky? Thanks anyhow, Willy, but I got bidness. On the Strip."

"Thought you was here to gamble."

"That too."

"I wouldn't be much of a host if I ask't you to stay at the Lucky. Hell, we got all sort 'a room. Don't we, Pete?"

Willy was right—the world was crazy—him along with it. Either that, or he was kidding about Art's purpose for being in Las Vegas. "Plenty of room," I said.

Willy took my bag from my hand. "Pete'll help you with your bags, and I won't hear a no, not even a shake 'a your head. Hell, you wouldn't wanna insult an ol Texas boy."

I fit Art's two suitcases in the trunk. Willy said we'd stop for a short bite at the Lucky. Though he seemed composed, Art was beginning to sweat, as evidenced by his armpits.

Art slept at the house and received Willy's undivided attention. The first night Willy kept him up until dawn drinking sour mash and trading stories. I stayed up until midnight, when finally Willy told me to go to bed. Art objected, saying there was no reason to send me off, but Willy told me to go on.

Willy left the business to George and devoted every waking moment to Art. The more hospitable he was toward Art, the more skeptical I became. I figured what Willy had claimed about Art was a gag. I enjoyed Art's stories about his days as a vice cop in Fort Worth and started liking him, and whenever I stood to leave, he would ask me to stay for another story, and Willy would motion for me to sit.

Betty flirted openly with Art, which didn't seem to affect Willy. Art and Stella discussed old acquaintances. He complimented her clothes, her garden, her taste in furniture and drapes, her hairdo—a charmer. Stella said she'd make him a special meal and ordered Betty and me to help take down Christmas decorations, after which she sent Jamita home and told Betty she would have to help serve dinner. Betty said she had a date, which meant nothing to Stella. Willy insisted that she stay, and Art seemed pleased with the idea of her being there. We sat staring at platters of lamb chops, cauliflower, and potatoes au gratin, Willy at the head of the table, Art to his immediate right. Stella sat opposite Willy, while Betty and I sat toward the center facing one another. Betty picked at her food, alternately looking at her watch and the door. Now and then she'd mention that she had planned all week to go out.

Willy became less talkative, almost sullen. Stella seemed a bit cooler toward Art. Betty was detached. Art talked nervously and picked at his food, now and then nodding to show approval. Near the end of the meal Willy asked, "Art, how do you like Stella's lamb chops?"

Art looked to get Stella's attention. "Mighty fine, ma'am."

"Thank you, Art. We miss Dallas. Don't we, Willy?"

"Sure do."

"Dad, can I go now?" Betty said.

Willy shook his head. "Not just yet, darlin. We got company."

Betty looked at Art. "If you ask me, he looks like he'd rather be somewhere else, too."

"Is 'at right, Art?" Willy asked. "You'd ruther be somewheres else?"

"Now, Willy, what kind'a question's 'at?" Stella said. "Peter, you want another chop?"

Art, thankful that Stella had come to his aid, cut off a bite of meat.

"Yes, ma'am," I said.

"Eats like he's two boys," Stella said to Art.

Art nodded, but it was obvious his mind was elsewhere. Betty watched me cut the lamb chop and shook her head. I held the meat on my fork and grinned before stuffing it in my mouth and chewing it with my mouth open.

"Disgusting," she said.

"Pete, close your mouth," Stella said. "Didn't your ma teach you nothin?"

I closed my mouth and chewed.

"Really, Dad, I'm late," Betty said.

"Darlin, don't bring it up again." Willy turned his attention back to Art. "It was a rude question I asked, Art, but I got another."

Art looked up from his plate. "Go ahead, Willy."

"You never did say what your bidness was."

"No, guess I didn't."

"Maybe I can help out. Maybe if your bidness don't go well, you can find work with me."

Art shook his head. "Got plenty 'a work, Willy."

"What exactly is it you're doin now, Art?"

Betty pushed her chair back and started to stand.

Willy aimed a finger at her and snapped, "Sit 'til I say otherwise."

She slouched down in her chair. I finished the last of my chop and folded my napkin.

"Willy," Stella said, "a handsome man like Art prob'ly sells jewelry or cars."

Willy shook his head. From beneath his coat he pulled out a Smith and Wesson .357 Magnum and held it up for Art to see. "Must be jewelry. Else why would he need this?" He opened the cylinder to show it was loaded, snapped it shut, and laid the gun before Art. "What is it, Art? Jewelry?"

Neither Betty nor I could move. Like Art, Betty stared at the revolver. Art swallowed and looked at the gun. Stella scooted her chair back and asked who wanted pecan pie.

Leaning back, Willy entwined his fingers behind his neck. "Art an me'll have some. Don't guess Betty wants any. Pete can take his upstairs an study. Boy has to study if he's gonna make it to lawyer school." Willy had taken to mentioning me and law school in one breath.

Like Betty and Art, I fixed my gaze on the revolver, while Willy and Stella seemed as casual as two picnickers discussing potato salad. When Betty and I stood to leave, Art said he had to go. Willy paid no mind, just kept his hands behind his neck, his elbows pointed to the sides. "After some pie, Art. You know, we ain't yet talked 'bout Tex. How's he doin these days? Must be a ol' man by now. Seventy or so."

His lips nearly white, Art swallowed hard. "Don't kill me, Willy. Don't." His hands were under the table out of sight, but it was obvious they were trembling.

Willy looked at the three of us. "We can have pie some other time," he said. "Y'all go on so's me an Art can talk."

. . . .

That spring, pressure from the IRS kept Willy inside the casino, where he met with politicians and poker players, told stories, walked among the patrons and shook hands, and smiled when a player with a million-dollar credit line asked to bet it all on a spin of the roulette ball.

"You want to spin the ball yourself?" Willy asked.

The gambler said, "No, I want you to spin it, Willy."

A pit boss stacked ten hundred-thousand-dollar marker buttons on the even. Willy set the ball on the rim of the wheel head and spun it so hard it whined for the first six rotations. When it finally descended twenty seconds later, it ticked a fret and dived into the six. Willy took eighty piles of greenbacks, twenty-five thousand in each, from three security guards and laid the money next to the million-dollar lammer button. "Care to let it ride?" he asked.

The high roller shook his head.

"Care to count it?" Willy asked.

"You ain't no banker, Willy. I trust you."

The event made headlines as the single biggest wager in history. Willy said he'd lost bigger bets than that, but those were in back rooms, and he wouldn't want revenuers to know about them because they might be business deductions. Reporters laughed at Willy's joke and took down every word.

Sin City, by B. Lawrence Karras, a best-seller in its first week, was published in May. A chapter devoted to Willy's exploits in Texas claimed he was connected to the underworld and had paid the Mafia to make hits, including the one on Sammy "the Slav" Lukovic, who once owned five percent of the old Sierra Club. The book didn't help Willy's image with the feds, but people flocked to the Lucky just to get a glimpse of him. For his part, Willy defended himself by saying that if anyone needed killing, he wasn't about to put up good money just to do public service.

I was the one who had to read to Willy the part where the author called him a splendidly ignorant hick and a splendidly stupid boor. Willy raised his finger for me to stop. "Man's a New Yorker. Never seen one who could play poker. Don't know how to bluff. They get the upper hand, they let you know right way. I never lost a penny to one in bidness, but many's the New Yorker lost to me. You keep the upper hand by letting 'em think they got it."

He laughed at the part about the Slav choking to death on a billiard ball held in place by a gag, said he always did bite off more than he could chew. Of course, the mystery to me was the same as the mystery to the author—why?

When I finished reading the last page of the book, Willy took it in hand and examined the dustcover. "He ain't no F. Scott Fitzgerald an this ain't no *Gatsby,*" he said, picked up the telephone, leaned back, and waited for his attorney to come on the line. He told the lawyer to draft a letter to B. Lawrence Karras telling him not to worry about a lawsuit, even though he'd told a few splendid whoppers, because business was up a splendid five or six points due to the splendid publicity. Willy added an invitation for Karras to come visit the Lucky at the casino's expense and, of course, sign a copy of the splendid book.

. . . .

Willy's tax lawyers, specialists from Los Angeles, started off optimistic about the case, then at a meeting in his office he berated them, saying he wasn't paying for optimism but results and so far it looked pretty sad to him. They made the mistake of looking to George for support. "Who you think's payin the tab here?" Willy said. Briefcases in hand, the lawyers skulked out of the casino. By firing that team and hiring a new firm from San Francisco, Willy was able to buy time. The next batch of attorneys focused on delays and legal maneuvers, a strategy that frustrated those around Willy, but not him. As the climax of the case neared, he acted as if nothing other than the next sunrise was pending.

His second team of lawyers weren't optimists, but they were arrogant. During dinner at the house he told them that income tax violated the Constitution and he aimed to stand up for the law. One asked how Willy had become an authority on the Constitution. He grinned and said he wasn't yet, but he sure would be by the time he got out of prison, which was where he was going because his lawyers "didn't know squat about the law." He laughed and poured himself a shot of whiskey. He was the only one who found this amusing.

. . . .

Willy's lawyers negotiated and his accountants cooked his books under the watchful eye of George. Still, the IRS had a case; it was a matter of degree and what kind of deal his attorneys could walk before a judge. The next day he surrendered to marshals, who said he'd be kept in isolation and closely observed until his case went to court. He was booked into the county jail and given a private cell with a television and a telephone. Two days later Willy pled guilty to one count of income-tax evasion.

. . . .

Summer set in, and despite continuous legal maneuvering on his behalf Willy remained incarcerated. He was made trusty without duties and allowed free rein of the third floor of the jail. Every afternoon he went outside and sat with a towel draped over his shoulder and smoked a cigar while other trusties washed and detailed patrol cars. Four evenings a week I brought him dinner and kept a book at hand to read.

. . . .

One evening as Willy was eating lamb chops and wild rice, six cops marched a prisoner past the cell. A tall, thick-bodied man with a mane of wheat-colored hair, he had a menacing look to him even though handcuffed and surrounded by half a dozen cops on his way to the booking cell. He looked, in fact, as if he was in charge of the procession. As he passed, he glared at me with his pale blue eyes. It was like looking at two blue dots in the hollow sockets of a skull.

When the cuffs were unlocked, he told one cop to keep his hands off and another to fuck himself. After that he stood silent and defiant as his belongings were inventoried and sealed in an envelope. When the booking officer asked his name, he said, "John Satan."

"Your real name."

"Lick my balls."

Willy was so well liked by inmates and the jailers that when it was slow, a cop or two would stop by for a little chitchat. A deputy named Fred Osterhaus strolled over after the prisoner was locked down. He carried a copy of the booking sheet, which he showed to Willy, apparently assuming Willy could read. Willy pretended to, but when he didn't react, the officer asked if he didn't think it was funny. Willy said show it to me. I knew to cover for him and read out loud the line where the deputy pointed. The booking officer had written in the prisoner's name as "Lick My Balls, a.k.a. John Satan." Willy offered up a belated laugh and said he missed that part. He asked what the man was booked for.

"Murder, Willy," Deputy Osterhaus said. "He robbed a dry cleaners and tied up the owner and two employees. Doused them with cleaning solvents and set fire to them. He hung around to piss on the wall. Told two witnesses he was trying to put out the blaze and laughed about it. Meanest sonofabitch I ever saw."

"Burned 'em alive?" Willy asked.

"Yes, sir."

Willy pushed the tray aside and shook his head. "Two of 'em just worked there?" I'd seen him angry before and knew him well enough to see he was upset.

"That's about it," the deputy answered.

Willy looked at the empty plate on his tray and back at the cop. "Fred, see if those folks had family. They did, get the names to George an he'll give 'em some money, say ten grand."

"You're serious."

"Serious as one of them atomic bombs they keep settin off."

"That's mighty generous, Willy."

"Never mind. Just do it an don't go tellin it around."

But Fred told, and maybe Willy intended for word of his generosity to circulate. I was never certain. He seemed to have some motive behind everything he did. No matter, the papers carried the story on the front page of the local section, and Willy's beneficence sparked others to initiate a trust fund providing support and college tuition for the victims' children. After half an hour of covering the first mass bombing of Hanoi, Cold War tensions, and a Titan 3 missile being launched with the thrust of 2,400,000 pounds from solid rocket fuel, the network news closed with a piece on Willy, who, though a prisoner, the anchorman said, "acted selflessly to help two families of men he'd never met."

The story captured the public's imagination for a week, and the publicity set off a chain reaction. Gross revenues at the Lucky increased forty percent the weekend following the broadcast. A man interviewed for the evening news said he knew he was going to lose and he'd rather it go to a gentleman like Willy. The governor, both senators, and the lone congressman from the state wrote on Willy's behalf to the U.S. attorney general and the judge who'd presided over the case. Included was a statement by Deputy Fred Osterhaus, who insisted he'd defied Willy's wishes to keep the donations confidential.

The judge agreed to reassess Willy's sentence and asked the U.S. attorney and Willy's lawyers to submit briefs. While his sentence was under review, Willy was released on bail and went home with every confidence that he would never again see jail from the inside. In one masterful stroke, he'd done for himself what a battery of high-priced attorneys couldn't accomplish.

DARRELL SPENCER [B. 1947]

By writing in a contemporary mode, Darrell Spencer manages to set works in Nevada without being labeled a regionalist writer. He is, in fact, one of Nevada's most prominent contemporary authors, winning the highly coveted $15,000 Drue Heinz Literature Prize in 2004 for his short story collection Bring Your Legs with You, *a series of linked stories that focus on a retired boxer in Las Vegas. In 1998 he won the prestigious Flannery O'Connor Award for Short Fiction for* Caution, Men in Trees (2000), *which reviewer Debra Monroe praises for its "dazzling verbal texture—syntax that contorts itself to serve up pleasure, . . . telling and idiosyncratic details," and "sentences full of gaps and light." Spencer's short story "Union Business" won the Lawrence Foundation Award for Fiction, and* So You Got next to the Hammer *won the 1998–99* Quarterly West *novella prize. Growing up in Las Vegas, where he played on the 1965 Las Vegas High School basketball team that won the state championship, Spencer at one time supported himself as a sign painter. Once he decided to write, however, he stuck with it, earning a* PHD *from the University of Utah. Currently the Stocker Professor of Creative Writing at Ohio University, Spencer teaches a graduate course on the theory of fiction, helping students understand what Miriam Clark in "Contemporary Short Fiction and the Postmodern Condition" means when she describes contemporary stories: "Read as reflections or displacements of the postmodern condition, these impossibilities of perception, these failures of coherence and accrual, have a different effect altogether," namely, "narrativity itself." These notions help to elucidate Spencer's own stories. Although he has earned a national reputation, Spencer says that his heart is still in Nevada, and he misses "the desert and endless blue sky, the big moons that come up at night. The smell of sagebrush after rain."*

My Home State of Nevada

She put the door in my face. I was coming in, and she was coming out. The door
was glass. She said, "Thank you." But she'd done the work.

The birthmark on her neck looked like my home state of Nevada.

So, I followed.

I galloped.

I said, "*Wie geht's?*"

She studied the sidewalk, me and my chutzpa, the jay-bird-blue sky, the olean-
ders behind us. She said, "*Trés bien,*" and an orange cat slinked by.

I thought, A multilingual family.

I could have said, I could have said, I could have said, and if I had, she'd have
raised a curtain of anger. I said, "God, I'm hungry. Lunch?"

We ate. We had children. They spoke Chinese, Portuguese, Pontiac, French,
Russian, and German. They went away, and they became Mormons.

With each birth her birthmark diminished until it was a red dot the shape of
Lake Mead. She had it lasered, and one day it wasn't here. Layer by layer, I undid
the bed, I combed the furrowed ground of the garden she'd worked row by row, I
flashlight-swept the shag carpet square foot by square foot, noodle by noodle.

What was gone was lost.

My home state of Nevada had a run of luck. Mount Oddie rained silver ore on
Tonopah, the sagebrush gave way and coats of grass rolled in, the rivers gained
depth and width, and every Christmas snow fell on Las Vegas, my hometown.

We moved to Sparks near enough to Reno and burned our bridges and rode
taxis. Money was no object.

Her hair leapt left and right from a part down the middle.

We got on. We did.

The lean years came, as they do, and we sat in Windsor chairs and looked fixedly
at the blue mountains and the dirt or we quarreled. Too often, it was *me first! me
first!* first thing in the morning.

Our oldest became a prophet.

We saw him on TV. His lips were wet, and he looked benign.

We zigzagged across the Great Basin without telling anyone when we expected
to return, not because we felt like tin gods or jackanapes or back-talking kids. We
showed our respect. We didn't skimp on water, we kept our clothes on, and we did
not put our feet or hands in places we couldn't see. Once she did sit down without
looking, and I prepared myself to suck venom from her wounds wherever they
might be.

We found a cave in Montana where you sit and absorb radon gas. We paid to get in and we sat and played hearts. There had been published disagreement. The scientists said we would die. The locals said we were cured.

She said, "In whom should we trust?", and the sun smacked us as we emerged.

STEVEN NIGHTINGALE [B. 1951]

*"The Great Basin is meant to be home for beautiful phrases and bright narratives," asserts Steven Nightingale. "It's where the light is animate; where heaven still comes round every now and then, to have a whiskey and spin some tales." Nightingale's two novels—*The Lost Coast *(1996) and its sequel,* The Thirteenth Daughter of the Moon *(1997)—spin bright desert tales that have been described by reviewers as "sensuous," "hyperkinetic," "wacky," "exuberant," and "raucous," a "rambunctious mix of the physical and metaphysical," in the style of Tom Robbins, with the transcendental magic of Pablo Neruda. These novels chronicle the adventures in love and soul of a zany cast of characters as they make a wild journey from the high desert of Eureka, Nevada, along Highway 50—"a long asphalt sentence spoken by the desert"—to the fabulous ocean coastline of California. As these merry travelers motor along, "moving through a desert that moved through them," they fall in love, encounter mystical animals, and find stories. Indeed, stories occupy a central place in Nightingale's cosmology, wherein we all tell stories, live by stories, live in stories, and in fact are ourselves stories. Steven Nightingale's own story is as idiosyncratic as those he invents for his characters. A Reno native, educated in computer science and literature at Stanford University, Nightingale has worked in the investment community for over two decades and lived for several years in Granada, Spain, with his wife and young daughter. For twenty years Nightingale wrote sonnets, stories, and novels without submitting them for publication. When St. Martin's accepted his debut novel* The Lost Coast, *he quickly became a literary light, publishing a sequel the next year, receiving the Silver Pen Award in 2001, and publishing* Cartwheels, *a sonnet collection, in 2004. His most recent sonnet collection is* The Planetary Tambourine *(2006). The following excerpt from* The Lost Coast, *fondly known to some as the baby lightning bolt story, is a favorite at Nightingale's public readings.*

From *The Lost Coast*

Our troupe was traveling along the west side of Pyramid Lake, past the cutoff to Reno and past Sutcliffe, toward the dirt roads that led to a pair of deserts in love:

the Smoke Creek and the Black Rock. As they came over the rise whence they looked over the Smoke Creek, Renato, up front with Ananda and Chiara said, "The world is a ragbag of beauties."

And, a raggedy bunch themselves, they went on north into the silence of the two biggest alkali plains of the Basin.

. . . .

Just at the beginning of the desert, in the southwest corner of the playa, they came upon a ranch.

Renato parked the truck beside the peacock, a common bird on rural Nevada ranches. There didn't seem to be anyone around, and so they spilled from the truck and sat down on some benches near the water pump, in the shade of a half-dozen black locusts.

The silence had changed. While Pyramid Lake had a silence rapt in power, as though the air held within itself heat lightning from another world, the Smoke Creek Desert had a winged silence, a silence that gave a weightlessness to the morning.

. . . .

And as if to confirm that ideas will only take us so far, just then behind them they saw grind to a halt a dilapidated ranch pickup with a rifle slung in the back window. Dust was spewed all over them.

"So thanks. Think I'll be moving along just now," said the peacock, as with haste he strutted away.

It was then our wanderers realized that the big muscular driver of the pickup was taking the rifle from the rack and stepping down into the dirt, where she took aim at them one by one, as if in drill for a mass shooting. But our dear travelers were getting tired of having guns pointed at them.

"We've seen it all before," said Chiara hotly.

"Besides, you look too much like Gertie," added Cookie.

The rifle-wielding woman smiled.

"My sister," she said gruffly. "She told me about you rip-snortin' crazy-ass bunch, and it don't surprise me to find you here messin' with the Peacocker."

"I must say I do love Nevada. You look every bit as sweet as our dear Gertie," said Renato ceremoniously.

"O fer blessed sakes!" said the woman, and she swung the rifle around and fired off a shot that rang the big bell by the barn; then three more shots to spin the weather vane at the top of her house; swiveling around, she squeezed off a pair that blew open the door to her chicken coop, releasing two fat hens she dropped with two quick shots; for lagniappe, she picked up the spinning in the vane again, whizzed a bullet through a little window in the house on the truck, picked the hood ornament off an ancient pickup abandoned near the corral, and for punctuation clanged the bell again three times.

"You ring a little bell, all the bells in the world want to get in the act," said Juha.

"Shut up," commented Beulah.

And she took a bullwhip from the cab of her truck.

"Maybe you should get into the act, meathead," said Beulah.

"Try me," challenged Juha.

"Toss that little bell into the air, I'll show you some swipin'," promised the big rancher.

Juha flung the tiny thing into the air.

Beulah all in one motion uncoiled the whip and smacked it so just the tip caught the bell, which catapulted high, then turned with little spins and descended light as a little chick back into Juha's hand. Beulah then pivoted—an awesome sight—and with several strokes snapped the latch off the barn door, wrenched on three valves to irrigate some alfalfa fields, and wrapped up the handles of two double-sided axes that with a jerk of the whip she sent cartwheeling toward her. As they went end-over-end through the dust, she dropped the whip, and snatched out of the air the two axes, one in each hand.

"I think I'm going to like this woman—" began Ananda.

But she was cut off by the ax that came rotating across the yard. Beulah had let go the first one with an over-the-head heave; as it spun the blade passed directly in front of our wanderers, who were of course standing at attention. With a terrific explosion of splinters, and a rocking of the whole fence, the edge slammed into a post just above the peacock's head.

The bird folded his tail. Color in the area was restored.

Beulah reared back with the second ax and whipped it toward the front of her house, so that instead of the blade the flat end of the ax head crashed into her front door and blew it wide open.

"Well," she said with a shrug, "it's a lucky thing I made all them raspberry pies this mornin'! Damn you all!" And with one sweep of her arm she herded them toward the house.

. . . .

Right about then Renato began to paint so much no one saw him except for an occasional meal. He would paint all day, and then at night in a tack room with some lights he had rigged, until he was too exhausted to stand. Then he would kneel down, spread out a bedroll, and sleep in front of his easel.

It was the way of working he loved best: painting souls.

Do souls become visible only when loved—like diamonds in a cave at night, ignited by the light of a torch?

Beulah would come to look at his doings.

"I'm keeping two of them things," she announced. "Room, board, and rent of the tack room." . . .

"Beulah, do you know any stories?" asked the painter. He surprised himself: but it had been too long.

Beulah considered him.

"I was goin' to tell you a story. Don't rush me."

"I'm not rushing you. No, ma'am. You take your sweet time."

"All the same, you *need* this story," continued Beulah. "I mean, when you need my boy the worst, that's when you'll see me again."

"Your boy?" asked Renato dubiously.

"Yes. My boy!" she said, taking the brush from his hand and pushing him into a saddle. And, leaning back against the side of the barn, she commenced to tell

The Story of the Infant Fallen from the Sky

"Sometimes when I was out on the desert I used to find little birds that had fallen from a nest, or had been attacked by some varmint, and I would take them back to the house and nurse the damn pecky little things back to health, even though I'd have to listen to all that peeping and chirruping. I liked it, though; I liked the little falcons the most. They had them bright eyes that made you think that they knowed everything that was goin' on outside the room and inside your head. I'm tellin' ya: falcons even when they're little can dive right into the middle of what you're thinkin' on and carry it away in their beaks. And a good thing too, since thinkin' is not so much damned use.

"One time, though, I was out in the east Smoke Creek and I saw this small gleamin', a little slip of sparkles, like a snake on fire. And I went over and there was this crooked little piece of light, I mean no longer than my forearm, but blazin'! I mean like dynamite goin' slow! Bright as a noontime packed in a stick—I mean if you took a rope and sowed gunpowder all though it so's it was more powder than rope, and lit the thing up, and it never stopped burnin', that's what it would be like 'cause this thing jes' kept firin' steady, crackin' and sizzlin' and singin' in its own heat."

Beulah paused and looked fiercely at Renato.

"Now what was I s'posed to do with the damn thing?"

"My guess is," said Renato, "that you're a good woman to have around when something weird happens."

"You're goddam right I am!" shouted Beulah, who looked like she was going to cuff Renato a hard one out of sheer happiness of recollection.

"And so this shining thing . . ." said Renato quickly, to get her back into the east Smoke Creek.

"And so," Beulah went on, "I was thinkin': now this ain't no rotten old bone, no old long horn all polished up, no sir, and it's the kind of thing that mebbe I could use to rout out some of my old pipes, and so what are you goin' to do, Beulah?"

The ranchwoman glared at Renato.

"And so what did you do, Beulah?"

"'Bout time you asked, pussyface!" she retorted. And she stepped up and leaned her muscle and gristle against a saddle and looked out the doorway as she talked.

"I roped the little sucker and dragged it back to the truck and hoisted it in the bed onto some blankets; I left it on the rope and tied it down and then headed out. And as I was drivin' back to the ranch, with this thing fizzin' and sparkin' all over the place, all of a sudden I started to hear."

"Hear?" inquired Renato with extreme courtesy.

"That's right, hear! Are you calling me a liar?"

Renato envisioned Beulah writing her name in his flesh with the horsewhip. But we recall that the painter loved women; and so he had the good sense to shout back: "Beulah, you're a rock of a woman; but I know it's rock candy. So knock off all this bullshit!"

Beulah, who had stood forth in fury, now leaned back again.

"Don't you tell nobody!" she said grudgingly.

"What do you mean, hear?"

"I couldn't help listenin' to all the fizzin', and it were pretty soon that I could start to make out it was sayin' somethin'; in the fits and bolts and burstin' out, I could start to hear what the little thing meant. And that's not all. Because the ornery little thing had slipped off the blankets in the back."

"How could you tell?"

"I could tell because the whole truck was glowin'! I looked like a comet comin' down the road! And then I knew! I knew what was what! It was a baby lightning bolt! The cute little thing had fallen out of a nest of clouds and jes' couldn't strike back up into the sky. And *now* what was it going to do? Come home with me, that's what . . . So's I had a big grin smack on my mug, I ain't never brung no lightning home off the range before. And then I thought, Beulah, you got a problem: how the hell am I going to get out of the truck without being fried?"

"It would take a lightning bolt to fry you, Beulah."

"I'll take that as a compliment."

Renato bowed.

"The trick is not to get grounded. And so when I pulled into the ranch I jes' threw open the door and hurled myself clean out of the cab, slammin' right down far out in the dust and rollin' away."

"Now *that* I would like to have seen," exclaimed Renato.

"And laying in the dirt I thought to myself: what does a woman do with a baby lightning bolt? Course, I knew right away what to do! 'Cause for the first time I was bustin' out with that mother-feelin'! Me, Beulah, I had got myself the baby meant for me. Mine! And there I was, all proud with lookin' at the way it made my truck shake, ripple, and glitter! My child!"

Slowly Renato got it.

"You mean that's what you've been doing out here all these years? Raising a lightning bolt?"

"You betcha!" said Beulah with satisfaction.

Renato paused to mull this one over.

"And so how many years ago was that?" he wondered.

"'Bout fourteen years now."

"So you have on your hands a teenage lightning bolt."

"Lanky. Wild. Strong," said Beulah with gusto.

"They say parents learn a lot from their children," he ventured.

"You betcha; he taught me how to strike out at things, if you know what I mean." And Beulah gave him a smile so hearty and strong that Renato felt like a little pipsqueak.

"And so . . ."

"It's a good life. I was supposed to be a mom. I done what I set out to do."

"And so where is he?" burst out Renato.

"Come with me," said Beulah, twirling Renato around and shoving him out of the door of the tack room.

. . . .

They walked, the painter and the ranchwoman, out in back of the ranch and straight through the sagebrush, moving toward some low hills.

"At first I didn't know what to do—hell, I hadn't had no kid around before. 'Sides, this was a boy that was goin' to take some figurin'. First thing: what the hell is his name? Well, what about Bolt? It says what it says. It is what he is. A good name for an impulsive boy, anyway! Next question: what does he eat? Then all at once it hit me. He eats everything standin'! If it stands, he'll eat it. Easy enough. So the next afternoon I took him out to where there was some little saplings in a draw of a canyon, and right there I jes' flipped him out of the blanket up in the air. It was kind of a windy day, the trees whippin' around, but that little bolt just hovered a minute and blammo! He made *ashes* of the tallest skinniest one! And I thought, don't turn this little sucker loose in town! You don't want to be the tallest cowboy in the room around my kid, nosirree!"

Renato measured his height against Beulah.

"And so I took him home and laid him out in some insulation in the back room, he was a sparklin' and a cracklin', the dear little thing, a sizzlin' and beamin', the sweet thing, that was my boy! Now I always did want a child with some energy, some zip. And there he was. And so's he and I jes' settled into our life together out here on the Smoke Creek. It's been good. This was the perfect spot—when you're raising up a lightning bolt, you need some room! It's jes' not something you could do in some piddlin' little house in town. What a little beauty he was. Wait till you see how he's grown! It's been wild. It's been a blowout. I don't know how it coulda been stranger."

Renato thought: every orphaned piece of lightning should have such an upbringing.

"There was one time early on when I took him out to the Sierra in the truck— already he was gettin' so big that he would barely fit in the bed of the pickup, and I had always to cover him up with blankets, otherwise his light would damn near blind me as I drove. I remember one time when a police car pulled me over for speedin' on one of those faraway straight roadways all over the state, and this cop he came a-stridin' up to the car and Bolt knew that he meant me no good. And he always was kinda protective. And so he started thrashin' around in the back of the truck, fizzin' and sparkin' heavy, clangin' on the sides of the bed, and the whole truck was shakin' with electricity, glowin' there in the road, the brightest thing in the Basin, in the middle of the day a star sittin' there in the high desert—the truck shinin' and buckin' and throwin' off sparks. There was a thumpin' in the air and the cop was standin' there wide-eyed and all of a sudden the thunder cracked right in the road, I mean *blasted* this guy, it was like thunder growed out of the ground and the cop turned and he hightailed it to his car and drove the hell out of there like somebody who had seen God! But it was jes' my boy Bolt! Sweet thing! How we laughed about that one for years! And what a day that was, like so many other days. We went out in some open valleys where no one would see us, and Bolt would dart around, jes' snap and zip around, rambunctious thing, what a beauty.

"Sometimes I would stay all day with him waitin', waitin': fer there ain't nothin' prettier than to see him play in the dark. I would jes' sit back, jes' sit back: and when twilight was gone he went sparklin', I mean sparklin' all through the valley and did his flashin' and jabbin' into the little canyons and shootin' down in caves, firin' back out, the black sky over us an' the whole valley singin' with light, my boy, my boy, he could *rock* those valleys, he could. He'd wear hisself out playin', he'd be plumb worn out and I would take him real soft and slow and I'd lay him in the back of the truck and cover him real careful and do a long slow drive back to the ranch. I don't know how I coulda been happier."

They were approaching the hills. Renato could see little whirlwinds of dust over soil and rock where it rose from the desert floor, and there was a movement—the whole hillside was rolling and steam piped from fissures in the stone.

Beulah smiled.

"Just how big is he now?" asked Renato as he heard the rumbling.

. . . .

Renato and Beulah stood at the base of the smoking hills. Before them, the entrance to a cave. Renato could see flares.

"Bolt!" called Beulah.

—Stampeding of air, shuddering of hillside, parting of sky: even with a story to ready his vision Renato could not keep his feet before the roaring of the light.

ART GIBNEY [B. 1952]

Most of the characters in Art Gibney's Skin of the Earth: Stories from Nevada's Back Country *(2002) live "halfway between nowhere and no place," on ranches where the closest towns are Hiko, Delamar, Caliente, and Pahrump. The omnipresent U.S. government looms over these stories like a dark cloud. Gibney, who spent several years in Nevada working for the U.S. Forest Service, nevertheless portrays the government through the eyes of folks who mostly resent it. The sagebrush empires of* Skin of the Earth *are criss-crossed by white government trucks that zip along dusty roads, dispensing film badges to ranchers to measure radioactive fallout. Strange characters populate the pages of Gibney's unsettling book, transforming Nevada's so-called blank spaces into a meeting ground of oddballs. One couple, for example, have never seen each other naked in twenty years of marriage; one man is pushing a shopping cart from Nevada to Jerusalem; one man named a town Adaven—"Nevada" spelled backwards—since, as he says, "Everything's upside down." If Gibney's style is realistic, then Nevada itself is surreal. Gibney is originally from the East Coast with an academic background in history and philosophy. He studied in the* MFA *program at the University of Arizona, and has published in* International Quarterly, South Dakota Review, ZYZZYVA, Story Quarterly, *and others. His story "The Bear Hunters" won the Edward Abbey Award for Ecofiction, and he was chosen to receive a 2000–2001 Individual Artist Grant from the Marin Arts Council. Gibney makes his home in Tiburon, in northern California, but he returns to the wild places of Nevada several times a year to listen to the quiet and to contemplate great spaces, where the self becomes lost in immensity. He is currently working on a novel set in Nevada, whose working title is* The Wildest Place in the West.

The Manure Spreader

We had three corrals, one for horses and two for cows, but that made no difference in the approach. First I piled it, starting with the horses because it was the smallest corral and the sweetest smelling. As soon as the horses saw the tractor crawling into their corral, they started running, not in a herd like mustangs, but every which way, and not because they were afraid of the tractor, but because they were happy and wanted to play. They knew exactly what was going on, because the tractor goes in the corral only once a year, in the spring, into the nearly knee-deep mixture of manure and earth, water and urine, and other ingredients, windblown, forgotten, and unseen, but still in there. When I pulled into the middle, I turned off the tractor and closed my eyes, listening to the animals pounding through the muck around me, feeling them all the way up through my seat, circling and snorting, crying out for me to begin.

All morning I moved manure. I pushed it and pulled it, scooped it and stacked it up in the middle of the corral, a huge pile by lunchtime, more than six feet high and four times as wide. The horses played on the pile like they did every year, playing king of the mountain, each one in turn standing up there still as a trophy, looking down on all the others from the top of the mound. Then I saw my father crossing the little wooden bridge over the irrigation ditch, carrying a long stick that I'd seen him use to help him walk sometimes, but now he held it in the middle and banged it against the fence posts, like he was checking their soundness as he passed. His face was yellow and waxy, and I could see the bones of his hips and knees through his jeans. By the time he reached the corral, I'd already backed out, closed the gate, and shut the engine down.

"You got the horses done," he said. I just shook my head. He knew I hated the job and that the worst part was still ahead.

"Jolina's happy," I said, pointing to the proud mare on the hill of manure.

"Been a good mare," he said, because Jolina was his mare that he had raised from a filly. He climbed up on the side of the tractor and hooked his arm around the post. I started up and we drove down to the shop, him hanging on to the side like I did when I was young. He just stood there staring out to the wind-carved hills that marked our place.

I knew a story was brewing when I saw him. He had more stories than anyone I ever met and he liked telling them, too. It didn't matter if it was just before lunch or just before bed or just before anything I'd rather be doing. He just started in and didn't stop until he was done and the story he told that day was one of the last ones he told in his life.

"Did I ever tell you about Murray the mailman?"

"Nope."

"Murray had the job of carryin' mail from Delamar to Hiko back in the days when Delamar was a mining town. He had a wagon and a team of horses he drove straight through Six Mile Valley, on the old road, around the hills to Hiko. Now, Murray was gettin' old. He must've been in his eighties or thereabouts, but he kept on doin' it. Well, it happened that one day he didn't show up in Hiko like usual and folks got to wonderin' where their mail was and where Murray went, so the next morning a few of them rode out around the hill and found him. He was sittin' in his wagon in the middle of the valley with his head down like he was sleeping, still holdin' the reins in his hands and the horses just standing there waitin' for him to tell them to move out. He just slowed down and died right there on his mail wagon."

"Horses just standing there," I said.

"All night long," he said.

"Murray still holding the reins," I said. "His batteries just ran out."

"Batteries run out," he said laughing, "That's good. Batteries run out just like that."

Back then, it seemed like everything that happened before I was born was just a story. And like all the stories my father told, each one had a beginning and an ending, told at different times for different reasons, pulled down from his memory as if it floated there like a balloon. Each was interesting and important by itself but had nothing to do with the others except the space they all floated in. I always thought that he told the stories only because he liked doing it, as a way of passing time or filling silence. I did not see back then that all the stories were simply snippets of a longer story, all connected just under the surface of the earth like rings of wild iris, which included me and could touch me like a long finger.

By the end of the day, I had made three mountains of manure. I saw the big bald-faced cow standing on one pile when I dumped silage in the trough at feeding time. Then, sometime after sunset, the cow got out through an old hole in the corral. I had patched the hole with baling wire years ago, but over time the wire had gotten rusty and brittle. She headed out along the ditch, over the little wooden bridge, across the cornfield and into the alfalfa, still a full month from swathing but leafy and green as she grazed out there under the moon until she started to swell. Until sometime before dawn, before the carved hills could be seen against the sky, she ate the fresh hay and finally stopped because she felt full, but it was too late. She stood there bellowing no doubt, way out between our house and the boneyard, but no one heard her as the calling pinched down to a whisper. We could not see her when she rolled over on her side and swelled until it killed her. In the morning, my father knew she was gone before I found her.

Weeds had grown up around the manure spreader in the spot I dropped it a year before, swearing I'd never touch it again. I hooked it to the tractor and pulled it back to the shop. My father was waiting with the grease gun. He kneeled down and braced his shoulder against the spreader and worked with a steadiness that was probably more for my benefit than anything else. "Calf bawlin' up there lost his mother," he said. "Big bald-face cow's gone." He pumped grease into the chopper bearings and into the bushings of the steel drum that moved the chains. I greased the square shaft, the driver—the heartbeat of the shitbox—and pulled it smoothly forward, locking it to the back of the tractor, holding it with both hands. And slowly, as each spot swelled with fresh grease, erupting from hidden spaces like wild iris, the boards warming in the sun as we limbered the stiff joints of forged steel, the manure spreader came back to life.

And then, carefully, expecting the whole cart to blow sky high, I lifted the lever below my seat and looked back over my shoulder at the square shaft as it turned slowly and turned the rusty drums and the chains and the choppers. My father gave a signal with his thumb and I bumped the throttle up a little. The spreader started rocking. With the side of my fist I tapped the throttle again and the old machine followed, striding in behind me, so I tapped again and brought it up to working speed, the diesel engine breathing and pushing, the shaft spinning, the whole contraption rocking and rocking the tractor as I sat there and watched my father move out of the way as the choppers flung chunks of old manure into the air and small stones and feathers and bits of paper and everything else that happened to fall in there.

I hopped off the tractor and stood with my father. We watched the machine, not looking for anything in particular, just looking, watching the parts move, listening to the squeaking and scraping and feeling somehow satisfied that we had done something right, that we had given life to something that had taken on a life of its own. Then my father reached up and throttled it down before turning the whole thing off.

"The chains can only give what they have," he said.

"They're old." I said.

"Everything on the place is old and wore out from workin'," he said.

"Not everything," I said. "Tractor's pretty new. And the trucks. The baler and swather aren't too old. The roof on the house—"

"The roof was leakin' and makin' streaks down the walls of the living room. We needed a new roof."

"Them chains've been breakin' every year since I can remember," I said.

"Breakin' from bein' overloaded," he said.

"They have more welding rod on 'em than they do steel they were made with," I said. "They're old."

"Old don't mean bad," he said.

"Not in people," I said. "But in machines it ain't good."

"I can spread all that manure without breakin' the chains once," he said, pointing to the corrals with his thumb.

"Take you four five days insteada three."

"Maybe *this* year you'll get a load on the field without bustin' the chains." I saw the muscles of his jaw flex and relax as he settled his weight evenly on both feet and set himself, like he set himself against a cold wind. Sometimes his determination boiled over to just plain stubborn.

I hated spreading manure. I hated smelling it, piling it, loading it, but mostly I hated shoveling it. I had to shovel it because the manure was too heavy, because I loaded too much in the spreader, not *way* too much, but just enough to break the chains that move the stuff back toward the choppers. But after feeding the horses, I got started.

The cows watched me. They waited to see if I'd push the spreader to its limit, but I didn't. "You want manure," I used to say, "I'll give you manure," and I'd load it up to within an inch of its life and pull it into the fields, but I did not say it this time. Something stopped me. It was something in the air, I think, or rather just the right mixture of many things at the right time that stopped me short. I looked over our place, across the fields to the hills and to the hills beyond them, the spine and the ribs of my whole world, where water gushed from a hole in the ground, giving water to us and everybody downstream from us, including the ducks and the geese and the fish, sending a thin streak of green across the loose brown dirt and pale green sage of that high Nevada desert. I thought of my father, a cowboy to the last drop, and the stamina he had, like a diesel engine, how he did not feel the cold as I did because he did not *look* cold or how he did not feel hunger or fatigue, because he always ate gracefully and with dignity no matter what time we sat down. He moved forward like the helmsman of a heavy ship, always taking care of everything, watching the horizon and making decisions, and we felt good because he was always in control of things. So I figured the least I could do now was to spread one load without snapping the chains, as a favor but not because I'd really learned anything.

And I pictured him gone, pictured the ranch, his empire, everything he had worked for since he was old enough to ride a horse or drive a tractor, falling squarely into my lap like a bucket-load of manure, and I swear it felt like someone grabbed me by the shoulders and shook me there in the seat of the tractor.

A few yellow birds blew in over the silo and landed on the top rail of the corral, then a few more, and then a whole flock flew in and ringed the corrals like candle flames with bright yellow bodies and scarlet heads, hundreds of them, side by side all around the rim, chirping and chattering, flitting around like fire. I figured then that something was happening, something that not only *involved* the birds and the manure spreader, my father and me, the missing bald-faced cow and the exact temperature and angle of the sun at that time, but something that could only happen once in anyone's lifetime when all those ingredients were thrown together in a way that no person could predict or plan.

The next hour unrolled like watching bread in the oven, checking on it from time to time to see that it moves closer to the only thing it can become, but not checking too often or too carefully, as the ingredients thrown together include gestures and songs and the feeling we get from very old stories and there is always something lost in the telling of it.

So I pulled the short load over the little wooden bridge and past the shop. My father saw that the spreader was not overloaded, assumed that for the first time in my life I had sense enough to work *with* the machine instead of *against* it, even though common sense had nothing to do with it. He waved as I headed out over the ditch, not a wave hello or good-bye but just a wave of recognition.

When I reached the far corner of the field, I eased up on the lever under my seat and the chopper started spinning, throwing moist chunks of manure every which way out the tail end as I moved forward over the stubble of last year's corn. The spreader rocked the tractor down the field, pushing me as much as I was pulling it, both forces working together perfectly. I expected the chains to snap at any time, but they didn't.

I swung wide at the lower end and looked back over my shoulder. The load was half gone. I slouched into my seat and let my head roll back so the sun hit my face. There I was, gently rolling over the flat field with the tractor and the spreader doing all the work, the steady drone of the machines falling back into the distance, the sun warming me and the shit flying like crazy. It was easy. I tapped my foot to the rhythm and closed my eyes because there was nothing I could hit even if I tried and it didn't matter where the manure fell as long as it hit the field. It felt good.

When I looped around by the lower field, I spotted the bald-faced cow, rolled over on her back with her legs sticking straight up like table legs, her whole body so swollen and stiff she didn't look like a cow at all, but rather like some creature that had simply fallen from the sky and landed there in our alfalfa. I drove directly to the shop and shut the engine down, waiting for my father. "Cow's bloated in the lower," I told him as he came out carrying a long six-by-six. He rested the timber on the rail of the spreader and looked inside, saw that the box was empty and that the chains had not snapped. He looked up at me and then back at the spreader and said, "I'll drag her to the boneyard. Load up and I'll meet you." And it was there by the shop, under the cottonwood tree, leaning against the manure spreader, that he decided to die. I saw it in the way he finally looked at me, with eyes that seemed to be made of glass. He didn't need words to explain the things he wanted to tell me. He always told stories about things that *happened* or things he *did*, but never about how he *felt*. Now he was scared. And he loved me.

With his pocketknife he worked at a splinter in the palm of his hand, holding the knife like he held a screwdriver or a dinner fork, digging at the sliver of wood with the same single-mindedness he did anything. My body went numb. I scrambled for something to say or something I could do to change his mind, to deflect him, but I had done what I had done and I could only watch him remove the splinter with his knife and with his teeth and then fold the knife against his hip and slip it back into his pocket where it stayed, as much a part of him as his boots or his hat or the look on his face when he made up his mind to do something. He wrapped one arm around the six-by-six and dragged it around the corner of the shop, leaving a furrow in the dirt and leaving me no choice but to do the only thing I could do.

I raced up to the corral and loaded the manure spreader full, packing it down with the tractor bucket until the side boards bulged. My father showed up with a long chain draped over his shoulder and let it fall into the bucket of the tractor. He didn't even notice the manure spreader, didn't look at the load as he drove off toward the wooden bridge. I pulled my heavy wagon through the muck, bouncing over the little bridge, chunks of manure dropping into the ditch. I stopped to grab a shovel, because I knew this load would pop the chains.

He was waiting for me as I came around the cottonwood into the lower field. He waved at me again, smiled a simple smile of recognition. I waved back. On the back of his tractor, I hooked the chain and wrapped the other end twice around the hind leg of the bald-faced cow. My father took up the slack and the big cow started to move, scraping over the hard stubble of corn, making a hollow sound like a big canvas bag full of air, leaving a trail to the boneyard.

By the time I reached the upper field and lined up where I left off, he was half-way to the hills. I bumped the engine up and lifted the lever under my seat. The tractor started to rock, manure flying into the sun, falling in pieces on the earth, the whole pile shaking and moving slowly until the chains popped. I jumped down and grabbed the shovel and climbed to the top of the pile. From there I could see my father entering the tall sagebrush at the boneyard. As I shoveled like a madman, throwing big scoops of manure into the air, throwing another scoop before the first one hit the ground, I heard the diesel engine on the wind and imagined my father in the boneyard. Just a windless wash protected and warmed by the sun, soundless except for the occasional reconnaissance flight of a fly, the entrance is lined with the skeletons of old trucks and broken machines, guardians of the small valley, their forged bones picked clean of moving parts.

I watched my father turn and cross the ditch. He was heading for the lower field. A few minutes later, he had swung around the wallow by the cottonwood tree and was heading straight at me. I dug down through the muck and found the chains and I followed them back, looking for the break when I heard the engine noise on the wind and saw that he had turned back, heading for the wallow again. I shoveled until sweat dripped off my face onto the manure. My father was now chugging toward the cottonwood very slowly, barely lugging along, moving through the shallow water and tall grass, inching forward as if his foot had fallen off the accelerator. The nose of the tractor touched the tree, gently, without a jolt. My father sat with both hands on the wheel as if he was crossing a long valley. His eyes were not *on* the horizon but *beyond* it.

I knew he was dead. I'd known it when he had crossed the water in the wallow and I had watched him from the top of the dung heap, but it took time for me to move. The tractor pushed against the cottonwood just enough so the wheels did not spin as the tree pushed back, the forces perfectly deadlocked. Finally I could jump from the spreader and run across the corn. The manure flew from my boots as I picked up speed and splashed through the shallow water.

A sudden little wind sent his old cowboy hat tumbling backward. But he still sat with his back straight as wild asparagus, both big hands on the wheel. I took him by the sleeve and pulled him slowly onto the ground. In the grassy water, I gave him my breath. I rested and told him that I had snapped the chains. I gave him my breath again, trying to start his heart as he rocked with me in the shallow water. But he had made his decision. I dragged him out of the water, onto the stubble of last year's corn, and carried him over the field and the ditch, through the high weeds and wild iris, into the house.

For three weeks, the manure spreader sat in the field with the shovel sticking out of it, marking the spot where I stopped. It rained once for a whole day, slowing things down, washing dust from the leaves and from the shingles of our house, settling the earth into the new grave across the street. Then I shoveled manure. I found the broken chains and welded the old steel back together again. I finished up.

A white government truck came up our road. It was Howard coming to check the air machine, to change the filter and take the used one back to the test site. I've seen the used filters. When we're haying, the filters are bright green, covered with particles of alfalfa. In midsummer, when it's dry and the hot wind blows out of the south, the filters are chocolate brown with dust. In winter, the filters are clean. Howard waved to me as he pulled up under the cottonwood. He walked over with his hands in his pockets. He is a nice man, always friendly, never a bad word to say about anyone, but he isn't a cowboy.

"Howdy, Justin," he said, shaking my hand.

"Hello, Howard," I said.

"How's your dad doing?"

"Dad died. Three weeks yesterday."

"Oh, I'm sorry to hear that," he said. "Keith was a good man, a very special man."

"That's a fact," I said. "So how's the air doing?"

"Clean as a whistle," he said, like he always said, and then, "Gonna be a test tomorrow ten o'clock."

"Okay," I said. Even though the test site was just over the hill from our valley, they tested those bombs so far down in the ground that nobody felt or heard a thing.

"Any visitors?" Howard asked. "Anyone staying any length of time?"

"Nope," I said. He always asked for the name of anyone staying longer than a visit. He had the names of everyone living within 150 miles of the place, and since people came and went, cowboys and miners just drifting in and out of little outfits tucked away in canyons all through the hills, Howard had his hands full keeping the list current. We talked for a few more minutes, about the weather and the manure, and then he left. Before driving away, he sat in his truck with the engine running and wrote something in his notebook. "Ten o'clock tomorrow," he said and headed up the road for Whipple's place. The next day, I loaded the manure spreader and pulled it into the field. It was the last load of that year and the last load of my life, although I didn't know it back then.

My mother and I decided to sell the ranch that summer. She thought of raising ostriches, but I don't trust birds bigger than me and I wasn't particularly partial to cows, either. When it came time to spread manure the next year, the cows belonged to someone else and the manure belonged to someone else and I was in Sacramento working in a hardware store and going to school.

At the far edge of the field, against the hills where our water gushed out of the ground through a hole as big as a bushel basket, I hopped off the tractor and dropped down on my hands and knees and pushed my whole face into the ice-cold water, sipping slowly, feeling the force of the water surging against me as it tumbled out of the earth. I opened my eyes underwater and tried to look past the sunlight, past the loose dirt, deep below the skin of the earth, to the black lake pressed firmly between layers of smooth stone. My father had told me about the lake. It used to be above the ground. He showed me fossils of ferns in the sagebrush. He traced the shoreline with his finger as we sat on horseback in the hills, looking out over the valley in the long shadows before sunset. Then the lake slowly dried, leaving the earth shaded only by sage, moistened by occasional rain, fed by springs hidden in the hills that only my father knew. "A thing can only give what it has," he'd said. I missed him. I looked for him in the water and I understood for the first time that nothing is worse than not being alive. Even grieving and suffering are better than nothing. As I came back up, reaching the light and the air again, feeling the sun on my face, deeply breathing the warm air that blew from the west, I felt a movement in the earth, a slow rolling and a gentle but certain thumping in the ground. I thought it might be the bomb test, shaking the deep rock below the lake. I looked at my watch. It was almost eleven o'clock. Howard had said the test would be at ten. They were never late. They were always exactly on time. It was something that we all counted on. So I stood up and got back on the tractor, starting my last pass across the cornfield.

MONIQUE LAXALT [B. 1953]

The Deep Blue Memory (1993) by Monique (Laxalt) Urza is an autobiographical novel about growing up in one of Nevada's most prominent families. Monique's father was Robert Laxalt, author of the classic story Sweet Promised Land, the book with the deep blue cover that recounted his Basque father's immigration to America. Monique's uncle, Paul Laxalt, was a Nevada governor and a two-term U.S. senator. Monique herself earned a BA in English at Stanford University, an MA in French literature, and a JD at the University of Iowa. A Reno native, Monique Laxalt was always aware of her family's otherness, their Basqueness. Yet when the Laxalt family spent two one-year periods in the Basque country when Monique was young, she became acutely conscious of her Americanness. Deep Blue Memory grapples with these dual-identity issues as the narrator observes her grandparents' Basque customs and enjoys the security of family solidarity yet feels the pull of personal freedom and self-expression. How can one write honestly about the complex dynamics among four generations of a close-knit and well-known family without breaking their trust? For a long time, Monique Laxalt, a loyal daughter and, moreover, a practicing lawyer, kept silent. When at last driven to write, she used "Urza" (her married name), called the work fiction, and developed a distinctive and beauti-

ful imagistic, incantatory—and elliptical—style. As the scholar of Basque studies William A. Douglass has noted, Deep Blue Memory *"revisits many of the same places and events that her father describes in his works. The result is a fascinating treatment of the Basque-American experience from a different generational and gendered perspective," and the works of father and daughter are interesting to read in tandem. In addition to* Deep Blue Memory, *Monique Laxalt coauthored* An Elegant Line: The Art of the Sheppard Family *(2000), has published several stories in magazines, and writes poetry.*

from *The Deep Blue Memory*

Under Grandma's dining room table it was dark and warm like the earth. The legs of the table were deep brown and thick. They were woven among one another, like the limbs of a jungle, leading everywhere and nowhere, within a circle. We played in them silently, timelessly.

The top of the table Grandma would have covered with a round tablecloth of white lace. She would set white, gold-rimmed cups and saucers around the circle, the cream and sugar in the center.

They would be seated around the table, drinking coffee and smoking cigarettes. The men wore khaki pants and wingtips, the women slim-fitting dresses and stockings and sleek shoes. They spoke intensely, in voices that rang with certainty and success. They were young, younger than we are now, and adult, more adult than we are now.

In the corner by the window, Grandma would sit and watch the afternoon Nevada snow fall quietly outside.

In the other corner, next to the blazing window of the stove, Grandpa would sit upright, straddling the oak straight-backed chair turned backwards.

Grandma would bring fresh coffee from the kitchen, and Grandpa would stand and add wood to the stove. The windows would steam up, and the room would fill with the smell of the coffee and the thick white cream, the smoke of the cigarettes, the warmth of the blazing stove.

In the dark of the underneath, the thick, interwoven legs of the table connected them. We could hear the pure, clear, crystalline ring of their voices. It sheltered, encircled the darkness, like a sphere.

In those days, Grandma was strong and sturdy, imposing. On Saturday, when they had left us for the weekend, she would be up early. We would awake to the smell of steaming chocolate, and bear claws warmed on the wood stove in the kitchen, lit hours before.

While we ate, Grandma would disappear into her bedroom. She would reappear in her elbow-sleeved dress made of black wool, looming above us, her hair braided neatly across the top of her head, wearing stockings and thick-heeled black shoes.

After we dressed, we would leave through the dark entryway at the front of the U-shaped house. We would listen in vain for sounds of the small Indian family who rented the other side of the U, living silently in what was called the "apartment."

We would emerge from the screened front porch of the old white frame house, and would walk the chilled back-street sidewalks of Carson City. Grandma would wear her black purse over the forearm of her left coat sleeve, her chin high and her face turned forward, and we would proceed at a march to Main Street, then left one block to Gilbert's Drug.

Once arrived, Grandma would browse in the birthday card section and visit formally with the proprietor or his wife while we scanned the toy section, made our selection, and brought it to her. We would choose such morbid things as a rubber tarantula on a string, and once home we would choose the moment to dangle it in front of her. She would start with fright, then scowl furiously. Then she would smile in her twinkling, mischievous way as we paraded the spider, on its string, through the house in search of Grandpa.

In the afternoon she would sit by the corner window, working her crochet needles quickly and mechanically, producing more and more of the round lace doilies that ornamented the house. We would play in the back porch area outside the kitchen, the small area between the two wings of the house that trapped the afternoon sun. We crept slowly, silently in the direction of the woodpile, in ever futile attempts to seize one of the wild kittens that lived there. Grandma would bring warm milk in bowls, and we would crouch inside the kitchen door, waiting, as the kittens ever so tenuously appeared, and approached, and began to drink. Then we would emerge in a burst of glee, and in a split second the kittens would vanish. We knew they were in the woodpile, and were watching.

In the evening, after dinner, Grandma would dress for bed at the same time as we. She would emerge from her bedroom in her long robe, her braids taken down, draped behind her shoulders, down to her waist. We would stand by her chair in the window corner where the shade was pulled down now, and we would brush out her hair from the braids. It spread in silver, crimped waves down the front of her robe, more beautiful than anything we knew.

In the later evening, we would crawl into the double bed in the large far-back bedroom, and would shiver under the covers. Grandpa would come with wood, and he would light a fire in the small alabaster fireplace not far from the foot of our bed. Lying there, in the glow of the fire, we could hear the distant, quiet, enchanted sound of the old language that we did not understand and that was a part of this house. Later, over the quiet sound of the fire, we could hear Grandpa rattling in his attic bedroom above us, and the floorboards in Grandma's room next to us creak as she got into bed. At some moment, in the still, pure air of the bedroom and amidst the glow of the fire, we would cross over into sleep.

We would awake to Sunday morning sunlight, the alabaster fireplace cold, the smell of hot rum permeating the house. Grandma would seat us at the dining room table, at the white lace tablecloth. She would bring rolled pancakes soaked in a blend of maple syrup and rum. They had a taste that like the distant sound of the old language went only with this house. We ate them voraciously, gluttonously, searching for the sweet taste of the syrup.

Grandma would help us wash and dress in the bathroom, and send us to the dining room to wait. She would appear in her black wool dress, a black wool scarf tied around her head. She would hand a rosary to each of us.

We would walk the back streets to Saint Theresa's Catholic Church. We would ascend the steps, and once inside we would reach up, into the marble basin that held the holy water, and cross ourselves. We would proceed in Grandma's wake, taking a pew toward the front of the church, and kneeling, and crossing ourselves, and taking the rosary beads from our pockets. In the quiet before Mass had begun, we would bow our heads like Grandma, fingering the rosary beads and mimicking the silent movement of her lips. At some point we would break into muffled, uncontrollable laughter, and she would throw a black scowl that went through us.

She would proceed, whispering, with the infinite succession of rosaries that stretched right on through the Mass. Grandpa would arrive late, and would stand at the back, even when the church was half empty. He would vanish just after Communion, and afterwards we would find him waiting outside, on the sidewalk, outside the little wrought-iron fence that bordered the churchyard.

We would walk the back streets home, some up front with Grandpa, some at Grandma's side. It was like this time and time again.

. . . .

In spring, we would make the hour's drive south twenty miles past Carson, then southeast through the little town of Wellington, pulling off the highway at mid-morning and heading down the straight strip of dirt road that led to one of the sheep ranches. We would find our grandfather there in the corrals, amidst the dust and the ewes and the new lambs.

He would take one of us up in one arm and a new lamb in the other, and standing there in his dust-covered Levi's and brown denim work shirt and round-toed work boots, his sun-darkened face and snow-white hair framed against the clear blue of the Nevada sky, he would break into a smile that was as radiant, as pure, as the spring sun.

In the warmth of the late morning, he would bottle feed milk to the bummer lambs, those whose mothers had died or rejected them, and they would take it in one swoosh, filling the bottle with foam.

We could smell the dust and the warmth of the Nevada desert, and the sun-cracked wood of the corral posts and the denim of our grandfather's work shirt, mixed in with the bleating of the newborns, with the sight of the snow-white wool and the spatterings of blood and the clear, clear blue of the Nevada sky.

At other times we would walk with Grandpa into a canyon that lay in the foothills of the Sierra just west of Carson, that smelled of sun-warmed sage and pine in fall, fresh snow and cold pine in winter. It had a wide, sagebrush-covered promontory that our father and mother dubbed the "peninsula," and a steep forest of straight pines that rose up just where the dirt road crossed the back of the peninsula. A wide band of aspen ran along the side of the peninsula and on up into the heart of the forest, following the path of a freshwater creek that wound down from the mountains beginning with the first snows. By late October the creek bed would be dry, its fine sand twinkling with specks of fool's gold. And the band of aspen would have turned, it stretched like a blaze of light up the depth of the canyon. It was family land.

Grandpa was like a young deer there. He knew the land, every inch of it; he knew the road in and the best place to leave the pickup and the best path across the peninsula, the place to be on the alert for rattlesnakes, the exact degree of coldness at which you no longer needed to watch for rattlers. He knew the best path up into the heart of the forest, and the best spot to stop and break out the picnic lunch, and the best spot for Christmas trees this year. He was like a solitary young deer that welcomed the company of our visit, that beamed with pride as he stooped and seized a piece of petrified wood and handed it to us. But at the same time like the young deer he would bound up the mountain free of us, disappearing from us, and with our father and mother we would follow with our slow, laboring steps.

It was what our father had written in the deep blue book. Our grandfather was at home here, his soul did not reside in any house, it could not be kept in any house, it was part of the land, it was one with the snow and the pines and the sage and the autumn blaze.

TERESA JORDAN [B. 1955]

Stories are like owner's manuals, Teresa Jordan once explained to an interviewer. If there are missing stories then we have lost part of our cultural instructions. Jordan grew up on a ranch in Wyoming and noticed that very few stories were passed down about rural women. Where were the stories that could provide instructive models for her own life? Since her family's ranch was so remote, Jordan was sent to boarding school in Colorado Springs for high school. There, surrounded by sophisticated students from wealthy urban families, Jordan felt ashamed of her own rural upbringing. She went east to Yale University, where she earned a BA in history. At Yale she rekindled ties with her rural past, writing an honors thesis entitled "Wyoming Ranchers during the Great Depression" and embarking upon an ambitious research project after graduation to interview more than one hundred ranch and rodeo women throughout the West, logging 60,000 miles on her old Honda Civic and writing her first book, Cowgirls: Women of the American West *(1982).* Cowgirls *launched Jordan's career, and she then wrote an evocative memoir* Riding the White Horse Home: A Western Family Album *(1993), edited* Graining the Mare: The Poetry of Ranch Women *(1994), and coedited* The Stories That Shape Us: Contemporary Women Write about the American West *(1995). More recently Jordan has combined writing and painting to create illustrated journals for her "Sketchbook Expeditions" series, with published volumes on the Grand Canyon and Yosemite. Jordan and her husband, folklorist and producer Hal Cannon, lived on a small ranch in Deeth, Nevada, for several years in the 1990s and now make their home in Salt Lake City, where Jordan continues to be a major force for community building in the West, collecting the stories that will help diverse groups work together toward a sustainable future.*

St. Francis of Tobacco

Horace McWallis and I were the only gringos at the funeral. I knew Horace would come since Francisco had worked for his family for more than sixty years. Horace's wife, Louise, would have been there, too, but her phlebitis was bad and she had to keep her feet up on a hassock.

There were maybe thirty of us in the little white church. Francisco's daughter Eléna, her husband, Jésus, and their four small daughters sat in the front row, the girls all dressed in white dresses, their dark hair hanging in thick shiny braids. I recognized an older couple who, like Francisco and his wife, had come up to Sky Valley from Mexico as young marrieds looking for work, and raised their children here. They never learned English so well, but their kids graduated from high school and some went on to college. Their oldest daughter practiced medicine in Reno. And then there were folks I recognized from restaurants and casinos in town, dark faces without names. I wished more of my neighbors had come to note the passing of someone who had lived among them for so long, but I guess to many of them Francisco was no different, just another dark face without a name.

Father Hernández drove over from Winnemucca and gave the mass in Spanish. His words were as foreign to me as Latin had been in high school the time I'd gone to Catholic church with Hazel O'Callahan. But I'm old enough to know something of love, and I got the meaning just fine.

We emerged from the service and, as Father Hernández crushed a flower over the grave, and then let fall a handful of dust, I felt old. I looked out over the valley shining in the clear autumn air, the gold meadows just melting from the morning's frost, the rusty lines of coyote willow, the pale stretches of desert dotted with sagebrush beyond the reach of the mountains' generous watershed. I knew that behind us, the Rubies were wearing their first shawls of snow, that white would blanket the meadows before long. After Father Hernández said the final prayer, I found myself drifting down to the fence of the small cemetery, resting my hand on the cold wrought iron.

I turned back to the chirping of young voices and saw Francisco's four granddaughters leaning over his grave, tossing in petals from their white floral crowns. Perched on the edge with their white dresses billowing out behind them, they reminded me of birds, ibis or swans. Angel birds, Francisco would have called them.

A different, more familiar sound drew my attention skyward, and I looked up to see two sandhill cranes. They looked ancient, almost prehistoric, with their long, thin bodies silhouetted black against the sun and their slender wings hesitating slightly at the top of each stroke. I'd never found words to describe their strange wooden cooing before, but that day they sounded like sad geese, gone hoarse from grief.

Francisco used to tell me things I thought might be true. "You know how hummingbirds go south?" he asked not so many weeks ago. It was the end of the summer, still hot, but the meadows had faded from green to gold and the aspen in the mountains were just starting to turn. We sat on the porch of his little shack, drinking lukewarm iced tea and watching the bright specks of birds hover to suck from the feeder he had made out of a plastic Mrs. Butterworth's bottle and some bright red ribbon. "Such tiny wings," he said, "so many miles. You ever wonder how they make it?"

I shook my head. There were a lot of things I'd never thought about.

"I don't know for sure," he said, "but I think they burrow in the feathers of snow geese and catch a ride. I had a friend once, he tell me he see this. So if I ever see a snow goose, I look, and maybe I see it too." He laughed, softly, and light caught in his dark, watery eyes. Then he started to cough, a wracking, phlegmy cough too strong for his thin body. He reached out blindly, adjusted the knob on the oxygen bottle next to his chair. It was on wheels and followed him everywhere, like a puppy on a leash. The coughing seemed to last forever, and I looked away, toward the mountains.

"No good, no good," he said when the spell was over. He gasped for breath, and I could see him consciously trying to remember to breathe through the little tubes strapped to his nostrils. He leaned his head back, closed his eyes. Tears streamed down his face.

When he had recovered, he reached in his pocket, pulled out a pouch of Bugle tobacco, started to roll a cigarette. "Francisco"—I couldn't help myself—"don't do that."

"Oh, it's bad for me, I know, but I learn too late. And now—what difference does it make?" He finished rolling the cigarette, reached over and turned off the oxygen, struck a wooden match with his thumbnail, and inhaled. He didn't cough, which surprised me. He blew out a thin stream of smoke. "I feel better," he said. "Don' worry."

A barn swallow flew onto the porch, landed on the arm of Francisco's chair. "*Hola, pájarito,*" he said as the bird cocked its head and looked at him through one eye. Then it plucked a flake of tobacco from his sweater and flew through an open window into the house.

"They will go south soon," he said, with a note of sadness in his voice. "I wish I could go too. Winter don' seem so good to me this year." I murmured in agreement and felt a wave of loss. I didn't think Francisco would see another spring.

Francisco had started living with the birds a couple of years earlier. He'd grown too weak to work, but Horace told him he could stay on. I like that about Horace and Louise, they have the sort of loyalty you don't see much anymore. Francisco was grateful. The Valley had been his home all his adult life. Years ago he'd told me he'd like to return to Mexico, but now that he was ill, the desire seemed to leave. "This is my home," he said to me. "I don' really remember the other anymore."

Horace and Louise worried about Francisco's ability to take care of himself. They talked Eléna's husband, Jésus, into coming to work on the ranch, and the young family moved in with Francisco. "I don' want to get in your way," he said after a few days, and he moved out to what had once been a grain shed. Eléna and Jésus were distraught. They wanted their daughters to know the old man and besides, people would think they had kicked him out. They enlisted Horace and

Louise, but Francisco held fast. "No, no, no, you need room," he insisted, and finally we all came to realize that he was the one who wanted privacy.

He cleaned the shed up slowly, as his breath would allow, sweeping out the
droppings of pack rats and spiders, sprinkling baking soda to soak up their musky
smells. But up in the rafters hung a line of mud cups, the nests of barn swallows,
and he left these alone. "This is their home," he said. "They don' need to worry
'bout me." He left his windows open from the time the birds first arrived in the
spring until they migrated south in the fall, and they flew in and out at their will.
"*Mi otra familia,*" he said with his soft laugh. To tell the truth, I think he moved out
of the house to be close to them.

"You know what this is?" he'd asked when I had visited him early in the summer. He showed me a handful of tiny feathers, the same buff color as my buckskin
mare. "These are *escrituras*––how you say?—deeds. Or maybe name tags." I looked
at him as if he were crazy. "No, really," he said. "Last fall, I watch as each bird, before she fly away, pluck one feather from her breast, leave it in her nest. And just
now, the birds, they come back, each one take up her nest, drop the feather on the
floor."

"Francisco . . ."

"Really," he said, his dark eyes twinkling. "Where else you think I got these?
This fall, you come see. And then you believe."

I'd known Francisco since I was sixteen and he was only a year or two older. It had
been the middle of the Depression and strangers roamed the country, dropping off
the freights, hitchhiking, looking for work or for food. My parents told me to be
careful and so I was afraid, especially of the men, and most especially of the Mexicans. I don't know how I got this last message so clear, but it came through.

I met Francisco during the first snowfall of the season, a nasty day, cold and
windy. I was driving the truck to town to lay in our winter groceries when I saw a
young Mexican couple on the road. The girl was pregnant and they looked so cold
and miserable, I stopped. They both started talking very fast, though I couldn't
understand anything they said. The girl burst into tears. She held her belly and the
boy kept pointing at it and talking louder, I made out the word "*médico.*"

"I'm going to town," I said. "I can take you." They looked at me blankly, but I
waved them into the truck and they understood. They climbed in and I realized
they were shivering. The girl wore a thin cotton dress with no stockings, and a
man's wool coat, several sizes too big. I guessed it belonged to the boy. It was filthy,
stained with mud and grease and I didn't know what else. I found myself inching
away from it. The boy wore no coat at all, just a dirty cotton shirt with a right-angle
tear on the shoulder, like he'd caught it when he ducked under a barbed wire fence.

The girl's teeth chattered and he held her hands to warm them. The truck had no heater, but I pulled a wool robe out from behind the seat, though I admit I hesitated for a minute before I handed it over. *Gracias, gracias,* they both said as they unfolded it.

Snow slicked the road. I had to keep stopping to clear ice from the windshield. Once the boy understood what I was doing, he'd hop out before I even had the truck stopped, and clear it with his bare hands. There was no arguing with him, even when his hands turned blue. I gave him my gloves and they fit fine.

Though I didn't speak their language and they didn't speak mine, I came to know a few things about them during that long ride to town. Their names were Francisco and María Sanchez. It was too early for the baby, but something was wrong. I thought I understood that María was bleeding. Francisco worked for Señor McWallis—that would have been Horace's father—and he feared McWallis would fire him for leaving.

"It's okay," I said. "I'll talk to him. My father will talk to him." I didn't think they understood.

Mostly, we drove in silence. I kept stealing glances at María. She looked so scared. She was no older than I was, maybe even younger. I tried to imagine what it would be like to be married, to be having a baby. But I couldn't.

By the time we reached town, María was pale and trembling all over. I took her to Dr. Phelps, who took care of our family. "Do you know these people?" his nurse asked me.

"No," I said. "They work for Mr. McWallis."

"Can they pay to see the doctor?"

"I don't know. I don't think so. Mr. McWallis will pay for it. Or my father will."

"Does your father know about this?"

"Oh, yes," I lied. "He sent me in."

"Well, all right, then . . ." She looked dubious, but she gestured for María to come into an examination room. Francisco followed along. The nurse tried to get him to stay in the waiting room, but he insisted and she gave up.

She came back in a few minutes. "She'll have to go into the hospital," she told me. "You might as well go home."

"And Francisco?"

"I don't think he'll leave her." I must have looked worried, because she added, "It'll be okay. We'll call the priest. There are other Mexican families in town. They won't be so alone."

I went back to the truck and climbed in. A small pool of blood marked the place where María had sat. It must have soaked clear through the coat. It was as red as my own.

"What were you doing, picking up people like that?" my mother demanded when I started to tell my folks about the day. "They might have killed you." But she calmed down as I told the whole story, and when I finished, my father said I'd done the right thing. He talked to McWallis, and he must have smoothed things over, because when Francisco finally came back from town, he still had a job.

I didn't learn for a long time that María had died. She hemorrhaged, I guess, and bled to death. She was my age, we'd been shoulder to shoulder, and now she was dead. They'd been able to save the baby, a little girl born five weeks premature. Francisco named her Eléna and a family in town took her in. I didn't speak to Francisco; even if I had had the language, I wouldn't have known what to say. Sometimes I'd see him from a distance, forking hay off the sled to the cattle or, when spring came, walking the irrigation ditches with a shovel in his hand. Always, he wore that dirty wool coat. It struck me it was all he had left.

The years whirl past, don't they? I graduated from high school, went to college for a couple of years, came back and married the boy next door, Isaac Place. We worked for his folks for a few years, and then, when my father died and Mom moved to town, we took over the home place. Isaac's folks died and we inherited half their ranch, bought the other half from Isaac's brother. Bought some more land, build up quite a spread.

Isaac loved land, loved buying and selling it. He loved buying and selling anything, really: cows, horses, ranches, building, stocks and bonds. Union Pacific, he loved Union Pacific, bought another share of it every time he had an extra dollar in his pocket. People said we were in the ranching business and it was true: Isaac was in business and I was on the ranch. He wasn't around much, always off chasing after one deal or another, and to tell the truth, that suited me fine. I was always glad to see him. He was loads of fun. The minute he'd get home, the house would fill with people, with stories and laughter and whiskey. And ideas. He always brought home a lot of ideas, of new machinery we could buy, improvements in irrigation, new breeds of cattle. For a while he wanted to build a new house, a real showplace. I liked living in the home place, in the house I grew up in. I let him talk me into a new kitchen—that didn't take much talking—and I loved my up-to-date appliances, but that was enough. Lucky for me, he had a short attention span and I was always glad to see him go, to let him put that energy into something else.

Isaac liked being known as a rancher, he just didn't like ranching, didn't like the cold or getting manure on his lizard-skin boots. There are a lot of people like that, men and women both, and I don't blame any of them. But I felt just the opposite. I liked manure. Well, not really, but I liked the critters that made manure, and I liked what manure did for the grass. As far as I was concerned, as long as I had my horses and cows, Isaac was welcome to all the fancy boots in the world.

That was the only real fight we ever had. Isaac liked to live on the edge, to wheel and deal, to *leverage,* to use one of his favorite words. I didn't know he'd "leveraged" this place, didn't know he could, until one day the banker showed up with a handful of papers and told me we no longer owned the ranch. I didn't even know where Isaac was—he was in Tucson, as it turned out—but I tracked him down and read him the riot act. I don't know what he sold or what he traded; things were nip and tuck for a year or two. But in the end we kept the ranch and, at my insistence, he put it in my name. I didn't care about anything else, any buildings or ranches or herds of cattle in distant places. I just wanted to know that *my* home and *my* herd were safe. I could sleep again. Isaac was a decent man. I think he would have done anything he could to make me happy. Except stay home or stop trading, and I never asked him to do either of those things

Francisco was invisible in those years. I'd see him sometimes if I went to help the McWallises brand, and sometimes when he was irrigating, I'd pass him on the road. We'd nod or wave at each other; well, everybody out here did that. But I was busy all the time, putting the ranch together, making things work. And then Isaac and I were trying to start a family.

I could get pregnant easy enough, but come the second or third month, I'd miscarry. The third time, Dr. Phelps said, "No more." If it happened again, he said, I might not survive. He took everything out. When I woke up from surgery, Isaac sat by my bed, holding my hand. He was sweet and kind, and he nursed me through the next few days. When I got back on my feet, he left again, though he called every other day or so and sent funny little gifts.

But I was feeling blue. Empty, you know, and sort of worthless. To make matters worse, my two-year-old sorrel filly, the one I was so proud of, ran through the barbed wire and impaled herself on a fence stay, ran it almost clear through her shoulder. The vet sewed her up and managed, for the most part, to prevent infection. But as the wound healed, it made proud flesh, sort of like it didn't know when to stop healing until she had this raw outgrowth on her shoulder the size of a grapefruit. The vet told me there was nothing much I could do about it. He could try to surgically remove it, but it would probably grow back.

I had just stepped into the corral to nurse the filly when Francisco rode in, trailing a couple of my heifers who'd walked the fence and turned up in McWallis's meadow. "Señora," he said—he always called me Señora now—"you got trouble?" He swung off his horse and looked at the filly. "*No problema,*" he said. "I come back in a little while." An hour or so later, he turned up with a poultice made out of cayenne and tobacco and I don't know what else. He put it on the wound and just held it there for a while as if warming it with his hands. Then he laid gauze over the swelling and taped it. Every day after that, he'd show up with more herbs, and I could see the proud flesh recede. The vet said it was impossible, and then he said it was a miracle. The red swelling disappeared almost entirely, just a faint ridge of scarring remained, and the filly's coat came back to cover it, only the hair came in white, shaped like a human hand. I joked about her war paint, but it made me think she healed more from Francisco's touch than from his herbs.

"Oh, yeah, Francisco's something," Horace said when I mentioned it to him. "He can fix anything. We hardly ever call the vet anymore." He told me that the Spanish have a word for someone who heals, *curandero*. It usually refers to someone who works with people, but Francisco was a *curandero de animales*. After that, I started calling on him every time I had a lame horse or a wire cut or a calf coming backwards. He always knew what to do. If he had to sew something up, his stitches were as fine and precise as a blue-ribbon quilter's. And no matter how frightened or how badly injured, the animal calmed down the minute Francisco came around. After he treated one of my critters, I always tried to pay him, but he never accepted it. I started baking him pies and rolls and cookies, giving him little gifts of coffee and tobacco, handing them to him when he was there, or sometimes taking them over.

I remember, that morning of the accident, I was mad at Isaac. He'd just called from Denver to tell me he'd made a deal on our steer calves—on *my* steer calves—and I was furious because he hadn't consulted me first. "You were going to sell them anyway," he said, "and I didn't think you could get a better deal." But they were *my* calves, *my* deals to make. We had plenty of hay that year, and I'd wanted to winter them over as yearlings. I was unleashing my temper on the chopping block, splitting a load of piñon into kindling. I looked up for a minute and saw Francisco coming down our drive with a big bird on his shoulder. It had to be the red-tailed hawk with the broken wing he'd been doctoring. Francisco had told me the bird was almost healed, and I figured he was bringing him down to show me before he let him go.

I kept swinging during the split second I looked up. I'll never know exactly what happened, but I missed the piece of wood and the axe hit the edge of the chopping block. The head broke off and I remember the blade soaring back through the air as if in slow motion, dark and heavy, clumsy, like a wounded pigeon. It landed deep in my thigh, just above the knee. Everything blurred from that point on. Francisco started to run. The hawk took off, and I remember feeling this great sense of exhilaration to see it fly. At the same moment, I saw the blood gushing out of my jeans, and I knew I had done something bad.

"Aye, Señora," Francisco said, and he whipped off the bandanna he wore wrapped around his neck. He ripped open my jeans and as he tied a tourniquet, I could see red red blood spurting out of an artery and, beside it, the white of my bone.

Dr. Phelps told me later that if Francisco hadn't been so quick to reattach the artery, I would have died, or at least risked losing my leg from the tourniquet by the time he could have gotten me to town. The doctor said he had never seen such an expert job of sewing. But what I remember is Francisco's great gentleness, the quiet murmur of his Spanish, the calm that washed over me, the sense that everything would be okay. And I remember, too, those next few days and nights in the hospital, a strange heat overtaking me, and while dreaming, images of exposed white bone, of hawks in blue sky, of Francisco and me together, riding, working with animals, touching. In waking I felt dizzy, almost drunk with a yearning for something I'd never required of Isaac.

Francisco came to see me. He held his hat in his hand, deferential as always. He motioned with his chin at my leg. "It is going to be okay, no?" he said. "You heal soon, yes?" He was formal and shy and I ached to have him close to me again, murmuring, caring for me.

"Francisco, you saved me," I said, and I found myself stammering on the words, flushing and giggling like a young girl. I reached out. I wanted to draw him close. But he looked at my hand, gripped the rim of his hat more tightly.

"Francisco, please, I want . . ."

I didn't know what I wanted. I did know what I wanted. Francisco knew, he had to know.

He said, "Señora . . ." and his voice trailed off.

"Anna," I said. "Don't call me Señora. I'm Anna."

He touched the bandage on my leg, softly, tenuously. "Señora," he said again. "You are my friend. My very good friend."

I could feel the heat of his hand through my bandage, or I thought that I could.

"Your leg heals fast, and we work together. I look forward to that time. But now, I must go." He took my hand then, for just a moment, and then he turned and walked out of my room. When the nurse checked in a while later, she found me sobbing hysterically. The same nurse had attended my hysterectomy, and she took hold of me with a hearty authority. "It's shock," she said, dabbing my face with a cool wet cloth. "You've been through a lot in the last few months."

Rules, even the unwritten ones—perhaps especially the unwritten ones—keep the walls of our ordered worlds from caving in. They are a scaffolding of sorts I guess, and we should probably be grateful for them. But sometimes they feel a lot like prison bars. I came home from the hospital. I used crutches for a while, but I healed up good. I didn't see Francisco for some weeks and then he showed up one day carrying a young cat with a bandaged leg. "Someone hit him on the road," he said. "I fix him up, but he needs a home." I took the cat and he leaned against my chest, started to purr. He was a fine black fellow with a pure white belly. I felt a sense of great relief. Things were as they always had been. We'd be okay.

So we went along, Francisco and I. He helped me with my animals, I helped him with his birds. He brought me tomatoes out of his garden, I gave him zucchinis out of mine. Isaac died, Francisco and I grew old, we could joke with each other more. "It's that handsome vaquero," I'd say when he arrived; he called me *Señora Pájarita Bonita*, Mrs. Pretty Little Bird. He smoked and wheezed, I complained about my arthritis, we both started having trouble remembering people's names.

And now Francisco is gone. Today is cold and overcast and spitting snow; I can't help thinking how much this air would have hurt his lungs. I visited his shack the other day, to see if the barn swallows had left, to sweep up the feathers and close his windows if they had. Maybe I was looking for the *escrituras,* the breast feathers that marked their departure. As I approached I saw that the meadow was filled with big white birds. Swans, I thought at first, but then I saw the black tips on their wings. Snow geese. I'd never seen them in the valley before. Most of them were hunched over with their beaks to the ground, pecking for grain or for grass, and they reminded me of something, though I couldn't put my finger on it. Then it came to me: Francisco's granddaughters at the graveside, angel birds. I watched for a while until, of a moment, the geese took flight, circling higher and higher, finally forming a vee, heading south.

SAM MICHEL [B. 1960]

Although he divides his time between South America and Massachusetts, where he holds a creative writing position at the University of Massachusetts, Amherst, Sam Michel grew up in Reno and has stated that Nevada "inhabits my fiction." Most of the fifteen stories in his first book, Under the Light *(1991), take place in Nevada. All of them feature a character named Harry Drake, the kind of psychologically wounded, hard-drinking, womanizing man one might find in a Hemingway story. Harry is not easy to like. How he came to be who he is and what it is like to be Harry Drake are central concerns of the fiction. Writer John Graves describes Michel's work as being "unsentimental to the point of bleakness at times, yet the lilt of his speech buoys and tempers—and can make you laugh whenever Michel decides he wants you to." Michel is attentive to what Robert Frost once called "the cave of the mouth," crafting prose that has the "sound sense" of poetry, where style and voice are as significant as the story line. Trained in philosophy at the University of California, Michel began focusing on writing in Montana, publishing in the* Quarterly, Cutbank, *and* Neon, *and receiving grants from the Sierra Arts Foundation and Nevada Arts Council. He studied under Gordon Lish, former editor at Knopf, whom Michel thanks "for pulling me out of the sage and teaching me how to speak." Michel earned an* MFA *from the University of Florida and served as a writer-in-residence at Phillips Academy, publishing in the* Massachusetts Review *and* Epoch. *His novel* Big Dogs and Flyboys *was published in 2007. He has completed a novel set in Winnemucca—Lincoln Dahl Turns Five—and is at work on a new novel whose first chapter won the Lidano Award at* New York Tyrant *magazine.*

Seeing Hunter Creek

Pete's Arm! Sixty-two years old, that arm was. Looking at it, Harry could not believe it, but it was, was sixty-two, and the rest of Pete, too—both legs, chest, liver, heart, the high-held shoulder from where that sided arm used to hang—all of it, Harry knew: sixty-two.

To see it work! To see that arm hammer and lift and dig! To see it—from Harry's fifteen-year-old's shoes—not shrivel and scale, but grow and shine: humping lumber, digging ditches, clearing scrap, doing the kind of work that sent high school and college students—even Mexicans—packing. To see it work the knife and cut the meat, shuffle up and deal the deck. To see it touch a woman's back! To see Pete's arm now, suddenly, after a lifetime, with rememberings of it, wonderings on it, expectations for it, was a thing as to fill Harry with fear and joy and hope.

It was a thing, to see Pete's arm reaching, then lifting, then standing those walls—how many walls?—that made Harry's heart rise to his throat and, if nobody was watching, pump his fist high in the air. It was the arm, in Harry's mind, at that time, the rope-muscled and dove-tattooed arm, that made Pete, made what he said true, or if not true, then at least believable, and if not that, then the arm, hammer-sharp pounding out punctuation to some story big and wild, made Harry want to forget what was and was not true, and for the time of Pete's speaking, believe in a world he, Harry, would wish could be.

"Watch out!" Harry shouted. "Watch him now! Give him room," he said. "He's got to have *breathing* room."

Harry had six takers on the bet, the bet to see if Pete could lift Harry's father's diesel Mercedes—it had taken four of the boys to do it—dollar a wager. Harry had positioned one of the takers on each side of the car, to help keep the balance.

"You didn't say he was going to need help," said one of the boys.

"I said he'd lift the damn thing," said Harry, "and he will. If you want to see him balance it," he said, "it'll cost you another buck."

The boys were quiet then as Pete settled into a squat at the business end of the car. Harry shifted his eyes back and forth from the boys to Pete, who was staring hard now at the bumper, a single shining spot on the bumper, and nothing else but that spot. Pete laid his hand on that spot, stroked it. He worked his hand, clenching and stretching his fingers, before sliding his hand under the bumper, and with set jaw, but no sound—no grunts, no air from his nose, none of it—Pete lifted, straight-backed, coming steadily out of the squat.

Nobody said a word until Pete reached his full height and stopped lifting, the Mercedes balanced, on the one hand, and with no help. Then the same boy who had spoken earlier said, "All's he used was his legs; you told us he'd do it with his arm," and Harry saw something change in Pete's eyes, and Pete began to do it: skin stretching tighter over his biceps, veins standing out on his forearm, the car rose higher, was raised to Pete's waist, balancing, never wavering, the boys standing on each side with their hands held up and their mouths slacked wide, Pete grinning, lowering the car back to the pavement; and as Harry watched, he recognized in Pete's eyes the same change he'd seen in the rodeo bull's eyes, when the animal has thrown a man, and has sighted him on his knees, scrambling to find his feet.

They were sitting in Pete's place, Harry and Pete, sipping Pete's medicine. It was a Sunday afternoon, hot. They had quit with the cards because of the heat and were taking turns looking through the telescope. Neither wore a shirt. Harry kept trying not to look at the scar-slicked purple of Pete's stump, tried watching instead the sweat beads rolling off the chilled bottle, Pete's hand gripping the neck. Harry was waiting for Pete to go back to the telescope, so he could get another shot at that bottle.

What Pete was saying, was how in this town, in his time, Pete's time, back when he had two arms, a guy could do anything whatever it was he wanted to do. Anything! he was saying. All of it! *Imagine it.* Say a guy wanted to fish, or get divorced quick. He could do that. Both of that. Divorce, sure, shit. But try to fish now, he was saying, and see what you pull out of that creek. Try to hunt. Look across this valley in winter, tell me what you see. We didn't know what a *temperature inversion* was, he was saying, because we'd never been able to see one! And the water, the water! Would you drink from a public swimming pool? There were ladies then, too, like there aren't ladies now. Ask one of the ladies down at the house to do you straight up—straight up!—for a Lincoln spot. And disease! You'd better double-bag it now, boy, because you'll catch yourself something a whole lot worse than the clap to brag on. For laughs, he was saying, try this: try stretching naked in the morning sun on your porch, your own damn back porch! Or say a man, a waiter, say, is rude, to your wife, say. Poke him in the nose, why don't you? Gather up his collar, poke him! See how many people you know down at the clubs, how many remember that that's your seat, by God, your lucky-for-blackjack seat, and see if a stranger will switch you when you tell him to. Tell me how many people who know who are from here, or have a head to stay here, or give a rat's ass about what's going on here? In his time, Pete was saying, a person couldn't beat this place for land or town or people.

"It's no good," said Pete, "when a thing's too good."

Pete raised his bottle, and Harry watched the swallow Pete's throat made. Pete set the bottle down, scratched at his stump, turned back to the telescope. Pete was focusing, Harry knew—his fingers so light on the dials—far up the mountain, focusing on a place even the power of the scope could not find from where they stood, a place Pete had told Harry about, the best Pete had ever built, but Harry—despite the number of times he'd been up there—had never yet seen, deep in the fir and pine tree forest, near an aspen stand, near Hunter Lake, a place Pete had built under the cool shade there, and kept secret.

Pete got himself twenty-eight stitches over his right eye. Three bones broken in his hand, he got, and his middle finger. One hundred and thirty-six stitches ran from the inside of his elbow, up across the dove tattoo, clear to the outside of his shoulder. The finger, Pete figured, came when he put his hand through the refrigerator case. The hand and the arm, he said, came from the front door that didn't give, and didn't give, then finally gave. His eye, Pete explained, came from the security guard and the clerk, who knocked him down, the counter corner catching him just there, just right.

"Why?" Harry asked.

"Because the guy couldn't speak English," said Pete. "Because the guy wouldn't change a hundred-dollar bill," he said. "Because," he said, "there was no*body* there. Because," Pete said, "if you are going to say something worth saying, you'd better make sure somebody hears it."

They looked to Harry like dinosaurs; monstrous, prehistoric things. They always had. Big, belching, ripping, roaring yellow things. Metal and rubber, oil and gas. Bucket-bellied and saber-toothed: this one tearing, that one hauling, the other dumping—one to digest, even, sucking up and spewing out, and another rolling around and around, pissing down the flying dust.

Harry stood next to Pete, watching the brush and curve of Hunter Creek hill flatten out and blow away. Harry was Pete's help now—now that Pete's hand and arm were the way they were—his assistant, his boy.

On break, at the burger joint, Harry watched Pete trying to eat, how slow it went for Pete. Harry ate his own fast, and had already started in on the second bag of fries, when things began dropping from Pete's hand. First a bit of onion. A pickle. Some mustard and ketchup. Then it happened that the whole thing split itself in half, just at Pete's mouth, and Harry saw the way Pete's other side, the no-armed side, moved—like to catch it.

They sat staring that way, at the mess there in the Styrofoam box, Pete's hand resting next to it—the cast, the splint. Nobody moved a thing an inch, and the music in that time seemed loud to Harry. Finally, something like a smile, Harry saw, came to Pete's lips, and Harry watched as Pete fished around in the paper sack, began lining out the little packets of ketchup and mayonnaise on the table.

Harry gave a jerk, and winced to see it, when Pete's fist came down on the first packet, and then the second, the third, the fourth, the stuff splattering everywhere.

"Senators!" Pete was shouting. "Infidelity! Japs and water meters! California!" he shouted. "New fucking York!"

. . . .

"Kill those lights," Pete said.

Harry switched off the pickup lights and the flat site went black. He rolled down his window, heard off in the brush the whine and buzz of the nighttime insects. Harry heard Pete loading shells.

Pete was saying, "I've been building all my life. I've built the best places in this town," he said. Pete said, "I've pulled enough sliver wood from my body to frame a whole house."

Harry watched Pete working the chamber, the .12 gauge pinched between his knees. Pete swigged from the medicine bottle, making the liquid-in-glass sound, and handed the bottle to Harry and got out of the pickup. Harry did not turn his head, but could feel Pete looking him over there through the open window. Harry could feel the shotgun barrel resting against the pickup door.

Pete said, "You're all right, boy? You know what to do?"

"Sure, I know," said Harry, and kept staring out, his palms wet on the wheel, trying not to think how it would look in the morning, in the light.

Pete said, "This town, boy, is hellbent for mediocrity."

To the east, across the valley and behind the mountains, Harry saw the first tip of the rising moon. He saw the yellow come back into the dark shapes of the tractors and trucks, and the alkali white of the laser-leveled, tractor-graded earth. By daylight, it had not seemed so big to Harry, but as the moon rose to quarter view, half, then full—the flat, luminous area appeared greater than five, ten, fifteen football fields, all pushed together, a giant stadium glowing under the bright reflected light, edged around by the tangled hedge of sage and bitter brush, wild peach, wild rose. It felt funny to Harry, seeing Hunter Creek hill stripped that way, and it made the hair stand up on his arms, as if he had seen a ghost, or a car-struck dog, not quite dead, never coming back.

Above himself Harry heard Pete's hand, tap-tapping on the pickup roof. From the brush he heard the dove's coo, the owl's hoot. From up the hill he could hear the down-spilling rush of Hunter Creek, making its way to the ditch below where Harry could hear the leaves of the cottonwood blowing brittle.

Then, from everywhere Harry looked, creeping in from around the perimeter, as if by signal, or else by magic—the rabbits. Rabbits moving two, three hops, crawling, almost, then stopping, raising noses, cocking ears, testing the air, then moving again toward the center of the clearing. Big and small, jack and cottontail, waves of rabbits, hundreds of rabbits, it seemed to Harry, moving toward the center, toward the open.

At Harry's ear, Pete said, he whispered, "Ready?" and Harry hit the brights, and the rabbits froze.

Pete stopped walking, asked Harry what time it was.

"About seven," said Harry.

Pete looked up at the sky, then east, down the tracks. Harry did the same, seeing the twin lines converging in the distance, the buildings—casinos and restaurants— rain-washed and sharp, and the clouds, already past them, headed for Utah and Idaho and beyond, still raining down, he saw, and colored the desert colors of sunset. Harry breathed deep, smelled the wet gravel and the pavement, felt the end-of-summer air, felt the sharp beginning of things changing.

It had been a good summer, and the building had gone well, it being hard already for Harry to tell what Hunter Creek hill had once looked like, hard even to remember, hard to care. Even Pete, Harry thought, seemed caught up in the fast-moving sweep of work. Harry looked at Pete—Pete's arm, the sun-leathered lines in his sixty-two-year-old face.

Pete said, "We'll go this way."

They walked along the tracks, on Commercial Street, and Harry felt great, his first one-hundred-dollar bill aflame in his pocket. They had been to cash their checks at the club, and Pete had loaned Harry five bucks to put on top of his ninety-five-dollar earnings, to let Harry get the big bill. Pete turned, leaving the street, and walked through the gravel, right up to the tracks. He knelt down in the gravel, put his hand on the rail. Then Pete stood up and asked Harry for a nickel. Harry gave Pete the nickel. Pete laid the nickel on the rail where his hand had been, took two steps back.

"Put your hand on that rail, boy," Pete said. "What do you feel?"

"It tickles," said Harry. "Feels like tickling."

When the train had passed, clacking and wranging and banging by two steps close—Harry had never stood so close—Pete had Harry go and find the nickel: flat, distorted, some old President's face—Jefferson's, Harry thought—a metal smear.

"That's it," Pete said, and wiggled the shoulder on the no-armed side. "Right here in this place. Right there on that spot," said Pete. "That's how I lost her."

Harry didn't like the weight of the tool bags hanging on his hips—the way they pulled his pants down, the impressions left on his skin—and he took them off, generally, when he did not need to use the things in them. He was standing on the roof, stacking sheets of plywood that Pete was sliding up to him on the two-by-four ramp—three-quarter-inch sheets, four feet by ten, sixty-two years old!—when Harry stopped to unclip the belt.

Pete said, "You leave those things on, boy."

"Why?" said Harry.

"Why," Pete said, "because they're lifesavers; that's why."

"Lifesavers?" Harry said.

"Your hammer," said Pete, "is your best friend in high places. Your hammer and your arm," Pete said.

Pete began to climb the ladder, one-arming his way up the rungs. Up top, next to Harry, Pete gathered together a fistful of sawdust, threw the sawdust all over a spot on the steep-sloped roof.

"Hold my hand," Pete said, "and you just go on ahead and put your foot out on that dust."

Harry did what Pete said, felt his feet begin to slide. He felt Pete's grip holding him back. Then, without a word between them, Harry saw Pete, Pete's hammer in his hand, his arm cocked out from his side—on the ready—step out onto the dust. Harry watched Pete slide, knees bent, to the edge, where Pete jumped, out and away from the house, and spun—in midair—his big arm holding the hammer high above his head, then bringing it down, claw side first, fast, and hard, the claw striking, but not sticking—the way Harry knew Pete thought it would—but bouncing: the arm, the hand, the hammer, everything going down, over the edge, and out of Harry's sight.

Harry went to the edge, saw Pete there on the ground, flat on his back. He could see Pete's mouth opening and closing, trying to get the air in, trying to get back all that had gone out. Harry could see Pete's eyes—wide and wild, finally afraid.

Snow had fallen in the night. Harry woke up and looked out on it, a thin-skinned layer of it, the season's first, lying white and silent, just outside the little lodgepole lean-to, way up on the mountain, in the secret place Pete had built, not a stone's throw from Hunter Lake. Harry had found the place easily—Pete had told about it so much before he had moved away. Harry could not believe he had never seen the place before, could not believe much of all of what he saw while seeing so high up, seeing for the very first time now something new in everything old.

Harry reached and touched one of the poles, touched the manzanita woven tight between the poles: so tight that no wind came in from the sides, so tight that neither rain nor snow nor anything would come down in from above.

Harry left the lodgepole lean-to, crossed through the woods—the first, the clean, pine scent—his steps making no sound in the new-fallen snow. He made his way to the lake, and once there was surprised to see how from where he stood the town was out of sight, just as this place had been out of sight from the telescope in town. Harry skirted the lake—the green reeds, the snow-covered cattails—to where the lake became a creek, Hunter Creek, that flowed down out of these woods and manzanita, through the sage and bitter brush, the wild peach and rose, on past the ravine and into the ditch below Hunter Creek hill. He followed the creek awhile, then turned off into the aspen grove—white-barked, quaking, yellow leaves against a cobalt sky. Harry began reading things etched into the bark of the aspen: names, promises, obscenities. JIM and LARRY, he read. SARAH 1982. LEN LOVES LAURIE. FUCK YOU and EAT SHIT. Harry kept walking, deeper into the grove, until he felt he must be in the center of it, and there was nothing he could see but the trunks and limbs and leaves and sky, lost in it, looking, now, on his own in it, and there, on what Harry guessed must have been the biggest tree of all, high up on the trunk, right where Pete said it would be, almost too high up to read, was carved PETE 1943, plain and bold, still alive, and growing.

JEFFREY CHISUM [B. 1979]

"To write about a place you have to hate it." This remark, which the critic Leslie Fiedler attributes to William Faulkner in conversation, strikes a chord with fiction writer Jeffrey Chisum, who hated Nevada while growing up, but who since then has found himself drawn to write about it with a degree of empathy that being at a safe distance makes possible. Chisum, whose family has lived in Nevada for generations, was born in Yerington and grew up in Fernley, with a devout Mormon mother and a moody, temperamental father. Eldest of five siblings, Chisum went to work at age eleven, doing a variety of jobs that afforded insight into the lives of the working class, small-town Nevadans who inhabit his fiction. Chisum's fiction takes place in a town named Lahontan, based on Fernley. His goal as a writer is to imaginatively lay claim to this Nevada locale in the same way that Faulkner created the fictional world of Yoknapatawpha County, Mississippi. For Chisum, Nevada literature is fundamentally "about confrontation with the void, or the great, empty space of the desert." It is, he continues, "about loneliness and isolation, violence, suffering, the harsh indifference of nature, human desperation, sin, immorality, and, more generally, about a grasping for spiritual meaning." A graduate of the University of Southern California, where he dual-majored in English and cinema-television, Chisum stayed on to earn an MA and a PHD in literature and creative writing, mentored by the novelist T. C. Boyle. Chisum has published in L.A. Weekly *and* Mississippi Review, *has twice won first place in the Edward W. Moses Fiction Contest, and is currently program coordinator for the USC Writing Program.*

The Middle of Nowhere

Bud Capps hadn't heard anything about his wife for a long time. One summer night, he was sitting behind the counter at the Lazy Inn watching TV, and the phone rang.

"Hello?" There was silence at the other end for a moment, and then a woman's voice said:

"Hi, Arthur."

He paused. It took him a moment to realize that it was her. Who else ever called him by his real name?

"Laurie? Um, hello." He rubbed his palm on the desktop, trying to think of something to say. "Where are you?"

"Nowhere. I was just calling." She sounded woozy and drugged.

"Well, are you coming home any time soon?"

"You're an idiot, Bud." The line went dead.

He held the phone in his hand for a few seconds and then hung it up. There was a pack of cigarettes sitting near an ashtray to his right, and he reached for it and took one out and lit it. He watched the smoke curl in thin wisps under the yellow, bug-spotted light.

Laurie was Bud's second wife, and when she left, he hadn't been surprised. What was strange though, was the way she had done it. There hadn't been any note, and she hadn't taken their car. Furthermore, nobody in town seemed to know anything about it; it was almost as if she'd vanished off the face of the earth.

At first, Bud considered the possibility that she'd been kidnapped, but then he figured that it was more likely that she'd simply gone off with some man who'd been staying at the motel. He had, after all, seen her talking comfortably with a number of men—usually roguish-looking types with long hair and tattoos. And, her complaints about 'being stuck in this desert dump' had become more and more frequent. So, when she finally left, it didn't come as much of a shock. That was almost ten months ago, though, and the whole affair was beginning to trouble Bud's mind more and more—especially the strange, infrequent phone calls. Most of all, Bud simply wanted all the questions in his head answered: Where've you been? Why did you leave? What did I do? He'd tried to reassure himself by telling himself that it was no fault of his own, but that never got him anywhere—the questions still kept him up at night.

There was a rustling at the door, and Bud's teen-aged son, Applehead, came shuffling through the door. The boy was wearing his tuxedo, as usual, but his hair had fallen a bit out of place. He stood stock-still inside the door frame and looked at Bud.

"Well, son, don't just stand there. Come in and sit down."

Applehead walked around to the back of the counter and took his seat in the corner.

"Laurie called." Bud didn't look at Applehead as he spoke. "I don't know what I should do. I think we should try and find her somehow. What do you think about that?"

Applehead didn't make any reply, which was nothing new—the boy rarely ever spoke. His face was slack and unmoving, and he shifted his thin shoulders underneath the jacket of his thrift-store tuxedo.

The boy was afflicted with some mental disorder that Bud had never troubled to investigate. He got along well enough, after all, and he was perfectly competent at his chores around the motel, and furthermore, he had an unnatural talent with numbers. But, he needed looking-after, and if he got upset, he sometimes had seizures, and strange outbursts of incoherent speech. Everyone who walked in the door knew that there was something odd about him, and that was the reason for the tuxedo—it somehow made them feel more relaxed. The boy's real name was Charles, but like his father, he was generally called by his nickname.

Bud rubbed his chin.

"Yeah. I think we need to try and find her somehow. She's out there somewhere, and I got a lot of questions I want to ask her." He looked at his boy, but Applehead just stared. "Well, don't you got anything to say about it?"

Applehead's mouth hung open, and then he said in his high, young voice:

"Daddy, what's her phone number?"

"I don't know, son." He looked down at his hands. "That might be an idea though." Bud lifted his head and looked out the windows at the parking lot. Through the screen, he could see the stars glimmering over the eastern horizon. "You're a smart boy, Charles. That's what we'll do. We'll get one of them things that shows you the phone number that calls. And then we'll go find her. I'm sick and tired of not bein' able to sleep because I don't know nothing."

The next day, Bud got in touch with his friend Nick Robbins, who worked for the phone company. Nick said he'd drop by at around ten o'clock. When he got there, Bud explained the whole situation to him.

"Jeez, that sounds kinda crazy, Bud. Besides, Laurie was a lousy wife anyhow. Hell, I would thank my lucky stars if Marcy would up and bail like that."

"Well, Nick, that's you." He rubbed the stubble on his face. "You ain't lost any wives, and this is the second that's run out on me. I want some goddamn questions answered."

"All right, then. I can get this caller ID set up for you, but I still don't think it'll give you much of a chance of finding her. These things don't work all that great, and plus, how do you know if she's ever gonna call again?"

"I'll worry about that."

Nick stood up and began to head out to his truck, but he stopped and turned back to Bud. "Hey. I'm really sorry about this whole Laurie thing. You didn't deserve any of it. You're a good man. She's just a bitch, you know? There's nothing more to say, I guess." He gave a half smile and walked out the door.

The whole operation didn't take more than fifteen minutes, and though Nick gave Bud a friendly discount, it still wasn't especially cheap. The device was a small white box with a grey digital window that registered the number of whoever was calling—usually. Even though it was some kind of special phone-company-issued reader, sometimes no number came up at all, and this made Bud nervous. He always stared at the little window whenever the phone rang, and sometimes he would miss the opening snatches of conversation because of this. And he always felt disappointed when the voice on the other line wasn't hers. It was all just a matter of waiting, he supposed.

He spent the rest of the day in room 107 working on a broken hot-water valve with Applehead. The boy sat on the bathroom floor and handed tools to Bud, who was lying on his back underneath the sink. Applehead had taken off his jacket, but he'd gotten black smudges all over his white dress-shirt. It was almost eight o'clock when Bud began to tighten down the last nut. He twisted the wrench all the way around the pipe, and then it popped, and water began to spout into the room.

"Dammit!"

Bud clamored to his feet and hurried out of the room with Applehead at his heels. As they charged towards the shut-off valve, they could hear the office phone ringing. "Go and answer that, son." Applehead looked at him confusedly for a second and then turned and ran towards the office. Bud's hands were shaking as he opened the door to the pump room and turned off the water main. As he walked back to 107, he looked down at his hand and saw a red gash on his knuckle. "It just gets worse," he said. He wiped the blood on his shirtfront and then gathered a bunch of towels and began sopping up the liquid mess in the bathroom.

Applehead came silently into the room and squatted behind Bud. The water was nearly all wiped up when Bud finally turned and saw him.

"Oh! There you are. I was just about to holler for you." He wiped the sweat from his brow and then leaned over the bathtub and wrung the towel out into it. "I need you to go and get me a length of pipe out of the tool room." He handed over a busted section of steel-colored pipe. As Applehead took it, the boy handed a small scrap of paper to Bud.

"What's this?"

"Laurie called. She didn't say very much, and that is her phone number."

"What? What did she say? How did you know it was her?"

Applehead's eyes were large and round and moist.

"I don't know. That is her phone number."

Bud stared at the numbers on the paper. He could feel his face getting hot.

"Well, don't you remember anything? Come on, boy! What did she say?"

"That's her phone number." Applehead said the words as though his mouth was full.

"For Christ's sake!" Bud stood up and put his wounded knuckle to his lips. He looked down at his son, who seemed to have shrunk. The boy's eyes were filling. "Aw, hey, I'm sorry, Charles." Bud moved over to his son and massaged his long, thin neck. "You did a good job. I'm glad you wrote down this number. Maybe we can find Laurie now, right?"

Applehead gulped and nodded slowly.

"Are you positive it was her? Absolutely sure?"

Applehead kept nodding.

"Now, I'm going to be upset if it wasn't her. Was it her?"

"Yes."

Bud rubbed the boy's short, pomaded hair.

"Okay, then. Let's get this sink finished." He walked back to the bathroom and got down underneath the sink. Applehead left the room, and then Bud got up and went to the phone at the side of the bed. He picked it up and dialed the number. It rang and rang, but nobody picked it up.

That night, Bud couldn't fall asleep. The sheets felt stiff and rough, and he could hear Applehead's breath coming soundly and peacefully from the other bed, and that only made matters worse. It reminded him of the last restful night he'd had—the night Laurie left. Since then, he'd spent his sleepless nights lying on his back going over everything in his head. He'd never been mean or aggressive with her. He'd yelled at her a couple of times, like the day he found her smacking Applehead because he had spilled soda on her shirt, but for the most part, Bud had always been kind to her. She didn't necessarily deserve it though, and his train of thought in the dead of night generally next shifted towards his wondering why'd he ever married her in the first place. He thought about her clean, pale skin, and the pleasant bulk of her thighs—large, but without cellulite. He also thought about the times, mostly during the first months of their marriage, when she would grab him by the wrist and pull him into one of the unoccupied rooms and kiss him ferociously. And then there were the quiet times, when they'd sit behind the counter and smoke cigarettes and drink beers, and she would go on and on about her days as a rodeo queen. She'd tell him all the details about how her hair had been and what she'd worn, and he would wonder how he'd gotten so lucky.

He coughed and sat up in his bed. A palpitation in his heart shuddered through him, and he swung his legs over and got out of bed. He put on his jeans and his slippers and walked towards the door. Applehead stirred and lifted himself up on his elbows.

"It's okay, son. I'm just going out to get some fresh air."

Applehead looked at him for a moment, his eyes big and wet in the moonlight, and then he lay back down and seemed to fall immediately asleep.

Bud shut the door quietly and walked out across the asphalt of the parking lot. The desert night air was cool, and Bud could smell the faint, sweet odor of sagebrush coming from across the railroad tracks. To the west, the Sierras sat dark and bulky and slightly backlit by all the round-the-clock neon and mercury of Reno's high-rise casinos. The weatherman had mentioned something about a meteor shower, and so Bud looked up into the blue-black of the nighttime sky. To the south, he could make out a few glimmers of moving light. They looked like fiery dust motes zipping to their deaths somewhere in the opaque, black distance. Everything was immensely quiet, as it always was in this little town, and Bud thought that this must be the worst place for an insomniac to live. He had spent nearly his entire life here, without much thought or care as to what lay beyond the ring of pale brown and purple mountains. And now he wondered if he should regret it. A breeze stirred the little windmill that was planted in the rock garden along Main Street. Bud shivered and then reminded himself that he could go to see Nick tomorrow. Maybe he could finally get some of his questions answered soon. He licked his lips and stuffed his hands into his pockets and then turned and went back into his room and tried to go to sleep.

The next day, Bud sat Applehead behind the desk, and then he walked out and got into his pickup and drove out of the lot. The July sun was bright and hot as he turned down Main Street and rolled past the China Chef and Fred McGregor's cowboy store. The phone company office was in a small two-story building on the left—just a couple buildings before one of the town's two stop lights. Bud climbed out of his truck and went through the glass door and walked up the stairs. He went into the phone company office and found Roxanne, the office secretary, sitting behind the desk and looking at a shopping website on her computer.

"Hi, Roxanne."

She swivelled in her chair to look at him: "Oh, hello, Bud."

"Is Nick around?"

"No, honey—he's out on a call." She smiled and leaned forward. "What was it that you needed? Do you want to leave a message for him?"

"Well, no . . . That's all right. I just—" he fingered the scrap of paper in his pocket. "Well, this is how it is. Do you think you could do me a favor? You see, I got this number." He laid the paper on the desk, and she immediately grabbed it.

"You want to know whose number this is?"

"Yeah. That should do it. Either who it is or where it is."

She looked at him and smiled softly.

"Well, buddy boy, we're not supposed to do this, and it might not turn up anything, but I'll go ahead and look it up for you."

"Thanks, Roxanne. I appreciate it."

She stared at the number and then began typing figures into her computer.

"You know," she said, "I think I've seen this number before. Like on a pay-phone or something."

"What do you mean?"

"You know how sometimes there's phone numbers graffitied on phone booths? Well, I think I saw this number before."

"Jeez. How could you remember that?"

"Please, Bud. I work with numbers all day long."

"I guess that's true." He didn't really believe her, though. He decided that she must have called the number herself for some reason, which perplexed him.

"It'll be up in a second." She held out her hands and looked at them. "How's Applehead?"

"He's good."

Bud tried to catch a glance at the screen. Roxanne tapped her long, gaudy fingernails on the desk. At last, the computer screen flickered. She twisted the screen over so he could see it.

"Well, here's your info."

He looked at the screen, and he realized that he was so nervous he couldn't read it.

"What does all that mean?" he said.

"It's one of ours—it's a pay phone. Way down somewhere in Nye County. Close to Area 51. What, are you hunting aliens or something? Don't tell me you're into all that UFO stuff, Bud."

"No. I ain't." He looked hard at the list on the screen. He knew that Roxanne wanted more information, that she was on to him, but he didn't care. "Hey, can I write that down or something?"

"Sure, sweetie." She handed him a pad and a pen. He wrote down the address: 1300 Syrinx Road, Rachel, Nevada. He tore off the piece of paper and put it in his breast pocket.

"Thanks again, Roxanne."

"No problem, Bud. See you later. And I hope you find whatever it is you're looking for."

He looked back at her over his shoulder, and he thought that he saw something like pity in her expression.

When he got back to the Lazy Inn, it was barely past eleven o'clock, and Bud went straight into his room and began packing. He piled clothes and toiletries into a suitcase, and then he packed a bag for Applehead. He had been incredibly tired earlier, but now, all his fatigue and frustration seemed to lift for a moment. The sound of someone's throat being cleared drifted in through the doorway, and Bud turned and saw Applehead staring at him.

"Hey, son." He smiled. "Well, I think I might know where Laurie is. We're gonna go for a trip. How does that sound?"

Applehead just stared.

"Come on. Let's go. Let's go close up the office. Did anybody stop in while I was gone?"

Applehead didn't say anything. Bud went into the office and double-checked the register, but it was blank—business had been unusually slow this summer. He closed the book and put it underneath the counter. Then, he walked out the door and locked it and checked to make sure it was secure. He figured that it would be at least a five-hour drive down to Rachel, but he was too excited to care. Applehead got in on the passenger side, and Bud slung their bags into the bed of the pickup and then climbed into the truck and drove away.

The two of them drove on and on, past red, rocky hills and long stretches of land that were blank save for sparse scatterings of sagebrush. They passed the time by listening to country tunes on the radio. Bud would say a thing or two to Applehead every so often, but the conversation was entirely one-sided. The route they took— via Highway 50—is the loneliest road in America, and Bud and Applehead did not pass more than three or four cars during their entire trip. When they finally saw a roadsign that read Rachel: 35 Mi., the sun had just barely begun its descent towards the peaks to the west. The sky stretched blue and blank between the mountains, and it was utterly devoid of any clouds.

Bud's truck came over a crest, and he and Applehead began a steep descent down into a valley. Far below, they could see trailers and small buildings alongside the road. As they neared the gathering of shacks and mobile homes, hard gusts began to whip the truck's antenna back and forth.

"God," said Applehead.

"Yeah, no kidding." Bud hunched forward over the steering wheel and adjusted the radio. "We're pretty close to Area 51. Keep and eye out for aliens. Or black jeeps."

"Okay." Applehead stared straight ahead.

Finally, they reached the bars and trailers and shops along the highway. The population of the place could not have been more than a hundred and fifty. One building was called "The Little A'Le'Inn." It seemed somehow familiar to Bud, and so he turned into the gravel driveway and killed the motor.

"Wait here, son. I'll be right back."

He got out of the truck and went through a dust-blotched screen door and into the office. An old woman with red hair and grey roots was reading a romance novel behind the desk.

"'Scuse me, ma'am."

She looked over the pages of her book, but she didn't put it down.

"Um, I was just wondering if you could tell me where Syrinx Road is."

She sneered at Bud and made a scolding noise through her teeth.

"So that's what it is, huh?" she said. "Well, you just go a couple blocks over yonder. It's a dirt road. You'll be drivin' a while before you get there, though."

"What do you mean?"

"You're going to the phone booth, ain't you? That's what you're looking for, right? I've always thought it was pretty stupid, but, if you want to see it for yourself, go ahead. It ain't much to look at, though."

Bud was confused, but he could see that the woman was irritated, and so he turned and walked out. He got back into the truck and sat next to Applehead. Bud stared for a long time out the window. Then he started up the engine and drove off.

The woman's directions turned out to be quite accurate, and within a few moments, the tires of Bud's pickup were sending a thin ribbon of yellow dust up into the air. Syrinx Road was unpaved and lined with deep ruts. After twenty minutes, Bud still couldn't see anything.

"God," said Applehead.

"What's that? Hey, why do you keep sayin' that?"

"I don't know."

Bud clicked off the radio and rolled down the window and spit out into the dust. He kept driving, and eventually, off in the distance, he could see the telephone wires stretching down to the earth. Then, up ahead, the last rays of the sun began to shine off of something small and rectangular. They drove for a few minutes more, until Bud stopped the truck next to the phone booth. He and Applehead climbed out and walked over to it.

The glass had been smashed out of one side of the thing, and the metal was etched with graffiti—both profane and nonsensical. Gravel crunched under Bud and Applehead's shoes as they approached. Bud put his hands on his hips and stared at the ruined booth.

"Hell."

A number of thoughts flashed rapidly through his head. He looked over at Applehead and forced a grin. The boy smiled back. "Why in the hell did I waste all my time? Roxanne told me it was a pay phone, didn't she?" Applehead made no reply. Bud walked around the booth and kicked at a jagged tooth of glass. "Damn it all to hell." He looked out at the mountains and the desert. Why, he wondered, would anyone put a phone booth clear out here in the middle of nowhere? And, why would Laurie make a call from it? He had hoped to learn something, anything, but instead, his mind was filled with a whole new set of questions. Bud went inside the booth and picked up the phone and listened to the dial tone. He wondered if the people at Area 51 ever monitored the line. Maybe they knew where Laurie was.

Applehead had taken off his tuxedo jacket, and now he slung it over his shoulder. Bud looked at him and it seemed as if the boy was listening to something.

"You hear something, Charles?"

Applehead started, as though he'd been woken out of a daydream. He lifted his arm and pointed to the phone wires that stretched up from the sand and led off in separate directions towards either horizon.

"What? They makin' a buzzin' sound or something?" Bud looked up at them and listened hard, but he couldn't hear anything. He walked over to Applehead and put his hand on the boy's shoulder. "Well, son, I guess we better go. This trip was a waste of time. Let's go see if they got anything to eat in Rachel."

"Okay, dad."

They drove back in silence, and Bud never once gestured towards the radio. The rough road jostled them, and Bud couldn't stop wondering why on earth Laurie had called from that strange phone booth. The truck turned back towards Rachel, and Bud parked it in front of a place called Bill's Buffalo Burgers.

Inside, each of them sat and ordered a steak dinner. Their waiter was a frail old man who was liver-spotted and kept looking at Applehead out of the corner of his eye. Applehead was eating very slowly, but he kept drinking his water down to the ice. The waiter came over to refill his glass.

"Wow, you sure are thirsty."

Applehead looked up at him.

"We had a long trip," said Bud. "We came clear down from Lahontan."

The waiter set the water pitcher on the table. It was beaded with droplets of water.

"Did you guys come to look for flying saucers or something?"

"No, it wasn't aliens we were looking for."

The waiter grinned a gapped smile.

"Well, why on earth would you want to come clear out here?"

"Oh, we were just looking for somebody."

The old man nodded his head. He picked up the water pitcher and then set it back down.

"You know," he said, "I would never think that this place would be good for finding much of anything, but I heard stranger things in my days. Especially here. I've lived here for thirty-five years."

"Really?"

"Oh, yeah. And you want to hear something really weird? This just goes to show you how strange the kids are these days. There's this phone booth all by itself clear out in the desert. Just out there in the middle of the desert—I think the military put it there in case anyone got lost on a training mission, cause, you know, Area 51 is just over yonder. And anyhow, these kids will drive out there and just sit around to see if anybody calls it. I go out there sometimes to just sit and think, and I seen cars with plates from California, and Arizona, and Utah, and one time, North Carolina. I don't see what the point is of just sittin' there and waiting for someone to call." The old man had a disapproving look on his face. "But one time, though, I gotta tell you, that thing started ringing. I about near wet my pants it scared me so bad. I went over there and answered it, but all it was was just some partyers. They asked me who I was and I just hung up."

"That's pretty weird, alright," said Bud.

"Yeah. You got that right. Anyhow. If you boys need anything, just holler."

"We'll do that."

Bud and Applehead finished their meals and Bud left a generous tip for the old waiter. They walked outside and climbed into the pickup and drove away. The sun had finally sunk down into the west outside Bud's window, and the stars began to wink in the nighttime sky. The road stretched on straight as an arrow, and before long, Applehead was asleep.

Bud still had a lingering curiosity about where Laurie was and what her calls meant. Still, he thought, what was the use in worrying about it? He couldn't pinpoint it, but something felt better inside him. He figured that he could go on wondering forever, and it would be okay. His body was very tired, and he looked forward to lying down in his bed. Way in the distance toward the east, he could see specks of light—meteors—streaking across the darkness and vanishing into nothingness. All the broad and lonesome landscape was still, but to the east, far off in the distance, it was raining starlight.

Bud thought that he might doze off, and so he reached down and turned on the radio. Naturally, the country singer was crooning about the wife who'd left him. Applehead stirred and sat up and blinked. The boy looked around for a moment and then settled back in the seat and folded his hands in his lap.

"Nope. We're not quite there yet," said Bud.

"Lost?" Applehead was staring at the side of Bud's head.

"No. We're not lost. We'll be home in a couple of hours."

"I'm sorry, dad."

Bud reached over and squeezed the boy's neck.

"You don't have anything to be sorry about, son."

After a while, Applehead fell asleep again. Bud turned the radio down so that it was little more than a whisper. The mountains rose and fell like waves against the nightscape, until finally, Bud could see the familiar curves of the desert as he neared home. He slowed the truck down to twenty miles per hour when he got into town, and he made a silent promise to himself that he would forget all about Laurie. In fact, he hoped that he would never hear another thing about her.

The truck turned into the parking lot of the Lazy Inn, and Bud parked in front of the office. He nudged Applehead, and the boy's eyes snapped open. The two of them got out of the truck and lumbered towards their room. Bud helped Applehead out of his tuxedo and tucked him into bed. Then he went into the bathroom and brushed his teeth, and he was about to shut off the bathroom light, but instead he put on his slippers and walked outside toward the office. In the distance, he could hear a train rumbling across the track. There was one last thing he wanted to do. Bud went to the office phone and picked it up and dialed the number of the mysterious phone booth. He held it to his ear and listened to it ringing. It would be out there, all solitary and strange in the middle of the desert, crying its metallic lamentation into the night. He held the phone in his hand, ringing, and after a while, he hung it back up, and after turning off the lights in the office, he went back to his bed where he began to settle himself amongst all the quiet and strange immensity of the universe.

THIRTEEN

WILD NEVADA

Lessons of the Land

E arly travelers, squinting under the sun glare across barren Nevada deserts, were sometimes fooled by mirages to see fantastic scenes that weren't really there. They saw vast sheets of water, shimmering lakes, ships at sea, entire Mediterranean villages. It took an effort of will to resist being seduced by these lovely phantasms and maintain stoic belief in a much bleaker reality. In a curious shift of perspective, the writers collected in this chapter suggest that the image of Nevada as a desolate wasteland is itself an illusion that has blinded us to the reality that Nevada's wild heart beats with abundant life and beauty. These pieces span more than one hundred years, modeling a range of styles of engagement, from recreation and adventure to nature observation, aesthetic appreciation, solitary contemplation, and concern for the future. They invite us to resee this most arid, most mountainous state through enlightened eyes, deepening our understanding and enjoyment of this remarkable place.

As you read these pieces, you'll notice a pattern in which authors contrast how Nevada seems at first glance against how it appears with greater knowledge. Many of the pieces open by proposing a hypothetical point of view—the Californian, the easterner, the driver on Interstate 80, the inexperienced observer, an ignorant generation. Through these eyes Nevada appears, above all, barren—ugly, fierce, and relentless. Having established this conventional view, the author then counterpoises a new way of seeing, a shifted perspective, from which the same place becomes luminous, fascinating, and valuable. The words *observe, notice, come to know* crop up repeatedly, implying that if we *pay attention* we will discover creatures and beauty that were present all along. Just as a class in wine appreciation educates our palette to more fully savor this common drink, equipping us with a vocabulary to distinguish and describe its properties, so, too, authors teach us a language of response to Nevada's special qualities. "Delicious solitude," "the vastness of time," "a great spatial silence," "a metropolis of nocturnal rodents," "the transcendent quiet of a vast Nevada night," "the grandeur of the everyday"—such phrases deepen our awareness of what we have taken for granted, what we have not seen.

In the effort to resee Nevada, science is a powerful tool, and the writers here draw upon geology, climatology, paleontology, botany, biology, ecology, and biogeography. John McPhee, for example, uses plate tectonics to explain that in Nevada the earth is active, that we stand on a thinning, spreading crust, afloat on a viscous mantle, a land where mountains are being made and where sparse vegetation is a blessing to geologists who gravitate to this geologically young state to read the naked mountains like a history book. Other writers teach us to perceive Nevada through the lens of biogeography, revealing a patchwork of habitats where we saw only uniform bleakness, charting transition zones that perhaps we hadn't noticed—between the Mojave and Great Basin deserts, for example—and suggesting that mountain ranges are biological islands separated by a sea of sagebrush, where evolutionary processes take place in relative isolation. Rambling botanizer John Muir praises the nondescript piñon pine—Nevada's state tree—a tree that many people can't identify and whose properties they don't know.

Science as a frame of understanding imbues the world with significance and restores our sense of wonder toward the mundane, posing questions we never thought to ask. Through the lens of science, Nevada's borders tend to melt away to be replaced by the outline of the Great Basin, a region understood not as a political entity but as a biophysical one, defined by interior drainage and species distribution. In important ways the scientific view resembles an indigenous one, with attention to habitats, water sources, plant and animal communities, and natural features. Thus, via science and aesthetics of the wild, we complete a full circle, hearkening back to Native American stories and returning to the landscape that engendered Nevada's literature in the first place.

MARK TWAIN [1835–1910]

For biographical information on Mark Twain, see p. 117. Ancestral summering grounds for the Washoe Indians, Lake Tahoe was first discovered by whites in 1844 when John Frémont saw and named it Bonpland after a French botanist. The lake, situated in the Sierra Nevada at elevation 6,229 feet, began to be called Bigler in 1853, named after the third governor of California. As early as 1859, the lake's scenic beauty was being publicly extolled. An article that year in San Francisco's Alta California *called Tahoe "one of the most interesting and agreeable resorts for pleasure and amusement" on the West Coast. Despite the lake's resort potential, Californians of the day raced by it, bound for the new gold and silver strikes in Virginia City. Intense demand for lumber on the Comstock meant that Tahoe's forests were valued more for timber than for natural beauty, and a sawmill was established at Glenbrook in 1861, the same year that Twain first visited the lake, as fondly recounted in* Roughing It *(1872). He and his friend Johnny K. spent several happy weeks there, marveling that the water's singular clarity created the illusion that their rowboat was a hot-air balloon. The two friends laid claim to three hundred acres near Carnelian Bay. The fantasy of owning lakeside property, however, literally went up in flames when Twain accidentally started a fire that burned up their provisions and their forest in a spectacular conflagration. In 1862 "Tahoe," derived from the Washoe word dá'aw, meaning "lake," began to replace "Bigler." Twain was livid. In an 1863 article for the* Territorial Enterprise *he lambasted "Tahoe" as being "repulsive to the ear," its "hideous, discordant syllables" unendurable, a "spoony, slobbering, summer-complaint of a name. . . . it sounds as weak as soup for a sick infant." "'Tahoe' be—forgotten!" he railed. But "Tahoe" took hold, formally recognized by the California legislature in 1945.*

from Roughing It

It was the end of August, and the skies were cloudless and the weather superb. In two or three weeks I had grown wonderfully fascinated with the curious new country, and concluded to put off my return to "the States" awhile. I had grown well accustomed to wearing a damaged slouch hat, blue woolen shirt, and pants crammed into boot tops, and gloried in the absence of coat, vest, and braces. I felt rowdyish and "bully" (as the historian Josephus phrases it, in his fine chapter upon the destruction of the Temple). It seemed to me that nothing could be so fine and so romantic. I had become an officer of the government, but that was for mere sublimity. The office was a unique sinecure. I had nothing to do and no salary. I was private secretary to His Majesty the Secretary and there was not yet writing enough for two of us. So Johnny K—— and I devoted our time to amusement. He was the young son of an Ohio nabob and was out there for recreation. He got it. We had heard a world of talk about the marvelous beauty of Lake Tahoe, and finally curiosity drove us thither to see it. Three or four members of the brigade had been there and located some timberlands on its shores and stored up a quantity of provisions in their camp. We strapped a couple of blankets on our shoulders and took an ax apiece and started—for we intended to take up a wood ranch or so ourselves and become wealthy. We were on foot. The reader will find it advantageous to go horseback. We were told that the distance was eleven miles. We tramped a long time on level ground, and then toiled laboriously up a mountain about a thousand miles high and looked over. No lake there. We descended on the other side, crossed the valley, and toiled up another mountain three or four thousand miles high, apparently, and looked over again. No lake yet. We sat down, tired and perspiring, and hired a couple of Chinamen to curse those people who had beguiled us. Thus refreshed, we presently resumed the march with renewed vigor and determination. We plodded on, two or three hours longer, and at last the lake burst upon us—a noble sheet of blue water lifted six thousand three hundred feet above the level of the sea, and walled in by a rim of snow-clad mountain peaks that towered aloft full three thousand feet higher still! It was a vast oval, and one would have to use up eighty or a hundred good miles in traveling around it. As it lay there with the shadows of the mountains brilliantly photographed upon its still surface, I thought it must surely be the fairest picture the whole earth affords.

We found the small skiff belonging to the brigade boys and, without loss of time, set out across a deep bend of the lake toward the landmarks that signified the locality of the camp. I got Johnny to row—not because I mind exertion myself, but because it makes me sick to ride backward when I am at work. But I steered. A three-mile pull brought us to the camp just as the night fell, and we stepped ashore very tired and wolfishly hungry. In a "cache" among the rocks we found the provisions and the cooking utensils, and then, all fatigued as I was, I sat down on a boulder and superintended while Johnny gathered wood and cooked supper. Many a man who had gone through what I had would have wanted to rest.

It was a delicious supper—hot bread, fried bacon, and black coffee. It was a delicious solitude we were in, too. Three miles away was a sawmill and some workmen, but there were not fifteen other human beings throughout the wide circumference of the lake. As the darkness closed down and the stars came out and spangled the great mirror with jewels, we smoked meditatively in the solemn hush and forgot our troubles and our pains. In due time we spread our blankets in the warm sand between two large boulders and soon fell asleep, careless of the procession of ants that passed in through rents in our clothing and explored our persons. Nothing could disturb the sleep that fettered us, for it had been fairly earned, and if our consciences had any sins on them they had to adjourn court for that night,

anyway. The wind rose just as we were losing consciousness, and we were lulled to
sleep by the beating of the surf upon the shore.

It is always very cold on that lake shore in the night, but we had plenty of blankets and were warm enough. We never moved a muscle all night, but waked at
early dawn in the original positions, and got up at once, thoroughly refreshed, free
from soreness, and brimful of friskiness. There is no end of wholesome medicine
in such an experience. That morning we could have whipped ten such people as we
were the day before—sick ones at any rate. But the world is slow, and people will
go to "water cures" and "movement cures" and to foreign lands for health. Three
months of camp life on Lake Tahoe would restore an Egyptian mummy to his
pristine vigor and give him an appetite like an alligator. I do not mean the oldest
and driest mummies, of course, but the fresher ones. The air up there in the clouds
is very pure and fine, bracing and delicious. And why shouldn't it be?—it is the
same the angels breathe. I think that hardly any amount of fatigue can be gathered
together that a man cannot sleep off in one night on the sand by its side. Not under
a roof, but under the sky; it seldom or never rains there in the summertime. I know
a man who went there to die. But he made a failure of it. He was a skeleton when he
came, and could barely stand. He had no appetite and did nothing but read tracts
and reflect on the future. Three months later he was sleeping out of doors regularly,
eating all he could hold, three times a day, and chasing game over mountains three
thousand feet high for recreation. And he was a skeleton no longer, but weighed
part of a ton. This is no fancy sketch, but the truth. His disease was consumption.
I confidently commend his experience to other skeletons.

JOHN MUIR [1838–1914]

*Carrying bread, tea, and a tin for boiling water, John Muir headed east over the Sierra en
route to Nevada in the fall of 1878. Accustomed to sauntering under towering sequoias, he was
momentarily stunned when the woods gave out before him as suddenly as if he had reached
the ocean. Undaunted, Muir pressed on and, despite the initial repugnance of Nevada's "barren
aspect," discovered a wilderness far richer than he had expected. This enthusiastic mountaineer
was born in the seacoast town of Dunbar, Scotland. When Muir was eleven, his father moved
the family to Wisconsin to clear a farm in the wilderness. As early as possible, Muir escaped the
domineering presence of his Calvinistic father and made his way west, where he gloried in what
he later called his "young mountain-climbing days." He married at age forty-one and raised a*

family while managing a fruit orchard in Martinez, California. Renowned as the father of the
movement for wilderness preservation, Muir founded the Sierra Club in 1892. In 1903 he took
President Theodore Roosevelt camping in Yosemite, which helped lead to federal protection for
the park. A reluctant but diligent writer, in later life Muir labored in his "scribble den" to cham-
pion preservation of wilderness. He published his first book, Mountains of California *(1894)*
at age fifty-six, followed by several more, including My First Summer in the Sierra *(1911),*
The Yosemite *(1912), and* The Story of My Boyhood and Youth *(1913). By the turn of the*
century Americans were beginning to take his message to heart. In Our National Parks *(1901)*
he wrote: "The tendency nowadays to wander in wilderness is delightful to see. Thousands of
tired, nerve-shaken, over-civilized people are beginning to find that going to the mountains is
going home." Steep Trails *(1918), the essay collection in which "Nevada Forests" appears, was*
published posthumously, edited by William Frederic Badè.

Nevada Forests

When the traveler from California has crossed the Sierra and gone a little way
down the eastern flank, the woods come to an end about as suddenly and completely as if, going westward, he had reached the ocean. From the very noblest
forests in the world he emerges into free sunshine and dead alkaline lake-levels.
Mountains are seen beyond, rising in bewildering abundance, range beyond range.
But however closely we have been accustomed to associate forests and mountains,
these always present a singularly barren aspect, appearing gray and forbidding and
shadeless, like heaps of ashes dumped from the blazing sky.

But wheresoever we may venture to go in all this good world, nature is ever
found richer and more beautiful than she seems, and nowhere may you meet with
more varied and delightful surprises than in the byways and recesses of this sublime
wilderness—lovely asters and abronias on the dusty plains, rose-gardens around
the mountain wells, and resiny woods, where all seemed so desolate, adorning the
hot foothills as well as the cool summits, fed by cordial and benevolent storms of
rain and hail and snow; all of these scant and rare as compared with the immea-
surable exuberance of California, but still amply sufficient throughout the barest
deserts for a clear manifestation of God's love.

Though Nevada is situated in what is called the "Great Basin," no less than
sixty-five groups and chains of mountains rise within the bounds of the State to a
height of about from eight thousand to thirteen thousand feet above the level of
the sea, and as far as I have observed, every one of these is planted, to some extent,
with coniferous trees, though it is only upon the highest that we find anything
that may fairly be called a forest. The lower ranges and the foothills and slopes
of the higher are roughened with small scrubby junipers and nut pines, while the

dominating peaks, together with the ridges that swing in grand curves between them, are covered with a closer and more erect growth of pine, spruce, and fir, resembling the forests of the Eastern States both as to size and general botanical characteristics. Here is found what is called the heavy timber, but the tallest and most fully developed sections of the forests, growing down in sheltered hollows on moist moraines, would be regarded in California only as groves of saplings, and so, relatively, they are, for by careful calculation we find that more than a thousand of these trees would be required to furnish as much timber as may be obtained from a single specimen of our Sierra giants.

The height of the timber-line in eastern Nevada, near the middle of the Great Basin, is about eleven thousand feet above sea-level; consequently the forests, in a dwarfed, storm-beaten condition, pass over the summits of nearly every range in the State, broken here and there only by mechanical conditions of the surface rocks. Only three mountains in the State have as yet come under my observation whose summits rise distinctly above the tree-line. These are Wheeler's Peak, twelve thousand three hundred feet high, Mount Moriah, about twelve thousand feet, and Granite Mountain, about the same height, all of which are situated near the boundary-line between Nevada and Utah Territory.

In a rambling mountaineering journey of eighteen hundred miles across the state, I have met nine species of coniferous trees—four pines, two spruces, two junipers, and one fir—about one third the number found in California. By far the most abundant and interesting of these is the *Pinus Fremontiana,* or nut pine. In the number of individual trees and extent of range this curious little conifer surpasses all the others combined. Nearly every mountain in the State is planted with it from near the base to a height of from eight thousand to nine thousand feet above the sea. Some are covered from base to summit by this one species, with only a sparse growth of juniper on the lower slopes to break the continuity of these curious woods, which, though dark-looking at a little distance, are yet almost shadeless, and without any hint of the dark glens and hollows so characteristic of other pine woods. Tens of thousands of acres occur in one continuous belt. Indeed, viewed comprehensively, the entire State seems to be pretty evenly divided into mountain-ranges covered with nut pines and plains covered with sage—now a swath of pines stretching from north to south, now a swath of sage; the one black, the other gray; one severely level, the other sweeping on complacently over ridge and valley and lofty crowning dome.

The real character of a forest of this sort would never be guessed by the inexperienced observer. Traveling across the sage levels in the dazzling sunlight, you gaze with shaded eyes at the mountains rising along their edges, perhaps twenty miles away, but no invitation that is at all likely to be understood is discernible. Every mountain, however high it swells into the sky, seems utterly barren. Approaching nearer, a low brushy growth is seen, strangely black in aspect, as though it had been burned. This is a nut pine forest, the bountiful orchard of the red man. When you ascend into its midst you find the ground beneath the trees, and in the openings also, nearly naked, and mostly rough on the surface—a succession of crumbling ledges of lava, limestones, slate, and quartzite, coarsely strewn with soil weathered from them. Here and there occurs a bunch of sage or linosyris, or a purple aster, or a tuft of dry bunch-grass.

The harshest mountain-sides, hot and waterless, seem best adapted to the nut pine's development. No slope is too steep, none too dry; every situation seems to be gratefully chosen, if only it be sufficiently rocky and firm to afford secure anchorage for the tough, grasping roots. It is a sturdy, thickset little tree, usually about fifteen feet high when full grown, and about as broad as high, holding its knotty branches well out in every direction in stiff zigzags, but turning them gracefully upward at the ends in rounded bosses. Though making so dark a mass in the distance, the foliage is a pale grayish green, in stiff, awl-shaped fascicles. When examined closely these round needles seem inclined to be two-leaved, but they are mostly held firmly together, as if to guard against evaporation. The bark on the older sections is nearly black, so that the boles and branches are clearly traced against the prevailing gray of the mountains on which they delight to dwell.

The value of this species to Nevada is not easily overestimated. It furnishes fuel, charcoal, and timber for the mines, and, together with the enduring juniper, so generally associated with it, supplies the ranches with abundance of firewood and rough fencing. Many a square mile has already been denuded in supplying these demands, but, so great is the area covered by it, no appreciable loss has as yet been sustained. It is pretty generally known that this tree yields edible nuts, but their importance and excellence as human food is infinitely greater than is supposed. In fruitful seasons like this one, the pine-nut crop of Nevada is, perhaps, greater than the entire wheat crop of California, concerning which so much is said and felt throughout the food-markets of the world.

The Indians alone appreciate this portion of Nature's bounty and celebrate the harvest home with dancing and feasting. The cones, which are a bright grass-green in color and about two inches long by one and a half in diameter, are beaten off with poles just before the scales open, gathered in heaps of several bushels, and lightly scorched by burning a thin covering of brushwood over them. The resin, with which the cones are bedraggled, is thus burned off, the nuts slightly roasted, and the scales made to open. Then they are allowed to dry in the sun, after which the nuts are easily thrashed out and are ready to be stored away. They are about half an inch long by a quarter of an inch in diameter, pointed at the upper end, rounded at the base, light-brown in general color, and handsomely dotted with purple, like birds' eggs. The shells are thin, and may be crushed between the thumb and finger. The kernels are white and waxy-looking, becoming brown by roasting, sweet and delicious to every palate, and are eaten by birds, squirrels, dogs, horses, and man. When the crop is abundant the Indians bring in large quantities for sale; they are eaten around every fireside in the State, and oftentimes fed to horses instead of barley.

Looking over the whole continent, none of Nature's bounties seems to me so great as this in the way of food, none so little appreciated. Fortunately for the Indians and wild animals that gather around Nature's board, this crop is not easily harvested in a monopolizing way. If it could be gathered like wheat the whole would be carried away and dissipated in towns, leaving the brave inhabitants of these wilds to starve.

Long before the harvest-time, which is in September and October, the Indians examine the trees with keen discernment, and inasmuch as the cones require two years to mature from the first appearance of the little red rosettes of the fertile flowers, the scarcity or abundance of the crop may be predicted more than a year in advance. Squirrels, and worms, and Clarke crows, make haste to begin the harvest. When the crop is ripe the Indians make ready their long beating-poles; baskets, bags, rags, mats, are gotten together. The squaws out among the settlers at service, washing and drudging, assemble at the family huts; the men leave their ranch work; all, old and young, are mounted on ponies, and set off in great glee to the nut lands, forming cavalcades curiously picturesque. Flaming scarfs and calico skirts stream loosely over the knotty ponies, usually two squaws astride of each, with the small baby midgets bandaged in baskets slung on their backs, or balanced upon the saddle-bow, while the nut-baskets and water-jars project from either side, and the long beating-poles, like old-fashioned lances, angle out in every direction.

Arrived at some central point already fixed upon, where water and grass is found, the squaws with baskets, the men with poles, ascend the ridges to the laden trees, followed by the children; beating begins with loud noise and chatter; the burs fly right and left, lodging against stones and sagebrush; the squaws and children gather them with fine natural gladness; smoke-columns speedily mark the joyful scene of their labors as the roasting-fires are kindled; and, at night, assembled in circles, garrulous as jays, the first grand nut feast begins. Sufficient quantities are thus obtained in a few weeks to last all winter.

The Indians also gather several species of berries and dry them to vary their stores, and a few deer and grouse are killed on the mountains, besides immense numbers of rabbits and hares; but the pine-nuts are their main dependence—their staff of life, their bread.

Insects also, scarce noticed by man, come in for their share of this fine bounty. Eggs are deposited, and the baby grubs, happy fellows, find themselves in a sweet world of plenty, feeding their way through the heart of the cone from one nut-chamber to another, secure from rain and wind and heat, until their wings are grown and they are ready to launch out into the free ocean of air and light.

ISRAEL C. RUSSELL [1852–1906]

Among wild Nevada's earliest admirers was the geologist Israel Cook Russell, who appreciated the West's vast expanses of unvegetated earth, where "the features of the naked land are fully revealed beneath a cloudless sky." Exposed landscapes beckoned like open books, wherein the trained observer could read the history of landforms, a study that Russell's generation called physiography, known today as geomorphology. Russell gained a reputation as a meticulous geographic explorer, amassing field data that supported theories about the formation of mountains, lakes, and climate change. Russell was born in New York State and attended East Coast schools, earning his BS and MS from the University of the City of New York and pursuing post-graduate studies at the School of Mines of Columbia University. Although he held a number of academic positions, including chair of geology at the University of Michigan, Russell most enjoyed fieldwork, where he displayed boundless energy and resourcefulness. He joined expeditions to New Zealand and Alaska, and he spent four years in the Great Basin in the early 1880s, working as a geologist for the U.S. Geological Survey, researching the geological history of the desert basins. His classic account Geological History of Lake Lahontan, a Quaternary Lake of Northwestern Nevada *(1885) established his scientific reputation. While that account includes detailed quantitative observations, other popular publications allowed Russell to express his artistic sensibilities, such as the 1888 article excerpted below from the* Overland Monthly. *For purely aesthetic enjoyment, he notes, the best time to view Nevada is the evening, when the drab mountains appear transfigured. Author of over one hundred scientific and popular papers, Russell also wrote books for a lay audience on North American lakes, glaciers, volcanoes, and rivers. At the time of his death in Ann Arbor, Michigan, Russell was president of the Geological Society of America. Mount Russell (14,088 feet), a mile north of Mount Whitney, is named after this attentive geologist.*

The Great Basin

A desert is generally considered as a barren waste of sand; probably on account of our familiarity with descriptions of the sandy deserts of Egypt. The American deserts however, are flat mud plains, the beds of ancient lakes, and are but seldom covered with drifting sand. During the dry season, when not a drop of rain falls on their surfaces for four, five, or even six months at a time, they become dry and hard, and broken in every direction by intersecting shrinkage cracks. At such times they bear a striking resemblance to some of the old Roman pavements made of small blocks of cream-colored marble.

When in this condition one may ride over them without leaving more than a faint impression of the horse's hoofs on their smooth, glossy surfaces. In the stillness of night—and no one can appreciate the stillness of a desert until he has slept alone with only the boundless plain about him—the hoof-beats of a galloping horse ring out as on the pavements of a city. As the summer's sun dries the desert mud, the salts that the waters bring to the surface in solution are left behind, and gradually accumulate until they are several inches thick, and make the deserts appear as if covered with snow. This illusion is especially marked when one traverses the deserts by moonlight.

During the long, hot days of summer, when the dome of blue is above the deserts, without a cloud the strange, delusive mirage transforms the landscape beyond all recognition, and makes it appear tenfold more strange and weird than it is in realty. At such times bright clear lakes, with rippling surfaces and willow-fringed banks, allure the unwary traveler, and would lead him to destruction should he believe them real. The mountains around the desert are also deformed by the mirage and made to assume the most extravagant and fantastic shapes.

During hot summer days the monotony of the desert is varied by dust columns, formed by small whirlwinds, which sometimes reach such magnitudes as to be decidedly uncomfortable to the traveler who chances to be in their path. Many times these columns are two or three thousand feet in height, and have an approximate diameter of from thirty to fifty feet. The fact that they are hollow, whirling columns of dust is indicated, even from a distance, by their spiral appearance and by a light line in the center of each. These bending and swaying columns moving here and there across the desert landscape, impart a novel feature to the plain, and call to mind the genii of Arabian tales.

. . . .

As we have said, the desert ranges are extremely rugged and angular, bare of vegetation, and as silent and lifeless as the deserts around them. Many of them are of volcanic origin, and unlike the deserts have nearly every combination of color that nature has been able to devise. We must say, however, that her taste has at times been extravagant and her colors bizarre.

Under the intense light of the midday sun, the soft mingling of gray and brown on the deserts, and the brilliantly contrasted colors of the mountains, are alike obscured and deadened by the glare of light. At such times the mountains seem wanting in relief and are not attractive in form or color; one may ride for hours among gorgeous hills and not be aware of the grandeur surrounding him. But as soon as the sun approaches the western horizon, and the shadows of the serrate range begin to creep across the plains, each mountain becomes a complete picture and reveals every shade of color that its rocks possess and each ravine and cañon that has been carved on its rugged sides. The distant peaks assume a purple tint, which deepens and seems to be reflected from range to range as the shadows lengthen, until every mountain mass in view is of the deepest and richest purple. In the dry air of the Great Basin, the colors of evening do not appear, as in more humid climes, to be caused by a curtain of blue, drawn in thicker and thicker folds about the hills until they are lost in the night, but the rich purple seems to emanate from the rocks themselves, and the mountains appear self-luminous. The reader is, of course, aware that the soft lovely blue of the Virginia hills and the deep royal purple of the Nevada mountains are due alike to atmospheric effects.

No scene in nature has ever appeared to the writer more attractive or more worthy a sacred corner in the memory than the bare, silent, lifeless deserts of the Great Basin as seen at sunset from some commanding pinnacle. The reader must not suppose, however, that these scenes are all desert and sky, like the familiar pictures of the country back from the Nile. On the contrary, rugged mountains are always in sight, and many times appear in serrate ranks stretching away, range after range, as far as the eye can reach. The colors that blend and harmonize with each other in these medleys of plains and mountains have a richness of color and depth of tone that is seldom if ever seen in moist, forest-covered regions. Late in the evening when the desert plains are seas of purple shadows, the mountains of brilliantly colored rock rise from out of the unfathomable depths, like the gilded spires and minarets of some dreamland city, and repose against the soft warm tints of the sky with a subdued grandeur that is all but supernatural. Long have I lingered on the cliffs commanding such a view as is suggested above, until the light has faded from the sky, and my camp fire shining out in the darkness far below called me to a wanderer's home.

So clear is the air in the desert regions that at night the sky overhead seems almost black, shading off to deep blue at the horizon. The stars shine out with great brilliancy even low down near the earth and when they vanish it is all at once; they are eclipsed in their full splendor by the mountains as the earth turns on its axis.

GEORGE R. STEWART [1895–1980]

Best known for his unsurpassed history of the Donner party, Ordeal by Hunger *(1936), his original study of the ways that places get named,* Names on the Land *(1945), and his haunting postapocalyptic novel* Earth Abides *(1949), George R. Stewart wrote seven novels and twenty-one nonfiction books in his distinguished career, many of which are at least partially set in Nevada. Stewart's parents moved the family from Pennsylvania to Southern California when he was twelve, and he developed a lifelong passion for western history, geography, and natural history. Nevertheless, his mother insisted that he go east to Princeton University for his undergraduate education. He returned west to earn an* MA *from the University of California, went east for a* PHD *in English at Columbia University, began teaching at the University of Michigan, married the university president's daughter, and brought her west, where they settled for his forty-year tenure at the University of California, Berkeley, 1923–62.* UC *Berkeley led the nation in studies of atomic physics, wildlife biology, National Parks, and cultural geography. Biographer Donald M. Scott notes that "Stewart learned well from his colleagues," adopting a multidisciplinary perspective that "wove human and natural sciences and history into remarkable 'Whole Earth' works long before Earth Day." Considering Stewart's novels* Storm *(1941),* Fire *(1948),* Earth Abides *(1949), and* Sheep Rock *(1951), Scott credits Stewart with being the first ecological novelist. Similarly, referring to* Sheep Rock *(1951), Wallace Stegner observes, "Twenty years before the Seventies made it fashionable, Stewart was writing an 'environmental' novel about return to the land."* Sheep Rock *imagines what would happen if a poet and his family spent a year on Nevada's Black Rock Desert ("Sheep Rock"). Humbled by the immensity of the land, the poet abandons his plan to write a poem about the place and instead allows the place to write itself on him.*

from *Sheep Rock*

I had thought to capture this place, this fortress, by storm. But now I know that it is not to yield before any noisy artillery of words or any tank-assault of emotion. No, there is spadework to be done, lines to be advanced slowly, positions to be consolidated, blood to flow. There must be, not only emotion, but also knowledge and wisdom.

I have gained a little knowledge and a little wisdom. As I look back, I can see the changes in my own attitude toward the place. First, it affected me almost with an exaltation. I sensed its beauty and its grandeur, its wildness, solitude, and vastness, until I was nearly overcome. Then later a kind of despair came over me at the place, and I sensed more its ugliness and fierceness and grim relentlessness. Now both of these have changed—in my mind. Now, as I look upon the place, I sense in my mind a kind of resignation, or stoicism, or neutrality. Now I am trying to see the place not as to what my relation is to it, and not as to what the relation of mankind is to it, but rather as to what the place itself may be. I am trying to see what it is, not to be like the man who went out to look at a pool of water and came back to describe only his own eyes and lips and nose.

Springtime is here now, but there is no wild profusion of flowering color on this desert. The yellow of winter has yielded to touches of green, except that mostly the gray of the flat and the black of the rock and the red of the mountains still prevail.

This morning, deceived by a cool breeze, I set out to walk. But the heat of the sun built up rapidly. By that time I was far away and had to walk back, taking punishment. Yet the walk was interesting. I noted the tracks of the kangaroo-rats in the sand of the dunes, and knew that they had returned to activity. I saw the lizards again. I noticed that the blackbirds had returned and were sitting here and there, red-winged on the tips of the bulrushes round the spring. Once, as I stepped across the top of a hummock, I surprised some little animal, and he went scurrying off thirty feet among the bushes until he popped into a hole. He was some kind of ground-squirrel, I suppose, and he ran with that bobbing motion that you have noticed in chipmunks.

I had unwisely come off without a hat, and the sun was now hot enough to fry my brains. Its glare was everywhere, dazzling my eyes. I felt myself suddenly pitying the little ground-squirrel, for having to live his whole life in such a place as this. Then suddenly I realized my new resolution, not to interpret this place in my own terms. I tried to imagine what this country was like, not to a man, but to a ground-squirrel. First of all, he must see it from a different point of view, from an eye scarcely more than an inch from the surface of the ground. So, on a whim, I lay down. Resting the side of my head on the earth I closed my upper eye, and indulged myself in a ground-squirrel's view.

Suddenly the whole country had a new aspect. No longer was it a desert, barren of growth, mercilessly beaten by the sun. Instead, it was like a beautiful parkland, generously spotted with magnificent shade-trees. Some of the little bushes, in fact, looked much like miniature oaks. They rose six inches, clear of branches, with thick gnarled trunks, and then branched out a foot in each direction, keeping to something of the proportion of an oak-tree. To a man, these bushes fail to reach his knee, and so the desert is hideously without shade. But to a ground-squirrel or a lizard or even to a rabbit, this desert is a beneficent checkerboard of sun and shade so that one can have the heat or be sheltered from it as one wishes, and doubtless their philosophers have theories that is the best of all possible worlds.

So also these creatures would not think of the desert as lacking water, for they are adjusted to go without water by some internal chemistry of their own. Many of them, I believe, never drink at all.

Or, consider what the desert must be to a purely nocturnal creature like the kangaroo-rat. He peeps from his hole in the deep twilight after the sun is below the horizon, and he withdraws in the gray dawn long before the sun has risen. He must know the moon well, in all its phases, but he can have no conception of the sun or of its heat. If you could penetrate a burrow and talk with an intelligent kangaroo-rat, you would undoubtedly find him highly sceptical of your story of the sun. "I have lived here all my life, and my father before me," he might say, "and I have never seen this thing you call the sun, and never heard tell of it. I am inclined to think, begging your pardon, that your story is pure moonshine." (Only, of course, he could not use such an expression as moonshine, because the moon is a plain reality to him.) I suppose also that these rats would be inclined to doubt the actuality of snow and the whistling cold winds, and perhaps the whole conception of winter, because at that time they are snug and cosy in their farthest burrows.

All this philosophy from seeing a ground-squirrel! And I am not even sure that it is a ground-squirrel!

Such a little creature, even if it escapes the coyote and the badger, lives only three or four years. "So little time!" we may say. Yet man's seventy years is not appreciably longer if we take it in comparison with the life of the land, as we can see it even here around the spring.

The raven is fabled to live past his century. Perhaps the ravens have seen the vegetation alter a little. One of them might say sagely: "Since I was a fledgling, the seepweed has worked out into the flat along the water-courses, yes, all of a hundred yards." But even the ravens could not claim to have seen the size of a meadow alter much or to have observed any great re-shaping of the hills.

Yes, since I have lived here, I have come to feel more and more the vastness of time, and with the vastness of time, also, space has seemed to expand. First, my mind was encompassed mostly by what I saw close by, the spring and the rock. And then it moved outward toward the beaches and the flat, and all their barrenness, and perhaps because of that I myself passed into despair. But now my eyes reach farther and I gain calm. I look out and see the red cliffs of the mountains and the gently rolling surface that lies above them, and the distant peak, and then whenever I raise my eyes higher still I see, over all, the greater vastness of the sky.

SESSIONS S. WHEELER [1911–1998]

The well-thumbed books of outdoorsman and career biology teacher Sessions S. "Buck" Wheeler occupy a special place on the bookshelves of many Nevadans. His novel Paiute *(1965) mixes fictional characters and real ones to narrate the discovery of the Comstock Lode and the ensuing 1860 Pyramid Lake Indian War from a standpoint sympathetic to the Indians. His popular nonfiction books* The Desert Lake: The Story of Nevada's Pyramid Lake *(1967),* The Nevada Desert *(1971), and* The Black Rock Desert *(1978) blend natural history, human history, photographs, and excerpts from primary sources to deepen our knowledge and enjoyment of Nevada's deserts. A native of Fernley, Nevada, Wheeler grew up in Reno, earned a BS in biology from the University of Nevada, Reno, and in 1935 became the eleventh student to receive a masters of science degree from UNR, with a thesis on shade-tree diseases. Wheeler began teaching in Fernley, then taught at Reno High School (1940–66), also teaching conservation at UNR during summers and from 1966 to 1972. An early leader in environmental education and eventual winner of several national education and conservation awards, Wheeler first displayed his penchant for writing in 1941 in the* Reno Evening Gazette's *weekly "Sage and Stream" column, which he coauthored until 1948. In 1949 he coauthored* Conservation and Nevada, *one of the first conservation textbooks in America, following that with* Nevada Conservation Adventure *in 1954. From 1947 to 1950 he took a leave of absence from teaching to serve as the first director of the Nevada State Fish and Game Commission. In addition to his portraits of Nevada deserts, Wheeler authored three biographies, one on Nevada sheepman Reginald Meaker, the others on prominent Nevadans Max C. Fleischmann and the Bliss family of Tahoe. The notes for his uncompleted autobiography,* Sagebrush, Pine Trees, and Youth, *along with Wheeler's professional papers in UNR's Special Collections Department, await a future scholar.*

from *The Nevada Desert*

In the temperate zones of the North American continent, a desert is usually defined as a region of hot daytime summer temperatures, higher than average evaporation rates, and—most important—less than ten inches of precipitation annually. In amounts of rain and snow falling on its rugged surface, Nevada is the driest—and has the largest percentage of its total area classified as desert—of all states in the Union.

Contributing to its uniqueness, nature divided it into two main desert regions. Most of the northern two-thirds of the state is included within the largest of the North American deserts, the Great Basin Desert which is often called Nevada's "high" or "cool" desert. The southern one-third of the state, where valley floors have lower elevations, is a portion of the Mohave Desert—the "low" or "warm" desert.

Each area has its distinctive beauty. During early mornings and evenings, the high desert's upland valleys and hillsides shine with the silvery gray of its dominant shrubs, the sagebrush and shad scale; and after a summer thunderstorm, the pleasant odor of sagebrush saturates the air. The Mohave, with its widely spaced creosote bushes, odd Joshua trees, and gray desert soil is probably more spectacular—the type of desert usually portrayed in motion pictures.

Except for the state's southern tip where drainage flows to the Colorado River, and its northeastern extreme where river waters eventually reach the Columbia, Nevada lies within the Great Basin—a land of interior drainage where streams lose their identity in lakes and marshes or beneath the ground instead of contributing their waters to the sea. Along the perimeters of the high desert's valleys, mountain canyons contain springs or small streams. Many of the streams flow only short distances beyond their canyon mouths before sinking from sight into valley floors; but others, fed by the rain and snow falling on larger high-elevation areas, provide irrigation water for the state's ranches. Originating from extensive watersheds in the Sierra Nevadas, the Truckee and Walker rivers flow eastward to desert lakes, and the Carson makes its way to its sink northeast of Fallon. The Humboldt is the state's longest river, originating in the mountains of northeastern Nevada and flowing westward through the high desert approximately three hundred miles to where its sink adjoins that of the Carson River. Because of its meandering, it is estimated that its water actually flows almost a thousand miles. People from less arid states are often amazed at a small size of some of the Nevada streams which official maps title rivers.

Mountain ranges, many of which rise more than ten thousand feet above sea level, extend their lengths in a general north-south direction and divide the state into a series of flat-floored valleys. In the high desert many of these valleys and their surrounding upland areas provide grazing for cattle and sheep; while others, once covered by prehistoric lakes or marshes, are flats of baked mud coated with alkali salts in which only specially adapted plants can survive. Early emigrants and settlers considered several of these playas as individual deserts and named them as such.

To some who hurry along Nevada highways, the country through which they pass seems almost barren of life. But to those who know it, the desert is the home of a myriad of living things—animals and plants capable of solving their problems of survival in intensely interesting ways.

The desert's mountain ranges provide climatic and biologic islands where juniper and piñon pines form the most widespread forests. Other species of conifers grow in limited areas, and shrubs and deciduous trees along streams and around springs offer shade and food to game mammals and birds.

The mountains of the southern desert have the largest number of Nelson desert bighorn sheep found in North America, and mule deer range over most of the state. Other large mammals include the pronghorn antelope and the interesting carnivores—the coyote, cougar, and bobcat. Sage grouse, chukar partridge, and other game birds and small game mammals exist in areas where the habitat is suitable for their needs; and several of the desert's sinks receive enough drainage water to form marshes which attract thousands of migratory waterfowl each year. Most of the lakes, rivers, and even the smaller streams contain trout and other fish, and of special interest to the naturalists are several endemic species such as the cui-ui of Pyramid Lake and certain minnows found in desert springs.

But in the most barren appearing areas are creatures which, in some ways, are the most interesting of all. Small mammals, such as the kangaroo rat, are largely nocturnal—carrying on most of their life processes at night, when the desert is cool. Underground-dwelling amphibians race through their complex life history of egg, tadpole, and adult before a thunderstorm's pool of water dries, and beautifully colored and distinctively marked lizards appear as miniatures of the great prehistoric reptiles. Various species of snakes, unusual birds, the desert tortoise, and odd insects make the desert a fascinating showcase of specialized animals ingeniously adapted to an arid land.

In the desert plants nature's unique devices for survival are also noticeable. Leaves are coated or specially constructed to minimize loss of water, and roots delve deep into the earth to reach underground water tables or form widely spreading, near-surface networks so as to absorb every possible drop of rain. Seeds, which remain dormant during years of insufficient moisture, quickly germinate after ample spring rains and grow rapidly to maturity so as to produce a new generation of their species before soils dry. Their flowers of brilliant colors bring the desert dazzling beauty.

. . . .

To those who love the desert, its beauty and primitive qualities are unique and precious. To them it is a world of stillness, of vast space, of great mountains with canyons so sharp and deep that the sun's rays hardly touch their floors. It is a region of brightness where rocks and plants, scrubbed by windblown sand, sparkle with their cleanliness. It is a land of mystery where ancient man left evidence of his visits thousands of years ago. It is a place of history where Indian warriors fought for their way of life, and where legends of the old West were born.

Because of man's alterations, the Nevada desert is no longer a true natural area; but it is still a refuge for some special living things—wild animals and plants which are unable to survive in a tamed environment. And to some men, those who love wilderness and need solitude, it is also a sanctuary.

"And he came to the desert, and there he found peace."

JOHN MCPHEE [B. 1931]

Two groups of people are drawn to Nevada as if by magnetic force: gamblers and geologists. Geologists trek to Nevada to see rocks not cloaked by shrubbery and to witness geological processes in action. The Great Basin is today's geological wonderland, the place where the vast forces of plate tectonics are pulling the earth apart and possibly opening a seaway. As Pulitzer Prize–winning journalist John McPhee explains in Basin and Range *(1981), "you can see it all in Nevada." For most people, however, geology is duller than dirt. The genius of John McPhee, as reviewer Thomas Turman has noted, is to turn rocks into rock music so that "the rhapsodic rise of range and lilting fall of basin become a beautiful harmonic landscape that plays itself before us everyday." McPhee characteristically brings his subject alive via a connoisseur's choice of language, savoring words on the page like wine in the mouth, and via vivid profiles of memorable individuals who serve as expert guides, such as Princeton geology professor Kenneth Deffeyes in* Basin and Range. *McPhee, who was born and raised in Princeton, New Jersey, has been a staff writer for the* New Yorker *since 1965 and has published more than twenty-five books, including* In Suspect Terrain *(1983),* Rising from the Plains *(1986), and* Assembling California *(1993), which appear with* Basin and Range *and* Crossing the Craton *in his edited compilation* Annals of the Former World *(1998), a geology quintet. McPhee's extraordinary productivity—frequently averaging a book a year—was jump-started by a high school English teacher who required that her students write three essays per week. The subjects of his books range widely—basketball, plate tectonics, Alaska, hydroelectric dams, birch-bark canoes, theoretical physics, and oranges—but their common denominator is McPhee's fascination with people who are engaged in "their thing, their activity, whatever it is," the calling that summons them into the world.*

from *Basin and Range*

Basin. Fault. Range. Basin. Fault. Range. A mile of relief between basin and range. Stillwater Range. Pleasant Valley. Tobin Range. Jersey Valley. Sonoma Range. Pumpernickel Valley. Shoshone Range. Reese River Valley. Pequop Mountains. Steptoe Valley. Ondographic rhythms of the Basin and Range. We are maybe forty miles off the interstate, in the Pleasant Valley basin, looking up at the Tobin Range. At the nine-thousand-foot level, there is a stratum of cloud against the shoulders of the mountains, hanging like a ring of Saturn. The summit of Mt. Tobin stands clear, above the cloud. When we crossed the range, we came through a ranch on the ridgeline where sheep were fenced around a running brook and bales of hay were bright green. Junipers in the mountains were thickly hung with berries, and the air was unadulterated gin. This country from afar is synopsized and dismissed as "desert"—the home of the coyote and the pocket mouse, the side-blotched lizard and the vagrant shrew, the MX rocket and the pallid bat. There are minks and river otters in the Basin and Range. There are deer and antelope, porcupines and cougars, pelicans, cormorants, and common loons. There are Bonaparte's gulls and marbled godwits, American coots and Virginia rails. Pheasants. Grouse. Sandhill cranes. Ferruginous hawks and flammulated owls. Snow geese. This Nevada terrain is not corrugated, like the folded Appalachians, like a tubal air mattress, like a rippled potato chip. This is not—in that compressive manner—a ridge-and-valley situation. Each range here is like a warship standing on its own, and the Great Basin is an ocean of loose sediment with these mountain ranges standing in it as if they were members of a fleet without precedent, assembled at Guam to assault Japan. Some of the ranges are forty miles long, others a hundred, a hundred and fifty. They point generally north. The basins that separate them—ten and fifteen miles wide—will run on for fifty, a hundred, two hundred and fifty miles with lone, daisy-petalled windmills standing over sage and wild rye. Animals tend to be content with their home ranges and not to venture out across the big dry valleys. "Imagine a chipmunk hiking across one of these basins," Deffeyes remarks. "The faunas in the high ranges here are quite distinct from one to another. Animals are isolated like Darwin's finches in the Galapagos. These ranges are truly islands."

Supreme over all is silence. Discounting the cry of the occasional bird, the wailing of a pack of coyotes, silence—a great spatial silence—is pure in the Basin and Range. It is a soundless immensity with mountains in it. You stand, as we do now, and look up at a high mountain front, and turn your head and look fifty miles down the valley, and there is utter silence. It is the silence of the winter forests of the Yukon, here carried high to the ridgelines of the ranges. As the physicist Freeman Dyson has written in *Disturbing the Universe,* "It is a soul-shattering silence. You hold your breath and hear absolutely nothing. No rustling of leaves in the wind, no rumbling of distant traffic, no chatter of birds or insects or children. You are alone with God in that silence. There in the white flat silence I began for the first time to feel a slight sense of shame for what we were proposing to do. Did we really intend to invade this silence with our trucks and bulldozers and after a few years leave it a radioactive junkyard?"

What Deffeyes finds pleasant here in Pleasant Valley is the aromatic sage. Deffeyes grew up all over the West, his father a petroleum engineer, and he says without apparent irony that the smell of sagebrush is one of two odors that will unfailingly bring upon him an attack of nostalgia, the other being the scent of an oil refinery. Flash floods have caused boulders the size of human heads to come tumbling off the range. With alluvial materials of finer size, they have piled up in fans at the edge of the basin. ("The cloudburst is the dominant sculptor here.") The fans are unconsolidated. In time to come, they will pile up to such enormous thicknesses that they will sink deep and be heated and compressed to form conglomerate. Erosion, which provides the material to build the fans, is tearing down the mountains even as they rise. Mountains are not somehow created whole and subsequently worn away. They wear down as they come up, and these mountains have been rising and eroding in fairly even ratio for millions of years—rising and shedding sediment steadily through time, always the same, never the same, like row upon row of fountains. In the southern part of the province, in the Mojave, the ranges have stopped rising and are gradually wearing away. The Shadow Mountains. The Dead Mountains, Old Dad Mountains, Cowhole Mountains, Bullion, Mule, and Chocolate Mountains. They are inselberge now, buried ever deeper in their own waste. For the most part, though, the ranges are rising, and there can be no doubt of it here, hundreds of miles north of the Mojave, for we are looking at a new seismic scar that runs as far as we can see. It runs along the foot of the mountains, along the fault where the basin meets the range. From out in the valley, it looks like a long, buff-painted, essentially horizontal stripe. Up close, it is a gap in the vegetation, where plants growing side by side were suddenly separated by several metres, where, one October evening, the basin and the range—Pleasant Valley, Tobin Range—moved, all in an instant, apart. They jumped sixteen feet. The erosion rate at which the mountains were coming down was an inch a century. So in the mountains' contest with erosion they gained in one moment about twenty thousand years. These mountains do not rise like bread. They sit still for a long time and build up tension, and then suddenly jump. Passively, they are eroded for millennia, and then they jump again. They have been doing this for about eight million years. This fault, which jumped in 1915, opened like a zipper far up the valley, and, exploding into the silence, tore along the mountain base for upward of twenty miles with a sound that suggested a runaway locomotive.

"This is the sort of place where you really do not put a nuclear plant," says Deffeyes. "There was other action in the neighborhood at the same time—in the Stillwater Range, the Sonoma Range, Pumpernickel Valley. Actually, this is not a particularly spectacular scarp. The lesson is that the whole thing—the whole Basin and Range, or most of it—is alive. The earth is moving. The faults are moving. There are hot springs all over the province. There are young volcanic rocks. Fault scars everywhere. The world is splitting open and coming apart. You see a sudden break in the sage like this and it says to you that a fault is there and a fault block is coming up. This is a gorgeous, fresh, young, active fault scarp. It's growing. The range is lifting up. This Nevada topography is what you see *during* mountain building. There are no foothills. It is all too young. It is live country. This is the tectonic, active, spreading, mountain-building world. To a nongeoloist, it's just ranges, ranges, ranges."

Most mountain ranges around the world are the result of compression, of segments of the earth's crust being brought together, bent, mashed, thrust and folded, squeezed up into the sky—the Himalaya, the Appalachians, the Alps, the Urals, the Andes. The ranges of the Basin and Range came up another way. The crust—in this region between the Rockies and the Sierra—is spreading out, being stretched, being thinned, being literally pulled to pieces. The sites of Reno and Salt Lake City, on opposite sides of the province, have moved apart fifty miles. The crust of the Great Basin has broken into blocks. The blocks are not, except for simplicity's sake, analogous to dominoes. They are irregular in shape. They more truly suggest stretch marks. Which they are. They trend north-south because the direction of the stretching is east-west. The breaks, or faults, between them are not vertical but dive into the earth at roughly sixty-degree angles, and this, from the outset, affected the centers of gravity of the great blocks in a way that caused them to tilt. Classically, the high edge of one touched the low edge of another and formed a kind of trough, or basin. The high edge—sculpted, eroded, serrated by weather—turned into mountains. The detritus of the mountains rolled into the basin. The basin filled with water—at first, it was fresh blue water—and accepted layer upon layer of sediment from the mountains, accumulating weight, and thus unbalancing the block even further. Its tilt became more pronounced. In the manner of a seesaw, the high, mountain side of the block went higher and the low, basin side went lower until the block as a whole reached a state of precarious and temporary truce with God, physics, and mechanical and chemical erosion, not to mention, far below, the agitated mantle, which was running a temperature hotter than normal, and was, almost surely, controlling the action. Basin and range. Integral fault blocks: low side the basin, high side the range. For five hundred miles they nudged one another across the province of the Basin and Range. With extra faulting, and whatnot, they took care of their own irregularities. Some had their high sides on the west, some on the east. The escarpment of the Wasatch Mountains—easternmost expression of this immense suite of mountains—faced west. The Sierra—the westernmost, the highest, the predominant range, with Donner Pass only halfway up it—presented its escarpment to the east. As the developing Sierra made its skyward climb—as it went on up past ten and twelve and fourteen thousand feet—it became so predominant that it cut off the incoming Pacific rain, cast a rain shadow (as the phenomenon is called) over lush, warm, Floridian and verdant Nevada. Cut it off and kept it dry.

We move on (we're in a pickup) into dusk—north up Pleasant Valley, with its single telephone line on sticks too skinny to qualify as poles. The big flanking ranges are in alpenglow. Into the cold clear sky come the ranking stars. Jackrabbits appear, and crisscross the road. We pass the darkening shapes of cattle. An eerie trail of vapor traverses the basin, sent up by a clear, hot stream. It is only a couple of feet wide, but it is running swiftly and has multiple sets of hot white rapids. In the source springs, there is a thumping sound of boiling and rage. Beside the springs are lucid green pools, rimmed with accumulated travertine, like the travertine walls of Lincoln Center, the travertine pools of Havasu Canyon, but these pools are too hot to touch. Fall in there and you are Brunswick stew. "This is a direct result of the crustal spreading," Deffeyes says. "It brings hot mantle up near the surface. There is probably a fracture here, through which the water is coming up to this row of springs. The water is rich in dissolved minerals. Hot springs like these are the source of vein-type ore deposits. It's the same story that I told you about the hydrothermal transport of gold. When rainwater gets down into hot rock, it brings up what it happens to find there—silver, tungsten, copper, gold. An ore-deposit map and a hot-springs map will look much the same. Seismic waves move slowly through hot rock. The hotter the rock, the slower the waves. Nowhere in the continental United States do seismic waves move more slowly than they do beneath the Basin and Range. So we're not woofing when we say there's hot mantle down there. We've measured the heat."

The basin-range fault blocks in a sense are floating on the mantle. In fact, the earth's crust everywhere in a sense is floating on the mantle. Add weight to the crust and it rides deeper, remove cargo and it rides higher, exactly like a vessel at a pier. Slowly disassemble the Rocky Mountains and carry the material in small fragments to the Mississippi Delta. The delta builds down. It presses ever deeper on the mantle. Its depth at the moment exceeds twenty-five thousand feet. The heat and the pressure are so great down there that the silt is turning into siltstone, the sand into sandstone, the mud into shale. For another example, the last Pleistocene ice sheet loaded two miles of ice onto Scotland, and that dunked Scotland in the mantle. After the ice melted, Scotland came up again, lifting its beaches high into the air. Isostatic adjustment. Let go a block of wood that you hold underwater and it adjusts itself to the surface isostatically. A frog sits on the wood. It goes down. He vomits. It goes up a little. He jumps. It adjusts. Wherever landscape is eroded away, what remains will rise in adjustment. Older rock is lifted to view. When, for whatever reason, crust becomes thicker, it adjusts downward. All of this—with the central image of the basin-range fault blocks floating in the mantle—may suggest that the mantle is molten, which it is not. The mantle is solid. Only in certain pockets near the surface does it turn into magma and squirt upward. The temperature of the mantle varies widely, as would the temperature of anything that is two thousand miles thick. Under the craton, it is described as chilled. By surface standards, though, it is generally white hot, everywhere around the world—white hot and solid but magisterially viscous, permitting the crust above it to "float." Deffeyes was in his bathtub one Saturday afternoon thinking about the viscosity of the mantle. Suddenly he stood up and reached for a towel. "Piano wire!" he said to himself, and he dressed quickly and went to the library to look up a book on piano tuning and to calculate the viscosity of the wire. Just what he guessed—10^{22} poises. Piano wire. Look under the hood of a well-tuned Steinway and you are looking at strings that could float a small continent. They are rigid, but ever so slowly they will sag, will slacken, will deform and give way, with the exact viscosity of the earth's mantle. "And that," says Deffeyes, "is what keeps the piano tuner in business." More miles, and there appears ahead of us something like a Christmas tree alone in the night. It is Winnemucca, there being no other possibility. Neon looks good in Nevada. The tawdriness is refined out of it in so much wide black space. We drive on and on toward the glow of colors. It is still far way and it has not increased in size. We pass nothing. Deffeyes says, "On these roads, it's ten to the minus five that anyone will come along." The better part of an hour later, we come to the beginnings of the casino-flashing town. The news this year is that dollar slot machines are outdrawing nickel slot machines for the first time, ever.

STEPHEN TRIMBLE [B. 1950]

"The Great Basin remains mostly unknown," photographer and writer Stephen Trimble once told a biographer, "and is thus always subject to shortsighted development and irredeemable destruction. We need to know the place, to care enough to save it. We cannot afford to let it remain unknown—a place no one knew well enough to fight for." In his award-winning The Sagebrush Ocean: A Natural History of the Great Basin *(1989), Trimble introduces the reader to the biogeography of this arid heart of the West, revealing what lives where and why in a land of subtle ecosystems, where the passing tourist may fail to discern a single living thing, but where a myriad of creatures carry on their cryptic lives. Wallace Stegner endorsed* The Sagebrush Ocean *as "a mine of information—more information, and more reliable, than has ever been gathered into one volume for the lay reader." But whereas a compendium of scientific information might be boring, Trimble, who honed his interpretive skills as a naturalist for the National Park Service, makes learning enjoyable, sharing his excitement and sprinkling in enough anecdotes that his readers, like pushy tour group members, jockey to stay close to their guide so they won't miss anything. While the Great Basin is alien to many, it is a favorite home landscape to Trimble, who grew up in Colorado, earned an MS in ecology and evolutionary biology from the University of Arizona, and has been a freelance writer, editor, and photographer, based in Salt Lake City, since the 1980s, specializing in the American West, natural his-*

tory, Native Americans, and education of children. Among his other books are Words from the Land: Encounters with Natural History Writing *(1988; expanded edition, 1995),* The People: Indians of the American Southwest *(1993),* The Geography of Childhood: Why Children Need Wild Places *(with Gary Paul Nabhan, 1994),* Earthtones: A Nevada Album *(with Ann Ronald, 1995), and* Testimony: Writers of the West Speak on Behalf of Utah Wilderness *(with Terry Tempest Williams, 1996).*

from *The Sagebrush Ocean*

As unvarying as it may seem at first glance from Interstate 80, as abrupt as many field guides are in their summary description of the Great Basin ("a monotonous stand of shrubs"), patterns in ecological communities mark this land. No one kind of plant can grow everywhere. Temperature, precipitation, soils, topography, inter-action with other living things—all these and more determine where plants grow. And the plants, in turn, determine where animals can live.

As I drive along, I look for the patterns. It is a humbling experience.

I spot black sagebrush and sit back behind the wheel, complacent with my identification. My mind wanders, and the next time I pull over to stroll through the shrubs, I have descended imperceptibly into vivid green greasewood and dusty-leaved shadscale; iodine bush is holding out at the shore of the barren playa a few feet away. Along a wash I stare at an almost lifeless and leafless shrub. I know I should recognize it, but a name won't come. Finally I say, "rabbitbrush!" The white-green stems should have given it away.

The nature of the plant communities changes with remarkable subtlety. Why does shadscale spread across this basin when sagebrush filled the valley back over the last pass? Why does juniper grow where it does? What about this stand of winterfat?

Such questions can keep botanists busy for a lifetime and still leave them stumped. Add the hundreds of vertebrate and thousands of invertebrate species that have their own distribution patterns and the challenge begins to come clear.

In trying to understand why a particular Great Basin species grows where it does, every theory leads to another, every explanation is incomplete, everything is interconnected. Groups of plants and animals that favor the same environment live and reproduce as single individuals, adapt and differentiate as species. But they also confront similar opportunities and difficulties in any one environment—and in some ways evolve together as a community.

U.S. Highway 50, roller-coastering across the basins and ranges, rises into piñon-juniper woodland, drops back into sagebrush, then plunges on even lower to salt deserts. Up to the next pass, through woodland again, past bands of mountain brush and open forest to within sight of the bare mountaintops: alpine tundra. These basic patterns are undeniable.

A bit of knowledge makes a profound difference in the way you perceive the Great Basin. Botanist James Reveal met a family moving from Tennessee to California as they pulled into Ely, Nevada. They remarked in amazement that they had not seen a single living thing for two hundred miles!

To anyone accustomed to the overwhelming greens of the eastern deciduous forest, to the sheer bulk of plants, their reaction is understandable. To Reveal: "These eastern visitors had looked upon the vast expanses I had always relished as desolated vistas; those grayish shrubs and sparse low trees, which I had always considered a teeming forest, signified to them a bleak struggle for existence in a barren land."

I remember my own delight when I discovered in college the individuality hidden in the mass of greenery around me in Colorado. Suddenly, these were not just plants but specific and separate identities. Not just conifers, but Douglas-fir and limber pine and Engelmann spruce. Not just grass, but blue grama and ricegrass and sacaton. Not just flowers, but pinks and lilies and vetches. Each had distinctive qualities that made it as easily recognized as a Blue Jay, a grizzly bear, or a movie star. Graceful seed heads, pointed, square-edged needles, flowers with spurs and keels.

As you come to know Great Basin plants, the mass of dull gray shrubs pops into sharp focus. As your eye sharpens, animals, too, begin to reveal themselves: a dune that seems sterile becomes a metropolis of nocturnal rodents and their predators when you look for tracks at dawn before the wind whisks them away.

Once you recognize the residents of this desert as distinct characters you begin to notice them repeatedly in the same environments: whitebark pines on windswept mountain ridges, muskrats in marshes, Pinyon Jays in piñon-juniper woodland. You expect to see them there; if they turn up somewhere else, you look for an explanation.

You have developed a naturalist's eye; you have begun to think like a biogeographer.

. . . .

When I was young, each year the *World Book Encyclopedia* came out with a set of transparent overlays in its yearbook that taught me some new piece of reality—the organ systems of "the visible man" or the physical and cultural resources of a distant continent. Layer by layer, the acetate films built on each other until the whole appeared from out of the parts, understood in a new way.

Understanding the distribution patterns of life in the Great Basin grows from a similar set of overlays. Each addition to the stack dictates rules to living things with the same sense of incontrovertibility as an encyclopedia.

Start with a topographic base map: the high Sierra and Wasatch on the west and east, the scatter of island ranges between. Relief shading indicates much better high-altitude connections from the Wasatch out to the central Basin ranges than from the Sierra, cut off by the Lahontan trough.

Over this lay a map of Pleistocene lakes for a sense of the toughest, saltiest lowland soils. A simplified geologic overlay shows the distinct difference between the overwhelmingly acidic, igneous rocks of the Sierra and the more diverse but largely basic rocks of the Great Basin and Rockies.

Next add two climatic overlays. One shows a broad line across the northern basin: behind this line to the north, frigid polar air hovers in winter. The second shades the area of summer rain, dark and important in the southeast, attenuated to the north and west until the northwestern section of the overlay is unshaded clear acetate—as clear as its summer skies.

Add a couple of decorative drawings in each corner, a ticking clock and a Clark's Nutcracker and Pinyon Jay, and the encyclopedia's promise comes true: in these overlays lie much of the story of Great Basin biogeography.

The Sierra casts its rain shadow eastward across these maps; it creates this desert. At the north edge, polar air intensifies, winters grow ever colder. Increasing elevation and latitude bring more snow; northward, the Great Basin Desert ends. Likewise, southward, with the sharp drop in elevation across south-central Nevada, cold-desert shadscale and sagebrush give way to hot deserts and creosote bush.

The clock symbolizes the remarkable recency of much of this desert; it marks off the alternating cycles of warming and cooling through the Pleistocene to the present. Shadscale flats of the Lahontan and Bonneville basins have appeared only in the last few thousand years where the Pleistocene lakes once filled the lowest valleys.

The clock began ticking at different moments for every range across the Basin. The Rockies are older than the Basin ranges, which in turn are older than the Sierra. Rocky Mountain plants thus had more time to emigrate into the Great Basin than Sierra Nevada plants. Sierran plants grow mostly in acidic soil, and this, too, has made it difficult for them to disperse eastward into the Basin.

Meanwhile, jays and nutcrackers flap across the map, caw-cawing. They pause here and there on mountain ranges. They leave behind sprouting groves of pines.

ANN HAYMOND ZWINGER [B. 1925]

In The Mysterious Lands *(1989), Ann Zwinger, award-winning author of* The Nearsighted
Naturalist *(1998), explores the four great deserts of the Southwest—the Chihuahuan, Sonoran, Mojave, and Great Basin deserts, lands that John C. Van Dyke in 1901 called "the
breathing-spaces of the west." With Zwinger as a friendly and knowledgeable teacher, the reader
learns to perceive the special qualities and characteristic plants and animals of each desert. In
the Mojave, for example, Zwinger highlights night lizards, singing dunes, Joshua trees, red-
spotted toads, alluvial fans, desert tortoises, and pupfish, while in the Great Basin she profiles
blackbrush, sagebrush, rattlesnakes, grouse locusts, greasewood, kangaroo mice, pronghorns,
glowworms, and spadefoot toads. In her more-than-a-dozen books, Zwinger combines an artist's eye, a researcher's insatiable curiosity, a scientist's understanding, and an optimist's zest
for life. Born in Muncie, Indiana, and educated in art history (Wellesley College,* BA, *Indiana
University,* MA*), Zwinger frequently illustrates her own and others' books. For the first half of
her adulthood, Ann Zwinger was a self-described housewife; married to an air force pilot, she
raised three daughters and was a Girl Scout leader. When her husband retired, the Zwing-
ers settled in Colorado Springs. There, in a chance encounter, Rachel Carson's literary agent
encouraged Zwinger to write a book on Colorado ecology. Flabbergasted, Zwinger nonetheless
wrote* Beyond the Aspen Grove *(1970), thus launching a postmidlife writing and adventuring career that has netted many honors, including the John Burroughs Memorial Association
award for* Run, River, Run: A Naturalist's Journey down One of the Great Rivers of the
American West *(1975) and the Western Arts Federation award for* Downcanyon: A Naturalist
Explores the Colorado River through the Grand Canyon *(1995). An active environmentalist,
Zwinger shapes her writing to delight rather than to preach, blazing enticing trails that help
readers establish their own relationship to the natural world.*

Of Blackbrush and Sagebrush

The wind twitches the short, stiff branches of somber blackbrush and sets them
scratching at my shins. Here, on this high ridge, the transition zone between the
Mojave and Great Basin deserts, the contrast between the warmer southern desert
and the cooler steppe desert could not be more marked. The giddy creosote bushes
with their graceful branches are replaced by these angular-branched shrubs with
twigs sprouting stiffly at right angles. Their color is darker green, more somber.

Even the sky is overcast. A mizzle falls. A cold wind bites the air. I miss the sunshine of the Mojave, the brilliance of the Sonoran, the glow of the Chihuahuan, as
I stand poised on the threshold of a far more severe and stringent landscape with
a different beauty.

Creosote bushes and Joshua trees persisted into Nevada. Then creosote bush disappeared, and with it the distinctive color and growth patterns so much a part of the three southern deserts. The landscape looked odd without creosote bush. Joshua trees still arrayed the hillsides, scattered and gesticulating, and then they too thinned out until only single stalks remained, sentinels without regiments. Along with those humanoid arboreal forms went a certain animation and spontaneity. With Joshua trees gone, the visual change was complete.

Although the northern Mojave greatly resembles the Great Basin in its limited life forms and the simple composition of most communities, the rise in altitude of the basin floor plus a latitudinal step northward shuts out the warmth-loving plants of the Mojave. Rainfall, on the increase, and temperature, on the decrease, control this transition zone in which I stand and shiver.

Blackbrush dominates here, a plant community restricted to the upper bajadas, occupying an intermediate position between the creosote bush of the Mojave and the big sagebrush of the Great Basin, replacing a more mesic juniper community some 7,500 years ago.

Boundaries like this one fascinate me. These visual boundaries augur the invisible ones: where stands the last creosote bush and where grows the first sagebrush? Where does the last saguaro become a mere armless post in the ground and finally give up its footing? Where does the kangaroo rat pause, one well-adapted desert foot poised in the air, nose twitching toward a wetter, lusher existence, and not cross over? Where is the line beyond which the desert cockroach does not tunnel? Where is the barrier that keeps the sidewinder and the fringe-toed lizard at home on the hot sands? Where does the desert tortoise blink its slow eyes and turn back to the only home it knows? In trying to define where a desert is not, one learns where it is.

The soaking mist that blurs the air molds a subtle series of silhouettes and softens the hard mountain outlines. Sixty percent of the year's moisture arrives during the long winters, falling on frozen ground, when it brings the least blessing; if spring or summer rain does fall, its amount and length are highly variable and unpredictable. Trapped in the interior of the continent, the Great Basin Desert suffers some of the most severe desert conditions in North America. Behind the rain shadow of the Sierra Nevada, barricaded from moisture coming in from the east by the Rocky Mountains, the Great Basin is an inland island desert. Although polar outbreaks bring temperatures below freezing, sometimes for extended periods, summer temperatures easily reach over 100 degrees F.

The clouds overhead shred for a moment and pallid shafts of light focus through the openings, highlighting a piece of mountain flank here, an outcrop there, like a good stage set, leaving the rest up to imagination. Then they close in again, a lowering ceiling. The gloomy, melancholy effect prompted Dr. James Schiel, surveying the Great Basin in 1853, to enter in his journal that "the shadows of small clouds obscuring the morning sun were the only living, moving thing in the landscape, and they seemed to heighten the feeling of utter gloom. If the eye of a man of ancient Greece had seen this sight, he would have located the entrance to the underworld here."

Flying over in September, from twelve thousand feet the Great Basin Desert has a past-finished aspect, as if all that could be done to it has been done, and now it is old and tired and worn-out, grizzled and gutted, faded and weatherbeaten. Sometimes the land has a worn velvet look, tucked with arroyos, pleated with mountains, a landscape seemingly without seasons or eternally half past autumn, a landscape left out to dry, forgotten, tattered with rain, wrinkled with sun, and yet, in a peculiar sense I cannot explain, always vital and never forlorn.

Because big sagebrush is the same color winter or summer, the landscape has a changelessness that grants it an aura of stability. It won't slide into the ocean. It may slip with a fault here and there, ooze with molten rock that darkens a slope with basalt, but it itself is the in-between, the middle, the hammock that holds the shores together, creases and adjusts with time to tensions and stresses, heaves up another mountain range, drops another graben, and just gets on with it.

. . . .

Garbed in a March morning, Sara and I hike a nameless sagebrush flat in far southwestern Utah. The incessant sagebrush looks like a collage of torn gray-green paper, one piece laid on top of the other, smallest in back, largest in front, compressed into two dimensions like a telephoto photograph. Winter lingers white under the big bushes. Simple plant communities characterize the Great Basin Desert, uniformly covering thousands of square miles—big sagebrush, saltbush, greasewood, rabbit brush, sometimes stretching as far as the eye can see. Sagebrush itself occupies over half the acreage of each of eleven western states, and has the largest range of any ecosystem in the western United States, spreading over nearly 300 million acres.

Like the other North American deserts, the Great Basin Desert evolved recently, between twelve thousand and five thousand years ago, as climate warmed and dried, and into this expanding aridity, its two major desert shrubs, sagebrush and saltbush, spread as well, laying a gray haze over the landscape. Hairiness provides intermittent protection from arid winds and drought for plants that tap a deep water supply, as sagebrush and saltbush do. Waxy or varnished leaves, such as those of creosote bush, or tiny leaves may be more effective at stopping water loss where water supply is more meager. Sagebrush covers all eventualities for water, with both a fibrous surface root system and a deep taproot.

From a distance, the terrain looks deceptively flat, but when we walk it, it is as hummocky and rough as a newly harrowed field. We speculate about how difficult it must have been for emigrants to jockey their wagons through, sagebrush close enough together to thwart easy wagon passage, wagon wheels raised and lowered in a cadence of jerks and bruising lurches. In July 1849, Bennett Clark, traveling from Missouri to California, had enough of it and wrote, "If we once get safely out of this great Basin we will not be cought [*sic*] here again in a hurry. The eye tires & mind wearies of this tasteless monotony of scenery." Still, the sight of big sagebrush was welcome; it indicated land that, if cleared, was suitable for agriculture, with a mean annual rainfall of at least eight inches and nonsaline soil.

The hoary, fragrant shrubs not only look old, they often are, enduring up to 150 years. High as my shoulder, a feathering of branches fans out of shaggy-barked, twisted trunks caused by eccentric growth rings. The growth pattern of big sagebrush is typical of Great Basin shrubs: multibranched, soft-wooded, leafed all year round, and spineless. And in the easy swiftness of my pace, I realize a great truth: there are no thorns to scratch and tear, no spines to lodge and pain, that sagebrush desert can be *friendly* desert.

DIANA KAPPEL-SMITH [B. 1951]

Diana Kappel-Smith's Desert Time: A Journey through the American Southwest *(1992) describes her travels across nine different American deserts, where she logged twenty-five thousand miles on her car, doing firsthand research. Before Kappel-Smith entered Nevada, she practiced pronouncing it, forming the central* a *to sound like the one in* gap *so she wouldn't instantly give herself away as an easterner. Indeed, this Connecticut-born writer's descriptions of Nevada's wild places—Pahranagat National Wildlife Refuge, Ash Meadows, the Santa Rosa Range, Wheeler Peak, Caliente, Lake Mead, and others—sparkle with the fresh vision of someone for whom this desert world is new and full of fascinating surprises. As a writer and illustrator, with a BS in biology, Kappel-Smith specializes in revealing the teeming life that is unseen, overlooked, and little known. For example,* Wintering *(1984) uncovers the hidden workings of nature on her Vermont farm in winter, a season when many people assume that nature is dormant. Similarly,* Night Life: Nature from Dusk to Dawn *(1990) sheds light on the nocturnal creatures who carry out their lives when most people slumber. By the same token, in* Desert Time *she introduces us to a lively host of plants and animals and people, past and present, who have made our deserts their home. A front page article in the* Los Angeles Times Book Review *states: "You come to trust her company and to savor her observations; she is the sort of guide who gestures at what you would otherwise step across—or on—without noticing. She calls her collection 'an introduction to particulars.' These she infuses with radiance." While primarily aimed at an eastern readership,* Desert Time, *which also received favorable reviews in the* Wall Street Journal *and the* New York Times Book Review, *may help westerners to see their home anew and to appreciate places that they have taken for granted.*

Fossil Water
Pahranagat National Wildlife Refuge, Nevada

When you come from the south there are the fluid shapes of mountains reflecting in dark double form, and the double brightness of—must be water, couldn't be anything else—set like a mirror in a frame of dusty no-account hills.

It is so strange to come on open water out here that at first it looks as if pieces of sky had fallen on the ground, and the frills of greenery around them look entirely false.

This is Pahranagat, an oasis that lies along a crease of the Mojave desert some eighty miles north of Las Vegas. At the south end is a wildlife refuge that runs for ten miles, including in its boundaries quantities of desert scrub, grasslands, meadows, cattail swamps, crops, pastures, and *seven hundred acres* of open water. Farther north, rich farm fields stretch for thirty-five more miles along the line of ponds and marshes, lush round shapes that lie in their crease of the hills like a string of pearls.

The water is pearl-colored in the evening light. Cottonwoods billow on the shores. Above ponds and swamps and cottonwoods are hillsides of average Mojave, meaning rocks and creosote and bursage with sometimes a spiky yucca. In a "normal" spring there would be wildflowers clothing the rocks and dust in ephemeral color, but this is the third and worst year of drought so wildflowers are out of the question. Their seeds are in the dust, monumentally patient.

This year only dark green yuccas stand out against the pale hills and bleached vegetation. The Mojave yucca tends to grow in clusters, little ones and big ones in cartoonish family bunches, each faceless member made of a substance like pineapples and scissorblades. Every yucca seems to be twisted to one side, like a maimed figure.

I have never been able to get used to the raw rocks lying where they have fallen from some outcrop. There they lie, unchanged over centuries. Somehow this is discouraging; these rocks express a kind of futility.

There are very few cacti in the Mojave. The Mojave is a cold desert, cold in winter, anyway. Not now. The rusty creosote bushes, with their twigs wriggling up and out, look as if they were the skeletons of fires.

So, among all this, coming to the oasis of Pahranagat, one heaves a sigh of happiness; this is a miracle, a wonder, and a mystery. Where is this water *from?*

On the pale surface of the first big lake is a freckling of shapes like pepper sprinkled: birds. Stopping there, squatting under a cottonwood tree, feeling the dance of water-flecked light on my face, I watch a muskrat paddle by in a wake of silver ripples. I hear the clurks and low mutters of mallards, the clicks, clucks, squeaks and rattle-squeals of coot, the bright loud warbles of a marsh wren, the watery flops as one coot chases another, head down like a black awl.

A wren is making a nest in an island of bulrush. He is full of self-importance and his tail sticks straight in the air. He sings with the passion of a diva. There is a caldron of turkey vultures boiling up over the north end of the lake, the dark birds circling slowly in their thermal tower to gain altitude. There are hundreds of cormorants and white egrets perched in the cottonwood trees.

By the time I make camp I've seen numbers of ring-necked ducks and northern shovelers, gadwalls, several pied-billed grebes and a half-dozen great blue herons, and two gulls too far off to identify.

In October, so I hear, serious numbers of ducks come through Pahranagat on their way from Canada to the southern coasts. Then there are thousands of northern pintails, green-winged teals, canvasbacks, wigeons. In winter there are hundreds of swans and Canada geese. There have been white pelicans at Pahranagat, and white-faced ibis, grebes and egrets of all kinds, even greater sandhill cranes. Now it is the tail end of the spring migration, and the coot and mallard are setting up housekeeping.

In the evening I set up mine, on a rocky hill above a lake.

When the sun is down and the air goes lavender and gold, I light a fire. Sturdy dry cottonwood branches the size of my arms make a good bright hot fire; it's the first one in a long time, the first fire larger than microscopic in weeks. It's the first place where there has been fuel for the taking. Now the smoke is coming over my shoulder, one pants leg is warm and one ear, my rump, one arm. The lake is alive even in the dark; there are trills, whistles, rustlings, and splashings. There are coyotes calling from up-country.

Twelve thousand years ago I would have been listening for other things. I would have been worried about a herd of mammoths stampeding over me in the darkness. Or horses, or camels. I would have been concerned about a sabertooth cat or a pack of dire wolves scenting me out, or a three-hundred-pound Shasta ground sloth or a giant beaver the size of a black bear blundering into my tent.

In the valley of Pahranagat there was a river in those days, it was called the

White River, and it ran all the way to the Colorado. This was a semiarid steppe with juniper trees and grasses instead of the yucca and the creosote.

Speaking of rains—this is the odd thing. The rains of that time charged the underwater aquifers, and gently canted impervious layers of rock have since guided that water for dozens and hundreds of miles, out at last into the light. A series of such ancient springs now feeds Pahranagat; there is no upstream of the White River anymore. What water is here now comes from long ago.

This is a fragment of Eden pinched off and saved.

The cottonwood trees have been saved, and the coots fussing, and the silver world of the muskrats.

This water has been down in the rock for a long time. According to experts in desert hydrodynamics, the water that fills Pahranagat now is from rain that fell twelve thousand years ago. It is known as fossil water. Here it comes. Here it is.

JOE ELY [B. 1957]

Joseph Homer Ely, known on the reservation as Homer, grew up on a cattle ranch outside of Nixon, on the Pyramid Lake Indian Reservation. After high school Ely moved to Reno and took a variety of jobs, including packing garbage for Reno Disposal Services, working as tribal historian for the Inter-Tribal Council of Nevada, doing maintenance for the Washoe County School District, and being a police officer for the Reno-Sparks Indian Colony. His favorite job though was buckarooing on the Ninety-Six Ranch in Paradise Valley, Nevada, a large cattle outfit committed to ranching in the old way. The chance availability of a reservation house brought Ely back to the Pyramid Lake Indian Reservation when he was still in his early twenties, where he worked "throwing skids" for a Southwest Gas pipeline job until being commissioned by Pyramid Lake High School to compile a glossary of the Pyramid Lake Paiute language. Modeling his glossary on the popular Charlie Brown Dictionary, *Joseph H. Ely produced* The Language of the Pyramid Lake Paiute: Part I, The Glossary *(1982). Subsequent jobs with the Pyramid Lake tribe's planning department and fish hatchery led to Ely's central involvement in the Truckee–Carson–Pyramid Lake Water Settlement of 1990, which successfully concluded thorny negotiations after eighty years of conflict. This settlement is of vital importance to the Pyramid Lake Paiute people and the people of northern Nevada, guaranteeing that enough water reaches Pyramid Lake to keep it a living lake with healthy fisheries. Ely has served as chairman of the Inter-Tribal Council of Nevada and chairman of the Pyramid Lake Paiute Tribe, twice reelected. He currently continues his work in Indian country, in Mesa, Arizona, as project coordinator for Stetson Engineers, where his writing is mostly limited to technical reports and his primary focus is ensuring that the firm's tribal clients receive the technical information they need to negotiate water issues.*

More Than Romance

I grip the back of the seat in anticipation as we pull over the bluff leading toward the mouth of the Truckee River where it spills into Pyramid Lake. I see the feverish activity below. People, mostly young men and boys about my age, are milling about cars, some attempting to unstick them from the sand, others laughing, visiting and catching up on lost time.

Approaching closer, we bump over the sand until stopping near the cars. I see the shore lined with fishermen. Wearing tennis shoes, jeans and T-shirts, those fishing from shore use standard-sized fishing poles with heavy line connected to large treble hooks. The older anglers, in loose work pants, khaki shirts and felt hats, stand knee to waist deep in the water. Their hooks are fastened to military surplus parachute cord tied around their wrists or to a belt hoop. Regardless of equipment, both shore and wading fishermen throw or cast the hooks as far as possible into the lake and retrieve them with several jerks to snag the gathering fish.

Sitting on the shore, not fishing, but very much a part of the harvest are women gossiping as they clean and dress the catch. With wise, deft hands, they move their knives up the soft belly of the carcass to a point just near the gills. With a couple of swift cuts, they pull the entrails and backbone from the flesh, leaving only the white meat with head attached. With the waste and bones discarded on a nearby pile, the edible portion, to be later cooked or dried, is added to the now swelling gunny sack.

Some of the younger women, and men who've grown tired of fishing, visit as they remove only the fat, white fillets from under the black skin, throwing the delicious flesh into various containers to be fried later that evening.

An air of celebration surrounds the harvest. Young voices fill the area as the children play among the fishermen and workers, hiding from each other and their favorite dogs while the gulls screech overhead and dive down to steal the scraps in the sand.

The Cui-ui run has begun; the annual spawn, a migration upstream to spawning grounds beginning five miles from where we stand to another 10–15 miles up the Truckee River.

I, not wanting to miss any of the excitement, untangle my pole from behind the seat of the blue station wagon, and move quickly to set up my fishing stand near the others. Within the first several casts, my hook abruptly stops near mid-jerk. I feel the familiar slow strength as the hooked Cui-ui defiantly pulls my line from the reel. Turning to alert my dad of the catch, my eyes fix on the long line of men and boys also tugging in their fish. A few minutes later it's over. My first catch of this run. Removing the hook from the fish's back, my thoughts are only of how wonderful it feels to be out here with all the people and excitement, being part of the run.

A couple of days later, a full week into the run, we return to the lake to take a few more fish before they turn soft and undesirable. The few fishermen now look a little tired. Although the air is still filled with something special, concern has now crept in to temper the excitement. I overhear conversations about the short duration of this run, and about the small harvest in comparison to previous years. I hear expressions of loss mixed with an unwillingness to let go.

Walking down the shore, now littered with bones and waste, surrounded by the clattering noise of the gluttonous gulls and buzzing flies, I begin to imagine past runs of the Cui-ui spoken about by my mother and grandparents. I imagine a time of several generations past of watching the Cui-ui move up the river in numbers so large they completely blackened the waters. Hiding the bottom, they gave the appearance of a large, single moving body surging and breathing as it moved from the lake's dark depths into the river on its mysterious journey upstream.

Recalling the stories, I see children among the Cui-ui as they move through the shallows, lying on the many backs like the shimmering tommy trout as the moving mass and opposite flowing water allows for the illusion of a ride upstream. And with the spawn complete, the river's flow made gray for days to follow, clogged with the fish's white eggs and newly hatched larvae.

The ride home is quiet, setting a pattern for the rest of the evening. An evening that marked the last day I would fish for and take the Cui-ui, nearly 25 years ago.

The Cui-ui, found only at Pyramid Lake, is the last of its species, the last of its genus. It is the most fragile component of the identity and existence of its name-sake, the "Cui-ui Tuccutta," Cui-ui eaters, known today as the Pyramid Lake Paiute Tribe.

The tribe is in a desperate struggle to recover the Cui-ui, currently listed on the nation's endangered species list. Much of the last 80 years has been devoted to this struggle, costing the tribe, federal and state governments, and many others touched by this effort, millions of dollars, and, comparatively speaking, as much time and turmoil.

At the heart of the struggle, which turned to battle, is water: water, the obvious element necessary to recover and sustain the existence of the Cui-ui. Just as obviously, water is the component necessary to sustain agriculture, municipal growth and human life in the area. When short sightedness and poor planning brought these interests into conflict, the stage was set for what would be the longest Indian water rights dispute in U.S. history: a dispute that would either directly or indirectly touch the lives of every individual drawing water from the Truckee River.

Why has this dispute taken so long to solve? Why has there been so much conflict over what would appear a simple progress-versus-nostalgia issue or, as it is sometimes further broken down, a fish-versus-people problem? Nearly every other time this type of problem has arisen, the solution has been swift with the romance of the past and wildlife clearly the losers. The answer isn't simple because the question isn't simple. We really don't have a fish-versus-people problem but instead a people-versus-people problem or maybe even a culture-versus-culture problem. What may be passed off as romance or nostalgia is, in fact, more accurately described as culture and tradition. The preservation of that culture and tradition is what is embraced as the heart of this struggle.

The history of western civilization adequately explains the position of progress and, in this case, the importance of agriculture and municipal growth, but little has been done to explain the other side, the other culture. To understand the culture and traditions of the Pyramid Lake Paiute is also to discover their source of courage and tenacity, and to understand why such a high level of effort is put forth to recover and preserve the Cui-ui.

The tribe has lived along the shores of Pyramid Lake since time immemorial. Anthropologists and oral historians suggest Indians have lived at the lake continually for about 10 thousand years. During that time, the tribe has experienced two conditions foreign to many other North American tribes: a stable homeland and relative prosperity. Any people dwelling in a land rich in natural resources for that long a time would acquire a strong relationship, in essence a kinship, with that area and its consequent way of life. Further, it would be difficult to erase thousands of years of tradition or the memory of that tradition in less than a century and a half. It is also unthinkable for any culture to give up its fight to maintain its traditions when only a comparatively short time separates the current evolutionary way of life from that of old.

The history of the "Cui-ui Tuccutta" is marked by many events stored in the minds of elders who, in turn, teach the children by telling stories and legends. The legend of the Stone Mother, the story of the tribe's origin, is the most often told story. Telling of the creation of the people, the lake, and the Cui-ui, it also sheds light on the importance of their existence.

Long ago, before Pyramid Lake and before our tribe, the earth as we know it was mostly inhabited by animals. There were the wolf, the lion, the bear, the coyote, and many lesser animals. The wolf was the leader of these animals for he knew of many things and was very wise. The wolf was respected by all except his younger brother the coyote, who was foolish and full of mischief. The coyote caused trouble and made problems for the wolf and the other animals.

Among these animals lived an Indian woman. She was beautiful and of pleasant nature. She took as her husband a bear, and they lived in a cave. Although they lived together for a long time, it was a difficult relationship for the woman. For the bear would at times become very mean and the woman feared his rage.

After time had passed, the woman began to hear stories of a great man who lived in a land far south of her home. She heard he was kind and gentle yet very strong and of noble character. It was told that he was like a god and his appearance in these lands had been a surprise. Little was known about where he came from.

This news made the woman very restless. As days passed, she wanted more and more to meet this man.

One day the bear became very angry and started to pick on the woman. A fight started between them. The woman was able to use a rock to hit the bear. She killed him.

Immediately she again began to long for the man she'd heard so much about. So with the bear now gone, she began her journey to the south: to the home of the great man. The journey took many months and was difficult. But the woman was determined. The prospect of meeting this man kept her going. Along the journey she had many experiences. One involved a giant who killed and ate people.

When the woman met the giant, she was very afraid. The giant, of course, was bold and tried to capture the woman. A struggle broke out, and the woman managed, with the help of a club, to slay the giant. She continued on her way.

After several more days and many miles, she came to the land surrounding the home of the great man. She looked here and there until one day she finally set eyes on him. She was in awe of his appearance and character. Afraid to go near him, she watched from a distance as he walked among the animals and creatures of the land. She was impressed by his strength and kindness. Her longing grew, but her shyness and apprehension kept her from meeting the man.

Gradually the man began to notice the beautiful woman. Each day he would see her hiding behind a rock or some other obstruction watching him as he went about his daily tasks. He tried to pay her little attention, but as time passed he could no longer ignore her beauty and watchful eyes.

One day he decided to offer her food in an attempt to draw her near him so he might talk with her. He wanted to tell her to not be afraid, that he, too was longing to meet. He approached her slowly offering her a bowl of soup. To his surprise, she accepted immediately, and they had soup together. For several days, they spent much time visiting and talking. After a short while, they fell in love and married.

They had many children. But their lives were not happy because of one child. The oldest son was mean and always caused fights among the other children. He would pick on them, and hurt them whenever he could. When he grew tired of hurting them himself, he would lie and cause them to fight and hurt each other. There was no peace in the home of the great man and beautiful woman.

One day, while the woman was out gathering food for her family, the man called his children together. He told the children that he could no longer tolerate all the fighting and dissension in his family. He told of his decision to split up the children and to send them separate ways. He said he, too, would then go away. He would go to the mountain top, and up into the sky where he would live from then on. He told them some day they would all come back to him, and they would dwell in peace. But now they must go separate ways.

Before the father sent them away in separate directions, he said he hoped they would learn a lesson from this. He hoped they would learn kindness and peace, not hurt and dissension. So he took a boy and a girl, and sent them west. They formed the Pit River Indian Tribe. Then he took another boy and girl, and sent them east. They became the Shoshone Tribe. Finally, he kept a boy and a girl, to stay with the mother. They became the "Cui-ui Tuccutta" or Pyramid Lake Paiutes. Then as he promised, he went away.

This made the mother very unhappy. Her children were gone and her husband, whom she loved very much, was also gone. She cried every day. She felt bad and cried for the Pit River Tribe because they were so poor. Although the Shoshone Tribe did all right, she cried because she missed them very much. The Paiutes did well and became large, but because of their numbers, they, too, risked becoming poor in the future.

Finally one day as the mother gathered food, she was completely overcome by her sorrow. Her legs could no longer hold her up, so she knelt down. In the sand she sat crying, no longer able to stop the tears. The tears fell about her and formed a puddle becoming larger and larger. She cried for days and days until all the water from her heart and body was gone.

She turned to stone. Her tears became "Cui-ui pah," Cui-ui water, Pyramid Lake. In the lake she provided the Cui-ui to sustain the growing population of "Cui-ui Tuccutta."

There are many significant aspects within the legend of the Stone Mother, but none as clear as the direct relationship between the Cui-ui, the people ("Cui-ui Tuccutta"), and the lake ("Cui-ui Pah," Pyramid Lake). These three creations become the three components that give name and identity to the Pyramid Lake Paiute Tribe. If one component is lost, the identity from creation and an immemorial tradition is completely erased.

The problem, therefore, is much larger than fish versus people. The tribe's past, future and very survival as a people and nation depends on the existence of these three components.

The willingness to engage in an all-out campaign to acquire and reserve enough water to restore and preserve the Cui-ui, the most fragile component, is backed up by thousands of years of tradition and history. The goal is attainable. It must be attained. The very existence of the "Cui-ui Tuccutta" depends on it.

The cool water laps at my ankles as I sit daydreaming in the shade of the evening shadows. In the distance, I hear the gulls cry as they search the shores for leftovers and scraps from the day's activity. Through the dusk, I can dimly make out the stoic shapes of the many gathering pelicans floating, searching the shallows for movement.

A slight spring breeze, now picking up, raises the hair on my neck, and spreads tiny bumps on the skin under my sleeves. The drifting smell of sagebrush fills the air. Newly hatched insects swarm overhead creating a ringing noise.

It's time for the Cui-ui run.

Scanning the shore at the mouth of the river, I see it's empty. No fishermen, no children, no air of celebration. Only the birds. Maybe tonight the coyote will take part in this year's spawn. There will be a spawn. A small one. Like nearly every year, the Cui-ui will make an attempt. If the water's there, some will succeed.

I wonder, will my sons, one now a young man and the other only a few years behind, ever know the thrill of snagging their first Cui-ui? Or participate in the harvest's laughter and celebration? Or really know what it's like to be "Cui-ui Tuccutta"?

Walking back to the car, somehow I feel confident that some day, in the near or distant future, I, along with my children, will again join in the spring harvest, and celebrate the return and run of the Cui-ui.

JIM SLOAN [B. 1956]

"The only way to explain Nevada is by telling stories about it," writes Jim Sloan. He might have added that in Nevada, truth is stranger than fiction, for in Nevada: True Tales from the Neon Wilderness *(1993) Sloan tells eleven stories that are factually accurate, yet as wildly imaginative and gripping as any fiction. Consider the story reprinted below, in which scientists kill the oldest living tree in the world in order to determine its age. Or read about how the infamous*

brothel owner Joe Conforte tried to frame a district attorney for statutory rape. These riveting stories, based on firsthand interviews, news reports, and court documents, favor Nevada noir, detailing the antics and schemes of charlatans, casino cheats, extortionists, bombers, imposters, prostitutes, mustang killers, and swindlers as they finagle ways to make good in Nevada. Jim Sloan was born in Connecticut, raised on the East Coast, and earned a degree in journalism from the University of Maine in 1978, whereupon he worked for a newspaper in New Hampshire, covering the presidential primaries and writing stories on the demise of weir-net fishing, whale watching, and oyster harvesting. In 1979 he took a job in South Lake Tahoe and has remained in the Reno-Tahoe area ever since, working for the Reno Gazette-Journal *since 1983, where he has risen through the ranks to senior editor, winning a national feature-writing award in 1990 for his profile of Joe Conforte. Author of a second book,* Staying Fit over 50: Conditioning for Outdoor Activities *(1999), Sloan himself stays fit by hunting chukar in Nevada's backcountry. Once berating Nevada as "a place of lost hope and meager offerings," he has come to think of it as "a place of great wealth and promise." The crooks in his stories would no doubt agree.*

The Oldest Living Thing

Don Cox is retired now. He left Ely several years ago and moved to Arizona for the heat and dry air. Every couple of years somebody calls him up and asks about the tree and he doesn't mind telling the story. It wasn't much to look at, he tells them; folks wouldn't walk an extra hundred yards to look at it. The truth is we had much better bristlecones, much prettier ones. This one was dead but for one branch, and that could have just as easily broken off in the next windstorm.

He laughs. The wind blew a hundred miles an hour up on that ridge sometimes, took rocks the size of Volkswagens right off the hillsides. It's a different world up there at ten thousand feet. People don't know. That tree could have died the next day, the next winter. Then nobody would have ever paid any attention.

You can hear the soft clink of ice in his glass as he sips a drink. He sighs, then chuckles softly, reminiscing privately.

Does he regret cutting it down?

I regret a lot of things, he says, but I can't regret learning. You've got to make the most of your mistakes. I regret losing my friend, though. That tree killed him. I would change that if I could. But cutting the tree down—no. I don't regret it. I'm not ashamed of it, either. I tell people. It was the oldest living thing in the world and we cut her down. Changed the course of history, I tell them. Changed the way we thought about things.

His voice trails off. He's thinking perhaps about the other men and what lessons they may have learned. He's remembering some of them as being reckless, lunging through life and missing too much. The others—the ones he admires—were more cautious and never let anything get by them. They were like that old bristlecone.

. . . .

Time, all progress, seemed to have slipped by Ely without touching it. It was 1963 and the world was changing, the nation was in upheaval. A war was brewing, and beautiful new suburbs were springing up everywhere with the glint of aluminum siding. But Ely stayed the same—sleepy, lost and forgotten. Folks liked it that way.

Cox was a district ranger in the Humboldt National Forest, which stretched all along the Snake Range on the Nevada-Utah border, an oasis in the Great Basin deserts that stretched from Salt Lake to the Sierra. The mountains were sharp, like the Earth's very teeth, and sometimes it was early August before the snow left the southeastern slopes. Families traveling through the West found it most often by accident, but they usually stayed longer than they intended, hiking up to explore the caves or fish in the streams that trickled out of the rocky faces like strings of jewels. The hardiest made it all the way to the ten-thousand-foot elevations, where the forests gave out and there was the rubble left behind from the glaciers that once thrived there, nibbling at the mountains and carving out the splendid gorges and cirques of the highest ridges. All that grew there were some simple lichen and the bristlecone pines, which stood like sentries, marking the passing of generations. They were ancient trees, and some said they were older than the sequoias. But most people were skeptical of that. They thought 3,000-year-old trees should be towering and cathedral, and as trees go, the bristlecones were not beautiful. They were stunted, and their thick trunks were twisted and pockmarked, ravaged by time and the harsh weather. In some eyes, they were pitiful, for they merely survived and never thrived. They had little stature. Most looked nearly dead, barely hanging on with a thin, troubled crown or a dangling branch. The soil around them was brutally rocky and dusty. How did they hang on? Many felt a sorrow in the trees, an elegiac calm; they hung on out of stubbornness, in memory of a time past.

Yet others found a patient beauty in the trees, a persistence. Some scientists had recently learned that some bristlecones in California were more than four thousand years old, and many who endured the breathless hike it took to reach them in the Snakes came to admire their strength. They had a haunting allure, a wizened character that gave great meaning to each twist in its trunk, each scar in its bark. They had survived droughts and mudslides and terrifying winters. They were already ancient when Christ was born. They bent with the wind, flourished in the warmth of an early spring, yet knew the waste of impetuosity. They'd learned to relish the Earth's meager offerings.

That summer a young man named Donald Currey arrived at the ranger station and told Cox and the other rangers that he was there to do some research. He was a graduate student doing some kind of project for a university in the East. He spoke in a clipped, measured way of one who chooses his words carefully, and he seemed extremely serious and intelligent. He talked to Cox of carbon dating and ice ages and glacial moraines and tree corings, but a lot of it went over the ranger's head and he didn't think much about it. Cox liked Currey, though. Unlike a lot of young people then, he seemed very conscientious, and Cox admired his sense of determination and discipline.

Although Currey was away for long stretches of time, he and Cox slowly got to know one another. Cox saw a puppy-dog eagerness in Currey, particularly when the young scientist talked about the bristlecones. He told Cox they'd sprouted from the debris left from the retreating glaciers, and he felt that if he could find out how old one of the trees was, he could more accurately tell when the sheets of ice from the last ice age had left the Great Basin. He said the rings of the old, ruined trees could also tell you when there were periods of drought or heavy rain or warm weather or ten-month winters. He might be able to tell something about major earthquakes, or floods, or rockslides that helped shape the mountains. It's all in the spacing, the depth of the rings, he said. They're like finding hidden diaries. Ancient treasure.

But they look dead, Cox told him.

They just look that way, Currey said. Sometimes it takes a century for the trunk to get just an inch thicker, and in most places the rings are so tightly packed you have to count them with a microscope. Currey locked his fingers together. The cells are so tightly packed that insects and rot can't get in there. That's why they live so long. The tougher it is for them, the better they like it. They've found scraps of bristlecone ten thousand years old that still smell of that fragrant resin it produces. Imagine that; a wood that doesn't rot in ten thousand years. It's like a diamond, this wood.

Cox was intrigued by the stories. He'd always liked the trees himself, but for reasons he never really understood. Currey, on the other hand, saw a brilliant, complex order to things and Cox couldn't help but think the young man's admiration of life was unusually textured and powerful.

But how do you find out how old the tree is? he asked.

Currey showed Cox a pencil-thin rod with a cross bar on it, like a lug wrench, only far more delicate. You bore into the tree with this and pull out a cross-section, he said. Then you mount it on another piece of wood and you count the rings under a microscope. It's really very simple. The tree survives.

. . . .

Currey returned the following summer. It had been a particularly harsh winter, and the upper passes were just losing their snow and allowing some of the hiking trails to open up. Cox was grateful for the warmer weather, but like most accustomed to living in the mountains, it also made him just a bit sad because he realized it wouldn't last long enough to suit him. Winter would return all too quickly.

Currey, after a winter of lab work and studying his maps, said he'd found just the right tree. It was growing out of the glacial rubble on a fairly stable crest, and it seemed extremely old, much older than the ones around it. The tree's trunk was symmetrical but oblong, and Currey told Cox he would have to bore through six feet of wood to get an accurate count of its rings.

Cox wished him luck, but several days later Currey returned from the mountain and said the coring had gone badly and that he didn't think he'd ever get an accurate measure of the rings. He said the rings were infuriating; sometimes they turned at ninety-degree angles and sometimes the wood was so dense that his coring tool wandered and missed the heart of the tree. It was almost as if the tree wanted to keep its secrets. And what made things worse was that it wasn't even that nice of a bristlecone. It was short and ugly and it was just barely hanging on. It was possible that Currey was the only person in the world interested in that tree and now he was being prevented from fully understanding it.

Cox felt sorry for him. After nearly two summers of work, it looked like his project would fail.

Unless they cut the tree down. Then it would be no problem counting the rings. They'd be right there, in all their twisted beauty, a road map of time, centuries of time.

Cox shrugged. Why not? It's all in the name of science, right? So he contacted his supervisor, who told him to head up there and take a look at the tree. Cox did.

He found a tree that had a certain quiet anguish about it. It was set off by itself, and it probably wouldn't even be missed: there were no sensitive bushes living in its meager shade; there was no sensitive soil being held back by its withering roots; and any hikers would head up the ridge to where there was a thicker stand of healthier trees. So Cox reported back: It's not even that good-looking, he said. It's mostly dead, it's off by itself, and if we cut her down nobody's even going to notice and we'll be doing a service to science.

So have at it, the supervisor said.

Cox took a crew of five rangers up the following week. It was a hot afternoon and the chainsaws were heavy and there was a lot of joking about who was going to be the first among them to have a heart attack. They found the tree without too much trouble and immediately set to work, sawing in shifts to give each other a chance to catch their breath in the thin mountain air. Their chainsaws wailed against the niggardly trunk, chips of the dense, inscrutable wood flying in the woodcutter's face as if in some kind of protest. The nearby community of bristlecones watched in a mocking silence. Finally the tree toppled, leaving a pained stillness on the ridge. The bare stump stared up at them like an indignant old woman who's just lost her wig, and the rangers moved about uneasily as they cut off a slab of the tree to carry down the mountain. One of the men, a young ranger named Fred Solace, complained of heartburn. He had to talk to his wife about that spaghetti she fixed.

They had begun making their way down the mountain, the slab of bristlecone in a canvas stretcher, when Solace collapsed, pawing at his chest. He stopped breathing, and then his heart stopped, and for two hours the rangers worked on him—pounding on his chest and breathing air into his lungs before they, too, fell away and collapsed, breathless and worn out by the grief and futility of it. Solace was dead. They rolled the slab of bristlecone off the stretcher and rolled Solace onto it. They would have to come back for the tree.

. . . .

A year or two later a short article was published in an obscure science journal. Research showing that the oldest living things in the world—the bristlecone pines—were restricted to the White Mountains of California was not entirely accurate. Pines of very great age have been discovered in eastern Nevada, along the Snake Range near Wheeler Peak. One tree in particular was found to be 4,900 years old, a full three centuries older than what till then had been considered the oldest thing in the world: a bristlecone east of Bishop, California, that had been named Methuselah, after the biblical patriarch held to have lived 969 years. The tree on Wheeler Peak had not been given a name. In a grim, ironic footnote, the author said the age of the tree had been determined by a complete cross-section of the tree. Some had to read the piece twice before the full impact was felt: the oldest living thing known to the world had been simultaneously discovered and killed.

Currey had suffered this epiphany alone, several days after the slab of bristlecone had been retrieved from the slopes of Wheeler Peak. The trunk had been cut into three-inch slabs, and after he had collected his from the Forest Service, Currey spent several evenings in the back yard of his motel room huddled over the wood with a magnifying glass, marking each decade of growth with a colored pin. It took him hours to reach the birth of Christ, then the Norman invasion, and then the discovery of America, but it was all there in the troop of pins snaking across the wood. The American Revolution, the Civil War, the Industrial Revolution. Through it all, the bristlecone had hung on monastically, its world a tiny, silent lip of the Earth's crust. Currey leaned back in his chair at last, all pins in place, time perfectly measured. Four thousand nine hundred years. How much more would the bristlecone have endured? No one would know. The clock had stopped.

Although the age of the tree was kept secret for a time, Currey finally wrote his article and word got out. The howls of protest were deafening. The fledgling environmental movement used the incident as a rallying point for why wilderness areas needed to be protected, and one outdoorsman called the tree-cutting "environmental terrorism" intended to kill the Wheeler Peak area's chances of becoming a national park. The Forest Service launched an investigation of the incident. The leftover slabs of bristlecone were confiscated and hidden away in a storage basement in Ogden, Utah, while Cox was sent back up to Wheeler Peak to "sanitize" the cutting area and make it look like there had never been a tree there in the first place. The stump was buried under some rock. Critics could not be reasoned with; the Forest Service pointed out that the tree was nearly dead when it was cut down, but the conservationists pointed out that the tree had probably looked dead since Stonehenge was erected. What had taken nearly five thousand years to create had been destroyed in about an hour.

Cox was called a monster. At times he didn't understand what all the fuss was about. Why were so many people upset about a tree they'd never seen? If they hadn't cut it down, nobody would have known how old it was and that tree would still be sitting up there with nobody paying any bit of attention to it. Sometimes he felt empty, like he'd been deceived. He was not a stupid man, and no one admired the trees as much as he did.

. . . .

The following summer Cox got a call from a university professor from Arizona named C. W. Ferguson. He had somehow acquired one of the bristlecone slabs and had been studying it for some time, and now he'd like to come out to the Humboldt Forest and meet Cox. He wanted to study the area some more and he needed a guide. Would Cox be interested? Cox was skeptical. Yes, Ferguson said, he understood that Cox had cut down the tree, but that didn't matter. Cox agreed.

They spent a week together in the backcountry, mostly wandering but also collecting a few samples and examining some of the remaining bristlecones. Ferguson, Cox found, was a calming, simple man who had a way of describing the most complex scientific notions in simple, elegant analogies. Although Cox had expected the scientist to be among those angry for the way the bristlecone was cut down, Ferguson actually sounded grateful. I've learned things from that slab that would have been impossible had it not been cut, Ferguson said. And though my work's not complete, I think it's going to dramatically change the way we look at history, the way we remember things. They visited the rocky slopes where the oldest tree had been cut, and Ferguson gazed over the scene as though he were able to imagine the saplings rising from the primordial muck of a melted glacier. That tree knew things that we didn't, he said. It had a better memory and it was smart enough to keep a careful record.

Cox didn't fully understand until sometime later, when Ferguson published his findings. Using a complicated radiocarbon-dating procedure on each ring of the tree, Ferguson discovered that some chunks of recorded history were off by as much as seven hundred years. It was a startling discovery. The great stone tombs of France and Spain were probably older than the Egyptian pyramids. Stonehenge was centuries older than similar structures elsewhere. Advancements in engineering and science may actually have originated in Europe rather than the Far East.

Cox looks back on it now as a vindication, if not a victory. Others made mistakes, too—mistakes that Ferguson and the bristlecone straightened out. You're never too old to learn.

He kept in touch with Ferguson until the scientist died. He's heard Currey's a teacher, and that he takes his geography students to Wheeler Peak every year to look at the caves. He's also heard that some scientists may have found a tree down in central Mexico that's older than the bristlecone, but he doesn't really care. He doesn't want to be let off the hook.

ANN RONALD [B. 1939]

"Why Don't They Write about Nevada?" asked literary scholar Ann Ronald in a 1989 essay of that title, observing that the major wilderness writers overlook Nevada, one of the wildest landscapes in the nation. Ronald herself, who grew up in the forested Pacific Northwest and earned her PHD at Northwestern University in Illinois, had to learn, as Wallace Stegner once admonished, to "get over the color green" when she was hired in 1970 to teach at the University of Nevada, Reno. Quick to adapt, Ronald began exploring Nevada's wild places and publishing scholarly essays on the women writers of Tonopah, Reno divorce novels, Idah Meacham Strobridge, and Walter Van Tilburg Clark. These essays and others are reprinted in Ronald's retrospective collection Reader of the Purple Sage: Essays on Western Writers and Environ-

mental Literature *(2003). Indeed, Ronald is one of the first critics to map Nevada's literary landscape, and she has held important leadership roles in both the Western Literature Association (president 1983–84, Exceptional Service Award 1999) and at* UNR *(chair of the English Department 1985–88, dean of the College of Arts and Science 1989–96), guiding both institutions toward greater environmental awareness. Ronald wrote the first book on Edward Abbey,* The New West of Edward Abbey *(1982), now in its second edition, and edited* Words for the Wild *(1987), a popular collection of nature writing. In the 1990s she began composing her own creative writing about the natural world, publishing* GhostWest: Reflections Past and Present *(2002), which ponders, in her words, "how the historic past dictates our sense of the present," and* Oh, Give Me a Home *(2006), which examines land use patterns in today's West that will affect sense of place in the future.* Earthtones: A Nevada Album *(1995), from which "Water" is excerpted, is a collaboration with photographer Stephen Trimble that takes the reader off the beaten path to Nevada's remote wild places, teaching us how to appreciate a land few people have loved. In 2006 Ronald was inducted into the Nevada Writers Hall of Fame.*

Water

Nevada state climatologist John James tells me that the term "average annual rainfall" is misleading in Nevada. While precipitation in the Silver State may average nine inches each year, that precipitation does not arrive in ways a Pacific Northwesterner might expect. Nevada receives no gentle rains spread over a season or a full twelve months. Instead, according to James, Nevada's basins and ranges receive episodes.

The dictionary defines the word "episode" in telling ways. An episode is an incident that is complete in itself. Or, an episode may be an event complete in itself but part of a larger whole—an installment in a drama, for example. The word, aptly enough, originated as a designation for the part of an ancient Greek tragedy between two choric songs. While I don't mean to imply that Nevada's weather episodes are necessarily tragic, I do mean to suggest that they often present a kind of climactic explosion in the midst of relative calm. A number of such energetic—and often startling—weather bursts comprise Nevada's average annual rainfall.

The Las Vegas area offers some stunning episodic examples. The only time I have seen the front of a flash flood begin its rampage occurred in the midst of an episode in this ordinarily dry desert country. It happened in March, twice. Camped beside a wash in Valley of Fire, high enough to be safe yet close enough to have a decent view, I sat and waited. Rain had deluged the park all week long, so the red earth was soggy and saturated. Already at least one flash flood had caromed down this particular canyon—I could see where the motion had churned and receded—

but the water hadn't risen far or done much damage. Given the current downpour, I assumed another flood would follow soon. It did.

It looked just like the descriptions I've read in books, a cauldron of roiling tomato soup spilling, fast. Caught in its lip, foam and sage and rocks turned upside down. Not as loud as a freight train, for my flood wasn't an especially large one, a guttural undertone nonetheless could be heard. As the water rose, I could see its power cutting banks where no banks had been before and pulling up bushes that had been growing for years. A hundred red waterfalls spewed off the high canyon walls, all feeding this little nameless wash that was on its way to becoming a river. The deeper the water, the larger the debris swept along by the force. Since the rain, though violent, was intermittent, the torrent fortunately wore itself out before it got too close. When the rains returned, however, the flood waters reappeared too.

The truck was never in any real danger, but I must admit that I fretted when the curving cut of the ever-deepening wash came closer and closer to where I had parked. Though I didn't move the truck that night, I thought about it a lot. Between twilight and dawn, I woke myself up a dozen times. The next morning, the truck still safely anchored, I investigated. Only a zigzag line of damp sand, sporadic piles of torn brush, some upended red rocks, and swirls of thickening mud marked the way of the water. First I walked up the canyon to examine the steaming, drying walls where the watercourse began. Then I followed the water's path—a trail of sucking quicksand in many places—down beyond my campsite to where the wash had careened alongside a cliff, chewed through a dirt road, and then dispersed harmlessly onto an open flat. Strolling the canyon today, half a dozen years later, I can hardly imagine the long-receded turbulence. Creosote has taken hold of the watercourse, and tourist footprints powder red dirt that looks like it's been dry for decades.

My Valley of Fire flash flood was by no means tragic or even traumatic, but episodes often are. After the storm, Las Vegas newspapers told stories of flooded streets, drowning underpasses, cars and people caught in the churning water. By then, however, bright sunshine gave an illusion of serenity and peace. The torrent I saw was a true episode in John James's sense of the word, an incident complete in itself but part of a larger pattern of rainfall and aridity. Only in dry desert country do flash floods so violently burst forth and then so quickly, so gently recede. A handful of such episodes, added together, total that meaningless statistic used by weather forecasters and their followers eager for facts on which to lean—average annual rainfall. Unabated aridity in Nevada is a kind of myth perpetuated by those who don't live in the desert. While ninety-nine days out of a hundred may bake under a burning sun, that hundredth day can offer up an unexpected episode.

A flash flood is one kind of episodic event; an off-season blizzard is another. The Las Vegas area is too far south for wintry surprises in summer, but the northern tier of the state can receive snow during any month of the year, snow that may be bracketed by summer days of eighty-degree temperatures. There is nothing more schizophrenic than setting out on a camping trip wearing shorts and T-shirt, then ending the outing in a blinding snowstorm. Backpacking in the Clan Alpines in June, when I was younger and more naive, I once woke to find my boots completely filled with snow. I didn't even have a pair of long pants to protect my legs on the slippery hike down out of the range.

I'm slightly smarter now, but no less astonished when summer skies begin to churn blackish-gray and sudden north winds drop a temperature more than a dozen degrees in just a few minutes. That's when a wise camper eats a hasty meal, goes to bed early, turns her boots upside down—or brings them inside the tent— and waits. One such episode in the Schell Creek Range outside of Ely changed July into a veritable winter wonderland. Since the Schells are the fourth-highest range in Nevada, I might have expected something. After setting up camp along Timber Creek and donning layers of extra clothes, I watched afternoon storm clouds build massively to the west. I cooked supper in a cold rain. Sometime that night, the temperature dropped lower still and the rain gave way to snow.

I planned to climb North Schell, a rather gentle 11,883-foot peak whose July slopes normally are covered with clusters of purple heather, green lichen, wild buckwheat, and thousands of tiny phlox. The elk transplanted to the Schells more than half a century ago often graze just below the crests and offer special entertainment to humans hiking nearby. From the top of North Schell, the highest mountain in the range but one of the easiest climbs—nothing more than a long walk, really—the panorama swings 360 degrees. On a clear summer day, I've seen Wheeler Peak and Moriah to the southeast, Ward Mountain and the mine at Ruth to the southwest, basins and ranges beyond and even the Ruby Mountains far to the north. Best of all, few other hikers clutter the view. The register on top once told me in late June that I was the first person to make the ascent since the previous September.

Another July, another story, however. That episode buried the route to the summit in a whiteout so thick that at times I couldn't' see more than half a dozen feet. Wisely, I didn't go as far as the exposed ridges, but I did wander up Timber Creek for a couple of miles. The thick sloppy white stuff stood nearly knee-deep, the young aspen bent sideways with the weight. At intervals, red Indian paintbrush stuck up through the snow, like Christmas ornaments out of season. Neither elk nor deer could be seen, though birds everywhere twittered disbelief at what July had precipitated.

I didn't reach the top of North Schell that year, just as I didn't challenge Mount Augusta in the Clan Alpines so many years earlier, just as I didn't climb Tohakum one April Sunday when, standing beside Pyramid Lake, I watched a disorienting snowburst hide the shoreline only two feet away. It's impossible to live in Nevada without experiencing episodes now and again, explosive and potentially tragic wet interludes in the midst of ongoing aridity, regular irregular climactic events. Anyone who spends time exploring the Silver State quickly learns to follow the Boy Scout motto and to expect the unexpected.

· · · · · · · ·

For many people, ongoing aridity connotes monotony. Yet I object to an easy label that tags the Great Basin inaccurately. While it is true that aridity counters conventional notions of what makes a place attractive, it is equally true that dryness generates beauty of its own. Often what I like best comes in response to water. A claret cactus flowering crimson cups after an April rain, or dark anvils clouding and lowering a Toiyabe horizon. Deer prints, large and small, tracking a worn path to an isolated canyon spring, or hexagonal snowflakes, melting on the dry playa of Winnemucca Lake. Because I like to think of the desert as a stage alive with dramatic characters and incidents, I perceive desert water as the engine that drives the life of the land, the energy that keeps things moving.

One Memorial Day I parked the truck on a divide between two of the five Sheep Peaks in northern Washoe County. The noonday sun had been hot, more like summer than late spring, and the afternoon seemed almost sultry. Watching heavy clouds build on both sides of the seven-thousand-foot divide and feeling the air grow more humid still, I knew a thunderstorm would break soon. Lightning began to streak the sky to the south, followed by low rumbles from every direction. I wanted to sit outside and watch the pyrotechnics, but with no trees or bushes in sight, the truck seemed a bit like a lightning rod. I drove off the crest to wait for the storm to blow past. Perhaps fifty yards beyond the divide, I found a semi-level spot and settled there. Soon the rumbles changed to a cacophony of cymbals and drums. Bolts of lightning—too many to count—split across the sky. If I couldn't count bolts, I thought I might count intervals, then realized there were no intervals. A simultaneous flash and what sounded like a sonic pop inside my head meant the storm was almost directly over the truck, a conclusion confirmed by the acrid smell of sulphur.

After the rain began to pummel the ground, it was more difficult to see through the truck windows. I kept peering uphill, though, trying to guess where the lightning had hit. Instead of a brush fire, I saw a herd of phantoms. The lead apparition, a magnificent palomino, stopped in midstride when he discovered the truck blocking the way. Head up, hoofs slipping on the muddy grass, he spun around to chase his harem back into the storm. They all reversed themselves and galloped up over the crest, manes and tails streaming in the hard-driving rain. If I have a picture in my imagination of an episodic interlude punctuating an arid desert landscape, it is a snapshot of that stallion, his mares, the electric moment of their flight, and the pungent smell of ozone and wet sage.

MICHAEL P. COHEN [B. 1944]

Michael Cohen—writer, thinker, historian, literary critic, professor, mountaineer, environmentalist—has been asking difficult questions for more than a quarter century. Originally trained as a chemist, Cohen then earned a PHD in literature, switching disciplines to ask broader kinds of questions. His first book, The Pathless Way: John Muir and American Wilderness *(1984), which won the Mark H. Ingraham Prize from the University of Wisconsin Press, is a groundbreaking work of ecological philosophy, tracing the evolution of John Muir's thought by posing fundamental questions, such as "What is the right relationship between Man and Nature, Civilization and Wilderness?" and analyzing the answers that Muir worked out in his own writing. Cohen's* The History of the Sierra Club, 1892–1970 *(1988) has been called "balanced, impartial, and unsparingly honest," although Cohen once quipped that the book "seemed to offend almost everyone." Indeed, Cohen is temperamentally provocative, goading us out of intellectual complacency. His* A Garden of Bristlecones: Tales of Change in the Great Basin *(1998), which inaugurated the Environmental Arts and Humanities Series of the University of Nevada Press and was a finalist for the Western States Book Award in nonfiction, is a cultural history of the world's oldest living trees, viewing bristlecone pines as a site where human interests collide, and examining the questions we pose to nature and the uses to which our answers are put. Cohen taught at Southern Utah University for twenty-seven years, driving across the Great Basin every year, bound for rock climbing in Yosemite or summering at a cabin flanked by the eastern Sierra. He is a pioneer of first ascents in the Sierra Nevada, a competitive cross-country skier, fly fisherman, kayaker, and has been a professional mountain guide. He and his wife, the painter and environmental activist Valerie Cohen, have made their home in Reno since 2000. The essay reprinted here originally appeared as the afterword to* A Vast and Ancient Wilderness: Images of the Great Basin *(1997), edited by Steve Roper with photographs by Claude Fiddler.*

The Future of the Great Basin

Sometime in the late afternoon, you might be driving down a good two-lane road in the Great Basin with no other cars in sight. Never mind the highway sign that calls this road an extraterrestrial highway. This land is so open, so uninhabited, that it seems like the original terra firma, the skeleton and bare bones of the earth. You can see a hundred miles, across the violet shadows creeping into a long valley, to a new range of mountains and a ridgeline so mysterious and fascinating that you are surprised you have never gone there before.

Certainly the Great Basin contains more ranges of mountains than any one person can ever know; and like all ranges, each one suggests the origin of the earth. This range in front of you has such a distinctive shape you are sure you have never seen it before; but while you have driven this road scores of times, you have never seen the geography revealed in this light. You stop the car, consult the map, and realize that you were walking up a canyon on the other side of the ridge only a few months ago.

Set apart by a distinctive geology and biogeography, and scarred by its recent human history, this region tests human perception, tricks human memory, and divines human desire. The past five decades of human behavior here include ultimate human horrors, yet this land has been inhabited for a much longer time by the human cultures and the biota that preceded those modern humans who have recently turned it to their own strange military needs.

Modern Americans have been here for such a short time, have experienced such a limited range of conditions, have asked such paltry questions! Coming here in the midst of an interglacial era, what they have seen in the Great Basin is a forbidding climate, a cold desert, some exposed minerals, a few shrubs and grasses, and an empty space. Not long ago, a paleontologist patiently explained a simple fact to me: The earth has spent 90 percent of the last two million years in glacial eras; and during those times, the Great Basin's valleys and mountains were the home of alpine forests. These two million years probably included about ten complete climate cycles, so the present climate thus represents only about 10 percent of recent history. Our era, in other words, is neither representative nor final.

Add the following fact: Modern humans have been on this earth for about 100,000 years; they have inhabited the earth through less than half of one glacial cycle. The evidence of modern humans in the Great Basin is certain from only some 11,500 years ago. This understanding is relevant to any future we might imagine for the region or ourselves.

Because the Great Basin seems to be mostly empty space, its future has been highly contested; it has been claimed most recently by traditional patterns of exploitation. The booming and busting mining eras of the last 150 years have left, and are still creating, monuments to a simple theory of history—that people find only what they seek, asking narrow economic questions and receiving limited answers. The ranching history of the past century leaves its own legacy of conflict between memory and desire, and after permanently altering the grasslands of the region, ranching continues to hang on as a marginal occupation. The military history here has been the most dramatic and most recent, a textbook case of the human mind confronting empty space as a repository of its worst nightmares. The concept of the Great Basin as a patchwork of bombing ranges, nuclear reserves, and secret installations comes from the earliest understanding of the region as a place of no exit, where everything flows in and nothing flows out. Proponents of the MX missile system of the early 1980s, in the ultimate expression of this idea, wanted to make the entire region a nuclear target capable of absorbing the weaponry of an evil empire.

The Great Basin is not an empty repository, but an archive of natural and human history full of all the wonderful and horrible things that make it a stark and complete picture of the world and of human ingenuity at work on the world. The results of military occupation must be preserved, but the real and viable future for the region resides in its natural history and natural beauty. An open and visible geology makes each mountain range a textbook for the study not only of the discipline itself, but of the meaning of geology as space.

The region's biological history has its own fascination. Here, for instance, bristlecone pines, the world's oldest living trees, grow at high altitudes on limestone ranges. The tree rings of old bristlecones, living and dead, embody ten thousand years of natural history; the forests are also an archive, a window into the climatic history of the entire postglacial era. These trees provide a record of terrestrial conditions that is of the same temporal span as human occupation. The bristlecone has, in the past forty years, acquired an additional value as modern sculpture, and the old groves are now preserved as exquisite and priceless sculpture gardens.

Here is what we might have learned, late in the twentieth century, from our recent devaluation of nuclear weapons and our reevaluation of bristlecone pines: A portion of the earth thought a desolate wasteland by one ignorant generation can become highly valued by the next, if the next generation grows wiser. The Great Basin is, at this very moment, on the cusp of such a transition of thought. Nobody would imagine this region to be an Eden, yet it no longer seems a desolate wasteland. We begin to notice that it is full of things that make it what it is. People come here in increasing numbers, attracted by its beauty, but hardly knowing yet what attracts them.

JON CHRISTENSEN [B. 1960]

Freelancer Jon Christensen, who once made his home at a former divorce ranch in Washoe Valley, may be described as a reincarnation of the legendary Comstock journalists. Like his newspaper predecessors Dan De Quille and Mark Twain, Christensen finds a gold mine of stories in Nevada, and he churns out columns of print almost as fast as quartz mills once processed ore. Christensen began his writing career in the 1980s as a journalist in San Francisco. He then began covering the Great Basin as a regional editor for High Country News, *also contributing Nevada-related stories to the* New York Times, Bloomsbury Review, Mother Jones, Outside *magazine, and others, including most of Nevada's newspapers. In the late 1990s Christensen produced* Nevada Variations *for Nevada Public Radio, an ambitious series of documentaries on each of the state's seventeen counties, covering topics such as Area 51, Basques in Nevada, holistic ranching, Las Vegas wilderness, Spirit Cave, Walker Lake, wildfires in Lander County, the Burning Man festival, Eureka, and Great Basin National Park. He is a pioneer of new media as well, establishing and serving as editor in chief for both* Great Basin *magazine and for* Great Basin Web *(www.greatbasinweb.com). Recently Christensen has been a Knight Professional Journalism Fellow at Stanford University (2002–2003) and a Steinbeck Fellow at San Jose State University (2003–2004). He is currently at Stanford University, where he is a research fellow in the Center for Environmental Science and Policy, working on a* PHD *focused on the history of conservation. The excerpt below is from Christensen's first book,* Nevada *(2001), a collaboration with photographer Deon Reynolds. The book reflects his long-standing engagement with environmental issues, such as sustainable ranching, water use, wilderness areas, biodiversity, and nuclear waste. By sharing his love for Nevada's secrets, "often hidden in plain sight," Christensen has helped Nevadans and a wider audience understand what's at stake in the Great Basin.*

from *Nevada*

When human beings first ventured into Nevada—sometime around ten thousand years ago as far as paleontologists have been able to discern—the climate was cooler and wetter than it is now. But as the last Ice Age ended, the weather grew hotter and drier, and the mountain ranges of Nevada became islands of moist montane habitat surrounded by a sea of sagebrush and desert scrub. Streams and springs in the desert basins became the last refuges for fish, as the waters that filled many basins in prehistoric times steadily retreated.

Now, unique communities of plants and animals survive in these isolated islands of habitat. Life is naturally precarious in this setting. Nevada is one of the top ten states in both biological diversity and vulnerability. The state has some three hundred "sensitive" animal and plant varieties that are already on federal and state lists of endangered and threatened species, or are prime candidates for listing. Some are found nowhere else.

Like the Galapagos Islands, Nevada's mountain ranges are a good place to study evolution and the extinction of species. Thus, Nevada has landed a significant role in the study of island biogeography, perhaps the most important development in ecology since Charles Darwin's *Origin of Species.*

The theory of island biogeography, first proposed by Edward O. Wilson and Robert MacArthur in 1963, provides a key to understanding not only islands in the ocean, but also habitat islands in places like Nevada (and, ultimately, most of the increasingly fragmented world that we live in). The idea is beautifully simple and easy to understand: First, larger islands harbor more species than smaller islands. This is called the species-area relationship. Second, islands that are closer to shore will be more easily colonized by mainland species. Third, each island will maintain a rough equilibrium in the number of species it hosts. If a species becomes extinct on an island, it will likely be replaced by another species, often occupying a similar ecological niche.

Edward O. Wilson and Daniel Simberloff tested the theory on small mangrove islands along the coast of Florida, and the theory held up. A decade later, in Nevada, a crucial piece was added to the puzzle, when James H. Brown discovered that boreal mammals—animals that prefer cool forests—were becoming extinct on the Great Basin's island mountaintops. Brown searched for fourteen mammals—including yellowbelly marmot, bushytail woodrat, ermine, and others—on seventeen mountains. He found that the species-area relationship held true. There were thirteen species on the Toiyabe-Shoshone range, which has 684 square miles above 7,500 feet, and only six species on the Diamond range, which has only 159 square miles of similarly montane habitat. But Brown found no relationship between the Great Basin's sky islands and the Sierra Nevada and Rocky Mountains, which he considered the "mainland," and the likeliest source of immigrating species. In fact, he could find no relationships among any of the ranges, even with their closest neighbors.

Brown surmised that the mammals must have first populated the ranges more than ten thousand years ago, when the intervening valleys were more hospitable, and central Nevada was blanketed with a wide belt of trees now found only on the mountaintops. Since then, the Great Basin sky islands have become completely isolated in "a vast sea of sagebrush desert," Brown concluded. Most of the mountains originally had a full complement of montane mammals. As they have become isolated, the islands have lost species—but they have not gained new species. There is no equilibrium, only extinction.

The presence of water makes for another kind of island habitat in the desert. Bathtub rings on the hills above desert lakes remind us that water was abundant here long ago. As the climate became warmer and drier, these waters retreated to isolated water holes.

Ash Meadows, in southern Nevada, is one such place: a low spot in the desert near Death Valley, where an underground aquifer comes to the surface in springs, lime-encrusted pools, small streams that flow all year, and swamps and seeps. The Ash Meadows National Wildlife Refuge is home to twenty-six plant and animal varieties found nowhere else—the greatest concentration of endemic species in the United States.

Islands are renowned as locales in which evolution struts its stuff. Fish are masters of evolution—so when fish live in aquatic islands, things get interesting real fast. Desert fishes "present one of the clearest illustrations of the evolutionary process in North America, rivaling the diversity of finches of the Galapagos Islands which first caused Charles Darwin to crystallize his ideas on the evolutionary process," according to biologists David Soltz and Robert Naiman.

In the thirteen thousand years since the lake that once covered Death Valley dried up, one species of Death Valley pupfish has evolved into four different species. One of these, the Devils Hole pupfish, "has evolved in probably the most restricted and isolated habitat of any fish in the world," according to Soltz and Naiman.

The usually aggressive pupfish are curiously peaceful in Devils Hole, perhaps as the result of isolation in an impoverished environment. Pairs mate and spawn without interference from others. The pupfish have abandoned the former ways of their kind to survive together on a rocky shelf that measures only six-and-a-half by thirteen feet.

Of course, water in the desert attracts humans, too. And Ash Meadows is a sight for sore desert eyes, as Louis Nussbaumer testified in his diary in 1849: "We arrived at a beautiful valley considerably lower than we had been before and quite a warm region so that we encountered flies, butterflies, beetles, etc. At the entrance to the valley to the right is a hole in the rocks which contains magnificent warm water and in which Hadapp and I enjoyed an extremely refreshing bath."

Unfortunately, not all of the subsequent interest in Ash Meadows has been as benign as Louis and Haddap's bath in Devils Hole. In the 1970s, irrigation pumps threatened to drain Ash Meadows dry, and the first sign of alarm concerned the Devils Hole pupfish. Devils Hole itself was protected as part of Death Valley National Monument. But the pumps were outside the monument. In 1976, the U.S. Supreme Court upheld an injunction prohibiting pumping that would lower the water level and endanger the pupfish, which the court ruled were "objects of historical and scientific interest."

In 1983, The Nature Conservancy bought the rest of Ash Meadows from developers who intended to build a planned community in the oasis, and Congress passed a bill making it a national wildlife refuge. Since then the refuge has been working to restore habitat. To understand just how much a little restoration can mean to an isolated species, consider this: restoring one hundred yards of a stream at Ash Meadows increased the total habitat on earth for an endangered aquatic insect by a factor of ten.

In Nevada, scientists distinguish between the hot, low-elevation Mojave Desert of cactus and creosote bush in the south, and the cold, high-elevation Great Basin desert dominated by sagebrush in the north. But the two deserts blend into each other.

You can see this around Goldfield, where a band of Joshua trees marks the transition zone. I'm confident this bit of specific sightseeing advice will remain true for a while. But even though this landscape may look as old as God, it is actually a young changeling. It is a landscape on the move.

Today, piñon forests drape the shoulders of the mountain ranges in a dusty green coat all the way from Las Vegas to Reno. The piñon produces delicious pine nuts. It is the most abundant tree in Nevada, and (not surprisingly) the state tree.

But the piñon forest is a relatively recent arrival in Nevada, especially in the north. Scientists have determined this by examining pollen, seeds, and other plant material in packrat middens. (Packrats stash a little bit of everything in these caches, which are preserved for thousands of years by packrat urine.) It turns out that piñon trees were first present in southern Nevada about ten thousand years ago, and the forest has been moving north at the rate of almost a foot per day, or a football field every year.

"It's still going north," says Robin Tausch, a scientist with the U.S. Forest Service research station in Reno. The story of Nevada is a story of change—constant, long-term change, says Tausch. "If you want to understand that change, you need to understand history."

Packrat middens show species on the move, appearing here, vanishing there. It is a relentless picture that conveys the grand sweep of change across the land. The changes have largely been driven by climate until the last century or so; but now the picture is getting complicated.

The pace of change seems to be accelerating rapidly. And it probably comes as no surprise that we seem to be the ones with our foot on the pedal. On a geological scale, people increased erosion in mountain canyons by bulldozing four-wheel-drive roads all over the place after World War II. We helped piñon forests spread by suppressing wildfires. And we spread weeds, such as cheat grass, by grazing cattle and building roads and power lines across the desert.

Natural forces are now amplified in unnatural ways. Wildfires help spread cheat grass, which sprouts quickly after fires and is rapidly replacing native sagebrush grasslands, fueling bigger and bigger wildfires. And unnatural forces contribute additional feedback loops: increased levels of carbon dioxide in the atmosphere contribute to global warming, and weeds grow faster with more carbon dioxide.

"In Nevada, many of our communities are global climate change canaries," Tausch warns. "And they're dropping dead."

Remember those three hundred or so Nevada animals and plants on the lists of endangered and threatened species? Many are on those lists because they are only found here, and in small numbers. That is their natural state—but one little push may be all it takes to send them to oblivion.

For a world throughout which people—with their cities and suburbs and roads—are turning wildlands into islands, the Great Basin offers valuable lessons. That's not surprising, given that it is, after all, a continental landscape that began turning into islands thousands of years ago.

What are those lessons? Change is inevitable. It's part of the landscape. And, extinction happens. That might sound harsh; but it does happen, on a large scale, over a very long period of time, and also in our own lifetimes. We can see both here.

In Great Basin National Park on the eastern edge of Nevada, one can hike through the bristlecone forest to the last remnant of the ice-age glacier that carved the cirque in Wheeler Peak. Close up, the bristlecone pine looks like a survivor. But from a wide-angle view, one that takes in deep time and island biogeography, the bristlecones look like they are clinging to their last redoubts in the Great Basin.

Bristlecone pine trees used to grow four thousand feet lower on the mountain. Now they are found in this isolated patch. One day in 1964, a graduate student in geography and a local ranger cut down a bristlecone that had survived in this grove for nearly five thousand years. The tree's rings can be read as a record of the climate change that drove bristlecone pines off the lower slopes and to this last stand.

As long as bristlecones survive, they will continue to record their own history. We are only a small part of their history so far. But we play a bigger and bigger role, accelerating change even as we try to figure out how to live in this changing place.

Protecting places like Devils Hole and Great Basin National Park will not guarantee the survival of the pupfish and bristlecone pines for all time, but it could ensure that people will not be directly responsible for their demise. By its very nature, understanding this land requires a close-up view of the pupfish in Devils Hole and a wide-angle view from Wheeler Peak looking west across basin and range, basin and range, as far as the eye can see.

The awful hand of fate is writ large on the face of the land. Yet life thrives in the strangest places.

ROBERT LEONARD REID [B. 1943]

Well known in mountaineering circles, Robert Reid has spent many a glorious day scaling peaks, kicking crampons into vertical ice sheets, and jamming fingers into crevices of unyielding rock faces, and many a restless night hunkering down as gale winds and sleet pummeled the thin nylon walls of his tent. Reid's passion for mountains drew him to the American West, led him to get involved in conservation efforts, and animates much of his writing. Originally from Pennsylvania, Reid majored in mathematics at Harvard, graduating in 1965 to spend the next ten years teaching math in New York City secondary schools. In 1975 Reid made the leap to professional writer, moved to Palo Alto, California, and supported himself by writing mathematics textbooks, squeezing in time to produce articles for some seventy-five periodicals, including Sierra, Westways, American West, Climbing, Off Belay, South Dakota Review, *and the* San Francisco Chronicle. *In the Bay Area, Reid became a leading wilderness activist and helped found Project Wilderness for the local Sierra Club chapter, for which he received the chapter's Conservation Award. He also pedaled regularly to the Stanford University library, where he researched* A Treasury of the Sierra Nevada *(1983), the first anthology of writings from 150 years of the Sierra Nevada's recorded history. Reid's essay collection* Mountains of the Great Blue Dream *(1991), a fine work of mountaineering literature, is part adventure tale and part lyrical meditation on the allure of mountains. Eight years in New Mexico provided material for* America, New Mexico *(1998), a travel book that explores the paradoxes of a country where rich and poor, natural beauty and ravaged lands are juxtaposed. Of all the literary locales he has inhabited, Reid prefers his current home of Nevada, where the lay of the land is "forthright and fundamental and true," a "breeding ground for plain, shameless speaking." A slightly different version of the following piece appears under the title "Earth, Sky, Invincible Wind" in* Wild Nevada: Testimonies on Behalf of the Desert *(2005), edited by Roberta Moore and Scott Slovic.*

West, to the Future

I live on the last street in the southwest corner of an unincorporated district south of Carson City called Indian Hills. Sweeping west from my house, first in a series of low hills carpeted in sagebrush, then in steep, thickly forested mountainsides, are the foothills of the Sierra Nevada. The view from my front yard is little different from what one might have seen from the same spot a thousand years ago. Between November, when the Tioga Road across Yosemite National Park closes for the winter, and May, when it reopens—that is, for half the year and more—only three roads, all of them cozy two-laners, lie between my house and Yosemite Valley, 110 miles away.

In the opposite direction the view could not be more dissimilar; nor, for someone like me who spends a good deal of his time railing against the juggernaut seemingly intent on paving the world in Starbucks and McDonald's, more unsettling. Home Depot and Target crown a hill. Beside them a freshly minted golf course opens the way to Carson Valley, a ferociously growing portion of the fastest-growing state in America. Highway 395 bisects the scene, at most any hour a crush of cars and trucks. New homes spring up overnight, some of them on land where magnificent, century-old farms stood until recently. At night the Johnson Lane area looks like a small city. Ten years, my neighbor predicts: ten years till the valley is choked in houses and shopping malls, ten miles, all the way to Minden.

Perhaps he is right. And yet, something about Nevada gives me hope that it is the view west from my house, not east, which provides the ultimate glimpse into the future. One or two evenings a week, just before retiring for the night, I step outside into my front yard. My neighbors kindly douse their porch lights soon after sundown, and quiet their dogs. Moments after I close the door behind me, the great Nevada wilderness sweeps me into its arms. Above in depths of space so deep they're scary, mysteries and omens barnstorm the heavens. Inscrutable mountains rise up around me, a coyote cries, the beguiling odor of sage fills the air, undocumented breezes report in from distant lands. Before long I'm smelling comets, I'm listening to spiders spinning their after-hours webs. My address is Carson City but it might as well be a cozy cave in the Paleolithic. In the transcendent quiet of a vast Nevada night, I'm rocked by a perception that sometimes eludes me during pedestrian daylight hours, a perception not of a withering landscape under final assault by land movers, pavers, and fast-food restaurants, but of a vibrant, tolerant, and infinitely strong omnipresence waiting patiently for the world to come to its senses.

The idea of an invincible wilderness just beyond my doorstep is a new one for me. Before emigrating to Nevada nearly a decade ago (and, yes, becoming part of the problem I now decry), I viewed the wild as an exotic, fragile place to which I traveled after months of dreaming and planning—the Tetons, where I went to climb summer after summer, the Bugaboos, Shasta, the High Sierra. I'd load up my backpack and drive two or three days. Hooray! Wilderness!

In Nevada, where we're understocked in Top-10 thrills like the Tetons and the Bugaboos but crammed to the rafters with the grandeur of the everyday, I've come to understand wilderness not as the stuff of *Arizona Highways* photographs but as the world I live in; not as spectacle but as air and sky and earth—as the taste and feel of Tuesday evening in my front yard. Here the veneer of civilization lies lightly over the landscape. On a sidewalk near the capitol building, indomitable desert plants press upward between the cracks. Ten minutes from my house I watch a team of badgers excavating an unlucky ground squirrel from its den. Turkey vultures cruise the skies, coyotes sun themselves in a nearby field daydreaming of rabbit chops. My friend in Jacks Valley returns home at the end of the day to find a pair of bald eagles perched on the roof of his house. In many parts of the country, civilization is crowding in on eagles. In Nevada, it's sometimes the other way around.

A Nevadan has an easy time understanding Robinson Jeffers's confidence in the steadfastness of nature. "It has all time," reflected the brooding poet of the Pacific:

> It knows the people are a tide
> That swells and in time will ebb, and all
> Their works dissolve. Meanwhile the image of the
>   pristine beauty
> Lives in the very grain of the granite,
> Safe as the endless ocean that climbs our cliff.

The people are a tide. For Jeffers, humans were the problem—all humans. Enraged by profit-driven development, he made the mistake of confusing the ravenous few with everyone else, and became an intolerable misanthrope. I wish he had known a few of the men and women who live on my street, who are not destroyers. Working-class one and all, they provide healthy antidotes to the bitterness and disengagement that come with living alone on a privileged rock, as Jeffers did, and a firm refutation of his thesis. They like unspoiled nature. They're kind to it. They walk their dogs in it. They fish it and hike it and swim it and picnic it. They turn off their porch lights at night and then go out and smell it. They believe in open space, and when a card-carrying ravager showed up recently to carve a BMX track into a cherished spread of sagebrush, the entire neighborhood joined forces to defeat the plan. I don't deny that my neighbors want their toys, their TVs, and their Starbucks; so do I. Americans, all of us, want and use too much. We need to work on this.

Meanwhile, it's time to trust each other again. Most Nevadans don't want to crush wild things. Wild things are in our hair and in our nostrils and in our dreams. Why should we want to crush them?

A few years ago, wildlife biologists in the Netherlands freed some European beavers whose forebears had lived in zoos for more than half a century. Scores of generations of the species had known only confinement behind iron bars; none had gnawed a tree or swum a stream. Yet, delivered into a forest, the newly liberated animals set to work at once building a dam. Their wildness could not be defeated; it lived in their genes and in their cultural memories, and perhaps in their spirits, as surely and as vividly as the view west from my house lives in my own.

I'm not sure what the mechanism of freeing ourselves from our own confinement will be. But I do believe that the future is in free-running rivers and snowy mountains and deserts so wide and so graceful they make you cry. If I'm right, the purpose of Nevada, where the wild and the beautiful are as familiar as day and night, may be to remind the world of the primacy and goodness of wilderness as a moral principle, and of the will of the people to live in it and to glory in it. The future is here.

FURTHER READING

To read more deeply into Nevada, start with the books from which the selections in this anthology are reprinted. The Sources and Credits section supplies publication information for each selection. If you find an author you like, read his or her other books. The headnotes name notable books by each author, and an Internet or library catalog search will often yield additional titles. If you like a particular book, look it up on amazon.com and review the "Customers who bought this book also bought" titles, and call up the book on the Library of Congress online catalog (www.loc.gov) and hit the Subject links.

Also check the Nevada Writers Hall of Fame Web site (www.library.unr.edu/friends/ hallfame/Default.htm) and the Nevada Writers Silver Pen Award site (www.library.unr .edu/friends/hallfame/silverpen.html) for biographies and bibliographies of outstanding Nevada writers. These sites are linked to the "Alumni and Friends" page of the University of Nevada, Reno, library Web site. Entering "Nevada Authors" and "Glotfelty" in a google.com search will take you to the "Nevada Authors" homepage (www.scsr.nevada.edu/~glotfelt/ nvauthors.html), a growing Web site of biographies and book reviews by students at UNR. Annotated lists of recommended books can be found on the "Nevada Books" link of the *Nevada* magazine Web site (www.nevadamagazine.com) and on the *Great Basin Web* site (www.greatbasinweb.com). See also the Web sites of the University of Nevada Press (www .nvbooks.nevada.edu), Black Rock Press (www.blackrockpress.org), and Huntington Press (www.huntingtonpress.com).

Browsing the local-interest shelves of bookstores and the Nevada shelves of Nevada's public libraries is a great way to stumble upon interesting books. Visiting the Special Collections departments of Nevada's college and university libraries offers the delicious opportunity to see rare and out-of-print books, first editions, and the personal papers of some authors.

Below, keyed to the chapters of this anthology, is a selective list of anthologies, critical studies, and histories that illuminate Nevada's literary heritage and whose bibliographies and works-cited sections will guide you to still more books. Also listed are some recommended literary works that could not be included in this anthology.

GENERAL RESOURCES

Paher, Stanley W. *Nevada: An Annotated Bibliography.* Las Vegas: Nevada Publications, 1980. 558 pp.

>   Annotates 2,544 books and pamphlets relating to the history and development of Nevada; includes a brief chronology of Nevada history; extensive index.

Reid, John B., and Ronald M. James, eds. *Uncovering Nevada's Past: A Primary Source History of the Silver State.* Reno: University of Nevada Press, 2004. 228 pp.

>   Collects more than fifty documents of historical interest; with helpful introductions.

Ronald, Ann. *Reader of the Purple Sage: Essays on Western Writers and Environmental Literature.* Reno: University of Nevada Press, 2003. 248 pp.

>   Engaging critical essays on western writers, including Strobridge, Clark, and Abbey, and literary studies of Tonopah and Reno.

Shepperson, Wilbur S. *Mirage-Land: Images of Nevada.* Reno: University of Nevada Press, 1992. 190 pp.

>   An interesting scholarly study of how image-makers have depicted Nevada in national newspapers, literature, and media.

Shepperson, Wilbur S., ed. *East of Eden, West of Zion: Essays on Nevada.* Reno: University of Nevada Press, 1989. 189 pp.

>   A fine set of interpretive essays by historians and novelists, reflecting on Nevada's past to understand its present at century's end.

VOICES FROM THE HOMELAND: NATIVE AMERICAN STORIES AND MYTHS

D'Azevedo, Warren L., ed. *Great Basin.* Vol. 11 of *Handbook of North American Indians,* general ed. William C. Sturtevant. Washington, DC: Smithsonian Institution, 1986. 852 pp.

>   Leading anthropologists contributed extensively researched essays to this definitive compendium on prehistory, ethnology, history, and special topics.

Newe: A Western Shoshone History. Reno: Inter-Tribal Council of Nevada, 1976. 143 pp.

>   A tribal history of the Western Shoshone written from their perspective; includes stories.

Numa: A Northern Paiute History. Reno: Inter-Tribal Council of Nevada, 1976. 132 pp.

>   A tribal history of the Northern Paiutes, written from their perspective; includes stories.

Nuwuvi: A Southern Paiute History. Reno: Inter-Tribal Council of Nevada, 1976. 177 pp.

>   A tribal history of the Southern Paiutes, written from their perspective; includes stories.

Wa She Shu: A Washo Tribal History. Reno: Inter-Tribal Council of Nevada, 1976. 120 pp.

>   A tribal history of the Washoe Indians, written from their perspective; includes stories.

GREAT BASIN RANGINGS: JOURNALS OF EXPLORATION

Bartlett, Richard A. *Great Surveys of the American West.* Norman: University of Oklahoma Press, 1962. 408 pp.

The story of the four great surveys of the American West after the Civil War, 1867–79: Hayden, King, Powell, and Wheeler; with lively quotes from original sources.

Cline, Gloria Griffen. *Exploring the Great Basin.* 1963. Rpt., Reno: University of Nevada Press, 1988. 254 pp.

A chronological overview of the earliest explorers, fur trappers, and emigrant parties, from Spanish explorations in the 1700s to John C. Frémont in 1843; with maps.

King, Clarence. *United States Geological Exploration of the Fortieth Parallel.* Washington, DC: Government Printing Office, 1877. 7 volumes.

Report of a survey conducted 1867–68; vol. 4, pt. 3, by Robert Ridgway, on ornithology, is a delight, enlivened by Ridgway's enthusiasm and captivating stories.

Preuss, Charles. *Exploring with Frémont: The Private Diaries of Charles Preuss.* Translated and edited by Erwin G. Gudd and Elisabeth K. Gudd. Norman: University of Oklahoma Press, 1958. 162 pp.

Frémont's cartographer, Charles Preuss, gripes about both Frémont and Nevada; an amusingly grumpy counterpoint to Frémont's report; illustrated, with maps.

Steiner, Harold. *The Old Spanish Trail across the Mojave Desert: A History and Guide.* Las Vegas: Haldor, 1999. 244 pp.

A history and guide to the Mojave section of the Old Spanish Trail, retracing the route and quoting from original accounts; includes maps and photos.

FEARFUL CROSSINGS: EMIGRANT ENCOUNTERS AND INDIAN RESPONSES

Bruff, Joseph Goldsborough. *Gold Rush: The Journals, Drawings, and Other Papers of J. Goldsborough Bruff.* New York: Columbia University Press, 1949. 794 pp.

The voluminous papers of Bruff, who traveled from Washington, DC, to California and back, April 1849–July 1851; notable for Bruff's detailed line drawings.

Curran, Harold. *Fearful Crossing: The Central Overland Trail through Nevada.* Las Vegas: Nevada Publications, 1982. 212 pp.

A wonderful book about the emigrant crossing of Nevada; quotes vivid excerpts from a wealth of primary accounts; maps, photos, and illustrations; extensive bibliography.

Delano, Alonzo. *Across the Plains and among the Diggings.* 1853. Rpt., New York: Wilson-Erickson, 1936. 192 pp.

Overland journey in 1849 via Applegate Cutoff and Black Rock Desert; a well-known account among historians; unusually readable, lively, and good-natured.

Hafen, LeRoy R., and Ann W. Hafen, eds. *Journals of Forty-Niners: Salt Lake to Los Angeles.*
Glendale, CA: Arthur H. Clark, 1954. 333 pp.

   History of the southern route of the forty-niners; reprints of diaries; maps and photos; excellent annotations.

Stewart, George R. *Ordeal by Hunger: The Story of the Donner Party.* 1960. Rpt., Lincoln:
University of Nebraska Press, 1986. 392 pp.

   The classic history of the legendary Donner party, who were trapped in the Sierra
   Nevada in 1846 and resorted to cannibalism to survive.

LITERARY RICHES FROM THE MINING FRONTIER

Berkove, Lawrence I. ed. *The Sagebrush Anthology: Literature from the Silver Age of the Old
West.* Columbia: University of Missouri Press, 2006. 392 pp.

   Sixty-eight selections from Nevada's "Sagebrush School," 1860s to early 1900s, including fiction, memoirs, nonfiction, letters, and poetry from Mark Twain, Dan De
   Quille, Sam Davis, Joe Goodman, Rollin Daggett, Arthur McEwen, Alf Doten, and
   Fred Hart, with informative introductions by Berkove, a leading authority on these
   writers.

Buck, Franklin A. *A Yankee Trader in the Gold Rush: The Letters of Franklin A. Buck.* Compiled by Katherine A. White. Boston: Houghton Mifflin, 1930. 286 pp.

   Fond letters from Buck to his sister in Maine about the settlement and early years of
   Pioche, 1869–80; covers trading, mining, milling, and cattle ranching.

Davis, Sam P., ed. *The History of Nevada.* Reno: Elms, 1913. 1,279 pp.

   This two-volume early history of Nevada includes a fifty-four-page chapter on journalism, offering tributes to Nevada's nineteenth-century writers by a contemporary.

Emrich, Duncan, ed. *Comstock Bonanza.* New York: Vanguard Press, 1950. 363 pp.

   A collection of eight Comstock humorists, originally published in period newspapers
   and magazines; includes biographical sketches.

Fisher, Vardis. *City of Illusion.* New York: Harper and Brothers, 1941. 382 pp.

   Epic historical novel about the rise and fall of Virginia City (1859–1903) and the
   changing fortunes of Comstock millionaires Eilley and Sandy Bowers.

Wilhelm, Walt. *Last Rig to Battle Mountain.* New York: Morrow, 1970. 308 pp.

   A memoir of Wilhelm's frontier childhood as one of eight children, whose parents
   prospected around the West in a covered wagon, 1896–1910; with maps and photos.

THE OTHER NEVADA: REFLECTIONS ON RURAL LIFE

Brown, J. P. S. *The Outfit: A Cowboy's Primer.* New York: Dial Press, 1971. 349 pp.

   A novel about the growing tension between cowboys who work on a rugged southern Nevada ranch and the Hollywood mogul who owns it; a mix of mustangs and
   fighter jets.

Kittredge, William. *The Willow Field.* New York: Knopf, 2006. 352 pp.

> Kittredge, well established as an essayist, memoirist, and story writer, has written an epic first novel that follows the life of a boy from Reno (son of a casino pit boss) who leaves home in the early 1930s to work on a Nevada ranch, and whose life then takes him across the rural West and through the sweeping landscape of the twentieth century.

Patterson, Edna B., Louise A. Ulph, and Victor Goodwin. *Nevada's Northeast Frontier.* 1969. Rpt., Reno: University of Nevada Press, 1991. 702 pp.

> Excellent history of the area—an important transportation route—covering Indians and other groups who settled there; enjoyable reading; profiles the region's authors.

Perkins, George Elwood. *Pioneers of the Western Desert: Romance and Tragedy along the Old Spanish or Mormon Trail and Historical Events of the Great West.* Los Angeles: Wetzel, 1947. 103 pp.

> The first part of this book is a history of southern Nevada's Mormon settlements; the second part features poems by Perkins; the Moapa Valley historical poem sequence is noteworthy.

Strobridge, Idah Meacham. *Sagebrush Trilogy.* 1904, 1907, 1909. Rpt., Reno: University of Nevada Press, 1990, with introduction by Richard A. Dwyer and Richard E. Lingenfelter. 432 pp.

> Beautiful facsimile reprints of Strobridge's three self-bound books; includes nonfiction desert writing and formula fiction; illustrated by Maynard Dixon; excellent introduction.

Ulph, Owen. *The Leather Throne.* Salt Lake City: Dream Garden Press, 1984. 469 pp.

> A novel about a year on a cowboy outfit in central Nevada in 1953, as told by a history-professor participant named Doc; portrays cowboys realistically; good dialogue.

A GATHERING OF COWBOY POETRY

Cannon, Hal, ed. *Cowboy Poetry: A Gathering.* Salt Lake City: Gibbs M. Smith, 1985. 201 pp.

> Ten thousand poems were winnowed for this landmark collection; one-third are classics, two-thirds are new; with introduction and extensive bibliography.

———. *New Cowboy Poetry: A Contemporary Gathering.* Salt Lake City: Gibbs Smith, 1990. 165 pp.

> An illustrated sampler of the best contemporary cowboy poetry, with biographies of the poets; Nevada poets are Rod McQueary, Waddie Mitchell, and Eric Sprado.

Cannon, Hal, and Thomas West, eds. *Buckaroo: Visions and Voices of the American Cowboy.* New York: Simon and Schuster, 1993. 123 pp.

> This artful coffee-table book includes a CD of poets reciting their own and classic poems; Nevadans are Jack Walther, Larry Schutte, Rod McQueary, and Waddie Mitchell.

Jordan, Teresa, ed. *Graining the Mare: The Poetry of Ranch Women.* Salt Lake City: Gibbs Smith, 1994. 152 pp.

> Rural women writing honestly and movingly about their lives; includes nationally known authors and new voices; writers in or near Nevada are Linda Hussa and Sue Wallis.

Widmark, Ann Heath, ed. *Between Earth and Sky: Poets of the Cowboy West.* New York: Norton, 1995. 218 pp.

> Widmark travels to the ranches of selected poets, describes where they live, and offers in-depth profiles of them along with a selection of their work; includes photographs.

THE BIGGEST LITTLE CITY: WRITINGS ABOUT RENO

Alger, Mike. *Snow Storm.* Baltimore: PublishAmerica, 2002. 279 pp.

> Written by the chief meteorologist at News Channel 2 in Reno, this suspense thriller embroils an unsuspecting weatherman in a drug cartel bust; good local and weather detail.

Bigger, Earl Derr. *Keeper of the Keys.* Indianapolis: Bobbs-Merrill, 1932. 307 pp.

> A Charlie Chan detective novel set at Lake Tahoe with a brief visit to Reno. Chan investigates the murder of a singer, whose four ex-husbands are suspects; depicts Reno as a divorce town.

Land, Myrick. *The Dream Buyers.* New York: W. W. Norton, 1980. 207 pp.

> Mystery novel about an addictive gambler who is hired to catch casino cheats; good look at "eye in the sky" casino security and the psychology of gambling.

Luce, Clare Boothe. *The Women.* New York: Random House, 1937. 215 pp.

> A satirical hit play on Broadway, *The Women* dissects the personal lives of five New York women, most of whom have bad marriages; includes a Reno divorce scene.

Rule, Jane. *Desert of the Heart: A Novel.* 1964. Rpt., Tallahassee: Naiad Press, 1985. 222 pp.

> Evelyn Hall, an English professor, comes to Reno for her divorce and falls in love with Ann Childs, fifteen years her junior, who works in a casino; good desert scenes.

Vlautin, Willy. *The Motel Life: A Novel.* New York: Harper Perennial, 2007. 240 pp.

> A debut novel about down-and-out, hard-luck characters who inhabit the seedy streets of Reno. Vlautin, who hails from Reno, has been called "the secret love child of Raymond Carver and Flannery O'Connor." Illustrated with pen-and-ink drawings of Reno's cheap motels.

LIVING LAS VEGAS: INSIDE THE ENTERTAINMENT CAPITAL OF THE WORLD

Dunne, John Gregory. *Vegas: A Memoir of a Dark Season.* New York: Random House, 1974. 288 pp.

> Fictionalized memoir about living in Las Vegas during an especially dark period in the author's life; features a private investigator, a prostitute, and a stand-up comic.

Freeman, Judith. *A Desert of Pure Feeling: A Novel.* New York: Pantheon, 1996. 274 pp.

> A gripping novel about a writer who goes to Las Vegas to digest her difficult past; she befriends a prostitute who has AIDS; good scenes in Moapa and Valley of Fire.

Logsdon, Richard, Todd Moffett, and Tina D. Eliopulos, eds. *In the Shadow of the Strip: Las Vegas Stories.* Reno: University of Nevada Press, 2003. 145 pp.

> Fourteen recent stories that explore facets of Las Vegas and its people—gamblers and pit bosses, a liquor store owner, a magician, golfers, a chimpanzee, and a murder planner.

Rothman, Hal K., and Mike Davis, eds. *The Grit beneath the Glitter: Tales from the Real Las Vegas.* Berkeley: University of California Press, 2002. 388 pp.

> Twenty-two essays and photo series by artists, critics, and scholars who discuss Las Vegas from the inside—trade unions, infrastructure, power grids, water wars, childhoods.

Tronnes, Mike, ed. *Literary Las Vegas: The Best Writing about America's Most Fabulous City.* New York: Henry Holt, 1995. 358 pp.

> Two dozen essays and book excerpts from superb writers—mostly journalists—whose imaginations have been captured by the Las Vegas spectacle; many classics.

IN OUR BACKYARD: NOTES FROM NUCLEAR NEVADA

Bergon, Frank. *The Temptations of St. Ed and Brother S.* Reno: University of Nevada Press, 1993. 305 pp.

> A dark comedy about two Cistercian monks trying to live a contemplative life while the Department of Energy plans a nuclear waste dump nearby; smart and thought-provoking.

Bradley, John, ed. *Atomic Ghost: Poets Respond to the Nuclear Age.* Minneapolis: Coffee House Press, 1995. 330 pp.

> An important collection of poems about atomic warfare and testing, a handful of which are set at the Nevada Test Site.

———. *Learning to Glow: A Nuclear Reader.* Tucson: University of Arizona Press, 2000. 317 pp.

> Essays by noted writers, academics, and activists on international nuclear weapons testing; includes haunting testimonies about the personal costs of radiation exposure.

Brown, Dale. *Battle Born.* New York: Bantam, 1999. 397 pp.

> A military techno-thriller about a world on the brink of World War III; includes a simulated air war over Fallon and mysterious goings on at Groom Lake.

Daugherty, Tracy. *What Falls Away.* New York: W. W. Norton, 1996. 219 pp.

> A chilling novel about an arts commissioner in a small military town near the Nevada Test Site who is at the center of a conflict between patriotism and art.

Day, Jim. *Screw Nevada! A Cartoon Chronicle of the Yucca Mountain Nuke Dump Controversy.* Las Vegas: Stephens Press, 2002. 112 pp.

> Trenchant editorial cartoons that ran in the *Las Vegas Review-Journal* from 1987 to 2002 protesting the selection of Yucca Mountain as the sole site to be considered for a national nuclear waste dump.

THE LONELIEST ROADS IN AMERICA: CONTEMPORARY TRAVEL WRITING

Banham, Reyner. *Scenes in America Deserta.* Salt Lake City: Gibbs M. Smith, 1982. 228 pp.

> A well-read architectural historian, originally from Britain, Banham shares his love for American deserts, especially the Mojave; names a dozen other important desert writers.

Baudrillard, Jean. *America.* 1986. Translated by Chris Turner. London: Verso, 1988. 129 pp.

> A modern-day Tocqueville, Frenchman Baudrillard searches for the essence of America, finding it in western deserts; urbane insights on Las Vegas and hyperreality.

Kreuter, Holly. *Drama in the Desert: The Sights and Sounds of Burning Man.* San Francisco: Raised Barn Press, 2002. 142 pp.

> Photographs by Kreuter, accompanied by poetry and prose by thirty-six writers; captures the essence of this popular annual phenomenon; with DVD and offbeat glossary.

Schultheis, Rob. *The Hidden West: Journeys in the American Outback.* New York: Random House, 1982. 176 pp.

> Schultheis, an MA in anthropology, travels the West focusing on each region's Native Americans—their early survival methods, culture, and current situation.

The WPA Guide to 1930s Nevada. Nevada Writers' Project of the Works Progress Administration. 1940. Rpt., Reno: University of Nevada Press, 1991. 315 pp.

> Organized by highway driving tours, this Depression-era guide remains a trove of valuable information and lore; includes maps and period photographs.

A DESERT BLOOMS: CONTEMPORARY POETRY

Fox, William L., ed. *Seven Nevada Poets.* Reno: Rainshadow Editions, 1991. 15 pp.

> Poems by seven contemporary poets living in Nevada: Elaine Dallman, Shaun Griffin, Gailmarie Pahmeier, Kirk Robertson, Gary Short, A. Wilber Stevens, William Wilborn.

———. *TumbleWords: Writers Reading the West.* Reno: University of Nevada Press, 1995. 377 pp.

> Poetry of seventy-two writers of the intermountain West who participated in a reading series for underserved communities; Nevada poets are Shaun Griffin, Stephen S. N. Liu, Gailmarie Pahmeier, Kirk Robertson, and Gary Short.

Griffin, Shaun T., ed. *Desert Wood: An Anthology of Nevada Poets*. Reno: University of Nevada Press, 1991. 250 pp.

Excellent collection of poems by forty-nine Nevada poets of the twentieth century; valuable biographies and bibliographies.

Sage in Bloom: An Anthology. Reno: Nevada Federation of Women's Clubs, 1950. 100 pp.

The Nevada Federation of Women's Clubs published an anthology of Nevada poetry in 1927 and this collection in 1950; poems by men and women about a range of subjects.

Short, Gary, and Roger Smith, eds. *The Nevada Poet*. Fallon: Frosty Morning Press, 1981. 202 pp.

The first systematic survey of the poetry of any western state, this book has two sections: poems by serious poets (with biographies) and miscellaneous other poems.

ANYTHING IS POSSIBLE: CONTEMPORARY FICTION

Betts, Doris. *The Sharp Teeth of Love*. New York: Knopf, 1997. 336 pp.

Psychological novel about a woman who ditches her fiancé in Reno and goes to Donner Lake to recover, where she meets the ghost of Tamsen Donner and adopts an abused boy.

Didion, Joan. *Play It As It Lays*. New York: Farrar, Straus and Giroux, 1970. 214 pp.

A devastating novel about a Hollywood woman who is falling apart; flashbacks to her childhood in "Silver Wells," Nevada; aimless wandering in Las Vegas and at Hoover Dam.

Griffin, Shaun T., ed. *The River Underground: An Anthology of Nevada Fiction*. Reno: University of Nevada Press, 2001. 349 pp.

Fiction by twenty-five contemporary writers with strong ties to Nevada; includes short stories and novel excerpts, established and new writers; good biographies and bibliographies.

Kingston, Maxine Hong. *China Men*. New York: Knopf, 1980. 308 pp.

Stories about Chinese and Chinese American men, from ancestral China to Vietnam; a stunning chapter on nineteenth-century railroad building through the Sierra Nevada.

Rock, Peter. *This Is the Place*. New York: Anchor, 1997. 244 pp.

Imagine *Lolita* in a Wendover trailer court—an aging blackjack dealer falls for a young Mormon girl; insightful depiction of the Nevada-Utah border culture.

WILD NEVADA: LESSONS OF THE LAND

Austin, Mary. *The Land of Little Rain*. 1903. Rpt., New York: Penguin, 1988. 107 pp.

A classic in the literature of desert appreciation; Austin expresses the distinctive beauty of the eastern Sierra and befriends sheepherders, prospectors, and Native peoples.

Grayson, Donald K. *The Desert's Past: A Natural Prehistory of the Great Basin.* Washington, DC: Smithsonian Institution Press, 1993. 356 pp.

An impressive synthesis of vast amounts of data on geology, hydrology, bioscience, archaeology, and anthropology of the Great Basin; a valuable reference work.

Lanner, Ronald M. *The Piñon Pine: A Natural and Cultural History.* Reno: University of Nevada Press, 1981. 208 pp.

A beautifully written profile of the piñon pine, covering its evolution, ecology, and relationship to humans; includes a map, drawings, photos, and recipes; don't miss it.

Moore, Roberta, and Scott Slovic, eds. *Wild Nevada: Testimonies on Behalf of the Desert.* Reno: University of Nevada Press, 2005. 171 pp.

Twenty-nine writers on Nevada's wilderness; diverse perspectives voiced by artists, scientists, ranchers, Native Americans, politicians, land managers, and environmentalists.

Roper, Steve, ed., Claude Fiddler, photog. *A Vast and Ancient Wilderness: Images of the Great Basin.* San Francisco: Chronicle Books, 1997. 120 pp.

Fiddler's outstanding landscape photography complements an unusually rich assortment of literary excerpts and an informative introduction; includes maps; a great book!

CHRONOLOGICAL LIST OF CONTENTS

Below is an alternative list of contents for those who prefer to trace the state's literary trail through time. This list will assist teachers who may wish to teach a literature of Nevada class that is organized chronologically rather than thematically. This ordering highlights the strong ties between Nevada's economic frontiers and its literary production. Accounts by explorers, emigrants, and early settlers are dated here by the year of the events depicted, rather than by year of publication, which in many cases occurred decades later. The first flowering of Nevada literature corresponds with the mining booms, beginning in 1859, with additional discoveries throughout the nineteenth century. Simply put, mining brought money, people, and statehood to Nevada, attracting literary talents, who in turn enjoyed a national market for their stories of the Wild West.

The growth of Reno in the early twentieth century—closely tied to the divorce industry during that period—again attracted talent and produced a body of literature that reflected the town's economy. The ascendancy of Las Vegas in the second half of the twentieth century shifted Nevada's literary center of gravity to the south as writers explored the ethical and existential issues surrounding gambling and nuclear testing. In the present day, with a strong, diversifying economy and rapid population growth, Nevada has become, for many, the next best place. An increasing number of writers—both those who call Nevada home and those who keep coming back—are imaginatively engaging its history, its natural and urban environments, and its subcultures. Nevada is both an ancient place and a future world, and its recent literary renaissance shows no sign of slowing.

NATIVE AMERICAN STORIES AND MYTHS: THE ORAL TRADITION

It is not possible to precisely date Native American stories and myths, but these stories from the oral tradition are in all likelihood far older than the other works in this anthology. See the Table of Contents for a list of these stories.

CROSSING THE DESERT: EARLY EXPLORATION AND EMIGRATION (1826–1850S)

JEDEDIAH S. SMITH
   from *The Southwest Expedition of Jedediah S. Smith* (1826–27)

PETER SKENE OGDEN
   from *Journal of the Snake Country Expedition, 1828–29*

ZENAS LEONARD
   from *Adventures of Zenas Leonard, Fur Trader* (1833)

JOHN C. FRÉMONT
   from *A Report of the Exploring Expedition to the Rocky Mountains in the Year 1842,*
   and to Oregon and North California in the Years 1843–44

VIRGINIA REED MURPHY
   Across the Plains in the Donner Party (1846)

J. QUINN THORNTON
   from *Oregon and California in 1848*

WILLIAM GRAHAM JOHNSTON
   from *Experiences of a Forty-Niner* (1849)

SARAH ROYCE
   from *A Frontier Lady* (1849)

ADDISON PRATT
   Diary (1849)

WILLIAM LEWIS MANLY
   from *Death Valley in '49* (1849)

JAMES H. SIMPSON
   from *Report of Explorations across the Great Basin of the Territory of Utah in 1859*

EARLY SETTLERS, MINING FRONTIERS, AND INDIAN RESPONSE (1859–1908)

HOWARD R. EGAN
   Mountain Rat, Food for Indians
   Pine-Nut Harvest
   Hunting for Water (1846–78)

MARYANN HAFEN
   A New Home in Nevada (1860)

J. ROSS BROWNE
   A Peep at Washoe (1860–61)

JOSEPH C. IVES
   from *Report upon the Colorado River of the West* (1861)

ALFRED DOTEN
   Nevada Correspondence (1864–67)

MARK TWAIN
   Information for the Millions (1868)
   from *Roughing It* (1872)

GEORGE M. WHEELER
   Cave in Cave Valley (1869)

DAN DE QUILLE
Underground Business Arrangements
Fun and Frolic (1876)

FRED H. HART
from *The Sazerac Lying Club* (1878)

JOHN MUIR
Nevada Forests (1878)

MARY MCNAIR MATHEWS
from *Ten Years in Nevada* (1880)

SAM DAVIS
The First Piano in Camp (1880)

SARAH WINNEMUCCA
from *Life among the Piutes* (1883)

ISRAEL C. RUSSELL
The Great Basin (1888)

WOVOKA
The Messiah Letter (1891)

IDAH MEACHAM STROBRIDGE
The Quest of Old Man Berry (1904)

MRS. HUGH BROWN
from *Lady in Boomtown* (1904)

ANNE ELLIS
from *The Life of an Ordinary Woman* (1907)

SARAH E. OLDS
from *Twenty Miles from a Match* (1908)

THE LITERARY EMERGENCE OF NORTHERN NEVADA (1900–1960)

JACK LONDON
Confession (1907)

ARTHUR RUHL
The Fight in the Desert (1910)

LESLIE CURTIS
Reno
Our Alphabet
As Others See Us (1924)

CORNELIUS VANDERBILT JR.
from *Reno* (1929)

WILL JAMES
from *Lone Cowboy: My Life Story* (1930)

MAX MILLER
> from *Reno* (1941)

WALLACE STEGNER
> Mormon Trees (1942)

WALTER VAN TILBURG CLARK
> from *The City of Trembling Leaves* (1945)

IRENE BRUCE
> Virginia City, Nevada
> Arrowhead (1950)

GEORGE R. STEWART
> from *Sheep Rock* (1951)

JILL STERN
> from *Not in Our Stars* (1957)

JOANNE DE LONGCHAMPS
> Snowmountain (1957)
> Bat (1981)
> Becoming Crippled (1993)

NELL MURBARGER
> Queen of the Black Rock Country (1958)

MILDRED BREEDLOVE
> What Hills Are These?
> Camping (1959)

HAROLD WITT
> Pyramid (1961)
> Light on the Subject at Lehman Caves (1967)

ARTHUR MILLER
> from *The Misfits* (1961)

JEAN MCELRATH
> Rabbit Fighter
> Natcherly Dumb (1964)

LAS VEGAS AND THE STIRRINGS OF MODERNITY (1960S AND 1970S)

SAMMY DAVIS JR., JANE BOYAR, AND BURT BOYAR
> from *Yes I Can: The Story of Sammy Davis Jr.* (1965)

FRANK WATERS
> from *The Woman at Otowi Crossing* (1966)

LUCIUS BEEBE
> Going for the Mail (1966)

OLEPHIA KING
> The Dappled Grey Mustang (1967)

GARY SNYDER
> Hitch Haiku (1968)
> Magpie's Song (1974)
> Old Woodrat's Stinky House (1996)

JOAN DIDION
> At the Dam (1970)

SESSIONS S. WHEELER
> from *The Nevada Desert* (1971)

HUNTER S. THOMPSON
> from *Fear and Loathing in Las Vegas* (1971)

THOMAS SANCHEZ
> from *Rabbit Boss* (1973)

WILLIAM J. PLUMMER
> from *A Quail in the Family* (1974)

WILLIAM STAFFORD
> Reno (1974)
> At the Bomb Testing Site (1977)

MARIO PUZO
> from *Inside Las Vegas* (1977)

WILLIAM L. FOX
> untitled poem from *Monody* (1977)
> from *Driving by Memory* (1999)
> untitled poem from *Reading Sand* (2002)
> disowning (2002)

ROLLAN MELTON
> Truckee Treasures (1978)
> Reno Visitors Center (1984)

JOANNE MESCHERY
> An Otherwise Happy Life (1978)

THE RISING WAVE OF CREATIVITY (1980S)

JIM HUSKEY
> Stone Koan
> Building the Pumphouse (1980)

JOHN McPHEE
> from *Basin and Range* (1981)

SUSAN BERMAN
> from *Easy Street* (1981)

OWEN ULPH
> The Critter (1981)

MOLLY FLAGG KNUDTSEN
    Preface to *Under the Mountain*
    A Flake of Flint, A Sherd of Earthenware (1982)
WILLIAM LEAST HEAT-MOON
    from *Blue Highways* (1982)
DENISE LEVERTOV
    Watching *Dark Circle* (1984)
ROBERT VASQUEZ
    Early Morning Test Light over Nevada, 1955 (1984)
GEORGIE CONNELL SICKING
    Nevada's Subtle Beauty (1985)
ERNIE FANNING
    The Vanishing Valley (1985)
CHARLES BOWDEN
    Tortoises (1986)
JACK WALTHER
    The Longhorn's Short Career (1987)
JAMES CONAWAY
    from *The Kingdom in the Country* (1987)
TOM ROBBINS
    The Real Valley of the Dolls (1988)
WILLIAM KITTREDGE
    In My Backyard (1988)
ROBERT LAXALT
    from *The Basque Hotel* (1989)
STEPHEN TRIMBLE
    from *The Sagebrush Ocean* (1989)
ANN HAYMOND ZWINGER
    Of Blackbrush and Sagebrush (1989)

NEVADA'S RENAISSANCE: THE EXTRAORDINARY 1990S

BERNARD SCHOPEN
    from *The Big Silence* (1989)
    from *The Desert Look* (1995)
    from *The Iris Deception* (1996)
ERIC SPRADO
    Wait 'til You Become a Man (1990)
SUE WALLIS
    Coyote Bitch (1991)
TERRY TEMPEST WILLIAMS
    The Clan of One-Breasted Women (1991)

SAM MICHEL
>   Seeing Hunter Creek (1991)

DIANA KAPPEL-SMITH
>   Fossil Water (1992)

JOE ELY
>   More Than Romance (1992)

ADRIAN C. LOUIS
>   Nevada Red Blues (1992)
>   excerpt from "Earth Bone Connected to the Spirit Bone" (1997)
>   Coyote's Circle (1997)
>   The Boy Hears Distant Drums from across the Sierras (2000)

ROD MCQUEARY
>   Life and Times (1993)

CAROLE GALLAGHER
>   from *American Ground Zero* (1993)

DARRELL SPENCER
>   My Home State of Nevada (1993)

MONIQUE LAXALT
>   from *The Deep Blue Memory* (1993)

JIM SLOAN
>   The Oldest Living Thing (1993)

SALLY ZANJANI
>   Making History (1994)

WADDIE MITCHELL
>   Story with a Moral
>   Typical (1994)

REBECCA SOLNIT
>   from *Savage Dreams* (1994)

SHAUN T. GRIFFIN
>   A Place of Stone (1994)
>   Trash Run (1999)
>   Those People (1999)
>   Nevada No Longer (1999)

GARY SHORT
>   Toward Morning (1994)
>   Flying over Sonny Liston (1996)
>   Tidings (1996)
>   What I Believed (2004)

LINDA HUSSA
>   Ride the Silence (1995)

ANN RONALD
>   Water (1995)

A. WILBER STEVENS
  Vegas: A Few Scruples
  Paradise Crest (1995)
STEPHEN S. N. LIU
  Monologue from the Chicken Ranch
  A Mid-July Invitation (1995)
  August Mirage (2000)
LYNN EMANUEL
  Chinoisserie
  For Me at Sunday Sermons, the Serpent
  What Ely Was
  The Planet Krypton (1995)
CORBIN HARNEY
  from *The Way It Is* (1995)
FRANK BERGON
  from *Wild Game* (1995)
R. GUILD GRAY
  In Defense of Cattlemen (1996)
PHYLLIS BARBER
  Mormon Levis (1996)
KIRK ROBERTSON
  Adjusting to the Desert
  Fallon
  Lure (1996)
STEVEN NIGHTINGALE
  from *The Lost Coast* (1996)
DAVID KRANES
  The Phantom Mercury of Nevada (1996)
MICHAEL P. COHEN
  The Future of the Great Basin (1997)
WILLIAM A. DOUGLASS
  The End of the Line (1997)
DAVE HICKEY
  A Home in the Neon (1997)
NILA NORTHSUN
  sweat preparation checklist (1997)
  lost in the woods (1997)
  i gotta be indian tomorrow (2007)
BILL COWEE
  More Than Worms Slip through Worm Holes
  To the Austrolorps in Wild Abandon (1997)

DAVID DARLINGTON
>   from *Area 51: The Dreamland Chronicles* (1997)

BRUCE STERLING
>   Greetings from Burning Man! (1997)

EMMA SEPÚLVEDA
>   Here Am I Now (1997)
>   If I Renounce the Word (1997)
>   from *From Border Crossings to Campaign Trail* (1998)

GAILMARIE PAHMEIER
>   The Promise of Good Food
>   When You Love Someone for a Long Time (1998)

DAYVID FIGLER
>   The Shrimp Manifesto
>   Zamboni (1998)

JOHN L. SMITH
>   "Flying Nun" Stunt Double Lands on Her Feet in Las Vegas
>   Kidney Caper: The Making of a Myth Nobody Can Miss (1999)

HARRY FAGEL
>   Jaywalker
>   L.S.D. (Street Talk Pt. 4) (1999)

DAVID THOMSON
>   from *In Nevada: The Land, the People, God, and Chance* (1999)

TOM MESCHERY
>   Trucks
>   Weeds—Teaching Poetry at Wittenburg Juvenile Hall (1999)

JANICE EMILY BOWERS
>   Remains of the Day (1999)

BRUCE ISAACSON
>   Life in Las Vegas (1999)
>   Lucky (2001)

INTO THE TWENTY-FIRST CENTURY

GREGORY MARTIN
>   from *Mountain City* (2000)

MARY WEBB
>   from *A Doubtful River* (2000)

RICHARD RAWLES
>   Coyote Learns to Glow (2000)

JAMES CONRAD
>   from *Making Love to the Minor Poets of Chicago* (2000)

BILL DONAHUE
>   Boomtown (2000)

CLAUDIA KEELAN
>   Blue Diamond
>   Relinquish (2000)

DENNIS PARKS
>   from *Living in the Country Growing Weird* (2001)

VERITA BLACK PROTHRO
>   Porched Suitcases (2001)

BILL BRANON
>   Seven-Out Sally Is Loose with the Rent (2001)

HART WEGNER
>   The Blue Line (2001)

CURTIS OBERHANSLY AND DIANNE NELSON OBERHANSLY
>   from *Downwinders: An Atomic Tale* (2001)

TERESA JORDAN
>   St. Francis of Tobacco (2001)

JON CHRISTENSEN
>   from *Nevada* (2001)

SOPHIE SHEPPARD
>   Airspace (2002)

CAROLYN DUFURRENA
>   from *Fifty Miles from Home* (2002)

JOHN H. IRSFELD
>   Stop, Rewind, and Play (2002)

ART GIBNEY
>   The Manure Spreader (2002)

DONALD REVELL
>   The Little River Wants to Kee (2002)
>   My Mojave (2003)

GREGORY CROSBY
>   The Long Shot (2002)

H. LEE BARNES
>   from *The Lucky* (2003)

ALIKI BARNSTONE
>   You Pray to Rain Falling in the Desert (2004)
>   The Lights of Las Vegas
>   Freeway Love Poem

ROBERT LEONARD REID
>   West, to the Future (2005)

ELAINE DALLMAN
    Sparks for a 24/7 Week
    Desert (2005)
BRUCE LAXALT
    Work in Progress
    Autumn Fire (2005)
DOUGLAS UNGER
    Second Chances (2007)
JEFFREY CHISUM
    The Middle of Nowhere (2008)

SOURCES AND CREDITS

Citations for "Voices from the Homeland: Native American Stories and Myths" are listed in the order in which the stories appear in the book. Citations for all other sections are listed in alphabetical order by author's last name.

EPIGRAPH

Welch, Lew. "Step out onto the Planet." From *Ring of Bone: Collected Poems 1950–1972*, edited by Donald Allen. Bolinas, California: Grey Fox Press, 1973. Reprinted by permission of Maria M. Cregg.

VOICES FROM THE HOMELAND: NATIVE AMERICAN STORIES AND MYTHS

WESTERN SHOSHONE

"Origin Tale," "Coyote Wants to Be Chief," "Bungling Host," and "Tso'apittse." From *Shoshone Tales*, edited by Anne M. Smith with assistance from Alden Hayes, 150–51, 76–77, 86–89, 82–83. Salt Lake City: University of Utah Press, 1993. Reprinted by permission of the University of Utah Press.

NORTHERN PAIUTE

"Stone Mother" and "Water Babies at Coo yu e Lake." From Nellie Shaw Harnar, *Indians of Coo-yu-ee Pah (Pyramid Lake): The History of the Pyramid Lake Indians*, 16–18, 18–20. 1974. Rpt., Sparks, NV: Western Printing and Publishing, 1978. Reprinted by permission of Curtis S. Harnar.

"Pa-o-ha." From *Anthropology of the Numa: John Wesley Powell's Manuscripts on the Numic Peoples of Western North America, 1868–1880*, edited by Don D. Fowler and Catherine S. Fowler. *Smithsonian Contributions to Anthropology* 14 (1971): 224–25, 285.

"Porcupine and Coyote" from "Northern Paiute Tales," by Isabel T. Kelly. From *Journal of American Folklore* 51, no. 202 (October–December 1938): 407–8. Reprinted by permission of the American Folklore Society (www.afsnet.org).

SOUTHERN PAIUTE

"The Creation of the Indians," "Cŭnā´waвⁱ," "Cŭnā´waвⁱ's Grandson," and "Salt." From
    Robert H. Lowie, "Shoshonean Tales." *Journal of American Folk-lore* 37, nos. 143–44
    (January–June 1924): 157–60, 160–61, 165–67, 199–200. Reprinted by permission of
    American Folklore Society.

WASHOE

"Wolf and Coyote—Origin of Death." From Robert H. Lowie, "Ethnographic Notes on the
    Washo." *University of California Publications in American Archaeology and Ethnology*
    36, no. 5 (1939): 333.
"*Damollale* and the Black Widow Spider," "*Damollale* and the Water Baby," and "Story of
    the *Ong.*" From Jo Ann Nevers, *Wa She Shu: A Washo Tribal History,* 30–33, 35–36.
    Reno: Inter-Tribal Council of Nevada, 1976. Reprinted by permission of Inter-Tribal
    Council of Nevada.

GREAT BASIN RANGINGS: JOURNALS OF EXPLORATION

Frémont, John Charles. Excerpts from *A Report of the Exploring Expedition to the Rocky
    Mountains in the Year 1842, and to Oregon and North California in the Years 1843–44,*
    573, 574, 575, 601–605, 607–10. Printed by order of the Senate of the U.S. Washington,
    DC: Gales and Seaton, Printers, 1945.
Ives, Joseph C. Excerpts from *Report upon the Colorado River of the West,* 70–72, 73, 78–79,
    80–84. Washington, DC: U.S. Government Printing Office, 1861.
Leonard, Zenas. Excerpts from *Adventures of Zenas Leonard, Fur Trader,* 64–65, 67–73. 1839.
    New ed., edited by John C. Ewers. Norman: University of Oklahoma Press, 1959. New
    edition copyright © 1959 by the University of Oklahoma Press, Publishing Division of
    the University. Reprinted by permission of the University of Oklahoma Press.
Ogden, Peter Skene. Excerpts from *Journal of the Snake Country Expedition, 1828–29.* In
    "The Peter Skene Ogden Journals; Snake Expedition, 1827–28 and 1828–29," ed. T. C.
    Elliott, *Quarterly of the Oregon Historical Society* 11, no. 4 (December 1910): 384–86.
Simpson, James H. Excerpts from *Report of Explorations across the Great Basin of the Ter-
    ritory of Utah in 1859.* Washington, DC: U.S. Government Printing Office, 1876. Rpt.,
    Reno: University of Nevada Press, 1983.
Smith, Jedediah S. Excerpts from *The Southwest Expedition of Jedediah S. Smith: His Per-
    sonal Account of the Journey to California, 1826–1827,* edited by George R. Brooks.
    Glendale, CA: Arthur H. Clark, 1977. Reprinted by permission of Jedediah Strong
    Smith Papers, Missouri Historical Society, St. Louis.
Wheeler, George M. "Cave in Cave Valley." From *Preliminary Report upon a Reconnaissance
    through Southern and Southeastern Nevada, Made in 1869.* By George M. Wheeler
    and D. W. Lockwood. Washington, DC: U.S. Government Printing Office, 1875.

FEARFUL CROSSINGS: EMIGRANT ENCOUNTERS AND INDIAN RESPONSES

Johnston, William Graham. Excerpts from *Experiences of a Forty-Niner.* Pittsburgh: William Graham Johnston, 1892.

Manly, William Lewis. Excerpts from *Death Valley in '49.* San Jose, CA: Pacific Tree and Vine, 1894.

Murphy, Virginia Reed. "Across the Plains in the Donner Party (1846)." *Century* 42, no. 3 (July 1891): 409–26.

Pratt, Addison. "Diary" [1849]. From *Journals of Forty-Niners: Salt Lake to Los Angeles,* edited by LeRoy R. Hafen and Ann W. Hafen. Glendale, CA: Arthur H. Clark, 1954.

Royce, Sarah. Excerpts from *A Frontier Lady: Recollections of the Gold Rush and Early California,* edited by Ralph Henry Gabriel. New Haven, CT: Yale University Press, 1932. Copyright © 1932 by Yale University Press; renewal copyright © 1960 by Ralph Henry Gabriel. All rights reserved. Reprinted by permission of Yale University Press.

Thornton, J. Quinn. Excerpts from *Oregon and California in 1848.* 2 vols. New York: Harper and Brothers, 1855.

Winnemucca [Hopkins], Sarah. Excerpts from *Life among the Piutes: Their Wrongs and Claims,* edited by Mrs. Horace Mann. 1883. Rpt., Reno: University of Nevada Press, 1994.

Wovoka, "The Messiah Letter." From James Mooney, "The Ghost-Dance Religion and the Sioux Outbreak of 1890." *14th Annual Report of the Bureau of American Ethnology 1892–93,* pt. 2. Washington, DC: U.S. Government Printing Office, 1896.

LITERARY RICHES FROM THE MINING FRONTIER

Beebe, Lucius. "Going for the Mail." From *The Lucius Beebe Reader,* edited by Charles Clegg and Duncan Emrich. Garden City, NY: 1967. Reprinted by permission of Ann Clegg Holloway.

Brown, Mrs. Hugh. Excerpts from *Lady in Boomtown: Miners and Manners on the Nevada Frontier.* Reno: University of Nevada Press, 1968. Copyright © 1968 by Marjorie Anne Brown. Reprinted with the permission of the University of Nevada Press.

Browne, J. Ross. "A Peep at Washoe." *Harper's Monthly,* December 1860, January/February 1861.

Davis, Sam. "The First Piano in Camp." From *The First Piano in Camp.* New York: Harper and Brothers, 1919.

De Quille, Dan. "Underground Business Arrangements" and "Fun and Frolic." From *History of the Big Bonanza.* San Francisco: A. L. Bancroft, 1876.

Doten, Alfred. "Nevada Correspondence." Published letters to *Old Colony Memorial and Plymouth Rock* newspaper, Plymouth, MA, 1864–1867.

Ellis, Anne. Excerpts from *The Life of an Ordinary Woman.* Boston: Houghton Mifflin, 1929.

Copyright 1929 by Anne Ellis; copyright © renewed by Neita Carey and Earl E. Ellis. Reprinted by permission of Houghton Mifflin Company. All rights reserved.

Hart, Fred H. "Life in a Mining Town." From *The Sazerac Lying Club: A Nevada Book.* San Francisco: Henry Keller, 1878.

Mathews, Mary McNair. Excerpts from *Ten Years in Nevada; or, Life on the Pacific Coast.* Buffalo: Baker, Jones, 1880. Rpt. Lincoln: U of Nebraska P, 1985.

Murbarger, Nell. "Queen of the Black Rock Country." From *Sovereigns of the Sage.* Palm Desert, CA: Desert Magazine Press, 1958. Reprinted by permission of Stanley W. Paher.

Strobridge, Idah Meacham. "The Quest of Old Man Berry." From *In Miners' Mirage-Land* (1904). In *Sagebrush Trilogy: Idah Meacham Strobridge and Her Works,* introduction by Richard A. Dwyer and Richard E. Lingenfelter. Reno: University of Nevada Press, 1990. Copyright © 1904 by Idah Meacham Strobridge.

Twain, Mark. Excerpts from *Roughing It.* 1872. Hartford, CT: American, 1898.

———. "Information for the Millions." From *The Celebrated Jumping Frog of Calaveras County, and Other Sketches.* New York: C. H. Webb, 1867.

Zanjani, Sally. "Making History." From *New Trails: Twenty-three Original Stories of the West from Western Writers of America,* edited by John Jakes and Martin H. Greenberg. New York: Doubleday, 1994. Reprinted by permission of Sally Zanjani.

THE OTHER NEVADA: REFLECTIONS ON RURAL LIFE

Dufurrena, Carolyn. Excerpts from *Fifty Miles from Home: Riding the Long Circle on a Nevada Family Ranch,* photographs by Linda Dufurrena, text by Carolyn Dufurrena. Reno: University of Nevada Press, 2002. Copyright © 2002 by Carolyn Dufurrena. Reprinted with the permission of the University of Nevada Press.

Egan, Howard R. "Mountain Rat, Food for Indians," "Pine-Nut Harvest," and "Hunting for Water." From *Pioneering the West, 1846 to 1878.* Richmond, UT: Howard R. Egan Estate, 1917.

Hafen, Mary Ann. "A New Home in Nevada." From *Recollections of a Handcart Pioneer of 1860: A Woman's Life on the Mormon Frontier.* 1938. Rpt., Lincoln: University of Nebraska Press, 1983.

James, Will. Excerpts from *Lone Cowboy: My Life Story.* New York: Charles Scribner's Sons, 1930. Published with permission of Will James Art Company, Billings, MT.

Knudtsen, Molly Flagg. "Preface" and "A Flake of Flint, A Sherd of Earthenware." From *Under the Mountain.* Reno: University of Nevada Press, 1982. Copyright © 1982 by Molly Flagg Knudtsen. Reprinted with the permission of the University of Nevada Press.

Martin, Gregory. Excerpts from *Mountain City.* New York: North Point Press, 2000. Copyright © 2000 by Gregory Martin. Reprinted by permission of North Point Press, a division of Farrar, Straus and Giroux, LLC.

McElrath, Jean. "Rabbit Fighter" and "Natcherly Dumb." From *Aged in Sage.* San Francisco:

Recorder Press, 1964. Copyright © 1964 by Jean McElrath. Reprinted by permission of Jean Wagner.

Olds, Sarah E. Excerpts from *Twenty Miles from a Match: Homesteading in Western Nevada.* Reno: University of Nevada Press, 1982. Copyright © 1978 by University of Nevada Press. Reprinted with the permission of the University of Nevada Press.

Parks, Dennis. Excerpts from *Living in the Country Growing Weird: A Deep Rural Adventure.* Reno: University of Nevada Press, 2001. Copyright © 2001 by Dennis Parks. Reprinted with the permission of the University of Nevada Press.

Sheppard, Sophie. "Airspace." from *Sharing Fencelines: Three Friends Write from Nevada's Sagebrush Corner,* by Carolyn Dufurrena, Linda Hussa, and Sophie Sheppard. Salt Lake City: University of Utah Press, 2002. Reprinted by permission of the University of Utah Press.

Stegner, Wallace. "Mormon Trees." From *Mormon Country.* New York: Duell, Sloan and Pearce, 1942. Copyright © 1942 by Wallace Stegner. Copyright renewed © 1970 by Wallace Stegner. Reprinted by permission of Brandt & Hochman Literary Agents, Inc.

Ulph, Owen. "The Critter." From *The Fiddleback: Lore of the Line Camp.* 1981. Rpt., San Francisco: Browntrout, 1995. Reprinted by permission of Wendover H. Brown, Publisher.

A GATHERING OF COWBOY POETRY

Fanning, Ernie. "The Vanishing Valley." From *Cowboy Poetry: A Gathering.* Ed. Hal Cannon. Salt Lake City: Gibbs M. Smith, 1985. Reprinted by permission of Ernie Fanning.

Gray, R. Guild. "In Defense of Cattlemen." From *Nature Sings: Great Basin Scenes with Verse.* Las Vegas: R. Guild Gray, 1996. Reprinted by permission of Irmalee Ross.

Hussa, Linda. "Ride the Silence." From *Ride the Silence.* Reno: Black Rock Press, 1995. Reprinted by permission of Linda Hussa.

King, Olephia "Leafy." "The Dappled Grey Mustang." From *Western Poems No. II.* Fallon, NV: Fallon Publishing, 1967. Reprinted by permission of Linda L. Jensen.

McQueary, Rod. "Life and Times." From *Buckaroo: Visions and Voices of the American Cowboy,* edited by Hal Cannon and Thomas West. New York: Simon and Schuster, 1993. Reprinted by permission of Callaway Arts & Entertainment.

Mitchell, Waddie. "Story with a Moral" and "Typical." From *Waddie's Whole Load: The Cowboy Poetry of Waddie Mitchell.* Salt Lake City: Gibbs Smith, 1994. Reprinted by permission of Waddie Mitchell.

Sicking, Georgie Connell. "Nevada's Subtle Beauty." From *Just Thinkin'.* Fallon, NV: Loganberry Press, 1985. Reprinted by permission of Georgie Connell Sicking.

Sprado, Eric. "Wait 'til You Become a Man." From *New Cowboy Poetry: A Contemporary Gathering,* edited by Hal Cannon. Salt Lake City: Gibbs Smith, 1990. Reprinted by permission of Eric Sprado.

Wallis, Sue. "Coyote Bitch." From *Graining the Mare: The Poetry of Ranch Women,* edited by Teresa Jordan. Salt Lake City: Gibbs Smith, 1994. Reprinted by permission of Sue Wallis.

Walther, Jack. "The Longhorn's Short Career." From *Ruby Mountain Rhymes.* Lamoille, NV: Jack Walther, 1987. Reprinted by permission of Jack H. Walther.

THE BIGGEST LITTLE CITY: WRITINGS ABOUT RENO

Clark, Walter Van Tilburg. Excerpts from *The City of Trembling Leaves.* Rpt., Reno: University of Nevada Press, 1991. Copyright © 1945 by Walter Van Tilburg Clark. Reprinted with the permission of the University of Nevada Press.

Curtis, Leslie. "Reno," "Our Alphabet," and "As Others See Us." From *Reno Reveries.* Reno: Armanko Stationery, 1924. Reprinted by permission of Suzette Kitselman.

Douglass, William A. "The End of the Line." From *Neon: Artcetera from the Nevada State Council on the Arts* (Spring 1997). Reprinted by permission of William A. Douglass.

London, Jack. "Confession." From *The Road.* New York: Macmillan, 1907.

Melton, Rollan. "Reno Visitors Center" and "Truckee Treasures." From *Nevadans.* Reno: University of Nevada Press, 1988. Copyright © 1988 by Rollan Melton. Reprinted with the permission of the University of Nevada Press.

Miller, Arthur. Excerpts from "The Misfits." From *Arthur Miller's Collected Plays, Vol. II.* by Arthur Miller, Copyright © 1981 by Arthur Miller, Introduction and compilation. Used by permission of Viking Penguin, a division of Penguin Group (USA) Inc.

Miller, Max. Excerpts from *Reno.* New York: Dodd, Mead, 1941.

Prothro, Verita Black. "Porched Suitcases." From *The River Underground: An Anthology of Nevada Fiction,* edited by Shaun T. Griffin. Reno: University of Nevada Press, 2001. Copyright © 2001 by the University of Nevada Press. Reprinted with the permission of the University of Nevada Press.

Ruhl, Arthur. "The Fight in the Desert." *Collier's,* July 9, 1910.

Sepúlveda, Emma. Excerpts from *From Border Crossings to Campaign Trail: Chronicle of a Latina in Politics.* Falls Church, VA: Azul Editions, 1998. Reprinted by permission of Azul Editions.

Sepúlveda-Pulvirenti, Emma. "Here Am I Now" and "If I Renounce the Word." From *Death to Silence: Muerte al silencio,* translated by Shaun T. Griffin. Houston: Arte Público Press—University of Houston; © 1997. Reprinted with permission from the publisher.

Stafford, William. "Reno." From *Going Places: Poems.* Reno: West Coast Poetry Review, 1974. Reprint granted by permission of the Estate of William Stafford.

Stern, Jill. Excerpts from *Not in Our Stars.* New York: David McKay, 1957. Copyright © 1957 by Jill Stern. Used by permission of McKay, a division of Random House, Inc.

Vanderbilt, Cornelius, Jr. Excerpts from *Reno.* New York: Macaulay, 1929. Used by permission of Vanderbilt University Special Collections.

Webb, Mary. Excerpts from *A Doubtful River,* by Mary Webb with photographs by Robert Dawson and Peter Goin. Reno: University of Nevada Press, 2000. Copyright © 2000 by Robert Dawson, Peter Goin, and Mary Webb. Reprinted with the permission of the University of Nevada Press.

LIVING LAS VEGAS: INSIDE THE ENTERTAINMENT CAPITAL OF THE WORLD

Barber, Phyllis. "Mormon Levis." From *Parting the Veil: Stories from a Mormon Imagination.* Salt Lake City: Signature Books, 1999. Reprinted by permission of Signature Books Publishing, LLC.

Berman, Susan. Excerpts from *Easy Street.* New York: Dial Press, 1981. Reprinted by permission of Julie Smith.

Branon, Bill. "Seven-Out Sally Is Loose with the Rent." From *Red Rock Review* 1, no. 9 (Winter 2001). Reprinted by permission of *Red Rock Review.*

Crosby, Gregory. "The Long Shot." Printed on a plaque at Poets Bridge, Lewis Avenue Corridor, Las Vegas, Nevada, dedicated 2002. Reprinted by permission of Gregory Crosby.

Davis, Sammy, Jr., Jane Boyar, and Burt Boyar. Excerpts from *Yes I Can: The Story of Sammy Davis Jr.* New York: Farrar, Straus and Giroux, 1965. Reprinted by permission of Burt Boyar.

Fagel, Harry. "Jaywalker" and "L.S.D. (Street Talk Pt. 4)." From *Street Talk.* Berkeley, CA: Zeitgeist Press, 1999. Reprinted by permission of Harry Fagel.

Figler, Dayvid. "The Shrimp Manifesto" (unpublished). "Zamboni" from *Las Vegas Weekly,* October 21, 1998. Reprinted by permission of Dayvid Figler.

Hickey, Dave. "A Home in the Neon." © 1997 The Foundation for Advanced Critical Studies, Inc. Originally published in *Art Issues* 35 (November/December 1994) and subsequently included in *Air Guitar: Essays on Art & Democracy,* by Dave Hickey. Los Angeles: Art Issues Press, 1997. Reprinted by permission.

Irsfeld, John H. "Stop, Rewind, and Play." *South Dakota Review* 12, no. 1 (1974). Reprinted from *Radio Elvis and Other Stories.* Fort Worth, TX: TCU Press, 2002. Reprinted by permission of *South Dakota Review.*

Isaacson, Bruce. "Life in Las Vegas." *Red Rock Review* 1, no. 6 (Summer 1999). Revised for *Ghosts among the Neon,* by Bruce Isaacson. Las Vegas, NV: Zeitgeist Press, 2005. Reprinted by permission of Bruce Isaacson.

———. "Lucky." *Red Rock Review* 1, no. 9 (Winter 2001). Revised for *Ghosts among the Neon,* by Bruce Isaacson. Las Vegas, NV: Zeitgeist Press, 2005. Reprinted by permission of Bruce Isaacson.

Plummer, William J. Excerpts from *A Quail in the Family.* 1974. Rpt., Greenwich, CT: Fawcett Crest, 1974. Reprinted by permission of William J. Plummer.

Puzo, Mario. Excerpts from *Inside Las Vegas.* New York: Grosset and Dunlap, 1977. © 1977 by Mario Puzo. Reprinted by permission of Donadio & Olson, Inc.

Smith, John L. "'Flying Nun' Stunt Double Lands on Her Feet in Las Vegas" and "Kidney Caper: The Making of a Myth Nobody Can Miss." From *On the Boulevard*. Las Vegas: Huntington Press, 1999. Reprinted by permission of *Las Vegas Review-Journal*.

Stevens, A. Wilber. "Paradise Crest" and "Vegas: A Few Scruples." From *From the Still Empty Grave: Collected Poems*. Reno: University of Nevada Press, 1995. Copyright © 1995 by University of Nevada Press. Reprinted with the permission of the University of Nevada Press.

Thompson, Hunter S. Excerpts from *Fear and Loathing in Las Vegas: A Savage Journey to the Heart of the American Dream*. New York: Random House, 1972. Copyright © 1972 by Hunter S. Thompson. Used by permission of Random House, Inc.

Unger, Douglas. "Second Chances." From *Southwest Review*, 2007. Reprinted by permission of Douglas Unger.

Wegner, Hart. "The Blue Line." From *Off Paradise: Stories*. Reno: University of Nevada Press, 2001. Copyright © 2001 by Hart Wegner. Reprinted with the permission of the University of Nevada Press.

IN OUR BACKYARD: NOTES FROM NUCLEAR NEVADA

Conrad, James. Excerpts from *Making Love to the Minor Poets of Chicago*. New York: St. Martin's Press, 2000. Copyright © 1999 by the author and reprinted by permission of St. Martin's Press, LLC.

Emanuel, Lynn. "The Planet Krypton." From *The Dig and Hotel Fiesta, Two Volumes of Poetry*. Urbana: University of Illinois Press, 1995. Reprinted by permission of Lynn Emanuel and the University of Illinois Press.

Gallagher, Carole. Excerpts from *American Ground Zero: The Secret Nuclear War*. Cambridge, MA: MIT Press, 1993. Reprinted by permission of Carole Gallagher.

Griffin, Shaun T. "Nevada No Longer." From *Bathing in the River of Ashes: Poems*. Reno: University of Nevada Press, 1999. Copyright 1989 by Shaun T. Griffin. Reprinted with the permission of the University of Nevada Press.

Harney, Corbin. Excerpts from *The Way It Is: One Water, One Air, One Mother Earth*. Nevada City, CA: Blue Dolphin, 1995. Reprinted by permission of Blue Dolphin Publishing, Inc.

Kittredge, William. "In My Backyard." *Harper's*, October 1988. Copyright © 1988 by Harper's Magazine. All rights reserved. Reproduced from the October issue by special permission.

Levertov, Denise. "Watching *Dark Circle*." From *Oblique Prayers*. New York: New Directions, 1984. Copyright © 1984 by Denise Levertov. Reprinted by permission of New Directions Publishing Corp.

Louis, Adrian C. "Nevada Red Blues." From *Among the Dog Eaters*. Albuquerque: West End Press, 1992. Reprinted by permission of Adrian C. Louis.

Oberhansly, Curtis, and Dianne Nelson Oberhansly. Excerpts from *Downwinders: An*

Atomic Tale. Salt Lake City: Black Ledge Press, 2001. Reprinted by permission of Dianne Nelson Oberhansly and Curtis Oberhansly.

Rawles, Richard. "Coyote Learns to Glow." From *Learning to Glow: A Nuclear Reader,* edited by John Bradley. Tucson: University of Arizona Press, 2000. © 2000 The Arizona Board of Regents. Reprinted by permission of the University of Arizona Press.

Short, Gary. "Tidings." From *Flying over Sonny Liston: Poems.* Reno: University of Nevada Press, 1996. Copyright © 1996 by Gary Short. Reprinted with the permission of the University of Nevada Press.

Solnit, Rebecca. Excerpts from *Savage Dreams: A Journey into the Landscape Wars of the American West.* New York: Random House, 1994. Reprinted by permission of Rebecca Solnit.

Stafford, William. "At the Bomb Testing Site." From *The Way It Is: New & Selected Poems.* Saint Paul, MN: Graywolf Press, 1998. Copyright 1960, 1998 by the Estate of William Stafford. Reprinted from *The Way It Is: New & Selected Poems* with the permission of Graywolf Press, Saint Paul, Minnesota.

Vasquez, Robert. "Early Morning Test Light over Nevada, 1955." From *At the Rainbow: Poems.* Albuquerque: University of New Mexico Press, 1995. Reprinted by permission of Robert Vasquez.

Waters, Frank. Excerpts from *The Woman at Otowi Crossing, Revised Edition.* Athens: Swallow Press/Ohio University Press, 1998. Reprinted with the permission of Swallow Press/Ohio University Press, Athens, Ohio.

Williams, Terry Tempest. "The Clan of One-Breasted Women." From *Refuge: An Unnatural History of Family and Place.* New York: Random House, 1991. Reprinted by permission of Random House, Inc.

THE LONELIEST ROADS IN AMERICA: CONTEMPORARY TRAVEL WRITING

Bowden, Charles. "Tortoises." From *Blue Desert.* Tucson: University of Arizona Press, 1986. © 1986 The Arizona Board of Regents. Reprinted by permission of the University of Arizona Press.

Bowers, Janice Emily. "Remains of the Day." From *Desert: The Mojave and Death Valley,* with photographs by Jack Dykinga. New York: Abrams, 1999. Published by Abrams, a division of Harry N. Abrams, Inc., New York. All rights reserved.

Conaway, James. Excerpts from *The Kingdom in the Country.* Boston: Houghton Mifflin, 1987. Reprinted by permission of James Conaway.

Darlington, David. Excerpt from *Area 51: The Dreamland Chronicles.* New York: Henry Holt, 1997. © 1997 by David Darlington. Reprinted by permission of Henry Holt and Company, LLC.

Didion, Joan. "At the Dam." From *The White Album.* New York: Simon and Schuster, 1979. Copyright © 1979 by Joan Didion. Reprinted by permission of North Point Press, a division of Farrar, Straus and Giroux, LLC.

Donahue, Bill. "Boomtown." From *Double Take* 5 (1999). Reprinted by permission of Bill Donahue.

Fox, William L. Excerpts from *Driving by Memory*. Albuquerque: University of New Mexico Press, 1999. Reprinted by permission of William L. Fox.

Heat-Moon, William Least. Excerpts from *Blue Highways: A Journey into America*. Boston: Little, Brown, 1982. Copyright © 1982, 1999 by William Least Heat-Moon. By permission of Little, Brown and Co., Inc.

Robbins, Tom. "The Real Valley of the Dolls." *Esquire,* December 1988. Reprinted by permission of Tom Robbins.

Sterling, Bruce. "Greetings from Burning Man!" *Wired,* November 1996. Reprinted by permission of Bruce Sterling.

Thomson, David. Excerpts from *In Nevada: The Land, the People, God, and Chance*. New York: Knopf, 1999. Copyright © 1999 by David Thomson. Used by permission of Alfred A. Knopf, a division of Random House, Inc.

A DESERT BLOOMS: CONTEMPORARY POETRY

Barnstone, Aliki. "You Pray to Rain Falling on the Desert." Copyright © 2004 by Aliki Barnstone. First published in *New Letters* 70, nos. 3/4 (Fall 2004). It is printed here with the permission of *New Letters* and the Curators of the University of Missouri–Kansas City.

———. "The Lights of Las Vegas" and "Freeway Love Poem." *The Drunken Boat* 6, nos. 3 and 4 (Fall/Winter 2006). Reprinted by permission of Aliki Barnstone and *The Drunken Boat* (www.thedrunkenboat.com).

Breedlove, Mildred. "What Hills Are These?" and "Camping." From *Those Desert Hills and Other Poems*. Los Angeles: Vogue House, 1959. Reprinted by permission of Kathy Petersen.

Bruce, Irene. "Virginia City, Nevada." From *Night Cry*. Reno: Poetry West, 1950.

———. "Arrowhead." From *Crag and Sand*. Reno: Reno Poetry Workshop, 1945.

Cowee, Bill. "More Than Worms Slip through Worm Holes" and "To the Austrolorps in Wild Abandon." From *Bones Set against the Drift*. Reno: Rainshadow Editions, 1997. Reprinted by permission of Bill Cowee.

Dallman, Elaine. "Sparks for a 24/7 Week" and "Desert." From *Nevadans*. Georgetown, KY: Finishing Line Press, 2005. Reprinted by permission of Elaine Dallman.

de Longchamps, Joanne. "Snowmountain." Originally published in *California Quarterly* (1954). Rpt. from *Eden under Glass*. Francestown, NH: Golden Quill Press, 1957. Reprinted by permission of William L. Fox.

———. "Bat." From *Warm-Bloods, Cold-Bloods: Poems & Collages*. Reno: West Coast Poetry Review, 1981. Reprinted by permission of William L. Fox.

———. "Becoming Crippled." From *Torn by Light: Selected Poems*, edited Shaun T. Griffin. Reno: University of Nevada Press, 1993. Reprinted by permission of William L. Fox.

Emanuel, Lynn. "Chinoisserie," "For Me at Sunday Sermons, the Serpent," and "What Ely Was." From *"The Dig" and "Hotel Fiesta": Two Volumes of Poetry*. Urbana: University of Illinois Press, 1995. Reprinted by permission of Lynn Emanuel and the University of Illinois Press.

Fox, William L. Untitled poem from *Monody*. Woodinville, WA: Laughing Bear Press, 1977. Reprinted by permission of William L. Fox.

————. Untitled poem and "disowning" from *Reading Sand: Selected Desert Poems, 1976–2000*. Reno: University of Nevada Press, 2002. Copyright © 2002 by William L. Fox. Reprinted with the permission of the University of Nevada Press

Griffin, Shaun T. "A Place of Stone." From *Snowmelt*. Reno: Rainshadow Editions, Black Rock Press, 1994. Reprinted by permission of Shaun T. Griffin.

————. "Trash Run" and "Those People." From *Bathing in the River of Ashes: Poems*. Reno: University of Nevada Press, 1999. Copyright © 1999 by Shaun T. Griffin. Reprinted with the permission of the University of Nevada Press.

Huskey, Jim. "Stone Koan." From *Portfolio I: Poems*. Fallon, NV: Sand Mountain Press, 1980. Reprinted by permission of Constance L. Hart.

————. "Building the Pumphouse." From *Desert Wood: An Anthology of Nevada Poets*, edited by Shaun T. Griffin. Reno: University of Nevada Press, 1991. Reprinted by permission of Constance L. Hart.

Keelan, Claudia. "Blue Diamond" and "Relinquish." From *Utopic*. Farmington, ME: Alice James Books, 2000. Copyright © 2000 by Claudia Keelan. Reprinted with the permission of Alice James Books.

Laxalt, Bruce. "Work in Progress" and "Autumn Fire." From *Songs of Mourning and Worship: Poems*. Reno: Rainshadow Editions, Black Rock Press, 2005. Reprinted by permission of Black Rock Press and Bruce Laxalt.

Liu, Stephen S. N. "A Mid-July Invitation." From *TumbleWords: Writers Reading the West*, edited by William L. Fox. Reno: University of Nevada Press, 1995. Copyright © 1977 by Stephen Shu-Ning Liu. Used by permission of the University of Nevada Press.

————. "August Mirage." From *My Father's Martial Art: Poems*. Reno: University of Nevada Press, 2000. Copyright © 1987 by Stephen Shu-Ning Liu. Reprinted with the permission of the University of Nevada Press.

————. "Monologue from the Chicken Ranch." By permission of Stephen S. N. Liu.

Louis, Adrian C. "Coyote's Circle." From *Wild Indians & Other Creatures*. Reno: University of Nevada Press, 1996. Copyright © 1996 by Adrian C. Louis. Reprinted with the permission of the University of Nevada Press.

————. Excerpt from "Earth Bone Connected to the Spirit Bone." From *Ceremonies of the Damned: Poems*. Reno: University of Nevada Press, 1997. Copyright © 1997 by Adrian C. Louis. Reprinted with the permission of the University of Nevada Press.

————. "The Boy Hears Distant Drums from across the Sierras." From *Ancient Acid Flashes Back: Poems*. Reno: University of Nevada Press, 2000. Copyright © 2000 by Adrian C. Louis. Reprinted with the permission of the University of Nevada Press.

Meschery, Tom. "Trucks" and "Weeds—Teaching Poetry at Wittenburg Juvenile Hall." From *Nothing We Lose Can Be Replaced: Poems.* Reno: Black Rock Press, 1999. Reprinted by permission of Tom Meschery.

northSun, nila. "sweat preparation checklist" and "lost in the woods." From *a snake in her mouth: poems, 1974–1996.* Albuquerque: West End Press, 1997. Reprinted by permission of West End Press.

———. "i gotta be indian tomorrow." From *love at gunpoint.* Penn Valley, California: R. L. Crow Publications, 2007. Reprinted by permission of R. L. Crow Publications.

Pahmeier, Gailmarie. "The Promise of Good Food." From *The House on Breakaheart Road: Poems.* Reno: University of Nevada Press, 1998. Copyright © 1998 by Gailmarie Pahmeier. Reprinted with the permission of the University of Nevada Press.

———. "When You Love Someone for a Long Time." From *The House on Breakaheart Road: Poems.* Reno: University of Nevada Press, 1998. Copyright © 1997 by Gailmarie Pahmeier. Reprinted with the permission of the University of Nevada Press.

Revell, Donald. "The Little River Wants to Kee." From *Arcady.* Middletown, CT: Wesleyan University Press, 2002. © 2002 by Donald Revell. Reprinted by permission of Wesleyan University Press.

———. "My Mojave." From *My Mojave.* Farmington, ME: Alice James Books, 2003. Copyright © 2003 by Donald Revell. Reprinted with the permission of Alice James Books.

Robertson, Kirk. "Adjusting to the Desert," "Fallon," and "Lure." From *Just Past Labor Day: Selected and New Poems, 1969–1995.* Reno: University of Nevada Press, 1996. Copyright © 1996 by Kirk Robertson. Reprinted with the permission of the University of Nevada Press.

Short, Gary. "Toward Morning." From *Theory of Twilight.* Boise: Ahsahta Press, Boise State University, 1994. Reprinted by permission of Gary Short.

———. "Flying over Sonny Liston." From *Flying over Sonny Liston: Poems.* Reno: University of Nevada Press, 1996. Copyright © 1996 by Gary Short. Reprinted with the permission of the University of Nevada Press.

———. "What I Believed." From *10 Moons and 13 Horses: Poems.* Reno: University of Nevada Press, 2004. Copyright © 2004 by Gary Short. Reprinted with the permission of the University of Nevada Press.

Snyder, Gary. "Hitch Haiku." From *The Back Country.* New York: New Directions, 1968. Copyright © 1968 by Gary Snyder. Reprinted by permission of New Directions Publishing Corp.

———. "Magpie's Song." From *Turtle Island.* New York: New Directions, 1974. Copyright © 1974 by Gary Snyder. Reprinted by permission of New Directions Publishing Corp.

———. "Old Woodrat's Stinky House." From *Mountains and Rivers Without End.* Washington, DC: Counterpoint, 1996. ISBN: 1887178201. Copyright © 1996 by Gary Snyder. Reprinted by permission of Counterpoint, a member of Perseus Books, LLC.

Witt, Harold. "Pyramid." From *Beasts in Clothes.* New York: Macmillan, 1961. Reprinted with the permission of Scribner, an imprint of Simon & Schuster Adult Publishing

Group, from *Beasts in Clothes* by Harold Witt. Copyright © 1961 by Harold Witt. All rights reserved.

———. "Light on the Subject at Lehman Caves." *New York Times,* August 15, 1967. Rpt. from *Desert Wood: An Anthology of Nevada Poets,* edited by Shaun T. Griffin. Reno: University of Nevada Press, 1991. Reprinted by permission of Jessamyn Witt Picton.

ANYTHING IS POSSIBLE: CONTEMPORARY FICTION

Barnes, H. Lee. Excerpts from *The Lucky.* Reno: University of Nevada Press, 2003. Copyright © 2003 by H. Lee Barnes. Reprinted with the permission of the University of Nevada Press.

Bergon, Frank. Excerpts from *Wild Game.* Reno: University of Nevada Press, 1995. Copyright © 1995 by Frank Bergon. Reprinted with the permission of the University of Nevada Press.

Chisum, Jeffrey. "The Middle of Nowhere." Reprinted by permission of Jeffrey Chisum.

Gibney, Art. "The Manure Spreader." Originally published in *Zyzzyva* 10, no. 4, issue 40 (Winter 1994). Rpt. in *Skin of the Earth: Stories from Nevada's Back Country.* Reno: University of Nevada Press, 2002. Copyright © 2002 by Art Gibney. Reprinted with the permission of the University of Nevada Press.

Jordan, Teresa. "St. Francis of Tobacco." From *The River Underground: An Anthology of Nevada Fiction,* edited by Shaun T. Griffin. Reno: University of Nevada Press, 2001. Copyright © 2001 by University of Nevada Press. Reprinted with the permission of the University of Nevada Press.

Kranes, David. "The Phantom Mercury of Nevada." From *Low Tide in the Desert: Nevada Stories.* Reno: University of Nevada Press, 1996. Copyright © by David Kranes. Reprinted with permission of the University of Nevada Press. All Rights reserved.

Laxalt [Urza], Monique. Excerpts from *The Deep Blue Memory.* Reno: University of Nevada Press, 1993. Copyright © 1993 by Monique Urza. Reprinted with the permission of the University of Nevada Press.

Laxalt, Robert. Excerpts from *The Basque Hotel.* Reno: University of Nevada Press, 1989. Copyright © 1989 by Robert Laxalt. Reprinted with the permission of the University of Nevada Press.

Meschery, Joanne. "An Otherwise Happy Life." *Fiction* 5, nos. 2 and 3 (1978). Reprinted by permission of Joanne Meschery.

Michel, Sam. "Seeing Hunter Creek." From *Under the Light.* New York: Alfred A. Knopf, 1991. Reprinted by permission of Sam Michel.

Nightingale, Steven. Excerpts from *The Lost Coast.* New York: St. Martin's, 1996. Copyright © 1996 by the author and reprinted by permission of St. Martin's Press, LLC.

Sanchez, Thomas. Excerpts from *Rabbit Boss.* New York: Vintage, 1973. Reprinted by permission of International Creative Management, Inc. Copyright © 1973 by Thomas Sanchez.

Schopen, Bernard. Excerpts from *The Big Silence*. 1989. Rpt., Reno: University of Nevada Press, 1989. Copyright © 1989 by Bernard A. Schopen. Reprinted with the permission of the University of Nevada Press.

———. Excerpts from *The Desert Look*. 1990. Rpt., Reno: University of Nevada Press, 1995. Copyright © 1989 by Bernard A. Schopen. Reprinted with the permission of the University of Nevada Press.

———. Excerpts from *The Iris Deception*. Reno: University of Nevada Press, 1996. Copyright © 1996 by Bernard A. Schopen. Reprinted with the permission of the University of Nevada Press.

Spencer, Darrell. "My Home State of Nevada." From *Our Secret's Out*. Columbia: University of Missouri Press, 1993. By permission of the University of Missouri Press. Copyright © 1993 Darrell Spencer.

WILD NEVADA: LESSONS OF THE LAND

Christensen, Jon. Excerpts from *Nevada*, by Jon Christensen with photography by Deon and Trish Reynolds. Portland, OR: Graphic Arts Center Publishing, 2001. © 2001, with the permission of Graphic Arts Center Publishing, an imprint of Graphic Arts Center Publishing Company.

Cohen, Michael P. "The Future of the Great Basin." © 1997 by Michael P. Cohen. Originally appeared in *A Vast and Ancient Wilderness: Images of the Great Basin*, ed. Claude Fiddler, photog. Steve Roper. San Francisco: Chronicle Books, 1997. © 1997 by Claude Fiddler and Steve Roper. Reproduced with permission from Chronicle Books LLC, San Francisco. Visit www.ChronicleBooks.com.

Ely, Joe. "More Than Romance." *Nevada Public Affairs Review* 1 (1992). Reprinted by permission of Joe Ely.

Kappel-Smith, Diana. "Fossil Water." From *Desert Time: A Journey through the American Southwest*. Boston: Little, Brown, 1992. Copyright © 1992 by Diana Kappel-Smith. Reprinted with permission of McIntosh & Otis, Inc.

McPhee, John. Excerpts from *Basin and Range*. New York: Farrar, Straus and Giroux, 1981. Copyright © 1980, 1981 by John McPhee. Reprinted by permission of Farrar, Straus and Giroux, LLC.

Muir, John. "Nevada Forests." *San Francisco Evening Bulletin* (1878). Rpt. from *Steep Trails: California, Utah, Nevada, Washington, Oregon, the Grand Cañon*, edited by William Frederic Badè. Boston: Houghton Mifflin, 1918.

Reid, Robert Leonard. "West, to the Future." From "Earth, Sky, Invincible Wild," in *Wild Nevada: Testimonies on Behalf of the Desert*, edited by Roberta Moore and Scott Slovic. Reno: University of Nevada Press, 2005. Copyright © 2005, 2007 by Robert Leonard Reid. Reprinted with the permission of the University of Nevada Press.

Ronald, Ann. "Water." From *Earthtones: A Nevada Album*, essays by Ann Ronald and photographs by Stephen Trimble. Reno: University of Nevada Press, 1995. Copyright © 1995 by the University of Nevada Press. Reprinted with the permission of the University of Nevada Press.

Russell, Israel C. "The Great Basin." *Overland Monthly,* 2nd ser., 11, no. 64 (April 1888).

Sloan, Jim. "The Oldest Living Thing." From *Nevada: True Tales from the Neon Wilderness.* Salt Lake City: University of Utah Press, 1993. Reprinted by permission of Jim Sloan.

Stewart, George R. Excerpts from *Sheep Rock.* New York: Random House, 1951.

Trimble, Stephen. Excerpts from *The Sagebrush Ocean: A Natural History of the Great Basin.* Reno: University of Nevada Press, 1989. Copyright © 1989, 1999 by University of Nevada Press. Reprinted with the permission of the University of Nevada Press.

Twain, Mark. Excerpts from *Roughing It.* 1872. Hartford, CT: American, 1898.

Wheeler, Sessions S. Excerpts from *The Nevada Desert.* 1971. Rpt., Caldwell, ID: Caxton Printers, 1989. Reprinted by permission of The Caxton Printers, Ltd.

Zwinger, Ann Haymond. "Of Blackbrush and Sagebrush." From *The Mysterious Lands: A Naturalist Explores the Four Great Deserts of the Southwest.* New York: E. P. Dutton, 1989. Reprinted by permission of Ann Haymond Zwinger and Susan Zwinger.

INDEX

Entries in boldface type refer to authors' names; page number *xxxvi* in italics refers to the place name on the map; and page *426* in italics refers to the photographs following page 426.

"Across the Plains in the Donner Party (1846)" (Murphy), 67–71

"Adjusting to the Desert" (Robertson), 580–81

Adventures of Zenas Leonard, Fur Trader (Leonard), 40–45

"Airspace" (Sheppard), 225–31

American Ground Zero (Gallagher), 450–53

"An Otherwise Happy Life" (J. Meschery), 637–44

Area 51, 520, 717, 718

Area 51: The Dreamland Chronicles (Darlington), 515–22

"Arrowhead" (Bruce), 554

Ash Meadows, 478, 779–80

"As Others See Us" (Curtis), 276–77

"At the Bomb Testing Site" (Stafford), 436

"At the Dam" (Didion), 487–89

"August Mirage" (Liu), 562

Austin, *xxxvi*

"Autumn Fire" (B. Laxalt), 594

Barber, Phyllis, 365, *426*

Barnes, H. Lee, *426*, 662

Barnstone, Aliki, 607–8

Basin and Range (McPhee), 741–46

Basque Hotel, The (R. Laxalt), 621–26

"Bat" (de Longchamps), 557–58

Battle Mountain, *xxxvi*, 162, 486, 627–28, 632–33

"Becoming Crippled" (de Longchamps), 558

Beebe, Lucius, 165, *426*

Bergon, Frank, *426*, 649–50

Berman, Susan, 355, *426*

Big Silence, The (Schopen), 645–46

Big Smoky Valley, *xxxvi*

Black Canyon, *xxxvi*, 52, 56

Black Rock Desert, *xxxvi*, 74, 143–44, 157–59, 227–30, 486, 523–31, 735–37

"Blue Diamond" (Keelan), 616

Blue Highways (Heat-Moon), 490–94

"Blue Line, The" (Wegner), 394–402

"Boomtown" (Donahue), 541–45

Boulder City, *xxxvi*

Boundary Peak, *xxxvi*

Bowden, Charles, 494–95

Bowers, Janice Emily, 545

Boyar, Burt, 343

Boyar, Jane, 343

"Boy Hears Distant Drums from across the Sierras, The" (Louis), 576–77

Branon, Bill, 392

Breedlove, Mildred, 554–55

Browne, J. Ross, 103

Brown, Mrs. Hugh, 149

Bruce, Irene, 553

"Building the Pumphouse" (Huskey), 591–92

"Bungling Host" (Western Shoshone), 7–9

Bunkerville, 186, 188

"Camping" (Breedlove), 555–56

Carson City, *xxxvi*, 180, 473, 531, 691–93

Carson River, *xxxvi*, 76–78, 83, 739

Carson Valley, 201

"Cave in Cave Valley" (G. Wheeler), 63–64

"Chinoisserie" (Emanuel), 584

Chisum, Jeffrey, 711

Christensen, Jon, 777

City of Trembling Leaves, The (Clark), 287–92

"Clan of One-Breasted Women, The" (Williams), 441–47

Clark, Walter Van Tilburg, 286–87, *426*

Clark County, 180, 339, 413, 428, 473

Cohen, Michael P., 774

Colorado River, *xxxvi*, 52–56, 478, 739

Comstock, The, 101–9, 111, 113, 125–26, 129, 133, 165–67, 176, 287, 316, 536, 552, 598, 725, 738, 777

Conaway, James, 500–501

"Confession" (London), 265–69

Conrad, James, 479–80

Cowee, Bill, 571–72

"Coyote Bitch" (Wallis), 261

"Coyote Learns to Glow" (Rawles), 476–79

"Coyote's Circle" (Louis), 577–79

"Coyote Wants to Be Chief" (Western Shoshone), 7

"Creation of the Indians, The" (Southern Paiute), 17–19

"Critter, The" (Ulph), 203–8

Crosby, Gregory, 423–24

"Cŭnä´waвⁱ" (Southern Paiute), 19–20

"Cŭnä´waвⁱ's Grandson" (Southern Paiute), 20–23

Curtis, Leslie, 273–74

Dallman, Elaine, 567

"*Damollale* and the Black Widow Spider" (Washoe), 25–26

"*Damollale* and the Water Baby" (Washoe), 26–27

"Dappled Grey Mustang, The" (King), 245–47

Darlington, David, 514

Davis, Sam, 133, *426*

Davis, Sammy, Jr. 343, *426*

Dayton, *xxxvi*

Death Valley in '49 (Manly), 88–92

Deep Blue Memory, The (M. Laxalt), 690–93

de Longchamps, Joanne, *426*, 556

Denio, *xxxvi*, 539–40

De Quille, Dan, 109, *426*

"Desert" (Dallman), 568–69

Desert Look, The (Schopen), 646–48

Devil's Gate, 104, 107–9

"Diary" (Pratt), 84–87

Didion, Joan, 487

"disowning" (Fox), 588–90

Donahue, Bill, 541

Doten, Alfred, 125

Doubtful River, A (Webb), 323–29

Douglass, William A., 306

Downwinders: An Atomic Tale (Oberhansly and Oberhansly), 460–64

Driving By Memory (Fox), 531–36

Dufurrena, Carolyn, 231

"Early Morning Test Light over Nevada, 1955" (Vasquez), 439–40

"Earth Bone Connected to the Spirit Bone" (Louis), 575–76

Easy Street (Berman), 355–63

Egan, Howard R., 181

Elko, *xxxvi*, 236, 243–44

Ellis, Anne, 153–54

Ely, *xxxvi*, 491, 764

Ely, Joe, 756–57

Emanuel, Lynn, 447, 583–84

"End of the Line, The" (Douglass), 306–14

Eureka, *xxxvi*

Experiences of a Forty-Niner (Johnston), 75–78

Fagel, Harry, 386

Fallon, *xxxvi*, 590

"Fallon" (Robertson), 581–82

Fanning, Ernie, 251–52

Fear and Loathing in Las Vegas (Thompson), 347–49

Fifty Miles from Home (Dufurrena), 231–35

"Fight in the Desert, The" (Ruhl), 270–73

Figler, Dayvid, 383

"First Piano in Camp, The" (Davis), 133–39

"Flake of Flint, A Sherd of Earthenware, A" (Knudtsen), 209–11

"'Flying Nun' Stunt Double Lands on Her Feet in Las Vegas" (John L. Smith), 379–81

"Flying over Sonny Liston" (Short), 602–3

"For Me at Sunday Sermons, the Serpent" (Emanuel), 584–85

"Fossil Water" (Kappel-Smith), 754–56

Fox, William L., *426*, 531, 586

"Freeway Love Poem" (Barnstone), 611–12

Frémont, John C., 45, *426*

From Border Crossings to Campaign Trail (Sepúlveda), 314–20

Frontier Lady, A (Royce), 79–83
"Fun and Frolic" (De Quille), 114–17
"Future of the Great Basin, The" (Cohen), 775–76

Gallagher, Carole, 450
Gibney, Art, 680–81
"Going for the Mail" (Beebe), 165–67
Goldfield, 153, 154–55, 162, 168–76, 264, 780
Grass Valley, 210–11
Gray, R. Guild, 247
Great Basin, 1–2, 45, 50, 59, 200, 287, 315, 501, 552, 673, 724, 728–29, 734, 738–52, 764–65, 773–82
"Great Basin, The" (Russell), 732–34
Great Basin National Park, *xxxvi*, 781
"Greetings from Burning Man!" (Sterling), 523–31
Griffin, Shaun T., 426, 473–74, 598
Groom Lake, *xxxvi*, 517, 519

Hafen, Mary Ann, 185–86
Harney, Corbin, 426, 465
Hart, Fred H., 139
Hawthorne, *xxxvi*, 486, 534–35
Heat-Moon, William Least, 489–90
Henderson, *xxxvi*
"Here Am I Now" (Sepúlveda), 320–21
Hickey, Dave, 373
Hiko, *xxxvi*
"Hitch Haiku" (Snyder), 564
"Home in the Neon, A" (Hickey), 373–78
Hoover Dam, *xxxvi*, 340, 487–89, 490
Humboldt Mountains, *xxxvi*, 61
Humboldt River, *xxxvi*, 5, 38–39, 65–66, 118, 739
"Hunting for Water" (Egan), 183–85
Huskey, Jim, 590–91
Hussa, Linda, 253

"If I Renounce the Word" (Sepúlveda), 322
"i gotta be indian tomorrow" (northSun), 596–97
"In Defense of Cattlemen" (Gray), 248
"Information for the Millions" (Twain), 121–25
"In My Backyard" (Kittredge), 469–73
In Nevada: The Land, the People, God, and Chance (Thomson), 537–41
Inside Las Vegas (Puzo), 341–42

Iris Deception, The (Schopen), 648–49
Irsfeld, John H., 402
Isaacson, Bruce, 389
Ives, Joseph C., 52–53

James, Will, 195, 426
Jarbidge, *xxxvi*
"Jaywalker" (Fagel), 386–87
Johnston, William Graham, 74–75
Jordan, Teresa, 694
Journal of the Snake Country Expedition, 1828–29 (Ogden), 37–39

Kappel-Smith, Diana, 753–54
Keelan, Claudia, 616
"Kidney Caper: The Making of a Myth Nobody Can Miss" (John L. Smith), 381–82
King, Olephia, 245
Kingdom in the Country, The (Conaway), 501–7
Kittredge, William, 468–69
Knudtsen, Molly Flagg, 208
Kranes, David, 626–27

Lady in Boomtown (Brown), 149–53
Lahontan, 749
Lake Mead, *xxxvi*, 370, 488
Lake Tahoe, *xxxvi*, 14, 23, 26–27, 324, 725
Las Vegas, *xxxvi*, 1, 84, 328, 339–433, 442, 447–54, 470–71, 478, 495, 530, 531–33, 608–10, 662–65, 672, 770–72. *See also* Hoover Dam; Pahrump
Laughlin, *xxxvi*, 495–500
Laxalt, Bruce, 592–93
Laxalt, Monique, 689–90
Laxalt, Robert, 426, 621
Lehman Caves, *xxxvi*
Leonard, Zenas, 40
Levertov, Denise, 437
Life among the Piutes (Winnemucca), 93–98
"Life and Times" (McQueary), 259–60
"Life in Las Vegas" (Isaacson), 389–90
Life of an Ordinary Woman, The (Ellis), 154–56
"Light on the Subject at Lehman Caves" (Witt), 560
"Lights of Las Vegas, The" (Barnstone), 609–10
Little High Rock Canyon, *xxxvi*, 650
"Little River Wants to Kee, The" (Revell), 605–6

Liu, Stephen S. N., *426, 560–61*
Living in the Country Growing Weird (Parks), 218–25
London, Jack, 265
Lone Cowboy: My Life Story (James), 195–99
"Longhorn's Short Career, The" (Walther), 249–50
"Long Shot, The" (Crosby), 424–25
Lost Coast, The (Nightingale), 673–80
"lost in the woods" (northSun), 596
Louis, Adrian C., *426, 448–49, 574*
"L.S.D. (Street Talk Pt. 4)" (Fagel), 388
"Lucky" (Isaacson), 390–92
Lucky, The (Barnes), 662–71
"Lure" (Robertson), 582–83

"Magpie's Song" (Snyder), 564–65
"Making History" (Zanjani), 168–77
Making Love to the Minor Poets of Chicago (Conrad), 480–83
Manly, William Lewis, 87
"Manure Spreader, The" (Gibney), 681–89
Martin, Gregory, 236
Mathews, Mary McNair, 129–30
McDermitt, *xxxvi, 539*
McElrath, Jean, *212, 426*
McPhee, John, 741
McQueary, Rod, 259
Melton, Rollan, *302, 426*
Mercury, *xxxvi*
Meschery, Joanne, 636
Meschery, Tom, 569
Mesquite, *xxxvi*
"Messiah Letter, The" (Wovoka), 99–100
Metropolis, 212–15
Michel, Sam, 703–4
"Middle of Nowhere, The" (Chisum), 711–22
"Mid-July Invitation, A" (Liu), 561–62
Miller, Arthur, *299–300, 426*
Miller, Max, 281
Misfits, The (A. Miller), 300–302
Mitchell, Waddie, *256, 426*
Moapa, *xxxvi*
Mojave Desert, *xxxvi, 16, 546–47, 738–39, 743, 750–51, 780*
Monody, untitled poem (Fox), 586
"Monologue from the Chicken Ranch" (Liu), 562–63
"More Than Romance" (Ely), 757–62

"More Than Worms Slip through Worm Holes" (Cowee), 572–73
"Mormon Levis" (Barber), 366–72
"Mormon Trees" (Stegner), 200–202
Mountain City, *xxxvi, 238, 240*
Mountain City (Martin), 236–41
"Mountain Rat, Food for Indians" (Egan), 181–82
Mount Charleston, *xxxvi, 430*
Mount Grant, *xxxvi, 533, 536*
Mount Moriah, *xxxvi, 729*
Mount Rose, 289, 290
Muddy River, *xxxvi*
Muir, John, *426, 727–28*
Murbarger, Nell, *157, 426*
Murphy, Virginia Reed, 67
"My Home State of Nevada" (Spencer), 672–73
"My Mojave" (Revell), 606–7

"Natcherly Dumb" (McElrath) 215–18
Nellis Air Force Range, *xxxvi, 427, 454, 522, 532*
Nevada (Christensen), 777–82
"Nevada Correspondence" (Doten), 126–29
Nevada Desert, The (S. Wheeler), 738–40
"Nevada Forests" (Muir), 728–32
"Nevada No Longer" (Griffin), 474–75
"Nevada Red Blues" (Louis), 449–50
"Nevada's Subtle Beauty" (Sicking), 251
Nevada Test Site, *xxix, xxxvi, 427–83, 517*
"New Home in Nevada, A" (Hafen), 186–89
Nightingale, Steven, 673
Northern Paiute. *See* Paiute, Northern
northSun, nila, *426, 594–95*
Not in Our Stars (Stern), 294–99

Oberhansly, Curtis, 459–60
Oberhansly, Dianne Nelson, 459–60
"Of Blackbrush and Sagebrush" (Zwinger), 750–53
Ogden, Peter Skene, 37
"Oldest Living Thing, The" (Sloan), 763–69
Olds, Sarah E., 190
"Old Woodrat's Stinky House" (Snyder), 565–67
Oregon and California in 1848 (Thornton), 72–74
"Origin Tale" (Western Shoshone), 5–6
"Our Alphabet" (Curtis), 274–75

Pahmeier, Gailmarie, 613
Pahranagat Valley, 754–56
Pahrump, *xxxvi, 541–45*

Paiute, Northern, 11
Paiute, Southern, 16–17
"Pa-o-ha" (Northern Paiute), 14–15
"Paradise Crest" (Stevens), 364–65
Paradise Valley, 539
Parks, Dennis, 218, *426*
Peavine Mountain, 290, 327–28
"Peep at Washoe, A" (Browne), 103–8
"Phantom Mercury of Nevada, The" (Kranes),
    627–36
Pilot Peak, *xxxvi*
"Pine-Nut Harvest" (Egan), 182–83
Pioche, *xxxvi*, 490
"Place of Stone, A" (Griffin), 598–99
"Planet Krypton, The" (Emanuel), 447–48
Pleasant Valley, 741–44
Plummer, William J., 349–50
"Porched Suitcases" (Prothro), 329–38
"Porcupine and Coyote" (Northern Paiute),
    15–16
Pratt, Addison, 83–84
"Promise of Good Food, The" (Pahmeier),
    613–14
Prothro, Verita Black, 329
Puzo, Mario, 341
Pyramid Lake, *xxxvi*, 11, 50, 282–86, 756–62
"Pyramid" (Witt), 559–60

Quail in the Family, A (Plummer), 350–54
"Queen of the Black Rock Country" (Mur-
    barger), 157–64
"Quest of Old Man Berry, The" (Strobridge),
    143–48
Quinn River, *xxxvi*

Rabbit Boss (Sanchez), 657–62
"Rabbit Fighter" (McElrath), 212–15
Rachel, *xxxvi*, 515–22, 717, 718
Rawles, Richard, 475–76
Reading Sand, untitled poem (Fox), 586–87
"Real Valley of the Dolls, The" (Robbins),
    508–14
Reese River, 205
Reese River Valley, *xxxvi*, 62
Reid, Robert Leonard, 782
"Relinquish" (Keelan), 617
"Remains of the Day" (Bowers), 545–49
Reno, *xxxvi*, 179, 191, 263–338, 744, 763, 769, 774,
    780

"Reno" (Curtis), 274
Reno (M. Miller), 281–86
"Reno" (Stafford), 293
Reno (Vanderbilt Jr.), 277–81
"Reno Visitors Center" (Melton), 302–4
*Report of Explorations across the Great Basin
    of the Territory of Utah in 1859* (Simpson),
    59–62
*Report of the Exploring Expedition to the Rocky
    Mountains in the Year 1842, and to Oregon
    and North California in the Years 1843–44, A*
    (Frémont), 45–52
Report upon the Colorado River of the West
    (Ives), 53–58
Revell, Donald, 605
Rhyolite, 545, 548–49
"Ride the Silence" (Hussa), 254
Robbins, Tom, 507
Robertson, Kirk, *426*, 579–80
Ronald, Ann, *426*, 769–70
Roughing It (Twain), 118–21, 725–27
Royce, Sarah, 78–79
Ruby Mountains, *xxxvi*, 695
Ruby Valley, 59
Ruhl, Arthur, 269–70
Russell, Israel C., 732

Sagebrush Ocean, The (Trimble), 747–49
Saint Thomas, 2, 23
"Salt" (Southern Paiute), 23
Sanchez, Thomas, 657
Sand Mountain, *xxxvi*, 492
Savage Dreams (Solnit), 454–58
Sazerac Lying Club, The (Hart), 139–42
Schell Creek Range, 772
Schopen, Bernard, 644–45
Schurz, 533
Searchlight, *xxxvi*
"Second Chances" (Unger), 410–23
"Seeing Hunter Creek" (Michel), 704–10
Sepúlveda, Emma, 314
"Seven-Out Sally Is Loose with the Rent" (Bra-
    non), 392–93
Sheep Rock (Stewart), 735–37
Sheldon Antelope Refuge, 540
Sheppard, Sophie, 225
Short, Gary, 458, 601
Shoshone, Western, 5–10
"Shrimp Manifesto, The" (Figler), 383–84

Sicking, Georgie Connell, 250–51, *426*
Sierra Nevada Mountains, *xxxvi*, 725, 744, 749, 783
Simpson, James H., 58–59
Simpson Park Canyon, 61–62
Sloan, Jim, 762–63
Smith, Jedediah S., 31
Smith, John L., 378–79
Smoke Creek Desert, *xxxvi*, 230
"Snowmountain" (de Longchamps), 556–57
Snyder, Gary, 563–64
Solnit, Rebecca, 453–54
Southern Paiute. *See* Paiute, Southern
Southwest Expedition of Jedediah S. Smith, The
    (Smith), 31–36
"Sparks for a 24/7 Week" (Dallman), 568
Spencer, Darrell, 671
Sprado, Eric, 254–55
Stafford, William, 293, 436
Stegner, Wallace, 200
Sterling, Bruce, 523
Stern, Jill, 294
Stevens, A. Wilber, 363–64, *426*
Stewart, George R., 735
"St. Francis of Tobacco" (Jordan), 694–703
"Stone Koan" (Huskey), 591
"Stone Mother" (Northern Paiute), 11–12
"Stop, Rewind, and Play" (Irsfeld), 403–9
"Story of the *Ong*" (Washoe), 27
"Story with a Moral" (Mitchell), 257–58
Strobridge, Idah Meacham, 142–43, *426*
"sweat preparation checklist" (northSun), 595

Ten Years in Nevada (Mathews), 130–32
Thompson, Hunter S., 346–47
Thomson, David, 536–37
Thornton, J. Quinn, 71–72
"Those People" (Griffin), 600
"Tidings" (Short), 458–59
Toiyabe Range, *xxxvi*, 778
Tonopah, *xxxvi*
"Tortoises" (Bowden), 495–500
"To the Austrolorps in Wild Abandon" (Cowee),
    573–74
"Toward Morning" (Short), 601–2
"Trash Run" (Griffin), 599–600
Trimble, Stephen, 746–47
Truckee Meadows, 251–52, 263, 323, 325, 328
Truckee River, *xxxvi*, 263, 264, 276, 279
"Truckee Treasures" (Melton), 304–5

"Trucks" (T. Meschery), 570
"Tso'apittse" (Western Shoshone), 9–10
Tuscarora, *xxxvi*, 219–20
Twain, Mark, 117–18, *426*, 725
Twenty Miles from a Match (Olds), 190–94
"Typical" (Mitchell), 258

Ulph, Owen, 202–3
"Underground Business Arrangements" (De
    Quille), 109–14
Under the Mountain, preface to (Knudtsen), 209
Unger, Douglas, 410
Unionville, *xxxvi*

Vanderbilt, Cornelius, Jr., 277
"Vanishing Valley, The" (Fanning), 252–53
Vasquez, Robert, 438–39
"Vegas: A Few Scruples" (Stevens), 364
Virginia City, *xxxvi*, 62, 101, 102, 105, 107-8, 122,
    126–29, 130–32, 166–67, 316, 506
"Virginia City, Nevada" (Bruce), 553
Virgin River, *xxxvi*

Wadsworth, *xxxvi*
"Wait 'til You Become a Man" (Sprado), 255–56
Walker Lake, *xxxvi*, 11
Walker River, *xxxvi*, 533, 739
Wallis, Sue, 260–61
Walther, Jack, 249
Washoe County, 180, 329
Washoe Indians, 23–24
"Watching *Dark Circle*" (Levertov), 437–38
"Water Babies at Coo yu e Lake" (Northern
    Paiute), 12–14
"Water" (Ronald), 770–74
Waters, Frank, 429
Way It Is, The (Harney), 465–68
Webb, Mary, 323
"Weeds—Teaching Poetry at Wittenburg Juve-
    nile Hall" (T. Meschery), 570–71
Wegner, Hart, 393–94
Wells, *xxxvi*
Wendover, *xxxvi*
"West, to the Future" (Reid), 783–85
Western Shoshone. *See* Shoshone, Western
"What Ely Was" (Emanuel), 585
"What Hills Are These?" (Breedlove), 555
"What I Believed" (Short), 603–5
Wheeler, George M., 62–63

Wheeler, Sessions S., *426*, 738

Wheeler Peak, *xxxvi*, 63, 729, 767–68

"When You Love Someone for a Long Time" (Pahmeier), 614–15

White Sides Mountain, 518–19

Wild Game (Bergon), 650–56

Williams, Terry Tempest, 440

Winnemucca, *xxxvi*, 486

Winnemucca, Sarah, 92–93, *426*

Witt, Harold, 558–59

"Wolf and Coyote—Origin of Death" (Washoe), 24

Woman at Otowi Crossing, The (Waters), 429–35

"Work in Progress" (B. Laxalt), 593–94

Wovoka, 98, *426*

Yes I Can: The Story of Sammy Davis Jr. (Davis Jr., Boyar, and Boyar), 343–46

"You Pray to Rain Falling on the Desert" (Barnstone), 608–9

Yucca Mountain, *xxxvi*, 428, 467, 470–73, 476, 477–78, 479, 480–83

"Zamboni" (Figler), 384–85

Zanjani, Sally, 168

Zwinger, Ann Haymond, 750